D0903357

THE SPINOZA BIBLIOGRAPHY

Compiled by Adolph S. Oko

Published under the Auspices of the
Columbia University Libraries

G. K. HALL & CO., 70 LINCOLN STREET, BOSTON, MASS.
1964

This publication is printed on Permalife paper, developed by W. J. Barrow under a grant from the Council on Library Resources.

PREFACE

It is difficult to say when Adolph S. Oko conceived the idea of a definitive bibliography of Spinozana. Since his first interest in the philosopher goes back to his fifteenth year, it can be said that it began at that time. He certainly started working on it seriously soon after he became librarian at the Hebrew Union College in 1906. He hoped to have it "completed" in time for the three-hundredth anniversary of Spinoza's birth in 1932. "Completed" is a term one can never use about a bibliography and in the case of a perfectionist like Adolph Oko this becomes an even greater impossibility. From the time he resigned as librarian in Cincinnati in 1932 until the time he became editor of the *Contemporary Jewish Record* in 1942, he concentrated on his Spinoza studies and especially on perfecting the *Bibliography*. He put these studies aside to give his attention to his new undertaking, but always with the intention of going back to his great love and his great task, as soon as possible. This was not to be.

At the time of his death on October 2, 1944, the *Bibliography* consisted of about 20,000 cards or notations collected in boxes. Among these were many unchecked items, many more duplicates, and unfinished entries and a small proportion of cards completed in Mr. Oko's clear and precise style of writing. The explanations for this unfulfilled hope are many — personal and less personal. But anyone seeing the bulk of material in hand did not have far to seek. To complete the work, it would have taken the lifetime of more than one person with the high standards which this scholar imposed upon himself. He aimed to examine every item which he was recording. With this in mind, he hoped to be able to go to Italy, Portugal, Russia, South America and even Japan. He had spent many days checking in the libraries of Germany, Holland, France and England. He might have been able to carry out some of these ambitious plans, had he lived long enough. After his death, the many inquiries about the "Spinoza Bibliography" convinced me that of the several unfinished works upon which my husband had been engaged, this was the one that should somehow be preserved, if not "completed." Certainly, I had no illusions that it could be completed as he would have wished it to be.

I was encouraged and given inestimable help throughout this undertaking by my husband's good friends, Harry A. Wolfson of Harvard University and Horace M. Kallen of the New School for Social Research. There have been many others who have helped in a great variety of ways — practically, scholarly and spiritually. Among these are James Guttman and Paul Kristeller of the Philosophy Department of Columbia University and Miss Altha Terry and Miss Elizabeth Abbott, catalogers at the Columbia University Libraries. To spell out the contribution of

Preface

each of these would be difficult in this short space but I must especially emphasize Miss Abbott's which was carried on with so much imagination, devotion and love that it would have delighted Mr. Oko's scholarly heart.

In addition to these many voluntary contributors, there were three whose work was paid for. Eugene Kuhlman, of the New School for Social Research, and Herbert Matsen, a graduate student at Columbia, each spent many hours verifying, searching, checking and arranging the entries. Mrs. Mary Hunt, who was engaged to prepare final copy, deserves especial mention because of the intelligence and care which she exercised on every phase of her work.

The continuing interest and wise guidance of Dr. Richard H. Logsdon, Director of the Columbia University Libraries, must be acknowledged particularly. It was his faith in the importance of completing this undertaking that overcame each new obstacle to publication. It is my hope that this faith will be rewarded by the appreciation of scholars and by their comments and criticisms. With these to build upon, a later edition might be brought nearer to the goal which Adolph Oko had set for himself.

This brings me to an explanation of the "Spinoza Bibliography" as it appears here. In order to bring this task to an end, adjustments had to be made, such as the following:

1. Examination of every item had to be abandoned. Instead, the entries in other libraries and other bibliographies had to be relied upon for bibliographical details. They were rendered as accurately as possible.
2. Many items in the original collection of cards had to be eliminated either because they were too incomplete to be located or identified or because upon examination they proved quite unrelated.
3. The special notations on many of the fully completed cards in Mr. Oko's handwriting could not be incorporated into the body of the bibliography for practical reasons. As many as possible have been reproduced in Appendix V.
4. The cut-off date for entries was established as 1942, but it will be noted that there are few entries dated later than 1940, when Mr. Oko began to turn his attention elsewhere.
5. Only one location is indicated for each item, although some may be available in several libraries. Preference was given to Columbia where the Oko-Gebhardt collection is located (the notation SPE-

Preface

CIAL COLLECTIONS - SPINOZA identifies items in this collection); next, to the Hebrew Union College in Cincinnati where the extensive Spinoza Library was built up by Mr. Oko; and then to other libraries more or less at random. Some errors crept into the transcribing of several location symbols so that in the end the library could not be identified. These have not been omitted in the hope that in due course these omissions can be rectified. There were also a few items for which the bibliographic details appeared adequate but for which no location was found. The absence of location symbol identifies these. Again it is the hope that they will in due course be located.

6. While the items are arranged generally according to the plan Mr. Oko had in mind, there have been some changes in detail. A few general categories had to be introduced to cover items for which the title gave no specific indication of content. It was decided to rely on the detailed subject classification scheme rather than attempt a detailed index. A clearer understanding of these points can be gained from the following explanation of the way the material has been arranged.

Explanation of Arrangement and Contents

A. *Bibliographies* contains bibliographies in printed catalogs and some books which list Spinoza's works and books on his philosophy, etc.

B. *Works:*

In original languages, arrangement is chronological; in translation, arrangement is by language, alphabetically, and then chronologically within each language.

1. Complete works are the "Opera Omnia."
2. Selected works, in addition to the "Opera Posthuma," include all in which several works are to be found in one volume.
3. Single works are arranged alphabetically under the Latin title except the "Stelkonstige Reeckening." Under "Epistolae" will be found the collected letters and also items dealing with single letters in which an original letter is reproduced.
4. "Selections" includes selections, excerpts and quotations from different works by Spinoza. These are arranged alphabetically as cataloged in the library holding the item, i.e., by editor, compiler, issuing agency or under the heading "Spinoza . . ." followed by title.

Preface

C. *Life, Contemporaries, Environment, etc.:*

1. "Life" contains straight biographies and other works dealing with aspects of his life.
2. "Environment and Contemporaries" includes books describing the times and places in which Spinoza lived, and dealing with some of his contemporaries. Because of their importance, Bayle and Rembrandt were singled out.
3. "Iconography" covers all illustrated materials, some photographs of portraits, statues, and other graphic materials related to Spinoza.

D. *Works on Spinoza's Philosophy:*

1. "General" and 2. "Sections or Chapters" include material dealing with Spinoza's philosophy as a whole.
3. "Studies . . ." includes material on specific works.
6. "Anniversary Commemorations" is for any speeches or articles which were prepared for occasions commemorating the philosopher's birth or death.

E. *Philosophical Works with References to Spinoza*" includes the many works in which some reference has been made to Spinoza or which have some connection with his philosophical thought. These are divided by periods; within each period some of the more important persons are singled out.

F. *Non-Philosophical Literature and Spinoza* contains books in literature, psychology, etc., in which Spinoza's ideas figure or books by authors who were influenced by Spinoza's philosophy although not themselves philosophers. There were many such but, since Lessing and Goethe were the outstanding examples, only these two were given separate headings.

G. *History and Spinoza* includes works of a general historical nature in which the ideas of Spinoza are either discussed or have some relationship. The secular and religious are divided.

H. Under *Influence in Different Countries* are books which deal with Spinozism as reflected in these countries.

I. The section on *Special Topics* is an attempt to make more readily accessible material on some of the specific areas of Spinoza's philosophy. Many other headings could have been included and items might have been placed under other headings, but it is hoped that these will prove a good starting point for scholars.

J. *Reviews.* No attempt was made to include all reviews. These were the reviews collected by Adolph S. Oko; they have been listed in this section generally under the author of the review.

K. *Notes about Authors* means that here are a few miscellaneous items about some of the Spinoza scholars whose books are included in the *Bibliography.*

L. *Fiction, Poetry and Drama:*

1. "Fiction" may include works in which Spinoza is one of the characters or where he has obviously been an influence.
2. "Poetry and Drama" is for works inspired by Spinoza, in which he may have been referred to, or in which he is one of the characters.

M. *Miscellaneous (re: Spinoza):*

1. "Spinoza's Library" refers to the books which were believed to have been in his own library. In addition to some of the specific books, not always in the precise edition, there are works about the library itself.
3. "Spinozahouses" includes anything about the various houses in which Spinoza lived, most of which later were made into museums.

Appendix:

IV. "Auxiliary Works" are those found in the original cards which do not have specific reference to Spinoza but which may prove useful to students in re-creating his intellectual environment.

V. In the section "A. S. Oko's Original Cards" we have included many of the cards in his own handwriting and some from the catalog of the Hebrew Union College. These were selected with two things in mind: to indicate Adolph S. Oko's way of working and to preserve some of the special notations which he had made on some of his completed cards.

Finally, we have had to place items within these categories largely on the basis of external evidence. If readers do not find an item under an expected category, we would suggest that they look elsewhere. If any items have been incorrectly arranged or omitted, we would welcome suggestions for changes and additions. Above all, we hope that this *Bibliography* will fulfill Adolph S. Oko's original purpose of stimulating further study of the works and influence of Benedictus de Spinoza.

Dorothy Kuhn Oko

CONTENTS

Page

Introduction xi

Subject Classification Scheme xv

Symbols Used in Bibliography xxi

The Spinoza Bibliography 1

Appendix 527

INTRODUCTION

This *Bibliography* is a work of piety and love. Begun by Adolph S. Oko as a boy of fifteen, it has been completed and provided for the use of students and devotees of Baruch Spinoza through the devoted concern of Mr. Oko's widow, Dorothy Kuhn Oko, twenty years after her husband's death. As nearly as possible, it embodies Adolph Oko's conception of bibliography as "the science which treats of books, their authors, subjects, history, classification, typography, materials (including paper, printing and binding, dates, editions, etc.)." But it is here a science religiously pursued. To Adolph Oko, Spinoza had been the "greatest thinker and saintliest of men," to be loved and followed for what he was as for what he taught; a philosopher in whom faith and works were one and reasoned — a rare condition indeed in the personal histories of the world's philosophers. "All I dare claim," Oko told an audience at Amherst College in 1932, "is that there are few who regard him with a deeper feeling of personal and ardent reverence than myself, or whose devotion goes back to earlier boyhood days." It is no accident that when Oko began to write, he took for his penname "S. Baruch."

S. Baruch's initiation into his Spinozist faith occurred in 1898, when he came upon the philosopher's essay *On the Improvement of the Understanding,* in a German translation. Born in Russia, in the town of Rudkov, in 1883, he was settled six years later in Germany, where he grew up and received his education, some of it at the University of Berlin. He was nineteen years old when he emigrated to the United States and found work in the Astor Library of New York City as a specialist in the literature of the Scandinavian countries. Four years later, in 1906, the twenty-three-year-old boy was invited to the Hebrew Union College in Cincinnati, there to organize its library. He continued as the College librarian for twenty-seven years, in due course getting naturalized, marrying, becoming the father of a son and a daughter, working at his vocation, involving himself in the affairs of his community, suffusing his institutional labors and extra-mural activities with his concern for Spinoza's personality, his works and the works about him.

As he built up the library's notable collections of Hebraica and Judaica, he also assembled for it a very distinguished collection of Spinozana, never to have for himself anything that appeared on the market unless it was already in the Hebrew Union College collection. Of an inheritance of Spinozana that had been left him by a friend, Oko kept only the duplicates, presenting the rest to the College. Oko's quest of Spinoza led to correspondence with collectors who shared his Spinozist faith, among them Carl Gebhardt in Germany and Sir Frederick Pollock in England. Both men came to count among his personal friends and to turn to him for counsel and guidance in the purchase of rare items, even in their writing about Spinoza. (Sir Frederick Pollock takes up much of his brief preface to his life of Spinoza, published in London in 1936, with his debt to Oko. The typescript of this little book, which Mrs. Oko had prepared for him and which he presented to her with its annotations and corrections, is also in the collection, a gift from her.)

Oko's correspondence with Gebhardt began in 1912. They did not come face to face until after World War I, and from then on served together as free will missioners of the Spinozistic faith. They collected Spinozana, with Oko acting as the book expert. They strove to unite the world's diversity of Spinoza lovers by exchanges of letters and occasional gatherings into the *Societas Spinozianum,* which became a fact in 1925. This was the year that Gebhardt (no academic — only a gentleman-scholar of some independence) published, in the form of a mosaic drawn from all of Spinoza's works, his notable exposition of Spinozistic doctrine and discipline, *Spinoza: von den Festen und Ewigen Dingen.* With Oko as Secretary of the *Societas,* they began to issue the *Chronicon Spinozanum,* which Oko edited. Against the two hundred and fiftieth anniversary of Spinoza's untimely death (February 21, 1677), Gebhardt raised enough money for the purchase price of the ruin of the house, then in the red light district of The Hague, where Spinoza died. The *Societas* arranged for its dedication on the twenty-first day of February 1927 as *Domus Spinozanum.* Carl Gebhardt, Sir Frederick Pollock and Adolph Oko were constituted its curatorium, to restore the house, to provide it with furniture of the period and with a library including as nearly as possible all the books Spinoza was believed to have owned or used, and to restore its garden in the back. It was their hope and desire that the *Domus* might be used more and more as a place where the world's Spinoza-lovers and Spinoza-scholars might meet to talk to each other about their researches, their beliefs and their projects.

Five years later, in 1932, came the three-hundredth anniversary of Spinoza's birth. An international assembly of scholars celebrated it at the *Domus,* among them Leon Brunschweig, Sir Frederick Pollock and George Santayana. Oko was in the chair for Santayana's address, *Ultimate Religion,* "before this chosen audience, in this consecrated place." A bust of Spinoza was unveiled in the garden of the *Domus.* All the proceedings were printed the following year under the title *Septimana Spinozana* (The Spinoza Week) and published by Nijhoff at The Hague. Sir Frederick Pollock later elaborated his own address into his interpretation of Spinoza's personal history for the Duckworth series of *Great Lives.* There is no record of Oko's words. He had long been gathering materials about the impact of Spinoza on the literary imagination of the West, and this would have been a theme appropriate to the occasion.

But there are left only his materials and notes and copies of his lectures at Amherst College and the University of Cincinnati when he returned home that year of 1932.

It was the following year that he made his second marriage and went with his wife to live in England, residing for a time in London and then in Surrey where four years later their son Benjamin was born. Oko gave all of the five years of their stay in England to the service of his Spinozist faith. He kept building up the *Bibliography*, writing letters and visiting persons and places as the work required. He kept gathering materials bearing on his conception of Spinoza's influence on the Western imagination. His hunt for Spinozana was increasing. So was his correspondence with Gebhardt, who had become too ill to receive visitors. When Gebhardt died in 1934, Oko was called to speak the needful words at the obsequies of his friend and brother in Spinoza. As Gebhardt's literary executor, he was also called upon to take responsibility for his collection, and for the ongoing problems of the financing of the *Domus Spinozana*. The added duties required more frequent meetings with octogenarian Sir Frederick Pollock who soon became a house-friend of the Okos. At his funeral, all too few years later, the only mourner not a member of the family who was invited to be present was Oko.

Meanwhile, the fascist, communist, Nazi and falangist eruptions had started to break up the order of the European world. In succession, Russia, Italy, Poland, Spain, Germany, Austria and Hungary fell under the heel of one variety or another of totalitarianism; as new political parties, totalitarianism reared its obscene hydra-head in every free country of the Western world. Between 1933 and 1939 the head and front of this "wave of the future" became Hitlerism, by 1939 launching its war for the enslavement of mankind. The Okos felt constrained to return to the United States where, after all, Adolph might serve his Spinozist mission with fewer anxieties. One such had been the security of the Gebhardt collection of Spinozana. It had had to be taken over, transported to England and then, together with the Oko collection, to the United States. The wear and tear of the times and the tasks, with the addition of communal Jewish responsibilities that Oko assumed when he returned home, taxed his system beyond endurance. His busy final years in his own country were years of mounting ill-health. In 1944 he died, his books to be written, his *Bibliography* unfinished, his Gebhardt-Oko collection unhoused, the future of the *Societas* and the *Domus* precarious indeed.

Of course other devoted Spinozists took over, with ambiguous effect so far as the salvaging of the *Societas* and the *Domus* were concerned. But a colleague in both, the late Simon Millner, author of *The Face of Benedictus Spinoza* (a reproduction of portraits and sculptures with an interpretive essay), opened negotiations with a number of universities for the disposal of the collection. Finally, through the generosity of Dr. Corliss Lamont and his mother, Mrs. Thomas W. Lamont, the Oko-Gebhardt collection of Spinozana came into the possession of Columbia University. On May 27, 1947, the collection was formally installed and dedicated, crowned with a bust of the philosopher-seer modelled by the eminent Anglo-American sculptress Phyllis Blundell, and presented to Columbia University by Mrs. Simon Kuhn of Cincinnati.

The collection is now housed and cataloged in a special department of the University's Butler Library, and is available to all students with a care for Spinoza. Finishing this *Bibliography* — which is designed not only to signalize what Spinoza himself wrote and what has been felt and written about him, but even more to help new generations of inquirers toward knowing and understanding him — presented a task more detailed and difficult than the others. To this Adolph Oko's widow, Dorothy Kuhn Oko, committed herself. She undertook to make sure that when the *Bibliography* was completed it would have a structure and functional readiness which would meet her husband's ideals. Doing this required greater resources and technical help than had been anticipated, or that could be found. Nevertheless, it has been done. The responsibility which Mrs. Oko assumed to bring to completion her husband's life-long endeavor has been so discharged that, together with the Gebhardt-Oko collection, it renders Columbia University one of the most practical working centers in the world for the study of Spinoza, his philosophy and his influence.

Horace M. Kallen

SUBJECT CLASSIFICATION SCHEME

A. Bibliographies
   1. Spinoza's Works
   2. Works on Spinoza

B. Works
   1. Complete
      a. Original language (arranged chronologically)
      b. Translations (arranged alphabetically by language and chronologically)
   2. Selected Works (several works in one volume)
      a. Original language — Opera Posthuma
      b. Translations — alphabetically by language, arranged chronologically
   3. Single Works (original language — if any — followed by translations, by language, arranged chronologically)
      a. Compendium Grammatices
      b. Epistolae
         1. collected
         2. individual — single letters or about individual letters
      c. Ethica
      d. Renati Des Cartes Principia and Cogitata Metaphysica
      e. Stelkonstige Reeckening (van de Regenboog en Reechening van Kanssen)
      f. Tractatus de Deo et Homine (Korte verrhandeling van God de mensch en deszelfs welstand) (short treatise on God, man and human welfare)
      g. Tractatus de Intellectus Emendatione et de Via (improvement of the understanding)
      h. Tractatus Politicus (a treatise on politics)
      i. Tractatus Theologico-Politicus (a treatise partly theological, partly political)
   4. Selections (includes selections from different books, excerpts, quotations, arranged as cataloged in library holding the item, i.e., by editor, compiler, issuing agency; or Spinoza, then title of book)

C. Life, Contemporaries, Environment, etc.
   1. Life (biographies and works about Spinoza's life)
      a. Colerus
      b. Lucas
      c. By others

2. Environment and Contemporaries (books about the general environment in which he lived and about his contemporaries)
   a. General
   b. Contemporary Jewish aspects
   c. Bayle
   d. Rembrandt
3. Iconography (about portraits, statues and other graphic material related to Spinoza)

D. Works on Spinoza's Philosophy
1. General (devoted entirely to Spinoza)
   a. Books
   b. Articles in periodicals, and collections
   c. Articles in encyclopedias, lexicons, etc.
2. Sections or Chapters in Histories of Philosophy
3. Studies of Works or Portions Thereof
   a. Selected Works (Opera Posthuma)
   b. Compendium Grammatices
   c. Epistola
   d. Ethica
   e. Renati Des Cartes Principia
   f. Tractatus de Deo
   g. Tractatus de Intellectus
   h. Tractatus Politicus
   i. Tractatus Theologico-Politicus
4. Works on Spinoza Sources
5. Works on Spinoza's System
6. Anniversary Commemorations

E. Philosophical Works with References to Spinoza by Periods with Special Sections on Important Authors
1. Before 1596
   a. General
   b. Socrates, Plato, Aristotle
   c. Maimonides, Moses Ben
   d. Crescas
   e. Machiavelli
   f. Bruno, Giordano
   g. Jewish medieval philosophy

- 2. 1596-1750
  - a. General
  - b. Hobbes, Thomas
  - c. Descartes, René
  - d. Malebranche, Nicolas
  - e. Leibniz, Gottfried Wilhelm
  - f. Toland, John
- 3. 1750-1850
  - a. General
  - b. Mendelssohn, Moses
- 4. 1850 to date
  - a. General
  - b. Brunner, Constantin

F. Non-Philosophical Literature and Spinoza

- 1. General
- 2. Lessing, Gotthold Ephraim
- 3. Goethe, Johann Wolfgang von

G. History and Spinoza

- 1. Secular
- 2. Religious
  - a. Christian and others
  - b. Anabaptist
  - c. Jewish
  - d. Kabbala
  - e. Sabbati Zevi

H. Influence in Different Countries

I. Special Topics in Spinoza's Philosophy

- 1. Aesthetics
- 2. Affects
- 3. Amor Dei
- 4. Atheism

Subject Classification Scheme

5. Attributes
6. Beatitude
7. Bible
8. Causality
9. Christianity (see also Christian religion, etc.)
10. Creation
11. Deism
12. Education
13. Emotions
14. Error
15. Essence
16. Eternity
17. Ethical Theory
18. Evolution
19. Free Thought
20. Free Will
21. God
22. Idea
23. Idealism
24. Immortality
25. Indeterminism
26. Individuality
27. Intuition
28. Judaism (see also Jewish religion, etc.)
29. Lex Humana
30. Logic
31. Materialism
32. Metaphysics
33. Methodology
34. Mind and Body
35. Miracles
36. Miscellaneous
37. Mode

38. Monism
39. Natural Rights
40. Naturalism
41. Nature
42. Ontological Argument
43. Pantheism
44. Political and Ethical Philosophy
45. Political Ideas
46. Psychology
47. Psychology and Ethics
48. Religion
49. Science
50. State and Religion
51. Substance
52. Teleology
53. Terminology
54. Theism
55. Theology
56. Theory of Knowledge
57. Truth

J. Reviews
   1. General
   2. Works in Translation

K. Notes about Authors (misc.)

L. Fiction, Poetry and Drama
   1. Fiction (Spinoza as one of the characters in story)
   2. Poetry and Drama (Spinoza inspired, referred to, or as one of characters)

Subject Classification Scheme

M. Miscellaneous (items related to Spinoza)

1. Spinoza's Library — books believed to be in his library, not necessarily the same edition — also material about Spinoza's library
2. Societas Spinozana
3. Spinozahouses, in Hague, Rijnsburg, etc.
4. Inedita Spinozana
5. Pseudo-Spinozana

Appendix:

- I. Leone Ebreo
- II. Acosta, Uriel
- III. De Tribus Impostoribus
- IV. Auxiliary Works (for recreating intellectual environment of Spinoza — useful for students)
- V. A. S. Oko's Original Cards

SYMBOLS USED IN BIBLIOGRAPHY

CBPac	....	Pacific School of Religion, Berkeley, California
CLU-C	....	William Andrews Clark Memorial Library, University of California, Los Angeles, California
CLSU	....	University of Southern California, Los Angeles, California
CU	....	University of California, Berkeley, California
CtY	....	Yale University, New Haven, Connecticut
DCU	....	Catholic University, Washington, D. C.
DFSA	....	Central Library, U. S. Federal Security Agency, Washington, D. C.
DLC	....	U. S. Library of Congress, Washington, D. C.
DLN	....	*
FCU	....	University of Miami, Coral Gables, Florida
ICJ	....	John Crerar Library, Chicago, Illinois
ICMILC	....	Midwest Inter-Library Center, Chicago, Illinois
ICN	....	Newberry Library, Chicago, Illinois
ICU	....	University of Chicago, Chicago, Illinois
IEN	....	Northwestern University, Evanston, Illinois
IU	....	University of Illinois, Urbana, Illinois
IaU	....	State University of Iowa, Iowa City, Iowa
LC	....	see DLC (Library of Congress)
MA	....	Amherst College, Amherst, Massachusetts
MB	....	Boston Public Library, Boston, Massachusetts
MBaT	....	Boston Athenaeum, Boston, Massachusetts
MH	....	Harvard University, Cambridge, Massachusetts
MWA	....	American Antiquarian Society, Worcester, Massachusetts
MWeLC	....	Wellesley College, Wellesley, Massachusetts
MdBj	....	Johns Hopkins University, Baltimore, Maryland
MdBP	....	Peabody Institute, Baltimore, Maryland
MiD	....	Detroit Public Library, Detroit, Michigan
MiGr	....	Grand Rapids Public Library, Grand Rapids, Michigan
MiU	....	University of Michigan, Ann Arbor, Michigan
MnCS	....	St. John's University, Collegeville, Minnesota
NBug	....	Grosvenor Library, Buffalo, New York
NN	....	The New York Public Library, New York, New York

* The institution represented by this symbol cannot be identified at present (see Preface).

Symbols Used in Bibliography

NNB	....	Association of the Bar of the City of New York, New York
NNC	....	Columbia University, New York, New York
NNG	....	General Theological Seminary of the Protestant Episcopal Church, New York, New York
NNJ	....	Jewish Theological Seminary of America, New York, New York
NNM	....	American Museum of Natural History, New York, New York
NNNAM	....	New York Academy of Medicine, New York, New York
NNUT	....	Union Theological Seminary, New York, New York
NNU-W	....	Washington Square Library, New York University, New York, New York
NNY	....	*
NNYi	....	YIVO Institute of Jewish Research, New York, New York
NN-YC	....	Yeshiva College, New York, New York
NUC	....	Usually refers to National Union Catalog, does not identify specific location
NcU	....	University of North Carolina, Chapel Hill, North Carolina
Nic	....	Cornell University, Ithaca, New York
NjNbS	....	Theological Seminary of the Reform Church in America, New Brunswick, New Jersey
NjP	....	Princeton University, Princeton, New Jersey
NjPT	....	Princeton Theological Seminary, Princeton, New Jersey
OC	....	Public Library of Cincinnati, Ohio
OCH	....	Hebrew Union College, Cincinnati, Ohio
OCLW	....	Western Reserve University, Cleveland, Ohio
OKU	....	University of Oklahoma, Norman, Oklahoma
OO	....	Oberlin College, Oberlin, Ohio
PHC	....	Haverford College Library, Haverford, Pennsylvania
PP	....	Free Library of Philadelphia, Philadelphia, Pennsylvania
PPDrop	....	Dropsie College for Hebrew and Cognate Learning, Philadelphia, Pennsylvania

* The institution represented by this symbol cannot be identified at present (see Preface).

Symbols Used in Bibliography

PPE	....	Pedagogical Library, Philadelphia Board of Public Education, Philadelphia, Pennsylvania
PPL	....	Library Company of Philadelphia, Philadelphia, Pennsylvania
PPLT	....	Krauth Library, Lutheran Theological Seminary, Philadelphia, Pennsylvania
PPM	....	Mercantile Library, Philadelphia, Pennsylvania
PPCP	....	College of Physicians, Philadelphia, Pennsylvania
PPPCP	....	Philadelphia College of Pharmacy and Science, Philadelphia, Pennsylvania
PPT	....	Temple University, Philadelphia, Pennsylvania
PU	....	University of Pennsylvania, Philadelphia, Pennsylvania
PV	....	Villanova University, Villanova, Pennsylvania
SPT	....	*
UCLA	....	see CLU (University of California at Los Angeles)
ViU	....	University of Virginia, Charlottesville, Virginia
YIVO	....	see NNYi (YIVO Institute of Jewish Research)

SPECIAL COLLECTIONS - SPINOZA in upper left-hand corner refers to the Oko-Gebhardt Collection, Columbia University.

*The institution represented by this symbol cannot be identified at present (see Preface).

The Spinoza Bibliography

A

BIBLIOGRAPHIES

 A1

Amzalak, Moses Bensabat, 1892–
... David Nieto, notícia biobibliográfica. Lisboa [Composto e impresso nas oficinas gráficas do Museu comercial] 1923.
37 p. incl. facsims. 2 port. 28 x 22cm.
"Edição de cem exemplares."
Includes a reference to Spinoza (p. 11)
Original paper cover bound in.
1. Nieto, David, 1654–1728—Bibl.

 A2

Baer, Joseph, & co., *Frankfurt am Main.*
... Spinoza; katalog einer sammlung seiner werke, der schriften seiner anhänger und schüler und der literatur über ihn, enthaltend u. a. die Spinoza-bibliothek des † herrn geheimrat Jacob Freudenthal ... Als ganzes zu verkaufen durch Joseph Baer & co. ... Frankfurt a. Main ... [Frankfurt am Main, 1911]
cover-title, 80 p. 21½ cm.
Katalog 598. Ms. notes by A. S. Oko, with indication of holdings in his Spinoza collection.
1. Spinoza, Benedictus de, 1632–1677—Bibl. 2. Catalogs, Booksellers'—Germany. I. Freudenthal, Jacob, 1839–1907.

A3

Bernfeld, Simon, 1860-1940.
Literarische Jahresrevue. [1913]
[21]-63 p.
In Jahrbuch für jüdische Geschichte und Literatur, 16. Bd., 1913.
Includes books about Spinoza.

 A4

Besant, Annie (Wood) 1847-1933.
The law of population: its consequences, and its bearing upon human conduct and morals. London, Freethought Publishing Company [1877?]
48, 8 p. 19cm.
Spinoza's name is included in list of "Half-hours with the freethinkers" on p. 7 of "Catalogue of works sold by the Freethought Publishing Company" (8 p. at end)

A5

Bradlaugh, Charles, 1833–1891.
Catalogue of the library of the late Charles Bradlaugh. London, Mrs. H. B. Bonner, 1891.
vi, [2], 137 p. front. 22cm.
Priced.
Pref. signed: Hypatia Bradlaugh Bonner.
1. Gt. Brit.—Pol. & govt.—Bibl. I. Bonner, Mrs. Hypatia (Bradlaugh) 1858–

 A6

Burgersdijk, firm, booksellers, Leyden.
Bulletin de la librairie ancienne Burgersdijk & Niermans à Leyde (Hollande) Nouvelle série, no. 6. 1911.
[193]-231 p. 24cm.
Lists books by and about Spinoza (p. 224-228)

 A7

Burgersdijk, firm, booksellers, Leyden.
Théologie, philosophie; catalogue de livres anciens et modernes aux prix marqués. Leyde, Burgersdijk & Niermans, 1900.
ii, 670 p. 25cm.
Lists works by and about Spinoza (p. 593-597) and a few other works in which he is of secondary interest.
On cover: Bibliotheca theologica et philosophica.

 A8

Burgersdijck, Franco Petri, 1590-1635.
Fr. Burgers Dijcki Idea politica cum annotationibus GeorgI HornI. Lugd. Batav., Apud Felicem Lopez de Haro, 1668.
[6], 225, [7] p. plates. 13cm.
Bound with Cunaeus, Petrus, 1586-1638. Petri Cunaei De republica Hebraeorum libri III. 1666.

 A9

Castro, David Henriques de, 1826–1898.
Catalogue de vente de la succession de feu M. D. Henriques de Castro Mz., sous la direction de MM. J. Vita Israel et Jacq. Lamed ... avril ... mai 1899. Amsterdam [1899]
xii, 231, [2] p. front., plates. 26½cm.
Includes items by and about Spinoza.
1. Jews—Bibl. 2. Hebrew literature—Bibl. 3. Manuscripts, Hebrew—Catalogs.

SPECIAL COLLECTIONS
SPINOZA
A10

Castro, David Henriques de, 1826-1898.
[Photostats of manuscripts relating to Spinoza, from the Castro collection]
[10] l. 43cm.

Manuscripts dated 1656-1873.

1. Spinoza, Benedictus de, 1632-1677.

NNC

A11

Constance. Von Wessenbergische Stadtbibliothek.
Katalog der v. Wessenbergischen Bibliothek, wissenschaftlich geordnet und aufgestellt von F. A. Kreuz. Juli 1862. Constanz, J. Stadler, 1863.
x, 439 p. 22 cm.

----- 1./2.-5. Fortsetzung des Kataloges. [Constanz, 1867-77]
4 v. 22 cm.

Includes works by and about Spinoza.

DLC

SPECIAL COLLECTIONS
SPINOZA
A12

Fabricius, Johann Albert, 1668-1736.
Jo. Alberti Fabricii ... Bibliographia antiqvaria, sive Introductio in notitiam scriptorvm, qvi antiqvitates hebraicas, graecas, romanas et christianas scriptis illvstravervnt. Editio secunda, auctior, & indice duplici rerum scriptorumque locupletata. Hambvrgi et Lipsiae, impensis Christiani Liebezeit, 1716.
[14], 664, [64] p. front. 22cm.

Includes reference to Spinoza (p. 236)

SPECIAL COLLECTIONS
SPINOZA
A13

Fock, Gustav, firm, booksellers, Leipzig.
Philosophie, einschliesslich Psychologie und Geheimwissenschaften, hierin auch Werke aus der Bibliothek des Professors der Philosophie I. Baumann, Göttingen. Leipzig [1912?]
249 p. 22cm.

"Antiquariatskatalog 423."
Lists books by and about Spinoza (p. 191-193)

SPECIAL COLLECTIONS
SPINOZA
A14

Fürst, Julius, 1805-1873.
Bibliotheca judaica. Bibliographisches Handbuch umfassend die Druckwerke der jüdischen Literatur einschliesslich der über Juden und Judenthum veröffentlichten Schriften, nach alfabetischer Ordnung der Verfasser bearb., mit einer Geschichte der jüdischen Bibliographie sowie mit Indices versehen und hrsg. von Julius Fürst. Neue Ausg. Leipzig, W. Engelmann, 1863.
3 v. in 2. 23cm.

Includes books by and about Spinoza (v. 3, p. 358-371)

SPECIAL COLLECTIONS
SPINOZA
A15

Fürst, Julius, 1805-1873.
Bibliotheca Judaica. Bibliographisches Handbuch der gesammten jüdischen Literatur, mit Einschluss der Schriften über Juden und Judenthum und einer Geschichte der jüdischen Bibliographie. Nach alfabetischer Ordnung der Verfasser bearbeitet von Dr. Julius Fürst. Leipzig, W. Engelmann, 1849-63.
3 v. 23cm.

Includes books by and about Spinoza (v. 3, p. 358-371)

A16

Goss, Charles William Frederick, 1864-
A descriptive bibliography of the writings of George Jacob Holyoake, with a brief sketch of his life, prefaced by Mrs. Holyoake-Marsh. London, Crowther & Goodman, 1908.
lxxxii, 118 p. 19 cm.

Lists Spinoza's Treatise on politics, ed. by G. J. Holyoake, London, 1853.

SPECIAL COLLECTIONS
SPINOZA
A17

Grunwald, Max, 1871-
Spinoza in Deutschland. Gekrönte Preisschrift. Berlin, S. Calvary, 1897.
iv, 380 p. 23cm.

Original paper cover bound in.
"Beiträge zur Spinoza-Bibliographie": p. [361]-370.

1. Spinoza, Benedictus de, 1632-1677.

SPECIAL COLLECTIONS
SPINOZA
A18

Hebrew Union College, Cincinnati. Library.
Annual report of the Librarian, May 31, 1913. [1913]
29 p. plates. 23cm.

Signed: Adolph S. Oko.
Includes a section "The Spinoza collection" (p. 14-20)

SPECIAL COLLECTIONS
SPINOZA
A19

Heidelberger Akademie der Wissenschaften.
Sitzungsberichte der Heidelberger Akademie der Wissenschaften. Stiftung Heinrich Lanz. Jahresheft 1913. Heidelberg, C. Winters Universitätsbuchhandlung, 1914.
xlvii p. 25cm.

Includes the note "Ausserdem wurde die Unterstützung einer Spinoza-Ausgabe von Herrn Gebhardt-Frankfurt a. M. im Prinzip angenommen" (p. xl)

NNC

Heims, Wilhelm, firm, booksellers, Leipzig.
Spinoza. ⌈1926⌉
8 p. 23cm.

"Katalog 109."

1. Spinoza, Benedictus de, 1632-1677 - Bibl.

Hellersberg, firm, booksellers, Berlin.
Philosophie. Berlin ⌈1927⌉
cover-title, 44 p. 23cm.

Katalog XVIII, Nachtrag zu Katalog XII/XIV.
Includes books by and about Spinoza (p. 38-39)

Hellersberg, firm, booksellers, Berlin.
Philosophie. Berlin ⌈192-⌉
cover-title, 103 p. 23cm.

Katalog VI.
Includes books by and about Spinoza (p. 87-91)

Hellersberg, firm, booksellers, Berlin.
Philosophie. Berlin ⌈1927⌉
cover-title, 50 p. 23cm.

Katalog XIV.
Includes books by and about Spinoza (p. 25-29)

Hertzberger, Menno, firm, booksellers, Amsterdam.
Literatuur en geschiedenis der Joden in Nederland. ⌈1930?⌉
cover-title, 15 p. illus., port., facsims. 18cm.

Includes works about Spinoza (p. 1, 15)

Index librorum prohibitorum.
Index librorum prohibitorum SS.mi D. N. Benedicti XIV. pontificis maximi jussu recognitus, atque editus. Cum appendicibus. Romae, Ex Typographia Rev. Cameræ Apostolicæ, 1770.
xxxxviii, 320 p. 19cm.

Includes two works of Spinoza (p. 257, 271)

International Antiquariaat (Menno Hertzberger & co.) n. v., Amsterdam.
Baruch de Spinoza (1632-1677) Catalogue no. 97. ⌈Amsterdam, 193-?⌉
14 p. port. 23cm.

List of books by and about Spinoza, with prices.

Israelitische Kultusgemeinde, Vienna. Bibliothek.
Zuwachsverzeichnis für die Jahre 1930 und 1931. Mit einer Beilage: Spinoza-Literatur, 2. Folge. Wien, Selbstverlag, 1932.
145, 14 p. 23cm.

1. Spinoza, Benedictus de, 1632-1677 - Bibl.

Kayserling, Meyer, 1829–1905.
Biblioteca española-portugueza-judaica. Dictionnaire bibliographique des auteurs juifs, de leurs ouvrages espagnols et portugais et des oeuvres sur et contre les Juifs et le judaïsme, avec un aperçu sur la littérature des Juifs espagnols et une collection des proverbes espagnols; par M. Kayserling. Strasbourg, C. J. Trubner ⌈Budapest, Impr. C. L. Posner et fils⌉ 1890.
1 p. l., xxi, 155 p. ~~25½cm.~~ 27cm.
Includes works by and about Spinoza.
1. Spanish literature—Bibl. 2. Hebrew literature—Bibl. 3. Portuguese literature—Bibl. 4. Jews in Spain—Bio-bibl. I. Title.

Knowlton, Charles, 1800–1850.
Fruits of philosophy, an essay on the population question. 2d new ed., with notes. London, Freethought Pub. Co. ⌈187-⌉
56 p. 19 cm.

A work on Spinoza included in list on p. 6 of "Catalogue of works sold by the Freethought Publishing Company" at end of volume.

1. Birth control. 2. Malthusianism. I. Title.

Knuttel, Willem Pieter Cornelis, 1854-1921.
Verboden boeken in de republiek der Vereenigde Nederlanden; beredeneerde catalogus door Dr. W. P. C. Knuttel ... 's-Gravenhage, M. Nijhoff, 1914.
xii, 140 p. 25½cm. (Added t.-p.: Bijdragen tot de geschiedenis van den Nederlandschen boekhandel. Uitg. door de Vereeniging ter bevordering van de belangen des boekhandels. XI)

Series title also on t.-p.
Includes books by Spinoza (p. 110-111, 115)

König, Georg Matthias, 1616-1699.
Bibliotheca vetus et nova, in qua Hebræorum, Chaldæorum, Syrorum, Arabum, Persarum, Ægyptiorum, Græcorum & Latinorum per universum terrarum orbem scriptorum, theologorum, JCtorum, medicorum, philosophorum, historicorum, geographorum, philologorum, oratorum, poëtarum, &c. patria, ætas, nomina, libri, sæpiùs etiam eruditorum de iis elogia, testimonia & judicia summa fide atq; diligentia ex quotidianâ autorum lectione depromta à prima mundi origine ad annum usq; M.DC.LXXIIX. ordine alphabetico digesta gratissima brevitate

(Continued on next card)

3-32884
[a33b1]

König, Georg Matthias, 1616-1699. Bibliotheca vetus et nova ... (Card 2)
recensentur & exhibentur à Georgio Matthia Königio ... Altdorfi, impensis W. Mauritii & hæredum J. A. Endterorum, typis H. Meyeri, 1678.
6 p. l., 888 p. 29cm.
Cover stamped: G. K. 1682.
Includes an article on Spinoza.

1. Bibliography—Universal catalogs. I. Title.

3-32884
Library of Congress Z1010.K65
[a33b1]

Land, Jan Pieter Nicolaas, 1834-1897.
Bibliographische Bemerkungen. III. Spinozistisches. [1894]
374-375 p.

In Archiv für Geschichte der Philosophie, Bd. 7, 1894.

Levi, Alessandro.
... Saggio di una bibliografia filosofica italiana dal 1.° gennaio, 1901 al 30 giugno 1908. Comp. sotto gli auspici della Società filosofica italiana da A. Levi e B. Varisco. Bologna-Modena, A. F. Formiggini, 1908.
2 p. l., [ix]-xii, 143 p., 1 l. 25cm. (Biblioteca di filosofia e di pedagogia)
"Offerto in omaggio agli intervenuti al III Congresso internazionale di filosofia in Heidelberg, XXXI agosto-V settembre MCMVIII."
Includes works about Spinoza (p. 38)

1. Philosophy, Italian—Bibl. I. Varisco, Bernardino, 1850- joint author. II. Società filosofica italiana.

10-1182
Library of Congress Z7129.I8L6

Librairie Lipschutz, Paris.
Philobiblion; catalogue illustré d'ouvrages modernes concernant le judaïsme. Paris [1937]
cover-title, 248 p. illus., ports., facsims. 16cm.

At head of title: XLVIIe année, N° 71, 1937.
Includes a list of books by and about Spinoza (p. 60-62) and a portrait of him (p. 59)

Linde, Antonius van der, 1833-1897.
Benedictus Spinoza; bibliografie. 's Gravenhage, M. Nijhoff, 1871.
viii, ii, 113 p. 23cm.

Volume of pamphlets.

Linde, Antonius van der, 1833-1897.
Benedictus Spinoza; bibliografie. 's Gravenhage, M. Nijhoff, 1871.
viii, ii, 113 p. 24cm.

Manuscript notes by Carl Gebhardt.

Linde, Antonius van der, 1833-1897.
Benedictus Spinoza; bibliografie. 's Gravenhage, M. Nijhoff, 1871.
viii, ii, 113 p. 24cm.

Manuscript notes by Adolph S. Oko.

Linde, Antonius van der, 1833-1897.
Benedictus Spinoza; bibliografie. 's Gravenhage, M. Nijhoff, 1871.
viii, ii, 113 p. 23cm.

Interleaved. Original paper covers bound in.

A 40

Linde, Antonius van der, 1833-1897.
Notiz zur Litteratur des Spinozismus. ₍1864₎ 301-305 p.

In Zeitschrift für Philosophie und philosophische Kritik, 45. Bd., 1864.

SPECIAL COLLECTIONS
SPINOZA
A 41

Lorentz, Alfred, firm, Leipzig.
Vademecum philosophicum. Kat. 216, 1913.
Leipzig ₍1913₎
cover-title, 332 p. 22cm.

Includes books by and about Spinoza (p. 285-289)

A 42

Meerman, Gerard, 1722-1771.
Bibliotheca Meermanniana; sive, Catalogus librorum impressorum et codicum manuscriptorum, quos maximam partem collegerunt viri nobilissimi Gerardus et Joannes Meerman; morte dereliquit Joannes Meerman, toparcha in Dalem et Vuren, etc. etc. Quorum publica fiet auctio die VIII sqq. junii, anni MDCCCXXIV Hagae Comitum in aedibus defuncti ... Per bibliopolas S. et J. Luchtmans, Lugduno-Batavos, fratres Van Cleef, Haganos et Amstelodamenses, et B. Scheurleer, Haganum. ₍Hagae Comitum, 1824₎
4 v. in 2. 22cm.
Vols. 1/2 and 3/4 have collective half-titles. Contents for v. 1-2 given in v. 1; v. 3-4, in v. 3.
Vol. 2 has half-title only; v. 3 has title abbreviated; v. 4: Bibliothecae Meermannianae tomus IV. sive Catalogus codicum manuscriptorum.
~~(Continued on next card)~~

NN

₍43d1₎ 13—11190-1

SPECIAL COLLECTIONS
SPINOZA
A 43

Mees-Verwey, M
De betekenis van Johannes van Vloten; een bibliografie met inleiding. Santpoort (N. H.) Uitgeverij C. A. Mees, 1928.
359 p. port., facsim. 26cm.

Includes a chapter on Van Vloten's work on Spinoza (p. 200-216) and entries connected with Spinoza (nos. 267-323) in bibliography.
Bibliography: p. ₍225₎-345.

SPECIAL COLLECTIONS
SPINOZA
A 44
193Sp4
AM4

Meijer, Willem, 1842-1926.
Spinozana 1897-1922, bevattende uittreksels uit de jaarverslagen van den secretaris der vereeniging Het Spinozahuis ₍W. Meijer₎ Benevens een levensbericht omtrent Dr. W. Meijer en eene lijst van diens geschriften. Curis Societatis Spinozanaê. Heidelberg, C. Winter; ₍etc., etc.₎ 1922.
xliv, 143, ₍1₎ p. front. (port.) 23x18cm.
(Half-title: Bibliotheca Spinozana curis Societatis Spinozanaê. t. I)

CONTINUED ON NEXT CARD

SPECIAL COLLECTIONS
SPINOZA
A 45

Mendelssohn, Moses, 1729-1786.
Verzeichniss der auserlesenen Büchersammlung des seeligen Herrn Moses Mendelssohn. Berlin, 1786. ₍Leipzig, F. A. Brockhaus, 1926₎
facsim. (56 p.), v p. 16cm.

Edited by Herrmann Meyer.
Fifth publication of the Soncino-Gesellschaft der Freunde des Jüdischen Buches e. V., Berlin.
Lists two books by Spinoza.

SPECIAL COLLECTIONS
SPINOZA
A 46

Murr, Christoph Gottlieb von, 1733-1811.
... Beschreibung der sämtlichen reichskleinodien und heiligthümer, welche in der des H. R. Reichs freyen stadt Nürnberg aufbewahret werden. Mit einer kupfertafel. Nürnberg, In commission der Bauer- und Mannischen buchhandlung, 1790.
2 p. l., 92 p. 1 illus., plates (part fold.) fold. diagr. 21cm.

1. Nuremberg - Antiquities.

SPECIAL COLLECTIONS
SPINOZA
A 47

Murr, Christoph Gottlieb von, 1733-1811.
... Beschreibung der vornehmsten Merkwürdigkeiten in des H. R. Reichs freyen Stadt Nürnberg und auf der hohen Schule zu Altdorf. Nebst einem chronologischen Verzeichnisse der von Deutschen, insonderheit Nürnbergern, erfundenen Künste, vom XIII Jahrhunderte bis auf jetzige Zeiten ... Nürnberg, J. E. Zeh, 1778.
₍16₎, 762, ₍2₎ p. fold. plates, fold. facsim. 18cm.

CONTINUED ON NEXT CARD

SPECIAL COLLECTIONS
SPINOZA
A 47

Murr, Christoph Gottlieb von, 1733-1811. ... Beschreibung der vornehmsten Merkwürdigkeiten in des H. R. Reichs freyen Stadt Nürnberg und auf der hohen Schule zu Altdorf. 1778. (Card 2)

Includes extensive notices of the libraries and museums, both public and private, with lists of the more important rarities (books, mss., etc.)

SPECIAL COLLECTIONS
SPINOZA
A 48

Murr, Christoph Gottlieb, 1733-1811.
Beschreibung der vonnehmsten Merkwürdigkeiten in der Reichsstadt Nürnberg, in deren Bezirke, und auf der Universität Altdorf. Nebst einem Anhange. 2. durchaus verm. Ausg. Mit einer Kupfertafel. Nürnberg, Wolf-Penkerische Kunst- und Buchhandlung, 1801.
iv, 718 p. fold. plates. 20cm.

Includes extensive notices of the libraries, both public and private, with lists of the more important rarities (books, mss., etc.)

SPECIAL COLLECTIONS
SPINOZA
A
50

Murr, Christoph Gottlieb von, 1733-1811.
Bibliothèque glyptographique. Dresde, Chez les Frères Walther, 1804.
294 p. 17cm.

1. Glyptics.

SPECIAL COLLECTIONS
SPINOZA
A
51

Murr, Christoph Gottlieb von, 1733-1811.
Catalogvs librorvm quos v. c. Christophorvs Theophilvs de Mvrr ... collegerat Noribergae a. MDCCCXII. d. VI. m. aprilis et diebus seqq publicae auctionis lege pro parata pecunia distrahendorum. Libros in classes disposuit b. poss. suasque annotatiunculas litterarias passim adspersit vitamque levi penicillo adumbratam praemisit Ioannes Ferdinandvs Rothivs ... Noribergae, in bibliopolio Lechneriano, 1811.
xxx p., 1 l., 365 p. 17cm.

Includes books by and about Spinoza.

SPECIAL COLLECTIONS
SPINOZA
A
52

Murr, Christoph Gottlieb von, 1733-1811.
Christophori Theophili de Murr Satira in paedantismum, thrasonismum et charlataneriam semi-eruditorum; sive, Laudatio funeralis in obitu viri excellentissimi, pereximii doctissimique domini magistri Gangolphi Unkepunz, poetae laureati, ludimagistri meritissimi et hypodidascali excelebеrrimi in illvstri schola octava, quae Bopfingae floret, una com lessu moestissimorum discipulorum ... Editio tertia, prioribus

CONTINUED ON NEXT CARD

SPECIAL COLLECTIONS
SPINOZA
A
53

Murr, Christoph Gottlieb von, 1733-1811.
Christophori Theophili de Murr Satira in paedantismum ... 1789. (Card 2)

multo auctior, et sic locupletata, ut novum opus videri possit. Norimbergae, Apud Iohannem Hoeschium, 1789.
40 p. 20cm.

SPECIAL COLLECTIONS
SPINOZA
A
54

Murr, Christoph Gottlieb von, 1733-1811.
Conspectvs bibliothecae glotticae vniversalis propediem edendae operis quinqvaginta annorvm. Avctore Christophoro Theophilo de Mvrr. Norimbergae, In bibliopolio Monath-Kvssleriano, 1804.
32 p. 21cm.

CONTINUED ON NEXT CARD

NNC

SPECIAL COLLECTIONS
SPINOZA
A
55

Murr, Christoph Gottlieb von, 1733-1811.
Inscriptio Arabica litteris cvficis avro textili picta in infima fimbria Pallii imperialis, Panormi A. C. 1133 confecti, inter S. R. Imp. Germ. Klinodia Norimbergae adservati. Delineata et explicata a Christophoro Theophilo de Mvrr. Cum sedecim tabvlis ligneis et dvabvs aeneis. Norimbergae, Apvd Adamvm Theophilvm Schneidervm, 1790.
28 p. illus., fold. plates. 27cm.

Includes bibliographical references.

NNC

A
56

Mylius, Johann Christoph, 1710-1757.
Bibliotheca anonymorvm et psevdonymorvm ad svpplendvm et continvandvm Vincentii Placcii Theatrvm et Christoph. Avg. Hevmanni schediasma de anonymis et psevdonymis, collecta et adornata à M. Joh. Christoph. Mylio ... cvm præfatione M. Gottlieb Stollii. Hamburgi, C. W. Brandt, 1740.
2 pt. in 1 v. 18cm.

1. Anonyms and pseudonyms. I. Placcius, Vincent, 1642-1699. II. Title.

NNUT
Library of Congress Z1041.M99 6—44955
[44b1]

SPECIAL COLLECTIONS
SPINOZA
A
57

New York. Public Library.
List of books relating to philosophy. New York, 1908.
cover-title, 93 p. 26cm.

"Reprinted from the Bulletin, July-August, 1908."
Works by and about Spinoza: p. 84-87; includes also other books containing references to him.
Manuscript notes by A. S. Oko.

SPECIAL COLLECTIONS
SPINOZA
A
58

Nijhoff, Martinus, firm, booksellers, The Hague.
Philosophie. La Haye, 1908.
cover-title, 77 p. 24cm.

At head of title: No. 362. Livres anciens et modernes en vente aux prix marqués.
Includes a list of books by and about Spinoza (p. 59-63)

SPECIAL COLLECTIONS
SPINOZA
A
59

Oko, Adolph S , 1883-1944.
The Spinoza collection in the Hebrew Union College Library. [1914]
p. 14. 26cm.

From the Union bulletin, v. 4, no. 2, March 1914.

1. Spinoza, Benedictus de, 1632-1677.

NNC

SPECIAL COLLECTIONS
SPINOZA

A 60

193Sp4
DP535

Peignot, Gabriel, 1767-1849.
Dictionnaire critique, littéraire, et bibliographique des principaux livres condamnés au feu, suprimés ou censurés: précédé d'un discours sur ces sortes d'ouvrages. Par G. Peignot ... Paris, A. A. Renouard, 1806.
2 v. in 1. 20cm.

Lists and describes books by and about Spinoza (v. 1, p. xxvii-xxxviii; v. 2, p. 131-135, 142-144)

SPECIAL COLLECTIONS
SPINOZA

A 65

Ravà, Adolfo,
Il matrimonio secondo il nuovo ordinamento italiano. Padova, CEDAM, 1929.
xii, 153 p. 23cm.

Presentation copy to Carl Gebhardt, with the author's inscription.
Includes a bibliographical reference to Spinoza (p. 155)

A 61

Peirce, Charles Santiago Sanders, 1839-1914.
Chance, love and logic; philosophical essays, edited with an introduction by Morris R. Cohen. With a supplementary essay on the pragmatism of Peirce by John Dewey. London, K. Paul, Trench, Trubner; New York, Harcourt, Brace, 1923.
xxxiii, 318 p. diagrs. 23 cm. (International library of psychology, philosophy and scientific method)

"Bibliography of Peirce's published writings" includes his reviews of works by and about Spinoza (pp. 315, 316, 317)

SPECIAL COLLECTIONS
SPINOZA

A 66

[Roos, S H de,]
Aankondiging van de Heuvelpers te Hilversum, Juni MCMXXVII. [1927]
[4] p. 24cm.

Signed: S. H. de Roos.
Announces a new edition of Spinoza's Tractatus politicus as the first work of the new publishing firm De Heuvelpers.

NNC

SPECIAL COLLECTIONS
SPINOZA

A 62

Pinto, Vivian de Sola, 1895–
Sir Charles Sedley, 1639–1701; a study in the life and literature of the restoration, by V. de Sola Pinto ... London, Constable & company ltd., 1927.
xi, 400 p. incl. geneal. tab. 2 port. (incl. front.) 22½ cm.
"Principal manuscript sources and bibliography": p. 363–388.
Includes references to works of Spinoza in the catalogue of Sir Charles Sedley's library (p. 326, 337)

1. Sedley, Sir Charles, bart., 1639?–1701.

PR3671.S4P5 28—5821

Library of Congress [a55e1]

A 67

Shepherd, Richard Herne, 1842-1895.
The bibliography of Coleridge. A bibliographical list, arranged in chronological order, of the published and privately-printed writings in verse and prose of Samuel Taylor Coleridge ... Rev., cor., and enl. by Colonel W. F. Prideaux. London, F. Hollings, 1900.
x p., 1 l., 95 p. 20 cm.

Includes a reference (p. 81) to an article by J. Dykes Campbell in The Athenaeum, May 22, 1897, on marginalia written by Coleridge on a copy of Spinoza's Works in the library of Manchester College, Oxford.

A 63

[Ravà, Adolfo]
Bibliografia degli scritti italiani relativi a Benedetto Spinoza pubblicati fino al 250° anniversario della sua morte. [1927]
[370]-375 p.

In Rivista di filosofia, anno 18, 1927.

SPECIAL COLLECTIONS
SPINOZA

A 68

Simons, Fanny
Haagsche bibliotheekgids. 's-Gravenhage, M. Nijhoff, 1913.
vii, 72 p. 20cm.

SPECIAL COLLECTIONS
SPINOZA

A 64

Ravà, Adolfo
Bibliografia degli scritti italiani relativi a Benedetto Spinoza pubblicati fino al 250° anniversario della sua morte. [1927]
[369]-375 p. 24cm.

From Rivista di filosofia, anno XVIII, n. 3, luglio-settembre 1927.
With manuscript notes by A. S. Oko.

A 69

Sleumer, Albert, 1876–
Index romanus. Verzeichnis sämtlicher auf dem römischen index stehenden deutschen bücher, desgleichen aller fremdsprachlichen bücher seit dem jahre 1870. Auf grund der neuesten vatikanischen ausgabe zusammengestellt und mit einleitung versehen von Dr. phil. Albert Sleumer ... Osnabrück, G. Pillmeyer, 1906.
76 p. 20½ cm.

Includes books by and about Spinoza.
1. Prohibited books. 2. Index librorum prohibitorum.

NN

Library of Congress Z1019.S55 6-40232

Smith, Simon Nowell
Mark Rutherford: a short bibliography of the first editions, by Simon Nowell Smith ... ⌊London, The Bookman's journal, 1931⌋
23 p. plates, facsims. 24½cm. (In Bibliographies. Third series)

"Supplement to 'The Bookman's journal', 1930"
Lists two works of Spinoza translated by Mark Rutherford.

Stonehill, Charles Archibald, 1900-
The Jewish contribution to civilization, with a preface by Stefan Zweig, edited by C. A. Stonehill, jr. A collection of books formed and offered by C. A. Stonehill, ltd. ⌊Birmingham, Printed at the press of F. Juckes, 1940⌋
198 p. illus., facsims. 22cm.

Lists books by and about Spinoza.

Sondheim, Moriz, 1860-
Gesammelte Schriften; Buchkunde, Bibliophilie, Literatur, Kunst, u. a. Frankfurt a. M., Für den Verfasser gedruckt, 1927.
xix, 418 p. illus., plates, port., facsim. 27cm.

Includes references to Spinoza (p. viii, xvii)
No. 141 of 200 copies.
Presentation copy to Carl Gebhardt with the author's inscription and initials.

Struve, Burckhard Gotthelf, 1671–1738.
Bibliothecae philosophicae Strvvianae emendatae continvatae atqve vltra dimidiam partem avctae a Lvd. Mart. Kahlio ... tomvs I ...⌈-II⌉ Gottingae, impensis Vandenhoeck et Cvnonis, 1740.
2 v. in 1. 21cm.

CONTENTS.—t. 1. Scriptores philosophiae contemplativae percensens.—t. 2. Scriptores philosophiae practicae percensens.
Includes works by and about Spinoza.

1. Philosophy—Bibl. I. Kahle, Ludwig Martin, 1712-1775. II. Title.

Spinozahuis, Leyden.
Catalogus van de boekerij der Vereeniging "Het Spinozahuis". ⌊'s-Gravenhage, Boekhandel vh. Gebr. Belinfante, 1914⌋
89 p. 29cm.
Ms. notes by Carl Gebhardt.

1. Spinoza, Benedictus de, 1632-1677 - Bibl.
I. Spinoza, Benedictus de, 1632-1677.

Weg, Max, firm, booksellers, Leipzig.
Bibliotheca Spinozana; eine überaus reichhaltige Sammlung von Schriften von und über Benedictus Spinoza. Nebst fast allen bekannten Bildnissen Spinozas. Leipzig, Max Weg, 1893.
cover-title, 18 p. port. 22cm.

"Katalog No. 29."
Interleaved.
Ms. notes by A. S. Oko.

Spinozahuis, Leyden.
Catalogus van de boekerij der Vereeniging "Het Spinozahuis". ⌊'s-Gravenhage, Boekhandel vh. Gebr. Belinfante, 1914⌋
89 p. 29cm.

1. Spinoza, Benedictus de, 1632-1677 - Bibl.
I. Spinoza, Benedictus de, 1632-1677.

Weg, Max, firm, booksellers, Leipzig.
Bibliotheca Spinozana; eine überaus reichhaltige Sammlung von Schriften von und über Benedictus Spinoza, nebst fast allen bekannten Bildnissen Spinozas. Leipzig, Max Weg, 1893.
42 l. 29cm.

"Katalog No. 29."
Typescript.

Stolle, Gottlieb, 1673-1744.
Kurtze Nachricht von den Büchern und deren Urhebern in der Stollischen Bibliothec ... Jena, In Verlegung Joh. Meyers seel. Wittve, 1733-43.
18 pts. in 2 v. 23cm.

Includes references to Spinoza.
Parts 8 and 16 have index and table of contents for pts. 1-8 and 9-16 respectively.
Parts 17 and 18 have title: Fortsetzung der Nachrichten von den Büchern der Stollischen Bibliothec.

Wolfenbüttel. Herzog-August Bibliothek.
Hundert Merkwürdigkeiten der Herzoglichen Bibliothek zu Wolfenbüttel. Für Freunde derselben aufgezeichnet von C. P. C. Schönemann. Hannover, F. Culemann, 1849.
71 p. 24 cm.

A
80

Zeitschrift für Philosophie und philosophische Kritik.
Register ... Band 1-150. Hrsg. von Hans und Hertha Schliebitz. Leipzig, J. A. Barth, 1914.
iv, 187 p. 26cm.

Lists articles about Spinoza.

1. Spinoza, Benedictus de, 1632-1677 - Bibliography.

B
WORKS

B-1
COMPLETE

B-1-a
ORIGINAL LANGUAGE

B-1-a
81

Spinoza, Benedictus de, 1632-1677.
Benedicti de Spinoza Opera qvae svpersvnt omnia. Itervm edenda cvravit, praefationes, vitam avctoris, nec non notitias, qvae ad historiam scriptorvm pertinent addidit Henr. Eberh. Gottlob Pavlvs ... Ienae, in Bibliopolio academico, 1802-03.
2 v. diagrs. 22½cm.

Signatures of Sainte-Beuve and A. S. Oko on flyleaf of v. 1.

1. Paulus, Heinrich Eberhard Gottlob, 1761-1851, ed.

Library of Congress B3958 1802 11-19532
[28d1]

B-1-a
82

Spinoza, Benedictus de, 1632-1677.
Benedicti de Spinoza Opera philosophica omnia. Edidit et praefationem adjecit A. Gfroerer ... Stuttgardiae, Typis J. B. Mezleri, 1830.
lxxviii, 664 p. 2 plates. 21cm.

Includes reproductions of title-pages of original editions.
Manuscript notes on fly-leaf.
Bibliographical footnotes.

B-1-a
83

Spinoza, Benedictus de, 1632-1677.
Benedicti de Spinoza Opera quae supersunt omnia. Ex editionibus principibus denuo edidit et praefatus est Carolus Hermannus Bruder ... Editio stereotypa. Lipsiae, typis et sumtibus Bernh. Tauchnitz jun., 1843-46.
3 v. diagrs. 16cm.

CONTENTS.—I. Principia philosophiae. Cogitata metaphysica. Ethica.—II. De intellectus emendatione. Tractatus politicus. Epistolae.—III. Tractatus theologico-politicus. Compendium grammatices linguae hebraeae.

1. Bruder, Karl Hermann, 1812-1892, ed.

Library of Congress B3958 1843 44-29100
[2]

B-1-a
84

Spinoza, Benedictus de, 1632-1677.
Ad Benedicti de Spinoza Opera quae supersunt omnia supplementum. Continens Tractatum hucusque ineditum de Deo et homine, Tractatulum de iride, epistolas nonnullas ineditas, et ad eas vitamque philosophi collectanea. Cum philosophi chirographo ejusque imagine photographica, ex originali hospitis H. van der Spijck. Amstelodami, Apud Fredericum Muller, 1862.
1 p. l., v, [1], 360 p. mount. port., fold. facsim. 16cm.

Ed. by J. van Vloten.
Signature of Carl Gebhardt on t.-p.

B-1-a
85

Spinoza, Benedictus de, 1632-1677.
Benedicti de Spinoza opera, quotquot reperta sunt. Recognoverunt J. van Vloten en J. P. N. Land ... Hagae Comitum, M. Nijhoff, 1882-83.
2 v. front. (port.: v. 2) illus., 2 fold. facsim. 24cm.

A. S. Oko's signature on flyleaf.

B-1-a
86

Spinoza, Benedictus de, 1632-1677.
Benedicti de Spinoza Opera quotquot reperta sunt; recognoverunt J. van Vloten et J. P. N. Land. Edito altera. Hagae Comitum, M. Nijhoff, 1895.
3 v.

Bibliographical footnotes.

B-1-a
87

Spinoza, Benedictus de, 1632-1677.
Benedicti de Spinoza Opera quotquot reperta sunt; recognoverunt J. van Vloten et J. P. N. Land. Editio tertia. Hagae Comitum, Apud Martinum Nijhoff, 1914.
4 v. 21cm.

Manuscript notes by Carl Gebhardt in margins.
Bibliographical footnotes.

CONTINUED ON NEXT CARD

B-1-a
88

Spinoza, Benedictus de, 1632-1677. Benedicti de Spinoza Opera quotquot reperta sunt. 1914. (Card 2)

Contents.--v. 1. Tractatus de intellectus emendatione. Ethica ordine geometrico demonstrata.--v. 2. Tractatus politicus. Tractatus theologico-politicus.--v. 2. Epistolae I-LXXXIII. Appendix Epistolae XLIX.--v. 4. Korte verhandeling van God, de mensch en deszelfs welstand. Renati des Cartes Principiorum

NNC CONTINUED ON NEXT CARD

SPECIAL COLLECTIONS
SPINOZA
B-1-a
89

Spinoza, Benedictus de, 1632-1677. Benedicti de Spinoza Opera quotquot reparta sunt. 1914. (Card 3)

philosophiae pars I et II. more geometrico demonstratae. Appendix, continens Cogitata metaphysica. Stelkonstige reeckening van den Regenboog. Reeckening van Kanssen.

B-1-b
TRANSLATIONS

SPECIAL COLLECTIONS
SPINOZA
B-1-b
90

Spinoza, Benedictus de, 1632-1677.
Oeuvres complètes de B. de Spinoza, traduites et annotées par J. G. Prat ... Paris, Librairie de L. Hachette et Cie, 1863-72.
2 v. illus., port., facsim. 18cm.

Complete in 2 v.? --cf. Bibl. Nat. Cat.
Contents.--1. sér. Vie de Spinoza, par Lucas. Vie de Spinoza, par Colérus. Principes de la philosophie de Descartes et Méditations métaphysiques.--2. sér. Traité théologico-politique.

SPECIAL COLLECTIONS
SPINOZA
B-1-b
91

Spinoza, Benedictus de, 1632-1677.
B. v. Spinoza's sämmtliche Werke. Aus dem Lateinischen mit dem Leben Spinoza's von Berthold Auerbach. Stuttgart, J. Scheible's Buchhandlung, 1841.
5 v. port., fold. facsim. 16cm.

SPECIAL COLLECTIONS
SPINOZA
B-1-b
92

Spinoza, Benedictus de, 1632-1677. B. v. Spinoza's sämmtliche Werke. 1841. (Card 2)

Contents.-- 1. bd. Das Leben Spinoza's, von Berthold Auerbach. Die Principien der Philosophie von Renatus Des Cartes.-- 2. bd. Theologisch-politischer Tractat.-- 3. bd. Die Ethik in geometrischer Reihenfolge dargestellt.-- 4. bd. Abhandlung über Politik. Abhandlung über die Ausbildung des Verstandes und über den Weg, am besten zur wahren Erkenntniss der Dinge zu gelangen.-- 5. bd. Briefwechsel.

SPECIAL COLLECTIONS
SPINOZA
B-1-b
93

Spinoza, Benedictus de, 1632-1677.
B. de Spinoza's sämmtliche Werke. Aus dem Lateinischen mit einer Lebensgeschichte Spinoza's von Berthold Auerbach. Mit dem Bildnisse Spinoza's. Zweite, sorgfältig durchgesehene und mit den neu aufgefundenen Schriften vermehrte Auflage. Stuttgart, Verlag der J. G. Cotta'schen Buchhandlung, 1871.
2 v. illus., port. 23cm.

SPECIAL COLLECTIONS
SPINOZA
B-1-b
94

Spinoza, Benedictus de, 1632-1677.
Spinoza's sämtliche Werke, übers. von J. H. v. Kirchmann, C. Schaarschmidt und O. Baensch. Leipzig, Verlag der Dürr'schen Buchhandlung [1905?]
2 v. 20cm.

Reissue of Bd. 91-96 of the Philosophische Bibliothek [1871]-1905.
Each work has special t.-p.

SPECIAL COLLECTIONS
SPINOZA
B-1-b
95

Spinoza, Benedictus de, 1632-1677.
Sämtliche Werke, herausgegeben von O. Baensch, A. Buchenau, C. Gebhardt, C. Schaarschmidt. Leipzig, Verlag von Felix Meiner, 1914.
3 v. port. 20cm.

Reissue of Bd. 91-95, 96a-b of the Philosophische Bibliothek, 1907-14.
Each work has special t.-p.

SPECIAL COLLECTIONS
SPINOZA
B-1-b
96

Spinoza, Benedictus de, 1632-1677.
... Sämtliche werke, in verbindung mit O. Baensch und A. Buchenau herausgegeben und mit einleitungen, anmerkungen und registern versehen von Carl Gebhardt. Leipzig, F. Meiner [19—]

3 v. illus., port., diagrs. 19½cm.

At head of title: Baruch de Spinoza.
Reissue of bd. 91-95, 96 a-b of the Philosophische bibliothek, 1914-22.

CONTENTS.—I. Kurze abhandlung von Gott, dem menschen und seinem glück, übertragen und hrsg. von C. Gebhardt. 1922. Ethik, übers. ... von O. Baensch. 10., mit der 7. gleichlautende aufl. 1922.—II. Theo-

(Continued on next card)

31—13868

[43b1]

SPECIAL COLLECTIONS
SPINOZA
B-1-b
97

Spinoza, Benedictus de, 1632-1677. ... **Sämtliche werke** ... [19—] (Card 2)

CONTENTS—Continued.

logisch-politischer traktat, übertragen und eingeleitet ... von K. Gebhardt. 4. aufl. 1921. Descartes' Prinzipien der philosophie auf geometrische weise begründet ... 4. aufl. neu übers. und hrsg. von dr. A. Buchenau. 1922. Abhandlung über die verbesserung des verstandes; Abhandlung vom staate. 4. aufl. neu übertragen und eingeleitet ... von C. Gebhardt. 1922.—III. Briefwechsel, übertragen ... von C. Gebhardt. [Neue ausg.] 1914. Lebensbeschreibungen und gespräche übertragen und hrsg. von C. Gebhardt. [Neue ausg.] 1914.

I. Gebhardt, Carl, 1881- ed. II. Baensch, Otto, 1878-1936, ed.
III. Buchenau, Artur, 1879- ed.

31—13868

B-2
SELECTED

B-2-a
ORIGINAL LANGUAGE

SPECIAL COLLECTIONS
SPINOZA
B-2-a
99

[**Spinoza, Benedictus de**] 1632-1677.
B. d. S. Opera posthuma ... [Amstelodami, J. Rieuwertsz] 1677.

20 p. l., 614, [34], 112, [8] p. diagrs. 21½ x 17cm.

Edited by J. Jellis; his preface, originally written in Dutch, translated by L. Meyer.

CONTENTS.—I. Ethica, more geometrico demonstrata.—II. Politica.—III. De emendatione intellectûs.—IV. Epistolæ, & ad eas responsiones.—V. Compendium grammatices linguæ hebrææ.

I. Jellis, Jarig, ed. II. Title.

11—19178

Library of Congress B3955.A18

[44e1]

SPECIAL COLLECTIONS
SPINOZA
B-2-a
98

Spinoza, Benedictus de, 1632-1677.
B. D. S. Opera posthuma ... 1677.
1 p. l., 752 p. port. 23cm.

Manuscript; handwriting varies.
Note by Carl Gebhardt: "Dies ist eine alte Copie des Opera Posthuma aus dem Ende des 17. Jahrhunderts, aus Amsterdam stammend."
Does not contain "Epistolae" and "Compendium grammatices linguae Hebraeae" as listed p. 51 and included in the printed edition.
Pages 53-54, 495-498, 681-684 are blank.

SPECIAL COLLECTIONS
SPINOZA
B-2-a
100

[Spinoza, Benedictus de] 1632-1677.
B. d. S. Opera posthuma ... [Amstelodami, J. Rieuwertsz] 1677.
20 p. l., 614, [34], 112, [8] p. diagrs. ~~21½ x 17cm.~~ 24cm.
Edited by J. Jellis; his preface, originally written in Dutch, translated by L. Meyer.
Large paper copy.
Contents.—I. Ethica, more geometrico demonstrata.—II. Politica.—III. De emendatione intellectûs.—IV. Epistolæ, & ad eas responsiones.—V. Compendium grammatices linguæ hebrææ.

I. Jellis, Jarig, ed. II. Title.

Library of C[ongress] 11—19178

B-2-b
TRANSLATIONS

SPECIAL COLLECTIONS
SPINOZA
B-2-b
101

Spinoza, Benedictus de, 1632-1677.
De Geschriften van Benedictus de Spinoza, vervattende I. Een verhandeling van God; den mensch, en deszelfs welstand. II. Godgeleerde staatkundige verhandelinge. Bijde met anteekeninge des schrijvers, en uijt het Latijn vertaald.
[9], 183 (i. e. 185), [1], 20 p. port. 23cm.

Photostat copy (positive) of manuscript in the Koninklijke Bibliotheek, The Hague.

CONTINUED ON NEXT CARD

SPECIAL COLLECTIONS
SPINOZA
B-2-b
102

Spinoza, Benedictus de, 1632-1677. De Geschriften van Benedictus de Spinoza ... (Card 2)

Photostats of recto and verso of each leaf are mounted to form pages as in the original.
Does not contain "II. Godgeleerde staatkundige verhandelinge."
Error in pagination: numbers 145-146 repeated.

SPECIAL COLLECTIONS
SPINOZA
B-2-b
103

[Spinoza, Benedictus de] 1632-1677.
De nagelate schriften van B. d. S. Als Zedekunst, Staatkunde, Verbetering van 't verstant, Brieven en antwoorden. Vit verscheide talen in de Nederlandsche gebragt. [n. p.] 1677.
24 p. l., 666, [2] p. diagrs. 21½ x 17 cm.
"Vertaling van Jan Hendriksz."—A. van der Linde, Benedictus Spinoza: bibliografie.
Author's initials on t.-p. supplemented in ink to Baruch d'es Spinoza.
I. Hendriksz, Jan, 17th cent., tr. II. Title.

B3955.A2 11—19179

Library of Congress [55c½]

SPECIAL COLLECTIONS
SPINOZA
B-2-b
104

[Spinoza, Benedictus de] 1632-1677.
De nagelate schriften van B. d. S. Als Zedekunst, Staatkunde, Verbetering van 't verstant, Brieven en antwoorden. Vit verscheide talen in de Nederlandsche gebragt. [n. p.] 1677.
24 x 19cm.
24 p. l., 666, [2] p. diagrs. ~~21½ x 17 cm.~~
"Vertaling van Jan Hendriksz."—A. van der Linde, Benedictus Spinoza: bibliografie.
Place of author's birth and death, with dates, penned on t.-p.
I. Hendriksz, Jan, 17th cent., tr. II. Title.

B3955.A2 11—19179

Library of Congress [55c½]

SPECIAL COLLECTIONS
SPINOZA
B-2-b
105

Spinoza, Benedictus de, 1632-1677.
The chief works of Benedict de Spinoza, tr. from the Latin with an introduction by R. H. M. Elwes ... London, G. Bell and sons, 1883-84.
2 v. 19 cm. (*Half-title:* Bohn's philosophical library)
Contents. — v. 1. Introduction. Tractatus theologico-politicus. Tractatus politicus.—v. 2. De intellectus emendatione. Ethica. Correspondence (abridged)

1. Philosophy—Collected works. I. Elwes, Robert Harvey Monro, 1853- tr.

B3958.E5 199.492 11—19176

Library of Congress [a53o1]

B-2-b
106

Spinoza, Benedictus de, 1632-1677.
The chief works of Benedict de Spinoza, translated with an introduction by R. H. M. Elwes. London, 1889.
2 v.

OCLW

SPECIAL COLLECTIONS
SPINOZA
B-2-b
107

Spinoza, Benedictus de, 1632-1677.
The chief works of Benedict de Spinoza, translated from the Latin, with an introduction by R. H. M. Elwes. London, G. Bell & sons, 1917-1919.
2 v. (Bohn's philosophical library)

Contents.--v. 1. Introduction, Tractatus theologico-politicus, Tractatus politicus.--v. 2. De intellectus emendatione, Ethica.
Rev. ed.

SPECIAL COLLECTIONS
SPINOZA
B-2-b
108

Spinoza, Benedictus de, 1632-1677.
Philosophy of Benedict de Spinoza. Translated from the Latin by R. H. M. Elwes. With an introduction by Frank Sewall, M. A. New York, Tudor publishing co., ~~1933.~~ c1936.
1 p. l., [v]-xxxiii, 427 p. 24 cm.
Previously issued under title: Improvement of the understanding, Ethics and Correspondence of Benedictus Spinoza.

1. Elwes, Robert Harvey Monro, 1853- tr.

Library of Congress B3958.E53 1933 33—21266

[49j5] 199.492

Spinoza, Benedictus de, 1632–1677.
Writings on political philosophy, by Benedict de Spinoza, edited by A. G. A. Balz ... New York, London, D. Appleton-Century company, incorporated [°1937]
xxxv, 197 p. 19½ cm. (*Half-title:* Appleton-Century philosophy source-books, S. P. Lamprecht, editor)
"The translation of the Tractatus politicus and of the selections from the Tractatus theologico-politicus employed in this volume is that of R. H. M. Elwes, Bohn's philosophical library, Chief works of Benedict de Spinoza, London, 1883."—Note.
1. Political science. 2. Philosophy and religion. 3. Free thought. I. Balz, Albert George Adam, 1887– ed. II. Elwes, Robert Harvey Monro, 1853– tr.
JC163.S73 1937 320.1 37—2018
Library of Congress [52n1]

Spinoza, Benedictus de, 1632–1677.
Œuvres de Spinoza, tr. par Émile Saisset ... avec une introduction du traducteur ... Paris, Charpentier, 1842.
2 v. in 1. 18cm.
CONTENTS.—1. sér. Introduction. Vie de Spinoza (par Colerus) Théologie de Spinoza.—2. sér. Éthique. Réforme de l'entendement. Correspondence.
I. Saisset, Émile Edmond, 1814–1863, tr. II. Colerus, Johannes, 1647–1707.
11—19175
Library of Congress B3959.S8 [a40b1]

Spinoza, Benedictus de, 1632–1677.
Œuvres de Spinoza, traduites par Émile Saisset ... avec une introduction critique. Nouv. éd. rev. et augm. ... Paris, Charpentier, 1861.
3 v. 18½cm.
CONTENTS.—t. I. Introduction critique.—t. II. Vie de Spinoza (par Colerus) Notice bibliographique (p. [lvi]–lxviii) Traité théologico-politique. Traité politique.—t. III. Éthique. De la réforme de l'entendement. Lettres.
Original paper covers bound in.
Ms. notes by Carl Gebhardt.
I. Saisset, Émile Edmond, 1814–1863, tr. II. °Colerus, Johannes, 1647–1707.
35—81054
Library of Congress G3959.S3 1861 [42b1] 198.9

Spinoza, Benedictus de, 1632-1677.
Oeuvres de Spinoza, traduites par Émile Saisset ... avec une introduction critique. Nouv. éd. rev. et augm. Paris, Charpentier, 1872.
3 v. 19cm.

Contents.--t. 1. Introduction critique.--t. 2. Vie de Spinoza. Notice bibliographique. Traité théologico-politique. Traité politique. --t. 3. Éthique. De la réforme de l'entendement. Lettres.

Spinoza, Benedictus de, 1632-1677.
Ouevres de Spinoza, traduites et annotées par Ch. Appuhn. Paris, Garnier frères [pref. 1904]
v. 1-2. (Classiques Garnier)

Contents.--v. 1. Court traité. Traité de la réforme de l'entendement. Principes de la philosophie de Descartes. Pensées métaphysiques.--v. 2. Traité théologico-politique.

Spinoza, Benedictus de, 1632-1677.
Oeuvres de Spinoza, traduites et annotées par Ch. Appuhn. Paris, Garnier frères, 1907.
v. 1. 20cm.

Contents.--v. 1. Court traité. Traité de la réforme de l'entendement. Principes de la philosophie de Descartes. Pensées métaphysiques.

Spinoza, Benedictus de, 1632-1677.
Oeuvres de Spinoza, traduites et annotées par Ch. Appuhn. Nouvelle édition, revue et corrigée d'après l'édition de Heidelberg. Paris, Librairie Garnier frères [1928]-29.
v. 1-3. 20cm. (Classiques Garnier)

Vol. 3 lacks edition statement and series note.
Contents.--v. 1. Court traité. Traité de la réforme de l'entendement. Principes de la philosophie de Descartes. Pensées métaphysiques.--v. 2. Traité théologico-politique.--v. 3. Traité politique. Lettres.

Spinoza, Benedictus de, 1632-1677.
Spinoza's philosophische Schriften ... Gera, bey Christoph Friedrich Bekmann, 1787-90.
v. 1-2. 22cm.

Each vol. has special t.-p. also; general t.-p. to v. 1 lacking.
Tr. by Schack Hermann Ewald.

CONTINUED ON NEXT CARD

Spinoza, Benedictus de, 1632-1677. Spinoza's philosophische Schriften. 1787-90. (Card 2)

Contents.--1. Bd. Benedikt von Spinoza über Heilige Schrift, Judenthum, Recht der höchsten Gewalt in geistlichen Dingen, und Freyheit zu philosophiren.--2. Bd. Spinoza's Ethik, erster Theil.
A copy of v. 3 is cataloged with another copy of v. 2 as an edition of Spinoza's Ethik, 1790-93.

Spinoza, Benedictur de, 1632-1677.
Die unvollendeten lateinischen Abhandlungen Spinoza's. Mit einer Einleitung herausgegeben von Hugo Ginsberg. Heidelberg, Georg Weiss (früher E. Koschny's Verlag in Leipzig) 1882.
[6], 73, xxiv, 256, [2] p. 21cm.

Original paper cover bound in: Spinozae Opera philosophica. Vol. IV.
Bound with Spinoza, Benedictus de. Der theologisch-politische Tractat Spinoza's. Leipzig, 1877.

Spinoza, Benedictus de, 1632-1677.
Tractatus de intellectus emendatione.
[Heidelberg, C. Winter, 1919-20]
308 p. 24cm.

Half-title.
Includes his Ethica.
Page proof of v. 2 of Spinoza. Opera, 1925, ed. by Carl Gebhardt.

Spinoza, Benedictus de, 1632-1677.
Spinoza, Opera; im Auftrag der Heidelberger Akademie der Wissenschaften herausgegeben von Carl Gebhardt. Heidelberg, Carl Winters Universitätsbuchhandlung [1925?]
4 v. ports. 23cm.

No. 12 of 50 copies.

Spinoza, Benedictus de, 1632-1677.
... Opera, im auftrag der Heidelberger akademie der wissenschaften herausgegeben von Carl Gebhardt. Heidelberg, C. Winter [1925]
4 v. fronts. (ports.) illus., diagrs. 22½ x 18½ cm.

At head of title: Spinoza.
Presentation copy to Adolphe S. Oko, with the translator's inscription and signature.

1. Gebhardt, Carl, 1881- ed.

B3953 1925 27—21552

Library of Congress [55c½]

Spinoza, Benedictus de, 1632-1677.
Spinoza, Tractatus de intellectus emendatione, Ethica. Heidelberg, Carl Winters Universitatsbuchhandlung [1926]
[4], 392 p. 23cm.

"Sonderdruck aus Spinoza, Opera herausgegeben von Carl Gebhardt."
Bibliographical references included in "Textgestaltung" (p. 309-392)

Spinoza, Benedictus de, 1632-1677.
Obras filosóficas de Spinoza, vertidas al castellano y precedidas de una introduccion por Emilio Reus y Bahamonde. [Tomo I] Tratado teologico-politico. Notas marginales al Tratado teologico-politico. Madrid, Biblioteca Perejo [1878]
cxvi, 367 p. 22cm. (Coleccion de filósofos modernos, no. 3)

No more published?
Bibliography: p. [cvii]-cxiv.

Spinoza, Benedictus de, 1632-1677.
Dzieła; przełożył Dr. Ignacy Halpern. Z dwoma portretami de Spinozy. Warszawa, Skład główny w Ksiegarni Gebethnera i Wolffa, 1914-16.
2 v. ports. 24cm. (Biblioteka filozoficzna, wydawana przez Henryka Goldberga)

Originally projected in 4 v., as a translation of Spinoza's complete works. No more published.
Bibliography: v. 1, p. xxxvi-xli.

CONTINUED ON NEXT CARD

Spinoza, Benedictus de, 1632-1677. Dzieła. 1914-16. (Card 2)

Presentation copy to Carl Gebhardt, with the translator's inscription and signature.
Ms. notes inserted preceding fly-leaf in v. 1.
Contents.--v. 1. Traktat o poprawie rozumu. Etyka.--v. 2. Traktat teologiczno-polityczny. Przypiski do Traktatu teologiczno-politycznego. Traktat polityczny.

Spinoza, Benedictus de, 1632-1677.
Dzieła; przełożył Ignacy Myślicki. Warszawa, Skład główny w Domu książki polskiej, 1927.
v. 1. port., facsim. 23cm.

"Wydanie jubileuszowe, w 250-ą rocznicę zgonu Spinozy."
Bibliographical footnotes.
Original paper cover bound in.
Presentation copy to Carl Gebhardt, with translator's inscription and signature.

B-3
SINGLE WORKS

B-3-a
COMPENDIUM GRAMMATICES

Spinoza, Benedictus de, 1632-1677.
Benedicti de Spinoza Compendium grammatices linguae Hebraeae. Podgórze-Kraków, Drukiem i nakładem J. Flessnera i Ski., 1905.
115 p. ports. 19cm.

Added t.-p. and text in Hebrew.
Translated into Hebrew by Solomon Rubin.

Spinoza, Benedictus de, 1632-1677.
Benedicti de Spinoza Compendium grammatices linguae Hebraeae. ⌊Translated into Hebrew by Solomon Rubin⌋ Podgórze-Kraków, Drukiem i nakładem J. Plessnera i Ski., 1905.
115 p. ports. 19cm.

Added t.-p. and text in Hebrew.
Translated into Hebrew by Solomon Rubin.

B-3-b-1
EPISTOLAE - COLLECTED

Spinoza, Benedictus de, 1632–1677.
Der briefwechsel des Spinoza im urtexte hrsg. und mit einer einleitung über dessen leben, schriften und lehre versehen von Hugo Ginsberg ... Angehängt ist: La vie de B. de Spinosa, par Jean Colerus. Leipzig, E. Koschny, 1876.
iv, 89, 252, (2) p. 20½cm. 18cm.

I. Ginsberg, Hugo, ed. II. Colerus, Johannes, d. 1707.

11-19195

Library of Congress B3964.G5G6

Spinoza, Benedictus de, 1632-1677.
Der Briefwechsel des Spinoza im Urtexte hrsg. und mit einer Einleitung über dessen Leben, Schriften und Lehre versehen von Hugo Ginsberg. Angehängt ist: La vie de B. de Spinoza, par Jean Colerus. Leipzig, E. Koschny, 1876.
iv, 89, 252, ⌊4⌋ p. 20cm.

The last two unnumbered pages contain "81. Epistola" to Ludwig Mayer and the beginning of "Epistola XXIII".

Spinoza, Benedictus de, 1632-1677.
Brieven van en aan Benedictus de Spinoza, benevens des schrijvers Vertoog over het zuivere denken. Amsterdam, S. L. van Looy, 1897.
xx, 390, xii, 63 p. fold. facsim. 19cm.
(Klassieke schrijvers)

Spinoza, Benedictus de, 1632–1677.
The correspondence of Spinoza, translated and edited with introduction and annotations by A. Wolf ... London, G. Allen & Unwin ltd. ⌊1928⌋
3 p. l., 9-502 p., 1 l. front., illus., ports., facsim., diagrs. 22 cm.
"Bibliographical": p. 64-69.

I. Wolf, Abraham, 1876- ed.

B3964.E5W6 28—20659

Library of Congress ⌊52e½⌋

Spinoza, Benedictus de, 1632-1677.
Lettres, inédites en français, traduites et annotées par J. G. Prat. Avec portrait et autographe. Paris, L. Baillière et H. Messager, 1884.
xv, 147 p. port., facsim. 19cm.

Original paper cover bound in.

Spinoza, Benedictus de, 1632-1677.
Lettres de B. de Spinoza, inédites en français, traduites et annotées par J. G. Prat. Avec portrait et autographe. 2. éd. Paris, C. Reinwald, 1885.
xv, 147 p. port., facsim. 19cm.

Original paper cover bound in.

Spinoza, Benedictus de, 1632-1677.
Spinozas Briefwechsel. Verdeutscht und mit Einleitung und Anmerkungen versehen von J. Stern. Leipzig, Verlag von Philipp Reclam jun. ⌊pref. 1904⌋
294 p. illus. 15cm. (Philipp Reclam's Universal-Bibliothek, 4553-55)

Spinoza, Benedictus de, 1632-1677.
Spinozas Briefwechsel. Verdeutscht und mit Einleitung und Anmerkungen versehen von J. Stern. Leipzig, Druck und Verlag von Philipp Reclam jun. ⌊pref. 1904⌋
295 p. illus. 14cm. ⌊Philipp Reclams Universalbibliothek. 4553-4555⌋

Manuscript notes of Carl Gebhardt, with his signature on t.-p.

Spinoza, Benedictus de, 1632-1677.
Spinoza: Briefwechsel; übertragen und mit Einleitung, Anmerkungen und Register versehen von Carl Gebhardt. Leipzig, F. Meiner, 1914.
xxxviii, 388 p. 20cm. (Philosophische Bibliothek, Verlag von Felix Meiner. ⌊Neue Aufl.⌋ Bd. 96a)

Ms. notes by Carl Gebhardt.

I. Gebhardt, Carl, 1881-1934, tr.

Spinoza, Benedictus de, 1632-1677.
Spinozas Briefwechsel und andere Dokumente.
Ausgewählt und übertragen von J. Bluwstein.
Leipzig, Im Insel-Verlag, 1916.
xxiii, 353 p. 21cm.

Manuscript notes by Carl Gebhardt.
Bibliographical footnotes.

Spinoza, Benedictus de, 1632-1677.
Der Briefwechsel Spinozas; ein Menschenbild.
Vom Verfasser des Spinoza redivivus und Augustinus redivivus. Halle (Saale) Weltphilosophischer Verlag, 1919-20.
2 v. 26cm. (Philosophische Weltbibliothek. 4. Bd.)

Auerbach's translation.
Spinoza redivivus attributed by A. S. Oko and Carl Gebhardt to Glatzel.

Spinoza, Benedictus de, 1632-1677.
Spinozas Briefwechsel und andere Dokumente.
Ausgewählt und übertragen von J. Bluwstein.
Leipzig, Im Insel-Verlag, 1923.
xxiii, 367 p. 22cm.

Spinoza, Benedictus de, 1632-1677.
Переписка. Перевод с латинского и голландского и примечания В. Брушлинского. Под ред. и со вступ. статьей В. Вандека и В. Тимоско.
Москва, Партийное изд-во, 1932.
274 p. illus., port. 23cm.

Title transliterated: Perepiska.
At head of title: Коммунистическая академия.
Институт философии.

EPISTOLAE – SELECTED

Spinoza, Benedictus de, 1632-1677.
Brief van Bened. de Spinoza, aan Dr. Lamb. van Veldhuysen. ⌈1844⌉
⌈159⌉-193 p. fold. facsims. 16cm.

From Utrechtsche Volks-Almanak voor 1844.
Includes Latin text and Dutch translation of the letter, and an essay signed: H. W. T.
Bibliographical footnotes.

Spinoza, Benedictus de, 1632-1677.
A letter expostulatory to a convert from Protestant Christianity to Roman Catholicism.
From the Latin. Ramsgate, T. Scott, 1869.
14 p.

A letter to Albert Burgh.

CtY

Spinoza, Benedictus de, 1632-1677.
A letter expostulatory to a convert from Protestant Christianity to Roman Catholicism; from the Latin. London, Trübner, 1869.
14 p.

A letter to Albert Burgh.

NN

Stern, Alfred, 1846-1936.
Ueber einen bisher unbeachteten Brief Spinozas und die Korrespondenz Spinozas und Oldenburgs im Jahre 1665. ⌈n. p., 1872?⌉
523-537 p. 19cm.

Presentation copy of Johann Jacoby with author's inscription and signature.
Bibliographical footnotes.

Spinoza, Benedictus de, 1632-1677.
Vervielfältigung eines eigenhändigen Briefes des Benedictus Despinoza an Joh. Georg. Graevius (Aufbewahrt in der Königlichen Bibliothek zu Kopenhagen) ⌈18--⌉
⌈4⌉ p. facsim. (in pocket) 25cm.

Includes a German translation of the letter and comments by W. Meijer.

Spinoza, Benedictus de, 1632-1677.
Die Briefe mehrerer Gelehrten an Benedict von Spinoza und dessen Antworten, soweit beide zum besseren Verständniss seiner Schriften dienen. Uebersetzt und erläutert von J. H. v. Kirchmann. Leipzig, Verlag der Dürr'schen Buchhandlung, 1897.
xiii, 258 p. 19cm. (Philosophische Bibliothek. Bd. 96)

Spinoza, Benedictus de, 1632-1677.
Vertoog over het zuivere denken, en de wijze waarop dit het best, tot de ware kennis der dingen kan geraken. Uit het Latijn door W. Meijer. Amsterdam, S. L. van Looy ₍1897₎
xii, 63 p. 19cm. (In Spinoza, Benedictus de. Brieven van en aan Benedictus de Spinoza, 1897)

Spinoza, Benedictus de, 1632-1677.
Nachbildung der im Jahre 1902 noch erhaltenen eigenhändigen Briefe des Benedictus Despinoza. Hrsg. von W. Meijer. Haag, Druck von Mouton & Co., 1903.
15 pts. XIII facsims. 35cm.

In portfolio.
Includes thirteen facsimiles, "Transcriptio und Uebersetzungen der facsimilierten Briefe des Benedictus Despinoza" (84 p.) and "Erläuterungen zu den facsimilierten Briefen des

CONTINUED ON NEXT CARD

Spinoza, Benedictus de, 1632-1677. Nachbildung der im Jahre 1902 noch erhaltenen eigenhändigen Briefe des Benedictus Despinoza. 1903. (Card 2)

Benedictus Despinoza" (20 p.) Each facsimile is enclosed in cover with special title stating the respective owners of the original letters.
Copy no. 90.

₍Langewiesche, Wilhelm₎ 1866-1934.
Das Unerkannte auf seinem Weg durch die Jahrtausende, die merkwürdigsten der guten Glaubens erzählten Fälle aus dem Gebiet des Übersinnlichen im Wortlaut der ersten Berichte. Ohne Deutungsversuche herausgegeben von Enno Nielsen ₍pseud.₎ Ebenhausen bei München, Wilhelm Langewiesche-Brandt, 1922.
326 p. 19cm. (Half-title: Die Bücher der Rose. Neue Friedensreihe)

CONTINUED ON NEXT CARD

₍Langewiesche, Wilhelm₎ 1866-1934. Das Unerkannte auf seinem Weg durch die Jahrtausende. 1922. (Card 2)

Includes a letter of Spinoza to Peter Balling in German translation (p. 179-181)
"Eine Fortsetzung ... erscheint unter dem Titel 'Das grosse Geheimnis'".

Spinoza, Benedictus de, 1632-1677.
Scientia intuitiva (Wahres Wissen) Spinoza's mathematisch-philosophischer Traktat "Ueber das Unendliche". Mit einem Vorwort von G. Gervai. Berlin, Carl Heymanns Verlag, 1930.
15 p. illus. 25cm.

Spinoza's letter to Ludwig Meyer of April 20, 1663, in the original Latin and in German translation.

Spinoza, Benedictus de, 1632-1677.
An addition to the correspondence of Spinoza ₍ed. by₎ A. Wolf. ₍1935₎
200-204 p. facsim. 25cm.

Part of a letter of Spinoza, contained in Oldenburg's letter to Sir Robert Moray of Oct. 7, 1665, in facsimile, transcript and English translation.
From Philosophy, the journal of the British Institute of Philosophy, vol. X, no. 38, April 1935.

B-3-c ETHICA

Spinoza, Benedictus de, 1632-1677.
Die Ethik des Spinoza im Urtexte, herausgegeben und mit einer Einleitung über dessen Leben, Schriften und Lehre versehen von Hugo Ginsberg ... Leipzig, Erich Koschny (L. Heimann's Verlag) 1875.
4, ₍4₎, ₍5₎-299 p. 19cm.

Bibliography: p. ₍51₎-56.
Pages 291-298 wanting.

Spinoza, Benedictus de, 1632-1677.
Die Ethik des Spinoza im Urtexte, herausgegeben und mit einer Einleitung über dessen Leben, Schriften und Lehre versehen von Hugo Ginsberg ... Leipzig, Erich Koschny (L. Heimann's Verlag) 1875.
4, ₍4₎, ₍5₎-299 p. 19cm.

Bibliography: p. ₍51₎-56.

Spinoza, Benedictus de, 1632-1677.
Benedicti de Spinoza Ethica, ordine geometrico demonstrata. Ex editione Operum quotquot reperta sunt quam curaverant J. van Vloten et J. P. N. Land seorsum repetita. Hagae Comitis, Apud Martinum Nijhoff, 1905.
₍8₎, ₍6₎, 180 p. 26cm.

Spinoza, Benedictus de, 1632-1677.
Benedicti de Spinoza Ethica, ordine geometrico demonstrata. Ex editione Operum quotquot reperta sunt quam curaverant J. van Vloten et J. P. N. Land seorsum repetita. Hagae Comitis, Apud Martinum Nijhoff, 1914.
[8], 180 p. 26cm.

Manuscript corrections in margins.

Spinoza, Benedictus de, 1632-1677.
Benedicti de Spinoza Ethica, ordine geometrico demonstrata; testo latino, con note di Giovanni Gentile. Bari, Laterza, 1915.
xviii, 385 p. 22cm. (Classici della filosofia moderna. a cura di B. Croce e G. Gentile. 22)

Original paper covers bound in.

Spinoza, Benedictus de, 1632-1677.
Benedicti de Spinoza Ethica, ordine geometrico demonstrata et in quinque partes distincta. [Muenchen, Rupprecht-Presse, 1920]
181 p. 28cm.

"Zehntes Buch der Rupprecht-Presse zu Muenchen, im Auftrage von Walther C. F. Hirth unter Druckleitung von F. H. Ehmcke."
No. 141 of 150 copies.

Spinoza, Benedictus de, 1632-1677.
Benedicti de Spinoza Ethica, ordine geometrico demonstrata; testo latino, con note di Giovanni Gentile. Seconda edizione, riveduta da Tommaso Fiore. Bari, Gius. Laterza & figli, 1933.
xviii, 385, [1] p. 22cm. (Classici della filosofia moderna; collana di testi e di traduzioni. XXII)

Bibliographical references included in "Note" (p. [289]-370)

Spinoza, Benedictus de, 1632-1677.
Rozprava o zdokonalení rozumu a Ethika po geometricku vyložená. Přeložili Frant. Krejčí, Čestmír Stehlík a Alois Stejskal. V Praze, Nákladem České akademie věd a umění, 1925.
xli, 339 p. 24cm. (Added t.-p.: Filosofická biblioteka, vydávaná I. Třídou České akademie věd a umění. Řada II. Číslo 4. Benedikta de Spinozy Spisy filosofické, I.)

Original paper cover, dated 1926, bound in.
Bibliography: p. [v]-viii.

Spinoza, Benedictus de, 1632-1677.
Etik. Oversat og forsynet med indledning og noter af S. V. Rasmussen. København, Levin & Munksgaards forlag, 1933.
xx, 319 p. 27cm.

At head of title: Baruch de Spinoza.
Original paper covers bound in.
Bibliographical references included in "Noter" (p. [211]-295)

Spinoza, Benedictus de, 1632-1677.
Ethica, op de wijze der meetkunde behandeld en verdeeld in vijf hoofdstukken welke handelen: I. Over God. II. Over den aard en den oorsprong van de ziel. III. Over den oorsprong en den aard der aandoeningen. IV. Over 's menschen dienstbaarheid of de macht der aandoeningen. V. Over de macht van het verstand of 's menschen vrijheid. Uit het Latijn door W. Meijer. Amsterdam, S. L. van Looy [189-?]
324 p. fold. table. 19cm.

Spinoza, Benedictus de, 1632-1677.
Ethica, op de wijze der meetkunde behandeld en verdeeld in vijf hoofdstukken welke handelen: I. Over God. II. Over den aard en den oorsprong van de ziel. III. Over den oorsprong en den aard der aandoeningen. IV. Over 's menschen dienstbaarheid of de macht der aandoeningen. V. Over de macht van het verstand of 's menschen vrijheid. Uit het Latijn door W. Meijer. Amsterdam, S. L. van Looy [1895]

CONTINUED ON NEXT CARD

Spinoza, Benedictus de, 1632-1677. Ethica. [1895] (Card 2)

324 p. fold. table. 19cm. (On cover: Klassieke schrijvers, 32-[36] Spinoza's werken. II)

Original paper cover of first part bound in.

Spinoza, Benedictus de, 1632-1677.
Ethica, van Benedictus de Spinoza. Vertaald door H. Gorter. 's-Gravenhage, Loman en Funke, 1895.
iii, 288 p. 25cm.

Spinoza, Benedictus de, 1632-1677.
Ethica, op meetkundige wijze uiteengezet en verdeeld in vijf hoofdstukken, handelende: [I.] Over God. II. Over den aard en den oorsprong der ziel. II. [!] Over den oorsprong en den aard der aandoeningen. IV. Over 's menschen dienstbaarheid of de krachten der aandoeningen. V. Over de kracht van het verstand of 's menschen vrijheid. Uit het Latijn door W. Meijer. Tweede druk. Amsterdam, S. L. van Looy, 1905.
xviii, 315 p. fold. tab. (On publisher's binding: Klassieke schrijvers)

Spinoza, Benedictus de, 1632-1677.
Benedictus de Spinoza, Ethica. Vertaald door J. C. Logemann. [Nieuwe uitg.] Amsterdam, Cohen zonen [1915]
276 p. 22cm. (De groote denkers der eeuwen; algemeene bibliotheek van wijsbegeerte [IV])

Spinoza, Benedictus de, 1632-1677.
Ethica, op meetkundige wijze uiteengezet. Uit het Latijn door Dr. W. Meijer. Derde druk. Amsterdam, S. L. van Looy, 1923.
liv, 333 p. port. 23cm.

Spinoza, Benedictus de, 1632-1677.
Ethica, in meetkundigen trant uiteengezet; vertaald, ingeleid en toegelicht door Jhr. Dr. Nico van Suchtelen. Tweede, herziene druk ... Met 2 portretten. [Amsterdam, Wereldbibliotheek, 1928.
xx, 405 p. ports. 19cm. (Wereldbibliotheek, 317)

Bibliographical footnotes.

Spinoza, Benedictus de, 1632–1677.
The Ethics of Benedict de Spinoza. Demonstrated after the method of geometers, and divided into five parts, in which are treated separately: I. Of God. II. Of the soul. III. Of the affections or passions. IV. Of man's slavery, or the force of the passions. V. Of man's freedom, or the power of the understanding. From the Latin. With an introductory sketch of his life and writings ... New York, D. Van Nostrand, 1876.
xxxvii, [1], 338 p. 22½cm.
Translator's preface signed: D. D. S. [Daniel Drake Smith?]
1. Ethics. I. Smith, Daniel Drake, supposed tr. II. Title.
11—19196
Library of Congress B3973.E5S5
[43d1]

Spinoza, Benedictus de, 1632-1677.
Ethic, demonstrated in geometrical order and divided into five parts, which treat I. Of God. II. Of the nature and origin of the mind. III. Of the origin and nature of the affects. IV. Of human bondage, or of the strength of the affects. V. Of the power of the intellect, or of human liberty. By Benedict de Spinoza. Translated from the Latin by William Hale White. London, Trübner & Co., 1883.
xxxviii, 297 p. 22cm. (The English and foreign philosophical library, vol. XXI)

Spinoza, Benedictus de, 1632-1677.
The Ethics of Benedict de Spinoza, demonstrated after the methods of geometers and divided into five parts in which are treated separately I. Of God, II. Of the soul, III. Of the affections or passions, IV. Of man's slavery, or the force of the passions, V. Of man's freedom, or the power of the understanding. From the Latin, with an introductory sketch of Spinoza's life and writings.

CONTINUED ON NEXT CARD

Spinoza, Benedictus de, 1632-1677. The Ethics of Benedict de Spinoza. 1888. (Card 2)

New York, D. Van Nostrand, G. P. Putnam's sons, 1888.
xxxvii, 338 p.

"Translator's preface" signed: D. D. S. [Daniel Drake Smith?]
Bibliographical footnotes.

Spinoza, Benedictus de, 1632-1677.
Ethic: demonstrated in geometrical order and divided into five parts, which treat (1) of God; (2) of the nature and origin of the mind; (3) of the nature and origin of the affects; (4) of human bondage, or of the strength of the affects; (5) of the power of the intellect, or of human liberty. Tr. from the Latin of Benedict de Spinoza by W. Hale White; translation revised by Amelia Hutchison Stirling. 2d ed., rev. and corr., with new preface. London, T. Fisher Unwin, 1894.
cv, 297 p. 23cm.
Manuscript notes in margins.

Spinoza, Benedictus de, 1632–1677.
Ethic demonstrated in geometrical order, and divided into five parts, which treat (1) of God; (2) of the nature & origin of the mind; (3) of the nature & origin of the affects; (4) of human bondage, or of the strength of the affects; (5) of the power of the intellect, or of human liberty. Translated from the Latin of Benedict de Spinoza by W. Hale White; translation revised by Amelia Hutchison Stirling ... 3d ed., rev. and corr. London, Duckworth & co., 1899.
cv, 297, [1] p. 23cm.
1. Ethics. I. White, William Hale, 1831-1913, tr. II. Stirling, Amelia Hutchison.
44-36296
Library of Congress B3973.E5W5 1899
[2]

Spinoza, Benedictus de, 1632–1677.

Ethic: demonstrated in geometrical order and divided into five parts, which treat (1) of God; (2) of the nature and origin of the mind; (3) of the nature & origin of the affects; (4) of human bondage, or of the strength of the affects; (5) of the power of the intellect, or of human liberty. Translated from the Latin of Benedict de Spinoza by W. Hale White; translation revised by Amelia Hutchison Stirling ... 4th ed., rev. and cor. London, New York [etc.] ~~H. Frowde, 1910.~~ H. Milford, 1923.

xcix, 297, [1] p. 23 cm.

1. Ethics. I. White, William Hale, 1831–1913, tr. II. Stirling, Amelia Hutchison, tr.

Newberry Library for Library of Congress [B3973.E5W] [a51k½] A 11—2579

Spinoza, Benedictus de, 1632–1677.

Ethic: demonstrated in geometrical order and divided into five parts, which treat (1) of God; (2) of the nature and origin of the mind; (3) of the nature & origin of the affects; (4) of human bondage, or of the strength of the affects; (5) of the power of the intellect, or of human liberty. Translated from the Latin of Benedict de Spinoza by W. Hale White; translation revised by Amelia Hutchison Stirling ... 4th ed., rev. and cor. London, New York [etc.] H. Frowde, 1910.

xcix, 297, [1] p. 23 cm.

1. Ethics. I. White, William Hale, 1831–1913, tr. II. Stirling, Amelia Hutchison, tr.

Newberry Library for Library of Congress [B3973.E5W] [a51k½] A 11—2579

Spinoza, Benedictus de, 1632–1677.

Spinoza's Ethics and "De intellectus emendatione." London, J. M. Dent & sons, ltd.; New York, E. P. Dutton & co. [1910]

xlviii, [1], 263 p. 17½ cm. (*Half-title:* Everyman's library, ed. by Ernest Rhys. [No. 481] Philosophy & theology)

"Translated by A. Boyle; introduction by George Santayana."

"Treatise on the correction of the understanding (Tratatus de intellectus emendatione) and on the way in which it may be directed towards a true knowledge of things": p. [225]–263.

"A list of the works of Spinoza": p. xxiii.

1. Ethics.

[B3973.E5B] A 11-32

Union Theol. Sem. Libr. for Library of Congress [a55c²1]

Spinoza, Benedictus de, 1632–1677.

Spinoza's Ethics and "De intellectus emendatione." London, J. M. Dent & sons, ltd.; New York, E. P. Dutton & co. ~~[1910]~~ c1913.

xlviii, [1], 263 p. 17½ cm. (*Half-title:* Everyman's library, ed. by Ernest Rhys. [No. 481] Philosophy & theology)

"Translated by A. Boyle; introduction by George Santayana."

"Treatise on the correction of the understanding (Tratatus de intellectus emendatione) and on the way in which it may be directed towards a true knowledge of things": p. [225]–263.

"A list of the works of Spinoza": p. xxiii.

1. Ethics.

[B3973.E5B] A 11-32

Union Theol. Sem. Libr. for Library of Congress [a55c²1]

Spinoza, Benedictus de, 1632–1677.

Ethic: demonstrated in geometrical order and divided into five parts, which treat (1) of God; (2) of the nature and origin of the mind; (3) of the nature & origin of the affects; (4) of human bondage, or of the strength of the affects; (5) of the power of the intellect, or of human liberty. Translated from the Latin of Benedict de Spinoza by W. Hale White; translation revised by Amelia Hutchison Stirling ... 4th ed., rev. and cor. London, New York [etc.] ~~H. Frowde, 1910.~~ H. Milford, Oxford University Press, 1927.

xcix, 297, [1] p. 23 cm.

1. Ethics. I. White, William Hale, 1831–1913, tr. II. Stirling, Amelia Hutchison, tr.

Newberry Library for Library of Congress [B3973.E5W] [a51k½] A 11—2579

Spinoza, Benedictus de, 1632–1677.

Spinoza's Ethics and "De intellectus emendatione." London, J. M. Dent & sons, ltd.; New York, E. P. Dutton & co. ~~[1910]~~ c1928.

xlviii, [1], 263 p. 17½ cm. (*Half-title:* Everyman's library, ed. by Ernest Rhys. [No. 481] Philosophy & theology)

"Translated by A. Boyle; introduction by George Santayana."

"Treatise on the correction of the understanding (Tratatus de intellectus emendatione) and on the way in which it may be directed towards a true knowledge of things": p. [225]–263.

"A list of the works of Spinoza": p. xxiii.

1. Ethics.

[B3973.E5B] A 11-32

Union Theol. Sem. Libr. for Library of Congress [a55c²1]

Spinoza, Benedictus de, 1632–1677.

Ethic: demonstrated in geometrical order and divided into five parts, which treat (1) of God; (2) of the nature and origin of the mind; (3) of the nature & origin of the affects; (4) of human bondage, or of the strength of the affects; (5) of the power of the intellect, or of human liberty. Translated from the Latin of Benedict de Spinoza by W. Hale White; translation revised by Amelia Hutchison Stirling ... 4th ed., rev. and cor. London, New York [etc.] ~~H. Frowde, 1910.~~ H. Milford, Oxford University Press, 1930.

xcix, 297, [1] p. 23 cm.

1. Ethics. I. White, William Hale, 1831–1913, tr. II. Stirling, Amelia Hutchison, tr.

Newberry Library for Library of Congress [B3973.E5W] [a51k½] A 11—2579

Spinoza, Benedictus de, 1632–1677.

Ethics [of] Spinoza. London, J. M. Dent & sons, ltd.; New York, E. P. Dutton & co., inc. [1934]

xlviii p., 1 l., 263 p. diagrs. 17½ cm. (*Half-title:* Everyman's library, ed. by Ernest Rhys. Philosophy & theology. [no. 481])

"First published in this edition 1910; reprinted ... 1934."

"Translated by A. Boyle; introduction by George Santayana."

"Treatise on the correction of the understanding (tractatus de intellectus emendatione) and on the way in which it may be directed towards a true knowledge of things": p. [225]–263.

"A list of the works of Spinoza": p. xxiii.

1. Ethics. I. Boyle, Andrew, tr.

36—37585

Library of Congress AC1.E8 no. 481 [50d1] 171

Spinoza, Benedictus de, 1632–1677.

Ethics [of] Spinoza. London, J. M. Dent & sons, ltd.; New York, E. P. Dutton & co., inc. ~~[1934]~~ c1938.

xlviii p., 1 l., 263 p. diagrs. 17½ cm. (*Half-title:* Everyman's library, ed. by Ernest Rhys. Philosophy & theology. [no. 481])

"First published in this edition 1910; reprinted ... 1934."

"Translated by A. Boyle; introduction by George Santayana."

"Treatise on the correction of the understanding (tractatus de intellectus emendatione) and on the way in which it may be directed towards a true knowledge of things": p. [225]–263.

"A list of the works of Spinoza": p. xxiii.

1. Ethics. I. Boyle, Andrew, tr.

36—37585

Library of Congress AC1.E8 no. 481 [50d1] 171

Spinoza, Benedictus de, 1632-1677.

De la droite manière de vivre, par B. de Spinoza. Traduite en français et annotée par J.-G. Prat. 2. éd., entièrement rev. et corr. Paris, G. Decaux, 1877.

x, 102 p. 14cm.

Original paper covers bound in.

An excerpt from the 4th book of the Ethics.

Spinoza, Benedictus de, 1632-1677.
Ethique; traduit et annotée par J. G. Prat. Paris, Librairie Hachette, 1880-83.
cover-title, 2 v. 28cm.

Contents.--v. 1. De Dieu.--v. 2. De l'âme.

Spinoza, Benedictus de, 1632-1677.
Éthique; traduction nouvelle de Raoul Lantzenberg, avec préface, table analytique et notes. Paris, E. Flammarion [1908]
viii, 345 p. facsim. 19cm.

Spinoza, Benedictus de, 1632-1677.
Éthique; traduction inédite du comte Henri de Boulainvilliers, publiée avec une introduction et des notes par F. Colonna d'Istria. Paris, A. Colin, 1907.
xliii, 374 p. 23cm.

"Bibliographie des ouvrages de Boulainvilliers qui ont été consultés pour cette édition": p. [372]-374.

Spinoza, Benedictus de, 1632-1677.
Éthique, démontrée suivant l'ordre géométrique et divisée en cinq parties. Texte latin soigneusement revu. Traduction nouvelle, notice et notes par Ch. Appuhn. Paris, Garnier frères, 1909.
710 p. 19cm.

Lettered in manuscript on spine: Oeuvres de Spinoza traduites par Ch. Appuhn. III.
Bibliothèque nationale catalogue lists a

CONTINUED ON NEXT CARD

Spinoza, Benedictus de, 1632-1677. Éthique. 1909. (Card 2)

1908 edition of Appuhn's translation of the Ethics as v. [4] of the Oeuvres de Spinoza.
Original paper cover bound in.

Spinoza, Benedictus de, 1632-1677.
Spinoza, Éthique. Introduction, traduction et notes par Gilbert Maire. Paris, La Renaissance du livre [1929]
181 p. port. 15cm. (Les cent chefs-d'oeuvre étrangers)

Original paper covers bound in.
Adolphe S. Oko's initials on paper cover.
Bibliography: p. 25-26.

Spinoza, Benedictus de, 1632-1677.
L'Éthique de Spinoza; traduction nouvelle par A. Guérinot, préface de Léon Brunschvicg. Paris, Éditions d'art Édouard Pelletan, 1930.
2 v. (xxxii, 732 p.) ports. 16cm. (Philosophes et moralistes, 11)

No. 658 of 1280 copies.

Spinoza, Benedictus de, 1632-1677.
... Éthique, démontrée suivant l'ordre géométrique et divisée en cinq parties; traduction nouvelle avec notice et notes par Charles Appuhn ... Paris, Garnier frères [1934]
2v. in 1. 19cm. (On cover: Classiques Garnier)

At head of title: Spinoza.
Latin and French on opposite pages.

1. Ethics. I. Appuhn, Charles, 1862- tr.

35-28553

Library of Congress B3971.A6
[2] 171

Spinoza, Benedictus de, 1632-1677.
B. v. S. Sittenlehre, widerleget von dem berühmten Weltweisen unserer Zeit Herrn Christian Wolf. Aus dem Lateinischen übersetzet. Frankfurt und Leipzig [Herold] 1744.
598, 128 p. port. 18cm.

Includes Spinoza's Ethics in German translation and Wolff's refutation.

Spinoza, Benedictus de, 1632-1677.
Spinoza's Ethik. Gera, In der Bekmannschen Buchhandlung, 1790-93.
2 v. in 1. 20cm. (His Philosophische Schriften, 2.-3. Bd.)

Spinoza, Benedictus de, 1632-1677.
Spinoza's Ethik ... Neue unveränderte Auflage. Leipzig, bey Adam Friedrich Böhme, 1796.
2 v. in 1. 20cm. (His Philosophische Schriften, 2.-3. Bd.)

Vol. 1 lacks series note.

Spinoza, Benedictus de, 1632-1677.
Benedikt von Spinoza's Ethik, nebst den Briefen, welche sich auf die Gegenstände der Ethik beziehen, aus dem Lateinischen übersetzt von Friedr. Wilh. Valent. Schmidt. 1. Bd. Die Ethik enthaltend. Berlin und Stettin, Bei Friedrich Nicolai, 1812.
viii, 431 p. 22cm.

No more published.

Spinoza, Benedictus de, 1632-1677.
Benedict von Spinoza's Ethik. Uebersetzt, erläutert und mit einer Lebensbeschreibung Spinoza's versehen von J. H. v. Kirchmann. Berlin, L. Heimann, 1868.
viii, 258 p. 20cm. (Philosophische Bibliothek. 4. Bd.)

Bound with the author's Kurzgefasste Abhandlung von Gott, dem Menschen und dessen Glück. 1869.

Spinoza, Benedictus de, 1632-1677.
Benedict von Spinoza's Ethik. Uebersetzt, erläutert und mit einer Lebensbeschreibung Spinoza's versehen von J. H. v. Kirchmann. 2. Aufl. Berlin, L. Heimann, 1870.
viii, 258 p. 20cm.

Added t.-p.: Benedict von Spinoza's Sämmtliche philosophische Werke, uebersetzt von J. H. von Kirchmann und Prof. Schaarschmidt. 1. Bd. Berlin, L. Heimann, 1868.
Original paper cover, dated 1872, bound in.

Spinoza, Benedictus de, 1632-1677.
Benedict von Spinoza's Ethik. Uebersetzt, erläutert und mit einer Lebensbeschreibung Spinoza's versehen von J. H. v. Kirchmann. 2. Aufl. Berlin, L. Heimann, 1870.
viii, 258 p. 20cm. (Philosophische Bibliothek. 4. Bd.)

Spinoza, Benedictus de, 1632-1677.
Benedict von Spinoza's Ethik. Uebersetzt, erläutert und mit einer Lebensbeschreibung Spinoza's versehen von J. H. v. Kirchmann. 4. verb. Aufl. Heidelberg, G. Weiss, 1886.
xv, 255 p. 19cm. (Philosophische Bibliothek. 4. Bd.)
Original paper cover bound in.

Spinoza, Benedictus de, 1632-1677.
Die Ethik; neu übersetzt und mit einem einleitenden Vorwort versehen von J. Stern. Leipzig, Reclam ⌊pref. 1887⌋
408 p. 15cm.

Ms. notes by Carl Gebhardt, with his signature on t.-p.

Spinoza, Benedictus de, 1632-1677.
Benedict von Spinoza's Ethik. Uebersetzt, erläutert und mit einer Lebensbeschreibung Spinoza's versehen von J. H. v. Kirchmann. 5. verb. Aufl. Berlin, Philos.-histor. Verlag ⌊1893⌋
x, 268 p. 20cm. (Philosophische Bibliothek. 4. Bd.)

Spinoza, Benedictus de, 1632-1677.
Ethik. Übersetzt und mit einer Einleitung und einem Register versehen von Otto Baensch. Leipzig, Verlag der Dürr'schen Buchhandlung, 1905.
xxvi, 311 p. 19cm. (Philosophische Bibliothek, Band 92)

Ms. notes by Carl Gebhardt, with his signature on t.-p.
Bibliographical references included in "Vorwort" (p. ⌊iii⌋-viii)

Spinoza, Benedictus de, 1632-1677.
Spinozas Ethik. In verkürzter Übersetzung herausgegeben von Dr. M. Kronenberg. ⌊Stuttgart, Greiner und Pfeffer ⌊1908⌋
201 p. illus. 20cm. (Bücher der Weisheit und Schönheit)

Title-page mutilated.

Spinoza, Benedictus de, 1632-1677.
Die Ethik, von Baruch Spinoza. Deutsch von Dr. Carl Vogl. Leipzig, Alfred Kröner Verlag ₍pref. 1909₎
148 p. 24cm. (Kröners Volksausgabe)

Original paper covers bound in.

Spinoza, Benedictus de, 1632-1677.
Die ethik, von B. Spinoza; neu übersetzt und mit einem einleitenden vorwort versehen von J. Stern. 2. aufl. Leipzig, P. Reclam jun. ₍1909₎
402 p. diagrs. 15cm.

1. Ethics. I. Stern, Jakob, 1843-1911, tr.

44-14058

Library of Congress B3973.G5S7 1909 ₍2₎

Spinoza, Benedictus de, 1632-1677.
Ethik. Übersetzt und mit einer Einleitung und einem Register versehen von Otto Baensch. 7. (der neuen Übersetzung 2., verb.) Aufl. Leipzig, Verlag von Felix Meiner ₍1910₎
xxix, 315 p. 19cm. (Philosophische Bibliothek, Band 92)

Bibliographical references included in "Vorwort zur ersten Auflage" (p. ₍iii₎-viii)
Ms. notes in margins.

Spinoza, Benedictus de, 1632-1677.
Ethik. ₍Nach der Übersetzung von Berthold Auerbach herausgegeben von Artur Buchenau₎ Berlin, Deutsche Bibliothek ₍1914₎
xii, 269 p. 18cm. ₍Deutsche Bibliothek, Bd. 87₎

Bibliography: p. ₍vii₎

Spinoza, Benedictus de, 1632-1677.
Ethik, übers. und mit einer Einleitung und einem Register versehen von Otto Baensch. 9., mit der 7. gleichlautende Aufl. Leipzig, Verlag von Felix Meiner, 1919.
xxix, 315 p. 20cm. (Der Philosophischen Bibliothek Bd. 92)

Original paper covers bound in.
On cover: Neunte, mit der siebenten und achten gleichlautende Auflage.

Spinoza, Benedictus de, 1632-1677.
Ethik; übersetzt von Otto Baensch. ₍Darmstadt, Ernst Ludwig Presse, 1920₎
320 p. 27cm.

"Sechsundzwanzigstes Buch der Ernst Ludwig Presse zu Darmstadt. Hergestellt in 150 Abzügen, davon 50 auf Japanbütten. Begonnen 1914 durch Ch. H. Kleukens. Beendet 1920 durch Karl Simon in Darmstadt."

Spinoza, Benedictus de, 1632-1677.
Ethik; übersetzt von Otto Baensch. ₍Darmstadt, Ernst Ludwig Presse, 1920₎
320 p. 27cm.

"Sechsundzwanzigstes Buch der Ernst Ludwig Presse zu Darmstadt. Hergestellt in 150 Abzügen, davon 50 auf Japanbütten. Begonnen 1914 durch Ch. H. Kleukens. Beendet 1920 durch Karl Simon in Darmstadt."
Printed on Japan paper.

Spinoza, Benedictus de, 1632-1677.
Benedictus de Spinoza, Die Ethik, nach Art der Geometrie dargestellt. Neu übersetzt von J. Stern. 3. Aufl. Mit einer Einleitung von Werner Schingnitz. Leipzig, Verlag von Philipp Reclam jun. ₍pref. 1923₎
420 p. 15cm. ₍Philipp Reclam's Universal-Bibliothek, 2361-64₎

Spinoza, Benedictus de, 1632-1677.
Die Ethik von Baruch Spinoza. Deutsch von Carl Vogl. Leipzig, Alfred Kröner Verlag, 1923.
272 p. 17cm. (Kröners Taschenausgabe, Band 24)

Spinoza, Benedictus de, 1632-1677.
Die Ethik. ₍Übertragen von Rudolf Borch, herausgegeben von Richard Hirsch₎ Berlin und Wien, Hans Heinrich Tilgner Verlag, 1924.
231 p. 22cm.

Presentation copy to Carl Gebhardt, with the translator's inscription and signature.

Spinoza, Benedictus, 1632-1677.
Die Ethik von Benedictus de Spinoza. Deutsch von Carl Vogl. Mit einer Einleitung von Friedrich Bülow. Leipzig, A. Kröner [1929]
xxxii, 274 p. port. (Króners Taschenausgabe, Band 24)

Spinoza, Benedictus de, 1632-1677.
חקר אלוה עם תורת האדם, מתורגם ... עם מבוא ... מאת
שלמה ראבין ... ויען, בדפוס של ג. בראג, תרמ"ה.
[Wien, 1885]
lxiv, 288 p. 19 cm.
"לוח המלות": p. [lvi]–lxiv.
Added t.-p.: Ethica ... Die Ethik (Tugendlehre), hebräisch übersetzt nebst ausführlicher Einleitung und erläuternden Noten von Dr. S. Rubin.

1. Ethics. I. Rubin, Salomon, 1823–1910, tr. II. Title.
Title transliterated: Ḥeḳer Eloah.

A 47-5117*

Spinoza, Benedictus de, 1632-1677.
תורת־המדות מאת ברוך שפינוזה, מתור־
גמה מרומית על־ידי יעקב קלצקין, בצרוף
הקדמה, הערות, מראה־מקומות, תרגומי
המונחים ובאוריהם. ליפסיה בהוצאת אב־
רהם יוסף שטיבל תרפ"ד.

[Leipzig, 1924]
xxi, 404 p. ports. 21cm. (כתבי ברוך
שפינוזה מתרגמים מן המקור)

Title transliterated: Tōrath ha-middōth.

Spinoza, Benedictus de, 1632-1677.
L'Etica. Della correzicne dell'intelletto. Traduzione sull'edizione di J. V. Vloten et J. P. N. Land di Mario Rosazza. Milano, Fratelli Bocca editori, 1913.
xxxi, 303 p. 24cm. (On cover: Biblioteca di scienze moderne, no. 61)

Original paper covers bound in.

Spinoza, Benedictus de, 1632-1677.
Ethica; parti I. e II. ed estratti delle parti III., IV. e V. con introduzione, commento e nota bibliografica a cura di Augusto Guzzo. Firenze, Vallecchi editore [1924]
230, [1] p. 20cm. (On cover: Testi filosofici commentati)

"Nota bibliografica": p. [203]-228.
Presentation copy to Carl Gebhardt, with editor's inscription and signature.

Spinoza, Benedictus de, 1632-1677.
L'Etica; esposta e commentata da Piero Martinetti. Torino, G. B. Paravia & C., 1928.
xii, 150 p. port. 20cm. (On cover: Piccola biblioteca di filosofia e pedagogia)

Original paper covers bound in.

Spinoza, Benedictus de, 1632-1677.
L'Etica. Nuova traduzione dall'originale latino con introduzione e note di Erminio Troilo. Milano, Casa editrice Bietti [1933]
339 p. 18cm.

Original paper covers bound in.

Spinoza, Benedictus de, 1632-1677.
L'Etica. Esposta e commentata da Piero Martinetti. Torino, G. B. Paravia & C. [1933]
xii, 150 p. port. 20cm. (On cover: Piccola biblioteca di filosofia e pedagogia)

Original paper covers bound in.

Spinoza, Benedictus de, 1632-1677.
Supinoza tetsugaku taikei (Echika) Obi Hanji yaku. [Tokyo] Iwanami shoten [1922]
5, 4, 510, 21 p. 23cm.

Spinoza, Benedictus de, 1632-1677.
Etik. Översättning med en inledning av Alf Ahlberg. Stockholm, Björck & Börjesson [1922]
299 p. port. 23cm. (On cover: Berömda filosofer. XX)

Original paper covers bound in.

B-3-c
228

Societatea Română de Filosofie.
B. Spinoza 250 ani dela moarte. Filosofia lui Spinoza, de Dr. I. Brucăr. B. Spinoza: Etica, traducere din limba latină de Prof. S. Katz. București, 1930.
clxxvii, vi, 223 p. port. 24cm. (Revista de filosofie, volumul XII (seria nouă))

The translation of the Ethics has special t.-p.
Bibliography: p. [clxxiii]-clxxvii.
Original paper covers bound in.

B-3-c
229

Spinoza, Benedictus de, 1632-1677.
Бенедикта Спинозы Этика изложенная геометрическимъ методомъ и раздѣленная на пять частей, въ коихъ разсуждается: I. О Богѣ. II. О природѣ и началѣ души. III. О началѣ и природѣ аффектовъ. IV. О рабствѣ человѣческомъ или о силѣ аффектовъ. V. О власти разума или о человѣческой свободѣ. Переводъ съ латинскаго подъ редакціею проф. В. И. Модестова. Изд. 4. С.-Петербургъ, Изданіе Л. Ф. Пантелѣева, 1904.
[6], 327 p. 23cm.

Title transliterated: Benedikta Spinozy Ėtika.

B-3-c
230

Spinoza, Benedictus de, 1632-1677.
Этика, доказанная въ геометрическомъ порядкѣ и раздѣленная на пять частей ... Переводъ съ латинскаго Н. А. Иванцова. Изд. 2-е. Москва, И. Н. Кушнеревъ, 1911.
384 p. port. 25cm. (Труды Московскаго психологическаго общества, вып. V)

Title transliterated: Etika.

B-3-c
231

Spinoza, Benedictus de, 1632-1677.
Этика, доказанная в геометрическом порядке и разделенная на пять частей ... [Набор сделан с издания, переведенного с латинского языка Н. А. Иванцовым. Ответственная редакция А. К. Топоркова] Москва, Гос. социально-эконом. изд-во, 1932.
222 p. port. 20cm.

Title transliterated: Etika.
Added t.-p. in Latin.

B-3-c
232

Spinoza, Benedictus de, 1632-1677.
... Ética. Versión castellana de Manuel Machado. París, Casa Editorial Garnier Hermanos [1920]
410 p. 19cm. (On cover: Biblioteca de autores célebres)

At head of title: Espinosa.
Original paper covers bound in.

B-3-c
233

Spinoza, Benedictus de, 1632-1677.
... Etica. Traducción de Juan Carlos Bardé. Prólogo y notas de V. E. Lollini. Madrid, Buenos Aires, Librería Perlado [©1940]
2 p. l., [vii]-xvii, 293 p., 2 l. diagrs. 16cm. (*Half-title:* Biblioteca clásica universal; dirección literaria de F. F. Corso. 6)
At head of title: Espinosa.
Bibliographical foot-notes.

1. Ethics. I. Bardé, Juan Carlos, tr. II. Lollini, V. E., ed. III. Title.

A 43-1979

Harvard univ. Library
for Library of Congress [2]

B-3-c
234

Spinoza, Benedictus de, 1632-1677.
די עטיק (דערוויזן אויף א געאמעט-
רישן אופן) אין פינף טיילן. יידיש:
ו. נאמאנסאן. שיקאגא, פארלאג "נייע
געזעלשאפט".
[Chicago, 1923]
317 p. mounted port. 25cm.

Title transliterated: Di etik.

B-3-c
235

Spinoza, Benedictus de, 1632-1677.
די עטיק (דערוויזן אויף א געאמעט-
רישן אופן) אין פינף טיילן [פון] ברוך
שפינאזא. יידיש: ו. נאמאנסאן. וואר-
שע, פארלאג "קולטור-ליגע" [1928]
[Warsaw, 1928]
317 p. port. 24cm.

Title transliterated: Di etik.

B-3-d
RENATI DES CARTES
PRINCIPIA AND COGITATA METAPHYSICA

B-3-d
236

Spinoza, Benedictus de, 1632-1677.
Renati Des Cartes Principiorum philosophiæ pars I, & II, more geometrico demonstratæ per Benedictum de Spinoza ... Accesserunt ejusdem Cogitata metaphysica, in quibus difficiliores, quæ tam in parte metaphysices generali, quàm speciali occurrunt, quæstiones breviter explicantur ... Amstelodami, apud Johannem Riewerts, 1663.
8 p. l., 140 p. illus. 21 x 16½cm.

1. Descartes, René, 1596-1650.

11-16419

Library of Congress B1875.S7
[39b1]

B-3-d
237

Spinoza, Benedictus de, 1632-1677.
Renatus des Cartes Beginzelen der wysbegeerte, I en II deel, na de meetkonstige wijze beweezen door Benedictus de Spinoza Amsterdammer. Mitsgaders des zelfs Overnatuurkundige gedachten, in welke de zwaarste geschillen, die zoo in't algemeen, als in't byzonder deel der overnatuurkunde ontmoeten, kortelijk werden verklaart. Alles uit 't Latijn vertaalt door P. B. t' Amsterdam, by Jan Rieuwertsz, 1664.
[12], 168, [6] p. 20cm.

Spinoza, Benedictus de, 1632-1677.
The principles of Descartes' philosophy, by Benedictus de Spinoza (the philosopher's earliest work) tr. from the Latin, with an introduction by Halbert Hains Britan, PH. D. Chicago, The Open court publishing company; [etc., etc.] 1905.
5 p. l., lxxxi, 177 p. port., diagrs. 19½ cm. (On cover: Philosophical classics. Religion of science library, no. 59)
"Appendix, containing Cogitata metaphysica ...": p. 113-177.

1. Descartes, René, 1596-1650. I. Britan, Halbert Hains, 1874-1945, tr.

Spinoza, Benedictus de, 1632-1677.
René Descartes' Prinzipien der Philosophie, erster und zweiter Theil. In geometrischer Weise begründet durch Benedict von Spinoza. Mit einem Anhang: Metaphysische Gedanken des Letztern ... Uebers. und erläutert von J. H. v. Kirchmann. Berlin, L. Heimann, 1871.
xxv, 170 p. 20cm. (Philosophische Bibliothek, 41. Bd.)

Bound with the author's Ethik. 1870.

Spinoza, Benedictus de, 1632-1677.
I. Descartes' Prinzipien der Philosophie auf geometrische Weise begründet. II. Anhang, enthaltend Metaphysische Gedanken. 3. Aufl. Neu übers. und hrsg. von Artur Buchenau. Leipzig, Verlag der Dürr'schen Buchhandlung, 1907.
viii, 190 p. diagrs. 19cm. (Philosophische Bibliothek; Verlag von Felix Meiner. Bd. 94)

Ms. notes by Carl Gebhardt.

Spinoza, Benedictus de, 1632-1677.
Descartes' Prinzipien der Philosophie auf geometrische Weise begründet. Anhang, enthaltend Metaphysische Gedanken. Neu übersetzt und herausgegeben von Dr. Artur Buchenau. 4. Aufl. Leipzig, Verlag von Felix Meiner, 1922.
viii, 190 p. diagrs. 19cm. (Der Philosophischen Bibliothek Band 94)

Bibliographical references included in "Anmerkungen" (p. [165]-177)

B-3-e

STELKONSTIGE REECKENING VAN DE REGENBOOG EN VAN KANSSEN

Spinoza, Benedictus de, 1632-1677.
Stelkonstige reeckening van den regenboog en Reeckening van kanssen. 's-Gravenhage, Martinus Nijhoff, 1883.
cover-title, 18 p. illus. 23cm.

"Afzonderlijke afdruk uit Benedicti de Spinoza Opera quotquot reperta sunt, recognoverunt J. van Vloten et J. P. N. Land, vol. II."
Includes reproduction of t.-p. of the original edition: 's-Gravenhage, Ter Druckerye van Levyn van Dyck, 1687.

Spinoza, Benedictus de, 1632-1677.
Benedictus de Spinoza, "Stelkonstige reeckening van den regenboog" and "Reeckening van kanssen". Two nearly unknown treatises. Leiden, Reimpression by Dr. D. Bierens de Haan, 1884.
[8], 20, 8 p. illus. 22cm.

Includes reproduction of t.-p. of original edition.
Dedicated to the University of Edinburgh at its tercentenary jubilee by D. Bierens de Haan.
Unbound copy with manuscript notes in margins.

Spinoza, Benedictus de, 1632-1677.
Benedictus de Spinoza, "Stelkonstige reeckening van den regenboog" and "Reeckening van kanssen". Two nearly unknown treatises. Leiden, Reimpression by Dr. D. Bierens de Haan, 1884.
[8], 20, 8 p. illus. 22cm.

Includes reproduction of t.-p. of original edition.
Dedicated to the University of Edinburgh at its tercentenary jubilee by D. Bierens de Haan.

B-3-f

TRACTATUS DE DEO ET HOMINE

Spinoza, Benedictus de, 1632-1677.
Benedicti de Spinoza Tractatus de Deo et homine eiusque felicitate lineamenta atque Adnotationes ad Tractatum theologico politicum; edidit et illustravit Eduardus Boehmer. Halae ad Salam, J. F. Lippert, 1852.
63 p. 27cm.

Latin text and Dutch translation in opposite columns.
Ms. notes by A. S. Oko on flyleaf.

Spinoza, Benedictus de, 1632-1677.
Benedicti de Spinoza "Korte verhandeling van God, de mensch en deszelfs welstand". Tractatuli deperditi De Deo et homine ejusque felicitate versio belgica. Ad antiquissimi codicis fidem edidit et praefatus est Car. Schaarschmidt. Cum Spinozae imagine chromolithographica. Amstelodami, Apud Fredericum Muller, 1869.
xxiv [i. e. xxxiv], 135 p. col. port. 25cm.

Bibliographical footnotes.
Ms. notes in pencil by Carl Gebhardt. Ms. notes in ink by A. v. d. Linde, former owner.

Spinoza, Benedictus de, 1632-1677.
Korte verhandeling van God, de mensch en deszelvs welstand. Oorspronkelijk in het Latijn geschreven door B(enedictus) D(e) S(pinoza), en thans uit een Neêrduitsche vertaling der 17de eeuw in de taal van onzen tijd overgebracht door W. Meijer. Amsterdam, S. L. van Looy, 1899.
2 p. l., xxv, 254, [1] p. 19cm.

On publisher's binding: Klassieke schrijvers.

Spinoza, Benedictus de, 1632-1677.
Korte verhandeling van God, de mensch en deszelvs welstand. Oorspronkelijk in het Latijn geschreven door B(enedictus) D(e) S(pinoza), en thans uit een Neêrduitsche vertaling der 17de eeuw in de taal van onzen tijd overgebracht door W. Meijer. Amsterdam, S. L. van Looy, 1899.
2 p. l., xxv, 254, [1] p. 19cm. (On cover: Klassieke schrijvers. Spinoza's werken. IV)

CONTINUED ON NEXT CARD

Spinoza, Benedictus de, 1632-1677. Korte verhandeling van God, de mensch en deszelvs welstand. 1899. (Card 2)

Original paper cover bound in.
Ms. notes by Carl Gebhardt; Gebhardt's signature on t.-p.

Spinoza, Benedictus de, 1632-1677.
Spinoza's Short treatise on God, man and human welfare; tr. from the Dutch by Lydia Gillingham Robinson. Chicago, The Open Court Publishing Co., 1909.
xxiv, 178 p. port. 20cm. (On cover: Philosophical classics. Religion of science library no. 62)

Original paper cover bound in.
A. S. Oko's signature on fly-leaf.

Spinoza, Benedictus de, 1632-1677.
Spinoza's Short treatise on God, man, & his well-being; translated and edited, with an introduction and commentary and a life of Spinoza by A. Wolf. London, A. and C. Black, 1910.
cxxviii, 246 p. plate, port., facsims. 22cm.

Bibliography: p. cxxvii-cxxviii.
Ms. notes by Carl Gebhardt. Presentation copy to Carl Gebhardt, with A. S. Oko's inscription and signature.

Spinoza, Benedictus de, 1632-1677.
Dieu, l'homme et la béatitude, traduit pour la première fois en français et précédé d'une introduction par Paul Janet. Paris, Librairie Germer Baillière et Cie, 1878.
li, 136 p. 18cm. (Bibliothèque de philosophie contemporaine)

At head of title: Supplément aux oeuvres de Spinoza.
Original paper cover bound in. Ms. notes.

Spinoza, Benedictus de, 1632-1677.
B. de Spinoza's kurzgefasste Abhandlung von Gott, dem Menschen und dessen Glück. Aus dem Holländischen zum ersten Male ins Deutsche übers. und mit einem Vorwort begleitet von C. Schaarschmidt. Berlin, L. Heimann, 1869.
xviii, 117 p. 19 cm. (Philosophische Bibliothek. 18. Bd.)

Spinoza, Benedictus de, 1632-1677.
B. de Spinoza's kurzgefasste Abhandlung von Gott, dem Menschen und dessen Glück. Aus dem Holländischen zum ersten Male ins Deutsche übers. und mit einem Vorwort begleitet von C. Schaarschmidt. Berlin, L. Heimann, 1869.
xviii, 117 p. 20 cm. (Philosophische Bibliothek. 18. Bd.)
Pages [xvii]-xviii bound at end.

Spinoza, Benedictus de, 1632-1677.
Benedict de Spinoza's Kurzer tractat von Gott, dem menschen und dessen glückseligkeit. Auf grund einer neuen, von dr. Antonius van der Linde vorgenommenen vergleichung der handschriften ins deutsche übersetzt mit einer einleitung, kritischen und sachlichen erläuterungen begleitet von dr. Christoph Sigwart ... Tübingen, H. Laupp, 1870.
lxiii, [1] p., 1 l., 232 p. 21cm.

1. Ethics. 2. God. I. Linde, Antonius van der, 1833-1897. II. Sigwart, Christoph von, 1830-1904.

Spinoza, Benedictus de, 1632-1677.
B. de Spinoza's Kurzgefasste Abhandlung von Gott, dem Menschen und dessen Glück. Aus dem Holländischen in's Deutsche übersetzt und mit einem Vorwort begleitet von C. Schaarschmidt. 2. verb. Aufl. Berlin, E. Koschny, 1874.
xiii, 117 p. 19cm. (Philosophische Bibliothek, 18. Bd.)

Title-page and preliminary pages lacking.
Bound with the author's Ethik. 1870.

Spinoza, Benedictus de, 1632-1677.
Benedict de Spinoza's Kurzer tractat von Gott, dem menschen und dessen glückseligkeit. Auf grund einer neuen von dr. Antonius van der Linde vorgenommenen vergleichung der handschriften ins deutsche übersetzt mit einer einleitung, kritischen und sachlichen erläuterungen begleitet von dr. Christoph Sigwart ... 2. ausg. Freiburg i. B. und Tübingen, J. C. B. Mohr (P. Siebeck) [1881].
lxiii, [1] p., 1 l., 232 p. 21cm.

Manuscript notes by Carl Gebhardt.

Spinoza, Benedictus de, 1632-1677.
Kurzgefasste Abhandlung von Gott, dem Menschen und dessen Glück. Aus dem Holländischen ins Deutsche übers. und mit einem Vorwort begleitet von C. Schaarschmidt. 3. verb. Aufl. Leipzig, Verlag der Dürr'schen Buchhandlung, 1907.
xi, 128 p. 20cm. (Philosophische Bibliothek, Bd. 91)

Ms. notes by Carl Gebhardt; Gebhardt's signature on t.-p.

Spinoza, Benedictus de, 1632-1677.
Kurze Abhandlung von Gott, dem Menschen und seinem Glück; übertragen und hrsg. von Carl Gebhardt. [4. Aufl.] Leipzig, F. Meiner, 1922.
xxviii, 156 p. 19cm. (Der Philosophischen Bibliothek Bd. 91)

Spinoza, Benedictus de, 1632-1677.
מאמר קצר/ על אלוה/ על האדם ואשרו,
חבר מאת ברוך שפינוזה, ומתורגם מהולנ־
דית על ידי ישעיהו בן יהודה ליב זנה,
בצירוף מבוא והערות. תל־אביב בהוצ'
אברהם, יוסף שטיבל תרצ"ה.
[Berlin, A. J. Stybel, 1935]
248 p. 23cm. (כתבי ברוך שפינוזה)

Title transliterated: Maʾămār qāṣēr ...
Hebrew translation of Tractatus de Deo et homine.

Spinoza, Benedictus de, 1632-1677.
די עטיק (דערוויזן אויף א געאמעט־
רישן אופן) אין פינף טיילן [פון ברוך
שפינאזא. יידיש: וו. נאטאנסאן. ווארר־
שע, פארלאג "קולטור־ליגע" [1928]
[Warsaw, 1928]
517 p. port. 24cm.

Title transliterated: Di etik.

B-3-g
TRACTATUS DE
INTELLECTUS EMENDATIONE
ET DE VIA

Spinoza, Benedictus de, 1632-1677.
Tractatus de intellectus emendatione et de via, qua optime in veram rerum cognitionem dirigitur. Translated from the Latin of Benedict de Spinoza by W. Hale White. Translation revised by Amelia Hutchison Stirling. London, T. Fisher Unwin, 1895.
xxx, 62 p. 19cm.

Spinoza, Benedictus de, 1632-1677.
Tractatus de intellectus emendatione et de via, qua optime in veram rerum cognitionem dirigitur. Translated from the Latin of Benedict de Spinoza by W. Hale White, translation revised by Amelia Hutchison Stirling. London, Duckworth, 1899.
xxx, 62 p. 19cm.

Spinoza, Benedictus de, 1632-1677.
Improvement of the understanding, Ethics and Correspondence of Benedict de Spinoza. Translated from the Latin by R. H. M. Elwes. With an introduction by Frank Sewall. New York, Willey Book Co. [c1901]
xxxiii, 427 p. 21cm.

Spinoza, Benedictus de, 1632-1677.
Improvement of the understanding, Ethics and Correspondence of Benedict de Spinoza. Translated from the Latin by R. H. M. Elwes. With an introduction by Frank Sewall. New York, Aladdin Book Company [c1901]
xxxiii, 427 p. 21cm.

Spinoza, Benedictus de, 1632-1677.
Improvement of the understanding, Ethics and Correspondence of Benedict de Spinoza. Translated from the Latin by R. H. M. Elwes, with an introduction by Frank Sewall. Washington, M. Walter Dunne [c1901]
xxxiii, 427 p. col. front. 24cm. (Universal classics library)

On spine: Edition de luxe.

Spinoza, Benedictus de, 1632-1677.
Improvement of the understanding, Ethics and Correspondence of Benedict de Spinoza. Translated from the Latin by R. H. M. Elwes, with an introduction by Frank Sewall. Washington, M. Walter Dunne [c1901]
xxxiii, 427 p. col. front. 24cm.

Spinoza, Benedictus de, 1632–1677.
... Traité de la réforme de l'entendement et de la meilleure voie à suivre pour parvenir à la vraie connaissance des choses; traduction et notes par A. Koyré ... Paris, J. Vrin, 1937.
2 p. l., [vii]-xxi, 114 p., 1 l. 19cm.
At head of title: B. de Spinoza.
French and Latin on opposite pages.
Bibliographical references in "Notes du traducteur" (p. [95]-114)
Original paper cover, dated 1938, bound in.
1. Science—Methodology. 2. Knowledge, Theory of. I. Koyré, Alexandre, 1892- ed. and tr.
Library of Congress B3955.K8 41-81844
[2] 199.492

Spinoza, Benedictus de, 1632-1677.
Abhandlung über die Verbesserung des Verstandes. Abhandlung vom Staate. 3. Aufl. Übertragen und eingeleitet nebst Anmerkungen und Register von Carl Gebhardt. Leipzig, Verlag der Dürr'schen Buchhandlung, 1907.
xxxii, 214 p. 19cm. (Philosophische Bibliothek. Bd. 95)
Bibliography: p. xxxi-xxxii.

CONTINUED ON NEXT CARD

Spinoza, Benedictus de, 1632-1677.
Benedikt von Spinoza. Zwey Abhandlungen über die Kultur des menschlichen Verstandes und über die Aristokratie und Demokratie. Herausgegeben und mit einer Vorrede begleitet von S. H. Ewald ... Leipzig, in der von Schönfeldschen Handlung, 1785.
xvi, viii, 263, 96 p. 17cm.

Spinoza, Benedictus de, 1632-1677. Abhandlung über die Verbesserung des Verstandes ... 1907. (Card 2)
Ms. notes by Carl Gebhardt, with his signature on t.-p. Imprint date on t.-p. changed in manuscript to 1906.

Spinoza, Benedictus de, 1632–1677.
Benedict von Spinoza's Abhandlung über die verbesserung des verstandes ... und desselben Politische abhandlung ... Uebers. und erläutert von J. H. v. Kirchmann. Berlin, L. Heimann, 1871.
xix, 151 p., 1 l. 19cm. (*Added t.-p.:* Philosophische bibliothek ... 44. bd.)
~~*With* Spinoza, B. de. René Descartes' Principien der philosophie ... Berlin, 1871.~~
1. Knowledge, Theory of. 2. Political science. I. Kirchmann, Julius Hermann von, 1802-1884, tr.
Library of Congress B23.P55 44. bd. 25-649
[2]

Spinoza, Benedictus de, 1632-1677.
[Abhandlung über die Verbesserung des Verstandes. 1907?]
19 l. 23cm.
Introduction and first chapters of Spinoza's treatise in a German translation, probably by Carl Gebhardt.
Typescript.

Spinoza, Benedictus de, 1632-1677.
Abhandlung über die Vervollkommung des Verstandes und über den Weg, auf welchem er am besten zur wahren Erkenntnis der Dinge geführt wird. Von B. Spinoza. Neu übersetzt von J. Stern. Leipzig, Druck und Verlag von Philipp Reclam jun. [pref. 1887]
61 p. 14cm. [Philipp Reclams Universal-bibliothek. 2487]
Ms. notes, by Carl Gebhardt.
Bound with Spinoza. Briefwechsel. [pref. 1904]

Spinoza, Benedictus de, 1632-1677.
Abhandlung über die Verbesserung des Verstandes. Abhandlung vom Staate. 4. Aufl., neu übertragen und eingeleitet, sowie mit Anmerkungen und Register versehen von Carl Gebhardt. Leipzig, F. Meiner, 1922.
xxxii, 214 p. 21cm. (Der Philosophischen Bibliothek Band 95)
Bibliography: p. xxxi-xxxii.

Spinoza, Benedictus de, 1632-1677.
Abhandlung über die Verbesserung des Verstandes. Abhandlung vom Staate. In 3. Aufl. neu übertragen und eingeleitet, sowie mit Anmerkungen und Register versehen von Carl Gebhardt. Leipzig, F. Meiner, 1907.
xxxii, 214 p. 20cm. (Der Philosophischen Bibliothek Bd. 95)
Bibliography: p. xxxi-xxxii.

Spinoza, Benedictus de, 1632-1677.
Abhandlung über die Läuterung des Verstandes und über den Weg, auf welchem er am besten zur wahren Erkenntnis der Dinge geführt wird. Übersetzt von J. Stern. Durchgesehen und eingeleitet von Dr. Werner Schingnitz. Leipzig, Verlag von Philipp Reclam jun. [pref. 1926]
63 p. 15cm.

Spinoza, Benedictus de, 1632-1677.
Spinoza: Vom Weg der Erkenntnis, mit Versen des Angelus Silesius [pseud.] Zusammengestellt von Carl Gebhardt. [Frankfurt am Main, Frankfurter Gutenbergpresse, 1929]
39 p. 26cm.

"Dritter Druck der Frankfurter Gutenberg Presse."
No. 35 of 400 copies.
Presentation copy to A. S. Oko with Carl Gebhardt's inscription and signature.

Spinoza, Benedictus de, 1632-1677.
מאמר על דבר השתלמות שכל האדם, מאת ברוך שפינוזא. מתרגם עברית מאת יצחק בן־מאיר מרגליות. ווארשא, בדפוס י. אלאפין, תרנ"ג.
[Warsaw, O. Alapin], 1893.
56 p. 19cm.

Title transliterated: Ma'ămār 'al dĕbhar hishtallĕmūth śekhel hā-ādhām.
Title-page in Hebrew and Russian.

CONTINUED ON NEXT CARD

Spinoza, Benedictus de, 1632-1677. מאמר על דבר השתלמות שכל האדם. 1893.
(Card 2)

On back-cover: Benedicti de Spinoza Tractatus de intellectus omendatione [!] Abhandlung über die Vervollkommnung des Verstandes, von B. Spinoza, hebräisch übersetzt von Isidor Margolis.

Spinoza, Benedictus de, 1632-1677.
De intellectus emendatione; a cura di Augusto Guzzo. Firenze, G. C. Sansoni, 1933.
49 p. 20cm. (On cover: Studi e testi, pubblicati a cura della R. Scuola normale superiore di Pisa. Serie seconda, vol. I)

Original paper cover bound in.

Spinoza, Benedictus de, 1632-1677.
Chisei kaizen-ron, Hatanaka Naoshi yaku. [Tokyo, Iwanami shoten [1931]
95 p. 16cm. (Iwanami bunko, 688)

Japanese translation of the Tractatus de intellectus emendatione.

Spinoza, Benedictus de, 1632-1677.
השתלמות שכל האדם במאתה ברוך שפינוזה. מתורגם לעברית מאת יצחק בן מאיר מרגליות. ורשה, הוצ' מ. ערליכמאן, תרצ"ה.
[Warsaw, M. Erlichman, 1935]
56 p. illus., ports. 19cm.

Title transliterated: Hishtallĕmūth śekhel hā-ādhām.
On verso of t.-p.: Benedicti de Spinoza Tractatus de intellectus omendatione [!]

B-3-h
TRACTATUS POLITICUS

Spinoza, Benedictus de, 1632-1677.
Benedictus de Spinoza. Tractatus politicus. [Hilversumi, Excudebat Sjoerd H. de Roos prelo suo, cui nomen Heuvelpers, 1928]
2 p. l., 111, [2] p. 25cm.

Imprint from colophon.
Edited by Tobie Goedewaagen.
No. 23 of 125 copies.

Spinoza, Benedictus de, 1632-1677.
Staatkundig vertoog, of Verhandeling waarin wordt aangetoond, hoe een maatschappij waar een vorst regeert zoowel als een gemeenschap waar de regeering aan eenige der aanzienlijkste burgers is toevertrouwd, moet worden ingericht om alle dwingelandij te voorkomen en ongestoorde rust en vrijheid aan alle burgers te waarborgen. Uit het Latijn door W. Meijer. Amsterdam, S. L. van Looy, 1901.
xxix, 174 p. 19cm. (On cover: Klassieke schrijvers, 70-74. Spinoza's werken, V)

CONTINUED ON NEXT CARD

Spinoza, Benedictus de, 1632-1677.
Staatkundig vertoog, of Verhandeling waarin wordt aangetoond, hoe een maatschappij waar een vorst regeert zoowel als een gemeenschap waar de regeering aan eenige der aanzienlijkste burgers is toevertrouwd, moet worden ingericht om alle dwingelandij te voorkomen en ongestoorde rust en vrijheid aan alle burgers te waarborgen. Uit het Latijn door W. Meijer. Amsterdam, S. L. van Looy, 1901.
xxix, 174 p. 19cm.

CONTINUED ON NEXT CARD

Spinoza, Benedictus de, 1632-1677. Staatkundig vertoog ... 1901. (Card 2)

On publisher's binding: Klassieke schrijvers.
Ms. notes by Carl Gebhardt: Gebhardt's signature on t.-p.

SPECIAL COLLECTIONS
SPINOZA B-3-h 288

Spinoza, Benedictus de, 1632-1677.
A treatise on politics. Translated from the Latin of Benedict Spinoza. By William MacCall. London, Holyoake and Co., 1854.
115 p. 17cm. (On cover: The Cabinet of reason, a library of freethought, politics and culture. Vol. V)

Original paper covers bound in.

SPECIAL COLLECTIONS
SPINOZA B-3-h 289

Spinoza, Benedictus de, 1632-1677.
A treatise on politics. Translated from the Latin of Benedict Spinoza. By William MacCall. London, Holyoake and Co., 1854.
115 p. 17cm.

Sir F. Pollock's copy with ms. notes.
Volume of pamphlets.

NNC

SPECIAL COLLECTIONS
SPINOZA B-3-h 290

Spinoza, Benedictus de, 1632-1677.
Traité politique de B. de Spinoza. Traduit en français pour la première fois, annoté, suivi d'un index analytique et accompagné de trois plans des trois différentes formes de gouvernement par J. G. Prat. Paris, 1860.
xl, 332 p. fold. tables. 18cm.

SPECIAL COLLECTIONS
SPINOZA B-3-h 291

Spinoza, Benedictus de, 1632-1677.
Der politische Traktat. Übersetzt und mit einem Vorwort versehen von J. Stern. Leipzig, Verlag von Philipp Reclam jun. [pref. 1906]
160 p. 15cm. [Philipp Reclam's Universal-bibliothek, 4752-53]

SPECIAL COLLECTIONS
SPINOZA B-3-h 292

Spinoza, Benedictus de, 1632-1677.
Der politische Traktat von B. Spinoza. Neu übersetzt und mit einem Vorwort versehen von J. Stern. Leipzig, Druck und Verlag von Philipp Reclam jun. [pref. 1906]
165 p. 15cm. (On cover: Universal-Bibliothek, 4752, 4753)

Ms. notes by Carl Gebhardt, with his signature on t.-p.

SPECIAL COLLECTIONS
SPINOZA B-3-h 293

Spinoza, Benedictus de, 1632-1677.
Tractatus politicus. Traduzione e prefazione di Antero Meozzi. Lanciano, R. Carabba [1934]
124 p. 20cm. (On cover: Cultura dell'anima. [55])

Original paper covers bound in.

B-3-i
TRACTATUS THEOLOGICO-POLITICUS

SPECIAL COLLECTIONS
SPINOZA B-3-i 294

[Spinoza, Benedictus de] 1632-1677.
Tractatus theologico-politicus continens dissertationes aliquot, quibus ostenditur libertatem philosophandi non tantum salva pietate, & reipublicae pace posse concedi: sed eandem nisi cum pace reipublicae, ipsaque pietate tolli non posse ... Hamburgi, Apud Henricum Künraht, 1670.
[12], 233, [1] p. 21cm.

First issue of 1st edition. -Cf. Baer,

CONTINUED ON NEXT CARD

SPECIAL COLLECTIONS
SPINOZA B-3-i 295

[Spinoza, Benedictus de] 1632-1677. Tractatus theologico-politicus. 1670. (Card 2)

Joseph, & Co. Spinoza: Katalog einer Sammlung [1911] no. 5. Also Gebhardt ed. of Spinoza's Opera, v. 3, p. 363 ff.
Fictitious imprint. Printed at Amsterdam by J. Rieuwertsz; also ascribed to C. Conrad.

SPECIAL COLLECTIONS
SPINOZA B-3-i 296

[Spinoza, Benedictus de] 1632-1677.
Tractatus theologico-politicus continens dissertationes aliquot, quibus ostenditur libertatem philosophandi non tantum salva pietate, & reipublicae pace posse concedi: sed eandem nisi cum pace reipublicae, ipsaque pietate tolli non posse ... Hamburgi, Apud Henricum Künraht, 1670.
[12], 233, [1] p. 20cm.

Second impression. -Cf. Baer, Joseph, & Co. Spinoza: Katalog einer Sammlung [1911] no. 6;

CONTINUED ON NEXT CARD

SPECIAL COLLECTIONS
SPINOZA B-3-i 297

[Spinoza, Benedictus de] 1632-1677. Tractatus theologico-politicus. 1670. (Card 2)

and Gebhardt ed. of Spinoza's Opera, v. 3, p. 363 ff.
Fictitious imprint. Printed at Amsterdam by J. Rieuwertsz; also ascribed to C. Conrad.
Manuscript notes in margins.

ₓSpinoza, Benedictus de, 1632-1677.
Tractatus theologico-politicus continens dissertationes aliquot, quibus ostenditur libertatem philosophandi non tantum salva pietate, & reipublicaê pace posse concedi: sed eandem nisi cum pace reipublicaê, ipsaque pietate tolli non posse ... Hamburgi, Apud Henricum Künrath, 1670.
[12], 233, [1] p. 20cm.

Third impression. -Cf. Baer, Joseph, & Co. Spinoza: Katalog einer Sammlung [1911] no. 7;

CONTINUED ON NEXT CARD

[Spinoza, Benedictus de] 1632-1677. Tractatus theologico-politicus. 1670. (Card 2)

and Gebhardt ed. of Spinoza's Opera, v. 3, p. 363 ff.
Fictitious imprint. Printed at Amsterdam by J. Rieuwertsz; also ascribed to C. Conrad.
Manuscript notes in margins.

[Spinoza, Benedictus de] 1632-1677.
Tractatus theologico-politicus continens dissertationes aliquot, quibus ostenditur libertatem philosophandi non tantum salva pietate, & reipublicaê pace posse concedi: sed eandem nisi cum pace reipublicaê, ipsaque pietate tolli non posse ... Hamburgi, Apud Henricum Künrath, 1670.
[12], 233 p. 21cm.

Fourth impression. -Cf. Baer, Joseph, & Co.

CONTINUED ON NEXT CARD

[Spinoza, Benedictus de] 1632-1677. Tractatus theologico-politicus. 1670. (Card 2)

Spinoza: Katalog einer Sammlung [1911] no. 8, and Gebhardt ed. of Spinoza's Opera, v. 3, p. 363 ff.
Fictitious imprint. Printed at Amsterdam by J. Rieuwertsz; also ascribed to C. Conrad.
Marginal manuscript notations.

[Spinoza, Benedictus de] 1632-1677.
Tractatus theologico-politicus continens dissertationes aliquot, quibus ostenditur libertatem philosophandi non tantum salva pietate, & reipublicaê pace posse concedi: sed eandem nisi cum pace reipublicaê, ipsaque pietate tolli non posse ... Hamburgi, Apud Henricum Künraht, 1672.
[12], 233, [1] p. port. 21cm.

Corresponds typographically to the second impression of the 1670 edition.

[Spinoza, Benedictus de] 1632-1677.
Danielis Heinsii P. P. Operum historicorum collectio prima [-secunda] Editio secunda, priori editione multo emendatior & auctior. Accedunt quaêdam hactenus inedita. Lugd. Batav., Apud Isaacum Herculis, 1673.
2 v. in 1. 18cm.

Part 1 is Spinoza's Tractatus theologico-politicus; part 2 is Philosophia S. Scripturae interpres, by Lodewijk Meyer.

[Spinoza, Benedictus de] 1632-1677.
Tractatus theologico-politicus, cui adjunctus est Philosophia S. Scripturaê interpres. Ab authore longé emendatior. [Amsterdam?] 1674.
[22], 334, [17], 182, [19] p. 17cm.

The Philosophia S. Scripturae interpres is by Lodewijk Meyer.
One leaf following p. 334 (first leaf of Philosophia S. Scripturae interpres) lacking.
Pages 315-330 bound between p. [16-17] at end

NNC

[Spinoza, Benedictus de] 1632-1677.
De rechtzinnige theologant, of godgeleerde staatkundige verhandelinge. Uit het Latijn vertaalt. Te Hamburg, by Henricus Koenraad, 1693.
14 p. l., 380 p. 21cm.
Translated by Jan Hendrik Glazemaker.
Ms. notes by Carl Gebhardt.

1. Philosophy and religion. 2. Free thought. I. Glazemaker, Jan Hendrik, tr. II. Title.

Spinoza, Benedictus de, 1632-1677.
Benedictus de Spinoza, Godgeleerd-staatkundig vertoog; uit het Latijn door W. Meijer, met inleiding van Prof. Dr. J. P. N. Land. Amsterdam, S. L. van Looy, H. Gerlings [pref. 1894]
422 p. 19cm. (On cover: Klassieke schrijvers. Spinoza's werken. I)

Original paper cover bound in.

[Spinoza, Benedictus de] 1632-1677.
A treatise partly theological, and partly political, containing some few discourses, to prove that the liberty of philosophizing (that is making use of natural reason) may be allow'd without any prejudice to piety, or to the peace of any commonwealth; and that the loss of public peace and religion it self must necessarily follow, where such a liberty of reasoning is taken away ... Translated out of Latin. London, 1689.
15 p. l., 452 p. 19cm.
Translation of Spinoza's "Tractatus theologico-politicus".
1. Philosophy and religion. I. Title.

ₑSpinoza, Benedictus de, 1632-1677.ₒ
A treatise partly theological, and partly political, containing some few discourses, to prove that the liberty of philosophizing (that is making use of natural reason) may be allowed without any prejudice to piety, or to the peace of any commonwealth. And that the loss of public peace and religion itself must necessarily follow, where such a liberty of reasoning is taken away ... Translated from the Latin of Spinoza. London, 1737.
15 p. l., 452 p.

PPL

ₑSpinoza, Benedictus de, 1632-1677.ₒ
La clef du santuaire par un sçavant homme de nôtre siecle ... A Leyde, Chez Pierre Warnaer, 1678.
ₑ30ₒ, 531, ₑ30ₒ, 30 p. 14cm.

A translation, by Gabriel de Saint-Glain, of the Tractatus theologico-politicus.
First impression. Also issued later in 1678 with title-pages reading: Reflexions curieuses d'un esprit des-interressé sur les matieres les plus importantes au salut ...

CONTINUED ON NEXT CARD

Spinoza, Benedictus de, 1632-1677.
Tractatus theologico-politicus: a critical inquiry into the history, purpose, and authenticity of the Hebrew Scriptures; with the right to free thought and free discussion asserted, and shown to be not only consistent but necessarily bound up with true piety and good government. By Benedict de Spinoza. From the Latin. With an introduction and notes by the editor ... London, Trübner & Co., 1862.
vii, 359 p. 22cm.

Translated by Robert Willis.

ₑSpinoza, Benedictus de, 1632-1677. La clef du santuaire. 1678. (Card 2)

A Cologne, Chez Claude Emanuel, 1678; and Traitté des ceremonies superstitieuses des Juifs ... A Amsterdam, Chez Jacob Smith, 1678.
"Remarques curieuses et necessaires pour l'intelligence de ce livre" (30 p. at end) is a translation of Spinoza's Adnotationes ad Tractatum theologico-politicum.
In this copy the imprint date has been altered with pen to read 1686.

Spinoza, Benedictus de, 1632-1677.
Tractatus theologico-politicus: a theological and political treatise, showing under a series of heads that freedom of thought and of discussion may not only be granted with safety to religion and the peace of the state, but cannot be denied without danger to both the public peace and true piety. From the Latin, with an introduction and a few notes by the translator. London, Williams and Norgate, 1868.
viii, 359 p. 23cm.

Translated by Robert Willis.

ₑSpinoza, Benedictus de, 1632-1677.ₒ
La clef du santuaire par un sçavant homme de nôtre siecle ... A Leyde, Chez Pierre Warnaer, 1678.
ₑ34ₒ, 531, ₑ30ₒ, 30 p. 15cm.

A translation, by Gabriel de Saint-Glain, of the Tractatus theologico-politicus.
Includes all three title-pages with which the work was variously issued in 1678. The 2d and 3d read: Reflexions curieuses d'un esprit des-interressé ... A Cologne, Chez

CONTINUED ON NEXT CARD

Spinoza, Benedictus de, 1632-1677.
Tractatus theologico-politicus, Tractatus politicus. Translated from the Latin, with an introduction by R. H. M. Elwes. London and New York, George Routledge and sons ₑ189-ₒ
xxxiii, 387 p. 19cm. (Sir John Lubbock's hundred books ₑ91ₒ)

Bibliographical footnotes.

ₑSpinoza, Benedictus de, 1632-1677. La clef du santuaire. 1678. (Card 2)

Claude Emanuel, 1678; and Traitté des ceremonies superstitieuses des Juifs ... A Amsterdam, Chez Jacob Smith, 1678.
Second impression of the text and title-pages. -Cf. Baer, no. 10-12.
"Remarques curieuses, et necessaires pour l'intelligence de ce livre" (30 p. at end) is a translation of Spinoza's Adnotationes ad Tractatum theologico-politicus.

Spinoza, Benedictus de, 1632-1677.
Tractatus theologico-politicus, Tractatus politicus. Translated from the Latin, with an introduction by R. H. M. Elwes. Revised edition. London, George Routledge and sons, 1895.
xxxiii, 387 p. 20cm. (Sir John Lubbock's hundred books. 91)

Bibliographical footnotes.

ₑSpinoza, Benedictus de, 1632-1677.ₒ
Reflexions curieuses d'un esprit des-interressé sur les matieres les plus importantes au salut, tant public que particulier. A Cologne, Chez Claude Emanuel, 1678.
ₑ32ₒ, 531, ₑ30ₒ, 30 p. 15cm.

A translation, by Gabriel de Saint-Glain, of the Tractatus theologico-politicus.
First issued 1678 with t.-p. reading: La clef du santuaire ... A Leyde, Chez Pierre Warnaer, 1678. Also issued later in 1678

CONTINUED ON NEXT CARD

[Spinoza, Benedictus de] 1632-1677. Reflexions curieuses ... 1678. (Card 2)

with t.-p.: Traittée des ceremonies superstitieuses des Juifs ... A Amsterdam, Chez Jacob Smith, 1678.
Includes the third t.-p.; text and title-pages are second impression. Baer no. 12.
"Remarques curieuses, et necessaires pour l'intelligence de ce livre" (30 p. at end) is a translation of Spinoza's Adnotationes ad Tractatum theologico-politicum.

[Spinoza, Benedictus de] 1632-1677.
Traitté des ceremonies superstitieuses des Juifs tant anciens que modernes. A Amsterdam, Chez Jacob Smith, 1678.
[30], 531, [30], 30 p. 14cm.

A translation, by Gabriel de Saint-Glain, of the Tractatus theologico-politicus.
Also issued earlier in 1678 with title-pages reading: La clef du santuaire ... A Leyde, Chez Pierre Warnaer, 1678; and Reflexions curieuses d'un esprit des-interressé

CONTINUED ON NEXT CARD

[Spinoza, Benedictus de] 1632-1677. Traitté des ceremonies superstitieuses des Juifs. 1678. (Card 2)

... A Cologne, Chez Claude Emanuel, 1678.
First impression of the text. -Cf. Baer, no. 10-12.
"Remarques curieuses, et necessaires pour l'intelligence de ce livre" (30 p. at end) is a translation of Spinoza's Adnotationes ad Tractatum theologico-politicum.
Manuscript notes on fly-leaf.

[Spinoza, Benedictus de] 1632-1677.
Traitté des ceremonies superstitieuses des Juifs tant anciens que modernes. A Amsterdam, Chez Jacob Smith, 1678.
[30], 531, [30], 30 p. 14cm.

A translation, by Gabriel de Saint-Glain, of the Tractatus theologico-politicus.
Also issued earlier in 1678 with title-pages reading: La clef du santuaire ... A Leyde, Chez Pierre Warnaer, 1678; and Reflexions curieuses d'un esprit des-interressé ... A

CONTINUED ON NEXT CARD

[Spinoza, Benedictus de] 1632-1677. Traitté des ceremonies superstitieuses des Juifs ... 1678. (Card 2)

Cologne, Chez Claude Emanuel, 1678.
Second impression of the text; cf. Baer, no. 10-12. Title-page also varies typographically from other example with this title.
"Remarques curieuses, et necessaires pour l'intelligence de ce livre" (30 p. at end) is a translation of Spinoza's Adnotationes ad Tractatum theologico-politicum.

Spinoza, Benedictus de, 1632-1677.
Benedikt von Spinoza über Heilige Schrift, Judenthum, Recht der höchsten Gewalt in geistlichen Dingen, und Freyheit zu philosophiren. Aus dem Lateinischen. Gera, bey Christoph Friedrich Bekmann, 1787.
xxii, [6], 456 p. 21cm.

Spinoza, Benedictus de, 1632-1677.
Benedikt's von Spinoza Theologisch-politische Abhandlungen. Neu übersetzt mit den von Hrn. v. Murr herausgegebenen Anmerkungen des Verfassers zu diesem Traktat, einer einleitenden Vorrede und einigen Anmerkungen begleitet von Carl Philipp Conz. Stuttgart, Bey Joh. Friedrich Steinkopf, 1805.
lxxvi, 16, 424 p. 19cm.

Table of contents and half-title of "Erster Abschnitt" bound between p. lxx-lxxi.

Spinoza, Benedictus de, 1632-1677.
Benedikt's von Spinoza Theologisch-politische Abhandlungen. Neu übersetzt mit den von Hrn. v. Murr herausgegebenen Anmerkungen des Verfassers zu diesem Traktat, einer einleitenden Vorrede und einigen Anmerkungen begleitet von Carl Philipp Conz. Stuttgart, Bey Joh. Friedrich Steinkopf, 1806.
lxxvi, 16, 424 p. 19cm.

Spinoza, Benedictus de, 1632-1677.
Theologisch-politische abhandlungen von Spinoza. Freye uebersetzung und mit anmerkungen begleitet von dr. J. A. Kalb. München, J. A. Finsterlin, 1826.
2 p. l., [iii]-xlviii, 432 p. 22½cm.

1. Philosophy and religion. 2. Free thought. I. Kalb, J. A., tr. II. Title.

Spinoza, Benedictus de, 1632-1677.
Benedict von Spinoza's Theologisch-politische Abhandlung ... Uebersetzt und erläutert von J. H. v. Kirchmann. Berlin, L. Heimann, 1870.
xii, 276 p. 20cm.

Added t.-p.: Benedict von Spinoza's Sämmtliche philosophische Werke, uebersetzt von J. H. von Kirchmann und Prof. Schaarschmidt. 2. Bd. Berlin, L. Heimann, 1869.
Original paper cover, dated 1872, bound in.
Bound with the author's Ethik. 1870.

SPECIAL COLLECTIONS
SPINOZA
B-3-i
328

Spinoza, Benedictus de, 1632-1677.
Benedict von Spinoza's Theologisch-politische Abhandlung ... Uebersetzt und erläutert von J. H. v. Kirchmann. Berlin, L. Heimann, 1870.
xii, 276 p. 20cm. (Philosophische Bibliothek. 35. Bd.)

Bound with the author's Kurzgefasste Abhandlung von Gott, dem Menschen und dessen Glück. 1869.

SPECIAL COLLECTIONS
SPINOZA
B-3-i
329

Spinoza, Benedictus de, 1632-1677.
Benedict von Spinoza's Theologisch-politische Abhandlung ... Uebersetzt und erläutert von J. H. v. Kirchmann. Berlin, Philosoph-histor. Verlag ꜀pref. 1870꜁
xii, 276 p. 20cm. (Philosophische Bibliothek. 35. Bd.)

Pencilled on t.-p.: 1892?

SPECIAL COLLECTIONS
SPINOZA
B-3-i
330

Spinoza, Benedictus de, 1632-1677.
Der theologisch-politische Tractat Spinoza's. Mit einer Einleitung herausgegeben von Hugo Ginsberg. Leipzig, Erich Koschny (L. Heimann's Verlag) 1877.
35, xvi, 336 p. 19cm.

Article on Spinoza from Bayle's Dictionaire historique et critique, 2d ed.: p. ꜀239꜁-336.
On spine: Spinoza Opera. III.

SPECIAL COLLECTIONS
SPINOZA
B-3-i
331

Spinoza, Benedictus de, 1632-1677.
Der theologisch-politische Tractat Spinoza's. Mit einer Einleitung herausgegeben von Hugo Ginsberg. Leipzig, Erich Koschny (L. Heimann's Verlag) 1877.
35, xvi, 336 p. 21cm.

Original paper cover bound in: Spinozae Opera philosophica. Vol. III. Der theologisch-politische Tractat Spinoza's im Urtexte herausgegeben und mit einer historischen Einleitung versehen von Hugo Ginsberg. Heidelberg, Georg Weiss, 1882.

CONTINUED ON NEXT CARD

SPECIAL COLLECTIONS
SPINOZA
B-3-i
332

Spinoza, Benedictus de, 1632-1677. Der theologisch-politische Tractat Spinoza's. 1877. (Card 2)

Article on Spinoza from Bayle's Dictionnaire historique et critique, 2d ed.: p. ꜀239꜁-336.

SPECIAL COLLECTIONS
SPINOZA
B-3-i
333

Spinoza, Benedictus de, 1632-1677.
Der Theologisch-politische Traktat von B. Spinoza. Neu übersetzt und mit einem biographischen Vorwort versehen von J. Stern. Leipzig, Druck und Verlag von Philipp Reclam jun. ꜀pref. 1886꜁
385 p. 15cm. (Philipp Reclam's Universal-Bibliothek, 2177-80)

Ms. notes by Carl Gebhardt; Gebhardt's signature on t.-p.

SPECIAL COLLECTIONS
SPINOZA
B-3-i
334

Spinoza, Benedictus de, 1632-1677.
Theologisch-politischer Traktat. 3. Aufl. Ubertragen und eingelautet nebst Anmerkungen und Registern von Carl Gebhardt. Leipzig, Verlag der Dürr'schen Buchhandlung, 1908.
xxxiv, 423 p. 19cm. (Philosophische bibliothek; verlag von Felix Meiner. Neue aufl. bd. 93)

Bibliography: p. xxx-xxxiv.
Ms. notes by Carl Gebhardt.

SPECIAL COLLECTIONS
SPINOZA
B-3-i
335

Spinoza, Benedictus de, 1632-1677.
Der Theologisch-politische Traktat von B. Spinoza. Neu übersetzt und mit einem biographischen Vorwort versehen von J. Stern. Zweite Auflage. Leipzig, Druck und Verlag von Philipp Reclam jun. ꜀pref. 1909꜁
384 p. 16cm. (On cover: Reclams Universal Bibliothek. Nr. 2177-2180)

Original paper cover bound in.

SPECIAL COLLECTIONS
SPINOZA
B-3-i
336

Spinoza, Benedictus de, 1632-1677.
Der theologisch-politische Traktat von B. Spinoza. Neu übersetzt und mit einem biographischen Vorwort versehen von J. Stern. Zweite Auflage. Leipzig, Druck und Verlag von Philipp Reclam jun. ꜀pref. 1909꜁
384 p. 16cm. (On cover: Universal-Bibliothek. 2177-2180)

Unbound copy.

SPECIAL COLLECTIONS
SPINOZA
B-3-i
337

Spinoza, Benedictus de, 1632-1677.
Der Theologisch-politische Traktat. 3. Aufl. Neu übersetzt und mit einem biographischen Vorwort versehen von J. Stern. Leipzig, Verlag von Philipp Reclam jun. ꜀pref. 1909꜁
384 p. 15cm. ꜀Philipp Reclam's Universal-bibliothek, 2177-80꜁

I. Stern, J Tr.

 B-3-i 338

Spinoza, Benedictus de, 1632-1677.
Tractatus theologico-politicus. [Heidelberg, C. Winter, 1920?]
431 p. 23cm.

Half-title.
Includes reproduction of t.-p. of the original edition (Hamburg, Künraht, 1670)
Page proof of v. 3 of Spinoza. Opera, 1925, ed. by Carl Gebhardt.

 B-3-i 339

Spinoza, Benedictus de, 1632-1677.
Theologisch-politischer traktat. Übertragen und mit Einleitung, Anmerkungen und Registern versehen von Carl Gebhardt. 4. Aufl. Leipzig, Verlag von Felix Meiner, 1922.
xxxvii, 423 p. 20cm. (Der Philosophischen Bibliothek Band 93)

Bibliographical references included in "Einleitung" (p. [v]-xxxvii)

 B-3-i 340

Spinoza, Benedictus de, 1632-1677.
Tratado teológico-politico compuesto por Benito Spinoza. Traducción de Julian de Vargas y Antonio Zozaya. (2.ª edición) Madrid, Dirección y administration, 1890-92.
3 v. in 1. 15cm. (Biblioteca económica filosófica, vol. VI-VIII)

Original paper covers bound in.
Error in series statement at head of title and on half-title in v. 1: Volúmen IV.

 B-3-i 341

Spinoza, Benedictus de, 1632-1677.
דער טעאלאגיש-פאליטישער טראקטאט
פון ברוך (בענעדיקט) שפינאזא.
פאלשטענדיק איבערזעצט דורך נ. פערעל-
מאן. ניו-יארק פארלאג מ. יאנקאוויטש.
[New York, 1925?]
375 p. 22cm.

Title transliterated: Der teologish-politisher traktat.

 B-3-i 342

Spinoza, Benedictus de, 1632-1677.
דער טעאלאגיש-פאליטישער טראקטאט
פון ברוך (בענעדיקט) שפינאזא.
פאלשטענדיק איבערזעצט דורך נ. פערעל-
מאן. ניו-יארק פארלאג מ. יאנקאוויטש.
[New York, 1925?]
375 p. 22cm.

Title transliterated: Der teologish-politisher traktat.

B-4 SELECTIONS

 B-4 343

Anthologie der neueren Philosophie; mit einer Einleitung von Paul Deussen. Berlin, Askanischer Verlag, 1919.
xvi, 552 p. 24cm. (Added t.-p.: Anthologie der Wissenschaften, hrsg. von Friedrich Ramhorst. 1. Bd.)

Includes a selection from Spinoza's Ethica (p. 21-55)

 B-4 344

Brown, Brian, 1881- *ed.*
The wisdom of the Hebrews; their philosophy and religious teachings, their sayings and proverbs, as taken from the Talmud, the lives of the rabbis, and the writings of Josephus, Spinoza, and the most learned of the Hebrews of the past, introduction by Maurice H. Farbridge ... edited with a preface, by Brian Brown. New York, Brentano's [°1925]
xxii p., 1 l., 280, [1] p. front., ports. 21cm.
"Bibliography and sources": p. [281]
Includes selections from Spinoza (p. 200-238)
1. Jews—Civilization. 2. Hebrew literature—Translations into English. 3. English literature—Translations from Hebrew. I. Title.
25—9536
Library of Congress DS113.B7
[44j1]

 B-4 345

Die heiligen Triebe; Gedichte. [19--]
46 l. 26x22cm.

Includes a quotation from Spinoza (leaf 1)
Reproduced from typewritten copy.

NNC

B-4 346

Douglas, Charles Noel, *comp.*
Forty thousand quotations, prose and poetical; choice extracts on history, science, philosophy, religion, literature, etc. Selected from the standard authors of ancient and modern times, classified according to subject. Comp. by Charles Noel Douglas. New York, Sully and Kleinteich, 1915.
2 p. l., 9-2000, [8] p. 21½ cm.
"This new and revised edition of Forty thousand quotations was first published as Forty thousand sublime and beautiful thoughts."—Introd. Also published by the Christian herald under the latter title.
1. Quotations, English. I. Title.
NNUT
Library of Congress PN6081.D6 1915a 15—18958
[50q½]

Feldmann, Joseph ed.
Schule der Philosophie; Auslese charakteristischer Abschnitte aus den Werken der bedeutendsten Denker aller Zeiten. Mit Unterstützung zahlreicher Philosophen und Pädagogen herausgegeben und mit einer Einführung und Erläuterungen versehen von Joseph Feldmann. Paderborn, F. Schöningh Verlag, 1925.
xi, 511 p. plate.

Includes selections from Spinoza (p. 204-217)
Bibliographical references.

Fleg, Edmond, 1874– ed.
... Anthologie juive ... Paris, Les Éditions G. Crès et cie., 1923.
2 v. 18½cm.
The notes include bio-bibliography.
CONTENTS.—v. [1] Des origines au moyen âge.—v. [2] Du moyen âge à nos jours.
Includes selections from Spinoza in French translation (v. 2, p. 77-90)
On original paper covers (bound in): 7. éd.
1. Jewish literature. I. Title.

Fleg, Edmond, 1874–
The Jewish anthology, by Edmond Fleg, translated by Maurice Samuel. New York, Harcourt, Brace and company [°1925]
vii p., 2 l., 3-399 p. 22½cm.

Includes selections from Spinoza (p. 204-208)

1. Jewish literature. I. Samuel, Maurice, 1895– tr. II. Title.

Fouillée, Alfred, 1838-1912.
Extraits des grands philosophes. Paris, Librairie Ch. Delagrave, 1877.
600 p. 23cm.

Includes selections from Spinoza's Ethics (p. 227-236)
Original paper covers bound in.

Leibniz, Gottfried Wilhelm, Freiherr von, 1646-1716.
Philosophischer Briefwechsel. Hrsg. von der Preussischen Akademie der Wissenschaften. Darmstadt, O. Reichl, 1926.
xxxiv, 579 p. (His Sämtliche Schriften und Briefe. 2. Reihe) 25½ cm.

Includes letters to and from Spinoza (p. 155, 184, 271) and also references to him.
Ms. notes by A. S. Oko on flyleaf.

Leitl, Emmeram, 1877-
Lateinbuch für Erwachsene, hervorgegangen aus Unterrichtskursen für Männer und Frauen aller Stände, von Dr. Emmeram Leitl. [München] Verlag Josef Kösel & Friedrich Pustet, Lehrmittelabteilung München, 1924.
v. 2.

Selections from Spinoza's Ethica in Latin and German: v. 2, p. 75-84.

Lindsay, James Alexander, 1856-1931.
Among the thinkers; leaves from my notebooks. London, H. K. Lewis, 1931.
ix, 197 p.

Includes quotations from Spinoza.

Müller, Johannes, 1801-1858.
Handbuch der Physiologie des Menschen, für Vorlesungen. Coblenz, J. Hölscher, 1840-44.
[v. 1, 1844]
2 v. illus. 23cm.

Vol. 1 is 4. verb. Aufl.
Includes excerpts from Spinoza's Ethics in German translation (v. 2, p. 543-548)
Includes bibliographies.

Murr, Christoph Gottlieb von, 1733-1811.
Versuch einer Geschichte der Juden in Sina. Nebst P. Ignaz Köglers Beschreibung ihrer heiligen Bücher in der Synagoge zu Kai-fong-fu, und einem Anhange über die Entstehung des Pentatevchs. Hrsg. von C. G. von Murr. Halle, J. C. Hendels Verlag, 1806.
136 p. 22cm.

Includes chapter 8 of Spinoza's Tractatus theologico-politicus in Karl Philipp Conze's German translation (p. 115-136)
Bibliography: p. [5]-12.

Rand, Benjamin, 1856– comp.
The classical moralists; selections illustrating ethics from Socrates to Martineau, comp. by Benjamin Rand ... Boston, New York [etc.] Houghton Mifflin company [°1909]
xix, 797, [1] p. 22½ cm.

1. Ethics—Hist. I. Title.

B-4
357

Roerich Society. Spinoza Center.
Erste Spinoza-Gruppe. [Unser Streben und unser Ziel. New York, 193-]
16 p. 16cm.

A statement of aims of the group, expressed through selected passages from Spinoza.

I. Spinoza, Benedictus de, 1632-1677.
cor. mk.: Selections. Ger.

B-4
358

Roerich Society. Spinoza Center.
The first Spinoza Community. [New York, 193-]
[7] p. port. 17cm.

"Extracts from Spinoza's correspondence": p. [5-7]

I. Spinoza, Benedictus de, 1632-1677.
cor. mk.: Selections. Eng.

B-4
359

Roerich Society. Spinoza Center.
First Spinoza group. [Our striving and our aim. New York, 193-]
16 p. 16cm.

A statement of aims of the group, expressed through selected passages from Spinoza.

I. Spinoza, Benedictus de, 1632-1677.
cor. mk.: Selections. Eng.

B-4
360

Schmidt, Nathaniel, 1862-
Our forerunners, III: Baruch Spinoza. [New York, 1916.
[185]-188 p. 26cm.

From the Standard, vol. 2, no. 7, April 1916.
"Sayings of Spinoza": p. 188.

B-4
361

Schuster, Max Lincoln, 1897- *ed.*
A treasury of the world's great letters from ancient days to our own time, containing the characteristic and crucial communications, and intimate exchanges and cycles of correspondence, of many of the outstanding figures of world history, and some notable contemporaries, selected, edited, and integrated with biographical backgrounds and historical settings and consequences, by M. Lincoln Schuster. New York, Simon and Schuster, 1940.
xlviii, 563 p. facsims. 24 cm.

~~"Third printing."~~ Includes Albert Burgh's letter to Spinoza and Spinoza's reply (p. 105-122)
1. Letters. I. Title.

B-4
362

Spinoza, Benedictus de, 1632-1677.
Benedictus de Spinoza, Wijsgeerige fragmenten; een bloemlezing uit zijn geschriften en brieven, uit het Latijn vertaald en toegelicht door Dr. N. van Suchtelen. Amsterdam, N. V. Mij. tot Verspreiding van Goede en Goedkoope Lectuur, 1932.
304 p. 19cm. (Wereldbibliotheek)

B-4
363

Spinoza, Benedictus de, 1632-1677.
Benoît Spinoza, par Philippe Borrell. Paris, Librairie Bould & Cie, 1911.
68 p. 15cm. (Philosophes et penseurs)

Original paper covers bound in.
Selections from Spinoza's works in French translation.
Bibliography: p. 64-65.

B-4
364

Spinoza, Benedictus de, 1632-1677.
De la droite manière de vivre. Appendice extrait de la IVe partie de l'Ethique, traduit en français et annoté par J. G. Prat. Paris, 1860.
72 p.

B-4
365

Spinoza, Benedictus de, 1632-1677.
Dio. A cura di Nicola Checchia. Lanciano, R. Carabba [pref. 1911]
126 p. 20cm. (On cover: Cultura dell'anima)

The first book of his Ethics in Italian translation.
Bibliography: p. [29]-35.
Original paper covers bound in.

B-4
366

Spinoza, Benedictus de, 1632-1677.
God as infinite substance. [1931]
76-113 p.

Selections from the Ethics.
From Selections from the literature of theism, ed. by Alfred Caldecott and H. R. Mackintosh, 3d ed., 1931.

Spinoza, Benedictus de, 1632-1677.
God, wereld, leven; gedachten van Benedictus de Spinoza. Verzameld door de Societas Spinozana (Afdeeling Nederland) Inleiding en toelichting van Dr. J. H. Carp, nabeschouwing van Dr. J. D. Bierens de Haan. 's-Gravenhage, Uitgave N. V. Drukkerij Albani, 1935.
192 p. port. 20cm.

Spinoza, Benedictus de, 1632-1677.
El pensamiento vivo de Spinoza, presentado por Arnold Zweig. [Traducción por Francisco Ayala] Buenos Aires, Editorial Losada [1939]
206 p. port. 19cm. (Half-title: Biblioteca del pensamiento vivo. 8)

Spinoza, Benedictus de, 1632-1677.
The living thoughts of Spinoza; presented by Arnold Zweig ... New York, Toronto, Longmans, Green and co., 1939.
3 p. l., 162 p. front. (port.) 19cm. (The Living thoughts library; edited by A. O. Mendel) [9]
Illustrations and text on lining-papers.
"The woodcut portrait of Spinoza was made by Professor Hans A. Mueller."
"Translation of the Introductory essay by Eric Katz and Barrows Mussey. The selections are from Improvement of the understanding, Ethics and Correspondence of Benedict de Spinoza translated by R. H. M. Elwes, published by M. Walter Dunne, New York, 1901."
"First edition."
I. Zweig, Arnold, 1887- ed. II. Katz, Eric, tr. III. Mussey, June Barrows, 1910- joint tr. IV. Elwes, Robert Harvey Monro, tr.
Library of Congress B3955.Z9 1939a 39-28991
[15] 199.492

Spinoza, Benedictus de, 1632-1677.
... The philosophy of Spinoza as contained in the first, second, and fifth parts of the "Ethics," and in extracts from the third and fourth, tr. from the Latin, and ed. with notes by George Stuart Fullerton ... 2d ed., enl. New York, H. Holt and company, 1907.
viii, 358 p. 20cm. (Series of modern philosophers)

Bibliography: p. [1]-4.

Spinoza, Benedictus de, 1632-1677.
The philosophy of Spinoza, selected from his chief works, with a life of Spinoza and an introduction, by Joseph Ratner ... New York, The Modern library [c1927]
lxx, 376 p., 1 l. 17 cm. (*Half-title:* The Modern library of the world's best books)

I. Ratner, Joseph, 1901- ed.
B3958.R3 27—6169
Library of Congress [58k1]

Spinoza, Benedictus de, 1632-1677.
Prophetie und Propheten. Leipzig, Verlag von Felix Meiner [1922]
[15]-57 p. 19cm. (Taschenausgaben der "Philosophischen Bibliothek", Heft 47)

"Sonderausgabe aus: Spinoza. Theologisch-politischer Traktat. Herausgegeben und eingeleitet von Carl Gebhardt (Der Philosophischen Bibliothek Band 93.)"

Spinoza, Benedictus de, 1632-1677.
... Selections, edited by John Wild ... New York, Chicago [etc.] C. Scribner's sons [c1930]
lxi, [2], 479 p. illus., diagrs. 17½ cm. (Half-title: The modern student's library. [Philosophy series])

At head of title: Spinoza.
Bibliography: p. lx-lxi.

Spinoza, Benedictus de, 1632-1677.
Spinoza-Brevier; zusammengestellt und mit einem Nachwort versehen von Arthur Liebert. Berlin, Verlag Reichl & Co., 1912.
190 p. 19cm.

Bibliography: p. 185.

Spinoza, Benedictus de, 1632-1677.
Spinoza-Brevier; zusammengestellt und mit einer Einleitung herausgegeben von Arthur Liebert. 2., mit veränderter Einleitung versehene Aufl. Leipzig, Verlag von Felix Meiner, 1918.
xxxiv, 169 p. 19cm.

Bibliography: p. 163-164.

Spinoza, Benedictus de, 1632-1677.
Spinoza, von den festen und ewigen Dingen; uebertragen und eingeleitet von Carl Gebhardt. Heidelberg, C. Winter, 1925.
xlix, 594 p. 18cm.

Presentation copy to A. S. Oko, with editor's inscription and signature.
Includes the Ethica and selections from other works in German translation.

Spinoza, Benedictus de, 1632-1677.
Staat und Recht. Leipzig, Verlag von Felix Meiner ₍1922₎
₍273₎-291 p. 19cm. (Taschenausgaben der "Philosophischen Bibliothek", Heft 50)

"Sonderausgabe aus: Theologisch-Politischer Traktat. Herausgegeben und eingeleitet von Carl Gebhardt (Der Philosophischen Bibliothek Band 93)"

Spinoza, Benedictus de, 1632-1677.
Theologie, Vernunft und Glaube. Leipzig, Verlag von Felix Meiner ₍1922₎
₍249₎-272 p. 19cm. (Taschenausgaben der "Philosophischen Bibliothek", Heft 49)

"Sonderausgabe aus: Spinoza. Theologisch-politischer Traktat. Herausgegeben und eingeleitet von Carl Gebhardt. (Der Philosophischen Bibliothek Band 93.)"

Spinoza, Benedictus de, 1632-1677.
Uit de Ethica. (Opmerking bij stelling XLV van het vierde deel) Vertaald door Nico van Suchtelen. ₍1915₎
345-346 p. port. 19cm.

From Gedenkboek der Wereldbibliotheek, 1905-1915.

Spinoza, Benedictus de, 1632-1677.
Uren met Spinoza; een keur van stukken uit zijne werken, vertaald en van een inleiding en aanteekeningen voorzien door Dr. J. D. Bierens de Haan. Tweede druk, Baarn, Uitgegeven door de Hollandia-drukkerij, 1917.
₍4₎, 218 p. 19cm. (Boeken van wijsheid en schoonheid)

Spinoza, Benedictus de, 1632-1677.
Von den festen und ewigen Dingen. ₍Das erste Buch von der Verbesserung des Verstandes.₎ Uebertragen und eingeleitet von Carl Gebhardt. Heidelberg, C. Winter, 1925.
18 l. 33cm.

Galley proof.
Manuscript letter from Carl Gebhardt to A. S. Oko bound at beginning.

Spinoza, Benedictus de, 1632-1677.
Von den Wundern. Sonderausgabe aus: Spinoza, Theologisch-politischer Traktat. Leipzig, Verlag von Felix Meiner ₍1922₎
₍110₎-132 p. 19cm. (Taschenausgaben der "Philosophischen Bibliothek", Heft 48)

Spinoza, Benedictus de, 1632-1677.
Vom wahren Leben. ₍1926₎
62-63 p. 23cm.

"Aus: Spinoza, von den festen und ewigen Dingen ₍uebertragen und eingeleitet von Carl Gebhardt₎ Heidelberg, Carl Winter, 1925."
From Luxemburger Volksbildungskalender, 1926.

Spinoza, Benedictus de, 1632-1677.
Vom wahren Leben. ₍1926₎
79-80 p. 23cm.

"Aus: Spinoza, Von den Festen und ewigen Dingen, Heidelberg, Carl Winter, 1925."
From Der Rheinische Christopher; Rhein-Mainischer Heimatkalender, 1926.

Tannenbaum, Eugen, 1890-1936, *comp.*
Philo Zitaten-Lexikon; Worte von Juden; Worte für Juden. Hrsg. und beendet von Ernst Fraenkel. Berlin, Philo Verlag, 1936 ₍°1937₎
207 p. 19 cm.
"Literaturnachweis": p. 11.
Includes quotations from Spinoza (p. 101-102)

1. Quotations, Jewish. I. Fraenkel, Ernst, ed. II. Title.

Thatcher, Oliver J ed.
The ideas that have influenced civilization in the original documents. Vol. VI: Advance in knowledge, 1650-1800. Boston, Roberts-Manchester Publishing Co. ₍c1902₎
427 p. illus., ports. 26ᶜᵐ.

English translation of a part of Spinoza's Ethica: p. 63-78.

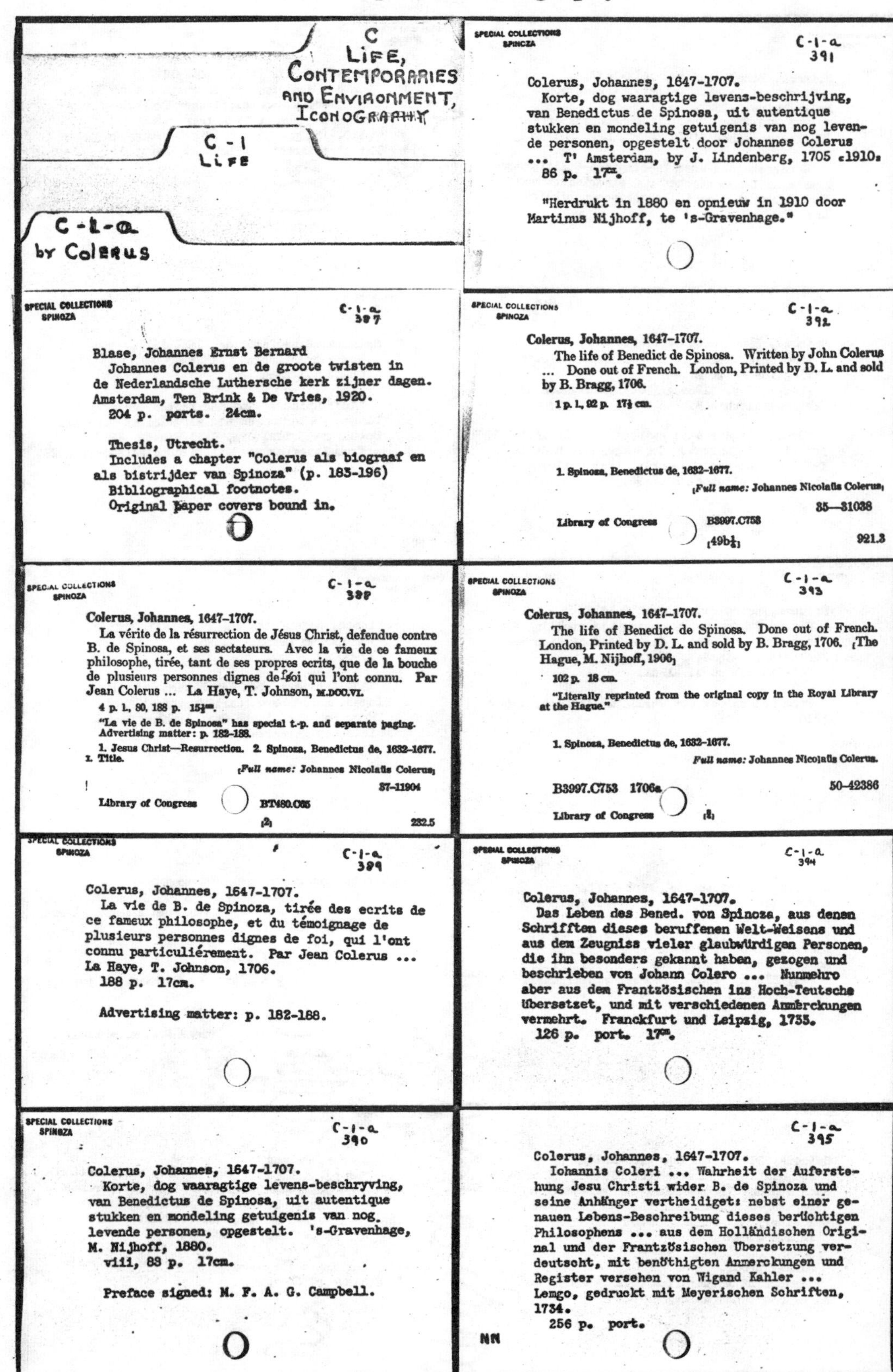

C
LIFE,
CONTEMPORARIES
AND ENVIRONMENT,
ICONOGRAPHY

C-1
LIFE

C-1-a
by COLERUS

SPECIAL COLLECTIONS
SPINOZA
C-1-a
391

Colerus, Johannes, 1647-1707.
Korte, dog waaragtige levens-beschrijving, van Benedictus de Spinosa, uit autentique stukken en mondeling getuigenis van nog levende personen, opgestelt door Johannes Colerus ... T' Amsteriam, by J. Lindenberg, 1705 [1910]
86 p. 17cm.

"Herdrukt in 1880 en opnieuw in 1910 door Martinus Nijhoff, te 's-Gravenhage."

SPECIAL COLLECTIONS
SPINOZA
C-1-a
387

Blase, Johannes Ernst Bernard
Johannes Colerus en de groote twisten in de Nederlandsche Luthersche kerk zijner dagen. Amsterdam, Ten Brink & De Vries, 1920.
204 p. ports. 24cm.

Thesis, Utrecht.
Includes a chapter "Colerus als biograaf en als bistrijder van Spinoza" (p. 183-196)
Bibliographical footnotes.
Original paper covers bound in.

SPECIAL COLLECTIONS
SPINOZA
C-1-a
392

Colerus, Johannes, 1647-1707.
The life of Benedict de Spinosa. Written by John Colerus ... Done out of French. London, Printed by D. L. and sold by B. Bragg, 1706.
1 p. l., 92 p. 17½ cm.

1. Spinoza, Benedictus de, 1632-1677.
[Full name: Johannes Nicolaüs Colerus]
35—31038
Library of Congress B3997.C753
[49b½]
921.3

SPECIAL COLLECTIONS
SPINOZA
C-1-a
388

Colerus, Johannes, 1647-1707.
La vérite de la résurrection de Jésus Christ, defendue contre B. de Spinosa, et ses sectateurs. Avec la vie de ce fameux philosophe, tirée, tant de ses propres ecrits, que de la bouche de plusieurs personnes dignes de foi qui l'ont connu. Par Jean Colerus ... La Haye, T. Johnson, M.DCC.VI.
4 p. l., 80, 188 p. 15½cm.
"La vie de B. de Spinosa" has special t.-p. and separate paging.
Advertising matter: p. 182-188.
1. Jesus Christ—Resurrection. 2. Spinoza, Benedictus de, 1632-1677. I. Title.
[Full name: Johannes Nicolaüs Colerus]
37-11904
Library of Congress BT480.C65
[2]
232.5

SPECIAL COLLECTIONS
SPINOZA
C-1-a
393

Colerus, Johannes, 1647-1707.
The life of Benedict de Spinosa. Done out of French. London, Printed by D. L. and sold by B. Bragg, 1706. [The Hague, M. Nijhoff, 1906]
102 p. 18 cm.
"Literally reprinted from the original copy in the Royal Library at the Hague."

1. Spinoza, Benedictus de, 1632-1677.
Full name: Johannes Nicolaüs Colerus.
B3997.C753 1706a 50-42386
Library of Congress [3]

SPECIAL COLLECTIONS
SPINOZA
C-1-a
389

Colerus, Johannes, 1647-1707.
La vie de B. de Spinoza, tirée des ecrits de ce fameux philosophe, et du témoignage de plusieurs personnes dignes de foi, qui l'ont connu particuliérement. Par Jean Colerus ... La Haye, T. Johnson, 1706.
188 p. 17cm.

Advertising matter: p. 182-188.

SPECIAL COLLECTIONS
SPINOZA
C-1-a
394

Colerus, Johannes, 1647-1707.
Das Leben des Bened. von Spinoza, aus denen Schrifften dieses beruffenen Welt-Weisens und aus dem Zeugniss vieler glaubwürdigen Personen, die ihn besonders gekannt haben, gezogen und beschrieben von Johann Colero ... Nunmehro aber aus dem Frantzösischen ins Hoch-Teutsche übersetzet, und mit verschiedenen Anmerckungen vermehrt. Franckfurt und Leipzig, 1733.
126 p. port. 17cm.

SPECIAL COLLECTIONS
SPINOZA
C-1-a
390

Colerus, Johannes, 1647-1707.
Korte, dog waaragtige levens-beschryving, van Benedictus de Spinosa, uit autentique stukken en mondeling getuigenis van nog levende personen, opgestelt. 's-Gravenhage, M. Nijhoff, 1880.
viii, 83 p. 17cm.

Preface signed: M. F. A. G. Campbell.

C-1-a
395

Colerus, Johannes, 1647-1707.
Iohannis Coleri ... Wahrheit der Auferstehung Jesu Christi wider B. de Spinoza und seine Anhänger vertheidiget: nebst einer genauen Lebens-Beschreibung dieses berüchtigen Philosophens ... aus dem Holländischen Original und der Frantzösischen Übersetzung verdeutscht, mit benöthigten Anmerckungen und Register versehen von Wigand Kahler ... Lemgo, gedruckt mit Meyerischen Schriften, 1734.
256 p. port.
NN

Colerus, Johannes, 1647-1707.
Das Leben des Bened. von Spinoza; hrsg. von Carl Gebhardt. Heidelberg, R. Weissbach, 1933.
[18], 126, [11] p. port. 19cm.

Facsimile (126 p.) has reproduction of the original title-page with imprint: Franckfurt und Leipzig, 1733. Preliminary pages and notes at end are mounted printed leaves. Manuscript title-page.
Apparently working copy for an edition which did not appear until 1952.

C-1-b
by LUCAS

[Lucas, Jean Maximilien] d. 1697, supposed author.
La vie de Spinosa, par un de ses disciples: nouvelle edition non tronquée, augmentée de quelques notes et du catalogue de ses ecrits, par un autre de ses disciples. &c. A Hambourg, Chez Henry Kunrath, 1735.
[4], 47, [12] p. 16cm.

Authorship variously ascribed to J. M. Lucas, to D. de Saint-Glain, and to a Hofrat Vroes.

CONTINUED ON NEXT CARD

[Lucas, Jean Maximilien] d. 1697, supposed author. La vie de Spinosa. 1735. (Card 2)

"The first part of the complete Le Vier edition [of La vie et l'esprit de Mr. Benoit de Spinosa, 1719] re-issued with a new title-page, and a modified preface": A. Wolf, ed., "The oldest biography of Spinosa", p. 29.
Catalogue des ouvrages de Mr. de Spinosa": p. 45-47.
"Recueil alphabetique des auteurs, et des ouvrages condamnés au feu, ou qui ont merité de l'être": [12] p. at end.

[Lucas, Jean Maximilien] d. 1697, supposed author.
The oldest biography of Spinoza, edited with translation, introduction, annotations, etc., by A. Wolf ... New York, Lincoln MacVeagh, The Dial Press, 1927.
3 p. l., [9]-196 p. ports., plates, facsims. 21cm.

Authorship variously ascribed to J. M. Lucas, to D. de Saint-Glain, and to a Hofrat Vroes.

CONTINUED ON NEXT CARD

[Lucas, Jean Maximilien] d. 1697, supposed author. The oldest biography of Spinoza. 1927. (Card 2)

First published 1719 in the Nouvelles litteraires, vol. X, p. 40-174, under title: La vie de Spinosa, and later in the same year as the first part of "La vie et l'esprit de m. Benoît de Spinosa."
"Select literature of Spinoza biography": p. 36-37.
Manuscript notes by A. S. Oko in margins.

[Lucas, Jean Maximilien] d. 1697, supposed author.
The oldest biography of Spinoza, edited with translation, introduction, annotations, etc., by A. Wolf ... London, G. Allen & Unwin Ltd. [1927]
3 p. l., [9]-196 p. ports., plates, facsims. 21cm.

Authorship variously ascribed to J. M. Lucas, to D. de Saint-Glain, and to a Hofrat Vroes.
Manuscript notes by A. S. Oko in margins.

C-1-c
by OTHERS

Aa, Abraham Jacob van der, 1792-1857.
Biographisch woordenboek der Nederlanden, bevattende levensbeschrijvingen van zoodanige personen, die zich op eenigerlei wijze in ons vaderland hebben vermaard gemaakt, door A. J. van der Aa ... Onder medewerking van de heeren: Mr. C. M. A. Simon van der Aa, Prof. P. O. van der Chijs ... en anderen ... Haarlem, J. J. van Brederode, 1852-78.
12 v. in 4. plates. 37 cm.

Includes an article on Spinoza.

Abraham, Philip
Curiosities of Judaism. [London] 1879.

Includes a biographical sketch of Spinoza (p. 280)

Ader, Jean Joseph, 1796-1859.
Plutarque des Pays-Bas; ou, Vies des hommes illustrés de ce royaume; précédé d'une introduction historique. Bruxelles, Laurent, 1828.
3 v.

Includes a section on Spinoza (v. 3, p. 155-170)

An account of the life and writings of Spinosa. To which is added, An abstract of his Theological political treatise. Containing I. His discourses of prophecy. II. Of prophets. III. Of the gift of prophecy to other nations as well as the Jewish. IV. Of ceremonies. V. Of miracles. VI. Of the dependency of religion, and all things relating to it, on the civil magistrate. VII. Of the liberty of thinking and speaking ... London, Printed for W. Boreham, 1720.
2 p. l., 96 p. 20cm.

Aschendorffsche Verlagsbuchhandlung, Münster i. Westf.
Der junge De Spinoza. Leben und Werdegang im Lichte der Weltphilosophie, von Stanislaus von Dunin-Borkowski, S. J. ₍1910?₎
₍5₎ p. 26cm.

Excerpts from reviews of Dunin-Borkowski's book published in various newspapers.

Auerbach, Berthold, 1812-1882.
... Briefe an seinen freund Jakob Auerbach. Ein biographisches denkmal. Mit vorbemerkungen von Friedrich Spielhagen und dem herausgeber ... Frankfurt a. M., Rütten & Loening, 1884.
2 v. front. (port.) 23cm.

Includes references to Spinoza and to his homes (v. 2, p. 304, 364-372)

Auerbach, Berthold, 1812-1882.
In Spinoza's home. ₍1884₎
₍3₎ col. 47cm.

Newspaper clipping.
Translated for the Jewish messenger from the author's Briefe an seinen Freund Jakob Auerbach, and includes entries for Sept. 5-8, and Sept. 10, 1878.

Bab, Arturo
Spinozas Ahnen. ₍1930₎
p. 321. 23cm.

From Jüdische Familien-Forschung, Jahrgang VI, Nr. 4, Dezember 1930.

1. Spinoza, Benedictus de, 1632-1677.

Der Bannspruch gegen Baruch Spinoza. ₍1862₎
623-624 p. 26cm.

From Allgemeine Zeitung des Judenthums, 26. Jahrgang, no. 44, 28. October 1862.
Includes the text of the excommunication edict issued against Spinoza in German translation.

Bannfluch gegen Spinoza. ₍Übertragung von L. Philippson. Darmstadt, Ernst Ludwig Presse, 1925₎
₍7₎ p. 28cm.

"Spinoza zu Ehren in einhundert fünfunddreissig Abzügen März 1925 hergestellt."

Bastian, Adolf, 1826-1905.
Schöpfung oder Entstehung. Aphorismen zur Entwicklung des organischen Lebens. Jena, H. Costenoble, 1875.
xxxi, 340 p.

Includes references to Spinoza.

Bennett, De Robigne Mortimer, 1818-1882.
The world's sages, infidels, and thinkers, being biographical sketches of leading philosophers, teachers, reformers, innovators, founders of new schools of thought, eminent scientists, etc. New York, Liberal and scientific publishing house, 1876.
1048 p. port. 21 cm.

Includes a section on Spinoza (p. 395-402)

Bersano, A
Per una notizia biografica su Spinoza. ₍1903₎
107-109 p.

In Rivista di filosofia e scienze affini, anno 5, v. 2, 1903.

Biographie universelle ancienne et moderne, ou Dictionnaire de tous les hommes qui se sont fait remarquer par leurs écrits, etc., depuis le commencement du monde jusqu'à ce jour ... Nouvelle ed. rev., corr., considérablement augm. ... par une société de gens de lettres et de savants. Bruxelles, H. Ode, 1843-47.
21 v. in 11. ports. 30cm.

Includes an article on Spinoza (v. 18, p. 267)

Betz, Hendrik Johan, 1842-1905.
Levensschets van Baruch de Spinoza, met een kort overzicht van zijn stelsel. 's Gravenhage, M. Nijhoff, 1876.
107 p. 22cm.

Bolin, Wilhelm, 1835-1924.
Спиноза. Біографическій и културно-историческій очеркъ. Переводъ с нѣмецкаго З. Н. Журавской и Д. В. Страндена. Подъ редакціей П. Струве. С.-Петербургъ, О. Н. Попова, 1899.
186 p. (Образовательная библіотека, сер. 2, № 5)

Title transliterated: Spinoza.
A translation of Spinoza, ein Kultur- und Lebensbild.

[Bradlaugh, Charles] 1833-1891.
Biographies of ancient and modern celebrated freethinkers. Reprinted from an English work, entitled "Half-hours with the freethinkers." By "Iconoclast." Collins [*pseud.*], & Watts. Boston. J. P. Mendum, 1877.
2 p. l., 344 p. 18 cm.
On cover: Half hours with freethinkers.
CONTENTS. — Thomas Hobbes. — Lord Bolingbroke. — Condorcet. — Spinoza.—Anthony Collins.—Des Cartes.—M. de Voltaire.—John Toland.—Compte de Volney.—Charles Blount.—Percy Byssche Shelley.—Claude Arian Helvetius. — Frances W. D'Arusmont. — Epicurus. — Zeno. — Matthew Tindal. — David Hume. — Dr. Thomas Burnet. — Thomas Paine.—Baptiste de Mirabaud.—Baron d'Holbach.—Robert Taylor.—Joseph Barker.
1. Rationalists. I. Collins, Anthony, pseud., joint author. II. Watts, John, joint author. III. Title. IV. Title: Half-hours with freethinkers.

[Bradlaugh, Charles] 1833-1891.
Biographies of ancient and modern celebrated freethinkers. Reprinted from an English work, entitled "Half-hours with the freethinkers." By "Iconoclast." New York, P. Eckler [1913?]
387 p. (Library of famous literature).

Includes a biography of Spinoza (p. 60-76)

[Bradlaugh, Charles] 1833-1891.
Half-hours with the freethinkers. Edited by Iconoclast, A. Collins [*pseud.*], & J. Watts ... 3d ed. London, F. Farrah, 1868.
1 p. l., 192 p. 19cm.
Contents differs slightly from that of 1st edition.
CONTENTS.—Des Cartes.—Volney.—Lord Bolingbroke.—Percy Bysshe Shelley.—Voltaire.—Anthony Collins.—Spinoza.—Thomas Paine.—Lord Shaftesbury. — Mirabaud and d'Holbach. — David Hume. — Thomas Hobbes.—Joseph Priestley.—Matthew Tindal.—Condorcet.—Epicurus.—Frances Wright D'Arusmont.—John Toland.—Zeno.—Helvetius.—Charles Blount.—Joseph Barker.—Robert Taylor.—Dr. Thomas Burnet.
1. Rationalism—Biog. I. Collins, Anthony, pseud., joint author. II. Watts, John, joint author. III. Title.

Browne, Lewis, 1897-
Blessèd Spinoza; a biography of the philosopher, by Lewis Browne ... New York, The Macmillan company, 1932.
xiii p., 3 l., 3-334 p. front., plates, ports., facsims. 22 cm.
"Selected bibliography": p. 321-328.
Presentation copy to A. S. Oko with the author's inscription and signature.

1. Spinoza, Benedictus de, 1632-1677.

Breza, Eugen Graf von
Gallerie der ausgezeichnetsten Israeliten aller Jahrhunderte, ihre Portraits und Biographien, hrsg. von Eugen Grafen Breza, redigirt von Richard Otto Spazier. Stuttgart, Fr. Brodhag'sche Buchhandlung, 1834-38.
5 pts. in 1 v. plate, ports. 28cm.

Parts [1-3] paged continuously.
Includes an essay on Spinoza (pt. [3], p. [87]-100.

Brucăr, I
Personalitatea lui Spinoza. [1928]
[50]-56 p. 24cm.

From Societatea de Studii Judaice din Romania. Sinai, anuar de studii Judaice, v. 1.

Brucăr, I
Spinoza, viața și filosofia. București, Editura Librăriei "Universala" Alcalay [1933]
193 p. 15cm. (Biblioteca pentru toti. 1334-1335)

Original paper cover bound in.

1. Spinoza, Benedictus de, 1632-1677.

Brunschvicg, Léon, 1869-1944.
Spinoza; vrij naar Léon Brunschvicg door W. G. van der Tak. 's-Gravenhage, J. P. Kruseman [1931]
189 p. plates, ports. (1 mount.) facsims. 25cm. (Helden van den geest. 1)

Carvalho, Joaquim de, 1892-
Sôbre o lugar de origem dos antepassados de Baruch de Espinosa. Coimbra, Imprensa da Universidade, 1930.
cover-title, 29 p.

At head of title: Miscelânea de estudos em honra de D. Carolina Michaëlis de Vasconcellos, professora da faculdade de letras da universidade de Coimbra.
Presentation copy to Carl Gebhardt with the author's inscription and signature.

Cingoli, Isacco Giuseppe
Baruch Spinoza; note critico-biografiche. ₍1911₎
296-297 p.

In Il Vessillo israelitico, anno 59, 1911.
With reference to the article Benedetto Spinoza e la teosofia ebraica, by "Discipulus" (Roberto Menasci)

Clark, Barrett Harper, 1890- *comp.*
Great short biographies of the world; a collection of short biographies, literary portraits, and memoirs chosen from the literatures of the ancient and modern world, by Barrett H. Clark. New York, R. M. McBride & company, 1928.
xiii, 1407 p. 24 cm.

Includes a biography of Spinoza by J. M. Lucas (p. 716-730)

1. Biography. I. Title. II. Title: Biographies of the world.

Cohn, Alexander Meyer, 1853-1904.
Die Autographen-Sammlung Alexander Meyer Cohn's. Mit einem Vorwort von Erich Schmidt. Berlin, J. A. Stargardt, 1905-06.
2 v. ports., facsims. 26cm.

"Versteigerung in Berlin vom 23. bis 28. Oktober 1905" und "vom 5. bis 10. Februar 1906."
No. 72 of 100 copies printed.
Includes a reference to Spinoza's autograph (no. 2513, v. 2, p. 223-224)

Cohon, Beryl David, 1898-
Spinoza - excommunicated saint. ₍1929₎
3-5 p. 23cm. (His Silhouettes from modern Jewish history. I)

Bibliography: p. 5.
From The Jewish Layman, v. 4, no. 3, November 1929.

Coleridge, Samuel Taylor, 1772-1834.
Biographia literaria. London, Dent; New York, Dutton ₍1910₎
xv, 334 p. 18cm. (Everyman's library. Essays. ₍no. 11₎)

Introduction by Arthur Symons.
Includes references to Spinoza.
Bibliography: p. xi-xii.

₍Costa, Isaac de₎ 1798-1860.
Adellijke geslachten onder de Israëlieten. ₍1857₎
210-217 p.

Signed: I - A.
In De Navorscher, 7. jaargang, 1857.
Includes references to the Spinoza family.

Costa, Isaac da, 1798-1860.
Noble families among the Sephardic Jews, with some account of the Capadose family (including their conversion to Christianity) by Bertram Brewster, and an excursus on their Jewish history, by Cecil Roth ... London, Oxford university press, 1936.
vi, 219 p. XLIV plates (incl. ports., facsims.) geneal. tables. 33 cm.

Includes sections on Spinoza (p. 89-91) and the Spinoza family (p. 115-116)

Couchoud, Paul Louis, 1879-
La jeunesse de Spinoza. ₍1901₎
318-330 p.

In Revue de philosophie, 1. année, 1901.
An excerpt from his Benoit de Spinoza.

Cresson, André, 1869-
... Spinoza; sa vie, son œuvre, avec un exposé de sa philosophie, par André Cresson. Paris, Alcan, Presses universitaires de France, 1940.
2 p. l., 142 p., 1 l. 18½cm. (Philosophes; collection dirigée par Émile Bréhier)

"Ces extraits sont généralement empruntés à la traduction de m. Appuhn ₍!₎"—p. ₍72₎
"Extraits": p. ₍73₎-135.
"Bibliographie": p. ₍137₎-139.

1. Spinoza, Benedictus de, 1632-1677. I. Spinoza, Benedictus de, 1632-1677. II. Appuhn, Charles, 1862- tr.

Damme, B
B. de Spinoza. Populaire bijdrage over zijn leven en leer. Met voorwoord van W. Meijer. Rotterdam, N. H. Luigies & Co., 1908.
107 p. port. 22cm.

[Davis, Mac], 1905-
From Moses to Einstein; they are all Jews. New York, Jordan publishing co. [c1937]
127 p. ports. 26 cm.

"Biographical sketches by Mac Davis with portraits by E. E. Claridge".
Includes a biography and portrait of Spinoza.

Diez, Heinrich Friedrich von, 1751-1817.
Benedikt von Spinoza nach Leben und Lehren. Dessau, 1783.
56 p.

Dubnov, Semen Markovich, 1860-
Die Geschichte des jüdischen Volkes in der Neuzeit; autorisierte Übersetzung aus dem russischen Manuskript von A. Steinberg. Berlin, Jüdischer Verlag [1927-28]
2 v. 24cm. (His Weltgeschichte des jüdischen Volkes, Bd. 6-7)

Vol. 2 includes a section "Der verbannte Baruch Spinoza" (p. 468-475) and other references to Spinoza.
Bibliography at end of each volume.

Dujovne, León
Spinoza; su vida, su época, su obra, su influencia. Buenos Aires, 1941-42.
v. 1-2. plates, ports., facsim. 24cm.

At head of title: Universidad de Buenos Aires. Facultad de filosofía y letras. Instituto de filosofía.
Contents.--I. La vida de Baruj Spinoza.--II. La época de Baruj Spinoza.

Dunin-Borkowski, Stanislaus, *graf* von, 1864-
Der junge De Spinoza. Leben und werdegang im lichte der weltphilosophie. Von Stanislaus von Dunin-Borkowski, s. J. Mit zwei vierfarbendrucken, dreizehn autotypien und sieben faksimiles. Münster i. W., Aschendorff, 1910.

xxiii, 633, [1] p. incl. 1 illus., plates, facsims. plates, ports. (2 col.; ~~incl. front.)~~ fold. facsims. 25cm.

Bibliography included in "Anmerkungen" (p. [521]-606) "Bibliographische notizen und wegweiser für die künftige forschung": p. [607]-608.

1. Spinoza, Benedictus de, 1632-1677.

[*Full name:* Graf Zbigniew Stanislaus Martin von Dunin-Borkowski]

Dunin-Borkowski, Stanislaus, Graf von, 1864-1934.
Der junge Spinoza. [1912]
165-170 p.

In Der Aar, Jahrgang 2, 1912.

Dunin-Borkowski, Stanislaus, Graf von, 1864-1934.
Nachlese zur ältesten Geschichte des Spinozismus. [1910]
61-98 p.

In Archiv für Geschichte der Philosophie, Bd. 24., 1910.

Dunin-Borkowski, Stanislaus, *graf* von, 1864- 1934.
... Spinoza ... Münster i. W., Aschendorff, 1933- 36.
4 v. plates, ports., facsims. (part fold.) 25cm.

Each volume has also special t.-p.

CONTENTS.—I. Der junge De Spinoza. 2. aufl.—II. Aus den tagen Spinozas. 1. t. Das entscheidungsjahr 1657.--III. Aus den tagen Spinozas. 2. t. Das neue leben.--IV. Aus den tagen Spinozas. 3. t. Das lebenswerk.

1. Spinoza, Benedictus de, 1632-1677.

[*Full name:* Graf Zbigniew Stanislaus Martin von Dunin-Borkowski]

Dunin-Borkowski, Stanislaus, Graf von, 1864-1934.
Spinoza. Münster i. W., Aschendorff, 1933-36.
4 v. plates, ports., facsims. (part fold.) 25cm.

Vol. 1-3 have special title-pages also.
Vol. 4 is proof copy, p. [77]-348 only.
Vol. 1-3, presentation copy to Carl Gebhardt, with author's inscription and signature in v. 1. Manuscript notes by A. S. Oko in v. 4.

SPECIAL COLLECTIONS SPINOZA C-1-c 446

Dunin-Borkowski, Stanislaus, *graf* von, 1864–
Spinoza nach dreihundert jahren, von Stan. von Dunin Borkowski, s. J. Berlin und Bonn, F. Dümmler, 1932.
204 p. 20cm.
CONTENTS.—Von den ahnen.—Der mensch und der denker.—Der nachlass.—Die erbschaft.—Buchkundliche nachschau.

1. Spinoza, Benedictus de, 1632-1677.
[*Full name:* Graf Zbigniew Stanislaus Martin von Dunin-Borkowski]
Title from Univ. of Minn. Printed by L. C. A C 33-147
[2]

C-1-c 451

Feller, François Xavier de, 1735-1802.
Biographie universelle, ou Dictionnaire historique des hommes qui se sont fait un nom par leur génie ... Nouvelle édition ... par M. Perennès. Besançon, Gauthier, 1833-38.
12 v.

MH

SPECIAL COLLECTIONS SPINOZA C-1-c 447

Dunin-Borkowski, Stanislaus, Graf von, 1864–
Zur Textgeschichte und Textkritik der ältesten Lebensbeschreibung Benedikt Despinozas. [1904]
34 p. 24cm.

From Archiv für Philosophie. I. Abteilung: Archiv für Geschichte der Philosophie. Neue Folge. XVIII. Band, 1. Heft."
Ms. notes by A. S. Oko.

SPECIAL COLLECTIONS SPINOZA C-1-c 452

Fernández Alonso, Benito, 1848-1922.
Los Judíos en Orense (siglos XV al XVII) Orense, A. Otero, 1904.
46 p. 21cm.

Includes references to Spinoza and his ancestors (p. 34-36)

SPECIAL COLLECTIONS SPINOZA C-1-c 448

Eberlin, Philipp
Antiphädon über die Natur. Von Philipp Eberlin ... Mannheim und Frankenthal, bey den Herausgebern der Sammlung historischer Schriftsteller, 1784.
77 p., [1] l. 18cm.

A short biographical sketch of Spinoza and a fictitious dialogue between him and his friend and disciple Georg Jelis.

C-1-c 453

[Fiorentino, Francesco] 1834-1884.
Vita e carattere di Benedetto Spinoza. [1870]
24-43 p.

Signed: F. Fiorentino.
In Rivista bolognese di scienze e lettere, anno 4, serie 2, 1870.

SPECIAL COLLECTIONS SPINOZA C-1-c 449

Ehrentheil, Moritz, 1825-1894, ed.
Jüdisches Familien-Buch ... 160 Lebens- und Charakterbilder der vorzüglichsten Gestalten der jüdischen Geschichte aus allen Zeitperioden und Staaten. Unter Mitwirkung bewährter Fachmänner hrsg. von M. Ehrentheil. Budapest, Pester Buchdruckerei-Actien-Gesellschaft, 1880.
576 p. 24cm.

Includes references to Spinoza.
Bibliographical footnotes.

SPECIAL COLLECTIONS SPINOZA C-1-c 454

Freudenthal, Jacob, 1839-1907, ed.
Die Lebensgeschichte Spinoza's in Quellenschriften, Urkunden und nichtamtlichen Nachrichten; mit Unterstützung der Königl. Preussischen Akademie der Wissenschaften hrsg. von J. Freudenthal. Leipzig, Veit, 1899.
xvi, 304 p. 24cm.

Original paper covers bound in.
Ms. notes by Carl Gebhardt.

SPECIAL COLLECTIONS SPINOZA C-1-c 450

Eisendraht, Maurice Nathan, 1902–
Spinoza, cursed in life; blessed in death. Toronto, Ont., Holy Blossom Synagogue [1932]
19 p. 19cm. (Holy Blossom pulpit, v. 3, no. 3, 1932-33)

SPECIAL COLLECTIONS SPINOZA C-1-c 455

Freudenthal, Jacob, 1839-1907.
Spinoza, leben und lehre ... Heidelberg, C. Winter; [etc., etc.] 1927.
xvi, 350, [2], 270 p. 22½ x 18cm. (*Half-title:* Bibliotheca Spinozana curis Societatis Spinozanae. t. v)
Bibliography: p. xii.
CONTENTS.—1. t. Das leben Spinozas, von J. Freudenthal. 2. aufl., hrsg. von Carl Gebhardt.—2. t. Die lehre Spinozas auf grund des nachlasses von J. Freudenthal, bearb. von Carl Gebhardt.

1. Spinoza, Benedictus de, 1632-1677. I. Gebhardt, Carl, 1881–
Library of Congress B3997.F8 1927 27-25517
[2]

Freudenthal, Jacob, 1839-1907.
Spinoza, sein Leben und seine Lehre. Erster Band: Das Leben Spinozas. Stuttgart, Fr. Frommanns Verlag (E. Hauff) 1904.
xiii, 349 p. 23cm.

No more published.
Ms. notes by Carl Gebhardt.
Bibliographical references included in "Anmerkungen" (p. [318]-349)

Freudenthal, Jacob, 1839-1907.
שפינוזה; קורות חייו ותוכן ספריו
במאת י. פריידינתאל, מעובד ומתורגם
מגרמניה ע"י מ. רבינזון. חלק ראשון.
ווילנה, הוצאת הירחון "ביבליאתיקה".
תרע"ג.

[Vilna] 1913.
221 p. 20cm.

Title transliterated: Spinoza.
No more published.

NNC

Freudenthal, Jacob, 1839-1907.
Über den Text der Lucasschen Biographie Spinozas. [1905]
189-208 p.

In Zeitschrift für Philosophie und philosophische Kritik, Bd. 126, 1905.

Friedländer, Michael, 1833-1910.
Spinoza. His life and philosophy. Two papers read before the Jews' College Literary Society, June 5th, 1887, and April 22nd, 1888. London, "Jewish Chronicle" Office, 1888.
32 p. 25cm.

Original paper covers bound in.
Author's inscription and signature on t.-p.

Friedländer, Michael, 1833-1910.
Spinoza. His life and philosophy. Two papers read before the Jews' College Literary Society, June 5th, 1887, and April 22nd, 1888. London, "Jewish Chronicle" Office, 1888.
32 p. 25cm.

Original paper covers bound in.
Author's inscription and signature on t.-p.

Fromer, Jakob, 1865-
Spinozas Persönlichkeit. [1926]
339-347 p. 25cm.

From Der Morgen, II. Jahrgang, 4. Heft, Oktober 1926.

1. Spinoza, Benedictus de, 1632-1677.

[Froude, James Anthony] 1818-1894.
The life of Spinoza. [1847]
387-427 p.

In Oxford and Cambridge review, v. 5, 1847.

CtY

Gebhardt, Carl, 1881-1934.
Der Name Spinoza. [Hagae Comitis, 1921]
[272]-276 p. 22cm.

Cover-title: Dissertatio ex Chronici Spinozani tomo primo separatim edita.

1. Spinoza, Benedictus de, 1632-1677.

Gebhardt, Carl, 1881-1934.
Spinoza; Lebensbeschreibungen und Gespräche. Übertragen und herausgegeben von Carl Gebhardt. Leipzig, F. Meiner, 1914.
xi, 147 p. port. 20cm. (Der Philosophischen Bibliothek. Bd. 96b)

Bibliographical notes: p. [133]-147.

Gebhardt, Carl, 1881-1934.
Spinoza in der Schule. [1930]
[170]-181 p. 26cm.

Reprint from Der philosophische Unterricht, Zeitschrift der Gesellschaft für philosophischen Unterricht. Bd. 1, Heft 4/5, 1930.

Gebhardt, Carl, 1881-1934.
Spinozas Bann. ⸢1927⸣
144-148 p. 25cm.

From Der Morgen, 3. Jahrgang, 2. Heft, Juni 1927.

Gebhardt, Carl, 1881-1934.
Spinozas Persönlichkeit. ⸢1932⸣
p. 1.

In Frankfurter Zeitung, Nov. 21, 1932.

NN

Ginsberg, Hugo, 1829-
Lebens- und Charakterbild Baruch Spinozas, nach den vorhandenen Quellen entworfen. Leipzig, E. Koschny, 1876.
45 p. 23cm.

Original paper covers bound in.

Gorelik, Schmarja, 1877-1942.
... Jüdische köpfe; lithographien von Joseph Budko. Berlin, F. Gurlitt, 1920.

114 p., 1 l. ports. 30 x 24cm.

At head of title: Sch. Gorelik.
"Aus dem jüdischen übersetzt von Stefania Goldenring und Nadia Strasser."
Includes a chapter on Spinoza (p. ⸢99⸣-114)
"Vorzugsausgabe" No. 2 of 100 copies, with the author's signature.

1. Jews—Biog. I. Budko, Joseph, 1888-1940, illus. II. Goldenring, Stefania, tr. III. Strasser, Nadia, joint tr. IV. Title.

44-10820

Library of Congress DS115.G64
⸢2⸣

Graetz, Heinrich, 1817-1891.
Baruch Spinoza; a biographical sketch. ⸢1868⸣
6 pts.

In The Israelite, v. 14, 1868.
From his Geschichte der Juden, Bd. 10. Leipzig, 1868.

OCH

Groyse mener.
גרויסע מענער (ביאגראפיעס) לעבענס־
בעשרייבונגען פון די גרעסטע מענער
פון אלע פעלקער און אלע צייטען. בעאר־
בייטעט נאך פארשידענע קוועלען.
New York, Star Hebrew Book Co. ⸢193-?⸣
1 v. (various pagings) 20cm.

Includes a chapter on Spinoza.

Gruenfeld, Karl Sigmund
Berühmte Männer und Frauen. Ein illustrirter Protest gegen den Antisemitismus. Hrsg. von C. S. Grünfeld. Illustrirt von C. E. von Stur. Ser. 1. Wien, M. Waizner, 1886.

Includes a biography and portrait of Spinoza.

OCH

⸢Guggenheim, M ⸣
Zum Leben Spinozas und den Schicksalen des Tractatus theologico-politicus. ⸢1896⸣
⸢121⸣-142 p. 23cm.

Signed: M. Guggenheim.
On cover: Vierteljahrsschrift für wissenschaftliche Philosophie. Sonderabdruck.

NNC

Goeree, Willem, 1635-1711.
De kerklyke en weereldlyke historien; uyt d'aal-ouwde aardbeschryving, en uytgezogte gedenk-penningen opgehelderd, door W. Goeree ... t'Amsteldam, By Gerardus en Jakobus Borstius, 1705.
⸢42⸣, 746, ⸢94⸣ p. illus., plates, ports., fold. maps, fold. geneal. table. 21cm.

Added engraved title-page.
Includes a section on Spinoza, with his portrait (p. 664-677)

NNC

Goeree, Willem, 1635-1711.
De kerklyke en weereldlyke historien; uyt d'aal-ouwde aardbeschryving, en uytgezogte gedenk-penningen opgehelderd, door W. Goeree ... Tweeden druk ... Te Leyden, By Johannes van Abkoude, 1730.
⸢44⸣, 746, ⸢94⸣ p. illus., ports., maps. geneal. table. 25cm.

Includes a section on Spinoza, with his portrait (p. 664-677)
Added title-page engraved.

C-1-c 476

Hallema, A
Spinoza in den hof van het Amsterdamsche Tuchthuis. Een schets van waarheid en verdichting. [1932]
p. 2.

In Nieuwe Rotterdamsche courant, Sept. 4, 1932.

DLC

C-1-c 477

How Spinoza lived. [1878-79]
p. 5.

In The Reformer and Jewish times, v. 10, no. 4, 1878-79.

NN

SPECIAL COLLECTIONS SPINOZA C-1-c 478

Ish-Kishor, Sulamith
The lens grinder of Amsterdam; the story of Baruch Spinoza. [1927]
2-3 p. illus., port. 31cm.

From the Young Judaean, March, 1927.

1. Spinoza, Benedictus de, 1632-1677.
I. Title.

C-1-c 479

Jäger, Johann Wolfgang, 1647-1720, praeses.
Spinocismus; sive, Benedicti Spinosae, famosi atheistae, vita et doctrinalia, quae pro materia disputationis praeside Joh. Wolfgango Jägero ... examini subjiciet J. J. Fladt ... Tubingae, Literis J. C. Reisi [1710]
32 p.

OCH

SPECIAL COLLECTIONS SPINOZA C-1-c 480

[Jones, Stephen] 1763-1827.
A new biographical dictionary; or, Pocket compendium: containing a brief account of the lives and writings of the most eminent persons in every age and nations ... London, Printed for G. G. and J. Robinson, J. Wallis, J. Scatcherd, and E. Newbery, 1794.
[4], 4, [422] p. 14cm.

Preface signed: S. J.
Includes an article on Spinoza.
Imperfect: pages lacking at end.

SPECIAL COLLECTIONS SPINOZA C-1-c 481

Jones, Stephen, 1763-1827.
A new biographical dictionary: containing a brief account of the lives and writings of the most eminent persons and remarkable characters in every age and nation. By Stephen Jones. The third edition, corrected: with very considerable additions. London; Printed by T. Bensley, for G. G. and J. Robinson [etc.] 1799.
viii, [424] p. 15cm.

Includes a paragraph on Spinoza (p. [383])

NNC

SPECIAL COLLECTIONS SPINOZA C-1-c 482

Jones, Stephen, 1763-1827.
A new biographical dictionary: containing a brief account of the lives and writings of the most eminent persons and remarkable characters in every age and nation. The seventh edition: with numerous additions and improvements. London, Printed for Longman, Hurst, Rees, Orme, and Brown [etc.] 1822.
443 p. 16cm.

Includes a paragraph on Spinoza (p. 394-395)

SPECIAL COLLECTIONS SPINOZA C-1-c 483

Jüdischer Plutarch; oder biographisches Lexicon der markantesten Männer und Frauen jüdischer Abkunft (aller Stände, Zeiten und Länder) mit besonderer Rücksicht auf das österreichische Kaiserthum. Von mehreren jüdischen und nichtjüdischen, in- und ausländischen Schriftstellern. Zweytes Alphabeth, oder zweyter Band. Wien, Verlag von Ulrich Klopf sen. und Alexander Eurich, 1848.
258 p. port. 18cm.

Includes a chapter on Spinoza (p. 229-234)

SPECIAL COLLECTIONS SPINOZA C-1-c 484

Kayser, Rudolf, 1889-
Spinoza; bildnis eines geistigen helden. Wien [etc.] Phaidon-verlag, 1932.
313 p., 1 l. plates, ports., facsim. 20½cm.
"Bibliographie": p. [309]-311.

1. Spinoza, Benedictus de, 1632-1677.

Library of Congress B3997.K3 33-13343
Copyright A—Foreign 20445 [2] 921.3

C-1-c 485

Kayser, Rudolf, 1889-
Spinozas Kinderzeit. [1932]
268-270 p.

In Gemeindeblatt der jüdischen Gemeinde zu Berlin, Jahrgang 22, 1932.
An excerpt from his Spinoza; Bildnis eines geistigen Helden.

NNJ

Kettner, Frederick, 1886-
Spinoza and the Spinoza Center. [1932]
138-139 p. illus., port. 30cm.

From B'nai B'rith Magazine, vol. 46, no. 5, February, 1932.

Klaar, Alfred, 1848-
Spinoza, sein Leben und seine Lehre. Berlin, Ullstein [c1926]
154 p. 18cm. (Wege zum Wissen. [59])

Bibliography: p. [155]

Klatzkin, Jacob, 1882-1948.
ברוך שפינוזה; חייו, ספריו, שטתו. מאת יעקב קלצקין. ליפסיה בהוצ' אברהם שטיבלם תרפ"ג.
[Leipzig, 1923]
193 p. port. (His כתבי ברוך שפינוזה, [v. 1.])

Title transliterated: Bārūkh Shpīnōzā.
Bibliography: p. [187]-193.

Klatzkin, Jacob, 1882-1948.
ברוך שפינוזה; חייו, ספריו, שטתו. מאת יעקב קלצקין. ליפסיה בהוצ' אברהם שטיבלם תרפ"ג.
[Leipzig, 1923]
193 p. port. (His כתבי ברוך שפינוזה, [v. 1.])

Title transliterated: Bārūkh Shpīnōzā.
Bibliography: p. [187]-193.
Presentation copy to A. S. Oko with the author's inscription and signature in Hebrew.

Kohler, Kaufmann, 1843-1926.
Baruch Spinoza. Sketch of the life and labors of the great philosopher. [1877-78]
p. 18.

In The Reformer and Jewish times, v. 9, no. 3, 1877-78.

[Lasker, Raphael]
Eminent Jewish authors and poets. [1903]
11-20 p. port.

In New era Jewish magazine, v. 2, 1903.
Includes biography and portrait of Spinoza.

Lazaron, Morris Samuel, 1888-
Seed of Abraham; ten Jews of the ages [by] Morris S. Lazaron. New York & London, The Century co. [°1930]
xiii, 327 p. front., plates, ports. 19cm. $2.50

CONTENTS.—Moses.—David.—Jeremiah.—Mary.—Jesus.—Spinoza.—Heinrich Heine.—Karl Heinrich Marx.—Benjamin Disraeli.—Theodor Herzl.

1. Jews—Biog. I. Title.

Lee, Arthur Bolles, 1849-1927.
Spinoza: the man and the philosopher. [1877]
567-602 p.

In Contemporary review, v. 29, 1877.

Lehmans, J B
Spinoza; sein Lebensbild und seine Philosophie. Würzburg, Druck von F. E. Thein, 1864.
vi, 127 p. 24cm.

Thesis, Würzburg.

Lehrer, David, 1898-
שפינאָזא-הויז אין ריינסבורג. [1930]
937-938 p.

Title transliterated: Shpinoza-hoyz in Raynsburg.
In Literarishe bleter, v. 6, 1930.

Lempriere, John, 1765?–1824.
Lempriere's universal biography; containing a critical and historical account of the lives, characters, and labours of eminent persons, in all ages and countries. Together with selections of foreign biography from Watkin's dictionary, recently published, and about eight hundred original articles of American biography. By Eleazar Lord. New York, R. Lockwood, 1825.
2 v. 22cm.
Includes an article on Spinoza (v. 2, p. 659)
1. Biography—Dictionaries. I. Lord, Eleazar, 1788–1871. II. Title.
19—3633

Letteris, Meir Halevi, 1800?-1871.
תולדות החכם החוקר ברוך די שפינא־
זא ז"ל, מאת מאיר הלוי לעטעריס.
Wien, Franz Edl. v. Schmidt & J. J. Busch, 1845.
27-33 l. 17cm.

Title transliterated: Tōlĕdhōth ...
From בכורי העתים החדשים (ed. by I. Reggio and I. Busch) neue Folge I.

Levensbeschryving van eenige voornaame meest Nederlandsche mannen en vrouwen ... Uit egte stukken opgemaakt. Te Amsterdam, By Petrus Conradi, Te Harlingen, By F. van der Plaats & Junior, 1774-83.
10 v. 23cm.

Vol. 2 includes a chapter on Spinoza.

Levinger, Elma (Ehrlich) 1887–
Great Jews since Bible times, for young people, by Elma Ehrlich Levinger ... New York city, Behrman's Jewish book shop, 1926.
158 p. illus. (incl. ports.) 19 cm.

Includes a section on Spinoza (p. 100-103)

1. Jews—Biog. 2. Biography—Juvenile literature. I. Title.

Lewes, George Henry, 1817–1878.
The biographical history of philosophy from its origin in Greece down to the present day. By George Henry Lewes ... Library ed., much enl. and thoroughly rev. New York, D. Appleton and company, 1857.
2 p. l., iii–xxxiv, 802 p. 22 cm.
CONTENTS.—pt. I. Ancient philosophy.—pt. II. Modern philosophy.
Includes a chapter on Spinoza.

1. Philosophers. I. Title.

Lewes, George Henry, 1817-1878.
A biographical history of philosophy. London, Routledge, 1894.
656 p. 19cm. (Sir John Lubbock's hundred books. 16)

Includes two chapters on Spinoza.

[Lewes, George Henry] 1817-1878, comp.
Life of Benedict Spinoza. [1851]
8 p.

In The Library of reason: articles from ancient and modern authors in favour of free inquiry, no. 3 [1851]
Compiled from his Spinoza's life and works.

[Lewes, George Henry] 1817-1878.
Spinoza's life and works. [1843]
530-549 p.

In Eclectic museum of foreign literature, science & art, v. 2, 1843.

[Lewes, George Henry] 1817-1878.
Spinoza's life and works. [1843]
372-407 p.

Signed: G. H. L.
In Westminster review, v. 39, 1843.

Lewes, George Henry, 1817-1878.
Spinoza. [1866]
257-292 p.

In Wetenschappelijke bladen, dl. 12, 1866.

Lopez-Trujillo, Clemente
Dialogo de sombras. ⌊1941⌋
p. 3.

In El Nacional, Mexico City, abril 5, 1941.
A sketch of Spinoza's life.

McCabe, Joseph, 1867-
A biographical dictionary of modern rationalists. London, Watts, 1920.
xxxii p., 934 numb. cols. 27 cm.

Includes an article on Spinoza (col. 753-754)

Maccall, William, 1812-1888.
Foreign biographies. London, Tinsley, 1873.
2 v. 21 cm.

Includes a biography "Benedict Spinoza" (v. 1, p. ⌊299⌋-320)

Mauthner, Fritz, 1849-1923.
Spinoza. Berlin, Schuster & Loeffler ⌊1906⌋
76 p. plate, ports., fold. facsim. (Die Dichtung. Bd. XLIII)

Carl Gebhardt's signature on t.-p.

Mauthner, Fritz, 1849–1923.
Spinoza; ein umriss seines lebens und wirkens, von Fritz Mauthner. Dresden, C. Reissner, 1921.
157 p. front. (port.) 19½cm.

"Die vorliegende ausgabe stellt eine erweiterte neubearbeitung der im jahre 1906 erschienenen schrift dar."

1. Spinoza, Benedictus de, 1632-1677.

Mauthner, Fritz, 1849-1923.
Spinoza; ein Umriss seines Lebens und Wirkens. 11. bis 16. Aufl. Dresden, C. Reissner, 1922.
157 p. port. 20cm. (Schöpferische Mystik)

Meijer, Willem, 1842-1926.
Spinoza. ⌊1911⌋
1480-1484 col. 27 cm.

From Molhuysen, Philip Christiaan. Nieuw Nederlandsch biografisch woordenboek, v. 1, 1911.

Meijer, Willem, 1842-1926.
Drie ambtelijke stukken betrekking hebbende op Spinoza's levensgeschiedenis. ⌊Hagae Comitis, 1921⌋
20-26 p. facsims. 22cm.

Cover-title: Dissertatio ex Chronici Spinozani tomo primo separatim edita.

1. Spinoza, Benedictus de, 1632-1677.

Meijer, Willem, 1842-1926.
Spinoza, een levensbeeld. Amsterdam, Ipenbuur & Van Seldam ⌊1915⌋
34 p. illus., ports. 27cm. (Populair wetenschappelijk Nederland. No. 14)

Original paper covers bound in.
Ms. notes by A. S. Oko.

1. Spinoza, Benedictus de, 1632-1677.

Meijer, Willem, 1842-1926.
Wer war Lucas? von W. Meyer. ⌊1898⌋
⌊270⌋-278 p. 24cm.

From Archiv für Philosophie. I. Abtheilung: Archiv für Geschichte der Philosophie. Neue Folge. XI. Band, 2. Heft.
Includes references to Spinoza.

C-1-c 516

Meinsma, Koenraad Oege, 1865-1929.
Die Unzulänglichkeit der bisherigen Biographien Spinoza's. [1896]
208-224 p.

In Archiv für Geschichte der Philosophie, Bd. 9., 1896.

SPECIAL COLLECTIONS SPINOZA C-1-c 517

Montor, Henry
The good life of Baruch Spinoza; with comments on Lewis Browne's biography. [1932]
2 p. ports. 35cm.

From the American Jewish world, vol. 21, no. 13, November 25, 1932.

SPECIAL COLLECTIONS SPINOZA C-1-c 518

[Nicéron, Jean Pierre] 1685-1738.
Mémoires pour servir à l'histoire des hommes illustres dans la république des lettres, avec un catalogue raisonné de leurs ouvrages ... Paris, Briasson, 1728-40.
v. 1-41 in 42. 17cm.

By Nicéron and others.
Includes sections on Spinoza (v. 13, p. 30-52; v. 20, p. 59-61)

C-1-c 519

Nicéron, Jean Pierre, 1685-1738.
Joh. Pet. Nicerons Nachrichten von den Begebenheiten und Schriften berümten [!] Gelehrten, mit einigen Zusätzen hrsg. von Siegmund Jacob Baumgarten. Halle, Verlag und Druck C. P. Franckens, 1749-77.
24 v. in 13. ports. 18cm.

Includes a section on Spinoza (v. 1, p. 265-283)

C-1-c 520

Nisselowitsch, Elieser Josef

מימי נעורי שפינוזה. [1872]
594-598 p.

Title transliterated: Miyemey ne'urey Shpinoza.
In ha-Karmel, v. 1, no. 11-12, 1872.

NNJ

C-1-c 521

Nouvelle biographie générale depuis les temps les plus reculés jusqu'à nos jours, avec les renseignements bibliographiques et l'indication des sources à consulter; publiée par mm. Firmin Didot frères, sous la direction de m. le dr. Hoefer. Paris, Firmin Didot, 1853-70.
46 v. 24 cm.

Includes a biography of Spinoza (v. 44, col. 336-346)

SPECIAL COLLECTIONS SPINOZA C-1-c 522

Paraira, Mozes Cohen
Gedenkschrift, uitgegeven ter gelegenheid van het 300-jarig bestaan der onderwijsinrichtingen Talmud Tora en Ets Haïm, bij de Portug. Israël. Gemeente te Amsterdam. Door M. C. Paraira en J. S. Da Silva Rosa. [Amsterdam, 1916]
83 p. illus., facsims. 29cm.

At head of title: 5376-5676.
Includes references to Spinoza and his family (p. 28, 69)

SPECIAL COLLECTIONS SPINOZA C-1-c 523

Payne, A H
Payne's biographisches Lexikon; nach den neuesten Quellen bearbeitet. Reudnitz bei Leipzig, A. H. Payne, 1884.
414 p. 27cm.

Includes a paragraph on Spinoza (p. 381)

SPECIAL COLLECTIONS SPINOZA C-1-c 524

[Philippson, Ludwig] 1811-1889.
Baruch Spinoza (eine Skizze) [1832]
327-336 p. 21cm.

Signed: Ludwig Philippson.
From Sulamith, eine Zeitschrift zur Beförderung der Kultur und Humanität unter den Israeliten, 17. Jahrg., 11. Heft.

SPECIAL COLLECTIONS SPINOZA C-1-c 525

Philipson, Moses, b. 1761.
Leben Benedikt's von Spinosa. Von M. Philipson ... Braunschweig, Verlag der Schulbuchhandlung, 1790.
120 p. 15½cm.

1. Spinoza, Benedictus de, 1632-1677.

7—18765

Library of Congress B3997.P5
[a40b1]

Pollock, Sir Frederick, bart., 1845-1937.
Spinoza: his life and philosophy. London, C. Kegan Paul & Co., 1880.
xlii, 467 p. port. 23cm.

Appendix A: The life of Spinoza, by Colerus (p. ₍409₎-445)

Pollock, *Sir* **Frederick,** *bart.*, 1845–1937.
Spinoza: his life and philosophy, by Sir Frederick Pollock ... 2d ed. ... London, Duckworth and co.; New York, The Macmillan company, 1899.

xxiv, 427 p. 23 cm.

Appendix: The life of Spinoza, by Colerus: p. ₍383₎–418.

1. Spinoza, Benedictus de, 1632–1677. I. Colerus, Johannes, d. 1707.

Pollock, Sir Frederich, bart., 1845-1937.
Spinoza: his life and philosophy. ₍2d ed., corrected and re-issued₎ London, Duckworth ₍1912₎
xxiv, 427 p. 23cm.

Appendix: The life of Spinoza, by Colerus (p. ₍383₎-418)

Pollock, *Sir* **Frederick,** *bart.*, 1845–
Spinoza, by Sir Frederick Pollock ... London, Duckworth ₍1935₎

143, ₍1₎ p. 19cm. (Great lives. ₍60₎)

"First published, 1935."
Bibliography: p. ₍144₎

Proof copy.

1. Spinoza, Benedictus de, 1632-1677.

Pollock, Sir Frederick, bart., 1845-
Spinoza. London, Duckworth ₍1935₎
143 p. 19cm. (Great lives. ₍60₎)

Proof copy with corrections indicated.
Bibliography: p. ₍144₎

Pollock, *Sir* **Frederick,** *bart.*, 1845–
Spinoza, by Sir Frederick Pollock ... London, Duckworth ₍1935₎

143, ₍1₎ p. 19cm. (Great lives. ₍60₎)

"First published, 1935."
Bibliography: p. ₍144₎
Ms. notes by A. S. Oko.

1. Spinoza, Benedictus de, 1632-1677.

Pollock, Sir Frederick, bart., 1845-1937.
Benedict de Spinoza. ₍1878₎
771-785 p. 23cm.

From Littell's living age, 5th series, vol. XXI; no. 1763, March 30, 1878.
Appeared originally in the Nineteenth century.

Rich, Elihu, 1819–1875, *ed.*
Appletons' cyclopædia of biography: embracing a series of original memoirs of the most distinguished persons of all times ... American ed., edited by Francis L. Hawkes ... New York, D. Appleton and company, 1856.

6, 1058 p. illus. 26½cm.

The basis of this work is the "Cyclopedia of biography" ed. by Elihu Rich in London. *cf.* Prelim. note.
Includes an article on Spinoza (p. 884-885)

1. Biography—Dictionaries. I. Hawks, Francis Lister, 1798–1866, joint ed. II. Title.

Rivaud, Albert, 1876-
Documents inédits sur la vie de Spinoza. ₍1934₎
253-262 p.

In Revue de métaphysique et de morale, 11. année, 1934.
A review of Spinoza, mercator et autodidactus, by A. M. Vaz Dias and Willem G. van der Tak.

Rombro, Jacob, 1858-1922.
Барухъ Спиноза; этюдъ. [1880-81]

Title transliterated: Barukh Spinoza.
In Разсвѣтъ, т. 2-3, 1880-1881.

[Rombro, Jacob] 1858–1922.
... ברוך ספינאזא: זיין לעבען און זיין פילאזאפיע. פון פיליפ קראנץ [pseud.]
[New York, International library publishing co., ©1905]
1 p. l., [5]–64 p. 17½cm. (On cover: די אינטערנאציאנאלע ביבליאטהעק)

On cover: Baruch Spinoza; biography by Ph. Krantz.
At head of title: לעבענסבעשרייבונגען פון בעריהמטע מענער
Title transliterated: Barukh Spinoza.

1. Spinoza, Benedictus de, 1632–1677. I. Title.

Title transliterated: Baruch Spinoza.

Rubin, Solomon, 1823-1910.
מורה נבוכים החדש; כולל שני ספרי החוקר הנשגב והנפלא ברוך די שפינוזה, לפי העתקת הצרפתי Emile Saisset ; עם תולדות חיי הפילוסוף, ממני שלמה ראבין. וויען, בבית הדפוס של יאזעף האלצווארטה, התרט"ז.
[Vienna, Joseph Holzwarth, 1856-57]
2 pt. in 1 v.

Title transliterated: Mōrē nĕbhūkhīm he-ḥādhāsh.
On Spinoza's life and philosophy.

Rubin, Solomon, 1823-1955.
שיטת שפינוזה בפילוסופיא. וויען, תרמ"ד.
[Wien, 1884]
243-262 p. 23cm.

Title transliterated: Shiṭṭath Spinoza.
From Haschachar (Die Morgenröthe) XII. Jahrgang, 4. Heft, 1884.

Rubin, Salomon, 1823-1910.
שיטת שפינוזה בפילוסופיא. [1884]
243-252 p.

Title transliterated: Shitath Shpinozah befilosofiya.
In ha-Shakhar, v. 12, no. 4, 1884.

Saintes, Amand, b. 1801.
Histoire de la vie et des ouvrages de B. de Spinosa, fondateur de l'exégèse et de la philosophie modernes. Par Amand Saintes. Paris, J. Renouard et cie, 1842.
2 p. l., xx, 390 p. front. (port.) 22½cm.

"Bibliographie Spinosiste": p. [xvii]-xx.
Original paper covers bound in.

Salinger, Richard, 1859-
Spinozas Berufung nach Heidelberg; ein Beitrag zur Geschichte der Denk- und Glaubensfreiheit. [1925]
320-321 p. 31cm.

From Der Schild; Zeitschrift des Reichsbundes jüdischer Frontsoldaten, E. V., 4. Jahrg., no. 22, September 3, 1925.

[Schaller, Prediger in Magdeburg]
Benedikt Spinoza. Geboren den 24. Nov. 1632. Gestorben den 21. Febr. 1677. [Halle, Waisenhaus-Buchhandlung, 1806]
[257]-316 p. 20cm.

From Der Biograph; Darstellungen merkwürdiger Menschen der drey letzten Jahrhunderte. 5. Bd.

1. Spinoza, Benedictus de, 1632-1677.

Scholz, Heinrich, 1884-
Spinozas Leben und Briefe. [1914]
379-384 p. 26cm.

From Die Grenzboten; Zeitschrift für Politik, Literatur und Kunst, Dec. 23, 1914.
A review of Carl Gebhardt's book Spinoza, Lebensbeschreibung und Gespräche, and of his translation of Spinoza's letters.

Schudt, Johann Jacob, 1664-1722.
Jüdische Merckwürdigkeiten vorstellende was sich curieuses und denckwürdiges in den neuern Zeiten bey einigen Jahr-hunderten mit denen in alle IV. Theile der Welt, sonderlich durch Teutschland, zerstreuten Juden zugetragen. Samt einer vollständigen Franckfurter Juden-Chronick, darinnen der zu Franckfurt am Mayn wohnenden Juden, von einigen Jahr-hunderten, biss auff unsere Zeiten merckwürdigste Begebenheiten enthalten. Benebst einigen, zur Erläuterung beygefügten Kupffern und Figuren.

CONTINUED ON NEXT CARD

Schudt, Johann Jacob, 1664-1722. Jüdische Merckwürdigkeiten. 1715. (Card 2)

Mit historischer Feder in drey Theilen beschrieben von Johann Jacob Schudt ... Franckfurt und Leipzig, Verlegts Samuel Tobias Hocker, 1715.
3 v. in 1. plates, ports. 21cm.

Includes a sketch of Spinoza's life (v. 1, p. 313-315)

Segond, Joseph, 1872-
La vie de Benoit de Spinoza. Paris, Librairie académique Perrin, 1933.
229 p. 19ᶜᵐ.

Original paper covers bound in.

Sehring, Ludwig
Spinoza, sein Leben und seine Philosophie. 2. Aufl. Berlin, H. Seemann Nachfolger ⌊1908?⌋
96 p. 24cm. (On cover: Kulturträger, Bd. 23)

Silberstein, Michael, b. 1834.
Spinoza's Grab. ⌊1890⌋
4 pts.

In Juedisches Litteratur-Blatt, Jahrgang 19, 1890.

Sobel, Isaac
תולדות שפינאזא ושטתו, מאת יצחק
בן יהודה ליב סאבעל. ס"ט פטרבורג,
ת'תרמ"ו.
⌊St. Peterburg⌋ 1885.
16 p. port. 25cm.

Title transliterated: Tōlĕdōt Spinoza ...
From Mispā, year 1, no. 4.
On Spinoza's life and philosophy.

Speidel, Ludwig, 1830-1906.
Persönlichkeiten; biographisch-literarische Essays. Berlin, Meyer, 1910.
xxiii, 380 p. port. (His Schriften, 1. Bd.)

Includes an essay "Ein Denkmal für Spinoza" (p. 23-30)

Spinozas Krankengeschichte; nach zeitgenössischen Berichten dargestellt von O. J. ⌊1926⌋
20-23 p. 23cm.

From Davoser revue, 1. Jahrgang, no. 7, 15. April 1926.

1. Spinoza, Benedictus de, 1632-1677. I. J., O.

Thomas, Henry, 1886-
Living biographies of great philosophers, by Henry Thomas and Dana Lee Thomas. Illustrations by Gordon Ross. New York, Garden City publishing co., inc. ⌊°1941⌋
viii, 335 p. front., ports. 23½ cm.

Includes an essay on Spinoza (p. ⌊115⌋-132)

1. Philosophers. I. Thomas, Dana Lee, 1916- joint author. II. Title.
Name originally: Henry Thomas Schnittkind.

B72.T34 1941 921 41-3760 rev
Library of Congress ⌊r55d1⌋

Tocco, Felice, 1845-1911.
Biografia di Benedetto Spinoza. ⌊1899⌋
233-264 p.

In Rivista d'Italia, anno 2, v. 1, 1899.

Tönnies, Ferdinand, 1855-1936.
Studie zur Entwicklungsgeschichte des Spinoza. ⌊1883⌋
⌊158⌋-183, ⌊334⌋-364 p. 22ᶜᵐ.

From Vierteljahrsschrift für wissenschaftliche Philosophie, 7. Jahrgang, 1883.

Valsecchi, Antonio, 1708-1791.
Ritratti o vite letterarie e paralleli di G. J. Rousseau e del sig. di Voltaire, di Obbes, e di Spinosa; e vita di Pietro Bayle. Opera posthuma. Venezia, Pasquali e Curti, 1816.
176 p.

Vaz Dias, A M. 1877-1939.
Spinoza, mercator & autodidactus. Oorkonden en andere authentieke documenten betreffende des wijsgeers jeugd en diens betrekkingen, verzameld door A. M. Vaz Dias, uitgegeven en toegelicht in overleg met W. G. van der Tak ... Met dertien facsimile's. 's-Gravenhage, M. Nijhoff, 1932.
xii, 68 p., 1 l. xi (i. e. 13) facsim. (part fold.) 29cm.

1. Spinoza, Benedictus de, 1632-1677. I. Tak, Willem Gerard van der, 1885- ed.

A C 33-3464

Title from Rochester Univ. B3997.V32a Printed by L. C.
[2]

Vloten, Johannes van, 1818-1883.
Benedictus de Spinoza, naar leven en werken, in verband met zijnen en onzen tijd. 2. herziene en vermeerderde druk. Schiedam, H. A. M. Roelants, 1871.
xiv, 288 p. 19cm.

Bibliographical footnotes.

Vexler, M
De l'"Apologie" de Spinoza. [1913]
231-242 p.

In Revue des études juives, t. 65., 1913.

Vloemans, Antoon
Het leven van Spinoza (de wijsgeer van de stilte) [1927]
289-299 p. 25cm.

From Het Nieuwe leven, 12e jaargang, afl. 11, Maart 1927.

1. Spinoza, Benedictus de, 1632-1677.

Villa, Emilio
La conversione di Spinoza (Commento alle prime pagine del "De intellectus emendatione"). [1927]
[361]-369 p.

In Rivista di filosofia, anno 18, 1927.

Vloten, Johannes van, 1818-1883.
Spinoza, de blijde boodschapper der mondige menschheid; toespraak bij de onthulling van zijn standbeeld. 's-Gravenhage, M. Nijhoff, 1880.
20 p. 25cm.

Bibliographical references included in "Aanteekeningen" (p. [19]-20)

[Vloten, Johannes van] 1818-1883.
Baruch d'Espinoza; zijn leven en schriften. in verband met zijnen en onzen tijd. Amsterdam, F. Muller, 1862.
x, 483 p. 19cm.

Original paper covers bound in.
Bibliographical footnotes.

Vloemans, Antoon
Spinoza; de mensch, het leven en het werk. 's-Gravenhage, H. P. Leopold, 1931.
xvi, 607 p. plates, ports., facsim. 24cm.

Bibliography: p. 585-595.
Ms. notes by Carl Gebhardt.

Vloten, Johannes van, 1818-1883.
Baruch d'Espinoza; zijn leven en schriften, in verband met zijnen en onzen tijd. Goedkoope uitgaaf. Amsterdam, K. H. Schadd, 1865.
x, 483 p. 20cm.

Bibliographical footnotes.

1. Spinoza, Benedictus de, 1632-1677.

[Vloten, Johannes van] 1818-1883.
Spinoza. Geboren 24 November 1632 te Amsterdam, gestorven 21 Februari 1677 te 's-Gravenhage. [1880?]
8 p. 26cm.

Pencilled on p. [1] by A. S. Oko: By J. van Vloten? The Hague? 1880?

1. Spinoza, Benedictus de, 1632-1677.

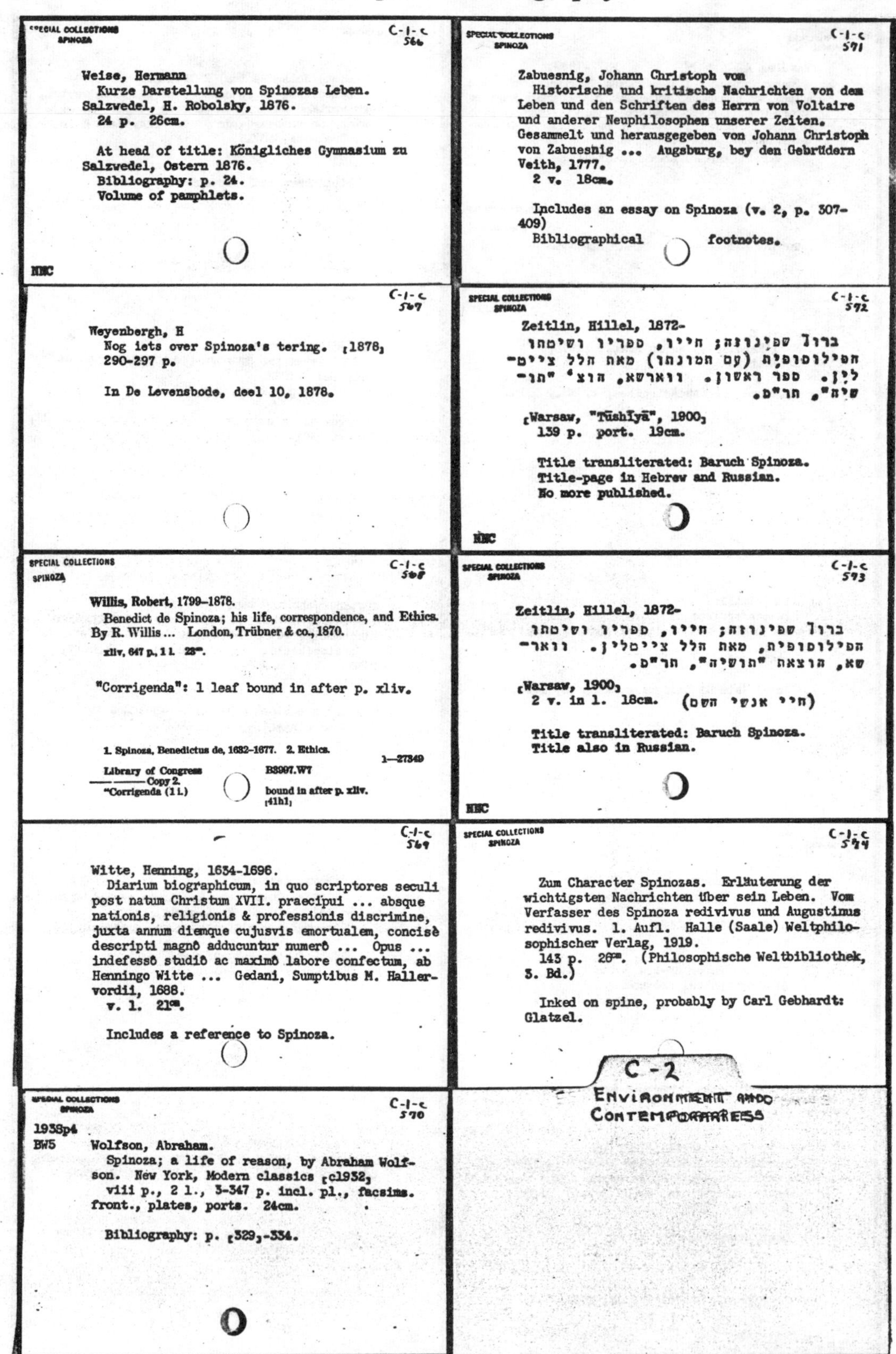

Weise, Hermann
Kurze Darstellung von Spinozas Leben. Salzwedel, H. Robolsky, 1876.
24 p. 26cm.

At head of title: Königliches Gymnasium zu Salzwedel, Ostern 1876.
Bibliography: p. 24.
Volume of pamphlets.

Weyenbergh, H
Nog iets over Spinoza's tering. ₍1878₎
290-297 p.

In De Levensbode, deel 10, 1878.

Willis, Robert, 1799–1878.
Benedict de Spinoza; his life, correspondence, and Ethics. By R. Willis ... London, Trübner & co., 1870.
xliv, 647 p., 1 l. 23cm.

"Corrigenda": 1 leaf bound in after p. xliv.

1. Spinoza, Benedictus de, 1632–1677. 2. Ethics.

Witte, Henning, 1634-1696.
Diarium biographicum, in quo scriptores seculi post natum Christum XVII. praecipui ... absque nationis, religionis & professionis discrimine, juxta annum diemque cujusvis emortualem, concisè descripti magnô adducuntur numerô ... Opus ... indefessô studiô ac maximô labore confectum, ab Henningo Witte ... Gedani, Sumptibus M. Hallervordii, 1688.
v. 1. 21cm.

Includes a reference to Spinoza.

Wolfson, Abraham.
Spinoza; a life of reason, by Abraham Wolfson. New York, Modern classics ₍c1932₎
viii p., 2 l., 3-347 p. incl. pl., facsims. front., plates, ports. 24cm.

Bibliography: p. ₍329₎-334.

Zabuesnig, Johann Christoph von
Historische und kritische Nachrichten von dem Leben und den Schriften des Herrn von Voltaire und anderer Neuphilosophen unserer Zeiten. Gesammelt und herausgegeben von Johann Christoph von Zabuesnig ... Augsburg, bey den Gebrüdern Veith, 1777.
2 v. 18cm.

Includes an essay on Spinoza (v. 2, p. 307-409)
Bibliographical footnotes.

Zeitlin, Hillel, 1872-
ברוך שפינוזה; חייו, ספריו ושיטתו הפילוסופית (עם תמונתו) מאת הלל צייטלין. ספר ראשון. ווארשא, הוצ׳ "תושיה", תר"ס.

₍Warsaw, "Tūshīyā", 1900₎
139 p. port. 19cm.

Title transliterated: Baruch Spinoza.
Title-page in Hebrew and Russian.
No more published.

Zeitlin, Hillel, 1872-
ברוך שפינוזה; חייו, ספריו ושיטתו הפילוסופית, מאת הלל צייטלין. ווארשא, הוצאת "תושיה", תר"ס.

₍Warsaw, 1900₎
2 v. in 1. 18cm. (חיי אנשי השם)

Title transliterated: Baruch Spinoza.
Title also in Russian.

Zum Character Spinozas. Erläuterung der wichtigsten Nachrichten über sein Leben. Vom Verfasser des Spinoza redivivus und Augustinus redivivus. 1. Aufl. Halle (Saale) Weltphilosophischer Verlag, 1919.
143 p. 20cm. (Philosophische Weltbibliothek, 3. Bd.)

Inked on spine, probably by Carl Gebhardt: Glatzel.

C-2
ENVIRONMENT AND CONTEMPORARIES

Alorna, João de Almeida Portugal, marques de Alorna, 1726-1802.
Des Herrn Marquis Johann von Alorna Beschreibung der Gefängnisse von Junqueira in Portugal; mit Nachrichten von dasigen Staatsgefangenen bis 1777. Aus dem Portugiesischen von Herrn Abbé Anselm von Eckart. Hrsg. von C. G. von Murr. Nürnberg, Monath und Kusslerische Buchhandlung, 1803.
80 p. 22cm.

Altkirch, Ernst, 1873-1926.
Maledictus und benedictus; Spinoza im urteil des volkes und der geistigen bis auf Constantin Brunner. Leipzig, F. Meiner, 1924.
211 p. 25cm.

Presentation copy to Carl Gebhardt, with the author's inscription and signature.

Altkirch, Ernst, 1873-1926.
Evremond und Spinoza. [1919]
88-96, 202-210, 313-319, 92-98, 204-212 p. 26cm.

From Nord und Süd, 43. Jahrgang, 168.-169. Bd., Januar - Mai 1919.

Baedeker, Karl, firm publishers.
Holland und Belgien; Handbuch für Reisende. 6. umgearb. Aufl. Coblenz, K. Baedeker, 1858.
v, 298 p. maps (part fold.) plans (part fold.) 17cm.

Includes a reference to Spinoza (p. 262)

NNC

Altkirch, Ernst, 1873-1926.
Die Freunde Spinozas. [1927]
37-44 p. 25cm.

From Der Morgen, III. Jahrgang, 1. Heft, April 1927.
Bibliographical footnotes.

Bernard, François, 1859-
La Hollande géographique, ethnologique, politique et administrative, religieuse, économique, littéraire, artistique, scientifique, historique, coloniale, etc. par MM. François Bernard, C.-H.-B. Boot [et autres] 222 gravures et 9 cartes. Paris, Librairie Larousse [1900]
463 p. illus. 22 cm. [États et colonies. Monographies encyclopédiques]

Includes a reference to Spinoza with his portrait (p. 255-257)

Altkirch, Ernst, 1873-1926.
Im Lande Spinozas. [1902]
[211]-222 p. illus., ports. 27cm.

1. Spinoza, Benedictus de, 1632-1677 - Homes and haunts.

Blok, Petrus Johannes, 1855-1929.
Geschiedenis van het Nederlandsche volk. Groningen, J. B. Wolters, 1892-1908.
8 v. ~~in 7.~~ maps. 25cm.

Vols. 7-8 have imprint: Leiden, Sijthoff.
References to Spinoza included in vols. 5 and 6.

NNC

Altkirch, Ernst, 1873-1926.
Im Lande Spinozas; ein Nachtrag. [1911]
429-434 cols. illus., port. 29cm.

A supplement to the author's article "Benedictus Spinoza", which appeared in Ost und West, v. 9-10.
From Ost und West, 11. Jahrg., Heft 5, Mai 1911.
Bound with Altkirch, Ernst, 1873-1926. Benedictus Spinoza. [1909-10]

Blok, Petrus Johannes, 1855-
Geschichte der Niederlande. Von P. J. Blok ... Im auftrage des verfassers verdeutscht durch pastor O. G. Houtrouw ... Gotha, F. A. Perthes, 1902-12.
v.1-5 21cm. (*Added t.-p.:* Geschichte der europäischen staaten. Hrsg. von A. H. L. Heeren, F. A. Ukert, W. v. Giesebrecht und K. Lamprecht ...)

Vol. 5 includes references to Spinoza.

1. Netherlands—Hist. I. Houtrouw, O. G., tr.

Library of Congress DJ109.B67 5—15605
[a29d1]

Bolin, Vilhelm, 1835-1924.
Spinoza: Zeit, Leben, Werk. 2. Aufl., neu bearb. von Carl Gebhardt. Darmstadt, E. Hofmann, 1927.
viii, 203 p. port. 20cm. (Geisteshelden, 9. Bd.)

"Zur Spinoza-Bibliographie", p. [199]-200.

Bontekoe, Cornelis, 1627-1685.
Tractaat van het excellenste kruyd thee ... 's Gravenhage, P. Hagen, 1679.
14 p. l., 367 p.

Includes references to Spinoza (p. 199, 349)

Bos, Lambert van den, 1610-1698.
Tooneel des oorlogs, opgerecht in de Vereenigde Nederlanden; door de wapenen van de koningen van Vrankryk en Engeland, Keulsche en Munstersche bisschoppen. Tegen de Staten der Vereenigde Nederlanden, en hare geallieerden ... Naaukeurig en waarachtig, uyt autentique schriften en sekere raporten, t'samengestelt. Door Lambert van den Bosch ... t'Amsterdam, By Jacob van Meurs, en Johannes van Someren, 1675.
4 v. in 2. plates, ports. 24cm.

CONTINUED ON NEXT CARD

Bos, Lambert van den, 1610-1698. Tooneel des oorlogs, opgerecht in de Vereenigde Nederlanden. 1675. (Card 2)

General t.-p. only; v. 2 has half-title, v. 3-4 have caption title only. Half-title of v. 2 bound preceding v. 3.
Added engraved t.-p.

Bowrey, Thomas, *ca.* 1650-1713.
The papers of Thomas Bowrey, 1669-1713, discovered in 1913 by John Humphreys ... and now in the possession of Lieut-Colonel Henry Howard ... edited by Lieut.-Colonel Sir Richard Carnac Temple, bt. ... London, Printed for the Hakluyt society, 1927.
xxx, 398 p. illus., IX pl. (incl. front., fold. plan, facsims.) maps (1 fold.) 22½ cm. (*Half-title:* Works issued by the Hakluyt society ... Second series, no. LVIII)
"Issued for 1925."
Bibliography: p. [363]-370.
CONTENTS.—Diary of a six weeks' tour in 1698 in Holland and Flanders.—The story of the Mary galley, 1704-1710.
1. Netherlands—Descr. & trav. 2. Mary galley (Ship) I. Temple, Sir Richard Carnac, bart., 1850-1931, ed.

Brandt, Geeraert, 1626-1685.
G. Brandts Historie der reformatie en andere kerkelyke geschiedenissen in en ontrent de Nederlanden ... Amsterdam, J. Rieuwertsz., H. en D. Boom, 1674-1704.
4 v. pl., ports. 21½cm.
Added t.-p., engr.
Vols. ~~2-3~~ 3-4, edited by Johannes Brandt, have imprint: Rotterdam, B. Bos.
CONTENTS.—1. deel. Met eenige aentekeningen en aenmerkingen. Naerder oversien, merklijk vermeerdert, en vervolgt tot het jaer 1600. 2. druk. 1677.—2. deel. Van het jaer 1600 tot het laetste van't jaer 1618. 1674.—3.-4. deel. 1618-1624. 1704.
1. Reformation—Netherlands. 2. Netherlands—Church history. I. Brandt, Johannes, 1660-1708, ed.
D-96 Revised

Brandt, Geeraert, 1626-1685.
G. Brandts Historie der reformatie, en andere kerkelyke geschiedenissen, in en ontrent de Nederlanden. Met eenige aentekeningen en aenmerkingen ... Tot Amsterdam, Voor Jan Rieuwertsz, Hendrik en Dirk Boom, 1674-1677 [v. 1, 1677]
2 v. ports. 21cm.

Vol. 1: Tweede druk.
Added title-page engraved.

Brandt, Geeraert, 1626-1685.
Leben und Thaten des fürtreflichen und sonderbahren See-Helden Herrn Michaels de Ruiter ... In Niederländischer Sprache beschrieben, durch Herrn Gerhard Brand ... Mit etliche schönen Kupferstichen gezieret. Aus der Niederländischen in die Hochdeutsche Sprache treulich übergesetzet. Zu Amsterdam, Bei Wolfgang, Waasbergen, Boom, von Someren, und Goethals, 1687.
2 v. in 1. double plates. 32cm.

Added t.-p., engr.

Braun, Johannes, 1628-1708.
La veritable religion des Hollandois. Avec une apologie pour la religion des Estats Generaux des Provinces Unies. Contre le libelle diffamatoire de Stoupe, qui a pour titre La religion des Hollandois, representée en plusieurs lettres écrites par un officier de l'armée du roy, à un pasteur & professeur en theologie à Berne. Par Jean Brun, ministre du roy des armées ... Cy est joint le Conseil d'extorsion ou la volerie des Francois. Exercée en la ville de Nimegue par le commissaire Methelet & des supôts. A

CONTINUED ON NEXT CARD

Braun, Johannes, 1628-1708. La veritable religion des Hollandois. 1675. (Card 2)

Amsterdam, Chez Abraham Wolfgank, 1675.
[40], 392, 197 (i.e. 143), [1] p. 14cm.

Includes references to Spinoza (p. 158-164, 289-291)
Bound with Stoppa, Giovanni Battista. La religion des Hollandois. 1673.

Brieven van verscheyde vermaerde en geleerde mannen deser eeuwe: voornamelijk van Jacobus Arminius, J. Uytenbogaert, Hugo de Groot, S. Episcopius, N. Grevinchovius, C. Niëlius, &c. Waer in veelderhande hoochwichtige theologische materien en saecken, den stand der kercken betreffende, verhandelt werden. Noyt voor desen gedruckt. T'Amsterdam, By Jan Rieuwertz, 1662.
[14], 96, 483, [1] p. 17cm.

Caan, Jacobus Janus de la Bassecour
Schets van den regeringsvorm der Nederlandsche republiek, van 1515-1795. 's-Gravenhage, Gebroeders Belinfante, 1862.
viii, 206 p. 25cm.

Bibliographical footnotes.

1. Netherlands - Politics and government.

Brunschvicg, Léon, 1869-1944.
Spinoza et ses contemporains. [1905-06] 673-705, 35-82, 691-732 p.

In Revue de métaphysique et de morale, 13.-14. année, 1905-06.

[Cattenbaert, Jasper]
Hollands op-komst, oft Bedenkingen, op de schaadelijke schriften, genaamt Grafelyke regeeringe, en Interest van Holland, uit-gegeven door V. D. H. Ten dienste van alle liefhebbers, die de waare interest des lands beminnen, vergadert door J. C. Tot Leyden, By Jan Princen, 1662.
262, [2] p. 15cm.

By Jasper Cattenbaert. Cf. Brit. Mus. Cat.

Brunschvicg, Léon, 1869-1944.
Spinoza et ses contemporains, par Léon Brunschvicg ... 3. éd., rev. et augm. Paris, F. Alcan, 1923.
2 p. l., ii p., 1 l., 495, [1] p. 22½ cm. (*On cover:* Bibliothèque de philosophie contemporaine)

"La première partie de cet ouvrage est la troisième édition du Spinoza que nous avions publié en 1894 ... La seconde partie est formée d'articles qui ont paru dans la Revue de métaphysique et de morale, de 1904 à 1906."—Avant-propos.

1. Spinoza, Benedictus de, 1632-1677. 2. Descartes, René, 1596-1650. 3. Pascal, Blaise, 1623-1662. 4. Malebranche, Nicolas, 1638-1715. 5. Fénelon, François de Salignac de La Mothe-, 1651-1716. 6. Leibniz, Gottfried Wilhelm, freiherr von, 1646-1716.

CONTINUED ON NEXT CARD

Clapmar, Arnold, 1574-1604.
Arn. Clapmarii De arcanis rerumpublicarum libri sex iteratò illustrati a Joan. Arn. Corvino ... Accessit ... Chr. Besoldi, de eadem materia discursus, nec non Arnoldi Clapmarii et aliorum conclusiones de ivre pvblico. Amsterodami, Apud Ludovicum Elzevirium, 1644.
[128], 323, [1], 51, [29], 114 p. 14cm.

"Arnoldi Clapmarii, Francisci Roselli et Wolfgangi Heinrici Ruprechti Conclusiones de ivre publico" (with special t.-p.): 114 p. at end.

Brunschvicg, Léon, 1869-1944. Spinoza et ses contemporains. 1923. (Card 2)

Presentation copy to Carl Gebhardt with the author's inscription and signature.
Original paper cover bound in.

Clark, George Norman, 1890-
The seventeenth century, by G. N. Clark ... Oxford, The Clarendon press, 1929.
xii, 372 p. vii fold. maps. 23 cm.

Includes a section on Spinoza (p. 258-260) and other references to him.

1. Europe—Civilization. I. Title.

Burman, Pieter, 1668-1741, *ed.*
Sylloges epistolarum a viris illustribus scriptarum tomi quinque, collecti et digesti per Petrum Burmannum. Nomina exhibebit post tomum quintum index primus. Leidæ, apud S. Luchtmans, 1727.
5 v. 2 fold. pl. 26½ x 21cm.
Preface to vol. I dated: 1724.
Vols. II-V have half-title only.
The general t.-p. and preface, issued with the 5th vol., are in the present copy prefixed to the 1st vol.
Correspondence of J. Lipsius, N. Heinsius, J. F. Gronovius, I. Vossius, J. G. Graevius, J. Perizonius and others.
Includes a reference to Spinoza (v. 4, p. 475)
I. Title.

Cohen, Gustave, 1879-
Écrivains français en Hollande, dans la première moitié du XVIIe siècle. Paris, Champion, 1920.
756 p. illus., plates, ports., map, plans, facsims. 26 cm. (Bibliothèque de la Revue de littérature comparée, v. 1)

Includes references to Spinoza.

Coronel, Samuel Mozes Senior, 1827-
Baruch d'Espinoza, in de lijst van zijn tijd. Zalt-Bommel, Joh. Noman en Zoon, 1871.
52 p. 24cm.

Coronel, Samuël Mozes Senior, 1827-1892.
Baruch Spinoza im rahmen seiner zeit. Von dr. S. Sr. Coronel. Aus dem holländischen. Basel, H. Richter, 1873.
71 p. 20½cm. 23 cm.

Original paper cover bound in.
Bound with Fischer, Kuno. Baruch Spinoza's Leben ... 1865.

1. Spinoza, Benedictus de, 1632-1677.

Library of Congress B3997.C8 6-22741
[a32c1]

Coste, Pierre. 1668-1747.
The life of Lewis of Bourbon, late prince of Conde. Digested into annals. With many curious remarks on the transactions of Europe for these last sixty years. Done out of French. London, T. Goodwin, 1693.
2 v. in 1. 19½cm.

Vol. 2 has no t.-p.
The dedicatory epistle is signed by the translator, N. Tate.

CONTINUED ON NEXT CARD

[Coste, Pierre] 1668-1747. The life of Lewis of Bourbon. 1693. (Card 2)

The third French edition appeared under the author's name. cf. Barbier, Quérard.
Includes reference to Spinoza (v. 2, p. 173-174)

[Court, Pieter de la] 1618-1685.
Consideratien en exempelen van staat, omtrent de fundamenten van allerley regeringe. Beschreven door V. H. t'Amsterdam, By Ian Iacobsz Dommekracht, 1660.
[28], 369 p. 17cm.

[Court, Jan de la] 1622-1660.
Consideratien van staat, oder Politische Wag Schale mit welcher die allgemeine Staats-Angelegenheiten Haupt-Gründe und Mängel aller Republicken wie sie von langer Zeit biss itzo her gewesen und zugleich die beständigste, nützlichste auch beste Art unf Form einer freyen politischen Regierung in gleicher Gegenhaltung erwogen, allen verständigen Politicis zu fernerer Betrachtung und geschickter Vollziehung dargestellet wird. Aus dem Holländischen

CONTINUED ON NEXT CARD

[Court, Jan de la] 1622-1660. Consideratien van staat. 1669. (Card 2)

ins Teutsche übersetzet von Christophoro Kormarten, Lipsiensi. Leipzig und Halle, In Fickischen Buchladen, 1669.
[28], 672 p. 16cm.

Added engraved title-page.

[Court, Pieter de la] 1618-1685.
Consideratien van staat, ofte Polityke weegschaal, waar in met veele, reedenen, omstandigheden, exempelen en fabulen werd ooverwoogen; welke forme der regeeringe, in speculatie gebouđ op de practijk, onder de menschen de beste zy. Beschreven door V. H. In deese derde editie naawkeurig ooversien, merkelik vermeerdert en in veelen klaarder gestelt. t'Amsterdam, Voor Dirk Dirksz. Boekverkooper, 1662.
[28], 670 p. fold. plates. 17cm.

Added t.-p., engr.

[Court, Pieter de la] 1618-1865
Consideratien van staat, ofte Polityke weegschaal, waar in met veele, reedenen, omstandigheden, exempelen en fabulen werd ooverwoogen; welke forme der regeeringe, in speculatie geboud op de practijk, onder de menschen de beste zy. Beschreven door V. H. In deese derde editie naawkeurig ooversien, merkelik vermeerdert, en in veelen klaarder gestelt. t'Amsterdam, Voor Dirk Dirksz., 1662.
[28], 670 p. fold. plates. 16cm.

NNC

[Court, Pieter de la] 1618-1685.
Consideratien van staat, ofte Politike weegschaal, waar in met veele redenen, omstandigheden, exempelen, en fabulen wert overwogen; welke forme der regeeringe, in speculatie gebourt op de practjck, onder de menschen de beste zy. Beschreven door V. H. In deze vierde editie naauwkeurig overzien, merkelik vermeerdert, en in veelen klaarder gestelt. t'Amsterdam, Voor Jacob Vinckel, 1662.
[34], 681 p. 14cm.

Added t.-p., engr.

[Court, Pieter de la] 1618-1685.
Het welvaren van Leiden. Handschrift uit het jaar 1659, uitgegeven met Duitsche vertaling, aanteekeningen en bibliographische bijzonderheden. Met 5 facsimiles. 's-Gravenhage, M. Nijhoff, 1911.
x, 172, 172, 43 p. facsims. 28cm.

"Voorrede" signed: Felix Driessen.
"Bibliographie": p. 1-35 at end.

[Court, Pieter de la] 1618-1685.
Historie der gravelike regering in Holland, beschreven door V: H. Waer by is gevoegd De oorsprong der Nederlandse troublen; wel eer beschrven [!] door Viglius Zuichemus ab Ayta, en nu eerst in t'ligt gebraght door V: H. [Amsterdam, 1670?]
[16], 264 p. 17cm.

"Grondig berigt van't Nederlands oproer ... beschreven in 't François: door ... Vigilius Zuichemus ab Ayta ... in de Nederduitsche tale overgeset, door V. H.": p. [207]-264.

[Court, Pieter de la] 1618-1685.
Interest van Holland, ofte gronden van Hollands-welvaren. Aangewezen door V. D. H. t'Amsterdam, By Joan. Cyprianus vander Gracht, 1662.
[16], 267, [5] p. 17cm.

Later published under title: Aanwysing der heilsame politike, gronden en maximen de Republike van Holland.
Includes material by Johan de Witt.

[Court, Pieter de la] 1618-1685.
Interest van Holland, ofte gronden van Hollands-welvaren. Aangewezen door V. D. H. t'Amsterdam, By Joan. Cyprianus vander Gracht, 1662.
[16], 267, [5] p. 18cm.

Differs from other 1662 edition: List of errata at end; different title vignette.
Bound with the author's Historie der gravelike regering in Holland. [1670?]

[Court, Pieter de la] 1618-1685.
Lucii Antistii Constantis [pseud.] De juri ecclesiasticorum, liber singularis. Quo docetur: quodcunque divini humanique iuris ecclesiasticis tribuitur, vel ipsi sibi tribuunt, hoc, aut falsô impièque illis tribui, aut non aliundè, quam à suis, hoc est, ejus reipublicae sivè civitatis prodiis, in qua sunt constituti, accepisse. Alethopoli [i.e. Amsterdam] Apud Cajum Valerium Pennatum, 1665.
[15], 162, [5] p. 16cm.

CONTINUED ON NEXT CARD

[Court, Pieter de la] 1618-1685. Lucii Antistii Constantis [pseud.] De jure ecclesiasticorum. 1665. (Card 2)

Fictitious imprint.
"By B. de Spinoza? or, more probably by P. de la Court?"--Brit. Mus. Cat.
Manuscript note in French ascribing the work to Spinoza appears on page facing t.-p.; "B. Spinosæ" inserted by hand after the pseudonym on t.-p.

[Court, Pieter de la] 1618?-1685.
Memoires de Jean de Wit, grand pensionnaire de Hollande. Tr. de l'original en françois. Par Mr. de * * *. 3 ed. Ratisbonne, E. Kinkius, 1709.
xxxvi, 332 p. incl. front. (port.) ~~16cm.~~ 14½cm.

A translation of parts of the author's "Aanwijsing der heilsame politieke gronden en maximen van de republieke van Holland". Johan de Witt probably wrote two chapters of the memoirs. *cf.* Winkler Prins' geïllustreerde encyclopaedie; Van der Aa, Biog. woordenboek der Nederlanden.

1. Witt, Johan de, 1625-1672. I. Zoutelandt, Mme. E. de, tr. II. Title.

Library of Congress DJ173.W7C8 13—24284
[a33b1]

[Court, Pieter de la] 1618-1685.
Naeuwkeurige consideratie van staet, wegens de heerschappye van een vrye en geheymen staets-regering over de gantsche aertbodem, Aengewezen door V. D. H. t'Amsterdam, By Ioan Cyprianus van der Graft, 1662.
162 (i.e. 192) p. 15cm.

Page 192 incorrectly numbered 162.

Bound with Cattenbaert, Jasper, Hollands opkomst.

[Court, Jan de la] 1622-1660.
... Politike discoursen, handelende in ses onderscheide boeken, van steeden, landen, oorlogen, kerken, regeeringen en zeeden, beschreeven door D. C. Tot Leyden, By P. Hackius, 1662.
[14], 516 p. 24cm.

By Jan de la Court. Cf. Brit. Mus. Cat.
Edited by Pieter de la Court.
Engraved title-page.
Ms. notes by Carl Gebhardt on flyleaf.

[Court, Jan de la] 1622-1660.
... Politike discoursen handelende in ses onderscheide boeken, van steeden, landen, oorlogen, kerken, regeeringen en zeeden, beschreven door D. C. t'Amsterdam, By. I. Ciprianus vandr Gracht, 1662.
[24], 344, 311, [1] p. 17cm.

By Jan de la Court. Cf. Brit. Mus. Cat.
Edited by Pieter de la Court.
Engraved title-page.

[Court, Pieter de la] 1618-1685.
Public gebedt, ofte Consideratien, over het nominatim bidden in de publicque kerken, voor de hooge en mindere overheden, en specialyk voor den laest overleden Heer Stadthouder. Door D. H. ... Vermeerdert met de resolutien van de heeren staaten van Hollandt en West-Frieslandt, op het selve subject genomen. In 'sGravenhage, By Engelbreght Boucquet, 1707.
3 v. in 1. 17cm.

Vols. 1-2 continuously paged; vol. 3 has separate t.-p. and paging.

[Court, Pieter de la] 1618-1685.
The true interest and political maxims of the republick of Holland and West-Friesland ... Written by John de Witt and other great men in Holland. Pub. by the authority of the States. London, Printed in the year 1702.
lvi, 492 p. incl. port. 20 cm.

Crommelin, Claude August, 1878-
Het lenzen slijpen in de 17e eeuw. Met 29 afb. Amsterdam, H. J. Paris, 1929.
vii, 45 p.

"Voordracht gehouden den 2den Juni 1929 te Leiden in de algemene vergadering der Vereeniging Het Spinozahuis".

De grafplaatsen der de Witten en Spinoza in de Nieuwe Kerk. [1889]
53-57 p.

In Haagsch jaarboekje voor 1889, année 1.

Delbrück, Hans, 1848-1929.
Weltgeschichte; Vorlesungen, gehalten an der Universität Berlin 1896/1920. Berlin, O. Stollberg, 1924-28.
5 v. 23 cm.
Vol. 5 is without subtitle.
Includes bibliographies.
CONTENTS.—1. T. Das Altertum.—2. T. Das Mittelalter.—3. T. Neuzeit bis zum Tode Friedrichs des Grossen.—4. T. Neuzeit, die Revolutionsperiode von 1789 bis 1852.—5. T. Neuzeit von 1852 bis 1888.
Includes references to Spinoza (v. 3, p. 510, 643)
1. History, Universal.

D20.D4 25-9347 rev*

Library of Congress [r48c1]

Denucé, Jean, 1878-
Bijdrage tot de geschiedenis van oud Spaansch-Portugeesche geslachten in de Nederlanden. [De afkomst van Anna de Milan (ca. 1548-1613) stammoeder van het geslacht Teixeira de Mattos. Baesrode-Dendermonde, R. Bracke-van Geert, 1928]
23 p. fold. geneal. table. 25cm.

"Overdruk uit het Antwerpsch archievenblad, 1928, nr. 1."

De vryheid op den troon gezet door de edele achtbaere Heeren Schepenen der stad Amsteldam. Den 20sten van herftmaand [!] 1743. Te Middelburg, By Kornelis Jakobsz, 1743.
124 p.

Die Haghe; kleine geschriften. [Amsterdam, 1913?]
2 pts. illus. 19x25cm. (pt. 2, 27cm.)

Contents.--I. Een eeuw slooperswerk in den Haag, 1813-1913, door H. E. van Gelder. Overdruk van artikel IV der reeks "Sloopend herboren Nederland" uit het geïllustreerd weekblad "Buiten".--II. Den Haag in den patriottentijd, door J. Smit.

Does, Jacob van der
'S Graven-Hage, met de voornaemste plaetsen en vermaecklijckheden, door Jacob vander Does ... In 's Gravenhage, by Hermannus Gael, 1668.
[16] 143, [1] p. plates, fold. plan. 24cm.

In verse.

1. Hague - Description.

[Driessen, Felix, *ed.*
De reizen der de la Courts; 1641-1700-1710. [Leiden, pref. 1928]
cover-title, 1 p. l., iv, 121 p. illus., 2 pl., port., facsim. 28cm.
"Voorrede" signed: Felix Driessen.
Diaries and letters written by Pieter de la Court, father and son, and Allard de la Court.

1. Court, de la, family. 2. Gt. Brit.—Descr. & trav. 3. Gt. Brit.—Soc. life & cust. 4. France—Descr. & trav. 5. France—Soc. life & cust. I. Court, Pieter de la, 1618-1685. II. Court, Pieter de la, 1664-1739. III. Court, Allard de la, 1688-1755. IV. Title.

31-31993

Library of Congress CS829.C65D7
[38c1] 914

SPECIAL COLLECTIONS SPINOZA C-2-a 635

Enden, Franciscus van den, 1602-1674.
Drie brieven van Franciscus van den Ende aan Johan de Witt, medegedeeld door N. Japikse. [Hagae Comitis, 1921]
113-117 p. 22cm.

Cover-title: Dissertatio Chronici Spinozani tomo primo separatim edita.
Includes a reference to Spinoza (p. 117)

SPECIAL COLLECTIONS SPINOZA C-2-a 640

Francès, Madeleine
Spinoza dans les pays néerlandais de la seconde moitié du XVIIe siècle. 1. partie. Paris, F. Alcan, 1937.
viii, 365 p. 23cm.

No more published?
Issued also as thesis, Paris.
Original paper covers bound in.
Bibliographical footnotes.

C-2-a 636

Fischer, Isidor, 1868-1943.
De geneesheeren onder Spinoza's vrienden. [1921]
1856-1873 p.

In Nederlandsch tijdschrift voor geneeskunde, 65. jaargang, 1921.

NNNAM

SPECIAL COLLECTIONS SPINOZA C-2-a 641

Frowein, J F L
Het raadhuis van 's Gravenhage. 's-Gravenhage, W. P. Van Stockum & Zoon, 1910.
16 p. illus. 27cm.

1. Hague. Raadhuis.

NNC

SPECIAL COLLECTIONS SPINOZA C-2-a 637

Fitzmaurice-Kelly, Julia (Sanders)
El Inca Garcilasso de la Vega, by Julia Fitzmaurice-Kelly ... [Oxford] Oxford university press, H. Milford, 1921.
vi, 99 p. 17cm. (*Half-title:* Hispanic notes & monographs; essays, studies, and brief biographies issued by the Hispanic society of America, II)

Includes references to Leo Hebraeus.

1. Garcilaso de la Vega, el Inca, 1539-1616. I. Title. 22—5877

Library of Congress F3444.G33 [a42o1]

SPECIAL COLLECTIONS SPINOZA C-2-a 642

Gebhardt, Carl, 1881-1934.
Das Schicksal Hollands. [1916]
2 p. 58cm.

From Frankfurter Zeitung. 61. Jahrg., Nr. 281, Erstes Morgenblatt, 10. Oktober 1916.
Includes material on Johan de Witt.

SPECIAL COLLECTIONS SPINOZA C-2-a 638

[Fonseca, Antonio Lopez de]
La Haye. Par un habitant. La Haye, M. Nijhoff, 1857.
2 v. 23cm.

Preface signed: Antonio Lopez de Fonseca.
Includes references to Spinoza (v. 1, p. 36; v. 2, p. 202, 204)

SPECIAL COLLECTIONS SPINOZA C-2-a 643

Gothein, Eberhard, 1853-1923.
Reformation und Gegenreformation. München, Duncker & Humblot, 1924.
290 p. 24cm. (His Schriften zur Kulturgeschichte der Renaissance, Reformation und Gegenreformation. Bd. 2)

Includes references to Spinoza.
Ms. notes by Carl Gebhardt.
Bibliographical notes: p. [276]-289.

C-2-a 639

[Fonseca, Antonio Lopez de]
La Haye. Par un habitant. La Haye, W. P. van Stockum, 1853.
2 v.

Includes references to Spinoza.

OCH

SPECIAL COLLECTIONS SPINOZA C-2-a 644

Gram, Johan, 1833-1914.
's-Gravenhage in onzen tijd. Met 80 illustratiën en 3 photo-chromo-drukken naar Apol, Bosboom, Henricus, Israëls, Kerling, Klinkenberg, Koster, Rochussen, Sadée, Verveer, Weissenbruch en Wenckebach. Amsterdam, J. L. Beijers, 1893.
285 p. illus., plates (part col.) 26½cm.

On cover: Uitgave van Het Nieuws van den tag.
Includes a section on Spinoza (p. 171-173)

Gram, Johan, 1833-1914.
's Gravenhage voorheen en thans, door Johan Gram. 's Gravenhage, M. M. Couvée, 1905.
274 p. illus. (incl. ports.) plans (1 double) 25½cm.

Includes references to Spinoza (p. 104)

1. Hague—Descr. 2. Hague—Soc. life & cust. I. Title.

Grondig bericht van de Godsdienst der Hollanders, strekkende tot wederlegging van zeker ongenoemt schryver, die in zes brieven, over enige maanden uit Uitrecht aan een professor der theologie te Bern in Switserlant geschreven, en door de druk gemeen gemaakt, de Hollanders, wegens hun Godsdienst, gelijk by die vertoont, tracht gehaat te maken. Daar voor by gevoegt is: Wat d'eigentlijke oorzaak van de Fransche oorlog tegen Hollant is; Wat

CONTINUED ON NEXT CARD

Grondig bericht van de Godsdienst der Hollanders. 1674. (Card 2)

interest andere vorsten en staten binnen en buiten deze oorlog hebben; en Wat de Switsers bezonderlijk daar in hebben t'aanmerken. Nieuwelijks in de hoogduitsche taal beschreven, en daar uit vertaalt. t'Amsteldam, 1674.
38 p. 19cm.

Includes a reference to Spinoza (p. 36)

Groppe,
Johan de Witt. [18--?]
496 p. 25cm.

Imperfect: title-page and pages after p. 496 lacking.
Ms. notes by Carl Gebhardt.
Bibliographical footnotes.

Gründtlicher Bericht der Hollander Religion und andere obschwebende Welt-Händel betreffend, uber sechss Epistelen, so vor etliche Monathen auss Utrecht an einem Professori Theologiae zu Bern in der Schweitz, geschrieben, und in der Welt verspreyt worden ... 1674.
1 p. l., 62 p. 21cm.

A reply to Stoppa's La religion des Hollandois.
Includes a reference to Spinoza (p. 57)

Gründtlicher Bericht der Hollander Religion und andere obschwebende Welt-Händel betreffend, uber sechss Epistelen, so vor etliche Monathen auss Utrecht an einem Professori Theologiae zu Bern in der Schweitz, geschrieben, und in der Welt verspreyt worden ... 1674.
1 p. l., 62 p. 19cm.

A reply to Stoppa's La religion des Hollandois.
Includes a reference to Spinoza (p. 57)

Hague.
's-Gravenhage en Scheveningen, uitgegeven in opdracht van het gemeentebestuur. [Den Haag, Drukkerij Moulton & co., 1913]
2 p. l., 178 p., 1 l. illus. (incl. plans) fold. map, diagrs. 22cm.

1. Hague—Descr. 2. Hague—Hist. 3. Scheveningen, Netherlands.

Hague.
's-Gravenhage; publication of the municipality. The Hague, Printing Office Mouton & Co. [192-?]
106 p. (chiefly illus.) 28cm.

1. Hague - Description - Views.

Hague. Gymnasium.
De inwijding van het nieuwe gebouw voor het Gymnasium te 's-Gravenhage. 's-Gravenhage, M. Nijhoff, 1908.
62 p. illus., music. 21cm.

Hauck, Karl, 1868-
Karl Ludwig, kurfürst von der Pfalz (1617-1680), von dr. Karl Hauck ... Leipzig, Breitkopf & Härtel, 1903.
6 p. l., 334 p. 2 port. 25½cm. (*Added t.-p.:* Forschungen zur geschichte Mannheims und der Pfalz, hrsg. vom Mannheimer alterthumsverein. IV)

Includes a reference to Spinoza (p. 207)

1. Karl Ludwig, elector palatine, 1617-1680. 2. Palatinate—Hist.—Charles Louis, 1648-1680.

Het leven van Philopater, opgewiegt in Voetiaensche talmeryen, en groot gemaeckt in de verborgentheden der Coccejanen. Een waere historie. Tot Groeningen, Voor Siewert van der Brug, 1691.
[16], 221 p. 14cm.

Deals with Dutch philosophical and theological ideas at the time of Spinoza.
Ms. note by Carl Gebhardt on flyleaf.
Actually published at Amsterdam by Aert Wolsgreen.--cf. Doorninck, J. I. Vermomde en naamlooze schrijvers.

Hubbard, Elbert, 1856-1915.
Little journeys to the homes of great philosophers ... written by Elbert Hubbard ... East Aurora, N. Y., The Roycrofters, 1904.
2 v. front., plates, ports. 20 cm. (*His* Little journeys, vol. XIV-XV)
"Borders, initials and ornaments designed by Roycroft artists."
CONTENTS.—[book 1] Socrates. Seneca. Aristotle. Marcus Aurelius. Spinoza. Swedenborg.—[book 2] Immanual Kant. Auguste Comte. Voltaire. Herbert Spencer. Schopenhauer. Henry D. Thoreau.
1. Philosophers. I. Title.

Hoeven, Emanuel van der, ca. 1660-1727.
Leeven en dood der doorlugtige heeren gebroeders Cornelis de Witt ... en Johan de Witt ... Beschreeven door Emanuel van der Hoeven ... T'Amsterdam, By Jan ten Hoorn, 1705.
2 pts. in 1 v. port. 21cm.

Added title-page engraved.

Huizinga, Johan, 1872-1945.
... Holländische kultur des siebzehnten jahrhunderts, ihre sozialen grundlagen und nationale eigenart. Jena, E. Diederichs [1933]
3 p. l., [3]-63, [1] p. 26 pl. (incl. ports.) on 13 l. 22½cm. (*Half-title:* Schriften des Deutsch-niederländischen instituts Köln, hft. 1)
At head of title: J. Huizinga.
"3.-4. tausend."
"Drei vorträge für das Deutsch-niederländische institut Köln gehalten ... januar, 1932."
Includes a reference to Spinoza (p. [3])
1. Netherlands—Civilization. I. Title.

Hooft, Pieter Corneliszoon, 1581-1647.
P. C. Hoofts Nederlandsche historien, seedert de ooverdraght der heerschappye van Kaizar Kaarel den Vyfden op Kooning Philips zynen zoon, tot de doodt des Prinsen van Oranje. Met het vervolgh tot het einde der landtvooghdye des graaven van Leicester. De 3. druk, naar des schryvers eigen handtschrift op ontallyke plaatzen verbeetert, met des zelfs leeven vermeerdert, en met printen versiert. T'Amsterdam, By J. van Someren [etc.] 1677.
9 p. l., 27, [1], 1242, [40] p., 1 l. fold. pl., ports. 33½cm.
Added t.-p. engraved.
"'t Leeven van ... Pieter Corneliszoon Hooft ... beschreeven door Geeraardt Brandt": 27 p.
First edition, Amsterdam, 1642.
1. Netherlands—Hist.—Wars of independence, 1556-1648. I. Brandt, Geeraert, 1626-1685.

[Huybert, Pieter de]
Verdediging van de oude Hollantsche regeringh onder een stadthouder en kapiteyn generael; waer in de daden en diensten van de doorluchtige heeren princen van Orangien hoogloffelijcker memorie, klaerlijck werden vertoont. t'Samen gestelt tot opweckingh van alle ware liefhebbers des vaderlants, en overtuygingh van alle tegensprekers. t'Amsterdam, By Johannes van Someren, 1672.
1 p. l., 244 p. 16cm.

Horn, Georg, 1620-1670.
Kerkelyke en wereldlyke historie van de scheppinge des werelts, tot't jaer des Heeren 1666. Amsterdam, 1739.

Ipsen, Alfred
Holland. Rejseindtryk og studier. Med illustrationer i teksten. Kobenhavn, Gyldendal, 1891.
4 p. l., 308, iii p. incl. illus. 23 cm.

Includes a section on Spinoza (p. 267-270)

Horn, Georg, 1620-1670.
Kerkelyke en wereldlyke historie van de scheppinge des werelts, tot 't jaer des Heeren 1666. In 't Latijn beschreven door Georgius Hornius ... In het Nederduyts vertaalt. Waer aen is bygevoegt de Kerkelyke en wereldlyke historie, sedert den jare 1666 tot 1684. Door Balthazar Becker ... Den derden druck. Nevens een derde vervolg tot den jare 1696. Door Melchior Leydekker. 't Amsterdam, By Abraham van Someren, 1696.
4 pts. in 1 v. illus.

Japikse, Nicolaas, 1872-1944.
Johann de Witt, der Hüter des freien Meeres. Deutsch von W. Heggen. Leipzig, J. M. Meulenhoff, 1917.
xv, 327 p. illus., ports., facsims. 24cm. (Aus der Völker Geschichte. 1)

Includes a portrait of Spinoza and references to him (p. 252-254)

C-2-a
665

193Sp4
FW836 Japikse, Nicolaas, 1872-1944.
Johan de Witt. Geïllustreerd onder toezicht van den schrijver. Amsterdam, Meulenhoff, 1915.
358 p. illus., ports., facsims. (Nederlandsche historische bibliotheek. 9)

Includes a portrait of Spinoza and references to him (p. 279-281)

NNC

C-2-a
666

Japikse, Nicolaas, 1872-
Spinoza en De Witt. 's-Gravenhage, M. Nijhoff, 1927.
16 p. 25cm.

"Overdruk uit 'Bijdragen voor vaderlandsche geschiedenis', deel VI, afl. 1 en 2, 1927."

C-2-a
667

Japikse, Nicolaas, 1872-
Spinoza en De Witt. [1927]
1-16 p. 25cm.

From Bijdragen voor vaderlandsche geschiedenis en oudheidkunde, VIe reeks, deel VI, afl. 1 en 2, 1927.

C-2-a
668

Karpeles, Gustav, 1848-1909.
Von der Reise. (Brief aus Holland über Spuren Spinozas). [1900]
467-468 p.

In Allgemeine Zeitung des Judentums, Jahrg. 64, 1900.

C-2-a
669

[Koerbagh, Adriaan] 1632-1669.
Een bloemhof van allerley lieflijkheyd sonder verdriet geplant door Vreederijk Waarmond [pseud.] ... Of Een vertaaling en uytlegging van al de Hebreusche, Griekshe, Latijnse, Franse, en andere vreemde bastaart-woorden on wijsen van spreeken ... inde Nederduytse taal gebruykt worden [gedaen door M^r. Adr. Koerbagh] ... Gedrukt te Leyden voor Goedaart onderwijs, 1668.
[18], 672 p. 15cm.

CONTINUED ON NEXT CARD

C-2-a
670

[Koerbagh, Adriaan] 1632-1669. Een bloemhof van allerley lieflijkheyd sonder verdriet ... 1668. (Card 2)

Caption title: Algemeen woorden-boek der bastaard-woorden.
Added title-page has imprint: t'Amsterdam, Gedrukt voor den schrijver, 1668.

C-2-a
671

Koerbagh, Adriaan, 1632-1669.
Een bloemhof van allerley lieflijkheyd sonder verdriet geplant door Vreederijk Waarmond [pseud.] ... Of Een vertaaling en eytlegging van al de Hebreusche, Griecksche, Latijnse, Franse, en andere vreemde bastaart-woorden en wijsen van spreeken ... inde Nederduytse taal gebruykt worden, gedaen door M^r. Adr. Koerbagh ... t'Amsterdam, Gedrukt voor den schrijver, 1668.
[16], 672 p. 15cm.

CONTINUED ON NEXT CARD

C-2-a
672

Koerbagh, Adriaan, 1632-1669. Een bloemhof van allerley lieflijkheyd sonder verdriet ... 1668. (Card 2)

Caption title: Algemeen woorden-boek der bastaard-woorden.

C-2-a
673

Lefèvre-Pontalis, Germain Antonin, 1830-1903.
Vingt années de république parlementaire au dix-septième siècle. Jean de Witt, grand pensionnaire de Hollande. Paris, E. Plon, Nourrit et c^ie, 1884.
2 v. port. 24cm.

1. Witt, Johan de, 1625-1672. 2. Netherlands - Hist. - 1648-1714.

C-2-a
674

Le guide, ou nouvelle description d'Amsterdam; enseignant aux voyageurs, et aux negocians, son origine, ses agrandissemens & son etat actuel ... Avec une description de sa belle Maison de ville, et de tout ce qu'elle renferme de curieux. Nouvelle edition, augmentée considérablement, & enrichie d'un grand nombre de tailles douces. A Amsterdam, Chez Covens & Mortier, 1753.
[12], 359, [8] p. fold. plates, fold. plan. 16cm.

Lives, English and forein ... including the history of England, and other nations of Europe, from the year 1550, to the year 1690. By several hands. ... London, Printed for B. Tooke, 1704.
2 v. 20 cm.

Lucassen, Th R Valck
Het geslacht Teixeira in Nederland's adelsboek. ₍1919₎
₍138₎-190 col. coats of arms. 30cm.

From Maandblad van het Genealogisch-heraldisch genootschap: "De Nederlandsche leeuw", XXXVIIe jaargang, no. 4, April 1919.

Maatschappij tot Bevordering der Bouwkunst, Amsterdam.
Beschrijving van de Grafelijke Zalen op het Binnenhof te 's Gravenhage. In opdracht van den Minister van Waterstaat bewerkt door de Commissie van Advies, en uitgegeven door de Maatschappij Tot Bevordering der Bouwkunst. ₍'s Gravenhage, Mouton₎ 1907.
223 p. (chiefly illus., plans) 36cm.

Meijer, Willem, 1842-1926.
De Rozekruisers of de vrijdenkers der 17de eeuw. Haarlem, De erven F. Bohn, 1916.
90 p. 22cm.

Original paper cover bound in.
Includes references to Spinoza.

₍Meijer, Willem₎ 1842-1926.
De strijd der refugié's in Holland tegen het staatsbeleid van Lodewijk XIV. ₍1904₎
16 p. 23cm.

Signed: W. Meijer.
"Overgedrukt uit de Tijdspiegel, 1904."
Includes references to Spinoza.
Volume of pamphlets.

₍Meijer, Willem₎ 1842-1926.
De woning van Despinoza op de Stille Veerkade. ₍1902₎
11 p.

In De Haghe, 1902.

Meijer, Willem, 1842-1926.
Wie sich Spinoza zu den Collegianten verhielt. ₍1901₎
31 p. 23cm.

"Sonderabdruck aus dem Archiv für Geschichte der Philosophie, XV. Band, 1. Heft, 1901."
Volume of pamphlets.

Meinsma, Koenraad Oege, 1865-1929.
Spinoza en zijn kring; historisch-kritische studiën over Hollandsche vrijgeesten. 's-Gravenhage, M. Nijhoff, 1896.
xxiv, 457, 22 p. 22cm.

Bibliographical footnotes.

Meinsma, Koenraad Oege, 1865-1929.
Spinoza und sein Kreis; historisch-kritische Studien über holländische Freigeister, deutsch von Lina Schneider. Vorher: Spinoza gegen Kant und die Sache der geistigen Wahrheit, von Constentin Brunner. Berlin, K. Schnabel, 1909.
539 p. port. 24cm.

Bibliographical footnotes.
Manuscript notes by Carl Gebhardt.
Original paper cover bound in.

Menzel, Adolf, 1857-
Spinoza und die Collegianten. ₍1902₎
277-298 p.

In Archiv für Geschichte der Philosophie, Bd. 15., 1902.

SPECIAL COLLECTIONS SPINOZA C-2-a 685

[Mist, Johannes Uytenhage de, b. 1636?
Apologie ofte verantwoordiginge van den ondienst der stadthouderlyke regeeringe. Tegens den hersteller van den Prins van Orangie tot stadthouder ende capiteyn generael der Vereenigde Nederlanden. Door ÆEsopum Stomachatvm [pseud.] ... t'Amsterdam, By Joan. Cyprianus van der Gragt, 1663.
[16], 335 p. 16cm.

Bound with Réponse aux questions d'un républicain. [172-?]

C-2-a 686

Muller, H C
Een en ander omtrent de verhoreding zusschen Spinoza en Johan de Witt. [1919]
419-421 p.

In Tijdschrift voor wijsbegeerte, jaargang 13, 1919.

NN

C-2-a 687

Overeenstemming tusschen den Heer Fredericus van Leenhof en Spinosa en Philopater, vertoont in eenige korte aanmerkingen over de antwoorden op de artikelen van 't Eerw. Classis van Zwolle ... en de veranderingen in syn E. Keten der Bybelse Godgeleertheit gemaakt. Zynde een afgeperste verdediging van twee gedigten door Jo. Sluiter. Amsteldam, by G. Borstius, 1704.

WU

SPECIAL COLLECTIONS SPINOZA C-2-a 688

[Parival, Jean Nicolas de, b. 1605.
Le vray l'Interet de la Hollande, elevé sur les ruines de celuy qui voit le jour sous le nom de V. D. H. Et dedié a la fille du temps, par I. N. D. P. ... [Paris?] Chez Pierre Gardier, 1662.
[8], 168 p. 17cm.

By de Parival. Cf. Quérard.

SPECIAL COLLECTIONS SPINOZA C-2-a 689
1938p4
FC753

[Parival, Jean Nicolas de, b. 1605.
Le vray l'Interet de la Hollande, elevé sur les ruines de celuy qui voit le jour sous le nom de V. D. H. Et dedié a la fille du temps, par I. N. D. P. ... [Paris?] Chez Pierre Gardier, 1662.
[8], 168 p. 17cm.

By de Parival. Cf. Quérard.
Bound with Court, Pieter de la. Interest van Holland. 1662.

SPECIAL COLLECTIONS SPINOZA C-2-a 690

[Parival, Jean Nicolas de, b. 1605.
Ware interest van Holland; gebouwt op de ruïnen van den Interest van Holland, onlangs uitgegeven door D. V. H. toegeeygent aen de dochter van de tijt. Door I. N. D. P. ... Tot Leyden, By Jan Princen, 1662.
208 p. 18cm.

By de Parival. Cf. Brit. Mus. Cat.

SPECIAL COLLECTIONS SPINOZA C-2-a 691

Pars, Adriaan, 1641-1719.
Catti aborigines Batavorum. Dat is: De Katten de voorouders der Batavieren, ofte de twee Katwijken, aan See en aan den Rijn. Met de huisen te Britten en Sand. Uit de beste schrijvers, en met kopere plaatkens opgehelderd ... Door Adrianus Pars. Met aantekeningen; nevens een verzameling van Katwyksche, Rynsburgsche, en andere Nederlandsche oudheden ... beschreeven door Mr. P. van der Schelling. Te Leiden, By Johannes Arnoldus Langerak, 1745.
[122], 604, [89] p. fold. plates, port., coats of arms. 21cm.

CONTINUED ON NEXT CARD

SPECIAL COLLECTIONS SPINOZA C-2-a 692

Pars, Adriaan, 1641-1719. Catti aborigines Batavorum. 1745. (Card 2)

Includes a description of Rijnsburg where Spinoza lived from 1660 to 1663.

C-2-a 693

Perrens, François Tommy, 1822-1901.
Les libertins en France au XVIIe siècle.
Paris, L. Chailley [1896]
428 p.

Includes references to Spinoza.

OCH

C-2-a 694

Perrens, François Tommy, 1822-1901.
Les libertins en France au XVIIe siècle.
Nouvelle éd. Paris, Lévy, 1899.
525 p. 19 cm.

Includes references to Spinoza.

SPECIAL COLLECTIONS SPINOZA C-2-a 695

[Peters, C H]
Een "In memoriam" gewijd aan de Amsterdamsche Veerkade, de Stille Veerkade en de Paviljoensgracht te 's-Gravenhage. [1902]
[218]-259 p. plates. 19cm.

Signed: C. H. Peters.
From Die Haghe; bijdragen en mededeelingen, 1902.
Includes references to Spinoza.
With Meijer, Willem. De woning van Despinoza op de Stille Veerkade. [1902]

NNC

SPECIAL COLLECTIONS SPINOZA C-2-a 700

Réponse aux questions d'un républicain.
A Paris, Aux dépens de l'auteur [172-?]
1 p. l., vi, 198, [1] p. 16cm.

SPECIAL COLLECTIONS SPINOZA C-2-a 696

Philippson, Martin, 1846-1916.
Das zeitalter Ludwigs des Vierzehnten. Von Dr. Martin Philippson ... Berlin, G. Grote, 1879.
3 p. l., 531 p. illus., plates, ports., 3 fold. facsim. 24½cm. (Added t.-p.: Allgemeine geschichte in einzeldarstellungen ... Hrsg. von Wilhelm Oncken. 3. hauptabth. 5. th)

Includes a section on Spinoza (p. 225-227)
Bound in 2 v.

SPECIAL COLLECTIONS SPINOZA C-2-a 701

[Rey, Henry E , ed.
The Hague and the Hotel des Indes [edited by Henry E. Rey. Berlin, 1931?]
40 p. illus., map. 23x12cm.

Text in English, French, Dutch and German.
Includes a reference to Spinoza's home (p. 29) and to his grave (p. 31)
Advertising matter included.

NNC

SPECIAL COLLECTIONS SPINOZA C-2-a 697

Prins, Izak, 1887–
De vestiging der Marranen in Noord-Nederland in de zestiende eeuw, door mr. Izak Prins. Amsterdam, M. Hertzberger, 1927.
x, 246 p. 21 cm.
"Alphabetische literatuurlijst": p. [206]-226.
Includes references to Spinoza (p. 13, 94)

1. Maranos in the Netherlands. 2. Jews in the Netherlands. 3. Portuguese in the Netherlands. I. Title.
Full name: Izak Maurits Prins.

DS135.N4P7 296.09492 40—17809
Library of Congress [57c1]

C-2-a 702

Rogge, Hendrik Cornelis, 1831-1905.
Het kerkelyk en godsdienstig leven te Amsterdam in de zeventiende eeuw. [Amsterdam, J. Emmering, 19-?]
108 p. illus. 42 cm.

Includes a portrait of Spinoza (p. 95)

NNUT

SPECIAL COLLECTIONS SPINOZA C-2-a 698

Priolo, Benjamin, 1602-1667.
Benj. Prioli Ab excessu Ludovici XIII. de rebus Gallicis, historiarum. Libri XII ... Nova editio. Amstelodami, Apud Ioannem Maximilianum Lucas, 1677.
[30], 508, [10] p.

One leaf following t.-p. (signature *2) lacking.

SPECIAL COLLECTIONS SPINOZA C-2-a 703

Roth, Leon, 1896-
The Abscondita sapientiae of Joseph del Medigo. [1922]
54-66 p. 22cm.

Cover-title: Dissertatio ex Chronici Spinozani tomo secundo separatim edita.
Includes references to Spinoza.
Bibliographical footnotes.

SPECIAL COLLECTIONS SPINOZA C-2-a 699

Rees, Otto van, 1825-1868.
Verhandeling over de: Aanwijsing der politike gronden en maximen van de Republike van Holland en West-Vriesland, van Pieter de la Court. Utrecht, B. Dekema, 1851.
lvi, 180 p. 23cm.

Added t.-p. in Latin.
Thesis, Utrecht.
Bibliographical footnotes.
Ms. notes by Carl Gebhardt.

SPECIAL COLLECTIONS SPINOZA C-2-a 704

Sande Bakhuyzen, Hendricus Gerardus van de, 1838-1923.
De toestand van de natuurwetenschappen in den tijd van Spinoza; rede gehouden in de Algemeene vergadering van het "Spinozahuis", 6 Juli 1911. 's-Gravenhage, Gedrukt bij F. J. Belinfante voorh.: A. D. Schinkel, 1911.
cover-title, 20 p. 22cm.

[Seeligmann, Sigmund] 1877-1941.
Spinoza Amstelodamensis. [1933]
29-30 p. 26cm.

Signed: Sigmund Seeligmann.
From Amstelodamum, 20ste jaargang, no. 3, Maart 1933.
With Vas Nunes, E. H. Spinoza Amstelodamensis. [1933]

[Seeligmann, Sigmund] 1877-1941.
Spinoza Amstelodamensis. [1933]
17-22 p. 26cm.

Signed: Sigmund Seeligmann.
From Amstelodamum; maandblad voor de kennis van Amsterdam, orgaan van het Genootschap Amstelodamum. 20. jaargang, no. 2. Februari 1933.

Seventeenth century studies presented to Sir Herbert Grierson. Oxford, Clarendon Press, 1938.
xv, 415 p. plates, port. 23cm.

Includes references to Spinoza.

1. Spinoza, Benedictus de, 1632-1677.

Severijn, Johannes
Spinoza en de gereformeerde theologie zijner dagen. Utrecht, J. van Druten, 1919.
238 p. 25cm.

Thesis, Utrecht.
Bibliographical footnotes.

Shatzky, Jacob, 1894–
... ספינאזא און זיין סביבה. ניו־יארק, [New York] 1927
334 p. front., illus. (ports.) 20cm.
Bibliography: p. 319-334.
Presentation copy to A. S. Oko, with author's inscription and signature on fly-leaf.

1. Spinoza, Benedictus de, 1632-1677.
Title transliterated: Spinoza ...

Simons, Pieter
Johan de Witt en zijn tijd. Amsterdam, J. van der Hey, 1832-42.
3 v. port. 24cm.

Vol. 3 has imprint: Amsterdam, J. C. van Kesteren, 1842.

Simons, Pieter
Johann de Witt und seine Zeit. Aus dem Holländischen übersetzt, und mit eigenen Anmerkungen und Erläuterungen versehen von Ferd. Neumann. Erfurt, F. W. Otto, 1835-36.
v. 1-2 in 1. 23cm.

Slee, Jacob Cornelis van, 1841-1929.
De Rijnsburger Collegianten; geschiedkundig onderzoek. Haarlem, De Erven F. Bohn, 1895.
xi, 455 p. fold. plate. 25cm.

Includes references to Spinoza.
Bibliographical footnotes.

Sleutel, ontsluytende de boecke-kas van de Witte bibliotheeck, met sijn appendix. Waer in de duystere namen der boecken klaerlijck werden vertoont en bekent gemaeckt. Door J. B. Bibliothecaris. In 's Gravenhage, By Nil Volentibus arduum, 1672.
16 p.

Includes references to Spinoza.

Smith, Henry.
Spinoza and his environment. A critical essay with a translation of the ethics, by Henry Smith ... Cincinnati, R. Clarke & co., 1886.
clxxix p., 1 l., 244 p. front. (port.) 24cm.

1. Spinoza, Benedictus de, 1632-1677.

Sokolow, Nahum, 1859–1936.
ברוך שפינוזה וזמנו; מדרש בפילוסופיה ובקורות העתים.
[Paris, 1928/29]
xvii, 434 p. illus., ports., facsims. 25 cm.
Added t. p.: Baruch Spinoza and his time; a study in philosophy and history.

1. Spinoza, Benedictus de, 1632–1677.
Title transliterated: Barukh Shpinozah u-zemano.

Stolle, Gottlieb, 1673-1744.
Beitrage zur Kenntniss des 17. u. 18. Jahrhunderts aus den handschriftlichen Aufzeichnungen Gottlieb Stolle's. Mitgetheilt von G. E. Guhrauer. [1847]
385-436; 481-531 p.

In Allgemeine Zeitschrift für Geschichte, Bd. 7, 1847.
Includes references to Spinoza.

Sokolow, Nahum, 1859-1936.
Baruch Spinoza the Jew and his time. [1932]
723-731 p.

In Avukah annual, 1932.

[Stoppa, Giovanni Battista] fl. 1672.
Der Hollander Religion. In unterschiedlichen Brieffen, welche ein Officirer aus der frantzósischen Armée, ahn einen Professoren Theol: der Statt Bern geschrieben, vorgestelt. [Utrecht, 1673]
98 p. 19cm.

Includes references to Spinoza.

Stempels, G J D C
De levensbeschouwing der naaste toekomst. Haarlem, H. D. Tjeenk Willink & Zoon, 1922.
196 p.

Includes "Spinoza in het licht van dezen tijd" (p. 31-77)

[Stoppa, Giovanni Battista] fl. 1672.
La religion des Hollandois, representée en plusieurs lettres écrites par un officier de l'armée du roy, a un pasteur & professeur en theologie de Berne. A Cologne, Chez Pierre Marteau, 1673.
144 p. 14cm.

Includes references to Spinoza (p. 65-67, 107-109)

Stockum, Wilhelmus Petrus van
's-Gravenhage in den loop der tijden. 's-Gravenhage, W. P. van Stockum, 1889.
2 v. in 1. 21cm.

Includes a section on Spinoza's homes (v. 2, p. 162-165), a passage on his monument (v. 2, p. 179) and references to persons connected with him.

[Stoppa, Giovanni Battista] fl. 1672.
The religion of the Dutch. Represented in several letters from a Protestant officer in the French army to a pastor and professor of divinity at Berne in Swisserland. Out of the French. London, Printed for Samuel Heyrick, 1680.
ii, 66 p.

Stockum, Wilhelmus Petrus van
's-Gravenhage in den loop der tijden. Goedkoope uitgaaf met een kaart van 's Gravenhage in 1570. 's-Gravenhage, W. P. van Stockum, 1911.
2 v. in 1. fold. plan. 20cm.

Includes a section on Spinoza's homes (v. 2, p. 162-165), a passage on his monument (v. 2, p. 179) and references to persons connected with him.

Tak, Willem Gerard van der, 1885-
De Ludovico Meyer. [1921]
91-100 p. 22cm.

Cover-title: Dissertatio ex Chronici Spinozani tomo primo separatim edita.
Includes references to Spinoza.

Teixeira de Mattos, E
Critiek op het artikel van Mr. R. Th. Valck Lucassen in "De Nederl. leeuw" d. d. Mei 1918, over het geslacht Teixeira in het Nederl. adelsboek; bijdrage tot de geschiedenis betreffende Oud-Spaansch-Portugeesche geslachten in Nederland. Uitsluitend naar authentieke en officieele bescheiden. [1918?]
93 p. plates, fold. geneal. table.

Includes references to Spinoza.
Bibliographical footnotes.

Teixeira de Mattos, E
De phrenesie van de oude jonkvrouw Jeanne de Spinosa, te Rijssel, tijdsbeeld uit het begin der 17de eeuw; behandeling en beloop van periodiek terugkeerende dwang- en waangedachten met reactieve handelingen bij tusschentijds ongerept verstand en goed geheugen. [1928]
cover-title, 12 p. geneal. table. 25cm.

"Overgedrukt uit het Nederl. Tijdschrift voor geneeskunde, Twee en zeventigste jaargang, 1928, Tweede helft, no. 40."

CONTINUED ON NEXT CARD

Teixeira de Mattos, E De phrenesie van de oude jonkvrouw Jeanne de Spinosa. [1928] (Card 2)

Asserts the improbability of a relationship of Jeanne de Spinosa to Benedictus de Spinoza. (p. 11)

[Teixeira de Mattos, E]
Laster met bedrog door achterhouding van een essentieel document, onder verzwarende omstandigheden gepleegd door W. A. Beelaerts v. Blokland ... in het Maandblad de Nederlandsche leeuw van April 1921. [1921]
[7] p. 28cm.

Signed: E. Teixeira de Mattos.

Temple, Sir William, bart., 1628-1699.
Remarques sur l'estat des Provinces Unies des Païs-Bas, faites en l'an 1672. Par Monsieur le chevalier Temple ... A La Haye, Chez Jean & Daniel Steucker, 1680.
[38], 270, [1] p. 14cm.

Translated into French by A. Le Vasseur.- cf. B. M.

Tepelius, Johannes, *b.* 1649.
M. Johannis Tepelii ... Historia philosophiæ Cartesianæ. Norimbergæ, apud Johannis Andreæ & Wolfgangi Endteri junioris hæredes, 1674.
12 p. l., 96 p. ~~13 x 7½~~ 15cm.

Includes a reference to Spinoza (p. 95)

1. Descartes, René, 1596-1650.

Toetze, op het laster-schrift, t'onrecht genaamt Stadhouderlyke regeeringe van Holland en West-Vriesland. VVaar in klaarlijk aangewesen werdt, dat de stadhouders ... alles in Holland en West-Vriesland hebben verricht ... Door D. P. E. Tot Leyden, By Jan Princen, 1662.
126, [2] p. 18cm.

Bound with Parival, Jean Nicolas de. Ware interest van Holland. 1662.

Valck Lucassen, Th R
Het geslacht Teixeira in Nederland's adelsboek. [1919]
[138]-190 col. coats of arms. 30cm.

From Maandblad van het Genealogisch-heraldisch genootschap: "De Nederlandsche leeuw", XXXVIIe jaargang, no. 4, April 1919.

1. Teixeira family.

Vaz Dias, A M 1877-1939.
De firma Bento y Gabriel de Spinoza, door A. M. Vaz Dias en W. G. van der Tak. Leiden, E. J. Brill, 1934.
23 p. facsims. 24cm. (Mededeelingen van wege het Spinozahuis, I)

Vas Nunes, E H
Spinoza Amstelodamensis. [1933]
p. 29. 26cm.

Signed: E. H. Vas Nunes.
From Amstelodamum, 20ste jaargang, no. 3, Maart 1933.

1. Spinoza, Benedictus de, 1632-1677.

[Veegens, D]
De woonplaats van Spinoza en Elsje van Houwe-ningen. [1867]
[108]-117, 197 p. 25cm.

From Mededeelingen van de Vereening ter beoefening der geschiedenis van 's-Gravenhage, 2. deel, 2. aflevering.
Bibliographical footnotes.

Vereeniging tot Bevordering van het Vreemdelingenverkeer, The Hague.
Officieele gids voor 's-Gravenhage, Scheveningen en omstreken. Uitgegeven door de Vereeniging tot Bevordering van het Vreemdelingenverkeer te 's-Gravenhage, Scheveningen en omstreken. ['s-Gravenhage, 1927]
71 p. illus., fold. map. 23x11cm.

Includes a reference to Spinoza's grave (p. 37) and to his home (p. 48)

NNC

Vereeniging tot Bevordering van het Vreemdelingenverkeer, The Hague.
Plattegrond van den Haag en Scheveningen. ['s-Gravenhage, 192-?]
[27] p. 13 maps (part fold.) plans. 25cm.

Includes a reference to Spinoza Straat on map no. 4.

NNC

Vervolg van 't leven van Philopater. Geredded uit de verborgentheeden der Coccejanen, en geworden een waaragtig wysgeer. Een waare historie. Tot Groeningen, Voor Siewert van der Brug, 1697.
292 p. 14cm.

Includes a reference to Spinoza (p. 2)
Actually published and in part written by Aert Wolsgreen, Amsterdam.--cf. Doorninck, J. I. Vermomde en naamlooze schrijvers.
Bound with Het leven van Philopater. 1691.

[Vloten, Johannes van] 1818-1883.
[An essay concerning Wittichius and Philopater. 18--]
4 p. 28cm.

Includes references to Spinoza.

NNC

Widerlegung eines Büchleins, so den andern Tag May dises 1674. Jahrs zu Handenkommen, dessen Titul ist: Wahrer Bericht von der Holländern Religion. Und unterschiedlichen jetzt schwebenden Welt-Geschäfften. Auch von des Auctors sechs Epistlen. 1674.
[2], 49 p. 21cm.

A reply to Gründtlicher Bericht der Hollander Religion. 1674.

CONTINUED ON NEXT CARD

Widerlegung eines Büchleins, so den andern Tag May dises 1674. 1674. (Card 2)

Bound with Gründtlicher Bericht der Hollander Religion. 1674.

Witt, Johan de, 1662–1701.
Catalogus bibliothecae luculentissimae, & exquisitissimis ac rarissimis in omni disciplinarum & linguarum genere libris, magno studio, dilectu & sumptu quaesitis, instructissimae, a Joanne de Witt, Joannis Hollandiae consiliarii & syndici, magnique sigilli custodis, filio. Illius auctio habebitur Dordraci, in aedibus defuncti, ~~20 octobris~~ ... 1701. Dordraci, apud Theodorum Goris, & Joannem van Braam [1701]
2 v. in 1. ~~15½~~ 18cm.

Each volume has ornamental half-title, engraved: Bibliotheca wittiana. Pars I-II

(Continued on next card)

33-32887

[2]

Witt, Johan de, 1662–1701. Catalogus bibliothecae luculentissimae ... [1701] (Card 2)

Vol. 2 has title: Bibliothecae wittianae pars secunda; sive, Numismatum ac operis prisci thesaurus ... Amstelædami, ex typographia F. Halmae, 1701.

Compiled and published by J. G. Graevius.

1. Bibliography—Rare books. 2. Manuscripts—Catalogs. 3. Numismatics—Bibl.—Catalogs. 4. Numismatics—Rome. I. Graevius, Joannes Georgius, 1632–1703. II. Title. III. Title: Bibliotheca wittiana.

33-32887

Library of Congress Z997.W827
[2] 016.09

Witt, Johan de, 1662-1701.
Catalogus van eene aanzienlijke en zeer zeldzaame verzameling van manuscripten ... en voor het grootste gedeelte nagelaaten door ... Johan de Witt ... en Cornelis de Witt ... En laatst toebehoord hevvende ... Jan de Witt ... Al het welk publiek aan de meestbiedende zal verkocht worden, op den 21 en 22 November 1791. Door A. en J. Honkoop, boekhandelaars te Leyden ... Tweede druk. [1791]
20, 19 p. fold. table. 18cm.

NNC

CONTINUED ON NEXT CARD

Witt, Johan de, 1662-1701. Catalogus ... van manuscripten. [1791] (Card 2)

"Additions au catalogue des livres manuscrits": 19 p. at end.
Bound with the author's Catalogus bibliothecae luculentissimae. [1701]

Altkirch, Ernst, 1873-1926.
Die portugiesische Synagoge in Amsterdam. [1911]
234-239 p. illus. 28cm.

From Ost und West, XI. Jahrgang, Heft 3, März 1911.
Contains a picture of the synagogue in Spinoza's time.

Zesen, Philipp von, 1619-1689.
Filips von Zesen Beschreibung der Stadt Amsterdam: darinnen von derselben ersten Ursprunge bis auf gegenwärtigen Zustand/ihr unterschiedlicher Anwachs/herliche Vorrechte/und in mehr als 70 Kupfer-stükken entworfene führnehmste Gebeue/zusamt ihrem Stahts-wesen/Kauf-handel/und ansehnlicher Macht zur See/wie auch was sich in und mit derselben merkwürdiges zugetragen/vor Augen gestellt werden ... Amsterdam, Joachim Noschen, 1664.
[8], 398, [22] p. plates (part fold.) fold. plans. 23cm.

Amsterdam. Portugeesch-Israëlietisch Seminarium "Ets Haïm". Bibliotheek.
אלפי מנשה: 1627—1 Januari—1927. Catalogus der tentoonstelling in het Portugeesch Israëlietisch Seminarium "Ets Haïm" te Amsterdam ter herinnering aan het driehonderd-jarig jubileum van het eerste door Menasseh Ben Israel te Amsterdam gedrukte Hebreeuwsche boek; samengesteld door J. S. da Silva Rosa. Amsterdam, 1927.
30 p. illus., ports., facsims. 27cm.

Title transliterated: Alfē Mĕnashshē.

Zuiden, D S van
Haagsche straatnamen, in hun afkomst en beteekenis nagespoord en toegelicht door D. S. van Zuiden. Onder toezicht en met een inleiding van H. E. van Gelder. Met een plattegrond van 's Gravenhage en Scheveningen aangevende de geleidelijke uitbreidingen tot heden. Gouda, G. B. van Goor Zonen, 1909.
xx, 108 p. fold. map. 22cm.

Includes a reference to "Spinozastraat" (p. 68)

Amsterdam. Portugeesch-Israëlietisch Seminarium "Ets Haïm". Bibliotheek.
Catalogus van de tentoonstelling van Joodsche oorlogslitteratuur, gehouden te Amsterdam in de Bibliotheek van het Portugeesch Israëlietisch Seminarium "Ets Haïm" ... van Zondag ... 15 April 1917 tot en met Vrijdag ... 20 April 1917, ten bate van het inzamelingswerk voor de Joodsche oorlogsslachtoffers. [Amsterdam, 1917]
cover-title, xxix, 42 p. 24cm.

"Deze catalogus is bewerkt door: J. S. da Silva Rosa."

C-2-b
CONTEMPORARY JEWISH ASPECTS

Amsterdam. Synagoge der Portugeesch-Israëlietische Gemeente.
Feestelijke herdenking van het 250-jarig bestaan van de Synagoge der Portugeesch-Israëlietische Gemeente te Amsterdam ... 31 Juli 1925. [Amsterdam, 1925]
32 p. illus., plates, facsims. 25cm.

Includes a reference to Spinoza (p. 23)

Abrahams, Israel, 1858-1925.
Chapters on Jewish literature, by Israel Abrahams ... Philadelphia, The Jewish publication society of America, 1899.
275 p. 19½ cm.
Bibliography at end of each chapter.
Includes material on Spinoza in chapter "Amsterdam in the seventeenth century" (p. [243]-252) and other references to him.

1. Jewish literature—Hist. & crit. I. The Jewish publication society of America.

Ancona, J d'
Was Dr. Abraham Pharar vrijzinnig? Een verklaring van het ontstaan van de Derde Port. Isr. gemeente Beth Jisraël te Amsterdam in het jaar 1618. [1938]
12 p. 21cm.

"Overdruk uit het 'Nieuw Israel. Weekblad' van 19 Augustus 1938, 74e jaargang, no. 16."
Includes references to Spinoza.
Bibliography: p. 12.

C-2-6
754

Apfelbaum, Abe

[רבי משה זכות ושפינוזה.] [1926]
p. 200.

Title transliterated: Zakutho u-Shpinozah.
In ha-Olam, v. 14, 1926.

NNJ

C-2-6
755

Argens, Jean Baptiste de Boyer, marquis de, 1704-1771.
The Jewish spy: being a philosophical, historical and critical correspondence, by letters which lately pass'd between certain Jews in Turkey, Italy, France ... Translated from the originals into French by the marquis d'Argens; and now done into English. Dublin, 1753.
4 v.

PPL

Includes references to Spinoza.

C-2-6
756

Argens, Jean Baptiste de Boyer, marquis d', 1704-1771.
Lettres juives, ou, Correspondance philosophique, historique & critique entre un Juif voyageur à Paris et ses correspondans en divers endroits ... Nouvelle édition augmentée. La Haye, P. Paupie, 1742.
6 v. 16 cm.

Includes references to Spinoza.

CtY

SPECIAL COLLECTIONS
SPINOZA

C-2-6
757

Aron, Maurice
Histoire de l'excommunication juive. Nimes, Imprimerie Clavel-Ballivet, 1882.
168 p. 19cm.

Original paper covers bound in.
Includes a chapter "Anathème contre Spinoza" (p. [129]-143)

SPECIAL COLLECTIONS
SPINOZA

C-2-6
758

Ashkenazi, Ṣebī Hirsch ben Jacob, 1658-1718.
Rechtfertigung des Rabbi David Nieto gegen den Vorwurf in seiner Predigt Spinozas Lehre zu verbreiten [von] Chacham Zewi Hirsch Aschkenasi. [Berlin?, Officina Serpentis] 1930.
7 p. 23cm.

"Dieses Responsum ... des 18. Jahrhunderts wurde als Handpressendruck der Officina Serpentis in 200 Exemplaren hergestellt und den Mitgliedern ... der Soncino-Gesellschaft ... gewidmet."

NNC

C-2-6
759

Aulisio, Domenico d', 1639-1717.
Delle scuole sacre libri due postumi ... pubblicati dal suo erede e nipote Niccolo Ferrara Aulisio, ne' quali tratta delle scuole sacre che furono fra gli Ebrei, e che sono fra i Christiani. Napoli, presso Francesco Ricciardi, 1723.
2 v.

NNJ

SPECIAL COLLECTIONS
SPINOZA

C-2-6
760

Balling, Pieter
Het licht op den Kandelaar. Door Pieter Balling ... t'Amsterdam, By Jan Rieuwertsz, 1684.
23 p. 14cm.

Photostat copy (positive)
Bound with Jelles, Jarig. Belydenisse der algemeenen en Christelyken geloofs. 1684.

SPECIAL COLLECTIONS
SPINOZA

C-2-6
761

Buxtorf, Johann, 1564-1629.
Schoole der Jooden. Begrijpende het geheele Joodze geloof en geloofs-oeffening, benevens deszelfs ceremonien, in-zettingen, zeden en gebruiken ... Noch een Bondig-bericht, van hun toekomende Messia. Mitsgaders een reedestrijd, tusschen een Iode en een Christen ... Eertijds ... beschreven door M. Johannem Bvxdorfivm ... doch nu, uit het Hoogin't Nederduitz', vertaald door Jan Zoet ... t'Amsterdam, Gedrukt by Tymon Hovthaak voor Nicolaas Fransz, 1650.
[16], 578, 42, [15] p. 16cm.

SPECIAL COLLECTIONS
SPINOZA

C-2-6
762

193Sp4 Castro, David Henriques de, 1826-1898.
FC19 De synagoge der Portugeesch-Israelietische gemeente te Amsterdam. Tot inleiding: Eenige geschiedkundige aanteekeningen betreffende de vroegere bedehuizen dezer gemeente. Een gedenkschrift ter gelegenheid van haar tweedeeeuwfeest, door D. H. de Castro. 's-Gravenhage, Gebroeders Belinfante, 1875.
66, lxxvii p. plate. 24cm.

At head of title: 1675-1876.
Includes references to Spinoza and his family.

NNC

C-2-6
763

Cousin, Victor, 1792-1867.
Fragments de philosophie moderne. Nouvelle éd. Paris, Didier, 1856.
517 p.

Includes a section "Spinoza et la synagogue des Juifs portugais à Amsterdam" (p. 57-62)

MH

Cousin, Victor, 1792-1867.
Fragments philosophiques. 3. éd. Paris, Ladrange, 1838.
2 v.

Includes a section "Spinoza et la synagogue des Juifs portugais à Amsterdam" (p. 163-166) and other references to Spinoza.

Hillesum, J M
Uri-ha-Levi, de eerste mohel, chazzan en predikant der Portugeesche Joden te Amsterdam in het jaar 1593. Amsterdam, van Creveld, 1904.
51 p. 18cm.

"Overdruk uit het Centraal blad v. Isr. in Nederland."
Includes a reference to Spinoza (p. 11)

Cunaeus, Petrus, 1586-1638.
Petri Cunæi De republica Hebræorum. libri III. Editio novissima ... Curiæ, Sumptibus Johannis Brendelii, typis Gottofredi Minzelii, 1666.
[32], 368 p. 13cm.

Added t.-p., engraved.

Hirschel, L
Een godsdienstdispuut te Amsterdam in het begin der 17de eeuw. Amsterdam, M. Hertzberger, 1929.
cover-title, 7 p. illus. 28cm.

"Overgedrukt uit 'De Vrijdagavond,' zesde jaargang."
"Godsdienstdispuut ... tusschen den Engelschen Hebraïcus Hugh Broughton en den Jood Dr. David Farar."

Dubnov, Semen Markovich, 1860-
An outline of Jewish history, by S. M. Doubnow ... authorized translation from the Russian ... New York, N. Y., M. N. Maisel, 1925.
3 v. 21½cm.
CONTENTS.—v. 1. Biblical epoch.—v. 2. The Maccabean and Talmudic eras.—v. 3. The middle ages and modern times.
Includes a section "The Netherlands - Acosta and Spinoza" (v. 3, p. 211-217)
1. Jews—Hist. I. Title.

Hirschel, L
Jan Pietersz. Beeldthouwer en de rabbijnen; bijdrage tot de geschiedenis der Joden te Amsterdam. Opgedragen aan Jeremias Meyer Hillesum bij zijn veertig-jarig jubileum als conservator der Bibliotheca Rosenthaliana. [1930]
210-211, 227-228 p. 35cm.

Includes a reference to Spinoza.
From De Vrydagavond; Joodsch weekblad, jrg. 6, no. 40-41, 1930.
Bibliographical footnotes.

Harris, Maurice Henry, 1859-1930.
Modern Jewish history from the renaissance to the world war. New York, 1910.
161 p.

Includes "Spinoza and his contemporaries" with a portrait of Spinoza (p. 63-70)

Koenen, Hendrik Jacob, 1809-1874.
Geschiedenis der Joden in Nederland; uitgegeven door het Provinciaal Utrechtsche Genootschap van Kunsten en Wetenschappen. Te Utrecht, Bij C. van der Post jr., drukker van het Provinciaal Utrechtsche Genootschap, 1843.
xvii, 519 p. 24cm.

Includes a section on Spinoza (p. 349-356) and other references to him.
Bibliographical footnotes.

[Hillesum, J M]
Bijdrage tot de bibliographie van Menasseh ben Israel's geschriften. ['s-Gravenhage, M. Nijhoff, 192-?]
[353]-363 p. illus., facsims. 25cm.

Signed: J. M. Hillesum.
"Overdruk uit 'Het boek'."

Koenen, Hendrik Jakob, 1809-1874.
Geschiedenis van de vestiging en den invloed der fransche vluchtelingen in Nederland. Leiden, S. en J. Luchtmans, 1846.
xvii, 451 p. front. 23cm.

[La Peyrère, Isaac de] 1594-1676.
Dv rappel des Ivifs. 1643.
[7], 375, [1] p. 17cm.

By I. de La Peyrère.--cf. Bibl. nat. cat.

Manasseh ben Joseph ben Israel, 1604-1657.
Menasseh ben Israel's mission to Oliver Cromwell: being a reprint of the pamphlets published by Menasseh ben Israel to promote the re-admission of the Jews to England, 1649-1656; ed. with an introduction and notes by Lucien Wolf. London, Pub. for the Jewish Historical Society of England by Macmillan, 1901.
lxxxviii, 190 p. ports. 27cm.

Includes a reference to Spinoza (p. xxxvi)

Manasseh ben Joseph ben Israel, 1604-1657.
מקוה ישראל Esto es, Esperança de Israel. Obra con suma curiosidad conpuesta por Menasseh ben Israel ... Trata del admirable esparzimiento de los diez tribus, y su infalible reducción con los de mas, a la patria; con muchos puntos, y historias curiosas, y declaracion de varias prophecias, por el author rectamente interpretadas. Dirigido a los señores Parnassim del K. K. de Talmvd Tora. En Amsterdam, En la imprension de Semvel ben Israel

CONTINUED ON NEXT CARD

Manasseh ben Joseph ben Israel, 1604-1657.
מקוה ישראל. (Card 2)

Soeiro, año 5410 [1650]
[14], 126 p. 16cm.

Title transliterated: Miḳwē Yisrā'ēl.

Morteira, Saul Levi, 1595 (ca.)-1660.
Libro yntitulado Providençia de dios con israel verdad y heternidad de la lei de moseh compuesto por ... Saul Levi Mortera ...
15, [2], 618, [1] l. ports. 28cm.

Manuscript. "Este libro fue cópiadc de su original por Abraham y dana, correcto el año de 1683": final leaf. Illustrated title-page.
Old (17th century) Dutch red morocco binding, gilt tooled with all edges gauffred; attributed to Magnus. Remnants of brass hinges and hasps.

[Orobio, Balthasar de] d. 1687.
Epistola invectiva contra Prado un philosopho medico, q'dudava, ô no crehia la verdad de la divina Escritura, y pretendió encubrir su malicia con la affecta confession de Dios, y ley de naturaleza.
43-147 p. 28cm.

"Photographic copy of the best of the 3 mss. in the Library of the Portuguese-Jewish Seminary at Amsterdam."--Oko's note inserted in the book.

Orobio, Balthasar de, *d.* 1687.
... La observancia de la divina ley de Mosseh; manuscrito do século XVII publicado pela primeira vez com um estudo prévio de Moses Bensabat Amzalak ... Coimbra, Imprensa da Universidade, 1925.
xl, 101 p., 1 l. facsims. 21cm.
At head of title: Isaac Orobio de Castro.
"Bibliografia": p. xviii-xxxix.
Includes references to Spinoza (p. xiv-xv)
1. Jews—Religion—Apologetic works. 2. Jews—Religion—Relations—Christianity. I. Amzalak, Moses Bensabat, ed. II. Title.

Schindler, Solomon, 1842-1915.
Dissolving views in the history of Judaism, by Rabbi Solomon Schindler ... Boston, Lee and Shepard; New York, C. T. Dillingham, 1888.
8 p. l., 340 p. 19½cm.
Lectures delivered 1887-88.
Includes a chapter "Baruch Spinoza and his time" (p. 215-227)
1. Jews—Hist. I. Title.

Seeligmann, Sigmund, 1877-1941.
Bibliographie en historie; bijdrage tot de geschiedenis der eerste Sephardim in Amsterdam. Amsterdam, H. Hertzberger, 1927.
62 p. facsims. 25cm.

Seeligmann, Sigmund, 1877-1941.
Het geestelijk leven in de Hoogduitsche Joodsche gemeente te 's-Gravenhage. 's-Gravenhage, 1914.
44 p. illus., facsim. 21cm.

"Overgedrukt uit D. S. Van Zuiden: Geschiedenis der Hoogduitsche Joden in 's-Gravenhage."

Seeligmann, Sigmund, 1877-1941.
Die Juden in Holland; eine Charakteristik.
[København, Hertz's bogtrykkeri, 1923]
v p. 23cm.

"Søertryk af Festskrift i anledning af Professor David Simonsens 70-aarige fødselsdag."

1. Jews in Netherlands.

Seeligmann, Sigmund, 1877-1941.
Het Marranen-probleem uit oekonomisch oogpunt. [1925]
36 p. 22cm.

"Overdruk uit Bijdragen en mededeelingen van het Genootschap voor de Joodsche Wetenschap in Nederland. III. Amsterdam, Menno Hertzberger, 1925."
Includes a reference to Spinoza (p. 20)

Silva Rosa, Jacob S da, 1886-
Een eigenhandige brief van Daniel Levi de Barrios; bijdrage tot eene biographie van dezen dichter-geschiedschrijver. [1923]
[106]-111 p. 23cm.

"Søertryk af Festskrift i anledning af Professor David Simonsens 70-aarige fødselsdag."
Presentation copy to Carl Gebhardt with the author's inscription and initials.

Silva Rosa, Jacob S da, 1886-
Geschiedenis der Portugeesche Joden te Amsterdam 1593–1925, door J. S. da Silva Rosa. Amsterdam, M. Hertzberger, 1925.
2 p. l., [vii]–xvi, 182 p. illus. (incl. ports., facsims.) 22½cm.
"Literatuur" at end of sections.
Includes references to Spinoza.

1. Jews in Amsterdam. I. Title: Portugeesche Joden te Amsterdam.

Silva Rosa, Jacob S da, 1886-
Iets over den Amsterdamschen opperrabbijn Isaäc Aboab. Amsterdam, Van Creveld, 1913.
19 p. 20cm.

"Overgedrukt uit het Centraal blad voor Israelieten in Nederland."

[Silva Rosa, Jacob S da] 1886-
Over de oudste Portugeese synagoges te Amsterdam. [Hagae Comitis, 1921]
[267]-272 p. illus. 23cm.

Signed: J. S. da Silva Rosa.
Cover-title: Dissertatio ex Chronici Spinozani tomo primo separatim edita.
Includes references to Spinoza.

[Silva Rosa, Jacob S da] 1886-
Van Marranen tot Portugeesche Joden te Amsterdam; een economisch of een religieus motief? [1933]
30-32 p. 26cm.

Signed: J. S. da Silva Rosa.
From Amstelodamum, 20ste jaargang, no. 3, Maart 1933.
Includes references to Spinoza.
Bound with Vas Nunes, E. H. Spinoza Amstelodamensis. [1933]

Simon, Richard, 1638-1712.
Histoire critique du Vieux Testament, par le R. P. Richard Simon ... Nouvelle edition, & qui est la premiere imprimée sur la copie de Paris, augmentée d'une apologie generale, de plusieurs remarques critiques & d'une réponse par un theologien protestant. On a de-plus ajoûté à cette edition une table des matieres, & tout ce qui a été imprimé jusqu'à présent à l'occasion de cette Histoire critique. A Rotterdam, Chez Reinier Leers, 1685.
[40], 667, [45] p. 25cm.

Sluys, D M
De oudste synagogen der Hoogduitsch-Joodsche Gemeente te Amsterdam (1635-1671) Amsterdam, Joachimsthal's Stoomdrukkerij, 1921.
30 p. 23cm.

Til, Salomon van, 1643-1713.
Het voor-hof der heydenen, voor alle ongeloovigen geopent, om de selve aldaar door een klare beschouwinge van de betoogde goddelykheyd van Mosis wet-boek tot een eerbiediger ingang in 't heyligdom van Gods wet toe te rusten, door Salomon van Til ... Tot Dordregt, By Dirk Goris, 1694.
[8], 394 p. 21cm.

Includes references to Spinoza.

Til, Salomon van, 1643-1713.
Het voor-hof der heydenen, voor alle ongeloovigen geopent, om deselve aldaar door een klare beschouwinge van de betoogde goddelykheyd van Mosis wet-boek tot een eerbiediger ingang in 't heyligdom van Gods wet toe te rusten, door Salomon van Til ... Tot Dordrecht, By Dirk en Casp. Joann. Goris, 1714.
[8], 392 p. 21cm.

Includes references to Spinoza.

Ullmann, Salomon
Geschichte der spanisch-portugiesischen Juden in Amsterdam im 17. Jahrhundert. [1907]
74 p.

In Jüdisch-literarische Gesellschaft, Frankfurt am Main. Jahrbuch, v. 5, 1907.
Includes references to Spinoza.

Van Marrano tot Joodsch apologeet, Dr. Isaac (Balthazar) Orobio de Castro (omstr. 1620-1687) [1926]
[21]-23 p. ports., facsim. 35cm.

From De Vrydagavond, jrg. 3, no. 28, 8 October 1926.
Includes references to Spinoza.
Bibliography: p. 23.

Weltmann, Lutz, 1901-
Spinoza, ein Jude im Europa des 17. Jahrhunderts. [1937]
47-83 p. 20cm.

From Jahrbuch für jüdische Geschichte und Literatur, 30. Bd., 1937.

1. Spinoza, Benedictus de, 1632-1677.

Bayle, Pierre, 1647-1706.
Analyse raisonnée; ou, Abrégé méthodique de ses ouvrages, particulierement de son Dictionnaire historique et critique, dont les remarques ont été fondues dans le texte, pour former un corps instructif & agréable de lectures suivies [par F. M. Marsy et J. B. R. Robinet] Londres, 1755-70.
8 v.

Includes a section "Du spinozisme" (v. 7, p. 1-101)

Bayle, Pierre, 1647-1706.
Analyse raisonnée de Bayle, ou Abrégé méthodique de ses ouvrages, particulierement de son Dictionnaire historique et critique ... Tome VII. Londres, 1770.
vi (i.e. xvi), 460 p. 18cm.

Includes a section "Du spinozisme" (p. [1]-101)

Bayle, Pierre, 1647-1706.
Dictionaire historique et critique: par Monsieur Bayle ... A Rotterdam, Chez Reinier Leers, 1697.
2 v. in 4. port. 39cm.

Title vignette.
Each volume in two parts.
Includes an article on Spinoza (v. 2, pt. 2, p. 1083-1100)

Bayle, Pierre, 1647-1706.
Dictionnaire historique et critique. Seconde édition, revue, corrigée et augmentée par l'auteur ... Rotterdam, Chez R. Leers, 1702.
3 v. 38 cm.

Includes an article on Spinoza (v. 3, p. 2767-2788)

Bayle, Pierre, 1647-1706.
Dictionaire historique et critique: par Monsieur Bayle. 3. éd., a laquelle on a ajoûté la vie de l'auteur, & mis ses additions & corrections à leur place. Rotterdam, 1715.
3 v. port. 40cm.

Title vignette.
Includes an article on Spinoza (v. 3, p. 610-631)

Bayle, Pierre, 1647-1706.
Dictionnaire historique et critique, par M^r^. Pierre Bayle. Troisième édition, revue, corrigée et augmentée par l'auteur. Rotterdam, Chez M. Bohm, 1720.
v. 3. 42^cm^.

Edited by P. Marchand. Cf. Brit. Mus. Cat.
Includes an article on Spinoza (v. 3, p. 2631-2649)

SPECIAL COLLECTIONS SPINOZA C-2-c 804

Bayle, Pierre, 1647-1706.
Dictionaire historique et critique, par mr. Pierre Bayle. 4. ed. rev., cor. et augm. avec la vie de l'auteur, par mr. Des Maizeaux ... Amsterdam, Chez P. Brunel; [etc., etc.] 1730.
4 v. front. (port.) 43cm.

Title vignette.
Edited by Prosper Marchand. cf. Brit. mus. Catalogue.
Includes an article on Spinoza (v. 4, p. 253-271)

SPECIAL COLLECTIONS SPINOZA C-2-c 805

Bayle, Pierre, 1647-1706.
Dictionaire historique et critique. 5. éd., rev., corrigée et augmentée de remarques critiques, avec la vie de l'auteur, par Mr. Des Maizeaux. Amsterdam, Par la Compagnie des libraires, 1734.
v. 5. 42cm.

Includes an article on Spinoza (v. 5, p. 201-226)

C-2-c 806

Bayle, Pierre, 1647-1706.
Dictionnaire historique et critique. Nouv. éd., augm. de notes extraites de Chaufepié, Joly, La Monnoie, Leduchat, L.-J. Leclerc, Marchand, etc., etc. Paris, Desoer, 1820.
16 v. 21 cm.

Includes an article on Spinoza (v. 13, p. 412-468)

NNC

C-2-c 807

Bayle, Pierre, 1647-1706.
The dictionary historical and critical of Mr. Peter Bayle. 2d ed. Carefully collated with the several editions of the original; in which many passages are restored, and the whole greatly augmented, particularly with a translation of the quotations from eminent writers in various languages. To which is prefixed The life of the author, revised, corrected and enlarged, by Mr Des Maizeaux ... London, Printed for J. J. and P. Knapton [etc.] 1734-38.
5 v. front. (port.) 36 cm.
Engraved frontispiece. Includes an article on Spinoza (v. 5, p. 199-224)
~~(Continued on next card)~~

NNC 25—5057 [48k1]

SPECIAL COLLECTIONS SPINOZA C-2-c 808

Bayle, Pierre, 1647-1706.
Herrn Peter Baylens ... Historisches und kritisches Wörterbuch, nach der neuesten Auflage von 1740 ins Deutsche übersetzt; auch mit einer Vorrede und verschiedenen Anmerkungen sonderlich bey anstössigen Stellen versehen, von Johann Christoph Gottscheden. Nebst dem Leben des Herrn Bayle vom Herrn Desmaizeau. Leipzig, B. C. Breitkopf, 1741-44.
4 v. port. 40cm.

Includes an article on Spinoza (v. 4, p. 260-279)

SPECIAL COLLECTIONS SPINOZA C-2-c 809

Bayle, Pierre, 1647-1706.
Herrn Peter Baylens ... Verschieden Gedanken bey Gelegenheit des Cometen, der im Christmonate 1680 erschienen, an einen Doctor der Sorbonne gerichtet. Aus dem Französischen übersetzet, und mit Anmerkungen und einer Vorrede ans Licht gestellet von Joh. Christoph Gottscheden ... Hamburg, bey sel. Felginers Wittwe und J. C. Bohn, 1741.
[48], 922, [22] p. 17cm.

Includes references to Spinoza.

SPECIAL COLLECTIONS SPINOZA C-2-c 810

Bayle, Pierre, 1647-1706.
Het leven van B. de Spinoza, met eenige aantekeningen over zyn bedryf, schriften, en gevoelens: door den Heer Bayle ... Nevens een Kort betoog van de waarheit des Christelyken Godtdiensts; en twee verhandelingen, I. Van de ziel. II. Van Godts wezentlykheit. Door den Heer Jaquelot ... Vertaalt door F. Halma. De voorreden behelscht eenige aanmerkingen tegens 't Levensvervolg van Philopater. T'Utr., by François Halma, Willem van de Water, 1698.
[192], 464, [15] p. 17cm.

SPECIAL COLLECTIONS SPINOZA C-2-c 811

Bayle, Pierre, 1647-1706.
Het leven van B. de Spinoza, met eenige aantekeningen over zyn bedryf, schriften, en gevoelens: door den Heere Bayle ... Nevens een Kort betoog van de waarheit des Christelyken Godsdiensts; en twee verhandelingen, I. Van de ziel. II. Van Gods wezentlykheit. Door den Heere Jaquelot ... Vertaald door F. Halma. De voorreden behelscht eenige aanmerkingen tegens t Levensvervolg van Philopater. Te Utrecht, by Willem Broedelet, 1711.
[192], 464, [15] p. 17cm.

Pages [15-16] lacking.

C-2-c 812

Bayle, Pierre, 1647-1706.
An historical and critical dictionary. Translated into English, with many additions and corrections, made by the author himself, that are not in the French editions. London, 1710.
4 v. 36 cm.

NN

SPECIAL COLLECTIONS SPINOZA C-2-c 813

Bayle, Pierre, 1647-1706.
Lettres choisies de Mr. Bayle, avec des remarques ... A Rotterdam, Chez Fritsch et Böhm, 1714.
3 v. 16cm.

"Publiées par Des Maizeaux, avec des remarques supplémentaires (de P. Marchand)"--Bibl. nat. cat.
Includes references to Spinoza.

Bayle, Pierre, 1647–1706.
Miscellaneous reflections, occasion'd by the comet which appear'd in December 1680. Chiefly tending to explode popular superstitions. Written to a doctor of the Sorbon, by Mr. Bayle. Translated from the French. To which is added, the author's life ... London, Printed, 1708.
2 v. 18cm.
Paged continuously.
Vol. 1 has imprint: London, Printed for J. Morphew, 1708.
Includes a reference to Spinoza (p. 375-376)
1. Comets. 2. Comets—1680. 3. Omens.

Bayle, Pierre, 1647-1706.
Pensées diverses ecrites à un docteur de Sorbonne a l'occasion de la comete qui parut au mois de decembre 1680. Par Mr. Bayle. Sixieme edition, Amsterdam, Chez Meinard Uytwerf, 1749.
4 v. 17cm.

Includes references to Spinoza.

Bayle, Pierre, 1647-1706.
Nouvelles lettres de Mr. P. Bayle ... La Haye, Van Duren, 1739.
2 v. plates. 18 cm.

Bayle, Pierre, 1647–1706.
... Pensées diverses sur la comète. Édition critique avec une introduction et des notes, publiée par A. Prat ... Paris, E. Cornély et cie, 1911–12.
2 v. 18½cm.
At head of title: Société des textes français modernes.
Includes a reference to Spinoza (v. 2, p. 134-135)

1. Comets. 2. Comets—1680. 3. Omens. I. Prat, A. II. Société des textes français modernes.

Bayle, Pierre, 1647-1706.
Oeuvres diversés de Mr. Pierre Bayle, contenant tout ce que cet auteur a publié sur des matières de theologie, de philosophie, de critique, d'histoire, & de litterature; excepté son Dictionnaire historique et critique. La Haye, Chez P. Husson [etc.] 1727.
3 v. 43cm.

Engraved title-page.
Includes references to Spinoza.

Bayle, Pierre, 1647-1706.
Peter Baylens philosophisches Wörterbuch, oder die philosophischen Artikel aus Baylens historisch-kritischem Wörterbuche in deutscher Sprache abgekürzt und herausgegeben zur Beförderung des Studiums der Geschichte der Philosophie und des menschlichen Geistes, von Ludwig Heinrich Jakob ... Halle und Leipzig, Bei Johann Gottfried Ruff, 1797.
2 v. 22cm.

Includes an article on Spinoza (v. 2, p. 703-764)

Bayle, Pierre, 1647-1706.
Pensées diverses, écrites à un docteur de Sorbonne, à l'occasion de la comète qui parut au mois de decembre 1680. À Rotterdam, chez Reinier Leers, 1683.
[4], 811, [15] p. 16cm.

Includes references to Spinoza.

Boullier, David Renaud, 1699-1759.
Essai philosophique sur l'âme des bêtes; où l'on traite de son existence & de sa nature, et où l'on mêle par occasion diverses réflexions sur la nature de la liberté, sur celle de nos sensations, sur l'union de l'âme et où l'on réfute diverses objections de Mr. Bayle. Amsterdam, F. Changuion, 1728.
300 p. 16 cm.

Bayle, Pierre, 1647-1706.
Pensées diverses, écrites à un docteur de Sorbonne, à l'occasion de la comete qui parut au mois de decembre 1680. Par Mr. Bayle. Cinquième édition ... A Amsterdam, Chez Herman Uytwerf, 1722.
2 v. ([30], 616, [18] p.) 16cm.

Includes a reference to Spinoza (v. 2, p. 374-375)

Feuerbach, Ludwig, 1804-1872.
Pierre Bayle; ein Beitrag zur Geschichte der Philosophie und Menschheit. Leipzig, A. Kröner [1924]
x, 212 p. port. 17cm. (Kröners Taschenausgabe. Bd. 31)

Includes references to Spinoza.

Feuerbach, Ludwig, 1804-1872.
Pierre Bayle, nach seinen für die Geschichte der Philosophie und Menschheit interessantesten Momenten dargestellt und gewürdigt. 2. Ausg. Leipzig, O. Wigand, 1844.
vi, 259 p. 22cm.

Includes references to Spinoza.

La Monnoye, Bernard de, 1641-1728.
Histoire de Mr. Bayle et de ses ouvrages. Nouvelle edition augmentée ... A Amsterdam, Chez Jaques Desbordes, 1716.
[16], 576 p.

Le Fèvre, J
Examen critique des ouvrages de Bayle. Paris, 1747.
2 v.

Pillon, François, 1830-1914.
L'évolution de l'idéalisme au XVIIIe siècle; les remarques critiques de Bayle sur le spinozisme. [1900]
55-145 p.

In L'Année philosophique, 1899. Paris, 1900.

Rencontre de Bayle, et de Spinosa dans l'autre monde. Cologne, P. Marteau, 1711.
viij, 64 p. 12½cm.

1. Bayle, Pierre, 1647-1706. 2. Spinoza, Benedictus de, 1632-1677.

Robinson, Howard, 1885-
Bayle the sceptic, by Howard Robinson ... New York, Columbia university press, 1931.
x, 334 p., 1 l. front. (port.) 23½ cm.
Bibliography: p. [310]-324.
Includes references to Spinoza.

1. Bayle, Pierre, 1647-1706. I. Title.
[Full name: James Howard Robinson]

Serrurier, C
Pierre Bayle en Hollande; étude historique et critique. Lausanne, Imprimerie cooperative La concorde, 1912.
224 p. port. 24cm.

Thesis, Lausanne.
Includes references to Spinoza.
Bibliography: p. [213]-215.

Sugg, Elisabeth Bernardine, 1901-
Pierre Bayle, ein Kritiker der Philosophie seiner Zeit. Leipzig, F. Meiner, 1930.
vi, 87 p. 24cm. (Forschungen zur Geschichte der Philosophie und der Pädagogik. 4. Bd., Heft 3)

Issued in part as thesis, Köln.
Includes references to Spinoza.
Bibliography: p. [v]-vi.

C-2-d
REMBRANDT

Amsterdam. Rijks-museum.
Rembrandt tentoonstelling. Ter plechtige herdenking van het 300-jarig bestaan der Universiteit van Amsterdam. Rijks-museum-Amsterdam 11 juni-4 september 1932. [Amsterdam, Druk de Bussy, 1932.
100 p. plates. 22cm.

Preface signed: F. Schmidt-Degener.

Bab, Julius, 1880-
Rembrandt und Spinoza. [1929]
393-397 p. 25cm.

From Der Morgen, V. Jahrgang, 4. Heft, Oktober 1929.

Bab, Julius, 1880-
Rembrandt und Spinoza; ein Doppelbildnis im deutsch-jüdischen Raum. Berlin, Philo Verlag, 1934.
102 p. illus. 19cm.

⌊Coppier, André Charles⌋ 1867-
Rembrandt et Spinoza. ⌊1916⌋
⌊160⌋-191 p. 25cm.

Signed: André-Charles Coppier.
From Revue des deux mondes, 86. année, 6. période, t. 31, 1916.

Dammann, Walter Heinrich, 1883-
Die Welt um Rembrandt; niederländische Novellen. Leipzig, Quelle & Meyer ⌊1920⌋
510 p. 22cm.

Includes references to Spinoza (p. 440)

Gebhardt, Carl, 1881-1934.
Rembrandt und Spinoza. ⌊1927?⌋
⌊161⌋-181 p. 24cm.

"Sonderdruck aus Kant-Studien, Band XXXII, Heft 1."
Author's inscription and signature on half-title.
Bibliographical footnotes.

⌊Gebhardt, Carl⌋ 1881-1934.
Rembrandt y Spinosa (contribución histórica al problema del barroco) ⌊1929⌋
⌊307⌋-340 p. 22cm.

Signed: Carl Gebhardt.
From Revista de occidente, año 7, no. 69, marzo 1929.

Huet, Coenraad Busken, 1826-1886.
Rembrandt's Heimath; Studien zur Geschichte der nordniederländischen Kultur im siebzehnten Jahrhundert. Autorisierte Übersetzung aus dem Holländischen von Marie Mohr. Herausgegeben von G. Frhr. von der Ropp. Leipzig, T. O. Weigel, 1886-87.
2 v. in 1. 21cm.

Includes references to Spinoza.
Bibliographical references included in "Anmerkungen" at end of each volume.

Kahn, Gustave, 1859-1936.
Spinoza et Rembrandt. ⌊1927⌋
86-87 p. illus. 32cm.

From Menorah, 6. année, no. 6, 15 mars 1927.
With Menorah. Le 250e anniversaire de Baruch Spinoza. ⌊1927⌋

1. Spinoza, Benedictus de, 1632-1677.
2. Rembrandt, Hermanszoon van Rijn, 1608-1669.

⌊Langbehn, Julius⌋ 1851-1907.
Rembrandt als Erzieher. Von einem Deutschen. 61.-66. Auflage. Autorisierte Neuausgabe, geordnet und gesichtet nach Weisungen des Verfassers. Leipzig, C. L. Hirschfeld ⌊c1925⌋
380 p. mount. port. 23cm.

Includes references to Spinoza (p. 362-363)

⌊Langbehn, Julius⌋ 1851-1907.
Rembrandt als Erzieher. Von einem Deutschen. 7. Aufl. Leipzig, C. L. Hirschfeld, 1890.
309 p. 24cm.

Includes a section on Spinoza (p. 48-51)

Peterson, Eugen
Rembrandts Verhältnis zum Judentum und zu Spinoza. Zur Erinnerung an des Künstlers Todestag (8 Oktober 1669). ⌊1919⌋
465-466 p.

In Allgemeine Zeitung des Judentums, Jahrgang 83, 1919.

Rembrandt and Spinoza; newly discovered ties between painter and philosopher. [1916]
p. 672, 741. 34cm.

From The American Hebrew and Jewish messenger, 37th year, September 29, 1916.
Signed: J. S.

Schmidt-Degener, Frederik, 1881-
Rembrandt und der holländische Barock. Deutsche Übersetzung von Alfred Pauli. Leipzig, R. G. Teubner, 1928.
53 p. 16 plates. 27cm. (Studien der Bibliothek Warburg, hrsg. von Fritz Saxl. IX)

A comparison of Rembrandt and Vondel.
"Diese Studie erschien in holländischer Sprache in Jahrgang 83 (1919) der Zeitschrift 'De gids'."
Includes references to Spinoza (p. 40)

Simmel, Georg, 1858-1918.
Rembrandt, ein kunstphilosophischer Versuch. Leipzig, K. Wolff, 1917.
viii, 205 p. 24cm.

Includes references to Spinoza.

Zwarts, Jacob
Haham Saul Levy Morteyra en zijn portret door Rembrandt. [1926]
1-17 p. plate, ports. 28cm.

From Oud Holland, tweemaandelijksch Nederlandsch kunsthistorisch tijdschrift, jaarg. 43, aflevering 1, 1926.

C-3
ICONOGRAPHY

Altkirch, Ernst, 1873-1926.
Benedictus Spinoza. [1909]
591-598, 653-664 col. ports. 28cm.

From Ost und West, IX. Jahrgang, Heft 10 and 11, 1909.

1. Spinoza, Benedictus de, 1632-1677 - Portraits. 2. Spinoza, Benedictus de, 1632-1677.

Altkirch, Ernst, 1873-1926.
Benedictus Spinoza. [1909-10]
3 pts. in 1 v. illus., ports., facsims. 29cm.

From Ost und West, 9. Jahrg., Heft 10, 11, Okt., Nov. 1909, und 10. Jahrg., Heft 2, Feb. 1910.
"Aus dem in Vorbereitung befindlichen Werke Ernst Altkirchs 'Spinoza im Porträt'."

Altkirch, Ernst, 1873-1926.
Die Bildnisse Spinozas. [1911]
370-380 p.

In Archiv für Geschichte der Philosophie, Bd. 24., 1911.
A reply to A. Levy's article "Spinozas Bildnis" in Archiv für Geschichte der Philosophie, Bd. 23., 1910.

Altkirch, Ernst, 1878-1926.
Die Bildnisse Spinozas. [1911]
[370]-380 p. 23cm.

"Sonderabdruck aus dem Archiv für Geschichte der Philosophie ... Vierundzwanzigster Band, 1911, Heft 3."
Newspaper clipping pasted in, with Altkirch's article "Spinozas Freunde".

Altkirch, Ernst, 1873-1926.
Ein unbekanntes Spinozabildnis. [1909]
176-179 p. port.

In Westermanns Monatshefte, 53. Jahrgang, 106. Bd., 1909.

Altkirch, Ernst, 1873-1926.
Spinoza im Porträt. Jena, E. Diederichs, 1913.
viii, 111 p. illus., 28 ports., facsim. 25cm.

Contents.--I. Das literarische Porträt Spinozas.--II. Die Bildnisse Spinozas.--III. Spinoza in anderen Werken der bildenden Kunst.--IV. Verzeichnis der in Büchern und Porträtwerken befindlichen und der als einzelblätter verbreiteten Bildnisse Spinozas.--V. Literatur (p. 109-111)

Berühmte Männer; ein Quartettspiel. Ravensburg, Verlag O. Maier ₍191-?₎
60 cards with ports. 14cm.

In box.
"Spielregeln für Quartettspiele" (₍4₎ p.) inserted.
Includes a portrait of Spinoza with short biographical sketch.

Bossu, L
La statue de Spinoza. Lettre à un bourgeois de La Haye. ₍1880₎
355-375 p.

In Revue catholique (Louvain. Université catholique) t. 52, 1880.

Brainin, Reuben, 1862-1939.
שפינוזה ואנטוקולסקי. (טיול במערכה מעשי-חרשים בברלין.) ₍1896₎
194-195 p.

Title transliterated: Shpinozah ve-Antokolski.
In ha-Magid, n. s., v. 5, 1896.

Brunner, Constantin, 1862-1937.
Ein Idealporträt Spinozas. ₍1913₎
27-43 p. plate.

In Nord und Süd, Jahrgang 37, 1913.

Chapman, Manuel
Enrico Glicenstein. ₍1930₎
11-13 p. illus. 30cm.

From B'nai B'rith Magazine, v. 45, no. 1, October, 1930.
Includes a picture of a status of Spinoza done by Glicenstein.

Een standbeeld voor Spinoza. ₍1876₎
₍3₎ p. 28cm.

Signed: Het Spinoza-comité: M. D. Graaf Van Limburg Stirum, Eere-voorzitter.

1. Spinoza, Benedictus de, 1632-1677.

Feest-bundel Dr. Abraham Bredius aangeboden den achttienden April, 1915. Amsterdam, Boek-, Kunst- en Handelsdrukkerij, v/h Gebroeders Binger ₍1915₎
2 v. front. (port.) 105 plates, fold. plan. 28cm.

Includes an article "De man ₍Spinoza?₎ met het vergrootglas, door Rembrandt" by J. Goekoop-de Jongh (v. 1, p. ₍53₎-60) and portraits illustrating the article (v. 2, plates 14-15)
Contents.--1. dell. Opstellen.-- 2. deel. Afbeeldingen.

Gebhardt, Carl, 1881-1934.
Spinoza im Portrait (aus dem Nachlass) ₍1937₎
₍399₎-401 p. 26cm.

Stamped at head of title: Belegexemplar aus "Philosophia".
Bound with Gebhardt, Carl. Spinoza in der Schule. ₍1930₎

Gebhardt, Carl, 1881-1934.
Spinoza im Porträt ₍und Das Geburtshaus Spinozas. Hagae Comitis, 1922₎
247-256 p. plates, port. 22cm.

Cover-title: Dissertatio ex Chronici Spinozani tomo secundo separatim edita.

Gorelik, Schmarja, 1877-1942.
... Jüdische köpfe; lithographien von Joseph Budko. Berlin, F. Gurlitt, 1920.

114 p., 1 l. ports. 30 x 24ᶜᵐ.

At head of title: Sch. Gorelik.
"Aus dem jüdischen übersetzt von Stefania Goldenring und Nadia Strasser."

Includes a chapter on Spinoza (p. ₍99₎-114)

1. Jews—Biog. I. Budko, Joseph, 1888-1940, illus. II. Goldenring, Stefania, tr. III. Strasser, Nadia, joint tr. IV. Title.

Gorelik, Schmarja, 1877-1942.
יידישע קעפ. דרעזדען, פארלאג
"וואסטאק", 1921.

[Dresden, Wostok, 1921]
132 p. 19cm.

Title transliterated: Yidishe kep.
Includes a chapter on Spinoza (p. 32-41)

Gunning, Johannes Hermanus, 1829-
Deze wereld of de toekomende? Een woord tot de gemeente naar aanleiding van het oprichten van een standbeeld voor Spinoza door J. H. Gunning, Jr. Utrecht, C. H. E. Breijer, 1880.
iv, 31 p. 23cm.

"Uitgegeven ten voordeele van de vierde School der hervormde Gemeente te 's-Gravenhage"
Includes references to Spinoza.
Bibliographical references included in "Aanteekeningen" (p. [26]-31)

Günther, Hans F K 1891-
Rassenkunde des jüdischen Volkes. Mit 305 Abbildungen und 6 Karten. München, Lehmann, 1930.
352 p. illus., maps. 24 cm.

Includes a portrait of Spinoza (p. 83)

Herbert, L M
Antokolsky's sculptures in America; will steps be taken to acquire the collection permanently for American Jewry? [1926.
p. 13, 49. illus. 34cm.

From The Jewish tribune, v. 89, no. 22, November 26, 1926.
Includes a picture and description of the statue of Spinoza by Antokolsky (p. 13)

החבר; לוח שמושי-ספרותי לתלמידים ול-
עם לשנת תרפ"ה (שנה שניה) ירו-
לים, הוצאת "שחר".

[Jerusalem, 1924]
208 p. illus., ports., tables. 17cm.

Title transliterated: he-Ḥābhēr.
Includes portrait of Spinoza with short note about him (p. 71)

Jacobs, Joseph, 1854-1916.
A newly discovered portrait of Spinoza. [1905]
377-378 p.

In The Athenaeum, Sept. 16, 1905.

Jüdischer illustrierter Kalender auf das Jahr 1926, 5686/5687. 2. Jahrg. Berlin, Jüdischer Kalender-Verlag [1926]
cover-title, [365] l. illus., ports. 15cm.

Includes a reference to Spinoza's death, Feb. 21, with his portrait, and to his excommunication, July 27.

Kohler, Rose
Art as related to Judaism. [19--]
16 p. 23cm.

Four paintings with Spinoza as subject included in "List of lantern slides" (p. 16)

Land, Jan Pieter Nicolaas, 1834-1897.
Over de nieuwe uitgave der werken en de portretten van Spinoza. Amsterdam, J. Müller, 1884.
cover-title, 15 p. 23cm.

"Overgedrukt uit de Verslagen en mededeelingen der Koninklijke Akademie van Wetenschappen, Afdeeling Letterkunde, 3de reeks, deel I. [p. [226]-239]"

Lavater, Johann Caspar, 1741-1801.
Essays on physiognomy, designed to promote the knowledge and the love of mankind. Illustrated by more than eight hundred engravings accurately copied; and some duplicates added from originals. Executed by, or under the inspection of, Thomas Holloway. Tr. from the French by Henry Hunter. London, J. Murray, 1789-98.
3 v. in 5. illus., plates, ports., facsims. 35 x 30 cm.

Includes Spinoza's name in "List of engraved portraits..." (v. 2, pt. 2, p. 433-440)

SPECIAL COLLECTIONS SPINOZA C-3 874

Levy, A
Spinozas Bildnis. [1910]
[117]-140 p. 23cm.

From Archiv für Geschichte der Philosophie, Bd. XXIII, Neue Folge, XVI. Bd.

1. Spinoza, Benedictus de, 1632-1677 - Portraits.

SPECIAL COLLECTIONS SPINOZA C-3 875

Levy, J
An unknown portrait of Spinoza. [1932]
317-320 p. ports. 28cm.

From the Connoisseur, vol. XC, no. 375, Nov. 1932.

1. Spinoza, Benedictus de, 1632-1677 - Portraits.

SPECIAL COLLECTIONS SPINOZA C-3 876

Lichtenstein, Isaac, 1888-
Spinoza; eight plates, by Isaac Lichtenstein. New York, Machmadim Art Editions, Inc., c1946.
[8] ports. (in portfolio) 46cm.

1. Spinoza, Benedictus de, 1632-1677 - Portraits.

C-3 877

Loewenberg, J
Wilhelm und Alexander von Humboldt im Verkehr mit ihren ältesten jüdischen Freunden, mitgetheilt von J. Loewenberg. [1866]
47-48 p.

In Wiener Jahrbuch für Israeliten, 5626 [1866]
Includes a reference to a portrait of Spinoza by Oeser.

NN

SPECIAL COLLECTIONS SPINOZA C-3 878

Mult és jövo.
Rendkivüli ajándék a Mult és jövő előfizetőinek. [1930]
33-[36] p. illus., ports. 29cm.

An announcement of a book, A Zsidók egyetemes története, by Ármin Kecskeméti, to be distributed to subscribers of Mult és jövő.
Includes a portrait of Spinoza (p. [34])
From Mult és jövő, XX. év, január 1930.

NNC

C-3 879

Nadel, Arno, 1878-
Eine Idealbüste Spinoza's. [1912]
525-532 p.

Concerning a bust by Georg Wienbrack.
In Ost und West, Bd. 12, 1912.

OCH

C-3 880

A new discovered portrait of Spinoza. [1905-06]
231-232 p.

In Reform advocate, v. 30, 1905-06.

OCH

SPECIAL COLLECTIONS SPINOZA C-3 881

Open Court Publishing Company, Chicago.
Philosophical portrait series ... Chicago, The Open Court Publishing Co., 1898-99.
2 pts. in 1 v. ports. 38cm.

Each part in three installments.
In portfolio.
Includes a portrait of Spinoza.
Contents.--pt. 1. Philosophers.--pt. 2. Psychologists.

NNC

SPECIAL COLLECTIONS SPINOZA C-3 882

Picard, Max, 1888-
... The human face, translated from the German by Guy Endore. New York, Farrar & Rinehart, incorporated [c1930]
8 p. l., 3-221 p. pl., ports. 25 cm.

Includes a portrait of Spinoza (p. 160)

1. Physiognomy. I. Endore, S Guy, 1901- tr. II. Title.

BF853.P485 138 30—28065
Library of Congress [a56e1]

C-3 883

Picard, Max, 1888-
... Das menschengesicht. München, Delphin-verlag [c1929]
223, [1] p. pl., ports. 26cm.

Includes a portrait of Spinoza (p. 186)

1. Physiognomy. I. Title.

30-12168
Library of Congress BF853.P48
Copyright A—Foreign 6294
[2]

C-3
884

Picciotto, Cyril ed.
A piece of mosiac, being the book of the Palestine exhibition and bazaar. Edited by Cyril Picciotto and C. M. Kohan. ⌊London, W. Clowes⌋ 1912.
82 p. illus., plates, port. 25cm.

Includes a reproduction of G. Bernard Solomon's etching "The excommunication of Spinoza" (p. 74)

C-3
885

Schwarz, Karl, 1885–
... Die Juden in der kunst; mit fünfzig tafeln in tiefdruck und neun textbildern. Berlin, Welt-verlag, 1928.
228 p. illus., plates (1 double) ports. 19cm.
Errata slip laid in.
Includes a picture of and reference to Mark Antokolski's statue of Spinoza (p. 182, 185-186)

1. Art, Jewish—Hist. I. Title.
Library of Congress N7415.S3 29-16451
Copyright A—Foreign 3097
[2]

C-3
886

Sneltjes, J K C
⌊Letter, offering bronze model of Miss R. van Dantzig's Spinoza statue for sale. n. p., 1910⌋
1 p. port. 25cm.

Bound with: Spinozahuis, Leyden. Verslag omtrent de lotgevallen ... 1896/99-1920/21.

C-3
887

Spinoza Denkmal. ⌊1880⌋
p. 331. 35cm.

Report about the unveiling of the Spinoza monument in The Hague.
From Der Zeitgeist; ein israelitisches Familienblatt, Jahrgang 1., 14. Oktober 1880.
With Von der Kabbalah zu Spinoza. ⌊1881⌋

C-3
888

Zwarts, Jacob
Joodsche archiefsprokkels; Uriel da Costa in Utrechtsche ballingschap (1627) ⌊1931⌋
61-64 p. illus. 35cm.

From De Vrydagavond; Joodsch weekblad, jrg. 8, no. 4, 24 April 1931.
Includes a reproduction of a painting of Spinoza with Uriel da Costa.

C-3
889

Wood, Wallace, d. 1916.
The hundred greatest men; portraits of the one hundred greatest men of history reproduced from fine and rare steel engravings. With general introduction by Ralph Waldo Emerson ... New York, D. Appleton and company, 1885.
3 p. l., [v]-viii, 504 p. illus. (ports.) 24cm.

Includes a biography and portrait of Spinoza (p. 232-235)
1. Biography. 2. Portraits. I. Emerson, Ralph Waldo, 1803-1882. II. Title.
A 33-1402
Title from H. E. Huntington Libr. CT104.W7
Printed by L. C.

D-1.
GENERAL

D-1-a
BOOKS

D-1-a
890

Acri, Francesco, 1836-1913.
Una nuova esposizione del sistema dello Spinoza. Firenze, G. Carnesecchi e figli, 1877.
87 p.

OCH

D-1-a
891

Alexander, Bernát, 1850–
Spinoza, von Bernhard Alexander ... München, E. Reinhardt, 1923.
178, [2] p. front. (port.) 20 cm. (Geschichte der philosophie in einzeldarstellungen. abt. IV. Die philosophie der neueren zeit I. bd. 18)
"Bibliographischer wegweiser": p. 167-168.
Ms. notes by Adolphe S. Oko.

1. Spinoza, Benedictus de, 1632-1677.
29-4146
Library of Congress B3997.A4
[2]

D-1-a
892

Appuhn, Charles, 1862-1942.
Spinoza. Paris, A. Delpeuch, 1927.
364 p. 20cm. (Civilisation et christianisme. 10)

Includes excerpts from Spinoza's works in French translation.

D-1-a 893

Arnoldson, Klas Pontus, 1844-1916.
Benedikt Spinoza. En uppsats. Upsala ₍1877₎
16 p. port. 19 cm.

CtY

D-1-a 894

Baltzer, August, 1864-
Spinozas Entwicklungsgang, besonders nach seinen Briefen geschildert. Kiel, Lipsius & Tischer, 1888.
169 p. 25cm.

Issued also as thesis, Kiel.
Includes bibliography.
Original paper covers bound in.

D-1-a 895

Baltzer, August, 1864-
Spinozas Entwicklungsgang, besonders nach seinen Briefen geschildert. Kiel, Lipsius & Tischer, 1888.
169 p. 25cm.

Issued also as thesis, Kiel.
Includes bibliography.
Manuscript notes by Carl Gebhardt.

D-1-a 896

Belaúnde, Victor Andrés, 1883-
La filosofía de Spinoza. ₍1940₎
₍123₎-139 p. 25cm.

From Mercurio peruano; revista mensual de ciencias sociales y letras, año 15, v. 22, no. 157, marzo 1940.

D-1-a 897

Bellangé, Charles
Spinoza et la philosophie moderne. Paris, H. Didier, 1912.
ii, 396 p. table. 23cm.

Original paper cover bound in.
Bibliographical footnotes.

D-1-a 898

Bergman, Sh
ברוך שפינאָזא,דער געניאַלער אפיקורס.
Warsaw, 1955.
55 p.

Title transliterated: Barukh Shpinoza, der geniyaler appikkores.

NNJ

D-1-a 899

Boer, Julius de
Spinoza. Baarn, Hollandia-Drukkerij ₍1911₎
cover-title, 48 p. (His Groote denkers. 3. serie, no. 5)

D-1-a 900

Boumann, Ludwig, b. 1802.
Explicatio Spinozismi. Berolini, Typis Feisterianis et Eisersdorffianis, 1828.
iv, 106 p. 21cm.

Thesis, Berlin.
Volume of pamphlets.

1. Spinoza, Benedictus de, 1632-1677.

NNC

D-1-a 901

Brasch, Moritz, 1843-1895.
Benedict von Spinoza's System der Philosophie nach der Ethik und den übrigen Traktaten desselben in genetischer Entwickelung dargestellt und mit einer Biographie Spinoza's versehen. Berlin, A. Wruck, 1870.
₍8₎, 192 p. 21cm.

D-1-a 902

Bröchner, H₍ans₎, 1820-1875.
Benedict Spinoza. En monographie. Kjöbenhavn, P. G. Philipsens forlag, 1857.
188 p. 20cm.

1. Spinoza, Benedictus de, 1632-1677.

Brucăr, I
Filosofia lui Spinoza. Bucureşti, Societatea Română de Filosofie, 1930.
184 p. 24cm.

Presentation copy to Carl Gebhardt with the author's inscription and signature.
Bibliography: p. [175]-179.

Brunschvicg, Léon, 1869–
Spinoza, par Léon Brunschvicg ... Paris, F. Alcan, 1894.
8 p. l., 224 p., 1 l. 23cm. (On cover: Bibliothèque de philosophie contemporaine)
"Ouvrage couronné par l'Académie des sciences morales et politiques."

Original paper covers bound in.

1. Spinoza, Benedictus de, 1632-1677.

Brunschvicg, Léon, 1869-1944.
Spinoza. 2. éd., rev. et augm. Paris, Alcan, 1906.
ii, 235 p. 23cm.

"Ouvrage couronné par l'Académie des sciences morales et politiques."

Caird, John, 1820-1898.
Spinoza. Philadelphia, J. B. Lippincott, 1888.
315 p. port. 18cm. (Philosophical classics for English readers, 12)

Caird, John, 1820-1898.
Spinoza. Edinburgh, W. Blackwood and Sons, 1888.
315 p. port. 18cm. (Philosophical classics for English readers, 12)

Caird, John, 1820-1898.
Spinoza. Cheap ed. Edinburgh, W. Blackwood, 1901.
315 p. 18cm. (Philosophical classics for English readers, 12)

Caird, John, 1820-1898.
Spinoza. New ed. Edinburgh, W. Blackwood, 1902.
315 p. 18cm. (Philosophical classics for English readers, 12)

Caird, John, 1820-1898.
Spinoza. Cheap edition. Edinburgh, W. Blackwood and Sons, 1910.
315 p. 18cm. (Philosophical classics for English readers, 12)

Caird, John, 1820-1898.
Spinoza. Cheap edition. Edinburgh, W. Blackwood and Sons, 1914.
315 p. 18cm. (Philosophical classics for English readers, 12)

Camerer, Theodor, 1833-1909.
Die Lehre Spinoza's. Stuttgart, J. G. Cotta, 1877.
xix, 300 p. 23cm.

Camerer, Theodor, 1833-1909.
Die lehre Spinozas, von Theodor Camerer. 2. aufl. (anastatischer neudruck) Stuttgart und Berlin, Cotta, 1914.
xix, [1], 300 p. 23½cm.
First published 1877.

1. Spinoza, Benedictus de, 1632-1677.
[Full name: Theodor Heinrich Camerer]

Carp, J H
Het Spinozisme als wereldbeschouwing; inleiding tot de leer van Benedictus de Spinoza. Arnhem, Van Loghum Slaterus, 1931.
227 p. plates, port. (Kleine bibliotheek van hedendaagsch cultuurleven)

Presentation copy to A. S. Oko with the author's inscription and signature.
Carl Gebhardt's manuscript note and signature on half-title page.

Carré, Jean Raoul, 1887-
... Spinoza. Paris, Boivin & cie, 1936.
3 p. l., 67 p., 2 l. 19cm. (Bibliothèque de la Revue des cours et conférences)

At head of title: J.-R. Carré.
Original paper covers bound in.

Chartier, Émile Auguste
Spinoza. Paris, Delaplane [1901]
122 p. 17 cm. (Les philosophes)

Chartier, Emile Auguste
Spinoza. 15. mille. Paris, Mellottée [1929?]
122 p. 19cm. (Les philosophes)

Bibliography: p. [121]-122.
Date pencilled on cover: 1929?
Original paper cover bound in.

Chatier, Émile.
... Spinoza, por Émile Chatier; traducción revisada por Rodrigo García Treviño. México, Editorial América, 1941.
2 p. l., 7-131 p. 17cm. (Biblioteca filosófica, II)
Cover-title: Spinoza, su vida, su obra, su pensamiento.

1. Spinoza, Benedictus de, 1632-1677. I. García Treviño, Rodrigo, tr.

Cipriani, Cipriano
Spinoza. Sassari, Tip. Libertà, 1914.
78 p.

Collins, Sir William Job, 1859-
Spinoza: the God-intoxicated man; a short account of his life and philosophy. Enfield, Meyers, Brooks, and Co., 1889.
21 p. 19cm.

Original paper covers bound in.

Couchoud, Paul Louis, 1879-
Benoît de Spinoza. Paris, F. Alcan, 1902.
xii, 305 p. 23cm. (Les grands philosophes)

Couchoud, Paul Louis, 1879-
Benoit de Spinoza. 2. éd., rev. Paris, F. Alcan, 1924.
xii, 308 p. 23cm. (Les grands philosophes)

 D-1-a 923

Cousin, Victor, 1792-1867.
Course of the history of modern philosophy. By M. Victor Cousin. Translated by O. W. Wight ... New York, D. Appleton & company, 1852.
2 v. 21 cm.

Includes reference to Spinoza (v. 2, p. 93-95)

1. Philosophy, Modern—Hist. 2. Philosophy—Hist. I. Wight, Orlando Williams, 1824-1888, tr.

B792.C9 1852 190 33—21843

Library of Congress [55e1]

D-1-a 924

Damiron, Jean Philibert, 1794-1862.
Mémoire sur Spinoza et sa doctrine. [1844] 164 p.

In Académie des sciences morales et politiques, Paris. Mémoires, série 2, t. 4, 1844.

 D-1-a 925

De Casseres, Benjamin, 1873-1945.
Spinoza, liberator of God and man, 1632-1932. New York, E. Wickham Sweetland [c1932]
xiv, 145 p. port. 21cm.

 D-1-a 926

Delbos, Victor, 1862-1916.
Le spinozisme; cours professé à la Sorbonne en 1912-1913. Paris, Société française d'imprimerie et de librairie, 1916.
214 p. 22cm.

1. Spinoza, Benedictus de, 1632-1677.

 D-1-a 927

Delbos, Victor, 1862-1916.
... Le spinozisme; cours professé à la Sorbonne en 1912-1913. 2. éd. Paris, J. Vrin, 1926.
214 p., 1 l. 22½cm. (*On cover:* Bibliothèque d'histoire de la philosophie)

Original paper covers bound in.

1. Spinoza, Benedictus de, 1632-1677.

[*Full name:* Étienne Marie Justin Victor Delbos]

36—6198

Library of Congress B3998.D38 1926 [39b1] 193.9

 D-1-a 928

Dessauer, Moritz
Der Sokrates der Neuzeit und sein Gedankenschatz. Sämmtliche Schriften Spinoza's gemeinverständlich und kurz gefasst mit besonderer Hervorhebung aller Lichtstrahlen, von Dr. M. Dessauer. Cöthen, Paul Schettler's Verlag, 1877.
iv, 182 p. 22cm.

Ms. notes by Carl Gebhardt.

 D-1-a 929

Dumrath, Oscar Heinrich, 1844-
... Spinoza, af O. H. Dumrath. Stockholm, H. Geber [1908]
64 p. 19½cm. (De största märkesmännen. VIII)
Portrait on cover.

1. Spinoza, Benedictus de, 1632-1677.

33-22630

Library of Congress B3997.D77 921.3

 D-1-a 930

Durant, William James, 1885-
... A guide to Spinoza [by] Will Durant ... Girard, Kan., Haldeman-Julius company [c1924]
96 p. 12½cm. (Little blue book, no. 520, ed. by E. Haldeman-Julius)
Advertising matter: p. 90-96.

1. Spinoza, Benedictus de, 1632-1677.

Library of Congress B3998.D85 CA 24-749 Unrev'd

Copyright A 782798

 D-1-a 931

Erhardt, Franz, 1864-1930.
Die Philosophie des Spinoza im Lichte der Kritik. Leipzig, O. R. Reisland, 1908.
vii, 502 p. 25cm.

Bibliographical footnotes.
Original paper cover bound in.
Carl Gebhardt's signature on t.-p.

 D-1-a 932

Erhardt, Franz, 1864-1930.
Die weltanschauung Spinozas, von dr. Franz Erhardt ... Stuttgart, Strecker und Schröder, 1928.
vii, [1], 159, [1] p. front. (port.) 21½cm.

1. Spinoza, Benedictus de, 1632-1677.

33-19425

Library of Congress B3998.E7 193.9

Fels, Wilhelm
Spinoza, der grosse Philosoph, als er römischkatholisch werden sollte. Leipzig, J. F. Glück, 1829.
44 p. 20cm.

Includes Albert Burch's letter to Spinoza and Spinoza's answer in German translation (p. [17]-44)

Ferrière, Émile, b. 1830.
La doctrine de Spinoza exposée et commentée à la lumière des faits scientifiques, par Émile Ferrière. Paris, F. Alcan [1899]
ix, 357 p. 28½ cm.

Original paper covers bound in.

1. Spinoza, Benedictus de, 1632-1677.

Fischer, Kuno, 1824-1907.
Барухъ Спиноза. [1865]
34 p.

Title transliterated: Barukh Spinoza.
In Заграничный вѣстникъ, т. 7, 1865.

Fischer, Kuno, 1824-1907.
Baruch Spinoza's Leben und Charakter; ein Vortrag. Mannheim, F. Bassermann, 1865.
iv, 52 p. 22cm.

Original paper covers bound in.
Bibliographical footnotes.

Fischer, Kuno, 1824-1907.
Spinozas Leben, Werke und Lehre. 4. neu bearb. Aufl. Heidelberg, C. Winter, 1898.
xvi, 573 p. 23cm. (His Geschichte der neuern Philosophie. Jubiläumsausgabe. 2. Bd.)

Fischer, Kuno, 1824-1907.
Spinozas Leben, Werke und Lehre. 5. Aufl. Heidelberg, C. Winter, 1909.
xvi, 635 p. 23cm. (His Geschichte der neuern Philosophie. 2. Bd.)

Fischer, Kuno, 1824-1907.
Spinozas Leben, Werke und Lehre. 6. Aufl. Heidelberg, C. Winter [191-?]
584 p. 23cm. (His Geschichte der neuern Philosophie, 2. Bd.)

T.-p. missing. Title from 5th ed.

Flottes, Jean Baptiste Marcel, 1789-1864.
Examen d'un ecrit intitulé: Spinosa. Montpellier, Boehm, 1845.
16 p.

Gans, M E
Spinozismus; ein Beitrag zur Psychologie und Kulturgeschichte des Philosophierens. Wien, J. Lenobel, 1907.
111 p. 22cm.

Original paper cover bound in.

Gebhardt, Carl, 1881-1934.
Spinoza. Leipzig, Verlag von Philipp Reclam jun., [c1932]
145 p. 16cm.

Presentation copy to A. S. Oko, with the author's inscription.
Includes selections from Spinoza's works in German translation.

Gebhardt, Carl, 1881-1934.
Spinoza; vier Reden. Heidelberg, C. Winter, 1927.
80 p. 23cm.

Handmade paper.

Gebhardt, Carl, 1881-1934.
Spinoza; vier Reden. Heidelberg, C. Winter, 1927.
80, 13 p. 23cm.

Reviews of works edited by Gebhardt: 13 p. at end.
The author's inscription and signature on leaf following t.-p.

Gebhardt, Carl, 1881-1934.
Spinoza; vier Reden. Heidelberg, C. Winter, 1927.
10, 13 l. 37x21cm.

Proof copy of two speeches. Contains manuscript corrections by Carl Gebhardt.
Contents.--Spinoza; Rede bei der Feier der Societas Spinozana, am 21. Februar 1927.--Spinoza, Judentum und Barok; Rede bei der Feier des Jüdischen Akademischen Philosophenvereins, am 12. August 1927.

Gebhardt, Carl, 1881-1934.
Spinoza; vier Reden von Carl Gebhardt. 1927.
5 pts. in 1 v. 22cm.

Holograph manuscript (with corrections and printing instructions) of the book published in Heidelberg, 1927.
Includes original German text and French translation of the second address, which was delivered in French.

Gebhardt, Carl, 1881-1934.
... Spinoza. Buenos Aires, Editorial Losada, s. a. [1940]
2 p. l., 7-174 p. 20cm. (Biblioteca filosófica, publicada bajo la dirección de Francisco Romero)

At head of title: Carlos Gebhardt.
"Traducción del alemán por Oscar Cohan."

1. Spinoza, Benedictus de, 1632-1677. I. Cohan, Oscar, tr.

Gebhardt, Carl, 1881-1934.
Was ist Spinozismus? Heidelberg, C. Winter, 1925.
xlix p. 19cm.

Original paper covers bound in.
"Sonderdruck aus: Spinoza, Von den festen und ewigen Dingen."

Gherasim, Versile
Activismul lui Spinoza (precedat de o expunere a genezei lui istorice) Cernăuţi, Institutul de arte grafice şi editură "Glasul Bucovinei", 1928.
148 p. port. 24cm.

Original paper cover bound in.
Presentation copy to Carl Gebhardt, with the author's inscription and signature.
Summary in German.
Bibliographical footnotes.

Gunn, John Alexander, 1896-
Benedict Spinoza, by J. Alexander Gunn ... Melbourne, Macmillan & co., ltd. in association with Melbourne university press, 1925.
xiii, 167 p. front. (port.) map. 19cm. [University of Melbourne. Publications. no. 5]
Bibliography: p. 129-154.

1. Spinoza, Benedictus de, 1632-1677. 2. Spinoza, Benedictus de, 1632-1677—Bibl.

Guzzo, Augusto, 1894-
Il pensiero di B. Spinoza. Firenze, Vallecchi [1924]
536 p. 20cm. (Il pensiero moderno; a cura di E. Codignola. XVIII)

Bibliographical footnotes.

Hatano, Seiichi
Supinoza kenkyū. Tokyo, Keisei-sha shoten [1910]
135, 22 p. 23cm.

1. Spinoza, Benedictus de, 1632-1677.

Høffding, Harold, 1843-1931.
Spinoza. [1927]
cover-title, 8 p. 24cm.

"Saertryk af 'Tilskueren', marts, 1927."

1. Spinoza, Benedictus de, 1632-1677.

Høffding, Harald, 1843-1931.
Spinozas liv og laere; et bidrag til taenkningens historie i det 17de aarhundrede. København, Klein, 1877.
v, 164 p. 21 cm.

Horner, Andreas
Zur Einführung in den Spinozismus. Leipzig, O. Wigand, 1891.
187 p. 23cm.

Original paper cover bound in.

1. Spinoza, Benedictus de, 1632-1677.

Inatomi, Eijirô
Supinoza no tetsugaku, kami no ninshiki no mondai o chûshin to shite. [Tokyo] Risô-sha shuppan-bu, 1930.
2, 2, 210, 11 p. port. 23cm.

1. Spinoza, Benedictus de, 1632-1677.

Jacobi, Friedrich Heinrich, 1743-1819.
Jacobis Spinoza Büchlein, nebst Replik und Duplik. Hrsg. von Fritz Mauthner. München, G. Müller, 1912.
xxvii, 344 p. 23cm. (Bibliothek der Philosophen. 2. Bd.)

Janet, Paul, 1823-1899.
Spinoza en het Spinozisme. s'Hertogenbosch, G. H. van der Schuyt [1868]
52 p.

Kaim, Julius Rudolf
Die Philosophie Spinozas. München, Rösl, 1921.
116 p. 17cm. (Philosophische Reihe. 35. Bd.)

Kant Gesellschaft. Afdeeling-Nederland.
Spinoza; gezamelijke redevoeringen, gehouden bij de Spinoza-herdenking door de Afdeeling-Nederland van de Kant-Gesellschaft op Donderdag, 29 December 1932 te Amsterdam ... door J. D. Bierens de Haan [et al.] Haarlem, De Erven F. Bohn, 1933.
viii, 78 p. 25cm.

CONTINUED ON NEXT CARD

Kant Gesellschaft. Afdeeling-Nederland.
Spinoza; gezamelijke redevoeringen. 1933.
(Card 2)

Contents.--Spinoza als metaphysicus, door J. D. Bierens de Haan.--Spinoza als ethicus, door Leo Polak.--Spinoza als mysticus, door J. H. Carp.--Spinoza als staats- en rechtsphilosoof, door J. J. von Schmid.--Spinoza en de Gereformeerde theologie, door H. W. van der Vaart Smit.

Kettner, Frederick, 1886-
Spinoza, the biosopher, by Frederick Kettner; introduction by Nicholas Roerich ... New York, Roerich museum press, 1932.
4 p. l., 263 p. 20cm. (*Half-title:* New era library. ser. III—"Heroica series", book III)

Manuscript notes by A. S. Oko on flyleaf.

1. Spinoza, Benedictus de, 1632-1677.

Kovner, Saveliĭ Grigor'evich, 1837-1896.
Спиноза, его жизнь и сочиненія; очеркъ, составленный С. Г. Ковнеромъ. Съ прибавленіемъ новѣйшей критики о Спинозѣ ... 2. (посмертное) доп. и испр. изд. Варшава, Изд. кн. маг. М. А. Ковнера, 1897.
xiv, [5]-173 p. ports. 19cm.

Title transliterated: Spinoza, ego zhizn' i sochineniia.
Original paper covers bound in.

Kühnemann, Eugen, 1868-
Über die Grundlagen der Lehre des Spinoza. Halle a. S., M. Niemeyer, 1902.
70 p. 25cm.

On original paper cover bound in: Sonderabzug aus: Philosophische Abhandlungen; Gedenkschrift für Rudolf Haym.
Carl Gebhardt's signature on t.-p.

Lasbax, Émile
La hiérarchie dans l'univers chez Spinoza. Paris, Alcan, 1919.
xii, 357 p. table.

Complementary thesis, Lyon.

Liebert, Arthur, 1878-1946.
Spinoza in den grundzugen seines systems; einleitung zur 3. aufl. des Spinoza-breviers. Leipzig, Felix Meiner verlag [1933]
cover-title, ix-xliv p. 19cm.

Linde, Antonius van der, 1833-1897.
Spinoza. Seine lehre und deren erste nachwirkungen in Holland. Eine philosophisch-historische monographie, von dr. Antonius van der Linde ... Göttingen, Van den Hoeck und Ruprecht, 1862.
xxxi, [1], 214 p., 1 l. 22½cm.

"Literatur des Spinozismus": p. [171]-214.
Thesis, Göttingen.

Loewenhardt, Siegismundus Eduard, 1796-1875.
Benedict von Spinoza in seinem Verhältniss zur Philosophie und Naturforschung der neueren Zeit. Berlin, W. Peiser, 1872.
xxv, 419 p. 25cm.
Original paper cover bound in.

Lotsij, Marius Cornelis Leendert
Spinoza's wijsbegeerte. Amsterdam, J. C. A. Sulpke, 1878.
263 p. 23cm.

Label pasted over imprint: Utrecht, H. A. J. Koezijnse.

1. Spinoza, Benedictus de, 1632-1677.

Luojola, Yrjö
Baruch Spinozan teologisen ajattelun filosofinen perusta. Helsinki, 1951.
154 p. 25cm.

Thesis, Helsinki.
Summary in German.
Bibliography: p. [139]-144.

1. Spinoza, Benedictus de, 1632-1677.

McKeon, Richard ~~Peter~~, 1900-
The philosophy of Spinoza; the unity of his thought, by Richard McKeon. New York [etc.] Longmans, Green and co., 1928.
ix, 345 p. front. (port.) 24½ cm.

Thesis (PH. D.)—Columbia university, 1928.
Vita.
Without thesis note.
Bibliography: p. 319-337.

1. Spinoza, Benedictus de, 1632-1677. 2. Spinoza, Benedictus de, 1632-1677—Bibl.

[Martin, Thomas Henri] 1813-1884.
Dissertatio de philosophicarum Benedicti de Spinoza, doctrinarum systemate, ex operibus ejus philosophicis omnibus expromto. [Cadomi, Excudebat Pagni, 1836]
93 p. 22cm.

Caption title.
Title-page reads: Universitas Regia. Facultas Litterarum in Academia Parisiensi. Thesis philosophica.
Thesis, Paris.

SPECIAL COLLECTIONS SPINOZA
D-1-a 973

Martineau, James, 1805-1900.
A study of Spinoza. London, Macmillan, 1882.
xi, 371 p. port. 20cm.

SPECIAL COLLECTIONS SPINOZA
D-1-a 974

Martineau, James, 1805-1900.
A study of Spinoza. 2d ed. rev. London, Macmillan, 1883.
xiii, 393 p. port. 19cm.

SPECIAL COLLECTIONS SPINOZA
D-1-a 975

Martineau, James, 1805-1900.
A study of Spinoza. 3d ed. London and New York, Macmillan, 1895.
xiii, 393 p. port. 19cm.

D-1-a 976

Matthias, Conrad
Benedicti Spinosae doctrina ex Ethica ejus recensita. Marburg, Krieger, 1829.
48 p.

Thesis, Marburg.

NN

SPECIAL COLLECTIONS SPINOZA
D-1-a 977

Mehlis, Georg, 1878–
... Spinozas leben und lehre. Freiburg i. B., E. Guenther, 1923.
102, [2] p. incl. front. (port.) 19cm.

1. Spinoza, Benedictus de, 1632-1677.

36-14182
Library of Congress B3997.M38 199.492

SPECIAL COLLECTIONS SPINOZA
D-1-a 978

[Meijer, Willem] 1842-1926.
Benedicti Despinozae philosophiae brevis commentatio. ['s-Gravenhage, Nijhoff, 1905]
20 p. 24cm.

1. Spinoza, Benedictus de, 1632-1677.

D-1-a 979

[Meijer, Willem, 1842-1926.
Benedicti Despinozae philosophiae commentatio.
[Hagae Comitis, 1906]
12 p.

OCH

SPECIAL COLLECTIONS SPINOZA
D-1-a 980

Meijer, Willem, 1842-1926.
Over de kenmerkende eigenschappen van de leer van Spinoza; Voordracht gehouden den 27sten April 1906 in de jaarvergadering der vereeniging: "Het Spinozahuis". [1906]
[153]-169 p. 25cm.

"Overgedrukt uit De XXe eeuw."
Original paper cover bound in.
Volume of pamphlets.

NNC

SPECIAL COLLECTIONS SPINOZA
D-1-a 981

[Oko, Adolph S] 1883-1944.
Spinoza, by S. Baruch [pseud. 1914-15]
3 pts. in 1 v. port. 24cm.

From Hebrew Union College monthly, November 1914-January 1915.
Bound with In defense of Spinoza. [1914]

NNC

SPECIAL COLLECTIONS SPINOZA
D-1-a 982

[Oko, Adolph S] 1883-1944.
Spinoza, by S. Baruch [pseud.] I. Prejudiced and partial? [1914]
[8] p. 24cm.

Reprinted from Hebrew Union College monthly, November 1914.
Bound with In defense of Spinoza. [1914]

NNC

D-1-a
983

[Oko, Adolph S] 1883-1944.
Spinoza, by S. Baruch [pseud.] [1914-15]
3 pts. port. 24cm.

From Hebrew Union College Monthly, November 1914-January 1915.
Bibliographical footnotes.

1. Spinoza, Benedictus de, 1632-1677.

NNC

D-1-a
984

Orelli, Konrad von, 1788-1854.
Spinoza's Leben und Lehre. Nebst einem Abrisse der Schelling'schen und Hegel'schen Philosophie. 2. durch einen Nachtrag verm. Aufl. Aarau, H. R. Sauerländer, 1850.
x, 412 p. 22cm.

Ms. notes by Carl Gebhardt.
Bibliographical footnotes.

D-1-a
985

Orelli, Konrad von, 1788-1854.
Spinoza's Leben und Lehre; nebst einem Abrisse der Schelling'schen und Hegel'schen Philosophie. Aarau, H. N. Sauerländer, 1843.
xii, 384 p. 22cm.

D-1-a
986

Ovink, Bernard Jan Hendrik, 1862-1944.
Spinoza. Baarn, Hollandia-Drukkerij, 1914.
cover-title, 48 p. 24cm. (Onze groote mannen. ser. 1, no. 5)

D-1-a
987

Pollock, Sir Frederick, bart., 1845-1937.
Benedict de Spinoza. [1879]
363-377 p.

In Royal Institution of Great Britain. Proceedings, v. 8, 1879.
A paper read before the Royal Institution of Great Britain, April 20, 1877.

NN

D-1-a
988

Pollock, Sir Frederick, bart., 1845-1937.
Spinoza. [1877]
15 p. 22cm.

At head of title: Royal Institution of Great Britain. Weekly evening meeting, Friday, April 20, 1877.
Bound with Kirchmann, Julius Hermann. Erläuterungen zu Benedict von Spinoza's Ethik. 1871.

NNC

D-1-a
989

Post, G P
Spinoza; eene volksvoordracht. 's-Gravenhage, W. A. Beschoor (firma S. van Velzen jr.) 1880.
28 p. 21cm.

1. Spinoza, Benedictus de, 1632-1677.

D-1-a
990

193Sp4
DR Radliński, Ignacy, 1843-1920.
Spinoza; rzecz historyczno-społeczna. Warszawa, Centnerszwer, 1910.
290 p.

"Wazniejsze prace autora": p. [291]-[293]

1. Spinoza, Benedictus de, 1632-1677.

D-1-a
991

193Sp4
DR4341 Ravà, Adolfo
Le opere di Spinoza. Milano, La Grafica moderna [1927]
48 p. 23cm.

"Estratto dalla Rivista di filosofia, n. 3, luglio-settembre 1927 (V)"
Presentation copy to Carl Gebhardt, with the author's inscription.

D-1-a
992

Rensi, Giuseppe, 1871-
Spinoza. Roma, A. F. Formiggini, 1929.
103 p. port. 16cm. (Profili, n. 107)

Robinson, Lewis
Метафизика Спинозы. СПБ., Шиповникъ, 1913.
421 p.

Title transliterated: Metafizika Spinozy.

OCH

Rosenkranz, Karl, 1805-1879.
De Spinozae philosophia dissertatio. Scripsit Dr. Carolus Rosenkranz. Halae et Lipsiae, Apud Reinickium et Comp., 1828.
59 p. 21cm.

Roth, Leon, 1896-
Spinoza. London, E. Benn ⌊1929⌋
xvi, 250 p. (Leaders of philosophy)

Roth, Leon, 1896–
Spinoza, by Leon Roth ... Boston, Little, Brown, and company, 1929.
3 p. l., ix-xvi, 250 p. 20 cm. (*Half-title:* Leaders of philosophy)
Printed in Great Britain.
"Bibliographical note": p. 239-241.

1. Spinoza, Benedictus de, 1632-1677.

Full name: Hyam Leon Roth.

Rubin, Solomon, 1823-1910.
הגיוני שפינוזה על האלהות, התבל ונפש האדם; או, שיטת הפילוסופיא של שפינוזה, מסודרת ומפורשת באר היטב בסגנון קל ונוח לחתבונן בלמודי הפי־לוסוף אשר בספר "חקר אלוה" עד היסוד בם. מאת S. Rubin . קראקא, בהוצאת אהרן פויסט, תרנ"ז.
Krakau, Verlag von A. Faust, 1897.
40 p. 16cm.

~~CONTINUED ON NEXT CARD~~

Rubin, Solomon, 1823-1910.
... הגיוני שפינוזה 1897. (Card 2)

Title transliterated: Heghyōnē Shpīnōzā.
On Spinoza's philosophy.
Cover-title in German: Die Philosophie Spinoza's populair dargestellt.

1. Spinoza, Benedictus de, 1632-1671.

Rupp, Julius, 1809-1884.
De Spinozae philosophia practica. Regimonti Prussorum, Impressit C. Paschke, 1832.
40 p.

Thesis, Königsberg.

NN

Saisset, Émile, 1814-1863.
Introduction aux oeuvres de Spinoza. Paris, Béthune et Plon, 1843.
ccx p. 22cm.

The introduction to the author's translation of Spinoza's works.
Original paper covers bound in.
"Bibliographie générale des oeuvres de Spinoza": p. ⌊ccv⌋-cviii ⌊i. e. ccviii⌋

Schlager, Benjamin
Spinoza. Zdjęcia z duszy heretyka. Kraków, "Wiedza i Sztuka", 1924.
250 p.

MID

Schlüter, Christoph Bernhard, 1801-1884.
Die Lehre des Spinosa in ihren Hauptmomenten, geprüft und dargestellt von C. B. Schlüter. Münster, Theissingsche Buchhandlung, 1836.
x, 107 p. 22cm.

1. Spinoza, Benedictus de, 1632-1677.

Schott, Andreas Heinrich, praeses.
Dissertatio historico-philosophica de Spinozismo. Quam praeside Andrea Henrico Schott ... pro obtinendis magisterii philosophici honoribus ... Sept. MDCCCIV. publice defendent Fridericus Gustavus Schoder ... [et al.] Tubingae, Litteris Reis- et Schmidianis [1804]
48 p. 20cm.

Schott, Andreas Heinrich, praeses.
Dissertatio historico-philosophica de variis Pantheismi formis. Quam praeside Andrea Henrico Schott ... pro obtinendis magisterii philosophici honoribus ... Sept. MDCCCV. publice defendent Christianus Ludovicus Liesching ... [et al.] Tubingae, Literis Schrammianis [1805]
40 p. 21cm.

Includes references to Spinoza.

Sérouya, Henri.
Spinoza, sa vie et sa philosophie, par Henri Sérouya ... Paris, Éditions Excelsior, 1933.
83 p., 2 l. incl. 1 illus., port. xxxII pl. (incl. front., ports., facsims.) 20½ x 10cm.
"Notice bibliographique": p. [77]-80.
Original paper covers bound in.

1. Spinoza, Benedictus de, 1632-1677.
Library of Congress B3997.S4
Copyright A—Foreign 21180
33-21509
[3]
921.2

Sigwart, Heinrich Christoph Wilhelm, 1789-1844.
Historische und philosophische Beiträge zur Erläuterung des Spinozismus. Tübingen, Gedruckt bei E. T. Eifert, 1838.
76 p. 21cm.

Bibliographical footnotes.

1. Spinoza, Benedictus de, 1632-1677.

Sigwart, Heinrich Christoph Wilhelm, 1789-1844.
Der Spinozismus historisch und philosophisch erläutert, mit beziehung auf ältere und neuere ansichten, von dr. H. C. W. Sigwart ... Tübingen, C. F. Osiander, 1839.
iv, [2], 265 p. 20cm.

1. Spinoza, Benedictus de, 1632-1677.
11-21424
[32c1]
Library of Congress B3998.S6

Spinoza redivivus; eine Fibel für Anfänger und Verächter der Philosophie. Mit 22 Figuren im Text. Berlin, M. Rockenstein, 1917.
135 p. illus., port. 28cm. [Neue philosophische Bibliothek, 1]

Inked on spine, probably by Carl Gebhardt: Glatzel.
Includes selections from Euclid's Elementa in German translation.

Spinoza redivivus; eine Fibel für Anfänger und Verächter der Philosophie. Mit 22 Figuren im Text. Halle (Saale) Weltphilosophischer Verlag [c1919]
135 p. illus. 27cm. (Philosophische Weltbibliothek, 1)

Includes selections from Euclid's Elementa in German translation.

Starcke, Carl Nicolai, 1858-1926.
Baruch de Spinoza. København, Kristiania, Gyldendal, 1921.
297, [3] p. 25 cm.

OCH

Starcke, Carl Nicolai, 1858-1926.
Baruch de Spinoza. Ins Deutsche übertragen von Karl Hellwig. København, Gyldendalske boghandel, 1923.
392 p. port. 24cm.

Original paper covers bound in.
Bibliography: p. [383]-389.

Stern, Jakob, 1843-1911.
Die Philosophie Spinoza's, erstmals gründlich aufgehellt und populär dargestellt. Stuttgart, J. H. W. Dietz, 1890.
viii, 184 p. port. 21cm.

Original paper covers bound in.

Stern, Jakob, 1843-1911.
Die Philosophie Spinoza's erstmals gründlich aufgehellt und populär dargestellt. 2., verb. Aufl. Stuttgart, J. H. W. Dietz, 1894.
viii, 192 p. port. ⌊Internationale Bibliothek, 8⌋

1. Spinoza, Benedictus de, 1632-1677.
I. Internationale Bibliothek. 8.

Stern, Jakob, 1843-1911.
Die Philosophie Spinozas, erstmals gründlich aufgehellt und populär dargestellt. 3., stark verb. Aufl. Stuttgart, J. H. W. Dietz Nachfolger, 1908.
viii, 192 p. port. 20cm. ⌊Internationale Bibliothek, 8⌋

Stern, Jakob, 1843-1911.
Die Philosophie Spinozas, erstmals gründlich aufgehellt und populär dargestellt. 4. Aufl. Stuttgart, J. H. W. Dietz Nachf., 1921.
viii, 192 p. port. 20cm. ⌊Internationale Bibliothek, 8⌋

Bibliographical footnotes.

Stupnicki, Saul J 1876-
ברוך שפּינאזא; זיין פילאזאפיע, בי־
בעל־קריטיק, שטאמפלערע און זיין בע־
דייטונג אין דער ענטוויקלונג פון מענ־
שליכען דענקען. פערפאסט פון ש. י. סטו־
פּניצקי. ווארשא, פערלאג "יודיש", תרע"ו
⌊Warsaw, 1916⌋
161 p. port. 22cm.

Title transliterated: Baruch Spinoza.

Tak, Willem Gerard van der, 1885-
Bento de Spinoza; zijn leven en gedachten over de wereld, den mensch en den staat. 's-Gravenhage, M. Nijhoff, 1928.
xii, 239 p. plates, port. 18cm.

Bibliography: p. ⌊234⌋-239.

1. Spinoza, Benedictus de, 1632-1677.

Thomas, Karl, d. 1873.
Spinozae systema philosophicum adumbratum. Regimontii Borussorum, Impressit Conradus Paschke ⌊1835?⌋
79 p. 21cm.

Thesis, Königsberg.
Published also without thesis note.

Tumarkin, Anna, 1875-
Spinoza; acht Vorlesungen gehalten an der Universität Bern. Leipzig, Quelle & Meyer, 1908.
89 p. 22cm. (Abhandlungen zur Philosophie und ihrer Geschichte, hrsg. von R. Falckenberg. Hft. 5)

Bibliographical footnotes.
Original paper covers bound in.

Turbiglio, Sebastiano, b. 1842.
Benedetto Spinoza e le trasformazioni del suo pensiero; libri tre. Roma, Tipografia G. B. Paravia, 1874.
307 p. 25cm.

Original paper covers bound in.

1. Spinoza, Benedictus de, 1632-1677.

Vandek, V
Очерк философии Б. Спиноза. Москва, Партийное издательство, 1932.
79 p.

Title transliterated: Ocherk filosofii B. Spinozy.
By V. Vandek and V. Timoshko.

NN

Vloemans, Antoon
De wijsbegeerte van Spinoza, haar plaats in het Nederlandsche denken en haar beteekenis voor de wereldphilosophie. Amsterdam, Wereldbibliotheek, 1932.
253 p. 19cm.

Bibliography: p. ⌊243⌋-249.

1. Spinoza, Benedictus de, 1632-1677.

D-1-a
1023

Wenzel, Alfred
Die Weltanschauung Spinozas. 1. Bd.: Spinozas Lehre von Gott, von der menschlichen Erkenntnis und von dem Wesen der Dinge. Leipzig, W. Engelmann, 1907.
viii, 479 p. 24cm.

No more published?
Ms. notes by Carl Gebhardt, with his signature on t.-p.
Original paper cover bound in.

D-1-a
1024

Wijck, Bernard Hendrik Cornelis Karel van der
Spinoza, door Jhr. van der Wijck. Groningen, J. B. Wolters, 1877.
48 p. 20cm.

D-1-a
1025

Wolf, Abraham, 1876-
Spinoza the conciliator. [Hagae Comitis, 1922]
13 p. 22cm.

Cover title: Dissertatio ex Chronici Spinozani tomo secundo separatim edita.

1. Spinoza, Benedictus de, 1632-1677.

D-1-a
1026

Wolfson, Harry Austryn, 1887–
The philosophy of Spinoza, unfolding the latent processes of his reasoning, by Harry Austryn Wolfson ... Cambridge, Mass., Harvard university press, 1934.
2 v. 23 cm.

"Into the fabric of this work, which in form follows the order of the 'Ethics,' we have also woven relevant passages from the other writings of Spinoza, so that the study of his philosophy herein presented is based upon his 'Ethics' as well as upon all his other writings in so far as they are related to the 'Ethics.'"—Pref., p. viii.
"List of editions of texts used": vol. II, p. [357]–364.

1. Spinoza, Benedictus de, 1632–1677. 2. Spinoza, Benedictus de, 1632–1677. Ethica. I. Title.

34—12012

Library of Congress B3998.W65

[49o1] 199.492

D-1-a
1027

Zuławski, Jerzy
Benedykt Spinoza: człowiek i dzieło.
Warszawa, 1902.
195 p.

NNJ

D-1-b

ARTICLES IN PERIODICALS AND COLLECTIONS

D-1-b
1028

[Adler, Marcus]
Mr. J. H. Levy on Spinoza. [1903]
8-9 p.

Signed: M. A.
In Jewish chronicle, London, Oct. 2, 1903.
A letter to the editor.

NNJ

D-1-b
1029

Archiv für Geschichte der Philosophie ...
Bd. 1-7.
1888-1894.
Bd. 8-41. (N. F., Bd. 1-[34])
1894-1932.
Berlin, 1888-[1932]

Includes articles on and references to Spinoza.

NNC

D-1-b
1030

Archiv für Geschichte der Philosophie ...
Bd. 1-3, 5, 7.
1888-1894.
Bd. 9, $11^{1, 3-4}$, 40^{1}. (N. F. Bd. 2, $4^{1, 3-4}$, [33^{1}])
1895-1931.
Berlin, 1888-1931.

Includes articles on and references to Spinoza.

D-1-b
1031

Arshovsky, Dov Bär
שפינוזה במאת דוב בער בן אהרן אר-
שובסקים קראקא, תרמ"ט-נ.
[Cracow, 1889-90]
[19]-22 p. 23cm.

Title transliterated: Shpīnōzā.
From Ōṣar ha-sifrūth, vol. 3.

1. Spinoza, Benedictus de, 1632-1677.

NNC

Baruch Spinoza. [1925]
p. 10. 25cm.

From The Jewish Religious Union bulletin, vol. X, no. 29, February 1925.

1. Spinoza, Benedictus de, 1632-1677.

Baruch Spinoza, 1632-1932. [1932]
[258]-261 p. 27cm.

From Observer, v. 22, no. 22, week of November 24, 1932.

1. Spinoza, Benedictus de, 1632-1677 - Anniversaries, etc., 1932.

Ben Rubin, M
Baruch, or Benedict Spinoza; a Jewish philosopher. [1853]
261-265, 300-304 p. 23cm.

From The Occident and American Jewish advocate, v. 11, no. 5 and 6, August and September 1853.

Benedict Spinoza. [1883]
57-64 p. port.

In Progress; a monthly magazine, v. 1, 1883.

Bergmann, Julius, 1840-1904.
Spinoza. Vortrag, gehalten im Goethe-Hause in Frankfurt zu der vom Freien Deutschen Hochstift veranstalteten Feier des Geburtstages Goethes. [1887]
129-164 p.

In Philosophische Monatshefte, 23. Bd., 1887.

Bernfeld, Simon, 1860-1940.
ברוך שפינוזה,אישיותו ותורתו.
לרגלי צאת כתביו בעברית. [1925-28]
411-419, 495-508 p.

Title transliterated: Barukh Shpinoza ...
In ha-Tkufah, v. 23-24, 1925-28.

Bernfeld, Simon, 1860-1940.
ברוך שפינוזה והיהדות. [1885]
4 pts.

Title transliterated: Barukh Shpinoza ...
In ha-Magid, v. 29, 1885.

Bierens de Haan, Johannes Diderik, 1866-1943.
Het Spinozisme als ontwikkelingsleer. [1914]
1-16 p.

In Tijdschrift voor wijsbegeerte, jaargang 8, 1914.

Boehmer, Eduard, 1827-1906.
Spinozana. [1860-70]
6 pts.

In Zeitschrift für Philosophie und philosophische Kritik, Bd. 36, 1860; Bd. 42, 1863; Bd. 57, 1870.

Boston daily advertiser.
The Spinoza revival. [1880]
p. 2.

Editorial of Oct. 2, 1880.

Bourget, Paul, 1852-1935.
Spinoza. [1912]

Translated by Jacques Mayer.
In The Sentinel; a weekly newspaper devoted to Jewish interests, 1912.

Browne, Lewis, 1897-1949.
Baruch Spinoza ... Vivid characterization of Spinoza. [1932]
p. [1] port. 33cm.

From American Hebrew and Jewish tribune, v. 132, no. 2, November 25, 1932.

1. Spinoza, Benedictus de, 1632-1677.

[Browne, James Henry]
Spinoza. [1874]
214-216 p.

In The Overland monthly, v. 13, 1874.

[Brunner, Constantin] 1862-1937.
Das Lamm Benedikt Spinoza. [1913]
414-425 p.

Signed: Konstantin Brunner.
In Die Zukunft, 84. Bd. [1913]

Brunschvicg, Léon, 1869-1944.
Sur l'interprétation du spinozisme. [1927]
84-86 p. illus. 32cm.

From Menorah, 6. année, no. 6, 15 mars 1927.
With Menorah. Le 250e anniversaire de Baruch Spinoza. [1927]

1. Spinoza, Benedictus de, 1632-1677.

Brunschvicg, Léon, 1869-1944.
Sur l'interprétation du spinozisme. [Hagae Comitis, 1921]
58-62 p. 22cm.

Cover-title: Dissertatio ex Chronici Spinozani tomo primo separatim edita.

1. Spinoza, Benedictus de, 1632-1677.

Busse, Ludwig, 1862-1907.
Beiträge zur Entwicklungsgeschichte Spinoza's.
Berlin, Schade [1885]
88 p. 26cm.

Thesis, Berlin.

Busse, Ludwig, 1862-1907.
Beiträge für Entwicklungsgeschichte Spinoza's. [1887]
50-88, 227-251 p. 22cm.

From Zeitschrift für Philosophie und philosophische Kritik, Neue Folge, 90.-91. Bd.
Bibliographical footnotes.

1. Spinoza, Benedictus de, 1632-1677.

Chronicon Spinozanum. Hagae Comitis, Curis Societatis Spinozanae, 1921-27.
5 v. illus., ports., facsims. 25cm.

Contributions in several languages.

Chronicon Spinozanum. Hagae Comitis, Curis Societatis Spinozanae, 1923-27.
v.3-5. illus., ports., facsims. 25cm.

Contributions in several languages.
Hand-made paper.

Cram, W A
Spinoza. [1867]
170-177 p.

In The Radical, Boston, v. 2, 1867.

NNUT

De Casseres, Benjamin, 1873-1945.
The liberator of God. [New York, 1930]
29-36 p. illus. 19cm.

From The Thinker, vol. 2, no. 3, July, 1930.
Later reprinted as chapter 3 of his Spinoza, liberator of God and man, 1632-1932.

De Dageraad.
jaarg. 1-10.
1879-1889.
Amsterdam [1879-89]

Includes articles on and references to Spinoza.

Durant, William, 1885-
Der Einfluss Spinozas. [1930]
8-9 p. illus.

In Jüdische Presszentrale Zurich und illustriertes Familienblatt für die Schweiz, 13. Jahrgang, 17. Januar 1930.

Edelstein, Samuel
Baruch Spinoza. [1930]
p. 22. 31cm.

From Young Israel, v. 22, no. 12, August 1930.

1. Spinoza, Benedictus de, 1632-1677.

Edman, Irwin, 1896-1954.
Spinoza's message for a world beset. [1932]
p. 5, 16. port.

In New York times. Magazine [section] Nov. 20, 1932.

Eickhoff, Richard,
Spinoza. [1927]
p. 31.

In Abwehrblätter. Mitteilungen aus dem Verein zur Abwehr des Antisemitismus, Jahrgang 37, 5/6, 1927.

OCH

Eickhoff, Richard
Spinoza und wir. [1920]

In Deutsche Revue, Stuttgart, Jahrgang 45, 1920.

NN

Feuer, Lewis Samuel, 1912-
The social motivation of Spinoza's thought. [1953]
36-42 p. 25cm.

On cover: Proceedings of the XIth International Congress of Philosophy. Vol. XIII.
Bibliographical footnotes.

1. Spinoza, Benedictus de, 1632-1677.

Fichman, Jacob, 1881-
משהו על שפינוזה. תל־אביב, תרצ"ג.
[1932]
14-15 p. 29cm.

Title transliterated: Mashshehū ʿal Shpīnōzā.
From Moznayim, vol. 4, no. 26, Dec. 15, 1932.
With Roth, Leon. Mishnāthō shel Shpīnōzā ... [1932]

NNC

ₑFreudenthal, Jacob, 1839-1907.
On the history of Spinozism. ₑ1895ₑ
17-70 p. 23cm.

Signed: J. Freudenthal.
From the Jewish quarterly review, vol. VIII, October, 1895.
Ms. notes by A. S. Oko.
Bibliographical footnotes.

ₑFreudenthal, Jacob, 1839-1907.
On the history of Spinozism. ₑ1895,
17-70 p. 23cm.

Signed: J. Freudenthal.
From the Jewish quarterly review, vol. VIII, no. 29, 1895.

1. Spinoza, Benedictus de, 1632-1677.

Freudenthal, Jacob, 1839-1907.
Spinozastudien. ₑ1896,
ₑ238,-282 p. 26cm.

"Sonderabdruck aus Zeitschrift für Philosophie und philosophische Kritik. 108. Bd."
Ms. notes by Carl Gebhardt.
Bibliographical footnotes.

1. Spinoza, Benedictus de, 1632-1677.

ₑFroude, James Anthony, 1818-1894.
Spinoza. ₑ1855,
37 p.

In The Westminster and foreign quarterly review, v. 64, 1855.

Gebhardt, Carl, 1881-1934.
Spinozismus und Transcendentalphilosophie.
ₑHagae Comitis, 1922,
118-129 p. 22cm.

Cover-title: Dissertatio ex Chronici Spinozani tomo secundo separatim edita.

Giornale critico della filosofia italiana.
anno $8^{2, 4-6}$, $12^{1-2, 4-5}$, 13^{2-6}.
1927-1932.
anno $14-16^{2, 4-6}$. (ser. 2, v. $1-3^{2, 4-6}$)
1933-1935.
Messina, G. Principato, 1927-35.

Editor: Jan. 1920- Giovanni Gentile.
Imprint varies.
Includes articles on and references to Spinoza.

Giornale critico della filosofia italiana.
anno 1-13.
genn. 1920-1932.
anno 14-25. (ser. 2, v. 1-12)
1933-1946.
Messina, G. Principato, 1920-46.

Editor: Jan. 1920- Giovanni Gentile.
Imprint varies.
Includes articles on and references to Spinoza.

Goldberg, Abraham, 1883-1942.
ברוך שפינוזה (במלאת 300 שנה להו-
לדתו) ניו-יורק, הרצ"ג.
ₑ1932,
ₑ49,-50 p. port. 32cm.

Title transliterated: Bārūkh Shpīnōzā.
From ha-Doar, vol. XIII, no. 4, Nov. 25, 1932.

Grot, Nikolaĭ Ī͡Akovlevich, 1852-1899.
Основные моменты въ развитіи новой философіи. III. Спиноза. [1891]
ₑ1ₑ-18 p.

Title transliterated: Osnovnye momenty v razvitii novoĭ filosofii. III. Spinoza.
In Вопросы философии и психологіи, т. 10, отдѣлъ 2, 1891.

Grunwald, Max, 1871-
Spinoza. Vortrag, gehalten in der Henry-Jones-Loge zu Hamburg. ₑ1897,
315-317, 326-327 p.

In Die Neuzeit, 37. Jahrgang, 1897.

Gunn, John Alexander, 1896-
Spinoza. [1924]
23-42 p.

In Australasian journal of psychology and philosophy, v. 2, 1924.

Guttman, Mrs. Louis
Spinoza: a study. [1896]
641-642 p.

In The American Hebrew, v. 58, 1896.
Excerpt from a paper read before the New York Council of Jewish Women, March 26, 1896.

Haagsche omtrekken.
Sept. 4, 1886-Aug. 27, 1887.
's-Gravenhage, W. P. van Stockum, 1886-87.
weekly.

Hartmann, Hans
Der Spinozismus; zugleich eine Betrachtung zum internationalen Spinozakongress. [1933]
39-49 p. 24cm.

Page 49 lacking; supplied in typescript.
From Preussische Jahrbücher, Januar 1933.

[Heavenrich, Edgar E]
Spinoza. [1887]
[120]-122 p. 26cm.

Signed: Edgar E. Heavenrich.
From The Menorah, vol. II, no. 3, March, 1887.

Hecke, Gustav
Benedikt Spinoza, ein Herold des Humanitätsgedankens. [1909]
53 p. 19cm.

From Asträa, Taschenbuch für Freimaurer auf das Jahr 1909. Neue Folge, 28. Bd.

1. Spinoza, Benedictus de, 1632-1677.

Heilikman, Tobiah, d. 1948.

באָרוך שפּינאָזע (1677-1927) [1927]
95-103 p.

Title transliterated: Borukh Shpinoze ...
In Di Roite welt, v. 4, no. 12, 1927.

Hirzenberg, S
Spinoza. [1908]
p. 37.

In Jewish chronicle, London, Sept. 25, 1908.

Hofstede de Groot, Petrus, 1802-1886.
Waarde van Spinoza's wijsbegeerte. (Naar aanleiding van J. van Vloten en A. van der Linde). [1862]
803-843 p.

In Waarheid in liefde, 1862.

De Humanist. Tijdschrift voor geloofsvrije menschelijke beschaving en veredeling, op onbepaalde tijden in 't licht gegeven door J. van Vloten.
deel 1.
Haarlem, I. de Haan, 1882-83.
1 v. 21cm.

Supersedes De Levensbode.
No more published.
Includes articles on Spinoza.

In defense of Spinoza. [1914]
2 p. 24cm.

From Hebrew Union College monthly, November 1914.

1. Spinoza, Benedictus de, 1632-1677.

[Jellinek, Adolf] 1821-1893.
Neuere Beurtheitungen [!] Spinoza's. [1851]
302-303 col.

Signed: Ad. Jellinek.
In Der Orient; Berichte, Studien und Kritiken, 12. Jahrgang, 1851.

Юбилеенъ сборникъ въ честь на Соломонъ А. Розанесъ по случай неговата седемдесетгодишнина. София, Издание на Общеграждански юбилеенъ комитетъ при Централната консистория на евреитѣ въ България, 1933.
100 p. ports. 24cm.

Title transliterated: I͡Ubileen sbornik ...
Title also in Hebrew and French; text in Bulgarian, French, Spanish, German or Hebrew.
Includes an essay "Missverständnisse in und um Spinoza" by Jacob Klatzkin (p. 67-75)

[Jodl, Friedrich] 1849-1914.
Zur Interpretation Spinozas. [1902]
[342]-350 p. 27cm.

Signed: Friedrich Jodl.
"Sonderabdruck aus der Festschrift für Theodor Gomperz. Wien, 1902."

1. Spinoza, Benedictus de, 1632-1677.

Jacobs, Maurice
Mr. J. H. Levy on Spinoza. [1903]
p. 6.

In Jewish chronicle, London, Sept. 25, 1903.
A letter to the editor.

Joël, David, 1815-1882.
דברים אחדים או הערות,השגות ותקונים.
[1865]
13 pts.

Title transliterated: Dvarim aʿhadim ...
In ha-Magid, v. 9, 1865.
Includes references to Spinoza.

Jacobs, Maurice
Mr. J. H. Levy on Spinoza. [1903]
p. 7.

In Jewish chronicle, London, Oct. 9, 1903.
A letter to the editor in reply to Marcus Adler.

Journal zur Kunstgeschichte und zur allgemeinen Litteratur.
Th. 4.
Nürnberg, J. E. Zeh, 1777.

At head of title: Christoph Gottlieb von Murr.

[Janet, Paul] 1823-1899.
Spinoza et le Spinozisme d'après les travaux récens. [1867]
[470]-498 p. 25cm.

Signed: Paul Janet.
From Revue des deux mondes, 2. période, t. 70, 15 juillet 1867.

Kahana, David, 1838-1915.
ברוך שפינוזה. [1911]
36-41, 137-143 p.

Title transliterated: Barukh Shpinozah.
In ha-Shiloah, v. 25, 1911.

D-1-b 1092

Kalischer, Zebi Hirsch, 1795-1874.

מצב הפלוסופיא בזמננו. ‏⌊1861⌋
165-166 p.

Title transliterated: Mazab ha-filosofiyaʿ ...
In ha-Magid, v. 5, 1861.
Includes references to Spinoza.

NNJ

D-1-b 1093

Kalischer, Zebi Hirsch, 1795-1874.

עת מלחמה ועת שלום.תשובה למלחמה בשלום.
⌊1861⌋
277, 285-286 p.

Title transliterated: ʿeth milkhamah ve-ʿeth shalom.
In ha-Magid, v. 5, 1861.

NNJ

D-1-b 1094

Kalischer, Zebi Hirsch, 1795-1874.

משיב מענה רך. ‏⌊1863⌋
13-14, 21-22 p.

Title transliterated: Meshib maʿaneh rakh.
In ha-Magid, v. 7, 1863.
Includes references to Spinoza.

NNJ

D-1-b 1095

Kantor, H R
Some humanistic elements in Spinoza's thinking, by H. R. and J. R. Kantor. ⌊1934⌋
14-23 p.

In Biosophical review, v. 4, no. 1, 1934.

SPECIAL COLLECTIONS SPINOZA
D-1-b 1096

Keyser, Cassius Jackson, 1862-1947.
Benedict Spinoza. ⌊1938⌋
33-56 p. port. 25ᶜᵐ.

From Scripta Mathematica, vol. V, no. 1, January 1938.

SPECIAL COLLECTIONS SPINOZA
D-1-b 1097

Klausner, Joseph, 1874-
ברוך שפינוזה. תל-אביב, תרצ"ג.
⌊1932⌋
8-10 p. 29cm.

Title transliterated: Bārūkh Shpīnōzā.
From Moznayim, vol. 4, no. 26, Dec. 15, 1932.
With Roth, Leon. Mishnāthō shel Shpīnōzā ... ⌊1932⌋

NNC

D-1-b 1098

Korsh, V O
Барухъ Спиноза. [1881]

Title transliterated: Barukh Spinoza.
In Восходъ, 1881, № 1, 5, 7, 8.

NNJ

SPECIAL COLLECTIONS SPINOZA
D-1-b 1099

Kroeger, Adolf Ernst, 1837-1882.
Spinoza. ⌊1875⌋
363-393 p. 25cm.

From the Journal of speculative philosophy, vol. IX, no. 3, July 1875.

D-1-b 1100

Lagneau, Jules
Quelques notes de Jules Lagneau sur Spinoza. ⌊1895⌋
375-416 p.

In Revue de métaphysique et de morale, 3. année, 1895.

D-1-b 1101

Lazarus, Moritz, 1824-1903.
Ueber Spinoza. ⌊1881⌋
p. 97.

In Zeitgeist, Milwaukee, Jahrgang 2, 1881.

NN

[Lee, Arthur Bolles] 1849-1927.
Spinoza: the man and the philosopher. [1877]
131-151 p. 23cm.

Signed: Arthur Bolles Lee.
From Littell's living age, April, 1877.
Appeared originally in the Contemporary review.

[Letter about Spinoza. 1702]

In Mercure galant, sept. 1702.

De Levensbode. Tijdschrift voor onbevooroordeelse waarheid en wetenschap op verstandelijk en zedelijk gebied ...
deel [1]-12.
Haarlem, I. de Haan, 1865-81.
12 v. 20-22cm.

Edited by J. van Vloten (with H. J. Betz, deel 8-12)
Superseded by De Humanist.
Includes numerous articles on Spinoza.

Levi, Ezekiel, 1814-1864.
שפינוזא.(פתרונים להמגיד) [1864]
p. 86.

Title transliterated: Shpinoza.
In ha-Magid, v. 8, no. 11, 1864.
Signed with the author's pseudonym: Hazkiel.

Levy, J H
A modern Spinoza. Interview for the Jewish Chronicle with J. H. Levy. [1908]
16-17 p.

In Jewish chronicle, London, July 17, 1908.

Levy, J H
Religion and theolatry. [1903]
p. 6.

In Jewish chronicle, London, Sept. 11, 1903.
A letter to the editor.

Levy, J H
Religion and theolatry. [1903]
p. 6.

In Jewish chronicle, London, Sept. 25, 1903.
A letter to the editor in reply to Sally Daiches.

Levy, J H
Religion and theolatry. [1903]
p. 6.

In Jewish chronicle, London, Oct. 9, 1903.
A letter to the editor in reply to Sally Daiches.

Luzzatto, Samuele Davide, 1800-1865.
Intorno a Spinosa. [1862]
34-37, 65-68 p.

In Il Corriere israelitico, anno 1, 1862.

[Lewes, George Henry] 1817-1878.
Spinoza. [1866]
385-406 p.

Signed: Editor.
In Fortnightly review, v. 4, 1866.

M.
Philosophy of Spinoza. [1850]
76-81 p.

In Southern quarterly review, v. 16, 1850.

Mal'ākhī, A R
שפינוזאי לא־ידוע במאת א. ר. מל־
אכי. ניו־יורק, תרצ"ג.

[1932]
55-56 p. 32cm.

Title transliterated: Shpīnōzā'ī lō-yādūa'.
From ha-Doar, vol. XIII, no. 4, Nov. 25, 1932.
With Goldberg, Abraham. Bārūkh Shpīnōzā.
[1932]

Mauthner, Fritz, 1849-1923.
Spinoza. [1905]
51-76 p.

In Süddeutsche Monatshefte, 2. Jahrgang,
1. Bd., 1905.

Meijer, Willem, 1842-1926.
Benedictus Despinoza. [1901]
735-748 p. illus.

In Elsevier's geïllustreerd maandschrift,
11. jaargang, 1901.

Meijer, Willem, 1842-1926.
Bestrijding van Professor Erhardt's kritiek
over de philosophie van Spinoza. [1909]
28 p. 25cm.

A discussion of Die Philosophie des Spinoza
im Lichte der Kritik, by Franz Erhardt.
"Overdruk uit het Tijdschrift voor wijsbegeerte."
Bound with Meijer, Willem. Benedicti Despinozae philosophiae brevis commentatio.
[1905]

Meijer, Willem, 1842-1926.
Johannes Casearius. [1902]
398-417 p.

In Nederlandsch archief voor kerkgeschiedenis,
dl. 1, 1902.

Meijer, Willem, 1842-1926.
Opheldering van een meestal verkeerd begrepen
uitspraak van Spinoza. [1919]
p. 199.

In Tijdschrift voor wijsbegeerte, jaargang 13,
1919.

[Meisel, Nachman] 1887-
ברוך שפינאזא. ווארשע, פארלאג
ב. קלעצקין, 1932.

[Warsaw, 1932]
[565]-567 p. illus., port. 32cm.

Title transliterated: Borukh Shpinoza.
Signed: Nachman Meisel.
From Literarishe bleter, 9. yorgang, no. 36.

Melamed, Samuel Max, 1885-1938.
Spinoza, the Jew. [1916]
633-635 p. port. 34cm.

From The American Jewish chronicle, v. 1,
no. 20, September 22-29, 1916.

1. Spinoza, Benedictus de, 1632-1677.

[Menasci, Roberto]
Ancora su Baruch Spinoza. [1911]
442-443 p.

By "Discipulus".
In Il Vessillo israelitico, anno 59, 1911.

Mikhailov, A

ברוך שפינאזא. [1895]
449-456 p. port.

Title transliterated: Barukh Spinoza.
In Di[c] Zukunft, v. 4, 1895.

Mind; a quarterly review of psychology and philosophy, ed. by George Croom Robertson.
Vol. I, 1876. London, Williams and Norgate, 1876.
viii, 578 p. 22cm.

Includes references to Spinoza.

Minkin, Jacob Samuel, 1885-
Benedict Spinoza; his life and teaching. [1916]
41-44, 73-76, 85 p. 32cm.

From the Reform advocate, v. 51, Feb. 19 and 26, 1916.

1. Spinoza, Benedictus de, 1632-1677.

Morris, George Sylvester, 1840-1889.
Spinoza - a summary account of his life and teaching. [1877]
[278]-299 p. 24cm.

From the Journal of speculative philosophy, vol. XI, no. 3, July, 1877.

De Nederlandsche spectator.
Jan. 6-Dec. 29, 1877, Jan. 3-Dec. 25, 1880, Jan. 7-Dec. 30, 1905.
1877-1905.
weekly.

Includes articles on Spinoza.

Neuhausen, Simon

צוואת רבי.
Budapest, 1928.
7 p.

Title transliterated: Zawaath rabi.
Includes a reference to Spinoza (p. 4)
Reprinted from ha-Zofeh lehakhmath yisrael, v. 12, no. 4, 1928.

Orshavsky, Dov-Ber

שפינאזה. [1889-90]
19-22 p.

Title transliterated: Shpinozah.
In [c]ozar ha-safruth, v. 3, 1889-90.

Padovani, Umberto Antonio, 1894-
Il problema fondamentale della filosofia di Spinoza. [1919-20]
4 pts.

In Rivista di filosofia neo-scolastica, anno 11-12, 1919-20.

Pearson, Karl, 1857-1936.
Spinoza. [1881]
155-156 p.

In Cambridge review, v. 2, 1880-81.

Petri, J
Over Spinoza. [1914]

In Ons tijdschrift, jaargang 19, 1914.

Die Philosophie der Gegenwart; eine internationale Jahresübersicht ...
Bd. 1-5.
1908-1913.
Heidelberg, Weiss, 1910-15.
5 v. 25cm.

Includes works by and about Spinoza.

CONTINUED ON NEXT CARD

Die Philosophie der Gegenwart ... (Card 2)

Added t. p.: The Philosophy of the present time; an international annual review. La Philosophie contemporaine; une revue annuelle internationale.
Arnold Ruge, editor.
No more published.

Philosophische Bibliothek.
Bd. 1-4.
Göttingen, J. C. Dieterich, 1788-91.
4 v. 19cm.

By J. G. H. Feder and C. Meiners.
No more published.
Includes articles on Spinoza.

Pollock, Sir Frederick, bart., 1845-1937.
Benedict de Spinoza. [1878]
444-458 p. 24cm.

From the Popular science monthly, Supplement no. XI, March 1878.
Appeared originally in the Nineteenth century.

[Pollock, Sir Frederick, bart.] 1845-1937.
Benedict de Spinoza. [1878]
330-354 p. 23cm.

Signed: F. Pollock.
From the Nineteenth century, February 1878.
Volume of pamphlets.

[Pollock, Sir Frederick] bart., 1845-1937.
Notes on the philosophy of Spinoza. [1878]
195-212 p.

Signed: Frederick Pollock.
In Mind, v. 3, 1878.

[Pollock, Sir Frederick, bart.] 1845-1937.
Notes on the philosophy of Spinoza. [1878]
195-212 p. 22cm.

Signed: Frederick Pollock.
From Mind, v. 3, 1878.
Bibliography: p. 211-212.
Bound with Read, Carveth. Modern philosophy from Descartes to Schopenhauer and Hartmann. [1878]

Quérido, Israël, 1872-1932.
Kantteekeningen over Spinoza; hoogten en laagten. [1929]
[273]-286, [353]-383 p. 26cm.

From NU, August-September, 1929.
First part of the article (sections I-XXI) lacking.
Bibliographical footnotes.

[Radliński, Ignacy] 1843-1920.
Spinoza; notatka historyczna. [1902]
[87]-90, [99]-105, [111]-116, [123]-129 p. 29cm.

Signed: I. Radliński.
From Poradnik dla czytajacych ksiazki, rok II, no. 8-11, 1902.

1. Spinoza, Benedictus de, 1632-1677.

Raff, Emil
Zur Wissenschaft des Spinozismus. [1910]
20-41 p.

In Archiv für systematische Philosophie, 16. Band, 1910.

D-1-b
1142

Rapaport, Benzion, d. 1943.

שני פלוסופים יהודים. ⌐1913⌐
13-15, 13-15 p.

Title transliterated: Shney pilosofim yehudim.
In ha-Olam, no. 40-41, 1913.
About Spinoza and Bergson.

NNJ

D-1-b
1143

⌐Ratner, Joseph⌐ 1901-
In defense of Spinoza. ⌐1926⌐
121-133 p. 25cm.

Signed: Joseph Ratner.
From the Journal of philosophy, v. 23, no. 5, March 4, 1926.
Bibliographical footnotes.

D-1-b
1144

Reis, Meir

דבר בעתו (בנוגע במצב הפילוסופיא בזמננו). ⌐1861⌐
93-103 p.

Title transliterated: Davar be itho ...
In ha-Magid, v. 5, 1861.
Includes references to Spinoza.

NNJ

D-1-b
1145

Reis, Meir

⌐1862⌐ מענה רך אל מהר"ה קאלישער.
237-238, 245-246 p.

Title transliterated: Maʿaneh rakh ʿel ... kolisher.
In ha-Magid, v. 6, 1862.
Includes references to Spinoza.

NNJ

D-1-b
1146

Renan, Ernest, 1823-1892.
Spinoza. ⌐1877⌐

In Journal de débats, 1 mars 1877.

MB

D-1-b
1147

Renan, Ernest, 1823-1892.
Spinoza. ⌐1877⌐
97-120 p.

In Philosophische Monatshefte, 13. Bd., 1877.

D-1-b
1148

⌐Robertson, John MacKinnon⌐ 1856-1933.
Spinoza. ⌐1900⌐
7-20 p. port.

Signed: John M. Robertson.
In The Reformer, London, v. 4, 1900.

DLC

D-1-b
1149

Roll, Israel, 1830-1892.

מלחמה בשלום. ⌐1861⌐
245-246, 253-254 p.

Title transliterated: Milkhamah be-shalom.
In ha-Magid, v. 5, 1861.
Includes references to Spinoza.

NNJ

D-1-b
1150

Rosen, Anna H
World-renowned Jews: Baruch Spinoza. ⌐1903⌐
5-6 p.

In Young men's Hebrew association. Bulletin, v. 4, 1903.

NN

D-1-b
1151

Rothschild, David, 1816-1892.
Spinoza. ⌐1883⌐
32-40 p.

In Adolf Bruell's populär-wissenschaftliche Monatsblätter, Jahrgang 3, 1883.

NNJ

D-1-b
1152

Rubin, Salomon, 1823-1910.

חליפת מכתבים(מכתב הח' ד"ר ש.רובין אל הח' ש"א הורודצקי ותשובת האחרון אליו).
[1899]
236-238 p.

Title transliterated: Halifath miktabim ...
In ha-ʿeshkol, v. 2, 1899.
Includes references to Spinoza in an exchange of letters between Rubin and S. A. Horodetzky.

NNJ

D-1-b
1153

S., S. F.
Mr. J. H. Levy on Spinoza. [1903]
p. 13.

In Jewish chronicle, London, Sept. 18, 1903.
A letter to the editor.

NNJ

D-1-b
1154

Saxton, C T
Spinoza. [1871]
p. 659.

In Jewish times, New York, v. 3, 1871.

NN

D-1-b
1155

Scharfman, I Leo
Baruch Spinoza. [1910]
p. 3.

In Jewish advocate, Boston, Feb. 25, 1910.

NN

D-1-b
1156

Scheffer, W
Spinoza, in een nieuwe gedaante. [1863]
35 p.

"Overdruk uit de Godgeleerde Bijdragen voor 1863."

NjNbS

D-1-b
1157

Schreiber, Emmanuel
Baruch Spinoza. [1887]
423-434 p.

In The Platonist, v. 3, 1887.

SPECIAL COLLECTIONS
SPINOZA
D-1-b
1158

Schwarz, A
Baruch Spinoza. [1892]
[45]-47, [49]-51, [53]-54, [57]-59 p. 30cm.

From Jüdisches Litteratur-Blatt, Jahrg. XXI, nos. 12-16, 1892.

1. Spinoza, Benedictus de, 1632-1677.

D-1-b
1159

[Sears, Edward Isidore] 1819-1876.
Spinoza and his philsophy. [1864]
332-347 p.

In The National quarterly review, v. 9, 1864.

SPECIAL COLLECTIONS
SPINOZA
D-1-b
1160

[Sérouya, Henri] 1895-
Spinoza. [1932]
[257]-313 p. 21cm.

Signed: Henri Sérouya.
From Mercure de France, 1-XII-1932.
Bibliographical footnotes.

1. Spinoza, Benedictus de, 1632-1677.

D-1-b
1161

Sheldon, Walter Lorenzo, 1858-1907.
Benedict Spinoza. [1892]
[3127]-3131, [3135]-3137 p.

In The Open court, v. 6, 1892.

D-1-b 1162

Shemueli, Ephraim, 1908-
[1939] הטרגדיה של ברוך שפינוזה.
449-458, 332-344 p.

Title transliterated: ha-Tragediyah shel Barukh Shpinoza.
In Moznayim, v. 8, no. 4-5, Feb.-Mar. 1939; v. 9, no. 3, July-Aug. 1939.

NNJ

SPECIAL COLLECTIONS SPINOZA
D-1-b 1163

Shemueli, Ephraim
הטרגדיה של ברוך שפינוזה. בתל-אביב, 1939]
[Tel-Aviv, 1939]
449-458 p. 25cm.

Title transliterated: ha-Tragēdīyā shel Bārūkh Shpīnōzā.
From Moznayim, vol. 8, no. 4-5, Feb.-Mar. 1939.

NNC

SPECIAL COLLECTIONS SPINOZA
D-1-b 1164

[Simon, Jules] 1814-1896.
Spinoza. [1843]
[756]-786 p. 24cm.

Signed: Jules Simon.
From Revue des deux mondes, 1 juin, 1843.

1. Spinoza, Benedictus de, 1632-1677.

NNC

SPECIAL COLLECTIONS SPINOZA
D-1-b 1165

Sinn, John
Baruch Spinoza, by John Sinn and Lillian Pushin. [1927]
p. 7. 23cm.

From the Rockdale scroll, vol. 1, no. 2, Purim number, March 1927.

SPECIAL COLLECTIONS SPINOZA
D-1-b 1166

Sokolov, Nahum, 1859-1936.
ברוך שפינוזה. לונדון, תרפ"ז.
[London, 1927]
13 pts. 33cm.

Title transliterated: Bārūkh Shpīnōzā.
From "Haolam", vol. 15, no. 9-22, March 4-June 3, 1927.

1. Spinoza, Benedictus de, 1632-1677.

NNC

D-1-b 1167

Sokolow, Nahum, 1859-1936.
Spinoza the Jew. [1933]
35-44 p.

In Jewish review, London, v. 1, no. 3, 1932-33.

NNJ

SPECIAL COLLECTIONS SPINOZA
D-1-b 1168

Soncino-Gesellschaft der Freunde des Jüdischen Buches, Berlin.
Mitteilungen der Soncino-Gesellschaft, Nr. 7-10, März 1931. [1931]
120 p. 21cm.

Includes references to Spinoza (p. 39-40, 75, 104-105)

NNC

SPECIAL COLLECTIONS SPINOZA
D-1-b 1169

Sorley, William Ritchie, 1855-
Spinoza. London, Pub. for the British Academy by H. Milford, Oxford University Press [1918]
20 p. 24½cm. (The British Academy. Third annual lecture on a mastermind. Henriette Hertz trust)

"From the Proceedings of the British Academy, vol. VIII."

SPECIAL COLLECTIONS SPINOZA
D-1-b 1170

Spinoza. [London, 1927]
4-8 p. 25cm.

From the Jewish Religious Union bulletin, vol. XII, no. 51, April 1927.

1. Spinoza, Benedictus de, 1632-1677.

D-1-b 1171

Spinoza and De Casseres. [1927]
92-93 p.

In Jewish missionary magazine, v. 7, 1927.

DLC

D-1-b
1172

Spinoza. ⌊1877⌋
124-152 p.

In The London quarterly and Holborn review, v. 48, 1877.

NN

SPECIAL COLLECTIONS
SPINOZA
D-1-b
1173

⌊Spillecke, ⌋
Benedikt Spinoza; oder Über Atheismus, Fatalismus und Mystizismus. Eine Vorl. in der Gesellsch. d. Freunde d. Humanität. ⌊1808⌋
30 p. 17cm.

Signed: Spillecke.
From Neue Berlinische Monatschrift, 20. Bd., Julius bis Dezember 1808.

D-1-b
1174

Steinschneider, Moritz, 1816-1907.
Spinoza. ⌊1889⌋
82-83 p.

In Jahrbücher für jüdische Geschichte und Litteratur, 9. Jahrgang, 1889.

D-1-b
1175

Stempels, G J D C
Het eeuwig-vrouwelijke. ⌊1916⌋
296-312 p.

In Tijdschrift voor wijsbegeerte, jaargang 10, 1916.
Includes references to Spinoza.

NN

SPECIAL COLLECTIONS
SPINOZA
D-1-b
1176

⌊Sternheim, Emanuel⌋
Spinoza; an essay. ⌊1907⌋
⌊36⌋-50 p. 25cm.

Signed: Emanuel Sternheim.
From the Monthly review, no. 81, XXVII, 3, June 1907.

D-1-b
1177

Stone, Robert
The lost life of Baruch Spinoza. ⌊1927⌋
p. 1.

In San Antonio Jewish weekly, v. 5, 1927.

NN

SPECIAL COLLECTIONS
SPINOZA
D-1-b
1178

Strauss, Joseph
Essays. 2d ed. London, New York, Walter Scott Publishing Co., 1911.
264 p. ports. 19cm.

Includes an essay "Benedictus Spinoza" (p. ⌊25⌋-72)

D-1-b
1179

Stupnitzky, Saul Isaac, 1876-1942.

ברוך שפינאָזא. ⌊1925⌋
p. 2.

Title transliterated: Barukh Shpinoza.
In Literarishe bleter, v. 1, no. 48, 1925.

NNJ

D-1-b
1180

Szylkarski, Wladimir
Polemika o filosofje Spinozy. ⌊1928⌋
319-322 p.

In Przegląd filozoficzny, 1928, zesz. 3.

NN

D-1-b
1181

Taylor, Alfred Edward, 1869-1945.
Some incoherencies in Spinozism. ⌊1937⌋
137-158, 281-301 p.

In Mind, n. s. v. 46, 1937.

Tönnies, Ferdinand, 1855-1936.
Studie zur Entwicklungsgeschichte des Spinoza.
[1883]
[158]-183, [334]-364 p. 22cm.

Frim Vierteljahrsschrift für wissenschaftliche Philosophie, 7. Jahrgang, 1883.

1. Spinoza, Benedictus de, 1632-1677.

Trezek, Joseph Aryeh
המאסף; או, ערך מלין המלאכותיות,
עם הערות, מאת יוסף אריה טרעצעק.
ווארשא, בדפוס יצחק גאלדמאן, תרמ"ו.
[Warsaw] 1880.
100 p. 17cm.

Title transliterated: Ha-Mĕ'assēf.
Title-page in Hebrew and Russian.
Includes an article on Spinoza (p. 98-100)

Trezek, Joseph Aryeh
המאסף; או, ערך מלין המלאכותיות,
עם הערות, מאת יוסף אריה טרעצעק.
ווארשא, בדפוס יצחק גאלדמאן, תרמ"ו.
[Warsaw] 1886.
100 p. 17cm.

Title transliterated: Ha-Mĕ'assēf.
Title-page in Hebrew and Russian.
Includes an article on Spinoza (p. 98-100)

Vanderbrummer; or, The Spinosist. [1821]
501-508 p.

In Blackwood's Edinburgh magazine, v. 10, 1821.

[Vloten, Johannes van] 1818-1883.
Dr. Spruyt en Spinoza. [1872]
[120]-123 p. 20cm.

From De Levensbode; tijdschrift op onbepaalde tijden, door J. van Vloten, 5. deel.

[Vloten, Johannes van] 1818-1883.
Een vermakelijke uitspraak. [1878]
487-490 p.

Signed: v. Vl.
In De Levensbode, deel 10, 1878.
Includes references to Spinoza.

Vogels, Isidor
Benedictus de Spinoza. [1897]
441-498 p.

In Studien op godsdienstig, wetenschappelijk en letterkundig gebied, jaargang 29, dl. 48, 1897.

[Vulliaud, Paul] 1875-
Spinoza. [1932]
129-130 p. 24cm.

Signed: Paul Vulliaud.
From La Révue juive de Genève, 1re année, no. 3, Décembre 1932.

1. Spinoza, Benedictus de, 1632-1677.

Windelband, Wilhelm, 1848-1915.
Спиноза. [1901]
246-261 p.

Title transliterated: Spinoza.
In Міръ Божій, № 7, 1901.

[Wise, Isaac Mayer] 1819-1900.
Spinoza. [1899]
3 l. 23cm.

"Copied from: The American Israelite, vol. 45, no. 41, p. 4, April 13, 1899."
Typescript.

1. Spinoza, Benedictus de, 1632-1677.

Wolf, Abraham, 1876-
Spinoza. [1927]
19 p. port. 25cm.

"Reprinted from the January number of the Journal of philosophical studies, vol. II, no. 5."

1. Spinoza, Benedictus de, 1632-1677.

Wolf, Abraham, 1876-
Spinoza; summary of an address given in the Liberal Jewish Synagogue on Sunday, November 27th. [1933]
61-62 p. 25cm.

From the Liberal Jewish monthly, vol. IV, no. 8, January, 1933.

1. Spinoza, Benedictus de, 1632-1677.

[Wolfson, Harry Austryn] 1887-
Towards an accurate understanding of Spinoza. [1926]
268-273 p. 25cm.

Signed: H. A. Wolfson.
From the Journal of philosophy, vol. XXIII, no. 10, May 13, 1926.

1. Spinoza, Benedictus de, 1632-1677.

Worms, René, 1869-
Spinoza; conférence faite à la Société des études juives le 27 janvier 1894. [1894]
[xli]-liv p. 25cm.

From Revue des études juives, 1894.

Worms, René, 1869-
Spinoza; conférence faite à la Société des études juives le 27 janvier 1894. [1894]
14 p. 25cm.

Presentation copy to Sir Frederick Pollock, with the author's inscription and signature.
Reprinted from Revue des études juives, 1894.

1. Spinoza, Benedictus de, 1632-1677.

ARTICLES IN ENCYCLOPEDIAS, LEXICONS, ETC.

Alembert, Jean Lerond d', 1717-1783.
Einleitung in die französische Enzyklopädie von 1751 (Discours préliminaire) Hrsg. und erläutert von Eugen Hirschberg. Leipzig, F. Meiner, 1912.
2 v. in 1. 19cm. (Philosophische Bibliothek, Bd. 140a-b)

Includes a section on Spinoza (v. 2, p. 114-122)

[Artaud]
Spinoza (Baruch, ou comme il traduisit lui-même ce nom, Bénédict) [1844]
445-448 p.

Signed: A-D.
From Encyclopédie des gens du monde, t. 21, 1844.

[Baeumker, Clemens] 1853-1924.
Spinoza. [1911]
1338-1356 col.

From Staatslexikon, 4. Aufl., 4. Bd., 1911.

Barral, Pierre, abbé, d. 1772.
Dictionnaire historique, littéraire et critique, contenant une idée abrégée de la vie & des ouvrages des hommes illustres en tout genre, de tout tems & de tout pays. Avignon, 1758-59.
6 v.

Includes an article on Spinoza (v. 6, p. 353-354)

D-1-c
1201

Bauer, Ludwig
Spinoza (auch d'Espinosa), Baruch de. [1937]
726-728 col.

From Lexikon für Theologie und Kirche, v. 9, 1937.

NNUT

D-1-c
1202

Bertrand, abbé
Dictionnaire universel, historique et comparatif, de toutes les religions du monde ... Rédigé par m. l'abbé Bertrand. Paris, J.-P. Migne, 1848-58.
4 v. (Encyclopédie théologique, t. 24-27)

Includes an article "Spinosisme" (v. 4, col. 627-629)

NNUT

SPECIAL COLLECTIONS
SPINOZA

D-1-c
1203

Brockhaus' Konversations-Lexikon.
Conversations-Lexikon; allgemeine deutsche Real-Encyklopädie. 12. umgearb., verb. und verm. Aufl. 13. Bd., Salz bis Stabilität. Leipzig, F. A. Brockhaus, 1879.
1020 p. 26cm.

Includes an article on Spinoza (p. 956-958)

NNC

D-1-c
1204

Brunschvicg, Léon, 1869-1944.
Spinoza. [1901]
391-399 p.

From La Grande encyclopédie, v. 30 [1901]

NNC

D-1-c
1205

Chambers, Ephraim, d. 1740.
Cyclopaedia; or, An universal dictionary of arts and sciences; containing an explication of the terms ... in the several arts ... and the several sciences, human and divine. The second edition, corrected and amended with some additions. London, Midwinter, 1738.
2 v. illus., plates, facsims., tables, diagrs. 43 cm.

Vol. 2 includes an article "Spinozism".

D-1-c
1206

Chambers, Ephraim, d. 1740.
Dizionario universale delle arti e delle scienze ... di Efraimo Chambers. Traduzione ... dall'inglese. Venezia, G. Pasquali, 1748-49.
v. 1-2, 4-5, 7-9.

Includes an article "Spinozismo" (v. 8, p. 132-163)

OCH.

SPECIAL COLLECTIONS
SPINOZA

D-1-c
1207

Chambers's encyclopaedia; a dictionary of universal knowledge for the people, with maps and numerous wood engravings. Rev. ed. unaltered and unabridged. Vol. VII. New York, P. F. Collier [1876]
780 p. illus. 29cm.

Includes an article on Spinoza (p. 362-363)

D-1-c
1208

[Chaudon, Louis Mayeul] 1737-1817.
Anti-Dictionnaire philosophique, pour servir de commentaire & de correctif au Dictionnaire philosophique ... Quatrieme édition corrigée, considérablement augmentée & entiérement refondue ... A Paris, Chez Saillant & Nyon, 1775.
2 v.

Includes an article on Spinoza (v. 2, p. 390-393)

D-1-c
1209

[Chaudon, Louis Mayeul] 1737-1817, ed.
Nouveau dictionnaire historique, ou Histoire abregée de tous les hommes qui se sont fait un nom par le génie, les talens, les vertus, les erreurs, &c. depuis le commencement du monde jusqu'à nos jours ... Par une société de gens-de-lettres. 4. éd., enrichie d'augmentations nombreuses & intéressantes, & purgée de toutes les fautes qui défiguroient les précédentes ... Caen, G. Le Roy, 1779.
6 v. 20 cm.

Includes an article on Spinoza (v. 6, p. 400-402)

D-1-c
1210

Chauffepié, Jacques Georges de, 1702-1786.
Nouveau dictionnaire historique et critique pour servir de supplement ou de continuation au Dictionnaire historique et critique de Mr. Pierre Bayle. Amsterdam, Z. Chatelain, 1750-56.
4 v. 40 cm.

[Chaudon, Louis Mayeul], 1737-1817, ed.
Nouveau dictionnaire historique; ou Histoire abrégée de tous les hommes qui se sont fait un nom par des talens, des vertus, des forfaits, des erreurs, &c. depuis le commencement du monde jusqu'a nos jours ... Avec des tables chronologiques pour réduire en corps d'histoire les articles répandus dans ce dictionnaire. Par une société de gens-de-lettres. Sixiéme édition, revue, corrigée, & considérablement augmentée ... A Caen, Chez G. Le Roy, 1785-91 [v. 1, 1786]
9 v. 20cm.

CONTINUED ON NEXT CARD

[Chaudon, Louis Mayeul], 1737-1817, ed. Nouveau dictionnaire historique. 1785-91.
[v. 1, 1786] (Card 2)

Vol. 9 has imprint: A Lyon, Chez Bruyset freres, 1791.
"Tome IX, tiré des editions de 1786 & 1789, & servant de supplément aux précédentes editions." Half-title to v. 9 reads: Troisieme supplément au Nouveau dictionnaire historique.
Includes an article on Spinoza (v. 8, p. 174-177)

The Columbia encyclopedia ... compiled and edited at Columbia university, Clarke F. Ansley, editor in chief. New York, Columbia university press, 1935.
3 p. l., 1949 p. 31 cm.

Includes an article on Spinoza (p. 1671)

1. Encyclopedias and dictionaries. I. Ansley, Clarke Fisher, 1869-1939, ed. II. Columbia university.

Compendiöses Gelehrten-Lexicon, darinnen die Gelehrten, als Fürsten und Staats-Leute, die in der Literatur erfahren, Theologi, Prediger, Juristen, Politici, Medici, Philologi, Philosophi ... kurtz und deutlich nach alphabetischer Ordnung beschrieben werden ... Nebst einer Vorrede Hn. D. Joh. Burchard Menckens ... Leipzig, Bey Johann Friedrich Gleditsch und Sohn, 1715.
[14] p., 2682 col., [3] p. plates. 22cm.

Includes an article on Spinoza (col. 2160-2161)

Conversations-Lexicon, oder Encyclopädisches Handwörterbuch für gebildete Stände. Neunter Band. Seetz bis Tiz. Stuttgart, A. F. Macklot, 1818.
840 p. 19cm.

Includes an article on Spinoza (p. 300-305)

Creighton, James Edwin, 1861-1924.
Spinoza. [1907]
[3] p. 27 cm.

From The Americana; a universal reference library, v. 14 [1907]

Dennert, F ed.
Dennert's Konversations-Lexikon; ein Nachschlage- und Belehrungsbuch für alle Fälle und Lagen des täglichen Lebens. Unter Mitwirkung von zahlreichen Fachgelehrten. Neue revidierte Ausg. Berlin, P. I. Oestergaard [191-?]
v. 2. 26cm.

Includes a paragraph on Spinoza (v. 2, col. 2292)

Dictionnaire des hommes et choses remarquables.
[336] p. 16cm.

Manuscript. Apparently compiled at various times, about 1765?
Most articles in German, some in French.
Includes an article on Spinoza (p. [244-245])
Blank leaves left between some sections.

Dunin-Borkowski, Stanislaus, Graf von, 1864-1934.
Spinoza (d'Espinosa, Despinoza), Benedict. [1912]
217-220 p.

From The Catholic encyclopedia, v. 14 [c1912]

Eisler, Rudolf, 1873-
Philosophen-Lexikon; Leben, Werke und Lehren der Denker. Berlin, E. S. Mittler, 1912.
v, 889 p. 25cm.

Includes an article on Spinoza (p. 694-705)

D-1-c
1221

Eisler, Rudolf, 1873–
Wörterbuch der philosophischen begriffe und ausdrücke, quellenmässig bearb. von dr. Rudolf Eisler. Berlin, E. S. Mittler und sohn, 1899.
vi, 956 p. 23cm.
Includes a paragraph "Spinozismus" (p. 723)

1. Philosophy—Dictionaries.

G—1009

D-1-c
1226

Encyclopédie, ou Dictionnaire universel raisonné des connoissances humaines. Mis en ordre par M. de Felice. Yverdon, 1770-80.
58 v.

MH

D-1-c
1222

Encyclopaedia Perthensis; or Universal dictionary of knowledge ... Perth, Mitchell, 1816.
23 v.

Includes an article on Spinoza (v. 21, p. 291-293)

MH

D-1-c
1227

Encyclopédie méthodique. Philosophie ancienne et moderne. Par M. Naigeon. A Paris, Chez Panckoucke, 1791-[94?]
3 v. 27cm.

Vol. 3 has imprint: A Paris, Chez H. Agasse, l'an deuxième de la République Française.
Includes articles "Spinosisme ou philosophie de Spinosa" (v. 3, p. 566-581) and "Spinosistes" (v. 3, p. 581) the latter by Diderot.

D-1-c
1223

Encyclopaedisch handboek van het moderne denken, onder redactie van A. C. Elsbach [et al.] Arnhem, Van Loghum Slaterus, 1931.
2 v. 28cm.

Includes references to Spinoza.
Contains bibliographies.

D-1-c
1228

Everett, Walter Goodnow, 1860-1937.
Spinoza, Benedict (1632-1677). [1921] 424-425 p.

From Mathews, Shailer, ed. A dictionary of religion and ethics, 1921.

D-1-c
1224

Encyclopédie, ou Dictionnaire raisonné des sciences, des arts et des métiers, par une société de gens de lettres. Mis en ordre & publié par M. Diderot; & quant à la partie mathematique, par M. d'Alembert ... A Paris, Chez Briasson [etc.] 1751-65.
17 v. fold. tab. 40 cm.

Includes articles "Spinosa, philosophie de" and "Spinosiste" (v. 15, p. 463-474)

D-1-c
1229

Franck, Adolphe, 1808-1893, ed.
Dictionnaire des sciences philosophiques. Par une société de professeurs de philosophie [sous la direction de M. Ad. Franck] Paris, Hachette, 1844-52.
6 v. 24 cm.

Includes an article on Spinoza (v. 6, p. 729-763)

D-1-c
1225

Encyclopédie, ou Dictionnaire raisonné des sciences, des arts et des métiers, par une société de gens de lettres. Mis en ordre & publié par M. Diderot; & quant à la partie mathématique, par M. d'Alembert. Edition exactement conforme à celle de Pellet ... A Lausanne et à Berne, Chez les Sociétés typographiques, 1780-82 [v. 1, 1781]
36 v. ports, fold. tables. 22 cm.

Includes a section on Spinoza (v. 3, p. 809-828) in article "Atheisme"; and articles "Spinosa" and "Spinosiste" (v. 31, p. 619)

D-1-c
1230

Franck, Adolphe, 1808-1893, ed.
Dictionnaire des sciences philosophiques, par une société de professeurs et de savants, sous la direction de M. Ad. Franck. 2. éd. Paris, Librairie Hachette, 1875.
xii, 1806 p. 25cm.

In double columns.
Includes an article on Spinoza (p. 1652-1668)
Bibliographies at end of many articles.

D-1-c
1231

Ginzburg, Benjamin, 1898-
Spinoza, Baruch. [1934]
299-301 p.

From Encyclopaedia of the social sciences, v. 14 [c1934]

D-1-c
1232

Goebel, Julius, 1857-1931.
Spinoza, Baruch de. [1891]
2228-2230 p.

From Schaff, Philip, ed. A religious encyclopaedia, v. 4. New York, Funk & Wagnalls, 1891.

D-1-c
1233

[Gottheil, Richard James Horatio] 1862-1936.
Levi ben Gershon. [1915]
898-900 p.

From Encyclopaedia of religion and ethics, v. 7, 1915.
Includes a reference to Spinoza (p. 898)

D-1-c
1234

[Guzzo, Augusto] 1894-
Spinoza, Benedetto. [1936]
381-384 p. port.

From Enciclopedia italiana di scienze, lettere ed arti, v. 32, 1936.

D-1-c
1235

Harris, William Torrey, 1835-1909.
Spinoza, (Baruch) Benedict. [1895]
670-671 p. 28 cm.

From Johnson's universal cyclopaedia; new ed., v. 7, 1895.

D-1-c
1236

[Holmes, George Frederick] 1820-1897.
Spinoza, Benedict de (Baruch). [1880]
934-940 p.

From McClintock, John. Cyclopaedia of Biblical, theological, and ecclesiastical literature, v. 9, 1880.

D-1-c
1237

[Jacobs, Joseph] 1854-1916.
Spinoza, Baruch (Benedict de Spinoza) [1905]
511-521 p. illus., col. port., facsim. 28 cm.

From The Jewish encyclopedia, v. 11. New York and London, Funk & Wagnalls, 1901-06.

SPECIAL COLLECTIONS
SPINOZA
D-1-c
1238

Jacobs, Joseph, 1854-1916.
The Jewish encyclopedia; a guide to its contents, an aid to its use, by Joseph Jacobs, D. LITT., revising editor. New York and London, Funk & Wagnalls company, 1906.
xviii, 162 p. illus. 18½ᶜᵐ.

Includes references to Spinoza (p. 75-76) and his portrait (p. 95)

1. The Jewish cyclopedia.

6—12175
Library of Congress DS102.8.J7
[45f1]

SPECIAL COLLECTIONS
SPINOZA
D-1-c
1239

Jöcher, Christian Gottlieb, 1694-1758.
Compendiöses Gelehrten-Lexicon, darinne die Gelehrten aller Stände so wohl männ-als weiblichen Geschlechts, welche vom Anfang der Welt bis auf jetzige Zeit gelebt ... Nach dem Entwurff des sel. D. Joh. Burckh. Menckens in alphabetischer Ordnung beschrieben werden. In zwey Theilen. Die dritte Auflage heraus gegeben von Christian Gottlieb Jöcher ... Leipzig, bey Johann Friedrich Gleditschens seel. Sohn, 1733.
2 v. front. 22cm.

CONTINUED ON NEXT CARD

SPECIAL COLLECTIONS
SPINOZA
D-1-c
1240

Jöcher, Christian Gottlieb, 1694-1758. Compendiöses Gelehrten-Lexicon ... 1733. (Card 2)

In double columns.
Includes an article on Spinoza (v. 2, col. 1300-1301)

D-1-c
1241

[Kellett, Ernest Edward] 1864-
Spinoza. [1921]
768-784 p.

From Encyclopaedia of religion and ethics, v. 11, 1921.

D-1-c
1242

Kilpatrick, William Heard, 1871-
Spinoza, Baruch de. [1913]
p. 403. 28 cm.

From Monroe, Paul, ed. A cyclopedia of education, v. 5, 1913.

D-1-c
1243

[Lewes, George Henry] 1817-1878.
Spinoza.- Spinozism. [1842]
350-353 p. 30 cm.

From The Penny cyclopaedia of the Society for the Diffusion of Useful Knowledge, v. 22, 1842.

D-1-c
1244

[Loewe, Herbert] 1882-
Judaism. [1915]
581-609 p.

From Encyclopaedia of religion and ethics, v. 7, 1915.
Includes a reference to Spinoza (p. 606)

D-1-c
1245

The London encyclopaedia, or Universal dictionary of science, art, literature, and practical mechanics. By the original editor of the Encyclopaedia metropolitana [T. Curtis] assisted by professional and other gentlemen. London, T. Tegg, 1829.
22 v.

Includes an article on Spinoza (v. 21, p. 12-14)

NN

D-1-c
1246

[McGiffert, Arthur Cushman] 1861-1933.
Immanence. [1915]
167-172 p.

From Encyclopaedia of religion and ethics, v. 7, 1915.
Includes a reference to Spinoza (p. 169)

SPECIAL COLLECTIONS
SPINOZA
D-1-c
1247

Moreri, Louis, 1643-1680.
Le grand dictionaire historique ou Le mélange curieux de l'histoire sacrée et profane, qui contient en abregé l'histoire fabuleuse des dieux & des heroes de l'artiquité payenne: les vies et les actions remarquables des patriarches; des juges; des rois de juifs; des papes ... des empereurs; des rois, des princes illustres; & des grands capitaines; l'établissement et le progrés des ordres religieux & militaires; & la vie de leur fondateurs: les genealogies de plusieurs familles illustres de France, &

CONTINUED ON NEXT CARD

SPECIAL COLLECTIONS
SPINOZA
D-1-c
1248

Moreri, Louis, 1643-1680. Le grand dictionaire historique ... (Card 2)

d'autres païs: la description des empires ... l'histoire des conciles generaux & particuliers, sous le nom des lieux où ils ont été tenus. Le tout enrichi des remarques, de dissertations & de recherches curieuses ... tirées de differents auteurs, & sur tout du Dictionaire critique de M. Bayle. Par Mre Louis Morery ... Nouv. et derniere ed. rev., cor. et augm. Paris, Chez D. Mariette, 1707.
4 v. 40cm.

CONTINUED ON NEXT CARD

SPECIAL COLLECTIONS
SPINOZA
D-1-c
1249

Moreri, Louis, 1643-1680. Le grand dictionaire historique ... (Card 3)

Includes an article on Spinoza (v. 4, p. 663)

---- Supplement aux anciennes editions du Dictionnaire historique de Moreri. Tiré de l'edition de l'an 1712. Paris, Chez J. B. Coignard, Imprimeur & Libraire ordinaire du roy & de l'Académie française, 1714.
[4], 935, [1] p. 40cm.

D-1-c
1250

Moréri, Louis, 1643-1680.
Le grand dictionnaire historique, ou Le mélange curieux de l'histoire sacrée et profane ... par m[re] Louis Moréri ... Nouv. éd. dans laquelle on a refondu les supplémens de m. l'abbé Goujet. Le tout rev., cor. & augm. par m. Drouet. Paris, Les libraires associés, 1759.
10 v. port. 41 cm.

Includes an article on Spinoza (v. 9, p. 541-542)

D-1-c
1251

Moréri, Louis, 1643-1680.
The great historical, geographical and poetical dictionary; being a curious miscellany of sacred and profane history ... Collected from the best historians, chronologers, and lexicographers ... but more specially out of Lewis Morery, his 6th edition corrected and enlarged by Monsieur Le Clerk ... Now done into English ... London, Printed for H. Rhodes, 1694.
623 l. 40 cm.

DLC Includes an article on Spinoza.

D-1-c
1252

Moréri, Louis, 1643-1680.
The great historical, geographical, genealogical and poetical dictionary; being a curious miscellany of sacred and prophane history ... Collected from the best historians, chronologers, and lexicographers ... but more specially out of Lewis Morery, his 8th ed. cor. and enl. by Monsieur Le Clerc ... The 2d ed. rev., cor. and enl. to the year 1688; by Jer. Collier. London, Printed for H. Rhodes, 1701.
2 v. port. 40 cm.

Volume 2 includes an article on Spinoza.

D-1-c
1253

Neu-vermehrtes historisch- und geographisches allgemeines Lexicon, in welchem das Leben, die Thaten, und andere Merckwürdigkeiten deren Patriarchen, Propheten ... vornehmer Gelehrten, und anderer sonst in denen Geschichten berühmter Männern ... zusammen gezogen ... Zweyte Auflage. Mehr Bericht von allem ist zu finden in denen Vorreden, von Jacob Christoff Iselin ... Basel, Brandmüller, 1728-29.
4 v. 36cm.

Includes an article on Spinoza (v. 4, p. 470-471)

D-1-c
1254

Rees, Abraham, 1743-1825.
The cyclopaedia; or, Universal dictionary of arts, sciences, and literature. By Abraham Rees with the assistance of eminent professional gentlemen. London, Longman, Hurst, Rees, Orme & Brown, 1819.
39 v. port., illus. 28 cm.

Vol. 33 includes an article "Spinozism".

SPECIAL COLLECTIONS
SPINOZA
D-1-c
1255

Reichls philosophischer Almanach auf das Jahr 1923. Hrsg. von Paul Feldkeller. Darmstadt, O. Reichl, 1923.
261 p. 20cm.

Includes references to Spinoza.

SPECIAL COLLECTIONS
SPINOZA
D-1-c
1256

Reichls philosophischer Almanach auf das Jahr 1924. Immanuel Kant zum Gedächtnis, 22. April 1924. Mit einem Jugendbildnis Immanuel Kants, gezeichnet um das Jahr 1755 von der Gräfin Charlotte Amalia Keyserling, geb. Gräfin Truchsess-Waldburg. Hrsg. von Paul Feldkeller. Darmstadt, O. Reichl, 1924.
479 p. port. 21cm.

Includes references to Spinoza.
Bibliographical footnotes.

D-1-c
1257

Seth Pringle Pattison, Andrew, 1856-1931.
Spinoza, Baruch. [1911]
687-691 p.

From The Encyclopaedia Britannica, 11th ed., v. 25, 1911.

SPECIAL COLLECTIONS
SPINOZA
D-1-c
1258

Spinoza. [1798]
693-697 p. 29cm.

From Encyclopaedia; or, A dictionary of arts, sciences, and miscellaneous literature, v. 17. Philadelphia, T. Dobson, 1798.

1. Spinoza, Benedictus de, 1632-1677.

D-1-c
1259

Stewart, Dugald, 1753-1828.
Dissertation first: exhibiting a general view of the progress of metaphysical and ethical philosophy, since the revival of letters in Europe. [1853]
289 p.

From Encyclopaedia britannica, 8th ed., v. 1, 1853.
Includes sections on Spinoza (p. 144-147, 264-266)

D-1-c
1260

Thomsen, Anton
Spinoza. [1906]
510-513 p.

From Salmonsens store illustrerede konversationsleksikon, v. 16.

MH

D-1-c 1261

Universal cyclopædia and atlas. A new ed. under direction of Charles Kendall Adams ... editor-in-chief, assisted by a corps of associate editors ... A newly rev. and enl. ed. Rossiter Johnson ... editor of revision ... New York, D. Appleton and co., 1901.

12 v. illus., col. pl., maps, plans. 28½cm.

Includes an article on Spinoza (v. 11, p. 62-63)

1. Encyclopedias and dictionaries. I. *Johnson, Rossiter, 1840-1931, ed. II. Adams, Charles Kendall, 1835-1902. III. Title.

Library of Congress AE5.U5 2—1144
—— Copy 2.
Copyright A 19572, 19583 [a37e1]

D-1-c 1262

[Webb, Clement Charles Julian] 1865-1954.
Idea. [1915]
81-86 p.

From Encyclopaedia of religion and ethics, v. 7, 1915.
Includes a reference to Spinoza (p. 85)

D-1-c 1263

[Wolf, Abraham] 1876-
Spinoza. [1929]
231-239 p.

From The Encyclopaedia britannica, v. 21. 14th ed. [c1929]

D-1-c 1264

Zedler, Johann Heinrich, 1706-1763.
Grosses vollständiges universal Lexikon aller Wissenschaften und Künste, welche bisshero durch menschlichen Verstand und Witz erfunden und verbessert worden ... Nebst einer Vorrede, von der Einrichtung dieses mühsamen und grossen Wercks Joh. Pet. von Ludewig ... Halle, J. H. Zedler, 1732-50.
64 v. in 43. ports. 36 cm.

Includes articles on Spinoza and Spinozism (v. 39, col. 75-86, 88-94)

D-2 CHAPTERS OR SECTIONS IN HISTORIES OF PHILOSOPHY

D-2 1265

Adam, Charles Ernest, 1857-
Études sur les principaux philosophes. Nouv. éd., complétée par M. Gérard-Varet. Paris, Hachette, 1903.
xvi, 575 p.

Includes a chapter on Spinoza (p. 249-272)

MH

SPECIAL COLLECTIONS
SPINOZA

D-2 1266

Adamson, Robert, 1852-1902.
The development of modern philosophy, with other lectures and essays, by Robert Adamson ... ed. by W. R. Sorley ... Edinburgh and London, W. Blackwood and sons, 1903.
2 v. front. (port.) 23cm.

CONTENTS.—vol. I. Preface. Memorial introduction. Bibliography. The development of modern philosophy: Introduction. pt. I. Descartes and intellectualism. pt. II. English empiricism. pt. III. The philosophy of Kant. pt. IV. Post-Kantian idealism. pt. V. Suggestions towards a theory of knowledge based on the Kantian.—vol. II. pt. I. Occasional addresses and essays: Inaugural address in the University of Glasgow. Giordano Bruno. Psychology and epistemology. Kant's views of psychology. Philosophy and the social problem. The basis of morality. The regeneration of Germany. pt. II. Principles of psychology: A. General analysis. B. The psychology of thinking. Index.

1. Philosophy, Modern—Hist. I. Sorley, William Ritchie, 1855-1935, ed.

Library of Congress B791.A3 3—12282
[a37k1] 190.4

D-2 1267

Adamson, Robert, 1852-1902.
The development of modern philosophy with other lectures and essays, edited by W. R. Sorley. Edinburgh, Blackwood, 1930.
364 p.

DLC

D-2 1268

Alexander, Archibald Browning Drysdale, 1855-1931.
A short history of philosophy. 3d ed., rev. and enl. Glasgow, Jackson, Wylie, 1934.
xv, 648 p. 21 cm.

DLC

SPECIAL COLLECTIONS
SPINOZA

D-2 1269

Alexander, Archibald Browning Drysdale, 1855-
A short history of philosophy. 2d ed., rev. and enl. Glasgow, J. Maclehose and Sons, 1908.
xxvi, 601 p. 22cm.

Includes references to Spinoza.
Bibliography: p. [xvii]-xxvi.

SPECIAL COLLECTIONS
SPINOZA
193Sp4
DA636

D-2 1270

Allgemeine Geschichte der Philosophie, von Wilh. Wundt, Herm. Oldenberg [et al.] Berlin, B. G. Teubner, 1909.
viii, 572 p. 26cm. (Die Kultur der Gegenwart, T. 1, Abt. V)

Includes a section on Spinoza (p. 434-442) and other references to him.

Allgemeine Geschichte der Philosophie; von Wilhelm Wundt [et al.] 2., verm. und verb. Aufl. Leipzig, B. G. Teubner, 1923.
ix, 620 p. 26cm. (Die Kultur der Gegenwart, Teil I, Abteilung V)

Includes a section on Spinoza (p. 483-490) and other references to him.
Includes bibliographies.

Alpern, Henry, 1895-
The march of philosophy. New York, Dial Press, 1934.
xviii, 381 p. ports.

Includes a chapter on Spinoza and other references to him.

Ast, Friedrich, 1778-1841.
Grundriss einer Geschichte der Philosophie. Landshut, J. Thomann, 1807.
xvi, 491 p. 20cm.

Includes a section on Spinoza (p. 369-378)
Includes bibliographies.

Ast, Friedrich, 1778-1841.
Hauptmomente der Geschichte der Philosophie. München, A. Weber, 1829.
iv, 75 p. 21cm.

Includes a section on Spinoza (p. 61-62)

Aster, Ernst von, 1880-
Geschichte der neueren Philosophie. [1925] 375-548 p.

From Dessoir, Max, ed. Lehrbuch der Philosophie, Bd. 1 [1925]
Includes a section on Spinoza.

Aster, Ernst von, 1880-
Geschichte der Philosophie. 2., verb. Aufl. Mit einem Anhang: Wie studiert man Philosophie? Leipzig, A. Kröner Verlag [1935]
xxiii, 468 p. 18cm. (Kröners Taschenausgabe. Bd. 108)

Contains a section on Spinoza's philosophy (p. 213-217)
Bibliography: p. [431]-441.

Aster, Ernst von, 1880-
Grosse Denker; unter Mitwirkung von E. von Aster, O. Baensch [u. a.] ... hrsg. von E. von Aster. Leipzig, Quelle & Meyer [1911]
2 v. ports. 24cm.

Includes a chapter "Spinoza" by Otto Baensch (v. 2, p. [1]-36)
Contains bibliographies.

Barbe, Eustache, b. 1802.
Cours élémentaire de philosophie à l'usage des établissements d'éducation ... comprenant l'histoire de la philosophie. 2. éd. Paris, 1871.

Bauch, Bruno, 1877-
Immanuel Kant. 2. verb. Aufl. Berlin, Göschen, 1916.
209 p. 16cm. (Geschichte der Philosophie, V)

Sammlung Göschen, Bd. 536.
Bibliography: p. [5]-6.

Bauch, Bruno, 1877-
Neuere Philosophie bis Kant. 2. verb. und erweiterte Aufl. Berlin, Göschen, 1913.
178 p. 16cm. (Geschichte der Philosophie, IV)

Sammlung Göschen, 394.
Includes a section on Spinoza (p. 92-106)
Bibliography: p. [3]-4.

Bauch, Bruno, 1877–
... Neuere philosophie bis Kant, von dr. Bruno Bauch ... 3., verb. aufl. Berlin und Leipzig, W. de Gruyter & co., 1919.
178, [1] p. 16cm. (Geschichte der philosophie. IV)
Sammlung Göschen. 394.
"Literatur": p. [3]–4.
Includes a section on Spinoza (p. 92-106)

1. Philosophy, Modern.

Bauer, Wilhelm
Geschichte der Philosophie für gebildete Leser, zugleich als Einleitung in das Studium der Philosophie. Halle, Schwetschke, 1863.
viii, 374 p. 22cm.

Includes a section on Spinoza (p. 184-194)
Original paper covers bound in.

Behn, Siegfried, 1884-
Die Wahrheit im Wandel der Weltanschauung; eine kritische Geschichte der metaphysischen Philosophie. Berlin, F. Dümmler, 1924.
321 p. 24cm.

Includes a section "Der pantheïstische Monismus (Baruch Spinoza)", p. 209-215.

Benn, Alfred William, 1843–1915.
The history of English rationalism in the nineteenth century, by Alfred William Benn ... London, New York [etc.] Longmans, Green, and co., 1906.
2 v. 22½ cm.
"List of officers referred to": v. 1, p. xxi–xxviii.
Includes a section on Spinoza (v. 1, p. 94-103) and other references to him.

1. Philosophy, English. 2. Rationalism.

Benn, Alfred William, 1843-1915.
History of modern philosophy. Issued for the Rationalist Press Association, Limited. London, Watts, 1912.
v, 154 p. front., ports. 19 cm. (The history of science series)

Includes a section on Spinoza with a portrait (p. 45-57) and other references to him.

Bierens de Haan, Johannes Diderik, 1866-1943.
Hoofdfiguren der geschiedenis van het wijsgeerig denken. (Tijdperk van Cartesius tot Kant) 2e druk. Haarlem, De erven F. Bohn, 1927.
247 p.

Includes a chapter on Spinoza (p. 20-86)

Bernays, Jacob, 1824-1881.
Gesammelte Abhandlungen, hrsg. von H. Usener. Berlin, Hertz, 1885.
2 v. 23cm.

Includes references to Spinoza.
"Chronologische Uebersicht über Jacob Bernays' schriftstellerische Thätigkeit": v. 1, p. [xi]-xvii.
"Verzeichnis des an die K. Universitäts-Bibliothek zu Bonn übergegangenen handschriftlichen Nachlasses von Jacob Bernays": v. 1, p. [xviii]-xxiv.

Bernfeld, Simon, 1860-1940.
בני עליה; קבץ מונוגרפיות. תל-
אביב, הוצאת "דביר",

[Tel-Aviv, "Dvir", 1931]
v. 2. 23cm.

Title transliterated: Bĕnē ʻAlīyā.
Includes a chapter on Spinoza (v. 2, p. [73]-129)

Bernfeld, Simon, 1860-1940.
דעת אלהים; תולדות הפלוסופיא
הדתית בישראל, מאת שמעון ברנפלד.
ווארשא, הוצ' חברת "אחיאסף". תרנ"ז-
[Warsaw] 1897-
v. 1. 21cm.

Title transliterated: Daʻath Ĕlōhīm.
Includes a chapter on Spinoza (p. 521-550).
Title-page in Hebrew and Russian.

Bertram, Johann Friedrich, 1699-1741.
Johann Friderich Bertrams ... Einleitung in die philosophische Wissenschaften, darinn von derselben Namen, Ursprung, Art, Eintheilung ... Gebrauch und Missbrauch wie auch Historie kurtze Nachricht gegeben wird. Braunschweig, Zu finden bey Simon Jacob Rengern, 1727.
[10], [3]-368 p. 17cm.

Includes a paragraph on Spinoza (p. 350-351) and other references to him.

D-2 1291

Blakey, Robert, 1795-1878.
History of the philosophy of mind: embracing the opinions of all writers on mental science from the earliest period to the present time. London, Longman, Brown, Green and Longmans, 1850.
4 v. 23 cm.

Includes two chapters on Spinoza (v. 2, p. 355-384, 455-460) and other references to him.

NN

SPECIAL COLLECTIONS SPINOZA D-2 1296

Bowen, Francis, 1811-1890.
Modern philosophy, from Descartes to Schopenhauer and Hartmann. New York, Scribner, Armstrong and Co., 1877.
xi, 484 p. 24cm.

Includes a chapter on Spinoza.

SPECIAL COLLECTIONS SPINOZA D-2 1292

Blücher, Max
Philosophen: Plato, Descartes, Spinoza, Kant, Schopenhauer. Leipzig, G. Weigel [1925?]
79 p. ports. 17cm. (Führende Männer, Bd. XI)

SPECIAL COLLECTIONS SPINOZA D-2 1297

Brasch, Moritz, 1843-1895.
Die Klassiker der Philosophie, von den frühesten griechischen Denkern bis auf die Gegenwart. Eine gemeinfassliche historische Darstellung ihrer Weltanschauung nebst einer Auswahl aus ihren Schriften von Moritz Brasch. Leipzig, Gressner & Schramm [1884-85]
3 v. (viii, 2720 p.) ports. 23cm.

Includes an essay on Spinoza and selections from his Ethica and Tractatus politicus in Auerbach's translation (v. 2, p. [893]-972)

SPECIAL COLLECTIONS SPINOZA D-2 1293

Bouillier, Francisque Cyrille, 1813–1899.
Histoire de la philosophie cartésienne, par Francisque Bouillier ... Paris, Durand; [etc., etc.] 1854.
2 v. 21cm.

Includes five chapters on Spinoza (p. [299]-408) and other references to him.

1. Descartes, René, 1596–1650.

Library of Congress B1873.B8 11—16423 [31d1]

SPECIAL COLLECTIONS SPINOZA D-2 1298

Bréhier, Émile, 1876-
Histoire de la philosophie. Tome II: La philosophie moderne. I. Le dix-septième siècle. Paris, F. Alcan, 1929.
314 p. 25cm.

Includes a chapter on Spinoza.
Original paper covers bound in.
Bibliography at end of each chapter.

NNUT D-2 1294

Bouillier, Francisque Cyrille, 1813-1899.
Histoire et critique de la révolution cartésienne. Lyon, L. Boitel, 1852.
vii, 448 p. 22 cm.

Includes a section on Spinoza (p. 201-235) and other references to him.

D-2 1299

Brockdorff, Cay Ludwig Georg Conrad, Baron von, 1874-
Die Geschichte der Philosophie und das Problem ihrer Begreiflichkeit. Mit 1 Tafel und vielen Figuren im Text sowie einem Schopenhauerschen Facsimile. 2., stark verm. Aufl. Osterwieck, A. W. Zickfeldt, 1908.
xx, 154 p. illus. 24 cm.

Includes references to Spinoza (p. 97-116)

MH

D-2 1295

Boutroux, Émile, 1845-1921.
La philosophie allemande au XVIIe siècle. Cours professé à la Sorbonne en 1887-1888. Les prédécesseurs de Leibniz: Bacon, Descartes, Hobbes, Spinoza, Malebranche, Locke, et la philosophie de Leibniz. Paris, Vrin, 1929.
242 p.

NNUT

SPECIAL COLLECTIONS SPINOZA D-2 1300

Brucker, Jakob, 1696-1770.
Erste Anfangsgründe der philosophischen Geschichte, als ein Auszug seiner grössern Wercke herausgegeben von Jacob Brucker. Zweyte Ausgabe. Ulm, bey Daniel Bartholomäi und Sohn, 1751.
[8], 554, [28] p.

Includes a section on Spinoza (p. 520-523)

Brucker, Jakob, 1696-1770.
Iakob Bruckers Eerste beginselen van de hisrorie [!] der filozofie, uit 't Hoogduitsch vertaeld door A. de Stoppelaar, en uitgegeven door Iakobus de Vos ... te Utrecht, By Gisbert Tiemon van Paddenburg en Abraham van Paddenburg, 1778.
[30], 884, 52 p. 23cm.

Includes a section on Spinoza (p. 840-843)

Brulez, Lucien, 1891-
... Holländische philosophie. Breslau, F. Hirt, 1926.
132 p. incl. illus., ports. 19½cm. (Added t.-p.: Jedermanns bücherei ... Abt.: Philosophie ...)
"Literatur": p. [117]-121.
Includes a chapter on Spinoza (p. 82-104) and other references to him.

1. Philosophy—Hist.—Netherlands. I. Title.

Brucker, Jakob, 1696-1770.
Iacobi Brvckeri ... Historia critica philosophiae a mvndi incvnabvlis ad nostram vsqve aetatem dedvcta. Lipsiae, Literis et impensis Bern. Christoph. Breitkopf, 1742-44.
4 v. in 5. port. 24cm.

Includes a section on Spinoza (v. 4², p. 682-706) and other references to him.
Bibliographical footnotes.

Buhle, Johann Gottlieb, 1763-1821.
Geschichte der neuern Philosophie seit der Epoche der Wiederherstellung der Wissenschaften. Göttingen, Roewer, 1800-1805.
6 v.

Includes a section on Spinoza (v. 3, p. 508-660)

Brucker, Johann Jakob, 1696-1770.
Iacobi Brvckeri ... Historia critica philosophiae a mvndi incvnabvlis ad nostram vsqve aetatem dedvcta. Editio secvnda. volvmine VI. accessionvm et svpplementorvm avctior ... Lipsiae, impensis haered. Weidemanni et Reichii, 1766-67.
6 v. 2 plates, port. 26cm.

Vols. 1 and 6 published 1767; v. 2-[5], 1766; v. 3-6 without edition note on t.-p.
Vol. 4 issued in 2 parts; pt. 2 afterwards

CONTINUED ON NEXT CARD

Buhle, Johann Gottlieb Gerhard, 1763-1821.
Lehrbuch der geschichte der philosophie und einer kritischen literatur derselben ... von Johann Gottlieb Buhle ... Göttingen, Vandenhöck und Ruprecht, 1796-1804.
8 v. in 9. 18cm.

Includes references to Spinoza (v. 6, p. 725-757)

1. Philosophy—Hist. 2. Philosophy—Bibl.

Brucker, Johann Jakob, 1696-1770. Iacobi Brvckeri ... 1766-67. (Card 2)

considered as v. 5 of the complete work. cf. v. 6, p. [805]
Includes references to Spinoza.

Busse, Ludwig, 1862-1907.
Die Weltanschauungen der grossen Philosophen der Neuzeit. 2. Aufl. Leipzig, B. G. Teubner, 1905.
vi, 164 p. (Aus Natur und Geisteswelt ... 56. Bändchen)

Königsberger Hochschulkurse, Band 1.
Includes a section on Spinoza (p. 24-36)

Brucker, Jakob, 1696-1770.
Jacob Bruckers Kurze Fragen aus der philosophischen Historie von Anfang der Welt ... Ulm, 1731-36.
7 v.

Includes references to Spinoza.

Busse, Ludwig, 1862-1907.
Die Weltanschauungen der grossen Philosophen der Neuzeit. 3. Aufl. Leipzig, B. G. Teubner, 1907.
vi, 164 p. 19cm. (Aus Natur und Geisteswelt ... 56. Bändchen)

Königsberger Hochschulkurse, Band 1.
Includes a chapter on Spinoza (p. 23-35)

D-2
1311

Busse, Ludwig, 1862–1907.
... Die weltanschauungen der grossen philosophen der neuzeit, von dr. Ludwig Busse ... 5. aufl. hrsg. von dr. R. Falckenberg ... Leipzig, B. G. Teubner, 1912.
vii, [1], 160 p. 18½cm. (Aus natur und geisteswelt ... 56. bdchen.)

Includes a section on Spinoza (p. 23-33)

1. Philosophy, Modern. 2. Life. I. Falckenberg, Richard Friedrich Otto, 1851– ed.

12—5164

Library of Congress B793.B8
Copyright A—Foreign 4592
[40b1]

D-2
1312

Calkins, Mary Whiton, 1863-
The persistent problems of philosophy; an introduction to metaphysics through the study of modern systems. 3d ed. rev. New York, London, Macmillan, 1912.
xxvi, 577 p. 21 cm.

Includes a chapter "Monistic pluralism: the system of Spinoza" (p. 277-306) and a section in Appendix "Baruch de Spinoza: the monistic pluralist" (p. 464-483)

D-2
1313

Carus, Paul, 1852–1919.
Primer of philosophy, by Dr. Paul Carus. Chicago, The Open court publishing company, 1893.
2 p. l., [iii]–vi, 232 p. 20 cm.
Includes references to Spinoza.

1. Philosophy.

10—28628

Library of Congress B945.C22P9
[49e1]

D-2
1314

Cohn, Jonas, 1869–
... Führende denker; geschichtliche einleitung in die philosophie, von Jonas Cohn ... mit 6 bildnissen. 2., durchgesehene aufl. Leipzig, B. G. Teubner, 1911.
2 p. l., 106, [2] p. 6 port. 18½cm. (Aus natur und geisteswelt ... 176. bdchen.)

Includes a section on Spinoza with a portrait of him (p. 50-64)
1. Philosophy—Hist. I. Title.

[Full name: Jonas Ludwig Cohn]

11-27792 Revised

DLC

Library of Congress B84.C6
Copyright A—Foreign 3684
[r38b2]

D-2
1315

Cohn, Jonas, 1869-
Führende Denker; geschichtliche Einleitung in die Philosophie. 5. durchgesehene Aufl. Leipzig, B. G. Teubner, 1928.
116 p. ports. 19cm. (Aus Natur und Geisteswelt. 176. Bd.)

Includes a section on Spinoza (p. 56-71)

D-2
1316

Cohn, Jonas, 1869-
Führende Denker; geschichtliche Einleitung in die Philosophie. 4. Aufl. Leipzig, B. G. Teubner, 1921.
116 p. (Aus Natur und Geisteswelt, 176. Bdchen.)

Includes references to Spinoza.

ICMILC

D-2
1317

Cousin, Victor, 1792-1867.
Course of the history of modern philosophy. Translated by O. W. Wight. N. Y., Appleton, 1893.
2 v.

Includes a reference to Spinoza (v. 2, p. 94-95)

PPE

D-2
1318

Cousin, Victor, 1792-1867.
Histoire générale de philosophie, depuis les temps les plus anciens jusqu'à la fin du XVIIIe siècle. Paris, Didier, 1863.
vii, 567 p. 22cm.

Includes a section on Spinoza (p. 408-436)

D-2
1319

Cousin, Victor, 1792-1867.
Histoire générale de la philosophie depuis les temps les plus anciens jusqu'au XIXe siècle. 8. éd. rev. et augm. Paris, Didier, 1867.
vii, 578 p. 22½cm.

Includes a section on Spinoza (p. 421-445)

D-2
1320

Cashman, Herbert Ernest, 1865-
A beginner's history of philosophy. Boston, Houghton Mifflin Company [c1910]
2 v. illus., ports., maps. 19cm.

Vol. 2 has imprint: London, G. Harrap.
Includes a section on Spinoza (v. 2, p. 81-108) and other references to him.
Contents.--v. 1. Ancient and mediaeval philosophy.--v. 2. Modern philosophy.

SPECIAL COLLECTIONS SPINOZA D-2 1321

Deslandes, André François Boureau, 1690-1757.
Histoire critique de la philosophie, ou l'on traite de son origine, de ses progrès, & des diverses révolutions qui lui sont arrivées jusqu'à notre tems. Nouvelle edition. Par M. Deslandes ... A Amsterdam, Chez François Changuion, 1756.
4 v. 17cm.

Includes references to Spinoza.

SPECIAL COLLECTIONS SPINOZA D-2 1322

Deter, Christian Gustav Johann, 1831-1898.
Kurzer Abriss der Geschichte der Philosophie. 5. Aufl. Berlin, W. Weber, 1892.
vi, 142 p. 21cm.

Includes a section on Spinoza (p. 63-66)

SPECIAL COLLECTIONS SPINOZA D-2 1323

Deussen, Paul, 1845-1919.
Die neuere Philosophie von Descartes bis Schopenhauer. 2. Aufl. Leipzig, F. A. Brockhaus, 1920.
xiv, 603 p. (His Allgemeine Geschichte der Philosophie mit besonderer Berücksichtigung der Religionen. 2. Bd., 3. Abt.)

Includes a chapter on Spinoza.

SPECIAL COLLECTIONS SPINOZA D-2 1324

Dresser, Horatio Willis, 1866-
A history of modern philosophy, by Horatio W. Dresser ... New York, Thomas Y. Crowell company [°1928]
xiv, 471 p. 20½ cm.
Contains bibliographies.

Includes a chapter on Spinoza.

1. Philosophy, Modern—Hist.

28—4631
Library of Congress B791.D7
[31d2]

SPECIAL COLLECTIONS SPINOZA D-2 1325

Drews, Arthur, 1865-
Die Philosophie im ersten Drittel des neunzehnten Jahrhunderts. Leipzig, Göschen, 1912.
120 p. 16cm. (Geschichte der Philosophie, VI)

Sammlung Göschen, Bd. 571.
Includes references to Spinoza.
Bibliography: p. [4]

SPECIAL COLLECTIONS SPINOZA D-2 1326

Dühring, Eugen, 1833-1921.
Kritische Geschichte der Philosophie von ihren Anfängen bis zur Gegenwart. Berlin, L. Heimann, 1869.
xi, 519 p. 22 cm.

Includes a chapter on Spinoza (p. 273-313)

D-2 1327

Durant, William James, 1885-
Die grossen Denker. Mit einem Vorwort von H. Driesch. Zürich, O. Füssli [c1930]
xxiv, 557 p. 23 pl.

Includes a section on Spinoza (p. 141-189)

OCH

D-2 1328

Durant, William James, 1885-
Vies et doctrines des philosophes. Introduction à la philosophie. Paris, Payot, 1932.
487 p. (Bibliothèque historique)

Includes a chapter on Spinoza.

OCH

SPECIAL COLLECTIONS SPINOZA D-2 1329

Durant, William James, 1885-
The story of philosophy; the lives and opinions of the greater philosophers, by Will Durant, PH. D. New York, Simon and Schuster, 1926.
xiii, 577 p. front., ports., diagrs. 24½ cm.
One leaf inserted between p. xii and xiii.
CONTENTS.—Plato.—Aristotle and Greek science.—Francis Bacon.—Spinoza.—Voltaire and the French enlightenment.—Immanuel Kant and German idealism.—Schopenhauer.—Herbert Spencer.—Friedrich Nietzsche.—Contemporary philosophers.—Contemporary American philosophers.
1. Philosophy. 2. Philosophers.

B72.D8 26—12314
Library of Congress [52z*2]

SPECIAL COLLECTIONS SPINOZA D-2 1330

Eisler, Rudolf, 1873-
Geschichte des Monismus. Leipzig, A. Kröner, 1910.
viii, 204 p. 24cm.

Includes two articles on Spinoza.
Bibliography: p. [193]-204.
Original paper covers bound in.

D-2 1331

Eisler, Rudolf, 1873-
Handwörterbuch der Philosophie. Berlin, 1913.

Includes an article "Spinozismus" (p. 637)

NNUT

D-2 1332

Elmendorf, John Jay, 1827-1896.
Outlines of lectures on the history of philosophy, by John J. Elmendorf ... New York, G. P. Putnam's sons, 1876.
x, 298 p. 19cm.

Includes a section on Spinoza (p. 181-189)

1. Philosophy—Hist.

NNUT

Library of Congress B74.E4 10-21979 Revised
Copyright 1876: 12553 [r28c2]

D-2 1333

Enfield, William, 1741-1797.
The history of philosophy, from the earliest periods: drawn up from Brucker's Historia critica philosophiae. London, Printed for T. Tegg, 1839.
xvi, 670 p. 24 cm.

Includes a section on Spinoza (p. 617-618)

CtY

D-2 1334

Enfield, William, 1741-1797.
The history of philosophy, from the earliest periods: drawn up from Brucker's Historia critica philosophiae. London, Printed for T. Tegg, 1837.
xvi, 670 p. 24 cm.

Includes a reference to Spinoza (p. 617-618)

D-2 1335

Enfield, William, 1741-1797.
The history of philosophy, from the earliest times to the beginning of the present century; drawn up from Brucker's Historia critica philosophiae. London, 1819.
2 v.

Includes a section on Spinoza (v. 2, p. 531-533)

NN

SPECIAL COLLECTIONS SPINOZA D-2 1336

Enfield, William, 1741-1797.
The history of philosophy, from the earliest times to the beginning of the present century; drawn up from Brucker's Historia critica philosophiae. By William Enfield ... In two volumes. Dublin, Printed for P. Wogan [etc.] 1792.
2 v. fold. table. 22cm.

Vol. 2 includes a section on Spinoza.
Bibliographical footnotes.

SPECIAL COLLECTIONS SPINOZA D-2 1337

Erdmann, Benno, 1851-1921.
Betrachtungen über die Deutung und Wertung der Lehre Spinozas. [Berlin, Weidmannsche Buchhandlung, 1910]
[227]-246 p. 24cm.

Half-title.
Cover-title: Sonderabdruck. Carl Robert zum 8. März 1910 Genethliekon. Überreicht von der Graeca Halensis.

D-2 1338

Erdmann, Johann Eduard, 1805-1892.
Grundriss der Geschichte der Philosophie. Neu bearbeitet und bis in die Gegenwart fortgeführt von Ferdinand Clemens. Berlin, Eigenbrodler-Verlag, 1930.
730 p.

MH

SPECIAL COLLECTIONS SPINOZA D-2 1339

Erdmann, Johann Eduard, 1805-1892.
Grundriss der Geschichte der Philosophie. Berlin, W. Hertz, 1866.
2 v. 23cm.

Includes a section on Spinoza (v. 2, p. 47-76)
Bibliographical references.
Contents.--1. Bd. Philosophie des Alterthums und des Mittelalters.--2. Bd. Philosophie der Neuzeit.

SPECIAL COLLECTIONS SPINOZA D-2 1340

Erdmann, Johann Eduard, 1805-1892.
Grundriss der Geschichte der Philosophie. 2. sehr verm. Aufl. Berlin, W. Hertz, 1870.
v. 2.

Includes a section on Spinoza (v. 2, p. 45-74)
Bibliographical references.

D-2
1341

Erdmann, Johann Eduard, 1805-1892.
Grundriss der Geschichte der Philosophie.
3. verb. Aufl. Berlin, W. Hertz, 1878.
2 v. 24cm.

Includes bibliographies.
Contains a section on Spinoza (v. 2, p. 45-77)
Contents.--v. 1. Philosophie des Altertums und des Mittelalters.--v. 2. Philosophie der Neuzeit.
Notes by C. Schiller? C. Schiller's and A. S. Oko's signatures on flyleaf.

D-2
1346

Erdmann, Johann Eduard, 1805-1892.
Versuch einer wissenschaftlichen Darstellung der Geschichte der neueren Philosophie. Riga und Dorpat, E. Frantzen, 1834-58.
3 v. 21 cm.

Includes a section on Spinoza (v. 1, pt. 2, p. 47-98)

NNUT

D-2
1342

Erdmann, Johann Eduard, 1805–1892.
Grundriss der geschichte der philosophie von Johann Eduard Erdmann ... 4. aufl. bearb. von Benno Erdmann. Berlin, W. Hertz, 1896.
2 v. 24½cm.

CONTENTS.—1. bd. Philosophie des altertums und des mittelalters.—2. bd. Philosophie der neuzeit. Anhang: Die deutsche philosophie seit Hegel's tode.

Includes a section on Spinoza (v. 2, p. 49-81) and other references to him.

1. Philosophy—Hist. I. Erdmann, Benno, 1851-1921, ed.

Library of Congress B2.E6 8—6829
[42g1]

D-2
1347

Eucken, Rudolf Christof, 1846–1926.
The fundamental concepts of modern philosophic thought, critically and historically considered. By Rudolph Eucken. Tr. by M. Stuart Phelps ... with additions and corrections by the author, and an introduction by Noah Porter ... New York, D. Appleton and company, 1880.
xii p., 1 l., 304 p. 20cm.

1. Philosophy, Modern—Hist. 2. Philosophy, Modern. I. Phelps, Moses Stuart, tr.

Library of Congress B808.E83 1880 10—29624
[44j1]

D-2
1343

Erdmann, Johann Eduard, 1805-1892.
A history of philosophy. English translation edited by Williston S. Hough. 4th ed. London, Sonnenschein, 1897-98 [v. 1, 1898]
3 v.

NNJ

D-2
1348

Eucken, Rudolf, 1846-1926.
Die Lebensanschauungen der grossen Denker. Eine Entwicklungsgeschichte des Lebensproblems der Menschheit von Plato bis zur Gegenwart. 6. verb. Aufl. Leipzig, Veit, 1905.
viii, 523 p.

Includes a section on Spinoza (p. 334-350)

NNJ

D-2
1344

Erdmann, Johann Eduard, 1805-1892.
A history of philosophy. English translation edited by Williston S. Hough. Third edition. London, Swan Sonnenschein; New York, Macmillan, 1892-93.
3 v. 25 cm. (Library of philosophy, ed. by J. H. Muirhead)

Includes a section on Spinoza (v. 2, p. 52-91)

D-2
1349

Eucken, Rudolf, 1846-1926.
Die Lebensanschauungen der grossen Denker. Eine Entwicklungsgeschichte des Lebensproblems der Menschheit von Plato bis zur Gegenwart. 9. vielfach umgestaltete Aufl. Leipzig, Veit, 1911.

Includes a section on Spinoza (p. 341-357)

NNUT

D-2
1345

Erdmann, Johann Eduard, 1805-1892.
A history of philosophy. English translation edited by Williston S. Hough. London, Sonnenschein; New York, Macmillan, 1890.
3 v. 25 cm. (Library of philosophy)

Includes a section on Spinoza (v. 2, p. 52-91)

NNUT

D-2
1350

Eucken, Rudolf, 1846-1926.
Die Lebensanschauungen der grossen Denker; eine entwickelungsgeschichte des Lebensproblems der Menschheit von Plato bis zur Gegenwart. Leipzig, Veit, 1890.
viii, 496 p. 23cm.

Includes a section on Spinoza (p. 392-411)

Eucken, Rudolf, 1846-1926.
Die Lebensanschauungen der grossen Denker; eine Entwicklungsgeschichte des Lebensproblems der Menschheit von Plato bis zur Gegenwart. 15. und 16. Aufl. Berlin, Vereinigung wissenschaftlicher Verleger W. de Gruyter & Co. 1921.
viii, 564 p. 24cm.

Includes a section on Spinoza (p. 344-360)

Eucken, Rudolf Christof, 1846-1926.
Die Lebensanschauungen der grossen Denker; eine Entwicklungsgeschichte des Lebensproblems der Menschheit von Plato bis zur Gegenwart. 17. und 18. Aufl. Berlin und Leipzig, W. de Gruyter, 1922.
viii, 564 p. 24 cm.

Includes a section on Spinoza (p. 344-360)

Eucken, Rudolf, 1846-1926.
The problem of human life as viewed by the great thinkers from Plato to the present time. Tr. from the German by Williston S. Hough and W. R. Boyce Gibson. New York, Scribner, 1909.
xxv, 582 p. 23cm.

Includes a section on Spinoza (p. 362-380)

Faguet, Émile, 1847-1916.
Initiation philosophique. Paris, Hachette [c1913]
165 p. 19 cm.

Includes a section on Spinoza (p. 108-113)

Faguet, Émile, 1847-1916.
Initiation philosophique. Paris, Hachette, 1920.
169 p. 19cm. (Collection des initiations)

Includes a section on Spinoza (p. 108-113)

Falckenberg, Richard, 1851-1920.
Geschichte der neueren Philosophie, von Nikolaus von Kues bis zur Gegenwart; im Grundriss dargestellt. Leipzig, Veit & Co., 1886.
viii, 493 p. 23cm.

Includes a section on Spinoza (p. 83-103)

Ms. notes by Carl Gebhardt.

Falckenberg, Richard, 1851-1920.
Geschichte der neueren Philosophie von Nikolaus von Kues bis zur Gegenwart, im Grundriss dargestellt. 2., verb. und verm. Aufl. Leipzig, Veit, 1892.
x, 530 p. 23cm.

Includes a section on Spinoza (p. 94-115)
Original paper covers bound in.
Bibliographical footnotes.

Falckenberg, Richard, 1851-1920.
Geschichte der neueren Philosophie von Nikolaus von Kues bis zur Gegenwart. 7. verb. und ergänzte Aufl. Leipzig, Veit, 1913.
xii, 692 p. 23 cm.

Includes a section on Spinoza (p. 107-133) and other references to him.

Falckenberg, Richard, 1851-1920.
Geschichte der neueren Philosophie von Nikolaus von Kues bis zur Gegenwart. 9. Aufl., von E. von Aster. Berlin, W. de Gruyter, 1927.
xi, 749 p.

Includes a section on Spinoza (p. 102-129)

Feuerbach, Ludwig, 1804-1872.
Geschichte der neuern Philosophie von Bacon von Verulam bis Benedict Spinoza. Ansbach, C. Brügel, 1833.
lxiv, 434 p.

Includes a section on Spinoza (p. 341-434)

D-2
1361

Feuerbach, Ludwig, 1804-1872.
Geschichte der neuern Philosophie von Bacon von Verulam bis Benedict Spinoza. Leipzig, O. Wigand, 1847.
392 p. 22 cm.

Includes a section on Spinoza.

DLC

D-2
1362

Feuerbach, Ludwig, 1804-1872.
Geschichte der neuern Philosophie von Bacon von Verulam bis Benedict Spinoza. 2. Ausg. Leipzig, O. Wigand, 1844.
lxiv, 434 p. 21cm.

Includes a section on Spinoza (p. 341-434)

D-2
1363

Fischer, Kuno, 1824-1907.
Geschichte der neuern Philosophie. 1. Bd. Das classische Zeitalter der dogmatischen Philosophie. Mannheim, Bassermann & Mathy, 1854.
xxii, 595 p. 21cm.

Includes lectures on Spinoza (p. ⌊233⌋-595)

D-2
1364

Fischer, Kuno, 1824-1907.
Geschichte der neuern Philosophie. 1. Band. Descartes und seine Schule. 2. völlig umgearbeitete Aufl. Mannheim, Bassermann, 1865.
2 v. 22 cm.

Contents.--1. Th. René Descartes.--2. Th. Descartes' Schule; Geulinx, Malebranche, Baruch Spinoza.

NN

D-2
1365

Fischer, Kuno, 1824-1907.
⌊Geschichte der neuern Philosophie. Bd. II. 5. Aufl.⌋ Anhang. ⌊Heidelberg, C. Winter, 1909⌋
⌊585⌋-635 p. 24cm.

Includes articles on Spinoza.
"Neuere Spinoza-Literatur": p. 622-624.

NNC

D-2
1366

Franck, Adolphe, 1809-1893.
Moralistes et philosophes. Paris, Didier, 1872.
viii, 484 p. 22 cm.

Includes a section on Spinoza (p. 229-255)

MH

D-2
1367

Fränkel, J
Kurzes Repetitorium der Geschichte der Philosophie; mit Zugrundelegung der Werke von Brandis, K. Fischer, Gomperz, Harnack, Hegel, F. A. Lange, Lewes, Mullach, Stöckl, Ueberweg, Zeller, Zimmermann u. A. Leipzig, M. Breitenstein ⌊1894⌋
112 p. 20cm. ⌊Breitensteins Repetitorien, no. 60⌋

Includes a section on Spinoza (p. 61-64)

D-2
1368

Fülleborn, Georg Gustav, 1769-1803.
Beyträge zur Geschichte der Philosophie; herausgegeben von Georg Gustav Fülleborn ... Iena, bey Friedrich Fromann ⌊1793⌋-99.
3 v.

Includes references to Spinoza.

D-2
1369

Gérando, Joseph Marie, baron de, 1772-1842.
Histoire comparée des systêmes de philosophie, relativement aux principes des connaissances humaines. A Paris, Chez Henrichs, 1804-47.
2 pts. in 7 v.

Includes sections on Spinoza (pt. 1, v. 2, p. 61-72 and pt. 2, v. 2, p. 398-435) and other references to him.

D-2
1370

Gérando, Joseph Marie de, baron, 1772-1842.
Histoire de philosophie moderne à partir de la renaissance des lettres jusqu'à la fin du dix-huitième siècle. Paris, A. Delahays, 1858.
4 v. 22cm.

Vol. 2 includes material on Spinoza (p. 398-435)
Includes bibliographies.

D-2
1371

Geschichte der Philosophie in Längsschnitten.
Heft 1-11. Berlin, Junker, 1931-36.
9 v. 25 cm.

Includes many references to Spinoza.

D-2
1372

Gioberti, Vincenzo, 1801-1852.
Introduzione allo studio della filosofia, per Vincenzo Gioberti. Ed. 2., riv. e cor. dall' autore ... Brusselle, Stampe di Meline, Cans e compagnia, 1844.
4 v. 24cm. (*Half-title:* Opere edite ed inedite di Vincenzo Gioberti. vol. I-IV)

Includes references to Spinoza.

1. Philosophy. I. Title.

30-8082

Library of Congress BD24.G5 1844

D-2
1373

Gioberti, Vincenzo, 1801-1852.
Introduzione allo studio della filosofia.
Firenze, Poligrafia italiana, 1847-48.
3 v.

NNUT

SPECIAL COLLECTIONS
SPINOZA

D-2
1374

Glockner, Hermann, 1896-
Zur Geschichte der neueren Philosophie; Literaturbericht 1920-23.
[131]-166 p. 24cm.

"Sonderabdruck aus 'Deutsche Vierteljahrsschrift für Literaturwissenschaft und Geistesgeschichte', Band II, Heft 1."
Includes a section on Spinoza literature (p. 153-154)

D-2
1375

Guillon, Marie Nicolas Silvestre, 1760-1847.
Histoire générale de la philosophie ancienne et moderne jusqu'à nos jours, ou Supplément à la Bibliothèque choisie des pères grecs et latins. Par M.-N.-S. Guillon ... Paris, Depélafol [etc.] 1835.
2 v. 21cm.

Includes a section on Spinoza (v. 2, p. 292-294)

1. Philosophy—Hist. 2. Fathers of the church.

DLC

10-21987†

Library of Congress B77.G82

SPECIAL COLLECTIONS
SPINOZA

D-2
1376

Guttmann, Julius, 1880-1950.
Die philosophie des judentums, von professor Julius Guttmann ... München, E. Reinhardt, 1933.

412 p. front. (port.) 20cm. (Geschichte der philosophie in einzeldarstellungen. abt. I. Das weltbild der primitiven und die philosophie des Morgenlandes. bd. 3)

"Bibliographischer wegweiser": p. 363-369.

Includes a section "Der Einfluss der jüdischen Philosophie auf das System Spinozas" (p. 278-300) and other references to Spinoza.
1. Philosophy, Jewish. 2. Jews—Religion.

33-30893

Library of Congress B155.G8
[2]
181.3

SPECIAL COLLECTIONS
SPINOZA

D-2
1377

Handbuch der philosophie, bearbeitet von Alfred Baeumler, Arthur Baumgarten ... [u. a.] herausgegeben von A. Baeumler und M. Schröter ... München und Berlin, R. Oldenbourg, 1927-31.
v. 2-3 ~~4 v.~~ 25½cm.

Each volume has also special t.-p.
Includes references to Spinoza.

1. Philosophy. I. Baeumler, Alfred, 1887- ed. II. Schroeter, Manfred, 1880- joint ed.

36-14980

Library of Congress B82.H3
——— Copy 2. [2]

D-2
1378

Handbuch der Philosophie, bearbeitet von Alfred Baeumler, Arthur Baumgarten ... [u.a.] herausgegeben von A. Baeumler und M. Schröter.
Abt. 1. Die Grunddisziplinen. München und Berlin, R. Oldenbourg, 1934.

Includes references to Spinoza.

SPECIAL COLLECTIONS
SPINOZA

D-2
1379

Harms, Friedrich, 1819-1880.
Die Philosophie in ihrer Geschichte. Berlin, Th. Grieben, 1878-81.
2 v. in 1. 23cm. (Bibliothek für Wissenschaft und Literatur, 18. Bd. Philosophische Abtheilung, 3. Bd.)

Includes references to Spinoza.
Contents.--1. Bd. Psychologie.--2. Bd. Geschichte der Logik.

SPECIAL COLLECTIONS
SPINOZA

D-2
1380

Hartmann, Eduard von, 1842-1906.
Geschichte der Metaphysik. Leipzig, H. Haacke, 1899.
v. 1. 24cm. (His Ausgewählte Werke, Bd. XI-XII)

Includes a section on Spinoza (p. 389-419)

D-2
1381

Hegel, Georg Wilhelm Friedrich, 1770-1831.
Lectures on the history of philosophy; tr. from the German by Elizabeth S. Haldane and Frances H. Simson. London, K. Paul, Trench, Trübner, 1892-96.
3 v. 22 cm. (The English and foreign philosophical library)

Includes a section on Spinoza (v. 3, p. 252-290) and other references to him.

DLC

D-2
1386

Heussner, Alfred, 1871-
Die philosophischen Weltanschauungen und ihre Hauptvertreter; erste Einführung in das Verständnis philosophischer Probleme. Zweite durchgesehene Auflage. Göttingen, Vandenhoeck & Ruprecht, 1912.
275 p.

Includes a section "Der Monismus. Spinoza" (p. 66-85)

OCH

D-2
1382

Hegel, Georg Wilhelm Friedrich, 1770-1831.
Vorlesungen über die Geschichte der Philosophie. Dritter Band. Mit einem Vorwort von K. L. Michelet. Stuttgart, Fr. Frommanns Verlag (H. Kurtz), 1928.
viii, 692 p. (His Sämtliche Werke, 19. Bd.)

Includes a section on Spinoza (p. 368-411)

MH

SPECIAL COLLECTIONS
SPINOZA

D-2
1387

Heussner, Alfred, 1871-
Die philosophischen Weltanschauungen und ihre Hauptvertreter; erste Einführung in das Verständnis philosophischer Probleme. 5. durchgesehene Aufl. Göttingen, Vandenhoeck & Ruprecht, 1919.
iv, 277 p. 19cm.

Includes a chapter "Der Monismus. Spinoza" (p. [64]-83)
Bibliography: p. 273-277.

SPECIAL COLLECTIONS
SPINOZA

D-2
1383

Henry, Caleb Sprague, 1804-1884.
An epitome of the history of philosophy. Being the work adopted by the University of France for instruction in the colleges and high schools. Translated from the French, with additions, and a continuation of the history from the time of Reid to the present day. New-York, Harper & Brothers, 1842.
2 v. in 1. 16cm.

Includes a section on Spinoza (v. 2, p. 72-76)

SPECIAL COLLECTIONS
SPINOZA

D-2
1388

Heussner, Alfred, 1871-
Die philosophischen Weltanschauungen und ihre Hauptvertreter; erste Einführung in das Verständnis philosophischer Probleme. 6., durchgesehene Aufl. Göttingen, Vandenhoeck & Ruprecht, 1921.
iv, 225 p. 19cm.

Includes a chapter on Spinoza (p. 53-69)
Bibliography: p. 218-222.

SPECIAL COLLECTIONS
SPINOZA

D-2
1384

Hermann, Konrad, 1819-1897.
Geschichte der Philosophie in pragmatischer Behandlung. Leipzig, F. Fleischer, 1867.
xvi, 563 p. 23cm.

Includes two sections on Spinoza: "Der Lehrbegriff des Spinoza" (p. 273-276) and "Der Spinozismus nach seiner weiteren geschichtlichen Bedeutung" (p. 276-278)

SPECIAL COLLECTIONS
SPINOZA

D-2
1389

Høffding, Harald, 1843-1931.
A brief history of modern philosophy, by Dr. Harold Höffding ... Authorized translation by Charles Finley Sanders ... New York, The Macmillan company [°1912]
x p., 1 l., 324 p. 19½ cm.
Includes a section on Spinoza (p. 67-78)

1. Philosophy—Hist. I. Sanders, Charles Finley, 1869- tr.
12—22145
Library of Congress B798.D5H68
[48o1]

D-2
1385

Heussler, Hans, 1855-
Der Rationalismus des siebenzehnten Jahrhunderts in seinen Beziehungen zur Entwicklungs-Lehre. Breslau, W. Koebner, 1885.
160 p.

Includes a chapter on Spinoza (p. 66-87) and other references to him.

D-2
1390

Høffding, Harald, 1843-1931.
A brief history of modern philosophy. Authorized translation by C. F. Sanders. New York, Macmillan, 1931.
xi, 324 p.

Includes a section on Spinoza (p. 67-78)

NNUT

D-2 1391

Høffding, Harald, 1843-1931.
Geschichte der neueren Philosophie. Eine Darstellung der Geschichte der Philosophie von dem Ende der Renaissance bis zu unseren Tagen. Unter Mitwirkung des Verfassers aus dem Dänischen ins Deutsche übersetzt von F. Bendixen. 2. Aufl. Leipzig, O. R. Reisland, 1921.
2 v. 23 cm.

Vol. 1 includes a chapter on Spinoza.

D-2 1392

Høffding, Harald, 1843-1931.
Geschichte der neueren Philosophie; eine Darstellung der Geschichte der Philosophie von dem Ende der Renaissance bis zu unseren Tagen. Unter Mitwirkung des Verfassers aus dem Dänischen ins Deutsche übers. von F. Bendixen. Leipzig, O. R. Reisland, 1895-96.
2 v. 22cm.

Includes a chapter on Spinoza (v. 1, p. 324-372)

D-2 1393

Høffding, Harald, 1843-1931.
Histoire de la philosophie moderne. Traduit de l'allemand par P. Bordier. Préface de M. V. Delbos. Paris, F. Alcan, 1906.
v. 1.

Includes a chapter on Spinoza (v. 1, p. 306-350)

D-2 1394

Høffding, Harald, 1843-1931.
A history of modern philosophy; a sketch of the history of philosophy from the close of the renaissance to our own day, by Dr. Harald Höffding ... tr. from the German ed. by B. E. Meyer ... London, Macmillan & co., limited; New York, The Macmillan company, 1900.
2 v. 23½cm.
Authorized translation.
Includes a section on Spinoza (v. 1, p. 292-331) and other references to him.
1. Philosophy, Modern—Hist. I. Meyer, B. Ethel, tr.

D-2 1395

Høffding, Harald, 1843-1931.
A history of modern philosophy; a sketch of the history of philosophy from the close of the Renaissance to our own day. Translated from the German edition by B. E. Meyer. Authorized translation. London, Macmillan, 1915.
2 v. 23cm.

Vol. 1 includes a chapter on Spinoza.
Bibliographical references included in "Notes" at end of each volume.

D-2 1396

Høffding, Harald, 1843-1931.
A history of modern philosophy; a sketch of the history of philosophy from the close of the renaissance to our own day. Translated from the German edition by B. E. Meyer. London, Macmillan, 1935.
2 v.

Volume 1 includes a chapter on Spinoza.

D-2 1397

Höffding, Harald, 1843-1931.
Lehrbuch der Geschichte der neueren Philosophie. 2. Ausg. Leipzig, O. R. Reisland, 1920.
x, 290 p. 23cm.

Original paper covers bound in.
Includes a section on Spinoza (p. 59-70)

D-2 1398

Høffding, Harald, 1843-1931.
Den nyere filosofis historie; en fremstilling af filosofiens historie fra Renaissancens slutning til vore dage. Kobenhavn, Philipsen, 1894-1895.
2 v.

Includes a section on Spinoza (v. 1, p. 269-308) and other references to him.

D-2 1399

Hönigswald, Richard, 1875-
Die Philosophie von der Renaissance bis Kant. Berlin, W. de Gruyter, 1923.
x, 300 p. 25cm. (Geschichte der Philosophie, dargestellt von Bruno Bauch, Nicolai Hartmann, Richard Hönigswald ... Bd. 6)

Includes a section on Spinoza (p. 103-127)

D-2 1400

[Huhle, Emil]
Philosophie. Leipzig, A. O. Paul [1920]
110 p. 12cm. (Miniatur-Bibliothek. 497-499)

Includes a section on Spinoza (p. 99-102)

SPECIAL COLLECTIONS SPINOZA

D-2 1401

Hurst, John Fletcher, bp., 1834-1903.
History of rationalism: embracing a survey of the present state of Protestant theology. With an appendix of literature. Rev. and enl. from the 3d American ed. London, Trübner, 1867.
xvii, 525 p. 21cm.

Includes a section on Spinoza (p. 84-91)
Bibliography: p. ⌊483⌋-511.

D-2 1402

Janet, Paul, 1823-1899.
Histoire de la philosophie; les problèmes et les écoles, par Paul Janet ⌊et⌋ Gabriel Séailles. Paris, Delagrave, 1921.
iii, 1084 p.

Includes a section on Spinoza (p. 1029-1032) and many other references to him.

MH

D-2 1403

Janet, Paul, 1823-1899.
Les maîtres de la pensée moderne. Paris, Calmann Lévy, 1883.
403 p.

Includes essays "Spinoza et la théologie spinoziste" (p. 49-103) and "Le spinozisme en France" (p. 105-146)

D-2 1404

Jansen, W
Geschiedenis der wijsbegeerte (in voordrachten). Zutphen, W. J. Thieme, 1920-23.
4 v.

Vol. 2 includes a chapter on Spinoza (p. 404-446) and other references to him.

MH

SPECIAL COLLECTIONS SPINOZA

D-2 1405

Joad, Cyril Edwin Mitchinson, 1891-1953.
Great philosophies of the world. London, E. Benn ⌊1928⌋
79, ⌊1⌋ p. 17cm. (Benn's sixpenny library, no. 24)

Includes a reference to Spinoza (p. 28)
Bibliography: p. ⌊80⌋

D-2 1406

Jodl, Friedrich, 1849-1914.
Geschichte der Ethik als philosophischer Wissenschaft. 3., verb. Aufl. Stuttgart, Cotta, 1920-23.
2 v. 23 cm.

Includes a chapter on Spinoza (v. 1, p. 468-485) and other references to him.

DLC

SPECIAL COLLECTIONS SPINOZA

D-2 1407

Jodl, Friedrich, 1849–1914.
Geschichte der ethik als philosophischer wissenschaft, von Friedrich Jodl ... 2. neu bearb. und verm. aufl. Stuttgart und Berlin, Cotta, 1906–12.
2 v. 23½cm.
Vol. 2. 2. vollständig, durchgearbeitete und vermehrte auflage.
Includes a chapter on Spinoza and other references to him.

1. Ethics—Hist. 2. Philosophy—Hist.

9—16794
Library of Congress BJ73.J6
⌊a37b1⌋

SPECIAL COLLECTIONS SPINOZA

D-2 1408

Jodl, Friedrich, 1849-1914.
Geschichte der Ethik als philosophischer Wissenschaft. II. Bd. Von Kant bis zur Gegenwart. 3., verb. und erweiterte Aufl. Stuttgart, J. G. Cotta'sche Buchhandlung Nachfolger, 1923.
xii, 724 p. 22cm.

Includes references to Spinoza.

SPECIAL COLLECTIONS SPINOZA

D-2 1409

Jodl, Friedrich, 1849-1914.
Geschichte der neueren Philosophie, aus dem Nachlass hrsg. von Dr. Karl Roretz. Wien, Rikola verlag, 1924.
780 p. port. 25cm.

Includes a chapter on Spinoza.

SPECIAL COLLECTIONS SPINOZA

D-2 1410

Kannegiesser, Karl Friedrich Ludwig, 1781-1864.
Abriss der Geschichte der Philosophie. Leipzig, F. A. Brockhaus, 1837.
viii, 168 p. 21cm.

Includes a section on Spinoza (p. 124-129)

Kirchner, Friedrich, 1840-1900.
Katechismus der Geschichte der Philosophie, von Thales bis zur Gegenwart. Leipzig, 1877.
viii, 356 p. 18cm.

Includes a chapter on Spinoza.

Kirchner, Friedrich, 1848-1900.
Katechismus der Geschichte der Philosophie, von Thales bis zur Gegenwart. 2. Aufl. Leipzig, J. J. Weber, 1884.
viii, 428 p. 17cm.

Includes a chapter on Spinoza (p. 283-294)

Knauer, Vincenz, 1828-1894.
Geschichte der Philosophie, mit besonderer Berücksichtigung der Neuzeit. Wien, W. Braumüller, 1876.
x, 387 p. 24cm.

Includes a section on Spinoza (p. [134]-138)

Kostyleff, Nicolas
Esquisse d'une évolution dans l'histoire de la philosophie; essais. Paris, F. Alcan, 1903.
224 p. 17 cm.

Includes a section on Spinoza (p. 135-154)

Kotzias, N
Ἱστορία τῆς φιλοσοφίας ἀπὸ τῶν ἀρχαιοτάτων χρόνων μέχρι τῶν καθ' ἡμᾶς. Ἐν Ἀθήναις, Ἐκ τοῦ τυπογραφείου τοῦ "Μέλλοντος", 1876-84.
6 v.

Includes a chapter on Spinoza (v. 4, p. 159-186)
Title transliterated: Historia tēs philosophias.

Kramer, Franz, 1883-
Repetitorium der Geschichte der neueren Philosophie (von Descartes bis Kant) Berlin, W. de Gruyter, 1921.
85 p. 22cm. (Wissenschaftliche Repetitorien. 6)

Includes references to Spinoza (p. 22-31)
Original paper covers bound in.

Krause, Karl Christian Friedrich, 1781-1832.
Grundriss der Geschichte der Philosophie; aus dem handschriftlichen Nachlasse des Verfassers hrsg. von Paul Hohlfeld und Aug. Wünsche. Leipzig, O. Schulze, 1887.
xiv, 481 p. 23cm.

Includes a section on Spinoza (p. 259-268)

Krug, Wilhelm Traugott, 1770-1842.
Allgemeines Handwörterbuch der philosophischen Wissenschaften, nebst ihrer Literatur und Geschichte. Nach dem heutigen Standpuncte der Wissenschaft bearb. und hrsg. von Wilhelm Traugott Krug. Leipzig, F. A. Brockhaus, 1827-29.
5 v. 21cm.

Half-title: Krug's encyklopädisch-philosophisches Lexikon.
Includes an article on Spinoza (v. 3, p. 745-755)

Krug, Wilhelm Traugott, 1770-1842.
Allgemeines Handwörterbuch der philosophischen Wissenschaften, nebst ihrer Literatur und Geschichte. Nach dem heutigen Standpuncte der wissenschaft bearb. und hrsg. von Wilhelm Traugott Krug. 2. verb. und verm. Aufl. Leipzig, F. A. Brockhaus, 1832-34.
4 v. 22cm.

Includes an article on Spinoza (v. 3, p. 828-839)

Lagenpusch, Emil
Grundriss der Geschichte der Philosophie. Breslau, E. Trewendt, 1900.
v. 2 15cm.

Includes a section on Spinoza (v. 2, p. 26-33)
Contents.--v. 1. Geschichte der alten Philosophie und der Philosophie des Mittelalters.--v. 2. Geschichte der neueren Philosophie.

Land, Jan Pieter Nicolaas, 1834-1897.
De wijsbegeerte in de Nederlanden. Vertaald en bezorgd door C. van Vollenhoven, met levensbericht van den schrijver, door C. B. Spruyt. 's-Gravenhage, M. Nijhoff, 1899.
230 p. port. 21cm.

Includes a chapter on Spinoza (p. [181]-230)

Lefèvre, André ~~Paul-Émile~~, 1834-1904.
Philosophy historical and critical, by André Lefèvre. Translated with an introduction by A. H. Keane, B. A. London, Chapman and Hall; Philadelphia, J. B. Lippincott and co., 1879.
xxiv, 598 p. 20½cm. (*Half-title:* Library of contemporary science)

Includes a section on Spinoza (p. 317-324)

1. Philosophy—Hist. 2. Philosophy.

10—21890

Library of Congress B79.L5
[44e1]

Levinsohn, Isaac Baer, 1788-1860.
בית יהודה. Warsaw, 1901.
156 p.

Title transliterated: Beʿth yehudah.
Includes a chapter on Spinoza (p. 127)

Lewes, George Henry, 1817-1878.
A biographical history of philosophy. London, Cox, 1852.
4 v. in 2. 15cm.

Vol. 3 includes chapters "Spinoza's life" (p. 111-128) and "Spinoza's doctrine" (p. 129-154)
Bibliography: v. 1, p. 8-10.
Contents.--v. 1-2. Series I, Ancient philosophy.--v. 3-4. Series II, From Bacon to the present day.

Lewes, George Henry, 1817-1878.
Geschichte der Philosophie von Thales bis Comte; deutsch nach der vierten Ausgabe von 1871. Zweiter Band: Geschichte der neueren Philosophie. Berlin, R. Oppenheim, 1876.
viii, 811 p. 23cm.

Includes a chapter on Spinoza (p. 171-234)
Bibliographical footnotes.

Lewes, George Henry, 1817-1878.
Исторія философіи отъ ея начала до настоящаго времени. С. Петербургъ, 1865.
816 p.

Title transliterated: Istorii͡a filosofii ...
A translation of The biographical history of philosophy from its origin in Greece down to the present day.
Includes a chapter "Жизнь и ученіе Спинозы" (p. 466-481)

DLC

Lewes, George Henry, 1817-1878.
The history of philosophy from Thales to Comte. By George Henry Lewes. 3d ed. ... London, Longmans, Green, and co., 1867.
2 v. 22cm.

Includes a chapter on Spinoza (v. 2, p. 160-225) and other references to him.

1. Philosophy—Hist.

10—20560

Library of Congress B72.L7
[44b1]

Lindsay, James
Studies in European philosophy. Edinburgh and London, Blackwood, 1909.
xxi, 370 p. 23 cm.

Includes a chapter "The philosophy of Spinoza" (p. 154-170) and other references to him.

Loewenthal, Eduard, 1836-1917.
Geschichte der Philosophie im Umriss für Studierende, sowie für jeden Gebildeten. Berlin, Hannemann, 1896.
55 p. 19cm.

Includes a section on Spinoza (p. 33-34) and other references to him.

Loewenthal, Eduard, 1836-1917.
Geschichte der Philosophie im Umriss für Studierende, sowie für jeden Gebildeten. 4. verm. und verb. Aufl. Berlin, M. Hannemann, 1898.
55 p. 19cm.

Includes a section on Spinoza (p. 33-34) and other references to him.

Lotze, Hermann, 1817-1881.
Geschichte der deutschen Philosophie seit Kant; Diktate aus den Vorlesungen von Hermann Lotze. 2. Aufl. Leipzig, S. Hirzel, 1894.
104 p. 22cm.

Includes a section on Spinoza (p. 8-11)

Lotze, Hermann, 1817-1881.
Geschichte der neueren Philosophie von Hermann Lotze (+1881)
1 p. l., 147 p. 22cm.

Manuscript.
On t.-p.: "P. Drews. 8. S. 1879."
The text is that of the "Geschichte der deutschen Philosophie seit Kant; Diktate aus den Vorlesungen von Hermann Lotze", published 1882, as given in the summer semester 1879.
Includes a section on Spinoza (p. 5-8)

Mannheimer, Adolf
Geschichte der Philosophie in übersichtlicher Darstellung. Zweiter Teil: Von der Entstehung des Christentums bis Kant. Frankfurt am Main, Neuer Frankfurter Verlag, 1904.
120 p. 24cm.

Includes a section "Die Versuche zur Bildung einer neuen Weltanschauung durch Descartes und Spinoza" (p. 83-98)

Maréchal, Joseph, 1878-
Le point de départ de la métaphysique; leçons sur le développement historique et théorique du problème de la connaissance. Cahier II. Le conflit du rationalisme et de l'empirisme dans la philosophie moderne, avant Kant. Bruges, C. Beyaert; Paris, F. Alcan ₌1923₌
x, 189 p. 23cm. (Museum Lessianum. Section philosophique. Publications ₌4₌)

Includes chapters on Spinoza.

Maréchal, Joseph, 1878-
Le point de départ de la métaphysique; leçons sur le développement historique et théorique du problème de la connaissance. Bruges, C. Beyaert; Paris, F. Alcan, 1923.
v. 2. (Museum Lessianum. Section philosophique. Publications ₌2₌)

Maréchal, Joseph
Précis d'histoire de la philosophie moderne. t. 1, De la renaissance à Kant. Louvain, Museum Lessianum, 1933.
307 p. 24 cm. (Museum Lessianum, Section philosophique, no. 16)

Includes a chapter on Spinoza (p. 103-148) and other references to him.

Maurice, Frederick Denison ~~i. e. John Frederick Denison,~~ 1805-1872.
Modern philosophy; or, A treatise of moral and metaphysical philosophy from the fourteenth century to the French revolution, with a glimpse into the nineteenth century. By the Rev. Frederick Denison Maurice, M. A. London, Griffin, Bohn, and company, 1862.
xvii, 676 p. 18½cm.
Includes a section on Spinoza (p. 372-432)

1. Philosophy, Modern—Hist.

Maurice, Frederick Denison, 1805-1872.
Moral and metaphysical philosophy. New ed. with preface. London, Macmillan; New York, Scribner, Welford, and Armstrong, 1872.
2 v.

Includes a section on Spinoza (p. 372-432) and other references to him.

Maurice, Frederick Denison, 1805-1872.
Moral and metaphysical philosophy. London, 1850-62.
4 v.

Maurice, Frederick Denison, 1805-1872.
Moral and metaphysical philosophy. New ed., with preface. London, 1872.
2 v.

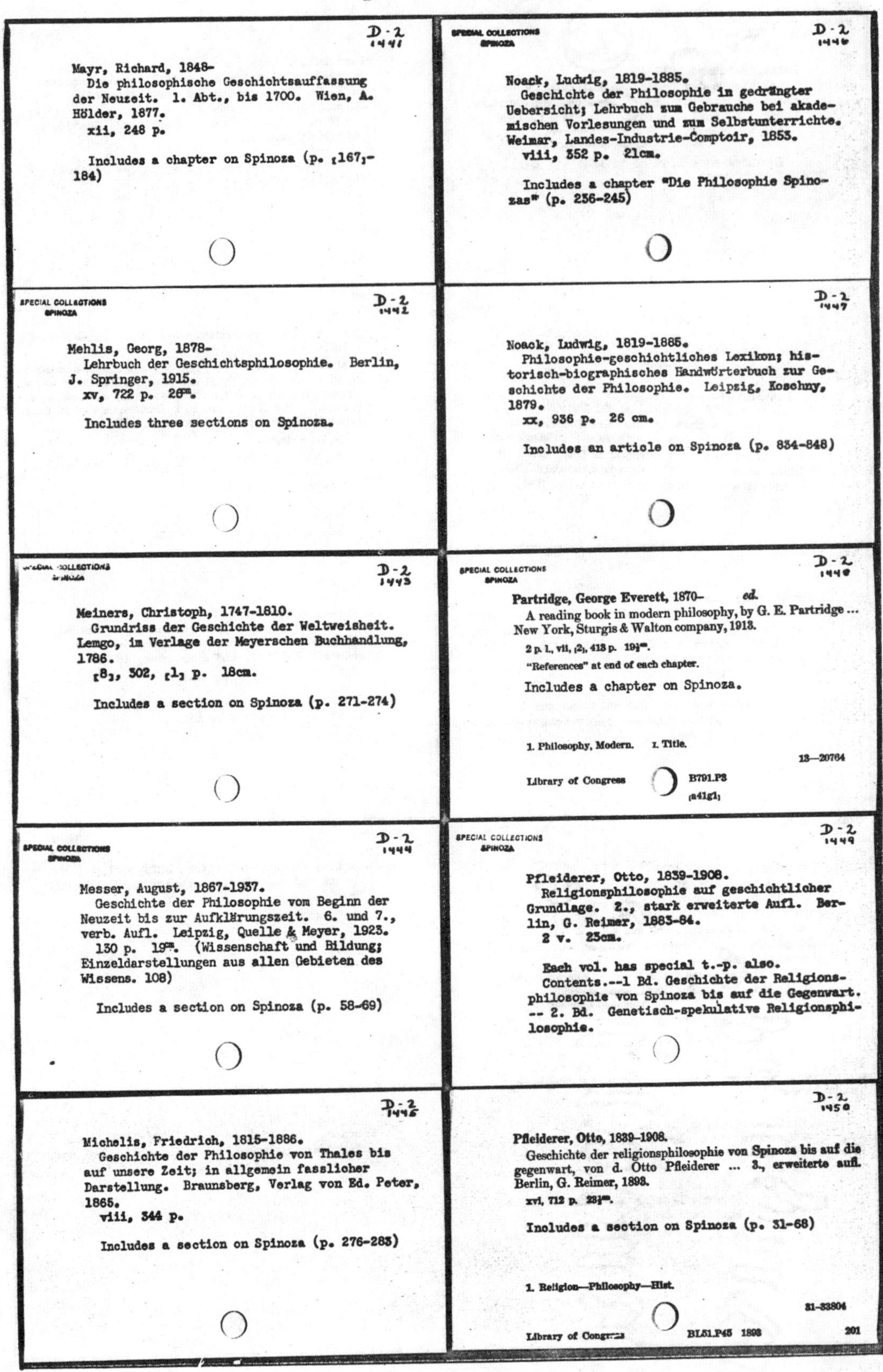

D-2 1441

Mayr, Richard, 1848-
Die philosophische Geschichtsauffassung der Neuzeit. 1. Abt., bis 1700. Wien, A. Hölder, 1877.
xii, 248 p.

Includes a chapter on Spinoza (p. [167]-184)

SPECIAL COLLECTIONS SPINOZA D-2 1442

Mehlis, Georg, 1878-
Lehrbuch der Geschichtsphilosophie. Berlin, J. Springer, 1915.
xv, 722 p. 26cm.

Includes three sections on Spinoza.

SPECIAL COLLECTIONS SPINOZA D-2 1443

Meiners, Christoph, 1747-1810.
Grundriss der Geschichte der Weltweisheit. Lemgo, im Verlage der Meyerschen Buchhandlung, 1786.
[8], 302, [1] p. 18cm.

Includes a section on Spinoza (p. 271-274)

SPECIAL COLLECTIONS SPINOZA D-2 1444

Messer, August, 1867-1937.
Geschichte der Philosophie vom Beginn der Neuzeit bis zur Aufklärungszeit. 6. und 7., verb. Aufl. Leipzig, Quelle & Meyer, 1923.
130 p. 19cm. (Wissenschaft und Bildung; Einzeldarstellungen aus allen Gebieten des Wissens. 108)

Includes a section on Spinoza (p. 58-69)

D-2 1445

Michelis, Friedrich, 1815-1886.
Geschichte der Philosophie von Thales bis auf unsere Zeit; in allgemein fasslicher Darstellung. Braunsberg, Verlag von Ed. Peter, 1865.
viii, 344 p.

Includes a section on Spinoza (p. 276-283)

SPECIAL COLLECTIONS SPINOZA D-2 1446

Noack, Ludwig, 1819-1885.
Geschichte der Philosophie in gedrängter Uebersicht; Lehrbuch zum Gebrauche bei akademischen Vorlesungen und zum Selbstunterrichte. Weimar, Landes-Industrie-Comptoir, 1853.
viii, 352 p. 21cm.

Includes a chapter "Die Philosophie Spinozas" (p. 236-245)

D-2 1447

Noack, Ludwig, 1819-1885.
Philosophie-geschichtliches Lexikon; historisch-biographisches Handwörterbuch zur Geschichte der Philosophie. Leipzig, Koschny, 1879.
xx, 936 p. 26 cm.

Includes an article on Spinoza (p. 834-848)

SPECIAL COLLECTIONS SPINOZA D-2 1448

Partridge, George Everett, 1870- ed.
A reading book in modern philosophy, by G. E. Partridge ... New York, Sturgis & Walton company, 1913.
2 p. l., vii, [2], 413 p. 19½cm.
"References" at end of each chapter.
Includes a chapter on Spinoza.

1. Philosophy, Modern. I. Title.

13-20764

Library of Congress B791.P3 [a41g1]

SPECIAL COLLECTIONS SPINOZA D-2 1449

Pfleiderer, Otto, 1839-1908.
Religionsphilosophie auf geschichtlicher Grundlage. 2., stark erweiterte Aufl. Berlin, G. Reimer, 1883-84.
2 v. 23cm.

Each vol. has special t.-p. also.
Contents.--1 Bd. Geschichte der Religionsphilosophie von Spinoza bis auf die Gegenwart. -- 2. Bd. Genetisch-spekulative Religionsphilosophie.

D-2 1450

Pfleiderer, Otto, 1839-1908.
Geschichte der religionsphilosophie von Spinoza bis auf die gegenwart, von d. Otto Pfleiderer ... 3., erweiterte aufl. Berlin, G. Reimer, 1893.
xvi, 712 p. 23½cm.

Includes a section on Spinoza (p. 31-68)

1. Religion—Philosophy—Hist.

31-33804

Library of Congress BL51.P45 1893 201

Philosophische Abhandlungen, dem Andenken Rudolf Hayms gewidmet von Freunden und Schülern. Halle a. S., M. Niemeyer, 1902.
xxvii, 560 p. 24cm.

Includes an essay "Über die Grundlagen der Lehre des Spinoza" by Eugen Kühnemann (p. [203]-272)

Pünjer, Bernhard, 1850-1885.
History of the Christian philosophy of religion from the reformation to Kant. Translated from the German by W. Hastie, with a preface by Robert Flint. Edinburgh, T. & T. Clark, 1887.
xix, 660 p. 23cm.

Includes a chapter on Spinoza (p. 407-434) and other references to him.

Rabus, Leonhard, 1835-1916.
Lehrbuch zur Einleitung in die Philosophie. Erlangen, A. Deichert, 1887-
v. 1. 24cm.

Includes a section on Spinoza (v. 1, p. 90-93) and other references to him.
Includes bibliographies.

Rehmke, Johannes, 1848-1930.
Grundriss der Geschichte der Philosophie. 2. Aufl. Leipzig, Quelle & Meyer, 1913.
vii, 289 p.

Includes a section on Spinoza (p. 115-131) and other references to him.

OCH

Rehmke, Johannes, 1848-1930.
Grundriss der geschichte der philosophie, von dr. Johannes Rehmke ... 3. aufl. Leipzig, Quelle & Meyer, 1921.
vii, 261 p. 22½cm.

Includes a section on Spinoza (p. 104-118)

1. Philosophy—Hist.

Reichenau, Wilhelm von, 1847-
Die monistische Philosophie von Spinoza bis auf unsere Tage. Gekrönte Preisschrift. Köln, E. H. Mayer, 1881.
xx, 348 p. 22cm.

Reichenau, Wilhelm von, 1847-
Die monistische Philosophie von Spinoza bis auf unsere Tage. Gekrönte Preisschrift. 2., mit einem neuen Vorwort verm. Aufl. Köln, E. H. Mayer, 1884.
xx, 348 p. 22cm.

Reinhold, Ernst, 1793-1855.
Handbuch der allgemeinen Geschichte der Philosophie für alle wissenschaftlich Gebildete ... Gotha, in der Hennins'schen Buchhandlung, 1828-30.
2 v. in 3. 21cm.

Includes a chapter "Spinoza's Pantheismus" (v. 2, p. [222]-286)
Contents.--1. Th. Geschichte der alten oder der griechischen Philosophie.--2. Th. Geschichte der neueren Philosophie. 2 v.

Reinhold, Ernst, 1793-1855.
Lehrbuch der Geschichte der Philosophie. Jena, F. Mauke, 1836.
xvi, 691 p. 22cm.

Includes a section on Spinoza (p. 412-441)

Reinhold, Ernst ~~Christian Gottlieb~~, 1793-1855.
Lehrbuch der geschichte der philosophie. Von Ernst Reinhold ... 2. verm. und verb. aufl. Jena, F. Mauke, 1839.
xx, 784 p. 21½cm.

First edition (2 v. in 3, Gotha, 1828-30) has title: Handbuch der allgemeinen geschichte der philosophie für alle wissenschaftliche gebildete.
Includes a section on Spinoza (p. 378-406)

1. Philosophy—Hist.

Reinhold, Ernst, 1793-1855.
Lehrbuch der Geschichte der Philosophie.
3. verbesserte Auflage. Jena, F. Mauke, 1849.
xx, 748 p.

Includes a section on Spinoza (p. 285-306)

Ritter, Heinrich, 1791-1869.
Die christliche Philosophie nach ihrem Begriff, ihren äussern Verhältnissen und in ihrer Geschichte bis auf die neuesten Zeiten.
Göttingen, Dieterich, 1858-59.
2 v. 22 cm.

Includes a section on Spinoza (v. 2, p. 260-274)

Ritter, Heinrich, 1791-1869.
Geschichte der Philosophie. Hamburg, Perthes, 1836-53.
12 v. 21cm.

Includes a section on Spinoza (v. 11, p. 169-291)

Ritter, Heinrich, 1791-1869.
Histoire de la philosophie moderne. Traduction française précédée d'une introduction par P. Challemel-Lacour. Paris, Ladrange, 1861.
3 v.

Ritter, Heinrich, 1791-1869.
Kleine philosophische Schriften. Kiel, Universitäts-Buchhandlung, 1839-40.
3 v. in 1. 22 cm.

Rixner, Thaddeus Anselm, 1766-1838.
Handbuch der geschichte der philosophie zum gebrauche seiner vorlesungen von Thaddä Anselm Rixner ... 2. verm. und verb. aufl. Sulzbach, J. E. von Seifel'sche buchhandlung, 1829.

3 v. 21cm.

CONTENTS.—I. bd. Allgemeine einleitung und geschichte der alterthümlichen, sowohl barbarischen als classischen philosophie.—II. bd. Geschichte der philosophie des mitteralters.—III. bd. Geschichte der philosophie der neueren und neuesten zeit.
Includes a section on Spinoza (v. 3, p. 56-82)
1. Philosophy—Hist.

Robertson, John Mackinnon, 1856-
A short history of morals, by J. M. Robertson. London, Watts & co., 1920.
vii, [1], 460 p. 23cm.
Includes a section on Spinoza (p. 240-253)

1. Ethics—Hist. I. Title.

Rogers, Arthur Kenyon, 1868-
A student's history of philosophy. New ed., rev. New York, Macmillan, 1923.
xiii, 511 p. 21 cm.

Includes references to Spinoza.

Rosenkranz, Karl, 1805-1879.
Neue Studien. Leipzig, E. Koschny, 1877.
v. 3. port. 22cm.

Includes an essay on Spinoza (v. 3, p. [3]-14)

Rosenthal, Ludwig A
Die monistische Philosophie; ihr Wesen, ihre Vergangenheit und Zukunft, für die Gebildeten aller Stände dargestellt. Berlin, C. Duncker's Verlag (C. Heymons) 1880.
v, 140 p. 22cm.

Includes three chapters on Spinoza: "Cartesius und sein Einfluss auf Spinoza", "Spinoza's Welteinheit" and "Leibnitz gegen Spinoza" (p. [7]-62)

Royce, Josiah, 1855-1916.
The spirit of modern philosophy; an essay in the form of lectures. Boston and New York, Houghton Mifflin [c1892]
xv, 519 p. 22cm.

Includes a section on the religious aspect of Spinozism (p. 41-67)

Ruggiero, Guido de, 1888-
La filosofia moderna. I. L'età cartesiana. 3. ed. Bari, Laterza, 1943.
362 p. 21 cm. (His Storia della filosofia, pt. 4, v. 1)

Includes a chapter on Spinoza (p. 169-258)

Ruggiero, Guido de, 1888-1948.
Modern philosophy, tr. by A. Howard Hannay and R. G. Collingwood. London, Allen [1921]
402 p. 22 cm. (Library of philosophy, J. H. Muirhead, ed.)

Saisset, Émile, 1814-1863.
Essai de philosophie religieuse. Paris, Charpentier, 1859.
xxviii, 489 p.

Includes a chapter "Le panthéisme de Spinoza" (p. 67-134)

NN

Saisset, Émile, 1814-1863.
Essai de philosophie religieuse. 2. éd. rev. et augm. d'éclaircissements. Paris, Charpentier, 1862.
2 v. in 1. 19cm.

Original paper covers bound in.
Includes a chapter "Le panthéisme de Spinoza" (v. 1, p. [111]-195)

Saisset, Émile, 1814-1863.
Essay on religious philosophy. Translated, with marginal analysis, notes, critical essay, and philosophical appendix. Edinburgh, T. & T. Clark, 1863.
2 v. 20cm.

Vol. 1 includes an essay on Spinoza.

Savérien, Alexandre, 1720-1805.
Histoire des philosophes modernes, avec leur portrait gravé dans le goût du crayon, d'apres les desseins des plus grands peintres. Par m. Saverien. Publiée par François, graveur des desseins du Cabinet du roi ... I. Partie. Contenant l'Histoire des metaphysiciens. Paris, Brunet, 1760.
111 p. plates.

Includes a section on Spinoza (p. 52-58)

Savérien, Alexandre, 1720-1805.
Histoire des philosophes modernes, par M. Savérien, avec leurs portraits gravés par François ... Paris, Chez Bleuet [etc.] 1773.
7 v. fronts., ports. 19cm.

Includes a section on Spinoza (v. 1, p. 171-193)

Sawicki, Franz, 1877-
Lebensanschauungen alter und neuer Denker. Dritter Band: Von der Renaissance bis zur Aufklärung. 1. und 2. Aufl. Paderborn, F. Schöningh, 1923.
198 p. 20cm.

Includes a chapter on Spinoza (p. [64]-93)
Includes bibliographies.

Schaller, Julius, 1810-1868.
Geschichte der Naturphilosophie von Baco von Verulam bis auf unsere Zeit. Leipzig, Wigand, 1841-46.
2 v. in 1. 21cm.

Vol. 2 has imprint: Halle, Schwetschke.
Added t.-p. to v. 2 reads: Darstellung und Kritik der kantischen Naturphilosophie.
Includes a section on Spinoza (v. 1, p. 326-343)

D-2 1481

Schellwien, Robert, 1821-
Der Geist der neueren Philosophie. Leipzig, Janssen, 1895.
2 v. in 1.

Includes a chapter "Uebergang vom Spinozismus zur späteren Entwicklung der Philosophie" (v. 2, p. [5]-10) and a section on Spinoza (v. 1, p. 73-163)

SPECIAL COLLECTIONS SPINOZA
D-2 1482

Scherr, Ignaz Thomas, 1801-1870.
Gemeinfassliche Geschichte der religiösen und philosophischen Ideen; mit besonderer Rücksicht auf das Leben und Wirken der Weisen aller Völker und Zeiten ... dargestellt von I. Thomas Scherr und Johannes Scherr. Schaffhausen, Brodtmann, 1842-43 [v. 1, 1843]
3 v. in 4. 20cm.

Includes a chapter on Spinoza (v. 3, p. 24-41)

D-2 1483

Schjelderup, Harald Krabbe, 1895-
... Filosofiens historie fra renaissancen til nutiden. Kristiania [etc.] Gyldendal, 1924.
5 p. l., 223 p. 22½cm.
At head of title: Harald K. Schjelderup.
Includes a section on Spinoza.

1. Philosophy, Modern—Hist.

DLC
Library of Congress B798.S3S3 25-7099
Copyright A—Foreign 26657
[2]

SPECIAL COLLECTIONS SPINOZA
D-2 1484

Schjelderup, Harald Krabbe, 1895-
Geschichte der philosophischen Ideen von der Renaissance bis zur Gegenwart. Berlin, W. de Gruyter, 1929.
viii, 232 p. 23cm.

Includes a section on Spinoza (p. 45-52)

D-2 1485

Schleiermacher, Friedrich Ernst Daniel, 1768-1834.
Geschichte der Philosophie. Aus Schleiermachers handschriftlichem Nachlasse hrsg. von H. Ritter. Berlin, Reimer, 1839.
311 p. (His Sämmtliche Werke, Bd. 27)

Includes "Kurze Darstellung des Spinozistischen Systems" (p. 283-311) and another section on Spinoza (p. 275-282)

D-2 1486

Schmidt, Eduard
Umrisse zur Geschichte der Philosophie. Berlin, F. Dümmler, 1839.

Includes a section on Spinoza (p. 233-245)

MH

D-2 1487

Schröder, Eric August, 1796-1849.
Handbok i philosophiens historia, af Eric August Schröder ... Upsala, Wahlström & c., på förf:s förlag, 1846-49.
3 v. 22cm.
Vol. III, pt. I, ed. by P. D. A. Atterbom.
Includes a section on Spinoza (v. 3, p. 305-334)

1. Philosophy—Hist. I. Atterbom, Per Daniel Amadeus, 1790-1855, ed.

10—21252
DLC
Library of Congress B99.S82S3
[a41b1]

SPECIAL COLLECTIONS SPINOZA
D-2 1488

Schwegler, Albert, 1819-1857.
Geschichte der Philosophie im Umriss; ein Leitfaden zur Uebersicht. 2. verb. Aufl. Stuttgart, Franckh, 1855.
iv, 216 p. 24cm.

Includes a section on Spinoza (p. 105-110)

SPECIAL COLLECTIONS SPINOZA
D-2 1489

Schwegler, Albert, 1819-1857.
Geschichte der philosophie im umriss. Ein leitfaden zur uebersicht. Von dr. Albert Schwegler. 4., verb. aufl. Nach dem tode des verfassers herausgegeben von dr. Karl Köstlin ... Stuttgart, Franck, ~~1861.~~ 1860.
vi, 241 p. 23cm.
Includes a section on Spinoza (p. 118-124)

1. Philosophy—Hist. I. Köstlin, Karl Reinhold von, 1819-1894, ed.
[Full name: Friedrich Karl Albert Schwegler]

33—31541
Library of Congress B84.S4 1861
[44b1] 109

D-2 1490

Schwegler, Albert, 1819-1857.
Geschichte der Philosophie im Umriss; ein Leitfaden zur Uebersicht. 5. verb. Aufl. Stuttgart, Franckh, 1863.
243 p. 24cm.

Includes a section on Spinoza (p. 118-124)

PU

Schwegler, Albert, 1819-1857.
Geschichte der Philosophie im Umriss; ein Leitfaden zur Uebersicht. 6. Aufl. Stuttgart, Franckh, 1868.
vi, 302 p. 23cm.

Includes a section on Spinoza (p. 147-153)

Schwegler, Albert, 1819-1857.
Geschichte der Philosophie im Umriss; ein Leitfaden zur Uebersicht. 9. Aufl. Stuttgart, C. Conradi, 1876.
viii, 302 p. 23cm.

Includes a section on Spinoza (p. 147-153)

Schwegler, Albert, 1819-1857.
Geschichte der Philosophie im Umriss. Ein Leitfaden zur Übersicht. Neue Ausg. Durchgesehen und ergänzt von J. Stern. Leipzig, P. Reclam jun. [189-?]
512 p. 14cm.

Includes a section on Spinoza (p. 241-249)

Schwegler, Albert, 1819-1857.
Geschichte der philosophie im umriss. Ein leitfaden zur uebersicht. Von dr. Albert Schwegler. 11. aufl., ergänzt durch eine darstellung der Schopenhauer'schen lehre, von dr. R. Koeber. Stuttgart, C. Conradi, 1882.
1 p. l., [vii]-viii, 320 p. 22½cm.

Includes a section on Spinoza (p. 147-153)

1. Philosophy—Hist. I. Koeber, Raphael Gustav von, 1848-
[Full name: Friedrich Karl Albert Schwegler]

Schwegler, Albert, 1819-1857.
Geschichte der Philosophie im Umriss; ein Leitfaden zur Übersicht. 14. Aufl., durchgesehen und ergänzt von R. Koeber. Stuttgart, C. Conradi, 1887.
iv, 372 p. 23cm.

Includes a section on Spinoza (p. 184-191)

Schwegler, Albert, 1819-1857.
Handbook of the history of philosophy; by Dr. Albert Schwegler. Tr. and annotated by James Hutchison Stirling ... 5th ed. ... cor. ... Edinburgh, Edmondston & Douglas, 1874.
xviii p., 1 l., 486 p. 18 cm.
Half-title: Schwegler's history of philosophy. Includes a chapter on Spinoza (p. 168-176) and other references to him.
1. Philosophy—Hist. I. Stirling, James Hutchison, 1820- ed. and tr.
Full name: Friedrich Karl Albert Schwegler.

Schwegler, Albert, 1819-1857.
Handbook of the history of philosophy. Tr. and annotated by James Hutchison Stirling. 7th ed. with additional corrections. Edinburgh, Edmonston, 1879.
xviii, 486 p.

Includes a chapter on Spinoza (p. 168-176) and other references to him.

Schwegler, Albert, 1819-1857.
A history of philosophy in epitome, by Dr. Albert Schwegler. Translated from the original German, by Julius H. Seelye. New York, London, D. Appleton and company, 1856.
xiv, [11]-365 p. 20cm.

Includes a section on Spinoza (p. 184-191)

1. Philosophy—Hist. I. Seelye, Julius Hawley, 1824-1895, tr.
[Full name: Friedrich Karl Albert Schwegler]

Schwegler, Albert, 1819-1857.
Overzicht van de geschiedenis der wijsbegeerte; een akademiesch handboek. Naar de vierde duitsche uitgave bewerkt door A. van der Linde. Utrecht, J. J. H. Kemmer, 1863.
viii, 374 p. 23cm.

Includes a section on Spinoza (p. 170-177)

Sengler, Jakob, 1799-1878.
Ueber das Wesen und die Bedeutung der spekulativen Philosophie und Theologie in der gegenwärtigen Zeit mit besonderer Rücksicht auf die Religionsphilosophie. Heidelberg, J. B. E. Mohr, 1837.
xix, 540 p.

Includes a section on Spinoza (p. 138-171)

D-2 1501

Shestov, Lev, 1866-1938.
На вѣсахъ Іова (странствованія по душамъ) Парижъ, 1929.
370 p.

Title transliterated: Na vi͡esakh Iova.
Includes a chapter on Spinoza (p. 235-257)

NNC

SPECIAL COLLECTIONS SPINOZA
D-2 1502

Siebert, Otto, 1869-
Geschichte der neueren deutschen Philosophie seit Hegel. Ein Handbuch zur Einführung in das philosophische Studium der neusten Zeit. Göttingen, Vandenhoeck und Ruprecht, 1898.
vii, [1], 496 p. 23cm.

Includes references to Spinoza.

SPECIAL COLLECTIONS SPINOZA
D-2 1503

Sigwart, Heinrich Christoph Wilhelm, 1789-1874.
Geschichte der Philosophie vom allgemeinen wissenschaftlichen und geschichtlichen Standpunkt. Stuttgart, Cotta, 1844.
3 v. 24cm.

Includes a section on Spinoza (v. 2, p. 203-292)
Bibliography: v. 1, p. 21-24, [375]-380.

D-2 1504

Sigwart, Heinrich Christoph Wilhelm von, 1789-1844
Handbuch der theoretischen Philosophie; ein Beytrag für Philosophie und Geschichte der Philosophie. Tübingen, C. F. Osiander, 1820.
vi, 442 p.

Includes a section "Spinozismus" (p. 209-222)

SPECIAL COLLECTIONS SPINOZA
D-2 1505

Snider, Denton Jaques, 1841-1925.
Modern European philosophy; the history of philosophy psychologically treated. St. Louis, Mo., Sigma Publishing Co. [1904]
829 p. 21cm.

Includes a chapter on Spinoza (p. 118-272)

D-2 1506

Socher, Joseph, 1755-1834.
Grundriss der Geschichte der philosophischen Systeme von den Griechen bis auf Kant. Zum Gebrauche öffentlicher Vorlesungen an der Kurfl. baierischen Landesuniversität bestimmt. München, J. Lentner, 1801.
5 p. l., 338 p., 1 l. 21 cm.

Includes a section on Spinoza (p. 229-234)

SPECIAL COLLECTIONS SPINOZA
D-2 1507

Sortais, Gaston
La philosophie moderne depuis Bacon jusqu'à Leibniz; études historiques. Paris, P. Lethielleux, 1920-22.
v. 1-2. plates, ports., facsim. 25cm.

Includes a section on Spinoza (v. 2, p. 461-480)

SPECIAL COLLECTIONS SPINOZA
D-2 1508

Spiegler, Gyula Samuel, 1838-
Geschichte der Philosophie des Judenthums. Nach den neuesten Forschungen dargestellt. Leipzig, W. Friedrich [1890]
xiii, 369 p. diagr. 21½cm.

Includes chapters on Spinoza (p. [318]-344)

D-2 1509

Stäudlin, Carl Friedrich, 1761-1826.
Geschichte der Moralphilosophie. Hannover, Helwing, 1822.
xxii, 1055 p.

Includes a section on Spinoza (p. 762-774)

D-2 1510

Stöckl, Albert, 1823-1895.
Lehrbuch der Geschichte der Philosophie. 3., verb. Aufl. Mainz, F. Kirchheim, 1888.
2 v. in 1.

Includes a section on Spinoza (v. 2, p. 154-169)

Strecker,
Spinoza, Benedikt. [1913]
836-839 col.

From Schiele, Friedrich Michael, ed. Die Religion in Geschichte und Gegenwart, Bd. 5, 1913.

Suabedissen, David Theodor August, d. 1835.
Resultate der philosophischen Forschungen über die Natur der menschlichen Erkenntniss von Plato bis Kant. Marburg, Verlag der neuen academischen Buchhandlung, 1805.
vi, 444 p.

Includes a chapter on Spinoza (p. 139-146)

Taylor, Henry Osborn, 1856-1941.
Human values and verities. New York, Macmillan, 1928.
xiv, 282 p. 24cm.

Includes a section on Spinoza (p. 163-178)

Tennemann, Wilhelm Gottlieb, 1761-1819.
Geschichte der philosophie, von d. Wilhelm Gottlieb Tennemann ... Leipzig, J. A. Barth, 1798-1819.
11 v. in 12. front. (port.: v. 10) 21½cm.
Contains bibliographies.
Includes a section on Spinoza (v. 10, p. 374-496)

1. Philosophy—Hist.

Tennemann, Wilhelm Gottlieb, 1761-1819.
Geschichte der Philosophie. [2. Aufl.] Mit berichtigenden, beurtheilenden und ergänzenden Anmerkungen und Zusätzen hrsg. von Amadeus Wendt. Erster Band: Die Geschichte der griechischen Philosophie bis auf Sokrates, nebst einer allgemeinen Einleitung in die Geschichte der Philosophie enthaltend. Leipzig, J. A. Barth, 1829.
lxxx, 558 p. 23cm.

No more published.
Contains bibliographies.

Tennemann, Wilhelm, Gottlieb, 1761-1819.
A manual of the history of philosophy, tr. from the German of Tennemann. By the Rev. Arthur Johnson ... Oxford, D. A. Talboys, 1832.
x, 494 p. 22cm.

Includes a section on Spinoza (p. 322-329)

1. Philosophy—Hist. I. Johnson, Arthur, 1798-1858, tr.

Tennemann, Wilhelm Gottlieb, 1761-1819.
A manual of the history of philosophy. Tr. from the German of Tennemann, by Arthur Johnson, rev., enl., and continued, by J. R. Morell. London, H. G. Bohn, 1852.
xii, 532 p. 19 cm. (Bohn's philological library)

Includes a section on Spinoza (p. 312-318)

Tennemann, Wilhelm Gottlieb, 1761-1819.
A manual of the history of philosophy, translated from the German of Tennemann, by the Rev. Arthur Johnson. Revised, enlarged, and continued by J. R. Morell. London, Bell & Daldy, 1873.
xii, 532 p. (Bohn's Philosophical library)

Includes a section on Spinoza (p. 312-318)

Tennemann, Wilhelm Gottlieb, 1761-1819.
Wilhelm Gottlieb Tennemann's Grundriss der Geschichte der Philosophie für den akademischen Unterricht. 4. verm. und verb. Aufl., oder zweite Bearbeitung von Amadeus Wendt. Leipzig, J. A. Barth, 1825.
xvi, 562 p. 21cm.

Includes a section on Spinoza (p. 337-344)
Includes bibliographies.

Tennemann, Wilhelm Gottlieb, 1761-1819.
Wilhelm Gottlieb Tennemann's Grundriss der Geschichte der Philosophie für den akademischen Unterricht. 5. verm. und verb. Aufl. oder 3. Bearbeitung, von Amadeus Wendt. Leipzig, J. A. Barth, 1829.
xvi, 607 p. 21cm.

Includes a section on Spinoza (p. 373-380)
Includes bibliographies.

Thilo, A
Kurze pragmatische Geschichte der neueren Philosophie. Cöthen, O. Schulze, 1874.
405 p. 23cm.

Includes sections on Spinoza (p. 69-89)

Trendelenburg, Friedrich Adolf, 1802-1872.
Historische Beiträge zur Philosophie. Berlin, G. Bethge, 1867.
v. 3.

Includes three essays on Spinoza.

Original boards.

Turbiglio, Sebastiano, b. 1842.
Storia della filosofia; Cartesio, Malebranche, Spinoza. Torino, Tipografia italiana, 1866.
88 p. 21cm.

Turner, William, *bp.*, 1871-1936.
History of philosophy, by William Turner, S. T. D. Boston and London, Ginn and company, 1903.
x, 674 p. 21½ cm.

CONTENTS.—pt. 1. Ancient philosophy.—pt. 2. Philosophy of the Christian era.

Includes a chapter on Spinoza (p. 466-485)

1. Philosophy—Hist.

Ueberweg, Friedrich, 1826-1871.
Friedrich Ueberwegs Grundriss der Geschichte der Philosophie. Dritter Teil: Die Neuzeit bis zum Ende des achtzehnten Jahrhunderts. 11. mit einem Philosophen- und Literatoren-Register versehene Aufl. bearbeitet und hrsg. von Dr. Max Frischeisen-Köhler. Berlin, Mittler, 1914.
xi, 439, 144 p. 24 cm.

Includes a section on Spinoza (p. 122-152) and other references to him.

Ueberweg, Friedrich, 1826-1871.
Friedrich Ueberwegs Grundriss der Geschichte der Philosophie. Dritter Teil: Die Neuzeit bis zum Ende des achtzehnten Jahrhunderts. 10, mit einem Philosophen- und Literatoren-Register versehene Aufl., bearb. und hrsg. von Max Heinze. Berlin, Mittler, 1907.
viii, 442 p. 24cm.

Added special t.-p.
Includes a section on Spinoza (p. 115-156)
Contains bibliographies.

Ueberweg, Friedrich, 1826-1871.
Friedrich Ueberwegs Grundriss der Geschichte der Philosophie. Dritter Teil: Die Philosophie der Neuzeit bis zum Ende des achtzehnten Jahrhunderts. 12., mit einem Philosophen- und Literatoren-Register versehene Aufl., völlig neubearb. von Max Frischeisen-Köhler und Willy Moog. Berlin, Mittler, 1924.
xv, 811 p. 24cm.

Added special t.-p.
Includes a section on Spinoza (p. 269-299)
Contains bibliographies.

Ueberweg, Friedrich, 1826-1871.
Grundriss der Geschichte der Philosophie. Dritter Theil. Die Neuzeit. 3., verb. und ergänzte, mit einem Philosophen- und Litteratoren-Register versehene Aufl. Berlin, Mittler, 1872.
xv, 391 p. 23cm.

Includes a section on Spinoza (p. 60-89) and other references to him.
Contains bibliographies.

Ueberweg, Friedrich, 1826-1871.
Grundriss der Geschichte der Philosophie. Zweiter Theil. Die mittlere oder die patristische und scholastische Zeit. 4., verb. und mit einem Philosophen- und Litteratoren-Register versehene Aufl., hrsg. von Rudolf Reicke. Berlin, Mittler, 1873.
viii, 262 p. 23cm.

Includes references to Spinoza.
Contains bibliographies.

Ueberweg, Friedrich, 1826-1871.
History of philosophy, from Thales to the present time. Tr. from the 4th German ed., by Geo. S. Morris, with additions, by Noah Porter. With a preface by the editors of the Philosophical and theological library. New York, Scribner, Armstrong, 1876.
2 v. 23 cm. (Theological and philosophical library ... Vols. I and II of the philosophical division)

Includes a section on Spinoza (v. 2, p. 55-78) and other references to him.

D-2 1531

Ulrici, Hermann, 1806-1884.
Das grundprincip der philosophie, kritisch und speculativ entwickelt von dr. Hermann Ulrici ... Leipzig, T. O. Weigel, 1845-46.
2 v. 21½cm.
L. C. set incomplete: v. 2 wanting.
CONTENTS.—1. th. Geschichte und kritik der principien der neueren philosophie.—2. th. Speculative grundlegung des systems der philosophie, oder die lehre vom wissen.
Includes a chapter on Spinoza (v. 1, p. 42-66)
1. Philosophy, Modern—Hist.
10-29943 Revised
Library of Congress B798.U4 [r84b2]

SPECIAL COLLECTIONS SPINOZA D-2 1536

Vorländer, Karl, 1860-
Geschichte der Philosophie. 3. Aufl. Leipzig, Dürr, 1911.
2 v. 20cm. (Philosophische Bibliothek, Bd. 105-106)

Includes a chapter on Spinoza (v. 2, p. 37-58) and other references to him.
Contains bibliographies.
Contents.--1. Bd. Altertum, Mittelalter und Übergang zur Neuzeit.--2. Bd. Philosophie der Neuzeit.

SPECIAL COLLECTIONS SPINOZA D-2 1532

Vaughan, Charles Edwyn, 1854-1922.
Studies in the history of political philosophy before and after Rousseau. Edited by A. G. Little. Manchester, University Press; London, New York, Longmans, Green, 1925.
2 v. port. 22cm. (Publications of the University of Manchester, no. 166-167)

Includes a chapter "The social contract: Spinoza" (v. 1, p. 62-129)

D-2 1537

Vorländer, Karl, 1860-
Geschichte der Philosophie. 4. Aufl. Leipzig, F. Meiner, 1913.
2 v. 20cm. (Philosophische Bibliothek; Verlag von Felix Meiner. Neue Folge, Bd. 105-106)

Includes a chapter on Spinoza (v. 2, p. 37-58) and other references to him.
Contents.--1. Bd. Altertum, Mittelalter und Ubergang zur Neuzeit.--2. Bd. Philosophie der Neuzeit.

NUC

SPECIAL COLLECTIONS SPINOZA D-2 1533

Verweyen, Johannes Maria, 1883-
Die philosophie des Mittelalters. Berlin, Vereinigung wissenschaftlicher Verleger, 1921.
x, 308 p. 24cm. (Added t.-p.: Geschichte der Philosophie ... Bd. 4)

Includes a section on Spinoza (p. 290-294)
Bibliographical footnotes.

SPECIAL COLLECTIONS SPINOZA D-2 1538

Vorländer, Karl, 1860-
Geschichte der Philosophie. 6. Aufl. Leipzig, F. Meiner, 1921.
2 v. 20cm.

Includes a chapter on Spinoza (v. 2, p. 37-58) and other references to him.
Contents.--v. 1. Altertum, Mittelalter und Übergang zur Neuzeit.--v. 2. Philosophie der Neuzeit.

SPECIAL COLLECTIONS SPINOZA D-2 1534

Vogel, August, 1842-
Geschichte der Philosophie, nebst einer tabellarischen Uebersicht und einer vergleichenden Zeittabelle. Gütersloh, C. Bertelsmann, 1873.
viii, 155 p. 20cm. (His Philosophisches Repetitorium, 1. Theil)

Includes a section on Spinoza (p. 82-87)

D-2 1539

Vorländer, Karl, 1860-
Geschichte der Philosophie. 7. Aufl. Leipzig, F. Meiner, 1927.
3 v. 20cm.

Includes a chapter on Spinoza (v. 2, p. 106-127) and other references to him.
Contents.--1. Bd. Altertum und Mittelalter.--2. Bd. Die Philosophie der Neuzeit bis Kant.--3. Bd. Die Philosophie des 19. und 20. Jahrhunderts.

NUC

D-2 1535

Voorthuysen, Hendrik du Marchie van, 1853-1885.
Nagelaten geschriften; uitgegeven door A. G. de Geer. Arnhem, P. G. Quint, 1886-87.
2 v.

Includes a section "De grondbeginselen van Spinoza's wijsbegeerte" (v. 2, p. 211-259)

MH

D-2 1540

Vossius, Gerardus Joannes, 1577-1649.
Gerardi Johannis Vossii De philosophorum sectis liber. Cum continuatione & supplementis Johannis Jacobi à Ryssel. Lipsiae, Impensis J. C. Meyeri, 1705.
4 p. l., 216 p., 2 l.

Includes a reference to Spinoza (p. 203)

OCH

Wahle, Richard, 1857-
Die Tragikomödie der Weisheit; die Ergebnisse und die Geschichte des Philosophierens. Ein Lesebuch. Wien und Leipzig, W. Braumüller, 1915.
vii, 415 p. 24cm.

Includes a section on Spinoza (p. 316-322)
Original paper covers bound in.

Willmann, Otto, 1839-1920.
Geschichte des Idealismus. Braunschweig, F. Vieweg, 1894-97.
3 v. 22 cm.

Includes a section on Spinoza (v. 3, p. 283-313)

Webb, Clement Charles Julian, 1865-
A history of philosophy, by Clement C. J. Webb. New York, H. Holt and company; ₍etc., etc., 1915₎
v, ₍7₎-256 p. 17 cm. (*Half-title:* Home university library of modern knowledge. No. 96)
Bibliography: p. 252-254.
Includes references to Spinoza.

1. Philosophy—Hist.

Willmann, Otto, 1839-1920.
Geschichte des Idealismus. 2. verb. und verm., mit Namen- und Sachregister und terminologischem Anhange versehene Aufl. Braunschweig, F. Vieweg, 1907.
3 v. 23cm.

Includes a section of Spinoza (v. 3, p. ₍287₎-318) and other references to him.

Weber, Alfred, 1835-1914.
Histoire de la philosophie européenne. 7. éd. augm. d'une préface. Paris, Fischbacher, 1905.
631 p.

Includes a section on Spinoza (p. 328-349)

Windelband, Wilhelm, 1848-1915.
Die Geschichte der neueren Philosophie; in ihrem Zusammenhange mit der allgemeinen Cultur und den besonderen Wissenschaften dargestellt. Leipzig, Breitkopf und Härtel, 1878-80.
2 v. 23cm.

Vol. 2 has also special t.-p.: Die Blüthezeit der deutschen Philosophie.
Includes a section on Spinoza (v. 1, p. 186-224)

Weber, Alfred, 1835-1914.
Histoire de la philosophie européenne. 8. éd. aug. d'un appendice bibliographique et d'une table alphabétique des noms propres. Paris, Fischbacher, 1914.
584 p. 25 cm.

Includes a section on Spinoza (p. 296-314) and other references to him.

Windelband, Wilhelm, 1848-1915.
Die Geschichte der neueren Philosophie in ihrem Zusammenhange mit der allgemeinen Kultur und den besonderen Wissenschaften. 1. Bd. Von der Renaissance bis Kant. 3., durchgesehene Aufl. Leipzig, Breitkopf und Härtel, 1904.
x, 588 p. 23cm.

Includes a section on Spinoza (p. 196-234)
Manuscript notes by Carl Gebhardt.

Weber, Alfred, 1835-1914.
History of philosophy, by Alfred Weber ... Authorized translation by Frank Thilly ... From the 5th French ed. New York, C. Scribner's sons, 1896.
xi, 630 p. 21cm.
"Sources": p. 6-16.
Bibliography: p. ₍605₎-611.
Includes a section on Spinoza (p. 323-343)

1. Philosophy—Hist. I. Thilly, Frank, 1865- tr.

₍*Full name:* Émile Alfred Weber₎

Windelband, Wilhelm, 1848-1915.
Die Geschichte der neueren Philosophie in ihrem Zusammenhange mit der allgemeinen Kultur und den besonderen Wissenschaften dargestellt. 7. und 8. unveränderte Aufl. Leipzig, Breitkopf & Härtel, 1922.
2 v. 23 cm.

Includes a section on Spinoza (v. 1, p. 200-239)

D-2
1551

Windelband, Wilhelm, 1848-1915.
Die Geschichte der neueren Philosophie in ihrem Zusammenhange mit der allgemeinen Kultur und den besonderen Wissenschaften. 6. unveränderte Aufl. Leipzig, Breitkopf & Härtel, 1919.
2 v. 24 cm.

Includes a section on Spinoza (v. 1, p. 200-239)

SPECIAL COLLECTIONS
SPINOZA

D-2
1552

Windelband, Wilhelm, 1848-1915.
תולדות הפילוסופיה החדשה, בחבורה עם התרבות הכללית ועם המדעים המיוחדים, מאת וילהלם וינדלבנד. כרך ראשון: הפילוסופיה של תקופת־התחיה. תרגם (בצרוף מבוא ורשימת המונחים ופירושיהם) ס. י. גליקסון. תל־אביב, הוצאת שטיבל, תרפ"ג.
[Tel-Aviv, 1933]
262 p. 23cm.

CONTINUED ON NEXT CARD

NNC

SPECIAL COLLECTIONS
SPINOZA

D-2
1553

Windelband, Wilhelm, 1848-1915. תולדות ה־ פילוסופיה החדשה. [1933] (Card 2)

Title transliterated: Tōlēdhōth ha-pīlōsōfīyā he-ḥădhāshā.
Includes a chapter on Spinoza (p. 212-248)

NNC

SPECIAL COLLECTIONS
SPINOZA

D-2
1554

Wundt, Wilhelm Max, 1832-1920.
Die nationen und ihre philosophie; ein kapitel zum weltkrieg, von Wilhelm Wundt. Leipzig, A. Kröner, 1915.
vi p., 1 l., 146 p. 22½cm.

Includes a section on Spinoza (p. 17-20)

1. Philosophy, Modern—Hist. 2. National characteristics. 3. European war, 1914-1918—Causes.

16—11702

Library of Congress B798.W8
[45b1]

SPECIAL COLLECTIONS
SPINOZA

D-2
1555

Wundt, Wilhelm Max, 1832-1920.
Die Nationen und ihre Philosophie; ein Kapitel zum Weltkrieg. Leipzig, A. Kröner, 1921.
154 p. 18cm. (Kröners Taschenausgabe)

Includes a section on Spinoza (p. 25-28)

D-2
1556

Wundt, William, 1832-1920.
Введеніе въ философію. Переводъ съ нѣмецкаго подъ редакціею Э. Л. Радлова. С.-Петербургъ, Брокгаузъ-Ефронъ, 1903.
vii, iii, 310 p.

Title transliterated: Vvedenie v filosofiŭ.
A translation of Einleitung in die Philosophie.
Includes a section on Spinoza.

NN

D-2
1557

Zerffi, George Gustavus, 1821-1892.
The historical development of idealism and realism. IV. Modern period: Descartes - Spinoza - John Locke. [1880]
331-355 p.

In Royal Historical Society, London. Transactions, v. 8, 1880.

SPECIAL COLLECTIONS
SPINOZA

D-2
1558

Zhitlowsky, Chaim, 1865-1943.
די פילאסאפיע, וואס זי איז און ווי זי האט זיך ענטוויקעלט. ארײנפיהר אין דאס שטודיום פון פילאסאפישע פראבלעמען: די געשיכטליכע ענטוויקלונג פון'ם פילאסאפישען געדאנק. פון דר. חיים זשיטלאווסקי ... ניו יארק, מייזעל עט קא. ...
Philosophy, its history and development. New York, 1910.
v. 1 22cm.
Includes a section on Spinoza (v. 1, p. 239-260)
Contains bibliographies.
1. Philosophy—Hist. I. Title. *Title transliterated:* Di filosofie.

B99.Y5Z5 47-38499

Library of

D-3
STUDIES OF WORKS OR PORTIONS THEREOF

D-3-a
SELECTED WORKS

SPECIAL COLLECTIONS
SPINOZA

D-3-a
1559

Leopold, J H
Ad Spinozae opera posthuma. Hagae Comitis, Apud Martinum Nijhoff, 1902.
92 p. 24cm.

Manuscript notes by Carl Gebhardt.
Original paper cover bound in.

D-3-a
1560

Stein, Ludwig, 1859-1930.
Neue Aufschlüsse über den litterarischen Nachlass und die Herausgabe der Opera posthuma Spinozas. [1888]
[553]-565 p. 23cm.

"Sonderabdruck aus dem Archiv für Geschichte der Philosophie ... Band I, Heft 4."
Original paper cover bound in.
Volume of pamphlets.

D-3-b
COMPENDIUM GRAMMATICES

D-3-b
1561

Chajes, Adolph
Ueber die Hebräische Grammatik Spinoza's. Promotions-Schrift. Breslau, F. W. Jungfer, 1869.
32 p. 23cm.

D-3-b
1562

Stern, Jakob, 1843-1911.
Dr. Salomon Rubin, sein Leben und seine Schriften. Krakau, F. H. Wetstein, 1908.
60 p. port. 21cm.

Includes a reference to his own book on Spinoza (p. 48) and discusses Rubin's translations of Spinoza's Ethica and Compendium grammatices into Hebrew (p. 31 and 39)
Original paper covers bound in.

D-3-c
EPISTOLAE

D-3-c
1563

Bluwstein, Jacob, 1880-
שפינוזה לאור מכתביו במאת י.
פלע. תל-אביב, תרצ"ג.
[1932]
11-13 p. 29cm.

Title transliterated: Shpīnōzā lĕ'ōr mikhtāvāw.
From Moznayim, vol. 4, no. 26, Dec. 15, 1932.
Extracts from the "Anmerkungen" to his edition of Spinozas Briefwechsel, 1916.
With Roth, Leon. Mishnāthō shel Shpīnōzā ... [1932]

NNC

D-3-c
1564

Jahrbuch für die Geschichte der Juden und des Judenthums. 2. Bd. Leipzig, O. Leiner, 1861.
xxiv, 407 p. fold. plate, facsim. 19cm.
(Added t.-p.: Schriften hrsg. vom Institute zur Förderung der israelitischen Literatur. 6. Jahr: 1860-1861)

"Baruch Spinoza, von Dr. Ludwig Philippson" (p. [189]-257) includes letters to and from Spinoza.

D-3-c
1565

Kirchmann, Julius Hermann von, 1802-1884.
Erläuterungen zu Benedict von Spinoza's Briefwechsel. Berlin, L. Heimann, 1872.
87 p. 20cm. (Philosophische Bibliothek. Bd. 47)

1. Spinoza, Benedictus de, 1632-1677. Epistolae.

D-3-c
1566

Land, Jan Pieter Nicolaas, 1834-1897.
De eerste uitgaven der brieven van Spinoza. Amsterdam, J. Muller, 1879.
12 p.

OCH

D-3-c
1567

Land, Jan Pieter Nicolaas, 1834-1897.
Over de eerste uitgaven der brieven van Spinoza. Amsterdam, J. Müller, 1879.
cover-title, 12 p. 24cm.

"Overgedrukt uit de Verslagen en mededeelingen der Koninklijke Akademie van Wetenschappen, Afdeeling Letterkunde, 2de reeks, deel IX."

1. Spinoza, Benedictus de, 1632-1677. Epistolae.

D-3-c
1568

Pollock, Sir Frederick, bart., 1845-1937.
Ms. letters of Spinoza in the Royal Society's Library. [1880]
569-570 p.

In The Athenaeum, Oct. 30, 1880.

D-3-c
1569

Voorst, Dirk Cornelis van, 1752-1833.
Catalogue raisonné de la précieuse collection de manuscrits et d'autographes de mm. D. C. van Voorst, père, et J. J. van Voorst, fils, pasteurs évangéliques à Amsterdam. Amsterdam, F. Muller, 1859.
viii, 224 p. 21 cm.

Includes entries for letters from Spinoza.

NN

D-3-d
ETHICA

D-3-d 1570

Barker, H
Notes on the second part of Spinoza's Ethics. [1938]
159-179, 281-302, 417-439 p.

In Mind, n. s. v. 47, 1938.

D-3-d 1575

Frankl, Wilhelm M
Zum Verständnis von Spinozas "Ethik". Ein Beitrag zur Naturgeschichte philosophischer Systeme. [1906]
218-224 p.

In Archiv für Geschichte der Philosophie, Bd. 19., 1906.

D-3-d 1571

Bierens de Haan, Johannes Diderik, 1866-1943.
De wereld-leer in Spinoza's Ethica. [1897]
143-170, 322-360 p.

In Tweemaandelijksch tijdschrift voor letteren, kunst, wetenschap en politiek, 3. jaargang, 1897.

DLC

SPECIAL COLLECTIONS SPINOZA D-3-d 1576

Garve, Christian, 1742-1798.
Ueber einen Satz aus der Ethik des Spinoza. [1845]
[45]-71 p. 11cm.

From Neue Miniatur-Bibliothek der deutschen Classiker, 99. Bändchen, 1. Theil.

1. Spinoza, Benedictus de, 1632-1677. Ethica.

SPECIAL COLLECTIONS SPINOZA D-3-d 1572

Dessoir, Max, 1867-1947.
Philosophisches lesebuch, hrsg. von Max Dessoir und Paul Menzer ... Stuttgart, Enke, 1903.
viii, 258 p. 22cm.

Includes selections from Spinoza's Ethica in Kirchmann's German translation (p. [82]-96)
Bibliographical references.

Original paper covers bound in.

D-3-d 1577

Garve, Christian, 1742-1798.
Vermischte Aufsätze welche einzeln oder in Zeitschriften erschienen sind. Neuherausgegeben und verbessert. Breslau, bey Wilhelm Gottlieb Korn, 1796-1800.
2 v. in 1.

Includes an essay "Ueber einen Satz aus der Ethik des Spinoza; ein Fragment" (v. 2, p. [357]-387)

SPECIAL COLLECTIONS SPINOZA D-3-d 1573

Dessoir, Max, 1867-1947, ed.
Philosophisches Lesebuch. Herausgegeben von Max Dessoir und Paul Menzer. Dritte, wiederum vermehrte Auflage. Stuttgart, Verlag von Ferdinand Enke, 1910.
viii, 321 p. 22cm.

Includes excerpts from Spinoza's Ethica in Kirchmann's German translation (p. [108]-122)

SPECIAL COLLECTIONS SPINOZA D-3-d 1578

Høffding, Harold, 1843-1931.
Das erste Buch der Ethica. [Hagae Comitis, 1922]
20-53 p. 22cm.

Cover-title: Dissertatio ex Chronici Spinozani tomo secundo separatim edita.
Bibliographical footnotes.

1. Spinoza, Benedictus de, 1632-1677. Ethica.

SPECIAL COLLECTIONS SPINOZA D-3-d 1574

Ettlinger, Max, 1877- ed.
Philosophisches lesebuch, hrsg. von dr. Max Ettlinger ... dr. Paul Simon ... [und] dr. Gottlieb Söhngen ... München, J. Kösel & F. Pustet k.-g. [1925]
443 p. illus. (ports.) 23cm.

Includes selections from Spinoza's "Ethica" (p. [232]-238)

1. Philosophy—Collections. 2. Philosophers. I. Simon, Paul, 1882- joint ed. II. Söhngen, Gottlieb, 1893- joint ed. III. Title.

25-15857

Library of Congress B80.E8
Copyright A—Foreign 28029
[2]

SPECIAL COLLECTIONS SPINOZA D-3-d 1579

Høffding, Harald, 1843-1931.
Spinoza's Ethica, analyse og karakteristik. København, A. F. Høst, 1918.
97 p. 27cm.

From D. Kgl. Danske vidensk. selsk. Skrifter, 7. raekke, Historisk og filosfisk afd. III. 3, p. [339]-433.
Presentation copy to Carl Gebhardt, with the author's inscription and signature.
Original paper cover bound in.

Høffding, Harald, 1843-1931.
Spinozas Ethica, Analyse und Charakteristik. Heidelberg, C. Winter, 1924.
146 p. 25cm. (Bibliotheca Spinozana curis Societatis Spinozanae, t. IV)

Høffding, Harald, 1843-1931.
Spinoza's Ethica, analyse og karakteristik. København, A. F. Høst, 1918.
97 p. 27cm.

From D. Kgl. Danske vidensk. selsk. Skrifter, 7. raekke, Historisk og filosfisk afd. III. 3, p. [339]-433.
Presentation copy to Carl Gebhardt, with the author's inscription and signature.
Original paper cover bound in.

Joachim, Harold Henry, 1868-1938.
A study of the Ethics of Spinoza (Ethica ordine geometrico demonstrata) by Harold H. Joachim ... Oxford, Clarendon press, 1901.
xiv, 316 p. 23 cm.
"References and abbreviations": p. xiii-xiv.

1. Spinoza, Benedictus de, 1632-1677—Ethica. 2. Ethics.

B3999.E8J6 2—7599

Library of Congress [55h1]

Kellermann, Benzion, 1869-
Die Ethik Spinozas; über Gott und Geist. Berlin, C. A. Schwetschke, 1922.
viii, 436 p. 23 cm.
Bibliographical footnotes.
Printed on "holzfreies Papier".

1. Spinoza, Benedictus de, 1632-1677. 2. Ethics.

B3999.E8K4 A 53-971

Columbia Univ. Libraries for Library of Congress [1]

Kellermann, Benzion, 1869-
Die Ethik Spinozas; über Gott und Geist. Berlin, C. A. Schwetschke, 1922.
viii, 436 p. 23 cm.
Bibliographical footnotes.

1. Spinoza, Benedictus de, 1632-1677. 2. Ethics.

B3999.E8K4 A 53-971

Columbia Univ. Libraries for Library of Congress [1]

Kirchmann, Julius Hermann von, 1802-1884.
Erläuterungen zu Benedict von Spinoza's Ethik. Berlin, L. Heimann, 1869.
viii, 186 p. 19cm. (Philosophische Bibliothek. 5. Bd.)

Bound with Spinoza, Benedictus de. Kurzgefasste Abhandlung von Gott, dem Menschen und dessen Glück. 1869

Kirchmann, Julius Hermann von, 1802-1884.
Erläuterungen zu Benedict von Spinoza's Ethik. 2. Aufl. Berlin, L. Heimann, 1871.
vii, 186 p. 19cm. (Philosophische Bibliothek. 5. Bd.)

Paper cover, bound in, has imprint: Heidelberg, G. Weiss, 1882.
Bound with Spinoza, Benedictus de. Ethik. 1886.

Kirchmann, Julius Hermann von, 1802-1884.
Erläuterungen zu Benedict von Spinoza's Ethik. 2. Aufl. Berlin, L. Heimann, 1871.
vii, 186 p. 20cm. (Philosophische Bibliothek. 5. Bd.)

Bound with Spinoza, Benedictus de. Ethik. 1870.

Kirchmann, Julius Hermann von, 1802-1884.
Erläuterungen zu Benedict von Spinoza's Ethik. 2. Aufl. Berlin, L. Heimann, 1871.
vii, 186 p. 22cm. (Philosophische Bibliothek. 5. Bd.)

Paper cover, bound in, has date 1870.

NNC

Kirchmann, Julius Hermann von, 1802-1884.
Erläuterungen zu Benedict von Spinoza's Ethik. 2. Aufl. Berlin, L. Heimann, 1871.
vii, 186 p. 19cm. (Philosophische Bibliothek. 5. Bd.)

Paper cover, bound in, has imprint: Heidelberg, G. Weiss, 1882.
Bound with Spinoza, Benedictus de. Ethik. 1886.

D-3-d
1590

Kirchmann, Julius Hermann von, 1802-1884.
Erläuterungen zu Benedict von Spinoza's Ethik. 3. Aufl. Leipzig, 1900.
186 p.

OCH

D-3-d
1595

Leibniz, Gottfried Wilhelm, Freiherr von, 1646-1716.
Hauptschriften zur Grundlegung der Philosophie. Übersetzt von A. Buchenau, durchgesehen und mit Einleitungen und Erläuterungen hrsg. von E. Cassirer. Leipzig, Dürr'schen Buchhandlung, 1904.
viii, 374 p. (His Philosophische Werke, 1. Bd.)

Philosophische Bibliothek, Bd. 107.
Includes a section "Zu Spinozas Ethik" (p. 355-374)

DLC

SPECIAL COLLECTIONS
SPINOZA
D-3-d
1591

[Kuffeler, Abraham Johannes] 1637-1694.
Specimen artis ratiocinandi naturalis & artificialis ad pantosophiâe principia manuducens ... Hamburgi, Apud Henricum Kunraht, 1684.
3 v. in 1. fold. plates. 16cm.

Includes a section against Willem van Blijenbergh's criticism of Spinoza's Ethica (v. 1, p. 119-127)
Vol. 2-3 have title: Principiorum pantosophiâe pars secunda [-tertia]

SPECIAL COLLECTIONS
SPINOZA
D-3-d
1596

Lewkowitz, Albert, 1883-
Die Ethik Spinozas in ihrem Verhältnis zum Judentum. [1926]
355-366 p. 24cm.

From Monatsschrift für Geschichte und Wissenschaft des Judentums, 70. Jahrgang, Heft 9/10, September/Oktober, 1926.

D-3-d
1592

Kuntze, Friedrich
Die Selbstbekenntnisse in der Ethik Spinozas. [1906]
409-423 p.

In Preussische Jahrbücher, 123. Bd., 1906.

D-3-d
1597

Lilla, Vincenzo, b. 1837.
Un saggio di critica objettiva delle sei definizioni del primo libro dell' Etica di B. Spinoza. [1896]
27 p.

In Accademia pontaniana, Naples. Atti, v. 26, 1896.

DLC

SPECIAL COLLECTIONS
SPINOZA
D-3-d
1593

Land, Jan Pieter Nicolaas, 1834-1897.
Over de uitgaven en den text der Ethica van Spinoza. Amsterdam, J Müller, 1881.
cover-title, 21 p. 23cm.

"Overgedrukt uit de Verslagen en mededeelingen der Koninklijke Akademie van Wetenschappen, Afdeeling Letterkunde, 2de reeks, deel XI."

1. Spinoza, Benedictus de, 1632-1677. Ethica

D-3-d
1598

Pulcini, Celestino
L'Etica di Spinoza. Studio critico, gnoseologico, storico; con prefazione di B. Varisco. Genova, A. F. Formíggini, 1914.
206 p. (Biblioteca di filosofia e di pedagogia)

MH

D-3-d
1594

Leibniz, Gottfried Wilhelm, Freiherr von, 1646-1716.
Die Bemerkungen, welche Leibnitz dem auf der Königlichen Bibliothek zu Hannover befindlichen Exemplare von Spinoza's Ethik (in B. d. S. Opera posthuma. 1677) beygefügt hat. [1830]
1265-1274 p.

In Göttingische gelehrte Anzeigen, 1830, Bd. 2.
Leibniz' notes to his copy of the Ethica, ed. by G. E. Schulze.

D-3-d
1599

Lindsay, James
Some criticisms on Spinoza's Ethics. [1905]
496-506 p.

In Archiv für Geschichte der Philosophie, Bd. 18., 1905.

Mielisch, Gustav, 1873-
Quae de affectuum natura et viribus Spinoza (Ethices p. III et IV) docuit, ita exponantur, ut quantum fieri potest, exemplis illustrentur. Halis Saxonum, Typis expressit "Wischan & Wettengel", 1900.
53 p. 22cm.

Thesis, Erlangen.

Philosophical essays in honor of James Edwin Creighton, by former students in the Sage school of philosophy of Cornell university, in commemoration of twenty-five years' service as teacher and scholar. New York, Macmillan, 1917.
xii, 356 p. 25 cm.

Includes "The confusion of categories in Spinoza's Ethics" by Ernest Albee (p. 1-25) and "Hegel's criticism of Spinoza" by Katherine E. Gilbert (p. 26-41)

Picton, James Allanson, 1832-1910.
Spinoza; a handbook to the Ethics. London, A. Constable, 1907.
ix, 264 p. 20cm.

Räder Hans, 1849-
Logische Prüfung der im ersten Buch von Baruch Spinoza's Ethik enthaltenen Definitionen. Wandsbeck, F. Puvogel, 1880.
vii p. 26cm.

At head of title: Gymnasium mit Höherer Bürgerschule in Wandsbeck. VII. Jahresbericht.

1. Spinoza, Benedictus de, 1632-1677. Ethica.

Rand, Benjamin, 1856- *comp.*
Modern classical philosophers; selections illustrating modern philosophy from Bruno to Spencer, comp. by Benjamin Rand ... Boston and New York, Houghton, Mifflin and company, 1908.
xiii, 740 p., 1 l. 22½ cm.
Includes a chapter of selections from Spinoza's Ethics (p. 148-198) and other references to Spinoza.

1. Philosophy, Modern—Hist. 2. Philosophy, Modern. I. Title.

Reyes, Alfonso, 1889-
El testimonio de Juan Peña (con tres dibujos de Manuel Rodríguez Lozano) ₍Rio de Janeiro, Villas Boas, 1930₎
₍49₎ p. illus. 28cm.

"Lo dedico a los dos o tres compañeros de mi vida que estudiaban conmigo la Ética, de Espinosa."

Robinson, Lewis.
Kommentar zu Spinozas Ethik, von Lewis Robinson ... Leipzig, F. Meiner, 1928-
v. 19½cm.

Manuscript notes by Carl Gebhardt.

1. Spinoza, Benedictus de, 1632-1677. Ethica.

Rogers, Arthur Kenyon, 1868-
Morals in review, by A. K. Rogers. New York, The Macmillan company, 1927.
xii p., 1 l., 456 p. 22½ cm.
Bibliography: p. 453-456.
Includes a chapter on Spinoza's Ethica (p. 159-190)

1. Ethics—Hist. I. Title.

Scheidemantel, Herman
Die Grundprobleme der Ethik Spinoza's. ("Der Begriff der actio im Gegensatz zu dem der passio in Spinoza's Ethik.") Preisschrift der Krug-Stiftung bei der Philosophischen Fakultät zu Leipzig. Leipzig, H. Haacke, 1898.
36 p. 23cm.

Scheler, Max, 1874-1928.
Spinozas Ethik; eine Einleitung. ₍München, 1923₎
30-38 p. port. 19cm.

From Almanach der Rupprechtpresse auf die Jahre 1923-25.

SPECIAL COLLECTIONS SPINOZA D-3-d 1610

Schmalz, Carl
Die Grundbegriffe des ersten Buches der Ethik Spinoza's. Berlin, M. Oldenbourg, 1892.
42 p. 27cm.

At head of title: Jahresbericht über das Königl. Joachimsthalische Gymnasium ...
Volume of pamphlets.

NNC

SPECIAL COLLECTIONS SPINOZA D-3-d 1611

Schmidt, Arnold, 1862-
Kritische Studie über das 1. Buch von Spinozas Ethik. Berlin, F. Schneider & Co. (H. Klinsmann) 1889.
28 p. 24cm.

Issued also as thesis, Berlin.
Original paper cover bound in.
Volume of pamphlets.

NNC

SPECIAL COLLECTIONS SPINOZA D-3-d 1612

Schmidt, Arnold, 1862-
Kritische Studie über das 1. Buch von Spinozas Ethik. Berlin, 1889.
28 p. 23cm.

Thesis, Berlin.

SPECIAL COLLECTIONS SPINOZA D-3-d 1613

Scholz, J
Über die geometrische Methode in der Ethik des Spinoza. Spremberg, C. F. Säbisch, 1863.
17 p. 27cm.

At head of title: Jahresbericht über die Stadtschule, insonderheit über die zukünftige Realschule zu Spremberg.
~~Volume of pamphlets.~~

SPECIAL COLLECTIONS SPINOZA D-3-d 1614

Schwarz, Friedrich, 1875-
Spinozas Ethik in ihrem Verhältnis zur Erfahrung. Cassel, Druck von L. Döll, 1902.
51 p. 21cm.

Thesis, Leipzig.

Bound with Kniat, Joseph. Spinoza's Ethik. 1888.

SPECIAL COLLECTIONS SPINOZA D-3-d 1615

Shanks, Alexander
An introduction to Spinoza's Ethic. London, Macmillan, 1938.
v, 103 p. 23cm.

SPECIAL COLLECTIONS SPINOZA D-3-d 1616

Shaw, Charles Gray, 1871-1949 ed.
Basic thoughts of philosophy & religion, edited by Charles Gray Shaw ... New York, The Sun dial press, inc., 1938.
5 p. l., 145 p. 21½cm.

"The intellectual love of God, from the Ethics of Spinoza": p. 31-34.

1. Philosophy. 2. Religion. I. Title.

38—29194
Library of Congress B29.S5
[44d1] 108.22

D-3-d 1617

Smith, J F
Ethics of Spinoza. [1870]
550-571 p.

In Theological review, v. 7, 1870.

NNUT

D-3-d 1618

Tukiewicz, Aleksander
O nietkórych zalozeniach Etyki Spinozy. [1925]
402-432 p.

In Kwartalnik filozoficzny, t. 3, 1925.

NN

SPECIAL COLLECTIONS SPINOZA D-3-d 1619

Wahle, Richard, 1857-
Kurze Erklärung der Ethik von Spinoza und Darstellung der definitiven Philosophie. Wien, W. Braumüller, 1899.
viii, 212 p. 20cm.

Weise, Hermann
Über das erste Buch der Ethik des Spinoza; Inauguraldissertation. Salzwedel, Buchdr. von H. Robolsky ₍1875₎
36 p. 23cm.

Bibliographical notes.

1. Spinoza, Benedictus de, 1632-1677. Ethica.

Wittich, Christoph, 1625-1687.
Christoph. Wittichii Anti-Spinoza; sive, Examen Ethices Benedicti de Spinoza, et Commentarius de Deo et ejus attributis. Amstelodami, Apud Joannem Wolters, 1690.
₍18₎, 7-424 p. 22cm.

Wrzecionko, Rudolf, 1865-
Der Grundgedanke der Ethik des Spinoza; eine Untersuchung über Inhalt und Methode der Metaphysik überhaupt und der Metaphysik des Spinoza im besonderen. Wien, W. Braumüller, 1894.
57 p. 24cm.

Original paper cover bound in.
Volume of pamphlets.

D-3-e
RENATI DES CARTES PRINCIPIA

Kirchmann, Julius Hermann von, 1802-1884.
Erläuterungen zu Benedict von Spinoza's Bearbeitung der Prinzipien der Philosophie des René Descartes. Berlin, L. Heimann, 1871.
112 p. 20cm. (Philosophische Bibliothek. 42. Bd.)

D-3-f
TRACTATUS DE DEO

Abrahams, Israel, 1858-1925.
Spinoza and the synagogue. ₍1910₎
18-19 p. port.

In Jewish chronicle, London, Feb. 11, 1910.
With reference to Spinoza's Short treatise on God, man, & his well-being, tr. and ed. with a life of Spinoza by Abraham Wolf.

Dunin-Borkowski, Stanislaus, Graf von, 1864-
Der erste Anhang zu de Spinozas Kurzer Abhandlung. ₍1921₎
63-80 p. 20cm.

Cover-title: Dissertatio ex Chronici Spinozani tomo primo separatim edita.

Freudenthal, Jacob, 1839-1907.
Spinozastudien. II. Über die dem kurzen Tractate eingefügten Dialoge. ₍1897₎
₍1₎-25 p. 27cm.

"Sonderabdruck aus Zeitschrift für Philosophie und philosophische Kritik. 109. Bd."
The first part of the article appeared in the same periodical, 108. Bd.

Freudenthal, Jacob, 1839-1907.
Spinozastudien. ₍1896-97₎
238-282, ₍1₎-25 p. 27cm.

From Zeitschrift für Philosophie und philosophische Kritik, 108.-109. Bd., 1896-97.
Contents.--I. Über den kurzen Tractat.--II. Über die dem kurzen Tractate eingefügten Dialoge.

Joël, Manuel, 1826-1890.
Zur genesis der lehre Spinoza's, mit besonderer berücksichtigung des kurzen traktats "Von Gott, dem menschen und dessen glückseligkeit", von dr. M. Joël ... Breslau, Schletter (H. Skutsch) 1871.
2 p. l., 74 p. 20½cm.

1. Spinoza, Benedictus de, 1632-1677. Tractatus de Deo et homine.

29-206

Sigwart, Christoph von, 1830-1904.
Spinoza's neuentdeckter Tractat von Gott, dem menschen und dessen glückseligkeit. Erläutert und in seiner bedeutung für das verständniss des spinozismus untersucht, von dr. Christoph Sigwart ... Gotha, R. Besser, 1866.
vi p., 1 l., 158 p. 22cm.

SPECIAL COLLECTIONS
SPINOZA

D-3-f
1630

Sigwart, Christoph von, 1830-1904.
Spinoza's neuentdeckter Tractat von Gott, dem menschen und dessen glückseligkeit. Erläutert und in seiner bedeutung für das verständniss des spinozismus untersucht, von dr. Christoph Sigwart ... Gotha, R. Besser, 1866.
vi p., 1 l., 158 p. 22cm.

1. Spinoza, Benedictus de, 1632-1677. Tractatus de Deo et homine.
44-18192

Library of Congress B3979.S5
[2]

D-3-f
1631

Wolf, Albert, 1890-
Die Bedeutung des kurzen Traktats und der Abhandlung über die Verbesserung des Verstandes für den Aufbau und die Entwicklung des Systems Spinozas. Breslau, Hochschulverlag [1919]
4 p.

Abstract of thesis, Breslau.

D-3 g
TRACTATUS DE INTELLECTUS

SPECIAL COLLECTIONS
SPINOZA

D-3-g
1632

[Bidney, David] 1908-
Joachim on Spinoza's Tractatus de intellectus emendatione.
47-65 p. 26cm.

Signed: D. Bidney.
"Reprinted from the Philosophical review, January, 1942."
Presentation copy to A. S. Oko with the author's inscription and signature.

SPECIAL COLLECTIONS
SPINOZA

D-3-g
1633

Elbogen, Ismar, 1874-1943.
Der Tractatus de intellectus emendatione und seine Stellung in der Philosophie Spinozas. Breslau, Preuss & Jünger, 1898.
90 p. 23cm.

Issued in part as thesis, Breslau.
Author's inscription and signature.
Original paper covers bound in.
Bibliographical footnotes.

SPECIAL COLLECTIONS
SPINOZA

D-3-g
1634

Elbogen, Ismar, 1874-1943.
Der Tractatus de intellectus emendatione und seine stellung in der philosophie Spinozas. Ein beitrag zur entwickelungsgeschichte Spinozas. 1. teil ... Breslau, Druck von T. Schatzky, 1898.
3 p. l., 33, [1] p., 1 l. 22cm.

Inaug.-diss.—Breslau.
Vita.

Published in full without thesis note.

1. Spinoza, Benedictus de, 1632-1677. 2. Tractatus de intellectus emendatione.
1—12608

Library of Congress B3984.E57
[a45b1]

SPECIAL COLLECTIONS
SPINOZA

D-3-g
1635

Gebhardt, Carl, 1881-1934.
Spinozas Abhandlung über die Verbesserung des Verstandes; eine entwicklungsgeschichtliche Untersuchung. I. Teil. Heidelberg, C. Winter's Universitätsbuchhandlung, 1905.
iv, 44 p. 23cm.

Thesis, Heidelberg.
Published in full without thesis note.
Bibliographical footnotes.

SPECIAL COLLECTIONS
SPINOZA

D-3-g
1636

Gebhardt, Carl, 1881-1934.
Spinozas Abhandlung über die Verbesserung des Verstandes; eine entwicklungsgeschichtliche Untersuchung. Heidelberg, C. Winter's Universitätsbuchhandlung, 1905.
117 p. 22cm.

Issued in part as thesis, Heidelberg.
Ms. notes by Carl Gebhardt, with his signature on t.-p.
Bibliographical footnotes.

SPECIAL COLLECTIONS
SPINOZA

D-3-g
1637

Gegenstand und Weise von Erfahrung und Transzendenz. Die Grundlagen der Philosophie. Vom Verfasser des Spinoza Redivivus und Augustinus redivivus. Halle (Saale) Weltphilosophischer Verlag, 1921.
296 p. 26cm. (Philosophische Weltbibliothek, 7. Bd.)

Pencilled on t.-p. by Carl Gebhardt: Glatzel.
Includes a chapter "Spinozas Abhandlung über die Verbesserung des Verstehens" (p. [116]-278)

SPECIAL COLLECTIONS
SPINOZA

D-3-g
1638

Joachim, Harold Henry, 1868-1938.
Spinoza's Tractatus de intellectus emendatione; a commentary by the late Harold H. Joachim ... Oxford, The Clarendon press, 1940.
xvi, 231, [1] p. 22½cm.
Edited by Sir David Ross. cf. Preliminary note.

1. Spinoza, Benedictus de, 1632-1677. Tractatus de intellectus emendatione. I. Ross, Sir William David, 1877- ed.

Library of Congress B3984.J6 41-14465
[6] 199.492

SPECIAL COLLECTIONS
SPINOZA

D-3-g
1639

Kirchmann, Julius Hermann von, 1802-1884.
Erläuterungen zu Benedict von Spinoza's Abhandlung über die Verbesserung des Verstandes und zu dessen Politischer Abhandlung. Berlin, L. Heimann, 1871.
136 p. 20cm. (Philosophische Bibliothek. 45. Bd.)

Original paper covers bound in.

Wenzel, Alfred
Zur Textkritik von Spinozas Tractatus de intellectus emendatione. [1909]
211-231 p. 26cm.

From Zeitschrift für Philosophie und philosophische Kritik, Bd. 134, Heft II, März 1909.
Bibliographical footnotes.

Wolf, Albert, 1890-
Die Bedeutung des kurzen Traktats und der Abhandlung über die Verbesserung des Verstandes für den Aufbau und die Entwicklung des Systems Spinozas. Breslau [1923]
83 p.

Thesis, Breslau.

D-3-h
TRACTATUS POLITICUS

[Goedewaagen, Tobie]
Spinoza's Tractatus politicus ... [Hilversum, Heuvelpers, 1928]
8 p. 25cm.

Signed: T. Goedewaagen.
Bound with Spinoza, Benedictus de. Tractatus politicus. [1928]

Goretti, Cesare
Il trattato politico di Spinoza. [1927]
[235]-247 p.

In Rivista di filosofia, anno 18, 1927.

Kühne, Alfred
Spinozas Tractatus politicus und die parteipolitischen Verhältnisse der Niederlande. [1906]
92-100 p.

From Philosophische Abhandlungen; Max Heinze zum 70. Geburtstage. Berlin, Mittler, 1906.

D-3-i
TRACTATUS THEOLOGICO-POLITICUS

Biedermann, Otto, 1879-
Die Methode der Auslegung und Kritik der biblischen Schriften in Spinozas Theologisch-politischem Traktat im Zusammenhang mit seiner Ethik. Erlangen, Druck der Universitäts-Buchdruckerei von E. T. Jacob, 1903.
70 p.

Thesis, Erlangen.
Volume of pamphlets.

Boulainvilliers, Henri, comte de, 1658-1722.
Analyse du Traité de la théologie politique de Spinoza, par Mr. le comte de Boulainvilliers.
56 p. 24 cm.

Manuscript.

[Boulainvilliers, Henri, comte de] 1658-1722.
[Analyse du Traité théologi-politique de Spinosa]
[3] l. 36cm.

Photostat copy (with title, Esprit de Spinoza) of prelim. leaf, p. 1 and 91 of manuscript in Library of Congress showing variations from copy printed in London, 1767.

Boulainvilliers, Henri, comte de, 1658-1722.
Doutes sur la religion, suivies de L'analyse du Traité theologi-politique de Spinosa, par le Comte de Boulainvilliers. Londres, 1767.
[4], 103 p. 16cm.

1. Spinoza, Benedictus de, 1632-1677. Tractatus theologico-politicus.

[Boulainvilliers, Henri, comte de] 1658-1722.
Exposition des sentiments de Spinosa.
[3] l. 36cm.

Photostat copy of p. 1, 3 and 169 of unidentified work included in a manuscript in Library of Congress and ascribed on cover to Boulainvilliers.

Bredenburg, Johannes, d. 1691.
Joannis Bredenburgii Enervatio Tractatus theologico-politici; unâ cum demonstratione, geometrico ordine dispositâ, naturam non esse deum: cujus effati contrario praedictus tractatus unicè innititur. Roterodami, Apud Isaacum Naeranum, 1675.
[6], 100 p. 21cm.

A reply to Spinoza's Tractatus theologico-politicus. Bound with a copy of the 1672 ed. of that work.

Chicago. College of Jewish Studies.
Rashi, 1040-1940 ... Exhibit on the occasion of the 900th anniversary of his birth to be held during the month of April, 1940. Chicago [1940]
[12] p. 21x11cm.

Includes a reference to Spinoza's Tractatus theologico-politicus (p. [9])
"The works of Rashi": p. [6-7]

Covotti, Aurelio
Relazione sul concorso pel premio annuale del 1912 sul tema: "Il Tractatus theologico-politicus dello Spinoza: attinenze della dottrina in esso svolta con l'Etica dello stesso autore. Rapporto della dottrina politica dello Spinoza con quella dell'Hobbes." [1914]
100-132 p.

In Accademia pontaniana di scienze morali e politiche, Naples. Rendiconto, anno 52, 1914.

[Dunin-Borkowski, Stanislaus, Graf von] 1864-
Randglossen zu Spinozas Schrift über die Freiheit des Philosophierens. [1910]
[521]-531 p. 24cm.

Signed: St. von Dunin-Borkowski.
From Stimmen aus Maria-Laach; katholische Blätter. Jahrgang 1910, 10. Heft. (LXXIX, 5).
Ms. notes by A. S. Oko.
Bibliographical footnotes.

Dunin-Borkowski, Stanislaus, Graf von, 1864-1934.
Randglossen zu Spinozas Schrift über die Freiheit des Philosophierens. [1910]
521-531 p.

In Stimmen aus Maria-Laach, Bd. 79, 1910.

[Earbery, Matthias] 1690-1740.
An answer to a book intitled, Tractatus theologico politicus. London, Printed for Charles Brome, 1697.
8 p. l., 189 p.

Earbery, Matthias, 1690-1740.
Deism examin'd and confuted. In an answer to a book intitled, Tractatus theologico politicus. London, Printed for Charles Brome, 1697.
8 p. l., 189 p.

Epistola ad amicum, continens censuram libri, cui titulus: Tractatus theologico-politicus, in quo demonstratur, &c. Ultrajecti, ex officinâ Cornelii Noenaert, anno 1671.
48 p. 21cm.

At head of title: J. M. V. D. M.

Guttmann. Julius, 1880-1950.
Mendelssohns Jerusalem und Spinozas Theologisch-politischer Traktat. Berlin, 1931.
[31]-66 p. 23cm.

At head of title: Achtundvierzigster Bericht der Hochschule für die Wissenschaft des Judentums in Berlin.
Original paper covers bound in.
Bibliographical references included in "Anmerkungen" (p. 63-[67])
Bound with another issue of the above.

J. M. V. D. M. Epistola ad amicum, continens censuram libri, cui titulus: Tractatus theologico-politicus, in quo demonstrantur, &c. Ultrajecti, Ex Officina Cornelii Noenaert, Bibliop., 1671.
48 p.

Possibly by Johannes Melchior.

Joël, Manuel, 1826-1890.
Beiträge zur Geschichte der Philosophie. Breslau, H. Skutsch, 1876.
2 v. in 1. 21cm.

Each article has separate t.-p. and pagination.
Includes sections on Spinoza's Tractatus theologico-politicus and Tractatus de Deo et homine.

Joël, Manuel, 1826-1890.
Spinoza's Theologisch-politischer Traktat, auf seine Quellen geprüft. Breslau, Schletter, 1870.
xi, 76 p. 21cm.

Bound with Joël, Manuel, 1826-1890. Don Chasdai Creskas' religionsphilosophische Lehren. 1866.

[Kaempf, Saul Isaac] 1818-1892.
B. v. Spinoza's Theologisch-politischer Tractat, von Isidor Kämpf. [1842]
4 pts.

In Der Orient; Literaturblatt, 1842.

Kirchmann, Julius Hermann von, 1802-1884.
Erläuterungen zu Benedict von Spinoza's Theologisch-politischer Abhandlung. Berlin, L. Heimann, 1871.
114 p. 19cm. (Philosophische Bibliothek. 36. Bd.)

Klein, Gottlieb, 1852-1914.
Ueber eine dunkle Stelle in Spinoza's theologisch-politischem Tractat. [1882]
427-430 p.

In Monatsschrift für Geschichte und Wissenschaft des Judenthums, 31. Jahrgang (n. F. 14. Jahrgang), 1882.

Land, Jan Pieter Nicolaas, 1834-1897.
Over vier drukken met het jaartal 1670 van Spinoza's Tractatus theologico-politicus. Amsterdam, J. Müller, 1881.
cover-title, 11 p. 23cm.

"Overgedrukt uit de Verslagen en mededeelingen der Koninklijke Akademie van Wetenschappen, Afdeeling Letterkunde, 2de reeks, deel XI."

Marcus, Ralph, 1900-
Spinosa on Judaism; notes on the Tractatus theologico-politicus, chapters I-III. [1926]
16-21 p. 26cm.

From the Jewish Institute quarterly, v. 2, no. 4, March 1926.

1. Spinoza, Benedictus de, 1632-1677. Tractatus theologico-politicus.

[Meijer, Willem] 1842-1926.
De voorgewende en de ware uitgever van het Tractatus theologico-politicus. [1911]
233-265 p.

In Tijdschrift voor boek- en bibliotheekwezen, jaargang 9, 1911.

Meijer, Willem, 1842-1926.
Over de beteekenis en de waarde van het godgeleerd-staatkundig vertoog van B. Despinoza. [1917]
[467]-483 p. 25cm.

From Tijdschrift voor wijsbegeerte, 11. jaarg., 4. aflevering, Oct. 1917.
Volume of pamphlets.

Meijer, Willem, 1842-
Over de beteekenis en de waarde van het Godgeleerd-staatkundig vertoog van B. Despinoza.
[467]-483 p. 25cm.

"Overdruk uit het Tijdschrift voor wijsbegeerte, 11e Jaargang, 4e alf."
Bound with Meijer, Willem. Benedicti Despinozae philosophiae brevis commentatio. [1905]

More, Henry, 1614-1687.
Henrici Mori Cantabrigiensis Opera omnia, tum quae Latinè, tum quae Anglicè scripta sunt, nunc vero Latinitate donata ... Londini, Typis impensa J. Macock, sumptibus autem J. Martyn et G. Kettilby, 1679.
2 v. 36 cm.

Vol. 1 includes a letter refuting Spinoza's Tractatus theologico-politicus (p. 563-635) and other references to Spinoza.

DLC

Musaeus, Johann, 1613-1681.
Spinosismus, hoc est, Tractatus theologico-politicus, quo Benedictus Spinoza, conatu improbo, demonstratum ivit, libertatem philosophandi, sive de doctrina religionis pro lubitu judicandi, sentiendi & docendi ... Ad veritatis lancem examinatus, A. M DC LXXIV. à Johanne Musæo ... Witebergæ, Apud Jo. Ludov. Meisel, 1708.
96 p. 20cm.

Musaeus, Johann, 1613-1681, praeses.
Tractatus theologico-politicus, quo auctor qvidam anonymus, conatu improbo, demonstratum ivit, libertatem philosophandi, h.e. de doctrina religionis prò lubitu judicandi, sentiendi & docendi, non tantùm salvâ pietate & rei publica pace posse concedi, sed eandem, nisi cum pace rei publicae ipsaq; pietate tolli non posse; ad veritatis lancem examinatus, præside DN. Johanne Musæo ... ventilationi publicæ submissus à Christiano Friderico Knorr ... ⌈Jenae⌉ Literis Bauhoferianis ⌈1674⌉
⌈8⌉, 96 p. 20cm.

CONTINUED ON NEXT CARD

NNC

Musaeus, Johann, 1613-1681, praeses. Tractatus theologico-politicus .. 1674. (Card 2)

Thesis, Jena (C. F. Knorr, respondent and author)
Against Spinoza's Tractatus theologico-politicus.

NNC

Royce, Josiah, 1855-1916.
Fugitive essays; with an introduction by J. Loewenberg. Cambridge, Harvard University Press, 1920.
429 p. port.

Includes an essay "Natural rights and Spinoza's essay on liberty ⌈the Tractatus theologico-politicus⌉" (p. ⌈290⌉-299)

Royce, Josiah, 1855-1916.
Fugitive essays. With an introduction by Dr. J. Loewenberg. Cambridge, Harvard University Press, 1925.
429 p. 21cm.

Includes an essay "Natural rights and Spinoza's essay on liberty ⌈the Tractatus theologico-politicus⌉" (p. ⌈290⌉-299)

Serrurier, Pierre, 17th cent.
Responsio ad exercitationem paradoxam anonymi cujusdam ... quâ philosophiam pro infallibili S. Literas interpretandi normâ orbi Christiano obtrudit ... Autore Petro Serario. Amstelodami, Typis Christophori Cunradi, 1667.
⌈22⌉, 82 p. 21cm.

A reply to Lodewijk Meyer's Philosophia S. Scripturae interpres. 1666.
Bound with ⌈Spinoza, Benedictus de⌉ Tractatus theologico-politicus. 1670.

⌈Sonne, Isaiah⌉ 1887-
Un manoscritto sconosciuto delle "Adnotationes" al Trattato teologico-politico di Spinoza. ⌈19--⌉
8 p. 25cm.

Signed: I. Sonne.
Manuscript note at head of title: Estratto dalla "Civiltà moderna."

NNC

Spanheim, Friedrich, 1632-1701.
Friderici Spanhemii F. Controversiarum de religione cum dissidentibus hodie Christianis, prolixè & cum Judæis, elenchus historico-theologicus. Rationem hujus elenchi præmissa series materiarum indicabit. Editio quæ novum opus videri possit. Amstelædami, Apud Joannem Wolters, 1694.
⌈24⌉, 682, ⌈2⌉ p. 17cm.

Includes a section on Spinoza's Tratatus theologico-politi- cus (p. 638-643)

Spinoza, Benedictus de, 1632-1677.
Aantekeningen van Benedictus de Spinoza op het Godgeleerd-staatkundig vertoog, door W. Meijer. Amsterdam, S. L. van Looy, 1901.
xiii, 32 p. 19cm. (On cover: Klassieke schrijvers. Spinoza's werken)

Carl Gebhardt's signature on t.-p.
Original paper cover bound in.
Bound with Spinoza, Benedictus de. Godgeleerd-staatkundig vertoog. ⌈pref. 1894⌉

Spinoza, Benedictus de, 1632-1677.
Benedicti de Spinoza Adnotationes ad Tractatum theologico-politicum. Ex autographo edidit ac praefatus est, addita notitia scriptorum philosophi, Christophorus Theophilus de Murr ... Cum imagine et chirographo. Hagae-Comitum, 1802.
44 p. port., facsim. 25cm.

Signature of Carl Gebhardt on t.-p.
Includes bibliographies.

Suckow, Gustav Friedrich Wilhelm
De ratione, qua se habeat Spinozae Tractatus theologico-politicus ad ejus Ethicam? Vratislaviae, Typis officinae R. Lucae [1849]
34 p. 21cm.

Thesis, Bratislava.

תפארת ישראל בחכמת הרפואה והפילוסופיא.
Diatriba de ortu et progressu facultatis, et formali constitutione artis medicinae per Iudaeos. Consequenter misera absurditas carnalis Sapientiae (quam philosophiam vulgò vocant) extra legem Dei constitutae, ad considerandum data, aliquot exemplis ex chymaerico Tractatu theologico-politico Spinosae edito. Ab antiquae veritatis studioso, veritatis amatoribus dicata. Hamburgi, anno 1670.
73 p.

Title transliterated: Tif'ereth Yiśrā'ēl ...

Volynskiĭ, A
Теологико-политическое ученіе Спинозу. [1885]

Title transliterated: Teologiko-politicheskoe uchenie Spinozy.
In Восходъ, 1885, № 10-12.

D-4
WORKS ON SPINOZA
SOURCES

Eisler, Moritz, 1818-1890.
Die Quellen des Spinozistischen Systems. [1882]
250-265 p.

In Zeitschrift für Philosophie und philosophische Kritik, 80. Bd., 1882.

Eisler, Moritz, 1818-1890.
Die Quellen des spinozistischen Systems. [1884]
100-111 p. 24cm.

From Das Jüdische Centralblatt, III. Jahrgang, III. Heft.

Hamelin, Octave, 1856-1907.
Sur une des origines du spinozisme. [1901]
15-28 p.

In L'Année philosophique, 1900. Paris, 1901.

Hartman, Nicolaas, 1677-1748.
De bedrieglijke philosoph ontdekt, uyt De nagelaten werken van Benedictus de Spinosa ... Te Zwolle, Gedrukt by D. Rampen en F. Clement, 1724.
4 p. l., 142 p.

McKeon, Richard, 1900-
Spinoza and medieval philosophy. [1928]
[129]-145 p. port. 23cm.

From the Open court, vol. XLII (no. 3) March, 1928.

Rietz, Johan Ernst, 1815-1868, praeses.
De Spinozismi fonte orientali; dissertatio academica, quam p. p. Joh. Ernestus Rietz, respondente Carolo A. Fürst. Lundae, typis excudit Carolus Fr. Berling, 1839.
18 p. 20cm.

Thesis, Lund.
Bibliographical footnotes.

Uhmeyer,
Quellen der Schriften Spinozas mit besonderer Berücksichtigung der Abhandlungen Joëls. Lemgo, F. L. Wagener, 1875.
16 p. 27cm.

At head of title: Jahresbericht über das Gymnasium zu Lemgo ...

1. Spinoza, Benedictus de, 1632-1677.

D-5
WORKS ON SPINOZA'S SYSTEM

Alberti, Herbert, 1884-
Die Grundlagen des Systems Spinozas im Lichte der kritischen Philosophie und der modernen Mathematik. Borna-Leipzig, Buchdruckerei R. Noske. 1910.
81 p. 23cm.

Thesis, Leipzig.
Bibliographical footnotes.

Grossbach, E
De vero sensu et veritate objectiva systematis Benedicti de Spinoza. Wirceburgi, 1829.
39 p.

Herder, Johann Gottfried von, 1744-1803.
Gott. Einige Gespräche über Spinoza's System, nebst Shaftesbury's Naturhymnus. [1879]
148 p. 17cm.

From Herder, Johann Gottfried. Herder's Werke [1879] v. 18.

Herder, Johann Gottfried von, 1744-1803.
Gott ... Einige Gespräche über Spinoza's System; nebst Shaftesburi's Naturhymnus, von J. G. Herder. Zweite, verkürzte und vermehrte Ausgabe. Gotha, Bei Karl Wilhelm Ettinger, 1800.
xxiv, 336 p. 16cm.

Includes references to Spinoza.

Humbert
Die wissenschaftliche Begründung des Wunders; Vortrag, im philomathischen Verein zu Oppeln gehalten am 2. Februar 1867. 2. Ausg. Oppeln, W. Clar's Buchhandlung (Tempeltey) 1869.
44 p. 22cm.

Bound with Brasch, Moritz, 1843-1895. Benedict von Spinoza's System der Philosophie. 1870.

Jariges, Philipp Joseph von, 1706-1770.
Examen du spinozisme et des objections de mr. Bayle contre ce systemé. [1746-48]
121-142, 295-316 p.

In Akademie der Wissenschaften, Berlin. Histoire de l'Academie royale des sciences et des belles lettres. Mémoires, t. 1-2, 1746-48.

Jariges, Philipp Joseph von, 1706-1770.
Ueber das System des Spinoza, und über Bayle's Erinnerungen gegen dieses System. Aus dem Französischen des Herrn de Jariges. [1782]
72 p.

In Magazin für die Philosophie und ihre Geschichte, 5. Bd., 1782.

Kaufmann, Fritz, 1891-
Spinoza's system as theory of expression. [1940]
[83]-97 p. 23cm.

"Reprinted from Philosophy and phenomenological research, September, 1940."

1. Spinoza, Benedictus de, 1632-1677.

MacQuesten, Rockwood
Higher criticism the philosophical outgrowth of Spinozism. 1893.
45 l.

Thesis, New York University.
Typescript.

Nordvall, Adolf Leonard
De Spinozismi initiis aphorismi ...
Upsaliae, Wahlströ, 1852.
14 p.

Poppo, Volckm Conrad
Spinozismvs detectvs, oder Vernünfftige Gedancken von dem wahren Unterscheid der philosophischen und mathematischen Methode oder Lehr Art, entworffen von M. Volckm. Conrad Poppo. Weimar, Gedruckt bey Johann Leonhard Mumbachen, 1721.
[16], 78 p. 17cm.

Rehberg, August Wilhelm, 1757-1836.
Ueber das Verhältniss der Metaphysik zu der Religion ... Berlin, bey August Mylius, 1787.
vi, 175, [1] p.

Includes a section "Wichtigkeit des Systemes des Spinoza" (p. 16-33) and other references to him (p. 33-64)

[Ritchie, Eliza]
The reality of the finite in Spinoza's system. [1904]
16-29 p.

Signed: E. Ritchie.
In Philosophical review, v. 13, 1904.

Samuel, Otto
Die Grundlehre Spinozas im Lichte der kritischen Philosophie. [1913]
252-270 p.

In Archiv für Geschichte der Philosophie, Bd. 26., 1913.

Thomas, Karl, d. 1873.
Spinozae systema philosophicum adumbratum. Regimontii Borussorum, Impressit Conradus Paschke [1835?]
79 p. 21cm.

Thesis, Königsberg.
Published also without thesis note.

Thomas, Karl, d. 1873.
Spinozae systema philosophicum delineavit Dr. Carolus Thomas. Regimontii Borussorum, Impressit Conradus Paschke, 1835.
79 p. 21cm.

Issued also as thesis, Königsberg.
Bound with the author's Spinozae systema philosophicum adumbratum. [1835?]

Thomson, James, 1834-1882.
Essays and phantasies. London, Reeves and Turner, 1881.
320 p. 19cm.

Includes an essay "A few words on the system of Spinoza" (p. 303-312)

Verdross, Alfred, 1890-
Das Völkerrecht im Systeme von Spinoza. [1928]
100-105 p.

In Zeitschrift für öffentliches Recht, Bd. 7, 1928.

D-6
ANNIVERSARY COMMEMORATIONS

Alexander, Samuel, 1859-1938.
Spinoza: an address delivered at the Liberal Jewish Synagogue, London, on Sunday, March 13th. 1927, by S. Alexander. [London] Published by the Jewish Religious Union [1927]
16 p. 19cm.

Alexander, Samuel, 1859-1938.
Spinoza; an address in commemoration of the tercentenary of Spinoza's birth. [Manchester] Manchester university press, 1933.
19 p. 20 cm. (Manchester university lectures, no. 29)

Altmann, Bruno
Benedikt Spinoza; zu seinem 300. Geburtstag. [1932]
[217]-223 p. 21cm.

From Abwehr-Blätter, 42. Jahrgang, no. 10, Dezember 1932.

1. Spinoza, Benedictus de, 1632-1677.

Amzalak, Moses Bensabat, 1892-
Spinoza. Lisboa [Of. Gráf. do Museu Comercial de Lisboa] 1927.
29 p. port. 23cm.

"Conferência realizada na Biblioteca Israelita da Lisboa, a convite da Associação de Juventude Israelita 'Hehaber', na noute de 20 de Fevereiro de 1927, em comemoração do 250.º aniversário da morte de Spinoza."

Antcliffe, Herbert
Spinoza's tricentennial celebrated; representatives of many sects and races honor Jewish philosopher at Hague. [1932]
p. 11. 35cm.

From The Jewish criterion, vol. 80, no. 23, October 14, 1932.

Appuhn, Charles, 1862-1942.
Troisième centenaire de la naissance de Spinoza. M. Ch. Appuhn présente à la Société de philosophie les observations ... [1932]
2 p. 24cm.

At head of title: Société française de philosophie. Séance du 26 novembre 1932.

1. Spinoza, Benedictus de, 1632-1677.

[B., A. E.]
The greatest Jew since St. Paul. Baruch de Spinoza: Nov. 24, 1632-Feb. 22, 1677. [1932]
625-626 p.

Signed: A. E. B.
In Church times, v. 108, 1932.

Baruch Spinoza. [1932]
p. 84. port. 29cm.

From B'nai B'rith magazine, vol. 47, no. 3, December, 1932.
Plans for the celebration in Chicago of the tercentenary of Spinoza's birth.

Baumgardt, David, 1890-
Spinoza. Zur 300. Wiederkehr seines Geburtstages am 24. November 1932. [1932]
266-268 p.

In Gemeindeblatt der jüdischen Gemeinde zu Berlin, Jahrgang 22, 1932.
An excerpt from his Spinoza und Mendelssohn.

Benedetto Spinoza nel CCL anno dalla morte, MDCXXXII-MDCLXXVII. [1927]
[205]-375 p. 24cm. (Rivista de filosofia, anno XVIII, n. 3, luglio-settembre, 1927)

Contents.--L'unità di Spinoza, da Adelchi Baratono.--Spinoza e la critica moderna della Bibbia, da Luigi Fossati.--Il Trattato politico di Spinoza, da Cesare Goretti.--Modi primitivi e derivati, infiniti e finiti, da Piero Martinetti.--Spinoza e la nozione del progresso umano, da Rodolfo Mondolfo.--Il principio del

Benedetto Spinoza nel CCL anno dalla morte, MDCXXXII-MDCLXXVII. [1927] (Card 2)

metodo sperimentale nella filosofia di Spinoza, da Annibale Pastore.--Le opere di Spinoza, da Adolfo Ravà.--La dottrina del contratto sociale in Spinoza, da Gioele Solari.--La necessità spinoziana e il determinismo contemporaneo, da Giuseppe Tarozzi.--La conversione di Spinoza, da Emilio Villa.--Bibliografia degli scritti italiani relativi a Benedetto Spinoza, da Adolfo Ravà.

Benedictus de Spinoza Amstelodamensis; drietal redenen ter gelegenheid van de 300ste verjaring zijner geboorte uitgesproken in de Agnietenkapel te Amsterdam door J. D. Bierens de Haan, H. Brugmans [en] W. G. van der Tak. Leiden, A. W. Sijthoff, 1932. vii, 59 p. port. 25cm.

Original paper covers bound in.
Bibliographical footnotes.

The bicentenary of Spinoza. [1877] p. 5.

In The Times, London, Feb. 28, 1877.
An account of an address by Ernest Renan at The Hague.

Benedictus de Spinoza Amstelodamensis. 1932. (Card 2)

Contents.--De beteekenis van het menschbegrip in Spinoza's wereldleer, door J. D. Bierens de Haan.--Spinoza en Amsterdam, door H. Brugmans.--Spinoza's persoonlijkheid, door W. G. van der Tak.

Bradish, Norman C.
The philosophy of Spinoza. [1932] p. 16.

In Chicago journal of commerce and La Salle street journal, Dec. 3, 1932.

Bergmann, Hugo, 1883-
Spinoza und unsere Zeit. Zum 300. Geburtstage des Philosophen. [1932] p. 3.

In Prager Presse, Nov. 24, 1932.

Brunschvicg, Léon, 1869-1944.
Spinoza. [1927] 142-148 p.

In Revue littéraire juive, v. 1, 1927.

Berkowitz, J H
Spinoza. (Written in commemoration of the 250th anniversary of the excommunication of Spinoza by the elders of Amsterdam, July 27, 1656; and inspired by E. E. Powell's Spinoza and religion.) [1907] p. 511.

In The Open court, v. 21, 1907.
A poem.

[Carp, J H]
Benedictus de Spinoza, 1632-1932. [1932] p. 11. illus., ports. 28cm.

Signed: J. H. Carp.
From De Radiogids, 6. jaargang, no. 44, 3 September 1932.

1. Spinoza, Benedictus de, 1632-1677.

Bernstein, Joseph Milton, 1908-
Homage to Spinoza, in the three hundredth year of his birth. [1932] p. 34. 25cm.

Poem.
From the Menorah journal, vol. XX, no. 1, April-June, 1932.

1. Spinoza, Benedictus de, 1632-1667 - Poetr[y]

Cohen, Gustave, 1879-
Saint-Evremond, Condé et Spinoza. A propos du 250e anniversaire de la mort de Spinoza. [1927] p. 4. port.

In Nouvelles littéraires, artistiques et scientifiques, 6. année, 26 février 1927.

SPECIAL COLLECTIONS
SPINOZA

D-6
1730

Cohn, Tobias
Spinoza am zweiten Säculartage seines Todes; Vortrag in der "Litterarischen Gesellschaft" zu Potsdam am Stiftungsfeste, den 23. Februar 1877, gehalten. Potsdam, Gropius, 1877.
34 p. 20cm.

D-6
1735

Felsenthal, Bernhard, 1822-1908.
Baruch Spinoza; Gedenkrede. [1877-78]
p. 6.

In The Reformer and Jewish times, v. 9, no. 1, 1877-78.

NN

D-6
1731

Dessauer, Moritz, 1842-1895.
Spinoza. 1) Festrede zu seiner 200 jährigen Todesfeier am 21. Februar, gehalten im Haag von Ernest Renan; übersetzt von Richard Lesser. 1877. 2) Zur Rechtfertigung seiner Philosophie und Zeit. Eine Denkschrift zum 200 jährigen Todestage von Dr. Rothschild. 1877. 3) Kurze Darstellung von Spinoza's Leben von Dr. Hermann Weise, Programmschrift des königl. Gymnasiums zu Salzwedel. Ostern, 1876. [1877]
81-82 p.

In Juedisches Litteratur-Blatt, Jahrgang 6, 1877.
A review of these works.

NNJ

D-6
1736

Finkelstein, Leo, 1895-1950.

די שפינאָזא־פײערונגען אין האג.
[1932]
74-83 p.

Title transliterated: Di Shpinoza-fayerungen in Hag.
In Globus, v. 1, no. 3, 1932.

NNJ

D-6
1732

Le 250e anniversaire de Baruch Spinoza. [1927]
83-87 p. illus.

In Menorah, Paris, année 6, 1927.

NN

D-6
1737

Fornari, Crescenzo
In margine ad un centenario: Spinoza e l'amore. [1932]
p. 3. port.

In Lavoro fascista, dic. 31, 1932.

DLH

SPECIAL COLLECTIONS
SPINOZA

D-6
1733

Eckstein, Walther, 1891-
Spinoza. Nach einem Vortrag, gehalten im Monistenbund in Österreich aus Anlass der zweihundertfünfzigsten Wiederkehr seines Todestages. Hamburg, Hamburger Verlag [1927]
cover-title, 38 p. 17cm. (Monistische Bibliothek. Kleine Flugschriften. 50/50a)

1. Spinoza, Benedictus de, 1632-1677.

SPECIAL COLLECTIONS
SPINOZA

D-6
1738

Freyer, Kurt
Spinoza, Führer der Irrenden; Gedenkschrift anlässlich der 250. Wiederkehr des Todestages Spinozas, 21. Februar 1927. [Berlin, Horodisch & Marx, 1927]
[32] p. 22cm.

"Gedruckt in 37 Exemplaren auf Kaiserlich Japan und 395 Exemplaren auf Van Gelder-Bütten Nummer XXVI."

D-6
1734

Falb, Virgil
Gedenkrede auf Spinoza. Gehalten am 21. Feber 1908 in der Loge "Verschwiegenheit" im Or. Pozsony. Pozsony, 1908.
19 p.

OCH

SPECIAL COLLECTIONS
SPINOZA

D-6
1739

[Galestin, A A]
Spinoza, 24 November 1632-20 Februari 1677. [1932]
15 p. 25cm. port.

Signed: A. A. Galestin.
"Overdruk uit de Broederketen."

1. Spinoza, Benedictus de, 1632-1677.

[Gebhardt, Carl] 1881-1934.
Annus Spinozanus MCMXXXII; eine Denkschrift.
[192-]
16 l. 31cm.

Proposals for the celebration of the tercentenary of Spinoza's birth in 1932.

1. Spinoza, Benedictus de, 1632-1677 - Anniversaries, etc., 1932.

[Gebhardt, Carl] 1881-1934.
Annus Spinozanus MCMXXXII; eine Denkschrift.
2. Ausg. [1929?]
16 l. 30cm.

Proposals for the celebration of the tercentenary of Spinoza's birth in 1932.
Reproduced from typewritten copy.
"Exemplar no. 95."

Gebhardt, Carl, 1881-1934.
Spinoza in unserer Zeit; Rede bei der Spinoza-Feier im Rolzaal in 's-Gravenhage am 5. September 1932. [1933]
[21]-27 p. 26cm.

"Reprint from Septimana Spinozana."
Bound with Gebhardt, Carl. Spinoza in der Schule. [1930]

Gentile, Giovanni, 1875-1944.
Benedetto Spinoza. [1927]
[237]-239 p. 25cm.

From Giornale critico della filosofia italiana, v. 8, fasc. 3, May 1927.
Reprinted from Corriere della sera, February 22, 1927.

Ginzburg, Benjamin, 1898-
Baruch Spinoza (1632-1677) [1927]
210-211 p.

In B'nai B'rith magazine, v. 41, 1927.

Ginzburg, Benjamin, 1898-
Spinoza: 1632-1932. [1932]
528-529 p.

In The Nation, v. 135, 1932.

Guttenbaum, Kalman, d. 1941.

שפינאָזא-מאָטיוון. (צום 300-סטן
יאָרצײַט פון ברוך שפינאָזא). [1932]
24 p.

Title transliterated: Shpinoza-motivn ...
In Globus, v. 1, no. 4, 1932.

Guzzo, Augusto, 1894-
Spinoza (1632-1932) Firenze, Tipografia E. Ariani, 1932.
cover-title, [530]-546 p. 25cm.

"Estratto da 'Scuola e cultura' (Annali della istruzione media) ... anno VIII, quaderno V-VI, 10 settembre-10 novembre 1932."

1. Spinoza, Benedictus de, 1632-1677.

Hamel, A G van
Spinoza, discours prononcé par Ernest Renan.
[1877]
19 p.

In Los en vast, dl. 13, 1877.

Hebrew University to observe Spinoza anniversary. [1927]
p. 7.

In Jewish times, New York, v. 15, Feb. 18, 1927.

D-6
1750

Heinze, Max, 1835-1909.
Zum Gedächtniss Spinozas an seinem zweihundertjährigen Todestage. [1877]
337-351 p.

In Im neuen Reich, 7. Jahrgang, Bd. 1, 1877.

D-6
1751

Das Helldunkel; von den Herren an Bord der Jacht "Rembrandt" gepflogene, dem Andenken Spinozas gewidmete Unterhaltungen. Zürich, Füssli [c1935]
526 p.

D-6
1752

Hessemer, Carl
Spinoza und wir. Zum Gedächtnis des 300. Geburtstages des Denkers am 24. November. [1932]
2 p.

In Beilage zur Karlsruher Zeitung, Nov. 19, 1932.
Includes a review of Spinoza, by Carl Gebhardt.

NN

D-6
1753

Hurwitz, Maximilian
A God-intoxicated man. The life of Baruch Spinoza, Dutch Jewish philosopher, the 250th anniversary of whose death occurs next Monday. [1927]
2, 16; 4, 11 p.

In New York Jewish tribune, v. 90, no. 7-8, 1927.

NNJ

D-6
1754

Israelitische Kultusgemeinde, Vienna. Bibliothek.
Spinoza-Literatur Verzeichnis; zum 250. Todestage Spinozas (21. Februar 1927) Wien, Selbstverlag, 1927.
23 p. 23cm.

1. Spinoza, Benedictus de, 1632-1677 - Bibl.

D-6
1755

Jacobsohn, Hermann, 1879-
Spinoza's 250th anniversary. [1927]
3-5, 49, 59-61 p.

In Jewish criterion, v. 69, no. 15, 1927.

OCH

D-6
1756

Kahana, David, 1838-1915.
משה קורדובירו וברוך שפינוזה.
ברלין, תרנ"ז.
[Berlin, 1897]
90-92 p. 24cm.

Title transliterated: Mōshē Qōrdōbhērō ū-Bhārūkh Shpīnōzā.
From ha-Shīlōaḥ, vol. 2, 1897.

NNC

D-6
1757

Kallen, Horace Meyer, 1882-
Spinoza: three hundred years after. [c1933]
6 p. 26cm.

From the Menorah journal, vol. XXI, no. 1, April-June, 1933.

D-6
1758

Kayser, Rudolf, 1889-
Baruch de Spinoza. Gestorben am 21. Februar 1677. [1927]
p. 1.

In Die literarische Welt, Jahrgang 3, Nr. 8, 1927.

MaBJ

D-6
1759

Klatzkin, Jacob, 1882-1948.
Missverständnisse in und um Spinoza; referat, gehalten im Haag auf dem Spinozakongress, 23. Februar 1927. [c1927]
p. 175.

In Jüdische Rundschau, Jahrgang 32, 1927.

NN

 D-6 1760

Knight, William, 1836-1916, ed.
Spinoza; four essays, by Land, Kuno Fischer, J. Van Vloten, and Ernest Renan. London, Williams and Norgate, 1882.
xiv, 170 p. 23cm.

Contents.--Introductory note by the editor.--In memory of Spinoza, by T. Land.--The life and character of Baruch Spinoza, by Kuno Fischer.--Spinoza, an oration, by J. Van Vloten.--Spinoza, 1677-1877, by Ernest Renan.

 D-6 1761

Kraus, Oskar, 1872-1942.
Über die Philosophie Spinozas; aus Anlass seines 250. Todestages. [1927]
[161]-172 p. 26cm.

From Euphorion, Zeitschrift für Literaturgeschichte, 28. Bd., 2. Heft.

1. Spinoza, Benedictus de, 1632-1677.

D-6 1762

Land, Jan Pieter Nicolaas, 1834-1897.
Ter gedachtenis van Spinoza. Uitgesproken in de akademische lessen van 24 Februarij 1877. Leiden, E. J. Brill, 1877.
68 p.

OCH

 D-6 1763

Land, Jan Pieter Nicolaas, 1834-1897.
Ter gedachtenis van Spinoza. Uitgesproken in de Akademische Lessen van 24 Februarij 1877. Leiden, E. J. Brill, 1877.
68 p. 25cm.

Original paper cover bound in.
Volume of pamphlets.

NNC

 D-6 1764

Lantzenberg, Raoul
Au Congrès spinoziste de La Haye. [1927]
[10]-20 p. 25cm.

From La Nouvelle revue, 4. série, t. 89, mars-juin 1927.

1. Spinoza, Benedictus de, 1632-1677 - Congresses.

D-6 1765

Leuthner, Karl
Benedikt de Spinoza. Zur Dreihundertjahrfeier seiner Geburt. [1932]
p. 7.

In Arbeiter-Zeitung, Vienna, Jahrgang 45, 1932.

DLC

 D-6 1766

Lewkowitz, Albert, 1883-
Der Spinozismus in der Philosophie der Gegenwart; zum 250. Todestage Spinozas (21. Februar 1677) [1927]
7 p. 23cm.

From Monatsschrift für Geschichte und Wissenschaft des Judentums, 71. Jahrg., Heft 1/2, Januar/Februar, 1927, p. 1-7.
"Neuere Spinoza-Literatur": p. 5-7.

D-6 1767

Lilli, Virgilio
Baruch Spinoza (1632-1932). [1932]
p. 3.

In La Tribuna, Rome, anno 50, 16 dicembre 1932.

DLC

 D-6 1768

Löwinger, Wilhelm
Spinoza; anlässlich der 250. Wiederkehr seines Todestages, 21. Februar 1677. [1927]
[117]-124 p. illus., ports. 25cm.

From Menorah, 5. Jahrg., Nr. 2, Februar 1927.

1. Spinoza, Benedictus de, 1632-1677.

D-6 1769

Maggiore, Giuseppe, 1882-
Due anniversari (Machiavelli e Spinoza) [1927]
207-209 p.

In Critica fascista, anno 5, 1927.

NN

D-6 1770

Magnin, Edgar F
The greatness of Spinoza. [1927]
3-4 p.

In B'nai B'rith messenger, v. 30, 1927.

NNJ

SPECIAL COLLECTIONS SPINOZA D-6 1771

Marbach, Gotthard Oswald, 1810-1890.
Gedächtnissrede auf Benedict von Spinoza, gehalten vor einer Versammlung seiner akademischen Mitbürger am 21. Februar 1831. Halle, F. Ruff, 1831.
31 p. 22cm.

SPECIAL COLLECTIONS SPINOZA D-6 1772

Marcus, D
Baruch Spinoza; conférence faite à la Loge de Constantinople. [1927]
[129]-142 p. port. 24cm.

From Hamenora; organe périodique des Béné Bérith du district d'Orient, no. XI, Vme année, no. 4, avril 1927.

1. Spinoza, Benedictus de, 1632-1677.

SPECIAL COLLECTIONS SPINOZA D-6 1773

Marcus, Hanna
Warum musste das traditionelle Judentum Spinoza ablehnen? Ein Nachtrag zur Spinoza-Feier. [Leipzig, 1927]
2 p. 33cm.

From Gemeindeblatt der israelitischen Religionsgemeinde. 3. Jahrgang, Nr. 16, 22. April 1927.

SPECIAL COLLECTIONS SPINOZA D-6 1774

Marcuse, Ludwig, 1894-
Als der Glaube an die Vernunft noch jung war. [1932]
1871-1877 p. 22cm.

An article about Spinoza.
From Das Tagebuch, Heft 48, Jahrgang 13, November 26, 1932.

SPECIAL COLLECTIONS SPINOZA D-6 1775

Mattuck, Israel Isidor, 1883 or 4-1954.
Spinoza; tercentenary addresses by Rabbi Dr. Israel I. Mattuck and Dr. Stanton Coit; being the fourth Horace Seal memorial lecture, given before the Ethical Union, London, on November 30th, 1932. London, Ethical Union, 1932.
cover-title, 21 p. 19cm.

D-6 1776

Melamed, Samuel Max, 1885-1938.
אשמתו של שפינוזה (למלאת מאתים וחמשים שנה לפטירתו) [1927]
241-245 p.

Title transliterated: Ashmotho shel Shpinozah.
In ha-Doar, v. 7, no. 17, 1927.

NNJ

SPECIAL COLLECTIONS SPINOZA D-6 1777

Menorah.
Le 250e anniversaire de Baruch Spinoza. [1927]
p. [83] port. 32cm.

From Menorah, 6. année, no. 6, 15 mars 1927.

1. Spinoza, Benedictus de, 1632-1677 - Anniversaries, etc., 1927.

NNC

SPECIAL COLLECTIONS SPINOZA D-6 1778

Milan. Università cattolica del Sacro Cuore. Facoltà di filosofia.
Spinoza nel terzo centenario della sua nascita; pubblicazione a cura della Facoltà di filosofia dell'Università cattolica del Sacro Cuore. Milano, Società editrice "Vita e pensiero", 1934.
210 p. port. 26cm.

At head of title: Rivista di filosofia neo-scolastica. Supplemento speciale al volume XXV. Agosto 1933.
Bibliographical footnotes.
Original paper covers bound in.

CONTINUED ON NEXT CARD

SPECIAL COLLECTIONS SPINOZA D-6 1779

Milan. Università cattolica del Sacro Cuore. Facoltà di filosofia. Spinoza nel terzo centenario della sua nascita. 1934. (Card 2)

Contents.--Introduzione di Agostino Gemelli. --La teoria spinoziana della sostanza e la metafisica tomistica, di S. Vanni-Rovighi.--Il Cusano e lo Spinoza, di Paolo Rotta.--Spinoza e Kant, di Mariano Campo.--Aporie del panlogismo (Spinoza e Hegel) di Leonida Gancikoff. --Schopenhauer, Spinoza e il panteismo, di U. A. Padovani.--La fisica spinoziana e la

CONTINUED ON NEXT CARD

Milan. Università cattolica del Sacro Cuore. Facoltà di filosofia. Spinoza nel terzo centenario della sua nascita. 1934. (Card 3)

fisica moserna, di Paolo Rossi.--Spinoza e l'idealismo contemporaneo, di Carlo Mazzantini.--Il diritto come potenza secondo Spinoza, di Guido Gonella.--La nullificazione della storia nella filosofia dello Spinoza, di Silvio Vismara.--La vita di Spinoza in rapporto al suo pensiero, di A. Bestetti.

Molden, Berthold
Spinoza. Zum 300. Geburtstag. [1932]
2 p.

In Neue freie Presse, Wien; Morgenblatt, Nov. 24, 1932.

Moritzen, Julius, 1863-1946.
The immortal Baruch. All lands to honor the memory of Spinoza, the lens-maker. [1927]
p. 500. port.

In The American Hebrew, v. 120, 1926-27.

Mutch, W J
Spinoza three centuries after. [1932]
347-351 p. 25cm.

From the Homiletic review, vol. 104, no. 5, November, 1932.

1. Spinoza, Benedictus de, 1632-1677.

[Myślicki, Ignacy]
Odrodzenie Spinozyzmu; sprawozdanie z obchodu 250-lecia zgonu Spinozy w hadze. [1927]
[86]-94 p. 25cm.

Signed: Ignacy Myślicki.
From Przeglad filosoficzny, 1927.

Neumann, Henry, 1882-
Spinoza, the man and the sage, after 250 years. [1927]
14-20 p. 26cm.

"An address before the Brooklyn Society for Ethical Culture, May, 1927."
From the Standard, vol. XIV, no. 1, July, 1927.

[Olgiati, Francesco] 1886-
Benedetto Spinoza nel 250° anniversario della sua morte. [1927]
193-198 p. 25cm.

Signed: Francesco Olgiati.
From Vita e pensiero, anno 13, v. 18, nuova serie, fascicolo 4, aprile 1927.

1. Spinoza, Benedictus de, 1632-1677.

[Osgood, Samuel] 1812-1880.
The centenary of Spinoza. [1877]
265-288 p.

Signed: Samuel Osgood.
In The North American review, v. 124, 1877.

Paraf, Pierre
Baruch de Spinoza. [1927]
124-125 p.

In Revue littéraire juive, v. 1, 1927.

La partecipazione della Società filosofica italiana al Congresso Spinozano ... [Roma? 1932?]
12 p. 25cm.

Cover-title: Notizie.
"Estratto da 'L'Archivio di filosofia' fasc. III, pp. 100-111, 1932. Anno XI."

SPECIAL COLLECTIONS SPINOZA D-6 1790

Philosophy club of Chicago.
Spinoza, the man and his thought; addresses delivered at the Spinoza tercentenary sponsored by the Philosophy club of Chicago, edited by Edward L. Schaub. Chicago, The Open court publishing company, 1933.
vi p., 2 l., 61 p. front. (port.) 23½cm.
CONTENTS.—Opening address, by C. W. Morris.—Address of the chairman, H. W. Chase.—Spinoza: his personality and his doctrine of perfection, by E. L. Schaub.—Spinoza's political and moral philosophy, by T. V. Smith.—Spinoza and religion, by S. B. Freehof.
Presentation copy to A. S. Oko from Freehof.
1. Spinoza, Benedictus de, 1632-1677. I. Schaub, Edward Leroy, 1881- ed. II. Title.

Library of Congress B3997.P55 33—11412
[a45f1] 199.492

SPECIAL COLLECTIONS SPINOZA D-6 1791

Pollock, Sir Frederick, bart., 1845-1937.
An address delivered at the opening meeting of the tercentenary celebration of Spinoza's birth, held at The Hague, September 1932. [1933]
[8]-12 p. 25cm.

"Reprint from Septimana Spinozana."

1. Spinoza, Benedictus de, 1632-1677.

SPECIAL COLLECTIONS SPINOZA D-6 1792

Ravà, Adolfo
Il congresso spinoziano dell'Aja e i principi filosofici dei rapporti tra le nazioni. Roma, 1933.
12 p. 24cm.

"Estratto dalla Rivista internazionale di filosofia del diritto, anno XIII, fasc. III."
Presentation copy of Carl Gebhardt, with the author's inscription and initials.

SPECIAL COLLECTIONS SPINOZA D-6 1793

Ravà, Adolfo
Descartes, Spinoza et la pensée italienne; communication faite le 26 février 1927 à la Sorbonne dans la séance de la Société française de philosophie pour la commémoration du deux cent cinquantième anniversaire de la mort de Spinoza. Paris, A. Colin, 1928.
23 p. 25cm.

Extract from Bulletin de la Société française de philosophie, 27e année, no. 2-3, juin 1927.

SPECIAL COLLECTIONS SPINOZA D-6 1794

[Ravà, Adolfo]
Il 250o anniversario della morte di Spinoza. [1927]
71-74 p. 25cm.

Signed: Adolfo Ravà.
From Giornale critico della filosofia italiana, anno ottavo, fascicolo primo, gennaio 1927.

SPECIAL COLLECTIONS SPINOZA D-6 1795

Ravà, Adolfo
Il pensiero di Spinoza nel terzo centenario della sua nascita; relazione sul congresso filosofico tenutosi all'Aja dal 5 al 10 settembre 1932. Lodi, G. Biancardi [1932]
11 p. 23cm.

"Estratto dalla Rivista di Filosofia, anno XXIII, No. 4."
Author's inscription and initials on t.-p.

SPECIAL COLLECTIONS SPINOZA D-6 1796

Ravà, Adolfo
Spinoza scrittore. Milano, Grafica moderna [1927]
14 p. 23cm.

"Estratto dalla Rivista di filosofia, n. 4, ottobre-dicembre 1927 (VI)"

1. Spinoza, Benedictus de, 1632-1677.

D-6 1797

Renan, Ernest, 1823-1892.
Nouvelles études d'histoire religieuse. 2. éd. Paris, Calmann, Lévy, 1884.
xxi, 533 p. 23 cm.

"Spinoza; conférence tenue à La Haye, le 12 février 1877; deux-centième anniversaire de la mort de Spinoza" (p. 499-533)

DLC

SPECIAL COLLECTIONS SPINOZA D-6 1798

Renan, Ernest, 1823-1892.
Spinoza; conférence tenue a la Haye, le 12 février 1877, deux-centième anniversaire de la mort de Spinoza. Paris, Ancienne maison M. Lévy frères, 1877.
26 p. 24cm.

SPECIAL COLLECTIONS SPINOZA D-6 1799

Renan, Ernest, 1823-1892.
Spinoza; discours prononcé à la Haye le 21 février 1877, à l'occasion du 200e anniversaire de sa mort. La Haye, M. Nijhoff, 1877.
31 p. 25cm.

Includes manuscript notes and corrections by Gebhardt; used for reprint in Chronicon Spinozanum, v. 5.

NNC

Renan, Ernest, 1823-1892.
Spinoza; discours prononcé à la Haye le 21 février 1877, à l'occasion du 200e anniversaire de sa mort. La Haye, M. Nijhoff, 1877.
31 p. 23cm.

"Publié au profit de l'oeuvre de la statue à ériger à Spinoza."
Volume of pamphlets.

Renan, Ernest, 1823-1892.
Spinoza: 1677 and 1877. [1877]
763-777 p.

In Contemporary review, v. 29, 1877.

Renan, Ernest, 1823-1892.
Spinoza. Festrede zu seiner 200jährigen Todesfeier am 21. Februar 1877 gehalten im Haag. Uebersetzt von Richard Lesser. Wien, A. Hartleben's Verlag, 1877.
32 p. 25cm. (Sammlung gemeinnützige populär-wissenschaftlicher Vorträge. 15. Heft)

Original paper cover bound in.
Volume of pamphlets.

Renan, Ernest, 1823-1892.
Spinoza. Oration delivered at the Hague, February 21, 1877. Tr. by M. Stuart Phelps. [1878]
763-781 p.

In The New Englander, v. 37, 1878.

Renan, Ernest, 1823-1892.
Spinoza. Rede am 21. Februar 1877 bei dessen zweihundertjähriger Todesfeier gehalten im Haag. Autorisirte Uebersetzung von C. Schaarschmidt. Leipzig, E. Koschny, 1877.
24 p. 25cm.

Original paper cover bound in.
Volume of pamphlets.

Renan, Ernest, 1823-1892.
Studies in religious history. New York, Scribner and Welford, 1887.
vi, 481 p. 20 cm.

Running title: New studies of religious history.
"Spinoza; a conference held at the Hague, February 12, 1877": p. [453]-481.

1. Religions—Addresses, essays, lectures. 2. Christianity—Addresses, essays, lectures. 3. Buddha and Buddhism. 4. Joachim, Abbot of Fiore, 1132 (ca.)-1202. 5. Francesco d'Assisi, Saint, 1182-1226. 6. Port Royal. 7. Spinoza, Benedictus de, 1632-1677. 8. Molinism.

Full name: Joseph Ernest Renan.

Renan, Ernest, 1823-1892.
Spinoza: 1677 and 1877. [1877-78]
p. 2-3, 2.

In The Reformer and Jewish times, v. 9, no. 14-15, 1877-78.

Rosenkranz, Hans, 1905-
Baruch Spinoza zum 21. Februar 1927. [Berlin, Soncino-Gesellschaft] 1927.
cover-title, [16] p. 24cm.

"Siegfried Alweiss druckte diesen Aufsatz für die Teilnehmer des Spinoza-Abends, den die Soncino-Gesellschaft, Berlin, anlässlich der 250. Wiederkehr von Spinoza's Todestag veranstaltete."

Renan, Ernest, 1823-1892.
Spinoza: 1677 and 1877. [1877]
216-230 p.

In Popular science monthly, v. 11, 1877.
First printed in Contemporary review.

Rothschild, David, 1816-1892.
Spinoza; zur Rechtfertigung seiner Philosophie und Zeit. Eine Denkschrift zum 200jährigen Todestage. Leipzig, E. Koschny, 1877.
32 p. 23cm.

Original paper cover bound in.
Volume of pamphlets.

1. Spinoza, Benedictus de, 1632-1677.

Sarton, George, 1884-1956.
Spinoza: 1632-1677. ⌊1928⌋
11-15 p. plates

In Isis, v. 10, 1928.

Sassen, Ferdinand, 1894-
Spinoza, 1677-1927. ⌊1927⌋
⌊145⌋-157 p. 19cm.

From Geloof en wetenschap, 2e jaargang, afl. 4, Juli-Aug. 1927.
Bibliographical footnotes.

Schlerath, Franz, 1894-
Die Spinozafeier im Haag. ⌊1927⌋
120-122 p. 25cm.

From Der Morgen, III. Jahrgang, 1. Heft, April 1927.
Bound with Altkirch, Ernst. Die Freunde Spinozas. ⌊1927⌋

⌊Schöler, Johannes⌋
Spinoza. Gezamelijke redevoeringen, gehouden bij de Spinoza-Herdenking door de Afdeeling Nederland van de Kant-Gesellschaft. ⌊1934⌋
70-73 p. 24cm.

Signed: Dr. Johannes Schöler.
Brief summaries of the lectures contained in the above-named work.
From Kant-Studien, Band XXXIX, Heft 1, 1934.

Schweiger, Lázár
Spinoza születésének tricentenáriumához. ⌊1933⌋
11-12 p. port. 29cm.

From Mult es jövö, XXIII. év, január 1933.

1. Spinoza, Benedictus de, 1632-1677.

Septimana Spinozana; acta conventus oecumenici in memoriam Benedicti de Spinoza diei natalis trecentesimi Hagae Comitis habiti. Curis Societatis Spinozanae edita. Hagae Comitis, M. Nijhoff, 1933.
xii, 321 p. port. 25cm.

(Continued on next card)

Septimana Spinozana. 1933. (Card 2)

Contents.--Openingsrede, door Leo Polak.--Address, by Sir Frederick Pollock.--Allocution, par Léon Brunschvicg.--Spinoza in unsrer Zeit, von Carl Gebhardt.--Il pensiero di Spinoza e i problemi dell'ora, di Adolfo Ravà.--De spinozistische gemeenschapsgedachte, door J. H. Carp.--Physique et métaphysique, par Léon Brunschvicg.--Physik und metaphysik, von J. Clay.--Physique et métaphysique, par Gaston Bachelard.

CONTINUED ON NEXT CARD

Septimana Spinozana. 1933. (Card 3)

--Die Physik Spinozas, von Stanislaus von Dunin Borkowski.--Ultimate religion, by George Santayana.--Wijsbegeerte en godsdienst, door Ferdinand Sassen.--Spinoza and philosophy of religion, by S. Alexander.--Religio metaphysica, von Carl Gebhardt.--Mysticisme et humanisme, par Charles Appuhn.--Poetic insight and religious truth, by Irwin Edman.--Philosophie et religion, par J. A. de Mattos Romão.--La

CONTINUED ON NEXT CARD

Septimana Spinozana. 1933. (Card 4)

philosophie du polisseur de verres, par J. Segond.--La pedagagia di Spinoza, di Adolfo Ravà.--Quelques remarques sur la notion d'essence dans les doctrines de Descartes et de Spinoza, par Albert Rivaud.--Hobbes und Spinoza, von Ferdinand Toennies.--Über den Grund der Beschränkung unserer Erkenntnis auf die Attribute des Denkens und der Ausdehnung bei Spinoza, von Julius Ebbinghaus.--Il concetto

CONTINUED ON NEXT CARD

Septimana Spinozana. 1933. (Card 5)

spinoziano dell'errore, di Pantaleo Carabellese.--Einflüsse Spinozas in der Literatur der englischen Romantik, von Johannes Hoops.--Spinozas Modell, von I. Myslicki.--Spinoza und Kant, von Leo Polak.--Benedict Spinoza, by H. F. Hallett.--Domus Spinozana, von Carl Gebhardt.

D-6
1920

[Sidersky, David] 1858-
Baruch de Spinoza (24 novembre 1632-21 février 1677) [1932]
9-16 p. port. 23cm.

Signed: D. Sidersky.
From Le Rayon, organe de l'Union libérale israelite, 14e année, nos. 1 et 2, octobre-novembre 1932.
Includes bibliography.

D-6
1921

Société française de philosophie.
Commémoration du deux cent cinquantième anniversaire de la mort de Spinoza. Séance du 26 février 1927. Paris, Librairie A. Colin, 1927.
cover-title, [25]-59 p. 26cm. (Its Bulletin, 27e année, nos. 2-3, juin 1927)

Carl Gebhardt's inscription and initials on p. [25]

D-6
1922

Souday, Paul, 1869-1929.
... La société des grands esprits. 5. éd. Paris, E. Hazan & cie [1929]
2 p. l., [7]-310 p., 2 l. 19½cm.
Contents. — Avant-propos. — Platon. — Les ruines de Delphes. — Démosthène et Clemenceau.—Les sceptiques grecs.—Le nouvel Anacharsis.—Rodin et les cathédrales.—Le sixième centenaire de Dante.—La renaissance et Walter Pater.—La statue de Rabelais.—Montaigne.—Descartes.—Le troisième centenaire de Pascal.—Le 250e anniversaire de Spinoza.—Voltaire démiurge.—La réligion de Jean-Jacques Rousseau.—Gœthe et Schiller.—Le germanisme et l'esprit humain.—Byron.—Berlioz, écrivain.—Le cinquantenaire de Michelet.—La science française.—Le centenaire de Bertholet.—Émile Meyerson.
1. Biography. 2. Philosophers. 3. Authors. I. Title.

30-30188
Library of Congress CT144.S65 1929
[42c1]

D-6
1923

Le souvenir d'un grand philosophe. [1927]
p. 227. illus. 40cm.

Signed: L. G. de G.
From L'Illustration, no. 4383, 85me année, 5 mars, 1927.
An account of the celebration of the 250th anniversary of Spinoza's death at the Hague.

NNC

D-6
1924

Spinoza 250th anniversary marked by B'nai B'rith. [1927]
p. 7.

In Jewish times, New York, v. 15, Feb. 18, 1927.

NN

D-6
1925

Spinoza. Zum 250. Todestag des Philosophen, 21. Februar 1927. [1927]
63-67 p. port. 23cm.

From Der Rheinische Christopher; Rhein-Mainischer Heimatkalender, 1927.
Includes "Spinoza-Worte", excerpts from Spinoza, von den festen und ewigen Dingen, übertragen von Carl Gebhardt.

D-6
1926

Spinoza. Zum 250. Todestag des Philosophen: 21. Februar 1927. [1927]
63-67 p. port. 23cm.

From Nassauer Landkalender, 1927.
"Spinoza-Worte" (from Spinoza, Von den festen und ewigen Dingen, übertragen von Carl Gebhardt): p. 67.

NNC

D-6
1927

Spinoza; zur dreihundertsten Wiederkehr seines Geburtstages (24. November 1932) Drei Aufsätze von Ernst Cassirer, Leo Baeck, David Baumgardt. [1932]
[323]-370 p. 25cm.

From Der Morgen, 8. Jahrgang, 5. Heft, Dezember 1932.

CONTINUED ON NEXT CARD

D-6
1928

Spinoza; zur dreihundertsten Wiederkehr seines Geburtstages. [1932] (Card 2)

Contents.--Spinozas Stellung in der allgemeinen Geistesgeschichte, von Ernst Cassirer.--Motive in Spinozas Lehre, von Leo Baeck.--Spinozas Bild im deutschen und jüdischen Denken, von David Baumgardt.

D-6
1929

Spinoza-Festheft; mit einem Bildnis des Philosophen. Berlin, Pan-Verlag R. Heise, 1927.
199 p. port. 24cm. (Kantstudien; philosophische Zeitschrift. Band XXXII, Heft 1)

Contents.--Benedictus de Spinoza, von Theodor Ziehen.--Die Verflechtung der Probleme in Spinozas Philosophie, von Harold Höffding.--Ewigkeit und Dauer bei Spinoza, von Otto Baensch.--Die Affektenlehre Spinozas, von Gertrud Jung.--Die religionsphilosophische Bedeutung des Spinozismus, von Albert Lewkowitz.--Rembrandt und

CONTINUED ON NEXT CARD

Spinoza-Festheft. 1927. (Card 2)

Spinoza, von Carl Gebhardt.--Spinoza und der deutsche Spinozismus, von David Baumgart.--Eine neue Spinoza-Ausgabe, von Paul Menzer.--Aufruf für das Spinoza-Haus, von der Societas Spinozana.

Spinoza-festschrift; herausgegeben von Siegfried Hessing, zum 300. geburtstage Benedict Spinozas (1632–1932) ... Heidelberg, Carl Winter [c1933]

xvi, 222, [2] p. ports. 24½cm.

"Das werk wurde in eintausend handnummerierten exemplaren gedruckt. Dieses exemplar trägt die nummer 404." 2".

CONTENTS.—Einleitung.—Hessing, S. Salve Spinoza!—Brucar, J. Spinoza und die ewigkeit der seele.—Buber, M. Spinoza und die chassidische botschaft.—Droop, F. Fünf szenen aus dem leben Spinozas.—Dubnow, S. Die gestalt.—Gebhardt, C. Der gotische Jude.—Gherasim, V. Die bedeutung der affektenlehre Spinozas.—Grunwald, M. Der lebensphilosoph Spinoza.—Hessing, S. Die glückseligkeit des freien menschen.—Klatzkin, J. Der missverstandene.—Klausner, J. Der jüdische charakter der lehre Spinozas.—Marcianu, M. Ein bekennt-

(Continued on next card)

A C 33-3181

[2]

Spinoza-festschrift; herausgegeben von Siegfried Hessing ... [c1933] (Card 2)

CONTENTS—Continued.

nis.—Myslicki, I. Spinoza und das ideal des menschen.—Niemirower, I. Spinozaverehrung eines nichtspinozisten.—Petrovici, I. Eine Spinoza huldigung.—Rolland, R. Der lichtstrahl Spinozas.—Sass, K. Spinozas Bibelkritik und Gottesbegriff.—Siegel, C. Vom grundlegenden dualismus in Spinozas system.—Sokolow, N. Der Jude Spinoza.—Zweig, A. Der schriftsteller Spinoza.—Ausserungen von: Alfred Einstein, Sigmund Freud und Jakob Wassermann.

Presentation copy to Carl Gebhardt with the editor's inscription and signature.

1. Spinoza, Benedictus de, 1632-1677. I. Hessing, Siegfried, 1903- ed.

A C 33-3181

Title from N. Y. Pub. Libr. Printed by L. C.

[2]

Spinoza institute of America, inc., *New York.*

Baruch Spinoza; addresses and messages delivered and read at the College of the city of New York, on the occasion of the tercentenary of Spinoza, November 23rd, 1932. New York, Spinoza institute of America, inc., 1933.

77 p. front. (port.) 24cm.

"Addresses and messages ... prepared for the Spinoza tercentenary celebration held by the Spinoza institute of America."—Introd. note.

CONTENTS.—Why honor Spinoza? By I. H. Muraskin.—Spinoza, apostle of freedom, by Isaac Husik.—Living in accordance with the philosophy of Spinoza, by G. R. Mason.—Spinoza and modern thought,

(Continued on next card)

33-9782

[a44c1]

Spinoza institute of America, inc., *New York.* Baruch Spinoza ... 1933. (Card 2)

CONTENTS—Continued.

by Jacob Shatzky.—The historic significance of Spinoza's philosophy, by Harry Waton.—Messages from Albert Einstein, Sir Frederick Pollock, Samuel Alexander, Constantin Brunner, Leo Polak, Carl Gebhardt [and] Leon Brunschvicg.—The Jewish question and Spinoza's philosophy, by Harry Waton.—Free will or determinism? By Walter Bernard.—Why a Spinoza institute? An address delivered on the occasion of the founding of the Spinoza institute of America, by Harry Waton.

1. Spinoza, Benedictus de, 1632-1677. I. New York. City college.

33-9782

Library of Congress B3961.S6

[a44c1] 921.2

Spinozas Stellung in der Vorgeschichte des dialektischen Materialismus; Reden und Aufsätze zur Wiederkehr seines 250. Todestages. Mit einem Vorwort von Hermann Duncker. Wien, Verlag für Literatur und Politik [1928]
118 p. 21cm. (Marxistische Bibliothek; Werke des Marxismus, Leninismus. Bd. 13)

At head of title: Thalheimer [und] Deborin [pseud.]
Bibliographical footnotes.

(Continued on next card)

Spinozas Stellung in der Vorgeschichte des dialektischen Materialismus. [1928] (Card 2)

Contents.--Vorwort, von Hermann Duncker.--Die Klassenverhältnisse und die Klassenkämpfe in den Niederlanden zur Zeit Spinozas, von A. Thalheimer.--Die Weltanschauung Spinozas, von A. Deborin.--Spinozas Einwirkung auf die klassische deutsche Literatur.

ספינאזא בוך, צום דרייהונדערטסטן
געבוירניאר פון בענעדיקטוס דע
ספינאזא, 1632-1932 רעדאקטירט
פון יעקב שאצקיס ניו יארק,
ארויסגעגעבן פון ספינאזא אינסטי-
טוט אין אמעריקע--יידישער אפטייל,
.1932

[New York, Spinoza Institute of America, 1932]
239 p. 34cm.

Title transliterated: Spinoza bukh.

CONTINUED ON NEXT CARD

ספינאזא בוך, צום דרייהונדערטסטן גע-
בוירניאר ... (Card 2)

Includes Spinoza's Tractatus de intellectus emendatione, translated into Yiddish by S. Wiener and I. Yudkoff (p. [185]-239)
Added t.-p.: Spinoza book, in commemoration of the tercentenary of Benedictus de Spinoza, 1632-1932, edited by Dr. Jacob Shatzky. New York, Published by the Yiddish Section of the Spinoza Institute of America, 1932.

CONTINUED ON NEXT CARD

ספינאזא בוך, צום דרייהונדערטסטן גע-
בוירניאר ... (Card 3)

Bibliography (works on Spinoza in Yiddish): p. 175-183.

Szemere, Samuel
Spinoza. Zur dreihundertsten Jahreswende seiner Geburt. [1932]
2 p.

In Pester Lloyd, nov. 24, 1932.

Tamari, Leo.
Die materie; ihr wesen, ihre trägheit und ihre schwere. Eine philosophisch-naturwissenschaftliche abhandlung, von Leo Tamari, herausgegeben anlässlich des 300. geburtsjahres Spinozas von einer gruppe von freunden dieser gedanken. Berlin, Carl Heymanns verlag, 1932.
142 p. 23cm.
"Anhang: Über die attribute bei Spinoza": p. [115]-142.

1. Matter. 2. Ether (of space) 3. Gravitation. 4. Spinoza, Benedictus de, 1632-1677.
A C 33-655
Title from N. Y. Pub. Libr. Printed by L. C.
[2]

The 300th anniversary of the birth of Baruch Spinoza. [1932]
840-843 p. 26cm.

From Religious education, vol. XXVII, no. 9, Nov. 1932.

1. Spinoza, Benedictus de, 1632-1677.

Van Son, A
World honors Spinoza; tercentenary of immortal philosopher observed universally. [1932]
p. 446. port. 33cm.

From American Hebrew and Jewish tribune, v. 131, no. 25, November 4, 1932.

Velada en honor de Benito Espinosa, celebrada en la Real Academia de Jurisprudencia y Legislación la noche del 21 de febrero de 1927 y organizada por Mario Méndez Bejarano con la cooperación de los catedráticos de filosofía Manuel Hilario Ayuso [et al.] Madrid, 1930.
118 p. ports. 20cm.

Original paper cover bound in.
Includes bibliographies (works of the speakers at the confer- ence)

Wachstein, Bernard, 1868-1935.
Spinoza (Zum 250. Todestage, 21. Februar 1927) [1927]
6 p. 23cm.

"Separatabdruck aus B'nai B'rith Mitteilungen für Österreich, Heft 3, März 1927, Jahrg. XXVII."

1. Spinoza, Benedictus de, 1632-1677.

Wachstein, Bernhard, 1868-1935.
Spinoza. (Zum 300. Geburtstage, 24. November 1932) [1932]
9 p. 23cm.

1. Spinoza, Benedictus de, 1632-1677.

Weichelt, Hans, 1873-
Spinoza. [1932]
873-877 p.

In Allgemeine deutsche Lehrerzeitung, Jahrgang 61, 1932.

Wendriner, Karl Georg, 1885-
Der Mensch Benedikt Spinoza. [1932]
2 p.

In Neue Züricher Zeitung; Morgenausgabe, Nr. 2187, Nov. 24, 1932.

Wiener, Max, 1886-
Spinoza. [1932]
263-266 p. port.

In Gemeindeblatt der jüdischen Gemeinde zu Berlin, Jahrgang 22, 1932.

D-6
1850

Windelband, Wilhelm, 1848-
Präludien; Aufsätze und Reden zur Einleitung in die Philosophie. 2. vermehrte Aufl. Tübingen, J. C. B. Mohr, 1903.
vii, 396 p.

Includes an essay "Zum Gedächtnis Spinozas" (An seinem zweihundertjährigen Todestage, 1877, gesprochen an der Universität Zürich), (p. 93-118)

MB

D-6
1851

Windelband, Wilhelm, 1848-1915.
Präludien; Aufsätze und Reden zur Einleitung in die Philosophie. Freiburg i. B., J. C. B. Mohr, 1884.
vi, 325 p. 22cm.

"Zum Gedächtniss Spinoza's (An seinem zweihundertjährigen Todestag gesprochen an der Universität Zürich)": p. [88]-111.

D-6
1852

Windelband, Wilhelm, 1848-1915.
Präludien; Aufsätze und Reden zur Einführung in die Philosophie. 4., verm. Aufl. Tübingen, J. C. B. Mohr (P. Siebeck) 1911.
2 v. 21cm.

Includes an essay "Zum Gedächtnis Spinozas (An seinem zweihundertjährigen Todestage gesprochen an der Universität Zürich) 1877" (v. 1, p. 88-111)

D-6
1853

Windelband, Wilhelm, 1848- 1915.
Präludien; Aufsätze und Reden zur Philosophie und ihrer Geschichte. 5., erweiterte Aufl. Tübingen, J. C. B. Mohr (P. Siebeck) 1915.
2 v. 23 cm.

Includes an essay "Zum Gedächtnis Spinozas (An seinem zweihundertjährigen Todestage gesprochen an der Universität Zürich) 1877" (v. 1, p. 88-111)

D-6
1854

Windelband, Wilhelm, 1848-1915.
Zum Gedächtniss Spinoza's. (An seinem zweihundertjährigen Todestage gesprochen an der Universität Zürich) [1877]
419-440 p.

In Vierteljahrsschrift für wissenschaftliche Philosophie, 1. Jahrgang, 1877.

D-6
1855

Windelband, Wilhelm, 1848-1915.
Прелюдіи; философскія статьи и рѣчи. Переводъ со 2-го нѣмецкаго изд. С. Франка. СПБ., Изд. Д. Е. Жуковскаго, 1904.
374 p. 23cm.

Title transliterated: Preliudii.
"Памяти Спинозы; рѣчь, произнесенная въ 1877 г. въ Цюрихскомъ университетѣ въ день 200-лѣтней годовщины его смерти": p. [71]-91.

D-6
1856

Wolfson, Abraham
"Spinoza's God is God of Israel". Entire world celebrates tercentenary of birth of one of the greatest philosophers: a liberal interpretation. [1932]
p. 35, 44. illus., port. 33cm.

From American Hebrew and Jewish tribune, v. 132, no. 2, November 25, 1932.
Includes a brief sketch of the author and his book: Spinoza: a life of reason.
Bound with Browne, Lewis. Baruch Spinoza. [1932]

D-6
1857

Wyslawski, Zebi, 1890-

ברוך שפינוצה ונדויו (קטעי הרהורים למלאות שלש מאות שנה להולדתו) [1932-33]
730-732, 746-748, 762-764, 2-4 p.

Title transliterated: Barukh Shpinozah u-neduyaw.
In ha-Olam, v. 20-21, 1932-33.

E
PHILOSOPHICAL WORKS WITH REFERENCES TO SPINOZA

E-1
BEFORE 1596

E-1-a
GENERAL

E-1-a
1859

Abravanel, Don Isaac ben Judah, 1437-1508.
Uma epístola de Isaac Abarbanel, publicada por Joaquim de Carvalho. Lisboa, 1928.
14 p. 24cm.

"Separata da Revista de estudos hebráicos, vol. I."
Presentation copy to A. S. Oko, with the editor's inscription and signature.
Bibliographical footnotes.

Adlerblum, Nima (Hirschensohn)
A study of Gersonides in his proper perspective. New York, Columbia University Press, 1926.
ix, 140 p. 20cm.

Issued also as thesis (Ph. D.) - Columbia University.
Includes a section on Spinoza (p. 126-130)
"List of Gersonides' works": p. 131-134.
Bibliography: p. 135-140.

Berlin. Jüdisches Museum.
Gedenkausstellung Don Jizchaq Abrabanel; seine Welt, sein Werk. Juni 1937. ₍Berlin, 1937₎
16 p. port., facsims. 21cm.

"Den Katalog hat Rahel Wischnitzer-Bernstein im Verein mit Dr. Josef Fried ... verfasst."
Includes a reference to Spinoza (p. 15)

Burgmann, Johann Christian, praeses.
Exercitatio philosophica de Stoa a Spinozismo et atheismo exculpanda. Wittenbergiae, Literis Gerdesianis ₍1721₎
₍2₎, 34 p. 20 cm.

Thesis, Wittenberg. (F. J. Helms and A. Holtermann, respondents)

Guttmann, Jacob, 1845-1919.
Die Philosophie des Salomon ibn Gabirol. Göttingen, Vandenhoeck & Ruprecht, 1889.
iv, 272 p. 22 cm.

Includes references to Spinoza.

Guyau, Jean Marie, 1854-1888.
La morale d'Epicure et ses rapports avec les doctrines contemporaines. 4. éd., rev. et augm. Paris, Alcan, 1904.
292 p.

Includes a section on Spinoza (p. 226-237)

Haneberg, Daniel Bonifacius, 1816-1876.
Ueber das Verhältnis von Ibn Gabirol zu der Encyclopädie der Ichwân uç çafâ. ₍1866₎
73-102 p.

In Akademie der Wissenschaften, Munich. Philosophisch-historische Klasse. Sitzungsberichte, Jahrgang 1866, Bd. 2.
Includes a reference to Spinoza (p. 98)

Hönigswald, Richard, 1875–
Denker der italienischen renaissance, gestalten und probleme, von Richard Hönigswald. Basel, Verlag Haus zum Falken, 1938.
248 p. 20cm.

1. Philosophy, Italian. 2. Philosophers, Italian. 3. Renaissance—Italy. I. Title.

A C 38-897

Yale univ. Library
for Library of Congress ₍2₎

Hoslett, Schuyler Dean
Spinoza and Lucretius. ₍1941₎
159-168 p. 26cm.

From The Personalist, vol. 22, no. 2, Spring, 1941.

Isaac Abravanel; six lectures by Paul Goodman, L. Rabinowitz ... ₍and others₎ with an introductory essay by H. Loewe; edited by J. B. Trend ... and H. Loewe ... Cambridge ₍Eng.₎ The University press, 1937.
xxvii, 157 p. port., facsims. 22½ cm.

Bibliography: p. 157.
Includes references to Spinoza.
CONTENTS.—Preface.—Isaac Abravanel and his age, by H. Loewe.—Introduction, by Paul Goodman.—Spain in the age of Abravanel, by I. González Llubera.—Abravanel's literary work, by M Gaster.—Abravanel as exegete, by L. Rabinowitz.—On Abravanel's philosophical tendency and political teaching, by L. Strauss.—Leone Ebreo and the renaissance, by A. R. Milburn.

~~(Continued on next card)~~
38—31613
₍a55f½₎

Jong, Karel Hendrik Eduard de, 1872-
Spinoza en de stoa. Leiden, E. J. Brill, 1939.
34 p. facsim. 24cm. (Mededeelingen van wege het Spinozahuis, V)

Maurice, Frederick Denison, 1805–1872.
Ancient philosophy: a treatise of moral and metaphysical philosophy anterior to the Christian era ... By the Rev. Frederick Denison Maurice, M. A. 4th ed. London, Griffin, Bohn, and company, 1861.
xi, 260 p. 18½cm.

1. Philosophy, Ancient.

Maurice, Frederick Denison, 1805-1872.
Mediaeval philosophy; or, A treatise of moral and metaphysical philosophy from the fifth to the fourteenth century. London, R. Griffin, 1857.
xi, 253 p. 20cm. (Encyclopaedia metropolitana; or, System of universal knowledge; on a methodical plan projected by Samuel Taylor Coleridge. Cabinet edition)

Maurice, Frederick Denison, 1805–1872.
Moral and metaphysical philosophy. Philosophy of the first six centuries. By the Rev. Frederick Denison Maurice ... 2d ed., rev. [London and Glasgow, R. Griffin and company, 1854]
viii, 157 p. 19cm. (*Added t.-p.:* Encyclopædia metropolitana: or, System of universal knowledge ... 2. ed., rev. First division. Pure sciences)

1. Philosophy, Ancient. 2. Fathers of the church—Hist. & crit.

Orschansky, L
Abraham Ibn-Esra als Philosoph, zur Geschichte der Philosophie im XII. Jahrhundert. Breslau, T. Schatzky, 1900.
40 p.

Thesis, Bern.
Includes a section "Der Einfluss Ibn-Esra's auf Spinoza" (p. 33-39)

Pico della Mirandola, Giovanni, 1463-1494.
Ausgewählte Schriften. Übersetzt und eingeleitet von Arthur Liebert. Jena, E. Diederichs, 1905.
293 p. port. 20cm.

Portugal. Sovereigns, etc., 1438-1481. (Affonso V)
[Copy of a letter of acquittance for Juda Abravanel, dated 1453, for money spent by him in the service of King Affonso V]
[12] p., 6 l. 30cm.

"Chancelery of Dom Affonso V. Book 3, folio 86 v."
Portuguese text (handwritten) and English translation (typescript)

Renan, Ernest, 1823-1892.
Averroès et l'averroïsme; essai historique. 3. éd., rev. et augm. Paris, Lévy, 1866.
xvi, 486 p. 23 cm.

Includes references to Spinoza.

Seyerlen, Rudolf, b. 1831.
Die gegenseitigen Beziehungen zwischen abendländischer und morgenländischer Wissenschaft mit besonderer Rücksicht auf Salomon ibn Gebirol und seine philosophische Bedeutung. Jena, G. Neuenhahn, 1899.
41 p.

Includes a reference to Spinoza (p. 24)

Vossius, Gerardus Joannes, 1577-1649.
Gerardi Johannis Vossii De philosophorum sectis liber. Cum continuatione & supplementis Johannis Jacobi à Ryssel. Lipsiae, Sumptibus J. C. Meyeri, 1690.
4 p. l., 216 p., [3] l.

Includes a reference to Spinoza (p. 203)

Xavier, Francisco, Saint, 1506-1552.
Sancti Francisci Xaverii Epistolarum liber primus [-quartus] ... [16--?]
468, [2] p. 11cm.

Imperfect copy: lacks title-page; first and last two pages mutilated.
Title from caption.

גאונים און גדולים (ביאגראפיעס) לע-
בענס-בעשרייבונגען פון אלע גאונים
און גדולים פון אידישען פאלק. בע-
ארבעט נאך פארשידענע קוועלען.
New York, Star Hebrew Book Co. ₍19--₎
1 v. (various pagings) 20cm.

Title transliterated: Geonim un gedolim.
Includes a life of Don Isaac Abravanel.

Ficino, Marsilio, 1433-1499.
Über die Liebe, oder Platons Gastmahl; übersetzt von Karl Paul Hasse. Leipzig, F. Meiner, 1914.
viii, 259 p. 20cm. (Der Philosophischen Bibliothek Bd. 154)

Bibliographical references included in "Anmerkungen" (p. ₍225₎-251)

Yeshuʿah ben Joseph ha-Levi, of Tlemsan, 15th cent.
הליכות עולם; עם, מבוא הגמרא:
sive, Clavis Talmvdica. Complectens formulas, loca dialectica & rhetorica priscorum Judaeorum. Latinè reddita per Constantinvm l'Empereur ab Oppyck ... Cum indicibus accuratissimis, & dissertatione, qua operis usus, utilitasque ostenduntur. Lugduni Batavorum, Ex Officina Elseviriorum, 1634.
₍40₎, 232, ₍24₎ p.

Title transliterated: Hălīkhōth ʿōlām.

Gebhardt, Carl, 1881-1934.
Spinoza und der Platonismus. ₍Hagae Comitis, 1921₎
178-234 p. 22cm.

Cover-title: Dissertatio ex Chronici Spinozani tomo primo separatim edita.

1. Spinoza, Benedictus de, 1632-1677.

E-1-b
SOCRATES, PLATO
ARISTOTLE

Aristoteles.
Opervm Aristotelis tomvs II. Librorvm Aristotelis qvi non extant, fragmenta quaedam. Item, indices duo ... Avreliae Allobrogvm, Apud Petrum de la Rouiere, 1606.
p. ₍1₎-142. 20cm.

Incomplete: pages after p. 142 lacking.
Includes only books I-VIII of the Nicomachean Ethics. The table of contents on verso of t.-p. lists the works of the complete volume.
Christoph Gottlieb von Murr's autograph on t.-p.

Guttmann, Julius, 1880-1950.
Spinozas Zusammenhang mit dem Aristotelismus. ₍Berlin, B. Cassirer, 1912₎
₍515₎-534 p. 25cm.

On paper cover bound in: Judaica; Festschrift zu Hermann Cohens siebzigstem Geburtstage.
Bibliographical footnotes.

Barthélemy-Saint-Hilaire, Jules, 1805-1895.
Traduction generale d'Aristote; table alphabétique des matières. Paris, Alcan, 1892.
2 v. 25 cm.

Includes references to "Spinosa" and "Spinosisme" (v. 2, p. 947-948)

Halévy, Elie, 1760-1826.
Socrate et Spinoza. ₍1818₎
p. 73.

In L'Israélite français, t. 2, 1818.

Burger, D Jr.
Homerus, Plato, Spinoza. Zutphen, W. Thieme, 1860.
43 p. 21cm.

Carl Gebhardt's manuscript note and initials on flyleaf.

Huit, Charles, 1845-1914.
Spinoza et Platon. ₍1904-05₎
302-315 p.

In Revue de l'Institut catholique de Paris, t. 9-10, 1904-05.

Judaica; Festschrift zu Hermann Cohens siebzigstem Geburtstage. Berlin, B. Cassirer, 1912.
viii, 721 p. 24cm.

Includes an essay "Spinozas Zusammenhang mit dem Aristotelismus" by Julius Guttmann (p. ⌊515⌋-534)

Klibansky, Raymond
Ein Proklos-Fund und seine Bedeutung. Heidelberg, C. Winter, 1929.
41 p. 25cm. (Sitzungsberichte der Heidelberger Akademie der Wissenschaften. Philosophisch-historische Klasse. Jahrgang 1928/29. 5. Abhandlung)

Includes fragments of a mediaeval Latin translation of Proclus' commentary on Plato's Parmenides.
Includes a reference to Spinoza (p. 13)
Bibliographical footnotes.

Kym, Andreas Ludwig, b. 1822.
Platon et Spinoza devant la science moderne; une antithèse historique. ⌊1873⌋
5-33 p.

In Bibliothèque universelle et revue suisse, nouv. période, t. 47, 1873.

Pater, Walter, 1839-1894.
Plato and Platonism; a series of lectures. New York and London, Macmillan, 1894.
vii, 256 p.

Includes a reference to Spinoza (p. 33)

Rader,
... Compendium phãe ũrlis. Dictatãe à R. P. Rader S. J. Conscriptum a me F. A. D'Lamezan 1756 ⌊?⌋
39, ⌊92⌋ p. diagrs. 17cm.

Manuscript.
Student's notebook of a course of natural philosophy, based on Aristotle, given by Rader.
Imperfect: of final leaf only a fragment remains.

Schaarschmidt, Karl Max Wilhelm, 1822-1906.
Plato et Spinoza philosophi inter se comparati. Berolini, Typis G. Schade ⌊1845⌋
52 p. 21cm.

Thesis, Berlin.

Sieveking, Karl, 1787-1847.
Die Geschichte der platonischen Akademie zu Florenz. Göttingen, H. Dieterich, 1812.
60 p. 16cm.

E-1-c
MAIMONIDES

Boer, Tjitze J de
Maimonides en Spinoza. Amsterdam, 1927.
cover-title, 50 p. 24cm. (Mededeelingen der Koninklijke Akademie van Wetenschappen, Afdeeling Letterkunde, deel 63, serie A, no. 2)

Brunner, Peter, 1900–
... Probleme der teleologie bei Maimonides, Thomas von Aquin und Spinoza, von Peter Brunner ... Heidelberg, C. Winter, 1928.
xii, 139 p. 23cm. (Beiträge zur philosophie. 13)
"Literaturverzeichnis": p. ⌊x⌋-xii.
Presentation copy to Carl Gebhardt with the author's inscription.

1. Teleology. 2. Moses ben Maimon, 1135-1204. 3. Thomas Aquinas, Sanit, 1225?-1274. 4. Spinoza, Benedictus de, 1632-1677.

Diesendruck, Zevi, 1890-1940.
Maimonides' theory of the negation of privation. New York, 1935.
cover-title, 13 p. 24cm.

Presentation copy to A. S. Oko, with the author's inscription and signature.
"Reprinted from the Proceedings of the American Academy for Jewish Research, vol. VI, 1934-1935 ⌊p. 139-151⌋"
Bibliographical footnotes.

E-1-c
1899

Diesendruck, Zevi, 1890-1940.
The philosophy of Maimonides. [1935]
13 p. 23cm.

"Reprinted from Yearbook, vol. XLV, the Central Conference of American Rabbis, 1935."
Presentation copy to A. S. Oko, with the author's inscription and signature.

E-1-c
1900

Gotthelf, Ezra Gerson, 1907-
Spinoza and the Moreh Nebuchim. [1928]
6-11 p.

In Jewish Institute quarterly, v. 5, 1928.

NNJ

E-1-c
1901

Kuntze, Friedrich, 1881-
Die Philosophie Salomon Maimons. Heidelberg, C. Winter, 1912.
xxvi, 532 p.

Includes a section "Leibniz und Spinoza" (p. 488-490) and other references to Spinoza.

NN

E-1-c
1902

Lévy, Louis Germain, 1870-
Maïmonide. Paris, F. Alcan, 1911.
284 p. 23cm. (Les grands philosophes)

Bibliography: p. [274]-284.
Includes material on Spinoza (p. 251-258)
Original paper covers bound in.

E-1-c
1903

Lévy, Louis Germain, 1870-
Spinoza et Maïmonide. [1911]
268-272, 300-303 p.

In L'Univers israélite, année 67, 1911-12.

NN

E-1-c
1904

Maimon, Salomon, 1754-1800.
Salomon Maimon: an autobiography. Translated from the German, with additions and notes, by J. Clark Murray. London, Gardner, 1888.
xv, 307 p.

Includes references to Spinoza.

E-1-c
1905

Mieses, Fabius, 1824-1898.

קורות הפילוסופיא החדשה. Leipzig, 1887.
160 p.

Title transliterated: Koroth ha-pilosofiya ha-hadashah.
Includes references to Spinoza in the chapter on Salomon Maimon (p. 100-103)

NNJ

E-1-c
1906

193Sp4
G05
v.3

Moses ben Maimon, 1135-1204.
Das jüdische Traditionswesen, dargestellt in des R. Moses Maimonides Einleitung in seinen Mischnahkommentar, namentlich zur Mischnahordnung Seraim. Gedachte Einleitung aus dem Hebräischen in's Deutsche übersetzt und mit sacherklärenden Anmerkungen versehen von R. J. Fürstenthal. Breslau, 1842.
75 p. 19cm.

Bound with Ōṣār neḥmādh, v. 3, 1860.

NNC

E-1-c
1907

Münz, Isak, 1857-
Moses ben Maimon (Maimonides); sein leben und seine werke, von dr. J. Münz. Frankfurt am Main, J. Kauffmann, 1912.
4 p. l., 385 p. 22cm.

Includes a reference to Spinoza (p. 239)

1. Moses ben Maimon, 1135-1204.

33-8836

Library of Congress BM755.M6M8 921.9

E-1-c
1908

Niemcewitsch, Leo
Crescas contra Maimonides. Lublin, Buchdruckerei Sch. Bromberg, 1912.
79 p. 21cm.

Includes references to Spinoza.
Thesis, Bern.
Original paper cover bound in.

Pearson, Karl, 1857–1936.
The ethic of freethought; a selection of essays and lectures, by Karl Pearson ... London, T. F. Unwin, 1888.
466 p., 1 l. 23 cm.

Includes a chapter "Maimonides and Spinoza" (p. ⌊137⌋–155)

1. Ethics. 2. Free thought. 3. Sociology—Addresses, essays lectures. I. Title.

Pearson, Karl, 1857–1936.
The ethic of freethought and other addresses and essays, by Karl Pearson ... 2d ed. (rev.) London, A. and C. Black, 1901.
xii p., 2 l., 431 p. 23 cm.

Includes a chapter "Maimonides and Spinoza" (p. ⌊125⌋–142)

1. Ethics. 2. Free thought. 3. Sociology—Addresses, essays, lectures. I. Title.

Pearson, Karl, 1857-1936.
Maimonides and Spinoza. ⌊1883⌋
⌊338⌋-353 p.
In Mind, v. 8, 1883.

Rubin, Solomon, 1823-1910.
Spinoza und Maimonides; ein psychologisch-philosophisches Antitheton. Wien, Herzfeld & Bauer, 1868.
50 p. 23cm.

Sachs, Senior, 1816-1892.
הערה. ⌊1854⌋
63-75 p.

Title transliterated: Haᶜarah.
In Kerem hemed, v. 8, 1854.
Includes arguments against Spinoza in a comparison with Maimonides.

⌊Saisset, Émile⌋ 1814-1863.
La philosophie des Juifs: Maimonide et Spinoza. ⌊1862⌋
⌊296⌋-334 p. 25cm.

Signed: Émile Saisset.
From Revue des deux mondes, 2. période, v. 37, 15 janvier, 1862.
Bibliographical footnotes.

Yellin, David, 1864–1941.
Maimonides; by David Yellin and Israel Abrahams. Philadelphia, Jewish publication society of America, 1903.
xii, 239 p. front. (port.) 8 pl., 2 facsim. 19 cm.
Based on Yellin's רבי משה בן מימון Warsaw, 1898. ("Tushiah" series)

Includes references to Spinoza.

1. Moses ben Maimon, 1135–1204. I. Abrahams, Israel, 1858–1925, joint author. II. Jewish publication society of America.

Coert, J
Spinoza en Grotius, met betrekking tot het volkenrecht. Leiden, E. J. Brill, 1936.
18 p. 24cm. (Mededeelingen van wege het Spinozahuis, III)

Grotius, Hugo, 1583-1645.
Des Hugo Grotius drei Bücher über das Recht des Krieges und Friedens, in welchem das Natur und Völkerrecht und das Wichtigste aus dem öffentlichen Recht erklärt werden. Aus dem Lateinischen des Urtextes übersetzt, mit erläuternden Anmerkungen und einer Lebensbeschreibung des Verfassers versehen von J. H. v. Kirchmann. Berlin, L. Heimann, 1869.
2 v. 19cm. (Philosophische Bibliothek, 15.-16. Bd.)

Grotius, Hugo, 1583-1645.
Hugo Grotius De veritate religionis Christianâe. Editio nova, additis annotationibus, in quibus testimonia. Lugduni Batavorum, Ex officinâ Joannis Maire, 1640.
2 pts. in 1 v. 13cm.

Pt. ⌊2⌋ has title: Hugonis Grotii Annotationes ad libros De veritate religionis Christianâe.

Grotius, Hugo, 1583-1645.
Hugo Grotius, Von der Gewissheit der christlichen Religion, sechs Bücher, mit den Anmerckungen, darin die Heil. Schrifft und die christliche lehre aus der Jüden und Mahumetisten eignem Gezeugniss behauptet ... Einem jeden einfältigen Christen, so der lateinischen Sprach nicht kündig ist, zu Nutz, und dem lateinischen Exemplar ins Teutsche gebracht, und mit kurtzen Summarien über jedes Buch, sammt einen nöthigen Zusatz, der reinen evangelischen Lehre halben, vermehret durch Valentinum Muscu-

CONTINUED ON NEXT CARD

Grotius, Hugo, 1583-1645. Hugo Grotius, Von der Gewissheit der christlichen Religion. 1696. (Card 2)

lum. Franckfurt und Leipzig [In Verlägung Johann Wiedemeyers, 1696.
[30], 475, [21] p. 16cm.

Title-page mutilated.
Added engraved t.-p.: H. Grotius. Von der wahren Religion. Lübeck, In Verlägung Johann Wiedemeyers.

Grotius, Hugo, 1583-1645.
Hugonis Grotii ... De imperio svmmarvm potestatvm circa sacra. Commentarius posthumus. Lvtetiae Parisiorvm, 1647.
[24], 391, [13] p. 17cm.

Grotius, Hugo, 1583–1645.
Verantvvoordingh van de vvettelijcke regieringh van Hollandt ende VVest-Vrieslant, midtsgaders eenigher nabuyrighe provincien, sulcx die was voor de veranderingh, gevallen in den jare 1618. geschreven by mr Hugo de Groot ... met wederlegginghe van de proceduren ende sententien, jegens den selven de Groot ende anderen ghehouden ende ghewesen. Den 2. druck, van nieus oversien, ende verbetert. 1623. [*Ornament*] Accordeert met het latijnsch, ghedruckt tot Parys ... 1622.
[~~n. p.~~] ~~1622.~~
15, 287 p. 19cm.
Numerous errors in paging.
1. Remonstrants. 2. Church and state in the Netherlands. [*Translation of:* Apologeticvs eorvm qvi Hollandiae Vvestfrisiae ...]
Library of Congress BX6195.G73 1622 41-40645
[2]

Molhuysen, Philip Christiaan, 1870-1944.
De briefwisseling van Hugo Grotius. Amsterdam, 1928.
cover-title, 29 p. 24cm.

"Mededeelingen der Koninklijke Akademie van Wetenschappen, Afdeeling Letterkunde, deel 66, serie B, no. 1." .

Vereeniging voor de Uitgave van Grotius, The Hague.
Grotiana.
1-3.
1928-1930.
's-Gravenhage, 1928-30.

E-1-d
CRESCAS

Joël, Manuel, 1826–1890.
Don Chasdai Creskas' religionsphilosophische lehren in ihrem geschichtlichen einflusse dargestellt von dr. M. Joël ... Breslau, Schletter (H. Skutsch) 1866.
iv, 83, [1] p. 19½ cm.
Includes references to Spinoza (p. [iii]-iv,9)

1. Chasdai ben Abraham Crescas, 1340–1410.
B759.C44J6 15–12239 rev
——— Copy 2. [*With* Frankel, Zacharias. Die eidesleistung der Juden. Dresden und Leipzig, 1847] BM720.O3F7 1847
Library of Congress [r47b1]

Joël, Manuel, 1826-1890.
תורת הפילוסופיה הדתית של רבי
(דון) חסדאי קרשקש, הרצאה מאת דר׳
עמנואל יואל, מתרגם ע"י צבי הר־שפר.
תל־אביב בדפוס השחר תרפ"ח.
[Tel-Aviv, 1928]
111 p.

Title transliterated: Tōrath ...
Includes references to Spinoza.

Luzzatto, Samuele Davide, 1800-1865.
Spinoza und Crescas. [1862]
163-164 p.

In Die Neuzeit, 2. Jahrgang, 1862.

Neumark, David, 1866-1924.
קרשקש ושפינוזה. [1909]
28 p.

Title transliterated: Kreskas u-Shpinozah.
In he-ʿAtid, v. 2, 1909.

Neumark, David, 1866-1924.
Crescas and Spinoza; a memorial paper in honor of the five-hundredth anniversary of the "Or Adonoi". [c1909]
277-318 p. 23cm. (In Year book of the Central Conference of American Rabbis, v. 18, 1908)

Neumark, David, 1866-1924.
Crescas and Spinoza; a memorial paper in honor of the five-hundredth anniversary of the "Or Adonoi". 1909.
72 p. 22cm.

"Reprint from the Year book of the Central Conference of American Rabbis [v. 18, 1908]"

Neumark, David, 1866-1925.
Essays in Jewish philosophy. [Cincinnati, O.] Central Conference of American Rabbis, 1929.
376 p. 26cm.

Includes an essay 'Crescas and Spinoza; a memorial paper in honor of the five hundredth anniversary of the 'Or Adonoi'" (p. [301]-346)
"Bibliography of Professor David Neumark": p. [369]-376.

Waxman, Meyer, 1884-
The philosophy of Don Hasdai Crescas. New York, Columbia University Press, 1920.
xii, 162 p. 25cm. (Columbia University Oriental studies, vol. XVII)

Issued also as thesis (Ph. D.) - Columbia University.
Includes references to Spinoza.
Bibliography: p. 157-158.

E-1-e
MACHIAVELLI

Machiavelli, Niccolò, 1469-1527.
Historie di Nicolo Macchiavelli, cittadino et secretario fiorentino ... Nvovamente ammendate, & con somma diligenza ristampate .. In Piacenza, Appresso gli heredi di Gabriel Giolito de Ferrari, 1587.
[12], 559, [9] p. 14cm.

Maggiore, Giuseppe, 1882-
Un regime e un'epoca. Milano, Treves, 1929.
232 p. 21 cm. (Biblioteca di cultura politica, v. 6)

Includes a section "Machiavelli e Spinoza" (p. 199-209)

[Pollock, Sir Frederick, bart.] 1845-1937.
Spinoza et le machiavelisme. [Traduit d'après le manuscrit anglais par M. G. Stempowski. 1919]
[3]-11 p. 25cm.

Signed: Sir Frederick Pollock.
From La Revue politique internationale, v. 11, janvier-juin 1919.
Copy presented to A. S. Oko by F. P.

[Pollock, Sir Frederick, bart.] 1845-1937.
Spinoza et le machiavelisme. [Traduit d'après le manuscrit anglais par M. G. Stempowski. 1919]
[3]-11 p. 25cm.

Signed: Sir Frederick Pollock.
From La Revue politique internationale, v. 11, janvier-juin 1919.

Ravà, Adolfo
Spinoza e Machiavelli; un contributo agli studi spinoziani. Modena, Società tipografica modenese, 1931.
cover-title, 15 p. 28cm.

"Estratto dagli 'Studi filosofico-giuridici dedicati a Giorgio del Vecchio'."
Presentation copy to Carl Gebhardt with the author's inscription and initials.
Ms. notes by Carl Gebhardt in margins.
Bibliographical footnotes.

Ravà, Adolfo
Un contributo agli studi spinoziani. Spinoza e Machiavelli. [1931]
299-313 p.

From Studi filosofico-giuridici dedicati a Giorgio del Vecchio, v. 2, 1931.

E-1-e
1939

Vorländer, Karl, 1860-1928.
Von Machiavelli bis Lenin; neuzeitliche Staats- und Gesellschaftstheorien. Leipzig, Quelle & Meyer, 1926.
286 p.

E-1-f
BRUNO

SPECIAL COLLECTIONS
SPINOZA

E-1-f
1940

Bergfeld, Max
Giordano Bruno. Berlin, Deutsche Bibliothek ⌈c1929⌉
215 p. 19cm. (Die Unsterblichen; die geistigen Heroen der Menschheit in ihrem Leben und Wirken. 5)

Includes references to Spinoza.

SPECIAL COLLECTIONS
SPINOZA

E-1-f
1941

Bruno, Giordano, 1548-1600.
Gesammelte Werke. Hrsg. von Ludwig Kuhlenbeck. ⌈Leipzig, E. Diederichs, 1904-09⌉
6 v. illus., port., diagrs. 21cm.

Each volume has also special t.-p.
"Ins deutsche übertragen von Ludwig Kuhlenbeck."
Includes a reference to Spinoza (v. 1, p. 2)

E-1-f
1942

Dilthey, Wilhelm, 1833-1911.
Giordano Bruno und Spinoza. ⌈1894⌉
269-283 p.

In Archiv für Geschichte der Philosophie, Bd. 7, 1894.

SPECIAL COLLECTIONS
SPINOZA

E-1-f
1943

Falkson, Ferdinand, 1820-1900.
Giordano Bruno. Hamburg, Hoffmann und Campe, 1846.
xvi, 312 p. 17cm.

Includes references to Spinoza (p. 262-263, 287-288)

E-1-f
1944

Lovejoy, Arthur Oncken, 1873-
The dialectic of Bruno and Spinoza. ⌈1904⌉
141-174 p.

In California university. Publications; philosophy, v. 1, 1904.

E-1-f
1945

McIntyre, James Lewis, 1868-
Giordano Bruno. London, New York, Macmillan, 1903.
xvi, 365 p. port. 23 cm.

Includes a discussion of Bruno's influence on Spinoza (p. 337-343) and other references to Spinoza.

E-1-g
JEWISH MEDIAEVAL PHILOSOPHY

E-1-g
1946

Efros, Israel Isaac, 1890-
... The problem of space in Jewish mediaeval philosophy, by Israel Isaac Efros ... New York, Columbia university press, 1917.
5 p. l., 125 p., 1 l. diagrs. 24½ cm. (Columbia university oriental studies. vol. XI)
Thesis (PH. D.)—Columbia university, 1916.
Vita.
Includes references to Spinoza.
1. Space and time. 2. Philosophy, Jewish. 3. Philosophy, Medieval. I. Title. II. Title: Space in Jewish mediaeval philosophy.

B757.S8E3 19—4883
Library of Congress ⌈a54f½⌉

SPECIAL COLLECTIONS
SPINOZA

E-1-g
1947

⌈Ferro, Andrea Alberto⌉ 1877-
La filosofia di Spinoza e la filosofia ebraica medievale. ⌈1935⌉
2 pts. 26cm.

Signed: A. Ferro.
From Giornale critico della filosofia italiana, anno XVI, seconda serie, vol. III., fasc. I, gennaio-febbraio 1935, p. ⌈50⌉-64, and fasc. II, marzo-aprile 1935, p. ⌈169⌉-180.

E-1-g
1948

Husik, Isaac, 1876-1939.
A history of mediaeval Jewish philosophy, by Isaac Husik ... New York, The Macmillan company, 1916.
4 p. l., vii-l p., 1 l., 462 p. 22½ cm.
Bibliography: p. 433-437.
Includes a reference to Spinoza (p. 398-399)

1. Philosophy, Jewish. 2. Philosophy, Medieval. I. Title. II. Title: Mediaeval Jewish philosophy, History of.

B755.H8 16—21233
Library of Congress ⌈58j½⌉

E-1-g
1949

Scheur, Schaje, 1887-
Spinoza und die juedische Philosophie des Mittelalters. Vorgelegt von Schaje Scheur recte Sonne. Firenze, Tip. Carpigiani & Zipoli, 1925.
53 p. 23cm.

Thesis, Zürich.
Bibliographical footnotes.

E-1-g
1950

Sonne, Isaiah, 1887-
Spinoza und die jüdische Philosophie des Mittelalters. Firenze, Carpigiani & Zipoli, 1925.
53 p.

Thesis, Zurich.

NNJ

E-1-g
1951

Sorley, William Ritchie, 1855-1935.
Jewish mediaeval philosophy and Spinoza. [1880]
362-384 p.

In Mind, v. 5, 1880.

E-1-g
1952

Sorley, William Ritchie, 1855-1935.
Jewish medieval philosophy and Spinoza. [1880]
23 p. 21cm.

"Reprinted from 'Mind', July, 1880."
Bibliographical footnotes.

E-1-g
1953

Wolfson, Harry Austryn, 1887-
Some guiding principles in determining Spinoza's mediaeval sources. Philadelphia, Dropsie College for Hebrew and Cognate Learning, 1937.
cover-title, 333-348 p. 25cm.

"Reprinted from the Jewish quarterly review. New series. Volume XXVII, number 4."

E-2
1596-1750

E-2-a
GENERAL

E-2-a
1954

Acta philosophorum; das ist, Gründl. Nachrichten aus der historia philosophica, nebst beygefügten Urtheilen von denen dahin gehörigen alten und neuen Büchern ...
t. 1[6]-3 (Stück 6-18)
Halle, Zu finden in der Rengerischen Buchhandl., 1716-[26]
2 v. illus., ports. 18cm.

"Nachricht von einem Spinozisten/Henrico Wirmarsio": Stück 7, p. 114-144.

E-2-a
1955

Andala, Ruardus, 1665-1727.
Ruardi Andala ... Dissertationum philosophicarum heptas ... Franequerae, Ex Officina W. Bleck, 1711.
[4], 292 p. 20cm. (His Syntagma theologico-physico-metaphysicum, pt. [3])

Includes references to Spinoza (p. 185-195)

NNC

E-2-a
1956

Anderson, George, 1676-1756.
A remonstrance against Lord Viscount Bolingbroke's philosophical religion, addressed to David Mallet, Esq., the publisher. Edinburgh, 1756.

CtY

E-2-a
1957

Argens, Jean Baptiste de Boyer, marquis de, 1704-1771.
The Jewish spy: being a philosophical, historical and critical correspondence, by letters which lately pass'd between certain Jews in Turkey, Italy, France, &c. Translated from the originals into French, by the Marquis d'Argens; and now done into English. London, Printed for D. Browne and R. Hett, 1739.
xii, 303, [45] p. port. 18cm.

Includes references to Spinoza.

[Argens, Jean Baptiste de Boyer, marquis d'] 1704-1771.
Lettres cabalistiques, ou, Correspondance philosophique, historique & critique, entre deux cabalistes, divers esprits élémentaires, et le seigneur Astaroth. Nouvelle edition, augmentée de nouvelles lettres & de quantité de remarques. La Haye, Chez Pierre Paupie, 1754
1 p. l., 368 p. 15cm.

Vol. 7 of a seven volume set.
Includes a reference to Spinoza (p. 118-119)

Argens, Jean Baptiste de Boyer, marquis d', 1703-1771.
La philosophie du bon-sens, ou Réflexions philosophiques sur l'incertitude des connoissances humaines, à l'usage des cavaliers et du beau-sexe: par Monsieur le Marquis d'Argens. A Londres, Aux dépens de la Compagnie, 1737.
xii, 444, [66] p. plates. 17cm.

Includes references to Spinoza.
Bibliographical footnotes.

Argens, Jean Baptiste de Boyer, marquis d', 1704-1771.
La philosophie du bon-sens; ou, Reflexions philosophiques sur l'incertitude des connoissances humaines, à l'usage des cavaliers & du beau-sexe. Nouvelle edition revue, corrigée & augmentée d'un examen critique des remarques de Mr. l'abbé d'Olivet ... Par Monsieur le marquis d'Argens.... A La Haye, Chez Pierre Paupie, 1746.
2 v. plate, port. 18cm.

Includes references to Spinoza.

Arnauld, Antoine, 1612-1694.
Oeuvres philosophiques. Nouv. éd., collationnée sur les meilleurs textes et précédée d'une introduction par Jules Simon. Paris, A. Delahays, 1843.
xlj, 563 p. 18 cm.

Includes references to Spinoza.

Bacon, Francis, viscount St. Albans, 1561-1625.
Fr. Baconi de Verulamio Sermones fideles, ethici, politici, œconomici: sive Interiora rerum. Accedit Faber Fortunæ, &c. Lug. Batavorum, Apud Franciscum Hackium, 1641.
439 (i.e. 417), [3] p. 13cm.

Page 169 incorrectly numbered 189; page 281 incorrectly numbered 181; numbers 52, 53, 171-190 not used.
Gibson 51.

Bacon, Francis, viscount St. Albans, 1561-1626.
Francisci Baconi ... opera omnia, quæ extant, philosophica, moralia, politica, historica ... in quibus complures alii tractatus, quos brevitatis causa prætermittere visum est, comprehensi sunt, hactenus nunquam conjunctim edita, jam vero summo studio collecta, uno volumine comprehensa, & ab innumeris mendis repurgata: cum indice rerum ac verborum universali absolutissimo. His præfixa est auctoris vita Francofvrti ad Moenvm, impensis J. B. Schonwetteri, 1665.

CONTINUED ON NEXT CARD

Bacon, Francis, viscount St. Albans, 1561-1626.
Francisci Baconi ... opera omnia. 1665.
(Card 2)

9 p. l., 1324 col., [29] p. 35½cm.

Each work has special t.-p., dated 1664.
Leaf following t.-p. missing.

Bacon, Francis, viscount St. Albans, 1561-1626.
Lord Franz Bacon ... über die Würde und den Fortgang der Wissenschafften. Verdeutschet und mit dem Leben des Verfassers und einigen historischen Anmerkungen herausgegeben von Johann Hermann Pfingsten ... Pest, im Verlag der Weingand und Köpfischen Handlung, 1783.
812 p. port. 23cm.

[Becker, Josef]
Untersuchungen zum Reisetagebuch des Gottlieb Stolle von 1703. [1930]
[261]-274 p. 25cm.

Signed: Josef Becker.
From Zentralblatt für Bibliothekswesen, Jahrgang 47, Juni 1930.
Includes references to Spinoza.
Bibliographical footnotes.

Becker, Theodor, 1851-
De philosophia Lockii et Humii, Spinozismi fructu, criticismi germine. Halis Saxonum, Formis Ploetzianis [1875]
31 p. 23cm.

Thesis, Halle.
Volume of pamphlets.

E-2-a
1968

Bentley, Richard, 1662–1742.
Sermons preached at Boyle's lecture; remarks upon a discourse of free-thinking; proposals for an edition of the Greek Testament; etc., etc. By Richard Bentley, D. D. Edited with notes, by the Rev. Alexander Dyce. London, F. Macpherson, 1838.
xvi, 546 p. 22ᶜᵐ. ~~(*Half-title:* The works of Richard Bentley ... vol. III. Theological writings)~~
CONTENTS.—Eight Boyle lectures.—Four letters from Sir Isaac Newton to Dr. Bentley.—Three sermons on various subjects: I. Of revelation and the Messias. II. Upon popery. III. Before King George I.—Visitation charge.—Remarks upon a discourse of free-thinking.—Proposals for printing a new edition of the Greek Testament.—Oratiuncula.
1. Church of England—Sermons. 2. Sermons, English. I. Dyce, Alexander, 1798–1869, ed. II. Newton, Sir Isaac, 1642–1727.
5-30698 Revised

E-2-a
1969

Berkeley, George, bp. of Cloyne, 1685-1753.
Berkeley's Commonplace book; edited with introduction, notes and index by G. A. Johnston. London, Faber & Faber [1930]
xxiv, 156 p. 20 cm.

Includes references to Spinoza.

E-2-a
1970

Berkeley, George, bp. of Cloyne, 1685-1753.
The works of George Berkeley ... Including his letters to Thomas Prior, esq., Dean Gervais, Mr. Pope, &c. &c. To which is prefixed an account of his life. In this edition the Latin essays are rendered into English, and the "Introduction to human knowledge" annotated, by the Rev. G. N. Wright. London, T. Tegg, 1843.
2 v.

E-2-a
1971

Berkeley, George, bp. of Cloyne, 1685-1753.
The works of George Berkeley. Collected and ed. with prefaces and annotations by Alexander Campbell Fraser. Oxford, Clarendon Press, 1871.
4 v. 23 cm.

Includes references to Spinoza.

E-2-a
1972

Berkeley, George, ***bp. of Cloyne,*** **1685–1753.**
The works of George Berkeley, D. D., bishop of Cloyne; ed. by George Sampson, with a biographical introduction by the Rt. Hon. A. J. Balfour ... London, G. Bell and sons, 1897–98.
3 v. fronts. (v. 1–2) 19ᶜᵐ. (*Half-title:* Bohn's philosophical library)

I. Sampson, George, 1873– ed. II. Balfour, Arthur James Balfour, 1st earl of, 1848–1930.
11—14616

E-2-a
1973

Blackall, Offspring, bp. of Exeter, 1654-1716.
The sufficiency of a standing revelation in general, and of the Scripture revelation in particular ... and that new revelations cannot reasonably be desired ... In eight sermons, preach'd ... at the lecture founded by the Honourable Robert Boyle Esq; in the year MDCC. By Ofspring Blackall ... London, Printed by J. Leake, for Walter Kettilby, 1700.
7 pts. in 1 v. 21cm.

Each sermon, except the fifth, has separate title-page with special title.

CONTINUED ON NEXT CARD

E-2-a
1974

Blackall, Offspring, bp. of Exeter, 1654-1716.
The sufficiency of a standing revelation ... 1700. (Card 2)

Bound with Bentley, Richard, 1662-1742. The folly and unreasonableness of atheism demonstrated. 1699.

E-2-a
1975

Blount, Charles, 1654-1693.
The oracles of reason: consisting of 1. A vindication of Dr. Burnet's Archiologiae. 2. The seventh and eighth chapters of the same. 3. Of Moses's description of the .riginal state of man, &c. 4. Dr. Burnet s appendix of the Brachmins religion. 5. An account of the deist's religion. 6. Of the immortality of the soul. 7. Concerning the Arrians, Trinitarians and councils. 8. That felicity consists in pleasure. 9. Of fate and fortune. 10. Of the

CONTINUED ON NEXT CARD

E-2-a
1976

Blount, Charles, 1654-1693. The oracles of reason ... 1693. (Card 2)

original of the Jews. 11. The lawfulness of marrying two sisters successively. 12. A political account of the subversion of Jewdaism, and original of the millenium. 13. Of the auguries of the ancients. 14. Natural religion as oppos'd to divine revelation. 15. That the soul is matter. 16. That the world is eternal, &c. In several letters to Mr. Hobbs and other

CONTINUED ON NEXT CARD

E-2-a
1977

Blount, Charles, 1654-1693. The oracles of reason ... 1693. (Card 3)

persons of eminent quality, and learning. By Char. Blount esq; Mr. Gildon and others. London, Printed 1693.
12 p. l., 226 (i. e. 228) p. 16cm.

Pages 119-120 repeated in paging.

NN E-2-a 1978

Blount, Charles, 1654-1693.
Religio laici, written in a letter to John Dryden, Esq. London, Printed for R. Bentley and S. Magnes, 1683.
11 p. l., 95 p.

MH E-2-a 1979

[Bonavino, Cristoforo] 1821-1895.
Letture su la storia della filosofia moderna. Bacone, Descartes, Spinoza, Malebranche. Per A[usonio] F[ranchi, pseud.] Milano, Ferrario, 1863.
2 v. 18cm.

E-2-a 1980

Boole, George, 1815-1864.
The laws of thought (1854) Chicago, The Open Court Pub. Co., 1940.
xvi, 448 p. 22 cm. (George Boole's Collected logical works, v. 2)

Includes a chapter "Analysis of Dr. Samuel Clarke's 'Demonstration of the being and attributes of God', and of the 'Ethica ordine geometrico demonstrata' of Spinoza".

DLC

E-2-a 1981

[Boyle, Robert] 1627-1691.
Reasons why a Protestant should not turn papist: or, Protestant prejudices against the Roman Catholic religion; propos'd, in a letter to a Romish priest. By a person of quality. London, Printed by H. Clark for John Taylor, 1687.
3 p. l., 32 p. 20 cm.

NNC

SPECIAL COLLECTIONS SPINOZA E-2-a 1982

Boyle, Hon. Robert, 1627-1691.
The works of the Honourable Robert Boyle. To which is prefixed the life of the author [by Thomas Birch] London, Printed for A. Millar, 1744.
5 v. fold. plates, port. 38cm.

E-2-a 1983

Brandl, Bened.
Die Überlieferung der "Schutzschrift" des Hermann Samuel Reimarus. Pilsen, C. Maasch [1907]
27 p. 25 cm.

NjP

SPECIAL COLLECTIONS SPINOZA E-2-a 1984

Buddeus, Johann Franz, 1667-1729.
Ioan. Francisci Bvddei ... Analecta historiae philosophicae. Halae Saxonvm, Sumptibus Orphanotrophii, 1706.
32, [30], 463 p. 18cm.

"Exercitatio historico-philosophica de Spinozismo ante Spinozam habita Halae Saxonvm die XX. Ivnii anno MDCCI. respondente Friderico Werder": p. [307]-359.
Bound with the author's Introdvctio ad historiam philosophiae Ebraeorvm. 1702.

SPECIAL COLLECTIONS SPINOZA E-2-a 1985

Buddeus, Johann Franz, 1667-1729, praeses.
... Dissertatio philosophica de Spinozismo ante Spinozam, quam ... praeside Io. Francisco Bvddeo ... pro gradv et privilegiis magistri philosophiae rite impetrandis ... submittit Ioannes Fridericvs VVerder ... Halae Magdeb., Typis Chr. Henckelii [1701]
32 p. 20cm.

NNC

E-2-a 1986

Buddeus, Johann Franz, 1667-1729.
Jo. Francisci Buddei Institutiones theologiae dogmaticae variis observationibus illustratae ... Lipsiae, ex officina T. Fritschii, 1723.
1816 p.

Includes references to Spinoza.

NNUT

SPECIAL COLLECTIONS SPINOZA E-2-a 1987

Burgersdijck, Franco Petri, 1590-1635.
Idea philosophiæ, moralis, sive Compendiosa institutio, auctore Francone Burgersdicio. Editio postrema, multis in locis emendata. Amstelodami, Apud Joannem Janssonium, 1660.
161 (i. e. 261), [2] p. 14cm.

E-2-a 1988

Campbell, Archibald, 1691–1756.

An enquiry into the original of moral virtue; wherein it is shewn (against the author of the "Fable of the bees", &c.,) that virtue is founded in the nature of things, is unalterable, and eternal ... With some reflections on a late book, entitled An enquiry into the original of our ideas of beauty and virtue. By Archibald Campbell ... Edinburgh, Printed for G. Hamilton, by R. Fleming and company, 1733.

2 p. l., xxxii, ⌊23⌋, 546, ⌊1⌋ p. 21cm.

1. Ethics. 2. Mandeville, Bernard, 1670–1733. The fable of the bees. 3. Hutcheson, Francis, 1694–1746. An enquiry into the original of our ideas of beauty and virtue. 4. Virtue.

NNUT

Library of Congress BJ1520.C2 1733 10–4538 ⌊a34b1⌋

SPECIAL COLLECTIONS SPINOZA

E-2-a 1989

193Sp4 DC136

⌊Campbell, Archibald⌋ 1691-1756.

'Αρετη-λογία; or, An enquiry into the original of moral virtue; wherein the false notions of Machiavel, Hobbes, Spinoza, and Mr. Bayle ... collected and digested by the author of The fable of the bees, are examin'd and confuted ... To which is prefix'd, a preparatory introduction, in a letter to that author. By Alexander Innes ... Westminster, Printed by J. Cluer and A. Campbell for B. Creake, 1728.

4 p. l., xli, ⌊1⌋, 333 p. 20½cm.

CONTINUED ON NEXT CARD

SPECIAL COLLECTIONS SPINOZA

E-2-a 1990

193Sp4 DC136

⌊Campbell, Archibald⌋ 1691-1756. 'Αρετη-λογία; or, An enquiry into the original of moral virtue. 1728. (Card 2)

Innes, "employed to make arrangements for its publication, appropriated it to himself." cf. Dict. nat. biog.

E-2-a 1991

Carroll, William

A letter to the Reverend Dr. Benjamin Prat ... wherein the dangerous errors in a late book ⌊by Anthony Collins⌋, intituled, An essay concerning the use of reason in propositions, the evidence whereof depends upon human testimony: are detected, confuted, etc. London, Richard Sare, 1707.

24 p.

CU

E-2-a 1992

⌊Carroll, William⌋

Remarks upon Mr. Clarke's sermons, preached at St. Paul's against Hobbs, Spinoza, and other atheists. London, Printed for Jonathan Robinson, 1705.

42 p. 20 cm.

E-2-a 1993

⌊Carroll, William⌋

Spinoza reviv'd: or, A treatise, proving the book, entitled, The rights of the Christian church, &c. (in the most notorious parts of it) to be the same with Spinoza's Rights of the Christian clergy, &c. and that both of them are grounded upon downright atheism. To which is added, A preliminary discourse relating to the said books, by the Reverend Dr. George Hicks ... London, Printed and to be sold by J. Morphew, 1709.

36 p. l., 179 p.

NNUT

SPECIAL COLLECTIONS SPINOZA

E-2-a 1994

Chevreau, Urbain, 1613-1701.

Chevraeana, ou Diverses pensées d'histoire, de critique, d'erudition et de morale. Recueillies & publiées par Mr. Chevreau. Amsterdam, Chez T. Lombrail, 1700.

2 v. fronts. (port.) 16cm.

Includes a paragraph on Spinoza (v. 2, p. 99-100)

E-2-a 1995

Chevreau, Urbain, 1613-1701.

Chevraeana. A Paris, Chez Florentin & Pierre Delaulne, 1697-1700.

2 v. 17 cm.

Includes a reference to Spinoza (v. 2, p. 105-106)

NN

E-2-a 1996

Clarke, Samuel, 1675-1729.

Demonstratio existentiae et attribvtorvm Dei, adversvs Hobbesivm et Spinosam ... Anglice conscripta à Samvele Clarkio ... Accedit interpretis Jenkini Thomasii Historia atheismi. Altdorffi Noricorvm, Apud Jodocvm Gvilielmvm Kohlesivm, 1713.

⌊16⌋, 174 p. 17 cm.

E-2-a 1997

Clarke, Samuel, 1675-1729.

A demonstration of the being and attributes of God: more particularly in answer to Mr. Hobbs, Spinoza, and their followers. Wherein the notion of liberty is stated, and the possibility and certainty of it proved, in oppostion to necessity and fate. Being the substance of eight sermons preach'd ... in the year 1704 at the lecture founded by R. Boyle, esq. London, Printed by W. Botham for J. Knapton, 1705.

8 p. l., 264 p. 19cm.

NNUT

E-2-a 1998

Clarke, Samuel, 1675-1729.
A demonstration of the being and attributes of God: more particularly in answer to Mr. Hobbs, Spinoza, and their followers: wherein the notion of liberty is stated, and the possibility and certainty of it proved, in opposition to necessity and fate. Being the substance of eight sermons preech'd ... in the year 1704 at the lecture founded by R. Boyle esq. The second edition, corrected. London, Printed by W. Botham for J. Knapton, 1706.
8 p. l., 206 p., 1 l.

ICU

E-2-a 1999

Clarke, Samuel, 1675-1729.
A demonstration of the being and attributes of God: more particularly in answer to Mr. Hobbs, Spinoza, and their followers ... The third edition. London, 1711.
xviii, 142 p.

NNUT

SPECIAL COLLECTIONS SPINOZA

E-2-a 2000

Clarke, Samuel, 1675-1729.
A discourse concerning the being and attributes of God, the obligations of natural religion, and the truth and certainty of the Christian revelation. In answer to Mr. Hobbs, Spinoza, the author of the Oracles of reason, and other deniers of natural and revealed religion. Being sixteen sermons, preach'd in the Cathedral-Church of St. Paul, in the years 1704, and 1705, at the lecture founded by the Honourable Robert Boyle, Esq; In which is

CONTINUED ON NEXT CARD

NNC

E-2-a 2001

Clarke, Samuel, 1675-1729.
A discourse concerning the being and attributes of God, the obligations of natural religion, and the truth and certainty of the Christian revelation. In answer to Mr. Hobbes, Spinoza and other deniers of natural and revealed religion. Being sixteen sermons preached ... in the years 1704 and 1705 at the lecture founded by the Honourable Robert Boyle esqr. The fourth edition. London, 1716.
3 pts.

IEN

E-2-a 2002

Clarke, Samuel, 1675-1729.
A discourse concerning the being and attributes of God, the obligations of natural religion, and the truth and certainty of the Christian revelation. In answer to Mr. Hobbs, Spinoza, the author of the Oracles of reason, and other deniers of natural and revealed religion. Being sixteen sermons preach'd ... in the years 1704 and 1705, at the lecture founded by the Honourable Rob. Boyle esq. The fifth edition, corrected. To which are added several letters to Dr. Clarke from a gentleman in Gloucester- -

MH

(Continued on next card)

E-2-a 2003

Clarke, Samuel, 1675-1729. A discourse concerning the being and attributes of God ... 1719. (Card 2)

shire, relating to the first volume; with the Drs answers. London, Printed by W. Botham for J. Knapton, 1719.
3 pts.

MH

E-2-a 2004

Clarke, Samuel, 1675-1729.
A discourse concerning the being and attributes of God, the obligations of natural religion, and the truth and certainty of the Christian revelation. In answer to Mr. Hobbs, Spinoza, and their followers ... The sixth edition, corrected. London, Printed by W. Botham for J. Knapton, 1725.
[24], 119 p.

NNUT

SPECIAL COLLECTIONS SPINOZA

E-2-a 2005

Clarke, Samuel, 1675-1729. A discourse concerning the being and attributes of God. 1732. (Card 2)

inserted a discourse concerning the connexion of the prophecies in the Old Testament, and the application of them to Christ. There is also, an answer to a seventh letter, concerning, the argument a priori, in proof of the being of God. By Samuel Clarke ... The eighth edition. London, Printed by W. Botham, for James and John Knapton, 1732.
[24], 504 p. 21cm.

NNC

SPECIAL COLLECTIONS SPINOZA

E-2-a 2006

Clarke, Samuel, 1675-1729.
A discourse concerning the being and attributes of God, the obligations of natural religion, and the truth and certainty of the Christian revelation. In answer to Mr. Hobbs, Spinoza, the author of the Oracles of reason, and other deniers of natural and revealed religion. Being sixteen sermons, preach'd in the Cathedral-church of St. Paul, in the years 1704, and 1705, at the lecture founded by the Honourable Robert Boyle, Esq; In which is inserted a Discourse concerning the connexion of

CONTINUED ON NEXT CARD

SPECIAL COLLECTIONS SPINOZA

E-2-a 2007

Clarke, Samuel, 1675-1729. A discourse concerning ... God. 1738. (Card 2)

the prophecies in the Old Testament, and the application of them to Christ. There is also, an answer to a seventh letter, concerning, the argument ... in proof of the being of God. By Samuel Clarke ... The ninth edition. London, Printed by W. Botham, for John and Paul Knapton, 1738.
[24], 504 p. 20cm.

E-2-a 2008

Clarke, Samuel, 1675-1729.
A discourse concerning the being and attributes of God, the obligations of natural religion, and the truth and certainty of the Christian revelation. In answer to Mr. Hobbs, Spinoza, the author of the Oracles of reason, and other deniers of natural and revealed religion. Being sixteen sermons, preach'd ... in the years 1704, and 1705, at the lecture founded by the Honourable Robert Boyle, esq. ... The tenth edition, corrected. London, Printed for John and Paul Knapton, 1749.
[24], 504 p.

SPECIAL COLLECTIONS SPINOZA E-2-a 2009

Clarke, Samuel, 1675-1729.
De l'existence et des attributs de Dieu: des devoirs de la religion naturelle, et de la verité de la religion chrétienne. Traitez qui sont le précis de XVI. sermons prononcez à Londres pour la lecture fondée par M. Boyle, par M. Clark ... Traduits de l'anglois par M. Ricotier ... À Amsterdam, Chez Jean Frederic Bernard, 1717.
2 v. in 1. 17cm.

Includes references to Spinoza.

E-2-a 2010

Clarke, Samuel, 1675-1729.
A discourse concerning the unchangeable obligations of natural religion, and the truth and certainty of the Christian revelation. Being eight sermons preach'd ... in the year 1705, at the lecture founded by the Honourable Robert Boyle esq. The third edition. London, Printed by W. Botham for J. Knapton, 1711.
20 p. l., 406 p., 1 l.

MH

E-2-a 2011

Clarke, Samuel, 1675-1729.
A discourse concerning the unchangeable obligations of natural religion, and the truth and certainty of the Christian revelation. The third edition. London, W. Botham, 1711.
351 p.

NNUT

SPECIAL COLLECTIONS SPINOZA E-2-a 2012

Clarke, Samuel, 1675-1729.
Oeuvres philosophiques de Samuel Clarke. Nouvelle édition, collationnée sur les meilleurs textes et précédée d'une introduction par Amédée Jacques. Paris, Charpentier, 1843.
xxxviii, 368 p. 19cm.

On paper covers (bound in): Avec notes et introduction par Émile Saisset.
Includes references to Spinoza.
Bibliographical footnotes.

E-2-a 2013

Clifford, Martin, d. 1677.
A treatise of humane reason. London, for Hen. Brome, 1674.
[2], 91 p. 13 cm.

NNUT

SPECIAL COLLECTIONS SPINOZA E-2-a 2014

[Condillac, Étienne Bonnot de] 1714-1780.
Traité des sistèmes, où l'on en démêle les inconvéniens & les avantages. Par l'auteur de l'Essai sur l'origine des connoissances humaines ... A La Haye, Chez Neaulme, 1749.
2 pt. in 1 v. ([10], 449, [1] p. 17cm.

Includes a chapter on Spinoza.

SPECIAL COLLECTIONS SPINOZA E-2-a 2015

Condillac, Étienne Bonnot de, 1714-1780.
Traite des systêmes, ou l'on en démèle les inconvénients et les avantages. Par M. l'Abbé de Condillac ... A Amsterdam, & a Leipsick, Chez Arkstée & Merkus, Libraires; et se vend, a Paris, Chez Jombert pere, 1771.
[4], 448 p. 17cm.

Includes a chapter on Spinoza.

SPECIAL COLLECTIONS SPINOZA E-2-a 2016

Conway, Anne (Finch) Conway, viscountess, 1631-1679.
Conway letters; the correspondence of Anne, viscountess Conway, Henry More, and their friends, 1642-1684, collected from manuscript sources & edited with a biographical account by Marjorie Hope Nicolson. London, Published by H. Milford, Oxford University Press, and to be sold in America by Yale University Press, 1930.
xxvii, 517 p. plates, ports., facsims. 26cm.

CONTINUED ON NEXT CARD

NNC

SPECIAL COLLECTIONS SPINOZA E-2-a 2017

Conway, Anne (Finch) Conway, viscountess, 1631-1679. Conway letters ... 1930. (Card 2)

"Published on the Kingsley Trust Association publication fund, established by the Scroll and Key Society of Yale College."
Includes a reference to Spinoza (p. 475) and to his Tractatus theologico-politicus, with marginal note by Oko (footnote, p. 429)

NNC

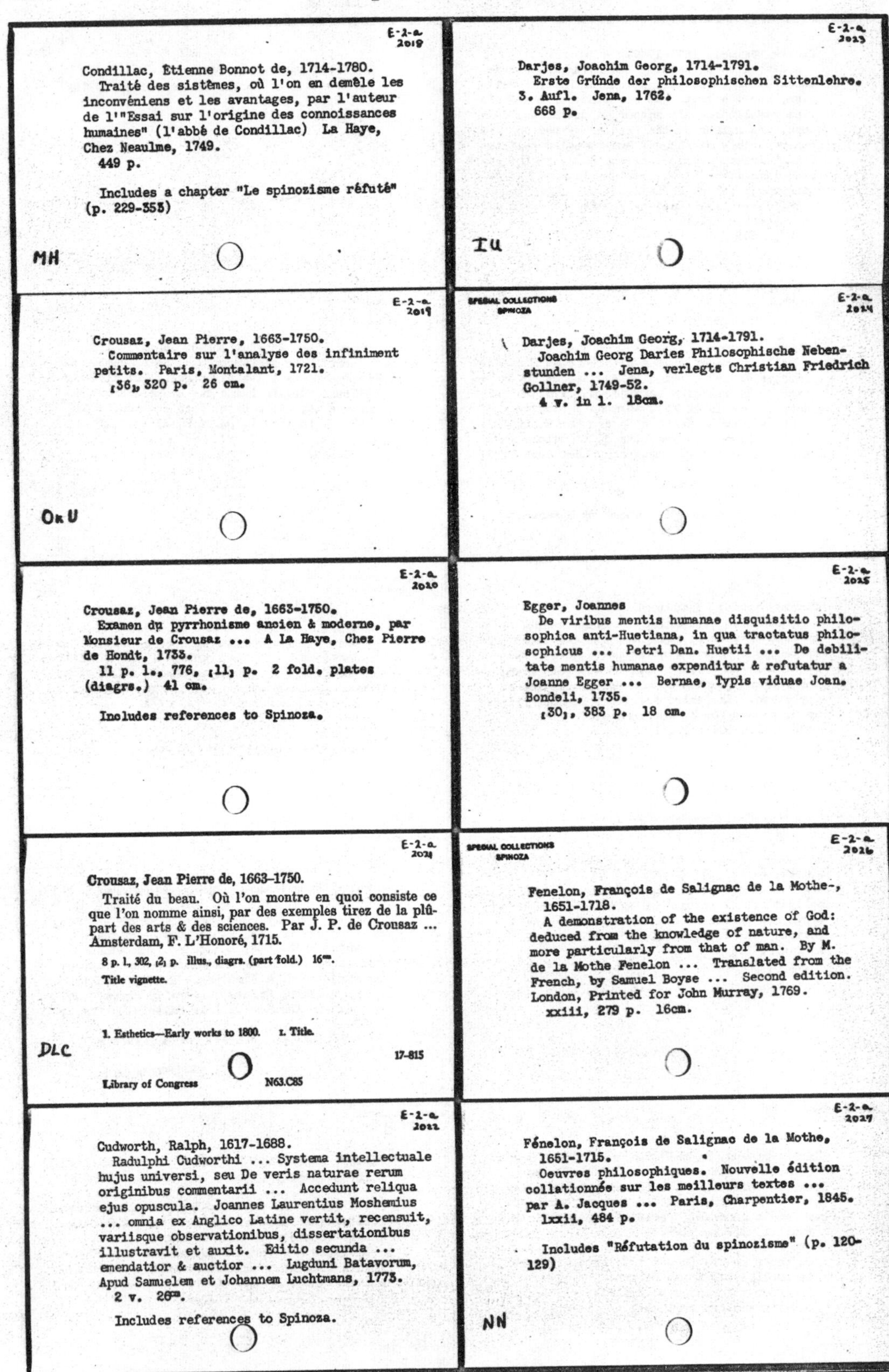

E-2-a
2018

Condillac, Étienne Bonnot de, 1714-1780.
Traité des sistêmes, où l'on en demêle les inconvéniens et les avantages, par l'auteur de l'"Essai sur l'origine des connoissances humaines" (l'abbé de Condillac) La Haye, Chez Neaulme, 1749.
449 p.

Includes a chapter "Le spinozisme réfuté" (p. 229-353)

MH

E-2-a
2019

Crousaz, Jean Pierre, 1663-1750.
Commentaire sur l'analyse des infiniment petits. Paris, Montalant, 1721.
[36], 320 p. 26 cm.

OkU

E-2-a
2020

Crousaz, Jean Pierre de, 1663-1750.
Examen du pyrrhonisme ancien & moderne, par Monsieur de Crousaz ... A La Haye, Chez Pierre de Hondt, 1733.
11 p. l., 776, [1] p. 2 fold. plates (diagrs.) 41 cm.

Includes references to Spinoza.

E-2-a
2021

Crousaz, Jean Pierre de, 1663-1750.
Traité du beau. Où l'on montre en quoi consiste ce que l'on nomme ainsi, par des exemples tirez de la plûpart des arts & des sciences. Par J. P. de Crousaz ... Amsterdam, F. L'Honoré, 1715.
8 p. l., 302, [2] p. illus., diagrs. (part fold.) 16cm.
Title vignette.

1. Esthetics—Early works to 1800. I. Title.

DLC

17-815

Library of Congress N63.C85

E-2-a
2022

Cudworth, Ralph, 1617-1688.
Radulphi Cudworthi ... Systema intellectuale hujus universi, seu De veris naturae rerum originibus commentarii ... Accedunt reliqua ejus opuscula. Joannes Laurentius Moshemius ... omnia ex Anglico Latine vertit, recensuit, variisque observationibus, dissertationibus illustravit et auxit. Editio secunda ... emendatior & auctior ... Lugduni Batavorum, Apud Samuelem et Johannem Luchtmans, 1773.
2 v. 26cm.

Includes references to Spinoza.

E-2-a
2023

Darjes, Joachim Georg, 1714-1791.
Erste Gründe der philosophischen Sittenlehre. 3. Aufl. Jena, 1762.
668 p.

IU

SPECIAL COLLECTIONS
SPINOZA

E-2-a
2024

Darjes, Joachim Georg, 1714-1791.
Joachim Georg Daries Philosophische Nebenstunden ... Jena, verlegts Christian Friedrich Gollner, 1749-52.
4 v. in 1. 18cm.

E-2-a
2025

Egger, Joannes
De viribus mentis humanae disquisitio philosophica anti-Huetiana, in qua tractatus philosophicus ... Petri Dan. Huetii ... De debilitate mentis humanae expenditur & refutatur a Joanne Egger ... Bernae, Typis viduae Joan. Bondeli, 1735.
[30], 383 p. 18 cm.

SPECIAL COLLECTIONS
SPINOZA

E-2-a
2026

Fenelon, François de Salignac de la Mothe-, 1651-1718.
A demonstration of the existence of God: deduced from the knowledge of nature, and more particularly from that of man. By M. de la Mothe Fenelon ... Translated from the French, by Samuel Boyse ... Second edition. London, Printed for John Murray, 1769.
xxiii, 279 p. 16cm.

E-2-a
2027

Fénelon, François de Salignac de la Mothe, 1651-1715.
Oeuvres philosophiques. Nouvelle édition collationnée sur les meilleurs textes ... par A. Jacques ... Paris, Charpentier, 1845.
lxxii, 484 p.

Includes "Réfutation du spinozisme" (p. 120-129)

NN

SPECIAL COLLECTIONS SPINOZA E-2-a 2028

Fénélon, François de Salignac de la Mothe-, 1651-1715.
Oeuvres philosophiques, ou demonstration de l'existence de Dieu, tirée de l'Art de la nature, dans la prémiere partie: et dans la seconde, des preuves purement intellectuelles, & de l'ideé de l'infini même. Par feu Messire François de Salignac de la Motte Fenelcn ... Nouvelle edition, où l'on a joint les lettres du même auteur sur divers sujets concernant la religion & la metaphysique, & ses sermons ...

CONTINUED ON NEXT CARD

SPECIAL COLLECTIONS SPINOZA E-2-a 2029

Fénélon, François de Salignac de la Mothe-, 1651-1715. Oeuvres philosophiques. 1731. (Card 2)

A Amsterdam, Chez Zacharie Chatelain, 1731.
2 v. 17cm.

Includes a chapter "Réfutation du spinozisme" (v. 1, p. 231-333) and also "Reflexions du Pere Tournemine, Jesuite, sur l'atheisme, sur la demonstration de Monseigneur de Cambrai, & sur le systême de Spinosa (v. 1, p. [337]-368)

E-2-a 2030

Fénelon, François de Salignac de la Mothe, 1651-1715.
Oeuvres philosophiques de Fénelon, comprenant le Traité de l'existence de Dieu, les Lettres sur divers sujets de métaphysique, la Réfutation su systême de Malebranche, précédées d'un essai sur Fénelon par m. Villemain. Paris, Hachette, 1843.
xxxvi, 460 p.

Includes a chapter "Réfutation du spinosisme" (p. 110-118)

E-2-a 2031

Fénelon, François de Salignac de la Mothe, 1651-1715.
Oeuvres philosophiques ... Par feu Messire François de Salignac de la Motte Fénelon. Paris, F. Delaulne, 1718.
12 p. l., 559, [2] p. 17 cm.

MH

SPECIAL COLLECTIONS SPINOZA E-2-a 2032

Fénelon, François de Salignac de La Mothe-, *abp.*, 1651-1715.
Réfutation des erreurs de Benoit de Spinosa, par M. de Fenelon ... le P. Lami ... & par m. le comte de Boullainvillers. Avec la vie de Spinosa, escrite par m. Jean Colerus ... augm. de beaucoup de particularités tirées d'une vie manuscrite de ce philosophe, faite par un de ses amis. Bruxelles, F. Foppens, 1731.

5 p. l., 158, 183 (*i. e.* 483), [2] p. 14½cm.

Edited by N. Lenglét Dufresnoy.

(Continued on next card)

11—19164 [a41d1]

SPECIAL COLLECTIONS SPINOZA E-2-a 2033

Fénelon, François de Salignac de La Mothe-, *abp.*, 1651-1715.
Réfutation des erreurs de Benoit Spinosa ... 1731. (Card 2)

"Certamen philosophicum propugnatæ veritatis divinæ ac naturalis adversus Joh: Bredenburg ... Quod religio nil rationi repugnans credendum proponit, evidenter ostenditur. Hæc meditabatur Ishak Orobio ... Amstelædami, ex autographo A. Theodori Ossaan, 1703 [1731]" (with special t.-p.) : p. [387]-[483]

1. Spinoza, Benedictus de, 1632-1677. 2. Bredenburg, Johannes. I. Lamy, François, 1626-1711, joint author. II. Boulainvilliers, Henri, comte de, 1658-1722, joint author. III. Lenglet, Dufresnoy, Nicolas, 1674-1755, ed. IV. Colerus, Johannes, 1647-1707. V. Lucas, Jean Maximilien, d. 1697. VI. Orobio, Balthasar de, d. 1687.

11—19164

Library of Congress B3998.F8 [a41d1]

SPECIAL COLLECTIONS SPINOZA E-2-a 2034

Flint, Robert, 1838-1910.
Vico. Philadelphia, Lippincott, 1884.
232 p. port. 18cm. (Philosophical classics for English readers. [v. 9])

Includes a reference to Spinoza (p. 121)

SPECIAL COLLECTIONS SPINOZA E-2-a 2035

Fraser, Alexander Campbell, 1819-1914.
Berkeley. Philadelphia, Lippincott, 1894.
viii, 234 p. port. 18cm. (Philosophical classics for English readers [v. 3])

Includes references to Spinoza.

SPECIAL COLLECTIONS SPINOZA E-2-a 2036

Fraser, Alexander Campbell, 1819-1914.
Locke. Philadelphia, Lippincott, 1890.
x, 299 p. port. 18cm. (Philosophical classics for English readers. [v. 15])

"Locke's works": p. 297-299.
Includes references to Spinoza.

E-2-a 2037

Geulincx, Arnold, 1624-1669.
Arnoldi Geulincx Compendium physicae, illustratum à Casparo Langenhert. Accedit hujusce Brutum cartesianum. Franequerae, Ex officinâ Leonardi Strick, 1688.
4 p. l., 21, [8], 247, [27] p. 17cm.

Includes a reference to Spinoza (p. 116)

Gore, Willard Clark.
... The imagination in Spinoza and Hume; a comparative study in the light of some recent contributions to psychology, by Willard Clark Gore, PH. D. Chicago, The University of Chicago press, 1902.
77 p. 24cm. (The University of Chicago Contributions to philosophy. vol. II, no. 4)
Appeared first as the author's thesis (PH. D.) University of Chicago, 1902.
1. Imagination. 2. Spinoza, Benedictus de, 1632-1677. 3. Hume, David, 1711-1776. I. Title.

Gracián y Morales, Baltasar, 1601-1658.
Der Mann von Welt, eingeweiht in die Geheimnisse der Lebensklugheit; ein nach Balthasar Gracian frey bearbeitetes, nachgelassenes Manuscript von Karl Heinrich Heydenreich. 2. neu durchgesehene Aufl. Reutlingen, J. J. Mäcken'sche Buchhandlung, 1805.
264 p. 17cm.

Added t.-p.: Taschenbuch für Freunde der Lebensklugheit; nach Gracian frey bearbeitet von Karl Heinrich Heydenreich. 1806.

Gronov, Jakob, 1645-1716.
Burcheri de Volder philosophiae & matheseos professoris laudatio, ab Jacobo Gronovio peracta. Ex decreto Rectoris Magnifici & Senatus Academici. A. d. XVII. Calendas Majas. Lugduni Batavorum, Apud Cornelium Boutestein, 1709.
[2], 38, [6] p. 22cm.

Hamann, Johann Georg, 1730-1788.
Schriften J. G. Hamanns, ausgewählt und hrsg. von Karl Widmaier. Leipzig, Insel-Verlag, 1921.
451 p. 24cm. (Der Dom; Bücher der deutschen Mystik)

Includes references to Spinoza.
"Bibliographie der Originalausgaben der Schriften Johann Georg Hamanns": p. [414]-425.
"Literatur": p. [426]-428.

Haym, Rudolf, 1821-1901.
Herder nach seinem Leben und seinen Werken. Berlin, R. Gaertner, 1880-85.
2 v. 23 cm.

Includes a section "Die Gespräche über Spinoza" (v. 2, p. 265-299)

Heineccius, Johann Gottlieb, 1681-1714.
Io. Gottl. Heineccii ... Elementa philosophiae rationalis et moralis. Praemissa est historia philosophica. Editio X. emendatior. Francofvrti cis Viadrum, Impens. Io. Christ. Kleibii, 1752.
xiiii, 352, [21] p. port. 19cm.

Includes a reference to Spinoza (p. 63)

Hooke, Robert, 1635-1703.
The diary of Robert Hooke, 1672-1680, transcribed from the original in the possession of the Corporation of the City of London (Guildhall Library) Edited by Henry W. Robinson and Walter Adams, with a foreword by Sir Frederick Gowland Hopkins. London, Taylor & Francis, 1935.
xviii, 527 p. illus., plates, facsims. 23cm.

Includes references to Spinoza (p. 353-368)

[Kames, Henry Home, lord] 1696-1782.
Essays on the principles of morality and natural religion. In two parts. Edinburgh, Printed by R. Fleming, for A. Kincaid and A. Donaldson, 1751.
3 p. l., 394 p. 21 cm.

King, William, abp. of Dublin, 1650-1729.
A defence of Dr. Clarke's Demonstration of the being and attributes of God ... Being an answer to a ... book entitul'd, A translation of Dr. King's Origin of evil, and some other objections. Together with a compendium of a demonstration of the being and attributes of God. London, 1732.

Land, Jan Pieter Nicolaas, 1834-1897.
Arnold Geulincx und seine philosophie. Von dr. J. P. N. Land ... Haag, M. Nijhoff, 1895.
x, 219 p. 20½cm.

Includes references to Spinoza.

1. Geulincx, Arnold, 1624-1669.

Lange, Joachim, 1670-1744.
Modesta disquisitio novi Philosophiae systematis de Deo, mundo et homine, et praesertim de harmonia commercii inter animam et corpus praestabilita ... Halae Saxonum, 1723.

Includes references to Spinoza.

⌊Le Clerc, Jean⌋ 1657-1736.
⌊Review of Histoire de la philosophie payenne, ou Sentimens des philosophes & des peuples payens, les plus célèbres, sur Dieu, sur l'ame, & sur les devoirs de l'homme. 1724. ⌊1724⌋
115-168 p.

In Bibliothèque ancienne et moderne, pour servir de suite aux Bibliothèques universelle et choisie, par Jean Le Clerc; t. 22, pour l'année 1724, 1. pte.
Includes a section on Spinoza (p. 134-136)

Ludovici, Carl Günther, 1707-1778.
Ausführlicher Entwurff einer vollständigen Historie der Wolffischen Philosophie, zum Gebrauch seiner Zuhörer herausgegeben von Carl Günther Ludovici ... Andere weitvermehrtere und mit Kupffern sowohl als dreyfachem Register versehene Auflage. Leipzig, verlegts Johann Georg Löwe, 1737.
3 v. in 1. port., plates. 17cm.

Includes references to Spinoza.

Mayer, Johann Friedrich, 1650-1712.
D. Joh. Frid. Mayeri ... Dissertationes selectae Kilonienses & Hamburgenses, varii & rarioris argumenti ... In gratiam veritatis evangelicae amantium prima vice conjunctim in lucem editae: adjecto sub finem necessario atque plenissimo indice. Francofurti ad Moenum, Cura Friderici Knochii, 1693.
⌊14⌋, 599, ⌊32⌋ p. port. 17cm.

CONTINUED ON NEXT CARD

Mayer, Johann Friedrich, 1650-1712. Dissertationes selectae Kilonienses & Hamburgenses. 1693. (Card 2)

"Ad lectiones publicas adversus Benedictum Spinosam bibliomastygem peramanter invitat Jo. Frid. Mayer": p. 418-421; other references to Spinoza.

Mellone, Sydney Herbert, 1869-
The dawn of modern thought; Descartes, Spinoza, Leibniz. With an introductory note by W. D. Ross. London, Oxford University Press, H. Milford, 1930.
124 p. 20cm.

Bibliography: p. ⌊119⌋-121.

Ménage, Gilles, 1613-1692.
Menagiana, ou, Les bons mots et remarques critiques, historiques, morales & d'érudition, de monsieur Ménage, recueillies par ses amis. Nouv. éd. Paris, Chez la veuve Delaulne, 1729.
4 v. 16½cm.

Includes references to Spinoza.

Meyer, Lodewijk, 1630-1681.
Disputatio philosophica inauguralis, de materia, ejusque affectionibus motu, et quiete; quam ... publice habebit Ludovicus Meyer ... Lugd. Batav., Ex Officinâ Francisci Hackii, 1660 ⌊Hagae Comitis, 1922⌋
⌊181⌋-184 p., facsim.: ⌊185⌋-195 p. 22cm.

Cover-title: Dissertatio ex Chronici Spinozani tomo secundo separatim edita.
Half-title: Scripta rediviva.
References to Spinoza included in pages preceding facsimile.

⌊Meyer, Lodewijk⌋ 1630-1681.
De philosophie, d'uytleghster der H. Schrifture. Een ... tractaet; daer in op een betoogende wijse betooght wordt, dat de ware philosophie d'onfeylbare regelmaet van de H. Schrift uyt te leggen, en te verklaren is, en de ghevoelens, die daer af verschillen, overwogen en wederleyt worden. Uyt het Latijn vertaelt. Te Vrystadt, 1667.
6 p. l., 139, ⌊1⌋ p.

⌊Meyer, Lodewijk⌋ 1630-1681.
De philosophie d'uytleghster der H. Schrifture. Een wonderspreuckigh tractaet; daer in op een betoogende wijse betooght wordt, dat de ware philosophie d'onfeylbare regelmaet van de H. Schrift uyt te leggen, en te verklaren is, en de ghevoelens, die daer af verschillen, overwogen en wederleyt worden. Uyt het Latijn vertaelt ... Te Vrystadt, Voor de liefhebbers van de ware uytlegginġh der H. Schrift, 1667.
⌊12⌋, 136 (i.e. 139), ⌊1⌋ p. 20cm.

CONTINUED ON NEXT CARD

⌐Meyer, Lodewijk⌐ 1630-1681. De philosophie d'uytleghster der H. Schrifture. 1667. (Card 2)

Also falsely ascribed to Spinoza and to Lambert van Velthuysen.--cf. Bibl. Nat. Cat.

⌐Meyer, Lodewijk⌐ 1630-1681.
Philosophia S. Scripturæ interpres; exercitatio paradoxa, in quâ, veram philosophiam infallibilem S. Literas interpretandi normam esse, apodicticè demonstratur, & discrepantes ab hâc sententiæ expenduntur, ac refelluntur ... Eleutheropoli ⌐Amstelodami⌐ ~~1666~~.1670.
⌐12⌐, 105, ⌐10⌐ p. 21cm.

Also falsely attributed to Spinoza and to Lambert van Velthuysen. -Cf. Bibl. Nat. Cat.
Bound with ⌐Spinoza, Benedictus de⌐ Tractatus theologicopoliticus. 1670.

⌐Meyer, Lodewijk⌐ 1630-1681.
Philosophia S. Scripturæ interpres; exercitatio paradoxa, in quâ, veram philosophiam infallibilem S. Literas interpretandi normam esse, apodicticè demonstratur, & discrepantes ab hâc sententiæ expenduntur, ac refelluntur ... Eleutheropoli ⌐Amstelodami⌐ ~~1666~~. 1672.
⌐12⌐, 105, ⌐10⌐ p. 20cm.

Also falsely attributed to Spinoza and to Lambert van Velthuysen. -Cf. Bibl. Nat. Cat.
Bound with ⌐Spinoza, Benedictus de⌐ Tractatus theologicopoliticus. 1672.

Moller, Daniel Wilhelm, 1642-1712.
Dan. Guil. Molleri Promissum de mulieribus hominibus exsolutum, cum epistola ad amicum. Altdorffl, Typis Johannis Henrici Schönnerstaedt, 1677.
⌐9⌐, 74 p. 14cm.

Bound with La Peyrère, Isaac de. Praeadamitae. 1655.

More, Henry, 1614–1687.
Philosophical writings of Henry More, edited with introduction and notes by Flora Isabel MacKinnon ... New York, London ⌐etc.⌐ Oxford university press, 1925.

xxvii, 333 p. illus. 23 cm. (The Wellesley semi-centennial series)

With reproductions of original title-pages.
Bibliography: p. ⌐233⌐–256.

CONTENTS.—Introduction.—Selections from the philosophical writings of More: I. The Antidote against atheism. II. The immortality of the soul. III. Enchiridion metaphysicum.—Bibliography.—Outline summary of More's philosophy.—Notes.
Includes references to Spinoza.
1. Philosophy. I. MacKinnon, Flora Isabel, ed.

⌐Nieto, David⌐ 1654-1728.
De la divina providencia, o sea naturaleza universal, o natura naturante, tratado theologico Divido en dos dialogos ... En Londres, Por James Dover, 5464 ⌐1704⌐
⌐4⌐, 89 ⌐1⌐ p. 21cm.

⌐Nieto, David⌐ 1654-1728.
De la divina providencia. O sea Naturaleza universal, o natura naturante. Tratado theologico, divido en dos dialogos, enlos quales, se prueva la identidad destos terminos, autenticada con autoridades dela Sagrada Biblia, del Talmud, Zohar, y Medrassim, y confirmada con irrefragables razones, deduzidas de las mismas autoridades. Segunda edicion corregida. En Londres, 5476 ⌐1716⌐
1 p. l., 9, ⌐2⌐, 176, ⌐1⌐ p. 19cm.

Nieuwentijdt, Bernard, 1654-1718.
Gronden van zekerheid, of de regte betoogwyse der wiskundigen so in het denkbeeldige, als in het zakelyke: ter wederlegging van Spinosaas denkbeeldig samenstel; en ter aanleiding van eene sekere sakelyke wysbegeerte, aangetoont, door Bernard Nieuwentyt, M. D. Tot Amsterdam, By Joannes Pauli, 1720.
⌐56⌐, 458 p. 27cm.

Nieuwentijdt, Bernard, 1654-1718.
Gronden van zekerheid, of de regte betoogwyse der wiskundigen so in het denkbeeldige, als in het zakelyke: ter wederlegging van Spinosaas denkbeeldig samenstel; en ter aanleiding van eene sekere sakelyke wysbegeerte, aangetoont, door Bernard Nieuwentyt M. D. Den tweden druk. Tot Amsterdam, By Joannes Pauli, 1728.
⌐56⌐, 456 p. 26cm.

Nieuwentijdt, Bernard, 1654-1718.
Gronden van zekerheid. Of de regte betoogwyse der wiskundigen so in het denkbeeldige, als in het zakelyke: ter wederlegging van Spinosaas denkbeeldig samenstel; en ter aanleiding van eene sekere sakelyke wysbegeerte aangetoont, door Bernard Nieuwentyt M. D. den derden druk. Tot Amsterdam, By Joannes Pauli, 1739.
⌐56⌐, 456 p. 26cm.

E-2-a 2068

Nourrisson, Jean Félix, 1825-1899.
Tableau des progrès de la pensée humaine depuis Thalès jusqu'à Leibniz, par M. Nourrisson. 2. éd. Paris, Didier et cᵉ, 1859.
2 p. l., iv, 526 p. 18ᶜᵐ.
Includes a section on Spinoza (p. 367-380)

DLC

1. Philosophy—Hist.

Library of Congress B79.N85 [28d1] 10—21991

E-2-a 2069

Oudin, Charles
Le spinozisme de Montesquieu; étude critique. Paris, Librairie générale de droit, 1911.
163 p.

DCU

E-2-a 2070

Paulinus, Martin, 1866-
Die Sittenlehre Geulincx', dargestellt in ihrem Zusammenhange mit der Metaphysik und beurteilt in ihrem Verhältnisse zu der Sittenlehre Spinozas. Pirna, Eberlein, 1892.
113 p. 23 cm.

Thesis, Leipzig.

E-2-a 2071

Poiret, Pierre, 1646-1719.
Petri Poiret ... Cogitationum rationalum de Deo, anima et malo libri quatuor ... Amstelodami, Apud Danielem Elsevirium, 1677.
298 p.

NNJ

SPECIAL COLLECTIONS SPINOZA

E-2-a 2072

Poiret, Pierre, 1646-1719.
Petri Poiret Cogitationum rationalium de Deo, anima, et malo libri quatuor. In quibus quid de hisce Cartesius, ejusque sequaces, boni aut secus senserint, omnisque philosophiæ certiora fundamenta, atque imprimis tota metaphysica verior, continentur; nec non Benedicti de Spinoza atheismus & exitiales errores funditus exstirpantur. Editio altera, priore plus duplo auctior. Amstelodami, Ex typographia Blaviana, 1685.
[52], 82, 808, [3] p. 22cm.

SPECIAL COLLECTIONS SPINOZA

E-2-a 2073

Poiret, Pierre, 1646-1719.
Petri Poiret Cogitationum rationalium de Deo, anima, et malo libri quatuor. In quibus quid de hisce Cartesius ejusque sequaces recte aut secus senserint, omnisque philosophiæ certiora fundamenta, atque imprimis tota metaphysica verior, continentur; nec non Benedicti de Spinoza atheismus & exitiales errores funditus exstirpantur. Editio tertia, novissime ab auctore recognita, emendata, & acta. Præmittitur dissertatio nova, ubi de duplici discendi methodo, deque simulato Petri

CONTINUED ON NEXT CARD

SPECIAL COLLECTIONS SPINOZA

E-2-a 2074

Poiret, Pierre, 1646-1719. Petri Poiret Cogitationum rationalium ... 1715. (Card 2)

Bælii contra Spinozæ atheismum certamine agitur. Amstelodami, Apud Joannem Pauli, 1715.
29, [43], 926, [12] p. 20cm.

E-2-a 2075

Polignac, Melchior de, Cardinal, 1661-1741.
Anti-Lucretius; sive, De Deo et natura, libri novem ... Melchioris de Polignac opus posthumum ... Abbatis Caroli d'Orleans de Rothelin curâ & studio editioni mandatum ... Parisiis, Apud Joannem-Baptistam Coignard, 1747.
2 v. port. 22ᶜᵐ.

Includes references to Spinoza.

SPECIAL COLLECTIONS SPINOZA

E-2-a 2076

Polignac, Melchior de, cardinal, 1661-1741.
Anti-Lucretivs, sive De Deo et natvra libri novem. Eminentissimi R. E. Cardinalis Melchioris de Polignac opvs posthvmvm; illvstrissimi Abbatis Caroli d'Orleans de Rothelin cvra et stvdio editioni mandatvm. Ad exemplar Parisinvm recensvit et de poetis philosophis, antiqvis aeqve ac recentioribvs praefatvs est Io. Christoph. Gottschedivs. Lipsiae, Apud Bernh. Christoph. Breitkopf, 1748.
[14], xlviii, 430, [18] p. port. 19cm.

Includes references to Spinoza.

SPECIAL COLLECTIONS SPINOZA

E-2-a 2077

Polignac, Melchior de, cardinal, 1661-1741.
Anti-Lucretius, sive De Deo et natura libri novem. Eminentissimi S. R. E. Cardinalis Melchioris de Polignac opus posthumum; illust. Abb. Caroli d'Orleans de Rothelin curâ & studio editioni mandatum ... Lugduni Batavorum, Typis Eliae Luzac, Jun., 1748.
2 v. in 1. (xxx, 372 p.) 17cm.

Includes references to Spinoza.

Polignac, Melchior de, cardinal, 1661-1741.
Anti-Lucretius, sive De Deo et natura libri novem. Eminentissimi S. R. E Cardinalis Melchioris de Polignac opus posthumum; illustriss. Abbatis Caroli d'Orleans de Rothelin curâ & studio editioni mandatum ... Parisiis, Apud Petrum-Ægidium Le Mercier, 1749.
2 v. in 1. 15cm.

Includes references to Spinoza.

Polignac, Melchior de, cardinal, 1661-1741.
L'anti-Lucrece, poëme sur la religion naturelle, composé par M. le cardinal de Polignac; traduit par M. de Bougainville ... A Paris, Chez Jean-Baptiste Coignard, & Antoine Boudet, ⌈et⌉ Pierre-Gilles Lemercier, 1749.
2 v. port. 21cm.

Includes references to Spinoza.

Ramsay, Andrew Michael, 1686-1743.
The philosophical principles of natural and revealed religion. Unfolded in a geometrical order by the Chevalier Ramsay ... Glasgow, Printed and sold by Robert Fouiis, 1748-49.
2 v. 20cm.

"Appendix to the foregoing work: containing a refutation of the first book of Spinosa's Ethics; by which the whole structure is undermined": v. 1, p. ⌈497⌉-541.

Reimarus, Hermann Samuel, 1694-1768.
Hermann Samuel Reimarus ... Abhandlungen von den vornehmsten Wahrheiten der natürlichen Religion. Fünfte Auflage, durchgesehen, und mit einigen Anmerkungen begleitet von Joh. Alb. Hinr. Reimarus ... Tübingen, Bey Chr. Gottl. Frank und Wilh. Heinr. Schramm, 1782.
⌈18⌉, ⌈3⌉-864, ⌈32⌉ p. 18cm. (Added t.-p.: Sammlung philosophischer Schriften. Zweyter Theil)

Includes a section on Spinoza (p. 248-251)

⌈Ricard, Ch L ⌉
Voltaire parmi les ombres ... A Genève, et se trouve à Paris, Chez P. G. Simon ⌈etc.⌉ 1776.
xii, ⌈13⌉-380 p. 17cm.

Ascribed to Ch. L. Ricard. cf. Quérard, Dictionnaire des ouvrages anonymes, vol. IV, col. 1054.
Includes a dialogue "Spinosa et Voltaire" (p. 355-373)

Royal Society of London.
Acta philosophica Societatis Regiæ in Anglia, anni M.DC.LXVII. Auctore Henrico Oldenburgio ... Anglicè conscripta, & in Latinum versa interprete C. S. Volumen secundum. Amstelodami, Apud Henricum & Theodorum Boom, 1672.
⌈4⌉, 392 p. fold. plates. 14cm.

Sabatier, Antoine, de Casgres, 1742-1817.
Apologie de Spinosa et du spinosisme; par M. Sabatier de Castres ... Altona, 1805.
122 p. 16cm.

"Lettre à M. L'abbé Sabatier de Castres, sur son ouvrage de la souveraineté," signed P. Motte, de Genève: p. 111-122.
Bound with Herder, Johann Gottfried von. Gott. 1800.

Samtleben, Gustav, 1861-
Geulincx, ein Vorgänger Spinozas. Halle a. S., Druck und Verlag von H. W. Schmidt, 1885.
48 p. 23cm.

Thesis, Halle.
Contents.--Geulincx' Verhältnis zu Descartes. --Geulincx' Verhältnis zu Spinoza.--Geulincx' Verhältnis zu Malebranche.
Volume of pamphlets.

Sarchi, Carlo.
Della dottrina di Benedetto de Spinoza e di Gian Battista Vico; discorsi. Milano, Bortolotti, 1877.
viii, 206 p. 23 cm.

Sonne, Isaiah, 1887-
Spinoza e Pascal. Como, Tipografia editrice E. Cavalleri, 1933.
10 p. port. 23cm.

"Estratto dalla rivista mensile L'Idea sionistica, Anno III, n. 6-7, ottobre-novembre 1932."

SPECIAL COLLECTIONS SPINOZA E-2-a 2088

Stolle, Gottlieb, 1673-1744.
Gottlieb Stolles ... Anleitung zur Historie der Gelahrheit, denen zum besten, so den freyen Künsten und der Philosophie obliegen, in dreyen Theilen nunmehr zum drittenmal, verbessert und mit neuen Zusätzen vermehret, herausgegeben ... Jena, In Verlegung Johann Meyers seel. Witwe, 1727.
[15], 778, [68], [8], 96, [24] p. plate. 21cm.

Includes references to Spinoza.

SPECIAL COLLECTIONS SPINOZA E-2-a 2089

Stolle, Gottlieb, 1673-1744.
Gottlieb Stolles ... Anleitung zur historie der gelahrheit, denen zum besten, so den freyen künsten und der philosophie obliegen, in dreyen theilen nunmehr zum viertenmal verbessert und mit neuen zusätzen vermehret, herausgegeben ... Jena, In verlegung J. Meyers seel. erben, 1736.
9 p. l., 798, [66] p. front. (port.) 22 x 17cm.
"Discours von dem nutzen der historiae et notitiae literariae": p. [783]-798.
CONTENTS.—1. th. Von der historia literaria überhaupt, und der freyen künste insonderheit.—2. th. Von der historia literaria der philosophie überhaupt, und der instrumental- und theoretischen philosophie insonderheit.—3. th. Von der historia literaria der practischen philosophie.

(Continued on next card)
34-18482

SPECIAL COLLECTIONS SPINOZA E-2-a 2090

Stolle, Gottlieb, 1673-1744. Gottlieb Stolles ... Anleitung zur historie der gelahrheit ... 1736. (Card 2)
—— Gottlieb Stolles Gantz neue zusätze und ausbesserungen der Historie der philosophischen gelahrheit. Jena, Zu finden bey J. Meyers seel. erben, 1736.
268, [28] p. 22 x 17cm. [With *his* Anleitung zu historie der gelahrheit. 4. aufl. Jena, 1736]

Includes references to Spinoza.

1. Literature—Hist. & crit. 2. Literature—Bibl.—Early. 3. Philosophy—Hist. I. Title.

34-18482

Library of Congress AZ203.S7 1736 001

SPECIAL COLLECTIONS SPINOZA E-2-a 2091

Til, Salomon van, 1643-1713.
Vervolg op't Voor-hof der heydenen, waar in de grond-stellingen van Mosis wet en wet-boek met de reden-leer werden vereffent, en haar vastigheyd regen de ongodisten nader tot versterkinge des geloofs netoogt. Door Salomon van Til ... Tot Dordregt, By Dirk Goris, 1696.
[10], 251, [13] p. 21cm.

Includes references to Spinoza.
Bound with Til, Salomon van. Het voor-hof der heydenen. 1694.

SPECIAL COLLECTIONS SPINOZA E-2-a 2092

Til, Salomon van, 1643-1713.
Vervolg op 't Voor-hof der heydenen, waar in de grond-stellingen van Mosis wet en wet-boek met de reden-leer werden vereffent, en haar vastigheyd tegen de ongodisten nader to versterkinge des geloofs betoogt. Door Salomon van Til ... Tot Dordregt, Goris, 1718.
[10], 251, [13] p. 21cm.

Includes a chapter "Het wanstaltig gevoelen van Spinoza ontmaskert" (p. 89-110)
Bound with the author's Het voor-hof der heydenen. 1714.

E-2-a 2093

Turretini, Jean Alphonsus, 1671-1737.
Opera omnia theologica, philosophica et philologica. Leovardiae et Franequerae, 1774-76.
3 v. 28 cm.

Includes a reference to Spinoza (v. 1, p. 4)

NNUT

SPECIAL COLLECTIONS SPINOZA E-2-a 2094

[Valk, Th de]
Spinoza en Vondel. [1921]
[440]-458 p. 25cm.

Signed: Th. de Valk O. P.
From De Beiaard. 6. jaargang, 2. deel, December 1921.

SPECIAL COLLECTIONS SPINOZA E-2-a 2095

Vollständige Sammlung aller derer Schrifften, welche in der Langischen und Wolffischen Streitigkeit im Monat Junio 1736. auf hohen Befehl abgefasset worden. Mit Veramanders [pseud.] Anmerckungen versehen, und zum Druck befördert von J. F. H. Marpurg, 1737.
264 p. 18cm.

Bound with Darjes, Joachim Georg. Philosophische Nebenstunden. 1749-52.
Includes a reference to Spinoza (p. 62)

SPECIAL COLLECTIONS SPINOZA E-2-a 2096

[Voltaire, François Marie Arouet de] 1694-1778.
Dictionnaire philosophique, portatif. Nouvelle edition revue, corrigée & augmentée de divers articles par l'auteur. Londres, 1765.
[10], 364 p. 17cm.

Includes a reference to Spinoza (p. 42)
Bound with Julianus, Apostata, emperor of Rome. Deffense du paganisme. 1764.

SPECIAL COLLECTIONS SPINOZA E-2-a 2097

Voltaire, François Marie Arouet de, 1694-1778.
Essays and criticisms by M. de Voltaire. Containing Letters on the Christian religion; The philosophy of history; The ignorant philosopher, and The Chinese catechism. New York, P. Eckler [1899]
1 v. (various pagings) plates, ports. 21cm.
(Library of liberal classics)

Each essay has special t.-p. and pagination.
Includes references to Spinoza.

SPECIAL COLLECTIONS SPINOZA
E-2-a 2098

Voltaire, François Marie Arouet de, 1694-1778.
Essays and criticisms by M. de Voltaire. Containing Letters on the Christian religion; The philosophy of history; The ignorant philosopher, and The Chinese catechism. New York, Peter Eckler Publishing Co., 1920.
1 v. (various pagings) plates, ports. 20cm.

Each essay has special t.-p. and pagination.
Includes references to Spinoza.

E-2-a 2099

Voltaire, François Marie Arouet de, 1694-1778.
Letters addressed to His Highness the Prince of XXX, containing comments on the writings of the most prominent authors, who have been accused of attacking the Christian religion. A new translation. London, R. Trophy, 1779.
2 p. l., 160 p. 19 cm.

NBuG

SPECIAL COLLECTIONS SPINOZA
E-2-a 2100

Voltaire, François Marie Arouet de, 1694-1778.
Mélanges littéraires. Paris, Armand-Aubrée, 1829.
2 v. 21cm. (His Oeuvres complètes, vol. 38-39)

Includes a letter "Sur Spinosa" (v. 1, p. 205-210)

E-2-a 2101

Voltaire, François Marie Arouet de, 1694-1778.
Oeuvres completes. [Kehl] Impr. de la Société littéraire-typographique, 1784-89.
70 v. ports., diagrs. 23 cm.

Includes a section on Spinoza (v. 32, p. 106-113) in "Le philosophe ignorant", and a letter on Spinoza (v. 47, p. 406-412)

E-2-a 2102

[Voltaire, François Marie Arouet de, 1694-1778.
The philosophical dictionary, for the pocket; translated from the French edition, corrected by the author. Catskill, Printed by T. & M. Croswell for selves and J. Fellows & E. Duyckinck, New York, 1796.
4 p. l., 336 p. 17^{m}.

Includes a reference to Spinoza (p. 23) in article "Atheist, atheism".

SPECIAL COLLECTIONS SPINOZA
E-2-a 2103

Voltaire, François Marie Arouet de, 1694-1778.
A philosophical dictionary. From the French of M. de Voltaire. London, W. Dugdale, 1843.
2 v. ports. 20^{m}.

Includes a reference to Spinoza (v. 2, p. 323)

E-2-a 2104

Voltaire, François Marie Arouet de, 1694-1778.
Oeuvres de Voltaire, avec préfaces, avertissements, notes, etc., par M. Beuchot. Paris, Lefèvre, 1829-40.
72 v. 21 cm.

Includes references to Spinoza.

SPECIAL COLLECTIONS SPINOZA
E-2-a 2105

Ward, Richard, 1657?-1723.
The life of the learned and pious D^{r}. Henry More, late fellow of Christ's college in Cambridge. To which are annex'd divers of his useful and excellent letters. By Richard Ward ... London, Printed and sold by Joseph Downing, 1710
[23], 362, [4] p. port. 19cm.

The letters (p. [241]-362) with title, "Select letters written upon several occasions", have special t.-p.
Imperfect copy: lacks portrait.

SPECIAL COLLECTIONS SPINOZA
E-2-a 2106

Weil, Gotthold Eliakim, 1882-
Aus einem Briefe John Lockes. [1926]
199-208 p. 32cm.

"Sonderabdruck aus den Soncino-Blättern; Beiträge zur Kunde des jüdischen Buches [v. 1, 1925/26]
Includes a reference to the correspondence between Spinoza and Oldenburg (p. 207)

SPECIAL COLLECTIONS SPINOZA
E-2-a 2107

[Whitby, Daniel] 1638-1726.
A dissuasive from enquiring into the doctrine of the Trinity: or, The difficulties and discouragements which attend the study of that doctrine. In a letter to a friend. London, Printed for John Baker, 1714.
43 p. 20cm.

Volume of pamphlets.

E-2-a
2108

Wolff, Christian, Freiherr von, 1679-1754.
Monitum ad commentationem luculentam de differentia nexus rerum sapientis et fatalis necessitatis, quo nonnulla sublimia metaphysicae ac theologiae naturalis capita illustrantur. Autore Christiano Wolfio ... Halae Magdeb., Officina Rengeriana, 1724.
36 p.

NNUT

E-2-b
Hobbes

E-2-b
2109

Battelli, Guido, 1869-
Le dottrine politiche dell' Hobbes e dello Spinoza. Firenze, S. Landi, 1904.
59 p.

MH

E-2-b
2110

1938Sp4
DB63863

Brockdorff, Cay Ludwig Georg Conrad, baron von, 1874-
... Eine Thomas Hobbes zugeschriebene handschrift und ihr verfasser. Ein verehrer Thomas Hobbes' als interpret des Aristoteles. Spinozas verhältnis zur philosophie des Ibn Tophail. Kiel, Karl J. Röszler, 1932.
32 p. 23½cm. (Veröffentlichungen der Hobbes-gesellschaft (Ortsgruppe Kiel), ₍I₎)

Bibliography included in "Anmerkungen": p. 7, 17-18, 32.

E-2-b
2111

Brockdorff, Cay Ludwig Georg Conrad, Baron von, 1874-
Hobbes als Philosoph, Pädagoge und Soziologe. 2. Aufl. Kiel, Lipsius & Tischer, 1929-
v. 1. 25cm.

Includes references to Spinoza.
Bibliographical references included in "Anmerkungen" (v. 1, p. ₍141₎-169)

E-2-b
2112

Clarendon, Edward Hyde, 1st earl of, 1609-1674.
A brief view and survey of the dangerous and pernicious errors to church and state, in Mr. Hobbes's book, entitled Leviathan. ₍Oxford₎ Printed at the Theater, 1676.
4 p. l., 322 p. 21 cm.

E-2-b
2113

Gaspary, Adolf, 1849-1892.
Spinoza und Hobbes. Berlin, Buchdruckerei G. Lange ₍1873₎
75 p. 23ᶜᵐ.

Thesis, Berlin.
Bibliographical footnotes.

E-2-b
2114

Hartenstein, Gustav, 1808-1890.
Historisch-philosophische Abhandlungen. Leipzig, L. Voss, 1870.
xii, 537 p. 21cm.

Bibliographical footnotes.
Includes an essay, "De notionum juris et civitatis, quas Bened. Spinoza et Thom. Hobbes proponunt, similitudine et dissimilitudine" (p. ₍217₎-240)

E-2-b
2115

Hobbes, Thomas, 1588-1679.
Hobbes's Leviathan. Reprinted from the ed. of 1651. With an essay by the late W. G. Pogson Smith. Oxford, Clarendon Press, 1909.
xxxi, 557 p. facsim. 20 cm.

Introductory essay "The philosophy of Hobbes" by W. G. Pogson Smith includes a reference to Spinoza (p. ₍vii₎)

E-2-b
2116

Hobbes, Thomas, 1588-1679.
Leviathan, sive, De materia, forma, & potestate civitatis ecclesiasticæ et civilis. Authore Thoma Hobbes ... Amstelodami, apud Joannem Blaeu, 1670.
2 p. l., 365, ₍13₎ p., 1 l. 20 x 15½ᶜᵐ.
Title vignette: J. Blaeu's device.

1. Political science. 2. State, The. I. Title.

43-21244

Library of Congress JC153.H657
₍2₎

E-2-b
2117

Honigsheim, Paul, 1885-
Neue Hobbes-Literatur. Baron Cay von Brockdorff: Hobbes als Philosoph, Pädagoge und Soziologe. I². Julius Lips: Thomas Hobbes, mit einer Einführung von Ferdinand Tönnies. ₍1930₎
₍325₎-329 p. 24cm.

"Aus Kölner Vierteljahrshefte für Soziologie. Jahrgang VIII, Heft 3."
A review of the two above-named works.

NNC

Hönigswald, Richard, 1875-
Hobbes und die Staatsphilosophie. Mit einem Bildnis des Hobbes. München, E. Reinhardt, 1924.
207 p., 1 l. port. 20 cm. (Geschichte der Philosophie in Einzeldarstellungen. Abt. V. Die Philosophie der neueren Zeit II. Bd. 21)

Includes references to Spinoza.

Iodice, Antonio
Le teorie di Hobbes e Spinoza studiate nella società moderna. Napoli, Detken, 1901.
viii, 316 p. 19 cm.

Laird, John, 1887-
Hobbes, by John Laird ... London, E. Benn limited [1934]
xii, 324 p. 22cm. (Half-title: Leaders of philosophy)

"Short bibliography": p. 318-319.
Includes references to Spinoza.

Robertson, George Croom, 1842-1892.
Hobbes. Edinburgh, W. Blackwood and Sons, 1886.
vii, 240 p. port. 18cm. (Philosophical classics for English readers. [v. 10])

Includes a reference to Spinoza (p. 225)

Sigwart, Heinrich Christoph Wilhelm von, 1789-1844
Vergleichung der Rechts- und Staats-Theorieen des B. Spinoza und des Th. Hobbes, nebst Betrachtungen über das Verhältniss zwischen dem Staate und der Kirche. Tübingen, T. F. Osiander, 1842.
vi, 153 p. 20 cm.

MH

Stephen, *Sir* Leslie, 1832-1904.
... Hobbes, by Sir Leslie Stephen. New York, The Macmillan company; London, Macmillan & co., ltd., 1904.
v, 243 p. 19½ cm. (*Half-title:* English men of letters, ed. by J. Morley)
Note at end signed: F. W. Maitland.
Series title also at head of t.-p.
Includes references to Spinoza.

1. Hobbes, Thomas, 1588-1679. I. Maitland, Frederic William, 1850-1906, ed.

B1246.S7 4—18613
Library of Congress [51z2]

Thayer, Vivian Trow, 1886-
A comparison of the ethical philosophies of Spinoza and Hobbes. [Chicago, 1922]
16 p. 23 cm.

Thesis, University of Wisconsin.

DLC

Tönnies, Ferdinand, 1855-1936.
Thomas Hobbes leben und lehre, von Ferdinand Tönnies ... 3. verm. aufl. ... Stuttgart, F. Frommann, 1925.
xxvii, 316 p. front. (port.) 21cm. (*Half-title:* Frommanns klassiker der philosophie ... II)
"Literatur": p. xx-xxii.
Includes references to Spinoza.

1. Hobbes, Thomas, 1588-1679.

29-21355
Library of Congress B1247.T6 1925

E-2-c DES CARTES

Andala, Ruardus, 1665-1727.
Apologia pro vera & saniore philosophia, quatuor partibus comprehensa, aucture Ruardo Andala ... Franequeraē, Ex officina Wibii Bleck, 1719.
[6], 210 p. 20cm.

A comparison of the philosophies of Descartes and Spinoza.
Includes bibliographical references.

Bordas-Demoulin, Jean Baptiste, 1798-1859.
Le cartésianisme, ou La véritable rénovation des sciences, suivi de la théorie de la substance et de celle de l'infini. Précédé d'un Discours sur la réformation de la philosophie au dix-neuvième siècle, pour servir d'introduction générale, par F. Huet. Paris, J. Hetzel, 1843.
2 v.

Includes a section on Spinoza (v. 1, p. 52-61)

NN

E-2-c 2128

Bordas-Demoulin, Jean Baptiste, 1798-1859.
Le cartésianisme; ou, La véritable rénovation des sciences, suivi de la théorie de la substance et de celle de l'infini. Nouv. éd. Paris, Gauthier, 1874.
iv, 682 p. 22 cm.

Includes a section on Spinoza (p. 42-50)

NNC

E-2-c 2129

Bouillier, Francisque, 1813-1899.
Histoire de la philosophie Cartésienne. 3. éd. Paris, Delagrave, 1868.
2 v. 21 cm.

Includes five chapters on Spinoza (v. 1, p. 315-428) and other references to him.

NNC

SPECIAL COLLECTIONS SPINOZA E-2-c 2130

Brockdorff, Cay Ludwig Georg Conrad, *baron* **von, 1874–**

Descartes und die fortbildung der kartesianischen lehre, von baron Cay v. Brockdorff ... Mit einem bildnis des Descartes. München, E. Reinhardt, 1923.

226, [2] p. front. (port.) 20 cm. (Geschichte der philosophie in einzeldarstellungen. abt. IV. Die philosophie der neueren zeit I. bd. 16/17)

"Bibliographischer wegweiser": p. 208-210.
Includes references to Spinoza.

1. Descartes, René, 1596-1650. 2. Philosophy, Modern.

B1875.B7 194.1 A 33—836
Rochester. Univ. Libr. for Library of Congress [a55d½]†

SPECIAL COLLECTIONS SPINOZA E-2-c 2131

Brunschvicg, Léon, 1869-1944.
Platon et Descartes. [1929]
[113]-126 p. 24cm.

"Overdruk uit het Tijdschrift voor wijsbegeerte, Jaargang 1929, afl. 2."
Includes references to Spinoza.

SPECIAL COLLECTIONS SPINOZA E-2-c 2132

Brunschvicg, Léon, 1869-1944.
René Descartes, par Léon Brunschvicg ... Paris, Les Éditions Rieder [c1937]
97 p., 1 l. XXXII pl. on 16 l. (incl. ports., facsims., diagrs.) 20½cm. (Half-title: Maîtres des littératures. 22)

Includes references to Spinoza.
Presentation copy to A. S. Oko, with the author's inscription and signature.
"Bibliographie sommaire": p. [87]-89.

E-2-c 2133

[Caird, Edward] 1835-1908.
Cartesianism. [1876]
142-159 p.

From Encyclopaedia britannica. 9th ed., v. 5, 1876.
Includes a section on Spinoza (p. 152-159)

E-2-c 2134

Cunningham, William, 1849-1919.
The influence of Descartes on metaphysical speculation in England; being a degree thesis. London & Cambridge, Macmillan, 1876.
xlviii, 188 p.

SPECIAL COLLECTIONS SPINOZA E-2-c 2135

Congrès international de philosophie. 9th, Paris, 1937.
Travaux du IXe Congrès international de philosophie, Congrès Descartes, publiés par les soins de Raymond Bayer. Paris, Hermann et cie, 1937.
pt. 1, 3, 5. 26cm. (Actualités scientifiques et industrielles, no. 530, 532, 534)

Parts 1, 3 and 5 include articles on Spinoza.

E-2-c 2136

[Cousin, Victor] 1792-1867.
De la philosophie de Descartes. [1860-61]
721-735; 29-47; 78-95 p.

Signed: V. Cousin.
In Journal des savants, année 1860, p. 721-735; année 1861, p. 29-47, 78-95.

E-2-c 2137

Cousin, Victor, 1792-1867.
Fragments de philosophie cartésienne. Paris, Charpentier, 1845.
xii, 470 p. 18 cm.

Includes a chapter "Des rapports du cartésianisme et du spinosisme" (p. 429-470)

Cousin, Victor, 1792-1867.
Fragments de philosophie cartésienne pour faire suite aux Fragments philosophiques. Paris, Didier, 1852.
xii, 470 p.

Includes a chapter "Des rapports du cartésianisme et du spinosisme" (p. 429-470)

NN

Cousin, Victor, 1792-1867.
Fragments philosophiques pour servir à l'histoire de la philosophie. 5. éd. Philosophie moderne, 1re partie. Paris, Didier, 1866.
487 p. 23cm.

Includes a chapter "Des rapports du cartésianisme et du spinozisme" (p. 259-296)
Original paper cover bound in.

Descartes, René, 1596-1650.
Correspondence of Descartes and Constantyn Huygens, 1635-1647, edited from manuscripts now in the Bibliothèque nationale, formerly in the possession of the late Harry Wilmot Buxton, F. R. A. S., by Leon Roth. Oxford, The Clarendon press, 1926.
2 p. l., iii-lxxv, 350, [1] p. facsims. (part fold.) diagrs. 30 x 23cm.
Bibliography: p. lxv. "List of authorities and abbreviations": p. lxxv.

I. Huygens, Constantijn, heer van Zuilichem, 1596-1687. II. *Roth, Leon, 1896- ed.

26-17870
Library of Congress B1873.A5
[a42d1]

Descartes, René, 1596-1650.
Geometria, à Renato Des Cartes anno 1637 Gallicè edita; nunc autem cum notis Florimondi de Beavne ... in linguam Latinam versa, & commentariis illustrata, operâ atque studio Francisci à Schootēn ... Lvgdvni Batavorvm, Ex officinâ Ioannis Maire, 1649.
[12], 336, [2] p. diagrs. 21cm.

NNC

Descartes, René, 1596-1650.
The Method, Meditations and selections from the Principles of Descartes. Translated from the original texts, with a new introductory essay, historical and critical, by John Veitch. 9th ed. Edinburgh and London, W. Blackwood and Sons, 1887.
clxxxi, 292 p. 19cm.

References to Spinoza included in the introduction (p. [ix]-clxxxi)
Bibliographical references included in "Notes" (p. [274]-292)

Descartes, René, 1596-1650.
Passiones animae, per Renatvm Des Cartes: gallicè ab ipso conscriptâe, nunc autem in exterorum gratiam latina civitate donatâe ab H. D. M. ... Amstelodami, Apud Ludovicum Elzevirium, 1650.
[24], 98, [5] p. 21cm. (In Descartes, René. Opera philosophica. 1650)

Descartes, René, 1596-1650.
Les passions de l'ame, of, De lydingen van de ziel; van Renatus Des Cartes in de Fransche taal beschreven, en door J. H. Glazemaker vertaalt. t'Amsterdam, Gedrukt by Tymon Houthaak, voor Jan Rieuwertsz., 1659.
[16], 99, [5] p. 21cm.

Bound with Descartes, René, 1596-1650. Principia philosophiae. 1657.

Descartes, René, 1596-1650.
Principia philosophiâe: of, Beginselen der wysbegeerte. Een werk, bequaam voor des zelfs naerstige betrachter, om door klare gronden tot de hoogste trap van wijsheit en wetenschap, die van't menschelijk verstant bereikt kan worden, op te klimmen, en tot de ware oorzaken der uitwerkingen aller stoffelijke dingen te geraken. Door Renatus Des Cartes beschreven, en van J. H. Glazemaker vertaalt. Amsterdam, I. Rieuwertsz., 1657.
[28], 380, [16] p. illus. 21cm.

Descartes, René, 1596-1650.
Renati des Cartes et Benedicti de Spinoza praecipua opera philosophica recognovit, notitias historico-philosophicas adjecit Dr. Carolus Riedel ... Lipsiae, Sumtibus Hermanni Hartung, 1843.
2 v. in 1. 16cm.

"Index librorum ad philosophiam Cartesianam et Spinozianam spectantium": v. 2, p. [277]-280.
Original paper covers bound in.

CONTINUED ON NEXT CARD

Descartes, René, 1596-1650. Renati des Cartes et Benedicti de Spinoza praecipua opera philosophica. 1843. (Card 2)

Contents.--v. 1. Renati des Cartes Meditationes de prima philosophia. Benedicti de Spinoza dissertationes philosophicae: De intellectus emendatione. Tractatus politicus. De jure ecclesiasticorum.--v. 2. Spinozae Ethica.

SPECIAL COLLECTIONS SPINOZA E-2-c 2148

Descartes, René, 1596-1650.
Renati Des Cartes Meditationes de prima philosophia, in quibus Dei existentia, & animæ humanæ a corpore distinctio, demonstrantur. His adjunctæ sunt variæ objectiones doctorum virorum in istas de Deo & anima demonstrationes; cvm responsionibvs avthoris. Tertia editio prioribus auctior & emendatior. Amstelodami, Apud Ludovicum Elzevirium, 1650.
[12], 164, 88 p.

SPECIAL COLLECTIONS SPINOZA E-2-c 2149

Descartes, René, 1596-1650.
Renati Des-Cartes Opera philosophica. Editio secvnda ab auctore recognita. [Amstelodami, Apud Ludovicum Elzevirium, 1650]
3 pts. in 1 v. 21cm.

Half-title; each part has special t.-p.
Contents.--pt. [1] Principia philosophiae.--pt. [2] Specimina philosophiae.--pt. [3] Passiones animae.

SPECIAL COLLECTIONS SPINOZA E-2-c 2150

Descartes, René, 1596-1650.
Renati Des-Cartes Principia philosophiæ. Amstelodami, Apud Ludovicum Elzevirium, 1650.
[40], 302 p. illus., diagrs. 21cm. (In Descartes, René. Opera philosophica. 1650)

SPECIAL COLLECTIONS SPINOZA E-2-c 2151

Descartes, René, 1596-1650.
Renati Des Cartes Specimina philosophiæ: sev Dissertatio de methodo rectè regendæ rationis, & veritatis in scientiis investigandæ: Dioptrice, et Meteora. Ex gallico translata, & ab auctore perlecta, variisque in locis emendata. Amstelodami, Apud Ludovicum Elzevirium, 1650.
[16], 316 p. illus., diagrs. 21cm. (In Descartes, René. Opera philosophica. 1650)

Translated by Étienne de Courcelles.

E-2-c 2152

Descartes, René, 1596-1650.
René Descartes: his life and Meditations. A new translation of the "Meditations," with introduction, memoir, and commentary, by Richard Lowndes ... London, F. Norgate, 1878.
2 p. l., iii, [3], 297 p. front. (port.) 20cm.

I. Lowndes, Richard, ed. and tr.

Library of Congress B1853.E5L6 11—16485 [38b1]

SPECIAL COLLECTIONS SPINOZA E-2-c 2153

Designatio scriptorvm editorvm et edendorvm a Christophoro Theophilo de Mvrr. Editio altera, auctior. Norimbergae, 1805.
16 p. 18cm.

Includes two works connected with Spinoza (p. 10, 13)

NNC

E-2-c 2154

Deventer, Charles Marius van, 1860-1931.
Spinoza's leer de natura corporum beschouwd in betrekking tot Descartes' mechanika. [1921]
265-293 p.

In Tijdschrift voor wijsbegeerte, jaargang 15, 1921.

NN

E-2-c 2155

Fischer, Kuno, 1824-1907.
Descartes and his school; tr. from the 3d and rev. German ed. by J. P. Gordy. Ed. by Noah Porter. New York, Scribner, 1887.
xvi, 589 p.

At head of title: History of modern philosophy.
Includes a section on Spinozism (p. 488-489) and other references to Spinoza.

SPECIAL COLLECTIONS SPINOZA E-2-c 2156

Fischer, Kuno, 1824-1907.
Descartes' Leben, Werke und Lehre ... 4. neu bearb. Aufl. Heidelberg, C. Winter, 1897.
xvi, 448 p. 22cm. (His Geschichte der neuern Philosophie, 1897-1904. Bd. 1.)

Includes a section "Spinozismus" (p. 440-441) and a reference to Spinoza (p. 429)

SPECIAL COLLECTIONS SPINOZA E-2-c 2157

Fischer, Kuno, 1824-1907.
Descartes und seine Schule. 3. neu bearb. Aufl. Heidelberg, C. Winter's Universitätsbuchhandlung, 1889.
2 v. 22cm. (His Geschichte der neuern Philosophie. Neue Gesammtausgabe. 1. Bd., 1-2. Theil)

Contents.--1. Theil. Allgemeine Einleitung. Descartes' Leben, Schriften und Lehre.--2. Theil. Fortbildung der Lehre Descartes'. Spinoza.

Gibson, Alexander Boyce, 1900-
The philosophy of Descartes. London, Methuen ,1932,
xiii, 382 p. 23 cm.

Includes references to Spinoza.

Grunwald, Max, 1871-
Varia zur Geschichte des Cartesianismus und Spinozismus. Aus der Wolfschen Briefesammlung. A) Spinoza. ,1897,
361-367 p.

In Archiv für Geschichte der Philosophie, Bd. 10., 1897.

Guttmann, Jacob, 1845-1919.
De Cartesii Spinozaeque philosophiis et quae inter eas intercedat ratione. Vratislaviae, Typis F. W. Jungferi ,1868,
58 p.

Thesis, Bratislava.

Haldane, Elizabeth Sanderson, 1862-
Descartes, his life and times. London, Murray, 1905.
xxviii, 398 p. ports., plate. 23 cm.

Includes references to Spinoza.

Hann, Franz Gustav, 1850-
Die ethik Spinozas und die philosophie Descartes, von dr. Franz Gustav Hann. Innsbruck, Wagner, 1875.
124 p. 22cm.

Original paper covers bound in.

1. Spinoza, Benedictus de, 1632-1677. 2. Descartes, René, 1596-1650. 3. Ethics.

Hatwig, J
Ueber das Verhältniss des Spinozismus zur cartesianischen Philosophie. Breslau, 1869.
32 p.

Iverach, James, 1839-1922.
Descartes, Spinoza and the new philosophy. Edinburgh, T. & T. Clark, 1904.
xii, 245 p. 20cm. (The World's epoch-makers. 19)

Keeling, Stanley Victor,
Descartes. London, Benn ,1934,
xi, 282 p. 22cm. (Leaders of philosophy)

Includes references to Spinoza.
"A Cartesian bibliography", p. 273-275.

Kohler, Sylvester
Jansenismus und Cartesianismus. Eine Studie zur Geschichte der Philosophie und zur Kirchengeschichte. Düsseldorf, O. Pflaum, 1905.
51 p.

Includes 1 reference to Spinoza (p. 17)

Laberthonnière, Lucien, 1860-1932.
Etudes sur Descartes. Paris, J. Vrin, 1935.
2 v. 23 cm. (His Oeuvres ,v. 1-2,)

Léon, Albert
Les éléments cartésiens de la doctrine spinoziste sur les rapports de la pensée et de son objet. Paris, Alcan, 1907.
294 p. 25cm.

Published also as thesis, Paris.
Bibliographical footnotes.

Lewkowitz, Julius, 1876-
Spinoza's Cogitata metaphysica und ihr Verhältnis zu Descartes und zur Scholastik. Breslau, Druck von T. Schatzky, 1902.
79 p. 24cm.

Issued also as thesis, Breslau.
Volume of pamphlets.

Lewkowitz, Julius, 1876-
Spinoza's Cogitata metaphysica und ihr Verhältnis zu Descartes und zur Scholastik. Breslau, Druck von Th. Schatzky, 1902.
79 p. 24cm.

Thesis, Breslau.
Volume of pamphlets.

Lewkowitz, Julius, 1876-
Spinoza's Cogitata metaphysica und ihr Verhältnis zu Descartes und zur Scholastik. Breslau, Druck von Th. Schatzky, 1902.
79 p. 23cm.

Thesis, Breslau.

Lindner, Ernst Otto, 1820-1867.
De relatione quae inter Spinozae Cogitata metaphysica et Cartesii doctrinam intercedit. Vratislaviae, Typis Fritzianis [1844]
31 p. 21cm.

Thesis, Bratislava.
Bibliographical footnotes.

Mahaffy, Sir John Pentland, 1839-1919.
Descartes. Philadelphia, J. B. Lippincott, 1887.
vi, 211 p. 18cm. (On cover: Blackwood's philosophical classics)

Includes a reference to Spinoza (p. 205-206)
Bibliographical footnotes.

Muller, P[ieter] L[odewijk]
Onze gouden eeuw; de republiek der Vereenigde Nederlanden in haar bloeitijd geschetst door ... P. L. Muller ... geïllustreerd onder toezicht van J. H. W. Unger ... Leiden, A. W. Sijthoff [1896-98]
3 v. fronts., illus., plates (partly col.) port., maps, facsims. 28½cm.
CONTENTS.—1. De opkomst.—2. De bloeitijd.—3. De laatste jaren.
Includes a section "Descartes en Spinoza" (v. 3, p. 319-324)
1. Netherlands — Hist. — Wars of independence, 1556-1648. 2. Netherlands—Hist.—1648-1714.

Müller, Johannes, 1864-
Der Begriff der sittlichen Unvollkommenheit bei Descartes und Spinoza. Leipzig, Akademische Buchhandlung (W. Faber) 1890.
61 p. 21cm.

Issued also as thesis, Leipzig.

Nieto, David, 1654-1728.
מטה דן כוזרי שני. Warsaw, 1884.
150 p.

Title transliterated: Matteh dan kuzari sheni.
Includes a disputation against the Cartesians and Spinozists.

Paris. Bibliothèque nationale.
Descartes; exposition organisée pour le IIIe centenaire du Discours de la méthode. Paris [Imprimerie J. Dumoulin] 1937.
xviii, 170 p. plates, ports., facsims. 21cm

At head of title: Bibliothèque nationale.
Edited by Marie-Thérèse d'Alverny.
Includes references to Spinoza (p. 141, 146)

Regius, Johannes, 1656-1738.
Cartesius verus Spinozismi architectus. Sive Uberior assertio & vindicatio tractatus, cui titulus Cartesius Spinosæ prælucens, antehac vernaculo sermone editi; quibus quam clarissime nec non certissime demonstratur, in Cartesio reperiri primaria fundamenta Spinozismi. Auctore Johanne Regio ... Amstelodami, Apud Balthazarum Lakeman, 1723.
[24], 230 p., [1] l. 17cm.

Ritter, Heinrich, 1791-1869.
Welchen Einfluss hat die Philosophie des Cartesius auf die Ausbildung der des Spinoza gehabt, und welche Berührungspunkte haben beide Philosophien mit einander gemein? Nebst einer Zugabe: Ueber die Bildung des Philosophen durch die Geschichte der Philosophie. Leipzig, F. A. Brockhaus, 1817.
viii, 120 p. 20cm.

Roth, Leon, 1896-
Spinoza and Cartesianism. [1923]
[12]-37, [160]-178 p. 22cm.

"Off-printed from Mind: a quarterly review of psychology and philosophy. Vol. XXXII, n. s., no. 125 [-126]"

Roth, Leon, 1896-
Spinoza, Descartes & Maimonides, by Leon Roth ... Oxford, The Clarendon press, 1924.
4 p. l., [7]-148 p. 19½ cm.

1. Spinoza, Benedictus de, 1632-1677. 2. Descartes, René, 1596-1650. 3. Moses ben Maimon, 1135-1204.
[*Full name:* Hyam Leon Roth]

Saisset, Émile, 1814-1863.
Précurseurs et disciples de Descartes. Paris, Didier, 1862.
xv, 466 p. 23cm.

Contents.--Roger Bacon.--La réforme de Ramus.--La vie et l'oeuvre de Descartes.--Spinoza et la philosophie des Juifs.--La personne de Malebranche.--Leibnitz et la dernière philosophie allemande.

Schaarschmidt, Karl Max Wilhelm, 1822-1906.
Des Cartes und Spinoza; urkundliche Darstellung der Philosophie beider. Bonn, A. Marcus, 1850.
204 p. 21cm.

Sigwart, Heinrich Christoph Wilhelm, 1789-1844.
Ueber den Zusammenhang des Spinozismus mit der cartesianischen Philosophie; ein philosophischer Versuch. Tübingen, C. F. Osiander, 1816.
viii, 152 p. 18cm.

Bibliographical footnotes.

Smith, Norman Kemp, 1872-
Studies in the Cartesian philosophy. London, New York, Macmillan, 1902.
xiv, 276 p. 20 cm.

Includes a section on Spinoza (p. 137-160) in chapter "The Cartesian principles in Spinoza and Leibniz".

Stölzle, Remigius, 1856-1921.
Descartes' Lebensende. [1890]
54-57 p.

In Archiv für Geschichte der Philosophie, Bd. 3, 1890.

Swarte, Victor de, 1848-
Descartes, directeur spirituel; correspondance avec la Princesse Palatine et la Reine Christine de Suède. Préface de m. Émile Boutroux. Paris, F. Alcan, 1904.
iii, 292 p. ports., plan, facsims., tables. 19cm.

Includes references to Spinoza.
Bibliography: p. 279-292.

SPECIAL COLLECTIONS SPINOZA E-2-c 2188

Wielenga, Bastiaan, 1873-
Spinozas "Cogitata metaphysica" als Anhang zu seiner Darstellung der cartesianischen Prinzipienlehre. Heidelberg, C. Winter's Universitätsbuchhandlung, 1899.
59 p. 24cm.

Thesis, Heidelberg.
Original paper cover bound in.
Bibliographical references included in "Anmerkungen" (p. 51-59)
VOLUME OF PAMPHLETS

NNC

SPECIAL COLLECTIONS SPINOZA E-2-c 2189

Wielenga, Bastiaan, 1873-
Spinozas "Cogitata metaphysica" als Anhang zu seiner Darstellung der cartesianischen Prinzipienlehre. Heidelberg, C. Winter's Universitätsbuchhandlung, 1899.
59 p. 24cm.

Issued also as thesis, Heidelberg.
Original paper cover bound in.
Bibliographical references included in "Anmerkungen" (p. 51-59)
VOLUME OF PAMPHLETS

NNC

SPECIAL COLLECTIONS SPINOZA E-2-c 2190

Wielenga, Bastiaan, 1873-
Spinoza's "Cogitata metaphysica" als Anhang zu seiner Darstellung der cartesianischen Prinzipienlehre. Heidelberg, C. Winter's Universitätsbuchhandlung, 1899.
59 p. 23cm.

Thesis, Heidelberg.
Bibliographical references included in "Anmerkungen" (p. 51-59)

E-2-d
MALEBRANCHE

SPECIAL COLLECTIONS SPINOZA E-2-d 2191

Böttger, Max
Malebranche's Occasionalismus und seine Beziehung auf die Lehre vom Schauen der Dinge in Gott. Gartz a. O., Karl Fiebelkorn [1910]
23 p. 23cm.

"Beigabe zum Jahresbericht des Gymnasiums zu Gartz a. O. von Ostern 1910."
Bibliography: p. 23.
Volume of pamphlets.

NNC

SPECIAL COLLECTIONS SPINOZA E-2-d 2192

Bridet, L.
... La théorie de la connaissance dans la philosophie de Malebranche, par L. Bridet ... Paris, M. Rivière, 1929.
5 p. l., [5]-367, [1] p. 23cm. (Bibliothèque de philosophie. Directeur: E. Peillaube. XIV)
Issued also as inaugural dissertation, Toulouse.
"Bibliographie": p. [349]-361.
Includes references to Spinoza (p. 271-272)

1. Malebranche, Nicolas, 1638-1715. 2. Knowledge, Theory of. I. Title.

36-18542
Library of Congress B1898.K5B7 1929
[2] [194.2] 121

SPECIAL COLLECTIONS SPINOZA E-2-d 2193

Erdmann, Johann Eduard, 1805-1892.
Malebranche, Spinoza und die Skeptiker und Mystiker des siebzehnten Jahrhunderts; Darstellung und Kritik ihrer Systeme. Leipzig, E. Frantzen, 1836.
xxii, 257, cx p. 23cm. (His Versuch einer wissenschaftlichen Darstellung der Geschichte der neueren Philosophie. Bd. 1, 2. Abth.)

SPECIAL COLLECTIONS SPINOZA E-2-d 2194

Glaser, Johann Karl, 1814-1894.
Vergleichung der Philosophie des Malebranche und Spinoza; ein Vortrag. Berlin, G. Bethge, 1846.
31 p. 23cm.

Bibliographical footnotes.

NNC

SPECIAL COLLECTIONS SPINOZA E-2-d 2195

Gouhier, Henri, 1898-
La philosophie de Malebranche et son expérience religieuse. Paris, Librairie philosophique J. Vrin, 1926.
431 p. 26cm. (Bibliothèque d'histoire de la philosophie)

Issued also as thesis, Paris.
Includes references to Spinoza.
Bibliography: p. [421]-424.

SPECIAL COLLECTIONS SPINOZA E-2-d 2196

Grunwald, Max, 1871-
Das Verhältnis Malebranches zu Spinoza. Breslau, Druck von Th. Schatzky, 1892.
40 p. 23cm.

Thesis, Rostock.
Bibliographical footnotes.

SPECIAL COLLECTIONS SPINOZA E-2-d 2197

Le Moine, Augustin, 1901-
Des vérités éternelles selon Malebranche. Paris, Librairie philosophique Vrin, 1936.
2 p. l., [7]-292 p., 1 l. 25½cm.

At head of title: A. Le Moine.
"Bibliographie": p. [9]-13.
Includes a chapter "Malebranche et Spinoza" (p. [275]-292)
Original paper covers bound in.

E-2-d
2198

Malebranche, Nicolas, 1638-1715.
Entretiens sur la métaphysique et sur la religion. 2e éd. Rotterdam, R. Leers, 1690.
2 p. l., 381 p.

CtY

E-2-d
2199

Malebranche, Nicolas, 1638-1715.
Entretiens sur la metaphysique, sur la religion, et sur la mort. Nouvelle éd., revue ... Paris, Chez M. David, 1711.
2 v. in 1. 18 cm.

MiU

E-2-d
2200

Malebranche, Nicolas, 1638-1715.
Méditations métaphysiques et correspondance avec J.-J. Dortous de Mairan, sur des sujets de métaphysique; publiées pour la première fois sur les manuscrits originaux. Paris, H. Delloye, 1841.
viii, 182 p. facsim.

Includes a section "Correspondance inédite sur la philosophie de Spinosa" (p. [89]-177)

E-2-d
2201

Pillon, François, 1830-1914.
L'évolution de l'idéalisme au XVIIIe siècle; la correspondance de Mairan et de Malebranche: spinozisme et malebranchisme. [1895]
85-199 p.

In L'Année philosophique, 1894. Paris, 1895.

SPECIAL COLLECTIONS
SPINOZA

E-2-d
2202

Uhlich, Rudolph, 1878-
Vergleichende Darstellung der Gotteslehren von Spinoza und Malebranche. Döbeln, Druck von A. Thallwitz, 1903.
60 p. 24cm.

Thesis, Leipzig.
Bibliography: p. 4.
Volume of pamphlets.

E-2-e
LEIBNIZ

SPECIAL COLLECTIONS
SPINOZA

E-2-e
2203

Bjerregaard, Carl Henrik Andreas, 1845-1922.
Spinoza, Leibnitz and Fichte.
5 p. 26cm.

From the New cycle, v. 11, no. 1, January 1900.

E-2-e
2204

Burns, Cecil Delisle, 1879-
The growth of modern philosophy, by C. Delisle Burns ... London, S. Low, Marston & company, ltd., 1909.
269, [1] p. 16 port. (incl. front.) 20cm.
Bibliography: p. 261-266.
Includes a chapter "Spinoza and Leibnitz" (p. 38-55)

1. Philosophy, Modern.

NNC
Library of Congress B791.B8 10—22781
[a21c1]

SPECIAL COLLECTIONS
SPINOZA

E-2-e
2205

Carr, Herbert Wildon, 1857-1931.
Leibniz, by Herbert Wildon Carr ... Boston, Little, Brown, and company, 1929.
vi p., 1 l., 3-222 p. 22cm. (*Half-title: Leaders of philosophy*)
Printed in Great Britain.
Bibliography: p. 219.
Includes references to Spinoza.

1. Leibniz, Gottfried Wilhelm, freiherr von, 1646-1716.

A 29—506
Stanford univ. Library for Library of Congress [B2597.C].
[a42e1]

E-2-e
2206

Colerus, Egmont, 1888-
... Leibniz; der lebensroman eines weltumspannenden geistes. Berlin [etc.] P. Zsolnay, 1934.
626, [1] p., 2 l. front. (port.) 20½cm.
"1.-5. tausend."

1. Leibniz, Gottfried Wilhelm, freiherr von, 1646-1716—Fiction. I. Title.

34-29376
Library of Congress PT2605.O4L4 1934
Copyright A—Foreign 25334
[2] 833.91

E-2-e
2207

Feuerbach, Ludwig, 1804-1872.
Darstellung, Entwicklung und Kritik der Leibniz'schen Philosophie. Zur neueren Philosophie und ihrer Geschichte. Durchgesehen und herausgegeben von Friedrich Jodl. Stuttgart, Fr. Fromann (E. Hauff), 1910.
xii, 448 p. (His Sämmtliche Werke, 4. Bd.)

Includes two sections on Spinoza (p. 27-35, p. 400-417)

Foucher de Careil, Louis Alexandre, comte, 1826-1891.
D'un commentaire de Leibniz sur l'Éthique de Spinoza; lettre inédite de Leibniz sur une lettre de Spinoza; véritables opinions religieuses de Leibniz. [1862]
[175]-191 p. 23cm.

From Mémoires de l'Académie impériale des sciences, arts & belles-lettres de Caen, 1862.

Foucher de Careil, Louis Alexandre, comte, 1826-1891.
Leibniz, Descartes et Spinoza. Avec un rapport par M. V. Cousin. Paris, Ladrange, 1862.
288 p. 23cm.

Foucher de Careil, Louis Alexandre, comte, 1826-1891.
A refutation recently discovered of Spinoza by Leibnitz. With prefatory remarks and introduction. Tr. by the Rev. Octavius Freire Owen. Edinburgh, Constable, 1855.
xix, 155 p. 18cm.

Gerhardt, Karl Immanuel, 1816-1899.
Leibniz und Spinoza. [1889]
6 p. 26cm.

From Sitzungsberichte der Königlich Preussischen Akademie der Wissenschaften zu Berlin, Bd. XLIX, 1889. Sitzung der Philosophisch-Historischen Classe vom 28. November.

Gomperz, Theodor, 1832-1912.
Essays und Erinnerungen. Mit dem Bildnis des Verfassers von Franz von Lenbach. Stuttgart und Leipzig, Deutsche Verlags-Anstalt, 1905.
x, 249 p. port. 25cm.

Includes an essay "Leibniz und Spinoza" (p. [144]-148)
Bibliographical references included in "Anmerkungen" (p. [228]-243)
Original paper covers bound in.

Guhrauer, Gottschalk Eduard, 1809-1854.
Gottfried Wilhelm Freiherr v. Leibnitz; eine Biographie. Zu Leibnitzens Säkular-Feier. Mit neuen Beilagen und einem Register. Breslau, F. Hirt, 1846.
2 v. in 1. port., 2 fold. facsims. 19cm.

Includes references to Spinoza.
Original paper covers bound in.

Heinze, Max, 1835-1909.
Leibniz in seinem Verhältniss zu Spinoza. [1875]
[921]-932 p. 23cm.

From Im neuen Reich, 5. Jahrgang, 1875, Bd. 2.
VOLUME OF PAMPHLETS

Helfferich, Adolph, 1813-1894.
Spinoza und Leibniz; oder, Das Wesen des Idealismus und des Realismus. Hamburg, F. und A. Perthes, 1846.
iv, 108 p. 23cm.

Original paper cover bound in.

Hissbach, Karl
Ist ein durchgehender Gegensatz zwischen Spinoza und Leibniz vorhanden? Weimar, Druck von R. Wagner, 1889.
56 p. 23cm.

Thesis, Jena.

Latta, Robert, 1865-
On the relation between the philosophy of Spinoza and that of Leibniz. [1899]
333-356 p.

In Mind, n. s. v. 8, 1899.

[Leibniz, Gottfried Wilhelm, freiherr von]
1646-1716.
Causa Dei asserta per justitiam ejus, cum caeteris ejus perfectionibus, cunctisque actionibus conciliatam. Amstaelodami, Apud Isacum Trojel, 1710.
46 p. fold. table. 20cm.

Bound with his Essais de théodicée sur la bonté de Dieu ... 1710.

Leibniz, Gottfried Wilhelm, Freiherr von,
1646-1716.
Herrn Gottfried Wilhelms Freyherrn von Leibnitz Theodicee, das ist, Versuch von der Güte Gottes, Freyheit des Menschen, und vom Ursprunge des Bösen, bey dieser vierten Ausgabe durchgehends verbessert, auch mit verschiedenen Zusätzen und Anmerkungen vermehrt von Johann Christoph Gottscheden ... Hannover und Leipzig, In Verlag sel. Nicol. Försters und Sohns Erben, 1744.
[24], 843, [53] p. fold. plate. 18 cm.
Includes references to Spinoza.

[Leibniz, Gottfried Wilhelm, freiherr von]
1646-1716.
Essais de theodicée sur la bonté de Dieu, la liberté de l'homme et l'origine du mal. A Amsterdam, Chez Isaac Troyel, 1710.
[54], 660, 99 p. 20cm.

Portrait of Leibniz inserted.
"Reflexions sur l'ouvrage que M. Hobbes a publié en anglois, de la liberté, de la necessité & du hazard": 99 p. at end.
Includes references to Spinoza.

Leibniz, Gottfried Wilhelm, Freiherr von, 1646-1716.
Herrn Gottfried Wilhelms Freyherrn von Leibnitz Theodicee, das ist, Versuch von der Güte Gottes, Freyheit des Menschen, und vom Ursprunge des Bösen, bey dieser vierten Ausgabe durchgehends verbessert, auch mit verschiedenen Zusätzen und Anmerkungen vermehrt von Johann Christoph Gottscheden ... Statt einer Einleitung ist die Fontenellische Lobschrift auf den Herrn von Leibnitz von neuem übersetzt.

CONTINUED ON NEXT CARD

Leibniz, Gottfried Wilhelm, Freiherr von,
1646-1716.
Essais de Théodicée sur la bonté de Dieu, la liberté de l'homme et l'origine du mal. Nouvelle édition, faite sur l'édition complète des oeuvres philosophiques de Leibniz, publiée par Mr. Erdmann. Berlin, G. Eichler, 1840.
2 v. fold. table. 16cm.

Includes references to Spinoza.

Leibniz, Gottfried Wilhelm, Freiherr von, 1646-1716. Theodicee. 1744. (Card 2)

Hannover und Leipzig, In Verlag sel. Nicol. Försters und Sohns Erben, 1744.
[24], 843, [53] p. fold. plate. 18cm.

Includes references to Spinoza.

Leibniz, Gottfried Wilhelm, *freiherr* **von, 1646-1716.**
Godofredi Guilielmi Leibnitii Tentamina theodicaeae de bonitate Dei, libertate hominis et origine mali. Versionis novae editio altera. Vita auctoris a Bruckero descripta, Kortholti Disput. de philosophia Leibnitii, &c., et variis observationibus aucta. Cum praefatione Aug. Frid. Boeckii ... Tubingae, Libraria bergeriana, MDCCLXXI.
2 v. front. (port.) fold. tab. 20cm.
Paged continuously.
Vol. II has half-title only. Includes references to Spinoza
1. Theodicy. 2. Theism. 3. Free will and determinism. I. Brucker, Johann Jakob, 1696-1770. II. Kortholt, Christian, 1633-1694.

Leibniz, Gottfried Wilhelm, Freiherr von,
1646-1716.
Lettres et fragments inédits sur les problèmes philosophiques, théologiques, politiques de la réconciliation des doctrines protestantes (1669-1704) publiés avec une introduction historique et des notes par Paul Schrecker. Paris, F. Alcan, 1934.
136 p. 23 cm. (Bibliothèque de philosophie contemporaine)

Leibniz, Gottfried Wilhelm, Freiherr von,
1646-1716.
Die Hauptwerke; zusamengefasst und übertragen von Gerhard Krüger. Mit einem Vorwort von Dietrich Mahnke. Leipzig, A. Kröner [c1933]
L, 301 p. port. 18cm. (Kröners Taschenausgabe, Bd. 112)

Includes references to Spinoza.

Leibniz, Gottfried Wilhelm, *freiherr* **von, 1646-1716.**
... The monadology and other philosophical writings, translated with introduction and notes by Robert Latta ... [London, New York, etc.] Oxford university press, H. Milford [1925]
x p., 1 l., 437 p. 20 cm.
At head of title: Leibniz.
"Parts II and III of the introduction were accepted by the University of Edinburgh as a thesis for the degree of doctor of philosophy."—Pref.
"Second impression 1925; first edition 1898."
"The works of Leibniz": p. 18-20.

~~(Continued on next card)~~

SPECIAL COLLECTIONS SPINOZA E-2-e 2228

Leibniz, Gottfried Wilhelm, *freiherr* **von, 1646–1716.**
The monadology of Leibniz, with an introduction, commentary & supplementary essays by Herbert Wildon Carr ... London, The Favil press, 1930.
ix, 213, [1] p. incl. mounted front. (port.) 22½ cm.
Includes references to Spinoza.
1. Monadology. I. Carr, Herbert Wildon, 1857–1931, ed.
31—15206
Library of Congress B2580.E5 1930 [50e½] [193.1] 113

SPECIAL COLLECTIONS SPINOZA E-2-e 2229

Leibniz, Gottfried Wilhelm, *freiherr* **von, 1646–1716.**
New essays concerning human understanding, by Gottfried Wilhelm Leibnitz; together with an appendix consisting of some of his shorter pieces; tr. from the original Latin, French and German, with notes by Alfred Gideon Langley ... New York, The Macmillan company; London, Macmillan & co., ltd., 1896.
xix, 861 p. 20½ cm.
"The work ... consists of a translation of the entire fifth volume of Gerhardt's Die philosophischen schriften von G. W. Leibniz, subentitled 'Leibniz und Locke,' consisting of an introduction by Gerhardt, several short pieces on Locke's Essay and the New essays on human
(Continued on next card)
4—3691
[51m1]

SPECIAL COLLECTIONS SPINOZA E-2-e 2230

Leibniz, Gottfried Wilhelm, *freiherr* **von, 1646–1716.** New essays concerning human understanding ... 1896. (Card 2)
understanding; and of an appendix containing a translation of other short pieces of Leibnitz bearing on the subjects discussed in the New essays or referred to therein."—Translator's pref.
Includes references to Spinoza.
1. Locke, John, 1632–1704. An essay concerning human understanding. 2. Knowledge, Theory of. I. Gerhardt, Karl Immanuel, 1816–1899. II. Langley, Alfred Gideon, tr.
4—3691
Library of Congress B2581.E5L5 [51m1] -193.1

E-2-e 2231

Leibniz, Gottfried Wilhelm, Freiherr von, 1646-1716.
Nouvelles lettres et opuscules inédits de Leibniz, précédés d'une introduction par A. Foucher de Careil. Paris, Durand, 1857.
ccxix, 440 p.

OCH

SPECIAL COLLECTIONS SPINOZA E-2-e 2232

Leibniz, Gottfried Wilhelm, Freiherr von, 1646-1716.
Otium hanoveranum sive Miscellanea, ex ore & schedis ... Godofr. Guilielmi Leibnitii ... qvondam notata & descripta, cum ipsi in colligendis & excerpendis rebus ad Historiam brunsvicensem pertinentibus operam navaret, Joachimus Fridericus Fellerus ... Additæ sunt ... Epistolæ gallicæ amoebeæ Leibnitii & Pelissonii de tolerantia religionum & de controversiis quibusdam theologicis, jampridem editæ,

SPECIAL COLLECTIONS SPINOZA E-2-e 2233

Leibniz, Gottfried Wilhelm, freiherr von, 1646-1716. Otium hanoveranum. 1718. (Card 2)
nunc recusæ ... Lipsiæ, Impensis Joann. Christiani Martini, 1718.
[28], 441, [23] p. port. 18cm.
Includes a paragraph on Spinoza (p. 221-222)

E-2-e 2234

Leibniz, Gottfried Wilhelm, *freiherr* **von, 1646–1716.**
The philosophical works of Leibnitz ... tr. from the original Latin and French. With notes by George Martin Duncan ... New Haven, Tuttle, Morehouse & Taylor, 1890.
4 p. l., 392 p., 1 l. 23½ᶜᵐ.
Notes (largely bibliographical): p. [366]–392.
Includes "Notes on Spinoza's Ethics" (p. [11]-26) and "Refutation of Spinoza" (p. [175]-184)
I. Duncan, George Martin, 1857–1928, ed.
11—19544
Library of Congress B2558.D8 [a44e1]

SPECIAL COLLECTIONS SPINOZA E-2-e 2235

Leibniz, Gottfried Wilhelm, *freiherr* **von, 1646–1716.**
The philosophical writings of Leibniz; selected and translated by Mary Morris. London & Toronto, J. M. Dent & sons ltd.; New York, E. P. Dutton & co. inc. [1934]
xxxiii, 284 p., 1 l. diagrs. 17½ᶜᵐ. (*Half-title:* Everyman's library, ed. by Ernest Rhys. Theology and philosophy. [no. 905])
"First published 1934."
Introduction by C. R. Morris.
"Bibliographical note": p. xxix–xxx.
CONTENTS.—The philosophical system of Leibniz.—The development of Leibniz's philosophy.—Miscellaneous extracts from Leibniz's philosophical writings. Includes references to Spinoza.
1. Monadology. I. Morris, Mary (De Selincourt) 1901– ed. and tr.
A 34-1591
Evansville, Ind. Public Library for Library of Congress AC1.E8 no. 905 [a45f3] 193.1

SPECIAL COLLECTIONS SPINOZA E-2-e 2236

Leibniz, Gottfried Wilhelm, Freiherr von, 1646-1716.
Philosophischer Briefwechsel. Hrsg. von der Preussischen Akademie der Wissenschaften. Darmstadt, O. Reichl, 1926.
xxxiv, 579 p. (His Sämtliche Schriften und Briefe. 2. Reihe)
Includes letters to and from Spinoza (p. 155, 184, 271) and also references to him.
Ms. notes by A. S. Oko on flyleaf.

SPECIAL COLLECTIONS SPINOZA E-2-e 2237

Leibniz, Gottfried Wilhelm, Freiherr von, 1646-1716.
Réfutation inédite de Spinoza par Leibniz, précédée d'un mémoire par A. Foucher de Careil. Paris, 1854.
cvi, 77 p. 22cm.
Text in Latin and French.
Original paper covers bound in.

Leibniz, Gottfried Wilhelm, Freiherr von, 1646-1716.
Viri illvstris Godefridi Gvil. Leibnitii Epistolae ad diversos, theologici, ivridici, medici, philosophici, mathematici, historici et philologici argvmenti; e msc. avctoris cvm annotationibvs svis primvm divvulgavit Christian. Kortholtvs. Lipsiae, Svmtv Bern. Christoph. Breitkopfii, 1734-42.
4 v. port. 19cm.

CONTINUED ON NEXT CARD

Leibniz, Gottfried Wilhelm, Freiherr von, 1646-1716. ... Epistolae ad diversos. 1734-42. (Card 2)

Includes a letter from Leibniz to Spinoza and Spinoza's reply (v. 4, p. [346]-349) and references to Spinoza.

Mackie, John Milton, 1813-1894.
Life of Godfrey William von Leibnitz. On the basis of the German work of Dr. G. E. Guhrauer. By John M. Mackie. Boston, Gould, Kendall and Lincoln, 1845.
xiii, [15]-288 p. 18cm.

Includes references to Spinoza.

1. Leibniz, Gottfried Wilhelm, freiherr von, 1646-1716. I. Guhrauer, Gottschalk Eduard, 1809-1854.

16-3259

Mahnke, Dietrich, 1884-1939.
Leibniz und Goethe; die Harmonie ihrer Weltansichten. Erfurt, K. Stenger, 1924.
82 p. 23cm. (Weisheit und Tat; eine Folge philosophischer Schriften. 4)

Includes a section "Goethes Wahlverwandtschaft mit Spinoza und Ideengemeinschaft mit Leibniz" (p. 7-8)
Bibliographical references included in "Anmerkungen" (p. 73-80)

Merz, John Theodore, 1840-1922.
Leibniz. Philadelphia, Lippincott, 1884.
vii, 216 p. port. 17cm. (Philosophical classics for English readers. 8)

On cover: Blackwood's philosophical classics)
Includes references to Spinoza.

Ritter, Paul
Neue Leibniz-Funde; Reisebericht. [1904]
47 p. 31cm.

From Akademie der Wissenschaften, Berlin. Abhandlungen. Anhang: Abhandlungen nicht zur Akademie gehöriger Gelehrter. Philosophische und historische Abhandlungen, 4, 1904.

Robertson, George Croom, 1842-1892.
Philosophical remains of George Croom Robertson ... with a memoir; ed. by Alexander Bain ... and T. Whittaker ... London and Edinburgh, Williams and Norgate, 1894.
xxiv, 481 p. front. (port.) 23½ cm.

Includes a chapter "Leibniz and Spinoza" (p. [334]-342) a discussion of Ludwig Stein's Leibniz und Spinoza.

I. Bain, Alexander, 1818-1903, ed. II. Whittaker, Thomas, 1856- joint ed.

1-12523

Russell, Bertrand Russell, *3d earl*, 1872-
A critical exposition of the philosophy of Leibniz, with an appendix of leading passages, by Bertrand Russell ... Cambridge [Eng.] The University press, 1900.
xvi p., 1 l., 311, [1] p. 23 cm.

Includes references to Spinoza.

1. Leibniz, Gottfried Wilhelm, freiherr von, 1646-1716. 2. Philosophy, Modern.
Full name: Bertrand Arthur William Russell, *3d earl Russell.*

A 28-2277

Schmalenbach, Herman, 1885-
Leibniz, von Herman Schmalenbach ... München, Drei masken verlag, 1921.
xv, 609, [1] p., 1 l. 24½cm.
Bibliographical foot-notes.
Includes references to Spinoza.

1. Leibniz, Gottfried Wilhelm, freiherr von, 1646-1716. 2. Metaphysics. 3. Philosophy, Modern.

23-3455

Sigwart, Heinrich Christoph Wilhelm, 1789-1844.
Die Leibniz'sche Lehre von der prästabilirten Harmonie in ihrem Zusammenhange mit früheren Philosophemen betrachtet. Tübingen, C. F. Osiander, 1822.
vi, 170 p. 18 cm.

Includes references to Spinoza.

E-2-e
2248

Somma, Ida.
... Il problema della libertà e del male in Spinoza e Leibniz. Napoli-Città di Castello, F. Perrella, 1933.
3 p. l., 137 p., 1 l. 25½cm. (Biblioteca di filosofia, diretta da Antonio Aliotta)

1. Spinoza, Benedictus de, 1632-1677. 2. Leibniz, Gottfried Wilhelm, freiherr von, 1646-1716. 3. Liberty. 4. Good and evil. I. Title.

Library of Congress B3998.S65 39-7334
[2] 199.492

SPECIAL COLLECTIONS
SPINOZA

E-2-e
2249

Stein, Ludwig, 1859-1930.
Leibniz in seinem Verhältniss zu Spinoza, auf Grundlage unedirten Materials entwickelungsgeschichtlich dargestellt. [1888]
13 p. 26cm.

From Sitzungsberichte der Königlich Preussischen Akademie der Wissenschaften, Philosophischhistorische Classe, Bd. XXV.

SPECIAL COLLECTIONS
SPINOZA

E-2-e
2250

Stein, Ludwig, 1859-1930.
Leibniz und Spinoza; ein Beitrag zur Entwicklungsgeschichte der Leibnizschen Philosophie. Mit neunzehn Ineditis aus dem Nachlass von Leibniz. Berlin, G. Reimer, 1890.
xvi, 362 p. 23cm.

E-2-e
2251

Stein, Ludwig, 1859-
Zwei ungedruckte Briefe von Leibniz über Spinoza. [1890]
72-78 p.

In Archiv für Geschichte der Philosophie, Bd. 3, 1890.

SPECIAL COLLECTIONS
SPINOZA

E-2-e
2252

Weber, Theodor, 1836-1906.
Spinozae atque Leibnizii philosophiae, ratione habita libri, cui nomen est: "Réfutation inédite de Spinoza par Leibniz préc. d'un mém. par A. Foucher de Careil. Paris 1854." critica commentatio. Bonnae, Formis C. Georgi, 1858.
24 p. 20cm.

Thesis, Bonn.

NNC

E-2-e
2253

Zimmermann, Robert, Edler von, 1824-1898.
Leibnitz und Lessing (Eine Studie). [1855]
326-391 p.

In Akademie der Wissenschaften, Vienna. Philosophisch-historische Classe. Sitzungsberichte, Bd. 16, 1855.
Includes references to Spinoza.

SPECIAL COLLECTIONS
SPINOZA

E-2-e
2254

Zimmermann, Robert, Edler von, 1824-1898.
Leibnitz bei Spinoza; eine Beleuchtung der Streitfrage. Wien, In Kommission bei F. Tempsky, 1890.
64 p. 25cm. (Sitzungsberichte der Kais. Akademie der Wissenschaften in Wien. Philosophisch-historische Classe. Band CXXII, II)

E-2-f
TOLAND

E-2-f
2255

An historical account of the life and writings of the late eminently famous Mr. John Toland ... By one of his most intimate friends ... London, J. Roberts, 1722.
102 p. 20 cm.

Includes references to Spinoza.

NNUT

SPECIAL COLLECTIONS
SPINOZA

E-2-f
2256

Benoist, Élie, 1640-1728.
Mélange de remarques critiques, historiques, philosophiques, theologiques sur les deux dissertations de M. Toland, intitulées l'une L'homme sans superstition, et l'autre, Les origines judaïques. Avec une dissertation, tenant lieu de préface, ou on examine l'argument tiré du consentement de tous les peuples, pour prouver l'existence de Dieu; & on refute les principales objections par lesquelles on a pretendu l'affoiblir. Par Élie Benoist ...

CONTINUED ON NEXT CARD

SPECIAL COLLECTIONS
SPINOZA

E-2-f
2257

Benoist, Élie, 1640-1728. Mélange de remarques critiques. 1712. (Card 2)

A Delf, Chez Adrien Beman, 1712.
374, [2] p. front. 20cm.

Berthold, Gerhard, 1834-
John Toland und der Monismus der Gegenwart. Heidelberg, C. Winter, 1876.
vii, 98 p. 24cm.

Includes references to Spinoza.
Bibliographical references included in "Anmerkungen" (p. [83]-98)
Original paper covers bound in.

Mangey, Thomas, 1688–1755.
Remarks upon Nazarenus. Wherein the falsity of Mr. Toland's Mahometan Gospel, and his misrepresentation of Mahometan sentiments, in respect of Christianity, are set forth; the history of the old Nazaræans clear'd up, and the whole conduct of the first Christians in respect of the Jewish law, explain'd and defended. By Thomas Mangey ... London, Printed for W. and J. Innys, MDCCXVIII. (i.e. 131)
4 p. l., 117 p. 19½cm. [With Toland, John. Nazarenus. London, 1718]

1. Toland, John, 1670–1722. Nazarenus. 2. Deism—Controversial literature. I. Title.

[Toland, John] 1670-1722.
An account of an Irish manuscript of the four Gospels; with a summary of the ancient Irish Christianity, before the papal corruptions and ursurpations: and the reality of the Keldees (an order of lay religious) against the two last bishops of Worcester ... London, Printed in the year 1718.
1 p. l., 57 p. 19cm. (In Toland, John. Nazarenus. 1718)

[Toland, John] 1670-1722.
Appendix. Containing I. Two problems, historical, political, and theological, concerning the Jewish nation and religion. II. A further account of the Mahometan Gospel of Barnabas, by Monsieur de La Monnoye ... III. Queries fit to be sent to any curious and intelligent Christians, residing or travelling in Mahometan countries; with proper directions and cautions in order to procure satisfactory answers. London: Printed in the year 1718.
1 p. l., 16 p. 19cm. (In Toland, John. Nazarenus. 1718)

Toland, John, 1670-1722.
A collection of several pieces of Mr. John Toland, now first publish'd from his original manuscripts: with some memoirs of his life and writings ... London, J. Peele, 1726.
2 v. 20½cm.

Includes references to Spinoza.

Ms notes by A. S. Oko on flyleaf of v.1.

Toland, John, 1670–1722.
... John Toland's Christianity not mysterious (Christentum ohne geheimnis) 1696, übers. von W. Lunde, eingeleitet und unter beifügung von Leibnizens Annotatiunculae, 1701, hrsg. von lic. Leopold Zscharnack ... Giessen, A. Töpelmann, 1908.
vii, 148 p. 23cm. (Studien zur geschichte des neueren protestantismus ... 3. quellenhft.)
Includes references to Spinoza.
Original paper covers bound in.
1. Deism. I. Zscharnack, Leopold, ed. II. Lunde, Wilhelm, tr. III. Leibniz, Gottfried Wilhelm, freiherr von, 1646–1716. IV. Title: Christianity not mysterious.

Toland, John, 1670–1722.
Letters to Serena: containing, I. The origin and force of prejudices. II. The history of the soul's immortality among the heathens. III. The origin of idolatry, and reasons of heathenism. As also, IV. A letter to a gentleman in Holland, showing Spinosa's system of philosophy to be without any principle or foundation. V. Motion essential to matter; in answer to some remarks by a noble friend on the confutation of Spinosa. To all which is prefixed, VI. a preface; being a Letter to a gentleman in London ... By Mr. Toland ... London, Printed for B. Lintot, 1704.
26 p. l., 239 p. 19½cm.
I. Title. II. Title: Serena, Letters to.

Toland, John, 1670–1722.
Lettres philosophiques sur l'origine des préjugés, du dogme de l'immortalité de l'ame, de l'idolâtrie & de la superstition; sur le systême de Spinosa & sur l'origine du mouvement dans la matiere. Tr. de l'anglois de J. Toland ... Londres [Amsterdam] 1768.
2 p. l., 267 p. 16½cm.

First published at London, 1704, under title: Letters to Serena. Translated by Baron d'Holbach and edited by J. A. Naigeon.

I. Holbach, Paul Henri Thiry, baron d', 1723–1789, tr. II. Naigeon, Jacques André, 1738–1810. III. Title.

Toland, John, 1670–1722.
Nazarenus: or, Jewish, gentile, and Mahometan Christianity. Containing the history of the antient Gospel of Barnabas, and the modern Gospel of the Mahometans, attributed to the same apostle: this last Gospel being now first made known among Christians. Also, the original plan of Christianity occasionally explain'd in the history of the Nazarens, whereby diverse controversies about this divine (but highly perverted) institution may be happily terminated. With the relation of an Irish manuscript of the four Gospels, as likewise a summary of the antient Irish Christianity, and the reality of the Keldees (an

(Continued on next card)

Toland, John, 1670–1722. Nazarenus ... (Card 2)
order of lay-religious) against the two last bishops of Worcester. By Mr. Toland ... London, Printed: and sold by J. Brown [etc.] 1718.
1 p. l., xxv, [1], 85 p., 1 l., 57 p., 1 l., 16 p. 19½cm.
"The relation of the Irish manuscript" has special t.-p. (and separate paging): An account of an Irish manuscript of the four Gospels; with a summary of the ancient Irish Christianity ...
"Appendix. Containing I. Two problems historical, political, and theological, concerning the Jewish nation and religion. II. A further account of the Mahometan Gospel of Barnabas, by Monsieur de La Monnoye ... III. Queries fit to be sent to any curious and intelligent Christians, residing or travelling in Mahometan countries; with proper directions and cautions in order to procure satisfactory answers" (with special t.-p.): 1 l., 16 p. at end.

~~(Continued on next card)~~

SPECIAL COLLECTIONS SPINOZA E-2-f 2268

[Toland, John] 1670-1722.
Pantheisticon sive Formula celebrandae sodalitatis Socraticae in tres particulas divisa, quae pantheistarum sive sodalium continet [!] 1. Mores et axiomata 2. Numen et philosophiam 3. Libertatem et non fallentem legem neque fallendam. Praemittitur de antiquis et novis eruditorum sodalitatibus, vt et de universo infinito et aeterno diatriba. Subiicitur de duplici pantheistarum philosophia sequenda, et de viri optimi et ornatissimi idea, disser-

CONTINUED ON NEXT CARD

SPECIAL COLLECTIONS SPINOZA E-2-f 2269

[Toland, John] 1670-1722. Pantheisticon. 1711 [!] (Card 2)

tatiuncula. Cosmopoli [London] 1711 [!]
1 p. l., 180 p. 18cm.

Manuscript.
"Lectori philomuso et philalethi f. p. Janus Junius Eoganesius [pseud.]" dated 1720.
Apparently a copy of the printed book, pub. 1720 (cf. half-title p. 106, where signature

CONTINUED ON NEXT CARD

SPECIAL COLLECTIONS SPINOZA E-2-f 2270

[Toland, John] 1670-1722. Pantheisticon. 1711 [!] (Card 3)

number of the printed book has been copied)
Without the notes and quotations in Greek. Numerous differences in capitalization and punctuation, some in spelling, and minor differences in text.

SPECIAL COLLECTIONS SPINOZA E-2-f 2271

Toland, John, 1670-1722.
Tetradymus. Containing I. Hodegus; or, The pillar of cloud and fire, that guided the Israelites in the wilderness, not miraculous: but, as faithfully related in Exodus, a thing equally practis'd by other nations, and in those places not onely useful but necessary. II. Clidophorus; or, Of the exoteric and esoteric philosophy, that is, of the external and internal doctrine of the ancients: the one open and public, accommodated to popular prejudices and the establish'd religions; the other private and secret, wherin, to the few capable and discrete, was taught the real truth stript of all disguises. III. Hypatia; or, The his-

(Continued on next card)

40—21020 [43c1]

SPECIAL COLLECTIONS SPINOZA E-2-f 2272

Toland, John, 1670-1722. Tetradymus ... (Card 2)
tory of a most beautiful, most virtuous, most learned, and every way accomplish'd lady; who was torn to pieces by the clergy of Alexandria, to gratify the pride, emulation, and cruelty of their Archbishop Cyril ... IV. Mangoneutes: being a defense of Nazarenus, address'd to the Right Reverend John, lord bishop of London; against his lordship's chaplain Dr. Mangey, his dedicator Mr. Patterson, and ... the Reverend Dr. Brett ... By Mr. Toland ... London, Printed: and sold by J. Brotherton and W. Meadows [etc.] MDCCXX.
1 p. l., xxii, 226 p., 1 l. 20½cm.
Includes references to Spinoza (p. 185-186)

40—21020 [43c1]

SPECIAL COLLECTIONS SPINOZA E-2-f 2273

Wiener, Max, 1886-
John Toland and Judaism. Cincinnati, 1941.
cover-title, [215]-242 p. 23cm.

"Offprint from Hebrew Union College annual, volume XVI."
Includes references to Spinoza.
Bibliographical footnotes.

SPECIAL COLLECTIONS SPINOZA E-2-f 2274

[Wotton, William] 1666-1726.
A letter to Eusebia: occasioned by Mr. Toland's Letters to Serena. London, Printed for Tim. Goodwin, 1704.
2 p. l., 75 p. 20cm.

Includes references to Spinoza.

E-3
1750-1850

E-3-a
GENERAL

SPECIAL COLLECTIONS SPINOZA E-3-a 2275

Adamson, Robert, 1852-1902.
Fichte. Philadelphia, Lippincott, 1881.
222 p. port. 18cm. (Philosophical classics for English readers. [v. 4])

Includes references to Spinoza.

E-3-a 2276

Baader, Franz von, 1765-1841.
Franz von Baader's sämmtliche Werke. Systematisch geordnete, durch reiche Erläuterungen von der Hand des Verfassers bedeutend vermehrte, vollständige Ausgabe der gedruckten Schriften sammt dem Nachlasse, der Biographie und dem Briefwechsel. Hrsg. durch einen Verein von Freunden des Verewigten ... Leipzig, H. Bethmann, 1850-60.
16 v. port., facsim. 21 cm.

Includes many references to Spinoza.

NNC

E-3-a 2277

Baader, Franz von, 1765-1841.
Ueber die Nothwendigkeit einer Revision der Wissenschaft natürlicher, menschlicher und göttlicher Dinge, in Bezug auf die in ihr sich noch mehr oder minder geltend machenden Cartesischen und Spinozistischen Philosopheme. Aus einem Sendschreiben an einen alten Freund. Erlangen, Palm und Enke, 1841.
45 p. 18 cm.

CLSU

Bartholmèss, Christian Jean Guillaume, 1815–1856.
Histoire critique des doctrines religieuses de la philosophie moderne, par Christian Bartholmèss ... Paris, C. Meyrueis et compagnie, 1855.
2 v. 22cm.

Includes a section "Renaissance du spinosisme" (v. 2, p. 29-82)

1. Philosophy and religion. 2. Philosophy, Modern—Hist.

Batteux, Charles, 1713–1780.
Histoire des causes premières, ou Exposition sommaire des pensées des philosophes sur les principes des êtres. Par M. l'abbé Batteux ... Paris, Saillant, 1769.
xx, 452 p. 20cm.
"Table chronologique des philosophes cités dans cet ouvrage": p. xv–xx.
Includes a section "Spinosa, Leibnitz, Newton" (p. 441-452)

1. Cosmology. 2. Causation.

Betz, Hendrik Johan, 1842-
Spinoza en Kant. 's Gravenhage, Nijhoff, 1883.
xx, 89 p. 22½cm.

Blakey, Robert, 1795-1878.
History of moral science. 2d ed. Edinburgh, J. Duncan, 1836.
2 v.

Blakey, Robert, 1795–1878.
Memoirs of Dr. Robert Blakey, professor of logic and metaphysics, Queen's college, Belfast ... Ed. by the Rev. Henry Miller ... London, Trübner & co., 1879.
ix p., 1 l., 252 p. 21½cm.

I. Miller, Henry, ed. II. Title.

Blei, Franz, 1871-
Avenarius, Philosoph in Zürich. [1930]
270-275 p. 24cm.

From Neue schweizer Rundschau, 23. Jahrg., Heft 4, April 1930.
Includes a reference to Spinoza (p. 272)

Borelius, Johan Jakob
I hvad afseende är Hegel Pantheist? Kritisk betraktelse, med anledning af prof. Ribbings skrift om pantheismen. Upsala, C. A. Leffler, 1851.
53 p. 22 cm.

Bowen, Francis, 1811-1890.
Critical essays on a few subjects connected with the history and present condition of speculative philosophy. Boston, H. B. Williams, 1842.
xxi, 352 p.

Includes references to Spinoza.

Brachmann, A
Spinozas und Kants Sittenlehren. [1901]
481-516 p.

In Archiv für Geschichte der Philosophie, Bd. 14., 1901.

Bryant, Jacob, 1715-1804.
An address to Dr. Priestly upon his Doctrine of philosophical necessity illustrated. London, Printed for T. Cadell, 1780.
136 p.

SPECIAL COLLECTIONS
SPINOZA

E-3-a
2288

Büchner, Georg, 1813-1837.
Sämtliche Werke und Briefe. [Hrsg. von Fritz Bergemann] Leipzig, Inselverlag, 1922.
834 p. 18cm.

Includes a section on Spinoza (p. [321]-352)

E-3-a
2289

Buhle, Johann Gottlieb, 1763-1821.
Einleitung in die allgemeine Logik und die Kritik der reinen Vernunft. Göttingen, Vandenhoeck und Ruprecht, 1795.
360 p. 18 cm.

MH

SPECIAL COLLECTIONS
SPINOZA

E-3-a
2290

Büsching, Anton Friedrich, 1724-1793.
D. Anton Friedrich Büschings ... Grundriss einer Geschichte der Philosophie und einiger wichtigen Lehrsätze derselben ... Berlin, Gedruckt und verlegt von Joh. George Bosse, 1772-74.
2 v. in 1 (xx, 966 p.) 18cm.

Includes references to Spinoza.
Bibliographical references.

SPECIAL COLLECTIONS
SPINOZA

E-3-a
2291

Carus, Friedrich August, 1770-1807.
Moralphilosophie und Religionsphilosophie. Nebst einer Vorrede vom Leben des Verfassers. Leipzig, bei I. A. Barth und P. G. Kummer, 1810.
334 p. 21cm.

Includes references to Spinoza.

E-3-a
2292

[Cassel, Paulus] 1821-1892.
Lessing's Christenthum und Philosophie gegen J. Jacoby. Ein gründlicher Nachweis, dass dem Dr. Jacoby selbst die Anfangsgründe in der Philosophie fehlen. Berlin, F. Heinicke, 1863.
63 p.

OCH

E-3-a
2293

Chamberlain, Houston Stewart, 1855-1927.
Immanuel Kant; a study and a comparison with Goethe, Leonardo da Vinci, Bruno, Plato and Descartes, by Houston Stewart Chamberlain; authorised translation from the German by Lord Redesdale ... with an introduction by the translator ... with eight portraits ... London, John Lane; New York, John Lane company; [etc., etc., 1914]

2 v. fronts., illus., ports., diagrs. 23 cm.
Includes references to Spinoza.
1. Kant, Immanuel, 1724-1804. 2. Goethe, Johann Wolfgang von, 1749-1832. 3. Leonardo da Vinci, 1452-1519. 4. Bruno, Giordano, 1548-1600. 5. Plato. 6. Descartes, René, 1596-1650. I. Redesdale, Algernon Bertram Freeman-Mitford, baron, 1837- tr.

B2798.C45 1914 14—15445

Library of Congress [56h½]

SPECIAL COLLECTIONS
SPINOZA

E-3-a
2294

Cousin, Victor, 1792-1867.
Fragmens philosophiques. Paris, A. Sautelet, 1826.
L, 438 p. 20cm.

Includes a reference to Spinoza (p. 431)

E-3-a
2295

Damiron, Jean Philibert, 1794-1862.
Observations sur Spinosa [par Jean Philibert Damiron et Adolphe Franck. 1861]
283-288 p.

In Académie des sciences morales et politiques, Paris. Revue des travaux et comptes-rendus de ses séances, 56. t., 1861.

E-3-a
2296

Delius, Johannes Friedrich, 1847-
Darstellung und Prüfung der Hauptgedanken von Friedrich Heinrich Jacobi. Halle, Plötz, 1878.
39 p.

Thesis, Halle.
Includes references to Spinoza.

SPECIAL COLLECTIONS
SPINOZA

E-3-a
2297

Delius, Rudolf von, 1878-
Hegel; eine einführung in seine philosophie, von Rudolf von Delius. Leipzig, P. Reclam jun. [°1928]
77, [1] p., 1 l. 16cm. (*On cover:* Reclams universal bibliothek. nr. 6849)

1. Hegel, Georg Wilhelm Friedrich, 1770-1831.

Library of Congress B2948.D4 28-24494
Copyright A—Foreign 39407
[2]

Feuerbach, Ludwig Andreas, 1804-1872.
Ludwig Feuerbach in seinem Briefwechsel und Nachlass, sowie in seiner philosophischen Charakterentwicklung, dargestellt von Karl Grün. Mit dem Bildniss Feuerbach's. Leipzig & Heidelberg, C. F. Winter, 1874.
2 v. port. 23 cm.

Includes references to Spinoza.

Fichte, Johann Gottlieb, 1762-1814.
Die Anweisung zum seeligen Leben, oder auch die Religionslehre. Durch Johann Gottlieb Fichte, in Vorlesungen gehalten zu Berlin, im Jahre 1806. Berlin, Im Verlage der Realschulbuchhandlung, 1806.
xiv, 352 p. 19cm.

Fischer, Kuno, 1824-1907.
Die Apologie meiner Lehre nebst Replik auf die "Abfertigung" des Herrn Schenkel. Mannheim, Bassermann & Mathy, 1854.
110 p. 22 cm.

Fischer, Kuno, 1824-1907.
Fichtes Leben, Werke und Lehre. 4. durchgesehene Aufl. Heidelberg, C. Winter, 1914.
xxii, 735 p. 24cm. (His Geschichte der neuern Philosophie. Gedächtnis-Ausgabe. 6 Bd.)

Includes references to Spinoza.
"Anhang: Neue Fichte-Literatur": p. [717]-729.

Fischer, Kuno, 1824-1907.
Hegels Leben, Werke und Lehre. 2. Aufl. Heidelberg, C. Winter, 1911.
2 v. (xx, 1265 p.) 23cm. (His Geschichte der neuern Philosophie, 8. Bd.)

Includes references to Spinoza.

Fischer, Kuno, 1824-1907.
Schellings Leben, Werke und Lehre. 4. Aufl. Heidelberg, C. Winter, 1923.
xxxii, 859 p. 24cm. (His Geschichte der neuern Philosophie. Gedächtnis-Ausgabe. 7. Bd.)

Includes references to Spinoza.
"Anhang: Neuere Schelling-Litteratur": p. [833]-849.

Fricker, Hermann
Die Philosophie des Friedrich Heinrich Jacobi, nach Disciplinen bearbeitet und kritisch beleuchtet. Augsburg, K. Kollmann, 1854.
iv, 74 p.

Includes a section (p. 37-41) comparing the theories of Spinoza and Jacobi.

[Friedrich II, der Grosse, king of Prussia] 1712-1786.
Des Philosophen von Sanssouci sämtliche Werke ... Neuübersezt ... Berlin, bei Arnold Wever, 1782-86 [v. 1, 1784]
4 v. port. 18cm.

Includes references to Spinoza (v. 2, p. [3]-4; v. 3, p. 175-176)

Frohschammer, Jakob, 1821-1893.
Ueber die Bedeutung der Einbildungskraft in der Philosophie Kant's und Spinoza's. München, T. Ackermann, 1879.
vii, 172 p. 24cm.

Original paper covers bound in.

Galluppi, Pasquale, barone, 1770-1846.
Alcune osservazioni sullo spinozismo. [1904]
225-226 p. 27 cm.

From Onoranze al prof. Vincenzo Lilla per suo 40. anno d'insegnamento. Messina, Tipografia d'Angelo, 1904.

E-3-a
2308

Galluppi, Pasquale, barone, 1770-1846.
Lettere filosofiche su le vicende della filosofia relativamente ai principi delle conoscenze umane da Cartesio sino a Kant inclusivamente ... Messina, 1827.
290 p. 21 cm.

CtY

E-3-a
2309

Galluppi, Pasquale, barone, 1770-1846.
Lettere filosofiche su le vicende della filosofia relativamente a' principi delle conoscenze umane da Cartesio sino a Kant inclusivamente, con introduzione e note di Augusto Guzzo. 2a ed., riveduta. Firenze, Vallecchi [1925]
L, 312 p.

Includes references to Spinoza.

MH

E-3-a
2310

Galluppi, Pasquale, barone, 1770-1846.
Saggio filosofico sulla critica della conoscenza, o sia analisi distinta del pensiere umano, con un esame delle piu importanti questioni dell'ideologia del Kantismo, e della filosofia transcendentale. 2a ed. corretta. Napoli, Raffaello, 1833.
6 v.

MB

E-3-a
2311

Galluppi, Pasquale, barone, 1770-1846.
Saggio filosofico sulla critica della conoscenza, o sia analisi distinta del pensiere umano, con un esame delle piu importanti questioni dell'ideologia del Kantismo, e della filosofia transcendentale. 1a ed. milanese. Milano, 1846.
5 v.

NN

E-3-a
2312

Galluppi, Pasquale, barone, 1770-1846.
Lettere filosofiche sulle vicende della filosofia relativamente ai principi delle conoscenze umane, da Cartesio sino a Kant inclusivamente ... Precedute da un discorso di Luigi Blanch. Edizione conforme all'ultima di Napoli. Firenze, P. Fraticelli, 1842.
352 p. 14 cm.

PV

E-3-a
2313

Galluppi, Pasquale, barone, 1770-1846.
Lettres philosophiques sur les vicissitudes de la philosophie relativement aux principes des connaissances humaines, depuis Descartes jusqu'à Kant. Tr. de l'italien sur la 2. éd. par L. Peisse. Paris, Librarie philosophique de Ladrange, 1844.
xii, 352 p. 23cm.

E-3-a
2314

Giessler, Richard, 1852-
Ethica Spinozae doctrina cum Kantiana comparatur. Halis Saxonum, 1878.
33 p. 19cm.

Thesis, Halle.

E-3-a
2315

Glockner, Hermann, 1896-
Hegel. Stuttgart, Frommann, 1929.
v. 1 port.

Includes a section on Spinoza (p. 176-182)

E-3-a
2316

Gottsched, Johann Christoph, 1700-1766.
Erste Gründe der gesammten Weltweisheit, darinn alle philosophische Wissenschaften, in ihrer natürlichen Verknüpfung, in zween Theilen abgehandelt werden ... Siebente vermehrte und verbesserte Auflage ... Leipzig, Verlegts Bernhard Christoph Breitkopf, 1762.
2 v. front., diagrs. 21 cm.

E-3-a
2317

Gottsched, Johann Christoph, 1700-1766.
Historische Lobschrift des ... Herrn Christians ... Freyherrn von Wolf ... Halle, in Verlegung der Rengerischen Buchhandlung, 1755.
152, 108 p. port. 26 cm.

Includes references to Spinoza.

E-3-a
2318

Green, Joseph Henry, 1791-1863.
Spiritual philosophy: founded on the teaching of the late Samuel Taylor Coleridge: by the late Joseph Henry Green ... Ed., with a memoir of the author's life, by John Simon ... London and Cambridge, Macmillan and co., 1865.

2 v. front. (port.) 23cm.

Includes a reference to Spinoza (v. 2, p. 44)

1. Coleridge, Samuel Taylor, 1772-1834. I. Simon, Sir John, 1816-1904, ed.

Library of Congress B1589.G73S7 11—16746
[44c1]

E-3-a
2319

Grupp, Georg, 1861-
Spinoza und Kant. [1891]
35-54, 210-227 p.

In Divus Thomas; Jahrbuch für Philosophie und spekulative Theologie, Bd. 5, 1891.

MH

E-3-a
2320

Harms, Friedrich, 1819-1880.
Ueber die Lehre von Friedrich Heinrich Jacobi. [1877]
17 p.

In K. Akademie der Wissenschaften, Berlin. Abhandlungen, aus dem Jahre 1876. Philologische und historische Klasse. Berlin, 1877.
Includes references to Spinoza.

E-3-a
2321

Hartmann, Eduard von, 1842-1906.
Schelling's philosohpisches [!] system. Von Eduard von Hartmann. Leipzig, H. Haacke, 1897.

xii, 224 p. diagrs. (1 fold.) 24cm.

"Chronologische uebersicht der wichtigeren schriften Schellings": p. [222]-224.
Includes a section on Spinoza (p. 7-14) and other references to him.

1. Schelling, Friedrich Wilhelm Joseph von, 1775-1854.

[Full name: Karl Robert Eduard von Hartmann]

Library of Congress B2898.H3 38-10153
[2] 193.4

SPECIAL COLLECTIONS
SPINOZA
E-3-a
2322

Hegel, Georg Wilhelm Friedrich, 1770-1831.
Georg Wilhelm Friedrich Hegel's Vorlesungen über die Geschichte der Philosophie; hrsg. von Karl Ludwig Michelet. Berlin, Duncker und Humblot, 1833.
2 v. 22cm. (His Werke, 13.-14. Bd.)

Bibliographical footnotes.

E-3-a
2323

Hegel, Georg Wilhelm Friedrich, 1770-1831.
Georg Wilhelm Friedrich Hegel's Werke; vollständige Ausgabe, durch einen Verein von Freunden des Verewigten: D. Ph. Marheineke, D. J. Schulze, D. Ed. Gans. Berlin, Duncker, 1832-87.
19 v. in 12. port., facsim. 22 cm.

Includes a section on Spinoza (v. 15, p. 332-369) and references to him in "Anmerkung" (v. 4, p. 187-193)

E-3-a
2324

Hegel, Georg Wilhelm Friedrich, 1770-1831.
Vorlesungen über die Geschichte der Philosophie. Hrsg. von Carl Ludwig Michelet. 2., verb. Aufl. Berlin, Duncker und Humblot, 1840-44.
3 v. (His Werke, 13.-15. Bd.)

Includes a section on Spinoza (v. 3, p. 332-369)

E-3-a
2325

Heman, Karl Friedrich, b. 1839.
Kant und Spinoza. [1900]
273-339 p.

In Kant-Studien, 5. Bd., 1900.

SPECIAL COLLECTIONS
SPINOZA
E-3-a
2326

Herbart, Johann Friedrich, 1776-1841.
Gespräche über das Böse. Königsberg, A. W. Unzer, 1817.
viii, 184 p. 18cm.

Includes references to Spinoza.

E-3-a
2327

Herbart, Johann Friedrich, 1776-1841.
Johann Friedrich Herbart's sämmtliche Werke, herausgegeben von G. Hartenstein. Leipzig, L. Voss, 1850-52.
12 v. port., fold. plates (music) 22 cm.

Includes "Die Lehre des Spinoza" and "Vergleichung zwischen Spinoza, Leibnitz und Kant" (v. 3, p. 158-194); and "Spinoza und Schelling, eine Skizze" (v. 12, p. 7-10)

Herbart, Johann Friedrich, 1776-1841.
Joh. Fr. Herbart's sämtliche Werke in chronologischer Reihenfolge hrsg. von Karl Kehrbach und Otto Flügel. Langensalza, Beyer, 1887-1912.
19 v. tables, diagrs., ports. 23 cm.

Includes a section "Spinoza und Schelling; eine Skizze" (v. 1, p. [9]-11)

Herbart, Johann Friedrich, 1776-1841.
Zur Lehre von der Freyheit des menschlichen Willens; Briefe an Herrn Professor Griepenkerl. Göttingen, Dieterichsche Buchhandlung, 1836.
xxiv, 255 p. 18cm.

Includes a letter about Spinoza (p. 100-117) and other references to him.

Herder, Johann Gottfried von, 1744-1803.
Gott ... Einige Gespräche von J. G. Herder. Gotha, bei Karl Wilhelm Ettinger, 1787.
viii, 252 p. 16cm.

Includes references to Spinoza.

[Hess, Moses]
Die europäische Triarchie. Leipzig, O. Wigand, 1841.
185 p.

Includes references to Spinoza.

[Hess, Moses] 1812-1875.
Die heilige Geschichte der Menschheit, von einem Jünger Spinoza's. Stuttgart, Hallberger'sche Verlagsbuchhandlung, 1837.
346 p. 18cm.

Includes references to Spinoza.
Original paper covers bound in.

Heuschkel, Hermann
Hat die grosse Übereinstimmung zwischen Spinoza und Fénelon statt, die Jakobi in seinem Sendschreiben an Fichte behauptet? Tremessen, L. Marten, 1906.
15 p.

At head of title: XXXX. Jahresbericht über das Königliche Progymnasium zu Tremessen ...

Heydenreich, Karl Heinrich, 1764-1801.
Grundsätze der moralischen Gotteslehre, nebst Anwendungen auf geistliche Rede- und Dichtkunst, von Karl Heinrich Heydenreich ... Leipzig, In der Weygandschen Buchhandlung, 1792.
xvi, 224 p. 22cm.

Includes references to Spinozism (p. 143-144)
Contains bibliographical references.

Heydenreich, Karl Heinrich, 1764-1801.
Karl Heinrich Heydenreich's ... Betrachtungen über die philosophie der natürlichen religion ... Leipzig, Weygand, 1790-91.
2 v. in 1. 21cm.
Title vignette.
Includes a section "Kritik und Widerlegung der ersten Gründe des Spinozismus" (v. 1, p. 258-272) and other references to him (v.2, p. 168-175)
1. Natural theology. 2. Philosophy and religion. 3. Knowledge, Theory of (Religion)

Heydenreich, Karl Heinrich, 1764-1801.
Karl Heinrich Heydenreichs ... Encyclopädische Einleitung in das Studium der Philosophie nach den Bedürfnissen unsers Zeitalters. Nebst Anleitungen zur philosophischen Litteratur. Leipzig, In der Weygandschen Buchhandlung, 1793.
xiv, 249 p. 21cm.

Includes bibliographies.
A few works by Spinoza listed in bibliographies.

Heydenreich, Karl Heinrich, 1764-1801.
Philosophisches Taschenbuch für denkende Gottesverehrer, von K. H. Heydenreich. Ister Jahrgang. Leipzig, Bey Gottfried Martini, 1796.
[10], 164 p., [1] l., 98, [2] p. front. 14cm.

[Hitchcock, Ethan Allen] 1798–1870.
The doctrines of Spinoza and Swedenborg identified; so far as they claim a scientific ground. In four letters. By *. *. *., United States army. Boston, Munroe & Francis; New York, C. S. Francis & co., 1846.
36 p. 22½cm.

1. Swedenborg, Emanuel, 1688–1772. 2. Spinoza, Benedictus de, 1632–1677. I. Title.

[Hitchcock, Ethan Allen] 1798-1870.
Swedenborg, a hermetic philosopher. Being a sequel to Remarks on alchemy and the alchemists. Showing that Emanuel Swedenborg was a hermetic philosopher and that his writings may be interpreted from the point of view of hermetic philosophy. With a chapter comparing Swedenborg and Spinoza. By the author of Remarks on alchemy and the alchemists. New York, D. Appleton, 1858.
352 p. 19 cm.

Hoffart, Elisabeth, 1892-
Herders "Gott". Halle a. S., M. Niemeyer, 1918.
xii, 96 p. 22cm. (Bausteine zur Geschichte der deutschen Literatur. 16)

Issued in part as the author's thesis, Erlangen.
Includes a section "Herder and Spinoza" (p. [70]-96)
Bibliography: p. [ix]-xii.

Hoffmann, Franz, 1804-1881.
Franz Baader im Verhältnisse zu Spinoza, Leibniz, Kant, Jacobi, Fichte, Schelling, Hegel, Herbart. Leipzig, H. Bethmann, 1851.
lxxiv p. 20cm.

"Besonderer Abdruck der Einleitung zu Franz von Baaders sämmtliche Werke, erste Hauptabtheilung, zweiter Band: Gesammelte Schriften zur philosophischen Grundwissenschaft oder Metaphysik."
Includes a section on Spinoza (p. xix-xxiv)

Hoffmann, Franz, 1804-1881.
Franz Baader im Verhältnisse zu Spinoza, Leibniz, Kant, Jacobi, Fichte, Schelling, Hegel, Herbart. Leipzig, H. Bethmann, 1851.
lxxiv p. 20cm.

"Besonderer Abdruck der Einleitung zu Franz von Baaders sämmtliche Werke, erste Hauptabtheilung, zweiter Band: Gesammelte Schriften zur philosophischen Grundwissenschaft oder Metaphysik."
Includes a section on Spinoza (p. xix-xxiv)
Original paper cover bound in.

Jacobi, Friedrich Heinrich, 1743-1819.
Friedrich Heinrich Jacobi wider Mendelssohns Beschuldigungen betreffend die Briefe über die Lehre des Spinoza ... Leipzig, bei Georg Joachim Goeschen, 1786.
vii, 127 p. front., illus. 18cm.

Jacobi, Friedrich Heinrich, 1743-1819.
Friedrich Heinrich Jacobi wider Mendelssohns Beschuldigungen betreffend die Briefe über die Lehre des Spinoza ... Leipzig, bei Georg Joachim Goeschen, 1786.
vii, 127 p. front., illus. 18cm.

Bound with Jacobi, Friedrich Heinrich. Uber die Lehre des Spinoza. 1785.

Jacobi, Friedrich Heinrich, 1743-1819.
Friedrich Heinrich Jacobi's Werke. 4. Bd. ... Leipzig, G. Fleischer, 1819.
2 v. in 1. 21cm.

Contents.--1. Abth. Ueber die Lehre des Spinoza, in Briefen an Herrn Moses Mendelssohn.--2. Abth. Beylagen zu den Briefen über die Lehre des Spinoza.

Jacobi, Friedrich Heinrich, 1743-1819.
Jacobi an Fichte ... Hamburg, bei Friedrich Perthes, 1799.
x p., 1 l., 106 p.

Includes references to Spinoza.

Jacobi, Friedrich Heinrich, 1743-1819.
Jacobis Gespräche mit Lessing. [1935]
167-182 p.

From Lessing, Gotthold Ephraim. Lessings Werke, v. 24. Berlin, Bong [1935]
Includes references to Spinoza.

Jacobi, Friedrich Heinrich, 1743-1819.
Sulla dottrina dello Spinoza; lettere al signor Mosè Mendelssohn. Tradotte da Francesco Capra. Bari, G. Laterza & figli, 1914.
vii, 231 p. 22cm. (Classici della filosofia moderna. 21)

Original paper cover bound in.

[Jacobi, Friedrich Heinrich] 1743-1819.
Ueber die Lehre des Spinoza in Briefen an den Herrn Moses Mendelssohn. Breslau, bey Gottl. Löwe, 1785.
[8], 215, [1] p. 16cm.

Dedication signed: Friedrich Heinr. Jacobi.
Controversy about Lessing's philosophic views, particularly with respect to Spinoza, including Jacobi's account of a conversation with Lessing in 1780 (p. 17-36)

[Jacobi, Friedrich Heinrich] 1743-1819.
Ueber die Lehre des Spinoza in Briefen an den Herrn Moses Mendelssohn. Neue verm. Ausg. ... Breslau, G. Lowe, 1789.
2 p. l., [iii]-li, [1], 440 p. port. 18cm.

Dedication signed: Friedrich Heinrich Jacobi.
Controversy about Lessing's philosophic views, particularly with respect to Spinoza, including Jacobi's account of a conversation with Lessing in 1780 (p. 19-44)

Kant, Immanuel, 1724-1804.
Critik der Urtheilskraft, von Immanuel Kant. Zweyte Auflage. Berlin, bey F. L. Lagarde, 1793.
lx, 482 p. 20cm.

Includes references to Spinoza.

Kant, Immanuel, 1724-1804.
Immanuel Kant's sämmtliche Werke. Hrsg. von Karl Rosenkranz und Friedr. Wilh. Schubert. Leipzig, L. Voss, 1838-42.
14 v. in 8. front., pl., diagrs. 22 cm.

Includes references to Spinoza in essay "Was heisst: sich im Denken orientiren?" (v. 1, p. 371-390)

Kausler, Carolus Ludovicus Fridericus
Dissertatio philosophica sistens disquisitiones quasdam in Spinozam quan ... publice defendet auctor Carolus Ludovicus Frider. Kausler ... Tubingae, Litteris Hopfferianis, 1803.
26 p. 20cm.

Thesis, Tübingen.

Kronenberg, Moritz, 1865-
Herder's Philosophie nach ihren Entwickelungsgang und ihrer historischen Stellung. Heidelberg, C. Winter, 1889.
xi, 116 p. 23cm.

Includes a section "Herder unter dem Einfluss von Leibniz und Spinoza" (p. 47-88)

Kuhn, Johannes von, 1806-1887.
Jacobi und die Philosophie seiner Zeit; ein Versuch, das wissenschaftliche Fundament der Philosophie historisch zu erörten. Mainz, bei F. Kupferberg, 1834.
xvi, 558 p., 1 l.

Includes references to Spinoza (p. 87-118)

Kühnemann, Eugen, 1868-
Herder. 2., neu bearb. Aufl. München, C. H. Beck, 1912.
xxiv, 670 p. port.

Includes references to Spinoza.

Kühnemann, Eugen, 1868-
Herders Persönlichkeit in seiner Weltanschauung; ein Beitrag zur Begründung der Biologie des Geistes. Berlin, F. Dümmler, 1893.
xvi, 269 p.

Includes references to Spinoza (p. 151-154)

Kühnemann, Eugen, 1868-
Kant, von Eugen Kühnemann ... München, Beck, 1923-24.
2 v. 22cm.

Includes a chapter "Moderne Metaphysik, Spinoza" (v. 1, p. [319]-382)
Contents.--1. t. Der europäische gedanke im vorkantischen denken.--2. t. Das werk Kants und der europäische gedanke.

Léon, Xavier
Fichte et son temps. Paris, A. Colin, 1922-27.
2 v. in 3. port. 25cm.

Vol. 2 includes references to Spinoza.
Bibliography: v. 2[2], p. [293]-319.

Levisohn, George, d. 1797.

שלש עשרה יסודי התורה.[יסוד התורה
להרמ"ג הרמב"ם]
Altoona, 1892.
210 p.

Title transliterated: Shelosh ʿesreh yesodey ha-torah ...
Includes an attack on and arguments against Spinoza (p. 40-41)

Lévy-Bruhl, Lucien, 1857-1939.
Jacobi et le spinozisme. [1894]
46-72 p.

In Revue philosophique de la France et de l'étranger, 19. année, t. 37, 1894.

Lévy-Bruhl, Lucien, 1857-1939.
La philosophie de Jacobi. Paris, F. Alcan, 1894.
xxviii, 263 p. 23cm.

Bibliographical note: p. xxvii-xxviii.
Includes a chapter on Spinoza.

Loewe, Johann Heinrich, 1808-1892.
Die Philosophie Fichte's nach dem Gesammtergebnisse ihrer Entwickelung und in ihrem Verhältnisse zu Kant und Spinoza. Mit einem Anhange: Ueber den Gottesbegriff Spinoza's und dessen Schicksale. Stuttgart, W. Nitzschke, 1862.
321 p. 22cm.

Lotze, Hermann, 1817-1881.
Geschichte der Aesthetik in Deutschland. München, Cotta, 1868.
viii, 672 p. 23 cm. (Geschichte der Wissenschaften in Deutschland. Neuere Zeit, 7. Bd.)

Lucka, Emil
Spinoza und Fichte. Eine Betrachtung über das Philosophieren. [1913]
193-216 p.

In Preussische Jahrbücher, 153. Bd., 1913.

Luzzatto, Moses Hayyim, 1707-1744.
שיר ידידות תהלה לישרים, מאת ...
משה חיים לוצאטו ליום חתונת הרופא שב־
תי מארינו; נמצא באוצר הספרים בעיר אקס־
פארד ... ויצא כעת ... ממני צבי אירש
עדעלמאן ... לונדון שנת עושר וכבוד לפ"ק.
[London, 1854]
15, [1] p.

Title transliterated: Shīr yĕdhīdhūth Tĕhillā layshārīm.
Bound with Ōsār nehmādh, v. 3, 1860.

Luzzatto, Samuele Davide, 1800-1865.
המשתדל; והוא פירוש על קצת מקומות
מן התורה, מלאכת שמואל דוד לוצאטו.
Vienna, Francesco Nobile di Schmidt ed I. I. Busch, 1847.
1 v. (various pagings) 22cm.

Title transliterated: ha-Mishtaddel.
Includes references to Spinoza.

E-3-a
2368

Luzzatto, Samuele Davide, 1800-1865.

Vienna, 1847. ...המשתדל
122 p.

Title transliterated: ha-Mishtadel.
Includes an introduction of four pages against Spinoza.

NNJ

E-3-a
2369

Luzzatto, Samuele Davide, 1800-1865.

מכתב רש"ד"ל אל ש"ז"ח"ה. [1864]
77-82 p.

Title transliterated: Miktab ...
In Yeshurun, v. 4, 1864.
About Spinoza, with reference to Isaac Mieses' attitude to him in his Zafnath paaneah.

NNJ

E-3-a
2370

Luzzatto, Samuele Davide, 1800-1865.
פניני שד"ל. [1888] (Card 2)

Added t.-p. in Italian: Scelta di scritti sparsi ebraici di Samuel David Luzzato, pubblicata da' suoi figli a cura di Eisig Gräber. Przemysl, 1888.

E-3-a
2371

McEachran, Frank, 1900–
The life and philosophy of Johann Gottfried Herder, by F. McEachran ... Oxford, The Clarendon press, 1939.

4 p. l., 98 p., 1 l. front. (port.) 23 cm. (*Half-title:* Oxford studies in modern languages and literature. General editor: H. G. Fiedler)

"Errata" slip between 3d and 4th prelim. leaves.
Bibliography: p. [88]–94.

Includes a section on Spinoza and Herder (p. 74-80) and other references to Spinoza.

1. Herder, Johann Gottfried von, 1744-1803.

PT2353.M2 193.9 40—7766

Library of Congress [57e½]

E-3-a
2372

Martin, Thomas Henri, 1813-1884.
Philosophie spiritualiste de la nature. Introduction à l'histoire des sciences physiques dans l'antiquité. t. 1. Paris, Dezobry et E. Magdeleine, 1849.
xxvii, 376 p.

Includes a section on Spinoza (p. 180-183)

OCH

E-3-a
2373

Medicus, Fritz Georg Adolf, 1876–
J. G. Fichte. Dreizehn vorlesungen gehalten an der Universität Halle von Fritz Medicus. Berlin, Reuther & Reichard, 1905.

viii, 269 p. 22cm.

Includes references to Spinoza (p. 198)

1. Fichte, Johann Gottlieb, 1762-1814.

39-16575

Library of Congress B2848.M37

[2]

E-3-a
2374

Meiners, Christoph, 1747-1810.
Grundriss der Geschichte der Weltweisheit ...
2. verb. Aufl. Lemgo, Meyer, 1789.
[9], 2-299 p. 17 cm.

Includes references to Spinoza.

CLSU

E-3-a
2375

Mieses, Izaak, 1802-1883.

מכתב ריב"ם אל שז"חה. [1864]
83-88 p.

Title transliterated: Miktav ...
In Yeshurun, v. 4, 1864.
Includes a letter to J. S. Halberstam against S. D. Luzzatto's attacks on Spinoza.

NNJ

E-3-a
2376

Minkin, Jacob Samuel, 1885-
Spinoza. [1915]
812-815 p.

In Reform advocate, v. 49, 1915.
With reference to the criticism of Spinoza in Immanuel Kant, by Houston S. Chamberlain.

NNJ

E-3-a
2377

Muzel, Philipp Ludwig
An den Verfasser der Resultate der Jacobischen und Mendelssohnschen Philosophie. [1793]
p. 342.

In Allgemeines Repertorium der Literatur, 1793, Bd. 1.

MH

Oischinger, Johann Nepomuk Paul, 1817–1876.
Die Günther'sche philosophie. Mit rücksicht auf die geschichte und das system der philosophie, sowie auf die christliche religion dargestellt und gewürdigt von dr. Joh. Nepomuk Paul Oischinger ... Schaffhausen, Hurter, 1852.
viii, 418 p. 20½cm.

Bound with Volkmuth, Peter. Der dreieinige Pantheismus von Thales bis Hegel. 1837.

1. Günther, Anton, 1783–1863. 2. Philosophy and religion. 3. Religion—Philosophy. I. Title.

Oischinger, Johann Nepomuk Paul, 1817-1876.
Speculative Entwicklung der Hauptsysteme der neueren Philosophie von Descartes bis Hegel. Schaffhausen, Hurter, 1853-54.
2 v.

Includes a section on Spinoza (v. 1, p. 134-206)

Ploucquet, Gottfried, 1716-1790.
Principia de substantiis et phaenomenis metaphysicae. Francofurti et Lipsiae, in Bibliopolio Bergeriano, 1764.
399, 72 p. 20 cm.

Includes a section on Spinoza (p. 203-236)

Rehberg, August Wilhelm, 1757-1836.
Sämmtliche Schriften. Erster Band. Hannover, Hahn'sche Hofbuchhandlung, 1828.
vii, 428 p. 23cm.

Includes a section on Spinoza (p. 7-12)

Reiff, Jakob Friedrich, 1810-1879.
Ueber den Spinozismus in der Kantischen Philosophie. [1856]
181-223 p.

In Zeitschrift für Philosophie und philosophische Kritik, 29. Bd., 1856.

[Reinhold, Karl Leonhard] 1758-1823.
Systematische Darstellung aller bisher möglichen Systeme der Metaphysik. [1794]
3-18, 235-256 p.

Signed: Reinhold.
In Der Neue teutsche Merkur vom Jahre 1794, 1. Bd.
Includes references to Spinoza.

Riehl, Alois, 1844–1924.
Führende denker und forscher, von Alois Riehl. 2. aufl. Leipzig, Quelle & Meyer, 1924.
4 p. l., 240 p. 21cm.

CONTENTS.—Plato.—Giordano Bruno.—Immanuel Kant.—Fichtes universitätsplan.—Gotthold Ephraim Lessing.—Rudolf Haym.—Galileo Galilei.—Robert Mayer.—Helmholtz.
Includes a reference to Spinoza in the section on Fichte (p. 104)

1. Philosophers. 2. Scientists. I. Title.

Ripley, George, 1802–1880, *comp.*
Philosophical miscellanies, translated from the French of Cousin, Jouffroy, and B. Constant. With introductory and critical notices. By George Ripley ... Boston, Hilliard, Gray, and company, 1838.
2 v. 19cm. (*Added t.-p.:* Specimens of foreign standard literature. Ed. by George Ripley. vol. I–II)

1. Philosophy, French. I. Cousin, Victor, 1792–1867. II. Jouffroy, Théodore Simon, 1796–1842. III. Constant de Rebecque, Henri Benjamin, 1767–1830. IV. Title.

[Rist, J]
Schönborn und seine Zeitgenossen; drei Briefe an ihn nebst einigen Zugaben aus seinem Nachlass und einer biographischen Skizze als Einleitung hrsg. von J. R. Hamburg, F. Perthes, 1836.
120 p. facsims. 22cm.

"Abriss einer Geschichte des Spinozismus" (p. [87]-120) falsely ascribed to Schönborn by Rist.-cf. Allgemeine deutsche Biographie v. 32, p. 281.

Ritter, Heinrich, 1791-1869.
Histoire de la philosophie. Traduite de l'allemand par C.-J. Tissot. 1. partie. Histoire de la philosophie ancienne. Paris, Ladrange, 1835-36.
4 v.

Saintes, Amand, b. 1801.
Histoire critique du rationalisme en Allemagne depuis son origine jusqu'à nos jours. 2. éd., rev. et augm. Paris, Librairie de Brockhaus et Avenarius, 1843.
xv, 572 p. 22cm.

Includes references to Spinoza.
Bibliographical footnotes.

Saitta, Giuseppe, 1881-
Il pensiero di Vincenzo Gioberti. Messina, Principato, 1917.
452 p. 22 cm. (Studi filosofici, diretti da Giovanni Gentile, VI)

Sarti, Christophorus
Christophori Sarti in Academia Pisana Philosophiae rationalis artis criticae ac metaphysicae p. p. specimen theologiae naturalis. Lucae, Typis Francisci Bonsignori, 1780.
xii, 173 p., 1 l.

Includes references to Spinoza.

OCH

Schelling, Friedrich Wilhelm Joseph von, 1775-1852.
Briefe über Dogmatismus und Kritizismus; hrsg. und eingeleitet von Otto Braun. Leipzig, F. Meiner, 1914.
20, 93 p. 19cm. (Hauptwerke der Philosophie in originalgetreuen Neudrucken. Bd. III)

Includes references to Spinoza.

Schelling, Friedrich Wilhelm Joseph von, 1775-1852.
F. W. J. Schelling's Denkmal der Schrift von den göttlichen Dingen &c. des Herrn Friedrich Heinrich Jacobi und der ihm in derselben gemachten Beschuldigung eines absichtlich täuschenden, Lüge redenden Atheismus. Tübingen, J. G. Cotta, 1812.
vi, 215 p. 21cm.

Includes references to Spinoza.

Schelling, Friedrich Wilhelm Joseph von, 1775-1854.
Friedrich Wilhelm Joseph von Schellings sämmtliche Werke. Erste Abtheilung. Zehnter Band. Stuttgart, J. G. Cotta, 1861.
viii, 453 p. 21cm.

Includes a chapter "Spinoza. Leibniz. Wolff" (p. 33-72)

Schelling, Friedrich Wilhelm Joseph von, 1775-1854.
Ideen zu einer Philosophie der Natur, als Einleitung in das Studium dieser Wissenschaft. Erster Theil. 2. durchaus verb. und mit berichtigenden Zusätzen verm. Aufl. Landshut, Ph. Krüll, 1803.
xvi, 492 p. 19cm.

No more published.
Includes a reference to Spinoza (p. 85-86)

Schelling, Friedrich Wilhelm Joseph von, 1775-1854.
Ueber die Gottheiten von Samothrace; eine Abhandlung in der zur Feyer des Allerhöchsten Namensfestes Sr. Majest. des Königes von Baiern gehaltenen öffentlichen Versammlung der Akademie der Wissenschaften, am 12. Oct. 1815 vorgelesen. Stuttgart, J. G. Cotta, 1815.
117 p. 27cm.

Includes bibliographical references.

Schirnhofer, Resa von, 1855-
Vergleich zwischen den lehren Schelling's und Spinoza's ... Zürich, Druck von Zürcher & Furrer, 1889.
vi, 85, [1] p. 22½cm.
Inaug.-diss.—Zürich.
Curriculum vitae.

1. Schelling, Friedrich Wilhelm Joseph von, 1775-1854. 2. Spinoza, Benedictus de, 1632-1677.

Schleiermacher, Friedrich Ernst Daniel, 1768-1834.
Grundlinien einer Kritik der bisherigen Sittenlehre, entworfen von F. Schleiermacher. Berlin, Im Verlage der Realschulbuchhandlung, 1803.
x, 489 p. 21cm.

Includes references to Spinoza.

E-3-a
2398

Schleiermacher, Friedrich Ernst Daniel, 1768-1834.
Friedrich Schleiermachers Reden über die Religion. Kritische Ausgabe, mit Zugrundlegung des Textes der ersten Auflage besorgt von G. C. B. Pünjer. Braunschweig, Schwetschke, 1879.
xv, 306 p.

E-3-a
2399

Schleiermacher und Spinoza. [1904]
249-250 p.

In Verein zur Abwehr des Antisemitismus. Mittheilungen, Jahrgang 14, 1904.

E-3-a
2400

[Schleiermacher, Friedrich Ernst Daniel] 1768-1834.
Über die Religion; Reden an die Gebildeten unter ihren Verächtern. Berlin, Bei Johann Friedrich Unger, 1799.
312 p. 21cm.

I. Title.

E-3-a
2401

Schleiermacher, Friedrich Ernst Daniel, 1768-1834.
Ueber die Religion; Reden an die Gebildeten unter ihren Verächtern. Mit Einleitung hrsg. von Carl Schwarz. Leipzig, F. A. Brockhaus, 1868.
xx, 254 p. 18cm. (Bibliothek der deutschen Nationalliteratur des achtzehnten und neunzehnten Jahrhunderts)

E-3-a
2402

Schleiermacher, Friedrich Ernst Daniel, 1768-1834.
Über die Religion; Reden an die Gebildeten unter ihren Verächtern. 7. Auflage. Berlin, Reimer, 1878.
xii, 242 p. 23 cm.

E-3-a
2403

Schleiermacher, Friedrich Ernst Daniel, 1768-1834.
Über die Religion; Reden an die Gebildeten unter ihren Verächtern. Zum Hundertjahr-Gedächtnis ihres ersten Erscheinens in ihrer ursprünglichen Gestalt neu herausgegeben und mit Übersichten und Vor- und Nachwort versehen von Rudolf Otto. Göttingen, Vandenhoeck & Ruprecht, 1899.
xii, 182 p. ports. 21cm.

Includes reproduction of t.-p. of 1799 ed.

E-3-a
2404

Schleiermacher, Friedrich Ernst Daniel, 1768-1834.
Werke, Auswahl mit einem Bildnis Schleiermachers und einem Geleitwort von Aug. Dorner, hrsg. und eingeleitet von Otto Braun und Joh. Bauer. Leipzig, Meiner [1910]-13.
4 v. port. (Philosophische Bibliothek, Verlag von Felix Meiner. Neue Aufl. Bd. 136-139)

Includes references to Spinoza.

E-3-a
2405

Schmid-Noerr, Friedrich Alfred, 1877-
Friedrich Heinrich Jacobis Religionsphilosophie. Heidelberg, C. Winter, 1905.
57 p. 23cm.

Habilitationsschrift - Heidelberg.

E-3-a
2406

Schmid, Friedrich Alfred
Friedrich Heinrich Jacobi, eine Darstellung seiner Persönlichkeit und seiner Philosophie als Beitrag zu einer Geschichte des modernen Wertproblems. Heidelberg, Winter, 1908.
viii, 366 p.

Includes references to Spinoza.

E-3-a
2407

Schmidt, Paul Wilhelm, 1845-1921.
Spinoza und Schleiermacher; die Geschichte ihrer Systeme und ihr gegenseitiges Verhältniss. Ein dogmengeschichtlicher Versuch. Berlin, G. Reimer, 1868.
viii, 198 p. 22cm.

Bibliographical footnotes.
Original paper cover bound in.

E-3-a 2408

Sohnehen, Wilhelm von, 1863-
Herders religiöse Weltanschauung. ‹1903›
83-93 p.

In Wartburgstimmen, Jahrgang 1, Heft 5, Nov. 1903.

DLC

E-3-a 2409

Schuetz, J W
Luzzatto über Spinoza. ‹1862›
89-90, 97-98 p.

In Ben Chananja, Jahrgang 5, 1862.

NNJ

SPECIAL COLLECTIONS SPINOZA

E-3-a 2410

Siegel, Carl, 1872-
Herder als philosoph, von dr. Carl Siegel ... Stuttgart und Berlin, Cotta, 1907.
xvi, 245, ‹1› p. 23cm.
Includes a section "Die Spinozagespräche" (p. ‹73›-82) and many other references to Spinoza.

1. Herder, Johann Gottfried von, 1744-1803.

32-4054

Library of Congress B3051.Z785 193.9

E-3-a 2411

Stewart, Dugald, 1753-1828.
The works of Dugald Stewart. Cambridge ‹Mass.› Hilliard and Brown, 1829.
7 v. 23 cm.

Includes a section on Spinoza (v. 6, p. 273-280)

E-3-a 2412

Stiedenroth, Ernst, 1794-1858.
Nova Spinozismi delineatio. Gottingae, C. Herbst, 1817.
40 p.

Thesis, Göttingen.

NN

SPECIAL COLLECTIONS SPINOZA

E-3-a 2413

Stockum, Theodorus Cornelis van, 1887-
Spinoza, Jacobi, Lessing; ein Beitrag zur Geschichte der deutschen Literatur und Philosophie im 18. Jahrhundert. Groningen, P. Noordhoff, 1916.
108 p. 25cm.

Thesis, Groningen.
Original paper cover bound in.
Volume of pamphlets.

NNC

SPECIAL COLLECTIONS SPINOZA

E-3-a 2414

Taine, Hippolyte Adolphe, 1828-1893.
De l'intelligence. 3. éd. corr. et augm. Paris, Hachette, 1878.
2 v. 19cm.

SPECIAL COLLECTIONS SPINOZA

E-3-a 2415

Trendelenburg, Friedrich Adolf, 1802-1872.
Über Spinoza's Grundgedanken und dessen Erfolg; vorgetragen in der Königlichen Akademie der Wissenschaften. Berlin, G. Bethge, 1850.
58 p. 28cm.

E-3-a 2416

Vollrath, Wilhelm, 1887-
Die Auseinandersetzung Herders mit Spinoza. Eine Studie zum Verständnis seiner Persönlichkeit. Darmstadt, Winter, 1911.
102 p.

Thesis, Giessen.

SPECIAL COLLECTIONS SPINOZA

E-3-a 2417

Volz, L
Der Einfluss Leibniz' und Spinozas auf Lessing. Heidelberg, Pädagogium Neuenheim-Heidelberg, 1910.
80 p. 25cm.

"Beilage zum Jahresbericht 1910."
Volume of pamphlets.

NNC

Vorländer, Karl, 1860-
Immanuel Kants Leben. Leipzig, F. Meiner, 1911.
xi, 223 p. port. 19cm. (Philosophische Bibliothek. 126. Bd.)

Includes a reference to Spinoza (p. 155)

Wagener, Bruno, 1890-
Über die Beziehungen Fichtes zu Spinoza und Leibniz; eine kritisch-philosophische Untersuchung. Borna-Leipzig, Druck von R. Noske, 1914.
viii, 69 p. 23cm.

Thesis, Erlangen.
Bibliography: p. [vii]-viii.

Wekhrlin, Wilhelm Ludwig, 1739-1792.
Hyperboreische Briefe. Nürnberg, Felssecker, 1788-90.
6 v. 17 cm.

Includes "Spinozism & anti-Spinozism" (v. 2, p. 171-177)

[Wizenmann, Thomas], 1759-1787.
Die Resultate der Jacobischen und Mendelssohnschen Philosophie; kritisch untersucht von einem Freywilligen ... Leipzig, bey G. J. Göschen, 1786.
1 p. l., 255 p. 16cm.

Includes references to Spinoza.
Ms. notes by Carl Gebhardt on fly-leaf.

Zerffi, George Gustavus, 1821-1892.
Immanuel Kant in his relation to modern history; paper read before the fellows of the Royal Historical Society on the 11th March 1875. London, T. Scott [1875]
28 p. 19cm.

Includes references to Spinoza.
Volume of pamphlets.

Zirngiebl, Eberhard
Friedrich Heinrich Jacobi's Leben, Dichten und Denken; ein Beitrag zur Geschichte der deutschen Literatur und Philosophie. Wien, W. Braumüller, 1867.
xiv, 367 p. port.

Includes references to Spinoza.

Zirngiebl, Eberhard
Der Jacobi-Mendelssohn'sche Streit über Lessing's Spinozismus; ein Bruchstück aus der von der philosophischen Fakultät der Ludwig-Maximilians-Universität München gekrönten Preisschrift "Quellenmässige Darstellung und Charakteristik der Philosophie von Friedr. Heinr. Jacobi". München, Druck von E. Stahl, 1861.
31 p. 21cm.

Inaugural-Abhandlung, Munich.

E-3-b
MENDELSSOHN

Akademie-Verlag, Berlin.
Moses Mendelssohn: Gesammelte Schriften, Jubiläumsausgabe. In Gemeinschaft mit F. Bamberger [et al.] hrsg. von I. Elbogen [et al.] [1929]
[8] p. port. 26cm.

A prospectus of a projected edition of Mendelssohn's works.

Auerbach, Jakob
Moses Mendelssohn und das Judenthum. [1887]
44 p.

In Zeitschrift für die Geschichte der Juden in Deutschland, Bd. 1, 1887.
Includes a reference to Spinoza (p. 33-34)

Baumgardt, David, 1890-
Spinoza und Mendelssohn; Reden und Aufsätze zu ihren Gedenktagen. [Berlin, Philo Verlag, 1932]
28 p. 25cm.

Original paper covers bound in.

Gedenkbuch für Moses Mendelssohn; herausgegeben vom Verbande der vereine für jüdische geschichte und literatur in Deutschland. Mit beiträgen von J. Bergmann ⌊und anderen⌋ Berlin, Poppelauer, 1929.
171 p. illus. (music) port. 23cm.

Includes references to Spinoza.

Guttmann, Julius, 1880-1950.
Mendelssohns Jerusalem und Spinozas Theologisch-politischer Traktat. ⌊Berlin, 1931⌋
⌊31⌋-66 p. 23cm.

Original paper covers bound in.
Presentation copy to A. S. Oko with the author's inscription and signature.
Bibliographical references included in "Anmerkungen" (p. 63-⌊67⌋)

Heydenreich, Karl Heinrich, 1764-1801.
Animadversiones in Mosis Mendelii filii refutationem placitorum Spinotzae. Scripsit et viro doctissimo Carolo Gottlob Sonntag ... summos in philosophia honores gratulatus est ... Carolus Henricus Heydenreich ... Lipsiae, Litteris Solbrigianis ⌊pref. 1787⌋
xv, ⌊1⌋ p. 24cm.

Kayserling, Meyer, 1829-1905.
Moses Mendelssohn; sein Leben und seine Werke. Nebst einen Anhange ungedruckter Briefe von und an Moses Mendelssohn. Leipzig, H. Mendelssohn, 1862.
viii, 569 p. 20cm. (Added t.-p.: Schriften hrsg. vom Institute zur Förderung der israelitischen Literatur. 7. Jahrgang: 1861-1862)

Includes a chapter "Mendelssohn und Spinoza" (p. 444-448)
Lacks series title.

Kayserling, Meyer, 1829-1905.
Moses Mendelssohn; sein Leben und Wirken. Mit authentischen Illustrationen und einem Facsimile. 2. verm. und neubearb. Aufl. Leipzig, H. Mendelssohn, 1888.
x, 548 p. plates, ports., fold. facsim. 21cm.

Includes references to Spinoza.

Kayserling, Meyer, 1829-1905.
Moses Mendelssohn's philosophische und religiöse Grundsätze, mit Hinblick auf Lessing dargestellt. Nebst einem Anhang, einige bis jetzt ungedruckte Briefe Moses Mendelssohn's enthaltend. Leipzig, H. Mendelssohn, 1856.
v, 163 p. 22cm.

Includes references to Spinoza.
Bibliographical footnotes.

Liebman, Joshua Loth, 1907-1948.
Mendelssohn shocked. ⌊1929⌋
10-13 p. 26cm.

From the Hebrew Union College monthly, vol. XVII, no. 1, Oct. 15, 1929.
Includes references to Spinoza.

Mendelssohn, Moses, 1729-1786.
An die Freunde Lessing's; ein Anhang zu Herrn Jacobi's Briefwechsel über die Lehre des Spinoza. Leipzig, F. A. Brockhaus, 1843.
36 p. (In his Gesammelte Schriften, 3. Bd.)

Mendelssohn, Moses, 1729-1786.
Moses Mendelssohn an die Freunde Lessings. Ein Anhang zu Herrn Jacobi Briefwechsel über die Lehre des Spinoza. Berlin, Bey Christian Friedrich Voss und Sohn, 1786.
xxiv, 87 p. 17cm.

Edited by J. J. Engel.
Differs from other issue of same year: p. 19, 5th line reads erzehlet.

Mendelssohn, Moses, 1729-1786.
Moses Mendelssohn an die Freunde Lessings. Ein Anhang zu Herrn Jacobi Briefwechsel über die Lehre des Spinoza. Berlin, Bey Christian Friedrich Voss und Sohn, 1786.
xxiv, 87 p. 16cm.

Edited by J. J. Engel.
Differs from other issue of same year: p. 19, 5th line reads erzählet.

Mendelssohn, Moses, 1729-1786.
Moses Mendelssohn an die Freunde Lessings. Ein Anhang zu Herrn Jacobi Briefwechsel über die Lehre des Spinoza. Berlin, bey Christian Friedrich Voss und Sohn, 1786.
xxiv, 87 p. 16cm.

Edited by J. J. Engel.
Bound with Jacobi, Friedrich Heinrich. Ueber die Lehre des Spinoza ... 1785.

Mendelssohn, Moses, 1729-1786.
Moses Mendelssohn, der Mensch und das Werk; Zeugnisse, Briefe, Gespräche, hrsg. und eingeleitet von Bertha Badt-Strauss. Berlin, Welt-Verlag, 1929.
xxiv, 264 p. plates, ports., facsim. 19cm.

Includes references to Spinoza.

1. Spinoza, Benedictus de, 1632-1677.

Mendelssohn, Moses, 1729-1786.
Moses Mendelssohn's gesammelte Schriften. Nach den Originaldrucken und Handschriften hrsg. von G. B. Mendelssohn. Leipzig, F. A. Brockhaus, 1843-45.
7 v. in 8. port. 19cm.

Includes a chapter "Spinozismus, Pantheismus, Alles ist Eins und Eins ist Alles, Widerlegung" (v. 2, p. [340]-349)

Mendelssohn, Moses, 1729-1786.
Moses Mendelssohns Morgenstunden, oder Vorlesungen über das Daseyn Gottes. Erster Theil. Berlin, Bey Christian Friedrich Voss und Sohn, 1785.
[14], [3]-330, xl p. 16cm.

No more published.
Includes a chapter on Spinoza (p. 213-234) and other references to him.

Mendelssohn, Moses, 1729-1786.
Moses Mendelssohns Morgenstunden, oder Vorlesungen über das Daseyn Gottes. Erster Theil. Frankfurt und Leipzig, 1786.
xvi, 368 p. 17cm.

No more published.
Includes a chapter on Spinoza (p. 211-232) and other references to him.

Mendelssohn, Moses, 1729-1786.
Moses Mendelssohns Morgenstunden, oder Vorlesungen über das Daseyn Gottes. Erster Theil. Veränderte Auflage. Frankfurt und Leipzig, 1790.
xvi, 368 p. 18cm.

No more published.
Includes a chapter on Spinoza (p. 211-232) and other references to him.

Mendelssohn, Moses, 1729-1786.
Phädon; oder, Über die Unsterblichkeit der Seele, in drey Gesprächen, von Moses Mendelssohn. Neueste Auflage. Frankfurt und Leipzig, 1778.
[10], 52, 222 p. front. 18cm.

Imperfect copy: pages after p. 222 lacking; page [7-8] of "Vorrede" mutilated.

Moses Mendelssohn zur 200jährigen Wiederkehr seines Geburtstages. Hrsg. von der Encyclopaedia Judaica. Berlin, L. Schneider, 1929.
137 p. plate, ports., facsim. 22cm.

Includes references to Spinoza.
Contents.--Moses Mendelssohn, von Bruno Strauss.--Die Philosophie Moses Mendelssohns, von Ernst Cassirer.--Moses Mendelssohns Wirken im Judentum, von Simon Bernfeld.--Mendelssohn Literatur, von Hermann Meyer.

Rawidowicz, Simon, 1893-
Moses Mendelssohn, the German and Jewish philosopher (in connection with his 150th "Jahrzeit", 1786-1936) [London, Taylor's Foreign Press, 1936]
472-487 p. 25cm.

"Reprint from Occident and Orient ... Gaster anniversary volume."
Includes references to Spinoza.

Rawidowitz, Simon, 1893-1957.
תרגום התהלים למנדלסון במאת
שמעון ראבידוביץ.
[1937]
283-301 p. 26cm.

Title transliterated: Targūm ha-Tĕhillīm ...
Reprint from Sefer Klausher, Tel-Aviv, 1937.

E-3-b
2448

Rawidowicz, Simon, 1893-
Zur "Jerusalem"-Polemik. Wien, 1937.
cover-title, 15 p. 24cm.

"Sonderabdruck aus der Kaminka-Festschrift ꞉p. ꞉103꞉-117꞉"

1. Mendelssohn, Moses, 1729-1786. Jerusalem.

E-3-b
2449

Rothman, Walter, 1898-
Mendelssohn's character and philosophy of religion. c1929.
43 p. 23cm.

Includes references to Spinoza.
"Reprinted from Yearbook, vol. XXXIX, The Central Conference of American Rabbis, 1929."
Author's inscription to A. S. Oko on first page.
Bibliographical footnotes.

E-3-b
2450

꞉Schulz, Johann Heinrich, called Zopfschulz꞉ 1739-1823.
Der entlarvte Moses Mendelsohn, oder Völlige Aufklärung des räthselhaften Todverdrusses des M. Mendelsohn über die Bekanntmachung des Lessingschen Atheismus von Jacobi. Amsterdam, 1786.
120 p. 19cm.

Includes references to Spinoza.

E-3-b
2451

꞉Schütz, Friedrich Wilhelm von꞉ 1758-1819.
Leben und Meinungen Moses Mendelssohn, nebst dem Geiste seiner Schriften in einem kurzen Abrisse dargestellet. Hamburg, Im Verlag der Möllerischen Buchhandlung, 1787.
꞉12꞉, 200 p. port. 16cm.

Includes references to Spinoza (p. 100-114)

E-3-b
2452

Wachstein, Bernhard, 1868-1935.
Moses Mendelssohn (Zum 200. Geburtstage, 6. September 1929) c1929.
12 p. 23cm.

Includes a reference to Spinoza.
"Sonderabdruck aus B'nai B'rith Mitteilungen für Osterreich, Heft 7, Jahrgang XXIX, September 1929."

E-3-b
2453

Walter, Hermann.
Moses Mendelssohn, critic and philosopher, by H. Walter ... New York, Bloch publishing co., 1930.
vii, 220 p. front., pl., ports. 19½cm.
Bibliography: p. 213-217.
Includes references to Spinoza.
Presentation copy to A. S. Oko with author's inscription.

1. Mendelssohn, Moses, 1729-1786.

E-3-b
2454

꞉Zöllner, J F ꞉
Ueber eine Stelle in Moses Mendelssohn's Schrift an die Freunde Lessings. ꞉1786꞉
271-275 p.

In Berlinische Monatsschrift, 7. Bd., Jan.-Jun. 1786.

E-4
1850 TO DATE

E-4-a
GENERAL

E-4-a
2455

Aimant, Bernard
Une des sources de la pensée moderne. L'évolution du spinozisme. ꞉1894꞉
260-275, 324-341 p.

In Annales de philosophie chrétienne, 64. année, 1894.

E-4-a
2456

Albert, Reinhard, 1880-
Die Philosophie Robinets. Leipzig, 1903.
xi, 83 p. 22cm.

Thesis, Leipzig.
Bibliography of Robinet's works: p. 6-8.

E-4-a
2457

Alexander, Samuel, 1859-1938.
Philosophical and literary pieces by Samuel Alexander ... edited, with a memoir, by his literary executor. London, Macmillan and co., limited, 1939.
viii, 389, ꞉1꞉ p. front. (port.) 22½ cm.
Preface signed: J. L. ꞉i. e. John Laird꞉
"Elenchus operum": p. 387-꞉390꞉
Includes two lectures on Spinoza: "Spinoza" (p. 332-348) and "Spinoza and time" (p. 349-385)
I. Laird, John, 1887- ed. II. Title.

Alexander, Samuel, 1859-1938.
Space, time, and deity, the Gifford lectures at Glasgow, 1916-1918, by S. Alexander ... London, Macmillan and co., limited, 1920.
2 v. 23 cm.
Vol. 2 includes references to Spinoza.

1. Space and time. 2. God. I. Title.

[Anderson, John Mueller] 1914-
Change and personality. [1938]
505-517 p.

Signed: John M. Anderson.
In Journal of philosophy, v. 35, 1938.
Includes references to Spinoza.

Andler, Charles, 1866-1933.
Nietzsche et ses dernières études sur l'histoire de la civilisation. [1928]
[161]-191 p. 26cm.

From Revue de métaphysique et de morale, t. XXXV, no. 2, 1928.
Includes a section on Spinoza (p. [161]-166)
Bibliographical footnotes.

Barth, Paul, 1858-1922.
Die stoa, von Paul Barth. 3. und 4., wiederum durchgesehene aufl. Stuttgart, F. Frommann, 1922.
294 p. 21½cm. (Half-title: Frommanns klassiker der philosophie ... XVI)

Includes references to Spinoza.

Barth, Paul, 1858-1922.
Die stoische Theodizee bei Philo. [1906]
14-33 p.

From Philosophische Abhandlungen; Max Heinze zum 70. Geburtstage. Berlin, Mittler, 1906.

Baumgardt, David, 1890-
Der kampf um den lebenssinn unter den vorläufern der modernen ethik, von David Baumgardt ... Leipzig, F. Meiner, 1933.
xi, 384 p. 23cm.
Bibliographical foot-notes.
Includes references to Spinoza.
Presentation copy to A. S. Oko with the author's inscription and signature.

1. Ethics. 2. Worth. 3. Life. 4. Philosophy, Modern. I. Title.

Baumann, Julius, 1837-1916.
Die lehren von raum, zeit und mathematik in der neueren philosophie nach ihrem ganzen einfluss dargestellt und beurtheilt von dr. Joh. Julius Baumann ... Berlin, G. Reimer, 1868-69.
2 v. diagrs. 23½cm.
CONTENTS.—I. Suarez, Descartes, Spinoza, Hobbes, Locke, Newton.—II. Leibniz, Leibniz und Clarke, Berkeley, Hume. Kurzer lehrbegriff von geometrie, raum, zeit und zahl. Schluss und regeln aus dem ganzen.

1. Space and time. 2. Mathematics—Philosophy. 3. Philosophy, Modern—Hist. I. Title.
[Full name: Johann Julius Baumann]

Beaussire, Émile, 1824-1889.
Antécédents de l'hégélianisme dans la philosophie française. Dom Deschamps, son système et son école d'après un manuscrit et des correspondances inédites du XVIIIe siècle. Paris, G. Baillière, 1865.
xvi, 233 p.

Includes a section "Réfutation courte et simple du système de Spinoza" (p. 39-43)

Beaussire, Émile, 1824-1889.
Les principes de la morale. Paris, Alcan, 1885.
307 p.

Bellaar Spruyt, Cornelis, 1842-1901.
Die Geschichte der Philosophie in Holland von 1878-bis 1888. [1890]
495-510 p.

In Archiv für Geschichte der Philosophie, Bd. 3, 1890.

Bellaar Spruyt, Cornelis, 1842-1901.
Geschiedenis der wijsbegeerte; naar de dictaten van wijlen Prof. C. B. Spruyt bewerkt door Ph. Kohnstamm, met medewerking van J. D. van der Waals Jr. en H. G. A. Leignes Bakhoven en met een voorbericht van I. J. de Bussy. Haarlem, V. Loosjes, 1905.
xxxvi, 600 p. port., fold. facsim. 24cm.

Includes a section on Spinoza (p. 386-388)

Benedict, Wayland Richardson, 1848-1915.
World views and their ethical implications. A syllabus of lectures in advanced ethics, by W. R. Benedict ... [Cincinnati] University press, 1902.
93 p. 19½cm. (University press, bulletin 20, series II, vol. II)

1. Ethics. I. Title.

5—30477

Library of Congress AS36.C45
——— Copy 2. BJ1025.B4
[a42b1]

NNC

Bergmann, Hugo, 1883-
ברוך שפינאזה. בירושלים, הרפ"ז
[Jerusalem, 1937]
[292]-303 p. port. 24cm.

Title transliterated: Bārūkh Shpīnōzā.
From "Mōledheth; yarnōn libhnē ha-ně ūrīm", vol. 9, 1937.

1. Spinoza, Benedictus de, 1632-1677.

NNC

Bergmann, Hugo, 1883-
שפינוזה ופני זמננו. [1920]
363-368 p.

Title transliterated: Shpinoza u-pene zemannenu.
In Ma'boroth, v. 2, 1920.

NNJ

Bergemann, Paul, 1862-
Ethik als Kulturphilosophie. Leipzig, Hofmann, 1904.
viii, 639 p. 24 cm.

Includes a section on Spinoza (p. 220-224) and other references to him.

NNC

Bergson, Henri Louis, 1859-1941.
Creative evolution, by Henri Bergson ... authorized translation by Arthur Mitchell, PH. D. New York, H. Holt and company, 1911.
xv, 370 p. 22½cm.
Includes a section "The metaphysical interpretation of modern science: Descartes, Spinoza, Leibniz" (p. 345-356)

1. Metaphysics. 2. Life. 3. Evolution. I. Mitchell, Arthur, tr.

NNC

Library of Congress B2430.B4E72 1911 11—8048
[a41m2]

Biedermann, Alois Emanuel, 1819-1885.
Ausgewählte Vorträge und Aufsätze, mit einer biographischen Einleitung von J. Kradolfer. Berlin, G. Reimer, 1885.
viii, 57, 457 p. port. 23 cm.

NNUT

Bierens de Haan, David, 1822-1895.
Bouwstoffen voor de geschiedenis der wis- en natuurkundige wetenschappen in de Nederlanden. No. XXIV, Twee zeldzame werken van Benedictus Spinoza. [1884]
78-84 p.

In K. Akademie van Wetenschappen, Amsterdam. Afdeeling Natuurkunde. Verslagen en mededeelingen, 2. reeks, 19. deel, 1884.

NNC

Bierens de Haan, Johannes Diderik, 1866-1943.
Nabeschouwing over: Het Spinozisme als ontwikkelingsleer. [1914]
186-199 p.

In Tijdschrift voor wijsbegeerte, jaargang 8, 1914.

NN

Bierens de Haan, Johannes Diderik, 1866-1943.
Vergezichten. Studies. Amsterdam, S. L. van Looy, 1921.
237 p.

MH

E-4-a
2478

Bierens de Haan, Johannes Diderik, 1866-1943.
Verweer tegen de nabeschouwing. [1914]
299-313 p.

In Tijdschrift voor wijsbegeerte, jaargang 8, 1914.

NN

E-4-a
2479

Bierens de Haan, Johannes Diderik, 1866-1943.
De weg tot het inzicht; een inleiding in de wijsbegeerte. Amsterdam, S. L. van Looy, 1909.
359 p.

Includes references to Spinoza.

NN-YC

E-4-a
2480

Bierens de Haan, Johannes Diderik, 1866-1943.
De weg tot het inzicht; een inleiding in de wijsbegeerte. 2e druk. Amsterdam, S. L. van Looy, 1917.
271 p.

Includes references to Spinoza.

MH

E-4-a
2481

Binkowitz, Aryeh Loeb
ספר חוקר עולם ... מאת אריה ליב
בינקאוויטץ מביאליסטאק. ווארשא,
בדפוס ר' נחן שריפטגיסער, תרנ"ה.
[Warsaw] 1895.
57 p. 17cm.

Title transliterated: Sefer Ḥōqēr ʿōlām.
Title also in Russian.
Includes references to Spinoza.

NNC

E-4-a
2482

[Blondel, Maurice] 1861-1949.
Un interprète de Spinoza: Victor Delbos, 1862-1916. [Hagae Comitis, 1921]
290-300 p. 22cm.

Signed: Maurice Blondel.
Cover-title: Dissertatio ex Chronici Spinozani tomo primo separatim edita.

E-4-a
2483

Boas, George, 1891-
The adventures of human thought; the major traditions of European philosophy, by George Boas ... New York and London, Harper & brothers, 1929.
5 p. l., 497, [1] p. diagr. 21½ cm.

First published under title: The major traditions of European philosophy.
Bibliography: p. 468-488.
Includes references to Spinoza.

1. Philosophy—Hist. I. Title.

B72.B65 1929a 30—2636

Library of Congress [53g½]

E-4-a
2484

Boer, Tjitze J de, 1866-1942.
Het Spinozisme van Santayana; een rede. [1928]
p. 2.

In Nieuwe Rotterdamsche courant, Juni 5, 1928.

DLC

E-4-a
2485

Bollnow, Otto Friedrich, 1903-
Die Lebensphilosophie F. H. Jacobis. Stuttgart, Kohlhammer, 1933.
viii, 254 p. 24cm. (Zweites Heft der Göttinger Forschungen; eine geisteswissenschaftliche Sammlung)

Includes references to Spinoza.

NNC

E-4-a
2486

Borelius, Johan Jakob
Den dogmatiska rationalismus strid mot den spekulativa filosofien. 1. häftet. Granskning af prof. Ribbings eristiska blad, I. Stockholm, Z. Haeggström, 1857.

MH

E-4-a
2487

Brandt, Frithiof, 1892- ed.
Den nyere filosofi: Spinoza, Hume, Rousseau, Schopenhauer, Comte, Darwin, Neitzsche. [København, Gyldendal, 1930]
233 p. port. 22cm. (Gyldendals bibliotek, no. 49)

Selections from Spinoza in Danish translation by S. V. Rasmussen: p. [17]-40.
Includes bibliographical references.

NNC

SPECIAL COLLECTIONS
SPINOZA
E-4-a
2488

Brockdorff, Cay Ludwig Georg Conrad, baron von, 1874-
Beiträge über das Verhältnis Schopenhauers zu Spinoza. Hildesheim, Druck und Verlag von G. Gerstenberg, 1900.
2 pts. in 1 v. 24cm.

Contents.--pt. 1. Revision des Urteils Schopenhauers über Spinoza auf Grund Schopenhauerscher Marginalien.--pt. 2. Vergleich der Individualitäten und der Lehren.
Bound with Rappaport, Samuel. Spinoza und Schopenhauer. 1899.

NNC

SPECIAL COLLECTIONS
SPINOZA
E-4-a
2489

Brucăr, I
Discurs asupra conceptului de filosofie a filosofiei. [Bucuresti] Societatea Română de Filosofie [pref. 1934]
107 p. 22cm.

Includes references to Spinoza.

SPECIAL COLLECTIONS
SPINOZA
E-4-a
2490

Brunschvicg, Léon, 1869-1944.
De la connaissance de soi, par Léon Brunschvicg ... Paris, F. Alcan, 1931.
3 p. l., [ix]-xi, 196 p., 2 l. 23cm. (*On cover:* Bibliothèque de philosophie contemporaine)
"Les dix chapitres de ce livre sont des leçons professées à la Sorbonne pendent l'hiver 1929-1930."—Avant-propos.
Bibliographical foot-notes.
References to Spinoza included in chapter "L'être spirituel" (p. [177]-196)
Presentation copy to Carl Gebhardt with the author's inscription and signature.
1. Consciousness. 2. Personality. I. Title.
A 32-1238 Revised
Columbia univ. Libraries for Library of Congress B2430.B77D4 [r41f2]
——— Copy 2. [159.923] 153.7

SPECIAL COLLECTIONS
SPINOZA
E-4-a
2491

Brunschvicg, Léon, 1869-1944.
Le progrès de la conscience dans la philosophie occidentale. Paris, F. Alcan, 1927.
2 v. (xxiii, 807 p.) 23cm. (Bibliothèque de philosophie contemporaine)

Includes a chapter on Spinoza (p. [162]-194) and other references to him.
Presentation copy to Carl Gebhardt with the author's inscription and signature.

E-4-a
2492

Bucke, Richard Maurice, 1837-1902.
Cosmic consciousness: a study in the evolution of the human mind, by Richard Maurice Bucke ... [4th ed., cor. and entirely re-set] New York, E. P. Dutton & company [1923]
xviii p., 1 l., 384 p. front. (port.) 25 cm.
"A list of some of the works quoted and referred to in this volume": p. [vii]-xv.
Includes a section on Spinoza (p. 276-282)
1. Consciousness. I. Title.
NNC
BF408.B8 1923 23—10521
Library of Congress [58g1]

SPECIAL COLLECTIONS
SPINOZA
E-4-a
2493

Burstein, N S
Ideas and ideals. Forward by Rabbi Professor Sir Hermann Gollancz. London, K. S. Bhat [1932]
xii, 210 p. 19cm.

Includes chapter on Spinoza.

SPECIAL COLLECTIONS
SPINOZA
E-4-a
2494

Busse, Ludwig, 1862-1907.
Die Weltanschauungen der grossen Philosophen der Neuzeit. Leipzig, B. G. Teubner, 1904.
164 p. 19cm. (Aus Natur und Geisteswelt ... 56. Bändchen)
Includes a section on Spinoza (p. 24-36)

E-4-a
2495

Caird, Edward, 1835-1908.
Essays on literature and philosophy. Glasgow, J. Maclehose, 1892.
2 v. 19 cm.

Includes a section on Spinoza (v. 2, p. 332-383) in essay "Cartesianism" and many other references to him.

SPECIAL COLLECTIONS
SPINOZA
E-4-a
2496

Camerer, Theodor, 1833-1909.
Spinoza und Schleiermacher; die kritische Lösung des von Spinoza hinterlassenen Problems. Stuttgart, J. G. Cotta'sche Buchhandlung Nachfolger, 1903.
vi, 179 p. 23cm.

E-4-a
2497

Caramella, Santino, 1902-
La formazione della filosofia giobertiana. Genova, Libreria editrice moderna, 1926.
314 p.

Includes a chapter "Tra Kant e Rosmini lo spinozismo di Gioberti" (p. 161-211)

MH

Carneri, Bartholomäus, ritter von, 1821-1909.
Entwickelung und Glückseligkeit; ethische Essays. Stuttgart, E. Schweizerbart, 1886.
469 p. 24 cm.

Chamberlain, Houston Stewart, 1855-1927.
Die Grundlagen des neunzehnten Jahrhunderts. München, F. Bruckmann, 1899.
2 v. (xvi, 1031 p.) 26cm.

Includes references to Spinoza.
Bibliographical footnotes.

Carp, J H
Carl Gebhardt en het Spinozisme. [1935]
227-238 p. 26cm.

"Overdruk uit het: Algemeen Nederlandsch tijdschrift voor wijsbegeerte en psychologie."
"Dit artikel is ontleend aan een voordracht, gehouden vanwege de Societas Spinozana in het Spinozahuis te 's-Gravenhage, ter herdenking van den op 25 Juli 1934 te Frankfurt a. M. overleden Spinozist Carl Gebhardt."
Volume of pamphlets.

Charles, Emile Auguste
Lectures de philosophie, ou, Fragments extraits des philosophes anciens et modernes, mis en ordre et annotés. Paris, Belin, 1873.
2 v. 22 cm.

Carritt, Edgar Frederick, 1876-
Morals and politics; theories of their relation from Hobbes and Spinoza to Marx and Bosanquet, by E. F. Carritt ... Oxford, The Clarendon press, 1935.
4 p. l., 216 p. 19½ cm.

1. Political ethics. I. Title.

Clark, Gordon Haddon
Readings in ethics, edited by Gordon H. Clark and T. V. Smith. New York, Crofts, 1931.
x, 405 p. 23 cm.

Cassirer, Ernst, 1874-1945.
Die Philosophie der Aufklärung. Tübingen, Mohr, 1932.
xviii, 491 p. 22 cm. (Grundriss der philosophischen Wissenschaften)
Bibliographical footnotes.
Includes a section on Spinoza (p. 247-256) and other references to him.

1. Enlightenment. 2. Philosophy, Modern. (Series)

Clemens, Ernst, 1869-
Schopenhauer und Spinoza. Leipzig, 1899.
72 p. 23cm.

Thesis, Leipzig.

Catlin, George Edward Gordon, 1896-
The story of the political philosophers, by George Catlin ... New York, London, Whittlesey house, McGraw-Hill book company, inc. [c1939]
xvii, 802 p. incl. front., diagr. ports. 24½ cm.
"Acknowledgments": p. xiii; "Bibliographical note" at end of each chapter; "Reading" at end of some of the chapters.
Includes a section on Spinoza (p. 248-254) and other references to him.

1. Political science—Hist. I. Title.

Cohen, Hermann, 1842-1918.
Der Begriff der Religion im System der Philosophie. Giessen, A. Töpelmann, 1915.
viii, 164 p. 23 cm. (Philosophische Arbeiten, 10. Bd., 1. Heft)
Includes references to Spinoza.

1. Philosophy and religion. (Series)

Cohen, Hermann, 1842-1918.
Ethik des reinen Willens. Berlin, B. Cassirer, 1904.
xvii, 641 p. 26 cm. (System der Philosophie, 2. T.)

Includes references to Spinoza.

Cohen, Morris Raphael, 1880–
Reason and nature, an essay on the meaning of scientific method, by Morris R. Cohen. New York, Harcourt, Brace and company [°1931]
xxiv, 470 p. 23½ cm.
"First edition."

Includes references to Spinoza.

1. Methodology. 2. Science—Philosophy. 3. Social sciences. I. Title.

Contemporary American philosophy; personal statements ... edited by George P. Adams and Wm. Pepperell Montague. New York, The Macmillan company, 1930.
2 v. fronts. (ports.) 22½ cm. [Library of philosophy, ed. by J. H. Muirhead]
"Principal publications" at end of each statement.

Includes a reference to Spinoza (v. 2, p. 431-433)

1. Philosophy, American. I. Adams, George Plimpton, 1882– ed. II. Montague, William Pepperell, 1873– joint ed.

Contemporary British philosophy; personal statements (first series) by J. B. Baillie, Bernard Bosanquet, C. C. Broad [and others] Edited by J. H. Muirhead. London, G. Allen & Unwin, New York, Macmillan [1924]
432 p. 22cm. (Library of philosophy, ed. by J. H. Muirhead)

Includes references to Spinoza.

Contemporary British philosophy; personal statements (first series) by J. B. Baillie, Bernard Bosanquet, C. D. Broad [and others] Edited by J. H. Muirhead. London, Allen & Unwin; New York, Macmillan [1925]
432 p. 22cm. (Library of philosophy, ed. by J. H. Muirhead)

Includes references to Spinoza.

Contemporary British philosophy; personal statements (second series) by James Ward, E. Belfort Bax, Douglas Fawcett [and others] ... Edited by J. H. Muirhead ... London, G. Allen & Unwin, ltd.; New York, The Macmillan company [1925]
3 p. l., 9-365, [1] p. 22 cm. (*Half-title:* Library of philosophy, edited by J. H. Muirhead)
Contains bibliographies.
Includes references to Spinoza.
CONTENTS.—Editor's preface to the second series.—A theistic monadism, by James Ward.—The analysis of reality, by E. Belfort Bax.—Imaginism, by Douglas Fawcett.—From idealism to realism, by

(Continued on next card)

Contemporary British philosophy ... [1925] (Card 2)

CONTENTS—Continued.

G. Dawes Hicks.—On Dawes Hicks.—On the way to a synoptic philosophy, by R. F. Alfred Hoernlé.—A realist philosophy of life, by C. E. M. Joad.—A defence of common sense, by G. E. Moore.—Philosophy as the development of the notion and reality of self-consciousness, by J. A. Smith.—Value and reality, by W. R. Sorley.—The freedom of man, by A. E. Taylor.—A biologist's philosophy, by J. Arthur Thomson.—Outline of a philosophy of religion, by Clement C. J. Webb.—Index.

1. Philosophy, English. I. Muirhead, John Henry, 1855-1940, ed.

Cornill, Adolph
Materialismus und Idealismus in ihren gegenwärtigen Entwickelungskrisen beleuchtet. Heidelberg, J. C. B. Mohr, 1858.
420 p. 21cm.

Includes a section on Spinoza (p. 346-355)

Cory, Charles Edward, 1878– *ed.*
Three philosophical studies, edited by Charles E. Cory ... St. Louis, 1931.
4 p. l., 7-81 p. 24½ cm. (Washington university studies. New series. Social and philosophical sciences. no. 3)
CONTENTS.—Spinoza and modern thought, by Lawson P. Chambers.—Existence and value, by George R. Dodson.—The realm of necessity, by Charles E. Cory.

1. Philosophy—Addresses, essays, lectures. I. Chambers, Lawson Powers. II. Dodson, George Rowland, 1865–

Cunynghame, *Sir* Henry Hardinge Samuel, 1848-1935.
Short talks upon philosophy, by Sir H. Cunynghame ... London [etc.] Constable & company limited, 1923.
4 p. l., 245, [1] p. 1 illus. 22½ cm.
Includes a chapter on Spinoza.

1. Philosophy—Addresses, essays, lectures. I. Title.

E-4-a
2518

Damme, B
Rijpe halmen byeengez. uit de werken v. Spinoza, Multatuli en Nietzsche. Rotterdam, J. Bedeaux, 1908.
ports.

UCLA

E-4-a
2523

Deutschthümler, Wilhelm
Ueber Schopenhauer zu Kant; ein kleines Geschichtsbild. Wien, Dirnböck, 1899.
136 p.

Includes a section on Spinoza (p. 35-38)

SPECIAL COLLECTIONS
SPINOZA

E-4-a
2519

De Burgh, William George, 1866-
Towards a religious philosophy, by W. G. De Burgh ... London, Macdonald & Evans, 1937.
xix, 260 p. 21½cm.

Some of the material has appeared in various periodicals. cf. Pref.
Includes references to Spinoza.

E-4-a
2524

Dewey, John, 1859-1952.
The quest for certainty: a study of the relation of knowledge and action, by John Dewey ... New York, Minton, Balch & company, 1929.
4 p. l., 3-318 p. 23 cm. (Gifford lectures. 1929)

Includes references to Spinoza.

1. Knowledge, Theory of. 2. Thought and thinking. 3. Science—Philosophy. I. Title.
BD161.D4 29—23500
Library of Congress [57w³3]

SPECIAL COLLECTIONS
SPINOZA

E-4-a
2520

Delbos, Victor, 1862-1916.
Figures et doctrines de philosophes: Socrate, Lucrèce, Marc-Aurèle, Descartes, Spinoza, Kant, Maine de Biran. Paris, Plon-Nourrit, 1918.
xii, 327 p. 19cm.

Original paper covers bound in.

SPECIAL COLLECTIONS
SPINOZA

E-4-a
2525

Dilthey, Wilhelm, 1833-1911.
Die Autonomie des Denkens, der konstruktive Rationalismus und der pantheistische Monismus nach ihrem Zusammenhang im 17. Jahrhundert. [1893]
[28]-91 p. 23cm.

"Sonderabdruck aus dem Archiv für Geschichte der Philosophie ... Band VII, Heft 1."
Includes references to Spinoza.
Original paper cover bound in.
Volume of pamphlets.

NNC

SPECIAL COLLECTIONS
SPINOZA

E-4-a
2521

Dernoscheck, Georg Alex, 1878-
Das Problem des egoistischen Perfektionismus in der Ethik Spinozas und Nietzsches. Annaberg, Druck von C. O. Schreiber, 1905.
64 p. 23cm.

Thesis, Leipzig.
"Litteraturangabe": p. [1-2]
Bound with Zinsser, August. Der ethische Intellektualismus Spinozas. 1892.

SPECIAL COLLECTIONS
SPINOZA

E-4-a
2526

Dilthey, Wilhelm, 1833-1911.
Briefwechsel zwischen Wilhelm Dilthey und dem Grafen Paul Yorck v. Wartenburg, 1877-1897. Halle (Saale) M. Niemeyer, 1923.
xi, 280 p. diagr. 24cm. (Added t.-p.: Philosophie und Geisteswissenschaften ... 1. Bd.)

Vorwort signed: Sigrid v. d. Schulenburg.
Includes references to Spinoza.

E-4-a
2522

[Dessauer, Moritz] 1842-1895.
Der Sokrates der Neuzeit [i. e. Spinoza] [1877]
148-151 p.

Signed: M. Dessauer.
In Die Gartenlaube, 1877.
An excerpt from his Der Sokrates der Neuzeit und sein Gedankenschatz.

SPECIAL COLLECTIONS
SPINOZA

E-4-a
2527

Dilthey, Wilhelm, 1833-1911.
Das Erlebnis und die Dichtung: Lessing, Goethe, Novalis, Hölderlin. Vier Aufsätze. Leipzig, B. G. Teubner, 1906.
405 p. 21cm.

Includes references to Spinoza.

Dilthey, Wilhelm, 1833–1911.
Leben Schleiermachers, von Wilhelm Diltheÿ. 1. bd. 2. aufl., vermehrt um stücke der fortsetzung aus dem nachlasse des verfassers, herausgegeben von Hermann Mulert. Berlin und Leipzig, W. de Gruÿter & co., 1922.
xxxii, 879 p. 23½cm.
No more published.
Includes a chapter "Shaftesbury and Spinoza" (p. 173-188)
1. Schleiermacher, Friedrich Ernst Daniel, 1768–1834. I. *Mulert, Hermann, 1879– ed.

Dilthey, Wilhelm, 1833-1911.
Weltanschauung und Analyse des Menschen seit Renaissance und Reformation; Abhandlungen zur Geschichte der Philosophie und Religion ... Leipzig, B. G. Teubner, 1914.
xi, 528 p. 25cm. (His Gesammelte Schriften. Bd. 2)

Includes references to Spinoza.
Manuscript notes by Carl Gebhardt.

Dilthey, Wilhelm, 1833-1911.
Weltanschauung und Analyse des Menschen seit Renaissance und Reformation; Abhandlungen zur Geschichte der Philosophie und Religion. 3. unveränderte Aufl. Leipzig, B. G. Teubner, 1923.
xi, 528 p. 25cm. (His Gesammelte Schriften, II. Bd.)

Includes references to Spinoza.

Draeger, Hans
Die deutsche Revisionsbewegung, ihre bisherige Entwicklung und künftigen Ziele. [Nowawes, Druck: Dr. Brönner, 1927?]
25 p. 23cm.

"Vortrag, gehalten auf der Reichstagung des Arbeitsausschusses Deutscher Verbände in Goslar, 5.-7. Juli 1927."
Includes reference to Spinoza (p. 23)

Dresser, Horatio Willis, 1866-1954.
Man and the divine order; essays in the philosophy of religion and in constructive idealism. New York, Putnam, 1903.
v, 448 p. 20cm.

Includes a chapter "Plotinus and Spinoza" (p. 201-222) and other references to Spinoza.

Drews, Arthur Christian Heinrich, 1865-1935.
Die deutsche Spekulation seit Kant mit besonderer Rücksicht auf das Wesen des Absoluten und die Persönlichkeit Gottes. Berlin, Maeter, 1893.
2 v.

Includes a section on Spinoza (v. 1, p. 42-47) and other references to him.

Druck, David, 1883-1943.
[New York, 1933] ר׳ לוי גינצבורג...
119 p.

Title transliterated: Reb Lewi Ginzburg.
Includes a section on Kuno Fischer and Spinoza (p. 54-56)

Drummond, James, 1835–1918.
The life and letters of James Martineau, LL. D., S. T. D., etc., by James Drummond ... and a survey of his philosophical work by C. B. Upton ... New York, Dodd, Mead and company, 1902.
2 v. fronts. (ports.) 23½ cm.
Includes a chapter on Martineau's "A study of Spinoza" (v. 2, p. 449-459) and other references to Spinoza.
1. Martineau, James, 1805–1900. I. Upton, Charles Barnes, 1831–1920, joint author.

Dumesnil, Georges Édouard, 1855–1916.
Du rôle des concepts dans la vie intellectuelle et morale; essai théorique d'après une vue de l'histoire ... Paris, Hachette et cie, 1892.
xvi, 250 p. 22½cm.
Thèse—Faculté des lettres de Paris.
Includes a section on Spinoza (p. 132-139)

1. Philosophy. 2. Reality. I. Title.

[Dunin-Borkowski, Stanislaus, Graf von] 1864-
Barockphilosophie. [1928]
[185]-202 p. 26cm.

Signed: Stanislaus v. Dunin Borkowski.
From Stimmen der Zeit, 59. Jahrgang, 3. Heft, 116. Band, Dezember 1928.
Deals with Spinoza as an example of baroque philosophy.
Bibliographical footnotes.

E-4-a
2538

Dunin-Borkowski, Stanislaus, Graf von, 1864-
Nachlese zur ältesten Geschichte des Spinozismus. [1910]
[61]-98 p. 23cm.

"Sonderabdruck aus dem Archiv für Geschichte der Philosophie ... Vierundzwanzigster Band, 1910, Heft I."

1. Spinoza, Benedictus de, 1632-1677.

E-4-a
2539

Duprat, Guillaume Léonce, 1872-
Morals: a treatise on the psycho-sociological bases of ethics. By Professor G. L. Duprat. Tr. by W. J. Greenstreet ... London and Newcastle-on-Tyne, W. Scott publishing co., ltd., 1903.
xv, 382 p. 19cm. (*Half-title:* The contemporary science series. [v. 44])
Bibliography: p. [371]-374.
Includes a section on Spinoza (p. 117-120) and other references to him.
1. Ethics, Evolutionary. 2. Social psychology. 3. Social ethics. I. Greenstreet, William John, 1861-1930, tr. II. Title.
4-5953
Library of Congress BJ1322.D9
[a38j1]

E-4-a
2540

Eleutheropulos, Abroteles, 1873-
Die Sittlichkeit und der philosophische Sittlichkeitswahn. Berlin, E. Hofmann, 1899.
viii, 135 p. 24cm. (His: Das kritische System der Philosophie. Grundlegung einer Sittenlehre (Ethik) die als Wissenschaft wird auftreten können. II. Abt.)

Original paper covers bound in.
Includes reference to Spinoza (p. 72)
Bibliographical footnotes.

E-4-a
2541

Elliot, Hugh Samuel Roger, 1881-
Modern science and the illusions of Professor Bergson, by Hugh S. R. Elliot ... With a preface by Sir Ray Lankester ... London, New York [etc.] Longmans, Green, and co., 1912.
xix, 257, [1] p. 20cm.
"It is not the purpose of the present work to furnish a detailed refutation of the philosophy of Professor Bergson. It is my purpose to investigate only those portions of it which profess to be founded on facts, and therefore to come within the province of science."—p. 1.
Includes references to Spinoza.
1. Bergson, Henri Louis, 1859-1941. 2. Science—Philosophy. 3. Knowledge, Theory of. I. Title.
12-22970
Library of Congress B2430.B43E5
[a42e1]

E-4-a
2542

Emerson, Ralph Waldo, 1803-1882.
Journals, 1820-1872, edited by Edward Waldo Emerson and Waldo Emerson Forbes. [Cambridge, Printed at the Riverside Press, 1909-14]
10 v. fronts., plates, ports., facsims. 23 cm.

Includes a reference to Spinoza (v. 10, p. 237)

E-4-a
2543

Erdmann, Benno, 1851-1921.
Bericht über neuere Philosophie bis auf Kant für die Jahre 1888 und 1889. Zweiter Teil. [1890]
[632]-646 p.

In Archiv für Geschichte der Philosophie, Bd. 3, 1890.
Includes a review of Spinozas Entwicklungsgang, besonders nach seinen Briefen geschildert, by A. Baltzer (p. 636-639)

E-4-a
2544

Essays in philosophy, by seventeen doctors of philosophy of the University of Chicago, edited by Thomas Vernor Smith and William Kelley Wright. Chicago, The Open Court Pub. Co. [c1929]
xvi, 337 p. 23 cm.

Reference to Spinoza (p. 297) included in "The grand strategy of evolution" by John Wild.

E-4-a
2545

Fairbairn, Andrew Martin, 1838-1912.
Studies in the philosophy of religion and history. New York, Lovell, Adam, Wesson [pref. 1876]
348 p. 20 cm.

Includes a section on Spinoza (p. 346-348)

E-4-a
2546

Falkenheim, Hugo, 1866-
Spinoza und Kuno Fischer. [Hagae Comitis, 1922]
220-232 p. 22cm.

Cover-title: Dissertatio ex Chronici Spinozani tomo secundo separatim edita.

E-4-a
2547

193Sp4
DR584
Festschrift für Alois Riehl von Freunden und Schülern zu seinem siebzigsten Geburtstage dargebracht. Halle, Niemeyer, 1914.
v, 522 p. port. 24cm.

Includes an essay "Spinozas Lebensgefühl" by Gustav Theodor Richter (p. [223]-247)

Festschrift Theodor Gomperz dargebracht zum siebzigsten Geburtstage am 29. März 1902, von Schülern, Freunden, Collegen. Wien, A. Hölder, 1902.
iv, 499 p. port. illus., fold. plate, facsims. 27cm.

Includes an essay "Zur Interpretation Spinoza's" by Friedrich Jodl (p. 342-350)

Fischer, Kuno, 1824-1907.
Das Interdict meiner Vorlesungen und die Anklage des Herrn Schenkel, Direktor des Heidelberger Prediger-Seminars, in der Darmstädtischen Kirchen-Zeitung. Mannheim, Bassermann & Mathy, 1854.
84 p. 22cm.

Includes references to Spinoza.

Feuerlein, Emil.
Die philosophische sittenlehre in ihren geschichtlichen hauptformen, von Emil Feuerlein ... Tübingen, L. F. Fues, 1857-59.
2 v. 21^{cm}.

Contents.— 1. t. Die sittenlehre des alterthums.— 2. t. Die sittenlehre der neueren culturvölker.
Vol. 2 includes references to Spinoza.

1. Title.

Fischer, Kuno, 1824-1907.
Mein Lebenslauf; Erinnerungen von Kuno Fischer, 1905 während seiner Krankheit diktiert. [1909]
37 l. 29cm.

On cover: Zum 23. Juli 1909.
Includes references to Spinoza.

Feyerabend, Wilhelm, 1884-
Schopenhauers Verhältnis zu Spinoza. Bonn, 1910.
105 p. 23cm.

Thesis, Bonn.
Bibliography: p. [5]-7.

Bound with Rappaport, Samuel. Spinoza und Schopenhauer. 1899.

Fischer, Ludwig, 1867-
Die natürliche Ordnung unseres Denkens und der Zusammenhang der Weltanschauungen. Leipzig, Meiner, 1927.
xi, 359 p. 24 cm. (Annalen der Philosophie. Beiheft, no. 7)

Includes references to Spinoza (p. 210-213)

Fiorentino, Francesco, 1834-1884.
La filosofia contemporanea in Italia; risposta al professore Francesco Acri. Napoli, D. Morano, 1876.
xv, 474 p.

Includes a section on Spinoza (p. 257-329)

Fisher, Mitchell Salem, 1903-
An excursion for sages: how through the centuries philosophers have sought the way of better understanding. [1928]
p. 766, 822-823, 837. ports. 33cm.

From The American Hebrew, April 6, 1928.
Includes references to Spinoza (p. 823 and 837) and a portrait of Spinoza (p. 766)

Fischer, Kuno, 1824-1907.
Die hundertjährige Gedächtnissfeier der Kantischen Kritik der reinen Vernunft. Johann Gottlieb Fichtes Leben und Lehre. Spinozas Leben und Charakter. 2. Aufl. Heidelberg, C. Winter, 1892.
[287]-378 p. 23^{cm}. (His Philosophische Schriften. 3)

Fleischer, Julius Wilhelm
Pierre Poiret als Philosoph; ein Beitrag zur Geschichte der Philosophie. [Falkenstein, Tischendorf, 1893]
53 p. 23 cm.

Thesis, Erlangen.
Includes references to Spinoza (p. 51-52)

SPECIAL COLLECTIONS SPINOZA E-4-a 2558

Fluegel, Maurice.
Philosophy, Qabbala and Vedānta. Comparative metaphysics and ethics, rationalism and mysticism, of the Jews, the Hindus and most of the historic nations, as links and developments of one chain of universal philosophy. Baltimore, H. Fluegel & Co., 1902.
v. 2.

Includes references to Spinoza.

E-4-a 2563

Fraser, Alexander Campbell, 1819-1914.
Biographia philosophica: a retrospect by Alexander Campbell Fraser ... Edinburgh and London, W. Blackwood and sons, 1904.
xiv, 335, [1] p. 23cm.

CONTENTS.—In the land of Lorne: early memories.—In Edinburgh: the enigma of the universe.—An ecclesiastical digression.—Return to philosophy: 'North British review.'—In the chair of Hamilton.—The University of Edinburgh.—Academical vacations.—In tenebris lux.
Includes references to Spinoza.

Library of Congress B1585.F73B4 1904 5—4440 [a34b1]

SPECIAL COLLECTIONS SPINOZA E-4-a 2559

Flügel, Otto, 1842-1914.
Die Probleme der Philosophie und ihre Lösungen; historisch-kritisch dargestellt. 3. Aufl. Cöthen, O. Schulze, 1893.
xiv, 272 p. 23cm.

Includes references to Spinoza.
Bibliographical footnotes.

E-4-a 2564

Fraser, Alexander Campbell, 1819-1914.
Rational philosophy in history and in system; an introduction to a logical and metaphysical course. Edinburgh, Constable, 1858.
xi, 143 p.

Includes references to Spinoza.

E-4-a 2560

Forest, Aimé
La réalité concrète et la dialectique. Paris, Vrin, 1931.
iii, 131 p. 23 cm.

Thesis, Paris, 1930.
Includes a reference to Spinoza (p. 50-52)

E-4-a 2565

[Fraser, Alexander Campbell] 1819-1914.
M. Saisset and Spinoza. [1863]
454-489 p.

In The North British review, v. 38, Edinburgh, 1863.
Includes a discussion of six works by Saisset.

E-4-a 2561

Forsberg, N A
Jemförande betraktelse af Spinozas och Malebranches metafysiska principer. Upsala, Edquist, 1864.
29 p. 23 cm.

Thesis, Upsala.

SPECIAL COLLECTIONS SPINOZA E-4-a 2566

Freudenthal, Jacob, 1839-1907.
Beiträge zur Geschichte der englischen Philosophie. [1891?]
[450]-477 p. 22cm.

First part of essay only.
"Sonderabdruck aus dem Archiv für Geschichte der Philosophie, IV. Band, 3. Heft. 1891."
Bibliographical footnotes.

E-4-a 2562

Fränkel, Nachman, 1833-188-?
ספר בקורת הדעות והאמונות.
Ein Kriterium der Vernunft- und Glaubenserkenntnisse. Drohobycz, A. H. Żupnik, 1901.
142 p.

Title transliterated: Sefer bikoreth ha-de'oth ...
Includes three chapters on Spinoza and other references to him.

NNJ

SPECIAL COLLECTIONS SPINOZA E-4-a 2567

Freudenthal, Jacob, 1839-1907.
[Pamphlets on philosophical subjects. 1860-91]
19 pamphlets in 1 v. 24cm.

Contents.--Der Gottesbegriff bei den Griechen und bei den Hebräern. [1865]--Ueber Princip und Gebiet der Präsumtionen nach talmudischer Lehre. 1860.--Eine Paraphrase des Erasmus von Rotterdam. [1868]--Glauben und Wissen: Vortrag. [1887]--Ueber die wissenschaftliche Thätigkeit Dr. M. Joels. [1890]--What is the original

NNC

CONTINUED ON NEXT CARD

Freudenthal, Jacob, 1839-1907. ₍Pamphlets on philosophical subjects. 1860-91₎ (Card 2)

language of the Wisdom of Solomon? ₍1891₎--Are there traces of Greek philosophy in the Septuagint? ₍1890₎--Johann Ludwig Havenreuter ₍und₎ Goclenius, Rudolph G., der ältere, aus der Allgem. deutschen Biographie abgedruckt. ₍1880?₎--Ueber den Begriff des Wortes Φαντασια bei Aristoteles. 1863.--Zur Kritik und Exegese von Aristoteles' Parva naturalia. 2 pts. ₍1870₎ --Zu Aristoteles De memoria 2. 452 a 17f.

CONTINUED ON NEXT CARD

Freudenthal, Jacob, 1839-1907.
Ueber die wissenschaftliche Thätigkeit Dr. M. Joels. ₍1890₎
589-592 p. 24cm. (In his ₍Pamphlets on philosophical subjects. 1860-91₎)

From Allgemeine Zeitung des Judenthums. 54. Jahrg., Nr. 46, 27. November 1890.
Includes references to Spinoza.

Freudenthal, Jacob, 1839-1907. ₍Pamphlets on philosophical subjects. 1860-91₎ (Card 3)

₍1883₎--Zur Geschichte der Anschauungen über die jüdisch-hellenistische Religionsphilosophie: Vortrag. ₍1869?₎--Zu Proklus und dem Jüngeren Olympiodor. ₍1881₎--Zu Phavorinus und der mittelalterlichen Florilegienlitteratur. ₍187-?₎ --Ueber die Lebenszeit des Neuplatonikers Proklus. ₍188-?₎--Zur Lehre des Xenophanes. ₍1888₎ --Spinoza und die Scholastik. ₍1887₎--Zur Beurtheilung der Scholastik. ₍1889₎--Beiträge

CONTINUED ON NEXT CARD

₍Fromer, Jakob₎ 1865-
Die Erneuung der Philosophie. ₍1913₎
355-364 p. 22cm.

Signed: Jakob Fromer.
From Die Zukunft, 21. Jahrg., nr. 50, 13. September 1913.
Includes references to Spinoza.

Freudenthal, Jacob, 1839-1907. ₍Pamphlets on philosophical subjects. 1860-91₎ (Card 4)

zur Geschichte der englischen Philosophie. 3 pts. ₍1891₎

Funck-Brentano, Théophile, 1830-1906.
Les sciences humaines, philosophie, médecine, morale, politique: la philosophie. Paris, Lacroix, 1868.
viii, ₍5₎-538 p.

Includes a section on Spinoza (p. 141-152)

Freudenthal, Jacob, 1839-1907.
Spinoza und die Scholastik. ₍1887₎
₍85₎-138 p. 23cm.

From Philosophische Aufsätze, Eduard Zeller zu seinem fünfzigjährigen Doctor-Jubiläum gewidmet.
Volume of pamphlets.

1. Spinoza, Benedictus de, 1632-1677.

Garello, Luigi
Levjathan. Richerche sulla natura morale dell'uomo. Torino, Bocca, 1910.
xvi, 429 p. 21 cm.

Includes a reference to Spinoza (p. 128-129)

Freudenthal, Jacob, 1839-1907.
Spinoza und die Scholastik. ₍1887₎
₍85₎-138 p. 24cm. (In his ₍Pamphlets on philosophical subjects. 1860-91₎)

From Philosophische Aufsätze, Eduard Zeller zu seinem fünfzigjährigen Doctor-Jubiläum gewidmet, 1887.

1. Spinoza, Benedictus de, 1632-1677.

₍Gebhardt, Carl₎ 1881-1934.
Dr. Willem Meijer. ₍Hagae Comitis, 1926₎
233-245 p. port. 23cm.

Signed: Carl Gebhardt.
Cover-title: Dissertatio ex Chronici Spinozani tomo quarto separatim edita.
Includes references to Spinoza.

Gebhardt, Carl, 1881-1934.
Schopenhauer gegen Augustinus. ₍1931₎
₍263₎-321 p. 23cm.

"Sonderdruck aus: Achtzehntes Jahrbuch der Schopenhauer-Gesellschaft, 1931."
Includes passages from Augustinus' De civitate Dei and Schopenhauer's critical remarks in Latin, with a German translation of both.

Gefen, Shem-Tob
תורת הנבואה הטהורה; או, הפלוסופיה
המתמתית של האין-סוף; מסה מתמתית המב-
ססת את הזיונות המכלל על סגלות המתמתי-
ות של האין-סוף במאת שם-טוב גפן.
במאמר שני: עיון בנבואה ובמופתים
קאירה, דפוס חיים ויזל, ה'תרפ"ג.
₍Cairo, 1923₎
cover-title, 57-128 p. 22cm.

Title transliterated: Tōrath ha-nĕvūʾā
...

CONTINUED ON NEXT CARD

Gefen, Shem-Tob תורת הנבואה
הטהורה ... ₍1923₎ (Card 2)

Title also in French: Philosophie mathématique de l'infini; essai mathématique basant les phénomènes de l'univers sur les propriétés mathématiques de l'infini.

1. Infinite.

Gentile, Giovanni, 1875-1944.
Rosmini e Gioberti. ₍1899₎
xii, 318 p.

In Pisa. Scuola normale e superiore. Annali; Filosofia e filologia, v. 13, 1899.
Includes references to Spinoza.

Gentile, Giovanni, 1875-1944.
Rosmini e Gioberti; saggio storico sulla filosofia italiana del Risorgimento. 2. ed. riveduta. Firenze, Sansoni, 1955.
xix, 326 p. (His Opere complete, vol. XVIII)

Includes references to Spinoza.

Gentile, Giovanni, 1875-1944.
Studi sul rinascimento. 2. ed. riveduta e accresciuta. Firenze, G. C. Sansoni, 1936.
311 p. 23cm. (His Opere complete, v. 10)

Includes references to Spinoza.
Bibliographical footnotes.

Gentile, Giovanni, 1875-1944.
Studi vichiani. Messina, G. Principato, 1915.
4 p. l., 458 p. 22cm. (Studi filosofici, diretti da Giovanni Gentile. III)

Includes references to Spinoza.
Bibliography: verso of 4th prelim. leaf.

Gentile, Giovanni, 1875-1944.
Studi Vichiani. 2. ed. riveduta ed accresciuta. Firenze, Le Monnier, 1927.
viii, 379 p. 23 cm. (Studi filosofici, diretti da Giovanni Gentile. 2. serie, I)

Includes references to Spinoza.

Glossner, Michael, b. 1837.
Zur Frage nach dem Einfluss der Scholastik auf die neuere Philosophie. ₍1889₎
486-493 p.

In Divus Thomas; Jahrbuch für Philosophie und spekulative Theologie, Bd. 3, 1889.
With reference to Spinoza und die Scholastik, by Jacob Freudenthal.

Golther, Ludwig von, 1823-1876.
Der moderne Pessimismus. Studie aus dem Nachlass des Staatsministers Dr. Ludwig von Golther. Mit einem Vorwort von Friedrich Theodor Vischer. Leipzig, F. A. Brockhaus, 1878.
xi, 224 p. 22cm.

Goltz, Alexander Wilhelm, Freiherr von der, 1800-1870.
Thomas Wizenmann, der Freund Friedrich Heinrich Jacobi's, in Mittheilungen aus seinem Briefwechsel und handschriftlichen Nachlasse, wie nach Zeugnissen von Zeitgenossen. Ein Beitrag zur Geschichte des innern Glaubenskampfes christlicher Gemüther in der zweiten Hälfte des 18. Jahrhunderts. Gotha, F. A. Perthes, 1859.
2 v. in 1 port., facsim.

Includes references to Spinoza.

Görland, Albert, 1869-
Religionsphilosophie als Wissenschaft aus dem Systemgeiste des kritischen Idealismus. Berlin, W. de Gruyter, 1922.
v, 334 p. 22 cm.

Includes a section on Spinoza (p. 274-276)

Grabo, Carl Henry, 1881-1955.
Spinoza and Shelley. [1942]
43-50 p. 28cm.

From the Chicago Jewish forum, vol. 1, no. 1, Fall, 1942.

Graham, William, 1839-1911.
English political philosophy from Hobbes to Maine. New York, Holt, 1899.
xxx, 415 p. 21 cm.

Graham, William, 1839-1911.
English political philosophy from Hobbes to Maine. London, Arnold, 1919.
xxx, 415 p. 21 cm.

Green, Thomas Hill, 1836-1882.
Works of Thomas Hill Green, ed. by R. L. Nettleship. London and New York, Longmans, Green, 1885-88.
3 v. port. 23 cm.

Includes a section on Spinoza (v. 2, p. 355-365) and other references to him.

Griffin, Edward Herrick, 1843-1929.
A comparison of Spinoza's "Ethics" and Spencer's "First principles". [1908]
101-102 p.

In The Psychological bulletin, v. 5, 1908.

Groeger, E M R
Expositio, ideam substantiae in recentiori philosophiae propius accessisse ad ideam subjecti. Vratislaviae, Typis Leopoldi Freund [1850?]
26 p.

Grunwald, Max, 1871-
Boullainvilliers. [1896]
165-168 p.

In Archiv für Geschichte der Philosophie, Bd. 9., 1896.
Includes references to works about Spinoza.

[H., F.]
Der Erlöser vom Egoismus [i.e. Spinoza]
Aus dem "Neuen Blatt". [1878]
11-14 p.

In Erziehungsblätter für Schule und Haus, Bd. 5, 1878.

E-4-a
2598

Hamberger, Julius
Die Cardinalpunkte der Franz Baader'schen Philosophie. Stuttgart, J. F. Steinkopf, 1855.
47 p. 20cm.

Bound with Hoffmann, Franz. Franz Baader im Verhältnisse zu Spinoza, Leibniz, Kant ... 1851.

E-4-a
2603

Hartmann, Eduard von, 1842-1906.
Zur Geschichte und Begründung des Pessimismus. 2., erweiterte Aufl. Leipzig, H. Haacke ₍1892₎
xxiii, 373 p. 22cm.

E-4-a
2599

Hamberger, Julius
Die Fundamentalbegriffe von Franz Baader's Ethik, Politik und Religions-Philosophie. Stuttgart, J. F. Steinkopf, 1858.
50 p. 20cm.

Bound with Hoffmann, Franz. Franz Baader im Verhältnisse zu Spinoza, Leibniz, Kant ... 1851.

E-4-a
2604

Hartshorne, Charles, 1897-
Beyond humanism; essays in the new philosophy of nature, by Charles Hartshorne ... Chicago, New York, Willett, Clark & company, 1937.
xiv p., 1 l., 324 p. 20 cm.
Bibliographical references in "Notes" appended to each chapter except the last.
Includes a section on Spinoza (p. 5-7) and other references to him.

1. Humanism—20th cent. 2. Religion—Philosophy. 3. Philosophy of nature. I. Title.

NNUT
B821.H36 144 38—11150
Library of Congress ₍53q1₎

E-4-a
2600

193Sp4
DH145

Hannequin, Arthur, 1856-1905.
Études d'histoire des sciences et d'histoire de la philosophie. Avec une préface de R. Thamin et une introduction de J. Grosjean. Paris, F. Alcan, 1908.
2 v. in 1. port. 24cm. (Bibliothèque de philosophie contemporaine)

Includes a chapter "Fragment d'une étude sur Spinoza" (v. 2, p. ₍1₎-16)

E-4-a
2605

Hazard, Paul, 1878-1944.
La crise de la conscience européenne (1680-1715). Paris, Boivin ₍1935₎
3 v. plates, ports. 23 cm.

Includes a section on Spinoza (v. 1, p. 183-195) with a portrait (v. 1, p. 184), and other references to him.

E-4-a
2601

Harte, Frederick Edward, 1872-
The philosophical treatment of divine personality from Spinoza to Hermann Lotze. With a foreword by Herbert L. Stewart. London, C. H. Kelly ₍1913₎
156 p.

Thesis, Queen's University, Belfast.

OCH

E-4-a
2606

Heinemann, Frederick Henry, 1889-
Neue wege der philosophie; geist, leben, existenz; eine einführung in die philosophie der gegenwart, von Fritz Heinemann ... Leipzig, Quelle & Meyer, 1929.
3 p. l., ₍ix₎-xxviii, 434 p. 24cm.

"Literatur": p. ₍411₎-417.
Includes references to Spinoza.

E-4-a
2602

Hartmann, Eduard von, 1842-1906.
Philosophie des Unbewussten. 7., erweiterte Aufl. Berlin, C. Duncker, 1876.
2 v. in 1. 23cm.

Vol. 2 includes references to Spinoza (p. 453 and p. 458)

E-4-a
2607

Heinrich, Wilhelm
Johannes Scotus Eriugena i Spinoza. ₍1910₎
53 p.

In Akademija Umiejetności, Krakow. Wydział historyczno-filozoficzny. Rozprawy, s. 2, t. 28, 1910.

NN

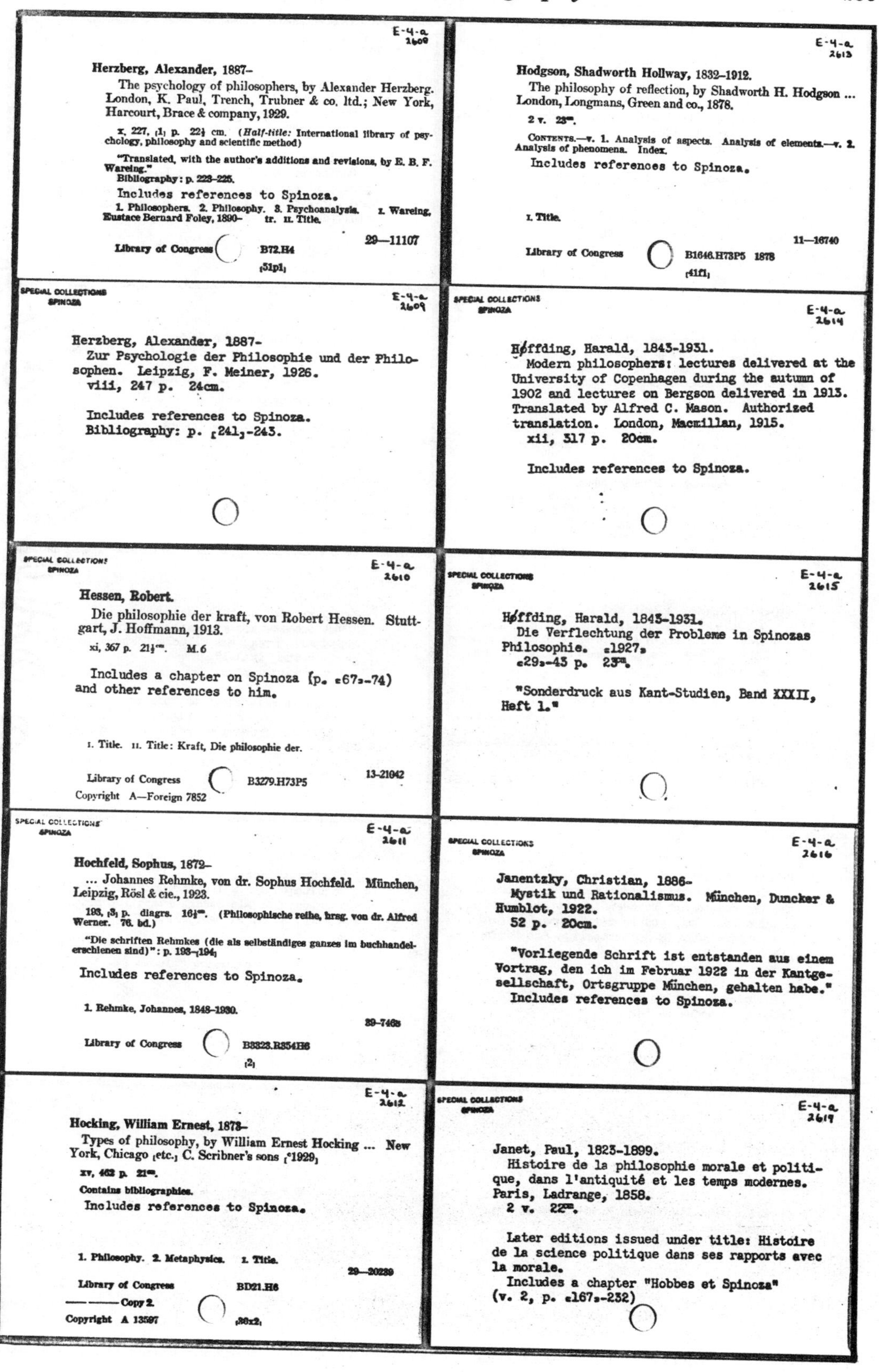

E-4-a
2608

Herzberg, Alexander, 1887-
The psychology of philosophers, by Alexander Herzberg. London, K. Paul, Trench, Trubner & co. ltd.; New York, Harcourt, Brace & company, 1929.
x, 227, [1] p. 22½ cm. (*Half-title:* International library of psychology, philosophy and scientific method)
"Translated, with the author's additions and revisions, by E. B. F. Wareing."
Bibliography: p. 223-225.
Includes references to Spinoza.
1. Philosophers. 2. Philosophy. 3. Psychoanalysis. I. Wareing, Eustace Bernard Foley, 1890- tr. II. Title.
Library of Congress B72.H4 29—11107
[51p1]

SPECIAL COLLECTIONS
SPINOZA
E-4-a
2609

Herzberg, Alexander, 1887-
Zur Psychologie der Philosophie und der Philosophen. Leipzig, F. Meiner, 1926.
viii, 247 p. 24cm.
Includes references to Spinoza.
Bibliography: p. [241]-243.

SPECIAL COLLECTIONS
SPINOZA
E-4-a
2610

Hessen, Robert.
Die philosophie der kraft, von Robert Hessen. Stuttgart, J. Hoffmann, 1913.
xi, 367 p. 21½cm. M.6
Includes a chapter on Spinoza (p. [67]-74) and other references to him.
I. Title. II. Title: Kraft, Die philosophie der.
Library of Congress B3279.H73P5 13-21042
Copyright A—Foreign 7852

SPECIAL COLLECTIONS
SPINOZA
E-4-a
2611

Hochfeld, Sophus, 1872-
... Johannes Rehmke, von dr. Sophus Hochfeld. München, Leipzig, Rösl & cie., 1923.
193, [3] p. diagrs. 16½cm. (Philosophische reihe, hrsg. von dr. Alfred Werner. 76. bd.)
"Die schriften Rehmkes (die als selbständiges ganzes im buchhandel erschienen sind)": p. 193-[194]
Includes references to Spinoza.
1. Rehmke, Johannes, 1848-1930.
Library of Congress B3323.R354H6 39-7468
[2]

E-4-a
2612

Hocking, William Ernest, 1873-
Types of philosophy, by William Ernest Hocking ... New York, Chicago [etc.] C. Scribner's sons [c1929]
xv, 462 p. 21cm.
Contains bibliographies.
Includes references to Spinoza.
1. Philosophy. 2. Metaphysics. I. Title.
Library of Congress BD21.H6 29—20239
——— Copy 2.
Copyright A 13597 [30x2]

E-4-a
2613

Hodgson, Shadworth Hollway, 1832-1912.
The philosophy of reflection, by Shadworth H. Hodgson ... London, Longmans, Green and co., 1878.
2 v. 23cm.
Contents.—v. 1. Analysis of aspects. Analysis of elements.—v. 2. Analysis of phenomena. Index.
Includes references to Spinoza.
I. Title.
Library of Congress B1646.H73P5 1878 11—16740
[41f1]

SPECIAL COLLECTIONS
SPINOZA
E-4-a
2614

Høffding, Harald, 1843-1931.
Modern philosophers: lectures delivered at the University of Copenhagen during the autumn of 1902 and lectures on Bergson delivered in 1913. Translated by Alfred C. Mason. Authorized translation. London, Macmillan, 1915.
xii, 317 p. 20cm.
Includes references to Spinoza.

SPECIAL COLLECTIONS
SPINOZA
E-4-a
2615

Høffding, Harald, 1843-1931.
Die Verflechtung der Probleme in Spinozas Philosophie. [1927]
[29]-43 p. 23cm.
"Sonderdruck aus Kant-Studien, Band XXXII, Heft 1."

SPECIAL COLLECTIONS
SPINOZA
E-4-a
2616

Janentzky, Christian, 1886-
Mystik und Rationalismus. München, Duncker & Humblot, 1922.
52 p. 20cm.
"Vorliegende Schrift ist entstanden aus einem Vortrag, den ich im Februar 1922 in der Kantgesellschaft, Ortsgruppe München, gehalten habe."
Includes references to Spinoza.

SPECIAL COLLECTIONS
SPINOZA
E-4-a
2617

Janet, Paul, 1823-1899.
Histoire de la philosophie morale et politique, dans l'antiquité et les temps modernes. Paris, Ladrange, 1858.
2 v. 22cm.
Later editions issued under title: Histoire de la science politique dans ses rapports avec la morale.
Includes a chapter "Hobbes et Spinoza" (v. 2, p. [167]-232)

E-4-a 2618

Janet, Paul, 1823-1899.
Histoire de la philosophie; les problèmes et les écoles, par Paul Janet ₍et₎ Gabriel Séailles. Paris, Delagrave, 1887.
iii, 1084 p. 22 cm.

Includes many references to Spinoza.

E-4-a 2619

Janet, Paul ~~Alexandre René~~, 1823-1899.
Histoire de la science politique dans ses rapports avec la morale, par Paul Janet ... 3. éd., rev., remaniée et considérablement augm. ... Paris, F. Alcan, 1887.
2 v. 22ᶜᵐ.

Includes a section on Spinoza (v. 2, p. 248-260) and references to him in "Index bibliographique" (v. 2, p. 761)

1. Political science—Hist. 2. Political ethics.

A 11—2655

Chicago. Univ. Library for Library of Congress JA81.J33 ₍a41e1₎

E-4-a 2620

Janet, Paul ~~Alexandre René~~, 1823-1899.
A history of the problems of philosophy, by Paul Janet ... & Gabriel Séailles; tr. by Ada Monahan; ed. by Henry Jones ... London, New York, Macmillan and co., limited, 1902.
2 v. 22½ cm.

CONTENTS.—vol. I. Introduction. pt. I. Psychology.—vol. II. pt. II. Ethics. pt. III. Metaphysics. pt. IV. Theodicy.
Vol. 2 includes many references to Spinoza.

1. Philosophy—Hist. I. Séailles, Gabriel, 1852-1922, joint author. II. Jones, Sir Henry, 1852-1922, ed. III. Monahan, Ada, tr.

B77.J3 3—12903

Library of Congress ₍53a1₎

SPECIAL COLLECTIONS SPINOZA E-4-a 2621

Jelinek, Ludwig
Kritische Geschichte der modernen Philosophie und Begründung der Nothwendigkeit der Schaffung einer neuen "Philosophie der Zukunft". Zdolbunow in Russland, Im Selbstverlage des Verfassers ₍1908₎
68 p. 21cm.

Includes a section on Spinoza (p. 17-20) and other references to him.

E-4-a 2622

Jerusalem, Wilhelm, 1854-1923.
Jerusalem, 1924. מבוא לתורת הפילוסופיה.
449 p.

Title transliterated: Mevoʿ letorath hapilosofiyah.
Includes references to Spinoza.

NNJ

SPECIAL COLLECTIONS SPINOZA E-4-a 2623

Jodl, Friedrich, 1849-1914.
Geschichte der Ethik in der neueren Philosophie. Stuttgart, J. G. Cotta, 1882-89.
2 v. 23ᶜᵐ.

Includes references to Spinoza.
Contents.--1. Bd. Bis zum Ende des 18. Jahrhunderts; mit einer Einleitung über die antike und christliche Ethik.--2. Bd. Kant und die Ethik im 19. Jahrhundert.

SPECIAL COLLECTIONS SPINOZA E-4-a 2624

Jodl, Friedrich, 1849-1914.
Ludwig Feuerbach. Stuttgart, F. Fromanns Verlag (E. Hauff) 1904.
135 p. port. 22ᶜᵐ. (Fromanns Klassiker der Philosophie, 27)

Includes references to Spinoza (p. 1)

SPECIAL COLLECTIONS SPINOZA E-4-a 2625

Jodl, Friedrich, 1849-1914.
Vom Lebenswege; gesammelte Vorträge und Aufsätze. Hrsg. von Wilhelm Börner. Stuttgart, Cotta, 1916-17.
2 v. port. 23cm.

Includes references to Spinoza.
"Verzeichnis der wichtigsten Veröffentlichungen von Friedrich Jodl": v. 2, p. ₍697₎-705.

SPECIAL COLLECTIONS SPINOZA E-4-a 2626

Joël, Karl, 1864-
Wandlungen der Weltanschauung; eine Philosophiegeschichte als Geschichtsphilosophie. Tübingen, J. C. B. Mohr, 1928-32.
v. 1-2¹⁻⁷.

Includes a section on Spinoza (v. 1, p. 492-515)

E-4-a 2627

Jong, Karel Hendrik Eduard de, 1872-
J. B. Morinus en Spinoza. ₍1921₎
556-560 p.

In De Nieuwe gids, jaargang 36, 1921.

NN

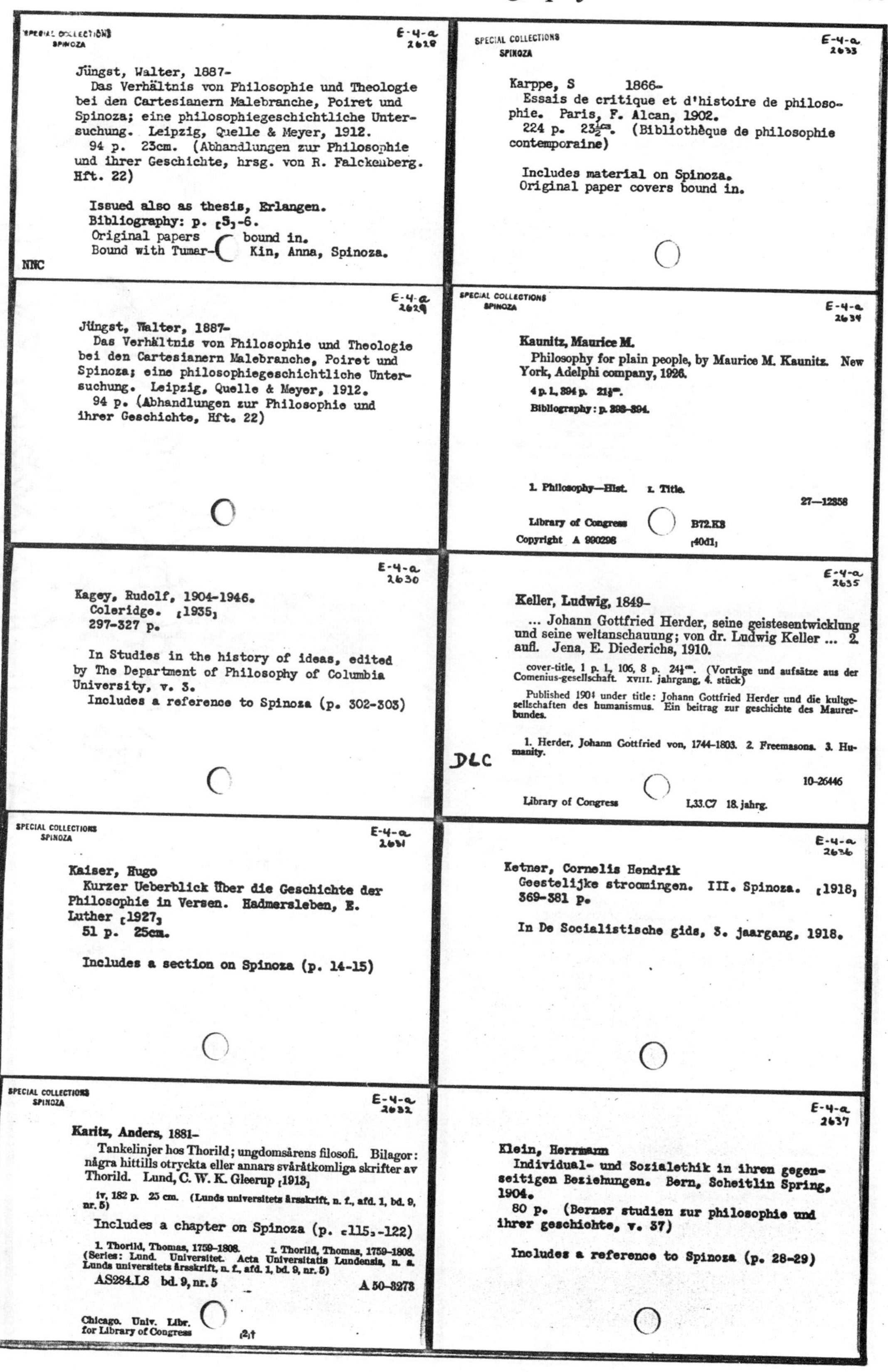

E-4-a
2628

Jüngst, Walter, 1887-
Das Verhältnis von Philosophie und Theologie bei den Cartesianern Malebranche, Poiret und Spinoza; eine philosophiegeschichtliche Untersuchung. Leipzig, Quelle & Meyer, 1912.
94 p. 23cm. (Abhandlungen zur Philosophie und ihrer Geschichte, hrsg. von R. Falckenberg. Hft. 22)

Issued also as thesis, Erlangen.
Bibliography: p. [5]-6.
Original papers bound in.
Bound with Tumarkin, Anna, Spinoza.
NNC

E-4-a
2629

Jüngst, Walter, 1887-
Das Verhältnis von Philosophie und Theologie bei den Cartesianern Malebranche, Poiret und Spinoza; eine philosophiegeschichtliche Untersuchung. Leipzig, Quelle & Meyer, 1912.
94 p. (Abhandlungen zur Philosophie und ihrer Geschichte, Hft. 22)

E-4-a
2630

Kagey, Rudolf, 1904-1946.
Coleridge. [1935]
297-327 p.

In Studies in the history of ideas, edited by The Department of Philosophy of Columbia University, v. 3.
Includes a reference to Spinoza (p. 302-303)

E-4-a
2631

Kaiser, Hugo
Kurzer Ueberblick über die Geschichte der Philosophie in Versen. Hadmersleben, E. Luther [1927]
51 p. 25cm.

Includes a section on Spinoza (p. 14-15)

E-4-a
2632

Karitz, Anders, 1881-
Tankelinjer hos Thorild; ungdomsårens filosofi. Bilagor: några hittills otryckta eller annars svåråtkomliga skrifter av Thorild. Lund, C. W. K. Gleerup [1913]
iv, 182 p. 25 cm. (Lunds universitets årsskrift, n. f., afd. 1, bd. 9, nr. 5)
Includes a chapter on Spinoza (p. [115]-122)

1. Thorild, Thomas, 1759-1808. I. Thorild, Thomas, 1759-1808. (Series: Lund. Universitet. Acta Universitatis Lundensis, n. s. Lunds universitets årsskrift, n. f., afd. 1, bd. 9, nr. 5)
AS284.L8 bd. 9, nr. 5 A 50-3273

Chicago. Univ. Libr. for Library of Congress [2]†

E-4-a
2633

Karppe, S 1866-
Essais de critique et d'histoire de philosophie. Paris, F. Alcan, 1902.
224 p. $23\frac{1}{2}$cm. (Bibliothèque de philosophie contemporaine)

Includes material on Spinoza.
Original paper covers bound in.

E-4-a
2634

Kaunitz, Maurice M.
Philosophy for plain people, by Maurice M. Kaunitz. New York, Adelphi company, 1926.
4 p. l., 394 p. $21\frac{1}{2}$cm.
Bibliography: p. 393-394.

1. Philosophy—Hist. I. Title.
27—12358
Library of Congress B72.K3
Copyright A 990298 [40d1]

E-4-a
2635

Keller, Ludwig, 1849-
... Johann Gottfried Herder, seine geistesentwicklung und seine weltanschauung; von dr. Ludwig Keller ... 2. aufl. Jena, E. Diederichs, 1910.
cover-title, 1 p. l., 106, 8 p. $24\frac{1}{2}$cm. (Vorträge und aufsätze aus der Comenius-gesellschaft. XVIII. jahrgang, 4. stück)
Published 1904 under title: Johann Gottfried Herder und die kultgesellschaften des humanismus. Ein beitrag zur geschichte des Maurerbundes.

1. Herder, Johann Gottfried von, 1744-1803. 2. Freemasons. 3. Humanity.
DLC
10-26446
Library of Congress L33.C7 18. jahrg.

E-4-a
2636

Ketner, Cornelis Hendrik
Geestelijke stroomingen. III. Spinoza. [1918]
369-381 p.

In De Socialistische gids, 3. jaargang, 1918.

E-4-a
2637

Klein, Herrmann
Individual- und Sozialethik in ihren gegenseitigen Beziehungen. Bern, Scheitlin Spring, 1904.
80 p. (Berner studien zur philosophie und ihrer geschichte, v. 37)

Includes a reference to Spinoza (p. 28-29)

Klencke,
Vom phantastischen Pessimismus zum freudigen Realismus: Schopenhauer und Spinoza. Von Dr. Klencke. Leipzig, Rossberg [1882]
cover-title, 55 p. 22cm.

Klyce, Scudder, 1879-
Universe, by Scudder Klyce, with three introductions by David Starr Jordan ... John Dewey ... Morris Llewellyn Cooke ... Winchester, Mass., S. Klyce, 1921.
2 p. l., iii-x, 251 p. diagrs. 32cm.
"First edition.—1000 copies.—Printed from type and no plates made."
"This book unifies or qualitatively solves science, religion, and philosophy—basing everything on experimental, verifiable evidence."—Pref.
CONTENTS.—Introductory remarks.—pt. 1. Formal unification; or theory of language.—pt. 2. Concrete unification; or physical science.—pt. 3. Spiritual unification; or humanics.
1. Cosmology. 2. Science. 3. Philosophy. I. Jordan, David Starr, 1851- II. Dewey, John, 1859- III. Cooke, Morris Llewellyn, 1872- IV. Title.
21—18106

Knauer, Vincenz, 1828-1894.
Die Hauptprobleme der Philosophie in ihrer Entwicklung und theilweisen Lösung, von Thales bis Robert Hamerling. Vorlesungen gehalten an der K. K. Wiener Universität. Wien, W. Braumüller, 1892.
xviii, 408 p. 25cm.

Includes a section on Spinoza (p. 258-262)

Knight, William, 1836-1916.
Hume. Philadelphia, Lippincott, 1886.
x, 239 p. port. 18cm. (Philosophical classics for English readers. [v. 11])

Includes references to Spinoza.

Knight, William, 1836-1916.
Varia; studies on problems of philosophy and ethics. London, J. Murray, 1901.
x, 196 p. 23cm.

Includes references to Spinoza.

Koester, Adolph
Spinoza - Goethe - Kant. [1910]
2-3 p.

In Der Zeitgeist; Beiblatt zum Berliner Tageblatt, Jan. 31, 1910.

Kohler, Josef, 1849-1919.
Lehrbuch der rechtsphilosophie, von Josef Kohler ... Berlin und Leipzig, W. Rothschild, 1909.
vi, 219, [1] p. 27cm.

Includes a reference to Spinoza (p. 155-156)

9-22011

Kohn-Bramstedt, Ernst
Über die Strukturidentität von Weltanschauung und Staatsauffassung bei Spinoza. [1928]
348-360 p. 24cm.

Manuscript note: Sonderdruck aus "Logos" XVII, 3.

1. Spinoza, Benedictus de, 1632-1677.

Kohut, Adolph, 1848-1917.
Johann Gottfried v. Herder und die Humanitätsbestrebungen der Neuzeit; eine literar-historische Studie. Tl. 1. Berlin, L. Gerschel, 1870.
95 p.

Includes a reference to Spinoza (p. 33-34)

Koigen, David, 1879-1933.
Der moralische Gott; eine Abhandlung über die Beziehungen zwischen Kultur und Religion. Berlin, Jüdischer Verlag, 1922.
218 p.

Includes a section on Spinoza (p. 65-68)

Korn, Alejandro, 1860-1936.
Obras. La Plata (Rep. Argentina) 1938-40.
v. 1-3 ports., facsim. 25 cm. (Universidad nacional de La Plata. Publicaciones oficiales)

Includes a section "Espinosa" (v. 2, p. 25-32)

Kotz, Wilhelm, Baron
Verschiedene Begriffsbildungen. Wien, J. Dirnböck, 1904.
219 p. 25cm.

Includes a section on Spinoza (p. 46-51) and other references to him.

Kraenzlin, Gerhard, 1877-
Die philosophie vom unendlichen menschen; ein system des reinen idealismus und zugleich eine kritische transzendental-philosophie, von Gerhard Kraenzlin. Leipzig, S. Hirzel, 1936.
1 p. l., [v]-viii, 664 p. 25½cm.

1. Idealism. I. Title.

[Krause, Ernst] 1839-1903.
Die allgemeine Weltanschauung in ihrer historischen Entwickelung; Charakterbilder aus der Geschichte der Naturwissenschaften, von Carus Sterne [pseud.] Stuttgart, O. Weisert, 1887.
402 p. illus., ports 23cm. (His Die alte und die neue Weltanschauung; Studien über die Rätsel der Welt und des Lebens)

Includes another t.-p., dated 1889.
Includes a section on Spinoza (p. 278-281)

Kreibig, Josef Clemens, 1863-
Geschichte und Kritik des ethischen Skepticismus. Wien, Hölder, 1896.
vi, 162 p.

Includes references to Spinoza.

Krochmal, Abraham, 1823-1895.
הכתב והמכתב לתורה נביאים וכתובים;
הכתב כתב אדם והמכתב מכתב אלהים.
הספר הזה הוא כ"י הנמצא חתום באבן סמוך
לעיר מעזבעז במחוז פאדאליע בארץ רייסין.
ונספח לו פירוש וביאור קצר ותרגום אשכנז.
ממני אב"ן הכהן קראכמאל. בלעמבערג
דרוק פאן קארל בודווייזער, 1874.
[Lemberg, 1874]
239, viii p. 18cm.

CONTINUED ON NEXT CARD

Külpe, Oswald, 1862-1915.
... Die philosophie der gegenwart in Deutschland. Eine charakteristik ihrer hauptrichtungen, nach vorträgen, gehalten im ferienkurs für lehrer 1901 zu Würzburg, von Oswald Külpe. Leipzig, B. G. Teubner, 1902.
3 p. l., 115 p. 18½cm. (Aus natur und geisteswelt. Sammlung wissenschaftlich-gemeinverständlicher darstellungen aus allen gebieten des wissens. 41. bd.)

Includes references to Spinoza.

1. Philosophy, German.

Külpe, Oswald, 1862-1915.
Die Philosophie der Gegenwart in Deutschland; eine Charakteristik ihrer Hauptrichtungen nach Vorträgen gehalten im Ferienkurs für Lehrer 1901 zu Würzburg. 3., verb. Aufl. Leipzig, B. G. Teubner, 1905.
125 p. 19cm. (Aus Natur und Geisteswelt ... 41. Bdch.)

Includes references to Spinoza.

Kuno Fischer, Geschichte der neueren Philosophie, im Urteil der Jahrzehnte 1852-1924. Zum 100. Geburtstag am 23. Juli 1924. Heidelberg, C. Winters Universitätsbuchhandlung, 1924.
84 p. 23cm.

Brief critical estimates of Fischer's work by various writers. Includes a section on Spinoza (p. 38-40)

Kutnik, Elijah Ṣĕvī
מורה דעת; ספר פילוסופי, בו יבאר
ויברר את כל השיטות של הפילוסופים
הנמצאים בעולם המדע, את כל טענותיהם
וסברותיהם למען נדע מה לקרב ומה לר-
חק.... המחבר אלי' צבי קוטניק.
[Kaunas, 1925]
112 p. port. 23cm.

Title transliterated: Mōrē daʿath.
Includes references to Spinoza.
Original paper covers bound in.

E-4-a
2658

Laffitte, Pierre, 1823-1903.
Cours philosophique sur l'histoire générale de l'humanité; discours d'ouverture. Paris, Dalmont, 1859.
179 p. tables 23 cm.

E-4-a
2659

Laffitte, Pierre, 1823-1903.
Les grands types de l'humanité; appréciation systématique des principaux agents de l'évolution humaine. Leçons rédigées par P. Dubuisson. Paris, E. Leroux, 1875-76.
2 v.

NN

E-4-a
2660

Laird, John, 1887-
The idea of value. Cambridge [Eng.] The University press, 1929.
xx, 384 p. 23 cm.

Includes a chapter "Spinoza's account of value" (p. 69-91) and other references to Spinoza.

NNUT

E-4-a
2661

Landauer, Gustav, 1870-1919.
Skepsis und Mystik. Versuche im Anschluss an Mauthners Sprachkritik. 2. Aufl. Köln a. R., Marcan-Block-Verlag, 1923.
73 p.

Includes references to Spinoza.

OCH

E-4-a
2662

Landmann, Edith
Die Transcendenz des Erkennens. Berlin, G. Bondi, 1923.
292 p. 24cm.

Includes references to Spinoza.

E-4-a
2663

Lange, Friedrich Albert, 1828-1875.
Geschichte des Materialismus und Kritik seiner Bedeutung in der Gegenwart. Wohlfeile Ausg., in der Reihe der Auflagen die vierte. Besorgt und mit biographischem Vorwort versehen von Prof. Hermann Cohen. Iserlohn, J. Baedeker, 1882.
xxx, 845 p. 23cm.

Includes references to Spinoza.

E-4-a
2664

Lange, Friedrich Albert, 1828-1875.
תולדות המטריאליסמוס ובקורת ערכו בזמנו. עם מבוא ביוגרפי ומאמר־בקורת מאת הרמן כהן. תרגום בר־טוביה. ספר ראשון. ניו־יורק, ווארשה, א. י. שטיבל, תרפ"ב.
[New York, Warszawa, 1921]
xvii, 430 p. 24 cm.

No more published?
Title transliterated: Toldot ha-materialismus.
Includes references to Spinoza.
1. Materialism. *Title transliterated:* Toldot ha-materialismus.

DLC

B825.L35 51-50418

Library of Congress [2]

E-4-a
2665

Lange, Friedrich Albert, 1828-1875.
Histoire du matérialisme et critique de son importance à notre époque. Traduit de l'allemand sur la 2e éd., par B. Pommerol, avec une introduction par D. Nolen. Paris, C. Reinwald, 1877-79.
2 v.

Includes references to Spinoza.

DCU

E-4-a
2666

Leatham, James
James Thomson ("B. V."), the laureate of pessimism. Cottingham, Yorks., The Gateway [1883?]
15 p. 22 cm.

NjP

E-4-a
2667

Leifchild, John R 1815-
The great problem. The higher ministry of nature viewed in the light of modern science, and as an aid to advanced Christian philosophy. With an introduction by Howard Crosby. New York, Putnam, 1872.
xvi, 543 p.

References to Spinoza included in two chapters (p. 149-196)

Lerminier, Jean Louis Eugène, 1803–1857.
Philosophie du droit, par E. Lerminier ... 3. éd., rev., cor. et augm. de plusieurs chapitres ... Paris, Guillaumin et c^ie, 1853.
2 p. l., xxxvi, 535 p. 19cm.

Includes a chapter on Spinoza (p. 291-306)

1. Law—Philosophy. I. Title.

Levine, Israel.
Faithful rebels; a study in Jewish speculative thought, by Israel Levine ... London, The Soncino press [1936]
viii, 146 p., 1 l. 23½cm.

CONTENTS.—The book of Job.—Ecclesiastes.—Philo and Maimonides.—Spinoza.—Marx.—Bergson.—Summary and conclusions.

1. Philosophy, Jewish. 2. Philosophers, Jewish. I. Title.

Lévy-Bruhl, Lucien, 1857-1939.
History of modern philosophy in France. With portraits of the leading French philosophers. Chicago, The Open Court Publishing Company, 1899.
x p., 1 l., 500 p. fronts., ports. 23 cm.

Translated by Miss G. Coblence.
Includes references to Spinoza.

Lewkowicz, Jakób, 1882-1910.
Z filozofji judaizmu. 1. Baruch Spinoza jako krytyk biblijny. 2. Fryderyk Nietzsche o zydach i judaizmie. Z przedmowa autora. Warszawa, Druk Kaniewskiego i Wasławowicza, 1909.
46 p.

Lipps, Gottlob Friedrich, 1865–1931.
... Mythenbildung und erkenntnis, eine abhandlung über die grundlagen der philosophie, von G. F. Lipps. Leipzig und Berlin, B. G. Teubner, 1907.
viii, 312 p. illus. 19½ cm. (Wissenschaft und hypothese. III)

Includes a section on Spinoza (p. 43-45)

1. Philosophy. I. Title.

Lovejoy, Arthur Oncken, 1873–
The great chain of being; a study of the history of an idea. The William James lectures delivered at Harvard university, 1933, by Arthur O. Lovejoy. Cambridge, Mass., Harvard university press, 1936.
ix p., 2 l., [3]–382 p. 23 cm.
Bibliographical references in "Notes" (p. [335]–373)
Includes "Plenitude and sufficient reason in Leibniz and Spinoza" (p. 144-182) and other references to Spinoza.
1. Continuity. I. Title. II. Title: Chain of being.

[Lowenthal, Marvin Marx]
Comparative study of Spinoza and neo-realism as indicated in Holt's "Concept of consciousness." [1915]
673-682, 701-713 p. 25cm.

Signed: Marvin Marx Lowenthal.
From the Journal of philosophy, psychology and scientific methods, v. XII, no. 25 and 25. Dec. 1915.

Luzzatti, Luigi, 1841-1927.
Freiheit des Gewissens und Wissens; Studien zur Trennung von Staat und Kirche. Einzig autorisierte Übersetzung von Dr. J. Bluwstein. Leipzig, Duncker & Humblot, 1911.
xiv, 155 p. port. 24cm.

Includes a chapter "Ein Heiliger der Philosophie als Verkünder der Freiheit des Gewissens und Wissens: Spinoza" (p. 94-108)
Original paper covers bound in.

Mach, Franz, 1845-1917.
Das Religions- und Weltproblem. Dogmenkritische und naturwissenschaftlich-philosophische Untersuchungen für die denkende Menschheit. Mit einer Selbstbiographie und dem Bildnisse des Verfassers. Dresden und Leipzig, E. Pierson, 1901.
2 v. port. 23 cm.

Includes references to Spinoza.

Magid, David, 1862-
הפרופיסור מרדכי בן מתתיהו אנטו־קולסקי; קצור תולדותיו ופרשת עבודתו בשדה מלאכת המחשבה עד היום הזה, חברו ד. מגיד. הוספה להצפירה בתור תשורה לחתומיה. ווארשה, בדפוס מ. לעווינסקי, שנת תרנ"ז לפ"ק.
[Warsaw, 1897.
224 p. illus., port. 20cm.

Title transliterated: ha-Professor ...
Includes references to Spinoza: p. 141-147.

E-4-a
2678

Manoloff, Philipp
Willensunfreiheit und Erziehungsmöglichkeit (Spinoza, Leibniz, Schopenhauer). Bern, Scheitlin Spring, 1904.
74 p. (Berner Studien zur Philosophie und ihrer Geschichte, Bd. 38)

E-4-a
2679

Martineau, James, 1805-1900.
Essays, reviews, and addresses. By James Martineau ... Selected and revised by the author ... London and New York, Longmans, Green and co., 1890-91.
4 v. 20 cm.
CONTENTS.—I. Personal: political.—II. Ecclesiastical: historical.—III. Theological: philosophical.—IV. Academical: religious.
Includes references to Spinoza.

1. Unitarian church—Collected works. 2. Theology—Collected works—19th cent.
BX9815.M28 208.1 35—32348
Library of Congress [55d½]

E-4-a
2680

Martineau, James, 1805-1900.
... Types of ethical theory; by James Martineau ... Oxford, At the Clarendon press, 1885.
2 v. 23 cm. (Clarendon press series)

Includes a chapter on Spinoza (v. 1, p. 234-369) and other references to him.

NNUT
1. Ethics—Hist.
BJ71.M4 10—2418
Library of Congress [58c1]

SPECIAL COLLECTIONS
SPINOZA
E-4-a
2681

Martineau, James, 1805-1900.
Types of ethical theory. 2d ed., rev. Oxford, Clarendon Press, 1886.
2 v. 23cm. (Clarendon Press series)

Includes a chapter on Spinoza (v. 1, p. [247]-393)

SPECIAL COLLECTIONS
SPINOZA
E-4-a
2682

Martineau, James, 1805-1900.
Types of ethical theory, by James Martineau ... 3d ed., rev. .. Oxford, Clarendon press, ~~1898~~ 1901.
~~2 v.~~ v. 1. 20cm. (Clarendon press series)

Includes a chapter on Spinoza (v. 1, p. [247]-393)

1. Ethics—Hist.
1—8414
Library of Congress BJ71.M43 [a41m1]

E-4-a
2683

Mauthner, Fritz, 1849-1923.
Beiträge zu einer Kritik der Sprache.
3. um Zusätze verm. Aufl. Leipzig, Meiner, 1923.
3 v. 23 cm.

Includes references to Spinoza.

SPECIAL COLLECTIONS
SPINOZA
E-4-a
2684

Mauthner, Fritz, 1849-1923.
Totengespraeche. Berlin, K. Schnabel, 1906.
127 p. 24cm.

Includes references to Spinoza.

SPECIAL COLLECTIONS
SPINOZA
E-4-a
2685

Mauthner, Fritz, 1849-1923.
Wörterbuch der Philosophie; neue Beiträge zu einer Kritik der Sprache. München, G. Müller, 1910.
2 v. 28cm.

Includes an article "Spinoza's 'Deus'" and many other references to Spinoza.

SPECIAL COLLECTIONS
SPINOZA
E-4-a
2686

Mauthner, Fritz, 1849-1923.
Wörterbuch der philosophie; neue beiträge zu einer kritik der sprache, von Fritz Mauthner. 2., verm. aufl. ... Leipzig, F. Meiner, 1923-24.
3 v. 22½ cm.

Includes references to Spinoza.

1. Philosophy—Dictionaries. I. Title.
B43.M3 1923 28—14297
Library of Congress [54c1]

SPECIAL COLLECTIONS
SPINOZA
E-4-a
2687

Meijer, Willem, 1842-1926.
Disputationem familiarem De republica habuit W. Meijer ... Latine edidit W. G. van der Tak. Amstelodami, Apud M. Hertzberger, 1926.
19 p. 22cm.

Includes references to Spinoza.

E-4-a
2688

Meijer, Willem, 1842-1926.
Over de overeenkomst van Spinoza's wereldbeschouwing met de Arabische wijsbegeerte. [1920]
64-72 p.

In Tijdschrift voor wijsbegeerte, jaargang 14, 1920.

NN

E-4-a
2689

Meijer, Willem, 1842-1926.
De wetenschap van Dr. G. Jelgersma en de wijsbegeerte van Benedictus de Spinoza.
's Gravenhage, Nijhoff, 1900.
50 p.

OCH

E-4-a
2690

Melamed, Samuel Max, 1885-1938.
Theorie, ursprung und geschichte der friedensidee. Kulturphilosophische wanderungen, von dr. Samuel Max Melamed. Stuttgart, F. Enke, 1909.
ix, [2], 262 p. 25cm.
Bibliographical foot-notes.
Includes references to Spinoza.

1. Peace.

Library of Congress JX1938.M4 20—10677
[s24b1]

SPECIAL COLLECTIONS
SPINOZA
E-4-a
2691

Menéndez y Pelayo, Marcelino, 1856-1912.
... Ensayos de crítica filosófica, por el doctor d. M. Menéndez y Pelayo ... Madrid, Est. tip. "Sucesores de Rivadeneyra," 1892.
397 p. 17cm. (Coleccion de escritores castellanos; criticos)

Title within ornamental border.

SPECIAL COLLECTIONS
SPINOZA
E-4-a
2692

Mieses, Fabius, 1824-1898.
מכתב מאת החכם פאביוס מיזעס
להחכם ר' שמואל פנחס הורוויץ בווין.
הובא לביה"ד ע"י עזריאל גינציג.
ברלין, בדפוס של צבי הירש איטצקאווס-
קי, תרנ"א.
[Berlin, 1891]
16 p.

Title transliterated: Mikhtav ...
Reprinted from ha-Maggid, 1890.
Includes a section on Spinoza.

E-4-a
2693

Mieses, Fabius, 1824-1898.

מכתב מאת החכם פאביוס מיזעס להחכם
ר' שמואל פנחס הורוויץ בווין.
Berlin, 1891.
16 p.

Title transliterated: Miktav me-... F. Mieses le-... S. P. Hurviz ...
About Spinoza and Nachman Krochmal.
Reprinted from ha-Magid, v. 34, 1890.

YIVO

E-4-a
2694

Miraglia, Luigi, 1846-1903.
... Comparative legal philosophy applied to legal institutions, by Luigi Miraglia ... tr. from the Italian by John Lisle ... with an introduction by Albert Kocourek ... Boston, The Boston book company, 1912.
2 p. l., [iii]-xl p., 1 l., 793 p. 21½ cm. (*Half-title:* The Modern legal philosophy series. III)
Series title also at head of t.-p.
Includes a section on Spinoza (p. 28-30)

1. Law—Philosophy. 2. Jurisprudence. I. Lisle, John, 1884-1915, tr.

Library of Congress [56g1] 12—9575

E-4-a
2695

Morgan, Conwy Lloyd, 1852-1936.
Emergent evolution; the Gifford lectures, delivered in the University of St. Andrews in the year 1922. London, Williams and Norgate, 1927.
xii, 313 p. diagrs. 22 cm.

Includes references to Spinoza.

SPECIAL COLLECTIONS
SPINOZA
E-4-a
2696

Morgan, Conwy Lloyd, 1852-1936.
Life, mind, and spirit; being the second course of the Gifford lectures, delivered in the University of St. Andrews in the year 1923 under the general title of Emergent evolution. London, Williams and Norgate, 1926.
xix, 316 p. 23cm.

Includes a section "Back to Spinoza!" (p. 26-30) and other references to Spinoza.

E-4-a
2697

Morgan, Conwy Lloyd, 1852-1936.
Mind at the crossways. New York, Holt, 1930.
xi, 275 p. 22 cm.

Muirhead, John Henry, 1855–1940.
Coleridge as philosopher, by John H. Muirhead ... London, G. Allen & Unwin ltd.; New York, The Macmillan company ₍1930₎
287, ₍1₎ p. front. (port.) 22 cm. (*Half-title:* Library of philosophy, ed. by J. H. Muirhead)
Appendixes: A. Materials for study in Coleridge's philosophy.—B. Joseph Henry Green's Spiritual philosophy.—C. Passages from ms. in the Henry E. Huntington library.
Includes a section "Berkeley and Spinoza" (p. 45-48) and other references to Spinoza.
1. Coleridge, Samuel Taylor, 1772–1834. I. Title.

₍Myślicki, Ignacy₎
Despinoza w nowym świetle; analiza dzieła Stanisława Dunin-Borkowskiego. ₍1913₎
403-427 p.

In Przegląd filozoficzny, 1913, no. 2-3.

Nasmith, David, 1829-1894.
Makers of modern thought, or, Five hundred years' struggle (1200 A. D. to 1699 A. D.) between science, ignorance and superstition. London, G. Philip & son, 1892.
2 v. 20cm.

"Spinoza": v. 2, p. 138-192, includes translation of part of the Ethics.

Nathanson, William, 1883-
שפינאזא און בערגסאן (א פאראלעל)
שיקאגא, פארלאג "נייע געזעלשאפט"
₍1923₎

₍Chicago, 1923₎
46 p. 22cm.

Title transliterated: Spinoza un Bergson.

Nathanson, William, 1883-
Spinoza and Bergson (a parallel) Translated from the Yiddish by David Wollins. ₍1925₎
117-122 p. 27cm.

From the Guardian; a literary monthly published in Philadelphia, vol. I, no. IV, February 1925.

Neumark, David, 1866-1924.
Lebensanschauung und Weltanschauung; historisch-philosophische Skizze. Krakau, Druck von J. Fischer, 1903.
44 p. 24cm.

Text in Hebrew.
"Separatabdruck aus dem 'Haschiloah', Band XI."
Includes a section on Spinoza (p. 30-39)
Original paper covers bound in.

Nir, Aaron
שניאור זק"ש. תל-אביב, הוצאת "כתו-
בים".

₍Tel-Aviv, 1928₎
88 p. port. 21cm.

Title transliterated: Shneur Sachs.
Includes reference to Spinoza (p. 38)
List of Sachs' publications: p. 83-88.

₍Noack, Ludwig₎ 1819-1885.
Das Buch der Weltweisheit; oder, die Lehren der bedeutendsten Philosophen aller Zeiten, dargestellt für die Gebildeten des deutschen Volkes. Leipzig, Avenarius & Mendelssohn, 1851.
2 v.

Includes a section on Spinoza (v. 2, p. 120-127)

Nossig, Alfred, 1864-
Ueber die bestimmende Ursache des Philosophirens; Versuch einer praktischen Kritik der Lehre Spinozas. Stuttgart, Deutsche Verlags-Anstalt, 1895.
ix, 84 p. 24cm.

1. Spinoza, Benedictus de, 1632-1677.

Oko, Adolph S 1883-1944.
William Hale White, 1831-1913. ₍1922₎
233-242 p. 22cm.

Cover-title: Dissertatio ex Chronici Spinozani tomo secundo separatim edita.

1. White, William Hale, 1831-1913.

Oldham, Alice.

An introduction to the study of philosophy; a series of lectures on ethics, metaphysics, and psychology delivered in Alexandra college, Dublin, by Alice Oldham. Dublin, Hodges, Figgis & co., ltd.; ₍etc., etc.₎ 1909.

3 p. l., v-xii p., 1 l., 370 p. diagr. 19½cm.

Preface signed: S. M.

Includes a lecture on Spinoza (p. 79-88)

1. Philosophy.

12-9863

Library of Congress BD21.O4

Paulsen, Friedrich, 1846-1908.

Friedrich Paulsen; an autobiography. Translated and edited by Theodor Lorenz, with a foreword by Nicholas Murray Butler. New York, Columbia University Press, 1938.

x, 514 p. plates, ports. 24cm.

Includes references to Spinoza.

Paulsen, Friedrich, 1846-1908.

Philosophia militans. Gegen klerikalismus und naturalismus. Fünf abhandlungen von Friedrich Paulsen. Berlin, Reuther & Reichard, 1901.

viii, 192 p. 21cm.

CONTENTS.—Das jüngste ketzergericht über die moderne philosophie.—Kant der philosoph des protestantismus.—Katholizismus und wissenschaft.—Fichte im kampf um die freiheit des denkens.—Ernst Haeckel als philosoph.

References to Spinoza included in chapter "Ernst Haeckel als Philosoph" (p. ₍119₎-192)

1. Philosophy, Modern—Hist. I. Title.

1-18278

Library of Congress B808.P35 ₍36e1₎

Paulsen, Friedrich, 1846-1908.

System der Ethik mit einem Umriss der Staats- und Gesellschaftslehre. Berlin, Hertz, 1889.

2 v. in 1. 23 cm.

Includes references to Spinoza.

Paulsen, Friedrich, 1846-1908.

Zur Ethik und Politik; gesammelte Vorträge u. Aufsätze. Berlin, Meelmeyer ₍1905₎

2 v. in 1. (Deutsche Bücherei, v. 31-32)

Includes a section on Spinoza (v. 31, p. 13-16)

Perrin, Raymond St. James, 1849-1915.

The evolution of knowledge; a review of philosophy. New York, Baker & Taylor ₍1905₎

xiii, 308 p. 21cm.

Includes a section on Spinoza (p. 129-135)

1. Spinoza, Benedictus de, 1632-1677.

Perrin, Raymond St. James, 1849-1915.

The religion of philosophy; or, The unification of knowledge: a comparison of the chief philosophical and religious systems of the world made with a view to reducing the categories of thought, or the most general terms of existence to a single principle, thereby establishing a true conception of God. London, Williams and Norgate, 1885.

xix, 566 p. 25cm.

Includes a section on Spinoza (p. 117-126).

Perry, Ralph Barton, 1876-

The approach to philosophy, by Ralph Barton Perry ... New York, C. Scribner's sons, 1905.

xxiv, 448 p. 19½cm.

Bibliography: p. 431-440.

Includes references to Spinoza.

1. Philosophy. I. Title.

5—16619

Library of Congress BD31.P4 ₍44a1₎

Perry, Ralph Barton, 1876-

Present philosophical tendencies, a critical survey of naturalism, idealism, pragmatism and realism together with a synopsis of the philosophy of William James, by Ralph Barton Perry ... New York ₍etc.₎ Longmans, Green, and co., 1912.

xv, 383 p. 22½ cm.

Includes two sections on Spinoza (p. 116-117 and 172-175) and references to Spinoza.

1. Philosophy, Modern. I. Title.

Z804.P3 12—5167

Library of Congress ₍54w1₎

Petzäll, Åke, 1901-

... Ethics and epistemology in John Locke's Essay concerning human understanding. By Åke Petzäll. Göteborg, Elanders boktryckeri aktiebolag, 1937.

83 p. 25cm. (Göteborgs högskolas årsskrift. XLIII. 1937: 2)

1. Locke, John, 1632-1704. Essay concerning human understanding. 2. Ethics. 3. Knowledge, Theory of.

A C 38-1526

Michigan. Univ. Library for Library of Congress AS284.G6 vol. 43, no. 2 [AS284.G6 vol. 43, no. 2] ₍4₎ (082)

Philosophische Aufsätze, Eduard Zeller zu seinem fünfzigjährigen Doctor-Jubiläum gewidmet. Leipzig, Fues's Verlag (H. Reisland) 1887.
482 p. 23cm.

Includes an essay "Spinoza und die Scholastik" by J. Freudenthal (p. ₍83₎-138)
Original paper covers bound in.
Bibliographical references.

Pichler, Hans, 1882-
Zur Entwicklung des Rationalismus von Descartes bis Kant. ₍1913₎
383-418 p.

In Kant-Studien, 18. Bd., 1913.
Includes references to Spinoza.

Pinto, Vivian de Sola, 1895-
Peter Sterry, Platonist and Puritan, 1613-1672; a biographical and critical study with passages selected from his writings. Cambridge ₍Eng.₎ The University Press, 1934.
xiii, 242 p. facsim. 23 cm.

Includes references to Spinoza.

Plumptre, Constance E
Natural causation; an essay in four parts. London, Unwin, 1888.
198 p. 23 cm.

Includes references to Spinoza.

Plümacher, O
Der Pessimismus in Vergangenheit und Gegenwart; geschichtliches und kritisches. 2. Ausg. Heidelberg, G. Weiss, 1888.
xii, 355 p. 23cm.

Includes references to Spinoza.

Polak, Leo
Zur sittlichen Rechtfertigung der Strafe. ₍1930₎
₍59₎-76 p. 24cm.

From Kant-Studien, Bd. XXXV, Hft. 1.
Includes a reference to Spinoza (p. 68)
Presentation copy to Carl Gebhardt with the author's inscription.

Poritzky, Jacob Elias, 1876-1935.
Franz Hemsterhuis, seine Philosophie und ihr Einfluss auf die deutschen Romantiker; eine Monographie. Berlin, Gebrüder Paetel, 1926.
146 p. 17cm. (Philosophische Reihe, hrsg. von Alfred Werner. 81)

Includes a reference to Spinoza (p. 93)

Pünjer, Bernhard, 1850-1885.
Geschichte der christlichen religions-philosophie seit der reformation. Braunschweig, C. A. Schwetschke und sohn, 1880.
v. 1 22cm.

Includes a chapter "Descartes und Spinoza" (v. 1, p. ₍288₎-330) and other references to Spinoza.

Raff, Emil
Die Monadenlehre in ihrer wissenschaftlichen Vervollkommung. ₍1910₎
99-127 p.

In Archiv für Geschichte der Philosophie, Bd. 24., 1910.
Includes references to Spinoza.

Rapaport, Benzion, d. 1943.

Berlin, 1929. .הכרה ומציאות
217 p.

Title transliterated: Hakarah u-meziᶜuth.
Includes two chapters on Spinoza (p. 1-20, 125-135)

Rappaport, Samuel, 1871-
Spinoza und Schopenhauer; eine kritisch-historische Untersuchung mit Berücksichtigung des unedierten schopenhauerschen Nachlasses dargestellt. Berlin, R. Gaertners Verlagsbuchhandlung H. Heyfelder, 1899.
148 p. 23cm.

Issued also as thesis, Halle.
Original paper covers bound in.
Bibliography: p. ₍147₎-148.

Rappaport, Samuel, 1871-
Spinoza und Schopenhauer. Halle a/S., 1899.
148 p. 23cm.

Thesis, Halle.
Published also without thesis note.
Bibliography: p. ₍147₎-148.

Rauwenhoff, Lodewijk Willem Ernst, 1828-1889.
Religionsphilosophie; uebers. und hrsg. von J. R. Hanne. 2. wohlf. Aufl. Braunschweig, C. A. Schwetschke, 1894.
xv, 607 p.

Ravà, Adolfo
La filosofia europea nel secolo decimonono. Padova, CEDAM, 1932.
146 p. 28cm.

"Estratto dall'opera L'Europa nel secolo XIX, diretta dai Proff. D. Donati e F. Carli. Volume III, Storia delle scienze."
Includes references to Spinoza.
Bibliography: p. 143-144.

Regensburg, Joseph, 1875- מההרצאות
... והנאומים ₍19--?₎ (Card 2)

Title transliterated: Mē-hā-harṣā'ōth ...
Includes reference to Spinoza (p. 6)

Reininger, Robert, 1869-
Philosophie des Erkennens. Leipzig, Barth, 1911.
464 p.

Renan, Ernest, 1823-1892.
The poetry of the Celtic races, and other studies, by Ernest Renan. Translated, with introduction and notes, by William G. Hutchison. London, W. Scott, ltd. ₍1896₎

xxxviii p., 1 l., 226 p. 17½ cm. (*Half-title:* The Scott library. ₍100₎)

CONTENTS.—Introduction.—The poetry of the Celtic races.—What is a nation?—Islamism and science.—Farewell to Tourgenief.—The deity of the bourgeois.—Intolerance in scepticism.—Marcus Aurelius.—Spinoza.—Henri-Frédéric Amiel.—Notes.

I. Hutchison, William G., 1873-1907, tr. II. Title.

Full name: Joseph Ernest Renan.

Renouvier, Charles Bernard, 1815-1903.
Introduction à la philosophie analytique de l'histoire. Les idées. Les religions. Les systèmes. Nouv. éd. rev. et considérablement augm. Paris, E. Leroux, 1896.
iii, 611 p. 28 cm.

Includes a reference to Spinoza (p. 41-42)

Ribbing, Sigurd, 1816-1899.
Försök till en framställning af spinozismens hufvudsatser. Upsala, P. Hanselli, 1851.
2 pts. in 1 (32 p.)

Thesis, Upsala.

Richter, Raoul Hermann Michael, 1871-1912.
Der Skeptizismus in der Philosophie. Leipzig, Verlag der Dürr'schen Buchhandlung, 1904-1908.
2 v. 24 cm.

Includes a section on Spinoza (v. 2, p. 169-177)

Richter, A
Worin weicht Thomas bei der Darstellung und Beurteilung Spinozas von Herbart ab? ⌊1909⌋
⌊365⌋-379 p. 24cm.

From Archiv für Geschichte der Philosophie, XXII. Bd.; Neue Folge, XV. Bd.
"Aus einer von der phil. Fakultät Jena gekrönten Preisarbeit."

Ritchie, David George, 1853-1903.
Philosophical studies, by David G. Ritchie ... Ed., with a memoir, by Robert Latta ... London, New York, Macmillan and co., limited, 1905.

xi, 355 p. 2 port. (incl. front.) 23 cm.

CONTENTS.—Memoir.—Cogitatio metaphysica.—The relation of logic to psychology ⌊Philosophical review, vol. v & vol. vi⌋—The relation of metaphysics to epistemology ⌊Philosophical review, vol. III⌋—The one and the many. ⌊Mind, n. s., vol. VII⌋—Confessio fidei.—Moral philosophy. On the method and scope of ethics.—Index.

Includes references to Spinoza.

1. Philosophy—Addresses, essays, lectures. 2. Ethics. I. Latta, Robert, 1865- ed.

Robertson, George Croom, 1842-1892.
Elements of general philosophy. Edited from notes of lectures delivered at the ⌊University⌋ College, ⌊London⌋, 1870-1892, by C. A. Foley Rhys Davids. London, Murray, 1905.
xvi, 365 p. (University extension manuals)

Includes 2 sections on Spinoza (p. 59-63, 274-295)

Rogers, Reginald Arthur Percy, 1874-
A short history of ethics, Greek and modern, by Reginald A. P. Rogers ... London, Macmillan and co., limited, ~~1911~~ 1913.

xxii, 303 p. 19 cm.

Includes a section "Rationalistic naturalism - Spinoza" (p. 143-146) and other references to Spinoza.

1. Ethics—Hist.

Rosmarin, *Mrs.* Trude Weiss, 1908-
Religion of reason; Hermann Cohen's system of religious philosophy, by Trude Weiss Rosmarin. New York, Bloch publishing company, 1936.

xi, 195 p. 21^cm.

Bibliography: p. ⌊177⌋-195.

Includes chapter on Spinoza.

1. Cohen, Hermann, 1842-1918. 2. Philosophy and religion. I. Title.

Roth, Leon, 1896-
The science of morals, an essay in method ⌊by⌋ Leon Roth. London, E. Benn limited ⌊1928⌋
141 p., 1 l. 19cm.

Includes a reference to Spinoza (p. 92)

1. Ethics.

Rousseau, Muriel
Some philosophers and some philosophies. ⌊1889⌋
30-35 p.

In The church review and ecclesiastical register, v. 53, April 1889.
Includes a reference to Spinoza (p. 31-32)

Roverelli, Giuseppe.
... Il pensiero spinoziano nell' idealismo moderno. Milano, Antonio Vallardi ⌊1934⌋

2 p. l., ⌊7⌋-118 p., 1 l. 20^cm.

Bibliographical foot-notes.

Original paper covers bound in.

1. Spinoza, Benedictus de, 1632-1677. I. Title.

Rubin, Salomon, 1823-1910.
תשובה נצחת.[להצדיק את ברוך שפינוזה
נגד טענות שד"ל].
Lemberg, 1859.
45 p.

Title transliterated: Teshubah Nizzahath.
Includes a reply to S. D. Luzzatto's attacks on Spinoza.

Rubin, Salomon, 1823-1910.
כל כתבי ד"ר שלמה רובין, ערוכים
וסדורים, מוגהים ומתוקנים בע"י א. ש.
הרשברג, עם תולדות חייו של המחבר מאת
יוסף קלוזנר. בורשה, "תושיה", תר"ע
⌊Warsaw, Tushiya⌋ 1910.
2 v. in 1. port. 21cm.

Title transliterated: Kol kithbhē ....
Includes references to Spinoza.
Title-page in Hebrew and Russian.

Ruggiero, Guido de, 1888-1948.
La filosofia contemporanea. Germania, Francia, Inghilterra, America, Italia. 2. ed., riveduta dall'autore ed accresciuta di un'appendice. Bari, Laterza, 1920.
2 v. 21 cm.

Includes references to Spinoza.

Ruggiero, Guido de, 1888-
La filosofia del Cristianesimo. Bari, Laterza, 1920.
3 v. 21 cm. (His Storia della filosofia, pt. 2)

Includes a reference to Spinoza (v. 3, p. 190)

Ruggiero, Guido de, 1888-
La filosofia greca. Bari, Laterza, 1921.
2 v. 21 cm. (His Storia della filosofia, pt. 1)

Russell, Bertrand Russell, 3d earl, 1872-
Mysticism and logic. ₍1914₎
780-803 p.

In Hibbert journal, v. 12, 1914.
Includes references to Spinoza.

Scheler, Max, 1874-1928.
Philosophische Weltanschauung. Bonn, F. Cohen, 1929.
158 p. 23cm.

Includes an essay on Spinoza (p. ₍124₎-139)
Bibliographical references included in "Anmerkungen" (p. 140-154)

Scheler, Max ~~Ferdinand~~, 1874-1928.
Die Stellung des Menschen im Kosmos. Darmstadt, O. Reichl, 1928.
114 p. 20cm.

Includes references to Spinoza.

1. Spinoza, Benedictus de, 1632-1677.

Schemann, Ludwig, 1852-1938.
Die Rasse in den Geisteswissenschaften; Studien zur Geschichte des Rassengedankens. ₍1.₎ Bd.₌ München, J. F. Lehmann, 1928.
xvi, 480 p. 23cm.

Includes references to Spinoza.
Bibliographical footnotes.

Schemann, Ludwig, 1852-1938.
Die Rasse in den Geisteswissenschaften; Studien zur Geschichte des Rassengedankens. München, J. F. Lehmann, 1928-31.
3 v. 24cm.

Includes references to Spinoza.

Schiller, Edward
Hand-book of progressive philosophy. New York, J. S. Redfield, 1871.
viii, 216 p. 19 cm.

Includes a reference to Spinoza (p. 150-151)

Schlatter, Adolf, 1852-1938.
Die philosophische Arbeit seit Cartesius nach ihrem ethischen und religiösen Ertrag. Gütersloh, Bertelsmann, 1906.
255 p. 22 cm. (Beiträge zur Förderung christlicher Theologie, v. 10)

Includes a section on Spinoza (p. 45-61)

Schoeler, Heinrich von, 1851-
Kritik der wissenschaftlichen Erkenntnis; eine vorurteilsfreie Weltanschauung. Leipzig, W. Engelmann, 1898.
viii, 677 p. 24cm.

Includes a chapter "Versuch einer intellektualen Weltanschauung durch Spinoza und Schelling (p. ˛148˛-158)

Seth, James, 1860-1924.
English philosophers and schools of philosophy, by James Seth ... London, J. M. Dent & sons, ltd.; New York, E. P. Dutton & co., 1912.
xi, 372 p. 20½ cm. (*Half-title:* The channels of English literature)

Includes a reference to Spinoza (p. 9)

1. Philosophy, English. I. Title.

Schulemann, Günther, 1889-
Philosophie als Wissenschaft und als Weisheit. ˛1928˛
4-16 p. 25cm.

From Blätter der Volkshochscnule Breslau, 7. Jahrgang, Heft 1/4, 1928/29.
Includes a reference to Spinoza (p. 15)

Seth, James, 1860-1924.
Essays in ethics and religion with other papers. Edited with a short memoir by A. Seth Pringle-Pattison. Edinburgh, Blackwood, 1926.
xxxviii, 208 p. ports. 21 cm.

Schultz, Julius August Heinrich, 1862-
Die philosophie am scheidewege; die antinomie im werten und im denken, von Julius Schultz. Leipzig, F. Meiner, 1922.
vii, 331 p., 1 l. 22cm.
"Zitierte autoren": p. ˛323˛-331.
Includes references to Spinoza.

1. Worth. 2. Philosophy, Modern. I. Title.

Seth Pringle Pattison, Andrew, 1856-1931.
The philosophical radicals and other essays, with chapters reprinted on the philosophy of religion in Kant and Hegel. Edinburgh and London, W. Blackwood and Sons, 1907.
x, 336 p.

Includes a reference to Spinoza (p. 108)

1. Spinoza, Benedictus de, 1632-1677.

Schwab, Andreas.
... Gespräche der genies über die menschheit ... Leipzig, Im selbstverlag des verfassers, bezug durch K. F. Koehlers antiquarium, 1922-23.
2 v. 20cm (v. 2: 18½cm)

Includes two sections referring to Spinoza (v. 1, p. 9-46)

I. Title.

Shaler, Sophia Penn Page
The masters of fate; the power of the will. New York, Duffield, 1906.
x, 358 p. 20cm.

Includes references to Spinoza.

Schweitzer, Albert, 1875-
Kultur und Ethik. Bern, P. Haupt, 1923.
xxiii, 280 p. (His Kulturphilosophie, 2. Teil)

"Olaus Petri Vorlesungen an der Universität Upsala."
Includes a chapter "Naturphilosophie und Weltanschauung bei Spinoza und Leibniz" (p. 113-121) and other references to Spinoza.
Bound with Schweitzer, Albert. Verfall und Wiederaufbau der Kultur. 1923.

Shestov, Lev, 1866-1938.
Сыновья и пасынки времени (исторический жребій Спинозы) ˛1925˛
˛316˛-342 p.

Title transliterated: Synov'ía i pasynki vremeni (istoricheskiĭ zhrebiĭ Spinozy)
In Современныя записки, кн. 25, 1925.

Sigwart, Christoph von, 1830–1904.
Kleine schriften, von Christoph Sigwart ... 1.–[2.] reihe ... Freiburg i B., Mohr, 1889.
2 v. 20½ᶜᵐ.
CONTENTS.—1. reihe. Zur geschichte der philosophie. Biographische darstellung. 2., berichtigte und verm. ausg.—2. reihe. Zur erkenntnisslehre und psychologie. 2., unveränderte ausg.
Includes references to Spinoza.
1. Philosophy—Addresses, essays, lectures.

Sigwart, Heinrich Christoph Wilhelm von, 1789-1844
Vermischte philosophische Abhandlungen.
Tübingen, H. Laupp, 1831.
Bd. 1.

Simon, Ernst, 1899-
Zu Hermann Cohens Spinoza-Auffassung. [1935]
181-194 p. 24cm.
From Maimonides-Festschrift. Monatsschrift für Geschichte und Wissenschaft des Judentums, 79. Jahrgang, Heft 2, März-April, 1935.

Simon, Jules, 1814-1896.
Victor Cousin; translated by Gustave Masson. London, G. Routledge and Sons, 1888.
192 p. port. 24cm. (Great French writers)
Includes references to Spinoza.

Singer, Edgar Arthur, 1873–
Modern thinkers and present problems; an approach to modern philosophy through its history, by Edgar A. Singer, jr.... New York, H. Holt and company, 1923.
vii, 322 p. 21½ cm.
CONTENTS.—Giordano Bruno, 1548–1600.—Benedict de Spinoza, 1632–1677.—A disciple of Spinoza (an illustration)—David Hume, 1711–1776.—Immanuel Kant, 1724–1804.—Arthur Schopenhauer, 1788–1860.—Friederich [!] Nietzsche, 1844–1900.—Pragmatism.—Progress.—Royce on love and loyalty.—Retrospect and prospect.
1. Philosophy—Hist. 2. Philosophers. I. Title.

Smith, Thomas Vernor, 1890–
Creative sceptics; in defense of the liberal temper, by T. V. Smith ... Chicago, New York, Willett, Clark & company, 1934.
vii, 270 p. 20½ cm.
Bibliography: p. 269-270.
Includes a chapter "Doubting one's way to spiritual peace, being a moral drawn from Benedict Spinoza (p. 67-105)
1. Skepticism. I. Title.

Sonne, Isaiah, 1887-
אנשים: שפינוזה ופסקל: למלאת שלש
מאות שנה ללדתו של פסקל. בווארשא,
[1932
[Warsaw, 1932]
[496]-498 p. 25cm.
Title transliterated: Anāshīm.
From ha-Tĕkūfā, vol. XX.
Deals with Spinoza and Pascal.

[Souriau, Paul] 1852-1928.
Louis Adelphe, 1879-1914. [1922]
243-244 p. 22cm.
Signed: Paul Souriau.
Includes references to Spinoza.
From Chronicon Spinozanum, v. 2.

Spaventa, Bertrando, 1817-1883.
La filosofia italiana nelle sue relazioni con la filosofia europea. Nuova ed., con note e appendice di documenti a cura di Giovanni Gentile. Bari, G. Laterza, 1908.
xxii, 317 p. 21 cm.
Includes references to Spinoza.

Spaventa, Bertrando, 1817-1883.
Saggi di critica filosofica, politica e religiosa. Vol. 1. Napoli, Ghio, 1867.
404 p.

E-4-a 2778

Spaventa, Bertrando, 1817-1883.
Scritti filosofici. Raccolti e pubblicati con note e un discorso sulla vita e sulle opere ... da Giovanni Gentile ... Prefazione di D. Jaja. Napoli, A. Morano, 1900.
cliii, 408 p.

Includes references to Spinoza.

MH

SPECIAL COLLECTIONS SPINOZA E-4-a 2779

Spengler, Oswald, 1880-1936.
Der Untergang des Abendlandes; Umrisse einer Morphologie der Weltgeschichte. München, Beck, 1920-22.
2 v. 24cm.

Includes references to Spinoza.
Contents.--1. Bd. Gestalt und Wirklichkeit. --2. Bd., Welthistorische Perspektiven.

SPECIAL COLLECTIONS SPINOZA E-4-a 2780

Spicker, Gideon, 1840-
Die Philosophie des Grafen von Shaftesbury nebst Einleitung und Kritik über das Verhältniss der Religion zur Philosophie und der Philosophie zur Wissenschaft. Freiburg i. B., C. Troemer, 1872.
xvi, 367 p. 21cm.

Includes a section on Kant and Spinoza (p. 14-19)

SPECIAL COLLECTIONS SPINOZA E-4-a 2781

Sprink, Walter, 1885-
Spinoza und Fechner; ein Beitrag zu einer vergleichenden Untersuchung der Lehren Spinozas und Fechners. Breslau, Druck von W. G. Korn, 1912.
63 p. 23cm.

Thesis, Breslau.
Bibliographical footnotes.

SPECIAL COLLECTIONS SPINOZA E-4-a 2782

Steckelmacher, Moritz, 1851-
Das Princip der Ethik, vom philosophischen und jüdisch-theologischen Standpunkte aus betrachtet. Mainz, Joh. Wirth, 1904.
255 p. 23cm.

Includes references to Spinoza.
Bibliographical footnotes.

E-4-a 2783

Stein, Ludwig, 1859-
Philosophische strömungen der gegenwart, von dr. Ludwig Stein ... Stuttgart, F. Enke, 1908.
xvi, 452 p. 25½cm.

Includes a section on Spinoza (p. 150-153) and other references to him.

1. Philosophy, Modern—Hist.

9—8890
Library of Congress B804.S7

E-4-a 2784

Stein, Ludwig, 1859-1930.
Der Sinn des Daseins; Streifzüge eines Optimisten durch die Philosophie der Gegenwart. Tübingen, J. C. B. Mohr, 1904.
xi, 437 p.

Includes references to Spinoza.

NN

E-4-a 2785

Stein, Ludwig, 1859-
Die soziale frage im lichte der philosophie; vorlesungen über soziologie und ihre geschichte, von dr. Ludwig Stein ... 3. und 4. umgearb. aufl. Stuttgart, F. Enke, 1923.
xx, 592 p. 24½cm.

Includes a section on Spinoza (p. 348-351) and other references to him.

1. Sociology. 2. Sociology—Hist. 3. Socialism. I. Title.

NNUT 25-25146
Library of Congress HM19.S8 1923

SPECIAL COLLECTIONS SPINOZA E-4-a 2786

Stein, Ludwig, 1859-1930.
Der soziale Optimismus. Jena, H. Costenoble, 1905.
vii, 267 p. 24cm.

Includes references to Spinoza.
Presentation copy to Carl Gebhardt, with the author's inscription.

E-4-a 2787

Stern, Viktor
Die Philosophie meines Vaters. [1910]
42-71 p.

In Archiv für systematische Philosophie, 16. Bd., 1910.
Includes a reference to Spinoza (p. 52-53)

E-4-a
2788

Stern, Wilhelm, 1844-
Kritische Grundlegung der Ethik als positiver Wissenschaft. Berlin, F. Dümmler, 1897.
471 p. 24 cm.

Includes a section on Spinoza (p. 207-217)

NNUT

E-4-a
2789

Strauss, David Friedrich, 1808-1874.
Gesammelte Schriften; nach des Verfassers letztwilligen Bestimmungen zusammengestellt. Eingeleitet und mit erklärenden Nachweisungen versehen von Eduard Zeller. Bonn, E. Strauss, 1876-78.
12 v. ports. 22cm.

Includes references to Spinoza (v. 5, p. 255-256 and v. 11, p. 159-160)

E-4-a
2790

Strong, Charles Augustus, 1862-1940.
Final observations. ⌈1941⌉
233-243 p.

In Journal of philosophy, v. 38, 1941.
Includes references to Spinoza.

SPECIAL COLLECTIONS
SPINOZA

E-4-a
2791

Stumpf, Karl, 1848-1936.
Spinozastudien. Berlin, Verlag der Akademie der Wissenschaften, in Kommission bei der Vereinigung wissenschaftlicher Verleger W. de Gruyter, 1919.
57 p. 29cm.

"Aus den Abhandlungen der Preussischen Akademie der Wissenschaften, Jahrgang 1919. Phil.-hist. Klasse. Nr. 4."

E-4-a
2792

Szylkarski, Wladimir
Nauka Spinozy o Bogu. ⌈1927⌉
27 p.

In Przegląd filozoficzny, 1927, zesz. 1.

NN

E-4-a
2793

Taylor, Alfred Edward, 1869-1945.
The faith of a moralist; Gifford lectures delivered in the University of St. Andrews, 1926-1928, by A. E. Taylor ... London, Macmillan and co., limited, 1930.

2 v. 22½ cm.

Bibliographical foot-notes.
CONTENTS.—The theological implications of morality.—Natural theology and the positive religions.
Includes many references to Spinoza.

1. Ethics. 2. Christian ethics. 3. Natural theology. 4. Philosophy and religion. I. Title.

BJ1011.T18 171 31—9511

Library of Congress ⌈57y1⌉

SPECIAL COLLECTIONS
SPINOZA

E-4-a
2794

Teitelbaum, Mordecai
הרב מלאדי ומפלגת חב"ד; חיי הרב, ספריו ושיטתו וקורות מפלגת חב"ד, מאת מרדכי טייטלבוים. ורשה, הוצאת "תושיה", תר"ע-תרע"ד.
⌈Warschau, Verlag "Tuschijah", 1910-13.
2v. in 1 port., facsim., music. 21cm.

Title transliterated: ha-Rabh ...
Added t.-p.: Der Rabh von Ladi ...
Includes references to Spinoza.

NNC

E-4-a
2795

Thilo, Christfried Albert
Die Wissenschaftlichkeit der modernen speculativen Theologie in ihren Principien beleuchtet. Leipzig, Fleischer, 1851.
xvi, 344 p. 22 cm.

Includes a chapter "Von einigen haupsächlichen allgemeinen philosophischen Meinungen des modernen Spinozismus" (p. 1-48)

NNUT

SPECIAL COLLECTIONS
SPINOZA

E-4-a
2796

Troeltsch, Ernst, 1865-1923.
Zur religiösen Lage, Religionsphilosophie und Ethik. 2. photomechanisch gedruckte Aufl. Tübingen, J. C. B. Mohr (P. Siebeck) 1922.
xi, 866 p. (His Gesammelte Schriften, 2. Bd.) 24cm.

Includes references to Spinoza.

SPECIAL COLLECTIONS
SPINOZA

E-4-a
2797

Türck, Hermann, 1856-1921.
Der geniale Mensch. 5. verm. Aufl. Berlin, F. Dümmler, 1901.
xii, 422 p. 23cm.

Includes a chapter "Genialität und Seelenfreiheit nach Schopenhauers und Spinozas Lehre" (p. ⌈197⌉-214)
Original paper covers bound in.

Türck, Hermann, 1856-1921.
Der geniale Mensch. 4. verm. Aufl. Berlin, Ferd. Dümmler, 1899.
x, 400 p. 23cm.

Includes a chapter "Genialität und Seelenfreiheit nach Schopenhauers und Spinozas Lehre" (p. ⌊195⌋-212)

Türck, Hermann, 1856-1921.
Der geniale Mensch. 7. verm. Aufl. Berlin, F. Dümmler, 1910.
xiv, 529 p.

Includes a section on Spinoza and other references to him.

Türck, Hermann, 1856-1921.
The man of genius. London, Black, 1923.
4 p. l., 483 p.

Includes a section on Spinoza (p. 208-214) and other references to him.

Türck, Hermann, 1856-1921.
The man of genius. ⌊1st English ed.⌋ Schwerin i. M., Stillersche Hofbuchhandlung (J. A. Strenge) 1914.
483 p. 25cm.

"Translated from the sixth edition of the German original by the late Professor George J. Tamson."
Includes a chapter "Genius and freedom of mind in Schopenhauer's and Spinoza's teachings" (p. 199-214)

Upton, Charles Barnes, 1831-1920.
Dr. Martineau's philosophy, a survey, by Charles B. Upton ... Rev. ed., with an introductory essay. London, J. Nisbet & co., limited, 1905.
xliii, 239, ⌊1⌋ p. 23cm.
First published as book II of the second volume of The life and letters of James Martineau, by James Drummond and C. B. Upton, 1902.
Includes references to Spinoza.

1. Martineau, James, 1805-1900.

Utitz, Emil, 1883-
... Die sendung der philosophie in unserer zeit. Leiden, A. W. Sijthoff, 1935.
ix, 159 p. 22½cm.

1. Philosophy. I. Title.

Vandek, V
Критика оценки механистами и меньшевиствующими идеалистами философии Спинозы. [1932]
128-159 p.

Title transliterated: Kritika otsenki mekhanistami i men'shevistvu͡ushchimi idealistami filosofii Spinozy.
By V. Vandek and V. Timoshko.
In Под знаменем марксизма, 1932, № 1-2.

Vassallo, Angel.
... Nuevos prolegómenos a la metafísica. Buenos Aires, Editorial Losada, s. a. ⌊1938⌋
2 p. l., 7-216 p. 21cm. ⌊Biblioteca filosófica, publicada bajo la dirección de Francisco Romero⌋
"Los estudios que forman este volumen (consignados en su estructura original de lecciones, disertación, ensayo), bajo la variedad cierta de los temas, viven unificados en la intención del autor."—Prólogo.
Includes an essay "El secreto de Spinoza" (p. 197-214)
Original paper covers bound in.
1. Metaphysics.

Verweyen, Johannes Maria, 1883-
Ehrenfried Walter von Tschirnhaus als Philosoph; eine philosophie-geschichtliche Abhandlung. Bonn, J. P. Hanstein, 1905.
137 p. 24cm.

Issued also as thesis, Bonn.
Includes references to Spinoza.
Original paper cover, dated 1906, bound in.
Bibliography: p. ⌊136⌋-137.

Volkelt, Johannes, 1848-1920.
Vorträge zur Einführung in die Philosophie der Gegenwart, gehalten zu Frankfurt a/M. im Februar und März 1891. München, C. H. Beck, 1892.
viii, 230 p. 21cm.

Includes references to Spinoza.

Vowinckel, Ernst, 1872-
Die Auswahl der philosophischen Lektüre in den Arbeitsgemeinschaften. [1931]
[40]-63 p. 24cm.

From Der Philosophische Unterricht; Zeitschrift der Gesellschaft für philosophischen Unterricht, Band 2, Heft 2/3, 1931.
Includes a reference to Spinoza (p. 61)

Wahle, Richard, 1857-
Beiträge zur Theorie der Interpretation philosophischer Werke. [1903]
64-72 p.

In Zeitschrift für Philosophie und philosophische Kritik, Bd. 122, 1903.
Includes references to Spinoza.

Wahle, Richard, 1857-
Geschichtlicher Überblick über die Entwicklung der Philosophie bis zu ihrer letzten Phase; ein Leitfaden für allgemein Gebildete und Studierende der Hoch- und Mittelschulen. Wien, W. Braumüller, 1895.
iv, 66 p. 23cm.

Includes a section on Spinoza (p. 57-58)

Walker, Leslie Joseph, 1877-
Theories of knowledge, absolutism, pragmatism, realism, by Leslie J. Walker. London, New York [etc.] Longmans, Green & co., 1910.
xxxix, 696 p. 19½ cm. (Stonyhurst philosophical series)
Thesis (M. A.)—University of London.
Includes references to Spinoza.

1. Knowledge, Theory of.
Full name: Leslie Joseph Ignatius Walker.

Wenley, Robert Mark, 1861-1929.
Aspects of pessimism, by R. M. Wenley ... Edinburgh and London, W. Blackwood and sons, 1894.
x, 337 p. 20cm.
Partly reprinted from various periodicals.
CONTENTS.—Jewish pessimism.—Mediaeval mysticism.—Hamlet.—The pessimistic element in Goethe.—Berkeley, Kant, and Schopenhauer.—Pessimism as a system.
Includes references to Spinoza.

1. Pessimism. I. Title.

Wenley, Robert Mark, 1861-1929.
Stoicism and its influence, by R. M. Wenley ... Boston, Mass., Marshall Jones company [c1924]
xi, 194 p. 19 cm. (*Half-title:* Our debt to Greece and Rome, [2] editors, G. D. Hadzsits ... D. M. Robinson)
Bibliography: p. 182-186.
Includes references to Spinoza.

1. Stoics.

Whittaker, Thomas, 1856-
Reason; a philosophical essay with historical illustrations (Comte and Mill, Schopenhauer, Vico, Spinoza) by Thomas Whittaker ... Cambridge [Eng.] The University press, 1934.
4 p. l., 217 p. 22½ cm.
On cover: Reason & other essays.
Each of the first three essays has a bibliography at end.

1. Philosophy—Addresses, essays, lectures. 2. Reason.

Wijck, Bernard Hendrik Cornelis Karel van der
[Reply to Gerardus Heymans' criticism of Spinoza in his Einführung in die Metaphysik. 1905]
129-157 p.

In Onze eeuw, 5. jaargang, 1905.

Windelband, Wilhelm, 1848-1915.
Die Blütezeit der deutschen Philosophie. 3., durchgesehene Aufl. Leipzig, Breitkopf und Härtel, 1904.
vi, 409 p. 23cm.

Added t.-p.: Die Geschichte der neueren Philosophie in ihrem zusammenhange mit der allgemeinen Kultur und den besonderen Wissenschaften. 2. Bd. Von Kant bis Hegel und Herbart.
Includes references to Spinoza.
Ms. notes by Carl Gebhardt.

Windelband, Wilhelm, 1848-1915.
A history of philosophy with especial reference to the formation and development of its problems and conceptions. Authorized translation by J. H. Tufts. New York, Macmillan, 1893.
xiii, 659 p. 24 cm.

Includes references to Spinoza.

E-4-a 2819

Windelband, Wilhelm, 1848-1915.
A history of philosophy with especial reference to the formation and development of its problems and conceptions. 2d ed., revised. New York, Macmillan, 1935.
xv, 726 p. 23 cm.

Includes references to Spinoza.

MH

SPECIAL COLLECTIONS SPINOZA

E-4-a 2823

Ziehen, Theodor, 1862-
Die Grundlagen der Religionsphilosophie (Nomotheismus) Leipzig, F. Meiner, 1928.
166 p. 20cm.

On cover: Acht Rundfunk-Vorträge.
Includes a section on Spinoza (p. 86-101)

E-4-a 2819

Windelband, Wilhelm, 1848-1915.
... Lehrbuch der geschichte der philosophie. Billige ausg. Mit einem schlusskapitel: Die philosophie im 20. jahrhundert, und einer übersicht über den stand der philosophiegeschichtlichen forschung herausgegeben von Heinz Heimsoeth ... Tübingen, Mohr, 1935.
xxxix, 642 p. 24½cm.

Includes many references to Spinoza.

1. Philosophy—Hist. I. Heimsoeth, Heinz, 1886- ed.

37-7558

Library of Congress B82.W5 1935
[3] 109

SPECIAL COLLECTIONS SPINOZA

E-4-a 2824

Zimmermann, Robert, Edler von, 1824-1898.
Samuel Clarke's Leben und Lehre; ein Beitrag zur Geschichte des Rationalismus in England. Wien, Kaiserlich-Königliche Hof- und Staatsdruckerei, 1870.
88 p. 28cm.

Includes references to Spinoza.
"Separatabdruck aus dem XIX. Bande der Denkschriften der philosophisch-historischen Classe der Kaiserlichen Akademie der Wissenschaften."

E-4-a 2820

Winkelmann, Elisabeth, 1903-
... Coleridge und die kantische philosophie; erste einwirkungen des deutschen idealismus in England, von Elisabeth Winkelmann. Leipzig, Mayer & Müller, g. m. b. h., 1933.
xii, 258 p. 23cm. (Palaestra 184)
"Quellennachweis": p. [256]-258.
Includes references to Spinoza.

1. Coleridge, Samuel Taylor, 1772-1834. 2. Kant, Immanuel, 1724-1804. 3. Idealism. 4. Literature, Comparative—German and English. 5. Literature, Comparative—English and German.

33-8837

Library of Congress PD25.P3 no. 184
[39c1] (808) 928.2

E-4-a 2825

Zuławski, Jerzy
Przed zwierciadłem prawdy; szkice filozoficzne. Warszawa, E. Wende i Spółka, 1914.
318 p.

NN

E-4-a 2821

Woltmann, Ludwig, 1871-1907.
Система моральнаго сознанія; въ связи съ отношеніемъ критической философіи къ дарвинизму и соціализму. Переводъ съ нѣмецкаго В. Михайлова и Г. Шпетта подъ редакціей М. М. Филиппова. С.-Петербургъ, Изд. Зябицкаго и Пятина, 1901.

Translation of System des moralischen Bewusstseins.
Includes a section on Spinoza.
Title transliterated: Sistema moral'nago soznaniia.

NN

E-4-a 2826

Zwick, Moses Isaac, 1899-
Berthold Auerbachs sozialpolitischer und ethischer liberalismus, nach seinen schriften dargestellt von M. I. Zwick. Stuttgart, W. Kohlhammer, 1933.
xv, [1], 124 p. 24cm.
Thesis (PH. D.)—Columbia university, 1933.
Thesis note on label mounted on t.-p. and "Curriculum vitae" mounted on p. 124.
"Literatur-verzeichnis": p. xiii-[xvi]
Includes a chapter "Spinozismus" (p. 26-34)

1. Auerbach, Berthold, 1812-1882.

34-684

[Library of Co]ngress Libr. PT1812.A3Z9 1933
[2] 928.3

SPECIAL COLLECTIONS SPINOZA

E-4-a 2822

Yoshioka, Kiyoshi,
Fusseru ni okeru kōsei-teki shikisai.
[1936]
15-57 p. 22cm.

From Tetsugaku zasshi, v. 46, July 1936.

1. Husserl, Edmund, 1859-1938.

NNC

E-4-b
BRUNNER

SPECIAL COLLECTIONS SPINOZA

E-4-b 2827

Altkirch, Ernst, 1873-1926.
Constantin Brunner (on the occasion of his 60th birthday) [1922]
229-235 p. 26cm.

From the Menorah journal, v. 8, no. 4, August 1922.
Includes references to Spinoza.

Altkirch, Ernst, 1873-1926.
Constantin Brunner. [1910]
279-284 col. port.

In Ost und West, 10. Jahrgang, 1910.
Includes references to Spinoza.

Aron, Willy
Constantin Brunner; a contribution to a bibliography of writings by and about him, by Willy Aron .. [1941]
7 p. 25½cm.

"Reprinted from Journal of Jewish bibliography ... September, 1941."
Includes items on Spinoza.

Bäumer, Eduard, 1870-
Constantin Brunner über die Prinzipien der Naturwissenschaft und der Aberglaube in der modernen Medizin. München, Verlag der Aerztlichen Rundschau O. Gmelin, 1911.
88 p. 24cm.

Includes references to Spinoza.

Bernard, Walter
The philosophy of Spinoza and Brunner. New York, Spinoza Institute of America, 1934.
239 p. 23cm.

Issued also as thesis (Ph. D.) - New York University.
Presentation copy to A. S. Oko, with the author's inscription and signature.
Bibliography: p. 235-237.

Bickel, Lothar
Erkenntniskritik und Relativitätslehre bei Constantin Brunner (zu seinem 70. Geburtstag am 28. August 1932) [1932]
310-313 p. 26cm.

From Kant-Studien, Bd. 37, 1932.

Brunner, Constantin, 1862-1937.
Aus meinem Tagebuch. Potsdam, G. Kiepenheuer, 1928.
405 p. 23cm.

Includes many references to Spinoza.

Brunner, Constantin, 1862-1937.
Goethes Verhältniss zu Spinoza. [1912]
386-389 p.

In Die Zukunft, 81. Bd., 1912.

Brunner, Constantin, 1862-1937.
Der Judenhass und die Juden. Berlin, Oesterheld, 1918.
xxxiii, 448 p. 23cm.

Includes references to Spinoza.

Brunner, Constantin, 1862-1937.
... Kunst, philosophie, mystik; gesammelte aufsätze. Zürich, Humanitas verlag [1940]
468 p., 2 l. front. (port.) 23 cm.
Foreword signed: Lothar Bickel.
"Verzeichnis der hauptwerke Constantin Brunners": 2d leaf at end.
CONTENTS.—Zum fünfundfünzigsten [!] geburtstage.—Kurze rechenschaft über die lehre von den geistigen und vom volk.—Künstler und philosophen.—Sokrates.—Das lamm Benedikt Spinoza.—Ein idealporträt Spinozas.—Goethes verhältnis zu Spinoza.—Eine Spinoza-gesellschaft?—Ruhm.—Traum.—Liliencron und alle seine unsterblichen dichter.—Zur technik des künstlerischen schaffens.—Natura sanat, medicus curat.—Über den aberglauben in der betrachtung von geisteskranken.—Faustischer geist und untergang des Abendlandes—eine

~~(Continued on next card)~~
A 41—3812
[49c1]

Brunner, Constantin, 1862-1937.
Die Lehre von den Geistigen und vom Volke. I, erster-[zweiter] Halbband. Berlin, K. Schnabel, 1908.
2 v. (1167 p.) port. 24cm.

No more published.
Includes many references to Spinoza.

Brunner, Constantin, 1862–
... Die lehre von den geistigen und vom volk ... 2. aufl. Potsdam, G. Kiepenheuer, 1927.
2 v. front. (port.) 22½cm.
Paged continuously.
Includes many references to Spinoza.

I. Title.
39-4401
Library of Congress B3213.B73L4 1927
[2]

Brunner, Constantin, 1862-1937.
Memscheleth sadon; letztes Wort über den Judenhass und die Juden. Berlin, Verlag Neues Vaterland [c1920]
111 p. 23cm.

Includes reference to Spinoza (p. 70)
Presentation copy to A. S. Oko, with the author's inscription and signature.

Brunner, Constantin, 1862-1937.
Spinoza contre Kant et la cause de la vérité spirituelle. Traduit et précédé d'un avant-propos par Henri Lurié. Paris, J. Vrin, 1932.
104 p. 22cm.

Brunner, Constantin, 1862-1937.
Spinoza gegen Kant und die Sache der geistigen Wahrheit. Berlin, K. Schnabel, 1910.
83 p. 23cm.

Brunner, Constantin, 1862-1937.
Eine Spinoza-Gesellschaft? [1910]
167-170 col. 28cm.

From Ost und West, X. Jahrg., Heft 3, 1910.

1. Spinoza, Benedictus de, 1632-1677.

Brunner, Constantin, 1862-1937.
Unser Christus; oder, Das Wesen des Genies. Berlin, Oesterheld, 1921.
725 p. 21½cm.

Includes references to Spinoza.

Brunner, Constantin, 1862–1937.
Vom einsiedler Constantin Brunner. Mein leben und schaffen. Unsre scholastische bildung. Das unglück unsres deutschen volkes und unsre "völkischen". Potsdam, G. Kiepenheuer, 1924.
151 p. 24cm.

Includes references to Spinoza.

I. Title.
27-23163
Library of Congress B3213.B74A3
Copyright A—Foreign 27208
[2]

Constantin Brunner-Gemeinschaft, Berlin.
Die Hauptwerke Constantin Brunners. Potsdam, G. Kiepenheuer Verlag [1927]
23 p. mount. port. 26cm.

Reviews, tables of contents and excerpts from Brunner's principal works.
Includes references to Spinoza.

Constantin Brunner-Gemeinschaft, Berlin.
Von Constantin Brunner und seinem Werk. Potsdam, G. Kiepenheuer [c1927]
79 p. port. 25cm. (Veröffentlichung der Constantin Brunner-Gemeinschaft, Berlin. 1927)

Includes references to Spinoza.

Gaulke, Johannes, 1869-
Constantin Brunner und die Geistigen. [c1915]
345-348 p. 23cm.

From Nord und Süd, Bd. 152, Jahrg. 39, 1915.
With Schnabel, Karl, firm, publishers, Berlin. Hinweis durch Urteile der Presse auf Constantin Brunner, Die Lehre von den Geistigen und vom Volke.

Kettner, Frederick, 1886-
Über Constantin Brunners Werk "Der Judenhass und die Juden", von Dr. Friedrich Kettner. Wien, R. Löwit, 1922.
52 p. 23cm.

Includes references to Spinoza.

Levy, Ernst
Von Constantin Brunners Werk. [1925]
578-585 p. 26cm.

From Kant-Studien, Bd. 30, 1925.
Includes references to Spinoza.

Moebius, A
Constantin Brunners Lehre, das Evangelium für die Gemeinschaft der geistig Lebendigen; eine Studie. Berlin, Im Verlage Neues Leben bei W. Borngraeber [1910]
75 p. 24cm.

Includes references to Spinoza.

Schnabel, Karl, firm, publishers, Berlin.
Hinweis durch Urteile der Presse auf Constantin Brunner, Die Lehre von den Geistigen und vom Volke. [191-]
16 p. 23cm.

Includes references to Spinoza.

Werthenau, E C
Constantin Brunners Bedeutung für die Jugend; Vortrag, gehalten in der Brunner-Gemeinschaft, Berlin. [192-]
19 p. 14cm.

"Sonderabdruck aus der Zeitschrift 'Das Bruderwort.'"
Includes references to Spinoza.

Werthenau, E C
Constantin Brunner und Friedrich Nietzsche, von E. C. Werthenau. Hamlet, ein Deutungsversuch auf Grund von Brunners Lehre, von Fritz Blankenfeld. Potsdam, G. Kiepenheuer [1928]
71 p. 26cm. (Veröffentlichung der Constantin Brunner-Gemeinschaft, Berlin. 1928)

Includes references to Spinoza.

F

Non-Philosophical Literature and Spinoza

F-1

General

Acton, John Emerich Edward Dalberg Acton, baron, 1834-1902.
Historical essays & studies, by John Emerich Edward Dalberg-Acton, first baron Acton ... ed. by John Figgis ... and Reginald Vere Laurence. London, Macmillan and co., ltd., 1919.
vii, 544 p. 24cm.

Includes references to Spinoza in the section on George Eliot's life (p. 278, 280, 286, 301)

Acton, John Emerich Edward Dalberg Acton, 1st baron, 1834-1902.
The history of freedom and other essays, by John Emerich Edward Dalberg-Acton, first baron Acton; ed., with an introduction, by John Neville Figgis and Reginald Vere Laurence. London, Macmillan, 1922.
xxxix, 638 p. port. 23cm.

Includes references to Spinoza (p. 48, 228)

Aešcoly, Aaron Ze'ev, 1901-1948.
שפינוזה בספרות היפה. תל־אביב, תרצ"ג.
[1932]
9-11 p. 29cm.

Title transliterated: Shpīnōzā bassifrūth ha-yāfā.
From Moznayim, vol. 4, no. 26, Dec. 15, 1932.
With Roth, Leon. Mishnāthō shel Shpīnōzā ... [1932]

Agoult, Marie Catherine Sophie de Flavigny, comtesse d', 1805-1876.
Mémoires 1833-1854, avec une introduction, de m. Daniel Ollivier. Paris, Calmann-Lévy [c1927]
xii, 246 p. 19 cm.

At head of title: Comtesse d'Agoult (Daniel Stern)

Alexander, Bernát, 1850-
Spinoza und die Psychoanalyse. [1928]
94-103 p. 18cm.

From Almanach des Internationalen Psychoanalytischen Verlages in Wien für das Jahr 1928.
"Aus dem im Februar 1927 zum 250. Todestag Spinozas im Haag erschienenen V. Band des 'Chronicon Spinozanum'."

Arnold, Matthew, 1822-1888.
Essays literary & critical. London, Dent; New York, Dutton [1909]
xv, 380 p. 18 cm. (Everyman's library. Essays.)

Includes an essay "A word more about Spinoza" (p. 174-185)

Arnold, Matthew, 1822-1888.
A word more about Spinoza. [1864]
136-142 p.

In Macmillan's magazine, v. 9, 1864.

Arnold, Matthew, 1822-1888.
A word about Spinoza. [1922]
36-53 p. 17cm.

From Modern English essays, vol. 1, 1922.

Athenaeum. Eine zeitschrift von August Wilhelm Schlegel und Friedrich Schlegel. 1.-3. bd.; 1798-1800. Berlin, Bey F. Vieweg dem älteren, 1798-1800.

3 v. 21cm.

Two numbers were issued annually. Vol. 2 and 3 with imprint "Berlin, bei Heinrich Frölich", have besides the general, a special t.-p. for the "erstes stück" of each respectively, and are paged continuously. The "zweites stück" of the 1st vol. in this copy, as probably in all the others, is without list of contents. The 3d vol. was ed. by Schleiermacher in place of F. Schlegel. *cf.* Houben, Zeitschriften der romantik.
No more published.

I. Schlegel, August Wilhelm von, 1767-1845, ed. II. *Schlegel, Friedrich von, 1772-1829, ed. III. Schleiermacher, Friedrich Ernst Daniel, 1768-1834.

Baldwin, James Mark, 1861-1934.
History of psychology; a sketch and an interpretation. Issued for the Rationalist Press Association, limited. London, Watts, 1913.
2 v. fronts., ports. 19 cm.

Includes a section on Spinoza (v. 1, p. 117-121)

Baltzer, Eduard, 1814-1887.

Neue propheten. Vorträge über deren leben, character und bedeutung von Eduard Baltzer. Nordhausen, F. Förstemann, 1852.

4 p. l., 228 p., 1 l. 23cm. (*Added t.-p.:* Alte und neue welt-anschauung ... 3. sammlung)

Contents.—I. Arnold von Brescia.—II. Wykliffe.—III. Huss.—IV. Gutenberg.—V. Savonarola.—VI. Kolumbus.—VII. Luther.—VIII. Zwingli.—IX. Dürer.—X. Hohenheim.—XI. Kopernikus.—XII. Keppler.—XIII. Galilei.—XIV. Bruno.—XV. Vanini.—XVI. Campanella.—XVII. Spinoza.—XVIII. Newton.—XIX. Thomasius.—XX. Woher und wohin?

I. Title.

[*Full name:* Wilhelm Eduard Baltzer]

Bastid, Paul, 1892-
Sieyès et sa pensée. [Paris] Hachette [c1939]
652 p. plates, ports. 26 cm.

Bernays, Michael, 1834-1897.
Briefe von und an Michael Bernays, mit einem Bildnis. Berlin, Behr, 1907.
xiv, 220 p. port. 20 cm.

Includes a reference to Spinoza (p. 193)

F-1
2867

Bernthsen, Sophie
Der Spinozismus in Shelley's Weltanschauung.
Heidelberg, Winter, 1900.
vii, 44 p. 23cm.

Thesis, Heidelberg.
Bound with non-thesis edition of same work.

F-1
2868

Bernthsen, Sophie.
Der Spinozismus in Shelley's Weltanschauung.
Heidelberg, Winter, 1900.
vii, 162 p. 23cm.

Issued in part as thesis, Heidelberg.

F-1
2869

Bick, Abraham
וועלט און היים; עסייען בפרון
הרב אברהם ביק. ניו-יארק, פארלאג
משה שמואל שקלארסקי, התש"ב.
[New York, M. S. Sklarsky, 1941]
191 p. 23½cm.

Title transliterated: Velt un haym.
Includes a chapter on Spinoza (p. 38-44)
Added t. p.: Welt un heim (World and home)
Essays. New York, M. S. Sklarsky, 1941.

F-1
2870

Bien, Hermann M 1831-1895.
Ben-Beor; a story of the Anti-Messiah, in two divisions. Pt. 1. Lunar intaglios. The man in the moon, a counterpart of Wallace's "Ben-Hur." Pt. 2. Historical phantasmagoria. The wandering gentile, a companion romance to Sue's "Wandering Jew." By H. M. Bien ... Baltimore, I. Friedenwald co., 1891.
ix, 528 p. 18½cm.

Includes a section on Spinoza (p. 453-456)

I. Title.

6-13122 Revised

Library of Congress PZ3.B477B
[r44e2]

F-1
2871

Blakey, Robert, 1795-1878.
The history of political literature, from the earliest times. London, R. Bentley, 1855.
2 v. 23 cm.

DLC

F-1
2872

Bolingbroke, Henry Saint-John, 1st viscount, 1678-1751.
The works of the late Right Honourable Henry St. John, lord viscount Bolingbroke. With the life of Lord Bolingbroke by Dr. Goldsmith, now enlarged by more recent information relative to his publick and personal character, selected from various authorities. A new ed. in eight volumes. London, J. Johnson, 1809.
8 v. port. 21 cm.

Includes references to Spinoza.

NNC

F-1
2873

Boswell, James, 1740-1795.
Boswell's Life of Johnson, including Boswell's Journal of a tour to the Hebrides and Johnson's diary of a journey into North Wales, ed. by George Birkbeck Hill. Oxford, Clarendon press, 1887.
6 v. port., map, facsim., fold. tab. 24 cm.

Includes references to Spinoza.

NNC

F-1
2874

Bourget, Paul, 1852-1935.
The disciple. London, Neely [c1898]
341 p.

Includes references to Spinoza.

NNC

F-1
2875

Bourget, Paul Charles Joseph, 1852-1935.
Le disciple. Illustrations de S. Macchiati. Paris, A. Lemerre [1899]
xi, 298 p. illus. 19cm. (Collection Guillaume-Lemerre)

Includes references to Spinoza.
Original paper covers bound in.

F-1
2876

Bourget, Paul Charles Joseph, 1852-
The disciple. By Paul Bourget. New York, C. Scribner's sons, 1901.
xvii, [1], 341 p. 19½cm.

Includes references to Spinoza.

I. Title.

1-30955 Revised

Library of Congress PZ3.B665D2
[r20c2]

F-1
2877

Brandes, Georg Morris Cohen, 1842-1927.
Recollections of my childhood and youth.
London, W. Heinemann, 1906.
5 p. l., 397 p. 23 cm.

Includes a reference to Spinoza (p. 101)

NN

F-1
2878

Brandes, Georg Morris Cohen, 1842-1927.
Reminiscences of my childhood and youth, by George Brandes. New York, Duffield & company, 1906.

5 p. l., 397 p. 23cm.
Includes a reference to Spinoza (p. 101)

NNC

Library of Congress PT8125.B8Z53 6—34030
[38l1]

F-1
2879

Brandes, Georg Morris Cohen, 1842-1927.
Spinoza. [1897]
4-6 p.

In Adolf Bruell's populär-wissenschaftliche Monatsblätter, Jahrgang 17, 1897.

NN

F-1
2880

Brandl, Alois, 1855-1940.
Samuel Taylor Coleridge and the English romantic school. English ed. by Lady Eastlake. (Assisted by the author.) London, J. Murray, 1887.
xvi, 392 p. port. 21 cm.

Includes references to Spinoza.

NNC

F-1
2881

Brandl, Alois, 1855-1940.
Samuel Taylor Coleridge und die englische Romantik. Berlin, R. Oppenheim, 1886.
xiii (i.e. xv), 437 p. 20 cm.

Includes references to Spinoza.

NNC

F-1
2882

Brenner, Joseph Ḥayyim, 1881-1921.
שכול וכשלון; או, ספר ההתלבטות. ניו־יורק, א. י. שטיבל, תר"ף.
[New York, 1920]

282 p. 20 cm.

Title transliterated: Shekhol ve-khishalon.
Includes references to Spinoza.

I. Title. *Title transliterated:* Shekhol ve-khishalon.

DLC

PJ5053.B7S5 21-8197 rev*

Library of Congress [r56b2]

F-1
2883

Brett, George Sidney, 1879-
A history of psychology ... by George Sidney Brett ... London, G. Allen & company, ltd., 1912-21.

3 v. 23 cm. (*Half-title:* Library of philosophy. Ed. by J. H. Muirhead)

Imprint varies: v. 2-3, London, G. Allen & Unwin ltd.—New York, The Macmillan company.
Bibliography: v. 1, p. 349-353; v. 2, p. 389-390; v. 3, p. 317-318.

CONTENTS.—[I] Ancient and patristic.—II. Mediæval & early modern period.—III. Modern psychology.

Vol. 2 includes references to Spinoza.

1. Psychology—Hist. 2. Philosophy, Ancient. 3. Psychology, Patristic.

NNC

BF81.B7 13—890

Library of Congress [54w1]

SPECIAL COLLECTIONS
SPINOZA

F-1
2884

[**Bridges, Robert Seymour**] 1844-1930, *ed.*
The spirit of man; an anthology in English & French from the philosophers & poets, made by the poet laureate in 1915 & dedicated by gracious permission to His Majesty the King. London, New York [etc.] Longmans, Green & co., 1916.

[336] p. 18 cm.
Includes selections from Spinoza.

1. English literature (Selections: Extracts, etc.) 2. French literature (Selections: Extracts, etc.) 3. Idealism in literature. I. Title.

PR1109.B65 16—6701

Library of Congress [55q1]

SPECIAL COLLECTIONS
SPINOZA

F-1
2885

Brown, Hugh
A philosopher's tragedy; Shakespeare and Spinoza. [1929]
299-313 p. 25cm.

From the Hibbert journal, v. 27, no. 2, Jan. 1929.

SPECIAL COLLECTIONS
SPINOZA

F-1
2886

Busch, Moritz, 1821-1899.
Unser Reichskanzler; Studien zu einem Charakterbilde. Leipzig, F. W. Grunow, 1884 [i. e. 1888]
2 v. 19cm. (Grenzboten-Sammlung. 2. Reihe, Bd. 1.-2)

Includes a reference to Spinoza (v. 1, p. 108)
Original paper covers bound in.

F-1
2887

Carvalho, Joaquim de, 1892-
A evolução espiritual de Antero (ensaio breve de interpretação) Lisboa, 1929.
109 p. 19cm.

"Separata de Seara nova."
Presentation copy to Carl Gebhardt, with the author's inscription and signature.
Includes references to Spinoza.

F-1
2888

Castro, Américo, 1885-
... El pensamiento de Cervantes, por Américo Castro. Madrid, Impr. de la librería y casa editorial Hernando (s. a.) 1925.
406 p. 25cm. (Revista de filología española.—Anejo VI)
At head of title: Junta para ampliación de estudios. Centro de estudios históricos.
Bibliographical foot-notes.
Errata slip inserted.
Includes a reference to Spinoza (p. 345)
1. Cervantes Saavedra, Miguel de, 1547-1616.
[Full name: Américo Castro y Quesada]
27—1984
Library of Congress PQ6351.C3
[37r33g1]

F-1
2889

Chekhov, Anton Pavlovich, 1860-1904.
Humoresken und Satiren von Anton Tschechow. Aus dem Russischen übersetzt von H. Röhl. Drittes Bändchen. Leipzig, Ph. Reclam [19--]
103 p. (Universal-Bibliothek, Bd. 5315) 14½cm.

References to Spinoza included in "Eine Schreckensnacht" (p. 19-29)

F-1
2890

Coert, H J
Spinoza's betrekking tot de geneeskunde en haar beoefenaren. Leiden, E. J. Brill, 1938.
18 p. 24cm. (Mededeelingen van wege het Spinozahuis, IV)

F-1
2891

Cohen, Max
Schiller and the Jews. [1905]
325-328 p.

In Reform advocate, v. 29, 1905.
Includes a reference to Spinoza.

NNJ

F-1
2892

Cohen, Mozes Herman, 1880-
Spinoza en de geneeskunde. [Amsterdam. de Bussy [1920]
xi, 74 p. 23½cm.

Original paper covers bound in.

F-1
2893

Coit, Thomas Winthrop, 1803-1885.
Benedict Spinoza. [1876]
507-508 p.

In The Churchman, v. 34, 1876.

NNUT

F-1
2894

Coleridge, Samuel Taylor, 1772-1834.
Coleridge on logic and learning, with selections from the unpublished manuscripts, by Alice D. Snyder ... New Haven, Yale university press; [etc., etc.] 1929.
xvi p., 1 l., 169 p. front., facsims., diagrs. 24 cm.
"Table of manuscripts and editions": p. [xi]-xiii.
Includes references to Spinoza from the works of Coleridge.

1. Logic. I. Snyder, Alice Dorothea, 1887- ed. II. Title.
BC71.C65 29—23816
Library of Congress [54e1]

F-1
2895

Conway, Moncure Daniel, 1832-1907.
The wandering Jew, by Moncure Daniel Conway ... New York, H. Holt and company, 1881.
4 p. l., [3]-292 p. 19cm.

Includes references to Spinoza.

I. Title.
NNJ Library of Congress 14—20108
——— Copy 2.
Copyright 1881: 10892 [37b1]

F-1
2896

Copeland, Arthur
Spinoza, apostle of emancipated thought. [1921]
p. 1.

In The American Israelite, v. 67, 1921.

OCH

Coralnik, Abraham
שריפטען פון אברהם קאראלניק.
ניו יארק, קאראלניק פארלאג קאמי-
טעט, 1938-

[New York, 1938-
v. 1 port., facsim. 24cm.

Title transliterated: Shriften.
Includes a chapter on Spinoza (v. 1, p. 41-50)

CONTINUED ON NEXT CARD

Coralnik, Abraham שריפטען.
[1938- (Card 2)

Contents.
1. בד. געשטאלטען און געדאנקען.--

Coralnik, Abraham

Warsaw, 1928. דאס בוך פון בלעטער.
2 v.

Title transliterated: Dos bukh fun bleter.
Includes an essay on Spinoza (v. 1, p. 5-[30])

Coulon, Marcel, 1873–
... L'enseignement de Remy de Gourmont; avec, en fac similé, des textes inédits de Gourmont et son portrait par Raoul Dufy. Paris, Éditions du siècle [1925]
10 p. l., 23-93 p., 1 l. incl. port., facsims. 16½cm.
"725 exemplaires sur vergé à la forme des papeteries d'Arches, numérotés de 26 à 750. Exemplaire ~~422~~ 259."
Includes references to Spinoza.
Original paper covers bound in.
1. Gourmont, Rémy de, 1858-1915. I. Dufy, Raoul, illus. II. Title.
25-22211
Library of Congress PQ2266.Z8C6

Cram, W A
Spinoza's doctrine. [1867]
543-549 p.

In The Radical, Boston, v. 2, 1867.

Critical remarks upon the late Lord Viscount Bolingbroke's letters on the study and use of history, as far as they regard sacred history. London, J. Woodyer, 1754.
[8], 67 p.

Cummings, Bruce Frederick, 1889-1919.
The journal of a disappointed man, by W. N. P. Barbellion [pseud.] with an introduction by H. G. Wells. New York, Doran [c1919]
viii, 312 p. 22 cm.

Includes a reference to Spinoza (p. 16)

Davis, Elmer, 1890-
The God of Hitler and Spinoza. [1940]
[186]-195 p. 26cm.

From Harper's magazine, July, 1940.

Davy, Sir Humphry, bart., 1778-1829.
Consolations in travel, or The last days of a philosopher. London, J. Murray, 1830.
vi, 281 p. 18cm.

Edited by John Davy.

De Casseres, Benjamin, 1873-1945.
Spinoza, one of the immortals. An appreciation of the great philosopher by one of his scions. [1927]
p. 1, 13.

In New York Jewish tribune, Feb. 18, 1927.

F-1
2907

De Casseres, Benjamin, 1873-1945.
Forty immortals. New York, J. Lawren ͼc1926ͽ
11-371 p. 23 cm.

Includes an essay on Spinoza (p. 51-56)

F-1
2908

De Morgan, Augustus, 1806-1871.
A budget of paradoxes. London, Longmans, Green, 1872.
vii, 511 p. 23 cm.

Includes references to Spinoza (p. 3, 29)

F-1
2909

De Quincey, Thomas, 1785-1859.
Essays. Including The confessions of an opium eater, Richard Bentley, Letters to a young man, John Paul Richter, etc., etc. With a brief memoir of the author. London, New York, Ward, Lock and Co. ͺ1886?ͺ
x, 488 p. port. 23cm.

Includes a reference to Spinosism in the section on Walking Stewart (p. 441)

NNC

F-1
2910

Deutsch-israelitischer gemeindebund.
Lessing-Mendelssohn-gedenkbuch. Zur hundertfünfzigjährigen geburtsfeier von Gotthold Ephraim Lessing und Moses Mendelssohn, sowie zur säcularfeier von Lessing's "Nathan". Mit 3 bildern in lichtbruck, initialen und vignetten in holzschnitt. Leipzig, Baumgärtner, 1879.
viii, 399 p. illus., ports.

Includes references to Spinoza.

F-1
2911

ͼDippel, Johann Conradͽ 1673-1734.
Analysis gramatis harmonici hyper-metaphysico-logico-mathematica, das ist: Chymischer Versuch zu destilliren per descensum, per ascensum et per latus, und in ihr Sal, Sulphur et Mercurium zu resolviren die drey harmonischen Systemata der heutigen Philosophie, nemlich des Cartesii, Spinosae und Leibnitzens ... In aller Freyheit, und nicht gezwungen, heraus gewickelt und wiederum gehörig zusammen gerollt durch Christianum Democritum ͼpseud.ͽ ... 1729.
88 p.

NN

F-1
2912

ͺDippel, Johann Conradͺ 1673-1734.
Christ. Democriti Vitae animalis morbus & medicina, suae vindicata origini disqvitisione physico-medica, qva simul mechanismi & Spinosismi deliramenta funditus deteguntur ... ex sanae rationis circulo deturbantur, & integrum universi motui systema concinnis vinculis nectitur. Lugduni Batavorum, Ex officina Luchtmanniana, 1711.
160 p. 17 cm.

IU-M

F-1
2913

ͺDippel, Johann Conradͺ 1673-1734.
Christiani Democriti Kranckheit und Artzney des animalischen Lebens. Wie beyde in einer physisch-medicinischen Untersuchung ihrem wahrem Ursprunge wieder zugeeignet, zugleich aber die Thorheiten des Mechanismi und Spinosismi aus dem Grunde entdeckt ... Aus dem Lateinischen von neuen übersetzt ... Franckfurth und Leipzig, Verlegts Johann Leopold Montag, 1736.
14 p. l., 412 p., 38 l.

PPCP

F-1
2914

ͺDippel, Johann Conradͺ 1673-1734.
Eröffneter Weg zum Frieden mit Gott und allen Creaturen, durch die Publication der sämtlichen Schrifften Christiani Democriti ͺpseud.ͺ ... Wozu noch kommt ein Anhang einiger noch nie gedruckten Stücken, so von ihm herkommen. Wie auch dessen Personalia. Mit einer kurtzen allgemeinen Vorrede des Auctoris, und einer andern von dem Herausgeber ... Berleburg, bey Johann Jacob Haug, 1747.
3 v.

PPLT

F-1
2915

ͼDippel, Johann Conradͽ 1673-1734.
Vitâe animalis morbus et medicina. Suâe vindicata origini disquisitione physico-medica, quâ simul mechanismi & Spinosismi deliramenta funditus deteguntur, & mathematicâ evidentiâ ex sanâe rationis circulo deturbantur, & integrum universi motus systema cocinnis vinculis nectitur. Auctore Christiano Democrito M. D. ͼpseud.ͽ Lugduni Batavorum, ex Officina Luchtmanniana, 1711.
160 p. 17cm.

F-1
2916

Dobell, Bertram, 1842-1914.
The laureate of pessimism: a sketch of the life and character of James Thomson ("B. V.") London, The author, 1910.
iv, 64 p. 19 cm.

SPECIAL COLLECTIONS SPINOZA F-1 2917

Doyle, John Andrew, 1844-1907.
Essays on various subjects. Edited by W. P. Ker, with an introduction by Sir William Anson. London, J. Murray, 1911.
xxviii, 333 p. port. 21cm.

Contents.--An idyll of education.--Freeman, Froude and Seeley.--The historical writings of Francis Parkman.--Trevelyan's "American revolution"--Ezra Stiles.--The poetry of sport.--Literature and the turf.--Racehorse breeding.--Modern rifle-shooting.--Harriers.

SPECIAL COLLECTIONS SPINOZA F-1 2918

Dunning, William Archibald, 1857-1922.
A history of political theories from Luther to Montesquieu, by William Archibald Dunning ... New York, The Macmillan company; London, Macmillan & co., ltd., ~~1905~~ 1919.
x p., 1 l., 459 p. 22½ cm.

"This volume carries forward to the middle of the eighteenth century the work begun in the History of political theories, ancient and mediæval" (1902)—Pref.
Bibliography: p. 435-448.
Includes a section on Spinoza (p. 309-317)

1. Political science—Hist.

JA81.D8 5—27137
Library of Congress ₍54o1₎

SPECIAL COLLECTIONS SPINOZA F-1 2919

Ebstein, Erich Hugo, 1880-1931.
Tuberkulose als Schicksal; eine Sammlung pathographischer Skizzen von Calvin bis Klabund, 1509-1928. Mit einer Einführung von Georg B. Gruber. Stuttgart, F. Enke, 1932.
vii, 184 p. ports. 23cm.

Includes a section on Spinoza (p. 36)
Bibliography: p. 177-178.

SPECIAL COLLECTIONS SPINOZA F-1 2920

Elger, Willem den, 1679-1703.
Twee minnebrieven van Mr. W. den Elger; met iets vooraf over den schrijver, door H. W. T. ₍1842₎
₍51₎-77 p. 16cm.

From Utrechtsche Volks-Almanak voor 1842.
Includes references to Spinoza (p. 54-55)

SPECIAL COLLECTIONS SPINOZA F-1 2921

Ellinger, Georg, 1859-
Angelus Silesius; ein Lebensbild. Breslau, W. G. Korn, 1927.
xii, 260 p. ports. 24cm.

Includes references to Spinoza.
Bibliographical references included in "Anmerkungen" (p. ₍231₎-253)

SPECIAL COLLECTIONS SPINOZA F-1 2922

Enelow, Hyman Gerson, 1876-1934.
Selected works of Hyman G. Enelow, with a memoir by Dr. Felix A. Levy ... ₍Kingsport, Tenn.₎ Priv. print. ₍Kingsport press, inc.₎ 1935.
4 v. front. (port.) 23½cm.

"Selected by Dr. Felix A. Levy."

Contents.—I. Memoir and sermons.—II. Sermons and reviews.—III. Collected writings.—IV. Scientific papers.
Includes a sermon "The spiritual value of Spinoza" (v. 2, p. 186-190)
1. Jews—Religion. I. Levy, Felix Alexander, 1884- ed.

36-18782
Library of Congress BM45.E6
₍5-5₎ 296.081

SPECIAL COLLECTIONS SPINOZA F-1 2923

Espinasse, Francis, 1823?-1912.
Literary recollections and sketches, by Francis Espinasse. London, Hodder and Stoughton, 1893.
xv, 426 p. ~~21½ cm.~~ 24cm.

"The contents of this volume are based on a series of articles, signed Φ, which appeared ... in the Bookman ..."—Note.

Includes references to Spinoza in the chapter on George Henry Lewe's early career (p. 274-276)

1. English literature—19th cent.—Hist. & crit. 2. Carlyle, Thomas, 1795-1881. 3. Hannay, James, 1827-1873. I. Title.

PR462.E7 820.903 4—17153
Library of Congress ₍57j1₎

SPECIAL COLLECTIONS SPINOZA F-1 2924

Etheridge, John Wesley, 1804-1866.
Jerusalem and Tiberias; Sora and Cordova: a survey of the religious and scholastic learning of the Jews; designed as an introduction to the study of Hebrew literature. London, Longman, Brown, Green and Longmans, 1856.
xi, 507 p. 19cm.

Includes section on Spinoza (p. 468-469)

SPECIAL COLLECTIONS SPINOZA F-1 2925

Evelyn, John, 1620-1706.
The diary of John Evelyn, from 1641 to 1705-6. With memoir. Edited by William Bray. London, Gibbings, 1895.
619 p. 25cm.

SPECIAL COLLECTIONS SPINOZA F-1 2926

Fahsel, Helmut, 1891-
Meine Vorträge. Freiburg im Breisgau, Herder, 1925.
34 p. 18cm.

Includes a paragraph on Spinoza (p. 28-29)

F-1
2927

Faulmann, Karl, 1835-1894.
Im Reiche der Geistes; illustrirte Geschichte der Wissenschaften anschaulich dargestellt. Wien, Hartleben, 1894.
xvi, 941 p. illus., plates, maps, facsims. 24 cm.

Includes a reference to Spinoza (p. 423-424)

F-1
2932

Fluegel, Maurice, 1831?-1911.
The Zend-Avesta and eastern religions; comparative legislations, doctrines, and rites of Parseeism, Brahmanism, and Buddhism; bearing upon Bible, Talmud, Gospel, Koran, their Messiah-ideals and social problems. By Maurice Fluegel ... Baltimore, H. Fluegel & co., 1898.
1 p. l., iii, 244 p. 24cm.
Includes a reference to Spinoza (p. 87)

1. Parsees. 2. Avesta. 3. Buddha and Buddhism. 4. Brahmanism. 5. Asia—Religions. I. Title.

Library of Congress BL1031.F6 98—1217
Copyright 1898: 57897 [a35e2] 290

F-1
2928

Fessler, Ignatius Aurelius, 1756-1839.
Dr. Fessler's Resultate seines Denkens und Erfahrens, als Anhang zu seinen Rückblicken auf seine 70jährige Pilgerschaft ... Breslau, W. G. Korn, 1826.
vii, 384 p. port. 22cm.

Includes references to Spinoza.

F-1
2933

Fontenelle, Bernard Le Bovier de, 1657-1757.
Oeuvres de Fontenelle, précédées d'une notice sur sa vie et ses ouvrages. Paris, Salmon, 1825.
5 v. plate, port. 21 cm.

F-1
2929

Fessler, Ignatius Aurelius, 1756-1839.
Abälard und Heloisa. Berlin, 1806.
2 v.

Includes a reference to Spinoza (v. 2, p. 591)

ViU

F-1
2934

France, Anatole, 1844-1924.
Monsieur Bergeret à Paris. Paris, Calmann-Lévy [1918]
404 p. 19 cm. (His Histoire contemporaine [t. 4])

Includes a reference to Spinoza (p. 254)

F-1
2930

Festschrift Th. G. Masaryk zum 80. Geburtstage 7. März 1930, 2. Teil: Th. G. Masaryk als Denker. Bonn, F. Cohen, 1930.
cover-title, vi, 25 p. port. 30cm.

"Sonderabdruck".
Includes "Un chef Thomas G. Masaryk", by Ad. Ferrière, "Präsident Masaryk", by R. N. Coudenhove-Kalergi and "Bibliographie über Th. G. Masaryk" by Boris Jakowenko.

F-1
2935

France, Anatole, 1844-1924.
A note on Spinoza. [1924]
p. 199. 26cm.

"Dictated by Anatole France, from his sick-bed, in response to a request of the American secretary of the Societas Spinozana, for publication in the third volume of the Chronicon Spinozanum."
From the Menorah journal, vol. X, no. 3, June-July 1924.

F-1
2931

Floerke, Gustav, 1846-1898.
Zehn Jahre mit Böcklin; Aufzeichnungen und Entwürfe. [Hrsg. von Hanns Floerke] München, F. Bruckmann, 1901.
255 p. plates, ports. 26cm.

Includes a reference to Spinoza (p. 171)

F-1
2936

France, Anatole, 1844-1924.
La vie littéraire. 3. série. Paris, Calmann-Lévy [1921]
xix, 406 p. 19cm.

The essay "La morale et la science: M. Paul Bourget"; (p. [54]-78) includes references to Spinoza.

SPECIAL COLLECTIONS SPINOZA

F-1 2937

Franck, Adolphe, 1809-1893.
Réformateurs et publicistes de l'Europe; dix-septième siècle. Paris, Calmann Lévy, 1881.
516 p. 22cm.

The second volume of the author's series entitled "Réformateurs et publicistes de l'Europe."
Includes a chapter on Spinoza (p. 410-429)

SPECIAL COLLECTIONS SPINOZA

F-1 2938

Frank, Waldo David, 1889-
Our America, by Waldo Frank. New York, Boni and Liveright [c1919]
xi, 3-232 p. 19 cm.
London edition published 1922, with title: The new America.
CONTENTS.—The land of the pioneer.—New England.—The chosen people.—The land of buried cultures.—Chicago.—The puritan says "yea."—New York.—The multitudes in Whitman.—The turning of the soil.
Includes a reference to Spinoza (p. 87)

1. U. S.—Civilization. 2. National characteristics, American. I. Title.

E169.1.F82 19—16552
Library of Congress [51k½]

SPECIAL COLLECTIONS SPINOZA

F-1 2939

Freehof, Solomon Bennett, 1892-
Stormers of heaven, by Solomon B. Freehof. New York and London, Harper & brothers, 1931.
viii p., 1 l., 225 p. 20cm.
"First edition."
Includes a section on Spinoza (p. 112-118)

1. Religions—Biog. 2. Religion—Hist. I. Title.

31—25273
Library of Congress BL72.F7
[a43h1] 922

F-1 2940

Freymüthige, lustige und ernsthafte, jedoch Vernunfft- und gesetzmässige Gedancken; oder, Monaths-Gespräche, über allerhand, fürnehmlich aber neue Bücher, durch alle zwölff Monate des 1688. und 1689. Jahres [Januarius-Aprilis des 1690 Jahres] durchgeführet von Christian Thomasius. Halle, C. Salfeld, 1688-90.
3 v.

Includes references to Spinoza.

CtY

SPECIAL COLLECTIONS SPINOZA

F-1 2941

1938p4
DF739
Friedell, Egon, 1878-1938.
Kulturgeschichte der Neuzeit; die Krisis der europäischen Seele von der schwarzen Pest bis zum Weltkrieg. Zweiter Band: Barock und Rokoko, Aufklärung und Revolution. 1. bis 6. Aufl. München, C. H. Beck, 1928.
xi, 536 p. 27cm.

Includes a section on Spinoza (p. 45-53) and other references to him.

F-1 2942

Friedlaender, David, 1750-1834.
An die Verehrer, Freunde und Schüler Jerusalem's, Spalding's, Teller's, Herder's und Löffler's. Hrsg. von Krug. Leipzig, C. H. F. Hartmann, 1823.
178 p. 20 cm.

Includes a reference to Spinoza (p. 54)

NN

F-1 2943

Friedrich, Otto
Weise von Zion. Bratislava, Prager, 1936.
218 p. ports. 20 cm.

Includes a section on Spinoza with a portrait (p. 83-120)

NN

F-1 2944

Fritzemeyer, Werner
Christenheit und Europa; zur Geschichte des europäischen Gemeinschaftsgefühls von Dante bis Leibniz. München, Oldenbourg, 1931.
170 p. 23 cm. (Historische Zeitschrift. Beiheft 23)

Includes a section on Spinoza (p. 131-136)

SPECIAL COLLECTIONS SPINOZA

F-1 2945

Froude, James Anthony, 1818-1894.
Essays in literature & history, by J. A. Froude ... London, J. M. Dent & co.; New York, E. P. Dutton & co. [~~1906~~19--]
xxiii, [1], 326 p. 17½ cm. (*Half-title:* Everyman's library, edited by Ernest Rhys. Essays and belles lettres. [no. 13])
Introduction by Hilaire Belloc.
List of J. A. Froude's published works: p. ~~xiv~~. [xxiv]
CONTENTS. — Introduction. — Arnold's poems. — Words about Oxford.—England's forgotten worthies.—The book of Job.—The lives of the saints.—The dissolution of the monasteries.—The philosophy of Christianity.—A plea for the free discussion of theological difficulties.—Spinoza.—Reynard the fox.—The commonplace book of Richard Hilles.
I. Title.

W 6—356
Washington, D.C. Pub. Library
for Library of Congress [55p1]

F-1 2946

Froude, James Anthony, 1818-1894.
Short studies on great subjects. By James Anthony Froude ... [First series] London, Longmans, Green, and co., 1867.
2 v. 19½cm.
CONTENTS.—[I] The science of history. Times of Erasmus and Luther. The influence of the reformation on the Scottish character. The philosophy of Catholicism. A plea for the free discussion of theological difficulties. Criticism and the gospel history. The book of Job.—II. Spinoza. The dissolution of the monasteries. England's forgotten worthies. Homer. The lives of the saints. Representative men. Reynard the Fox. The cat's pilgrimage. Fables: I. The lions and the oxen. II. The farmer and the fox. Parable of the bread-fruit tree. Compensation.
I. Title.

DLC
25-15722
Library of Congress PR4706.S4 1867

F-1
2947

Froude, James Anthony, 1818-1894.
Short studies on great subjects. 3d ed.
London, Longmans, Green, 1868.
vi, 440 p. 23cm.

Includes an essay "Spinoza" (p. 223-264)

F-1
2948

Froude, James Anthony, 1818-1894.
Short studies on great subjects. By James Anthony Froude ... ⌐First series¬ New York, C. Scribner and company, 1868.
534 p. 19 cm.
CONTENTS.—The science of history.—Times of Erasmus and Luther.—The influence of the reformation on the Scottish character.—The philosophy of Catholicism.—A plea for the free discussion of theological difficulties.—Criticism and the gospel history.—The book of Job.—Spinoza.—The dissolution of the monasteries.—England's forgotten worthies.—Homer.—The lives of the saints.—Representative men.—Reynard the Fox.—The cat's pilgrimage.—Fables: I. The lions and the oxen. II. The farmer and the fox.—Parable of the bread-fruit tree.—Compensation.
I. Title.

NNJ

PR4706.S4 1868 25—15723

Library of Congress ⌐56c½¬

F-1
2949

Froude, James Anthony, 1818-1894.
Short studies on great subjects. Third series. New York, Scribner, Armstrong & Co., 1877.
400 p. 20cm.

F-1
2950

Froude, James Anthony, 1818-1894.
Short studies on great subjects. New York, Scribner, Armstrong & Co., 1877.
534 p. 20cm.
Includes an essay "Spinoza" (p. ⌐274¬-323)

F-1
2951

Froude, James Anthony, 1818-1894.
Short studies on great subjects. Second series. New York, Scribner, Armstrong and Co., 1878.
472 p. facsim. 20cm.

Includes a reference to Spinoza (p. 323)

F-1
2952

Froude, James Anthony, 1818-1894.
Short studies on great subjects, by James Anthony Froude. First series. London, New York ⌐etc.¬ H. Milford, Oxford university press ⌐1924¬
3 p. l., 465 p. 15½ cm. (*Half-title:* The World's classics. 269)
"... Published in two volumes in 1867. In 'The World's classics' it was first published in 1924."
CONTENTS.—The science of history.—Times of Erasmus and Luther.—The influence of the reformation on the Scottish character.—The philosophy of Catholicism.—A plea for the free discussion of theological difficulties.—Criticism and the Gospel history.—The book of Job.—Spinoza.—The dissolution of the monasteries.—England's forgotten worthies.—Homer.—The lives of the saints.—Representative men.—Reynard the Fox.—The cat's pilgrimage.—Fables: I. The lions and the oxen. II. The farmer and the fox.—Parable of the bread fruit-tree.—Compensation.
I. Title.
Library of Congress AC8.F7 1924 25—26578
⌐50f½¬

F-1
2953

Fruin, Robert, 1857-1935.
Geschiedenis der staatsinstellingen in Nederland tot den val der Republiek. Uitgegeven door H. T. Colenbrander. 's-Gravenhage, M. Nijhoff, 1901.
xvi, 416 p. 25cm.

Includes bibliographies.

F-1
2954

Gizycki, Paul von, 1856-1908.
Vom Baume der Erkenntnis; Fragmente zur Ethik und Psychologie aus der Weltlitteratur, gesammelt und hrsg. von Paul von Gizycki. Berlin, Dümmler, 1896.
x, 829 p. 24 cm.

Includes references to Spinoza.

F-1
2955

The God-intoxicated Spinoza. ⌐1945¬
p. 102. 22cm.

From the Jewish family almanac, 1945.

1. Spinoza, Benedictus de, 1632-1677.

F-1
2956

Greef, Guillaume Joseph de, 1842–
Le transformisme social; essai sur le progrès et le regrès des sociétés, par Guillaume de Greef ... Paris, F. Alcan, 1895.
3 p. l., 520 p. 22½cm. (*On cover:* Bibliothèque de philosophie contemporaine)
"Liste d'ouvrages relatifs au transformisme social": p. ⌐515¬-518.
Includes a reference to Spinoza (p. 138-139)

1. Civilization. 2. Sociology. I. Title.

17-16614

Library of Congress HM101.G8 1895

Greenslet, Ferris, 1875-
Walter Pater, by Ferris Greenslet ... New York, McClure, Phillips & co., 1903.
viii p., 1 l., 163 p. front. (port.) 18½ cm. (*Added t.-p.:* Contemporary men of letters series)
Chronology: p. 153-163.
Includes a reference to Spinoza. (p. 83)
1. Pater, Walter Horatio, 1839-1894.
PR5136.G7 1903 -928.2 3—25326
Library of Congress ₍51d1₎

Grunsky, Karl, 1871-
... Richard Wagner und die Juden, von dr. K. Grunsky. München, Deutscher volksverlag ₍1920₎
96 p. 23½cm. (Deutschlands führende männer und das judentum. bd. II)
"Schrifttum": p. ₍5₎
Includes a reference to Spinoza (p. 30-31)
1. Wagner, Richard, 1813-1883. 2. Music—Jews.
NN
Library of Congress ML410.W19G88 24-601
₍2₎

Gundling, Nicolaus Hieronymus, 1671-1729.
Collegium historico-literarium; oder, Ausführliche Discourse über die vornehmsten Wissenschaften. Bremen, 1738-1743.
2 v.

Includes references to Spinoza.

NNUT

Guttmann, Julius, 1880-1950.
Religion und Wissenschaft im mittelalterlichen und im modernen Denken. Berlin, Philo Verlag, 1922.
72 p. 24cm.

Includes references to Spinoza.
Bibliographical footnotes.
Original paper cover bound in.

Haight, Gordon Sherman.
George Eliot & John Chapman, with Chapman's Diaries, by Gordon S. Haight. New Haven, Yale university press; London, H. Milford, Oxford university press, 1940.
xi p., 3 l., ₍3₎-261 p. 2 port. (incl. front.) facsims. 24 cm.
"Published on the Louis Stern memorial fund."
Bibliographical foot-notes.
Includes references to Spinoza.
1. Eliot, George, pseud., *i. e.* Marian Evans, afterwards Cross, 1819-1880. 2. Chapman, John, 1822-1894. I. Chapman, John, 1822-1894.
Library of Congress PR4683.H3 40—35116
₍49r41v2₎ 928.2

Hall, Granville Stanley, 1844-1924.
Founders of modern psychology, by G. Stanley Hall ... New York and London, D. Appleton and company, 1912.
vii p., 2 l., 3-470, ₍1₎ p. front., ports. 21½ cm.
CONTENTS.—Eduard Zeller.—Rudolph Hermann Lotze.—Gustav Theodor Fechner.—Eduard von Hartmann.—Hermann L. F. von Helmholtz.—Wilhelm Wundt.
Includes references to Spinoza.
1. Zeller, Eduard, 1814-1908. 2. *Lotze, Hermann, 1817-1881. 3. Fechner, Gustav Theodor, 1801-1887. 4. *Hartmann, Eduard von, 1842-1906. 5. Helmholtz, Hermann Ludwig Ferdinand von, 1821-1894. 6. Wundt, Wilhelm Max, 1832-1920.
Library of Congress BF103.H3 12—17650
₍49b²1₎

Hallam, Henry, 1777-1859.
Introduction to the literature of Europe, in the fifteenth, sixteenth and seventeenth centuries. 3d ed. London, J. Murray, 1847.
3 v. 23cm.

Includes references to Spinoza.
Bibliographical footnotes.

The Harvard classics, ed. by Charles W. Eliot.
New York, Collier ₍c1909-10₎
50 v. plates 21 cm.

Includes references to Spinoza.

₍**Harvey,** *Sir* **Paul**₎ 1869-
The concise Oxford dictionary of English literature. Oxford, The Clarendon press, 1939.
4 p. l., 567, ₍1₎ p. 17½ cm.
An abridgment of Sir Paul Harvey's Oxford companion to English literature prepared by John Mulgan. *cf.* Pref.
Includes an article on Spinoza (p. 494-495)
1. English literature—Dictionaries. 2. English literature—Bio-bibl. 3. American literature—Dictionaries. 4. American literature—Bio-bibl. I. *Mulgan, John, 1911-1945, ed. II. Title.
Full name: Sir Henry Paul Harvey.
PR19.H32 820.3 40—27031
Library of Congress ₍a57b²1₎

Hausenstein, Wilhelm, 1882-
Vom Geist des Barock. München, R. Piper, 1924.
135 p. plates. 24cm.

Includes a reference to Spinoza (p. 48)

F-1
2967

Hauser, Philippe, 1832-1925.
Évolution intellectuelle et religieuse de l'humanité. Paris, Alcan, 1920-21.
2 v.

Includes references to Spinoza (v. 1, p. 688-700, 755-758)

NN

F-1
2968

SPECIAL COLLECTIONS SPINOZA

Hauser, Philippe, 1832-1925.
Les Grecs et les Sémites dans l'histoire de l'humanité. Paris, A. Maloine [1910]
xv, 504 p. 25cm.

Includes a section on Spinoza (p. 223-234)
Original paper covers bound in.

F-1
2969

Heine, Heinrich, 1797-1856.
Religion and philosophy in Germany: a fragment. Translated by John Snodgrass. London, Trübner, 1882.
x, 177 p. 21 cm.

Includes a section on Spinoza (p. 69-74) and other references to him.

F-1
2970

SPECIAL COLLECTIONS SPINOZA

Heine, Heinrich, 1797-1856.
Religion and philosophy in Germany: a fragment. Translated by John Snodgrass. 2d ed. London, K. Paul, Trench, Trübner, 1891.
x, 177 p. (The English and foreign philosophical library)

Includes a section on Spinoza (p. 69-74) and other references to him.

F-1
2971

SPECIAL COLLECTIONS SPINOZA

Heine, Heinrich, 1797-1856.
Der Salon. Hamburg, Hoffmann und Campe, 1834-35.
v. 1-2 in 1. 17cm.

Includes a section on Spinoza (v. 1, p. 112-123)

F-1
2972

Heine, Heinrich, 1797-1856.
Zur Geschichte der Religion und Philosophie in Deutschland. Halle a. d. S., O. Hendel, 1887.
132 p. front. 18 cm.

References to Spinoza included in bk. 2 "Von Luther bis Kant" (p. 48-82)

F-1
2973

Heller, Ágost, 1843-1902.
Geschichte der physik von Aristoteles bis auf die neueste zeit, von August Heller ... Stuttgart, F. Enke, 1882-84.
2 v. in 1. 25cm.

CONTENTS.—1. bd. Von Aristoteles bis Galilei.—2. bd. Von Descartes bis Robert Mayer.
Includes a section on Spinoza (v. 2, p. 97-102)

1. Physics—Hist.

Library of Congress QC7.H5 3—5882
[s27e1]

F-1
2974

Herbert, Edward Herbert, baron, 1583-1648.
The autobiography of Edward, lord Herbert of Cherbury, with introduction, notes, appendices, and a continuation of the life, by Sidney L. Lee. London, J. C. Nimmo, 1886.
lxiv, 369 p. 4 port., geneal. tab. 24 cm.

NN

F-1
2975

SPECIAL COLLECTIONS SPINOZA

Herder, Johann Gottfried von, 1744-1803.
... God, some conversations; a translation with a critical introduction and notes by Frederick H. Burkhardt. New York, Veritas press, 1940.
2 p. l., vii-xiv, 247 p. 22cm.

At head of title: Johann Gottfried Herder.
Issued also as thesis (PH. D.) Columbia university.
Bibliographical references in "Notes to the translation" (p. 220-231)
"Selected bibliography": p. 233-241.

1. God. I. Burkhardt, Frederick Henry, 1912- tr.

Library of Congress BT100.H36 1940 a 40-14928
——— Copy 2.
Copyright [5] 231

F-1
2976

Heron, Denis Caulfield, 1826-1881.
An introduction to the history of jurisprudence. London, Parker, 1860.
viii, 846 p. 23 cm.

Includes a section on Spinoza (p. 480-482)

Hettner, Hermann, 1821-1882.
Literaturgeschichte des achtzehnten Jahrhunderts. 4. verbesserte Aufl. Braunschweig, Druck und Verlag von F. Vieweg und Sohn, 1881.
v. 1-2. 22cm.

Includes references to Spinoza (v. 1, p. 38-39, 175)

~~CONTINUED ON NEXT CARD~~

[Hilty, Karl] 1833-1909.
Saul von Tarsus und Baruch Spinoza. [1907]
62 p. 19cm.

"Separatabdruck aus dem Politischen Jahrbuch der Schweizerischen Eidgenossenschaft (Jahrgang 1907)"

Historische und diplomatische Nachricht von der alten Thüringischen Stadt Walterthausen, dem dabey gelegenen fürstlichen Schlosse Tennenberg und dem Dorffe Ibenhayn. Gotha, gedruckt bey Johann Christoph Reyher, 1763.
1 p. l., 260, [5] p. 22cm.

Includes references to Spinoza (p. 172, 177)

Holmes, Oliver Wendell, 1841-1935.
Collected legal papers, by Oliver Wendell Holmes. New York, Harcourt, Brace and Howe, 1920.
1 p. l., v-vii p., 1 l., 316 p. 23cm.

"This collection has been made by the kindness of ... Mr. Harold J. Laski."--Pref.
Includes a reference to Spinoza (p. 305)

Holmes, Oliver Wendell, 1841-1935.
Justice Oliver Wendell Holmes; his book notices and uncollected letters and papers, edited and annotated by Harry C. Shriver, introduction by Harlan Fiske Stone. New York, Central Book Co., 1936.
xiii, 280 p. 22cm.

Includes references to Spinoza.

Holyoake, George Jacob, 1817-1906.
The life and character of Richard Carlile. London, J. Watson,
40 p. 17cm.

Volume of pamphlets.

Holyoake, George Jacob, 1817-1906.
Organisation: not of arms - but ideas. London, J. Watson, 1853.
viii, 26 p. 17cm.

Volume of pamphlets.

Holyoake, George Jacob, 1817-1906.
Rationalism: a treatise for the times. London, J. Watson, 1845.
47 p. 17cm.

Volume of pamphlets.

1. Rationalism - Addresses, essays, lectures.

Howe, John, 1630-1705.
The works of John Howe. With a general preface by Henry Rogers. London, The Religious Tract Society [1862?-1874?]
6 v. 23 cm.

Hudson, William Henry, 1841-1922.
The purple land, by W. H. Hudson; introduction by William McFee. New York, The Modern library [c1927]
xvi, 389 p. 16 cm. (*Half-title:* The Modern library of the world's best books)

Includes a reference to Spinoza (p. 368-369)

1. Uruguay—Descr. & trav. I. Title.

F-1 2987

Hughes, A M D
The theology of Shelley. ₍1938₎
₍191₎-203 p. (Warton lecture on English poetry)

In Proceedings of the British academy, ₍v. 24₎ 1938.
Includes references to Spinoza.

F-1 2988

Hugo, Victor Marie, *comte*, 1802-1885.
Victor Hugo's intellectual autobiography (Postscriptum de ma vie); being the last of the unpublished works and embodying the author's ideas on literature, philosophy and religion; translated with a study of the last phase of Hugo's genius, by Lorenzo O'Rourke. New York and London, Funk & Wagnalls company, 1907.
lxx p., 1 l., 73-400 p. front. 19½cm.
Includes a reference to Spinoza (p. lxv)

I. O'Rourke, Lorenzo, tr.

NN

F-1 2989

Huxley, Thomas Henry, 1825-1895.
Collected essays. ₍Authorized ed.₎ New York, Appleton, 1894-98. ₍v. 1, 1896₎
9 v. illus. 19 cm.

F-1 2990

Jacoby, Daniel, 1844-
Nicolaus Lenau. ₍1883₎
242-249 p.

From Allgemeine deutsche Biographie, v. 18.
Includes references to Spinoza.

F-1 2991

Jacoby, Johann, 1805-1877.
Der freie Mensch. Rück- und Vorschau eines Staatsgefangenen. Berlin, J. Springer, 1866.
46 p.

Includes a section "Der homo liber des Paraklet Spinoza" (p. 1-35)

NN

F-1 2992

Janus, Daniel Friedrich, 1683-1760.
M. D. F. Jani ... De fatis dedicationum librorum; sive, Von den Zuschriften derer Gelehrten. Dissertatio historica et litteraria. Vitembergae, 1718.

Includes a reference to Spinoza (p. 6)

PU

F-1 2993

Jellinek, Adolf, 1821-1893.
Aus der Zeit. Tagesfragen und Tagesbegebenheiten. I. Serie. Budapest, S. Márkus, 1884.

References to Spinoza included in an article on A. Foucher de Careil (p. 81-85)

NNJ

F-1 2994

Joachim, Joseph, 1831-1907.
Briefe von und an Joseph Joachim, gesammelt und hrsg. von Johannes Joachim und Andreas Moser. Berlin, J. Bard, 1911-13.
3 v. plates, ports., facsims. 22 cm.

F-1 2995

Jørgensen, Adolf Ditlev, 1840-1897.
Nils Stensen. Et mindeskrift af A. D. Jørgensen. København, Udgivet af Samfundet til den danske literaturs fremme, B. Lunos Kgl. hof-bogtrykkeri, 1884.
2 p. l., 231 p. 21 cm.

Includes a section on Spinoza (p. 51-57)

F-1 2996

Jowett, Benjamin, 1817-1893.
Sermons, biographical and miscellaneous. Edited by W. H. Fremantle. New York, Dutton, 1899.
x, 370 p. 20cm.
Includes a sermon "John Bunyan and Benedict Spinoza" (p. ₍44₎-64)

Klausner, Joseph, 1874-
פילוסופים והוגי־דעות; מסות ומחקרים. מאת יוסף קלוזנר. תל־אביב, הוצאת דביר, תרצ"ד-
[Tel-Aviv, 1934-]
v. 1.

Title transliterated: Pilosofim ...
Includes a chapter on Spinoza.

Landauer, Gustav, 1870-1919.
Gustav Landauer, sein lebensgang in briefen, unter mitwirkung von Ina Britschgi-Schimmer herausgegeben von Martin Buber ... Frankfurt a. M., Rütten & Loening, 1929.
2 v. 2 port. (incl. front.) facsims. (part fold.) 20cm.

Includes references to Spinoza.

I. Buber, Martin, 1878- ed. II. Britschgi-Schimmer, Ina, joint ed.

Klinke, Hans, 1907-
William Hale White (Mark Rutherford) Versuch einer Biographie mit besonderer Berücksichtigung der Einflüsse von Dichtern, Denkern und Ereignissen mit vielem unveröffentlichten Material dargestellt. Frankfurt (Oder) Buchdruckerei W. Bohn, 1930.
143 p. 23cm.

Thesis, Greifswald.
Includes reference to White's translation of Spinoza's Ethica (p. 76-77)
Bibliography: p. 137-142.

Landauer, Gustav, 1870-1919.
... Shakespeare dargestellt in vorträgen ... Frankfurt am Main, Rütten & Loening, 1920.
2 v. 22½cm.
"Im letztwilligen auftrag des verfassers herausgegeben von Martin Buber."

Includes references to Spinoza.

1. Shakespeare, William—Criticism and interpretation. I. Buber, Martin, 1878- ed.

Külpe, Oswald, 1862-1915.
Die Realisierung; ein Beitrag zur Grundlegung der Realwissenschaften. Leipzig, S. Hirzel, 1912-20.
v. 1-2 23 cm.

Lanzky, Paul, 1852-
Abendröte. Psychologische Betrachtungen. Berlin, Duncker, 1887.
134 p.

Includes references to Spinoza.

Lachower, Fishel, 1883-
הוכוח על שפינוזה בספרות העברית. תל־אביב, תרצ"ג.
[1932]
13-14 p. 29cm.

Title transliterated: ha-Wikkūaḥ ʿal Shpīnōzā bassifrūth ha-ʿivrīth.
From Moznayim, vol. 4, no. 26, Dec. 15, 1932.
With Roth, Leon. Mishnāthō shel Shpīnōzā ... [1932]

[La Place, Pierre Antoine de, 1707-1793, comp.
Pieces intéressantes et peu connues, pour servir a l'histoire et a la littérature. Par M. D. L. P. ... Nouvelle édition. A Bruxelles, Chez Prault, 1790.
v. 8. 17cm.

Lachower, Fishel, 1883-1947.
הוכוח על שפינוזה בספרות העבריה.
[1932]
13-14 p.

Title transliterated: ha-Wikuah ʿal Shpinozah.
In Moznayim, v. 4, no. 26, 1932.

Laspeyres, Etienne, 1834-1913.
Geschichte der volkswirthschaftlichen Anschauungen der Niederländer und ihrer Litteratur zur Zeit der Republik. Leipzig, Hirzel, 1863.
xiv, 334 p. 28 cm. (Fürstlich Jablonowski-sche Gesellschaft der Wissenschaften. Preisschriften. 11)

Includes a section on Spinoza (p. 21-24) and other references to him.

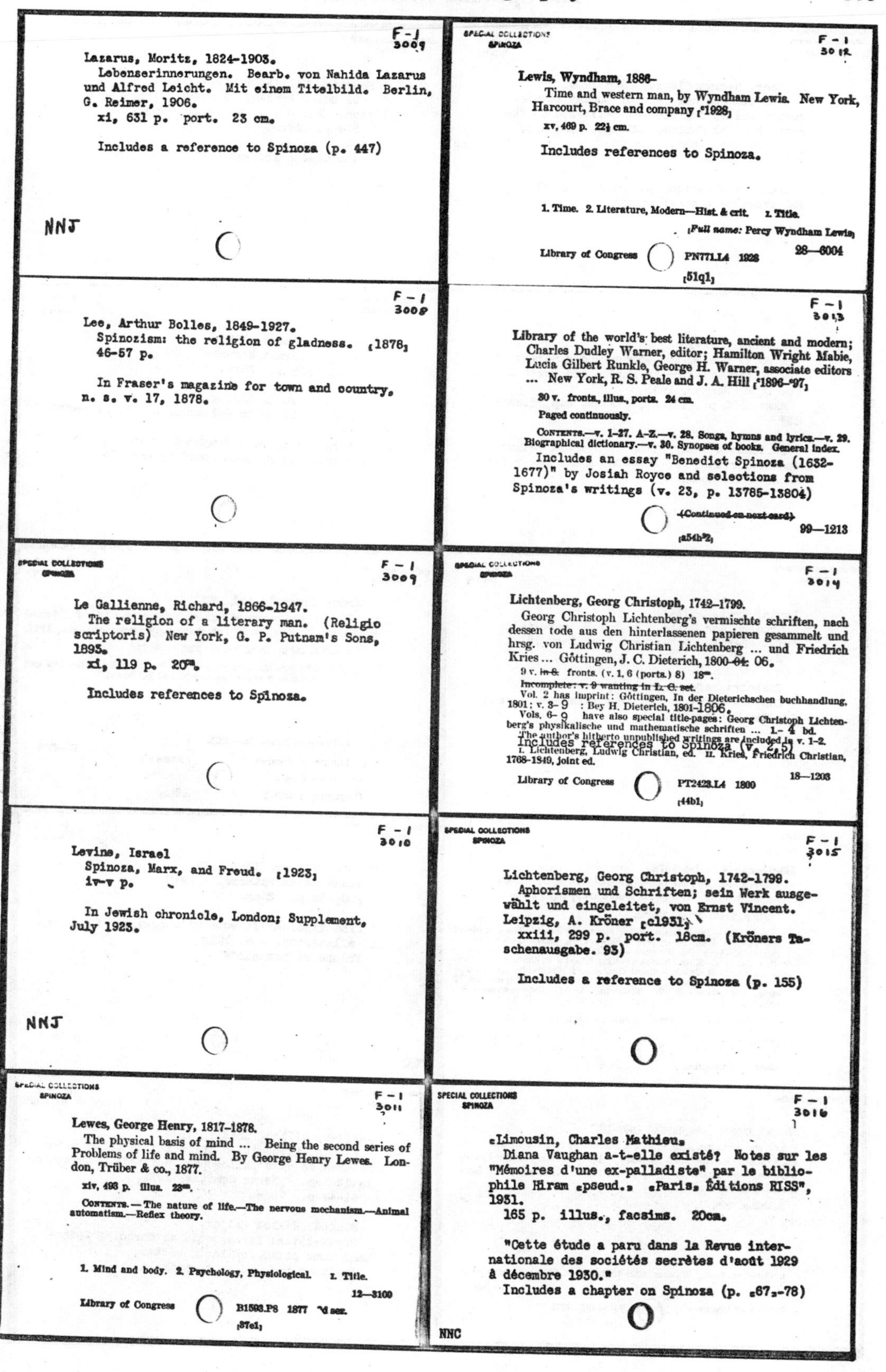

F-1 3007

Lazarus, Moritz, 1824-1903.
Lebenserinnerungen. Bearb. von Nahida Lazarus und Alfred Leicht. Mit einem Titelbild. Berlin, G. Reimer, 1906.
xi, 631 p. port. 23 cm.

Includes a reference to Spinoza (p. 447)

NNJ

F-1 3008

Lee, Arthur Bolles, 1849-1927.
Spinozism: the religion of gladness. [1878]
46-57 p.

In Fraser's magazine for town and country, n. s. v. 17, 1878.

SPECIAL COLLECTIONS SPINOZA

F-1 3009

Le Gallienne, Richard, 1866-1947.
The religion of a literary man. (Religio scriptoris) New York, G. P. Putnam's Sons, 1893.
xi, 119 p. 20cm.

Includes references to Spinoza.

F-1 3010

Levine, Israel
Spinoza, Marx, and Freud. [1923]
iv-v p.

In Jewish chronicle, London; Supplement, July 1923.

NNJ

SPECIAL COLLECTIONS SPINOZA

F-1 3011

Lewes, George Henry, 1817-1878.
The physical basis of mind ... Being the second series of Problems of life and mind. By George Henry Lewes. London, Trübner & co., 1877.
xiv, 493 p. illus. 23cm.

CONTENTS.—The nature of life.—The nervous mechanism.—Animal automatism.—Reflex theory.

1. Mind and body. 2. Psychology, Physiological. I. Title.

12—3100

Library of Congress B1593.P8 1877 2d set.
[37e1]

SPECIAL COLLECTIONS SPINOZA

F-1 3012

Lewis, Wyndham, 1886-
Time and western man, by Wyndham Lewis. New York, Harcourt, Brace and company [1928]
xv, 469 p. 22½ cm.

Includes references to Spinoza.

1. Time. 2. Literature, Modern—Hist. & crit. I. Title.
[Full name: Percy Wyndham Lewis]

Library of Congress PN771.L4 1928 28—6004
[51q1]

F-1 3013

Library of the world's best literature, ancient and modern; Charles Dudley Warner, editor; Hamilton Wright Mabie, Lucia Gilbert Runkle, George H. Warner, associate editors ... New York, R. S. Peale and J. A. Hill [1896-97]
30 v. fronts., illus., ports. 24 cm.
Paged continuously.
CONTENTS.—v. 1-27. A-Z.—v. 28. Songs, hymns and lyrics.—v. 29. Biographical dictionary.—v. 30. Synopses of books. General index.
Includes an essay "Benedict Spinoza (1632-1677)" by Josiah Royce and selections from Spinoza's writings (v. 23, p. 13785-13804)

~~(Continued on next card)~~ 99—1213
[a54b²2]

SPECIAL COLLECTIONS SPINOZA

F-1 3014

Lichtenberg, Georg Christoph, 1742-1799.
Georg Christoph Lichtenberg's vermischte schriften, nach dessen tode aus den hinterlassenen papieren gesammelt und hrsg. von Ludwig Christian Lichtenberg ... und Friedrich Kries ... Göttingen, J. C. Dieterich, 1800-~~04~~ 06.
9 v. ~~in 8.~~ fronts. (v. 1, 6 (ports.) 8) 18cm.
~~Incomplete: v. 9 wanting in L. C. set.~~
Vol. 2 has imprint: Göttingen, In der Dieterichschen buchhandlung, 1801; v. 3-9 : Bey H. Dieterich, 1801-1806.
Vols. 6-9 have also special title-pages: Georg Christoph Lichtenberg's physikalische und mathematische schriften ... 1.-4 bd.
The author's hitherto unpublished writings are included in v. 1-2.
Includes references to Spinoza (v. 2,5)
I. Lichtenberg, Ludwig Christian, ed. II. Kries, Friedrich Christian, 1768-1849, joint ed.

Library of Congress PT2423.L4 1800 18—1203
[44b1]

SPECIAL COLLECTIONS SPINOZA

F-1 3015

Lichtenberg, Georg Christoph, 1742-1799.
Aphorismen und Schriften; sein Werk ausgewählt und eingeleitet, von Ernst Vincent. Leipzig, A. Kröner [c1931]
xxiii, 299 p. port. 18cm. (Kröners Taschenausgabe. 93)

Includes a reference to Spinoza (p. 155)

SPECIAL COLLECTIONS SPINOZA

F-1 3016

[Limousin, Charles Mathieu]
Diana Vaughan a-t-elle existé? Notes sur les "Mémoires d'une ex-palladiste" par le bibliophile Hiram [pseud.] [Paris] Éditions RISS", 1931.
165 p. illus., facsims. 20cm.

"Cette étude a paru dans la Revue internationale des sociétés secrètes d'août 1929 à décembre 1930."
Includes a chapter on Spinoza (p. [67]-78)

NNC

Lorimer, George Claude, 1838-1904.
Isms old and new; winter Sunday evening sermon-series for 1880-81 delivered in the First Baptist Church, Chicago. Chicago, S. C. Griggs, 1881.
367 p. 19cm.

Includes a section on Spinoza (p. 65-70) and other references to him.

Lowenthal, Marvin
A world passed by; scenes and memories of Jewish civilization in Europe and North Africa. New York, Harper, 1933.
xxxv, 500 p. illus., plates, map, facsims. 23cm.

Includes a description of Spinoza relics in the Netherlands (p. 203-206) and other references to Spinoza.

Lucka, Emil, 1877-
Grenzen der Seele. 3. bis 5. erweiterte Aufl. Berlin, Schuster & Loeffler, 1917.
2 v. 21cm.

Includes references to Spinoza.
Contents.--v. 1. Das Tragische.--v. 2. Stufen der Genialität.

MacLaurin, Charles, 1872-
Mere mortals; medico-historical essays, by C. MacLaurin ... New York, George H. Doran company [c1925]
xiii p., 1 l., 17-291 p. 19½ cm.

CONTENTS.—Dr. Johnson.—King Henry the Saint.—The tragedy of the Tudors: King Henry VIII. Edward VI. Mary Tudor. Queen Elizabeth.—Ivan the Terrible.—Luther's devil.—Henry Fielding.—King James I.—King Charles I.—King Charles II, Catherine of Braganza and Nell Gwynn.—Henri Quatre and Marguerite de Valois.—Frederick the Great.—The children's crusade.—Some epidemics of social importance.—F. W. Nietzsche.—Arthur Schopenhauer.—Baruch Spinoza.

1. Biography—Addresses, essays, lectures. I. Title.

Mansel, Henry Longueville, 1820-1871.
Letters, lectures, and reviews, including the Phrontisterion; or, Oxford in the 19th century. By the Very Rev. Henry Longueville Mansel ... Ed. by Henry W. Chandler ... London, J. Murray, 1873.
vii, 408 p. 22cm.

I. Chandler, Henry William, 1828-1889, ed. II. Title: Phrontisterion.

Maugham, William Somerset, 1874-
Of human bondage; a novel. [Cheaper edition] London, W. Heinemann [1927]
648 p. 19cm.

Includes a reference to Spinoza (p. 272)

[Maurois, André] 1885-
Ce que dirait Baruch. [1915]
[283]-289 p. 26cm.

Signed: Emile Herzog.
From La Revue de Hollande, no. 3, septembre 1915.
Purports to be a fragment of an essay on war and peace by Spinoza found by Maurois.

Meeker, James Edward, 1890-
The life and poetry of James Thomson (B. V.) by J. Edward Meeker ... New York, Yale university press; [etc., etc.] 1917.
x p., 1 l., 148 p. front. (port.) 21cm. $1.75

"Published from the fund presented to the university by the 1914 and 1915 editorial boards of the Yale banner and Pot pourri."

1. Thomson, James, 1834-1882.

Meijer, Willem, 1842-1926.
Bismarck en Spinoza. [1912]
[60]-66 p. 25cm.

From Tijdschrift voor wijsbegeerte, 6. jaarg. 1. aflevering, Jan. 1912.
Volume of pamphlets.

[Meijer, Willem] 1842-1926.
Nicolai Stenonis ad novae philosophiae reformatorem de vera philosophia epistola. Epistolae latibulum. [Hagae Comitis, 1921]
41-44 p. 22cm.

Signed: Willem Meijer.
Cover-title: Dissertatio ex Chronici Spinozani tomo primo separatim edita.
Includes references to Spinoza.

SPECIAL COLLECTIONS SPINOZA
F-1 3027
193Sp4 AM4

Meijer, Willem, 1842-1926. Spinozana 1897-1922 ... 1922. (Card 2)

"Aan Dr. W. Meijer wordt ter gelegenheid van diens 80sten verjaardag als een blijk van hoogachting en hulde dit werk aangeboden door zijne vrienden."
Cover lettered: W. Meijer, Spinozana 1897-1922.

F-1 3032

Miscellanea Lipsiensia, ad incrementum rei litterariae edita cum praefatione J. F. Buddei. Lipsiae, Sumpt. Haered. Lanckisianorum, 1716-1723.
12 v. illus.

Includes a section on Spinoza (v. 12, p. 310-318)

NN

F-1 3028

Menage, Gilles, 1613-1692.
Menagiana, ou Bons mots, rencontres agréables, pensées judicieuses et observations curieuses. 3. éd. augm. Amsterdam, P. de Coup, 1713-16.
4 v. 13 cm.

Includes references to Spinoza.

ICU

F-1 3033

Mosheim, Johann Lorenz, 1694?-1755.
Institutes of ecclesiastical history, ancient and modern, in four books, much corrected and enlarged ... a new and literal translation from the original Latin, with copious additional notes, original and selected, by James Murdock. 3d ed. rev. and enl. New York, Harper, 1845-49.
3 v. 24 cm.

Includes references to Spinoza.

F-1 3029

Ménage, Gilles, 1613-1692.
Menagiana, ou Les bons mots et remarques critiques, historiques, morales & d'érudition, de monsieur Menage, recueillies par ses amis ... 3. ed., plus ample de moitié, & plus correcte que les précédentes. Paris, Florentin Delaulne, 1715.
4 v. 18 cm.

Includes references to Spinoza.

NN

SPECIAL COLLECTIONS SPINOZA
F-1 3034

Murry, John Middleton, 1889-
... Things to come; essays. [New York] The Macmillan company, 1928.
318 p. 22cm.
"A sequel to a previous volume, 'To an unknown God'."—Pref.
Includes references to Spinoza.

I. Title.

28-24841
Library of Congress PR6025.U8T5 1928 a [40f1]

F-1 3030

Michelis, Heinrich, 1878-
Monistische Charakterköpfe. Beiträge zu einer Entwicklungsgeschichte des monistischen Denkens in Einzeldarstellungen. Leipzig, Verlag Unesma, 1914.
vi, 94 p. ports.

Includes a section on Spinoza (p. 14-23)

OCH

SPECIAL COLLECTIONS SPINOZA
F-1 3035

Mussolini, Benito, 1883-
... Gli accordi del Laterano, discorsi al Parlamento. (2. ed. con appendice) Roma, Libreria del Littorio [1929]
4 p. l., 164 p. facsims. (1 fold.) 21½cm.
Includes reference to Spinoza (p. 120)

1. Concordat of 1929. 2. Roman question. 3. Church and state in Italy. I. Title.

31-19731
Library of Congress BX1545.M8 1929 a [2] 262.132

SPECIAL COLLECTIONS SPINOZA
F-1 3031

Middleton, Charles S
Shelley and his writings. London, Thomas Cautley Newby, 1858.
2 v. fold. facsim. 20cm.

SPECIAL COLLECTIONS SPINOZA
F-1 3036

Neuss, Heinrich Georg, 1654-1716.
Probatio spiritus et doctrinae Democriti, das ist, Prüfung des geistes und der lehre Christiani Democriti, sonst Dippel genandt, auff Verlangen christlicher Freunde, uber dessen summarisches und auffrichtiges Glaubens-Bekäntniss, welches nebst dessen Lebens-Lauff, um mehrer Erleuterung willen, diesem Tractat beygefüget worden. In der Furcht des Herrn angestellet durch Heinrich Georg Neuss ... Franckfurt am Mayn und Leipzig, Zu finden in Henning Grossens

NNC
CONTINUED ON NEXT CARD

Neuss, Heinrich Georg, 1654-1716. Probatio spiritus et doctrinae Democriti. 1701. (Card 2)

Buchhandlung; Halberstadt, Gedruckt bey Johann David Bergmann, 1701.
[7], 4-126 p. 35cm. (In Historia von denen Wider Tauffern. [1705?])

Neuss, Heinrich Georg, 1654-1716.
Probatio spiritus et doctrinae Democriti, das ist: Prüfung des Geistes und der Lehre Christiani Democriti, sonst Dippel genannt, auf Verlangen christlicher Freunde, uber dessen summarisches und aufrichtiges Glaubens-Bekäntniss, welches nebst dessen Lebens-Lauff, um mehrer Erläuterung willen diesem Tractat beygefüget worden. In der Furcht des Herrn angestellet durch Henrich Georg Neuss. 1702.
[7], 4-118 p. 34cm.

Newman, Francis William, 1805-1897.
Anthropomorphism. A comment by F. W. Newman on some poetry sent him by a lady. Ramsgate, T. Scott, 1870.
6 p. 19cm.

Volume of pamphlets.

Nicoll, Sir William Robertson, 1851-1923.
A bookman's letters. New York, Hodder and Stoughton, 1913.
xi, 438 p. 22cm.

Includes references to Spinoza.

Oeser, Hermann, 1849-1912.
Briefwechsel zwischen Hermann Oeser und Dora Schlatter; hrsg. von Emmy Oeser und Salomon Schlatter, mit Einleitung von Paul Jaeger. 5. Aufl. Heilbronn am Neckar, E. Salzer, 1922.
239 p. 21cm.

[Pariset, Georges, 1865-1927.
Sieyès et Spinoza. [1906]
309-320 p.

Signed: G. Pariset.
In Revue de synthèse historique, t. 12, 1906.

Pater, Walter Horatio, 1839-1894.
Gaston de Latour; an unfinished romance by Walter Pater ... prepared for the press by Charles L. Shadwell ... New York, The Macmillan company; London, Macmillan & co., ltd., ~~1896~~. 1897.
ix, 206 p. 18cm.

Includes a reference to Spinoza (p. 191-192)

I. Shadwell, Charles Lancelot, 1840-1919, ed. II. Title.

Pater, Walter Horatio, 1839-1894.
Imaginary portraits, by Walter Pater. London, Macmillan and co., limited, ~~1910~~. 1914.
2 p. l., 153, [1] p. 23 cm.
~~"First edition 1887 ... Library edition 1910."~~

CONTENTS.—A prince of court painters [Antony Watteau]—Denys L'Auxerrois.—Sebastian van Storck.—Duke Carl of Rosenmold.
Includes references to Spinoza.

I. Title.

Pattison, Mark, 1813-1884.
Essays by the late Mark Pattison, sometime rector of Lincoln college; collected and arranged by Henry Nettleship ... Oxford, Clarendon press, 1889.
2 v. 23cm.

Includes references to Spinoza.

1. Spinoza, Benedictus de, 1632-1677.

Pepys, Samuel, 1633-1703.
The diary of Samuel Pepys ... with notes by Richard, Lord Braybrooke. A verbatim reprint of the 1848-1849 edition, with an index. London, Routledge; New York, Dutton, 1906.
viii, 844 p. 23cm.

F-1
3047

Perry, Ralph Barton, 1876-1957.
The futility of absolutism. [1910]
621-640 p.

In Hibbert journal, v. 8, 1910.
Includes references to Spinoza.

F-1
3048

Peterson, Houston, 1897-
Havelock Ellis, philosopher of love.
Boston, Houghton Mifflin [1928]
ix, 432 p. front., ports., facsim. 22 cm.

Thesis, Columbia university, 1929.
Includes references to Spinoza.

SPECIAL COLLECTIONS
SPINOZA

F-1
3049

Peterson, Houston, 1897-
Havelock Ellis, philosopher of love, by Houston Peterson ... Boston and New York, Houghton Mifflin company, 1928.
ix p., 2 l., 432 p. front., ports., facsim. 22½ cm.
"Commonplace books, 1875-1885": p. [367]-393.
Bibliography: p. [394]-417.
Includes references to Spinoza.

1. *Ellis, Havelock, 1859-1939.

PR6009.L8Z8 1928 28—14155
Library of Congress [a56e4]

F-1
3050

Phillips, T M
The influence of Spinoza on modern literature.
[1921]
49-57 p.

In Manchester quarterly, year 40, 1921.

NN

F-1
3051

Plotke, Georg Jakob, 1888-
Heinrich Heine als Dichter des Judentums; ein Versuch. Dresden, Reissner, 1913.
111 p. 23 cm.

Includes a reference to Spinoza (p. 60-61)

F-1
3052

Pope, Alexander, 1688-1744.
Alexandre Pope ... Commentatio poëtica de homine, ex Anglico idiomate in Latinum translata, et carmine heroico expressa, notisque subjunctis illustrata, per Jo. J. G. Am-Ende. Editio nova et accuratior. Lugduni Batavorum, Apud Cornelium de Pecker, 1751.
16 p. l., 136 p. 22 cm.

Includes references to Spinoza.

IU

SPECIAL COLLECTIONS
SPINOZA

F-1
3053

Powys, John Cowper, 1872-
Confessions of two brothers, John Cowper Powys [and] Llewellyn Powys. Rochester, Manas Press, 1916.
265 p. 19cm.

Includes references to Spinoza.

F-1
3054

Prévost-Paradol, Lucien Anatole Prévost, called, 1829-1870.
Essais de politique et de littérature, ser. 1-3. Paris, Lévy, 1863-65.
3 v.

Includes a section on Spinoza (ser. 2, p. 290-303)

OCH

F-1
3055

Quérido, Israël, 1872-1932.
Meditaties over literatuur en leven. Deel I. 's-Gravenhage, Loman & Funke, 1898.
viii, 232 p.

Includes a section "Spinoza, systeemvorming, levenspantomime" (p. 57-63)

MH

F-1
3056

Rader, Melvin Miller, 1903-
... Presiding ideas in Wordsworth's poetry, by Melvin M. Rader ... Seattle, Wash., University of Washington press, 1931.
4 p. l., p. 121-215. 22½cm. (University of Washington publications in language and literature. v. 8, no. 2)
Thesis (PH. D.)—University of Washington, 1929.
Without thesis note.
Bibliography: p. 207-212.
Includes references to Spinoza.

1. Wordsworth, William, 1770-1850. I. Title.

Library of Congress PR5888.R3 1929 31-27893
Univ. of Washington Libr.
——— Copy 2. [3] 821.71

F-1
3057

Ragnisco, Pietro, 1839-1920.
Tommaso Rossi e Benedetto Spinoza; saggio storico-critico. Salerno, Migliaccio, 1873.
52 p.

F-1
3058

Rathbun, Constance
On certain similarities between Spinoza and psychoanalysis. [1934]
14 p.

In Psychoanalytic review, v. 21, 1934.

F-1
3059

Ravitch, Melech, 1893-
בענעדיקט דע שפינאָזא סוב ספעציע פּאָעזיע. 1927.
137-139 p.

Title transliterated: Benedikt de Shpinoza sub spetsye poezye.
In Literarishe bleter, v. 3, 1927.

F-1
3060

Regensburg, Joseph, 1875-
מההרצאות והנאומים שהרצה ד"ר למיד'
ולפיל' יוסף רגנסבורג בבית המדרש הג-
בוה לחכמת ישראל, למדעי הרוח והטבע
(בזמן הכבוש האשכנזי), באוניברסיטה
העממית על יד "הרבות" ובחברת הסטודנ-
טים העברים בוילנה. מוצא לאור על ידי
תלמידיו. וילנה, בית-דפוס "עקספרעס".
[Vilna, 19--?]
46 p. 17cm.

CONTINUED ON NEXT CARD

F-1
3061

Reichlin-Meldegg, Karl Alexander, Freiherr von, 1801-1877.
Heinrich Eberhard Gottlob Paulus und seine Zeit nach dessen literarischem Nachlasse, bisher ungedrucktem Briefwechsel und mündlichen Mittheilungen dargestellt. Stuttgart, Verlags-Magazin, 1853.
2 v.

F-1
3062

Reinhardt, Curt, 1855-1940.
Tschirnhausens Forschungslaboratorium für Porzellan in Dresden. [1929]
[131]-151 p. 25cm.

From Neues lausitzisches Magazin, Bd. 105, 1929.
Bibliographical footnotes.

F-1
3063

Reinhardt, Curt, 1855-1940.
Tschirnhaus oder Böttger? Eine urkundliche Geschichte der Erfindung des Meissner Porzellans. [1912]
162 p. plates, port. 25cm.

From Neues lausitzisches Magazin, Bd. 88, 1912.
Includes a reference to Spinoza (p. 5)
Bibliographical notes: p. [135]-162.

F-1
3064

Richter, Helene, 1861-
Percy Bysshe Shelley. Weimar, E. Felber, 1898.
640 p. port. 24cm.

Includes references to Spinoza.

F-1
3065

Robertson, John Mackinnon, 1856-1933.
Charles Bradlaugh. London, Watts, 1920.
vi, 122 p. ports. 19cm. (Life-stories of famous men)

Includes references to Spinoza (p. 27-28, 121)

F-1
3066

Robinson, Henry Crabb, 1775-1867.
Diary, reminiscences, and correspondence, selected and edited by Thomas Sadler. London, Macmillan, 1869.
3 v. port., facsim. 22 cm.
Errata slip inserted in v. 1.
Includes references to Spinoza.

1. Authors — Correspondence, reminiscences, etc. I. Sadler, Thomas, 1822-1891, ed.

F-1 3067

Rogers, Henry, 1806-1877.
The life and character of John Howe, M. A., with an analysis of his writings. By Henry Rogers. A new edition. London, The Religious tract society, 1863.
xii, 454 p. front. (port.) 22½cm.

1. Howe, John, 1630-1705. I. Religious tract society, London.

DLC

F-1 3068

Rosin, Heinrich, 1855-1927.
Bismarck und Spinoza, Parallelen ihrer Staatsanschauung. [1911]
[383]-420 p. 25cm.

"Sonderabdruck aus der Otto Gierke zum 70. Geburtstag von Schülern, Freunden und Verehrern dargebrachten Festschrift."

F-1 3069

Saint-Évremond, Charles de Marguetel de Saint Denis, seigneur de, 1613-1703.
The letters of Saint Evremond, Charles Marguetel de Saint Denis, seigneur de Saint Evremond. Edited with an introduction and notes by John Hayward. London, Routledge, 1930.
lxii, 383 p. front., 1 illus., ports. 23cm.
[Broadway diaries, memoirs & letters]

Includes reference to Spinoza (p. 201)

F-1 3070

Saint-Evremond, Charles de Marguetel de Saint Denis, seigneur de, 1613-1703.
Oeuvres de Monsieur de Saint-Evremond, publiées sur les manuscrits de l'auteur. Nouvelle édition revûë, corrigée & augmentée de la vie de l'auteur ... A Londres, Chez Jacob Tonson, 1725.
7 v. 17cm.

Includes references to Spinoza.

F-1 3071

Saint Évremond, Charles de Marguetel de Saint Denis, seigneur de, 1613-1703.
Oeuvres de Saint-Évremond, mises en ordre et publiées avec une introduction et des notices par René de Planhol. Paris, La Cité des livres, 1927.
3 v. 21cm.

Includes references to Spinoza.

F-1 3072

Saint-Evremond, Charles de Marguetel de Saint Denis, seigneur de, 1613-1703.
Oeuvres meslées de Mr de Saint-Evremond. Seconde édition reveüe, corrigée & augmentée de la vie de l'auteur. A Londres, Chez Jacob Tonson, 1709.
3 v.

Includes a reference to Spinoza (v. 1, p. xxix)

MB

F-1 3073

Scott, Evelyn, 1893-
Narcissus, by Evelyn Scott. New York, Harcourt, Brace and company [1922]
3 p. l., 3-263 p. 19½cm.

Includes a reference to Spinoza (p. 30)

I. Title.

[Real name: Elsie (Dunn) Wellman afterwards Metcalfe]

F-1 3074

Schweitzer, Albert, 1875-
Verfall und Wiederaufbau der Kultur. Bern, P. Haupt, 1923.
64 p. (His Kulturphilosophie, 1. Teil)

"Olaus Petri Vorlesungen an der Universität Upsala."

F-1 3075

Seligmann, Raphael
Vom moralischen und künstlerischen Typus. (Eine Parallele zwischen Juden- und Christentum). [1914]
675-697 p.

In Die Freistatt; Alljüdische Revue, Jahrgang 1, 1914.
Includes references to Spinoza.

NNJ

F-1 3076

Seume, Johann Gottfried, 1763-1810.
Rückerinnerungen von Seume und Münchhausen. Frankfurt am Mayn, bei Varrentrapp und Wenner, 1797.
[10], 96 p. plate. 18cm.

Bound with Heydenreich, Karl Heinrich. Gedichte. [1802]

[Shaftesbury, Anthony Ashley Cooper, 3d earl of] 1671-1713.
Characteristicks of men, manners, opinions, times. In three volumes ... [London] Anno 1711.
3 v. 20 cm.

Shaftesbury, Anthony Ashley Cooper, 3d earl of, 1671-1713.
Characteristics of men, manners, opinions, times, etc. Ed., with an introduction and notes, by John M. Robertson. London, G. Richards, 1900.
2 v. 21 cm.

Includes references to Spinoza.

Shelley, Percy Bysshe, 1792-1822.
Letters 1812 to 1818, ed. by Roger Ingpen. London, Pub. for the Julian editions by E. Benn; New York, Scribner, 1926.
xi, 348 p. 25 cm. (His Complete works, v. 9)

Includes references to Spinoza (p. 33-34, 39-40)

Shelley, Percy Bysshe, 1792-1822.
The poetical works of Percy Bysshe Shelley, with memoir, explanatory notes, etc. London, J. Finch [19--?]
xvi, 656 p. port. 20cm.

Shelley, Percy Bysshe, 1792-1822.
The prose works of Percy Bysshe Shelley; reprinted from the original editions and edited by Richard Herne Shepherd. Fine-paper edition. London, Chatto & Windus, 1912.
2 v. ports. 17cm.

Includes a quotation from Spinosa. Tract. theologico-pol., chap. i, p. 14 (v. 1, p. 328)

Shelley, Percy Bysshe, 1792-1822.
A selection from the poems of Percy Bysshe Shelley. Edited with a memoir by Mathilde Blind. Leipzig, B. Tauchnitz, 1872.
xl, 334 p., 1 l. 16cm. (*Half-title:* Collection of British authors. Tauchnitz edition. v. 1207)
"Authorities": p. [v]

I. Blind, Mathilde, 1841-1896, ed.

[Shestov, Lev] 1866-1938.
Les favoris et les déshérités de l'histoire: Descartes et Spinoza. [Traduit du texte russe inédit par J. Exempliarsky. 1923]
640-674 p. 23cm.

Signed: L. Chestov.
From Mercure de France, no. 600, 34e année, t. CLXIV, 15 juin 1923.
Published in German in Die Kreatur, Jahrgang II, Heft 4, 1928, with title: Kinder und Stiefkinder der Zeit.

Shestov, Lev, 1866-1938.
In Job's balances; on the sources of the eternal truths, by Leo Chestov, translated by Camilla Coventry and C. A. Macartney. London, Dent [1932]
xxxi, 413 p. 24cm.

Includes a chapter "Children and stepchildren of time; Spinoza in history" (p. 247-273)

Shestov, Lev, 1866-1938.
Kinder und Stiefkinder der Zeit (Das historische Los Spinozas) [Berlin, 1928]
369-396 p. 25cm.

From Die Kreatur, Jahrgang II, Heft 4, 1928.
Published in French in Mercure de France of June 15, 1923 with title: Les favoris et les déshérités de l'histoire: Descartes et Spinoza.

Sichel, Walter Sydney, 1855-1933.
Bolingbroke and his times. London, J. Nisbet, 1901-02.
2 v. plates, ports., facsim. 23 cm.

Sichel, Walter Sydney, 1855-
Types and characters; a kaleidoscope, by Walter Sichel ... London, Hutchinson & co. [1925]
xix, [21]-317 p. incl. front. (port.) 24cm.

1. Characters and characteristics. I. Title.

Siegfried, Carl, 1830-1903.
Festrede gehalten in der Universitätskirche zu Jena zur akademischen Preisvertheilung am 15. Juni 1895. Jena, G. Neuenhahn, 1895.
37 p.

Sinclair, May
Arnold Waterlow; a life. New York, Macmillan, 1924.
446 p. 20cm.

Includes references to Spinoza.

Sinclair, May
Mary Oliver: a life. New York, Macmillan, 1919.
380 p. 20cm.

Includes references to Spinoza.

Slochower, Harry, 1900-
Richard Dehmel, der Mensch und der Denker; eine Biographie seines Geistes im Spiegelbild der Zeit. Mit einem Geleitwort von Julius Bab. Dresden, C. Reissner, 1928.
289 p. 22cm.

Issued also as thesis (Ph. D.) Columbia University.
Includes references to Spinoza.
Bibliography: p. 276-282.

Smith, Maurice Hamlin, 1870-
Spinoza's anticipation of recent psychological developments. Cambridge [Eng.] University Press [1925]
cover-title, [257]-278 p. 26cm.

"Reprinted from the British journal of medical psychology, vol. V, part IV, 1925."
Author's inscription on cover.

Sophie, *consort of Ernest Augustus, elector of Hanover*, 1630-1714.
Briefwechsel der herzogin Sophie von Hannover mit ihrem bruder, dem kurfürsten Karl Ludwig von der Pfalz, und des letzteren mit seiner schwägerin, der pfalzgräfin Anna. Hrsg. von Eduard Bodemann. Veranlasst und unterstützt durch die K. Archiv-verwaltung. Leipzig, S. Hirzel, 1885.
xix, 492 p. 24½cm. (*Added t.-p.:* Publicationen aus den K. Preussischen staatsarchiven. 26. bd.)
Text in French. Includes references to Spinoza.
1. Palatinate—History—Sources. I. Karl Ludwig, elector palatine, 1617-1680. II. Gonzaga, Anna, princess palatine, 1616-1684. III. Bodemann, Eduard, 1827-1906, ed.

[Sorley, William Ritchie, 1855-1935.
Berkeley and contemporary philosophy. [1933]
312-340 p.

From Cambridge history of English literature, v. 9. N. Y., Macmillan; Cambridge, Univ. press, 1933.
Includes references to Spinoza.

Spitzel, Gottlieb, 1639-1691.
Felix literatus ex infelicium periculis et casibus, sive De vitiis literatorum commentationes historico-theosophicae, quibus infelicium ex animo, H. E. vitiosorum literatorum calamitates et miseriae, conquisitis exemplis et documentis selectioribus exponuntur, atque eruditis, ad verae et imperturbatae felicitatis sedem tendentibus via tutissima ostenditur. Authore Theophilo Spizelio ... Augustae Vindelicorum, Apud Theophilum Goebelium,

(Continued on next card)

Spitzel, Gottlieb, 1639-1691. Felix literatus ex infelicium periculis ... 1676. (Card 2)

Literis Koppmayerianis, 1676.
1184 p. port. 17 cm.

Includes a section on Spinoza (p. 143-145)

F-1 3097

Steffens, Henrich, 1773-1845.
Was ich erlebte. Aus der Erinnerung niedergeschrieben. Breslau, J. Max, 1840-44.
10 v. in 5 17 cm.

Includes a reference to Spinoza (v. 3, p. 283)

SPECIAL COLLECTIONS SPINOZA F-1 3098

Stephen, Sir Leslie, 1832-1904.
George Eliot. New York, Macmillan, 1913.
vi, 213 p. 19cm. (Half-title: English men of letters, ed. by John Morley)

Includes references to Spinoza.

F-1 3099

Struve, Burkhard Gotthelf, 1671-1738.
Bibliotheca historiae litterariae selecta, olim titvlo Introdvctionis in notitiam rei litterariae et vsvm bibliothecarvm insignita cvivs primas lineas dvxit Bvrc. Gotthelf Strvvivs ... Post variorvm emendationes et additamenta opvs ita formavit vt fere novvm dici qveat Iohannes Friderievs Ivgler ... Ienae, svmtibvs C. H. Cvnonis, 1754-63.
3 v. 21 cm.

Includes references to Spinoza.

DLC

SPECIAL COLLECTIONS SPINOZA F-1 3100

Stummer, Friedrich, 1886-
Die Bedeutung Richard Simons für die Pentateuchkritik. Münster i. W., Aschendorffsche Verlagsbuchhandlung, 1912.
vi, 146 p. 24cm. (Alttestamentliche Abhandlungen. III. Band, 4. Heft)

Includes a section on and other references to Spinoza.
Original paper covers bound in.
Bibliography: p. [iv]-vi.

SPECIAL COLLECTIONS SPINOZA F-1 3101

[Taylor, Alfred Edward] 1869-1945.
The novels of Mark Rutherford. [1914]
[51]-74 p. 22cm.

From Essays and studies by members of the English Association, v. 5, 1914.
Includes references to Spinoza.

SPECIAL COLLECTIONS SPINOZA F-1 3102

Thomson, *Sir* John Arthur, 1861-1933.
Introduction to science, by J. Arthur Thomson ... New York, H. Holt and company; [etc., etc., °1911]
256 p. 18cm. (*Half-title:* Home university library of modern knowledge, no. 21)
"Reference to books": p. 251-253.

1. Science. I. Title.

12—233
Library of Congress Q159.T42
[43p2]

SPECIAL COLLECTIONS SPINOZA F-1 3103

Thomson, William Hanna, 1833-1918.
Brain and personality; or, The physical relations of the brain to the mind, by William Hanna Thomson ... New York, Dodd, Mead & company, 1910.
4 p. l., 335 p. front., illus. 19½ cm.
"Published, September, 1906."
Includes a reference to Spinoza (p. 256)

1. Mind and body. 2. Brain. I. Title.

BF161.T42 1910 41—37842
[159.9122] 131.22
Library of Congress [54c1]

F-1 3104

Thorild, Thomas, 1759-1808.
Thomas Thorilds samlade skrifter; utgifna af P. Hanselli. Upsala, Hanselli, 1874.
2 v.

NcD

SPECIAL COLLECTIONS SPINOZA F-1 3105

Timmermans, Bernardus
Le spinozisme de Maeterlinck. Zalt-Bommel, Van de Garde & Co's drukkerij, 1924.
x, 196 p. 25cm.

Thesis, Groningen.
Bibliography: p. [vii]-x.
Original paper covers bound in.

SPECIAL COLLECTIONS SPINOZA F-1 3106

Tolstaia, Aleksandra L'vovna, grafinia, 1884-
Tolstojs Flucht und Tod; geschildert von seiner Tochter Alexandra. Mit den Briefen und Tagebüchern von Leo Tolstoj, dessen Gattin, seines Arztes und seiner Freunde. Hrsg. von René Fülöp-Miller und Friedrich Eckstein. Berlin, B. Cassirer [1925]
250 p. plates, ports. 19cm.

Traill, Henry Duff, 1842-1900.
Coleridge. London, Macmillan, 1912.
xi, 218 p. 19cm. (English men of letters, ed. by John Morley)

Trilling, Lionel, 1905–
Matthew Arnold, by Lionel Trilling. New York, W. W. Norton & co. [°1939]
4 p. l., vii–xiv, 15–465 p. front. (port.) 22½ cm.
"First edition."
"References": p. 407–435. Bibliography: p. 436–438. "General bibliography": p. 439–447.
Issued also as thesis (PH. D.) Columbia university.
Includes references to Spinoza.

1. Arnold, Matthew, 1822–1888.

Velthuysen, Lambert van, 1622-1685.
Tractatus duo medico-physici, unus de liene, alter de generatione. Authore Lamberto Velthusio ... Trajecti ad Rhenum, Typis Theodori ab Ackersdijck, & Gisberti à Zyll, 1657.
[56], 162, 286, [1] p. 13cm.

Vermehren, Konrad
Die neuen Urtheile und Nachrichten über Benedictus Spinoza. [1863]
481-493, 540-545 p.

In Deutsches Museum. Zeitschrift für Literatur, Kunst und öffentliches Leben, 1863.

Viereck, George Sylvester, 1884–
... Meine ersten 2000 jahre; autobiographie des Ewigen Juden, übersetzt von Gustav Meyrink. Leipzig, P. List [°1928]
3 p. l., iii–vii, [1], 632, [1] p. 19½cm.
At head of title: G. S. Viereck und P. Eldridge.
Includes a chapter "Ich spreche mit Spinoza über Gott" (p. 528-539) and other references to Spinoza.

1. Wandering Jew. I. Eldridge, Paul, 1888– joint author. II. Meyrink, Gustav, 1868–1932, tr. III. Title.

Viereck, George Sylvester, 1884-
My first two thousand years; the autobiography of the Wandering Jew [by] George Sylvester Viereck [and] Paul Eldridge. New York, Macaulay, 1928 [i. e. 1929]
xiii, 501 p. 21cm.

Includes a chapter "I discuss God with Spinoza" (p. 420-428) and other references to Spinoza.

Wallas, Graham, 1858-1932.
The life of Francis Place, 1771-1854. [Rev. ed.] London, G. Allen & Unwin [1918]
xiv, 415 p. port. 23cm.

Walter, Hermann.
Heinrich Heine, a critical examination of the poet and his works, by H. Walter ... London & Toronto, J. M. Dent & sons limited; New York, E. P. Dutton & co. inc. [1930]
xii, 322 p. front., pl., ports. 22cm.
"Errata" slip inserted.
Bibliography: p. 311–318.
Includes a section on Spinoza (p. 146-148)

1. Heine, Heinrich, 1797–1856.

Wanke, Georg
Psychoanalyse; Geschichte, Wesen, Aufgaben und Wirkung. Für Arzte, Geistliche und Juristen, sowie für Eltern, Lehrer und Erzieher. Halle a. S., C. Marhold, 1924.
xvi, 304 p. 24cm.

Includes references to Spinoza.

Warburton, William, bp. of Gloucester, 1689-1779.
A critical and philosophical commentary on Mr. Pope's Essay on man, in which is contain'd a vindication from the misrepresentations of Mr. De Resnel and Mr. De Crousaz. London, J. and P. Knapton, 1742.
xx, 188 p. 17 cm.

Ward, *Sir* **Adolphus William, 1837-1924.**
The Electress Sophia and the Hanoverian succession, by Adolphus William Ward ... London, Paris, New York, Goupil & co., 1903.

2 p. l., v, 254 p., 1 l. 12 illus., 34 pl. (incl. col. front., ports., facsims.) 38cm.

Title in red and black; initials.
"There have been printed of this work one thousand copies on fine paper ... no. ~~166~~ 553."
Includes a reference to Spinoza (p. 53)

1. Sophie, elector of Hanover, consort of Ernest Augustus, 1630-1714. 2. Gt. Brit.—Kings and rulers—Succession.

Weininger, Otto, 1880-1903.
Sex & character, by Otto Weininger. Authorised translation from the 6th German ed. London, W. Heinemann; New York, G. P. Putnam's sons [1906?]

xxii p., 1 l., 356 p. 22½ cm.

Includes references to Spinoza (p. 316-317)

1. Sex. 2. Sexual ethics. 3. Character. I. Title.

Waterhouse, Gilbert, 1888-
The literary relations of England and Germany in the seventeenth century, by Gilbert Waterhouse ... Cambridge, University press, 1914.

xx, 190 p. 22½ cm.

Bibliography: p. [145]-179.

1. Literature, Comparative—English and German. 2. Literature, Comparative—German and English. I. Title.

Weissel, Josefine
James Thomson der Jüngere, sein Leben und seine Werke dargestellt. Wien und Leipzig, W. Braumüller, 1906.
vi, 159 p. 23 cm. (Wiener Beiträge zur englischen Philologie, 24. Bd.)

Includes a reference to Spinoza (p. 113)

Watson, Foster, 1860-1929.
Luis Vives, el gran Valenciano (1492-1540) by Foster Watson ... With eight illustrations. [Oxford] Oxford university press, H. Milford, 1922.

viii, 126 p. front., plates, facsim. 17 cm. (*Half-title:* Hispanic notes & monographs; essays, studies, and brief biographies issued by the Hispanic society of America. IV)

1. Vives, Juan Luis, 1492-1540.

Werfel, Franz V 1890-1945.
... Geheimnis eines menschen, novellen. Berlin [etc.] P. Zsolnay, 1927.

315, [1] p. 20cm.

At head of title: Franz Werfel.
"1. bis 10. tausend."

CONTENTS.—Die entfremdung.—Geheimnis eines menschen.—Die hoteltreppe.—Das trauerhaus.
References to Spinoza included in "Das Trauerhaus."
I. Title.

Wedgwood, Julia, 1833-1913.
Nineteenth century teachers and other essays, by Julia Wedgwood. London, Hodder and Stoughton, 1909.

viii, 419 p. 24 cm.

CONTENTS.—Samuel Taylor Coleridge.—Frederick Denison Maurice.—Thomas Erskine of Linlathen.—Life of Charles Kingsley.—Arthur Penrhyn Stanley.—The Cambridge apostles of 1830.—Richard Holt Hutton.—A study of Carlyle.—The majority.—James Fitzjames Stephen.—The moral influence of George Eliot.—John Ruskin.—Laurence Oliphant.—Count Leo Tolstoi.—Morals and politics.—Ethics and science.—Biography.—The relation of memory to will.—The vanity of men of letters.—Invalids.—Apologies.—Henry Thomas Buckle.—The unfaithful steward.—Brothers, an address to female students.—De Senectute.—The drawbacks of the intellectual life.

~~(Continued on next card)~~

Werfel, Franz, 1890-1945.
Das Trauerhaus; Novelle. [1927]
[239]-283 p. 25cm.

From Die neue Rundschau. XXXVIII. Jahrgang, 9. Heft, September 1927.
Includes references to Spinoza.

Weimarer historisch-genealoges Taschenbuch des gesamten Adels jehudäischen Ursprunges ... 1912, erster Jahrgang. Weimar, Kyffhäuser-Verlag [1912]
lxii, 607 p. illus., port. 16cm.

Includes an article about Spinoza.

White, Dorothy Vernon (Smith)
The Groombridge diary, by Dorothy V. White. London, New York, [etc.] H. Milford, Oxford university press, 1924.

4 p. l., 503 p. front., plates, ports. 19½cm.

Includes references to Spinoza.

1. White, William Hale, 1831-1913. I. Title.

White, William Hale, 1831-1913.
Coleridge on Spinoza. ⌈1897⌉
680-681 p. 32cm.

From The Athenaeum. No. 3630, May 22, 1897.

1. Spinoza, Benedictus de, 1632-1577.
I. Coleridge, Samuel Taylor, 1772-1834.

White, William Hale, 1831-1913.
The early life of Mark Rutherford (W. Hale White) by himself. London, H. Milford; ⌈etc., etc.⌉ 1913.
91 p. front., plates, ports. 17½cm.
Foreword signed: W. Hale White.

I. White, William Hale, 1857- II. Title.

A 14—736

Princeton univ. Library
for Library of Congress ⌈a40d1⌉

⌈White, William Hale⌉ 1831-1913.
Last pages from a journal, with other papers, by Mark Rutherford ⌈pseud.⌉ (Edited by his wife) London, New York, H. Milford, Oxford University Press, 1915.
viii, 321 p. front. 17cm.

Includes references to Spinoza.

White, William Hale, 1831-1913.
Letters to three friends, by William Hale White ("Mark Rutherford") London, New York ⌈etc.⌉ H. Milford, Oxford university press, 1924.
3 p. l., 404 p. front., pl., ports., facsim. 20cm.
Edited by Mrs. Dorothy Vernon White.
CONTENTS.—To Mr. and Mrs. Colenutt, 1872-1908.—To Miss Partridge, 1893-1912.—To Mr. Philip Webb, 1894-1913.—Index.
Includes references to Spinoza.

I. White, Mrs. Dorothy Vernon (Smith) ed. II. Title.

24—16800

Library of Congress PR5795.W7Z58
⌈a36d1⌉

⌈White, William Hale⌉ 1831-1913.
More pages from a journal, with other papers, by Mark Rutherford ⌈*pseud.*⌉ London, New York ⌈etc.⌉ H. Frowde, 1910.
viii, 303 p. 17cm.

Includes a reference to Spinoza (p. 234)

A 11—520

Michigan. Univ. Library
for Library of Congress ⌈a40b1⌉

⌈White, William Hale⌉ 1831-1913.
Pages from a journal; with other papers, by Mark Rutherford ⌈pseud.⌉ London, T. F. Unwin, 1901.
vi, 283 p. 19cm.

Includes a chapter on Spinoza (p. 32-58)

⌈White, William Hale⌉ 1831-1913.
Pages from a journal, with other papers, by Mark Rutherford ⌈pseud.⌉ 2d ed. London, New York, H. Frowde, Oxford University Press, 1910.
vi, 343 p. 17cm.

Includes a chapter on Spinoza (p. 32-58)

Williams, Edward Ellerker, 1793-1822.
Journal of Edward Ellerker Williams, companion of Shelley and Byron in 1821 and 1822. With an introduction by Richard Garnett ... London, E. Mathews, 1902.
4 p. l., 67, ⌈1⌉ p. pl., 2 port. (incl. front.) 20cm.

Includes references to Spinoza (p. 8, 25-26)

1. Shelley, Percy Bysshe, 1792-1822. 2. Byron, George Gordon Noël Byron, 6th baron, 1788-1824. I. Garnett, Richard, 1835-1906, ed.

3-1344

Library of Congress CT788.W755.A32
⌈36c1⌉

Wijck, Bernard Hendrik Cornelis Karel van der
Levensbericht van Cornelis Bellaar Spruyt. Amsterdam, J. Müller, 1904.
cover-title, 28 p. 27cm.

"Overgedrukt uit het Jaarboek der Koninklijke Akademie van Wetenschappen, 1904."
Includes references to Spinoza.

⌈Wijck, Bernard Hendrik Cornelis Karel van der⌉
Spinozabespiegelingen. ⌈1900⌉
270-293 p.

In De Gids, v. 64, 4. serie, 18. jaargang, 4. deel, 1900.

F-1
3137

Wolbe, Eugen, 1873-
Berthold Auerbach; ein Lebensbild. Berlin, Neufeld & Henius [1907]
144 p. plates, ports. (Jugendbibliothek, Bd. 82)

Includes a section "Spinoza und Mendelssohn" (p. 45-52)

NNJ

F-2
LESSING

F-2
3142

Bartels, Adolf, 1862-
Lessing und die Juden; eine Untersuchung. Dresden, C. A. Koch, 1918.
380 p. 23cm.

Original paper covers bound in.
Includes references to Spinoza.

F-1
3138

[Wolf, Abraham] 1876-
The late poet laureate [Robert Bridges] and Spinoza. [1930]
p. 3.

Signed: A. Wolf.
In Jewish guardian, London, May 2, 1930.
A letter to the editor.

NN

F-2
3143

Berger, Arnold Erich, 1862-
Lessings geistesgeschichtliche Stellung. Darmstadt, E. Hofmann, 1929.
45 p. 22cm.

"Erweiterter Abdruck eines zur Zweihundertjahrfeier von Lessings Geburtstag im Januar 1929 im Städtischen Saalbau zu Darmstadt gehaltenen Festvortrags."
Includes a reference to Spinoza (p. 9)

F-1
3139

Zamenspraken van Spinoza, Bolingbroke, Pitt, Canning en Benjamin Constant in den tusschenstaat van het doodenrijk, over hunne verschillende bedrijven en derzelver gevolgen voor hen en anderen. 's Gravenhage, A. P. van Langenhuyzen, 1831.
132 p.

NIC

F-2
3144

Dembowski, Johannes
Studien über Lessings Stellung zur Philosophie. Teil 1. Königsberg, Hartung, 1888.
32 p. 26 cm.

"Beilage zum 13. Jahresbericht 1887/88 des Wilhelms-Gymnasium Königsberg."
Includes a reference to Spinoza (p. 22)

NIC

F-1
3140

Zielenziger, Kurt, 1890-
Theodor Ludwig Lau. Ein Beitrag zur deutschen Wirtschaftsgeschichte. [1924]
22-34 p.

In Jahrbücher für Nationalökonomie und Statistik, 122. Bd., 1924.
Includes a reference to Spinoza.

F-2
3145

Denecke, Arthur, 1851-
Lessings Spinozismus. [1914]
807-823 p.

In Zeitschrift für den deutschen Unterricht, 28. Jahrgang, 1914.

F-1
3141

Zuverlässige Nachricht von des Herrn Edelmanns Aufenthalt in Berlin. Franckfurth und Leipzig, 1747.
24 p. 17cm.

Bound with Süssmilch, Johann Peter. Die Unvernunft und Bosheit des berüchtigsten Edelmanns ... 1747.

F-2
3146

Drbal, Mathias Amos
Ueber den gegenwärtigen Stand der Frage nach Lessing's Spinozismus. Mit Beziehung auf R. Zimmermanns Leibnitz und Lessing. Wien, Edler v. Ghelen'schen Erben, 1856.
24 p.

OCH

Fittbogen, Gottfried, 1878-
Die Religion Lessings. Leipzig, Mayer & Müller, 1923.
viii, 325 p. 25 cm. (Palaestra, 141)

Includes a section on Spinoza (p. 226-269)

Guhrauer, Gottschalk Eduard, 1809-1854.
Lessing's Erziehung des Menschengeschlechts, kritisch und philosophisch erörtert. Eine Beleuchtung der Bekenntnisse in W. Körte's: Albrecht Thaer. Berlin, A. Hirschwald, 1841.
232 p. 18cm.

Includes references to Spinoza.

Hebler, Karl, 1821-1898.
Lessing-Studien. Bern, Korber, 1862.
195 p. 21 cm.

Includes many references to Spinoza in chapter "Lessing's Philosophie" (p. 116-143)

Hoops, Johannes, 1865-1949.
Lessings Verhältnis zu Spinoza. [1891]
28 p.

In Archiv für das Studium der neueren Sprachen und Litteraturen, Bd. 86, 1891.

Horovitz, Aurelie
Beiträge zu Lessings Philosophie. Bern, Scheitlin, Spring, 1907.
89 p. (Berner Studien zur Philosophie und ihrer Geschichte, Bd. 55)

Includes a reference to Spinoza (p. 88)

Jacoby, Johann, 1805-1877.
G. E. Lessing der Philosoph. Berlin, Guttentag, 1863.
66 p.

Jacoby, Johann, 1805-1877.
Gesammelte schriften und reden von dr. Johann Jacoby ... Hamburg, O. Meissner, 1872.
2 v. 20½cm.

Includes many references to Spinoza in "Lessing der Philosoph" (v. 2, p. 145-191)

Lessing, Gotthold Ephraim, 1729-1781.
Das Buch Lessing: Briefe, Schriften, Berichte, hrsg. von Heinrich Schneider. Ebenhausen bei München, W. Langewiesche-Brandt [c1929]
309 p. illus., port., facsim. 19cm. (Die Bücher der Rose)

Includes "Gespräch über Spinoza" (p. 292-299) and other references to Spinoza.

Lessing, Gotthold Ephraim, 1729-1781.
Die Erziehung des Menschengeschlechts ... Herausgegeben von Gotthold Ephraim Lessing. Berlin, Bey Christian Friedrich Voss und Sohn, 1780.
90 p. 16cm.

Kayser, Rudolf, 1889-
Lessing und Spinoza. [1929]
3-4 p.

In Die literarische Welt, Jahrgang 5, Nr. 3, 1929.

F-2
3157

Kayser, Rudolf, 1889-
Dichterköpfe. Wien, Phaidon-Verlag, 1930.
203 p. 21cm.

Includes two essays "Baruch de Spinoza" and "Lessing und Spinoza" (p. 7-18)

1. Spinoza, Benedictus de, 1632-1677.

F-2
3158

Kuckhoff, Adam, 1887-1943.
Lessing - und kein Anfang! [1929]
[721]-728 p. 24cm.

From Die Tat, XX. Jahrgang, 10. Heft, Jan. 1929.
Includes references to Spinoza.

F-2
3159

Leisegang, Hans, 1890-1951.
Lessings Weltanschauung. Leipzig, F. Meiner, 1931.
xi, 205 p. 24cm.

Includes a chapter "Die Gespräche über Spinoza" (p. [159]-179)
Bibliography: p. [199]-205.

F-2
3160

Lessing, Gotthold Ephraim, 1729-1781.
Lessings Briefe; in Auswahl herausgegeben von Julius Petersen. Leipzig, Insel-Verlag, 1911.
xvi, 298 p. 19cm.

Bibliographical footnotes.

F-2
3161

Lessing, Gotthold Ephraim, 1729-1781.
Gotthold Ephraim Lessings Gespräche nebst sonstigen Zeugnissen aus seinem Umgang; zum erstenmal gesammelt und hrsg. von Flodoard Freiherrn von Biedermann. Berlin, Propyläen-Verlag, 1924.
vi, 435 p.

Includes references to Spinoza.

F-2
3162

Oehlke, Waldemar, 1879-
Lessing and seine Zeit. München, Beck, 1919.
2 v. ports. 22cm.

Includes references to Spinoza.

F-2
3163

[Rauwenhoff, Lodewijk Willem Ernst] 1828-1889.
Was Lessing Spinozist? [1868?]
62 p. 22cm.

Signed: L. W. E. Rauwenhoff.

F-2
3164

Rehorn, Karl, 1840-1921.
G. E. Lessing's Stellung zur Philosophie des Spinoza. Frankfurt am Main, M. Diesterweg, 1877.
54 p. 22cm.

F-2
3165

Ritter, Heinrich, 1791-1869.
Ueber Lessing's philosophische und religiöse Grundsätze. Göttingen, Vandenhoeck und Ruprecht, 1847.
73 p. 22cm.

"Abgedruckt aus den Göttinger Studien, 1847."
Includes references to Spinoza.
Original paper cover bound in.

F-2
3166

Schmidt, Erich, 1853-1913.
Lessing. Geschichte seines Lebens und seiner Schriften. 2. veränderte Aufl. Berlin, Weidmann, 1899.
2 v. ports. 25 cm.

Includes references to Spinoza.

Schmidt, Erich, 1853-1913.
Lessing; Geschichte seines Lebens und seiner Schriften. 3. durchgesehene Aufl. Berlin, Weidmann, 1909.
2 v. ports. 23cm.

Includes references to Spinoza.

Schrempf, Christof, 1860-
Lessing als Philosoph. Stuttgart, Fr. Frommanns Verlag (E. Hauff) 1906.
203 p. 22cm. (Frommanns Klassiker der Philosophie. XIX)

Includes references to Spinoza.
Original paper cover bound in.

Schrempf, Christof, 1860-
Lessing als Philosoph. 2. Aufl. Stuttgart, Fr. Frommann, 1921.
193 p. port. 22cm. (Frommanns Klassiker der Philosophie. XIX)

Includes references to Spinoza.

Schrempf, Christof, 1860-
... Lessing, von dr. Christoph Schrempf ... Mit einem titelbild. Leipzig und Berlin, B. G. Teubner, 1913.
iv, 127, [1] p. front. (port.) 18½cm. (Aus natur und geisteswelt ... 403. bdchn.) M. 1.25

Includes references to Spinoza.

1. Lessing, Gotthold Ephraim, 1729-1781.

Sime, James, 1843-1895.
Lessing. By James Sime ... London, Trübner & co., 1877.
2 v. fronts. (ports.) 21 cm. (*Half-title:* The English and foreign philosophical library. Extra series. vol. I-II)

Includes references to Spinoza.

1. Lessing, Gotthold Ephraim, 1729-1781.

Stahr, Adolf, 1805-1876.
G. E. Lessing; sein Leben und seine Werke. Verm. und verb. Volks-Ausg. 4. Aufl. Berlin, J. Guttentag, 1866.
2 v. 16cm.

Volume 2 includes a chapter on Spinoza.

F-3 GOETHE

Arnim, Bettina (Brentano) von, 1785-1859.
Goethes Briefwechsel mit einem Kinde. Seinem Denkmal. Mit einer Einleitung von Franz Brümmer. Leipzig, Ph. Reclam jun. [1890]
583 p. plate. 15cm.

Astrada, Carlos, 1894-
Goethe y el panteismo spinoziano. Santa Fé, Rep. Argentina, Instituto Social de la Universidad Nacional del Litoral, 1933.
23 p. 24cm. (Publicaciones del Instituto Social)

Bayer, Josef
Göthe's Verhaltniss zu religiösen Fragen; Vortrag gehalten im Deutschen Casino am 15. April 1869. Prag, H. Mercy, 1869.
42 p.

Includes references to Spinoza (p. 30-32)

Bergmann, Julius, 1840-1904.
Zur Feier von Goethes Geburtstag: Spinoza. [1885]
8-13 p.

In Freies Deutsches Hochstift, Frankfurt a. M. Berichte, n. F. Bd. 2, 1885-86.

SPECIAL COLLECTIONS SPINOZA F-3 3177

ʀBerthelot, René, 1872-
La sagesse de Goethe et la civilisation de l'Europe moderne. ʀ1927ʀ
34 p. 25cm.

Signed: René Berthelot.
From Revue de métaphysique et de morale, 34. année, no. 1, janvier-mars, 1927.
Includes a section "Spinoza, Kant et l'idéal de la sagesse" (p. 1-5)

SPECIAL COLLECTIONS SPINOZA F-3 3178

Beutler, Ernst, 1885-
Goethe und die Natur. ʀ1929ʀ
ʀ129ʀ-143 p. 25cm.

From Natur und Museum; Senckenbergische naturforschende Gesellschaft, 59. Bericht, Heft 3.
Includes references to Spinoza.

SPECIAL COLLECTIONS SPINOZA F-3 3179

Bielschowsky, Albert, 1847-1902.
Goethe, sein Leben und seine Werke. München, C. H. Beck'sche Verlagsbuchhandlung, 1908.
2 v. ports. 22cm.

Vol. 1 is 15. Aufl., vol. 2, 13. Aufl.
Includes references to Spinoza.
Bibliographical references included in "Anmerkungen" at end of each volume.

F-3 3180

Bielschowsky, Albert, 1847-1902.
The life of Goethe. Authorised translation from the German, by William A. Cooper. New York and London, Putnam, 1905-08.
3 v. plates, ports. 25 cm.

References to Spinoza included in chapter "Goethe and philosophy" (v. 2, p. 156-181)

NNC

F-3 3181

ʀBruell, Adolfʀ
Göthe und Spinoza. ʀ1887ʀ
58-61 p.

In Adolf Bruell's populär-wissenschaftliche Monatsblätter, Jahrgang 7, 1887.

NNJ

F-3 3182

ʀCaro, Elmeʀ 1826-1887.
La philosophie de Goethe. I. Histoire de son esprit.- Goethe et Spinoza. ʀ1865ʀ
846-880 p.

Signed: E. Caro.
In Revue des deux mondes, 35. année, 2. période, t. 59, 1865.
An excerpt from his La philosophie de Goethe.

SPECIAL COLLECTIONS SPINOZA F-3 3183

Caro, Elme Marie, 1826-1887.
La philosophie de Goethe, par E. Caro. Paris, L. Hachette et cie, ~~1886.~~ 1866.
2 p. l., viii, 430 p., 1 l. 22½cm.
"Extraits et fragments philosophiques des œuvres de Goethe": p. ʀ363ʀ-427.
Includes a chapter "Goethe et Spinoza" (p. ʀ34ʀ-66)

1. Goethe, Johann Wolfgang von—Philosophy.

25—7711

Library of Congress PT2193.C25 ʀ42b1ʀ

F-3 3184

Caro, Elme, 1826-1887.
La philosophie de Goethe. 2. éd. Paris, Hachette, 1880.
vi, 398 p.

Includes chapter "Goethe et Spinoza" (p. 31-60)

SPECIAL COLLECTIONS SPINOZA F-3 3185

Carp. J H
Spinoza en Goethe. 's-Gravenhage, W. P. v. Stockum & Zn., 1932.
64 p. 21cm.

Presentation copy to A. S. Oko with the author's inscription and signature.

SPECIAL COLLECTIONS SPINOZA F-3 3186

Carus, Paul, 1852-1919.
Goethe, with special consideration of his philosophy. Containing one hundred and eighty-five portraits and other historical illustrations. Chicago, The Open court publishing company, 1915.
xi, 357 p. illus., ports., facsims. 24cm.

"Miscellaneous epigrams and poems" (tr. by the author): p. ʀ327ʀ-346.
Includes references to Spinoza (p. 29, 185)

F-3
3187

Danzel, Theodor Wilhelm, 1818-1850.
Ueber Goethe's Spinozismus; ein Beitrag zur tiefern Würdigung des Dichters und Forschers. Hamburg, J. A. Meissner, 1843.
iv, 138 p. 21cm.

1. Goethe, Johann Wolfgang von, 1749-1832.
2. Spinoza, Benedictus de, 1632-1677.

F-3
3188

Danzel, Theodor Wilhelm, 1818-1850.
Ueber Goethe's Spinozismus; ein Beitrag zur tiefern Würdigung des Dichters und Forschers. Neue wohlfeile Ausg. Hamburg, J. A. Meissner, 1850.
iv, 138 p. 21cm.

F-3
3189

Davidson, Thomas, 1840-1900.
The philosophy of Goethe's Faust. Ed. by Charles M. Bakewell. Boston, Ginn [1906]
iv, 158 p. 22 cm.

F-3
3190

Dilthey, Wilhelm, 1833-1911.
Aus der Zeit der Spinoza-Studien Goethe's. [1894]
317-341 p.

In Archiv für Geschichte der Philosophie, Bd. 7, 1894.

F-3
3191

1938Sp4
FG539 Ernst, Adolf Wilhelm, 1866-
Goethes Religion; eine Studie. Hamburg, C. Kloss, 1895.
62 p. 19cm.

Imperfect: p. 33-62 lacking.

1. Goethe, Johann Wolfgang von - Theology.

F-3
3192

Goethe, Johann Wolfgang von, 1749-1832.
Aus meinem Leben. Dichtung und Wahrheit, von Goethe. [1. Abth.] Dritter Theil. Tübingen, J. G. Cotta, 1814.
538 p. 18cm.

Includes references to Spinoza (p. 441-443)

1. Spinoza, Benedictus de, 1632-1677.

F-3
3193

Goethe, Johann Wolfgang von, 1749-1832.
Aus meinem Leben. Wahrheit und Dichtung. 4. Theil. [1851]
[197]-303 p. (In his Sämmtliche Werke, 18. Bd., 1851)

Includes references to Spinoza (p. 201-205)

F-3
3194

Goethe, Johann Wolfgang von, 1749-1832.
The auto-biography of Goethe. Truth and poetry: from my own life. London, H. G. Bohn, 1848-49.
2 v. 19 cm. [Goethe's Works, v. 1-2]

Volume 2 includes references to Spinoza in Book 16.

F-3
3195

Goethe, Johann Wolfgang von, 1749-1832.
Briefwechsel zwischen Goethe und F. H. Jacobi; hrsg. von Max Jacobi. Leipzig, Weidmann'sche Buchhandlung, 1846.
viii, 274 p.

Includes references to Spinoza.

F-3
3196

Goethe, Johann Wolfgang von, 1749-1832.
Goethe on Spinoza. [1914]
282-285 p.

From Pollak, Gustav. International perspective in criticism. New York, Dodd, Mead, 1914.

Goethe, Johann Wolfgang von, 1749-1832.
Goethes Gespräche; Gesamtausgabe, neu hrsg. von Flodoard Frhr. von Biedermann, unter Mitwirkung von Max Morris, Hans Gerhard Gräf und Leonhard L. Mackall. Leipzig, F. W. v. Biedermann, 1909-11.
5 v. 22 cm.

Includes references to Spinoza.

Goethe, Johann Wolfgang von, 1749-1832.
Goethes Philosophie aus seinen Werken; ein Buch für jeden gebildeten Deutschen. Mit ausführlicher Einleitung hrsg. von Max Heynacher. Leipzig, Dürr, 1905.
viii, 428 p. (Philosophische Bibliothek. Bd. 109)

Includes sections on Spinoza.

Goethe, Johann Wolfgang von, 1749-1832.
Goethes philosophie aus seinen werken; ein buch für jeden gebildeten Deutschen, mit ausführlicher einleitung, hrsg. von Max Heynacher; 2. verb. aufl. ... Leipzig, Felix Meiner, 1922.
cxxxi, 319 p. diagr. 19cm. (Der philosophischen bibliothek, bd. 109)

Includes sections on Spinoza.

I. Heynacher, Max, ed.

Goldschmidt, Ludwig, 1853-
War Goethe Spinozist? [1909]
2 p.

In Frankfurter Zeitung, Okt. 23, 1909.

Hering, Robert, 1866-1946.
Spinoza im jungen Goethe. Leipzig, 1897.
71 p. 23cm.

Thesis, Leipzig.
Bibliographical footnotes.

Heyder, Karl
Über das Verhältnis Goethe's zu Spinoza. [1866]
261-283 p.

In Zeitschrift für die gesammte Lutherische Theologie und Kirche, Bd. 27, 1866.

Hoffmann, Heinrich, 1874-
Die Religion des Goetheschen Zeitalters. Tübingen, J. C. B. Mohr (P. Siebeck) 1907.
37 p. 23cm. (Sammlung gemeinverständlicher Vorträge und Schriften aus dem Gebiet der Theologie und Religionsgeschichte. 81)

"Als Berner Hochschulvortrag am 9. Februar 1917 gehalten, mit einigen Veränderungen und Erweiterungen gedruckt."
Includes references to Spinoza (p. 20-21)
Original paper covers bound in.

Hoffmann, Paul
Untersuchungen über Goethes Ewigen Juden. [1891]
116-152 p.

In Vierteljahrschrift für Litteraturgeschichte, 4. Bd., 1891.
Includes references to Spinoza.

Jellinek, Georg, 1851-1911.
Ausgewählte Schriften und Reden. Mit einem Geleitwort von Wilhelm Windelband. Berlin, O. Häring, 1911.
2 v. ports. 23cm.

Edited by Walter Jellinek.
Includes a chapter "Die Beziehungen Goethes zu Spinoza" (v. 1, p. [179]-207)

Jellinek, Georg, 1851-1911.
Die Beziehungen Goethe's zu Spinoza. Vortrag, gehalten im Vereine der Literaturfreunde zu Wien. Wien, A. Hölder, 1878.
28 p.

Kappstein, Theodor, 1870-
Goethes Weltanschauung. München, Rösl, 1921.
201 p. 17cm. (Philosophische Reihe, hrsg. von Alfred Werner. 6. Bd.)

Includes references to Spinoza.
Bibliography: p. 199-201.

[Kaufmann, M]
Spinoza, Goethe, and the moderns. [1912]
390-412 p. 22cm.

Signed: M. Kaufmann.
From the Quarterly review, vol. 217, no. 433, Oct. 1912.
Ms. notes by A. S. Oko.
Bibliography: p. 390.

Key, Ellen, 1849-1926.
Människor. Stockholm, A. Bonnier [1899]
335 p. 20cm.

The essay "Goethehaus i Weimar" includes references to Spinoza (p. 325-326)

Kronenberg, Moritz, 1865-
Die All-Einheit; Grundlinien der Welt- und Lebensanschauung im Geiste Goethes und Spinozas. Stuttgart, Strecker und Schröder, 1924.
xiv, 103 p. 19cm.

Leisegang, Hans, 1890-
Goethes denken, von Hans Leisegang ... Leipzig, F. Meiner, 1932.
xii, 182 p. incl. front. (diagr.) 23½cm.

Includes references to Spinoza.

1. Goethe, Johann Wolfgang von—Philosophy. I. Title.

Lewes, George Henry, 1817-1878.
The life of Goethe. 2d ed., partly rewritten. London, Smith, Elder, 1864.
xviii, 575 p. port. 23cm.

Includes references to Spinoza.

Melzer, Ernst, 1835-1899.
Goethes philosophische Entwickelung; ein Beitrag zur Geschichte der Philosophie unserer Dichterheroen. Neisse, Verlag der Josef Graveur'schen Buchhandlung, 1884.
72 p. 23cm.

"Separatabdruck aus dem 22. Bericht der wissenschaftlichen Gesellschaft Philomatie in Neisse."
Includes a chapter "Goethe als Philosoph von

CONTINUED ON NEXT CARD

Melzer, Ernst, 1835-1899. Goethes philosophische Entwicklung. 1884. (Card 2)

der genaueren Kenntnisnahme Spinozas bis zu seinem Tode, 1784-1832" (p. 32-69)

Menzel, Alfred, 1883-
Goethes Welt- und Lebensanschauung. Ein Vortrag gehalten am 22. Februar 1919 in Hamburg. Hamburg, Pfadweiser, 1919.
39 p. 23 cm.

Includes references to Spinoza.

Meyer, Richard Moritz, 1860-1914.
Goethe. Mit zwei Bildnissen und einer Handschrift. 3. verm. Aufl. Berlin, E. Hofmann, 1905.
3 v. (xv, 911 p.) ports., fold. facsim. 20cm.

Includes references to Spinoza.
Bibliography: v. 3, p. [865]-879.

F-3 3217

Muckermann, Friedrich
Goethe. Bonn, Verlag der Buchgemeinde, 1931.
259 p.

Includes a section on Spinoza (p. 24-44)

WaU

SPECIAL COLLECTIONS SPINOZA F-3 3218

Paris. Bibliothèque nationale.
Goethe, 1749-1832. Exposition organisée pour commémorer le centénaire de la mort de Goethe. [Paris, Éditions des Bibliothèques nationales de France, 1932.
vii, 233 p. plates, ports., facsims. 21cm.

Avant-propos signed: Julien Cain.
Catalogue prepared by Henri Moncel.
"Visages et paysages dans le souvenir de Goethe", par Charles Andler: p. 1-14.
Includes references to Spinoza (p. 69-70, 91)

NNC

F-3 3219

Schaub, Edward Leroy, 1881-
Goethe and philosophy. [1933]
131-158 p.

From Chicago. University. Goethe centenary papers. Chicago, The Open court publishing company, 1933.

Includes references to Spinoza.

SPECIAL COLLECTIONS SPINOZA F-3 3220

Schneege, Gerhard, 1857-
Goethes Spinozismus. [1911]
[449]-462, [505]-517, 578-586, 632-650 p. 24cm.

From Zeitschrift für Philosophie und Pädagogik, 18. Jahrgang, 1911.

NNC

SPECIAL COLLECTIONS SPINOZA F-3 3221

Schneege, Gerhard, 1857-
Goethes Spinozismus. Langensalza, H. Beyer & Söhne (Beyer & Mann) 1911.
72 p. 21cm. (Pädagogisches Magazin; Abhandlungen vom Gebiete der Pädagogik und ihrer Hilfswissenschaften. 455. Heft)

Bibliographical footnotes.

SPECIAL COLLECTIONS SPINOZA F-3 3222

Schneege, Gerhard, 1857-
Goethes Verhältnis zu Spinoza und seine philosophische Weltanschauung. Pless, A. Krummer, 1890.
21 p. 24cm.

At head of title: Siebzehntes Programm der Evangl. Fürstenschule zu Pless.

F-3 3223

[Schneege, Gerhard] 1857-
Goethes Verhältnis zu Spinoza und seine philosophische Weltanschauung. [1891]
385-409, 513-527 p.

Signed: G. Schneege.
In Philosophische Monatshefte, 27. Bd., 1891.

SPECIAL COLLECTIONS SPINOZA F-3 3224

Schneege, Gerhard, 1857-
Zu Goethes Spinozismus. Breslau, Druck von O. Gutsmann, 1910.
26 p. 26x21cm.

"Wissenschaftliche Beilage zum Programm des Königl. König-Wilhelms-Gymnasiums zu Breslau für das Schuljahr 1909/1910."
Bibliographical footnotes.

F-3 3225

Splettstösser, Willi
Der Grundgedanke in Goethes Faust.
Berlin, G. Reimer, 1911.
viii, 191 p. 21 cm.

CtY

F-3 3226

Springer, Robert, 1816-1885.
Essays zur Kritik und Philosophie und zur Goethe-Litteratur. Minden i. W., J. C. C. Bruns, 1885.
xvi, 404 p.

Includes an essay "Goethe und Spinoza" (p. 214-239)

Strong, Augustus Hopkins, 1836-1921.
The great poets and their theology. Philadelphia, The Griffith & Rowland Press [c1897]
xvii, 531 p. 23cm.

Contents.--Homer.-- Virgil.--Dante.--Shakespeare.--Milton.--Goethe.--Wordsworth.--Browning.--Tennyson.
Includes references to Spinoza in section on Goethe.

[Suphan, Bernhard] 1845-1911.
Aus der Zeit der Spinoza-Studien Goethes, 1784-85. [1891]
[3]-12 p. 25cm.

A short essay by Goethe, followed by a commentary signed: B. Suphan.
At head of title: Mittheilungen aus dem Goethe- und Schiller-Archiv.
From Goethe-Jahrbuch, 12. Bd., 1891.

Suphan, Bernhard, 1845-1911.
Goethe und Spinoza, 1783-86. [1881]
[159]-193 p. 24cm.

From Festschrift zu der zweiten Säcularfeier des Friedrichs-Werderschen Gymnasiums zu Berlin.
Original paper covers bound in.
Bibliographical footnotes.

Teweles, Heinrich, 1856-1927.
... Goethe und die Juden. Hamburg, W. Gente, 1925.
205 p. 19½cm
The "Register" (p. [145]-205) includes brief biographical notices.
Includes references to Spinoza.

1. Goethe, Johann Wolfgang von—Political and social views. 2. Jews in Germany. I. Title.

Thomas, Calvin, 1843-1919.
Goethe. New York, Holt, 1917.
xii, 368 p. 20cm.

Includes references to Spinoza.
"Bibliography and notes": p. 355-361.

Trampe, Adolf, 1886-
Goethe und Spinoza; ein Beitrag zur Darstellung der Goethe'schen Weltanschauung. [Fulda, Druck und Kommissionsverlag der Fuldaer Actiendruckerei [1909?]
33 p. 25cm.

Trampe, Adolf, 1886-
Goethe und Spinoza, ein Beitrag zur Darstellung der Goetheschen Weltanschauung. [1911]
71-103 p.

In Philosophisches Jahrbuch, 24. Jahrgang, 1911.

Türck, Hermann, 1856-1921.
Eine neue Faust-Erklärung. 4. unveränderte Aufl. Berlin, O. Elsner, 1906.
150 p. 21cm.

Includes a chapter "Spinoza und Goethes 'Faust'" (p. [101]-128)

Türck, Hermann, 1856-1921.
Eine neue Faust-Erklärung. Berlin, O. Elsner, 1901.
82 p. 19cm.

Includes references to Spinoza.

[Türck, Hermann] 1856-1921.
Neue Spinoza-Elemente im "Faust". [1902]
92-100 p. 26cm.

Signed: Dr. Hermann Türck.
From Die Kultur, I. Jahrgang, 2. Juliheft, 1902.

Vogel, Theodor
Nüchterne Erwägungen über Goethes Spinozismus. [1901]
73-79 p.

In Zeitschrift für den deutschen Unterricht, 15. Jahrgang, 1901.

Vorländer, Karl, 1860-1928.
Goethes Verhältnis zu Kant in seiner historischen Entwicklung. [1896]
[60]-99 p. 24cm.

From Kantstudien, Band 1, Heft 1.
On cover: Ausgegeben am 25. April 1896.
Stamped on cover: Probenummer.
Includes references to Spinoza.

Wagner,
Goethes Weltanschauung im Lichte der neueren Forschung. [1927]
[129]-131 p. 27cm.

From Unsere Welt, illustrierte Zeitschrift für Wissenschaft und Weltanschauung, 19. Jahrg., Heft 5, Mai 1927.
Includes a reference to Spinoza.

Waldman, Mark, 1878-
Goethe and the Jews; a challenge to Hitlerism, by Mark Waldman ... New York, London, G. P. Putnam's sons, 1934.
xvi p., 1 l., 19-295 p. front. (port.) pl., facsims. 21 cm.

Includes references to Spinoza.

1. Goethe, Johann Wolfgang von—Political and social views. 2. Goethe, Johann Wolfgang von—Knowledge—Bible. 3. Goethe, Johann Wolfgang von—Religion and ethics. 4. Jews in Germany. 5. Jews in literature. I. Title.

Walter van der Bleek, Curt Heinrich Bruno Leo, 1877-
Giordano Bruno, Goethe und das Christusproblem. Naturwissenschaft und Bibel. Berlin, Borngräber, 1911.

Warnecke, Friedrich, 1837-1894.
Goethe, Spinoza und Jacobi. Weimar, H. Böhlaus Nachfolger, 1908.
59 p. 24cm.

Includes sections "Kriterien für die Entwickelung von Goethes Spinozismus" (p. 39-48) and "Spinoza-Zitate in Goethes Briefen" (p. [50]-54) and other references to Spinoza.
Original paper covers bound in.
Bibliography: p. [60]

Zilchert, Robert, 1867-
Goethe als Erzieher. 1. und 2. Aufl. Leipzig, J. C. Hinrichs, 1921.
vi, 187 p. 19cm.

G HISTORY AND SPINOZA

G-1 SECULAR

Adler, Felix, 1851-1933.
Creed and deed; a series of discourses by Felix Adler ... New York, Pub. for the Society for ethical culture, by G. P. Putnam's sons, ~~1877~~. 1890.
iv p., 1 l., 243 p. 20½cm.

CONTENTS.—Immortality.—Religion.—The new ideal.—The priest of the ideal.—The form of the new ideal.—The religious conservatism of women.—Our consolations.—Spinoza.—The founder of Christianity.—The anniversary discourse.—Appendix: The evolution of Hebrew religion.—Reformed Judaism, I, II, III.

1. Ethics. 2. Ethical culture movement. I. New York society for ethical culture. II. Title.

Anti-Spinoza. Ein Protest gegen die modern-scholastische romanisch-juristische Denkweise in Sachen der Philosophie ... Potsdam, In Commission bei R. Cabos, 1868.
24 p. fold. table, diagrs. 23cm.

1. Spinoza, Benedictus de, 1632-1677.

Arnold, Matthew, 1822-1888.
The bishop and the philosopher. [1863]
241-256 p.

In Macmillan's magazine, v. 7, 1863.
Includes references to Spinoza.

G-1
3247

Aubry, Jean Baptiste
Questions philosophiques sur la religion naturelle, dans lesquelles on propose et on résout avec les seules lumières de la raison les objections des athées, des matérialistes, des pyrrhoniens et des déistes. Paris, Th. Barrois, 1782.

CtY

G-1
3248

Bender, Wilhelm
Johann Konrad Dippel. Der Freigeist aus dem Pietismus; ein Beitrag zur Entstehungsgeschichte der Aufklärung. Bonn, Weber, 1882.
viii, 221 p.

NNUT

SPECIAL COLLECTIONS SPINOZA

G-1
3249

Blunt, John Henry, 1823–1884.
Dictionary of sects, heresies, ecclesiastical parties, and schools of religious thought. Edited by the Rev. John Henry Blunt ... London [etc.] Rivingtons, 1874.
viii, 647, [1] p. 27½cm.

Includes a section on Spinoza (p. 570-577)

1. Theology—Dictionaries. 2. Sects. I. Title.

7-13531

Library of Congress BR95.B6 1874 [a34b1]

G-1
3250

Bomble, Florentinus
Tweede briefe aan den Heer F. van Leenhof, behelsende noodige aanmerkingen over 't eerste deel van den opgehelderen Hemel op aarde. Tot wederlegging van de ongegronde berispingen en bewys datter geene ophelderinge in gevonden wordt. T' Amsteldam, by G. Borstius, 1706.

NIC

G-1
3251

[Bonnier, Charles]
Spinoza et Marx. [1904]
38-55 p.

In Le Mouvement socialiste, v. 12, January 1904.

NNC

SPECIAL COLLECTIONS SPINOZA

G-1
3252

Brandl, Alois, 1855-1940.
Samuel Taylor Coleridge und die englische Romantik. Berlin, R. Oppenheim, 1886.
xiii (i. e. xv), 437 p. 20cm.

Includes references to Spinoza.

SPECIAL COLLECTIONS SPINOZA

G-1
3253

193Sp4 FB559
Bredvold, Louis Ignatius, 1888-
The intellectual milieu of John Dryden; studies in some aspects of seventeenth-century thought, by Louis I. Bredvold ... Ann Arbor, University of Michigan press, 1934.
viii, 189 p. 23½cm. (Half-title: University of Michigan publications. Language and literature. vol. XII)

Includes references to Spinoza (p. 105)
"The bibliography of Roman Catholic controversy in England in the seventeenth century": p. 157-158.

SPECIAL COLLECTIONS SPINOZA

G-1
3254

Buddeus, Johann Franz, 1667-1729.
Herrn Io. Franc. Bvddei ... Lehr-Sätze von der Atheisterey und dem Aberglauben mit gelehrten Anmerckungen erläutert, und zum Behueff seiner Auditorum in lateinischer Sprache heraus gegeben, wegen des daraus zu hoffenden Nutzens aber zu iedermanns Gebrauch ins Teutsche übersetzet durch Theognostvm Evsebivm ... 2. Aufl. Jena, J. F. Bielcken, 1723.
[28], 734, [46] p. front. 17cm.

Includes a section on Spinoza (p. 144-159)

SPECIAL COLLECTIONS SPINOZA

G-1
3255

Buddeus, Johann Franz, 1667-1729.
Historische und theologische Einleitung in die vornehmsten Religions-Streitigkeiten, aus Hrn. Johann Francisci Buddei Collegio herausgegeben, auch mit Anmerckungen erläutert und vielen Zusätzen vermehret, von Joh. Georg Walchen. Jena, Zu finden in dem Meyerischen Buchladen, 1724.
[26], 743, [21] p. 17cm.

A projected second part, referred to in the author's preface, apparently never published.

SPECIAL COLLECTIONS SPINOZA

G-1
3256

Carp, J H
Spinoza als mysticus. [1933]
[31]-49 p. 25cm.

From Kant Gesellschaft. Afdeeling-Nederland. Spinoza; gezamelijke redevoeringen, 1933.

1. Spinoza, Benedictus de, 1632-1677.

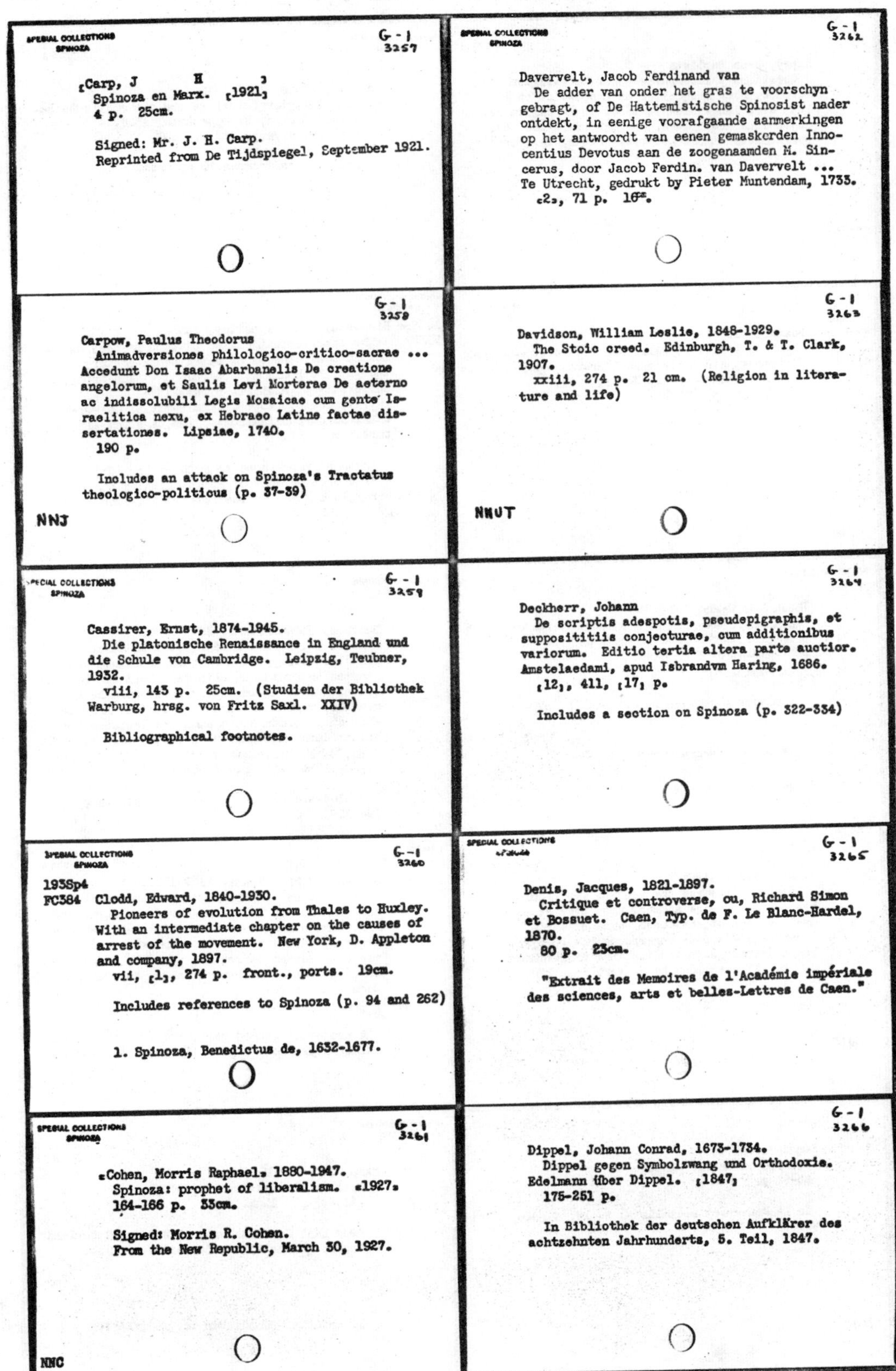

G-1
3257

[Carp, J H]
Spinoza en Marx. [1921]
4 p. 25cm.

Signed: Mr. J. H. Carp.
Reprinted from De Tijdspiegel, September 1921.

G-1
3262

Davervelt, Jacob Ferdinand van
De adder van onder het gras te voorschyn gebragt, of De Hattemistische Spinosist nader ontdekt, in eenige voorafgaande aanmerkingen op het antwoordt van eenen gemaskerden Innocentius Devotus aan de zoogenaamden M. Sincerus, door Jacob Ferdin. van Davervelt ... Te Utrecht, gedrukt by Pieter Muntendam, 1733.
[2], 71 p. 16cm.

G-1
3258

Carpow, Paulus Theodorus
Animadversiones philologico-critico-sacrae ... Accedunt Don Isaac Abarbanelis De creatione angelorum, et Saulis Levi Morterae De aeterno ac indissolubili Legis Mosaicae cum gente Israelitica nexu, ex Hebraeo Latine factae dissertationes. Lipsiae, 1740.
190 p.

Includes an attack on Spinoza's Tractatus theologico-politicus (p. 37-39)

NNJ

G-1
3263

Davidson, William Leslie, 1848-1929.
The Stoic creed. Edinburgh, T. & T. Clark, 1907.
xxiii, 274 p. 21 cm. (Religion in literature and life)

NNUT

G-1
3259

Cassirer, Ernst, 1874-1945.
Die platonische Renaissance in England und die Schule von Cambridge. Leipzig, Teubner, 1932.
viii, 143 p. 25cm. (Studien der Bibliothek Warburg, hrsg. von Fritz Saxl. XXIV)

Bibliographical footnotes.

G-1
3264

Deckherr, Johann
De scriptis adespotis, pseudepigraphis, et supposititiis conjecturae, cum additionibus variorum. Editio tertia altera parte auctior. Amstelaedami, apud Isbrandvm Haring, 1686.
[12], 411, [17] p.

Includes a section on Spinoza (p. 322-334)

G-1
3260

193Sp4
FC384 Clodd, Edward, 1840-1930.
Pioneers of evolution from Thales to Huxley. With an intermediate chapter on the causes of arrest of the movement. New York, D. Appleton and company, 1897.
vii, [1], 274 p. front., ports. 19cm.

Includes references to Spinoza (p. 94 and 262)

1. Spinoza, Benedictus de, 1632-1677.

G-1
3265

Denis, Jacques, 1821-1897.
Critique et controverse, ou, Richard Simon et Bossuet. Caen, Typ. de F. Le Blanc-Hardel, 1870.
80 p. 23cm.

"Extrait des Memoires de l'Académie impériale des sciences, arts et belles-Lettres de Caen."

G-1
3261

[Cohen, Morris Raphael, 1880-1947.
Spinoza: prophet of liberalism. [1927]
164-166 p. 33cm.

Signed: Morris R. Cohen.
From the New Republic, March 30, 1927.

NNC

G-1
3266

Dippel, Johann Conrad, 1673-1734.
Dippel gegen Symbolzwang und Orthodoxie. Edelmann über Dippel. [1847]
175-251 p.

In Bibliothek der deutschen Aufklärer des achtzehnten Jahrhunderts, 5. Teil, 1847.

G-1
3267

Dräseke, Johannes, 1844-1916.
Spinoza als Bahnbrecher auf dem Gebiete altt. Wissenschaft. [1901]
35-39 p.

In Neue Kirchliche Zeitschrift, Bd. 12, 1901.

NNUT

G-1
3268

Edelmann, Johann Christian, 1698-1767.
Die Begierde nach dre [!] Vernünfftigen Lautern Milch an einigen Säuglingen der ewigen Liebe bewundert, bey oeffentlicher Beantwortung eines hertzlichen Ermunterungs-Schreibens einiger so ungenannter, als unbekannter Brüder, denen seine unverfälschte Gegen-Liebe zu bezeugen vor seine Schuldigkeit erachtet, ihr ergebenster Mit-Bruder Johan Christian Edelmann. Zweyte Auflage. 1747.
258, [69] p.

MH

SPECIAL COLLECTIONS
SPINOZA

G-1
3269

Edelmann, Johann Christian, 1698-1767.
Christus und Belial, wie solche nie zusammenstimmen, in einem theologischen Brieff-Wechsel zwischen unten benanntsn auctore und Bruder Ludwig von Zinzendorff, Gott und Wahrheit liebenden Seelen zu geheiligter Prüfung vor Augen gelegt von Johann Christian Edelmann. [Freyburg?] 1741.
[64], 176 p. 17cm.

Bound with Edelmann, Johann Christian. Moses mit aufgedeckten Angesichte. [1740]

SPECIAL COLLECTIONS
SPINOZA

G-1
3270

Edelmann, Johann Christian, 1698-1767.
Die Göttlichkeit der Vernunft, in einer kurtzen Anweisung zu weiterer Untersuchung der ältesten und vornehmsten Bedeutung des Wortes λόγος, nebst einigen, in diese Materie einschlagenden Briefen, und einem Anhange: Von der Vernunfftmässigkeit des Christenthums, allen nach einer vernünfftigen lautern Milch begierigen und nach der Wiederherstellung eines vernünfftigen Gottesdienstes schon lange im Verborgenen seufftzenden Gemüthern

CONTINUED ON NEXT CARD

SPECIAL COLLECTIONS
SPINOZA

G-1
3271

Edelmann, Johann Christian, 1698-1767. Die Göttlichkeit der Vernunft. [1742?] (Card 2)

zur Ermunterung, den unbekannten Gott etwas näher kennen zu lernen, aus Liebe vorgestellet von Johann Christian Edelmann ... [Berlenburg, 1742?]
607, [52] p. 17cm.

Includes references to Spinoza.
Imprint from Brit. Mus. Cat.

SPECIAL COLLECTIONS
SPINOZA

G-1
3272

Edelmann, Johann Christian, 1698-1767.
Historische Nachrichten von Joh. Chr. Edelmanns, eines berüchtigten Religionsspötters, Leben, Schriften und Lehrbegrif, wie auch von den Schriften, die für und wider ihn geschrieben worden, gesamlet und mitgetheilet von Joh. Hinr. Pratje ... Hamburg, Christian Wilhelm Brandt, 1753.
[16], 275, [5] p. 18cm.

Pages 209-239 incorrectly numbered 193-223.
Includes reference to Spinoza.

SPECIAL COLLECTIONS
SPINOZA

G-1
3273

Edelmann, Johann Christian, 1698-1767.
Johann Christian Edelmanns Abgenöthigtes, jedoch Andern nicht wieder aufgenöthigtes Glaubens-Bekentniss. Aus Veranlassung unrichtiger und verhuntzter Abschrifften desselben, dem Druck übergeben und vernünfftigen Gemüthern zur Prufung vorgeleget von dem Auctore. 1746.
328, [48] p. 21cm.

Includes a reference to Spinoza (p. 230)

SPECIAL COLLECTIONS
SPINOZA

G-1
3274

Edelmann, Johann Christian, 1698-1767.
Johann Christian Edelmanns schuldigstes Dancksagungs-Schreiben an den Herrn Probst Süssmilch vor Dessen, Ihm unbewusst erzeigte Dienste. 1747.
31 p. 17cm.

Bound with Süssmilch, Johann Peter. Die Unvernunft und Bosheit des berüchtigsten Edelmanns ... 1747.

SPECIAL COLLECTIONS
SPINOZA

G-1
3275

[Edelmann, Johann Christian] 1698-1767.
Moses mit aufgedeckten Angesichte von zwey ungleichen Brüdern, Lichtlieb und Blindling, beschauet nach Art der unschuldigen Wahrheiten in einem freymüthigen Gespräche abgehandelt, und Licht- und Klarheit-liebenden Gemüthern zu Gott geheiligter Bewundrung und Ergötzung vorgestellt ... [Freyburg?] 1740.
3 pts. in 1 v. 17cm.

Vol. 1 without imprint date.
Includes references to Spinoza.

CONTINUED ON NEXT CARD

SPECIAL COLLECTIONS
SPINOZA

G-1
3276

[Edelmann, Johann Christian] 1698-1767. Moses mit aufgedeckten Angesichte. 1740. (Card 2)

Inspired by Spinoza's Tractatus theologico-politicus.--cf. Allgemeine deutsche Biographie, v. 5, p. 639.

Faber, Geoffrey Cust, 1889-
Oxford apostles; a character study of the Oxford movement. London, Faber and Faber [1933]
xxiii, 467 p. ports. 23cm.

"Principal authorities": p. [xxi]-xxiii.

Fichte, Johann Gottlieb, 1762-1814.
The way towards the blessed life; or, The doctrine of religion. Translated from the German, by William Smith. London, J. Chapman, 1849.
xvi, 221 p. 20 cm. (The Catholic series)

Fabricius, Johann Albert, 1668-1736.
Jo. Alberti Fabricii ... Delectus argumentorum et syllabus scriptorum qui veritatem religionis Christianae adversus atheos, Epicureos, deistas seu naturalistas, idolatras, Judaeos et Muhammedanos lucubrationibus suis asseruerunt ... Hamburgi, Sumtu Theodori Christophori Felginer, 1725.
[10], 755, [27] p. front. 22cm.

Includes a chapter "Adversus Spinosam & alios mundum aeternum confingentes ..." (p. 355-366)

Flint, Robert, 1838-1910.
Agnosticism, by Robert Flint ... New York, C. Scribner's sons, 1903.
2 p. l., vii-xviii, 664 p. 21 cm.

1. Agnosticism.

[Fassmann, David] 1683-1744.
Gespräche in dem Reiche derer Todten, hundert sechs und sechtzigste Entrevuë, zwischen dem berühmten Schweitzer Wilhelm Tell, der sehr viel zur Freyheit seines Vaterlandes contribuiret, und dem neapolitanischen Fischer Masaniello, so anno 1647. die Rebellen zu Neapolis en Chéf commandiret hat, worinnen, unter vielen besonderen Discursen, die wunderlichen Fata dieser beyden Männer, folglich sehr merckwürdige Begebenheiten enthalten. Samt dem Kern derer

Flint, Robert, 1838-1910.
Philosophy as scientia scientiarum, and A history of classifications of the sciences; by Robert Flint ... Edinburgh and London, W. Blackwood and sons, 1904.
x, 340 p. 23½ cm.

1. Classification of sciences. 2. Philosophy.

[Fassmann, David] 1683-1744. Gespräche in dem Reiche derer Todten. 1732. (Card 2)

neuesten Merckwürdigkeiten, und darüber gemachten curieusen Reflexionen. Leipzig, verlegts Wolffgang Deer, 1732.
1 p. l., [397]-464 p. front. 21cm.

Francke, Georg Samuel
Versuch über die von der erlauchten Königlich-Dänischen Gesellschaft der Wissenschaften zu Kopenhagen im Jahr 1805 bekannt gemachte Preisfrage: "Quaenam fuére recentiore ac recentissimo aevo fata Spinozismi, si tamen verus est, qui hodie a quibusdam perhibetur Spinozismus. Nocuitne an profuit rei philosophicae in universum et speciatim philosophiae de Deo?" Oder: Über die neuern Schicksale des Spinozismus und seinen Einfluss auf die Philosophie

CONTINUED ON NEXT CARD

Fassoni, Liberato, d. 1767.
De miraculis adversus Benedictum Spinozam; dissertatio theologica, quae prolusionis loco est publice habita ab Joanne Vincentio ... auctore Liberato Fassonio ... Editio altera auctior. Romae, Ex typographia Joannis Zempel, 1755.
65 p. 25 cm.

Francke, Georg Samuel Versuch ... 1808. (Card 2)

überhaupt und die Vernunfttheologie insbesondre ... Eine Schrift, welche den für 1805 ausgesetzten Preis erhalten hat, verfasst von Dr. G. S. Francke ... Schleswig, Gedruckt in der Kön. priv. Serringhausenschen Buchdruckerey, 1808.
xvi, 98 p. 19cm.

Fränkel, Nachman, 1833-188-?

שטת שפינאזא והמקובלים ודת היהודים.
[1865-66]
10 pts.

Title transliterated: Shitath Shpinoza ve-ha-mekubalim.
In ʿibri anokhi, v. 2, 1865-66.

Frothingham, Octavius Brooks, 1822–1895.
... George Ripley, by Octavius Brooks Frothingham. Boston, New York, Houghton, Mifflin and company, ~~1882.~~ [c1882]
320, [1] p.
vi, ~~321 p.~~ front. (port.) 18 cm. (*Half-title:* American men of letters. Ed. by C. D. Warner)

Series title also at head of t.-p.

Includes references to Spinoza.

1. Ripley, George, 1802–1880.

Frothingham, Octavius Brooks, 1822–1895.
Transcendentalism in New England; a history, by Octavius Brooks Frothingham ... New York, G. P. Putnam's sons, 1876.
ix, 395 p. front. (port.) 20½ cm.

Includes references to Spinoza.

1. Transcendentalism (New England) I. Title.

Gebhardt, Carl, 1881-1934.
Spinoza gegen Clapmarius. [Hagæ Comitis, 1923]
344-347 p. 22cm.

Cover-title: Dissertatio ex Chronici Spinozani tomo tertio separatim edita.

Gide, Charles, 1847-1932.
A history of economic doctrines from the time of the physiocrats to the present day, by Charles Gide and Charles Rist. Authorised translation from the 2d rev. and augm. ed. of 1913, under the direction of the late Professor William Smart, by R. Richards. Boston, New York, Heath [19--]
xxiii, 672 p. 23 cm.

Reprint of the 1915 edition.

Gordon, Adamus Bernardus Smits
Dissertatio philosophica inauguralis De origine mundi, quam ... submittit Adamus Bernardus Smits Gordon ... Hardervici, Apud Johannem Moojen, 1758.
[6], [3]-87, [25] p. 23cm.

Thesis, Harderwijk.
Includes a section on Spinoza (p. 57-87)

Graeber, Isacque, 1905-
The founder of European skepticism: Francis Sanchez, a Marano Jew, profoundly influenced Descartes and Spinoza. [1927]
p. 20, 60. port. 33cm.

From the Jewish Tribune, September 23, 1927.

Grunwald, Max, 1871-
Spinoza und die Reaktion. [1927]
52-61 p. illus., ports. 24cm.

From Hickl's Illustrierter jüdischer Volkskalender für das Jahr 5688-1927/28, 27. Jahrgang.

Guyot, Henri
L'infinité divine depuis Philon le Juif jusqu'à Plotin ... avec une introduction sur le même sujet dans la philosophie grecque avant Philon le Juif. Paris, Alcan, 1906.
xii, 260 p.

Includes a reference to Spinoza (p. 252)

Guzzo, Augusto, 1894-
Il primo critico dello Spinoza. [1922]
226-242 p.

In Giornale critico della filosofia italiana, anno 3, 1922.

Hagenbach, Karl Rudolf, 1801-1874.
Lehrbuch der Dogmengeschichte. 3. verb. Aufl. Leipzig, S. Hirzel, 1853.
xxii, 771 p. 24 cm.

Includes references to Spinoza.

Heidegger, Johann Heinrich, 1633-1698.
Joh. Henrici Heideggeri ... Exercitationes Biblicae, Capelli, Simonis, Spinosae & aliorum sive aberrationibus, sive fraudibus oppositae; accedunt historia vitae & dissertationes tres de religione communi, & de peste. Tiguri, D. Gessner, 1700.

Heil, Heinrich
Das Freidenkertum; Beiträge zur Geschichte und Beurteilung des Kampfes um die Weltanschauung. Paderborn, Bonifacius-Druckerei, 1922.
195 p. 22cm.

Includes references to Spinoza (p. 16-17)

Heller, Bernard, 1896-
Spinoza and the enlightenment. ₍1948₎
₍2₎, 139-147 p. port. 26cm.

"Reprinted from Michigan alumnus quarterly review, March 13, 1948, vol. LIV, no. 16."

1. Spinoza, Benedictus de, 1632-1677.

Herbertz, Richard, 1878-
Spinoza als Vorläufer Einsteins. ₍1925₎
24-26 p. 29cm.

From Das Weltall; bildergeschmückte Zeitschrift für Astronomie und verwandte Gebiete. 25. Jahrgang, 2. Heft, November 1925.

Heymans, Gerardus, 1857-1930.
Spinozistisch en modern Parallelisme. ₍1914₎
160-175 p.

In K. Akademie van Wetenschappen, Amsterdam. Afdeeling Letterkunde. Verslagen en mededeelingen, 5. reeks, deel 1, 1914.

Historie der ketteren in eene alphabethische ordre geschikt, behelzende den oorsprongk en voortgang der voornaamste ketteren en vreemde gezindheden, die zig van tyd tot tyd hebben opgedaan ... Met een aanhangsel der voornaamste geestelyke orders in de Roomsch-Catholyke-Kerk. Te Dordrecht, By Abraham Blusse, 1755.
₍4₎, 463 p. 16cm.

Includes a section on Spinoza (p. 367-376)

₍Hoffmann, Heinrich₎ 1874-
de Spinoza, Benedictus (1632-77). ₍1931₎
696-698 col.

From Die Religion in Geschichte und Gegenwart, Handwörterbuch für Theologie und Religionswissenschaft. 2. völlig neubearb. Aufl., v. 5, 1931.

Howe, John, 1630-1705.
The living temple: or, A designed improvement of that notion that a good man is the temple of God ... by John Howe ... London, Printed by J. H. for R. Clavell, J. Robinson, and A. and J. Churchill, 1702.
2 v. port. 19cm.

Huber, Johannes, 1830-1879.
Kleine Schriften. Leipzig, Duncker & Humblot, 1871.
vi, 447 p. 23cm.

Contents.--Lamennais.--Jacob Böhme.--Spinoza.--Communismus und Socialismus.--Die Nachtseiten von London.--Deutsches Studentenleben.
Original paper covers bound in.

Hulsius, Paulus, 1653-1712.
Spinosismi depulsio, nominatim circa corporum peccata et poenas. Quam, cum justae defensionis tum necessariae instructionis causa, instituit Paulus Hulsius ... Groningae, Typis Joh. Lens, 1702.
58 p.

Hutton, Richard Holt, 1826-1897.
Essays on some of the modern guides to English thought in matters of faith. London, Macmillan, 1888.
343 p.

Hylkema, C B
Reformateurs; geschiedkundige studiën over de godsdienstige bewegingen uit de nadagen onzer gouden eeuw. Haarlem, H. D. Tjeenk Willink & Zoon, 1900-02.
2 v. port. 24cm.

Includes references to Spinoza.
Ms. notes by Carl Gebhardt.
Bibliographical footnotes.

Institute essays. Read before the "Ministers' Institute", Providence, R. I., October, 1879. With an introduction by Henry Whitney Bellows. Boston, G. H. Ellis, 1880.
280 p.

Includes references to Spinoza (p. 31-35) in an essay "The relation of modern philosophy to liberalism" by C. C. Everett.

Janet, Paul, 1823-1899.
Histoire de la science politique dans ses rapports avec la morale. 2e édition de l'Histoire de la philosophie morale. Paris, Ladrange, 1872.
2 v.

Includes a section on Spinoza (v. 2, p. 365-378)

Jenichen, Gottlob, Friedrich, 1680-1735.
Historia Spinozismi Leenhofiani pvblica in Belgio avctoritate novissime damnati ex avthenticis docvmentis collecta a Gottlob Friderico Jenichen. Lipsiae, Sumptibus Jo. Herebordi Klosii, 1707.
[20], 234 p. 17cm.

Jones, Rufus Matthew, 1863-1948.
Geistige Reformatoren des sechzehnten und siebzehnten Jahrhunderts. Autorisierte Uebersetzung von E. C. Werthenau. Berlin, Quäkerverlag, 1925.
lxiii, 449 p. 23cm.

Includes a section on Spinoza (p. 156-167)

[Jung, Alexander] 1799-1884.
Baruch Spinoza und Baruch Börne. [1844] col. 207.

In Der Orient; Literaturblatt, 1844.
An excerpt from his Vorlesungen über sociales Leben und höhere Geselligkeit.

Kammari, M D
Спиноза и диалектический материализм. [Москва, 1932]
[39]-60 p. $25\frac{1}{2}$cm.

Title transliterated: Spinoza i dialekticheskiĭ materializm.
From Bol'shevik, no. 21, Nov. 15, 1932.
At head of title: M. Каммари, П. Юдин.

Kaufmann, M
Latitudinarianism and pietism. [1908]
2 l. 28cm.

Typescript.
From the Cambridge modern history, v. 5, p. 754-755, New York, 1908.
About Spinoza and the Dutch pietists.

G-1
3317

Kessler, Harry, graf von, 1868-1937.
Walther Rathenau; sein Leben und sein Werk. Mit zweiunddreissig Abbildungen in Kupfertiefdruck. Berlin-Grunewald, H. Klemm ⌊1928⌋
377 p. plates, ports., facsims.

Includes a section on Spinoza (p. 90-96)

G-1
3318

Kiesewetter, Karl, 1854-1895.
Die geheimwissenschaften. Von Kārl Kiesewetter. 2. aufl. Leipzig, W. Friedrich ⌊1902?⌋
iii-xxvii p., 1 l., 749, ⌊1⌋ p. illus., 2 port. 22cm.

First edition, Leipzig, 1895.
Forms second part of the author's: Geschichte des neueren occultismus.

CONTENTS.—Die alchymie.—Die astrologie und das divinationswesen.—Das hexenwesen in seiner geschichte und seinen erscheinungen.—Die weisse magie. Die theurgie. Die nekromantie.—Vergleichung der spiritistischen phänomene mit den geheimwissenschaftlichen.

Includes a reference to Spinoza (p. 145-146)

1. Occult sciences.

G-1
3319

Klencke,
Spinoza mit Rücksicht auf Kant, Schopenhauer, Göthe und die moderne Naturwissenschaft. Von Dr. Klencke. Leipzig, 1882.
55 p. 22 cm.

OCH

G-1
3320

Kranz, Philip, pseud.
שבתי צבי, דער פאלשער משיח מים
זיינע קאבאליסטישע נביאים און פאר-
עהרער אין אזיען, אפריקא און איי-
ראפא. פון פיליפ קראנץ.
New York, Star Hebrew Book Co. ⌊192-?⌋
78 p. 19cm.

Title transliterated: Shabsay Tsvi.

NNC

G-1
3321

⌊Lau, Theodor Ludwig⌋ 1670-1740.
Zwey seltene antisupernaturalistische Manuscripte eines Genannten und eines Ungenannten. Pendants zu den Wolfenbüttelschen Fragmenten. Berlin, 1792.
94 p. 14 cm.

OCH

G-1
3322

Lecky, William Edward Hartpole, 1838-1903.
History of the rise and influence of the spirit of rationalism in Europe. Rev. ed. New York, D. Appleton, 1879.
2 v. 21 cm.

Includes a reference to Spinoza (v. 1, p. 305)

G-1
3323

Lecky, William Edward Hartpole, 1838-1903.
History of the rise and influence of the spirit of rationalism in Europe. New edition. London, Longmans, Green, 1890.
2 v. 18cm.

Includes a reference to Spinoza (v. 1, p. 299)

G-1
3324

Leenhof, Frederik van, 1647-1713.
Artikelen tot satisfactie van de Eerw. Kerken Raad van Zwolle, voorgestelt aan Dr. Fred. van Leenhof, en by syn Eerw. ondertekent, wegens syn uitgegeven boeken, genaamt den Hemel op aarden, desselvs opheldering, en korte andwoord. Zwolle, Gerrit Tydeman, 1704.
20 p.

NN

G-1
3325

Leenhof, Frederik van, 1647-1713.
Trouhartige waarschouwing aan alle slag van menschen: wegens de over-eenstemminge tusschen den Hemel op aarden, beschreven door Fredericus van Leenhof, en de schriften van den godverzaker Benedictus de Spinoza, ten opsigte van verscheidene voornaame stellingen en spreekwyzen. Amsteldam, G. Borstius, 1704.
xii, 98 p.

NN

G-1
3326

Leenhof, Frederik van, 1647-1713.
De geest en conscientie des menschen, in haar eygen wezen en werkingen eenvoudiglijk verklaart, tegens de verwarde gedagten en valsche meeningen van veele, byzonder van die geene, welke hedendaags drijven dat de conscientie des menschen dwalen kan. Door Fredericus van Leenhof ... Den vierden druk nader overgezien en uitgebreid. Te Rotterdam, By Barent van Santbergen, 1691.
26 p. 15cm.

Leenhof, Frederik van, 1647-1713.
De geest en conscientie des menschen, in haar eigen wezen en werkingen eenvoudig verklaart, tegens de verwarde gedagten en valsche meeningen van veele, byzonder van die geene, welke hedensdaags drijven dat de conscientie des menschen dwalen kan. Door Fredericus van Leenhof ... Den vierden druk, van den autheur nader overzien en kragtiger uitgebreid. Te Zwolle, By Barent Hakvoord, 1700.
31 p. 16cm.

Leenhof, Frederik van, 1647-1713.
Den hemel op aarden, of een korte en klaare beschrijvinge van de waare en stantvastige blydschap: zoo naar de heden, als de H. Schrift, voor alle slag van menschen, en in allerlei voorvallen. Zaamen-gestelt door Fredericus van Leenhof ... Te Zwolle, By B. Hakvoord, 1703.
[8], 151 p. 16cm.

Leenhof, Frederic van, 1647-1713.
De keten der Bybelsche Godgeleertheit, soo als die in haar draad en samen-hang van de eerste waarheid af, door alle de wegen Gods aan een geschakelt is ... Samen-gesteld door Fredericus van Leenhof ... Den derden druk, van den autheur selfs oversien en vermeerderd. Begreepen in twee deelen. Waar nieuwelijks bygevoegd is, een beknopte ontledinge van de boeken des N. Testam. als mede een verandwoordschrift en verdediging bysonder van de Keten, tegens de E. Broederen des Clas. van Seven-

CONTINUED ON NEXT CARD

Leenhof, Frederic van, 1647-1713. De keten der Bybelsche Godgeleertheit. 1684. (Card 2)

wolden: door den selven autheur ... t'Amsterdam, By Wilhelmus Goeree, 1684.
4 pts. in 1 v. 17cm.

Part [4] has separate t.-p.: Zedig en Christelijk verandwoordschrift aan het eerwaarde classis van Seven-Wolden, daar in Cocceji God-geleerdheid met de Keten verdedigd ...

Leenhof, Frederik van, 1647-1713.
Joh. Cocceji God-geleertheit verdedigt en opengelegt, tegens de hedensdaagse misduidingen en voor-oordeelen: waar in, nevens de bysonderste grond-artijkelen der Christelijke religie, de bedeelinge der tijden, klaar ontvouwen, en den sleutel der Prophetien aangewesen werd. t'Samen-gestelt door Fredericus van Leenhof ... Den sesden druk, van den autheur nader overzien en verbetert. Te Zwolle, By Barent Hakvoord, 1700.
256 p. 16cm.

Leenhof, Frederik van, 1647-1713.
Het leven van den wijzen en magtigen Konink Salomon, leerzaamelijk voorgedragen in een kort ontwerp, van zijn geslagte, geboorte, opvoedinge, wijsheit, heerschappy, daden, heerlijkheit en verval des Rijks tot zijn dood toe, en daar na. Door Fredericus van Leenhof ... Te Zwolle, By Barent Hakvoord, en te Amsterdam, By de Wed: van Gysbert de Groot, 1700.
[8], 172, [1] p. plate. 17cm.

Added t.-p. engraved.

Leenhof, Frederik van, 1647-1713.
De Prediker van den wijzen en magtigen Konink Salomon, kort en leerzamelijk verklaart, en op onze tijden en zeden toegepast. Door Fredericus van Leenhof ... Te Zwolle, by Barent Hakvoord, en te Amsterdam, By de Wed: van Gysbert de Groot, 1700.
[8], 440 p. 17cm.

Bound with Leenhof, Frederik van. Het leven van den wijzen en magtigen Konink Salomon. 1700.

Leenhof, Frederic van, 1647-1713.
Zedig en Christelijk verandwoordschrift aan het eerwaarde classis van Seven-Wolden, daar in Cocceji God-geleerdheid met de Keten verdedigd ... door Fredericus van Leenhof ... Tweede druk van den autheur op nieus oversien. t'Amsterdam, By Wilhelmus Goeree, 1684.
136 p. 17cm. (In his De keten der Bybelsche Godgeleertheit. 1684, pt. [4])

Leenhof, Frederik van, 1647-1713.
Zedig en Christelijk verantwoord-schrift aan het Eerwaarde Classis van Seven-Wolden, daar in Cocceji God-geleertheit mit de Keten verdedigt, en veele voorname waarheden, soo de nature, als de H. Schrift rakende, samen-geschakelt en verklaart worden. Door Fredericus van Leenhof ... Te Zwolle, By Barent Hakvoord [1700?]
127 p. 16cm.

Includes a reference to Spinoza (p. 39)

CONTINUED ON NEXT CARD

Leenhof, Frederik van, 1647-1713. Zedig en Christelijk verantwoord-schrift ... [1700?] (Card 2)

Bound with the author's Joh. Cocceji Godgeleertheit verdedigt en opengelegt. 1700.

Leland, John, 1691-1766.
A view of the principal deistical writers that have appeared in England in the last and present century: with observations upon them, and some account of the answers that have been published against them. In several letters to a friend. London, R. Ogle, 1808.
2 v. port. 22cm.

Includes references to Spinoza.

LeLarge de Lignac, Joseph Adrien
Le témoignage du sens intime et de l'expérience, opposé à la foi profane et ridicule des fatalistes modernes ... Auxerre, Chez F. Fournier, 1760.
3 v. 19 cm.

Le Maître de Claville, Charles François Nicolas, 1670-1740.
Traité du vrai merite de l'homme, considéré dans tous les âges & dans toutes les conditions: avec des principes d'education, propres à former les jeunes gens à la vertu. Par M. Le Maitre de Claville ... Quatriéme edition, revûë, corrigée & considérablement augmentée par l'auteur. ... A Amsterdam, Par la Compagnie, 1737.
2 v. 17cm.

Reference to Spinoza: v. 2, p. 192.

Lilly, William Samuel, 1840-1919.
Many mansions, being studies in ancient religions and modern thought. London, Chapman & Hall, 1907.
xi, 260 p. 22cm.

Includes a chapter "Spinoza and modern thought" (p. 155-187)

Lilly, William Samuel, 1840-1919.
Spinoza and modern thought. [1907]
43-61 p.

In Fortnightly review, n. s. v. 81, 1907.

Lintz, Heinrich
Entwurf einer Geschichte der Rechtsphilosophie, mit besonderer Rücksicht auf Socialismus und Communismus. Danzig, Gerhard, 1846.
129 p. 23cm.

Includes a section on Spinoza (p. 71-74)
Pages 81-129 lacking.

Literarischer Ratgeber des Dürerbundes ... in Verbindung mit zahlreichen Gelehrten ... bearbeitet von Wolfgang Schumann. München, Callwey, 1919.
xi p., 1024 col., 1025-1053 p.

Includes a reference to Spinoza (col. 723)
Fifth edition.

Lunacharskiĭ, Anatoliĭ Vasil'evich, 1876-1933.
От Спинозы до Маркса; очерки по истории философии как миросозерцания. [Москва] "Новая деревня", 1925.
133 p. 23cm.

Title transliterated: Ot Spinozy do Marksa.

Lund. Universitet. ***Litteraturhistoriska seminariet.***
Till Thorilds minne den 1 oktober 1908, af Litteraturhistoriska seminariet i Lund. Lund, H. Ohlssons boktr., 1908.
vi, 107, [1] p. 25 cm. (Lunds universitets årsskrift, n. f., afd. 1, bd. 4, nr. 1)
CONTENTS.—Litterära strömningar vid den sydsvenska högskolan under Thorilds tid, af E. Wrangel.—Thorild och Young, af A. Forsvall.—Några ord om stämning och stil i Thorilds diktning, af H. Borelius.—Swedenborg, Thorild och Höijer, af B. Liljekrantz.—Thorild och hans filosofi, af A. Karitz.—Bilagor: 1. Allblick, af Thorild. 2. Das System der Systeme, af Thorild. --Includes references to Spinoza.
1. Thorild, Thomas, 1759-1808. I. Title. (Series: Lund. Universitet. Acta Universitatis Lundensis, n. s. Lunds universitets årsskrift, n. f., afd. 1, bd. 4, nr. 1)

Luzzatti, Luigi, 1841-1927.
God in freedom; studies in the relations between church and state, by the late Luigi Luzzatti ... translated from the Italian by Alfonso Arbib-Costa, with American supplementary chapters by President William H. Taft, Hon. Irving Lehman ... [and others] ... New York, The Macmillan company, 1930.
xxxix, 794 p. front. (port.) 24 cm.
Editor's preface: Max J. Kohler.
"Issued in commemoration of the one hundred and fiftieth anniversary of the constitutional establishment of religious liberty."
Includes a section "Spinoza and the precursors of freedom of conscience" (p. 115-125)
~~(Continued on next card)~~

G-1
3347

Luzzatti, Luigi, 1841-1927.
Liberté de conscience et liberté de science; études d'histoire constitutionnelle. Tr. par J. Chamard. Paris, Giard, 1910.
453 p. 23 cm.

Includes a section "Spinoza et les précurseurs de la liberté de conscience" (p. 217-233)

SPECIAL COLLECTIONS
SPINOZA
G-1
3348

Luzzatti, Luigi, 1841-1927.
La libertà di coscienza e di scienza; studi storici costituzionali. Milano, Fratelli Treves, 1909.
444 p. 21cm.

Includes a chapter on Spinoza.

G-1
3349

Luzzatti, Luigi, 1841-1927.
Spinoza e i precursori della libertà di coscienza. [1877]
592-604 p.

In Nuova antologia di lettere, scienze ed arti, 2. serie, v. 5, 1877.

G-1
3350

Manning, Jacob Merrill, 1824-1882.
Half truths and the truth. Lectures on the origin and development of prevailing forms of unbelief. Boston, Lee & Shepard, 1872.
xii, 398 p.

Includes a section "Spinoza and other masters" (p. 39-73) and other references to him.

NNUT

G-1
3351

Melchior, Johannes, 1646-1689.
Johannis Melchioris ... Opera omnia theologica, exegetica, didactica, polemica, duobis tomis absoluta, quibus Veteris ac Novi Testamenti libri conferuntur, explicantur, illustrantur: veritatis religionis Christianae argumentis validissimis asseritur, defenditur: triplici indice locupletata. Herbornae Nassoviorum, Typis et sumptibus J. N. Andreae, 1693.
2 v.

NJNbS

SPECIAL COLLECTIONS
SPINOZA
G-1
3352

Meli, Fausto, 1908-1931.
... Spinoza e due antecedenti italiani dello spinozismo. Prefazione di Giuseppe Saitta. Firenze, G. C. Sansoni, 1934.
viii, 197 p., 1 l. 24cm. (*Half-title:* Pisa. R. Scuola normale superiore. Studi di lettere, storia, e filosofia. III)

Deals with Benedictus de Spinoza, Fausto Soccino, and Giacomo Aconcio.
Bibliographical foot-notes.

1. Spinoza, Benedictus de, 1632-1677. 2. Soccino, Fausto, 1539-1604. 3. Aconcio, Giacomo, 1492?-1566?

A C 35-1519

Title from Stanford Univ. Printed by L. C.

[2]

G-1
3353

Menzel, Adolf, 1857-
Spinoza in der deutschen Staatslehre der Gegenwart. [1907]
[35]-48 p.

In Schmollers Jahrbuch für Gesetzgebung, Verwaltung und Volkswirtschaft im Deutschen Reich, 31. Jahrgang, 2. Heft, 1907.

SPECIAL COLLECTIONS
SPINOZA
G-1
3354

Merz, John Theodore, 1840-1922.
A history of European thought in the nineteenth century. Edinburgh, Blackwood; Chicago, University of Chicago Press, 1912-23.
4 v. 21cm.

Vol. 1, 4th unaltered edition, 1923; v. 2, 2d unaltered edition, 1912; v. 3-4, 1912-14.
Includes references to Spinoza.

G-1
3355

Montefiore, Claude Joseph Goldsmid, 1858-1938.
Liberal Judaism and Hellenism. London, Macmillan, 1918.
xi, 328 p.

Includes references to Spinoza.

NN

G-1
3356

[Montesquieu, Charles Louis de Secondat, baron de la Brède et de] 1689-1755.
Défense de l'Esprit des loix, à laquelle on a joint quelques éclaircissemens ... A Genève, Chez Barrillot et fils, 1750.
207 p.

Includes references to Spinoza.

OCH

G-1
3357

Montesquieu, Charles Louis de Secondat, baron de la Brède et de, 1689-1755.
Oeuvres. Paris, A. Belin, 1817.
2 v.

References to Spinoza (v. 1, p. [596]-608) included in "Défense de l'Esprit des lois".

G-1
3358

Müller, Johann Heinrich, 1671-1731, praeses.
De miraculis adversus Spinosam dissertatio. Altdorf, 1714.

CtY

SPECIAL COLLECTIONS
SPINOZA

G-1
3359

Murray, Robert Henry, 1874-
The history of political science from Plato to the present. New York, Appleton, 1926.
vii, 435 p. 22cm.

Includes references to Spinoza.
Bibliography: p. 403-405.

G-1
3360

Murry, John Middleton, 1889-1957.
The necessity of communism. New York, Seltzer, 1933.
136 p.

Includes a reference to Spinoza (p. 31)

SPECIAL COLLECTIONS
SPINOZA

G-1
3361

Newman, Francis William, 1805-1897.
Ancient sacrifice. London, T. Scott, 1874.
12 p. 19cm.

Volume of pamphlets.

NNC

SPECIAL COLLECTIONS
SPINOZA

G-1
3362

Nieuhoff, Bernardus
Bernardus Nieuhoff over Spinozisme. Te Harderwijk, Bij J. van Kasteel, 1799.
3 p. l., 372 p. 23cm.

SPECIAL COLLECTIONS
SPINOZA

G-1
3363

Nieuwentijdt, Bernard, 1654-1718.
Het regt gebruik der werelt beschouwingen, ter overtuiginge van ongodisten en ongelovigen aangetoont, door Bernard Nieuwentyt ... Den derden druk. Tot Amsterdam, By Joannes Pauli, 1720.
[14], 916, [17] p. port., tables. 26cm.

Added engraved t.-p. has inprint: Te Amsterdam by de weduwe J. Wolters en J. Pauli, 1715.
Includes references to Spinoza (p. 6-7, 9-10)

SPECIAL COLLECTIONS
SPINOZA

G-1
3364

Nieuwentijdt, Bernard, 1654-1718.
Het regt gebruik der werelt beschouwingen, ter overtuiginge van ongodisten en ongelovigen aangetoont, door Bernard Nieuwentyt, M. D. ... Den vierden druk. Tot Amsterdam, By Joannes Pauli, 1725.
[16], 916, [17] p. 28 fold. plates, port. 26cm.

Added engraved t.-p.
Includes references to Spinoza (p. 6-7, 9-10)

SPECIAL COLLECTIONS
SPINOZA

G-1
3365

Nieuwentijdt, Bernard, 1654-1718.
Het regt gebruik der werelt beschouwingen, ter overtuiginge van ongodisten en ongelovigen aangetoont, door Bernard Nieuwentyt ... Den sesden druk. Tegens de eerste origineele geconfronteert en van seer veele drukfouten gesuivert. Tot Amsterdam, By Joannes Pauli, 1740.
[12], 916, [17] p. fold. plates. 26cm.

Added engraved t.-p. has imprint: a Amsterdam chez Jean Pauli, 1727.
Includes references to Spinoza (p. 6-7, 9-10)

G-1
3366

Nieuwentijdt, Bernard, 1654-1718.
Het regt gebruik der werelt beschouwingen, ter overtuiginge van ongodisten en ongelovigen aangetoont, door Bernard Nieuwentyt ... Den sevenden druk. Tegens de eerste origineele geconfronteert en van seer veele drukfouten gesuivert. Te Amsterdam, By Adrianus Douci, 1759.
[14], 916, [17] p. fold. plates, port. 26cm.

Includes references to Spinoza (p. 6-7, 9-10)

Noack, Ludwig, 1819-1885.
Die Freidenker in der Religion, oder, Die Repräsentanten der religiösen Aufklärung in England, Frankreich und Deutschland. Berlin, Jent und Reinert, 1853-55.
3 v. 19cm.

Each volume has also special t.-p.
Contents.--v. 1. Die englischen Deisten.--v. 2. Die französischen Freidenker.--v. 3. Die deutsche Aufklärung.

Nourrisson, Jean Félix, 1825-1899.
Spinoza et le naturalisme contemporain, par Nourrisson. Paris, Didier et c^ie^, 1866.
2 p. l., xii, 305 p., 1 l. 18cm.

1. Spinoza, Benedictus de, 1632-1677. 2. Naturalism.

Ornstein, Martha, 1879-1915.
The rôle of scientific societies in the seventeenth century, by Martha Ornstein. Chicago, Ill., The University of Chicago press [1928]
xiv, 308 p. 23cm.
First published as thesis (PH. D.) Columbia university, 1913.
Bibliography: p. 271-288.
Includes references to Spinoza (p. 179, 228)

1. Scientific societies. 2. Science—Hist.

Owen, John, 1833-1896.
The skeptics of the French renaissance, by John Owen ... London, S. Sonnenschein & co.; New York, Macmillan & co., 1893.
2 p. l., vii-xv p., 1 l., [421]-830 p. 22cm.
A companion volume to the author's "The skeptics of the Italian renaissance", and paged consecutively with that work.
Reference to Spinoza in "Sanchez" (p. 639)
CONTENTS.—Montaigne.—Peter Ramus.—Charron.—Sanchez.—La Mothe-le-Vayer.—Pascal.—Index to literary references.—Index to subjects.

1. Skepticism. 2. Renaissance—France. 3. Philosophy, French.

Pape, Georg, 1877-
Christoph Wittichs Anti-Spinoza. [Berlin, Blanke, 1910]
112 p. 23cm.

Thesis, Rostock.
Bibliographical footnotes.

Paterson, James
Anti-Nazarenus. By way of answer to Mr. Toland; or, A treatise proving the divine original and authority of the Holy Scriptures against atheists, Jews, heathens, Mahometans, papists, Spinoza and other modern errors. London, S. Butter [1718?]

APM

Pflaum, Heinz, 1900-
Rationalismus und Mystik in der Philosophie Spinozas. [1926]
[127]-143 p. 23cm.

From Deutsche Vierteljahrsschrift für Literaturwissenschaft und Geistesgeschichte, 4. Jahrg., Heft 1, 1926.
Original paper covers bound in.

Pflaum, Heinz, 1900-
Rationalismus und Mystik in der Philosophie Spinozas. [1926]
[127]-143 p. 23cm.

"Sonderabdruck aus 'Deutsche Vierteljahrsschrift für Literaturwissenschaft und Geistesgeschichte', Band 4, Heft 1"
Presentation copy to Carl Gebhardt with the author's inscription.
Original paper cover bound in.

Plenkers, Wilhelm, 1851-
Der Däne Niels Stensen; ein Lebensbild, nach den Zeugnissen der Mit- und Nachwelt entworfen. Freiburg im Breisgau, St. Louis, Mo., Herder, 1884.
2 pt. in 1 v. (viii, 206 p.) port. 24cm. (Ergänzungshefte zu den "Stimmen aus Maria-Laach". [VII. Bd.] 25-26)

Includes references to Spinoza.
Ms. notes by Carl Gebhardt.
Bibliography: p. [v]-viii.

Pluquet, François André Adrien, 1716-1790.
Dictionnaire des hérésies, des erreurs et des schismes, ou Mémoires pour servir à l'histoire des égarements de l'esprit humain par rapport à la religion chrétienne ... Continué jusqu'à nos jours pour toutes les matières qui en font le sujet, comme pour le discours préliminaire, revu et corrigé d'un bout à l'autre; par m. l'abbé J.-Jh Claris ... Publiée par m. l'abbé Migne ... Paris, J.-P. Migne, 1847-53.
2 v. 29 cm. (Encyclopédie théologique, t. 11-12)

Includes an article "Spinosisme" (v. 2, col. 128-133)

Polignac, Melchior de, cardinal, 1661-1741.
L'anti-Lucrece, poëme sur la religion naturelle, composé par M. le cardinal de Polignac; traduit par M. de Bougainville ... A Paris, Chez Desaint & Saillant, 1750.
2 v. 15cm.

Includes references to Spinoza.

Pollock, Sir Frederick, bart., 1845-1937.
Spinoza. [1892]
709-723 p.

In Religious systems of the world. 2nd ed., 1892.
A lecture delivered at South Place Institute.

Pollock, Sir Frederick, bart., 1845-1937.
Spinoza. [1911]
709-723 p.

In Religious systems of the world. 10th ed., 1911.
A lecture delivered at South Place Institute.

Popper, Josef, 1838-1921.
Fürst Bismarck und der Antisemitismus. Wien, R. Löwit-Verlag, 1925.
154 p. 25cm.

At head of title: Josef Popper-Lynkeus.
"Ein unveränderter Abdruck der im Jahre 1886 beim Verlag Hugo Engel, Wien ... erschienenen Broschüre."
Includes references to Spinoza (p. 63-64)

Porter, Noah, 1811-1892.
The human intellect: with an introduction upon psychology and the soul. 4th ed. New York, Scribner Armstrong, 1877.
xvii, 673 p. 24cm.

Includes references to Spinoza.

Pratje, Johann Heinrich, 1736-1789.
Historische Nachrichten von Joh. Chr. Edelmanns, eines berüchtigten Religionsspötters, Leben, Schriften und Lehrbegrif, wie auch von den Schriften, die für und wider ihn geschrieben worden, gesamlet und mitgetheilet von Joh. Hinr. Pratje ... Hamburg, bey Christian Wilhelm Brandt, 1753.
[16], 275, [5] p. 18cm.

Pages 209-239 incorrectly numbered 193-223.
Includes references to Spinoza.

Pratje, Johann Heinrich, 1736-1789.
Historische Nachrichten von Joh. Chr. Edelmanns, eines berüchtigten Religionsspötters, Leben, Schriften und Lehrbegrif, wie auch von den Schriften, die für und wider ihn geschrieben worden, gesamlet und mitgetheilet von Joh. Hinr. Pratje ... Zwote verbesserte und sehr vermehrte Auflage. Hamburg, bei Christian Wilhelm Brandt, 1755.
[14], 376, [12] p. 17cm.

Includes references to Spinoza.
Bibliographical references.

Raats, Johannes Adrianus
Korte en grondige betoginge dat 'er in de natuur of het Geheel-al, meer als eene zelfstandigheid aanweezig is; tegen de valsche gronden en stellingen van Spinosa, die beweert dat 'er maar eene zelfstandheid aanwezig is. Mitsgaders, dat 'er meer als eene denkende zelfstandigheid gevonden word; tegen de valsche betoginge van Deurhof, die beweert dat 'er maar eene denkende zelfstandigheid van God geschapen is. In 's Gravenhage, by Johannes de Cros, 1743.
xl, 320 p. port.

Randall, John Herman, 1899-
The making of the modern mind; a survey of the intellectual background of the present age [by] John Herman Randall, jr. ... Boston, New York [etc.] Houghton Mifflin company [°1926]
x, 653 p. 21 cm.
"References" and "Selected reading lists" at end of most of the chapters.
Includes a section on Spinoza (p. 244-248) and other references to him.
1. Civilization—Hist. 2. Europe—Civilization. I. Title.

Reimarus, Johann Albert Heinrich, 1729-1814.
Ueber die Gründe der menschlichen Erkentniss und der natürlichen Religion ... Hamburg, C. E. Bohn, 1787.
[16], 172 p. 18cm.

Religious systems of the world, a contribution to the study of comparative religion; a collection of addresses delivered at South Place Institute, now revised and in some cases rewritten by the authors, together with some others specially written for this volume. [7th ed.] London, S. Sonnenschein, 1904.
viii, 824 p.

Preface signed: Wm. Sheowring, Conrad W. Thies, hon. secs. Institute committee.
Includes references to Spinoza.

Robertson, John Mackinnon, 1856-1933.
Pioneer humanists; by John M. Robertson. Issued for the Rationalist press association, ltd. London, Watts & co., 1907.
4 p. l., 399 p. 20½cm.
CONTENTS.—Machiavelli.—Bacon.—Hobbes.—Spinoza.—Shaftesbury.—Mandeville.—Gibbon.—Mary Wollstonecraft.

1. Humanism. I. Title.

W 7—154

Renan, Ernest, 1823-1892.
Leaders of Christian and anti-Christian thought. Translated from the French by W. M. Thomson. London, Mathieson [1891]

Includes a section on Spinoza (p. 47-71)

Robertson, John Mackinnon, 1856-1933.
A short history of freethought, ancient and modern, by John M. Robertson. London, S. Sonnenschein & co. ltd; New York, The Macmillan co., 1899.
xv, 447 p. 23cm.
Bibliographical foot-notes.
Includes a section on Spinoza (p. 332-335) and references to Spinoza.

1. Free thought—Hist.

46-30357

Riley, Isaac Woodbridge, 1869-1933.
American thought from Puritanism to pragmatism, by Woodbridge Riley ... New York, H. Holt and company, 1915.
viii, 373 p. 20 cm.
Bibliography: p. 361-367.
Includes references to Spinoza (p. 62, 146)

1. Philosophy, American. I. Title.

Robertson, John Mackinnon, 1856-1933.
A short history of freethought ancient and modern. 2d ed. rewritten and greatly enlarged. New York, G. P. Putnam's Sons, 1906.
2 v. 23cm.

Bibliographical notes.
Includes a section on Spinoza (v. 2, p. 198-203) and other references to Spinoza.

Riley, Isaac Woodbridge, 1869-1933.
Men and morals; the story of ethics, by Woodbridge Riley. Garden City, N. Y., Doubleday, Doran & company, inc., 1929.
viii p., 2 l., 3-425 p. front., plates, ports. 23½ cm.
"First edition."
Includes a section on Spinoza (p. 219-229) and other references to him.

1. Ethics—Hist. I. Title.

Robertson, John Mackinnon, 1856-1933.
A short history of freethought, ancient and modern. 3d ed., rev. and expanded. London, Watts & Co., 1915.
2 v. 24cm.

Includes a section on Spinoza (v. 2, p. 133-141) and other references to him.

Robertson, John Mackinnon, 1856-1933.
A history of freethought in the nineteenth century, by J. M. Robertson ... London, Watts & co. [1929]
2 v. fronts., ports. 22½ cm.
Paged continuously.
"The present volume is a new work—a rewriting, with manifold expansion, of the short section on the nineteenth century at the close of 'A short history of freethought' (3rd ed., 2 vols., 1915)."—Pref.
Includes a paragraph on Sir Frederick Pollock's "Spinoza" (v. 2, p. 414) and other references to Spinoza.
1. Free thought. 2. Rationalism. 3. Philosophy, Modern. 4. Philosophy and religion.

Ross, Alexander, 1590-1654.
Der Wunderwürdige Juden- und Heiden-Tempel ... Anfangs vom A. Rossen in Englischer Sprach beschrieben, nunmehro aber verbessert, und, mit vielem Zusatz vermehret, ausgeführt von D. Nerreter. Samt dessen Bericht vom Ursprung der Abgötterey, wie auch von denen poetischen Fabeln, und deren Bedeutung ... Nürnberg, W. M. Endter, 1701.
1195, [83] p. 17 cm.

Includes a reference to Spinozism (p. 254)

[Roth, Leon] 1896-
Spinoza in recent English thought. [1927]
[205]-210 p. 22cm.

Signed: L. Roth.
"Off-printed from Mind: a quarterly review of psychology and philosophy. Vol. XXXVI, n.s., no. 142."

Samter, N
Johann Peter Spaeth (Moses Germanus), der Proselyt. Ein Culturbild aus dem siebzehnten Jahrhundert. [1895]
178-187, 221-230, 271-281 p.

In Monatsschrift für Geschichte und Wissenschaft des Judenthums, 39. Jahrgang (n. F. 3. Jahrgang), 1895.
Includes references to Spinoza.

Schmidt, Conrad
Spinoza, ein Vorkämpfer der neuen Weltanschauung. Vortrag, gehalten in der freireligiösen Gemeinde zu Berlin am 23. Februar 1890. Berlin, W. Robenow, 1890.
16 p. 20cm.

Volume of pamphlets.

Schmidt, Conrad
Spinoza, ein Vorkämpfer der neuen Weltanschauung. Vortrag, gehalten in der freireligiösen Gemeinde zu Berlin am 23. Februar 1890. Berlin, W. Robenow, 1890.
16 p. 20cm.

Schmidt, Ferdinand Jakob, 1860-
Herder's pantheistische weltanschauung ... Berlin, Mayer & Müller [1888?]
2 p. l., 51, [3] p. 20½cm.

Inaug.-diss.—Berlin.
Vita.
Includes references to Spinoza.

1. Herder, Johann Gottfried von, 1744-1803.

Schmoldt, Hans, 1913-
Der Spinozastreit. Würzburg, K. Triltsch [1938]
114 p. 22cm.

Issued also as thesis, Berlin.
Original paper covers bound in.
Bibliographical footnotes.

Scholten, Johannes Henricus, 1811-1885.
Manuel d'histoire comparée de la philosophie et de la religion. Traduit du hollandais par A. Réville. Paris, Treuttel & Wurtz, 1861.
183 p. 24cm.

Includes a section on Spinoza (p. 74-76)

Schwarz, Karl Heinrich Wilhelm, 1811-1885.
Gotthold Ephraim Lessing als Theologe dargestellt. Ein Beitrag zur Geschichte der Theologie im 18ten Jahrhundert. Halle, C. E. M. Pfeffer, 1854.
x, 232 p.

Includes a chapter "Der philosophische Hintergrund der Lessing'schen Theologie; der Spinozismus Lessings" (p. 68-98)

Schweitzer, Albert, 1875-
Die mystik des apostels Paulus, von Albert Schweitzer ... Tübingen, Mohr, 1930.
xv, 407 p. 24cm.

"Das kapitel, das der 'Mystik des apostels Paulus' als einleitung dienen sollte, wuchs sich zu einem buche aus und erschien 1911 als 'Geschichte der paulinischen forschung'."—Vorrede.

1. Paul, Saint, apostle. 2. Mysticism. 3. Bible. N. T. Epistles of Paul—Theology. 4. Bible—Theology—N. T. Epistles of Paul. I. Title.

Schwellenbach, Robert, 1870-
Das Gottesproblem in der Philosophie Friedrich Paulsens und sein Zusammenhang mit dem Gottesbegriff Spinozas. Berlin, W. Blankenfeldt, 1911.
69 p. 22cm.

Thesis, Münster.
Bibliography: p. [70-71]

Seeberg, Erich, 1888–
Gottfried Arnold, die wissenschaft und die mystik seiner zeit, studien zur historiographie und zur mystik, von d. Erich Seeberg ... Meerane i. Sa., E. R. Herzog, 1923.
viii, 611 p. 23½cm.

1. Arnold, Gottfried, 1666-1714. 2. Church history—Historiography. 3. Mysticism—Germany. I. Title.

Süssmilch, Johann Peter, 1707-1767.
Die Unvernunft und Bosheit des berüchtigten Edelmanns durch seine schändliche Vorstellung des Obrigkeitlichen Amts aus seinem Moses dargethan und zu aller Menschen Warnung vor Augen gelegt von Johann Peter Süssmilch ... Berlin, bey A. Haude, und Joh. Carl Spener, 1747.
150 p. 17cm.

Includes a reference to Spinoza (p. 17)

Seeck, Otto, 1850-1921.
Geschichte des Untergangs der antiken Welt. Stuttgart, J. B. Metzler, 1920-22 [v. 1, 1921]
6 v. 21cm.

Edition varies.
Includes references to Spinoza (v. 1, p. 298; v. 6, p. 2)
--- --- Anhang. Stuttgart, J. B. Metzler, 1921-23 [v. 1, 1922]
6 v. 21cm.

Edition varies.

Swift, Lindsay, 1856-1921.
Brook Farm; its members, scholars, and visitors, by Lindsay Swift. New York, The Macmillan company; London, Macmillan & co., ltd., 1900.
x p., 1 l., 303 p. 18½ cm. (*On verso of half-title:* National studies in American letters)
"List of books and magazine articles cited or used": p. 283-292.
Includes a reference to Spinoza (p. 59)

1. Brook Farm.

Southwell, Charles
Socialism made easy; or, A plain exposition of Mr. Owen's views. London, J. Watson, 1840.
16 p. 17cm.

Sully, James, 1842-1923.
Pessimism, a history and a criticism. 2d ed. with new preface. New York, D. Appleton, 1891.
xv, 477 p. 22cm.

Includes references to Spinoza (p. 52, 54)
Bibliography: p. [xvii]-xix.

Stawell, Florence Melian
The making of the Western mind; a short survey of European culture, by F. Melian Stawell and F. S. Marvin. London, Methuen; New York, Doran [1923]
xiii, 353 p. plates. 20cm.

Includes references to Spinoza.

Taylor, Henry Osborn, 1856-1941.
Thought and expression in the sixteenth century, by Henry Osborn Taylor ... New York, The Macmillan company, 1920.
2 v. 22½ cm.
Bibliographical foot-notes.
CONTENTS.—vol. I. book I. The humanism of Italy. book II. Erasmus and Luther. book III. The French mind.—vol. II. book IV. England. book V. Philosophy and science.

1. Europe—Intellectual life. 2. Humanism. 3. Sixteenth century. I. Title.

Stephen, Sir Leslie, 1832-1904.
History of English thought in the eighteenth century. London, Smith, Elder, 1876.
2 v. 23cm.

Includes a section on Spinoza (v. 1, p. 30-33) and other references to him.

Tönnies, Ferdinand, 1855-1936.
Spinoza und Marx. [1924]
34-38 p. 24cm.

From Judentum, Judenvolk, Judenland; eine Sammelbroschürenreihe. Nichtjuden über den Kulturwert des Judentums. 1. Folge, 1924.

Travis, Henry
English socialism. London, A. Heywood & Co., 1880.
[a]-h, viii, 88 p. 17cm.

At head of title: Parts I. & II.
Volume of pamphlets.

1. Socialism in Gt. Brit.

G-2
RELIGIOUS

G-2-a
CHRISTIAN AND OTHERS

Van Loon, Hendrik Willem, 1882-1944.
The liberation of mankind; the story of man's struggle for the right to think. London, G. G. Harrap [1926]
307 p. plates (1 col.) 24cm.

Includes a chapter on Spinoza (p. [225]-235)
American edition (New York, Boni & Liveright, 1925) has title: Tolerance.

Abbadie, Jacques, 1654?-1727.
Traité de la verité de la religion chrétienne. Rotterdam, R. Leers, 1684.
2 v.

Van Loon, Hendrik Willem, 1882-
Tolerance, by Hendrik Willem Van Loon ... New York, Boni & Liveright, 1925.
viii p., 1 l., 11-399 p. 23 cm.

Includes a chapter on Spinoza (p. 292-306)

1. Toleration. I. Title.

Abbadie, Jacques, 1654?-1727.
Traité de la verité de la religion chrétienne. 2e éd. Rotterdam, R. Leers, 1689.
2 v.

Zerffi, George Gustavus, 1821-1892.
Ethics and aesthetics; or, Art and its influence on our social progress. A lecture delivered before the Sunday Lecture Society, St. George's Hall, Langham Place, on ... 5th March, 1876. London, T. Scott, 1876.
24 p. 19cm.

Volume of pamphlets.

[Alletz, Pons Augustin] 1703-1785.
Dictionnaire théologique-portatif, contenant l'exposition et les preuves de la révélation; de tous les dogmes de la foi et de la morale; les points de controverse; les hérésies les plus célebres; les opinions differentes des principaux théologiens scholastiques, et de leur plus fameuses ecoles ... A Paris, Chez Didot [etc.] 1761.
vi, [2], 530 p. 17cm.

Includes an article "Spinosistes" (p. 482-483)

Zerffi, George Gustavus, 1821-1892.
The spontaneous dissolution of ancient creeds. A lecture delivered before the Sunday Lecture Society, St. George's Hall, Langham Place, on ... 23rd January, 1876. London, T. Scott, 1876.
31 p. 19cm.

Volume of pamphlets.

Arnold, Gottfried, 1666-1714.
Gottfrid Arnolds Unparteyische Kirchen- und Ketzer-Historie, von Anfang des Neuen Testaments biss auff das Jahr Christi 1688. Franckfurt am Mayn, bey Thomas Fritsch, 1699-1700.
2 v. 36cm.

Vol. 2 has title: Gottfrid Arnolds Fortsetzung und Erläuterung oder dritter und vierdter Theil der unpartheyischen Kirchen- und Ketzer-Historie ...
Includes sections on Spinoza (v. 1, p. 611-614)

Arnold, Gottfried, 1666-1714.
Gottfried Arnolds Unpartheyische Kirchen- und Ketzer-Historie, vom Anfang des Neuen Testaments biss auf das Jahr Christi 1688 ... Franckfurt am Mayn, bey Thomas Fritschens sel. Erben, 1729.
2 v. 29cm.

Vol. [2] has title: Gottfried Arnolds Fortsetzung und Erläuterung oder dritter und vierdter Theil der unpartheyischen Kirchen- und Ketzer-Historie ...
Includes a section on Spinoza (v. 1, p. 1071-1072)

Augsburg confession.
Concordia pia et unanimi consensu repetita Confessio fidei et doctrinae electorum, principum et ordinum Imperii atque eorundem theologorum, qui Augustanam confessionem amplectuntur: cui e Sacra Scriptura ... quorundam articulorum, qui post D. Martini Lutheri felicem ex hac vita exitum in controversiam venerunt, solida accessit declaratio ... Cum appendice tripartita, novis indicibus ... Editio nova a mendis denuo repurgata. Lipsiae, In officina Grossiana, 1742.
[28], 878, [30], 92, [12], 314, [22] p. double plate. 17cm.

(Continued on next card)

Augsburg confession. Concordia pia et unanimi consensu repetita Confessio fidei et doctrinae. 1742. (Card 2)

"Confutatio articulorum Confessionis pontificia ... in publico concilio imperiali anno MDXXX producta et lecta, una cum Augustana confessione, a Philippo Melanchthone anno MDLX variata": 92 p.
"Appendix tripartita isagogica ad libros Eclasiae Lutheranae symbolicos ... a D. Adam.

(Continued on next card)

Augsburg confession. Concordia pia et unanimi consensu repetita Confessio fidei et doctrinae. 1742. (Card 3)

Rechenberg. Editio octava auctior. Lipsiae, In officina Grossiana, 1740": 314 p.
Includes a reference to Spinoza (p. 272 of the "Appendix tripartita")

Augustinus redivivus. Des heiligen Kirchenvaters philosophisches Weltbild. In Umrissen gezeichnet nach den Bekenntnissen. Vom Verfasser des Spinoza redivivus. Halle (Saale) Weltphilosophischer Verlag, 1919.
189 p. 25cm. (Philosophische Weltbibliothek. 2. Bd.)

Original paper cover bound in.
Includes references to Spinoza.
Inked on spine, probably by Carl Gebhardt: Glatzel.

Baltzer, Eduard, 1814-1887.
Zeugnisse aus und für die freie Religions-Gemeinde; Vorträge. Nordhausen, Selbstverlag des Verfassers, 1859.
iv, 332 p. 22cm.

Bound with the author's Neue Propheten. 1852.

Batalerius, Jacobus.
Dissertatio de Israelitarum conversione a Divo Paulo ad Romanos undecimo capite praedicta: auctore Jacobo Batalerio ... Hagae, Ex officina Danielis Geselle, 1669.
[12], 240, [11] p. 14cm.

Bound with Clemens I, Saint, Pope. Ad Corinthios epistola. 1669.

Batalerius, Jacobus,
Jacob & Esau, sive Dilucida & plena ex Sacris ipsis literis explicatio veri & germani sensus D. Pauli in Epistola ad Romanos capite nono, quo loco agit de Jacobi electione et Esavi rejectione ... Auctore Jacobo Batalerio ... Amstelodami, Sumptibus Henrici Boom, 1664.
[48], 114, [3] p. 14cm.

Bound with Clemens I, Saint, Pope. Ad Corinthios epistola. 1669.

Batalerius, Jacobus.
Vindiciae miraculorum per quae divinae religionis & fidei Christianae veritas olim confirmata fuit, adversus profanum auctorem. Tractatus theologico-politici. Auctore Jacobo Batalerio. Amstelaedami, Apud Joannem Janszonium à Waesberge, 1674.
103 p. 14cm.

Bound with Clemens I, Saint, Pope. Ad Corinthios epistola. 1669.

Baxter, Richard, 1615-1691.
The autobiography of Richard Baxter. London, J. M. Dent & sons, ltd.; New York, E. P. Dutton & co., inc. [1931]
xl, 312 p. 17½ cm. (*Half-title:* Everyman's library, ed. by Ernest Rhys. Biography. [no. 868])

"Edited with introduction & notes by J. M. Lloyd Thomas."
"First published in this edition, 1931."
Appendices: Last trial and death (p. 257-266) Love-story and marriage (p. 267-277)
Bibliography: p. xxxiv.

I. Thomas, Joseph Morgan Lloyd, 1868- ed.

G-2-a 3436

Baxter, Richard, 1615-1691.
The difference between the power of magistrates and church-pastors, and the Roman kingdom & magistracy under the name of a church ... London, Printed for Nevil Simmons, 1671.
2 p. l., 59 p. 20 cm.

MH

G-2-a 3437

Baxter, Richard, 1615-1691.
The practical works of the Rev. Richard Baxter: with a life of the author, and a critical examination of his writings, by William Orme. London, J. Duncan, 1830.
23 v. port.

NNC

SPECIAL COLLECTIONS SPINOZA
G-2-a 3438

Baxter, Richard, 1615-1691.
Richard Baxter's Catholick theologie: plain, pure, peaceable: for pacification of the dogmatical word-warriours ... In three books ... London, Printed by Robert White, for Nevill Simmons, 1675.
2 v. in 1. port. 32cm.

The third book was never published.
The first book is in three parts, with sepatate title-pages and pagination.
Includes references to Spinoza (book 1, part 3, p. 108, 114, 118)

SPECIAL COLLECTIONS SPINOZA
G-2-a 3439

Bekker, Balthasar, 1634-1698.
D. Balthasar Bekkers ... Bezauberte Welt. Neu übersetzt von Johann Moritz Schwager ...; durchgesehen und vermehrt von D. Johann Salomo Semler ... Leipzig, In der Weygandschen Buchhandlung, 1781-82.
3 v. in 2. fold. plate. 21cm.

Portrait on title-page.

SPECIAL COLLECTIONS SPINOZA
G-2-a 3440

Bekker, Balthasar, 1634-1698.
De betoverde weereld, zynde een grondig ondersoek van 't gemeen gevoelen aangaande de geesten, derselver aart en vermogen, bewind en bedryf: als ook 't geene de menschen door derselver kraght en gemeenschap doen. In vier boeken ondernomen van Balthasar Bekker ... t'Amsterdam, By Daniel van den Dalen, 1691-93.
4 v. in 2. 20cm.

Vols. 2-4 have special title-pages.

SPECIAL COLLECTIONS SPINOZA
G-2-a 3441

Bekker, Balthasar, 1634-1698.
Die bezauberte Welt: oder, Eine gründliche Untersuchung des allgemeinen Aberglaubens, betreffend, die Arth und das Vermögen, Gewalt und Wirckung des Satans und der bösen Geister über den Menschen, und was diese durch derselben Krafft und Gemeinschafft thun: so aus natürlicher Vernunfft und H. Schrifft in 4 Büchern zu bewehren sich unternommen hat Balthasar Bekker ... Nebenst des authoris generale Vorrede über diese seine 4 Bücher ... Aus dem

CONTINUED ON NEXT CARD

SPECIAL COLLECTIONS SPINOZA
G-2-a 3442

Bekker, Balthasar, 1634-1698. Die bezauberte Welt. 1693. (Card 2)

Holländischen nach der letzten vom Authore vermehrten Edition. In die teutsche Sprache übersetzet. Gedruckt zu Amsterdam, bey Daniel von Dahlen, 1693.
39, [1], 136, 270, [2], 179 (i.e. 195), [3], 308, [4] p. plate. 22cm.

G-2-a 3443

Bekker, Balthasar, 1634-1698.
Kort begryp der algemeine kerkelyke historien, zedert het jaar 1666, daar Hornius eindigt, tot den jare 1684. t'Amsterdam, B. Boekholt, 1685.
4 p. l., 62 p., 1 l.

Includes a section on Spinoza (p. 38-39)

OCH

SPECIAL COLLECTIONS SPINOZA
G-2-a 3444

Benthem, Henrich Ludolf, 1661-1723.
Henrich Ludolff Benthems P. C. und S. Holländischer Kirch- und Schulen-Staat. Franckfurt und Leipzig, In Verlegung Nicolaus Försters, Buchhändl: in Hannover; Merseburg, Druckts Christian Gottschick, 1698.
2 pts. in 1 v. plates, ports. 18cm.

Includes references to Spinoza.

G-2-a 3445

Bernis, François Joachim de Pierre de, comte de Lyon, cardinal, 1715-1794.
Oeuvres de François Joachim de Pierre, Cnal de Bernis. On y a joint le poëme de la Religion vengée, ouvrage posthume de l'auteur. A Paris, De l'imprimerie de P. Didot l'aîné, 1797.
524 p.

Beverland, Adriaan, 1654?-1712.
Hadriani Beverlandi ... De peccato originali, κατ' ἐξοχὴν sic nuncupato, dissertatio ... ⌈Leyden⌉, Ex typographeio, 1679.
⌈20⌉, 157, ⌈1⌉ p. 17cm.

Includes references to Spinoza.

Blunt, John Henry, 1823-1884.
Dictionary of doctrinal and historical theology. 2d ed. London, Rivingtons, 1872.
825 p. 28 cm.

Includes an article "Spinozism" (p. 707-710) and other references to Spinoza.

Blyenburg, Willem van
De kennisse Godts en Godts-dienst, beweert tegen d'uytvluchten der atheisten: in welcke met klare en natuurlijcke reden getoont wert dat Godt een Godts-dienst in-geschapen en geopenbaert heeft, dat Godt volgens de selve oock wil gedient wesen ... In vier boecken verdeelt, door Willem Van Blyenburg. Tot Leyden en Amsterdam, By Daniel, Abraham en Adriaen van Gaesbeeck, 1671.
⌈12⌉, 490, ⌈12⌉ p. 14cm.

Added title-page, engraved.

Blyenbergh, Willem van, 17th cent.
De waerheyt van de Christelijcke Godts-dienst en de authoriteyt der H. Schriften, beweert tegen de argumenten der ongodtsdienstige, of een wederlegginge van dat Godt-lasterlijcke boeck, genoemt Tractatus theologico-politicus ... Door Willem van Blyenbergh ... Gedruckt tot Leyden, By Daniel van Gaesbeeck, 1674.
⌈32⌉, 467, ⌈1⌉ p. 21cm.

Bomble, Florentinus
Brief aan den Heer Fredericus van Leenhof, predikant te Swolle: behelsende noodige aanmerkingen over desselvs Hemel op aarden; tot omsichtiger onderscheiding der ware blydschap van de ydele en bedrieglyke: door Florentinus Bomble ... Tot Amsteldam, by Gerardus Borstius, 1703.
⌈8⌉, 70 p. 16cm.

Bowen, Francis, 1811-1890.
Lowell lectures, on the application of metaphysical and ethical science to the evidences of religion; delivered before the Lowell institution in Boston, in the winters of 1848-49. By Francis Bowen. Boston, C. C. Little and J. Brown, 1849.
xviii p., 1 l., 465 p. 25½cm.

1. Christianity—Evidences. 2. Philosophy and religion. I. Lowell institute lectures, 1848-49. II. Title.

Bowman, Archibald Allan, 1883-1936.
Studies in the philosophy of religion, by Archibald Allan Bowman ... edited with a memorial introduction by Norman Kemp Smith ... London, Macmillan and co., limited, 1938.
2 v. 22½ cm.
Bibliography: v. 1, p. xiv-xlviii.
Includes references to Spinoza.

1. Religion—Philosophy. I. Smith, Norman Kemp, 1872- ed. II. Title.

Brown, James Baldwin, 1820-1884.
Stoics and saints; lectures on the later heathen moralists, and on some aspects of the life of the mediaeval church. By the late James Baldwin Brown ... Glasgow, J. Maclehose and sons, 1893.
viii, 296 p. 23cm.

"Note by the editor" signed: E. B. B. ⌈i. e. Elizabeth Baldwin Brown?⌉

⌈Bryant, Jacob⌉ 1715-1804.
A treatise upon the authenticity of the Scriptures, and the truth of the Christian religion. 2d ed. Cambridge, Printed by J. Archdeacon for T. Cadell, and P. Elmsly, London, 1793.
xv, 278 p. 22cm.
"Advertisement" signed: J. Bryant.

1. Apologetics—18th cent. I. Title.

Calamy, Edmund, 1671-1732.
The inspiration of the Holy Writings of the Old and New Testament consider'd and improv'd. In fourteen sermons preach'd at the merchants lecture at Salters Hall. By Edmund Calamy ... To which is added a single sermon in vindication of the divine institution of the office of the ministry, preach'd at the same lecture. London: Printed for T. Parkhurst ⌈etc.⌉, 1710.
⌈16⌉, 422, ⌈2⌉ p. 20cm.

An answer to Leclerc's Five letters concerning ... the Holy Scriptures.

G-2-a
3456

Carpenter, Joseph Estlin, 1844-1927.
James Martineau, theologian and teacher; a study of his life and thought. Boston, American Unitarian Association, 1905.
xv, 596 p.

NNUT

G-2-a
3457

Catholic church. Catechisms.
Catechismus Concilii Tridentini, Pii V. Pontif. Max. jussu promulgatus; sincerus & integer, mendisque repurgatus operâ P. D. L. H. P. A quo est additus apparatus ad Catechismum, in quo ratio, auctoritas, approbatores & usus declarantur. Editio novissima. Parisiis, Sumptibus bibliopolarum P. Witte, E. F. Savoye ac V. Henri, 1738.
[44], 520, [34] p. 13cm.

NNC

G-2-a
3458

Charpentier, Louis, 18th cent.
Lettres critiques, sur divers ecrits de nos jours, contraires à la religion & aux moeurs, par M. C***. ... Londres, 1751.
2 v. in 1. 16 cm.

Includes three letters on Spinoza (part 2, p. 149-222)

G-2-a
3459

Clemens I, Saint, Pope, 1st cent.
Τοῦ ἐν ἁγίοις πατρὸς ἡμῶν καὶ ἱερομάρτυρος Κλήμεντος πρὸς Κορινθίους ἐπιστολή. S. Patris & Martyris Clementis ad Corinthios epistola. Oxoniae, Excudebat A. & L. Lichfield, Acad: typograph: 1669.
[22], 133, [69] p. 14cm.

Wing C4631.

NNC

G-2-a
3460

Cremer, Bernard Sebastiaan, 1683-1750.
De wonderwerken van onsen Heere Jesus Christus, in haare waarheyt, goddelykheyt, ende geestsykheyt, opengelegt en verdedigt tegen Thomas Woolston ende Willem Deurhof, nevens derselver dierbaarheyt ende nuttigheyt, ter bevindinge van een levend geloof en evangelische godsvrucht, aangedrongen, door Bernard Sebastiaan Cremer ... Te Amsterdam, By Hendrik Vieroot, 1741.
17 p. l., 502 p.

G-2-a
3461

Daiches, Sally, 1880-
Religion and theolatry. [1903]
p. 13.

In Jewish chronicle, London, Sept. 18, 1903.
A letter to the editor in reply to J. H. Levy.

NNJ

G-2-a
3462

Daiches, Sally, 1880-
Religion and theolatry. [1903]
p. 8.

In Jewish chronicle, London, Oct. 2, 1903.
A letter to the editor in reply to Maurice Jacobs.

NNJ

G-2-a
3463

Dorn, Johann Christoph, d. 1752.
Dissertatio historico litteraria de doctis impostoribus ... Ienae, Litteris Mvllerianis, 1703.
76 p.

Thesis, Jena.

G-2-a
3464

Durocampo, J S de
Prodromus dissertationis theologico-politicae De propaganda fide & unione ecclesiastica inter Protestantes. Authore J. S. de Durocampo. [172-?]
1 p. l., 22 p. 20cm.

Bound with Meditationes succinctae de existentia Dei ... 1724.

NNC

G-2-a
3465

Edelmann, Johann Christian, 1698-1767.
Der neu eröffnete Edelmann; oder, Auswahl aus Edelmanns Schriften. Bern, Jenni, 1847.
87 p. 20 cm.

CLSU

Evans, John, 1767-1827.
A sketch of the denominations of the Christian world; accompanied with a persuasive to religious moderation ... 8th ed., with material corrections and improvements. London, B. Crosby, 1813.
xxxiv, 263 p. plate.

Includes a reference to Spinoza (p. 3)

Farrar, Adam Storey, 1826-1905.
A critical history of free thought in reference to the Christian religion. Eight lectures preached before the University of Oxford, in the year M.DCCC.LXII. On the foundation of the late Rev. John Bampton ... By Adam Storey Farrar ... London, J. Murray, 1862.
lix, [1], 684 p., 1 l. 22cm. (*Half-title:* Bampton lectures, 1862)

Includes a section on Spinoza (p. 147-162)

1. Free thought.

Farrar, Adam Storey, 1826-1905.
A critical history of free thought in reference to the Christian religion. Eight lectures preached before the University of Oxford, in the year M.DCCC.LXII., on the foundation of the late Rev. John Bampton ... By Adam Storey Farrar ... New York, D. Appleton and company, 1863.
xlvi, 487 p. 21 cm.

Includes references to Spinoza.

1. Free thought—Hist.

Farrar, Frederic William, 1831-1903.
History of interpretation; eight lectures preached before the University of Oxford in the year MDCCCLXXXV on the foundation of the late Rev. John Bampton. London, Macmillan, 1886.
li, 553 p. 23cm. (Bampton lectures 1885)

Flint, Robert, 1838-1910.
On theological, biblical, and other subjects, by Robert Flint ... Edinburgh and London, W. Blackwood and sons, 1905.
x, 459 p. 19½ cm.
CONTENTS.—Advice to students of divinity—Paper on the Book of Amos.—The theology of the Epistle of James.—The theology of St. Peter.—Christ our king.—Christ's teaching as to the kingdom of God.—The wisest of the ancient Greeks, Socrates.—The idea of God in the religion of ancient Egypt.—Idea of the divine in Chinese thought.—The Biblical idea of God.—Duties of the people of Scotland to the church of Scotland.

1. Theology—Addresses, essays, lectures.

Forster, Charles, d. 1871.
Spinoza redivivus; or, The reappearance of his school and spirit in the volume entitled "Essays and reviews". A sermon delivered in Canterbury Cathedral on Monday, May 6, 1861. Lonson [!] Spottiswood, 1861.

[Fourmont, Étienne], 1683-1745.
Lettre de R. Ismael Ben Abraham, juif converti, a M. l'abbé Houteville, sur son livre intitulé, La religion chrétienne prouvée par les faits. A Paris, Chez C. L. Thiboust, 1722.
xxviii, [4], 205 p. 15cm.

Includes references to Spinoza.

Fr. Leenhofs boek, strijdende tegen het Christendom en in het byzonder tegen den Gereformeerden Godsdienst. Amsterdam, 1704.

[Francès, Madeleine]
La morale de Spinoza et la doctrine calvinienne de la prédestination. [Strasbourg, 1933]
8 p. 25cm.

Signed: Madeleine Francès.
On cover: Revue d'histoire et de philosophie religieuses. Extrait.

Fülöp-Miller, René, 1891-
Macht und Geheimnis der Jesuiten; kulturhistorische Monographie. Leipzig, Grethlein [c1929]
xiv, 576 p. plates, ports., facsims. 25cm.

Includes references to Spinoza (p. 144,146)
Bibliography: 24 p. in pocket at end.

Fuessli, Johann Conrad
Johann Conrad Füesslins ... Neue und unpartheyische Kirchen- und Ketzerhistorie der mittlern Zeit ... Frankfurt und Leipzig, bey Christian Gottlob Hilschern, 1770-74.
3 v. 19cm.

Vol. 3 includes references to Spinoza.

Funus philosophico theologicum; dat is filozoofsche godsgeleerde uitvaart over de leere des geloofs, en geheimen van d'hervormde natuurkunde. Op het toneel der onbekende dwalingen dezer eeuwe vertoont. En uyt het grondbeginzel van den redelijken godsdienst herroepen en gesteuit in het Testament of zeeuwsche nagedachten van Johan Ruyter ... Tot Groningen, Gedrukt voor den auteur, by Johannes van Velsen, 1708.
48 l., 476 p.

Includes two letters on Spinoza (p. 1-149)

Geschiedenis der Christelijke kerk in Nederland, in tafereelen, onder redactie van B. ter Haar, W. Moll en E. B. Swalue. Met medewerking van P. Hofstede de Groot [et al.] Rotterdam, D. Bolle [1864-69]
2 v. 27cm.

Includes an essay "Het Spinozisme" (v. 2, p. 471-475) and a section on Spinoza (v. 2, p. 499-506)
Imprint dates from "Naschrift" at end of each vol.

[Goodwin, Timothy, abp. of Cashel] 1670?-1729, supposed author.
The life and character of that eminent and learned prelate, the late Dr. Edw. Stillingfleet ... together with some account of the works he has publish'd. London, Mortlock, 1710.
149 p. 19 cm.

Halfmann, Wilhelm
Christian Kortholt; ein Bild aus der Theologie und Frömmigkeit im Ausgang des orthodoxen Zeitalters. [1930]
82 p.

In Verein für Schleswig-Holsteinische Kirchengeschichte, Kiel. Schriften, Reihe 1, Heft 17, 1930.

[Hare, Francis, bp. of Chichester] 1671-1740.
The difficulties and discouragements which attend the study of the Scriptures in the way of private judgment ... In a letter to a young clergyman. By a presbyter of the Church of England. The second edition. London, Printed for John Baker, 1714.
47 p. 20cm.

Volume of pamphlets.

[Hering, Johann Gottfried]
Compendieuses Kirchen- und Ketzer-Lexicon, in welchem alle Ketzereyen, Ketzer, Secten, Sectirer ... auffs deutlichste erkläret, und insonderheit deren Urheber und Stiffter jeder Secte angezeiget werden ... zusammen getragen. Und mit einer Vorrede versehen von J. G. H. Schneeberg, bey C. W. Fulden, 1731.
3 p. l., 569 col.

Includes a section on Spinoza (col. 491-493)

[Hering, Johann Gottfried]
Compendieuses Kirchen- und Ketzer-Lexicon, in welchem alle Ketzereyen, Ketzer, Secten, Sectirer, geistliche Orden und viele zur Kirchen-Historie dienende Termini auffs deutlichste erkläret, und insonderheit die Urheber und Stiffter jeder Secte angezeiget werden, denen angehenden Studiosis Theologiae zu Erleichterung der Theologiae Polemicae, wie auch Ungelehrten zu einiger Bestärckung in der Erkändniss der Wahrheit zur Gottseeligkeit herausge-

[Hering, Johann Gottfried] Compendieuses Kirchen- und Ketzer-Lexicon. 1734. (Card 2)

geben von J. G. H. Andere und verbesserte Auflage. Schneeberg, Zu finden bey Carl Wilhelm Fulden, 1734.
[12] p., 848 columns, [2] p. front. 17cm.

Interleaved.
Includes a section on Spinoza (columns 724-727)

Hickes, George, 1642-1715.
Two treatises, one of the Christian priesthood, the other of the dignity of the episcopal order. Formerly written, and now published to obviate the erroneous opinions, fallacious reasonings, and bold and false assertations, in a late book, entituled, The rights of the Christian church. With a large prefatory discourse, wherein is contained an answer to the said book. All written by George Hickes D. D. London, Printed by W. B. for Richard Sare, 1707.
[16], ccxli, [5], 335 p. 20cm.

Huber, Marie, 1695-1753.
The world unmask'd: or, The philosopher the greatest cheat; in twenty-four dialogues ... To which is added, The state of souls separated from their bodies ... In answer to ... An enquiry into origenism ... Translated from the French. London, Printed for A. Millar, 1736.
viii, 446 p. 21 cm.

Translated by B. Mandeville.

[Hylkema, C B]
Luyken toch van den ouden stempel? [1909]
437-465 p.

In De Gids, v. 73, 4. serie, 27. jaargang, 2. deel, 1909.
Includes references to Spinoza.

[Jamin, N]
Heylsahme Ermahnungen zu den unbescheidenen Verehrern der seeligen Jungfrawen Mariâe, und schrifftmässige Betrachtungen, wie man den Drey-Einigen Gott in Geist und Warheit anbeten, seine Hülff und Trost, Heyl und Seligheit, allein durch Christum suchen und erlangen solle ... Zu Amsterdam, Gedrukt bey die Witwe von Christoffel Conradus, 1689.
[48], 96 p. 16cm.

"Zuschrifft" signed: N. Jamin.

CONTINUED ON NEXT CARD

Kahnis, Karl Friedrich August, 1814-1888.
Der innere Gang des deutschen Protestantismus seit Mitte des vorigen Jahrhunderts. 2. Aufl. Leipzig, Dörffling und Franke, 1860.
xii, 284 p. 20cm.

Includes a section on Spinoza (p. 8-10) and other references to him.

Kemp, Carel Maria van der, 1799-1861.
De eere der Nederlandsche Hervormde Kerk gehandhaafd tegen Ypey en Dermout. Rotterdam, Meer & Verbruggen, 1830-33.
3 v. in 1. 23 cm.

Kirkman, Thomas Penyngton, 1806-1895.
Clerical intemperance; a letter to the Rev. Canon Bardsley. Ramsgate, T. Scott, 1871.
7 p. 19cm.

Volume of pamphlets.

Kirkman, Thomas Penyngton, 1806-1895.
On church pedigrees. Ramsgate, T. Scott, 1871-72.
2 pts. in 1 v. 19cm.

Volume of pamphlets.

Kirkman, Thomas Penyngton, 1806-1895.
On the infidelity of orthodoxy. Ramsgate, T. Scott, 1870.
2 pts. in 1 v. 19cm.

Volume of pamphlets.

[La Peyrère, Isaac de] 1594-1676.
Praêadamitaê. Sive Exercitatio super versibus duodecimo, decimotertio, & decimoquarto, capitis quinti Epistolaê D. Pauli ad Romanos. Qvibvs indvcvntvr primi homines ante Adamum conditi. [Amsterdam, Elzevir] 1655.
2 pts. in 1 v. map. 21cm.

Place of publication and printer from Willems, Alphonse. Les Elsevir. 1880.
Part [2] has title: Systema theologicvm ex Praê-Adamitarvm hypothesi. Pars prima.

(Continued on next card)

[La Peyrère, Isaac de] 1594-1676. Praêadamitaê. 1655. (Card 2)

"Synagogis Ivdaeorvm vniversis": 8 p. at end of pt. [2] Pages 7-8 lacking.

[La Peyrère, Isaac de] 1594-1676.
Praeadamitae. Sive Exercitatio super versibus duodecimo, decimotertio, & decimoquarto, capitis quinti Epistolae D. Pauli ad Romanos. Qvibvs indvcvntvr primi homines ante Adamum conditi. [Amsterdam, Elzevir] 1655.
2 pts. in 1 v. fold. map. 14cm.

Place of publication and printer from Willems, Alphonse. Les Elsevir. 1880.
Part [2] has title: Systema theologicvm ex Praeadamitarvm hypothesi. Pars prima.

(Continued on next card)

[La Peyrère, Isaac de] 1594-1676. Praeadamitae. 1655. (Card 2)

"Synagogis Ivdaeorvm vniversis": [7] p. at end of pt. [2]

[La Peyrère, Isaac de] 1594-1676.
Systema theologicvm, ex Praeadamitarvm hypothesi. Pars prima. [Amsterdam, Elzevir] 1655.
[14], 317, [7] p. fold. map. 14cm. (In his Praeadamitae, 1655. pt. [2])

I. Title.

[La Peyrère, Isaac de] 1594-1676.
Systema theologicum, ex Prae-Adamitarum hypothesi. Pars prima. [Amsterdam, Elzevir] 1655.
[16], 297, 8 p. map. 21cm. (In his Praeadamitae, 1655. pt. [2])

Pages 7-8 at end lacking.

[La Peyrère, Isaac de] 1594-1676.
Praeadamiten, of Oeffening over het 12, 13, en 14. vers des vijfden capittels van den Brief des Apostels Pauli tot den Romeynen. Waer door geleert wort: datter menschen voor Adam geweest zijn. 1661.
2 pts. in 1 v. ([8], 516 p.) map. 14cm.

Part [2] has title: Theologische samen-stelling, uyt de voorstelling der Praeadamiten. Het eerste deel.

[La Peyrère, Isaac de] 1594-1676.
Theologische samen-stelling, uyt de voorstelling der Praeadamiten. Het eerste deel. 1661.
[79]-515 p. map. 14cm. (In his Praeadamiten, 1661. pt. [2])

I. Title.

[Le Prieur, Philippe] 17th cent.
Opmerkingen over 't boek der Praeadamiten, in welke den schrijver wederleyt wort, en vast staende gehouden wordt, dat Adam den eersten mensch geweest is. Door Eusebius Romanus [pseud.] ... 1661.
[12], 96 p. 14cm.

Bound with La Peyrère, Isaac de. Praeadamiten. 1661.

Leslie, Charles, 1650-1722.
A short and easie method with the deists. Wherein the certainty of the Christian religion is demonstrated ... In a letter to a friend. The sixth edition, corrected and enlarg'd, with a letter from the author to a deist ... To which is added a second part to the Jews: and also The truth of Christianity vindicated; with a dissertation on private judgment: and a defence of the short method with the deists prefix'd. By Mr. Charles Leslie. London, Printed for Geo. Strahan [1727?]
4 pts. in 1 v. front. 21cm.

(CONTINUED ON NEXT CARD)

Leslie, Charles, 1650-1722. A short and easie method with the deists ... [1727?] (Card 2)

Each part has special t.-p.
Contents.--[pt. 1] A short and easie method with the deists. 6th ed., 1726.--[pt. 2] A short and easie method with the Jews. 7th ed. corr., 1727.--[pt. 3] The truth of Christianity demonstrated. 6th ed., 1726.--[pt. 4] A dissertation concerning private judgment and authority. 3d ed. corr., 1726.

Leydekker, Melchior, 1642-1721.
Den ingebeelden hemel op der aarde, beschreven door D. F. Leenhof, verdweenen door den waarachtigen hemel op der aarde. Tot Utrecht, Gedrukt by Herman Hardenberg. 1704.
54 p.

SPECIAL COLLECTIONS SPINOZA
G-2-a 3506

Lindeborn, Jan, 1630-1696.
De leeder Jacobs. De maegden, die Godt met opzet van eeuwige reinigheit, in de weereld dienen, toe-gepast van den eerw. heere Joannes Lindeborn. Uit het Latijn, door den autheur van nieuws oversien ende verbetert, in het Nederduidsch vertaelt. Door den eerw. heere Adrianus Terlou ... T'Antwerpen, by Michiel Cnobbert voor Joachim à Metelen, 1670.
[22], 389, [4] p. plate. 17cm.

Added engraved t.-p. reads: De leeder van Jacob ...

G-2-a 3507

[Manen, W C van]
Pontiaan van Hattem; een bladzijde uit de geschiedenis der Gereformeerde Kerken dezer landen. [1885]
357-429; 84-115 p.

Signed: W. C. van Manen.
In De Gids, v. 3, 4. serie, 1885, 3. deel, p. 357-429; 4. deel, p. 84-115.
Includes references to Spinoza.

G-2-a 3508

Massillon, Jean Baptiste, bp., 1663-1742.
Oeuvres. Paris, Gaume Frères, 1848.
3 v.

Includes references to Spinoza (v. 1, p. 692) in sermon "Des doutes sur la religion" and (v. 1, p. 841) in an analysis of the sermon.

G-2-a 3509

Massillon, Jean Baptiste, 1663-1742.
Oeuvres choisies de Massillon. Paris, Delestre-Boulage, 1823-25.
6 v. 21 cm.

Includes a sermon against Spinoza (v. 2, p. 408-429)

NBuG

G-2-a 3510

Massillon, Jean Baptiste, bp., 1663-1742.
Oeuvres complètes. Paris, Raymond, 1821.
13 v.

Includes references to Spinoza in sermon "Des doutes sur la religion" (v. 4, p. 213-256) and in an analysis of the sermon (v. 4, p. 455-461)

MdBP

SPECIAL COLLECTIONS SPINOZA
G-2-a 3511

Melamed, Samuel Max, 1885-
Spinoza and Buddha; visions of a dead God, by S. M. Melamed. Chicago, Ill., The University of Chicago press [°1933]
xi, 391 p. 23½cm.
"Notes and bibliography": p. 367-382.

1. Spinoza, Benedictus de, 1632-1677. 2. Buddha and Buddhism. 3. Jews—Religion—Relations—Buddhism. 4. Christianity and other religions—Buddhism. I. Title.

33-33467

Library of Congress B3998.M4
[a45n1] 199.492

SPECIAL COLLECTIONS SPINOZA
G-2-a 3512

Meyer, Eduard, 1855-1930.
Ursprung und Anfänge des Christentums. Stuttgart, J. G. Cotta'sche Buchhandlung Nachfolger, 1921-24 [v. 1, 1924]
3 v. 24cm.

Vol. 1, 4. und 5. Aufl.; v. 2 and 3, 1.-3. Aufl.
Includes a reference to Spinoza (v. 2, p. 280)

G-2-a 3513

[Molkenboer, Bernardus Hilarius, Father, 1879-1948]
Met Spinoza in conjunctie. [1932]
172-178 p.

Signed: B. H. M.
In Vondel-kroniek, 3. jaargang, 1932.

G-2-a 3514

Mosheim, Johann Lorenz, 1694?-1755.
Institutes of ecclesiastical history, ancient and modern ... much corrected, enlarged and improved from the primary authorities. By John Lawrence von Mosheim. A new and literal translation, from the original Latin, with copious additional notes ... by James Murdock. 2d ed.
3 v. 24 cm.

LC

G-2-a 3515

Mosheim, Johann Lorenz, 1694?-1755.
J. L. von Mosheims Vollständige Kirchengeschichte des Neuen Testaments ... Heilbronn, Class, 1770-1784.
4 v.

Translated from the Latin by J. R. Schlegel.
Includes a section on Spinoza (v. 4, p. 53-60)

MH

Mosheim, Johann Lorenz, 1694?-1755.
Sämmtliche heilige Reden über wichtige Wahrheiten der Lehre Jesu Christi. Hamburg, J. C. Bohn, 1765.
3 v.

Newman, Francis William, 1805-1897.
Against hero-making in religion. Reprinted ... for private circulation. London, Printed by C. W. Reynell, 1865.
34 p. 19cm.

Volume of pamphlets.

Newman, Francis William, 1805-1897.
The controversy about prayer. London, T. Scott, 1873.
13 p. 19cm.

Volume of pamphlets.

Newman, Francis William, 1805-1897.
Divergence of Calvinism from Pauline doctrine Ramsgate, T. Scott, 1871.
10 p. 19cm.

Volume of pamphlets.

Newman, Francis William, 1805-1897.
On this and the other world. London, T. Scott [1875]
20 p. 19cm.

Volume of pamphlets.

Newman, Francis William, 1805-1897.
The religious weakness of Protestantism. Ramsgate, T. Scott, 1866.
45 p. 19cm.

Volume of pamphlets.

Newman, Francis William, 1805-1897.
The true temptation of Jesus. Ramsgate, T. Scott [1871]
22 p. 19cm.

Volume of pamphlets.

Nielen, Josef Maria
Augustinus: ein Gedenkwort zu seinem 1500. Todestag. [1931]
[7]-19 p. 26cm.

"Sonderabdruck aus den Neuen Jahrbüchern. Jahrgang 1931. Erstes Heft."

Norton, Andrews, 1786-1853.
A discourse on the latest form of infidelity; delivered at the request of the "Association of the alumni of the Cambridge theological school," on the 19th of July, 1839. With notes. Cambridge, J. Owen, 1839.
64 p. 23 cm.

Norton, Andrews, 1786-1853.
Remarks on a pamphlet entitled "'The latest form of infidelity' examined." By Andrews Norton. Cambridge, J. Owen, 1839.
72 p. 21½cm.

1. Skepticism. 2. "The latest form of infidelity" examined.

G-2-a 3526

Norton, Andrews, 1786-1853.
Tracts concerning Christianity. Cambridge, J. Bartlett, 1852.
392 p.

NNUT

G-2-a 3527

Outrein, Johannes d', 1662-1722.
Noodige aanmerkingen over een boeksken, dat tot sijn op-schrift draagt, de eenige gereformeerde waarheid, enz. ofte Christelyke kinderleer ... Opgesteld en uitgegeven door het collegie, het welke men den naam geeft van Hebreen. Benevens een na-reden tegen D. Fredericus van Leenhof. Door Johannes D'Outrein. Dordrecht, J. van Braam, 1704.
xxiv, 82 p.

NN

SPECIAL COLLECTIONS SPINOZA G-2-a 3528

Pearson, Thomas
Infidelity; its aspects, causes and agencies; being the prize essay of the British Organization of the Evangelical Alliance. New York, R. Carter & Brothers, 1854.
xi, 620 p. 23cm.

Includes references to Spinoza (p. 134 and 136)

SPECIAL COLLECTIONS SPINOZA G-2-a 3529

Petrejus, Alexander
Paraenesis, of te vermaninge om te vermijden de Socinianerije. Gestelt tegen het onzedigh ende Goddeloos Antwoordt van N. N. sich valschelijck noemende ... een Gereformeert Hollander. Door Alexand. Petreium ... Uyt het Latijn vertaelt ... Gedruckt tot Rotterdam, by Arnout Leers, 1655.
36 p. 21cm.

Bound with Blyenbergh, Willem van. De waerheyt van de Christelijcke Godts-dienst. 1674.

G-2-a 3530

Post, Jacobus
Het masker der Hattemisten afgeligt; zynde een catechismus dier vrygeesten ... Tot vereideling der klachten van Hendrik Woutelaars ... Te Amsterdam, By Reinier en Josua Ottens, 1734.
114 p. front.

UCLA

SPECIAL COLLECTIONS SPINOZA G-2-a 3531

Pythius, Joannes
Responsio exetastica ad tractatum, incerto autore, nuper editum, cui titulus Praeadamitae. Libri duo. Avtore J. Pythio ... Lvgd. Batav., Apud Johannem Elsevirivm, 1656.
[14], 414 p. 13cm.

Printer's device on t.-p.

G-2-a 3532

[Quinet, Edgar] 1803-1875.
De la Vie de Jésus par le docteur Strauss. [1838]
585-629 p.

Signed: E. Quinet.
In Revue des deux mondes, t. 16, 4. série, 1838.
Includes references to Spinoza.

G-2-a 3533

Radliński, Ignacy, 1843-1920.
Jezus, Paweł, Spinoza. Rzecz historyczno-społeczna. Warszawa, L. Bogusławski, 1912.
533 p.

OCH

SPECIAL COLLECTIONS SPINOZA G-2-a 3534

Die Religionen des Orients und die altgermanische Religion. Von Edv. Lehmann [et al.] 2., verm. und verb. Aufl. Leipzig, B. G. Teubner, 1913.
x, 287 p. 26cm. (Die Kultur der Gegenwart. T. 1, Abt. 3l)

Includes bibliographies.

G-2-a 3535

Renan, Ernest, 1823-1892.
Vie de Jésus. 22. éd. rev. et augm. Paris, Lévy, 1893.
cv, 552 p. 23 cm. (Histoire des origines du christianisme, livre 1)

Includes a reference to Spinoza (p. 51)

Réville, Albert, 1826-1906.
Histoire du dogme de la divinité de Jésus-Christ. 2. éd. Paris, Germer, Baillière, 1876.
xx, 184 p.

Includes a reference to Spinoza (p. 155-156)

Ryssen, Leonardus, fl. 1680.
L. Ryssenii Justa detestatio libelli A. Beverlandi de peccato originali ... Accedit descriptio poetica creationis et lapsus, versibus ex plerisque poetis concinnata ... Gorinchemi, 1680.
2 pts.

Sand, Christoph, 1644-1680.
Bibliotheca anti-trinitariorum, sive Catalogus scriptorum, & succincta narratio devita eorum auctorum, qui praeterito & hoc seculo, vulgo receptum dogma de tribus in unico Deo per omnia aequalibus personis vel impugnarunt, vel docuerunt solum patrem D. N. J. Christi esse illum verum seu altissimum Deum. Opus posthumum Christophori Chr. Sandii. Accedunt alia quaedam scripta ... Quae omnia simul juncta compendium historiae ecclesiasticae Unitariorum, qui Sociniani vulgo audiunt, exhibent. Freistadii, apud J. Aconium, 1684.
8 p. l., 296 p. 16 cm.

Schad, Johann Baptist, 1758-1834.
Lebens- und Klostergeschichte, von ihm selbst beschrieben. Neue Aufl. Altenburg, Hofbuchdruckerei, 1828.
3 v. 22 cm.

Schütz, Friedrich Wilhelm von, 1758-1819.
... Dispvtatio inavgvralis De haeresivm in ecclesia vtilitate, qvam ad illvstrandam partem commatis XIX. posteriorem 1. Ad Corinth. C. XI. ... pvblice proposvit Frider. Gvilelm. Schvtz ... Lipsiae, Literis Immanvelis Titii [1724]
71, [1] p. 20cm.

Thesis, Leipzig.
Bound with Meditationes succinctae de existentia Dei ... 1724.

Schwarz, Samuel
Os cristãos-novos em Portugal no século XX, com um prefácio: Pro Israel, do Ricardo Jorge. Lisboa, Empresa portuguesa de livros [1925]
xxiii, 110 p. illus. (incl. music) plates (incl. ports., facsim.) 26cm.

"Separata do IV volume da 'Arqueologia e história', publicação da Associação dos arqueologos portuguêses."
Includes references to Spinoza (p. xv, 22)

Schweitzer, Albert, 1875-
Das Christentum und die Weltreligionen. [2. Aufl.] München, Beck, 1925.
58 p. 22cm.

Includes a reference to Spinoza (p. 49)

Shedd, William Greenough Thayer, 1820-1894.
A history of Christian doctrine. New York, C. Scribner, 1863.
2 v. 23 cm.

Includes references to Spinoza.

Sherlock, Thomas, bp. of London, 1678-1761.
A vindication of the corporation and test acts, in answer to the Bishop of Bangor's reasons for the repeal of them, to which is added a second part concerning the religion of oaths. London, Pemberton, 1718.
116 p. 19 cm.

Skelton, Philip, 1707-1787.
The complete works of Philip Skelton. To which is prefixed Burdy's Life of the author. Edited by Robert Lynam. London, Richard Baynes, Hutchard & son; Oxford, Parker, 1824.
6 v. 22 cm.

Soccino, Fausto, 1539-1604.
Tractaet van de avctoriteyt der H. Schrifture. Eerst in't Italiaens beschreven, door Favstvs Socinvs van Siena. Naderhant in't Latijn ende Francois getranslateert. Mitsgaders het boeck van de Goddelijckheydt onses Heeren Jesu Christi. In't Latijn uytgegeven, door Valentinus Smalcius van Gotha ... Beyde getrouwelijck verduytscht, uytde iongste Latijnsche editien. Gedruckt tot Rakavv, By Sebastiaẽ Sternatzki ⌊1623⌋
2 p. l., 72, ⌊8⌋, 5-212 p. 20cm.

CONTINUED ON NEXT CARD

Soccino, Fausto, 1539-1604. Tractaet van de avctoriteyt der H. Schrifture. ⌊1623⌋
(Card 2)

"Tractaet van de Goddelijckheydt des herren Jesu Christi ... door Valentinus Smalcius" has separate title-page and paging.

Sozzini, Fausto, 1539-1604.
Fausti Socini van Siena Brieven aan zijn vrienden geschreeven. In welken van meest alle hoofstukken der Christelijke religie word gehandelt, en voor een van zijn voornaamste werken worden geacht. Nooit in het Nederlands voor deezen gedrukt. Hier is bygevoegt 1. Des zelfs Theologische lessen ... 2. N. N. Verklaring over het 53ste kap. van Esaias ⌊door Theophilus Eleutherius⌋ 3. De Schriftuurlijke lessen, van de geloofwaardigheyt der H. Schriftuur ...

CONTINUED ON NEXT CARD

Sozzini, Fausto, 1539-1604. Fausti Socini van Siena Brieven aan zijn vrienden geschreeven. 1666. (Card 2)

4. Tractaat van de geloofwaardigheyt der H. Schriftuur ... Na het jaar onzes Heeren, 1666.
5 pts. in 1 v. 25cm.

Each part except the first has special t.-p.

Stackhouse, Thomas, 1677-1752.
A defence of the Christian religion from the several objections of modern antiscripturists; wherein the literal sense of the prophecies contained in the Old Testament, and of the miracles recorded in the New, is explained and vindicated, in which is included the whole state of the controversy between Mr. Woolston and his adversaries ... Second edition, corrected. London, Printed for Edward Symon, 1733.
⌊36⌋, 509, ⌊3⌋ p.

Stillingfleet, Edward, Bp. of Worcester, 1635-1699.
Brief aan een ongodist; waar in de H. Schriftuur, van alle tegensprekingen gesuyvert werd; door Bisschop Stillingfleet. Mitsgaders: Moses, tegens Spinosa, Hobs, verdedigt; door Bisschop Kidder. Uyt het Engels vertaalt. Tot Delft, Gedrukt by Adriaan Beman, 1697.
⌊16⌋, 88, 46 ⌊i.e. 64⌋ p. 17cm.

Stillingfleet, Edward, bp., 1635-1699.
The works of that eminent and most learned prelate, Dr. Edw. Stillingfleet, late lord bishop of Worcester. Together with his life and character. London, Printed by J. Heptinstall, for Henry and George Mortlock, 1709-10.
6 v. port.

Includes references to Spinoza.

⌊Stoppa, Giovanni Battista⌋ fl. 1672.
De Gods-dienst der Hollanders, vertoont in verscheide brieven, geschreven door een amptenaar in 's Konings leger, aen leeraar ende professor in de God-geleertheid der stad Berne. Uit de Fransche-taal in het Neder-landsch overgezet. t'Amsterdam, By Cyprianus vander Gracht, 1673.
48 p. 19cm.

Includes references to Spinoza (p. 25-26, 39-40)

Stosch, Friedrich Wilhelm, 1646-1704?
Concordia rationis et fidei; sive, Harmonia philosophiae moralis et religionis Christianae. Amstelodami, 1692.
xvi, 124, ⌊34⌋, ⌊23⌋ p.

Strauss, David Friedrich, 1808-1874.
Hermann Samuel Reimarus und seine Schutzschrift für die vernünftigen Verehrer Gottes. Leipzig, F. A. Brockhaus, 1862.
xvi, 288 p.

Includes references to Spinoza.

Strimes, Samuel
Samuelis Strimesii ... Tractatus duo, De unione Euangelicorum ecclesiastica: quorum prior unionis hujus fundamentum; posterior naturam & indolem exponit, a duobus moderationi theologicae addictissimis ex Germanica lingua in Latinam versi. Lugduni Batavorum, Apud Joh: du Vivié, 1711.
[14], 89 p. 20cm.

Bound with Meditationes succinctae de existentia Dei ... 1724.

Trueblood, David Elton, 1900-
The influence of Emerson's Divinity School address. [1939]
41-56 p.

In Harvard theological review, v. 32, January, 1939.

Thomassin, Louis, 1619-1695.
Dogmata theologica. Editio nova ... adnotationibus illustrata, opera et studio P. F. Ecalle. Parisiis, Apud L. Vivès, 1864-72.
7 v.

Thudichum, Friedrich, 1831-1913.
Kirchliche Fälschungen. Stuttgart, F. Frommann, 1898-1906.
2 v. 22 cm.

References to Spinoza included in v. 2.

Unamuno y Jugo, Miguel de, 1864-1936.
Die Agonie des Christentums. [Berechtigte deutsche Übertragung von Otto Buek] München, Meyer & Jessen [1928]
184 p. 20cm.

Includes a reference to Spinoza (p. 31)

[Vloten, Johannes van] 1818-1883.
De geschiedenis van een messias. [1871]
332-406 p.

In De Levensbode, 4. deel, 1871.
Includes references to Spinoza.

Vloten, Johannes van, 1818-1883.
Over de leer der Hervormde Kerk en hare toekomst. Schiedam, H. A. M. Roelants, 1849.
94 p. 23cm.

Includes references to Spinoza.

Vollenhoven, Dirk Hendrik Theodoor, 1891-
Het Calvinisme en de reformatie van de wijsbegeerte. Amsterdam, H. J. Paris, 1933.
319 p. 25 cm.

Wallace, Robert, 1791-1850.
Antitrinitarian biography; or, Sketches of the lives and writings of distinguished antitrinitarians; exhibiting a view of the state of Unitarian doctrine and worship in the principal nations of Europe, from the Reformation to the close of the seventeenth century ... London, E. T. Whitfield, 1850.
3 v. 23cm.

Includes references to Spinoza.

White, Andrew Dickson, 1832-1918.
A history of warfare of science with theology in Christendom. New York, Appleton, 1914.
2 v. 23cm.

Includes references to Spinoza.
Contains bibliographies.

G-2-a
3566

Wielenga, Bastiaan, 1873-
Calvinisme en Spinozisme. [1911-12]
665-684, 811-833 p.

In Stemmen des tijds, 1. jaargang, 1911-12.

MH

G-2-a
3567

Wendland, Johannes, 1871-
Die neue Diesseitsreligion. Tübingen, J. C. B. Mohr (P. Siebeck) 1914.
47 p. 20 cm. (Religionsgeschichtliche Volksbücher für die deutsche christliche Gegenwart, 5. Reihe, 13. Heft)

Includes a reference to Spinoza (p. 9-11)

NNJ

G-2-a
3568

Witsius, Hermann, 1636-1708.
Hermanni Witsii Miscellaneorum sacrorum libri IV. Quibus de prophetis & prophetia ... diligenter & prolixe disseritur. Trajecti ad Rhenum, Apud Franciscum Halmam, 1692.
13 p. l., 859, [49] p.

Includes references to Spinoza.

NNJ

SPECIAL COLLECTIONS
Spinoza

G-2-a
3569

Wittich, Christoph, 1625-1687.
Christoph. Wittichii Theologia pacifica defensa. In qua theologiae pacificae capita, quae celeberrimus Samuel Maresius in annotationibus ad systematis sui theologici editionem novam impugnavit, singula vindicatur, & veritates non paucae aliae istis affines eruntur atque illustrantur. Amstelaedami, Apud Johannem Wolters, 1689.
[8], 1104 p. 20cm.

Includes a reference to Spinoza (p. [7] of first group)

G-2-a
3570

Wolle, Christoph, 1700-1761.
M. Christophori Wollii ... Commentatio philologica de parenthesi sacra. Accedunt duae dissertationes, prior de usu et abusu Αυξησεως nominum divinorum sacrae, posterior de loco Dan Genes. XIV. com. XIV contra Spinozam. Praefationem praemisit Christian. Frider. Boernerus. Lipsiae, Sumtibus Io. Frid. Gleditschii B. Filii, 1726.
8 p. l., 200 p., [4] l.

NN

G-2-a
3571

Ypey, Annaeus, 1760-1837.
Geschiedenis der Nederlandsche hervormde kerk; door A. Ypeij en I. J. Dermout. Breda, van Bergen, 1819-1827.
4 v. 23 cm.

Includes a section on Spinoza (v. 2, p. 573-579) and other references to him.

G-2-b
ANABAPTIST

SPECIAL COLLECTIONS
SPINOZA

G-2-b
3572

Alte und neue Schwarm-Geister-Bruth, und Quäcker-Greuel, das ist Gründliche Vorstellung und glaubwürdige Erzehlung von denen alten Quackern und neuen Frey-Geistern ... Alles zu gleich mit wahrhafftigen Exempeln erwiesen, aus Heiliger Schrifft gründlich und ausführlich widerleget ... 1702.
[16], 367 p. illus., ports. 35cm. (In Historia von denen Wider Tauffern. [1705?])

In two parts.

CONTINUED ON NEXT CARD

NNC

SPECIAL COLLECTIONS
SPINOZA

G-2-b
3573

Alte und neue Schwarm-Geister-Bruth ... 1702. (Card 2)

Part [2] has title: Quäcker-Greuel, das ist: Abscheuliche ... Irthum der neuen Schwermer ... 1702.
Includes a reference to Spinoza (p. [14])

NNC

SPECIAL COLLECTIONS
SPINOZA

G-2-b
3574

Anabaptisticum et enthusiasticum Pantheon und geistliches Lüst-Hauss, wider die alten Quacker, und neuen Frey-Geister, welche die Kirche Gottes zeithero verunruhiget, und bestürmet ... mit vielen zur Sache dienlichen und nützlichen Kupffern, bloss zu Gottes Ehre und Erhaltung seiner Christlichen Kirchen, auch den Geistlichen, Weltlichen und Hausstande zur Nachricht, Nutz und besten zusammen getragen und auffgerichtet. 1702.
18 p. 35cm. (In Historia von denen Wider Tauffern. [1705?])

NNC

SPECIAL COLLECTIONS
SPINOZA

G-2-b
3575

Eenige aanmerkingen voor den Philosopherenden boer, met eenige vragen aan den zelven. Voorgestelt door die gene, diemen spots-gewijse noemt Quakers. Tot Rotterdam, Gedrukt by Pieter van Wijnbrugge, 1676.
1 p. l., 13 p. 20cm.

Imperfect copy: p. 11-12 lacking.
Bound with Kuyper, Frans. Den philosopherenden boer, eerste deel. 1677.

NNC

Erschröckliche Brüderschafft der alten und neuen Wiedertäuffer, Quäcker, Schwärmer und Frey-Geister, mit denen Heil- und Gottlosen Juden. Darinnen bezeiget wird, wie diese Gesellschafft sich sehr wohl zusamen vergleichen, so wohl in Lehr, als auch Leben und Wandel einerley Sinnes und Vorhabens sind, deshalben sich alle fromme Christen, vor ihnen, als für dem Teuffel selbst zu hüten ... 1702.

24 p. 35cm. (In Historia von denen Wider Tauffern. [1705?])

Fürstellung vier neuer Welt-Weisen, nahmentlich, I. Renati Des Cartes, II. Thomae Hobbes, III. Benedicti Spinosa, IV. Balthasar Beckers, nach ihrem Leben und fürnehmsten Irrthümern. 1702.

16 p. 35cm. (In Historia von denen Wider Tauffern. [1705?])

Historia von denen Wider Tauffern. [Cöthen? 1705?]

15 pts. in 1 v. illus., ports. 35cm.

By Zacharias Theobald and others. Cf. Holzmann.

"A reissue, in one volume and with a collective title-page, of various tracts against the Anabaptists and Quakers, published at Cöthen and Frankfort in 1701 and 1702."--Brit. Mus. cat., v. 4, 1932, col. 296.

CONTINUED ON NEXT CARD

Historia von denen Wider Tauffern. [1705?]
(Card 2)

Contents.--Anabaptisticum et enthusiasticum Pantheon und geistliches Lust-Hauss.--Der alten und neuen Schwärmer [von Z. Theobald]--Historia fanaticorum.--Des Qvedlinburgischen Ertz-Schwermers ... Heinrich Kratzensteins Geschichte.--Königliche, chur- und fürstliche Edicta ... wider die neuen einschleichenden Schwärmer.--Alte und neue Schwarm-Geister-

Continued on Next Card

Historia von denen Wider Tauffern. [1705?]
(Card 3)

Bruth, und Quäcker-Greuel (2 parts)--Der verschmitzte Welt-Mann und scheinheilige Tyranne in Engelland, Olivier Cromwel.--Fürstellung vier neuer Welt-Weisen.--Die Geschichte von dem grossen Betrieger ... Sabatai-Sevi von Smirna.--Novus in Belgio Judaeorum rex Oliger Paulli.--Greuel der falschen Messien, von J. C. Müller.--Erschröckliche Brüderschafft der

Continued on Next Card

Historia von denen Wider Tauffern. [1705?]
(Card 4)

alten und neuen Wiedertäuffer.--Die Herrlichkeit Jesu Christi, von Friedrich Ragstadt von Weille.--Probatio spiritus et doctrinae democriti, von H. G. Neuss.

Includes a section on Spinoza ([pt. 9] p. 9-11) and other references to him in [pts. 2 and 6] and a portrait of him in [pt. 2]

Königliche, chur- und fürstliche Edicta, und Verordnungen, wider die neuen einschleichenden Schwärmer, auch wie bey denen hin und wieder sich ereigenden Neuerungen, und falschen Meynungen, der Enthusiasten, Chiliasten, und Quacker ... desgleichen denen Verächtern des öffentlichen Gottesdienstes ... Anjetzo männiglichen zur Warnung, und Nachricht dargestellet, und zum Druck befördert. Cöthen, Gedruckt bey Wilhelm Andreas Meyern, 1701.

[8], 5-44 p. ports. 35cm. (In Historia von denen Wider Tauffern. [1705?])

Knight, Rachel, 1878-1921.

The founder of Quakerism; a psychological study of the mysticism of George Fox, by Rachel Knight, PH. D. London, The Swarthmore press ld. [1922]

280 p. front., port., diagrs. 22½cm.

"Written as a thesis for the degree of doctor of philosophy at the University of Iowa [1919]."
Bibliography: p. 278-280.
"Introductory note" on the author, by A. Barratt Brown: p. 5-6.

Includes a section on Spinoza (p. 245-249)

1. Fox, George, 1624-1691.

22-7569

Library of Congress BX7795.F7K5
[a35c1]

Kratzenstein, Heinrich

Des Qvedlinburgischen Ertz-Schwermers und Qvaker-Propheten, Heinrich Kratzensteins Geschichte. Aus seinen eigenhändigen Brieffen und Schrifften, auch andern gewissen Uhrkunden zusammen gezogen ... Dem ist beygefüget Die Rede über dessen Absterben, so ihm seine lieben Mit-Brüder ... und Anführer zum unsterblichen Ehren-Gedächtnis verfertiget ... Zum Druck befördert im Jahr Christi 1701.

84 p. port. 35cm. (In Historia von denen Wider Tauffern. [1705?])

Kuyper, Frans, 1629-ca. 1692.

De diepten des Satans, of Geheymenissen der atheisterij, ontdekt en vernielt. Waar in der Godverzaakers, en der vyanden van de Christelijke Godsdienst, allergeheymste teegenwerpingen en bewijzen ... naaktelijk worden verklaart en weerleyd. Beneffens een nieuw richtsnoer, om de verschillen in de Godsdienst te beflechten, en de H. Schrift te verklaaren. Dienende met eenen tot onderrechting van de geenen, diemen heedensdaags noemt Kartezianen en Quaakers. By form van saamenspraak, tusschen een

CONTINUED ON NEXT CARD

SPECIAL COLLECTIONS
SPINOZA G-2-b 3586

Kuyper, Frans, 1629-ca. 1692. De diepten des Satans. 1677. (Card 2)

filosoof, Quaaker en boer. Zijnde een vervolg, of darde deel, van de Filosofeerende boer, de filosofie betreffende, en het by hem aangeweezene, volkoomender verhandelende en verklaarende; gelijk he tweede deel de Quaakerij, naaktelijk heeft ontdekt, en ontbloot. Door Frans Kuyper ... Tot Rotterdam, By Isaak Naeranus, 1677.
[8], 184, [8] p. 20cm.

CONTINUED ON NEXT CARD

NNC

SPECIAL COLLECTIONS
SPINOZA G-2-b 3587

[Kuyper, Frans] 1629-ca. 1692.
Den philosopherender boer, handelende van de dwalingen der hedendaagse Christenen, philosophen, Cartesianer en Quaakers, &c. In verscheyden onvermeynde zaaken begrepen in een samenspraak tusschen een boer, philosooph en Quaker. Door S. I. B. Gedrukt voor de Cartesianen en Quakers om de oogen te openen, 1676.
51 p. 20cm.

NNC

SPECIAL COLLECTIONS
SPINOZA G-2-b 3588

[Kuyper, Frans] 1629-ca. 1692.
Den philosopherenden boer, eerste deel. Handelende van de dwalingen der hedensdaagse Christenen, philosophen, Cartesianen en Quaakers, &c. In verscheyden onvermeynde zaaken. Begrepen in een samenspraak, tusschen een boer, philosooph en Quaker. Door S. I. B. De tweeden druk, merkelijk verbetert en vermeerdet, ook met een korte verhandeling, hoe de Christenen, in haar Christelijke vergaaderingen, haar zelfs behooren te draagen. Gedrukt voor de Cartesianen en Quakers, 1677.
56 p. 20cm.

NNC

SPECIAL COLLECTIONS
SPINOZA G-2-b 3589

Kuyper, Frans, 1629-ca. 1692.
Tweede deel of vervolg van de Philosopheerende boer. In welk de geheyme gevoelens der Quaakers, uyt haar eygen schriften, en met haar eygen woorden, ontdekt worden, in meest al de 28 vraagen, in de Philosopheerende boer aan de Quaakers voorgestelt. Tot beantwoording van der Quaakers aanmerkingen, voor den Philosopheerende boer. Door Frans Kuyper. Tot Rotterdam, By Isaak Naeranus, 1676.
[8], 43 p. 20cm.

CONTINUED ON NEXT CARD

NNC

SPECIAL COLLECTIONS
SPINOZA G-2-b 3590

Kuyper, Frans, 1629-ca. 1692. Tweede deel of vervolg van de Philosopheerende boer. 1676. (Card 2)

Bound with the author's Den philosopherenden boer, eerste deel. 1677.

SPECIAL COLLECTIONS
SPINOZA G-2-b 3591

Müller, Johann Christoph
Greuel der falschen Messien, wie auch, Schatz-Kammer des wahren Messiâe Jseu Christi. Das ist: Eine ziemliche Lista der jenigen falschen Messien, so von Anfang der Welt, biss auff diese jetzige Zeit haben können in Erfahrung gebracht werden ... Denen Jüden zur Erkäntnis und Reue, allen rechtschaffenen Christen aber zum Trost ans Licht gegeben, von Johann Christoph Müllern ... 1702.
48 p. plate. 35cm. (In Historia von denen Wider Tauffern. [1705?])

NNC

SPECIAL COLLECTIONS
SPINOZA G-2-b 3592

Novus in Belgio Judâeorum rex Oliger Paulli, multis editis monumentis literariis clarus. Das ist Der neue Juden-König, Oliger Paulli, in Niederland, durch viele heraus gegebene Schrifften bekannt. 1702.
38 p. 35cm. (In Historia von denen Wider Tauffern. [1705?])

1. Pauli, Oliger, b. 1644.

NNC

SPECIAL COLLECTIONS
SPINOZA G-2-b 3593

[Theobald, Zacharias] 1584-1627.
Der alten und neuen Schwärmer, Widertäuferischer Geist, das ist, glaubwürdiger, und historischer Bericht, was Jammer ... die alten Schwärmer und Widertäuffer, gestifftet und angerichtet haben; daraus zu schliessen, was man von denen jetziger Zeit, aufs neue einschleichenden Schwärmern ... zugewarten habe ... Denen beygefüget sind: Hoher Potentaten, Scharffe ... Befehle, wider solche Ketzer, und Schwärmer, desgleichen einige über sie, ihre

CONTINUED ON NEXT CARD

NNC

SPECIAL COLLECTIONS
SPINOZA G-2-b 3594

[Theobald, Zacharias] 1584-1627. Der alten und neuen Schwärmer ... 1701. (Card 2)

Lehre ... von Hoch-löblichen Universitäten, als Marburg ... gestellte Bedencken, und eingehohlte Urtheile ... Cöthen, Gedruckt bey W. A. Meyern, 1701.
[12], 186 p. plates, ports. 35cm. (In Historia von denen Wider Tauffern. [1705?])

Dedication signed: M. Zacharias Theobaldus.
Includes references to Spinoza and a portrait of him.

NNC

SPECIAL COLLECTIONS
SPINOZA G-2-b 3595

Der verschmitzte Welt-Mann und scheinheilige Tyranne in Engelland, Olivier Cromwel. Nebenst zween seiner geheimesten Räthe und Creaturen Hugo Petersen und John Coocken. Samt einem Anhange von Johann Labadie. 1702.
44 p. ports. 35cm. (In Historia von denen Wider Tauffern. [1705?])

NNC

Weile, Friedrich Ragstat von
Die Herrlichkeit Jesu Christi des wahren Messiâe und Heyland der Welt ... Kräfftiglich wieder die Juden ... bewiesen und verthädiget, von Friedrich Ragstadt von Weille ... Wegen der ungemeinen Fürtreffligkeit aus dem Holländischen ins Hochdeutsche übergesetzet von Johann Christoph Müllern ... 1702.
[8], 28 p. 35cm. (In Historia von donen Wider Tauffern. [1705?])

G-2-c
JEWISH

Akademie für die Wissenschaft des Judentums. Forschungs-Institut.
Bericht des wissenschaftlichen Vorstands. [1925]
[43]-47 p. 26cm.

From Korrespondenzblatt des Vereins zur Gründung und Erhaltung einer Akademie für die Wissenschaft des Judentums, 6. Jahrgang, 1925.
Includes references to Spinoza (p. 46)

Abbott, George Frederick.
Israel in Europe, by G. F. Abbott ... London, Macmillan and co., limited; New York, The Macmillan company, 1907.
xix, 538 p. fold. map. 22½ cm.
"Authorities": p. [xi]-xiv.
Includes a section on Spinoza (p. 251-254) and other references to him.

1. Jews in Europe. 2. Jews—Political and social conditions. 3. Jews—Hist. I. Title.

Akademie für die Wissenschaft des Judentums. Forschungs-Institut.
Bericht des wissenschaftlichen Vorstandes. [1929]
[38]-40 p. 26cm.

From Korrespondenzblatt des Vereins zur Gründung und Erhaltung einer Akademie für die Wissenschaft des Judentums, 10. Jahrgang, 1929.
Includes a reference to Spinoza (p. 39)

Adams, Henry Cadwallader, 1817-1899.
The history of the Jews from the war with Rome to the present time. London, The Religious Tract Society, 1887.
412 p.

Includes a section on Spinoza (p. 295-298)

Alexander, Hartley Burr, 1873-1939.
The Hebrew contribution to the Americanism of the future; the first annual Zunz Memorial Lecture, Dec. 28, 1919. [1920]
1-10, 65-74 p.

In The Menorah journal, v. 6, 1920.
Includes a reference to Spinoza (p. 71-72)

Adams, Hannah, 1755-1832.
Die Geschichte der Juden von der Zerstörung Jerusalems an bis auf die gegenwärtigen Zeiten. Aus dem Englischen übersetzt. Leipzig, In der Baumgärtnerschen Buchhandlung, 1819-20.
2 v. in 1. 21cm.

Publisher's lists included in paging at end of each volume.
Includes a section on Spinoza (v. 2, p. 155-157)

Alexander, J
The Jews: their past, present, and future: being a succinct history of God's ancient people in all ages; together with a brief account of the origin and formation of the Talmud. London, Partridge, 1870.
218 p.

Includes a reference to Spinoza (p. 189-190)

Adler, Felix, 1851-1933.
Two addresses delivered before the Society for Ethical Culture at Chickering Hall, December 19 and 26, 1880. [New York, 1881]
52 p. 22cm.

Includes a reference to Spinoza (p. 28) in address "The anti-Jewish agitation in Germany".

Altman, *Mrs.* Addie (Richman)
The story of Israel for children, glimpses of Jewish history, by Addie Richman Altman ... Unabridged school ed. New York, Bloch publishing company, 1916.
3 p. l., 5-133 p. 19cm.

Includes a reference to Spinoza (p. 112)

1. Jews—History, Juvenile. I. Title.

Azevedo, João Lucio d'.
... Historia dos christãos novos portugueses. Lisboa, Livraria clássica editora de A. M. Teixeira, 1921.
x, 518 p., 2 l. 23cm.

At head of title: J. Lucio d'Azevedo.
On cover: Lisboa, 1922.
Presentation copy to Carl Gebhardt, with the author's inscription and signature.

Balaban, Majer, 1877-1943.
Historja i literatura zydowska. Lwów, 1920-25.
v. 3

Includes a section on Spinoza with his portrait (p. 301-305)

Basnage, Jacques, *sieur de Beauval,* **1653-1723.**
The history of the Jews, from Jesus Christ to the present time: containing their antiquities, their religion, their rites, the dispersion of the ten tribes in the East and the persecutions this nation has suffer'd in the West. Being a supplement and continuation of the History of Josephus. Written in French by Mr. Basnage. Translated into English by Tho. Taylor, A. M. London, Printed for T. Bever and B. Lintot [etc.] 1708.
x p., 3 l., 759, [1] p. front. 40cm.

Title in red and black.
Includes a section on Spinoza (p. 741-743)
1. Jews—Hist. 2. Jews—Religion. I. Taylor, Thomas, of Magdalen college, Oxford, tr.

Basnage, Jacques, sieur de Beauval, 1653-1723.
Histoire des Juifs, depuis Jesus-Christ jusqu'a present. Pour servir de continuation a l'Histoire de Joseph. Nouvelle édition augmentée. La Haye, H. Scheurleer, 1716.
9 v. in 15. plates, tables. 17 cm.

Includes a chapter "Véritable origine du spinosisme" (v. 7, p. 128-158)

Berk, Matthew A
The history of the Jews from the Babylonian captivity to the present time ... Boston, 1847.
476 p. plates.

Includes a section on Spinoza (p. 287-288)

Berk, Matthew A
The history of the Jews, from the taking of Jerusalem by Titus, to the present time. Boston, Berk, 1846.

Includes a section on Spinoza (p. 204-205)

Bernstein, Simon Gerson, 1884-
בחזון הדורות; מסות ורשומות, מאת
ש. ברנשטיין. ניו-יורק, הוצאת-הספרים
של בלוך, תרפ"ח.
[New York, Bloch Publishing Company] 1928.
233 p. 24cm.

Title transliterated: Baḥăzōn ha-dōrōth.
Includes references to Spinoza (p. 41)

Bernstein, Simon Gerson, 1884-
"ראשונים" שלא מדעת; דמדומי הרעי-
ון הלאומי הישראלי בהשקפת-עולמם של
אוריאל אקוסטה וברוך שפינוזה, מאת
שמעון ברנשטיין. ניו-יורק, 1940.
[New York, 1940]
12 p. 23cm.

Title transliterated: "Rīshōnīm" shellō midda'ath.
Reprinted from Biṣṣārōn, no. 4, 1940.

Bildersee, Adele, 1883-
Jewish post-Biblical history through great personalities from Jochanan ben Zakkai through Moses Mendelssohn, by Adele Bildersee ... Cincinnati, The Union of American Hebrew congregations, 1918.
3 p. l., ix-xi p., 1 l., 283 p. front. (double map) illus. (incl. ports.) 20cm.
Bibliography: p. 271-272.
Includes material on Spinoza.

1. Jews—Biog. 2. Jews—Hist.—A. D. 70-1789. I. Title.

Blogg, Solomon Ephraim, d. 1858.
Binyan shelomoh. Aedificium Salomonis ... eine vollständige Geschichte der hebräischen Sprache, des Thalmuds und vieler merkwürdiger Begebenheiten des Altertums. Hannover, Telgener, 1831.
xv, 143 p. 23 cm.

Includes a reference to Spinoza (p. 110)

NNJ G-2-c 3616

Blüher, Hans, 1888-
Secessio Judaica. Philosophische Grundlegung der historischen Situation des Judentums und der antisemitischen Bewegung. Berlin, Weisse Ritter Verlag, 1922.
66 p.

Includes references to Spinoza (p. 22, 24)

G-2-c 3617

Box, George Herbert, 1869-
Hebrew studies in the reformation period and after: their place and influence. [1927]
315-375 p.

From Bevan, Edwyn Robert. The legacy of Israel.
Includes a section on Spinoza (p. 366-368)

NNC

G-2-c 3618

Brann, Marcus, 1849-1920.
Geschichte der Juden und ihrer Literatur. 3. Ausg. Breslau, Marcus, 1910-1913.
3 v.

Includes a section on Spinoza (v. 3, p. 63-64)

NN

G-2-c 3619

Brown, Bernard Joseph.
From Pharaoh to Hitler, "What is a Jew?" [By] Bernard J. Brown ... Chicago, Consolidated book publishers, inc. [1933]
xii p., 1 l., 217 p. incl. front. plates, port. 22½ cm.
"This first edition ... consists of two thousand copies."
Includes a section on Spinoza (p. 123-125)

1. Jewish question. 2. Jews—Political and social conditions. 3. Judaism. 4. Jews. I. Title.

NN DS141.B865 296 33—11468
Library of Congress [a55d½]

G-2-c 3620

Brown, Brian, 1881- *ed.*
The wisdom of the Hebrews; their philosophy and religious teachings, their sayings and proverbs, as taken from the Talmud, the lives of the rabbis, and the writings of Josephus, Spinoza, and the most learned of the Hebrews of the past, introduction by Maurice H. Farbridge ... edited with a preface, by Brian Brown. New York, Brentano's [°1925]
xxii p., 1 l., 280, [1] p. front., ports. 21cm.
"Bibliography and sources": p. [281]

1. Jews—Civilization. 2. Hebrew literature—Translations into English. 3. English literature—Translations from Hebrew. I. Title.

NNUT 25—9536
Library of Congress DS112.B7
[44j1]

G-2-c 3621

Buber, Martin, 1878-
Der Chassidismus als Antwort auf Spinoza. [1932]
p. 452.

In Jüdische Rundschau, Jahrgang 37, 1932.

NN

SPECIAL COLLECTIONS SPINOZA G-2-c 3622

Buber, Martin, 1878-
... Deutung des chassidismus; drei versuche. Berlin, Schocken verlag, 1935.
98 p., 1 l. 19½cm. (*Half-title:* Bücherei des Schocken verlags. [43])
Includes chapter on Spinoza.

1. Hasidism. I. Title.

37-5883
Library of Congress BM198.B78
[2] 296

SPECIAL COLLECTIONS SPINOZA G-2-c 3623

Buber, Martin, 1878-
Die chassidischen Bücher. Hellerau, J. Hegner, 1928.
xxxi, 717 p. 20cm.

Includes references to Spinoza.

SPECIAL COLLECTIONS SPINOZA G-2-c 3624

Buddeus, Johann Franz, 1667-1729.
Io. Francisci Bvddei P. P. Introdvctio ad historiam philosophiae Ebraeorvm. Accedit dissertatio de haeresi Valentiniana ... Halae Saxonvm, Typis & impensis Ophanotroph Glavcha-Halensis, 1702.
[16], 594 (i.e. 564), [26] p. 18cm.

SPECIAL COLLECTIONS SPINOZA G-2-c 3625

Buddeus, Johann Franz, 1667-1729.
Io. Francisci Bvddei ... Isagoge historico-theologica ad theologiam vniversam singvlasqve eivs partes. Lipsiae, Ex officina Thomae Fritschii, 1727.
2 v. ([14], 1844, [104] p.) illus. 22cm.

Includes references to Spinoza.

Cohen, Hermann, 1842-1918.
Hermann Cohens Jüdische Schriften. Mit einer Einleitung von Franz Rosenzweig hrsg. von Bruno Strauss. Berlin, Schwetschke, 1924.
3 v. port. 24cm. (Veröffentlichungen der Akademie für die Wissenschaft des Judentums)

Each vol. has special t.-p. also.
Includes an essay on Spinoza.
Contents.--1. Bd. Ethische und religiöse Grundfragen.--2. Bd. Zur jüdischen Zeitgeschichte.--3. Bd. Zur jüdischen Religionsphilosophie und ihrer Geschichte.

Cohen, Hermann, 1842-1918.
Die religiösen Bewegungen der Gegenwart; ein Vortrag. Leipzig, G. Fock, 1914.
31 p. 24cm. (Schriften hrsg. von der Gesellschaft zur Förderung der Wissenschaft des Judentums ₍18₎)

Includes references to Spinoza.

Costa, Isaac da, 1788-1860.
Israel and the gentiles; contributions to the history of the Jews from the earliest times to the present day. London, Nisbet, 1850.
xii, 628 p. 21cm.

Translated by Mary J. Kennedy.
Includes material on Spinoza (p. 425-430)

Costa, Isaac da, 1798-1860.
Israel en de volken; overzicht van de geschiedenis der Joden tot op onzen tijd, door Mr. Isaac da Costa. 2. druk. Met een voorrede van Dr. A. W. Bronsveld. Haarlem, A. C. Kruseman, 1873.
xvi, 550 p. 20cm.

Includes a section on Spinoza (p. 277-280)

Costa, Isaac da, 1798-1860.
Israel und die Völker. Eine Uebersicht der Geschichte der Juden bis auf unsere Zeit. Aus dem Holländischen von einer Freundin des göttlichen Wortes ins Deutsche übertragen und zum Drucke befördert von K. Mann. Frankfurt a. M., H. L. Brönner, 1855.
xvi, 446 p. 21cm.

Error in paging: p. 304 numbered 204.
Includes a section on Spinoza (p. 204 ₍i.e. 304₎-307)

The Dearborn independent.
The international Jew, the world's foremost problem, being a reprint of a series of articles appearing in the Dearborn independent from May 22 to October 2, 1920. ₍Dearborn, Mich., The Dearborn publishing co.₎ 1920.
1 p. l., ₍5₎-235 p. 19 cm.
Includes a reference to Spinoza (p. 164-165)

1. Jewish question. 2. "Protocols of the wise men of Zion." I. Title.

DeCasseres, Benjamin, 1873-
Spinoza against the rabbis, by Benjamin DeCasseres. New York city, B. DeCasseres at the Blackstone publishers ₍°1937₎
3 p. l., ₍9₎-58 p. 19½cm.
On cover: Book no. 14.

1. Spinoza, Benedictus de, 1632-1677.

De Solla, Jacob Mendes.
The Jewish student's companion. First part: Post Biblical history. Second part: Explanation of Mosaic commands. By J. Mendes De Solla ... New York, Hebrew book union, 1880.
x, 241 p. 19 cm.

References to Spinoza (p. 129-131) included in section "Eminent scholars of Holland".

1. Jews—Hist. 2. Jewish law. I. Title.

Dessauer, Emil
Die jüdische Geschichte im Zeitbilde grosser Kulturstufen. Für höhere Schulen und zur Selbstbelehrung dargestellt. Frankfurt am Main, J. Kauffmann, 1905.
v, 104 p.

Includes a reference to Spinoza (p. 76-77)

Dessauer, Julius Heinrich
Geschichte der Israeliten, mit besonderer Berücksichtigung der Kulturgeschichte derselben, von Alexander dem Grossen bis auf gegenwärtige Zeit, nach den besten Vorhandenenquellen bearbeitet. Erlangen, Palm, 1846.
xxi, 593 p. port. 21 cm.

Includes references to Spinoza (p. 457-461)

Deutsch, Gotthard, 1859-1921.
Does reform lead to apostacy? A rejoinder to the Chief Rabbi. ⌊1914⌋
p. 24.

In Jewish chronicle, London, June 26, 1914.
Includes a reference to Spinoza.

Deutsch, Gotthard, 1859-1921.
Dogging Moses and damning orthodoxy. ⌊1914⌋
p. 4.

In American Israelite, v. 60, no. 44, 1914.
A letter to the editor, including a reference to Spinoza.

Deutsch, Gotthard, 1859-1921.
The share of the Jewish people in the culture of the various nations and ages. ⌊1894⌋
175-192 p.

From Judaism at the World's Parliament of Religions. Cincinnati, R. Clarke, 1894.
Includes a reference to Spinoza (p. 187-188)

Deyling, Salomon, 1677-1755.
Observationum sacrarum pars prima ⌊-tertia⌋ in qua multa scripturae Veteris ac Novi Testamenti dubia vexata solvuntur, loca difficiliora ex antiquitate, et variae doctrinae apparatu, illustrantur, atque ab audaci recentiorum criticorum depravatione solide vindicantur ... Editio tertia emendatior, ac tertia parte auctior. Lipsiae, Sumptibus Haeredum F. Lanckisii, 1735-57.
3 v.
Includes references to Spinoza.

Diesendruck, Zevi, 1890-1940.
Saadya's formulation of the time-argument for creation. ⌊1935⌋
cover-title, 145-158 p. 24cm.

"Reprinted from Jewish studies in memory of George A. Kohut, New York, 1935."
Presentation copy to A. S. Oko, with the author's inscription and signature.
Includes references to Spinoza.
Bibliographical footnotes.

Drachman, Bernard, 1861-1945.
Should Jews honor Spinoza? Rabbi questions propriety of tercentenary observance: an ʻorthodox viewpoint. ⌊1932⌋
p. 34, 40. 33cm.

From American Hebrew and Jewish tribune, v. 132, no. 2, November 25, 1932.
Bound with Browne, Lewis. Baruch Spinoza. ⌊1932⌋

Farbridge, Maurice Harry, 1896-
The renewal of Judaism. London, E. Goldston, 1932.
320 p. 23 cm.

Includes a reference to Spinoza (p. 146-147)

Feiwelsohn, Elijah Meir
נצח ישראל; מאמרים על אודות דב־
רים הקומדים ברומו של עמנו, מאת
אליהו מאיר פייוולזאהן. ווארשא,
הוצ' חובבי נצח ישראל, תרע"ד.
⌊Warsaw, 1914⌋
354 p. 23cm.

Title transliterated: Neṣaḥ Yiśrāʾēl.
Includes references to Spinoza (p. 63-64)

Fichman, Jacob, 1881-1958.

דמות שפינוזה. ⌊1929⌋
621-622 p.

Title transliterated: Demuth Shpinozah.
In ha-Tekufah, v. 25, 1929.

Fromer, Jakob, 1865-
Du ghetto à la culture moderne; histoire d'une vie. Traduit de l'allemand par Louis de Chauvigny. Paris, J. Povolozky ⌊192-⌋
133 p. 20cm.

On cover: 2e édition.
Includes references to Spinoza.

Fromer, Jakob, 1865–
... Der Talmud; geschichte, wesen und zukunft. Berlin, P. Cassirer, 1920.
viii, 348 p. 23cm.
"Anhang: Monographische notizen zur geschichte des Talmud alphabetisch geordnet": p. [163]–348.
Contains bibliographies.
References to Spinoza included in Chapter XII (p. 145-157)

1. Talmud.
22—813
Library of Congress BM504.F7
[36b1]

Fuchs, Hugo, 1878–
Lehrbuch der jüdischen Geschichte. Frankfurt am Main, J. Kauffmann, 1922.
v, 272 p. 22cm.

Includes a section on Spinoza (p. 157-159)

Fuenn, Samuel Joseph, 1818-1890.
כנסת ישראל; זכרונות לתולדות גדולי ישראל הנודעים לשם בתורתם, בחכמתם, ובמעשיהם, מימות הגאונים עד הדור הזה, מאת שמואל יוסף בר״א פין ... בחלק ראשון ווארשא, בדפוס א. בוימריטער וג. גאנשאר, הרמ״ז. [Warsaw, 1886]
704 p. 23cm.

Title transliterated: Kĕnęsęth Yiśrā'ēl.
No more published.

Continued on Next Card
NNC

Fuenn, Samuel Joseph, 1818-1890. כנסת ישראל. [1886] (Card 2)

Added title in Russian.
Includes article on Spinoza (p. 198-201)
Contents.-- חלק א׳: א׳–י׳.

NNC

Feuer, Abraham
ספר זכרון אברהם ... במאתה אברהם בן שלמה מאיר פייער.
New York, Accomodating Press [1924]
116 p. port. 24cm.

Title transliterated: Sefer Zikhron Abhraham.
Includes essay on Spinoza (p. 16-18)

Gaster, Moses, 1856–1939.
... History of the Ancient synagogue of the Spanish and Portuguese Jews, the cathedral synagogue of the Jews in England, situate in Bevis Marks. A memorial volume written specially to celebrate the two-hundredth anniversary of its inauguration, 1701–1901. With illustrations and facsimiles of deeds and documents. By the Rev. the Haham, Dr. Moses Gaster ... London, 5661—1901.
3 p. l., 201 p. illus. (incl. facsims.) port., fold. geneal. tab. 28cm.
At head of title: קהל קדוש ספרדים שער השמים יצ״ו התס״א–התרס״א
Title vignette. Reference to Spinoza (p. 106)
"Not published. For presentation only."
1. London. Bevis Mark's synagogue. 2. Jews in London.
31—23606
Library of Congress BM295.B4G3
[a43b1] 296

[Gebhardt, Carl] 1881-1934.
Pieter Ballings Het licht op den kandelaar.
[Hagae Comitis, 1926]
187-192 p. 23cm.

Signed: C. G.
Cover-title: Dissertatio ex Chronici Spinozani tomo quarto separatim edita.
Includes references to Spinoza.

Geiger, Abraham, 1810–1874.
Abraham Geiger's Nachgelassene schriften. Hrsg. von Ludwig Geiger ... Berlin, L. Gerschel; [etc., etc.] 1875–78.
5 v. in 3. 22 cm.
The 5th vol. includes, with separate title-pages in German and in Hebrew: ... Nachgelassene schriften ... 5. bd., 1. abth.; Abhandlungen in hebräischer sprache, zusammengestellt von R. K. [Raphael Kirchheim] Berlin, 1877.
Includes references to Spinoza.

1. Judaism—Collected works. 2. Jews in Germany. 3. Jewish question. I. Geiger, Ludwig, 1848–1919, ed. II. Kirchheim, Raphael, 1804–1889.
BM45.G4 22—19200
Library of Congress [a55d½]

Goldblatt, David.
... Is the Jewish race pure? An examination of the evidence against and a statement of facts in its favor, by David Goldblatt ... New York, The Goldblatt publishing co. [°1933]
351, [1] p. illus. (incl. ports.) 21cm.
Bibliography: p. 343-346.
Includes a section on Spinoza (p. 278-281) and other references to him.

1. Jews. I. Title. II. Title: The Jewish race.
33-17413
NNJ Library of Congress GN547.G6
——— Copy 2.
Copyright A 63295 [2] [296] 572.892

Graetz, Heinrich, 1817-1891.
Volkstümliche Geschichte der Juden, in drei Bänden. 3. Bd. Von den massenhaften Zwangstaufen der Juden in Spanien bis in die Gegenwart. Leipzig, O. Leiner [1889]
808 p. port. 22cm.

Includes a chapter "Spinoza und Sabbatai Zewi" (p. 437-477)

Graetz, Heinrich, 1817-1891.
ספר דברי ימי ישראל (מיום היות ישראל לעם עד ימי הדור האחרון) מאת דר. צבי גראטץ, מתורגם בתוספות הערות והארות, חדושים ומלואים מאת שאול פינחס ראבינא־וויץ; עם הערות ומלואים מאת א. א. הרכבי. חלק שמיני, ספר ראשון (מן ימי התישבות יהודי ספרד באמשטרדם עד אחרית ימי התקו־פה הראשונה להתנועה השבתאית: שפ"נ־ת"מ) ווארשא, בדפוס שולדבערג ושותפו, תרנ"ט.

Graetz, Heinrich, 1817-1891. ספר דברי ימי ישראל. 1899. (Card 2)

[Warsaw] 1899.
x, 674 p.

Title transliterated: Sefer Dibhrē yĕmē Yiśrā'ēl.
Includes chapter on Spinoza: p. 193-228.

Graetz, Heinrich, 1817-1891.
ספר דברי ימי ישראל (מימי היותו לעם עד דורות העת החדשה) מאת ד"ר צבי גראטץ. מתורגם עברית בתוספות הערות והארות, חדושים ומלואים מאת שאול פינחס ראבינא־וויטץ, עם הערות ומלואים מאת א. א. הר־כבי. חלק שמיני, ספר שני, חוברת רביעית. בווארשא הוצאת אלכסנדר ז. כהן.
[Warsaw] 1900.
531-592 p. 23cm.

CONTINUED ON NEXT CARD

Graetz, Heinrich, 1871-1891. ספר דברי ימי ישראל. 1900. (Card 2)

Title transliterated: Sefer Dibhrē yĕmē Yiśrā'ēl.
Includes notes on Spinoza (p. 534-536)
Title-page in Hebrew and Russian; added t.-p. in German.

Graetz, Heinrich, 1817-1891.
די יודישע פאלקס-געשיכטע. [1901]
6 v.

Title transliterated: Di yudishe folks-geshikhte.
Includes a chapter on Spinoza (v. 3, p. 256-287)

Graetz, Heinrich, 1817-1891.
יודישע געשיכטע. צווייטע אויפלאגע.
Warsaw, 1913.
11 v.

Title transliterated: Yudishe geshikhte.
Includes a chapter on Spinoza (v. 7, p. 245-282)

Grinshpan, Avigdor
שיטת שפינוזה ותורת היהדות. ניו־יורק, תרצ"ג.
[1932]
51-52 p. 32cm.

Title transliterated: Shiṭṭath Shpīnōzā ...
From ha-Doar, vol. XIII, no. 4, Nov. 25, 1932.
With Goldberg, Abraham. Bārūkh Shpīnōza. [1932]

Grunsky, Hans Alfred, 1902-
Baruch Spinoza. [Hamburg, Hanseatische Verlagsanstalt, 1937]
[88]-115 p. 25cm.

From Forschungen zur Judenfrage, Bd. 2, 1937.
Bibliographical footnotes.

Grunwald, Max, 1871-
Das Judentum bei Oswald Spengler., Berlin, Philo-Verlag u. Buchhandlung, 1924.
46 p. 24cm.

Includes a section on Spinoza (p. 24-26)
Original paper covers bound in.

Grunwald, Max, 1871-
Spinoza - Jude? 1894.
[121]-125 p. 23cm.

From Populär-wissenschaftliche Monatsblätter zur Belehrung über das Judentum für Gebildete aller Konfessionen. 14. Jahrgang, Nummer 6, 1. Juni 1894.

1. Spinoza, Benedictus de, 1632-1677.

Hagani, Baruch, 1885-
L'émancipation des Juifs. Avec une préface de Charles Guignebert. Paris, Rieder, 1928.
270 p. (Judaïsme, études pub. sous la direction de P.-L. Couchoud. 8)

Includes a reference to Spinoza (p. 81-82)

Herford, Robert Travers, 1860-
Die Pharisäer. Autorisierte Übersetzung aus dem Englischen von Walter Fischel. Leipzig, G. Engel, 1928.
296 p. 23cm.

Includes a reference to Spinoza (p. 142)
Bibliographical footnotes.

Harper's weekly.
Zionism's crisis. ₍1914₎
p. 289

In Harper's weekly, v. 59, 1914.
An editorial including a reference to Spinoza.

Hirsch, Emil Gustav, 1852-1923.
Some modern problems and their bearing on Judaism. Chicago, Reform Advocate ₍1903₎
78 p.

Includes a reference to Spinozism (p. 35)

Hauser, Otto, 1876-
Geschichte des Judentums. Weimar, A. Duncker Verlag, 1921.
vii, 535 p. 24cm.

Includes references to Spinoza.

Holberg, Ludvig, baron, 1684-1754.
Juedische Geschichte ... Aus dem Dänischen ins Deutsche übersetzt von G. A. Dethardinq. Altona, Gebrüdere Korte, 1747.
2 v. port.

Includes "Geschichte des Spinoza" (v. 2, p. 681-683)

Hedge, Frederic Henry, 1805-1890.
The primeval world of Hebrew tradition. 2d ed. Boston, Roberts, 1872.
283 p.

Includes a reference to Spinoza (p. 276)

Hosmer, James Kendall, 1834-1927.
... The story of the Jews, ancient, mediæval, and modern; by James K. Hosmer ... New York and London, G. P. Putnam's sons, 1887.

xviii, ₍2₎, 381 p. front., illus., pl., 2 fold. maps. 20cm. (The story of the nations)

Later edition appeared under title: "The Jews, ancient, mediæval, and modern ..."

Includes a chapter referring chiefly to Spinoza (p. 215-231) and a portrait of him.
1. Jews—Hist.

Heman, Karl Friedrich, 1839-
Geschichte des jüdischen Volkes seit der Zerstörung Jerusalems. Stuttgart, Calwer Vereinsbuchhandlung, 1908.

Includes a section on Spinoza (p. 445-450)

Höxter, Julius, 1873-
Quellenbuch zur jüdischen Geschichte und Literatur. IV. Teil. Europäische Länder in der Neuzeit. Frankfurt am Main, J. Kauffmann, 1928.
vii, 169 p. 22cm.

Includes references to Spinoza.

[Huie, James A]
The history of the Jews, from the taking of Jerusalem by Titus, to the present time ... with an account of the various efforts made for their conversion. 2d American, from the 1st Edinburgh edition, greatly enlarged ... with a preface by William Jenks. Andover, Pub. by M. A. Berk, 1843.
395 p. 18 cm.

Includes a reference to Spinoza (p. 225-226)

Hulsius, Antonius, 1615-1685.
Non-ens Prae-Adamiticum, sive, Confutatio vani & Socinizantis cujusdam somnii, quo S. Scripturae praetextu incautiorious nuper imponere conatus est quidam anonymvs, fingens. Ante Adamum primum homines fuisse in mundo. Avtore Antonio Hvlsio. Lvgd. Batav., Apud Johannem Elsevirivm, 1656.
[12], 250 p. 13cm.

Printer's device on t.-p.

Iliowizi, Henry, 1850-1911.
Jewish dreams and realities contrasted with Islamitic and Christian claims. Philadelphia, 1890.
279 p.

[Jacobs, Joseph] 1854-1916.
The God of Israel: a history. [1879]
481-503 p.

In The Nineteenth century, v. 6, Sept. 1879.
Includes references to Spinoza.

Jacobs, Joseph, 1854-1916.
Jewish ideals, and other essays, by Joseph Jacobs ... London, D. Nutt; New York, Macmillan and co., 1896.
xviii p., 1 l., 242 p. incl. illus., tab. fold. plan. 22½cm.
"The following essays have appeared in various periodicals during the past eighteen years."—Pref.
"The Hagin family": geneal. tab., p. 185.
CONTENTS.—Jewish ideals.—The God of Israel: a history.—Mordecai: a protest against the critics.—Browning's theology.—The true, the only, and the complete solution of the Jewish question.—Jehuda Halévi, poet and pilgrim.—Jewish diffusion of folk-tales.—The London Jewry, 1290.—Little St. Hugh of Lincoln.—"Aaron, son of the devil."—Jewish history: its aims and methods.
1. Jews. 2. Jewish question. 3. Hagin family. I. Title.
Includes references to Spinoza.

Jäger, Johann Wolfgang, 1647-1720.
Historia ecclesiastica, cum parallelismo profanae, in qua Conclavia Pontificum Romanorum fidelitur aperiuntur, et sectae omnes recensentur ... Hamburgi, 1709-17.
2 v.

[Jamin, N] Heylsahme Ermahnungen zu den unbescheidenen Verehrern der seeligen Jungfrawen Mariae. 1689. (Card 2)

Bound with Wachter, Johann Georg. Der Spinozismud in Jüdenthumb. 1699.

Jews' College Literary Society.
Papers read before the Jews' College Literary Society during the session 1886-7. London, Office of the "Jewish chronicle", 1887.
193 p. 26cm.

"Reprinted from the 'Jewish chronicle'."
Includes essays "The influence of Judaism over ancient, mediaeval and modern philosophy: Philo, Ibn-Gebirol and Spinoza" by H. Behrend (p. [13]-27) and "Spinoza, his life and philosophy" by M. Friedländer (p. 163-177)

Josephus, Flavius
The Jewish history, from the creation of the world, to this present time. Being an abridgment of Roger L'Estrange's Josephus. With a continuation from the most authentick records ... London, S. Briscoe, R. Burrough & J. Baker, E. Curll & A. Collins, 1708.
v. 2.

Includes a reference to Spinoza.

Jost, Isaac Marcus, 1793-1860.
Geschichte des Judenthums und seiner Secten. Leipzig, Dörffling und Franke, 1857-59.
3 v. 22cm.

Includes a paragraph on Spinoza (v. 3, p. 201-202)

1. Spinoza, Benedictus de, 1632-1677.

Kagan, Solomon Robert, 1881-1955.
Researches in Hebrew literature. Spokane, Wash., M. N. Janton, 1929-30.
2 v. port. 23 cm.

Vol. 2 includes references to Spinoza.

Kamelhar, Jekuthiel
ספר דור דעה; ארבע תקופות גאוני בתראי בשנות ת"ק-ת"ר; סקירה כללית ופעולות נושאי דגל התורה, פרי עטו של הגאון ר' יקותיאל ארי' קאמעלהאר. פי-עטרקוב, בדפוס חנוך הענ'ך פאלמאן, הרצ"ה.
[Pietrkov, 1935]
239 p. 23cm.

Title transliterated: Sefe. Dōr dēʻā.
Includes references to Spinoza.

Kaufmann, M E
Gehört Spinoza zum Judentum? [Replik. 1908]
4-5 p.

In Die Wahrheit, Jahrgang 28, Nr. 8, 1908.

Kayserling, Meyer, 1829-1905.
Geschichte der Juden in Portugal. Von dr. M. Kayserling. Leipzig, O. Leiner, 1867.

xi, 367, [1] p. 20½cm. (*Added t.-p.:* Schriften hrsg. vom Institute zur förderung der israelitischen literatur ... 12. jahr: 1866-1867)
Added t.-p. lacking.
Includes references to Spinoza.

1. Jews in Portugal—Hist.

35—23381

Library of Congress DS135.P7K3
[40b1] 296.09469

Kirschstein, Arthur J.
The Jew; his contribution to modern civilization. Denver, The Western Jewish advocate, 1930.
v. 1. illus. 24 cm.

Includes a section on Spinoza (p. 21-23)

Kobler, Franz, 1882- comp.
Juden und judentum in deutschen briefen aus drei jahrhunderten; herausgegeben und erläuten von Franz Kobler. Wien, Im Saturn-verlag, 1935.

415, [1] p. 22cm.

CONTENTS.—Vorwort zur ersten auflage.—Vorwort zur zweiten auflage.—Einleitung.—I. t. Das ende des jüdischen mittelalters (1648-1750)—II. t. Aufklärung (1751-1790)—III. t. Geschlossene tore—offene salontüren (1790-1814)—IV. t. Vom Wiener zum Baseler kongress (1814-1897)—V. t. Krise der assimilation (1897-1922)—Nachwort.—Quellen- und literaturnachweis.—Verzeichnis der briefschreiber.

1. Jews in Germany. 2. German letters. I. Title.

A C 36-407 Revised

New York. Public library for Library of Congress DS135.G3K66
[r44c2]† 296

Kohut, Adolph, 1848-1917.
Berühmte israelitische männer und frauen in der kulturgeschichte der menschheit; lebens- und charakterbilder aus vergangenheit und gegenwart; ein handbuch für haus und familie. Mit zahlreichen porträts und sonstigen illustrationen; von dr. Adolph Kohut ... Leipzig-Reudnitz, A. H. Payne [1900-01]
2 v. front., illus., pl., port. 25½cm.
Includes a section on Spinoza.

1. Jews—Biog.

2—9028

Library of Congress DS115.K79
[a27c1]

Kohut, Adolph, 1848-1917.
Geschichte der deutschen Juden; ein hausbuch für die jüdische familie, von dr. Adolph Kohut. Illustriert von Th. Kutschmann. Berlin, Deutscher verlag (ges. m. b. h.) [1898-99]

808, [22], xviii p. col. front., illus., plates, ports., facsims. (part illum.) 26½cm.

Illuminated initials and borders.
Issued in 10 pts., 1898-99.
Includes a reference to Spinoza (p. 697)

1. Jews—Hist.—A. D. 70- 2. Jews in Germany. I. Kutschmann, Theodor, illus.

9—8742

Library of Congress DS135.G3K7
[43e1]

Kottek, H
Geschichte der Juden. Frankfurt a. M., Jüdisch-Literarische Gesellschaft, 1915.
ix, 457 p. 23cm.

Includes a chapter on Spinoza.

Krochmal, Abraham, 1823-1895.
אבן הראשה: ... ; ומשתי את עון הארץ נגד הפלסוף רבנו ברוך די שפינוזא ז"ל ביום אחד, כאשר עשה אחד מחסידי או"ה החכם הפלסוף האשכנזי הערדער ז"ל, מאת אב"ן הכהן קראכמאל, עם פתח דבר מאת פרץ בן משה סמאלענסקין. ווין, בדפוס יוזעף האלצוואַרטה, ה'תרל"א.
[Vienna, 1871]
67 p. 23cm.

Title transliterated: Ebhen ha-rōshā.

G-2-c
3696

Lamparter, Eduard, 1860–
Das judentum in seiner kultur- und religionsgeschichtlichen erscheinung, von Eduard Lamparter. Gotha, L. Klotz, 1928.
viii, 340 p. 23 cm.

Includes a section on Spinoza (p. 120-124)

1. Judaism. I. Title.

NNJ
DS113.L3 29—16795
Library of Congress ₍a52c½₎

G-2-c
3701

Magnus, Katie, lady, 1844-1924.
Outlines of Jewish history, from B. C. 586 to C. E. 1885 ... Revised by M. Friedländer. Republished for the Council of the Jewish war memorial. London, Myers, 1924.
xxiv, 343 p. port., maps, tables.

Includes a chapter on Spinoza.

NN

SPECIAL COLLECTIONS
SPINOZA
G-2-c
3697

Leimdörfer, David, 1851-1922.
Nachbiblische Geschichte für die israelitische Jugend. 4. verm. und verb. Aufl. Hamburg, Rothschild, Behrens, 1896.
121 p. 22cm.

Includes a reference to Spinoza (p. 82-83)

G-2-c
3702

Magnus, Katie, lady, 1844-1924.
Spinoza. ₍1903₎
p. 15.

In Jewish comment, v. 17, 1903.
Adapted from her Outlines of Jewish history.

NNJ

G-2-c
3698

Levinger, Elma (Ehrlich) 1887–
The story of the Jew for young people, by Elma Ehrlich Levinger ... and Rabbi Lee J. Levinger ... New York, Behrman's Jewish book shop, 1929.
ix, ₍1₎ p., 1 l., 13-302 p. illus. (incl. maps) diagrs. 20 cm.
Second edition, revised and enlarged.
Bibliography at end of each chapter.
Includes a section on Spinoza (p. 161-163)

1. Jews—History, Juvenile. I. Levinger, Lee Joseph, 1890– joint author.

DLC
DS118.L48 1929 29—5276
Library of Congress ₍57r36f½₎

G-2-c
3703

Magnus, Laurie, 1872-1933.
The Jews in the Christian era, from the first to the eighteenth century, and their contribution to its civilization. London, E. Benn ₍1929₎
432 p. 22 cm.

Includes a chapter on Spinoza (p. 330-363)

G-2-c
3699

Lewkowitz, Albert, 1883–
Das Judentum und die geistigen Strömungen der Neuzeit. II. Die Aufklärung. ₍1929₎
97-251 p.

From Festschrift zum 75jährigen Bestehen des Jüdisch-theologischen Seminars Fraenckelscher Stiftung, v. 1. Breslau, Marcus, 1929.
Includes references to Spinoza (p. 139-169)

G-2-c
3704

Malo, Charles, 1790-1871.
Histoire des Juifs, depuis la destruction de Jérusalem jusqu'à ce jour. Paris, Leroux, 1826.
viii, 548 p.

Includes a section on Spinoza (p. 396-398)

SPECIAL COLLECTIONS
SPINOZA
G-2-c
3700

1933Sp4
DM37
Magnus, Katie (Emanuel) lady, 1844-1924.
Outlines of Jewish history, from B. C. 586 to C. E. 1890. With three maps. By Lady Magnus. Revised by M. Friedländer, PH. D. Philadelphia, The Jewish publication society of America, 1890.
xxi, 388 p. front., 3 maps. 19cm. (Jewish publication society of America. ₍Publications₎)

Chapters 41-43 not written by Lady Magnus.
Includes a chapter on Spinoza.

SPECIAL COLLECTIONS
SPINOZA
G-2-c
3705

Marcus, Jacob Rader, 1896–
The Jew in the medieval world, a source book, 315-1791. Cincinnati, Sinai Press, 1938.
xxvi, 504 p. 24cm. ₍Jewish history source books₎

Chapter on Spinoza (p. 334-342) consists mainly of an English translation of Colerus' life of Spinoza.

G-2-c
3706

Margoshes, Joseph, 1866-1955.
ברוך שפינאָזאַ: דער אידישער פערפאָלגטער
פילאָזאָף (צו זיין געבורטס־טאָג). [1914]
p. 5.

Title transliterated: Barukh Shpinoza: der idisher ferfolgter filozof.
In Der Tog, New York, Nov. 24, 1914.

NNJ

G-2-c
3707

Maybaum, Siegmund, 1844-1919.
Die Methodik des jüdischen Religionsunterrichtes. Breslau, M. & H. Marcus, 1896.
xii, 126 p.

Includes a reference to Spinoza (p. 44)

NNJ

G-2-c
3708

Meisels, Samuel
Judenköpfe. Wien, Verlag Die Neuzeit, 1926.
271 p. 21cm.

Includes a chapter on Spinoza.

G-2-c
3709

Melamed, Samuel Max, 1885-1938.
Psychologie des jüdischen Geistes; zur Völker- und Kulturpsychologie. 2., verb. und verm. Aufl. Berlin, C. A. Schwetschke & Sohn, 1921.
xv, 222 p. 23cm.

Includes a chapter on Spinoza (p. 216-222)

1. Spinoza, Benedictus de, 1632-1677.

G-2-c
3710

Melamed, Samuel Max, 1885-
Psychologie des jüdischen Geistes, zur Völker- und Kulturpsychologie. Berlin, C. A. Schwetschke [1912]
ix, 224 p.

Includes a section on Spinoza (p. 212-220)

NNJ

G-2-c
3711

Melamed, Samuel Max, 1885-1938.
שפינוזה היהודי. [1911]
573-581 p.

Title transliterated: Shpinozah ha-yehudi.
In Hashiloah, v. 25, 1911.

NNJ

G-2-c
3712

Melamed, Samuel Max, 1885-1938.
Spinoza, the Jew; an interpretation of his philosophy. [1927]
218-220 p.

In The New Palestine, v. 12, 1927.

G-2-c
3713

[Menasci, Roberto]
Benedetto Spinoza e la teosofia ebraica. [1910-11]
538-540, 4-8 p.

By "Discipulus".
In Il Vessillo israelitico, anno 58-59, 1910-11.

NN

G-2-c
3714

Mieses, Isaak, 1802-1883.
Beitrag zur Würdigung der Wirren im Judenthume. Leipzig [J. H. Nagel] 1845.
x, 70 p.

Includes a reference to Spinoza (p. 65-66)

OCH

G-2-c
3715

Mocatta, Frederic David, 1828-1905.
The Jews of Spain and Portugal and the Inquisition. London, Longmans, Green, and Co., 1877.
viii, 99 p. 20cm.

Includes a section on Spinoza (p. 93-95)

G-2-c
3716

Mueller, Samuel
Jüdische Geschichte von der Zerstörung des II. Tempels bis zur Gegenwart in Charakterbildern dargestellt. Stuttgart, J. B. Metzler, 1911.
333 p. ports.

Includes a section on Spinoza (p. 166-175)

OCH

G-2-c
3717

Müller, Samuel
Jüdische Geschichte, von der Zerstörung des I. Tempels bis zur Gegenwart, in Charakterbildern dargestellt. Grosse Ausgabe. Stuttgart, J. B. Metzlersche Buchhandlung, 1913.
iv, 410 p. 20cm.

Includes a section on Spinoza.

G-2-c
3718

Murr, Christoph Gottlieb von, 1733-1811.
An Rabeners Schatten. Von C. G. von Murr ... Frankfurt und Leipzig, bey Johann Adam Lochner, 1771.
48 p. 16cm.

NNC

G-2-c
3719

Neumark, David, 1866-1924.

שפינוזה ע"ד עתידות ישראל. [1897]
277-288 p.

Title transliterated: Shpinozah ʿal doar ʿatidoth yisrael.
In ha-Shiloah, v. 2, 1897.

NNJ

G-2-c
3720

Palmer, Edward Henry, 1840-1882.
A history of the Jewish nation; from the earliest times to the present day. Rev. ed. edited by S. F. Smith. Boston, D. Lothrop; Dover, N. H., G. T. Day [1875]
119 p. illus., plates, 3 maps, plan. 24 cm.

Includes a reference to Spinoza (p. 117)

NN

G-2-c
3721

Perles, Felix, 1874-
Jüdische Skizzen. 2. Aufl. Leipzig, Engel, 1920.
viii, 266 p. 24 cm.

Includes references to Spinoza.

G-2-c
3722

Philippson, Phöbus, 1807-1870.
Die Vertreibung der Juden aus Spanien und Portugal, historische Skizze aus den Zeiten des fünfzehnten Jahrhunderts. [1834]
373-391 p.

In Israelitisches Predigt- und Schul-Magazin, Bd. 1, 1834.
Includes a reference to Spinoza.

OCH

G-2-c
3723

Pick, Ludwig
Die Weltanschauung des Judentums. Berlin, C. Boas, Nachfolger, 1912.
93 p. 24cm.

Includes a chapter on Spinoza.
Original paper cover bound in.

G-2-c
3724

[Plantier, Jacques]
Réflexions sur l'histoire des Juifs ... pour servir de preuves à la vérité de la religion chrétienne. Avec un abrégé préliminaire de l'histoire des Juifs, depuis qu'ils tombèrent sous la domination des Romains, jusqu'à la ruine entière de leur république, et une description abrégée de leur schisme et de leurs sectes ... Genève, Fabri & Barrillot, 1721.
2 v.

Vol. 2 includes references to Spinoza.

OCH

G-2-c
3725

Prinz, Joachim.
... Jüdische geschichte. Mit 16 illustrationen. Berlin, Verlag für kulturpolitik, 1931.
279 p. illus., plates, ports., facsim. 21½cm.
"Bibliographie": p. 270-272.
Includes a reference to Spinoza (p. 144-145)

1. Jews—Hist. I. Title.

31—11709

Library of Congress DS117.P7
Copyright A—Foreign 11241
[40c1]

296

NNJ

Raisin, Jacob Salmon, 1877–1946.
The Haskalah movement in Russia, by Jacob S. Raisin ... Philadelphia, The Jewish publication society of America, 1913.
355 p. front., ports. 21 cm.
Bibliography: p. 331–337.
Includes references to Spinoza.

1. Jews in Russia. I. Title.

Reinach, Théodore, 1860-1928.
Histoire des Israélites, depuis l'époque de leur dispersion jusqu'à nos jours. Paris, Hachette [1855]
xviii, 423 p. 18cm.

Includes a section on Spinoza (p. 242-245)

Ringer, Ernst
Geisteskämpfe im heutigen Judentum. [1933]
[110]-129 p. 25cm.

From Hochland; Monatsschrift für alle Gebiete des Wissens, der Literatur u. Kunst, 31. Jahrgang, 2. Heft, November 1933.
Includes a reference to Spinoza (p. 115)

Rosenberg, Alfred, 1893-1946.
Die Spur des Juden im Wandel der Zeiten. München, Deutscher Volks-Verlag, 1920.
163 p.

Includes a reference to Spinoza (p. 136-137)

Roth, Cecil, 1899-
Anglo-Jewish letters (1158-1917) edited by Cecil Roth. London, Soncino press, 1938.
xix, 332, [1] p. 23½cm. (Soncino Jewish publication society. Publication no. 6)

"Select bibliography of Jewish private letters": p. xix.
Includes a reference to Spinoza (p. 89)

Roth, Cecil, 1899–
The Jewish contribution to civilisation, by Cecil Roth. London, Macmillan and co., limited, 1938.
xv, 357, [1] p. front., plates, ports., map, facsim. 20½ cm.
"First edition February 1938. Reprinted April 1938."
Bibliography: p. 323–328.
Includes a section on Spinoza (p. 163-165) and other references to him.

1. Jews—Civilization. I. Title.

Roth, Leon, 1896-
המחשבה הישראלית בעולם המודרני.
[1928]
86-112 p.

Title transliterated: ha-Mahshabah ha-yisraelith ...
In Eyim, v. 1, pt. 1, 1928.
Includes a section on Spinoza (p. 97-101)

[Roth, Leon] 1896-
Jewish thought in the modern world. [Oxford, 1927]
[433]-472 p. plates, ports. 19cm.

From Bevan, Edwyn Robert. The legacy of Israel. 1927.
Includes a section on Spinoza (p. 449-457)

Roth, Leon, 1896-
משנתו של שפינוזה ביהדות. תל־אביב.
תרצ"ג.
[1932]
3-7 p. illus. 29cm.

Title transliterated: Mishnāthō shel Shpīnō-zā ...
From Moznayim, vol. 4, no. 26, Dec. 15, 1932.

Roth, Léon, 1896-
La pensée juive dans le monde moderne.
[1929]
6-15, 56-64 p. 28cm.

"Traduction de Juliette Gourfinkel."
From Palestine, nouvelle revue juive, revue mensuelle internationale. 2. année, janvier, février 1929.
Includes a section on Spinoza (p. 56-60)

G-2-c
3736

Sakheim, Arthur, 1884–
Das jüdische element in der weltliteratur; sieben vorträge, von Arthur Sakheim. Hamburg, Verlag Hazoref, Buchhandlung Goldschmidt, g. m. b. h., 1924.
190, [1] p. 22cm.
Errata slip laid in.
"Literaturverzeichnis": p. 189–[191]
Includes a reference to Spinoza (p. 66-67)

I. Title.

26-897

Library of Congress
Copyright A—Foreign 26875
[2]

SPECIAL COLLECTIONS
SPINOZA

G-2-c
3741

Schudt, Johann Jacob, 1664-1722.
Jüdische Merckwürdigkeiten vorstellende was sich curieuses und denckwürdiges in den neuern Zeiten bey einigen Jahr-hunderten mit denen in alle IV. Theile der Welt, sonderlich durch Teutschland, zerstreuten Juden zugetragen. Sammt einer vollständigen Franckfurter Juden-Chronick, darinnen der zu Franckfurt am Mayn wohnenden Juden, von einigen Jahr-hunderten, bis auff unsere Zeiten, merckwürdigste Begebenheiten enthalten. Benebst einigen, zur Erläuterung beygefügten Kupffern und Figuren.

CONTINUED ON NEXT CARD

G-2-c
3737

Samter, N.
Was thun? Ein epilog zu den judentaufen im 19. jahrhundert. Von dr. N. Samter. Breslau, Druck von T. Schatzky [1900]
42 p. 21½cm.
Bibliographical foot-notes.
Includes a section on Spinoza.

1. Jews—Religion. 2. Jews—Political and social conditions. I. Title. II. Title: Judentaufen.

22—4469

DLC

Library of Congress DS143.S2
[41b1]

SPECIAL COLLECTIONS
SPINOZA

G-2-c
3742

Schudt, Johann Jacob, 1664-1722. Jüdische Merckwürdigkeiten. 1714. (Card 2)

Mit historischer Feder in drey Theilen beschrieben von Johann Jacob Schudt ... Franckfurt und Leipzig, 1714.
3 v. in 1. plates, ports. 22cm.

Includes a sketch of Spinoza's life (v. 1, p. 313-315)

SPECIAL COLLECTIONS
SPINOZA

G-2-c
3738

Scholl, Carl, 1820-1907.
Das Judenthum und seine Weltmission. Leipzig, R. Friese, 1880.
26 p. 22cm.

"Separatabdruck aus 'Es werde Licht! Monatsblätter zur Förderung der Humanität', Jahrg. XI (1880), Februarheft."
Includes references to Spinoza.

SPECIAL COLLECTIONS
SPINOZA

G-2-c
3743

Schulman, Samuel, 1865-
The synagogue and the God-intoxicated Spinoza; an address read at a meeting of the Association of Reform Rabbis of New York City and vicinity, May 9, 1933. [New York, 1933]
15 p. 17cm.

G-2-c
3739

Schreiner, Martin, 1863-1926.
Der Kalâm in der jüdischen Literatur; wissenschaftliche Beigabe zum XIII. Bericht der Lehranstalt für die Wissenschaft des Judenthums zu Berlin. Berlin, Itzkowski, 1895.
67 p.

Includes a reference to Spinoza (p. 27)

MH

SPECIAL COLLECTIONS
SPINOZA

G-2-c
3744

Schwarz, A
Baruch Spinoza; Vortrag im Verein für jüdische Geschichte und Litteratur in Karlsruhe am 1. Februar 1892. Magdeburg, Verlag der "Israelitischen Wochenschrift", 1892.
26 p. 22cm.

1. Spinoza, Benedictus de, 1632-1677.

SPECIAL COLLECTIONS
SPINOZA

G-2-c
3740

Schröder, Johann Joachim, 1680-1756, praeses.
Dissertatio philologico-critica de annis Achasiae Jvdaeorum regis, ad concilianda loca S. Scripturae 2. Reg. VIII, 26. & 2. Chron. XXII, 2., qvam praeses Joh. Joach. Schröderus ... ad diem XXVI. Octobr. MDCCXV. examinandam exhibet, respondente Johanne Christiano Böhmio ... Marbvrgi Cattorvm, Typis Philippi Casimiri Mülleri [1715]
16 p. 20cm.

Thesis, Marburg an der Lahn.

SPECIAL COLLECTIONS
SPINOZA

G-2-c
3745

Seligmann, Raphael
Probleme des Judentums. Wien, R. Löwit, 1919.
155 p. 24cm.

Includes a chapter "Spinoza und die Weltanschauung des Judentums" (p. 18-25)
Original paper covers bound in.

G-2-c 3746

Seligmann, Raphael
Spinoza und die Weltanschauung des Judentums. ⌈1910⌉
846-848 p.

In Die Welt, Vienna, 14. Jahrgang, 1910.
An excerpt from his Probleme des Judentums.

OCH

G-2-c 3747

Setzer, Samuel Hirsch, 1882-
רב ישראל בעל-שם-טוב: זיין לעבען, לעהרע און ווירקען. New York, 1919.
2 v.

Title transliterated: Reb Yisrael Baal-Shem-Tov ...
Includes a section on Spinoza (v. 1, p. 227-251)

SPECIAL COLLECTIONS SPINOZA G-2-c 3748

Sonnenschein, S H
The three greatest Hebrews: Moses, Jesus, Spinoza. St. Louis, H. Feldrush, printer, 1886.
13 p. 19cm. ("Temple Israel" Sunday-lectures, no. 2)

SPECIAL COLLECTIONS SPINOZA G-2-c 3749

Spanheim, Friedrich, 1632-1701.
Friderici Spanhemii F. Selectiorum de religione controversiarum, etiam cum Graecis & orientalibus, et cum Judaeis, nuperisque antiscripturariis, elenchus historico-theologicus, errorum fontes ubique aperiuntur, insertis dissertationibus quae sunt hujus temporis. Lugd. Batav., Apud Felicem Lopez, 1687.
⌈22⌉, 5-695, ⌈1⌉ p. 14cm.

Includes a section on Spinoza (p. 665-671)

SPECIAL COLLECTIONS SPINOZA G-2-c 3750

Steckelmacher, Moritz, 1851-
H. Graetz als Darsteller der Systeme der jüdischen Religionsphilosophen. ⌈1918⌉
⌈125⌉-151 p. 23cm.

From Monatsschrift für Geschichte und Wissenschaft des Judentums. 62. Jahrg., Heft 4/6, April-Juni 1918)
Includes references to Spinoza (p. 146-150)

G-2-c 3751

Sterling, Ada, *d.* 1939.
The Jew and civilization, by Ada Sterling ... New York city, Aetco publishing co., 1924.
330 p. 24 cm.
Bibliography: p. 322-324.
Includes a section on Spinoza (p. 291-295)

1. Jews—Civilization. 2. Jewish question. I. Title.

Library of Congress DS141.S75 24—2180
⌈50f⌉

SPECIAL COLLECTIONS SPINOZA G-2-c 3752

Tedesche, Sidney S
Jewish champions of religious liberty. ⌈1926⌉
181-212 p. 24cm.

From Central Conference of American Rabbis. Yearbook, vol. XXXVI, 1926.
Includes references to Spinoza.

NNC

SPECIAL COLLECTIONS SPINOZA G-2-c 3753

Tharaud, Jérôme, 1874–
The chosen people; a short history of the Jews in Europe, by Jerome and Jean Tharaud; translated by Frances Wilson Huard; decorations by Charles O. Naef. London, New York ⌈etc.⌉ Longmans, Green and co., 1929.
240 p. incl. front., illus. 19½cm.

Includes references to Spinoza.

1. Jews in Europe. 2. Jews—Hist. 3. Jews—Soc. life & cust. I. Tharaud, Jean, 1877– joint author. II. Huard, Frances (Wilson) 1885– tr. III. Title. *Translation of* Petite histoire des Juifs.

29—5588
Library of Congress DS118.T53
⌈a44q1⌉

G-2-c 3754

Tharaud, Jérôme, 1874-
Petite histoire des Juifs ⌈par Jérôme et Jean Tharaud⌉ Paris, Plon ⌈1927⌉
vii, 282 p. 19 cm.

Includes a reference to Spinoza (p. 129-130)

SPECIAL COLLECTIONS SPINOZA G-2-c 3755

⌈Tharaud, Jérôme⌉ 1874-
Petite histoire des Juifs. ⌈1927⌉
⌈652⌉-669 p. 26cm.

Signed: Jérôme et Jean Tharaud.
Chapters 3 and 4 of their book with the same title.
From La Revue universelle, June 15, 1927.
Includes a reference to Spinoza (p. 657)

Theodores, T
The Talmud. [1874]
330-378 p. 23 cm.

From Essays and addresses, by professors and lecturers of the Owens college, Manchester. London, Macmillan, 1874.
Includes a reference to Spinoza (p. 334-335)

Verein jüdischer Hochschüler Bar Kochba, Prague.
Vom Judentum; ein Sammelbuch, hrsg. vom Verein jüdischer Hochschüler Bar Kochba in Prag. [3. Aufl.] Leipzig, K. Wolff, 1914.
ix, 284 p. 24cm.

Includes an essay "Spinoza und das jüdische Weltgefühl" by Margarete Susman (p. 51-70)
Ms. notes by Carl Gebhardt.

Wachter, Johann Georg, 1673-1757.
Der Spinozismus im Jüdenthumb, oder, Die von dem heütigen Jüdenthumb, und dessen geheimen Kabbala vergötterte Welt, an Mose Germano, sonsten Johann Peter Speeth, von Augsburg gebürtig, befunden und widerleget von Johann Georg Wachter. Amsterdam, Bey Johann Wolters, 1699.
[14], 256, 77, [1] p. fold. plate. 16cm.

Wagner, Albert
Gehört Spinoza zum Judentum? [1908]
3-4 p.

In Die Wahrheit, Jahrgang 28, Nr. 3, 1908.

Weltsch, Felix, 1884-
Probleme des Judentums. [1920-21]
435-436 p.

In Der Jude; eine Monatsschrift, Jahrgang 5, 1920-21.

Wiener, Max, 1886-
שאול אשער און די טעאריע וועגן
יידנטום ווי א רעליגיע. ניו־יארק.
c1944
[New York, 1944]
55-79 p.

Title transliterated: Shoul Asher ...
Reprint from Yivo bleter; journal of the Yiddish Scientific Institute.
Includes references to Spinoza.

Wiener, Max, 1886-
Spinoza's contribution to anti-Semitism. [1942]
9-[11] p. 26cm.

From the Reconstructionist, vol. VIII, no. 11, October 2, 1942.

1. Spinoza, Benedictus de, 1632-1677.

Wolf, Johann Christoph, 1683-1739.
Jo. Christophori Wolfii ... Bibliotheca Hebræa, sive Notitia tvm avctorvm Hebr. cvjvscvnqve ætatis, tvm scriptorvm, qvæ vel Hebraice primvm exarata vel ab aliis conversa svnt, ad nostram ætatem, dedvcta ... [Pars I.] Hamburgi & Lipsiæ, Impensis Christiani Liebezeit, 1715.
[6], 1161, [35], 24 p. front. 22cm.

Includes an article on Spinoza (p. 239-242)

Wolf, Lucien, 1857-1930.
Les Marranes ou Crypto-Juifs du Portugal. Paris, Alliance israélite universelle, 1926.
23 p. 22cm.

Zeitlin, Aaron
וואס אידען האבען ביי־געטראגען צו
וועלט־פילאזאפיע. ניו־יארק 1943.
[New York, 1943]
p. 5. 58cm.

Title transliterated: Wos Iden hoben baygetrogen tsu velt-filozofye.
From Der Morgen zhurnal. Jewish journal. June 6, 1943.
Includes references to Spinoza.

Zhitlowsky, Chaim, 1865-1943.

New York, 1912. געזאמעלטע שריפטען.
10 v.

Title transliterated: Gezamelte shriften.
Includes a discussion of the relation of Moses Hess to Spinoza (v. 3, p. 198)

Ziegler, Ignaz, 1861-
Die Geschichte des Judenthums von dem babylonischen Exile bis auf die Gegenwart; ein Familienbuch. Prag, Brandeis, 1900.
vi, 244 p. 24 cm.

Includes references to Spinoza.

Zinberg, Israel, 1873-
The history of the Jewish literature. Vilno, "Tomor", 1929-33.
4 v. 22 cm.

Added title-pages and text in Yiddish.
Includes a section on Spinoza, v. 4, p. 407-415.

Zweifel, Eliezer Zebi, 1815-1888.
שלום על ישראל. זיטאמיר, בדפוס א. ש. שאדאוו.
Житомиръ, ~~1868-78.~~ 1875.
v.3 ~~4 v. in 2.~~ 21 cm.

Vol. 3 published in Vilna.
Title-page lacking, supplied in manuscript.
Includes references to Spinoza.

1. Hasidism. *Title transliterated:* Shalom 'al Yisrael.

G-2-d
KABBALAH

Aešcoly, Aaron Ze'ev, 1901-1948.
Introduction à l'étude des hérésies religieuses parmi les Juifs: la Kabbale, le hassidisme; essai critique. Paris, Geuthner, 1928.
ii, 202 p. 26 cm.

At head of title: A.-Z. Aešcoly-Weintraub.
Includes references to Spinoza.

Benamozegh, Elijah, 1822-1900.
Spinoza et la Kabbale. [1863-64]
5 pts.

In L'Univers israélite, v. 19-20, 1863-64.

Bischoff, Erich, 1865-1936.
Die Kabbalah; Einführung in die jüdische Mystik und Geheimwissenschaft. Leipzig, Th. Griebens Verlag (L. Fernau), 1903.
vii, 126 p. illus., ports. 19cm.

Includes references to Spinoza.

Bloch, Philipp, 1841-1923.
Geschichte der Entwickelung der Kabbala und der jüdischen Religionsphilosophie, kurz zusammengefasst. Trier, 1894.
165 p. 24 cm.

Includes a reference to Spinoza (p. 164-165)

Franck, Adolphe, 1809-1893.
Die Kabbala, oder die Religions-Philosophie der Hebräer. Aus dem Französischen übersetzt, verbessert und vermehrt von Ad. Gelinek. Leipzig, H. Hunger, 1844.
xvi, 296 p. diagr.

Includes references to Spinoza (p. 19-22)

Franck, Adolphe, 1809-1893.
The kabbalah; or, The religious philosophy of the Hebrews. Rev. and enl. translation by Dr. I. Sossnitz. New York, The Kabbalah Publishing Company, 1926.
3 p. l., ix-lx p., 1 l., 63-326 p. port., diagr. 23 cm.

Includes references to Spinoza.

Freystadt, M
Philosophia cabbalistica et pantheismus; ex fontibus primariis adumbravit atque inter se comparavit M. Freystadt. Regimontii Prussorum, In commissis apud fratres Borntraeger, 1832.
xv, 143 p. 21cm.

Includes a section "Spinozismus" (p. 95-98) and other references to Spinoza.

Gelbhaus, Sigmund
Die Metaphysik der Ethik Spinozas im Quellenlichte der Kabbalah. Wien, Jüdischer Buch- und Kunstverlag M. Hickl, 1917.
108 p. 24cm.

Original paper covers bound in.

Heller, Bernard, 1896-
Spinoza and the Kabbalah. [1928]
9-15 p.

In Jewish Institute quarterly, v. 4, 1928.

Hirsch, Benzion J
Verspreide opstellen. Amsterdam, De Bussy, 1927.
66 p. illus., ports., facsim.

No. 29 of 60 copies.
"Overdruk uit het weekblad 'De Vrijdagavond' jaargang 2 en 3."
Includes a section "Spinoza en de Kabbala" (p. 59)

Horodezky, Samuel Aba, 1871-
אלהים והזויה בתורת שפינוזה. לונ-
דון, תרפ"ז.
[London, 1927]
577-579 p. 33cm.

Title transliterated: Ĕlōhīm ...
From "Haolam", vol. 15, no. 29, July 22, 1927.
Deals with Spinoza.
With Sokolov, Nahum. Peraqim. [1927] pt. 1.

Joel, David, 1815-1882.
מדרש הזוהר. Die religionsphilosophie des Sohar und ihr verhältniss zur allgemeinen jüdischen theologie. Zugleich eine kritische beleuchtung der Franck'schen "Kabbala." Von D. H. Joël ... Leipzig, Fritzsche, 1849.
xxii, [2], 394 p., 1 l. incl. diagr. 20cm.

Includes references to Spinoza.
Title transliterated: Midrash ha-zohar.
Bibliographical footnotes.

Kaufmann, H E
Philosophisches in der Kabbala. Vortrag, gehalten am 14. März 1901 im Vereinslocal des Wiener jüdischen Schulvereines. Pressburg, A. Alkalay, 1901.
18 p.

Includes a reference to Spinoza (p. 12)

Malachi, Eliezer Raphael, 1895-
מקובלים אין ארץ ישראל. ניו יארק, פארלאג "כנרת."
[New York] 1928.
191 p. 21 cm.

Includes references to Spinoza (p. 30-31)

1. Cabala—Biog. I. Title.
Title transliterated: Mekubalim in Erets Yisrael.
Name originally: Eliezer Raphael Engelmann.

[Mieses, Isaak] 1802-1883.
Spinoza und die Kabbala. [1869]
359-367 p.

In Zeitschrift für exacte Philosophie im Sinne des neuern philosophischen Realismus, 8. Bd., 1869.

Milo, Johann Wilhelm, praeses.
Exercitatio rabbinico-metaphysica de Kabbala recentiori Spinozismi genitrice, qvam ... pvblico ervditorvm examini svbiicit M. Iohannes Wilhelmvs Milo ... respondente Paulo Friderico Ruhig ... Regiomonti, Litteris Revsnerianis [1745]
37 p.

Thesis, Königsberg.

SPECIAL COLLECTIONS SPINOZA G-2-d 3786

Pistorius, Johann, 1546-1608, comp.
Artis cabalisticae: hoc est, reconditae theologiae et philosophiae, scriptorvm: tomus I. In quo praeter Pavli Ricii theologicos & philosophicos libros sunt Latini penè omnes & Hebraei nonnulli praestantissimi scriptores ... Opvs omnibvs theologis, et occvltae abstrvsae qve philosophiae stvdiosis pernecessarium ... Ex D. Ioannis Pistorii ... Basileae, Per Sebastianvm Henricpetri ⌊1587⌋
⌊52⌋, 979, ⌊1⌋ p. 33cm.

CONTINUED ON NEXT CARD

SPECIAL COLLECTIONS SPINOZA G-2-d 3787

Pistorius, Johann, 1546-1608, comp. Artis cabalisticae ... tomus I. ⌊1587⌋ (Card 2)

No more published. Cf. Brit. mus. cat.
Date from colophon.
Printer's mark on title-page and at end.
Several errors in paging.

CONTINUED ON NEXT CARD

SPECIAL COLLECTIONS SPINOZA G-2-d 3788

Pistorius, Johann, 1546-1608, comp. Artis cabalisticae ... tomus I. ⌊1587⌋ (Card 3)

Contents.--Pavli Ricii De coelesti agricvltvra libri IIII.--Rabi Iosephi De porta Lvcis.--Leonis Hebraei De amore dialogi tres.--Ioannis Revchlini De arte cabalistica libri III; De verbo mirifico. libri III.--Archangeli Bvrgonovensis Interpretationes in selectiora obscurioraq; cabalistarum dogmata.--Abrahami De creatione & cabalistinis, Hebraicè Sepher iezira, liber.

SPECIAL COLLECTIONS SPINOZA G-2-d 3789

Von der Kabbalah zu Spinoza. Von einem deutschen Rabbiner. ⌊1881⌋
p. 6, 27, 42-43. 35cm.

From Der Zeitgeist; ein israelitisches Familienblatt, Jahrgang 2., Nr. 1-3, 1881.

SPECIAL COLLECTIONS SPINOZA G-2-d 3790

Wachter, Johann Georg, 1673-1757.
Elucidarius cabalisticus, sive Reconditae Hebraeorum philosophiae brevis & succincta recensio, epitomatore Joh. Georgio Wachtero ... Romae, 1706.
1 p. l., 78, ⌊1⌋ p. 16cm.

Includes a chapter "De consensu Cabalae et Spinozae" (p. 39-70)

G-2-d 3791

Waite, Arthur Edward, 1857-
The doctrine and literature of the Kabalah. London, The Theosophical pub. co., 1902.

Includes a reference to Spinoza (p. 322)

NNJ

SPECIAL COLLECTIONS SPINOZA G-2-d 3792

Waton, Harry.
The kabbalah and Spinoza's philosophy as a basis for an idea of universal history, by Harry Waton ... New York, Spinoza institute of America, inc., 1931-32.
2 v. illus. 24cm.
CONTENTS.—v. 1. The philosophy of the kabbalah.—v. 2. The philosophy of Spinoza.

1. Cabala. 2. Spinoza, Benedictus de, 1632-1677. 3. History—Philosophy. I. Spinoza institute of America, inc., New York.

31-11187 Revised
Library of Congress BM525.W35
⌊r45c2⌋ 181.3

G-2-d 3793

Zohar.
Kabbala denudata: the Kabbalah unveiled, containing the following books of the Zohar: 1. The book of concealed mystery. 2. The Greater Holy assembly. 3. The Lesser Holy assembly. Translated into English from the Latin version of Knorr von Rosenroth, and collated with the original Chaldee and Hebrew text by S. L. MacGregor Mathers. London, G. Redway, 1887.
viii, 359 p. illus., plates, fold. tables.

Includes references to Spinoza (p. 38-41)

G-2-e
SABBATI ZEVI

SPECIAL COLLECTIONS SPINOZA G-2-e 3794

Die Geschichte von dem grossen Betrieger, oder falschen Juden Könige Sabatai-Sevi von Smirna, der sich anno 1666. für einen König der Juden in der Türckey auffgeworffen, nach dem aber den mahometischen Glauben angenommen und im 1676sten Jahr zu Constantinopel als ein Türck gestorben. 1702.
18 p. plates, port. 35cm. (In Historia von denen Wider Tauffern. ⌊1705?⌋)

NNC

G-2-e 3795

Graetz, Heinrich, 1817-1891.
Историа евреев. Одесса, 1906-09.
12 v. ports.
Title transliterated: Istoriia evreev.
Includes Спиноза и Сабатай Цеви (v. 11, p. 149-227)

NNJ

Graetz, Heinrich, 1817-1891.
Geschichte der Juden von den ältesten Zeiten bis auf die Gegenwart. Aus den Quellen neu bearbeitet. Leipzig, O. Leiner, 1855-75.
11 v.

Includes "Spinoza und Sabbataï Zewi" (v. 10, p. 168-258)

NNJ

Baeck, Leo, 1873-
Spinozas erste einwirkungen auf Deutschland. Von Leo Bäck ... Berlin, Mayer & Müller, 1895.
2 p. l., 91 p. 23½cm.
Bibliographical foot-notes.

1. Spinoza, Benedictus de, 1632-1677.

[Katzenstein, Julius] 1890-
The messiah of Ismir, Sabbatai Zevi, by Joseph Kastein [pseud.] translated by Huntley Paterson. New York, The Viking press, 1931.
4 p. l., 3-346 p. front., plates, ports. 22cm.
Bibliography: p. 341-343.
Includes references to Spinoza.

1. Shabbethai Zebi, 1626-1676. I. Paterson, Huntley, tr. II. Title.
Translation of Sabbatai Zewi, der messias von Ismir.

Boer, Tjitze J de
Spinoza in England. [1916]
[331]-336 p. 25cm.

From Tijdschrift voor wijsbegeerte, 10. jaarg., 3. aflevering, Juli 1916.
Manuscript notes by Adolphe S. Oko.

[Katzenstein, Julius] 1890-1946.
Sabbatai Zewi, der Messias von Ismir [von] Josef Kastein [pseud.] Berlin, E. Rowohlt, 1930.
385 p. plates, ports. 21 cm.
"Bibliographie": p. 382-384.
Includes references to Spinoza.

1. Shabbethai Zebi, 1626-1676.

Braun, Otto, 1885-1922.
Spinoza und sein Einfluss auf die deutsche Literatur. [1918]
4 p. 27cm.

From Deutsche Zeitung während des grossen Krieges herausgegeben von den in Holland internierten Deutschen, Reihe 1, Nummer 2, 1. Juli 1918.

Sluys, D E
Handboek voor de geschiedenis der Joden, door D. E. Sluys en Jacob Hoofiën. Amsterdam, J. B. de Mesquita, 1870-73.
3 v.

Includes "Spinoza en Sabbataï Tsewi" (v. 3, p. 424-460)

H
INFLUENCE IN DIFFERENT COUNTRIES

Chmaj, Ludwik
De Spinoza a Bracia polscy. Kraków, Krakowska Spólka Wydawnicza, 1924.
42 p. 24cm.

From "Reformacji w Polsce", Nr. 9/10, 1924.
Bibliographical footnotes.
Original paper covers bound in.

Antal, G von
Die holländische Philosophie im neunzehnten Jahrhundert; eine Studie. Utrecht, C. H. E. Breijer, 1888.
112 p. 22cm.

Includes references to Spinoza.

Cohen, Gustave, 1879-
Le séjour de Saint-Évremond en Hollande et l'entrée de Spinoza dans le champ de la pensée française. Paris, Champion, 1926.
96 p. 24cm.

H 3806

Damiron, Jean Philibert, 1794-1862.
Essai sur l'histoire de la philosophie en France, au XVIIe siècle. Paris, Hachette, 1846.
2 v. 22 cm.

Includes a section on Spinoza (v. 2, p. 177-351)

SPECIAL COLLECTIONS SPINOZA H 3807

Frank, Semen Liudvigovich, 1877-1950.
Die russische Philosophie der letzten fünfzehn Jahre. [1926]
[89]-104 p. 26cm.

From Kant-Studien, Bd. 31, 1926.
Includes references to Russian works and articles about Spinoza.

SPECIAL COLLECTIONS SPINOZA H 3808

Hashagen, Justus
Spinoza am Rhein. [1911]
92-93 p. 23cm.

From Monats-Hefte für rheinische Kirchengeschichte, 5. Jahrgang, Heft 3.

1. Spinoza, Benedictus de, 1632-1677.

SPECIAL COLLECTIONS SPINOZA H 3809

[Janet, Paul] 1823-1899.
French thought and Spinozism. [1877]
[1072]-1091 p. 23cm.

Signed: Paul Janet.
From Contemporary review, v. 29, May 1877.
Volume of pamphlets.

1. Spinoza, Benedictus de, 1632-1677.

H 3810

Janet, Paul, 1823-1899.
Le spinozisme en France. [1882]
109-132 p.

In Revue philosophique de la France et de l'étranger, 7. année, t. 13, 1882.

SPECIAL COLLECTIONS SPINOZA H 3811

Krakauer, Moses, 1853-
Zur Geschichte des Spinozismus in Deutschland während der ersten Hälfte des achtzehnten Jahrhunderts. Breslau, Druck von S. Schottlaender [1881]
51 p. 23cm.

Thesis, Breslau.
Bibliographical footnotes.

SPECIAL COLLECTIONS SPINOZA H 3812

Lehmann, Friedrich
Beitrag zur Geschichte und zur Kritik des Spinozismus. Siegen, Druck von W. Vorländer, 1898.
37 p. 22cm.

"Beilage zum 61. Jahresberichte des Realgymnasiums zu Siegen."
Bibliographical footnotes.

SPECIAL COLLECTIONS SPINOZA H 3813

Myślicki, Ignacy
Jonston i de Spinoza. Jonston et de Spinoza; l'influence supposée d'un Polonais sur de Spinoza. Varsaviae, Cura et sumptibus Universitatis Liberae Polonae, 1922.
cover-title, 23 p. 24cm. (Bibliotheca Universitatis Liberae Polonae, a. 1922, fasc. 3)

Resumé in French.

SPECIAL COLLECTIONS SPINOZA H 3814

Myślicki, Ignacy
Jonston et de Spinoaz [!] par Ignace Myślicki (Halpern) [Traduit du manuscrit par T. Warynski. Hagae Comitis, 1921]
118-157 p. 22cm.

Cover-title: Dissertatio ex Chronici Spinozani tomo primo, separatim edita.
Bibliographical footnotes.

SPECIAL COLLECTIONS SPINOZA H 3815

[Rullmann, W]
Die Anfänge des Spinozismus in Deutschland und die Wiederaufnahme desselben durch Johann Christian Edelmann. [1867]
[10]-38 p. 22cm.

From Einladung zu der am 17. (5.) und 18. (6.) Juny stattfindenden Prüfung und Schlussfeierlichkeit der Unterrichts- und Erziehungs-Anstalt (vormals Behmsche Schule) des Dr. Ferd. Zeidler zu Widburg, 1867.
Bibliographical footnotes.

SPECIAL COLLECTIONS SPINOZA H 3916

Spinoza in America.
v. 1-2.
Autumn 1931-Summer 1933.
New York, 1931-33.
quarterly.

SPECIAL COLLECTIONS SPINOZA H 3917

Stockum, Theodorus Cornelis van, 1887-
Spinoza's beoordeeling en invloed in Duitschland van 1677 tot 1750; eerste openbare les, gehouden bij de aanvaarding van het privaat-docentschap in de geschiedenis der nieuwere wijsbegeerte aan de Rijksuniversiteit te Groningen, op 10 October 1916. Groningen, P. Noordhoff, 1916.
20 p. 25cm.

H 3918

Ueber Spinoza. [1899]
p. 952.

In Dr. Bloch's oesterreichische Wochenschrift, Jahrgang 16, 1899.
Refers to Spinoza und die modernen Denker Deutschlands, a lecture by Jacob Freudenthal at Vienna, Dec. 9, 1899.

NN

H 3919

Wendriner, Karl Georg, 1885-
Spinoza und der deutsche Geist. [1936]
p. 1-2, 1.

In Neue Züricher Zeitung; Morgenausgabe, Nr. 1080, 1084, Juni 23, 1936.

DLC

SPECIAL COLLECTIONS SPINOZA H 3920

Wybrands, Aemilius Willem, 1838-1886.
Marinus Adriaansz. Booms; eene bladzijde uit de geschiedenis der Spinozisterij in Nederland. [1884]
78 p. 23cm.

"Overgedrukt uit het Archief voor Nederlandsche kerkgeschiedenis, dl. I, afl. 1, 's-Grav. 1884, blz. 51-128."
Bibliographical footnotes.

I SPECIAL TOPICS IN SPINOZA'S PHILOSOPHY

I-1 AESTHETICS

I-1 3921

Bergh van Eysinga, Henri Willem Philippus Elize van den
Bij denkers en dichters; studies in schoonheid en wijsheid. Amsterdam, L. J. Veen [1915]
224 p. port.

Includes a section on Spinoza.

MiD

SPECIAL COLLECTIONS SPINOZA I-1 3922

Schlerath, Franz, 1894-
Spinoza und die Kunst. Hellerau bei Dresden, Buchdruckerei J. Hegner, 1920.
83 p. 25cm.

Thesis, Münster.
Bibliography: p. [6]
Original paper cover bound in.

1. Spinoza, Benedictus de, 1632-1677.

I-2 AFFECTS

SPECIAL COLLECTIONS SPINOZA I-2 3923

Dörffling, Max
Die Ansichten Spinozas über das Wesen der Affecte und ihre gegenseitigen Verhältnisse; eine Studie. Zerbst, C. F. Dörffling, 1873.
27 p. 24cm.

Issued also as thesis, Rostock.
Original paper cover bound in.
Volume of pamphlets.

NNC

SPECIAL COLLECTIONS SPINOZA I-2 3924

Dörffling, Max
Die Ansichten Spinozas über das Wesen der Affecte und ihre gegenseitigen Verhältnisse. 1873.
27 p. 23cm.

Thesis, Rostock.
Volume of pamphlets.

Gordon, Abraham
Spinoza's Psychologie der Affekte mit Rücksicht auf Descartes. Breslau, Druck von H. Sulzbach, 1874.
iv, 86 p. 23cm.

Thesis, Leipzig.
Incomplete: pages after p. 86 missing.
Volume of pamphlets.

Hartmann,
Die Lehre des Cartesius De passionibus animae, und des Spinoza de affectibus humanis, dargestellt und verglichen. Wohlau, A. Leuckart, 1878.
16 p. 26cm.

At head of title: V. Programm des Städtischen Gymnasiums zu Wohlau.

Jung, Gertrud, 1894-
Spinozas Affektenlehre. ⌊Berlin, 1926⌋
70 p. 23cm.

Part of thesis, Berlin.
"Nur der erste Teil der Dissertation ... Der zweite Teil soll (in verkürzter Form) 1927 im Spinoza-Heft der Kantstudien veröffentlicht werden."
Bibliography: p. 67-69.

Jung, Gertrud, 1894-
Die Affektenlehre Spinozas; ihre Verflechtung mit dem System und ihre Verbindung mit ler Überlieferung. ⌊1927⌋
⌊85⌋-150 p. 23cm.

Second part, abridged, of thesis, Berlin.
"Sonderdruck aus Kant-Studien, Band XXXII, Heft 1."
Presentation copy to Carl Gebhardt, with author's inscription and signature.
Bibliographical footnotes.

Kellermann, Benzion, 1869-
Die Ethik Spinozas, dritter Teil: Ueber den Ursprung und die Natur der Affekte. ⌊1927⌋
107-117 p.

From Festschrift zum 70. Geburtstage von Moritz Schaefer. Berlin, Philo ⌊1927⌋

Mendelssohn, Moses, 1729-1786.
Ueber die Empfindungen. ⌊1777⌋
⌊xvii⌋-xxii, 190 p.

From his Philosophische Schriften, 1. Theil, 1777.

Mielisch, Gustav, 1873-
Quae de affectuum natura et viribus Spinoza (Ethices p. III et IV) docuit, ita exponantur, ut quantum fieri potest, exemplis illustrentur. Halis Saxonum, Typis expressit "Wischan & Wettengel", 1900.
53 p. 22cm.

Thesis, Erlangen.
Volume of pamphlets.

Nenitescu, Ioan, 1854-1901.
Die Affectenlehre Spinoza's. Leipzig, Bär & Hermann, 1887.
vi, 132 p. 23cm.

Thesis, Leipzig.
Volume of pamphlets.

I-3
AMOR DEI

Boer, Tjitze J de, 1866-1942.
Eenige opmerkingen over Spinoza's amor Dei intellectualis. ⌊1918⌋
⌊380⌋-395 p. 25cm.

"Voordracht, op de jaarvergadering van de vereeniging 'Het Spinozahuis' 30 Juni l.l. te Amsterdam gehouden."
From Tijdschrift voor wijsbegeerte, jaarg. 12, 1918.

Cohen, Morris Raphael, 1880-1947.
Amor Dei intellectualis. ⌊1923⌋
19 p. 22cm.

Cover-title: Dissertatio ex Chronici Spinozani tomo tertio separatim edita.
"Read before the American Philosophical Association, December, 1922."
Presentation copy with the author's inscription.

SPECIAL COLLECTIONS SPINOZA I-3 3835

Cohen, Morris Raphael, 1880-1947.
Amor Dei intellectualis. [1923]
10 l. 34cm.

"Read before the American Philosophical Association, December, 1922."
Proof sheets for Chronicon Spinozanum, v. 3.

NNC

SPECIAL COLLECTIONS SPINOZA I-3 3836

Cohen, Morris Raphael, 1880-1947.
The intellectual love of God. [1925]
332-341 p. 26cm.

From the Menorah journal, v. 11, no. 4, August 1925.
Article on Spinoza's ideal of the intellectual love of God.

I-3 3837

Dyroff, Adolf, 1866-1943.
Zur Entstehungsgeschichte der Lehre Spinozas vom Amor Dei intellectualis. [1917]
28 p.

In Archiv für Geschichte der Philosophie, 31. Bd., Okt. 1917-Juli 1918.

SPECIAL COLLECTIONS SPINOZA I-3 3838

Gunning, Johannes Hermanus, 1829-
De eenheid des levens, naar Spinoza's amor intellectualis. Nijmegen, H. ten Hoet, 1903.
156 p. 24cm.

Original paper covers bound in.
Bibliographical footnotes.

SPECIAL COLLECTIONS SPINOZA I-3 3839

Lülmann, Christian, 1861-
Ueber den begriff Amor Dei intellectualis bei Spinoza ... von C. Lülmann ... Jena, Frommannsche buchdr. (H. Pohle) 1884.
2 p. l., 46 p. 22cm.
Inaug.-diss.—Jena.

1. Spinoza, Benedictus de, 1632-1677. 2. God. 3. Pantheism.

11-21423 Revised
Library of Congress B3999.G6L8 [r45c2]

I-3 3840

Malapert, Paulin, 1862-
L'amour intellectuel de Dieu d'après Spinoza. [1888]
245-258 p.

In Revue philosophique de la France et de l'étranger, 13. année, t. 26, 1888.

I-3 3841

Wyneken, Gustav Adolf, 1875-
Amor Dei intellectualis; eine religionsphilosophische Studie. Greifswald, J. Abel, 1898.
68 p.

MH

I-4 ATHEISM

SPECIAL COLLECTIONS SPINOZA I-4 3842

L'athéisme folie dangereuse ... A Francfort sur le Main, Chez la veuve Knoch et J. G. Eslinger, 1753.
[8], 80 p. 19cm.

Dedication signed: R----s.
Includes references to Spinoza.

NNC

SPECIAL COLLECTIONS SPINOZA I-4 3843

[Aubert de Versé, Noël] d. 1714.
L'impie convaincu, ou Dissertation contre Spinosa. Dans laquelle on refute les fondemens de son athéisme. L'on trouvera dans cet ouvrage non seulement la refutation des maximes impies de Spinosa, mais aussi celle des principales hypotheses du cartesianisme, que l'on fait voir être l'origine du spinosisme. A Amsterdam, Chez Jean Crelle, 1684.
[12], 274, [1] p. 16cm.

NNC

CONTINUED ON NEXT CARD

SPECIAL COLLECTIONS SPINOZA I-4 3844

[Aubert de Versé, Noël] d. 1714. L'impie convaincu. 1684. (Card 2)

Title-page lacking, supplied in part in manuscript. Title from A. van der Linde. Benedictus Spinoza.

NNC

I-4 3845

Aubert de Versé, Noël, d. 1714.
L'impie convaincu; ou, Dissertation contre Spinoza, dans laquelle l'on refute les fondemens de son atheisme ... Amsterdam, Chez Jean Crelle, 1685.
[12], 275 p.

NN

I-4 3850

Buddeus, Johann Franz, 1667-1729.
Joan. Francisci Buddei ... Theses theologicae de atheismo et superstitione variis observationibus illustratae. Quibus suas annotationes adjecit Joannes Lulofs. Lugduni Batavorum, apud J. Le Mair, 1767.
xxxiv, 568 p.

Includes references to Spinoza.

NN

SPECIAL COLLECTIONS SPINOZA

I-4 3846

Bentley, Richard, 1662-1742.
The folly and unreasonableness of atheism demonstrated from the advantage and pleasure of a religious life, the faculties of humane souls, the structure of animate bodies, & the origin and frame of the world: in eight sermons preached at the lecture founded by the Honourable Robert Boyle ... in the first year, MDCXCII. By Richard Bentley ... The fourth edition corrected. London, Printed by J. H. for H. Mortlock, 1699.
[4], 280 p. 21cm.

SPECIAL COLLECTIONS SPINOZA

I-4 3851

Buddeus, Johann Franz, 1667-1729.
Traité de l'athéisme et de la superstition, par feu Mr. Jean-François Buddeus ... Avec des remarques historiques et philosophiques. Traduit en françois par Louis Philon ... et mis au jour par Jean-Chretien Fischer ... A Amsterdam, Chez Pierre Mortier, 1740.
[30], 368, [20] p. port. 20cm.

Includes a section on Spinoza (p. 233-238)

I-4 3847

Buchanan, James
Modern atheism. Boston, Gould & Lincoln, 1857.

Includes "The system of Spinoza" (p. 142-161)

NNUT

I-4 3852

Cairns, John, 1818-1892.
Unbelief in the eighteenth century as contrasted with its earlier and later history; being the Cunningham lectures for 1880. Edinburgh, Black, 1881.
ix, 309 p.

Includes a section on Spinoza (p. 50-59)

NNJ

I-4 3848

Buddeus, Johann Franz, 1667-1729.
Ioan. Francisci Buddei ... Theses theologicae de atheismo et superstitione variis observationibus illustratae et in usum recitationum academicarum editae. Suas quoque observationes et dissertationem contra atheos adjecit Hadrianus Buurt. Traiecti ad Rhenum, Apud I. H. Vonk van Lynden, 1737.
18 p.l., 625 p., [10] l.

Includes references to Spinoza.

NNUT

I-4 3853

Carroll, William,
A dissertation upon the tenth chapter of the fourth book of Mr. Locke's Essay, concerning humane understanding. Wherein that author's endeavours to establish Spinoza's atheistical hypothesis, more especially in that tenth chapter, are discover'd and confuted ... London, Printed by J. Matthews, 1706.
3 p. l., xv, 292 p.

SPECIAL COLLECTIONS SPINOZA

I-4 3849

Buddeus, Johann Franz, 1667-1729.
Ioan. Francisci Bvddei ... Theses theologicae de atheismo et svperstitione variis observationibvs illvstratae et in vsvm recitationvm academicarvm editae. Ienae, apud Ioan. Felic. Bielckivm, 1717.
[48], 816, [72] p. 14cm.

Includes a section on Spinoza (p. 163-179)

SPECIAL COLLECTIONS SPINOZA

I-4 3854

Conjectures philosophiques sur le sejour des ames décédées. à Francfourt & Leipsic, Chés Jean George Trausold, 1752.
24 p. 19cm.

Bound with L'athéisme folie dangereuse ... 1753.

NNC

 I-4 3855

Cudworth, Ralph, 1617-1688.
The true intellectual system of the universe: wherein all the reason and philosophy of atheism is confuted, and its impossibility demonstrated, with a treatise concerning eternal and immutable morality. To which are added the notes and dissertations of Dr. J. L. Mosheim, tr. by John Harrison. London, Printed for Thomas Tegg, 1845.
3 v. 23cm.

Includes references to Spinoza.

 I-4 3856

Cuperus, Franciscus
Arcana atheismi revelata, philosophice & paradoxè refutata, examine Tractatus theologico-politici. Per Franciscum Cuperum ... Roterodami, Apud Isaacum Naeranum, 1676.
[16], 304 p. 20cm.

Against Spinoza's Tractatus theologico-politicus.

I-4 3857

Derodon, David
David Derodons Widerlegter Atheismus worinnen aus der Vernunft erwiesen wird, dass ein Gott sey. Aus dem Frantzöschen übersetzt, mit einer Vorrede von des Auctoris Leben und Schrifften nebst benöthigten Anmerckungen und Register herausgegeben von Wigand Kahler. Lemgo, Gedruckt mit Meyerischen Schriften, 1733.
13 p. l., 252 p., 4 l. 1 plate.

Includes a reference to Spinoza (p. 25)

OCH

I-4 3858

[Dippel, Johann Conrad] 1673-1734.
Fatum Fatuum, dat is het dwase noodlot: sijnde een sonneklaar bewijs, dat alle tegensprekers van de vrye wil des menschen ... gedwongen sijn, de vryheidt Gods insgelijx weg te nemen: of de atheisterey van Spinosa vast te stellen. By welke gelegentheidt de geheymenissen der Cartesiaansche philosophie klaar ontdekt en wederlegt worden ... Nevens een geschrift ... genaamt, Een herder en eene kudde. Beyde ... door Christianus Democritus. Utrecht, en sijn te bekomen by G. en R. Wetstein in Amsterdam, 1709.
7 p. l., 328 p.

OCH

I-4 3859

Edwards, John, 1637-1716.
Some thoughts concerning the several causes and occasions of atheism, especially in the present age, with some brief reflections on Socinianism, and on a late book, entituled, "The reasonableness of Christianity as deliver'd in the Scriptures" [by J. Locke] London, Printed for J. Robinson, 1695.
4 p. l., 126 [i. e. 142] p. 18 cm.

MA

 I-4 3860

Flint, Robert, 1838-1910.
Anti-theistic theories; being the Baird lecture for 1877, by Robert Flint ... Edinburgh and London, W. Blackwood and sons, 1879.

xi, 555 p. 19 cm.

CONTENTS.—Atheism.—Ancient materialism.—Modern materialism.—Contemporary or scientific materialism.—Positivism.—Secularism.—Are there tribes of atheists?—Pessimism.—History of pantheism.—Pantheism.—Appendix.
Includes material on Spinoza (p. 358-379)

1. Natural theology. 2. Theism. I. Title.

BL200.F55 211 12—32185

Library of Congress [55g1]

I-4 3861

Flint, Robert, 1838-1910.
Anti-theistic theories; being the Baird lecture for 1877. 4th ed. Edinburgh and London, Blackwood, 1889.
xi, 555 p. 19 cm.

Includes a section on Spinoza (p. 358-375)

 I-4 3862

Flint, Robert, 1838-1910.
Anti-theistic theories; being the Baird lecture for 1877. 6th ed. Edinburgh, W. Blackwood and Sons, 1899.
xi, 554 p. 20cm.

Includes a section on Spinoza (p. 359-379)

 I-4 3863

[Frey des Landres, J Rodolphe]
Essai lyrique sur la religion. Francfort sur le Main, Chez la veuve Knoch et J. G. Eslinger, 1753.
[8], 78 p. 19cm.

"Avertissement" signed: J. E. R....s.
Attributed by Quérard to Frey des Landres.
Bound with L'athéisme folie dangereuse ... 1753.

NNC

 I-4 3864

Harris, John, 1667?-1719.
The atheistical objections, against the being of a God, and His attributes, fairly considered, and fully refuted. In eight sermons, preach'd in the Cathedral-Church of St. Paul, London, 1698. Being the seventh year of the lecture founded by the Honourable Robert Boyle, Esq; By John Harris ... London, Printed by J. L. for Richard Wilkin, 1698.
1 v. (various pagings) 21cm.

Each sermon has separate t.-p. and pagination
Includes references to Spinoza.

Heydenreich, Karl Heinrich, 1764-1801.
Briefe über den Atheismus. Herausgegeben von Karl Heinrich Heydenreich. Leipzig, bei Gottfried Martini, 1796.
3 p. l., [3]-168, [1] p. 18cm.

1. Atheism. I. Title.

Jäger, Johann Wolfgang, 1647-1720, praeses.
Franciscus Cuperus Amstelod. mala fide, aut ad minimum frigide atheismum Spinozae oppugnans pro materia disputationis praeside D. Joh. Wolfg. Jägero ... propositus a M. Georgio Frider. Mauritio Beuttler ... Tubingae, Typis Viduae G. H. Reisii [1710]
16 p.

Kirkman, Thomas Penyngton, 1806-1895.
Church cursing and atheism. Ramsgate, T. Scott, 1869.
iv, 72 p. 19cm.

Volume of pamphlets.

Kőbor, Thomas
Ein Gottesleugner? [i.e. Spinoza. c1922]
104-111 p.

In Concordia. Bibliothek für Freimaurer, Bd. 13 [c1922]

[Lamy, François] 1636-1711.
Le nouvel atheisme renversé, ou Refutation du sistême de Spinosa, tirée pour la plûpart de la conoissance de la nature de l'homme. Par un religieux benedictin de la Congrégation de Saint Maur. A Paris, Chez Jean de Nully, 1696.
[38], 540, [2] p. 17cm.

Lange, Joachim, 1670-1744.
Caussa Dei et religionis naturalis adversus atheismum, et, quae eum gignit, aut promovet, pseudophilosophiam veterum ac recentiorum, praesertim stoicam et Spinozianam ac Wolfianam: una cum nova systematis Wolfiani analysi; e genuinis verae philosophiae principiis methodo demonstrativa adserta. 2. ed. Halae Saxonum, Litteris et Impensis Orphanotrophi, 1727.
22 p. l., 560 p., 8 l. plate.

Lange, Joachim, 1670-1744.
Caussa Dei et religionis natvralis adversus atheismum, et, quae evm gignit, aut promovet, pseudophilosophiam veterum et recentiorum, praesertim stoicam et Spinozianam, e genuinis verae philosophiae principiis methodo demonstrativa adserta, auctore D. Ioachimo Langio ... Halae, Saxonum, Impensis Orphanotrophei, 1723.
11 p. l., 248 p. 1 pl.

Includes a section on Spinoza (p. 54-69)

[Leuckfeld, Johann Georg] 1668-1726.
Der verführische Atheisten Hauffe und das ungöttliche Wesen unter den Christen, worinnen so wohl der Sinn- und thätlichen Atheisterey ausführliche Beschreibungen, als auch drey sonderbare Haupt-Quellen ... mit einigen Exempeln und dienlichen Anmerckungen dargestellet und gewiesen werden. Auf Veranlassung des itzo in der Christenheit seyenden verwirten Zustandes verfertiget, und mit Genehmhaltung einiger Freunde zum Druck übergeben von J. G. L. Auff

CONTINUED ON NEXT CARD

[Leuckfeld, Johann Georg] 1668-1726. Der verführische Atheisten Hauffe. 1699. (Card 2)

Unkosten Henrici Theophili Steins. Franckfurth, Gedruckt bey Joh. Gottlieb Wahrhafft, 1699.
[27], 698 (i.e. 702) p. 18cm.

Includes a passage on Spinoza (p. 82-83)

Lindau, Hans, 1875- ed.
Die Schriften zu J. G. Fichte's Atheismus-Streit; hrsg. von Hans Lindau. München, G. Müller, 1912.
xxix, 387 p. 22cm. (Bibliothek der Philosophen, geleitet von Fritz Mauthner. 4. Bd.)

Includes references to Spinoza.
Bibliography: p. 387.

I-4
3875

Litman, Alexander, 1899-
Man's value and destiny; moral atheism in Spinoza. [1935]
77-85 p.

In American scholar, v. 4, 1935.

I-4
3876

Maréchal, Pierre Sylvain, 1750-1803.
Dictionnaire des athées anciens et modernes. Paris, chez Grabit [1800]
lxxii, 524 p.

Includes an article on Spinoza (p. 446-449)

NN

I-4
3877

Maréchal, Pierre Sylvain, 1750-1803.
Dictionnaire des athées anciens et modernes. Deuxième édition, augmentée des supplémens de J. Lalande; de pusieurs articles inédits, et d'une notice nouvelle sur Maréchal et ses ouvrages, par J. B. L. Germond. Bruxelles, Chez l'éditeur, 1833.
23, xxxix, 328, 85 p. 24 cm.

Includes an article on Spinoza (p. 279-261)

I-4
3878

Nieuwentijdt, Bernard, 1654-1718.
Die Erkänntniss der Weissheit, Macht und Güte des Göttlichen Wesens ... zur Ueberzeugung derer Atheisten ... Mit eine Vorrede von Christian Wolff, übersetzt von W. C. Baumann. Frankfurt, 1732.

CU

I-4
3879

Nieuwentijdt, Bernard, 1654-1718.
Het regt gebruik der werelt beschouwingen ter overtuiginge van ongodisten en ongelovigen aangetoont, door Bernard Nieuwentijdt. Den vijfden druk. Amsterdam, J. Pauli, 1730.
916 p.

OCH

I-4
3880

Nieuwentijdt, Bernard, 1654-1718.
Rechter Gebrauch der Welt-Betrachtung zur Erkentnis der Macht, Weisheit und Güte Gottes, auch Ueberzeugung der Atheisten und Ungläubigen. In einer freien Uebersetzung abermal ans Licht gestellet, und mit einigen Anmerkungen erläutert, von D. Joh. Andreas Segner ... Jena, bei Christian Heinrich Cuno, 1747.
11 p. l., 605, [23] p. 19 tables.

Includes references to Spinoza.

NN

I-4
3881

Nieuwentijdt, Bernard, 1654-1718.
The religious philosopher: or, The right use of contemplating the works of the Creator ... designed for the conviction of atheists and infidels ... throughout which, all the late discoveries in anatomy, philosophy, and astronomy ... are most copiously handled by that learned mathematician, Dr. Nieuwentyt. Translated from the original by John Chamberlayne ... To which is prefix'd, a letter to the translator, by the Reverend J. T. Desaguliers ... London, Printed for J. Senex [etc.] 1718-19.
3 v. fold. plates, fold. diagrs. 21cm.
~~(Continued on next card)~~

DLC

30-24904
[3881]

I-4
3882

Pensées sur la religion dirigées à la reunion des Chretiens ... 1749.
32 p. 19cm.

Bound with L'athéisme folie dangereuse ... 1753.

NNC

I-4
3883

Philipps, Jenkin Thomas, d. 1755.
Dissertatio historico-philosophica de atheismo. Sive Historia atheismi in qua multi scriptores vetusti & recentiores, impietatis falsò postulati, liberantur à turpi atheismi stigmate: alii verò qui de supremo Numine sentire videntur minus rectè, corripiuntur meritò. Authore J. Thomasio Philipps. Londini, Sumptibus authoris, 1716.
[12], 155 p. 20cm.

Includes a section on Spinoza (p. 128-136)

I-4
3884

Philipps, Jenkin Thomas, d. 1755.
Dissertatio historico-philosophica de atheismo. Sive Historia atheismi in qua multi scriptores vetusti & recentiores, impietatis falsò postulati, liberantur à turpi atheismi stigmate: alii verò qui de supremo Numine sentire videntur minus rectè, corripiuntur meritò. Authore J. Thomasio Philipps. Londini, Sumptibus authoris, 1716.
[12], 155 p. 18cm.

Includes a section on Spinoza (p. 128-136)

(Continued on next card)

Philipps, Jenkin Thomas, d. 1755. Dissertatio historico-philosophica de atheismo. 1716. (Card 2)

Six pages (leaves A2, A5-6) missing at beginning. Ms. notes by A. S. Oko.

Philipps, Jenkin Thomas, d. 1755.
Historia atheismi breviter delineata à Jenkino Thomasio...cui accedit Samvelis Clark tractatvs eximivs De existentia et attribvtis Dei, contra Spinosam atqve Hobbesivm Anglice conscriptis, jam autem Latine redditus, cvm praefatione Christiani Gotlib. Schvvarzii. Altorfi Noricorvm, apud Jod. Gvil. Kohlesivm, 1713.
286 (i.e. 288), 174 p. 17 cm.

Includes a section "De Benedicto Spinosa principe atheorum" (p. 227-241)

Reimmann, Jacob Friedrich, 1668-1743.
Iac. Frid. Reimmanni ... Historia vniversalis atheismi et atheorvm falso & merito suspectorum apud Jvdaeos, ethnicos, Christianos, Mvhamedanos, ordine chronologico descripta & a suis initiis usque ad nostra tempora deducta ... Hildesiae, Apud Lvdolphvm Schroeder, 1725.
[32], 562, [22] p. 19cm.

Includes references to Spinoza.

Sabatier, Antoine, de Castres, 1742-1817.
Apologie de Spinosa et du spinosisme, contre les athées, les incrédules et contre les théologiens scolastiques-platoniciens. Paris, Fournier, 1810.
iv, 136 p.

Scheppelin, Joh. Anton
Spinocismus, sive Benedicti Spinosae famosi atheistae vita et doctrinalia ... Tubingae [1710]

Thesis, Tübingen.

Staalkopff, Jacobus
Ab impiis detorsionibus Thomae Hobbesii et Benedicti de Spinoza, oraculum Paulinum, Per ipsum vivimus, movemur et sumus, Act. XVII, 28 asseret ... Gryphiswaldiae, Typis G. H. Adolphi [1707]
28 p.

Thesis, Greifswald.

Staalkopff, Jacobus, praeses.
Dissertatio de atheismo Benedicti de Spinoza ... adversus Joan. Geo. Wachterum ... Gryphiswaldiae, Typis D. B. Starkii [1707]
16 p.

Thesis, Greifswald (H. Ehlers, respondent)

Stichtelyke klaag-sangen, op-geheven over de goddelose spotternyen en lasteringen der snode Spinosisten; op een aller hemel-tergenste wyze uytgebraakt tegens God, zyn Heilig Woord, getrouwe en godvruchtige leeraren en waare belyderen van het Zalig Evangelium in Nederland. Ook zyn hier bygevoegd by wegen van kant-tekeningen, eenige korte aanmerkingen op het eer- en- faam-rovend libel van Henrik Hakvoord, genaamt Noodsakelyk

CONTINUED ON NEXT CARD

Stichtelyke klaag-sangen ... 1726. (Card 2)

bericht; enkelyk daar toe gericht, om in de aarde te treden de naam van den eerwaarden en zeer godvruchtigen heere Henricus Ravesteyn, predikant te Zwolle. Door een Liefhebber der waarheid. Te Zwolle, Gedrukt by D. Rampen en F. Clement, 1726.
36 p. 19cm.

Triller, Daniel Wilhelm, 1695-1782.
Hippocrates atheismi falso accusatus. Contra Nicol. Hieron. Gundlingium. Auctore D. W. T. D. Rudolstadii, Litteris Urbanianis, 1719.
112, [4] p. 18 cm.

Includes references to Spinoza.

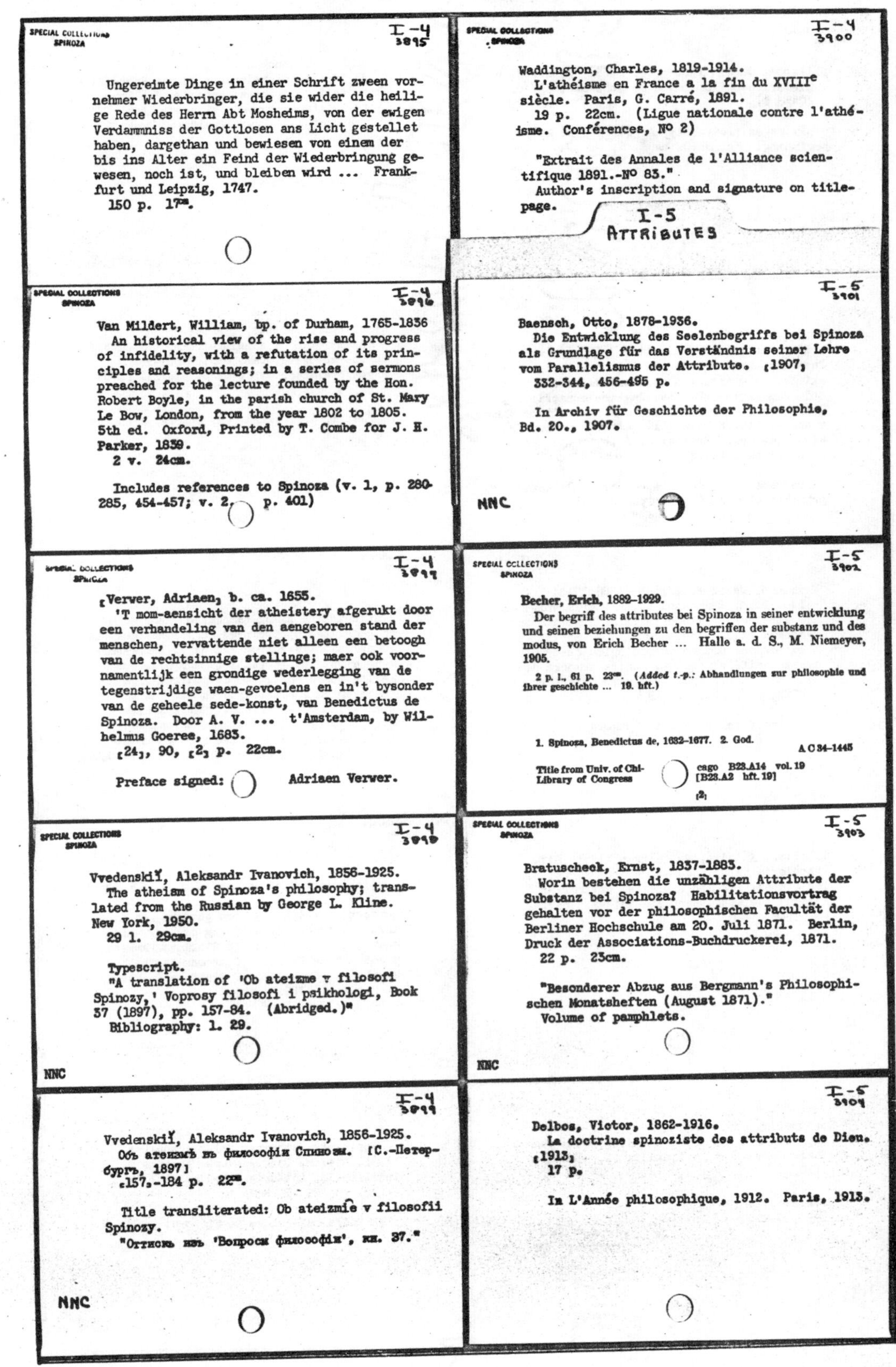

I-4
3895

Ungereimte Dinge in einer Schrift zween vornehmer Wiederbringer, die sie wider die heilige Rede des Herrn Abt Mosheims, von der ewigen Verdammniss der Gottlosen ans Licht gestellet haben, dargethan und bewiesen von einem der bis ins Alter ein Feind der Wiederbringung gewesen, noch ist, und bleiben wird ... Frankfurt und Leipzig, 1747.
150 p. 17cm.

I-4
3896

Van Mildert, William, bp. of Durham, 1765-1836
An historical view of the rise and progress of infidelity, with a refutation of its principles and reasonings; in a series of sermons preached for the lecture founded by the Hon. Robert Boyle, in the parish church of St. Mary Le Bow, London, from the year 1802 to 1805. 5th ed. Oxford, Printed by T. Combe for J. H. Parker, 1839.
2 v. 24cm.

Includes references to Spinoza (v. 1, p. 280-285, 454-457; v. 2, p. 401)

I-4
3897

[Verwer, Adriaen] b. ca. 1655.
'T mom-aensicht der atheistery afgerukt door een verhandeling van den aengeboren stand der menschen, vervattende niet alleen een betoogh van de rechtsinnige stellinge; maer ook voornamentlijk een grondige wederlegging van de tegenstrijdige waen-gevoelens en in't bysonder van de geheele sede-konst, van Benedictus de Spinoza. Door A. V. ... t'Amsterdam, by Wilhelmus Goeree, 1683.
[24], 90, [2] p. 22cm.

Preface signed: Adriaen Verwer.

I-4
3898

Vvedenskiĭ, Aleksandr Ivanovich, 1856-1925.
The atheism of Spinoza's philosophy; translated from the Russian by George L. Kline. New York, 1950.
29 l. 29cm.

Typescript.
"A translation of 'Ob ateizme v filosofi Spinozy,' Voprosy filosofi i psikhologi, Book 37 (1897), pp. 157-84. (Abridged.)"
Bibliography: l. 29.

I-4
3899

Vvedenskiĭ, Aleksandr Ivanovich, 1856-1925.
Объ атеизмѣ въ философіи Спинозы. [С.-Петербургъ, 1897]
[157]-184 p. 22cm.

Title transliterated: Ob ateizmie v filosofii Spinozy.
"Оттискъ изъ 'Вопросы философіи', кн. 37."

I-4
3900

Waddington, Charles, 1819-1914.
L'athéisme en France a la fin du XVIIIe siècle. Paris, G. Carré, 1891.
19 p. 22cm. (Ligue nationale contre l'athéisme. Conférences, No 2)

"Extrait des Annales de l'Alliance scientifique 1891.-No 83."
Author's inscription and signature on title-page.

I-5 ATTRIBUTES

I-5
3901

Baensch, Otto, 1878-1936.
Die Entwicklung des Seelenbegriffs bei Spinoza als Grundlage für das Verständnis seiner Lehre vom Parallelismus der Attribute. [1907]
332-344, 456-495 p.

In Archiv für Geschichte der Philosophie, Bd. 20., 1907.

I-5
3902

Becher, Erich, 1882-1929.
Der begriff des attributes bei Spinoza in seiner entwicklung und seinen beziehungen zu den begriffen der substanz und des modus, von Erich Becher ... Halle a. d. S., M. Niemeyer, 1905.
2 p. l., 61 p. 23cm. (*Added t.-p.:* Abhandlungen zur philosophie und ihrer geschichte ... 19. hft.)

1. Spinoza, Benedictus de, 1632-1677. 2. God.

A C 34-1445

Title from Univ. of Chicago B23.A14 vol. 19
Library of Congress [B23.A2 hft. 19]
[2]

I-5
3903

Bratuscheck, Ernst, 1837-1883.
Worin bestehen die unzähligen Attribute der Substanz bei Spinoza? Habilitationsvortrag gehalten vor der philosophischen Facultät der Berliner Hochschule am 20. Juli 1871. Berlin, Druck der Associations-Buchdruckerei, 1871.
22 p. 23cm.

"Besonderer Abzug aus Bergmann's Philosophischen Monatsheften (August 1871)."
Volume of pamphlets.

I-5
3904

Delbos, Victor, 1862-1916.
La doctrine spinoziste des attributs de Dieu. [1913]
17 p.

In L'Année philosophique, 1912. Paris, 1913.

I-5
3905

Ebbinghaus, Julius, 1885-
Über den Grund der Beschränkung unserer Erkenntnis auf die Attribute des Denkens und der Ausdehnung bei Spinoza. [1932]
420-421 p.

In Forschungen und Fortschritte, Jahrgang 8, Nov. 20, 1932.

I-5
3906

Frank, Semen Liudvigovich, 1877-1950.
Ученіе Спинозы объ атрибутахъ. [1912]
[523]-567 p.

Title transliterated: Uchenie Spinozy ob attributakh.
In Вопросы философіи и психологіи, годъ 23, № 4, 1912.

I-5
3907

Henke,
Die Lehre von den Attributen bei Spinoza. Perleberg, F. Jacobson [1875]
18 p. 28cm.

At head of title: Programm der städtischen Realschule erster Ordnung zu Perleberg ...

1. Spinoza, Benedictus de, 1632-1677.

I-5
3908

Krösche, Kurt, 1881-
Wie weit stimmt die Lehre Spinozas vom Parallelismus der göttlichen Attribute überein mit der Theorie vom psychisch-physischen Parallelismus bei Fechner und Fr. Alb. Lange? Berlin, Druck von W. Pormetter, 1910.
52 p. 26cm.

Thesis, Erlangen.
Bibliography: p. [6]

I-5
3909

Petersdorff, Egon von, 1892-
Spinoza's unendliche Attribute Gottes. [Hagae Comitis, 1922]
67-91 p. 22cm.

Cover-title: Dissertatio ex Chronici Spinozani tomo secundo separatim edita.

I-5
3910

Tumarkin, Anna, 1875-
Zu Spinozas Attributenlehre. [1907]
322-331 p.

In Archiv für Geschichte der Philosophie, Bd. 20., 1907.

I-5
3911

Vanni-Rovighi, Sofia
L'attributo spinoziano e la dimostrazione dell'unicità della sostanza. [1933]
164-166 p.

In Rivista di filosofia neo-scolastica, anno 25, 1933.

I-5
3912

Wolfson, Harry Austryn, 1887-
Spinoza's mechanism, attributes and panpsychism. [1937]
cover-title, 307-314 p. 25cm.

"Reprinted from the Philosophical review, May, 1937."
Ms. notes by A. S. Oko.

1. Spinoza, Benedictus de, 1632-1677.

I-6
BEATITUDE

I-6
3913

[Boeuf, Marie] 1870-1907.
La béatitude chez Spinoza et chez Fichte, par Camille Bos [pseud. 1905]
413-420 p.

In Archiv für Geschichte der Philosophie, Bd. 18., 1905.

I-6
3914

Vloemans, Antoon
Hoe Spinoza God zocht en de gelukzaligheid vond. [1927]
321-330 p. 25cm.

From Het Nieuwe leven, 12e jaargang, afl. 12, April 1927.

1. Spinoza, Benedictus de, 1632-1677.

 I-6 3915

Wahle, Richard, 1857-
Die Glückseligkeitslehre der "Ethik" des Spinoza. Wien, In Commission bei F. Tempsky, 1889.
44 p. 25cm. (Sitzungsberichte der Kais. Akademie der Wissenschaften in Wien. Philosophisch-historische Classe. Bd. CXIX, XI)

I-7
BIBLE

I-7 3916

Arnold, Matthew, 1822-1888.
Essays in criticism. [2d ed.] Boston, Ticknor and Fields, 1866.
xv, [2], 506 p. 19 cm.

First series.
Includes an essay "Spinoza" (p. 237-252)

NNC

 I-7 3917

Arnold, Matthew, 1822-1888.
Essays in criticism. Boston, James R. Osgood and Company, 1874.
xv, 506 p. 19cm.

Includes an essay, "Spinoza" (p. [237]-252)

I-7 3918

Arnold, Matthew, 1822-1888.
Essays in criticism, by Matthew Arnold. London and New York, Macmillan and co., 1889.
xi p., 1 l., 379 p. 18½ cm.
First series.
CONTENTS.—The function of criticism at the present time.—The literary influence of academies.—Maurice de Guérin.—Eugénie de Guérin.—Heinrich Heine.—Pagan and mediæval religious sentiment.—A Persian Passion play.—Joubert.—Spinoza and the Bible.—Marcus Aurelius.
1. Criticism. 2. *Guérin, Maurice de, 1810-1839. 3. Guérin, Eugénie de, 1805-1848. 4. Heine, Heinrich, 1797-1856. 5. Joubert, Joseph, 1754-1824. 6. Spinoza, Benedictus de, 1632-1677. 7. Aurelius Antoninus, Marcus, emperor of Rome.

DLC PR4022.E3 1889 4—20112
Library of Congress [55a1]

I-7 3919

Arnold, Matthew, 1822-1888.
Essays in criticism. London and New York, Macmillan, 1891.
xi, 379 p. 19 cm.

First series.
Includes an essay "Spinoza and the Bible" (p. 317-343)

NNC

 I-7 3920

Arnold, Matthew, 1822-1888.
Essays in criticism. New York, Macmillan, 1883-
v. 1.

Includes an essay "Spinoza and the Bible" (v. 1, p. [307]-343)

 I-7 3921

Arnold, Matthew, 1822-1888.
Essays in criticism. With introduction by Walter Raleigh. London, Gowans and Gray, 1912.
xvi, 350 p. port. 15cm. (Pocket masterpieces, 2)

Includes an essay "Spinoza" (p. [296]-313)

I-7 3922

Arnold, Matthew, 1822-1888.
Essays, including Essays in criticism, 1865; On translating Homer (with F. W. Newman's reply) and five other essays now for the first time collected. London, Milford, 1914.
487 p. port. 21 cm.

Includes an essay "Spinoza and the Bible" (p. 192-216)

NNC

I-7 3923

Arnold, Matthew, 1822-1888.
Literature & dogma; an essay towards a better apprehension of the Bible. New York, Macmillan, 1873.
xxxvi, 388 p. 19 cm.

NNC

 I-7 3924

Bonifas, Henri
Les idées bibliques de Spinoza. Mazamet, Imprimerie V. Carayol, 1904.
98 p. 24cm.

Thesis, Montauban.
Bibliography: p. [4]

1. Spinoza, Benedictus de, 1632-1677.

I-7 3925

[Bradlaugh, Charles] 1833-1891.
The Bible: what it is; its authorship & authenticity. Book 1. By Iconoclast. London, Austin, 1870.

OCH

I-7 3926

Briggs, Charles Augustus, 1841-1913.
General introduction to the study of Holy Scripture; the principles, methods, history and results of its several departments and of the whole. New York, Scribner, 1900.
xxii, 688 p. 23 cm.

Includes references to Spinoza (p. 274-276) in chapter "History of the higher criticism of Holy Scripture".

MNC

I-7 3927

Carpzov, Johann Gottlob, 1679-1767.
I. G. Carpzovii critica sacra Veteris Testamenti, parte I. circa textum originalem. II. circa versiones. III. circa pseudo-criticam Guil. Whistoni ... Lipsiae, sumtibus I. C. Martini, 1748.
7 p. l., 987 p., [48] l. port.

Includes references to Spinoza.

NNJ

SPECIAL COLLECTIONS
SPINOZA
I-7 3928

Cornill, Carl Heinrich, 1854-1920.
Einleitung in das Alte Testament. Freiburg i. B., J. C. B. Mohr (P. Siebeck) 1891.
xii, 325 p. 23cm. (Grundriss der theologischen Wissenschaften. [1. Reihe] 2. Theil, 1. Bd.)

Includes references to Spinoza.

I-7 3929

Cornill, Carl Heinrich, 1854-1920.
Introduction to the canonical books of the Old Testament, by Carl Cornill ... tr. by G. H. Box ... London, Williams and Norgate; New York, G. P. Putnam's sons, 1907.
xii, 556 p. 22½cm. (*Half-title:* Theological translation library. vol. xxiii)

First edition of German original published Freiburg i. B., 1891, under title: Einleitung in das Alte Testament. *cf.* Pref.

Includes references to Spinoza.

1. Bible. O. T.—Introductions. 2. Bible—Introductions—O. T. I. Box, George Herbert, 1869- tr.

8—3645

NNUT
Library of Congress BS1140.C7
[a39j1]

I-7 3930

Duff, Archibald, 1845-1934.
... History of Old Testament criticism, by Archibald Duff ... New York and London, G. P. Putnam's sons, 1910.
xiii, 201 p. front., illus. (ports.) 16½cm. (A history of the sciences)

Bibliography: p. 189-193.

Includes a section "The Old Testament criticism of Baruch Spinoza" (p. 129-136), a portrait of Spinoza (p. 108), and other references to him.

1. Bible. O. T.—Criticism, interpretation, etc.—Hist. 2. Bible—Criticism, interpretation, etc.—Hist.—O. T.

10—16088

Library of Congress BS1160.D6 1910 a
——— Copy 2.
Copyright A 268582 [39h2]

SPECIAL COLLECTIONS
SPINOZA
I-7 3931

[Faydit, Pierre Valentin] 1640?-1709.
Remarques sur Virgile et sur Homere, et sur le style poétique de l'Écriture-Sainte; où l'on refute les inductions pernicieuses que Spinosa, Grotius & Mr le Clerc en ont tirées. Et quelques opinions particulières du Pere Mallebranche, du Sieur l'Elevel, & de Monsieur Simon. A Paris, Chez Jean & Pierre Cot, 1705.
[16], 506, [38] p. 17cm.

I-7 3932

[Filleau de la Chaise, Jean] 1630 (ca.)-1693.
An excellent discourse proving the divine original and authority of the five books of Moses. Written originally in French by Monsieur Du Bois de la Cour [pseud.] ... To which is added a second part, or an examination of ... Père Simon's Critical history of the Old Testament, wherein all his objections, with the weightiest of Spinosa's, against Moses's being the author of the first five books of the Bible are answered ... By W. L. London, Printed for Tho. Parkhurst, 1682.
20 p. l., 168 p.

UCLA

I-7 3933

Fossati, Luigi
Spinoza e la critica moderna della Bibbia. [1927]
[217]-234 p.

In Rivista di filosofia, anno 18, 1927.

I-7 3934

Gilbert, George Holley, 1854-1930.
Interpretation of the Bible; a short history. New York, Macmillan, 1908.
vii, 309 p. 21 cm.

Includes a section on Spinoza (p. 241-244)

NNUT

I-7
3935

Ginzberg, Asher, 1856-1927.
Jerusalem, 1923-25. אגרות אחד-העם.
6 v.

Title transliterated: ᶜigeroth Ahad-ha-ᶜam.
Includes a letter to Joseph Klausner, with reference to Spinoza's attitude toward the Gospels (v. 4, p. 216) .

NNJ

I-7
3936

Gottheil, Richard James Horatio, 1862-1936.
Some early Jewish Bible criticism. ₍1904₎
12 p.

In Journal of Biblical literature, v. 23, 1904.
Includes references to Spinoza.

SPECIAL COLLECTIONS
SPINOZA

I-7
3937

Gray, Edward Dundas McQueen, 1854-
Old Testament criticism, its rise and progress from the second century to the end of the eighteenth. A historical sketch. New York, Harper ₍1923₎
252 p. 21cm.

Includes a chapter on Spinoza (p. 86-100)
Bibliography: p. ₍193₎-205.

SPECIAL COLLECTIONS
SPINOZA

I-7
3938

Grew, Nehemiah, 1641-1712.
Cosmologia sacra: or a discourse of the universe as it is the creature and kingdom of God. Chiefly written, to demonstrate the truth and excellency of the Bible; which contains the laws of his kingdom in this lower world. In five books. By Dr. Nehemiah Grew ... London, Printed for W. Rogers, S. Smith, and B. Walford, 1701.
₍14₎, xviii, 372 p. port. 32cm.

Includes references to Spinoza (p. 179-180, 203)

SPECIAL COLLECTIONS
SPINOZA

I-7
3939

Husik, Isaac, 1876-1939.
Maimonides and Spinoza on the interpretation of the Bible. ₍1935₎
22-40 p. 26cm.

"Reprinted from Journal of the American Oriental Society, Supplement no. 1, September, 1935."
Presentation copy to A. S. Oko, with the author's inscription and signature.

NNC

I-7
3940

Kahana, David, 1838-1915.
מסרת סיג למקרא.(ראיות...כי נוסחת כתבי הקדש אשר בידינו...היא העיקרית,וכי המסורה קדומה מאד והיא סיג למקרא...).
₍Vienna, 1882₎
134 p.

Title transliterated: Masoreth syag la-mikra.
Includes a section on Spinoza (p. 5)

NNJ

SPECIAL COLLECTIONS
SPINOZA

I-7
3941

Karppe, S 1866-
Quam Spinoza methodum scripturae interpretandae proposuerit. Lutetiae Parisiorum, Typis mandabat L. Maretheux, 1901.
55 p. 25cm.

Thesis, Paris.
Bibliographical footnotes.

SPECIAL COLLECTIONS
SPINOZA

I-7
3942

Krochmal, Abraham, 1823-1895.
הכתב והמכתב. ₍1874₎ (Card 2)

Title transliterated: ha-Kĕthabh ...
Added t.-p. in German: Haksaw wehamichtow; oder, Schrift und Urschrift. Eine zur Bibelerklärung wichtige alte Handschrift, welche der Sage nach identificirt wird mit dem von Herder erwähnten Bibelkomentare des Baruch Benedict Spinoza, erläutert und in deutscher Uibersetzung herausgegeben von Abraham Krochmal. Lemberg, Druck von Carl Budweiser, 1875.
Introduction in German.

NNC

I-7
3943

La Mothe, Claude Grostête, sieur de, 1647-1715?
The inspiration of the New Testament asserted and explained, in answer to some modern writers. London, Printed for Tho. Bennet, 1694.
₍11₎, 178 p. 18 cm.

NNUT

I-7
3944

₍Le Clerc, Jean₎ 1657-1736.
Sentimens de quelques théologiens de Hollande sur l'Histoire critique du Vieux Testament composée par le P. Richard Simon de l'Oratoire. Où en remarquant les fautes de cet auteur, on donne divers principes utiles pour l'intelligence de l'Ecriture Sainte. A Amsterdam, chez Henry Desbordes, 1685.
viii, 457 p.

Includes references to Spinoza.

NNUT

I-7
3945

Lee, William, 1815-1883.
The inspiration of Holy Scripture, its nature and proof: eight discourses, preached before the University of Dublin. Fourth edition. Dublin, Hodges, Smith, 1865.
607 p. 23 cm.

Includes references to Spinoza.

MH

I-7
3946

Le Long, Isaäc, *b.* 1683.
Boek-zaal der nederduytsche Bybels, geopent, in een historische verhandelinge van de oversettinge der Heylingen Schrifture in de nederduytsche taale ... Met een omstandig bericht, van meer dan hondert oude handtschriften, van Bybels en bybelsche boeken des Ouden en Nieuwen Testaments, tot op de vindinge van de drukkonst ... Doormengt met ... aanmerkingen ... door Isaac Le Long. Amsterdam, Hendrik Vieroot, 1732.
8 p. l., 898, [11] p. 21½cm.
Includes a reference to Spinoza (p. 845)
1. Bible. Dutch—Bibliography.
A 10-376
Union theol. sem. Libr. for Library of Congress [a37b1]

I-7
3947

Le Rossignol, James Edward, 1866-
Spinoza as a Biblical critic. [1895]
52-60 p.

In Canadian Methodist quarterly, v. 7, 1895.

NNUT

I-7
3948

Lipman, Armand

תורה ה׳ תמימה. Authenticité du Pentateuque; ou, La critique devant la tradition. Paris, E. Leroux, 1929.
xii, 292 p.

Includes a section on Spinoza (p. 126-128)

NNJ

SPECIAL COLLECTIONS
SPINOZA

I-7
3949

Löw, Leopold, 1811-1875.
המפתח Praktische einleitung in die Heilige Schrift und geschichte der schriftauslegung, ein lehrbuch für die reifere jugend, ein handbuch für gebildete. Von Leopold Löw ... Erster theil. Allgemeine einleitung und geschichte der Schriftauslegung. Gross-Kanischa, Druck von J. Markbreiter, 1855.
2 p. l., ix, [3]-355 p., 1 l. 20cm.
No more published.
Imperfect: p. 321-355 lacking.
Includes a section on Spinoza (p. 293-300)
1. Bible. O. T.—Criticism, interpretation, etc.—Hist.
Title transliterated: ha-Maftea*h*.
Library of Congress BS1160.L6 44-52670
[2]

SPECIAL COLLECTIONS
SPINOZA

I-7
3950

Löwenstein, Leopold, 1843-1924, supposed author.
Spinoza als Bibelkritiker.
79 p. 20cm.

Manuscript in ink, with a few notes in pencil. Notation by Carl Gebhardt on title-page attributes the manuscript to Löwenstein and the pencilled notes tentatively to Kuno Fischer.
Some sections in Hebrew.

I-7
3951

Lowth, William, 1661-1732.
A vindication of the divine authority and inspiration of the writings of the Old and New Testament. In answer to a treatise lately translated out of French, entituled, Five letters concerning the inspiration of the Holy Scriptures [by Jean Le Clerc]. Oxford, Printed at the Theater, 1692.
18 p. l., 288 p. 17 cm.

Includes references to Spinoza.

MWA

SPECIAL COLLECTIONS
SPINOZA

I-7
3952

Margival, Henri
Essai sur Richard Simon et la critique biblique au XVIIe siècle. Paris, Maillet, 1900.
xxviii, 336 p. 25cm.

Includes references to Spinoza.

SPECIAL COLLECTIONS
SPINOZA

I-7
3953

Matthes, Jan Carel
De Bijbelcritiek van Spinoza. [1909]
cover-title, 23 p. 25cm.

"Overgedrukt uit Teyler's Theologisch tijdschrift, zevende jaargang, aflevering 2."

I-7
3954

Moore, George Foot, 1851-1931.
The literature of the Old Testament. London, Williams [c1913]
256 p. 18 cm. (Home university library of modern knowledge, no. 65)

Includes references to Spinoza.

SPECIAL COLLECTIONS SPINOZA I-7 3955

Pick, Bernhard, 1842-1917.
Spinoza and the Old Testament. [1893]
113-122, 194-203 p. 23cm.

From The Biblical world, August-September 1893.

I-7 3956

Picton, James Allanson, 1832-1910.
Man and the Bible, a review of the place of the Bible in human history. London, Williams and Norgate, 1909.
334 p. 22 cm.

Includes references to Spinoza.

NNJ

I-7 3957

Pillon, François, 1830-1914.
Les origines de l'exégèse moderne: Spinoza. [1876]
337-349; 389-398 p.

In La Critique philosophique, politique, scientifique, littéraire, t. 5, 29 juin 1876.

SPECIAL COLLECTIONS SPINOZA I-7 3958

Siegfried, Carl, 1830-1903.
Spinoza als Kritiker und Ausleger des Alten Testaments; ein Beitrag zur Geschichte der alttestamentlichen Kritik und Exegese. Naumberg, Druck von H. Sieling, 1867.
53 p. 27cm.

"Einladungsprogramm zu der ... Stiftungsfeier der Königlichen Landesschule Pforta."
~~Volume of pamphlets.~~

NNC

I-7 3959

Simon, Richard, 1638-1712.
Histoire critique du texte du Nouveau Testament, où l'on établit la verité des actes sur lesquels la religion chrétienne est fondée. Par Richard Simon, prêtre. 2. éd. rev. & cor. par l'auteur. A Rotterdam, chez R. Leers, 1689.
8 p. l., 298 p. 26 cm.

Includes a section referring to Spinoza (p. 190-192) and a chapter "Examen des objections de Spinosa contre l'inspiration des livres du Nouveau Testament" (p. 207-211)

SPECIAL COLLECTIONS SPINOZA I-7 3960

Strauss, Leo, 1899-
Cohens Analyse der Bibel-Wissenschaft Spinozas. [1924]
295-314 p. 23cm.

From Der Jude, VIII. Jahrgang, Heft 5/6, Mai/Juni 1924.
A discussion of Hermann Cohen's "Spinoza über Staat und Religion, Judentum und Christentum".

SPECIAL COLLECTIONS SPINOZA I-7 3961

Strauss, Leo, 1899-
Die religionskritik Spinozas als grundlage seiner Bibelwissenschaft; untersuchungen zu Spinozas Theologisch-politischem traktat, von Leo Strauss. Berlin, Akademie-verlag, 1930.
3 p. l., ix-xii p., 1 l., 288 p. 24cm. (*Added t.-p.:* Veröffentlichungen der Akademie für die wissenschaft des judentums. Philosophische sektion. 2. bd.)

Ms. notes by Carl Gebhardt.

1. Spinoza, Benedictus de, 1632-1677. Tractatus theologico-politicus. I. Title. 30-19841

Library of Congress B3985.G5S7
Copyright A—Foreign 7224
[2]

SPECIAL COLLECTIONS SPINOZA I-7 3962

Strauss, Leo, 1899-
Zur Bibelwissenschaft Spinozas und seiner Vorläufer. [1926]
[3]-22 p. 25cm.

From Korrespondenzblatt des Vereins zur Gründung und Erhaltung einer Akademie für die Wissenschaft des Judentums, 7. Jahrgang, 1926.

SPECIAL COLLECTIONS SPINOZA I-7 3963

Trattner, Ernest Robert, 1898-
Unravelling the Book of books; being the story of how the puzzles of the Bible were solved, and its documents unravelled, by Ernest R. Trattner. New York, C. Scribner's sons, 1929.
xvi, 325 p. plates, facsims. 20½ cm.

Includes references to Spinoza.
Bibliography: p. 315-320.

1. Bible—Criticism, interpretation, etc. 2. Bible—Criticism, interpretation, etc.—Hist. I. Title.

BS520.T7 220 29—10663
Library of Congress [54n½]

I-7 3964

Veil, Charles Marie de, d. 1690.
A letter to the honourable Robert Boyle, esq., defending the divine authority of the Holy Scripture, and that it alone is the rule of faith. In answer to Father Simon's Critical history of the Old Testament... London, Printed for Thomas Malthus, 1683.
[1], 18 p. 19 cm.

NNUT

Vexler, M
Spinoza et l'authorité de la Bible. Paris, Librairie Durlacher, 1912.
31 p. 25cm.

"Extrait de la Revue des études juives, année 1912."

I-8
CAUSALITY

Brown, Thomas, 1778-1820.
Inquiry into the relation of cause and effect. Edinburgh, A. Constable, 1818.
xvi, 569 p.

Brown, Thomas, 1778-1820.
Inquiry into the relation of cause and effect. By Thomas Brown ... 4th ed. London, H. G. Bohn; [etc., etc.] 1835.
1 p. l., [v]-xvi, 461, [1] p. 22cm.

CONTENTS.—Introduction.—On the real import of the relation of cause and effect.—On the source of illusion with respect to the relation.—On the circumstances, in which the belief of the relation arises.—On Mr. Hume's theory of our belief of the relation.

1. Causation. 2. Hume, David, 1711-1776.

Guenther, W
Der Kausalitätsbegriff bei Spinoza. Wolgast, 1905.
24 p.

Programm -Wilhelmsschule, Wolgast.

Günther, W
Der Kausalitätsbegriff bei Spinoza. Wolgast, E. Hoffmann, 1905.
24 p. 26cm.

At head of title: Jahresbericht des Real-Progymnasiums (Wilhelmsschule) zu Wolgast. Ostern 1905.

Lamberty, Paul, 1885-
Die Ursache von allem erkannt; das Ende der Relativitätstheorie. [Haag, Selbstverlag des Verfassers, 1925?]
98 p. 22cm.

Includes a reference to Spinoza (p. 77)

Mann, Wilhelm
Causalitäts- und Zweckbegriff bei Spinoza. [1901]
437-480 p.

In Archiv für Geschichte der Philosophie, Bd. 14., 1901.

Mehlberg, Henryk
Essai sur la théorie causale du temps. [1935]
119-260 p.

In Studia philosophica, v. 1, 1935.
Includes a reference to Spinoza (p. 125)

Nagel, Fr
Über den Begriff der Ursache bei Spinoza und Schopenhauers Kritik desselben. [1898]
252-266 p.

In Zeitschrift für Philosophie und philosophische Kritik, n. F. 111. Bd., 1898.

Rackwitz, Max, 1858-
Studien über Causalität und Identität als Grundprincipien des Spinozismus; ein kritischer Versuch. Halle, Karras, 1884.
34 p. 24cm.

Thesis, Halle.
Title-page lacking.

1. Spinoza, Benedictus de, 1632-1677.

I-8
3975

Seligkowitz, Benzion, 1864-
Causa sui, causa prima et causa essendi. Mit besonderer Berücksichtigung von Schopenhauer's Kritik Spinoza's. [1892]
322-336 p.

In Archiv für Geschichte der Philosophie, Bd. 5, 1892.

I-8
3976

Tarozzi, Giuseppe, 1866-
La necessità spinoziana e il determinismo contemporaneo. [1927]
[354]-360 p.

In Rivista di filosofia, anno 18, 1927.

I-8
3977

Thilo, Christfried Albert
Über den Begriff der Kausalität bei Plato und Spinoza. [1893]
304-319 p.

In Zeitschrift für exacte Philosophie, Bd. 19, 1893.

I-9
CHRISTIANITY

I-9
3978

Beverland, Adriaan, 1654?-1712.
Le péché originel, traduit librement du latin d'Adrien Beverland par J.-Frédéric Bernard. Réimpression sur l'édition la plus complète de 1741; notice bio-bibliographique par un bibliophile. Paris, Librairie de l'Académie des bibliophiles; Bruxelles, C. Muquard, 1868.
2 p. l., xiv p., 1 l., [17]-184 p. 19cm.

"Tirage à 237 exemplaires numérotés: 2 papier de Chine, 235 papier de Hollande. No. 20."

1. Sin, Original. I. Bernard, Jean Frédéric, d. 1752, tr. II. Un bibliophile. III. Title.
41-89047
Library of Congress BT720.B5 1868
[2]

NN

I-9
3979

[François, Laurent] 1698-1782.
Preuves de la religion de Jésus-Christ contre les spinosistes et les déistes, par M. L. F. Paris, Veuve Estienne et fils, 1751.
3 v. in 4.

NN

SPECIAL COLLECTIONS SPINOZA

I-9
3980

Gallucci, G
La concezione del cristianesimo nel "Trattato teologico-politico" ed il panteismo di Spinoza; memoria approvata dalla R. Accademia di scienze morali e politiche della Società reale di Napoli. Napoli, Prem. stab. tipografico F. Sangiovanni & figlio, 1915.
11 p. 24cm.

"Estratto dal vol. XLIV (parte seconda) degli Atti della R. Accademia di scienze morali e politiche di Napoli."

SPECIAL COLLECTIONS SPINOZA

I-9
3981

Hess, Moses, 1812-1875.
Rom und Jerusalem, die letzte Nationalitätsfrage; Briefe und Noten. 2. unveränderte Aufl. Mit einem Bilde des Verfassers und einer Vorrede von Dr. Bodenheimer. Leipzig, M. W. Kaufmann, 1899.
xxii, 201 p. port. 21cm.

Includes a chapter "Christus und Spinoza" (p. [113]-134)

I-9
3982

Hess, Moses, 1812-1875.
Rom und Jerusalem, die letzte Nationalitätsfrage. Briefe. Wien, R. Löwit, 1919.
231 p. (Jüdische Handbücher, 3-5)

Includes references to Spinoza.

NNJ

I-9
3983

Hess, Moses, 1812-1875.

Warsaw, 1899. רומא וירושלים.
2 v. in 1. (154 p.)

Title transliterated: Roma ve-Yerushalayim.
Includes a chapter on Christ and Spinoza and other references to Spinoza.

NNJ

I-9
3984

Hess, Moses, 1812-1875.

New York, 1916. רוים און ירושלים.
253 p.

Title transliterated: Roym ʿun Yerusholayim.
Includes a chapter on Christ and Spinoza (p. 169-196) and other references to Spinoza.

NNJ

I-9
3985

Hofstede de Groot, Petrus, 1802-1886.
Spinoza over Jezus Christus en zijne opstanding. [1863]
14 p.

In Waarheid in liefde, 1863.

NjPT

I-9
3986

Homan, Reinhart Kruizinga, 1831-1885.
Christus of Spinoza? Godsdienst of geen godsdienst? Leeuwarden, 1868.
30 p.

NIC

I-9
3987

Meijer, Willem, 1842-1926.
Over de verhouding van Spinozisme, Boeddhisme en Christendom. [1908]
[331]-354 p. 25cm.

From Tijdschrift voor wijsbegeerte, 2. jaarg. 4. aflevering, Aug. 1908.
Volume of pamphlets.

NNC

I-9
3988

Meijer, Willem, 1842-1926.
Spinozas demokratische Gesinnung und sein Verhältnis zum Christentum. [1901]
[455]-485 p. 23cm.

"Sonderabdruck aus dem Archiv für Geschichte der Philosophie. XVI. Band, 4. Heft, 1903."
Volume of pamphlets.

NNC

I-9
3989

Roelofsz, Catharina
De beteekenis van Christus voor Spinoza. Met een voorwoord van J. H. Carp. Zeist, J. Ploegsma, 1938.
70 p.

CLU

I-9
3990

Rottenberg, J
Joodsche stemmen over Christus en Christendom. Met een inleidend woord van J. H. Gunning. Rotterdam, Bredée, 1932.
171 p.

Includes a section on Spinoza (p. 80-86)

OCH

I-9
3991

Voigtländer, Johan. Andr.
Entwickelung des Christenthums zur Welt- und Staatsreligion in Fragmenten nach Spinoza; ein Beitrag zu gerechter Würdigung seiner Theologie und Philosophie. Halle, Kümmel, 1836.
67 p.

I-10 CREATION

I-10
3992

Colliber, Samuel, fl. 1718-1737.
Free thoughts concerning souls, in four essays: I. Of the humane soul consider'd in its own nature, II. Of the humane soul compared with the souls of brutes, III. Of the supposed prae-existent state of souls, IV. Of the future states of souls, to which is added, An essay on creation ... London, Robinson, 1734.
xiii, [1], 168 p. 19 cm.

References to Spinoza included in "An essay on creation" (p. 134-168)

I-10
3993

Rubin, Salomon, 1823-1910.
מַעֲשֵׂה מֶרְכָּבָה.(ספר ראשון:הנבואה).
Vienna, 1883.
42 p.

Title transliterated: Maʿaseh merkabah ...
Includes references to Spinoza.

NNJ

I-11 DEISM

I-11
3994

Gildon, Charles, 1665-1724.
The deist's manual: or, A rational enquiry into the Christian religion. With some considerations on Mr. Hobbs, Spinoza ... &c. To which is prefix'd a letter, from the author of The method with the Deists. London, Printed for A. Roper, Fran. Coggan [etc.] 1705.
xvi, 301 p. 20 cm.

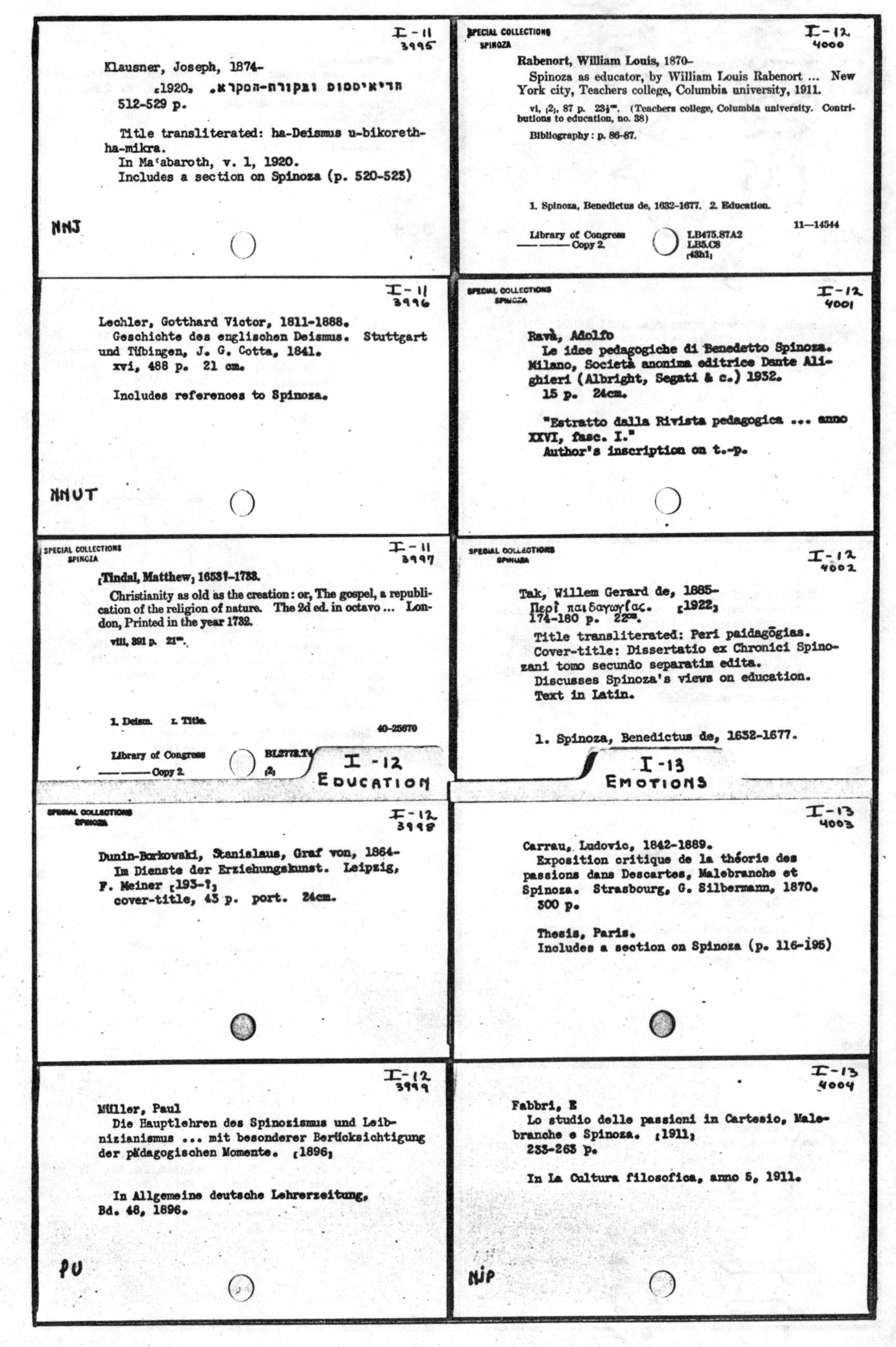

I-11
3995

Klausner, Joseph, 1874-
₍1920₎ הדיאיסמוס ובקורת-המקרא.
512-529 p.

Title transliterated: ha-Deismus u-bikoreth-ha-mikra.
In Maʻabaroth, v. 1, 1920.
Includes a section on Spinoza (p. 520-523)

NNJ

I-11
3996

Lechler, Gotthard Victor, 1811-1888.
Geschichte des englischen Deismus. Stuttgart und Tübingen, J. G. Cotta, 1841.
xvi, 488 p. 21 cm.

Includes references to Spinoza.

NNUT

SPECIAL COLLECTIONS
SPINOZA

I-11
3997

₍Tindal, Matthew₎ 1653?-1733.
Christianity as old as the creation: or, The gospel, a republication of the religion of nature. The 2d ed. in octavo ... London, Printed in the year 1732.
viii, 391 p. 21ᶜᵐ.

1. Deism. I. Title.

40-25670

Library of Congress BL2773.T4
——— Copy 2. ₍2₎

I-12
EDUCATION

SPECIAL COLLECTIONS
SPINOZA

I-12
3998

Dunin-Borkowski, Stanislaus, Graf von, 1864-
Im Dienste der Erziehungskunst. Leipzig, F. Meiner ₍193-?₎
cover-title, 43 p. port. 24cm.

I-12
3999

Müller, Paul
Die Hauptlehren des Spinozismus und Leibnizianismus ... mit besonderer Berücksichtigung der pädagogischen Momente. ₍1896₎

In Allgemeine deutsche Lehrerzeitung, Bd. 48, 1896.

PU

SPECIAL COLLECTIONS
SPINOZA

I-12
4000

Rabenort, William Louis, 1870-
Spinoza as educator, by William Louis Rabenort ... New York city, Teachers college, Columbia university, 1911.
vi, ₍2₎, 87 p. 23½ᶜᵐ. (Teachers college, Columbia university. Contributions to education, no. 38)
Bibliography: p. 86-87.

1. Spinoza, Benedictus de, 1632-1677. 2. Education.

11-14544

Library of Congress LB475.S7A2
——— Copy 2. LB5.C8
₍43h1₎

SPECIAL COLLECTIONS
SPINOZA

I-12
4001

Ravà, Adolfo
Le idee pedagogiche di Benedetto Spinoza. Milano, Società anonima editrice Dante Alighieri (Albright, Segati & c.) 1932.
15 p. 24cm.

"Estratto dalla Rivista pedagogica ... anno XXVI, fasc. I."
Author's inscription on t.-p.

SPECIAL COLLECTIONS
SPINOZA

I-12
4002

Tak, Willem Gerard de, 1885-
Περὶ παιδαγωγίας. ₍1922₎
174-180 p. 22ᶜᵐ.
Title transliterated: Peri paidagōgias.
Cover-title: Dissertatio ex Chronici Spinozani tomo secundo separatim edita.
Discusses Spinoza's views on education.
Text in Latin.

1. Spinoza, Benedictus de, 1632-1677.

I-13
EMOTIONS

I-13
4003

Carrau, Ludovic, 1842-1889.
Exposition critique de la théorie des passions dans Descartes, Malebranche et Spinoza. Strasbourg, G. Silbermann, 1870.
300 p.

Thesis, Paris.
Includes a section on Spinoza (p. 116-195)

I-13
4004

Fabbri, E
Lo studio delle passioni in Cartesio, Malebranche e Spinoza. ₍1911₎
233-263 p.

In La Cultura filosofica, anno 5, 1911.

NjP

I-13 4005

Labriola, Antonio, 1843-1904.
Scritti varii editi e inediti di filosofia e politica raccolti e pubblicati da B. Croce. Bari, Laterza, 1906.
viii, 507 p. port. 20 cm.

Includes an essay "Origine e natura delle passioni secondo l'Etica di Spinoza" (p. 35-87)

I-13 4006

Lange, Carl Georg, 1834-1900.
The emotions, by Carl Georg Lange and William James. Baltimore, Williams & Wilkins, 1922.
135 p. diagr. 24 cm. (Psychology classics; a series of reprints and translations, ed. by K. Dunlap, v. 1)

Includes references to Spinoza (p. 83, 90)

I-13 4007

Schlesing, Emil, 1868-
Das Verhältnis zwischen Leidenschaften und Freiheit in der Lehre des Spinoza. Heidelberg, J. Hörning, 1899.
83 p. 23cm.

Thesis, Heidelberg.
Bibliography: p. [1].

I-13 4008

Schlesing, Emil, 1868-
Das Verhältnis zwischen Leidenschaften und Freiheit in der Lehre des Spinoza. Heidelberg, J. Hörning, 1899.
83 p. 23cm.

Thesis, Heidelberg.
Bibliography: p. [1]
Volume of pamphlets.

I-14 ERROR

I-14 4009

Brochard, Victor Charles Louis, 1848-1907.
De l'erreur, par Victor Brochard ... Troisième édition. Paris, Félix Alcan, 1926.
3 p. l., 286 p., 1 l. 22½cm. (On cover: Bibliothèque de philosophie contemporaine)

Includes a chapter on Spinoza.
Original paper covers bound in.

1. Truth. I. Title.

A 39-945

I-14 4010

Levi, Adolfo, 1878-
Il problema dell'errore nella filosofia di B. Spinoza. Palermo, Industrie riunite editoriali siciliane, 1933.
17 p. 26cm.

"Estratto dalla rivista 'Sophia', aprile-giugno 1933, A. 11."

1. Spinoza, Benedictus de, 1632-1677.

I-14 4011

Mahler, Karl, 1887-
Die Entstehung des Irrtums bei Descartes und bei Spinoza. Leipzig, Druck von O. Heller, 1910.
41 p. 23cm.

Thesis, Leipzig.
Bibliography: p. [43]

I-15 ESSENCE

I-15 4012

Busse, Ludwig, 1862-1907.
Ueber die Bedeutung der Begriffe "essentia" und "existentia" bei Spinoza. Ein Beitrag zur Entwickelungsgeschichte Spinoza's. [1886]
283-306 p.

In Vierteljahresschrift für wissenschaftliche Philosophie, Jahrgang 10, 1886.

I-15 4013

Rivaud, Albert, 1876-
Les notions d'essence et d'existence dans la philosophie de Spinoza. Paris, F. Alcan, 1906.
viii, 216 p. 23cm.

Issued also as thesis, Paris.
Original paper cover bound in.
Carl Gebhardt's signature on t.-p.
Bibliography: p. [5]-7.

I-16 ETERNITY

I-16 4014

Grzymisch, Siegfried, 1875-
Spinoza's Lehren von der Ewigkeit und Unsterblichkeit. Breslau, Druck von Th. Schatzky, 1898.
59 p. 23cm.

Issued in part as thesis, Breslau.
Original paper covers bound in.

I-16 4015

Hallett, Harold Foster.
Aeternitas; a Spinozistic study, by H. F. Hallett. Oxford, The Clarendon press, 1930.
xix, 344 p. front. (port.) 23 cm.
Bibliographical foot-notes.

1. Eternity. 2. Time. 3. Spinoza, Benedictus de, 1632-1677. I. Title.
B3999.E78H3 193.9 31—10514
Library of Congress [35h1]

I-17 4020

Delbos, Victor, 1862-1916.
Le problème moral dans la philosophie de Spinoza. [1893]
126-139 p.

In Revue de métaphysique et de morale, 1. année, 1893.
An excerpt from his Le problème moral dans la philosophie de Spinoza et dans l'histoire du spinozisme.

I-17
ETHICAL THEORY

I-17 4016

Barth, Heinrich, 1890-
Ethische Grundgedanken bei Spinoza, Kant und Fichte; akademischer Vortrag gehalten in Basel am 9. Januar 1923. Tübingen, Mohr, 1923.
32 p. (Sammlung gemeinverständlicher Vorträge und Schriften aus dem Gebiet der Theologie und Religionsgeschichte. 105)

I-17 4021

193Sp4
DD15433
Delbos, Victor, 1862-1916.
Le problème moral dans la philosophie de Spinoza et dans l'histoire du spinozisme, par Victor Delbos ... Paris, F. Alcan, 1893.
3 p. l., xii, 569 p. 22½cm. (On cover: Bibliothèque de philosophie contemporaine)
Original paper covers bound in.

1. Spinoza, Benedictus de, 1632-1677.

I-17 4017

Bierens de Haan, Johannes Diderik, 1866-1943.
Levensleer naar de beginselen van Spinoza. 's-Gravenhage, M. Nijhoff, 1900.
x, 404 p. 20cm.

Original paper cover bound in.

1. Spinoza, Benedictus de, 1632-1677. Ethics

I-17 4022

[Dunin-Borkowski, Stanislaus, Graf von, 1864-1934.
Soziale Aufrichtigkeit und soziale Demut. [1923]
[281]-288 p. 26cm.

Signed: Stanislaus v. Dunin-Borkowski.
"Sonderabdruck aus den 'Stimmen der Zeit', Juli 1923, Band 105, Heft 10."

NNC

I-17 4018

Broad, Charlie Dunbar, 1887-
Five types of ethical theory, by C. D. Broad ... London, K. Paul, Trench, Trubner & co., ltd.; New York, Harcourt, Brace & company, 1930.
xxv, 288 p. 22 cm. (*Half-title:* International library of psychology, philosophy and scientific method)
"Five typical theories of ethics, viz., those of Spinoza, Butler, Hume, Kant, and Sidgwick."—p. 1.

1. Ethics. I. Title.
BJ71.B7 30—8851
Library of Congress [54k²2]

I-17 4023

Ferrari, Giuseppe Michele
L'Etica di B. Spinoza: appunti. Napoli, Pierro e Veraldi, 1902.
viii, 157 p.

MH

I-17 4019

Brochard, Victor, 1848-1907.
Le Traité des passions de Descartes et l'Éthique de Spinoza. [1896]
512-516 p.

In Revue de métaphysique et de morale, 4. année, 1896.

NNC

I-17 4024

Friedländer, Julius, 1813-1884.
Spinoza, ein Meister der Ethik. Nach einem Vortrage gehalten in der Deutschen Gesellschaft für ethische Kultur in Berlin. Berlin, C. R. Dreher's Verlag, 1895.
30 p. 24cm.

Original paper covers bound in.

I-17 4025

Handyside, John, 1883-1916.
The historical method in ethics and other essays, by John Handyside ... Liverpool, University press; [etc., etc., 1920]
xvi, 97 p. 22½cm.
CONTENTS.—Biographical note.—The historical method in ethics.—The absolute and 'intellect.'—System and mechanism.
Includes a section on Spinoza (p. 40-45)
1. Ethics—Addresses, essays, lectures. 2. Philosophy—Addresses, essays, lectures. 3. Intellect. I. Title.

DLC

Library of Congress B1646.H15H5 [32c2] 20-19515

I-17 4026

Henning, Leopold von
Principien der Ethik in historischer Entwickelung. Zum Gebrauch bei akademischen Vorlesungen. Berlin, F. A. Herbig, 1824.
xvi, 217 p. 20 cm.
Includes a section on Spinoza (p. 133-149)

PU

I-17 4027

Jelski, S
Spinoza's Tugendlehre. [1899]
In Vossische Zeitung, 1899, Nr. 15.

NN

I-17 4028

Jouffroy, Théodore Simon, 1796-1842.
Introduction to ethics, including a critical survey of moral systems. Translated from the French of Jouffroy, by William H. Channing. Boston, Hilliard, Gray, 1840.
2 v. 21 cm. (Specimens of foreign standard literature. Edited by George Ripley. Vol. V-VI)
Includes two lectures on Spinoza (v. 5, p. 145-199)

SPECIAL COLLECTIONS SPINOZA

I-17 4029

Jouffroy, Théodore Simon, 1796-1842.
Introduction to ethics, including a critical survey of moral systems, tr. from the French of Jouffroy. By William H. Channing ... Boston, J. Munroe and company, 1848.
2 v. 18cm.
Includes two chapters on Spinoza.
1. Ethics. 2. Ethics—Hist. I. Channing, William Henry, 1810-1884, tr.

Library of Congress BJ802.J8 [39e1] 10-4688

I-17 4030

Juvalta, Erminio
Osservazioni sulle dottrine morali di Spinoza. [1929]
297-328 p.
In Rivista di filosofia, anno 20, 1929.

SPECIAL COLLECTIONS SPINOZA

I-17 4031

Kniat, Joseph, 1858-
Spinoza's Ethik gegenüber der Erfahrung. Posen, 1888.
47 p. 21cm.
Thesis, Leipzig.
1. Spinoza, Benedictus de, 1632-1677. Ethica

I-17 4032

Kropotkin, Petr Alekseevich, kníaz, 1842-1921.
Этика. Петербург, "Голос труда", 1922.
v. 1. port.
Includes references to Spinoza.
Title transliterated: Ėtika.

NNC

I-17 4033

Lazarus, Moritz, 1824-1903.
Die Ethik des Judenthums. Frankfurt am Main, Kauffmann, 1899.
xxv, 469 p. 24 cm.
Includes a section on Spinoza (p. 438-442) in "Anhang" and other references to him.

I-17 4034

Lemonnier, Charles
Entretiens et conférences de la rue Scribe. La morale de Spinosa. [1866]
313-320, 335-344, 346-351 p.
In Revue des cours littéraires de la France et de l'étranger, 3. année, 1865-66.

Lénström, Carl Julius, 1811-1893.
De principiis philosophiae practicae Spinozae. Gevaliae, typis A. P. Landin, 1843.
26 p. 22cm.

1. Spinoza, Benedictus de, 1632-1677.

Leonhardt, Kurt, 1880-
Der Selbsterhaltungstrieb als Grundlage für die Ethik bei Spinoza. Leipzig, Buchdruckerei von H. John, 1907.
58 p. 23cm.

Thesis, Leipzig.
Bibliography: p. [5]
Bound with Zinsser, August. Der ethische Intellektualismus Spinozas. 1892.

Lewkowitz, Albert, 1883-
Die Ethik Spinozas in ihrem Verhältnis zum Judentum. [1926]
355-366 p. 24cm.

From Monatsschrift für Geschichte und Wissenschaft des Judentums, 70. Jahrgang, Heft 9/10, September/Oktober, 1926.

Lust, L
Das sittliche Ideal nach Spinoza. Berlin, G. Lange, 1873.
30 p. 27cm.

At head of title: Friedrichs-Realschule. Jahresbericht ...
Volume of pamphlets.

1. Spinoza, Benedictus de, 1632-1677.

Meurling, Harry, 1878-
Fullkomlighetsbegreppet i Spinozas filosofi. Uppsala, Almqvist & Wiksell, 1928.
viii, 139 p. 24cm.

Thesis, Uppsala.
Original paper cover bound in.
Bibliography: p. [140]

Meyer, Metellus, 1862-
Die Tugendlehre Spinoza's. Flensburg, Druck von J. B. Meyer, 1885.
81 p. 22cm.

Thesis, Leipzig.
Volume of pamphlets.

Molthan, Agnes, 1882-
Über das normative und das deskriptive Element in der Ethik Spinozas. Borna-Leipzig, Druck von R. Noske, 1917.
viii, 77 p. 23cm.

Thesis, Erlangen.
Bibliography: p. [vii]-viii.

Montbeillard, Léon de
De l'Éthique de Spinosa. Paris, Joubert, 1851.
iv, 166 p. 22cm.

Original paper covers bound in.

[Pollock, Sir Frederick, bart.] 1845-1937.
Spinoza as a moral teacher. [1888]
[416]-419 p. 23cm.

Signed: Frederick Pollock.
"Notes of a lecture given at Toynbee Hall, March 4th, 1888."
From Time, London, v. 18, 1888.

Rivaud, Albert, 1876-
Les per se nota dans l'Éthique. [Hagae Comitis, 1922]
138-154 p. 22cm.

Cover-title: Dissertatio ex Chronici Spinozani tomo secundo separatim edita.

Rogers, Reginald Arthur Percy, 1874–
A short history of ethics, Greek and modern, by Reginald A. P. Rogers ... London, Macmillan and co., limited, 1911.
xxii, 303 p. 19 cm.

Includes a section "Rationalistic naturalism - Spinoza" (p. 143-146) and other references to Spinoza.

1. Ethics—Hist.

Salinger, Richard, 1859-
Spinozas Lehre von der Selbsterhaltung. Berlin, Schade [1881.
78 p.

Thesis, Berlin, 1881.

Santayana, George, 1863-1952.
Ethical doctrine of Spinoza. [1886]
144-152 p.

In Harvard monthly, v. 2, 1886.

Schindler, C F
Ueber den Begriff des Guten und Nützlichen bei Spinoza. Jena, Druck von A. Neuenhahn, 1885.
42 p. 23cm.

Thesis, Jena.
Bibliographical footnotes.

Schindler, C F
Ueber den Begriff des Guten und Nützlichen bei Spinoza. Jena, A. Neuenhahn, 1885.
20 p. 27cm.

At head of title: Jahresbericht der Pfeiffer'schen Lehr- und Erziehungs-Anstalt zu Jena ...
Issued also as thesis, Jena.
Volume of pamphlets.

Selung, Bruno, 1900-
Mitleid, Demut und Reue in der Machtethik Spinozas und Nietzsches; ein historisch-kritischer Vergleich. Grossenbaum, 1926.
72 p. 22cm.

Thesis, Bonn.
Bibliography: p. 3.

[Smith, Thomas Vernor] 1890-
Spinoza's political and moral philosophy. [1933]
23-39 p.

Signed: T. V. Smith.
In The Monist, v. 43, 1933.

Strümpell, Ludwig, 1812-1899.
Die sittliche Weltanschauung des Spinoza. [1840]
1233-1235, 1237-1238, 1241-1243 p.

In Blätter für litterarische Unterhaltung, Jahrgang 1840, Bd. 2.

[Waddington, Charles] 1819-1914.
La morale de Spinoza; rapport sur le concours pour le prix Bordin à décerner en 1891. [Orléans, Imp. Paul Girardot, 1891?]
20 p. 22cm.

Signed: Charles Waddington.

1. Spinoza, Benedictus de, 1632-1677.

Wennerberg, Gunnar, 1817-1901.
Num recte et vere de Spinozismo judicavit Hegelius? Disquisitio critica quam p. p. Gunnar Wennerberg et M. N. Berling. Upsaliae, Wahlström, 1848.
33 p.

Wolff, Christian, Freiherr von, 1679-1754.
De differentia nexus verum sapientis et fatalis necessitatis, nec non systematis harmoniae praestabilitae et hypothesium Spinosae luculenta commentatio in qua simul genuina Dei existentiam demonstrandi ratio expenditur et multa religionis naturalis capita illustrantur. Halae Magdeb., Officina Rengeriana, 1724.
[8], 80 p.

Woltmann, Ludwig, 1871-1907.
System des moralischen Bewusstseins mit besonderer Darlegung des Verhältnisses der kritischen Philosophie zu Darwinismus und Socialismus. Düsseldorf, H. Michel, 1898.
xii, 391 p.

Includes a section on Spinoza (p. 242-245)

Worms, René, 1869-
La morale de Spinoza; examen de ses principes et de l'influence qu'elle a exercée dans les temps modernes. Paris, Hachette, 1892.
334 p. 19cm.

Bibliographical footnotes.

Wundt, Wilhelm, 1832-1920.
Ethical systems. Tr. by Margaret Floy Washburn. London, S. Sonnenschein; New York, Macmillan, 1897.
viii, 196 p. 23cm. (His Ethics: an investigation of the facts and laws of the moral life, v. 2)

Includes a section on Spinoza (p. 92-97) and other references to him.

Wuttke, Adolf, 1819-1870.
Christian ethics; with a special preface by Dr. Riehm. Translated by John P. Lacroix. New York, Nelson & Phillips, 1876.
2 v.

Includes a section on Spinoza (v. 1, p. 281-290) and other references to him.

Yarros, Victor S
Ethics and the Spinoza revival. [1922]
[714]-720 p. 23cm.

From the Open court, vol. XXXVI, no. 12, December, 1922.

1. Spinoza, Benedictus de, 1632-1677.

Zimmermann, from Olmütz
Ueber einige logische Fehler der spinozistischen Ethik. [1850]
451-464 p. 24cm.

From Sitzungsberichte der Philosophisch-historischen Klasse der K. Akademie der Wissenschaften in Wien, Jahrgang 1850, II. Bd., II. Hft.

Zinsser, August, 1867-
Der ethische Intellektualismus Spinozas. Leipzig, Druck von Pöschel & Trepte, 1892.
44 p. 23cm.

Thesis, Leipzig.

1. Spinoza, Benedictus de, 1632-1677. Ethica.

I-18
EVOLUTION

Meijer, Willem, 1842-1926.
De ontwikkelinsleer en het Spinozisme. [1914]
176-199 p.

In Tijdschrift voor wijsbegeerte, jaargang 8, 1914.

Mondolfo, Rodolfo, 1877-
Spinoza e la nozione del progresso umano. [1927]
[262]-266 p.

In Rivista di filosofia, anno 18, 1927.

Nordau, Max Simon, 1849–1923.
Morals and the evolution of man, by Max Nordau; a translation of "Biologie der ethik," by Marie A. Lewenz ... New York, Funk and Wagnalls company, 1922.
4 p. l., 278 p. 22½cm.

Includes a section on Spinoza (p. 13-18) and other references to Spinoza (p. 36, 37, 93)
1. Ethics, Evolutionary. I. Lewenz, Marie Adèle, 1876– tr. II. Title.
[Name originally: Max Simon (Simḥah Meïr) Südfeld]
22-17396

Bury, John Bagnell, 1861–1927.
A history of freedom of thought, by J. B. Bury ... London, Williams and Norgate [1913]
v, 7–256 p. 17 cm. (Added t.-p.: Home university library of modern knowledge. New York, H. Holt and company)
Bibliography: p. [253]
Includes references to Spinoza.

1. Free thought. 2. Rationalism. I. Title: Freedom of thought, A history of.
13—18502

I-19
FREE THOUGHT

[Aubert de Versé, Noël] d. 1714.
Traité de la liberté de conscience, ou de l'autorité des souverains sur la religion des peuples. Opposé aux maximes impies de Hobbes & de Spinosa, adoptées par le Sieur Jurieu dans son Histoire du papisme & dans son système de l'Eglise. A Cologne, Chez Pierre Marteau, 1687.
[44], 304 p. 14cm.

The Christian free-thinker; or, An epistolary discourse concerning freedom of thought; in which are contained observations on the lives and writings of Epicurus, Lucretius, Petronius, Cardan, Bruno, Vanini, and Spinosa. 2d ed. London, printed for J. Roberts, 1740.
vi, 66 p. 22 cm.

[Bentley, Richard] 1662-1742.
Remarks upon a late discourse of free-thinking: in a letter to F. H. ... by Phileleutherus Lipsiensis [pseud.] ... London: Printed for John Morphew, 1713.
2 v. in 1. 20cm.

Volume of pamphlets.

[Cockman, Thomas] b. 1678.
Free-thinking rightly stated; wherein a discourse (falsely so call'd) is fully consider'd ... London: Printed for George Strahan, 1713.
1 p. l., 131 p. 20cm.

Includes a reference to Spinoza (p. 38)

[Bentley, Richard] 1662-1742.
Remarks upon a late discourse of free-thinking [by Anthony Collins] in a letter to N. N. [Francis Hare, D. D.] By Phileleutherus Lipsiensis [pseud.] The seventh edition. London, W. Thurlbourn, 1737.
2 pts. in 1 v.

[Collins, Anthony] 1676-1729.
A discourse of free-thinking, occasion'd by the rise and growth of a sect call'd free-thinkers ... London, 1713.
vi, 3-178 p. 20cm.

Volume of pamphlets.

Biedermann, Alois Emanuel, 1819-1885.
Die freie Theologie oder Philosophie und Christentum in Streit und Frieden. Tübingen, L. F. Fues, 1844.
273 p. 22 cm.

Farrar, Adam Storey, 1826–1905.
A critical history of free thought in reference to the Christian religion. Eight lectures preached before the University of Oxford, in the year M.DCCC.LXII., on the foundation of the late Rev. John Bampton ... By Adam Storey Farrar ... New York, D. Appleton and company, 1876.
xivi, 487 p. 20½cm. (Bampton lectures, 1862)

Includes references to Spinoza.

1. Free thought—Hist.
25—24719

Lettre d'un medecin arabe a un fameux professeur de Halle en Saxe. Sur les reproches faits a Mahomet, de son recours aux armes, de la pluralité des femmes, de l'entretien des concubines, et de l'idée de son paradis. Traduitte de l'Arabie anno 1738.
[53] p. 23cm.

Manuscript.

CONTINUED ON NEXT CARD

Lettre d'un medecin arabe ... (Card 2)

The letter was published with the French translation of Anthony Collins' Discourse of free thinking, 1714, and was attributed to him by S. J. Baumgarten in Nachrichten, v. 2, p. 133 and 145.
Some pages (incl. t.-p.) closely cropped.
Bound with [Mirabaud, Jean Baptiste de] Opinion des anciens sur le nature de l'ame Anno 1738.

Taylor, Henry Osborn, 1856-1941.
Freedom of the mind in history, by Henry Osborn Taylor. London, Macmillan and co., limited, 1923.
xii, 297 p. 19½ cm.
Includes a reference to Spinoza (p. 176)

1. Civilization. 2. Progress. 3. Learning and scholarship. I. Title. II. Title: Mind in history.

Trinius, Johann Anton, 1722-1784.
... Freydenker-lexicon, oder, Einleitung in die geschichte der neuern freygeister, ihrer schriften, und deren widerlegungen. Nebst einem Bey- und nachtrage zu des seligen Herrn Johann Albert Fabricius Syllabo scriptorum, pro veritate religionis christianae. Leipzig und Bernburg, C. G. Cörner, 1759.
4 p. l., 876 p. 20cm.
Includes a section on Spinoza (p. 417-444)

1. Free thought—Bibl. I. Fabricius, Johann Albert, 1668-1736. Delectus argumentorum et syllabus scriptorum. II. Title.

[Voelkel, Titus] 1849-
Einführung in die Geschichte des freien Gedankens, in hundert Lebensabrissen seiner Vorkämpfer. Von S. E. Verus [pseud.] Frankfurt a. M., Neuer Frankfurter Verlag, 1914.
xvi, 224 p. 24cm.

Includes a section on Spinoza (p. 61-62) and other references to him.
Bibliography: p. [xvi]

Wehle, J H ed.
Das Toleranz-Buch. Aufsätze und Aussprüche über die Freiheit der Meinungsäusserung aus dem 17., 18. und 19. Jahrhundert. Herausgegeben von J. H. Wehle. Wien, Verlag von R. v. Waldheim, 1879.
xvi, 242 p. 16cm.
"Spinoza: Die Denk- und Redefreiheit": p. 1-18.

I -20
FREE WILL

Betz, Hendrik Johan, 1842-1905.
Spinoza en de vrijheid; eenige bedenkingen tegen de Spinoza-studie van den Heer J. H. Gunning, Jr. 's Gravenhage, M. Nijhoff, 1877.
96 p. 24cm.

Original paper cover bound in.
Bound with Bellaar Spruyt, Cornelis. Van Vloten's Benedictus de Spinoza. 1876.

Boutroux, Emile, 1845-1921.
Exposition de la doctrine de Spinoza sur la liberté. [1924]
505-542 p.

In Revue de métaphysique et de morale, 31. année, 1924.

Carr, Herbert Wildon, 1857-1931.
The unique status of man, by Herbert Wildon Carr ... New York, The Macmillan company, 1928.
216 p. 19½ cm. (The New era lectureship, University of Southern California, 1927)
Includes references to Spinoza.

1. Free will and determinism. I. Title.

Dienstfertig, Marcus
Die menschliche Freiheit nach Spinoza. 1. Theil. Der freie Mensch. Breslau, F. W. Jungfer, 1872.
31 p. 23cm.

Thesis, Breslau.
"Der zweite Theil dieser Dissertation nebst Anhang wird später unter dem Titel 'Die menschliche Freiheit als moralische Idee' im Druck erscheinen."
Bibliographical footnotes.

Dittes, Friedrich, 1829-1896.
Ueber die sittliche Freiheit, mit besonderer Berücksichtigung der Systeme von Spinoza, Leibnitz, Kant. Nebst einer Abhandlung über den Eudämonismus. Leipzig, J. Klinkhardt, 1860.
iv, 128 p. 21cm.

Bound with Hebler, Karl. Spinoza's Lehre vom Verhältniss der Substanz zu ihren Bestimmtheiten. 1850.

[Fowle, Thomas Welbank] 1836-
The place of will in evolution. [1879]
[385]-404 p. 23cm.

Signed: T. W. Fowle.
From the Nineteenth century, no. XXV, March 1879.
Includes references to Spinoza.
Volume of pamphlets.

Kaeser, Walter
Die Bedeutung und Stellung des Begriffs der menschlichen Freiheit im System Spinozas. Frankfurt a. M., Universitätsdruckerei Werner u. Winter [1926]
[4] p. 24cm.

Abstract of thesis, Frankfurt a. M.
Presentation copy to Carl Gebhardt, with the author's inscription.

Kecskes, P
Das Problem der sittlichen Freiheit nach Spinoza und Thomas von Aquin. Budapest, 1923.

Keller, Franz
Spinoza und Leibnitz über die Freiheit des menschlichen Willens. Erlangen, F. Enke, 1847.
iv, 78 p. 24cm.

Lackner, Otto, 1871-
Wie unterscheidet sich das Sittengesetz vom Naturgesetz? Ein versuch zur Lösung des Freiheitsproblems mit besonderer Berücksichtigung von Spinoza, Kant und Schleiermacher. Königsberg, Hartung, 1897.
64 p. 21 cm.

Thesis, Konigsberg.

Luzzatto, Samuele Davide, 1800-1865.
Gegen den Determinismus bei Spinoza. [1862]
223-224 p.

In Die Neuzeit, 2. Jahrgang, 1862.

Martinetti, Piero, 1872-
... La libertà. Milano, Libreria editrice lombarda, 1928.
499 p., 2 l. 24cm. (On cover: Collezione "Isis")
Includes a section on Spinoza (p. 271-282) and other references to him.

1. Free will and determinism. I. Title.
Library of Congress B3636.M33L5 1928 29-16906
Copyright A—Foreign 2379
[2]

Naudé, Philippe, 1654-1729.
Examen de deux traittez ... mis au jour par M. La Placette; dont le premier a pour titre, Réponse à une objection qu'on applique à divers sujets ... et le second, Eclaircissemens sur quelques difficultez qui naissent de la consideration de la liberté necessaire pour agir moralement. Avec une addition, où l'on prouve contre Spinoza que nous sommes libres. Amsterdam, E. Roger, 1713.
2 v.

Palmedo, Kurt
Der Freiheitsbegriff in der Lehre Spinozas. Ein Beitrag zur Geschichte der ethischen Prinzipien. Weida i. Thür., Thomas & Hubert, 1920.
65 p.

Thesis, Leipzig.

Pluquet, François André Adrien, 1716-1790.
Examen du fatalisme, ou Exposition et réfutation des différents systèmes de fatalisme qui ont partagé les philosophes sur l'origine du monde, sur la nature de l'âme et sur le principe des actions humaines. Paris, Didot, 1757.
3 v. 17 cm.

Includes references to Spinoza.

Roe, Edward Drake, 1859-1929.
The probability of freedom: a critique of Spinoza's demonstration of necessity. [1894]
641-659 p.

In The Bibliotheca sacra, v. 51, 1894.

Scholten, Johannes Henricus, 1811-1885.
Der freie Wille; kritische Untersuchung. Deutsche Ausgabe. Nach einer vom Verfasser revidirten und verbesserten Redaction aus dem Holländischen übersetzt von C. Manchot. Berlin, 1874.
xx, 286 p.

Includes a reference to Spinoza (p. 20-21)

Scholten, Johannes Henricus, 1811-1885.
Die vrije wil; kritisch onderzoek. Leiden, P. Engels, 1859.
xlvi, 400 p.

Includes references to Spinoza.

Urtel, Friedrich
Spinozae doctrina de voluntatis humanae natura exponitur et examinatur. Halis Saxonum, Formis Orphanotrophei, 1868.
37 p. 23cm.

Thesis, Halle.
Bibliographical footnotes.

1. Spinoza, Benedictus de, 1632-1677.

Watts, Isaac, 1674-1748.
An essay on the freedom of will in God and in creatures ... London, J. Roberts, 1732.
106 p.

Wiessner, Karl, 1871-
Die Freiheit bei Spinoza. Osterwieck/Harz, Druck von A. W. Zickfeldt, 1902.
50 p. 22cm.

Thesis, Jena.
Original paper cover bound in.

Wijnaendts Francken, Cornelis Johannes, 1863-
Het vraagstuk van den vrijen wil. Haarlem, H. D. Tjeenk Willink & Zoon, 1912.
116 p. 24cm.

Includes references to Spinoza.
Bibliographical footnotes.

Wijnaendts Francken, Cornelis Johannes, 1863-
Spinoza's oordeel over de wilsvrijheid. [1912]
[68]-72 p. 26cm.

From De Nieuwe gids, XXVIIe jaarg., 7[e] afl., Juli 1912.

1. Spinoza, Benedictus de, 1632-1677.

Wittenstein, Oscar Jürgen
Von der Macht des Verstandes oder von der menschlichen Freiheit. Stuttgart [Strecker und Schröder] 1921.
vii, 247 p. 26½cm.

Includes a section "Die Definition der Liebe bei Spinoza" (p. 137-140) and many other references to him.
Original paper covers bound in.

I - 21
GOD

SPECIAL COLLECTIONS
SPINOZA
I-21
4105

Abū Bakr ibn al-Tufail, Abū Ja'far, *al-Ishbīlī*, d. 1185.
The improvement of human reason, exhibited in the life of Hai ebn Yokdhan: written in Arabick above 500 years ago, by Abu Jaafar ebn Tophail ... newly translated from the original Arabick, by Simon Ockley ... With an appendix, in which the possibility of man's attaining the true knowledg of God, and things necessary to salvation, without instruction, is briefly consider'd. London, Printed and sold by E. Powell, 1708.
6 p. l., 195 p. front., plates. 20 cm.
The appendix ... by Simon Ockley (p. [163]-195) has special t.-p.
A Latin translation by Edward Pococke was published in 1671 under title: Philosophus autodidactus sive epistola Abi Jaafar ebn Tophail ...
1. Philosophy, Arabic. I. Ockley, Simon, 1678-1720, tr. II. Title.
B748.A33R5 1708 189.3 18—21887
Library of Congress [56r42d½]

I-21
4106

Antweiler, Anton
Unendlich, eine Untersuchung zur metaphysischen Wesenheit Gottes auf Grund der Mathematik, Philosophie, Theologie. [1934]
200 p.

In Freiburger theologische Studien, Heft 38, 1934.
Includes references to Spinoza.

NNUT

I-21
4107

Brochard, Victor, 1848-1907.
Le Dieu de Spinoza. [1908]
129-163 p.

In Revue de métaphysique et de morale, 16. année, 1908.

NNC

SPECIAL COLLECTIONS
SPINOZA
I-21
4108

Brunschvicg, Léon, 1869-1944.
Dieu et la pensée contemporaine. [Résumé de la conférence de M. Brunschvicg dans l'École des hautes études sociales, le 13 janvier 1929. 1929]
14 p. 24cm.

From Bulletin de l'Union de libres penseurs et de libres croyants pour la culture morale, 2. sér., 1929: IVe année, no. 1.
Includes references to Spinoza.
Copy inscribed to Carl Gebhardt by the author.

NNC

SPECIAL COLLECTIONS
SPINOZA
I-21
4109

Caro, Elme Marie, 1826-1887.
L'idée de Dieu et ses nouveaux critiques. 3. éd. Paris, Hachette, 1865.
508 p. 19cm.

Includes references to Spinoza.

SPECIAL COLLECTIONS
SPINOZA
I-21
4110

Caro, Elme, 1826-1887.
L'idée de Dieu et ses nouveaux critiques. Paris, Hachette, 1864.
506 p. 23cm.

Includes references to Spinoza.

I-21
4111

Der christlich ergänzte Spinozismus, die allein mögliche Vorstellung vom wahrhaft göttlichen Sein. Eine Skizze in vier Abtheilungen. Würzburg, P. Halm, 1858.
24 p.

SPECIAL COLLECTIONS
SPINOZA
I-21
4112

[Colliber, Samuel] fl. 1718-1737.
An impartial enquiry into the existence and nature of God; being a modest essay towards a more intelligible account of the divine perfections. With remarks on several authors both ancient and modern; and particularly on some passages in Dr. Clarke's Demonstration of the being and attributes of God. In two books. With an appendix concerning the nature of space and duration. By S. C. ... London, Printed; and sold by the booksellers, 1718.
230 p. 20cm.
Includes references to Spinoza.

I-21
4113

Colliber, Samuel, fl. 1718-1737.
An impartial enquiry into the existence and nature of God; being a modest essay towards a more intelligible account of the divine perfections. With remarks on several authors both ancient and modern; and particularly on some passages in Dr. Clarke's Demonstration of the being and attributes of God. In two books. With an appendix concerning the nature of space and duration. The third edition. With considerable additions and improvements, made

NNUT
(Continued on next card)

I-21
4114

Colliber, Samuel, fl. 1718-1737. An impartial enquiry into the existence and nature of God. 1735. (Card 2)

partly with regard to some objections of the Reverend Mr. Jackson. London, Printed for R. Robinson, 1735.
276 p.

Includes references to Spinoza.

I-21
4115

[Dunin-Borkowski, Stanislaus, Graf von] 1864-
Gott und die menschliche Sprechweise.
[1929]
[174]-181 p. 26cm.

Signed: Stanislaus v. Dunin Borkowski.
"Sonderabdruck aus den Stimmen der Zeit; Monatsschrift für das Geistesleben der Gegenwart, Dezember 1929, Band 118, Heft 3."
Includes a reference to Spinoza (p. 176)

I-21
4116

Ewyck, G van
Difficultas maxima, orta ex concatenationibus idearum, quas vir clarissimus D. Jacobus Wittichius ... concinnavit in disputatione sua de natura Dei. Cui difficultati ut publicè satisfiat, quùm & plurium mentes non parùm eâ torqueri possint, publicitus illam quoque proponere, nec non simul axioma Spinosisticum primarium penitùs subvertere, voluit G. van Ewyck, J. U. D. Lugduni Batavorum, Prostat apud Johannem vander Linden [1719]
56 p. 21cm.

CONTINUED ON NEXT CARD

I-21
4117

Ewyck, G van Difficultas maxima ... [1719] (Card 2)

Bound with Poiret, Pierre. Cogitationum rationalium ... libri quatuor. 1715.

I-21
4118

Fénelon, François de Salignac de la Mothe, 1651-1715.
A demonstration of the existence and attributes of God, drawn from the knowledge of nature, from proofs purely intellectual, and from the idea of the Infinite himself. Harrisburgh, W. Gillmor, 1811.
263 p. 17 cm.

Includes "A refutation of the principles of Spinoza" (p. 190-240) and "The reflections of Father Tournemine, a Jesuite upon atheism; upon my lord of Cambray's Demonstration, and upon Spinoza's system" (p. 242-263)

DLC

I-21
4119

Fénelon, François de Salignac de la Mothe, 1651-1715.
A demonstration of the existence and attributes of God ... translated from the French, by A. Boyer. Glasgow, R. Urie, 1754.
xx, 182 p.

NN

I-21
4120

Fénelon, François de Salignac de la Mothe, 1651-1715.
A demonstration of the existence, wisdom, and omnipotence of God ... Translated from the French [by A. Boyer] London, 1713.

NNUT

I-21
4121

Fénelon, François de Salignac de la Mothe, 1651-1715.
Démonstration de l'existence de Dieu, tirée de la connoissance de la nature, et proportionnée à la foible intelligence des plus simple. Amsterdam, 1713.

CtY

I-21
4122

Fénelon, François de Salignac de la Mothe, 1651-1715.
De l'existence et des attributs de Dieu. Entretiens sur la religion, Discours philosophique sur l'amour de Dieu, Lettre sur divers sujets de métaphysique et de religion, Dialogues sur l'éloquence, Mémoire et lettre sur les occupations de l'Académie française, Lettre sur les anciens et les modernes, Discours de réception à l'Académie française, Lettre à Louis XIV. Paris, Firmin Didot, 1846.
572 p. port. 18 cm.

(Continued on next card)

I-21
4123

Fénelon, François de Salignac de la Mothe, 1651-1715. De l'existence et des attributs de Dieu... 1846. (Card 2)

Includes a section "Extrait d'une lettre sur la réfutation de Spinoza" (p. 310-315)

Fischer, Kuno, 1824-1907.
Ученіе Спинозы о Богѣ. [1861]
117-140 p.

Title transliterated: Uchenie Spinozy o Bogie.
In Время, журналъ литературный и политическій, т. 5, 1861.

Fraysse, E. Albert
L'idée de Dieu dans Spinosa. Paris, C. Meyrueis, 1870.
116 p. 24cm.

Geldart, Edmund Martin, 1844-1885.
The living God. Ramsgate, T. Scott [1872]
11 p. 19cm.

Volume of pamphlets.

Gillett, Ezra Hall, 1823-1875.
God in human thought; or, Natural theology traced in literature, ancient and modern, to the time of Bishop Butler. With a closing chapter on the moral system, and an English bibliography, from Spenser to Butler. New York, Scribner, Armstrong, 1874.
2 v. 24 cm.

Paged continuously.
Includes a section on Spinoza (p. 537-544)

Gottfried, Mordechai

אלהי ישראל לא אלהי ברוך שפינוזה.
[Vienna, 1920]
11-16 p.

Title transliterated: ʿelohey yisrael loʾ ʿelohey Barukh Shpinozah.
With the author's Makhshavah u-ma aseh.

Hayyun, Nehemiah Hiyya ben Moses, 1650?-1730?
עוז לאלהים ובית קדש הקדשים.([מהימנותא דפלא]... להביר הבורא בדרך רחבה וקצרה...). [Berlin, 1713]
3 p. l., 7, 88 p.

Title transliterated: ʿoz le-ʾelohim u-beth kodesh ha-kadashim ...

Heidenfeld, Albrecht Friedrich Theodor, 1834-
Darstellung der von Cartesius, Spinoza und Leibnitz gegebenen beweise für das dasein Gottes ... 1. theil. Breslau, Druck von H. Lindner [1855]
2 p. l., 34 p., 1 l. 19½cm.

Inaug.-diss.—Breslau.
Vita.

1. God—Proof. 2. Descartes, René, 1596-1650. 3. Spinoza, Benedictus de, 1632-1677. 4. Leibniz, Gottfried Wilhelm, freiherr von, 1646-1716.

Herder, Johann Gottfried von, 1744-1803.
Gott ... Einige Gespräche. [1887]
[401]-580 p. (In his Sämmtliche Werke, 16. Bd. Berlin, Weidmann, 1887.)

Includes references to Spinoza.

Hirsch, Samuel, 1815-1889.
Gott, Persönlichkeit, Sünde, Vergebung. [1871-72]

In Jewish times, New York, v. 3, 1871-72.
Includes a reference to Spinoza (p. 297)

Hölters, Hans, 1914-
Der spinozistische Gottesbegriff bei M. Mendelssohn und F. H. Jacobi und der Gottesbegriff Spinozas. Emsdetten, H. & J. Lechte, 1938.
92 p. 25cm. (Universitas-Archiv. Philosophische Abteilung. Bd. 97)

Issued also as thesis, Bonn.
Bibliography: p. 90-92.

I-21
4134

Huan, Gabriel
Le Dieu de Spinoza. Arras, Imprimerie Schoutheer frères, 1913.
338 p. 25cm.

Thesis, Paris.
Published also without thesis note.
Bibliography: p. ⌊305⌋-336.

1. Spinoza, Benedictus de, 1632-1677.

I-21
4135

Huan, Gabriel
Le Dieu de Spinoza. Paris, F. Alcan, 1914.
338 p. 25cm.

Issued also as thesis, Paris.
Original paper cover bound in.
Bibliography: p. ⌊305⌋-336.

I-21
4136

"I believe in Spinoza's God." ⌊1932⌋
4-5 p. 31cm.

From Opinion; a journal of Jewish life and letters, vol. III, no. 1, November, 1932.

1. Spinoza, Benedictus de, 1632-1677.

I-21
4137

Inge, William Ralph, 1860-
God and the astronomers; containing the Warburton lectures, 1931-1933, by William Ralph Inge ... London, New York ⌊etc.⌋ Longmans, Green and co., 1933.
xiii, 308 p. 22½ cm.

CONTENTS.—Warburton lectures, introductory.—The new götterdämmerung.—The problem of time.—God in history.—The world of values.—God and the world.—The eternal world.

Includes references to Spinoza.

1. Religion and science—1900- 2. Religion—Philosophy. I. Title.

BL240.I 5 215 33—36225
Library of Congress ⌊52k1⌋

I-21
4138

Jacobi, Friedrich Heinrich, 1743-1819.
Von den göttlichen Dingen und ihrer Offenbarung. Leipzig, bey Gerhard Fleischer dem Jüngern, 1811.
viii, 222 p. 18cm.

Includes references to Spinoza.

I-21
4139

Jaquelot, Isaac, 1647-1708.
Dissertations sur l'existence de Dieu où l'on demontre cette verité par l'histoire universelle de la premiere antiquité du monde: par la refutation du systeme d'Epicure et de Spinosa: par les caracteres de divinité qui se remarquent dans la religion des Juifs; et dans l'atablissement du christianisme. On y trouvera aussi des preuves convaincantes de la révélation des livres sacrez. Par Mr. Jaquelot. A La Haye, Chez Etienne Foulque, 1697.
⌊42⌋, 705 p. 22cm.

NNC

I-21
4140

1938p4
DJ394

Jaquelot, Isaac, 1647-1708.
Dissertations sur l'existence de Dieu. Par M. Jaquelot. Nouvelle edition, augmentée de la vie de l'auteur, & de quelques lettres concernant la même matiere ... A Paris, Chez François Didot ⌊et⌋ Jacq. Barois, 1744.
3 v. 17cm.

Edited by Abbé Pérau.-cf. Bibl. Nat. Cat.
Includes a chapter "Où l'on fait voir la fausseté des principes de la démonstration de Spinosa" (v. 2, p. 422-441)

I-21
4141

Kohler, Kaufmann, 1843-1926.
For or against the personal God? To defend and defy. ⌊1871-72⌋
419-421, 435-437 p.

In Jewish times, New York, v. 3, 1871-72.
Includes references to Spinoza.

NNJ

I-21
4142

Kohler, Kaufmann, 1843-1926.
Für oder wider den persönlichen Gott? Zum Schutz und Trutz. ⌊1871-72⌋
393-394, 409-411 p.

In Jewish times, New York, v. 3, 1871-72.
Includes references to Spinoza.

NNJ

I-21
4143

Lachièze-Rey, Pierre
Les origines cartésiennes du Dieu de Spinoza. Paris, F. Alcan, 1932.
288 p. 23cm. (On cover: Bibliothèque de philosophie contemporaine)

Original paper covers bound in.
"Bibliographie": p. ix.

Lau, Theodor Ludwig, 1670-1740.
Meditationes philosophicae de Deo: mundo: homine. ⌊Frankfurt⌋ 1717.
48 p.

Levi ben Gershon, 1288-1344.
... Die kämpfe Gottes, von Lewi ben Gerson. Uebersetzung und erklärung des handschriftlich revidierten textes von Benzion Kellermann ... Berlin, Mayer & Müller, 1914-16.

2 v. 25cm. (*Added t.-p.:* Schriften der Lehranstalt für die wissenschaft des judentums, bd. III, hft. 1-2 (*i. e.* 3), bd. V, hft. 1-3)

Series title also at head of t.-p.

Includes references to Spinoza (v. 1, p. xii-xiii)

I. Kellermann, Benzion, 1869- ed. and tr. II. Title.

Lewkowicz, Jakob
Nauka Spinozy o Bogu w oswietleniu krytycznym. ⌊1903⌋
283-292 p.

In Przeglad filozoficzny, rok 6, 1903.

Lilla, Vincenzo, b. 1837.
Massima relazione fra Dio e il mondo e breve saggio critico sulle dottrine di Spinoza e di Bruno. ⌊1903⌋
178-191 p.

In R. Accademia peloritana, Messina. Atti, v. 18, 1903.

Lommatzsch, Bernhard Heinrich Carl
De Deo Spinozae, commentatio critica. Jenae, 1815.
30 p.

Thesis, Jena.

Mason, Gabriel Richard
Spinoza and Schelling; an inquiry into the relation of the God of Spinoza to the absolute of Schelling. 1911.
77 l.

Thesis, New York University.
Typescript.

Mazzantini, Carlo, 1895-
Spinoza e il teismo tradizionale. Torino, V. Bona, 1933.
74 p. 25cm.

Bibliography: p. ⌊71⌋-74.
Original paper covers bound in.

McGiffert, Arthur Cushman, 1861-1933.
The God of Spinoza as interpreted by Herder. ⌊1905⌋
706-726 p. 25cm.

From the Hibbert journal, vol. III, no. 4, July 1905.

Meditationes succinctâe de existentia Dei, de origine mali, de fundamentis juris naturâe, Ordine debito, methodoqve demonstrativa propositâe, et curis eruditorum ulterioribus subjectâe a veritatis amatore sincero. Halâe Magdeb., Impensis Jo. Christiani Hendelii, 1724.
24 p. 20cm.

Nieuwentijdt, Bernard, 1654-1718.
L'existence de Dieu démontrée par les merveilles de la nature. Paris, Jacques Vincent, 1725.
xxvij, ⌊1⌋, 681 p.

Translated by P. Noguez.

Powell, Elmer Ellsworth, 1861-
Spinozas Gottesbegriff. Halle a. S., M. Niemeyer, 1899.
ix, [1], 113 p. 24cm. (Added t.-p.: Abhandlungen zur Philosophie und ihrer Geschichte ... 12. hft.)

Enlarged from the author's inaugural dissertation, Bonn, 1899.
Original paper cover bound in.

[Ritchie, Eliza]
Notes on Spinoza's conception of God. [1902]
15 p.

Signed: E. Ritchie.
In Philosophical review, v. 11, 1902.

Powell, Elmer Ellsworth, 1861-
Über Spinozas Gottesbegriff. Halle a. S., Druck von E. Karras, 1899.
38 p. 24cm.

Thesis, Bonn.
Published also without thesis statement under title: Spinozas Gottesbegriff.
Volume of pamphlets.

Schwarz, Hermann, 1864-
Der Gottesgedanke in der Geschichte der Philosophie. 1. Teil, Von Heraklit bis Jacob Böhme. Heidelberg, Winter, 1913.
viii, 612 p. 21 cm. (Synthesis; Sammlung historischer Monographien philosophischer Begriffe, Bd. 4)

[Ratner, Joseph]
Spinoza on God. [1930]
56-72, 153-177 p.

In Philosophical review, v. 39, 1930.

Seth Pringle-Pattison, Andrew, 1856-1931.
The idea of God in the light of recent philosophy; the Gifford lectures delivered in the University of Aberdeen in the years 1912 and 1913. New York, Oxford University Press, 1917.
xvi, 425 p. 23cm.

Includes material on Spinoza.

Ratner, Joseph, 1901-
Spinoza on God, by Joseph Ratner. New York, H. Holt and company [°1930]
xiv, 88 p. 19½ cm.
"This essay is directly a contribution to the textual analysis, and only indirectly to the philosophical interpretation of the Ethica."—Pref.

1. Spinoza, Benedictus de, 1632-1677. Ethica. 2. Ethica. 3. God.

Sorley, William Ritchie, 1855-1935.
Moral values and the idea of God; the Gifford lectures, delivered in the University of Aberdeen in 1914 and 1915. Cambridge [Eng.] University Press; New York, Putnam, 1919.
xix, 534 p.

Includes references to Spinoza.
Bibliographical footnotes.

Régis, Pierre Sylvain, 1632-1707.
L'usage de la raison et de la foy, ou l'Accord de la foy et de la raison ... Réfutation de l'opinion de Spinoza touchant l'existence et de la nature de Dieu. Paris, J. Cusson, 1704.
1 p. l., [22], 500, [26] p. 25 cm.

Töllner, Johann Gottlieb, 1724-1774.
Die göttliche Eingebung der Heiligen Schrift untersucht. Mitau, J. F. Hinz, 1772.
xvi, 487, [1] p. 21 cm.

Includes references to Spinoza.

 I-21 4164

₍Vloten, Johannes van₎ 1818-1883.
Mr. Lotsy en Spinoza's Godsbegrip. ₍1872₎
₍601₎-605 p. 20cm.

From De Levensbode; tijdschrift op onbepaalde tijden, door J. van Vloten, 5. deel.
With Vloten, Johannes van. Dr. Spruyt en Spinoza. ₍1872₎

 I-21 4165

Wegener, Richard, 1843-
Begriff und Beweis der Existenz Gottes bei Spinoza. Berlin, Nauck, 1873.
55 p.

 I-21 4166

Wittichius, Jacobus.
Difficultas maxima, orta ex concatenationibus idearum, quas vir clarissimus D. Jacobus Wittichius ... concinnavit in disputatione sua de natura Dei. Cui difficultati ut publicè satisfiat, quùm & plurium mentes non parùm eâ torqueri possint, publicitus illam quoque proponere, nec non simul axioma Spinosisticum primarium penitùs subvertere, voluit G. van Ewyck, J. U. D. Lugduni Batavorum, Prostat apud Johannem vander Linden ₍1719₎
56 p. 21cm.

CONTINUED ON NEXT CARD

 I-21 4167

Wittichius, Jacobus. Difficultas maxima ... ₍1719₎ (Card 2)

Bound with Poiret, Pierre. Cogitationum rationalium ... libri quatuor. 1715.

I-21 4168

Wolff, Christian, Freiherr von, 1679-1754.
Natürliche Gottesgelahrtheit nach beweisender Lehrart abgefasst. Ins Deutsche übers. von G. F. Hagen. Halle, in Verlegung der Rengerischen Buchhandlung, 1742-45.
2 v. 21 cm.

 I-21 4169

Wolfson, Harry Austryn, 1887-
Spinoza e le prove dell'esistenza di Dio. Roma ₍1933₎
cover-title, ₍193₎-236 p. 24cm.

"Estratto da 'Ricerche religiose', vol. IX, n. 3."
Bibliographical footnotes.

I -22
IDEA

I-22 4170

Balz, Albert George Adam, 1887-
Idea and essence in the philosophies of Hobbes and Spinoza, by Albert G. A. Balz ... New York, Columbia university press, 1918.
2 p. l., 86 p., 1 l. 24½cm.

Thesis (PH. D.)—Columbia university, 1916.
Vita.
Published also as Archives of philosophy, no. 10.

1. Hobbes, Thomas, 1588-1679. 2. Spinoza, Benedictus de, 1632-1677.

I-22 4171

Blanche, F
L'ambiguité de la notion d'idée chez Spinoza. ₍1913₎
663-679 p.

In Revue des sciences philosophiques et théologiques, 7. année, 1913.

 I-22 4172

Busolt, Georg, 1850-1920.
Spinozas lehre von den ideen ... Berlin, Druck von E. S. Mittler & sohn, 1875.
2 p. l., 56 p., 2 l. 22½cm.

Inaug.-diss.—Königsberg.
Vita.
§ 1-4 der von der Albertus-universität gekrönten preisschrift: Grundzüge der erkenntnisztheorie und metaphysik Spinozas, Berlin, 1874.

1. Spinoza, Benedictus de, 1632-1677. 2. Knowledge, Theory of.

I-22 4173

Hillebrand, Joseph, 1788-1871.
Der Organismus der philosophischen Idee in wissenschaftlicher und geschichtlicher Hinsicht. Dresden und Leipzig, in der Arnoldischen Buchhandlung, 1842.
viii, 477 p.

Includes a section on Spinoza (p. 407-418)

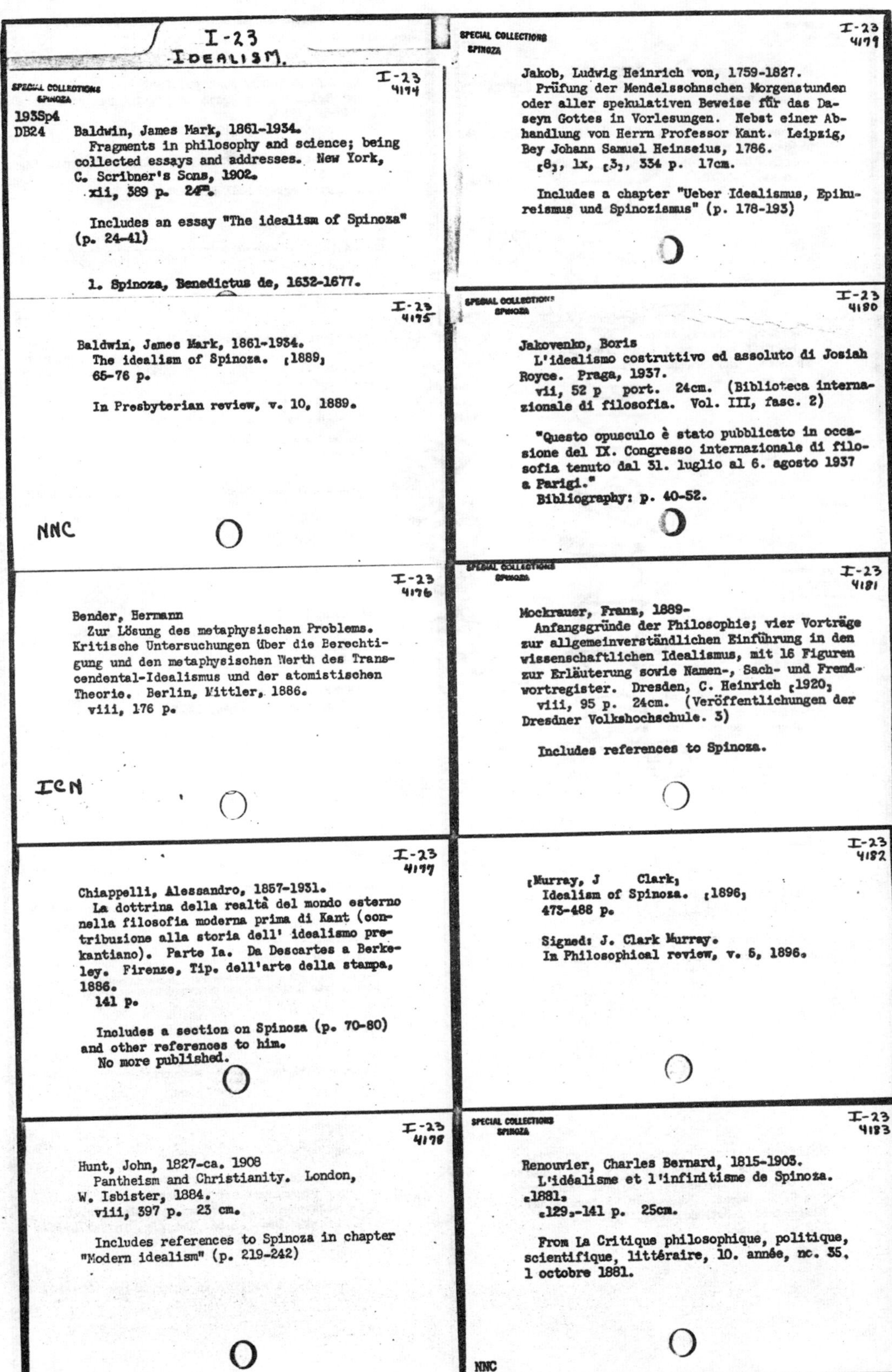

I-23
IDEALISM.

SPECIAL COLLECTIONS
SPINOZA
193Sp4
DB24

I-23
4174

Baldwin, James Mark, 1861-1934.
Fragments in philosophy and science; being collected essays and addresses. New York, C. Scribner's Sons, 1902.
xii, 389 p. 24cm.

Includes an essay "The idealism of Spinoza" (p. 24-41)

1. Spinoza, Benedictus de, 1632-1677.

I-23
4175

Baldwin, James Mark, 1861-1934.
The idealism of Spinoza. [1889]
65-76 p.

In Presbyterian review, v. 10, 1889.

NNC

I-23
4176

Bender, Hermann
Zur Lösung des metaphysischen Problems. Kritische Untersuchungen über die Berechtigung und den metaphysischen Werth des Transcendental-Idealismus und der atomistischen Theorie. Berlin, Mittler, 1886.
viii, 176 p.

ICN

I-23
4177

Chiappelli, Alessandro, 1857-1931.
La dottrina della realtà del mondo esterno nella filosofia moderna prima di Kant (contribuzione alla storia dell' idealismo prekantiano). Parte Ia. Da Descartes a Berkeley. Firenze, Tip. dell'arte della stampa, 1886.
141 p.

Includes a section on Spinoza (p. 70-80) and other references to him.
No more published.

I-23
4178

Hunt, John, 1827-ca. 1908
Pantheism and Christianity. London, W. Isbister, 1884.
viii, 397 p. 23 cm.

Includes references to Spinoza in chapter "Modern idealism" (p. 219-242)

SPECIAL COLLECTIONS
SPINOZA

I-23
4179

Jakob, Ludwig Heinrich von, 1759-1827.
Prüfung der Mendelssohnschen Morgenstunden oder aller spekulativen Beweise für das Daseyn Gottes in Vorlesungen. Nebst einer Abhandlung von Herrn Professor Kant. Leipzig, Bey Johann Samuel Heinseius, 1786.
[8], lx, [3], 334 p. 17cm.

Includes a chapter "Ueber Idealismus, Epikureismus und Spinozismus" (p. 178-193)

SPECIAL COLLECTIONS
SPINOZA

I-23
4180

Jakovenko, Boris
L'idealismo costruttivo ed assoluto di Josiah Royce. Praga, 1937.
vii, 52 p port. 24cm. (Biblioteca internazionale di filosofia. Vol. III, fasc. 2)

"Questo opusculo è stato pubblicato in occasione del IX. Congresso internazionale di filosofia tenuto dal 31. luglio al 6. agosto 1937 a Parigi."
Bibliography: p. 40-52.

SPECIAL COLLECTIONS
SPINOZA

I-23
4181

Mockrauer, Franz, 1889-
Anfangsgründe der Philosophie; vier Vorträge zur allgemeinverständlichen Einführung in den wissenschaftlichen Idealismus, mit 16 Figuren zur Erläuterung sowie Namen-, Sach- und Fremdwortregister. Dresden, C. Heinrich [1920]
viii, 95 p. 24cm. (Veröffentlichungen der Dresdner Volkshochschule. 3)

Includes references to Spinoza.

I-23
4182

[Murray, J Clark]
Idealism of Spinoza. [1896]
473-488 p.

Signed: J. Clark Murray.
In Philosophical review, v. 5, 1896.

SPECIAL COLLECTIONS
SPINOZA

I-23
4183

Renouvier, Charles Bernard, 1815-1903.
L'idéalisme et l'infinitisme de Spinoza. [1881]
[129]-141 p. 25cm.

From La Critique philosophique, politique, scientifique, littéraire, 10. année, no. 35, 1 octobre 1881.

NNC

I-23 4184

193Sp4
FS3184 Schelling, Friedrich Wilhelm Joseph von, 1774-1854.
System des transscendentalen idealismus, von Friedr. Wilh. Joseph Schelling. Tübingen, Cotta, 1800.
xvi, 486 p. 21½cm.

1. Idealism.

I-24 4189

Brochard, Victor, 1848-1907.
L'éternité des âmes dans la philosophie de Spinoza. [1901]
688-699 p.

In Revue de métaphysique et de morale, 9. année, 1901.

NNC

I-23 4185

Spaventa, Bertrando, 1817-1883.
La filosofia di Gioberti. Napoli, F. Vitale, 1863.
xiii, 543 p.

Includes a section "Contenuto della formola ideale (Spinozismo)" (p. 313-415)

MH

I-24 4190

Delille, Jacques Montanier, called, 1738-1813.
Dithyrambe sur l'immortalité de l'âme, suivi du Passage du St.-Gothard, poëme traduit de l'anglais par Jacques Delille. Paris, Giguet et Michaud, 1082 [i. e. 1802]
115 p. 21cm.

Le passage du St.-Gothard is a translation of The passage of the Saint Gothard by Georgiana, duchess of Devonshire.

I-23 4186

Wedde, Herwig, 1885-
Elemente des erkenntnistheoretischen Idealismus bei Spinoza; eine historisch-kritische Abhandlung. [Zwönitz, Buchdruckerei C. B. Ott, 1910]
80 p. 22cm.

Thesis, Jena.
Bibliographical footnotes.

I-24
IMMORTALITY

I-24 4191

Floss, Heinrich Joseph, 1819-1881.
De animorum immortalitate; disputatio philosophica. Bonnae, Typis C. Georgii, 1841.
98, 12 p. 21cm.

Thesis, Bonn.
Includes a reference to Spinoza (p. 80)
Bound with Volkmuth, Peter. Der dreieinige Pantheismus von Thales bis Hegel. 1837.

I-24 4187

Baxter, Andrew, 1686?-1750.
An enquiry into the nature of the human soul; wherein the immateriality of the soul is evinced from the principles of reason and philosophy ... London, Printed by James Bettenham, for the author [1733]
6 p. l., 376 p.

Includes references to Spinoza.

NNC

I-24 4192

Fullerton, George Stuart, 1859-1925.
... On Spinozistic immortality, by George Stuart Fullerton ... Philadelphia, Pub. for the University, 1899.
viii, [9]-154 p. 24cm. (Publications of the University of Pennsylvania. Series in philosophy. no. 3)

Manuscript notes by Carl Gebhardt, with his signature on t.-p.

1. Spinoza, Benedictus de, 1632-1677. 2. Immortality.

11-21402

Library of Congress B3999.I 4F8 [43f1]

I-24 4188

Blount, Charles, 1654-1693.
Anima mundi: or, An historical narration of the opinions of the ancients concerning man's soul after this life: according to unenlightened nature. By Charles Blount, gent. ... London, Printed in the year, 1679.
72, 85-133 p. 26 cm. (In his The miscellaneous works of Charles Blount ... 1695)

NNC

I-24 4193

Grzymisch, Siegfried, 1875-
Spinozas Lehren von der Ewigkeit und Unsterblichkeit. Breslau, Druck von Th. Schatzky, 1898.
32 p. 23cm.

Thesis, Breslau.
Published in full without thesis note.

I-24
4194

Lucka, Emil, 1877-
Grenzen der Seele. Berlin und Leipzig, Schuster & Loeffler, 1916.
430 p. 25 cm.

Includes references to Spinoza.

SPECIAL COLLECTIONS
SPINOZA

I-24
4195

Matthes, Ewald, 1865-
Die Unsterblichkeitslehre des Benedictus Spinoza. Heidelberg, Universitäts-Buchdruckerei von J. Hörning, 1892.
63 p. 22cm.

Thesis, Heidelberg.

1. Spinoza, Benedictus de, 1632-1677.

SPECIAL COLLECTIONS
SPINOZA

I-24
4196

[Mirabaud, Jean Baptiste de] 1675-1760.
Opinion des anciens sur la nature de l'ame. Anno 1738.
[100] p. 23cm.

Manuscript; handwriting varies.
A version of his De l'ame et de son immortalité, which was published in 1751 as [pt. 2] of his Le monde, son origine et son antiquité. Comparison with 2. éd., Londres, 1778, reveals extensive textual differences. Manuscript does not contain the notes and Conclusion.

SPECIAL COLLECTIONS
SPINOZA

I-24
4197

[Mirabaud, Jean Baptiste de] 1675-1760.
Sentimens des philosophes sur la nature de l'ame. Anno 1738.
[79] p. 23cm.

Manuscript.
By J. B. Mirabaud (cf. Bibl. Nat. Cat.)
Published in Nouvelles libertés de penser. Amsterdam [Paris] 1743.
"Sentiment de Spinosa": p. [47-59]
Pages [66-67] blank, cancelled.
Bound with his Opinion des anciens sur la nature de l'ame. Anno 1738.

I-24
4198

Robinson, Lewis
L'immortalité spinoziste. [1932]
445-469 p.

In Revue de métaphysique et de morale, 39. année, 1932.

I-24
4199

Ross, Alexander, 1590-1654.
The philosophical touch-stone: or Observations upon Sir Kenelm Digbie's discourses of the nature of bodies and of the reasonable soul; and Spinoza's opinion of the mortality of the soul. London, 1645.

NNUT

I-24
4200

Rubin, Salomon, 1823-1910.
Podgorze, 1908. השארת הנפש.
38 p.

Title transliterated: ha-Sh'arath ha-nefesh.
Includes references to Spinoza.

NNJ

I-24
4201

Taylor, Alfred Edward, 1869-1945.
The conception of immortality in Spinoza's Ethics. [1896]
145-166 p.

In Mind, n. s. v. 5, 1896.

I-25
INDETERMINISM

SPECIAL COLLECTIONS
SPINOZA

I-25
4202

Leroux, Emmanuel, 1883-1942.
L'indéterminisme latent de Spinoza. Napoli, F. Perrella, 1924.
10 p. 24cm.

"Estratto dagli Atti del V Congresso internazionale di filosofia ... 5-9 maggio 1924."

1. Spinoza, Benedictus de, 1632-1677.

SPECIAL COLLECTIONS
SPINOZA

I-25
4203

Leroux, Emmanuel, 1883-1942.
L'indéterminisme latent de Spinoza. Paris, F. Alcan [1924]
cover-title, [303]-308 p. 25cm.

Reprinted from Revue philosophique de la France et de l'étranger, septembre-octobre, 1924.

1. Spinoza, Benedictus de, 1632-1677.

 I-25 4204

Mabille, Paul
Controverses sur le libre arbitre au XVIIe siècle. Dijon, E. Jobard, 1879.
375 p. 25cm.

Includes a section on Spinoza (p. 78-88) and other references to him.
Original paper cover bound in.

I 26 INDIVIDUALITY

I-26 4205

Appuhn, Charles, 1862-1942.
La théorie de l'épigénèse et l'individualité du corps dans Spinoza. [1905]
764-772 p.

In Congrès international de philosophie. 2d, Geneva, 1904. Rapports et comptes rendus, 1905.

NNC

I-26 4206

Blumberg, Selma
Individualismus bei Spinoza. [1912]
681-689 p.

In Der Monismus, 7. Jahrgang, 1912.

MH

 I-26 4207

Thomas, Karl, d. 1873.
Spinoza's Individualismus und Pantheismus. Königsberg, In Commission bei A. Samter, 1848.
39 p. 23cm.

1. Spinoza, Benedictus de, 1632-1677.

 I-26 4208

Volkelt, Johannes, 1848-1930.
Pantheismus und Individualismus im Systeme Spinoza's; ein Beitrag zum Verständnisse des Geists im Spinozismus. Leipzig, In comm. bei H. Fritzsche's Buchhdlg. (A.Lorentz) 1872.
89 p. 20cm.

Thesis, Leipzig.
Published also without thesis note.

NNC

I-27 INTUITION

 I-27 4209

Brown, Alfred Barratt, 1887-
Intuition. [1914]
282-293 p. 25cm.

From The International journal of ethics. vol. 24, no. 3, April, 1914.
Includes a paragraph on Spinoza (p. 285)

I-28 JUDAISM

 I-28 4210

Ashkenazi, Ṣĕbī Hirsch ben Jacob, 1658-1718.
David Nieto and the orthodoxy of Spinozism. [1921]
278-282 p. 23cm.

"The eighteenth of the published Responsa of the Hhacham Zevi (Rabbi Zevi Aschkenazi)"
Signed: Leon Roth.
Cover-title: Dissertatio ex Chronici Spinozani tomo primo separatim edita.

NNC

I-28 4211

Baumgardt, David, 1890-
Spinozas jüdische Sendung. [1932]
451-452 p.

In Jüdische Rundschau, Jahrgang 37, 1932.

NN

I-28 4212

Behrend, Henry
The influence of Judaism over ancient, mediaeval and modern philosophy: Philo, Ibn-Gebirol and Spinoza. A paper read before the Jews' College literary society, Nov. 21, 1886. [1886]
11-12, 11, 14-15 p.

In Jewish chronicle, London; Nov. 26, Dec. 3, and Dec. 10, 1886.

NNJ

 I-28 4213

[Berman, David]
La foi de Spinoza. [1930]
4-8 p. 21cm.

Signed: David Berman.
From Le Rayon; organe mensuel de l'Union liberale israélite, 11. année, no. 5, février 1930.

Borrell, Philippe
Spinoza, interprète du judaïsme et du christianisme. [1912]
50-84, 113-131, 267-298 p.

In Annales de philosophie chrétienne, 4. sér., t. 14, 1912.

Chicago. Hebrew Theological College.
Ohel Moed; a volume of essays in Jewish studies issued by the Hebrew Theological College of Chicago. Edited by Rabbi Israel Gerstein and Carl L. Manello. St. Louis, Mo., Moinester Printing Co. [1927?]
(various pagings) 26cm.

Added t.-p. in Hebrew; articles in Hebrew or English.
Includes an article "Judaism and Spinoza's philosophy" by Simon G. Kramer.

Cohen, Hermann, 1842-1918.
Spinoza über Staat und Religion, Judentum und Christentum. [1915]
[56]-150 p. 20cm.

From Jahrbuch für jüdische Geschichte und Literatur, 18. Bd., 1915.

Eisendraht, Maurice Nathan, 1902-
Spinozism and Judaism. Toronto, Ont., Holy Blossom Synagogue [1932]
17 p. 19cm. (Holy Blossom pulpit, v. 2, no. 4, 1932-33)

"Address delivered ... December 11th, 1932."
Bound with the author's Spinoza, cursed in life, blessed in death. [1932]

Festgabe zum zehnjährigen Bestehen der Akademie für die Wissenschaft des Judentums, 1919-1929. Berlin, Akademie-Verlag [1929?]
91 p. port. 26cm.

Original paper covers bound in.
Contents.--Die Akademie für die Wissenschaft des Judentums, von Julius Guttmann.--Gustav Bradt, von Leo Baeck.--Ein ungedruckter Vortrag Hermann Cohens über Spinozas Verhältnis zum Judentum; eingel[ei]tet von Franz Rosenzweig.--Zum Problem der jüdischen Literatur-

CONTINUED ON NEXT CARD

Festgabe zum zehnjährigen Bestehen der Akademie für die Wissenschaft des Judentums. [1929?]
(Card 2)

geschichte, von Ismar Elbogen.--Ursprung und Wesen des Antisemitismus im Altertum, von Isaak Heinemann.

Franck, Adolphe, 1809-1893.
Philosophie et religion. Paris, Didier, 1867.
xv, 451 p. 22cm.

Includes a chapter "Moïse expliqué par Spinoza" (p. [265]-279)

Franck, Adolphe, 1809-1893.
Philosophie et religion. 2. éd. Paris, Didier, 1869.
xv, 451 p. 19cm.

Includes a chapter "Moïse expliqué par Spinoza" (p. [265]-279)
Original paper covers bound in.

Ginzburg, Benjamin, 1898-
Spinoza and the Jewish tradition. [1927]
19 p. port. 26cm.

From The Menorah journal, vol. XIII, no. 1, February, 1927.

1. Spinoza, Benedictus de, 1632-1677.

Gliksman, Abraham, 1883-
ברוך שפינוזה היהודי. לונדון,
תרפ"ד.
[London, 1924]
5 pts. in 1 v. 33cm.

Title transliterated: Bārūkh Shpīnōzā.
From "Haolam", vol. 11, no. 22-26, May 31-June 27, 1924.

Gossel, Josef, 1852- ed.
Populär-wissenschaftliche Vorträge über jüdische Geschichte und Literatur. 1. Band. Frankfurt a. M., J. Kauffmann, 1902.
vi, 372 p. 21cm.

Includes an essay "Spinoza und seine Stellung zum Judentum" by S. Richter (p. [262]-275)

Heller, Bernard, 1896-
Is Spinozism compatible with Judaism? New York, Bloch, 1927.
40 p. 23cm.

"Reprinted from Yearbook, vol. XXXVII, the Central Conference of American Rabbis."

Heller, Bernard, 1896-
Spinoza and Judaism; paper read at 38th Conference American rabbis at Cape May, N. J. [1927]
p. [1], 5. 41cm.

From the American Israelite, vol. 74. no. 7, August 11, 1927.

Hirsch, Benzion J
Spinoza's verhouding tot het Jodendom, aan hand van zijn "Godgeleerd staatkundig vertoog". [1928]
14 pt. illus., ports., facsim. 35cm.

From De Vrydagavond; Joodsch weekblad, jrg. 5, no. 9-16, 18-21, 23-24, 1928.
Bibliographical footnotes.

Hirsch, Benzion J
Spinoza's verhouding tot het openbarings-Jodendom, aan de hand van zijn wereld- en levensleer, beschreven in zijn Ethica (7 stellingen) Amsterdam, A. T. Kleerekoper, 1932.
67 p. port., facsim. 28cm.

1. Spinoza, Benedictus de, 1632-1677. Ethica.

Kalischer, Alfred Christlieb, 1842-1909.
Benedikt (Baruch) von Spinoza's Stellung zum Judenthum und Christenthum; als Beitrag zur Lösung der "Judenfrage". Berlin, C. Habel [1884]
88 p. 21cm.

On cover: Deutsche Zeit- und Streit-Fragen. Jahrgang XIII. Heft 193/194.

Kertész, Antal
Spinoza B. Viszonya a zsidósághoz és a kereszténységhez; észrevételek egy rabbi két predikációjához. Košice, "Globus" [1927?]
52 p. 17cm.

Klausner, Joseph, 1874-
האופי היהודי של תורת־שפינוזה; הר־צאה, שהורצתה מטעם האוניברסיטה העברית בירושלים כשמלאו 250 שנה לפטירתו של ברוך שפינוזה (1677--21 לפברואר--1927) הוצאה מיוחדת מן המאסף "כנסת". תל־אביב, תרפ"ט.
[Tel-Aviv, 1929]
179-199 p.

Title transliterated: ha-Ofi ...
Bibliographical footnotes.

Kramer, Simon G
Judaism and Spinoza's philosophy. [1930]
p. 19,67,69,71,73,75,77,79.

From the Eighth anniversary banquet journal of the Hebrew Theological College, Chicago.

Lefkowitz, David, 1875-
The relation of the life and philosophy of Spinoza to Judaism. [1928]
30-36 p. port. 24cm.

From the Kallah; an annual convention of Texas rabbis, vol. I, 1928.

Lippe, Karpel, 1830-1915.
ספר חדשים גם ישנים, מכיל: א) תו-
רת העוברין במעי אמן לפי חכמי התלמוד;
ב) שיטת שפינוזא ודעת חז"ל, מאת דר.
ק. ליפא. יאסי, בוכ- אונד שטיינדרו-
קעריי געבר. שאראגא בעמס י. י. לייבא-
וויטש בתרס"א

[Jassy] 1900.
cover-title, 30 p. 23cm.

Title transliterated: Sefer Ḥădhāshīm ....
Includes a section on Spinoza (p. 18-30)

Luzzatto, Samuele Davide, 1800-1865.
פניני שד"ל; והוא מבחר פזורי מכ-
תבי שד"ל ז"ל, שבניו הוציאו לאור
בהשתדלות שאלתיאל אייזיק גראבער
מיאראסלוי. פרזעמישל, דרוק זופ-
ניק, קנאללער עם האממערשמיד, תרמ"ח.
[Przemysl, 1888]
xv, 460 p. 22cm.

Title transliterated: Pĕnīnē ...
Includes two articles concerning Spinoza.

CONTINUED ON NEXT CARD

Mattuck, Israel Isidor, 1883 or 4-1954.
Spinoza and Judaism. [1932]
50-52 p. 25cm.

From the Liberal Jewish monthly, vol. IV, no. 7, December, 1932.

Meyerwitz, Arthur
Spinoza, his philosophy and its relation to Judaism. [1932]
p. 1, 5. 46x31cm.

From the American Israelite, v. 79, no. 21, Thursday, Nov. 23, 1932.

1. Spinoza, Benedictus de, 1632-1677.

Rakhman, D
Спиноза и юдаизм. [1923]
[85]-95 p.

Title transliterated: Spinoza i i͡udaizm.
From Trudy Instituta krasnoĭ professury, t. 1.

1. Spinoza, Benedictus de, 1632-1677.

Rivals, Georges
Notes sur le judaïsme libéral (de 1750 à 1913). Paris, 1913.
144 p.

Includes 2 sections on Spinoza (p. 29-34, 117-119)

Shemueli, Ephraim
מסרת ומהפכה; ארבע מונוגרפיות מאת
אפרים שמואלי. ניו־יורק, "ספרים",
תש"ב.

[New York, 1942]
xiv, [2], 318 p., 1 l. 22½cm.

Title transliterated: Massoreth ŭmahpēkhā.
Includes essay "Judaism and the world in Spinoza's teaching" (p. 163-240) in Hebrew.

Sokolow, Nahum, 1859-1936.
Spinoza et le judaïsme. [1927]
126-141 p.

In Revue littéraire juive, v. 1, 1927.

Sonne, Isaiah, 1887-
L'ebraismo di Spinoza. Firenze, "La Nuova Italia" [1933]
8 p. 28cm.

"Estratto dalla rivista 'La Nuova Italia', N. 7, 20 luglio 1933."
Bibliographical footnotes.

1. Spinoza, Benedictus de, 1632-1677.

Sonne, Isaiah, 1887-
יהדותו של שפינוזה. [1934]
7-8, 22-23, 56, 60, 70-71 p.

Title transliterated: Yahadutho shel Shpinozah.
In ha-Doar, v. 13, no. 1-2, 4-5, 1934.

 I-28 4244

Waxman, Meyer, 1884-
Baruch Spinoza's relation to Jewish philosophical thought and to Judaism. Philadelphia, Dropsie College for Hebrew and Cognate Learning, 1929.
cover-title, 411-430 p. 24cm.

"Reprinted from the Jewish quarterly review, New series, volume XIX, number 4."
Presentation copy to A. S. Oko, with the author's inscription and initials.
Bibliographical footnotes.

 I-28 4245

Waxman, Meyer, 1884-
Baruch Spinoza's relation to Jewish philosophical thought and to Judaism. [1929]
411-430 p. 24cm.

From the Jewish Quarterly Review, New Series, vol. XIX, no. 4, April, 1929.
Bibliographical footnotes.

I-28 4246

Weill, Julien, 1872 or 3-1950.
Spinoza et le judaïsme. [1904]
161-180 p.

In Revue des études juives, t. 49, 1904.
A review of Spinoza, sein Leben und seine Lehre, by Jacob Freudenthal.

I-29
LEX HUMANA

I-29 4247

Adelphe, Louis.
Comment la notion de "loi humaine" conçue par Spinoza peut-elle être déduite de sa philosophie générale? ... Nancy, A. Crépin-Leblond, 1905.
85 p., 1 l. 21½cm.
Thèse—Univ. de Nancy.

DLC

Library of Congress 7-13313

I-29 4248

Asturi, Francesco
Diritto e politica in B. Spinoza. [1926]
550-557 p.

In Rivista internazionale di filosofia del diritto, anno 6, 1926.

NNC

I-29 4249

Carp, J H
Spinozisme en rechtsphilosophie. [1932]
705-710 p.

In Nederlandsch juristenblad, jaargang 7, 1932.

I-29 4250

Eckstein, Walther, 1891-
Die rechtsphilosophischen Lehren Spinozas im Zusammenhang mit seiner allgemeinen Philosophie; zur Erinnerung an den 300jährigen Geburtstag Spinozas. [1933]
157-167 p.

In Archiv für Rechts- und Wirtschafts-Philosophie, Bd. 26, 1932-33.

I-29 4251

Jhering, Rudolph von, 1818-1892.
Der Zweck im Recht. Leipzig, Breitkopf & Härtel, 1877-1883.
2 v.

Vol. 1 includes references to Spinoza.

CtY

I-29 4252

Lioy, Diodato, 1839-
Della filosofia del diritto; opera di cultura generale. 4. ed. riveduta ed ampliata. Padova, Verona, Fratelli Drucker, 1906.
2 v. in 1. 25 cm.

I-29 4253

Lioy, Diodato, 1839-1912.
La philosophie du droit par Diodato Lioy ... Tr. de l'italien avec l'autorisation de l'auteur par Louis Durand ... et précédé d'une préface par Louis Durand et Jean Terrel ... Paris, Chevalier-Marescq et cie, 1887.
cxxxvi, 587 p. 23cm.

I. Durand, Louis, 1859- tr. II. Terrel, Jean.

NN 13-20252 Revised

Library of Congress [r44b2]

I-29
4254

Lioy, Diodato, 1839-1912.
The philosophy of right, with special reference to the principles and development of law. By Diodato Lioy ... Tr. from the Italian by W. Hastie ... London, K. Paul, Trench, Trübner, & co., ltd., 1891.
2 v. 21½cm. (Half-title: The English and foreign philosophical library)
"Bibliography of the principal works on the philosophy of right, published in Italy, from Vico to the present day": v. 2, p. [378]-392.
1. Ethics. 2. Natural law. 3. Law—Philosophy. I. Hastie, William, 1842-1903, tr. II. Title. III. Title: Right, Philosophy of.
12-19412
Library of Congress [a44h1]

I-29
4255

Lorimer, James, 1818-1890.
The institutes of law; a treatise of the principles of jurisprudence as determined by nature. 2d ed., rev. and enl. Edinburgh, Blackwood, 1880.
xx, 572 p. 23 cm.
Includes references to Spinoza.

I-30
LOGIC

I-30
4256

Boole, George, 1815-1864.
An investigation of the laws of thought, on which are founded the mathematical theories of logic and probabilities. London, Walton and Maberly, 1854.
5 p. l., 424 p., 2 l. 22 cm.
Includes a chapter "Clarke and Spinoza" (p. 185-218)
NNC

I-30
4257

Brunschvicg, Léon, 1869-1944.
La logique de Spinoza. [1893]
453-467 p.
In Revue de métaphysique et de morale, 1. année, 1893.
NNC

I-30
4258

Crousaz, Jean Pierre, 1663-1750.
La logique; ou, Système de réflexions qui peuvent contribuer à la netteté & à l'étendue de nos connoissances ... 3. éd. rev. ... Amsterdam, L'Honoré et Châtelain, 1725.
4 v. illus. 17 cm.

I-30
4259

Dubislav, Walter, 1895-
Über die Definition. 2. verb. Aufl. Berlin-Schöneberg, Weiss, 1927.
MH

I-30
4260

Dubislav, Walter, 1895-
Die definition, von Walter Dubislav. Dritte, völlig umgearbeitete und erweiterte auflage. Leipzig, F. Meiner, 1931.
viii, 160 p. 24½cm. [Beihefte der "Erkenntnis" ... 1]
"Literaturverzeichnis": p. [149]-157.
Includes a section on Spinoza (p. 66-68)
1. [Definition (Logic)]
A C 33-118
John Crerar library for Library of Congress [42c1] [42c1]

SPECIAL COLLECTIONS SPINOZA
I-30
4261

Greca, Carlo
L'esistere quale oggetto di scienza e di storia (dissertazione di logica formale) Parte prima: L'esistenza come intuizione. Girgenti, Tipografia Dima, Di Caro, 1925.
105 p. 28cm.
Includes a reference to Spinoza (p. 48)

SPECIAL COLLECTIONS SPINOZA
I-30
4262

Harms, Friedrich, 1819-1880.
Geschichte der Logik. Berlin, Th. Hofmann, 1881.
viii, 240 p. 23cm. (His Die Philosophie in ihrer Geschichte. 2. Theil)
Includes a section on Spinoza (p. 192-202)

SPECIAL COLLECTIONS SPINOZA
I-30
4263

Haserot, Francis Samuel, 1895-
Essays on the logic of being, by Francis S. Haserot. New York, The Macmillan company, 1932.
xiii, 641 p. 24 cm.
The second part of the essays is devoted to value as an ontological category. cf. Pref.
Includes references to Spinoza.
1. Ontology. 2. Worth. I. Title. II. Title: Logic of being.
BD311.H3 111 32-9768
Library of Congress [551½]

Holyoake, George Jacob, 1817-1906.
Rudiments of public speaking and debate: or, Hints on the application of logic. London, Watson, 1849.
vii, 90 p. 17cm.

Volume of pamphlets.

Keckermann, Bartholomäus, 1571-1608.
Systema logicae, tribvs libris adornatvm, pleniore praeceptorvm methode, & commentariis scriptis ad praeceptorum illustrationem & collationem cum doctrina Aristotelis, atque aliorum tum veterum, tum recentium logicorum sententiis ac disputationibus, a Bartholomaeo Keckermanno ... Editio postrema, ab avthore recognita & emendata. Cvm rervm et verborvm indice locupletissimo. Avreliopoli, Excudebat Samuel Mozetus, 1615.
[32], 575, [50] p. fold. tables. 18cm.

Lesbazeilles, Paul
De logica Spinozae. Parisiis, Apud Leopoldum Cerf, 1883.
108 p. 22cm.

Thesis, Paris.
Manuscript notes by Carl Gebhardt.
Original paper cover bound in.

1. Spinoza, Benedictus de, 1632-1677.

Saltus, Edgar, 1855-1921.
The anatomy of negation. London, Williams and Norgate, 1886.
226 p.

Includes a section on Spinoza (p. 112-121)

Trendelenburg, Friedrich Adolf, 1802-1872.
Logische Untersuchungen. Berlin, G. Bethge, 1840.
2 v. in 1. 22 cm.

Trendelenburg, Friedrich Adolf, 1802-1872.
Logische Untersuchungen. 2. ergänzte Aufl. Leipzig, S. Hirzel, 1862.
2 v.

Trendelenburg, Friedrich Adolf, 1802-1872.
Logische Untersuchungen. 3. verm. Aufl. Leipzig, S. Hirzel, 1870.
2 v. 24 cm.

Includes references to Spinoza.

Watts, Isaac, 1674-1748.
Logick: or, The right use of reason in the enquiry after truth. With a variety of rules to guard against error, in the affairs of religion and human life, as well as in the sciences. The 7th ed., cor. London: Printed for Richard Hett and James Brackstone, 1740.
[6], 365, [4] p. 19 cm.

Zimmermann, Robert, *edler* von, 1824-1898.
Studien und kritiken zur philosophie und aesthetik. Von Robert Zimmermann ... Wien, W. Braumüller, 1870.
2 v. in 1. 24½ cm.
Each volume has also special t.-p.
CONTENTS.—1. bd. Zur philosophie.—2. bd. Zur aesthetik.
Includes an essay "Ueber den logischen Grundfehler der spinozistischen Ethik" (v. 1, p. [36]-60)
1. Philosophy — Addresses, essays, lectures. 2. Aesthetics — Addresses, essays, lectures. I. Title.

Zimmermann, from Olmutz
Ueber einige logische Fehler der spinozistischen Ethik. [1850]
14 p. 23cm.

"Aus dem October-Hefte des Jahrganges 1850 der Sitzungsberichte der philos.-histor. Classe der kaiserl. Akademie der Wissenschaften besonders abgedruckt."
Volume of pamphlets.

I-31
MATERIALISM

I-31
4274

Bergier, Nicolas Sylvestre, 1718-1790.
Examen du materialisme; ou, Réfutation du Système de la nature. Paris, Humblot, 1771.
2 v.

An answer to Holbach's Système de la nature.

I-31
4275

Chuchmarev, Vladimir
Материализм Спинозы; к переоценке идеалистической традиции. Москва, Московский рабочий, 1927.
131 p. port. 20cm.

Title transliterated: Materializm Spinozy.

1. Spinoza, Benedictus de, 1632-1677.

I-31
4276

Hecker, Julius Friedrich, 1881-
Moscow dialogues; discussions on red philosophy. With a foreword by John Macmurray. London, Chapman and Hall [1933]
xvi, 284 p. 22 cm.

Includes a discussion of Spinoza's relation to dialectical materialism in Dialogue V (p. 55-63) and other references to Spinoza.

I-31
4277

[Ioffe, Abram Moiseevich] 1881-
שפינאזא דער פארגייער (אין ליכט פון מאטעריאליזם) כפון א. דעבארין [pseud.] יידיש: ב. גאלדבערג.ווארשע, ביבליאטעק מארק ראקאווסקי, 1930.
[Warsaw, R. Rakowski, 1930]
24 p. 23cm. (1 :ווינס)

Title transliterated: Shpinoza der forgayer.

I-31
4278

Karev, N
Спиноза и материализм (по поводу статьи Л. Аксельрод "Надоело!") [1927]
[190]-207 p.

Title transliterated: Spinoza i materializm.
In Красная новь, 1927.

NN

I-31
4279

Lange, Friedrich Albert, 1828-1875.
Geschichte des Materialismus und Kritik seiner Bedeutung in der Gegenwart. Iserlohn, J. Baedeker, 1866.
xvi, 563 p. 21cm.

Includes references to Spinoza.

I-31
4280

Lenin, Vladimir Il'ich, 1870-1924.
Materialismus und Empiriokritizismus; kritische Bemerkungen über eine reaktionäre Philosophie. Wien, Verlag für Literatur und Politik [1927]
xxxi, 486 p. port. 24cm. (His Sämtliche Werke. Bd. 13)

"Übertragen unter Redaktion von N. Borowski."
Includes a reference to Spinoza (p. 378)
Bibliography: p. 403-483.

I-31
4281

Man'kovskiĭ, L A
Спиноза и материализм. Москва, Государственное издательство, 1930.
205 p. port. 17cm. (Философская библиотека пропагандиста)

Title transliterated: Spinoza i materializm.

I-31
4282

Picton, James Allanson, 1832-1910.
The mystery of matter and other essays. London, Macmillan, 1873.
xii, 492 p. 20 cm.

NNUT

I-31
4283

Sommer, Hugo, b. 1839.
Die Lehre Spinoza's und der Materialismus. [1879]
1-30, 209-238 p.

In Zeitschrift für Philosophie und philosophische Kritik, 74. Bd., 1879.

I-32
METAPHYSICS

Alexander, Samuel, 1859-1938.
Spinoza and time. With an afterword by Viscount Haldane. London, G. Allen & Unwin [1921]
80 p. 17cm. (Arthur Davis memorial lecture. 4)

Bader, F E
Benedicti de Spinoza de rebus singularibus doctrina. Berlin, C. A. Schiementz, 1858.
28 p. 27cm.

At head of title: Jahresbericht über die Königstädtische Realschule ...
Volume of pamphlets.

Baratono, Adelchi
L'unità di Spinoza. [1927]
[205]-216 p.

In Rivista di filosofia, anno 18, 1927.

Bender, Wilhelm, b. 1845.
Metaphysik und Asketik; ein Beitrag zur Geschichte der Moralphilosophie. [1893]
1-42, 208-224, 301-331 p.

In Archiv für Geschichte der Philosophie, Bd. 6, 1893.
Includes references to Spinoza (p. 220-224)

[Bidney, David]
... Value and reality in the metaphysics of Spinoza ... [New York, 1936]
p. 229-244. 24cm.

"This article is based on a doctoral dissertation accepted by Yale university in 1932 entitled 'The idea of value in the metaphysics of Spinoza'."—p. 229.
Caption title.
Signed: D. Bidney.
Reprint from the Philosophical review, v. 45, no. 3, whole no. 267, May, 1936.
Presentation copy to A. S. Oko.
1. Spinoza, Benedictus de, 1632-1677. I. Title.

Blewett, George John
The study of nature and the vision of God: with other essays in philosophy. Toronto, W. Briggs, 1907.
ix, 358 p. 24 cm.

Includes an essay "The metaphysic of Spinoza" (p. 111-199)

Cohn, Jonas, 1869-
Geschichte des unendlichkeitsproblems im abendländischen denken bis Kant, von Jonas Cohn ... Leipzig, W. Engelmann, 1896.
vii p., 1 l., 261, [1] p. 22½cm.

Bibliography: leaf preceding p. [1]
Bibliographical foot-notes.
Includes a section on Spinoza (p. 152-159) and other references to him.

[Daumal, René, 1908-1944.
Le non-dualisme de Spinoza; ou, La dynamite philosophique. [1934]
[767]-787 p. 23cm.

Signed: René Daumal.
From La Nouvelle revue française, 22e année, no. 248, 1er mai 1934.

1. Spinoza, Benedictus de, 1632-1677.

Gebhardt, Carl, 1881-1934.
Religio metaphysica. [1933]
[134]-144 p. 26cm.

"Reprint from Septimana Spinozana."
Bound with Gebhardt, Carl. Spinoza in der Schule. [1930]

1. Spinoza, Benedictus de, 1632-1677.

Heymans, Gerardus, 1857-1930.
Einführung in die Metaphysik auf Grundlage der Erfahrung. Leipzig, Barth, 1905.
viii, 348 p.

Includes references to Spinoza.

Lasbax, Emile
La hiérarchie dans l'univers chez Spinoza. Nouvelle édition augmentée d'une préface sur l'application de la méthode d'intuition vitale à l'histoire de la philosophie. Paris, J. Vrin, 1926.
xxiv, 357, vii p. table. 23cm. (Bibliothèque d'histoire de la philosophie)

Original paper covers bound in.

Ludowici, August, 1866-
Das genetische prinzip; versuch einer lebenslehre, von August Ludowici ... München, F. Bruckmann a.-g., 1913.
299 p. fold. col. diagr. 23 cm.
"Literatur-angaben": p. [289]-298.

Includes references to Spinoza.

1. Metaphysics. 2. Life. 3. Evolution. I. Title.

13—26701

Library of Congress BS299.L8G5
[a50b½]

Meijer, Willem, 1842-1926.
De consensu metaphysicae Spinozanae cum philosophia Arabica sive Moslemitica. [Hagae Comitis, 1922]
14-19 p. 22cm.

Cover-title: Dissertatio ex Chronici Spinozani tomo secundo separatim edita.

1. Spinoza, Benedictus de, 1632-1677.

Myers, Henry Alonzo, 1906-1955.
Systematic pluralism in Spinoza and Hegel. [1935]
237-263 p.

In The Monist, v. 45, 1935.

Renouvier, Charles Bernard, 1815-1903.
Histoire et solution des problèmes métaphysiques. Paris, F. Alcan, 1901.
2 p. l., ii, 477 p. 23 cm. (Bibliothèque de philosophie contemporaine)

Includes references to Spinoza.

Robinson, Lewis
Untersuchungen über Spinozas Metaphysik. [1906]
297-332, 451-485 p.

In Archiv für Geschichte der Philosophie, Bd. 19., 1906.

Schwarz, Hermann, 1864-
Spinozas Identitätsphilosophie. [1906]
[226]-245 p. 24cm.

From Philosophische Abhandlungen Max Heinze zum 70. Geburtstage gewidmet. Berlin, 1906.

1. Spinoza, Benedictus de, 1632-1677.

Thomas, Karl, d. 1873.
Herbart - Spinoza - Kant, dornige Studien und Versuche; historische Beiträge zur Philosophie. Langensalza, H. Beyer, 1875.
xvii, 300 p. 23cm.

Includes an essay "Spinoza als metaphysiker und der Tractat von Gott" (p. [141]-256)

Thomas, Karl, d. 1873.
Spinoza als Metaphysiker, vom Standpunkte der historischen Kritik. Königsberg, Gräfe und Unzer, 1840.
vi, 176 p. 23cm.

Original paper covers bound in.

1. Spinoza, Benedictus de, 1632-1677.

Whittaker, Thomas, 1856-1935.
Transcendence in Spinoza. [1929]
[293]-311 p. 23cm.

From Mind, vol. XXXVIII, no. 151, July, 1929.

1. Spinoza, Benedictus de, 1632-1677.

I-33
METHODOLOGY

Adam, Charles Ernest, 1857-
De methedo apud Cartesium, Spinozam et Leibnitium. Lutetiae, Apud bibliopolam Hachette et socios, 1885.
115 p. 23cm.

Thesis, Paris.

Bertauld, Pierre Auguste, 1829-
De la méthode; méthode spinosiste et méthode hégélienne. 2. éd. Paris, Alcan, 1891.
384 p. 19cm. (His Introduction à la recherche des causes premières, I)

Beyer, Hermann
Mathematisch-naturwissenschaftliche Denkweise in der Philosophie des Spinoza. Zeulenroda [1908]
39 p. 26 cm.

Programm - Städtische Realschule, Zeulenroda.

Brunschvicg, Léon, 1869-1944.
Les étapes de la philosophie mathématique. 2. éd. Paris, F. Alcan, 1922.
xi, 591 p. 23cm. (Bibliothèque de philosophie contemporaine)

Includes a section "La philosophie mathématique de Spinoza" (p. 138-151)

Iriarte, Joaquín
La filosofía "geométrica" en Descartes, Spinoza y Leibniz. [1938]
481-497 p.

In Gregoriamm, anno 19, v. 29, 1938.

Kirchmann, Julius Hermann von, 1802-1884.
Ueber die Anwendbarkeit der mathematischen Methode auf die Philosophie; ein Vortrag. Halle a. S., Pfeffer, 1883.
70 p. illus. 23 cm. ([Philosophische Vorträge, n. F., Heft 4])

Includes references to Spinoza.

McKeon, Richard, 1900-
Causation and the geometric method in the philosophy of Spinoza. [1930]
cover-title, 178-189, 275-296 p. 25cm.

"Reprinted from The Philosophical review, vol. XXXIX, no. 2, March, 1930, and no. 3, May, 1930."

1. Spinoza, Benedictus de, 1632-1677.

Pastore, Annibale, 1868-
Il principio del metodo sperimentale nella filosofia di Spinoza. [1927]
[267]-272 p.

In Rivista di filosofia, anno 18, 1927.

Polovtsov, V N
Къ методологіи изученія философіи Спинозы. В. Н. Половцова. Москва, 1913.
84 p.

Title transliterated: K metodologii izuchenii͡a filosofii Spinozy.

1. Spinoza, Benedictus de, 1632-1677.

Popoff, Boris, 1886-
Versuch eines historischen Ueberblickes über die ethischen Methoden in den philosophischen Systemen von Plato bis Kant; ein Beitrag zur Geschichte der ethischen Methodologie. [Berlin, Ebering, 1914]
138 p. 23 cm.

Thesis, Berlin.
Includes a section on Spinoza (p. 61-72)

Richter, Raoul, 1871-1912.
Essays. Leipzig, F. Meiner, 1913.
xiii, 416 p. 19cm.

Includes a chapter "Die Methode Spinozas" (p. ₍55₎-91)

Richter, Raoul, 1871-1912.
Die Methode Spinozas. ₍1898₎
₍12₎-37 p. 25cm.

"Sonderabdruck aus Zeitschrift für Philosophie und philosophische Kritik. 113. Bd."
Bibliographical footnotes.

1. Spinoza, Benedictus de, 1632-1677.

Selsam, Howard, 1903-
Spinoza: art and the geometric order. ₍New York, 1935₎
₍253₎-269 p. 21cm.

From Studies in the history of ideas, edited by The Department of Philosophy of Columbia University, vol. III.

1. Spinoza, Benedictus de, 1632-1677.

₍Snow, Adolph Judah₎ 1894-
Spinoza's use of the "Euclidean form" of exposition. ₍1923₎
₍473₎-480 p. 23cm.

Signed: A. J. Snow.
From the Monist, vol. XXXIII, no. 3, July 1923.
Bibliographical footnotes.

Wahle, Richard, 1857-
Ueber die geometrische Methode des Spinoza. Wien, F. Tempsky, 1888.
24 p. 25cm.

"Aus dem Jahrgange 1888 der Sitzungsberichte der phil-hist. Classe der kais. Akademie der Wissenschaften (CXVI. Bd., I. Hft. S. 431) besonders abgedruckt."

Wolff, Christian, Freiherr von, 1679-1754.
Theologia naturalis methodo scientifica pertractata ... Auctore Christiano Wolfio ... Francofurti & Lipsiae, Prostat in Officina Libraria Rengeriana, 1737-39 ₍v. 1, 1739₎
2 v. 22cm.

Vol. 1 is "Editio nova".
Vol. 2 includes references to Spinoza.

I-34 MIND AND BODY

Busse, Ludwig, 1862-1907.
Geist und Körper, Seele und Leib. 2. Aufl. Mit einem ergänzenden und die neuere Literatur zusammenfassenden Anhang von Ernst Dürr. Leipzig, F. Meiner, 1913.
x, 566 p. 24cm.

Includes references to Spinoza.
Bibliography: p. ₍549₎-566.

Colsenet, Edmond
De mentis essentia Spinoza quid senserit. Parisiis, Germer Baillière, 1880.
57 p. 25cm.

Thesis, Paris.
Bibliographical footnotes.
Original paper cover bound in.

Dräseke, Johannes, 1844-1916.
In welchem Verhältnis steht Spinozas Lehre von Leib und Seele zu der seiner Vorgänger? ₍1916₎
144-168 p.

In Archiv für Geschichte der Philosophie, Bd. 29., Okt. 1915-Juli 1916.

Erdmann, Johann Eduard, 1805-1892.
Leib und Seele nach ihrem Begriff und ihrem Verhältniss zu einander; ein Beitrag zur Begründung der philosophischen Anthropologie. Halle, C. A. Schwetschke und Sohn, 1837.
viii, 133 p. 21cm.

Includes references to Spinoza.

Freudenthal, Jacob, 1839-1907.
Über die Entwicklung der Lehre vom psychophysischen Parallelismus bei Spinoza. Leipzig, W. Engelmann, 1907.
cover-title, ⌊73⌋-85 p. 23cm.

"Sonderabdruck aus 'Archiv für die gesamte Psychologie', IX. Bd., 1. Heft."
Bibliographical footnotes.

Kramer, Paul Matthias, b. 1842.
De doctrina Spinozae de mente humana. Halis Saxonum, Formis Orphanotrophei ⌊1865⌋
38 p. 20cm.

Thesis, Halle.

1. Spinoza, Benedictus de, 1632-1677.

Regensburg, Joseph, 1875-
Über die Abhängigkeit der Seelenlehre Spinoza's von seiner Körperlehre und über die Beziehungen dieser beiden zu seiner Erkenntnistheorie. Riga, Druck von Schnakenburg, 1900.
97, vii p. 23cm.

Thesis, Giessen.

Ricardou, A
De humanae mentis aeternitate apud Spinozam. Lutetiae Parisiorum, Edebat F. Alcan, 1890.
87 p. 23cm.

Thesis, Paris.

1. Spinoza, Benedictus de, 1632-1677.

White, William Hale, 1831-1913.
Spinoza's doctrine of the relationship between mind and body. ⌊1896⌋
515-518 p.

In International journal of ethics, v. 6, Oct. 1895-July 1896.

I-35 MIRACLES

⌊Blount, Charles⌋ 1654-1693.
Miracles, no violations of the lawvs of nature ... London: Printed for Robert Sollers, 1683.
⌊6⌋, 31 p. 20cm.

In the main a translation of the sixth chapter of Spinoza's Tractatus theologico-politicus, with a translation of a part of the chapter on miracles from Hobbes' Leviathan.

⌊Browne, Thomas⌋ 1654?-1741.
Miracles work's above and contrary to nature: or, An answer to a late translation out of Spinoza's Tractatus theologico-politicus, Mr. Hobb's Leviathan, &c. Published to undermine the truth and authority of miracles, Scripture, and religion, in a treatise entituled Miracles no violation of the laws of nature ... London, S. Smith, 1683.

1 p. l., 68 p. 19½cm. ⌊With Blount, Charles. Miracles, no violations of the laws of nature. London, 1683⌋

1. Blount, Charles, 1654-1693. Miracles, no violations of the laws of nature. 2. Miracles—Controversial literature. 3. Miracles—Early works to 1800. I. Title.

Library of Congress BT97.A2B5 41-35218
⌊2⌋

Wright, Charles James, 1888-
Miracle in history and in modern thought; or, Miracle and Christian apologetic. New York, Holt ⌊c1930⌋
ix, 433 p. 23cm.

Includes a section on Spinoza (p. 192-200) and other references to him.
Bibliography: p. 407-424.

I-36 MISCELLANEOUS

Bierens de Haan, Johannes Diderik, 1866-1943.
Wijsgeerige studies. 's-Gravenhage, Nijhoff, 1904.
236 p. 20cm.

Contents.--Spinoza. Vrijheid. Godsdienst. De menschelijke aktie. Logos. Eleaten. Grieksche sceptiek.

Brochard, Victor, 1848-1907.
Études de philosophie ancienne et de philosophie moderne; recueillies et précédées d'une introduction par V. Delbos. Nouvelle éd. Paris, J. Vrin, 1926.
xxviii, 559 p. 25cm.

Includes three chapters on Spinoza: "Le Traité des passions de Descartes et l'Éthique de Spinoza" (p. ⌊327⌋-331), "Le dieu de Spinoza" (p. ⌊332⌋-370) and "L'éternité des âmes dans la philosophie de Spinoza" (p. ⌊371⌋-383)

I-36
4334

Congrès international de philosophie. 3d, Heidelberg, 1908.
Bericht über den III. Internationalen kongress für philosophie zu Heidelberg 1. bis 5. september 1908 hrsg. von professor dr. Th. Elsenhans. Heidelberg, C. Winter, 1909.
xv, 1138 p. illus., ports. 25½cm.

Includes two essays: "La notion de substance et la notion de Dieu dans la philosophie de Spinoza", by Victor Delbos (p. 256-262) and "Spinoza als Politiker" by Carl Gebhardt (p. 263-267)

I-36
4335

Sander, Franz, 1897-
Die entwicklung der raumtheorien in der 2. hälfte des 17. jahrhunderts ... von Franz Sander ... Halle (Saale) Buchdruckerei H. John, 1931.
383, ⌊1⌋ p. 22½cm.
Inaug.-diss.—Halle.
Lebenslauf.
"Literaturverzeichnis": p. ⌊379⌋-383.
Includes a section on Spinoza (p. 196-209)
1. Space and time. I. Title.
⌊Full name: Friedrich Karl Franz Sander⌋

DLC 34-9096

I-37
MODE

I-37
4336

Hicks, George Dawes, 1862-1941.
The "modes" of Spinoza and the "monads" of Leibniz. ⌊1918⌋
329-362 p.

In Aristotelian Society. Proceedings, n. s. v. 18, 1918.

I-37
4337

Hicks, George Dawes, 1862-1941.
The "modes" of Spinoza and the "monads" of Leibniz. ⌊1932⌋
29-46 p.

From Losskiĭ, Nikolaĭ Onufrievich. Festschrift N. O. Losskij zum 60. Geburtstage. Bonn, Cohen, 1932.

I-37
4338

Martinetti, Piero, 1872-1943.
Modi primitivi e derivati, infiniti e finiti. ⌊1927⌋
⌊248⌋-261 p.

In Rivista di filosofia, anno 18, 1927.

I-37
4339

Schmitt, Elisabeth, 1877-
Die unendlichen Modi bei Spinoza. Leipzig, J. A. Barth, 1910.
viii, 135 p. 25cm.

Thesis, Heidelberg.
Bibliographical footnotes.
Volume of pamphlets.

NNC

I-37
4340

Schmitt, Elisabeth, 1877-
Die unendlichen Modi bei Spinoza. ⌊1910⌋
1-81, 129-182 p.

In Zeitschrift für Philosophie und philosophische Kritik, Bd. 140, 1910.

I-37
4341

Schmitt, Elisabeth, 1877-
Zur Problematik der unendlichen Modi. ⌊1922⌋
155-173 p. 22cm.

Cover-title: Dissertatio ex Chronici Spinozani tomo secundo separatim edita. Hagae Comitis, 1922.

I-38
MONISM

I-38
4342

Abate Longo, Giovanni
Il monismo nelle diverse forme di esistenza e nella libertà umana. Catania, Panzini, 1893.

MH

I-38
4343

Calkins, Mary Whiton, 1863-1930.
The persistent problems of philosophy; an introduction to metaphysics through the study of modern systems, by Mary Whiton Calkins ... New York, The Macmillan company; London, Macmillan & co., ltd., 1907.
xxii, 575 p. 21 cm.
CONTENTS.—Introduction.—Systems of numerical pluralism.—A criticism of preceding systems.—Systems of numerical monism.—Conclusion.—Appendix: Biographies and bibliographies of modern writers on philosophy, together with summaries and discussions of certain texts (p. 457-564)
Includes a chapter on Spinoza
1. Philosophy, Modern—Hist. 2. Metaphysics. I. Title.

NNUT B791.C2 7—11605
Library of Congress ⌊57m½⌋

Calkins, Mary Whiton, 1863-1930.
The persistent problems of philosophy; an introduction to metaphysics through the study of modern systems. 2d ed. New York, Macmillan, 1910.
xxiv, 558 p.

Includes a chapter "Monistic pluralism: The system of Spinoza" (p. 277-306) and other references to Spinoza.

Drews, Arthur, 1865- ed.
Der Monismus, dargestellt in Beiträgen seiner Vertreter. Jena, E. Diederichs, 1908.
2 v. 23cm.

Includes references to Spinoza.
Contents.--1. Bd. Systematisches.--2. Bd. Historisches.

Haeckel, Ernst, 1834-1919.
Gott-Natur (Theophysis) Studien über monistische Religion. 2. Aufl. Leipzig, A. Kröner, 1914.
71 p. 24ᶜᵐ. tables.

Includes references to Spinoza.

Klimke, Friedrich
Der Monismus und seine philosophischen Grundlagen. Freiburg im Breisgau, Herder, 1911.
xxiii, 620 p.

Maltese, Felice, 1839-1911.
Monismo o nichilismo; proposta di una riforma scientifica. Vittoria, Sicilia, Velardi, 1887.
2 v. 19 cm.

Noiré, Ludwig, 1829-1889.
Der monistische Gedanke; eine Concordanz der Philosophie Schopenhauer's, Darwin's, R. Mayer's und L. Geiger's. Leipzig, Veit, 1875.
xxvi, 366 p. 22cm.

Includes a reference to Spinoza (p. 7)

[Opitz,]
Spinoza als Monist, Determinist und Realist [1876]
193-204 p.

Signed: Opitz.
In Philosophische Monatshefte, 12, Bd., 1876.

Pawlicki, Stefan
Spinoza i dzisiejszy monizm. Kraków, Nakładem Towarzystwa Filozoficznego, 1912.
24 p. (Towarzystwo Filozoficzne w Krakowie. Wydawnictw no. 5)

Vaynes van Brakell Buys, Willem Rudolf de, 1905-
Het Godsbegrip bij Spinoza; een inleiding tot het monisme, door dr. W. R. van Brakell Buys. Utrecht, E. J. Bijleveld, 1934.
147 p., 1 l. 24ᶜᵐ.

"Literatuur": leaf at end.
Issued also as thesis, Utrecht.
Original paper covers bound in.

1. Spinoza, Benedictus de, 1632-1677. 2. God. I. Title.

Library of Congress B3999.G6V3 38-35410
[2] 199.492

Veitch, John, 1829-1894.
Dualism and monism, and other essays. With an introduction by R. M. Wenley. Edinburgh, W. Blackwood and Sons, 1895.
xlii, 221 p. 20cm. (Half-title: Essays in philosophy, 2d series)

"List of Professor Veitch's works": p. [ix]-x.
The third essay was originally published in "Wordsworthiana."
Includes references to Spinoza (p. 98-99, 101)

CONTINUED ON NEXT CARD

SPECIAL COLLECTIONS
SPINOZA

I-38
4354

Waton, Harry
A true monistic philosophy; comprehending the absolute, God, existence, man, society and history. [New York] Spinoza Institute of America [1947]
v. 1. port. 24cm.

Includes references to Spinoza.

I-39
NATURAL RIGHTS

SPECIAL COLLECTIONS
SPINOZA

I-39
4355

Carp, J H
Naturrecht und Pflichtbegriff nach Spinoza. [1921]
81-90 p. 22cm.

Cover-title: Dissertatio ex Chronici Spinozani tomo primo separatim edita.

SPECIAL COLLECTIONS
SPINOZA

I-39
4356

Krug, Wilhelm Traugott, 1770-1842.
Spinozae de ivre natvrae sententia denvo examinata; symbolarvm ad historiam philosophiae particvla qvarta qva philosophiae doctorvm et LL. AA. magistrorvm creationem annvam d XVII. Febr. a. MDCCCXXV ... nvntiat Gvilielmvs Travgott Krvg ... Lipsiae, Literis Staritii [1825]
15 p. 23cm.

I-40
NATURALISM

I-40
4357

Covotti, Aurelio, 1874–
... Spinoza, la trasformazione della dottrina di Cartesio, il puro naturalismo. Napoli, S. I. E. M., stabilimento industrie editoriali meridionali, 1935.
80 p. 25½cm.

1. Spinoza, Benedictus de, 1632-1677. 2. Descartes, René, 1596-1650.

37—13598

DLC

Library of Congress B3998.C87
[45c1] 199.492

I-40
4358

Herbart, Johann Friedrich, 1776-1841.
Allgemeine Metaphysik, nebst den Anfängen der philosophischen Naturlehre. Königsberg, A. W. Unzer, 1828-29.
2 v.

Includes a section "Die Lehre des Spinoza" (v. 1, p. 128-168) and other references to him.

I-40
4359

Hoffmann, A
Zur geschichtlichen Bedeutung der Naturphilosophie Spinozas. [1905]
163-186 p.

In Zeitschrift für Philosophie und philosophische Kritik, Bd. 125, 1905.

I-40
4360

[Holbach, Paul Henri Thiry, baron d'] 1723-1789.
Système de la nature, ou Des loix du monde physique & du monde moral. Par M. Mirabaud ... Londres, 1770.

Wrongly attributed on t.-p. to M. de Mirabaud.
Vol. 2 includes references to Spinoza.

I-40
4361

Kwiatkowski, Wincenty
De Spinozy modernistyczny naturalizm w Biblji. Poznań, Nakład Księgarni Św. Wojciecha, 1924.
28 p. (Sprawy Biblijne. Zeszyt 8)

OCH

I-40
4362

Ledinský, Franz
Die Philosophie Spinoza's im Lichte der modernen Naturforschung. Budweis, J. Krupička, 1871.
33 p.

Promotionsschrift, Rostock.

MH

I-40
4363

Nourrisson, Jean Félix, 1825-1899.
Spinoza et le naturalisme contemporain, par Nourrisson. Paris, Didier et cie, 1866.
2 p. l., xii, 305 p., 1 l. 18cm.

1. Spinoza, Benedictus de, 1632-1677. 2. Naturalism.

1-18914 Revised

Library of Congress B3998.N8
[r43b2]

I-40
4364

Paulsen, Friedrich, 1846-1908.
Philosophia militans; gegen Klerikalismus und Naturalismus. 3. u. 4. durchgesehene und verm. Aufl. Berlin, Reuther & Reichard, 1908.
ix, 233 p. 22cm.

Includes a reference to Spinoza (p. 81)
Original paper covers bound in.

I-40
4365
Simon, Jules, 1814-1896.
Natural religion. By M. Jules Simon. Translated by J. W. Cole. Edited, with preface and notes, by the Rev. J. B. Marsden ... London, R. Bentley, 1857.
xliv, 266 p. 20cm.
From the third French edition?
Includes references to Spinoza.
CONTENTS.—The nature of God.—Providence.—Immortality.—Worship.

1. Natural theology. 2. God. I. Marsden, John Buxton, 1803-1870, ed. II. Cole, John William, d. 1870, tr. III. Title.

[Name originally: François Jules Suisse]

30-24934

Library of Congress BL181.S52 210

I-40
4366

Simon, Jules, 1814-1896.
La religion naturelle. 5. éd. Paris, Hachette, 1860.
xxxi, 412 p. 19 cm.

NN

I-40
4367

Sorley, William Ritchie, 1855-
On the ethics of naturalism. Edinburgh, Blackwood, 1885.
xii, 292 p. 20 cm. (Shaw fellowship lectures, 1884)

I-40
4368

Ward, James, 1843-1925.
Naturalism and agnosticism; the Gifford lectures delivered before the University of Aberdeen in the years 1896-1898. London, Black, 1899.
2 v. 21 cm.

Includes references to Spinoza.

I-41
NATURE

I-41
4369

Alexander, Hartley Burr, 1873-1939.
Nature and human nature; essays metaphysical and historical, by Hartley Burr Alexander. Chicago, London, The Open court publishing company, 1923.
ix p., 2 l., 3-529 p. 22 cm.
Includes a section on Spinoza (p. 488-489)

1. Psychology—Addresses, essays, lectures. I. Title.

NNC 23-11340

I-41
4370

[Carlile, William Warrand]
Natura naturans. [1895]
624-640 p.

Signed: William W. Carlile.
In Philosophical review, v. 4, 1895.
Includes references to Spinoza.

I-41
4371

Delisle de Sales, Jean Claude Izouard, called, 1741-1816.
De la philosophie de la nature, ou, Traité de morale pour l'espèce humaine tiré de la philosophie et fondé sur la nature. 3. édition, et la seule conforme au manuscrit original. Londres, 1777.
6 v. front., 12 plates. 20 cm.

Includes references to Spinoza.

MH

I-41
4372

[Delisle de Sales, Jean Claude Izouard, called]
1741-1816.
De la philosophie de la nature ... A Amsterdam, Chez Arkstée & Merkus, 1770.
3 v. fronts. 18cm.

Includes references to Spinoza.

I-41
4373

Hayduck, Waldemar
De Spinozae natura naturante et natura naturata dissertationem metaphysicam scripsit Waldemarus Hayduck ... Vratislaviae, L. F. Maske, 1867.
52 p. 25cm.

Volume of pamphlets.

1. Spinoza, Benedictus de, 1632-1677.

NNC

Heydenreich, Karl Heinrich, 1764-1801.
Betrachtungen über die Philosophie der natürlichen Religion. 2. verb. Auflage. Leipzig, Weygand, 1804.
2 v.

Includes a section "Kritik und Widerlegung der ersten Gründe des Spinozismus" (v. 1, p. 258-272) and other references to him (v. 2, p. 168-175)

MH

Schelle, Karl Gottlob
Karl Heinrich Heydenreichs ... Charakteristik als Menschen und Schriftstellers. Entworfen von Karl Gottlob Schelle ... Leipzig, G. Martini, 1802.
xvi, 499, [1] p. port. 20cm.

Includes a section on Heydenreich's Natur und Gott nach Spinoza (p. 234-272)

Heydenreich, Karl Heinrich, 1764-1801.
Natur und Gott nach Spinoza. Von Karl Heinrich Heydenreich ... 1. Band ... Leipzig, in der Joh. Gottfr. Müllerschen Buchhandlung, 1789.
lxxx, 224 p. 19cm.

No more published.

Siebeck, Hermann, 1842-1921.
Ueber die Entstehung der Termini natura naturans und natura naturata. [1890]
370-378 p.

In Archiv für Geschichte der Philosophie, Bd. 3, 1890.
Includes references to Spinoza.

I-42
ONTOLOGICAL ARGUMENT

Holland, Georg Jonathan von, 1742-1784.
Réflexions philosophiques sur le Systême de la nature. A Paris, Chez Valade, 1773.
2 v. in 1.

Apel, Walter, 1883-
Spinozas Verhältnis zum ontologischen Beweise. Leipzig, Druck von Hartmann & Wolf, 1911.
77 p.

Thesis, Leipzig.
Bibliographical footnotes.

[Lucks, Henry Albert] 1901-
Natura naturans - natura naturata. [1935]
24 p.

Signed: Henry A. Lucks.
In The New scholasticism, v. 9, 1935.
Includes references to Spinoza.

Fischer, Friedrich, 1801-1853.
Der ontologische Beweis für das Daseyn Gottes und seine Geschichte. Basel, Schweighauser, 1852.
18 p. 25 cm.

Academic programme.
Includes a reference to Spinoza (p. 9-10)

[Robinet, Jean Baptiste René] 1735-1820.
De la nature. Amsterdam, E. van Harrevelt, 1761-66.
4 v. plates. 20cm.

Friedländer, Hans
Vom ontologischen Gottesbeweis. [1938]
[119]-135 p. 22cm.

From Festschrift für Leo Baeck, 1938.
Includes references to Spinoza.
Bibliographical footnotes.

I-42
4384

Petronievics, Branislav, 1875-
Der ontologische Beweis für das Dasein des Absoluten. Leipzig, H. Haacke, 1897.
29 p.

NN

I-42
4385

SPECIAL COLLECTIONS
SPINOZA

Silberstein, Solomon Joseph, 1845-
The disclosures of the universal mysteries ... By Solomon J. Silberstein. New York, P. Cowen, 1896.
viii, [5]-297, [1] p. diagrs. 19cm.

CONTENTS.—The idea of God: absolute intellectuality.—The creation: absolute emanation.—Matter and force: the universe in its potentiality and actuality.—The universal mechanism: motion and its transformations.

Includes references to Spinoza.

1. Ontology. 2. Cosmology. I. Title.

Library of Congress BD701.S5 11—24658
Copyright 1896: 49728 [a24e1]

I-42
4386

[Watts, Isaac] 1674-1748.
Philosophical essays on various subjects, viz. space, substance, body, spirit ... with some remarks on Mr. Locke's essay on the human understanding. To which is subjoined A brief scheme of ontology, or The science of being in general with its affections. By I. W. London: Printed for Richard Ford at the Angel, and Richard Hett at the Bible and Crown, 1733.
xii, [4], 403, [1] p. 20 cm.

I-43 PANTHEISM

I-43
4387

SPECIAL COLLECTIONS
SPINOZA

Avenarius, Richard, 1843-1896.
Ueber die beiden ersten Phasen des spinozischen Pantheismus und das Verhältniss der zweiten zur dritten Phase. Nebst einem Anhang: Ueber Reihenfolge und Abfassungszeit der älteren Schriften Spinoza's. Leipzig, E. Avenarius, 1868.
viii, 105 p. 23cm.

Ms. notes by Carl Gebhardt.

I-43
4388

Balthasar, N
Le panthéisme spinoziste; à la poursuite de l'unité métaphysique. [1926]
455-468 p.

In Revue neo-scolastique de philosophie, 28. année, 2. série, 1926.

NNC

I-43
4389

[Berlin, H J]
Het pantheismus, wijsgeerig stelsel onzer dagen, naar de groote wijsgeeren Jezus van Nazareth en Baruch van Spinoza. Geschetst en voorgedragen door een lid der vereeniging "De Dageraad" gedurende het eerste jaar harer bijeenkomsten. Amsterdam, R. C. Meijer, 1857.
206 p.

OCH

I-43
4390

Biedermann, Alois Emanuel, 1819-1885.
Unsere junghegelsche Weltanschauung oder der sogenannte neuste Pantheismus ... Zürich, Schulthess, 1849.
iv, 207 p. 23 cm.

NNU-W

I-43
4391

SPECIAL COLLECTIONS
SPINOZA

Biese, Alfred, 1856-1930.
Goethes dichterischer Pantheismus. [1893]
3-25 p. 22cm.

On cover: Sonderabdruck aus den Berichten des Freien Deutschen Hochstiftes zu Frankfurt am Main.
Presentation copy to Ferdinand Avenarius, with the author's inscription and signature.
Includes references to Spinoza.

I-43
4392

Buddingh, Steven Adriaan, 1811-1869.
Geschiedenis en beoordeeling van het pantheïsme of Algodendom. [1849]
41 p.

In Bataviaasch Genootschap van Kunsten en Wetenschappen, Batavia. Verhandelingen, dl. 22., 1849.
Includes references to Spinoza.

NNC

I-43
4393

SPECIAL COLLECTIONS
SPINOZA

[Cohen, Louisa Emily]
Pantheism, and other essays, by L. E. C. London, K. Paul, Trench, Trubner & Co., 1926.
7 p. l., 103 p. 19cm.

Letter from the author's daughter to A. S. Oko inserted.

SPECIAL COLLECTIONS SPINOZA I-43 4394

Cooley, William Forbes, 1857-
Spinoza's pantheistic argument. [1918] [171]-187 p. 21cm.

From Studies in the history of ideas, ed. by the Department of Philosophy, Columbia University, vol. I.

1. Spinoza, Benedictus de, 1632-1677.

NNC

I-43 4395

Danielo, M J
Du panthéisme, et du mosaïsme et du christianisme, dans leurs rapports avec les sociétés humaines et les gouvernements. Paris, B. Duprat, 1848.
93 p.

NN

I-43 4396

Dewey, John, 1859-1952.
The pantheism of Spinoza. [1882] 249-257 p.

In Journal of speculative philosophy, v. 16, 1882.

I-43 4397

Fraser, Alexander Campbell, 1819-1914.
Philosophy of theism; being the Gifford lectures delivered before the University of Edinburgh in 1894-95, first series. New York, Scribner, 1895.
3 p. l., 303 p. 21 cm.

Includes a lecture "Pantheistic necessity and unity: Spinoza" (p. 163-189) and other references to Spinoza.

I-43 4398

Gisler, Anton
Zwei Väter des Pantheismus. [1907] 335-346 p.

In Schweizerische Rundschau, Stans, Jahrgang 7, 1906-07.
Includes references to Spinoza.

DLC

I-43 4399

Hanne, Johann Wilhelm, b. 1813.
Die Idee der absoluten Persönlichkeit, oder: Gott und sein Verhältnisz zur Welt, insonderheit zur menschlichen Persönlichkeit. Eine speculativtheolog. Untersuchung über Wesen, Entwickelung und Ziel des christlichen Theismus. Hannover, C. Rümpler, 1861-62.
2 v.

Includes "Die Gestaltung der neueren Philosophie als vollendeter, akosmistischer Pantheismus beim Spinoza" (v. 2, p. 30-52)

NNUT

I-43 4400

Hittell, John Shertzer, 1825-1901.
A plea for pantheism. By John S. Hittell. New York, C. Blanchard, 1857.
x, 56 p. 18½cm.

Contents.—Preface.—Physiology vs. a future state.—Pantheism vs. anthropomorphism.—Moral responsibility.—Absolute truth unattainable by man.

1. Pantheism.

NNUT 30-28768
Library of Congress BL220.H5 212

SPECIAL COLLECTIONS SPINOZA I-43 4401

Holmes, Edmond, 1850-1936.
All is one; a plea for the higher pantheism. New York, E. P. Dutton [192-]
114 p. 20cm.

SPECIAL COLLECTIONS SPINOZA I-43 4402

Hugenholtz, Petrus Hermannus, 1834-1911.
Ethisch pantheïsme; een studie. Amsterdam, Van Holkema & Warendorf, 1903.
291 p. 20cm.

Includes a section on Spinoza (p. [175]-179)

SPECIAL COLLECTIONS SPINOZA I-43 4403

Hunt, John, 1827-ca. 1908.
An essay on pantheism. Rev. ed. London, Gibbings, 1893.
viii, 397 p. 23cm.

Includes a section on Spinoza (p. 219-242)

Hunt, John, 1827-ca. 1908.
An essay on pantheism. London, Longmans, Green, Reader & Dyer, 1866.
xxiv, 382 p.

Includes a section on Spinoza (p. 213-240)

Jacobi, Friedrich Heinrich, 1743-1819.
Die Hauptschriften zum Pantheismusstreit zwischen Jacobi und Mendelssohn. Hrsg. und mit einer historisch-kritischen Einleitung versehen von Heinrich Scholz. Berlin, Reuther & Reichard, 1916.
cxxviii, 364, 22 p. 22cm. (Neudrucke seltener philosophischer Werke, hrsg. von der Kantgesellschaft. Bd. 6)

Includes chapters on Spinoza.

[Jäsche, Gottlieb Benjamin] 1762-1842.
Ansichten des Pantheismus nach seinen verschiedenen Hauptformen. [1816]
[125]-185 p. 19cm.

From Dörptische Beyträge für Freunde der Philosophie, Litteratur und Kunst. 2. Bd., Jahrgang 1814.
Includes references to Spinoza.

Jäsche, Gottlob Benjamin, 1762-1842.
Der Pantheismus nach seinen verschiedenen Hauptformen, seinem Ursprung und Fortgange, seinem speculativen und praktischen Werth und Gehalt; ein Beitrag zur Geschichte und Kritik dieser Lehre in alter und neuer Philosophie. Berlin, Reimer, 1826-32.
3 v.

Includes a section "Der Pantheismus der neuern realistisch-dogmatischen Metaphysik, als Spinozismus" (v. 2, p. 221-325)

Kalisch, Marcus Moritz.
Path and goal. A discussion on the elements of civilisation and the conditions of happiness. By M. M. Kalisch ... London, Longmans, Green and co. [Leipzig printed] 1880.
3 p. l., 510, 138 p. 23cm.

Chapter IX. Pantheism (p. [377]-417) includes references to Spinoza.

1. Philosophy and religion. 2. Religion. I. Title.

Kellogg, Samuel Henry, 1839-1899.
The Jews; or, Prediction and fulfilment: an argument for the times. New York, A. D. F. Randolph [1883]
xx, 279 p. 20 cm.

Includes a section "The Jews and modern pantheistic rationalism - Spinoza - Maimonides" (p. 190-199)

Kerlen, J
Spinoza, der Pantheïst. [1901]
211-228 p.

In Studien. Tijdschrift voor godsdienst, wetenschap en letteren, jaargang 34, dl. 57, 1901.

Luzzatto, Samuele Davide, 1800-1865.
דברי החכם מונק על הפאנטעאיזמוס וקצת תשובה לקיקיון יונה. [1865]
p. 133.

Title transliterated: Divrey ... munk ʿal ha-panteʿizmus.
In ha-Magid, v. 9, 1865.
About Spinoza.

Maret, Henri Louis Charles, 1805-1881.
Essai sur le panthéisme, dans les sociétés modernes. 2e éd., revue et augmentée. Paris, 1841.

Maret, Henri Louis Charles, 1805-1881.
Essai sur le panthéisme dans les sociétés modernes. 3. éd., rev. et augm. Paris, Méquignon Junior et J. Leroux, 1845.
xxxii, 494 p. 22cm.

Includes a section on Spinoza (p. 165-172)
Original paper covers bound in.

Mauthner, Fritz, 1849-1923.
Der Atheismus und seine Geschichte im Abendlande. Stuttgart, Deutsche Verlagsanstalt, 1920-23.
4 v. 26cm.

Includes a chapter "Spinoza - Pantheismus" (v. 2, p. 346-371) and many other references to Spinoza.

Mendelssohn, Moses, 1729-1786.
Morgenstunden; oder, Vorlesungen über das Dasein Gottes. Leipzig, F. A. Brockhaus, 1843.
233-409 p. (In his Gesammelte Schriften, 2. Bd.)

Includes a chapter "Spinozismus.-Pantheismus.-Alles ist eins und Eins ist Alles.-Widerlegung." (p. ⌊340⌋-349)

Merten, J
Der sel. Frings und sein Freund als Antigüntherianer. Trier, Fr. Lintz, 1852.
83 p. 21cm.

Bound with Volkmuth, Peter. Der dreieinige Pantheismus von Thales bis Hegel. 1837.

Neuwirth, Samu
Pantheismus und Individualismus im Systeme der Schopenhauer'schen Philosophie. Würzburg, Becker, 1894.
58 p.

Thesis, Würzburg.
Includes references to Spinoza.

Pantheism - from the Vedas to Spinoza. ⌊1877⌋
41 p.

In Church quarterly review, v. 4, April 1877.

Picton, James Allanson, 1832-1910.
Pantheism; its story and significance, by J. Allanson Picton ... London, A. Constable & co ltd, 1905.
96 p. 17½cm. (*Half-title:* Religions ancient and modern)
"Selected works bearing on pantheism": p. 96.
Includes a chapter on Spinoza.

1. Pantheism.

Picton, James Allanson, 1832-
Pantheism; its story and significance. London, Constable, 1914.
96 p. 18cm. (Religions ancient and modern)

"Selected works bearing on pantheism": p. 96.
Includes a chapter on Spinoza.

Pillon, François, 1830-1914.
L'évolution de l'idéalisme au XVIIIe siècle; la critique de Bayle: critique du panthéisme spinoziste. ⌊1899⌋
85-143 p.

In L'Année philosophique, 1898. Paris, 1899.

Plumptre, Constance E
General sketch of the history of pantheism. London, Gibbings, 1878.
2 v. 22cm.

Contents.--v. 1. From the earliest times to the age of Spinoza.--v. 2. From the age of Spinoza to the commencement of the nineteenth century.

Plumptre, Constance E
General sketch of the history of pantheism. London, Trübner ⌊1881⌋
2 v.

Contents.--v. 1. From the earliest times to the age of Spinoza.--v. 2. From the age of Spinoza to the commencement of the nineteenth century.

I-43
4424

Rapaport, Benzion, d. 1943.

סבע ואלהות. ‹1929›
307-311 p.

Title transliterated: Teba ve-ʿelahuth.
In Seneh, v. 1, no. 3, 1929.
About Spinoza and the pantheists.

NNJ

I-43
4425

Repke, Johannes, 1859-
Pantheistischer und theistischer Monismus. ‹1912›
279-316 p.

In Biblische Zeit- und Streitfragen, 7. Serie, 8. Heft, 1912.
Includes references to Spinoza.

NNUT

I-43
4426

Richter, Franz Wilhelm, 1801-1875.
Ueber Pantheismus und Pantheismusfurcht; eine historisch-philosophische Abhandlung. Leipzig, R. Hartmann, 1841.
71 p. 22cm.

Includes a section on Spinoza (p. 34-42)
Original paper covers bound in.
Bibliographical footnotes.

I-43
4427

Ritter, Heinrich, 1791-1869.
Die Halb-Kantianer und der Pantheismus; eine Streitschrift, veranlasst durch Meinungen der Zeit und bei Gelegenheit von Jäsche's Schrift über den Pantheismus. Berlin, Trautwein, 1827.
viii, 91 p. 21 cm.

Includes references to Spinoza (p. 8, 19-22)

I-43
4428

Romang, J P
Der neueste Pantheismus, oder die junghegelsche Weltanschauung nach ihren theoretischen Grundlagen und praktischen Consequenzen. Allen Denkenden gewidmet. Bern, Schulthess, 1848.
xiv, 277 p.

CtY

I-43
4429

Romang, J P
System der natürlichen Religionslehre. Aus den ursprünglichsten Bestimmtheiten des allgemein religiösen Bewusstseins entwickelt. Zürich, Schulthess, 1841.

MH

I-43
4430

Rosmini-Serbati, Antonio, 1797-1855.
Vincenzo Gioberti e il panteismo: lezioni filosofiche. Milano, Perelli e Mariani, 1847.
109 p.

MH

I-43
4431

Rosmini Serbati, Antonio, 1797-1855.
Vincenzo Gioberti e il panteismo. Saggio di lezioni filosofiche, con altri opuscoli. Lucca, Giusti, 1853.
291 p. table.

Includes references to Spinoza (p. 91, 116-117)

MH

I-43
4432

Schwarz, Hermann, 1864-
Die Entwicklung des Pantheismus in der neueren Zeit. ‹1915›
20-80 p.

In Zeitschrift für Philosophie und philosophische Kritik, Bd. 157, 1915.
Includes many references to Spinoza.

I-43
4433

Schwarz, Hermann, 1864-
Über Gottesvorstellungen grosser Denker; sechs Hochschulvorträge. München, Rösl, 1922.
159 p. 17cm. (Philosophische Reihe, hrsg. von Alfred Werner. 12. Bd.)

Includes a lecture "Allerlei Pantheismus, insonderheit der Spinozismus" (p. 50-71)

Seligmann, Caesar
Judentum und moderne Weltanschauung; fünf Vorträge. Frankfurt a. M., J. Kauffmann, 1905.
117 p. 19cm.

References to Spinoza included in chapter "Pantheismus und Judentum" (p. ⌊28⌋-49)

Seling, Joh Mathias
Vernunftwissenschaft, besonders eine vernunftwissenschaftliche Menschen- und Gotteslehre, mit einem Anhange über die Ewigkeit der Zeit auf Seite Gottes. Osnabrück, In Commission bei L. Overwetter, 1857.
xxiv, 279 p. 21cm.

Bound with Volkmuth, Peter. Der dreieinige Pantheismus von Thales bis Hegel.

Sengler, Jakob, 1799-1878.
Die Idee Gottes. Erster historisch-kritischer Theil. Heidelberg, J. C. B. Mohr, 1845.
xxiv, 565 p. 22cm.

Includes a chapter "Der substanzielle Pantheismus" (p. 116-131) which discusses Spinoza's philosophy.

Siwek, Paul
Spinoza et le panthéisme religieux. Paris, Dusclée de Brouwer ⌊1937⌋
xxxi, 293 p. 21cm. (On cover: Bibliothèque française de philosophie. 3. sér.)

Original paper covers bound in.
Bibliography: p. ⌊xxi⌋-xxxi.

Stokes, G J
Gnosticism and modern pantheism. ⌊1895⌋
320-333 p.

In Mind, n. s. v. 4, 1895.

Urquhart, William Spence, 1877-
The fascination of pantheism. ⌊1911⌋
313-326 p. 25cm.

From The International journal of ethics, v. 21, no. 3, April, 1911.
Includes a reference to Spinoza (p. 313)

Volkelt, Johannes, 1848-1930.
Pantheismus und Individualismus im Systeme Spinoza's. Leipzig, A. Lorentz, 1872.
89 p. 20cm.

Bound with Horn, I. E., originally Ignaz Einhorn. Spinoza's Staatslehre. 1863.

1. Spinoza, Benedictus de, 1632-1677.

Volkmuth, Peter
Der dreieinige Pantheismus von Thales bis Hegel. Köln, J. Lumscher, 1837.
xvi, 306 p. 21cm.

Includes a section "Der Spinozistische Gott h. Geist" (p. 298-306) and other references to Spinoza.

Weissenborn, Georg
Vorlesungen über Pantheismus und Theismus. Marburg, R. C. Elwert, 1859.
243 p.

I-44
POLITICAL AND ETHICAL PHILOSOPHY

Duff, Robert Alexander.
Spinoza's political and ethical philosophy, by Robert A. Duff ... Glasgow, J. Maclehose and sons, 1903.
xii, 516 p. 24cm.

Ms. notes by Carl Gebhardt in margins, with his signature on t.-p.

Durant, William James, 1885-
Philosophy and the social problem. New York, Macmillan, 1917.
x, 272 p. 20cm.

Issued also as thesis (Ph.D.) Columbia University.
Includes a chapter "Spinoza on the social problem" (p. 90-116)

Solari, Gioele, 1872-1952.
La dottrina del contratto sociale in Spinoza. ͺ1927ͺ
ͺ317ͺ-353 p.

In Rivista di filosofia, anno 18, 1927.

Durant, William James, 1885-
Philosophy and the social problem. ͺ2d ed.ͺ New York, Simon & Schuster, 1927.
x, 272 p.

Includes a chapter "Spinoza on the social problem" (p. 90-116)

Strümpell, Ludwig, 1812-1899.
Abhandlungen aus dem Gebiete der Ethik, der Staatswissenschaft, der Asthetik und der Theologie. 1. Heft. Leipzig, A. Deichert, 1895.
iii, 53 p. 25cm.

Original paper cover bound in.
Contents.--H. Heine's Bericht "Zur Geschichte der Religion und Philosophie in Deutschland" an die Franzosen i. J. 1835.--Die sittliche Weltansicht des Spinoza.--Die Freiheit des logischen Denkens.

VOLUME OF PAMPHLETS

Durant, William James, 1885-
Philosophy and the social problem. London, Allen & Unwin ͺ1928ͺ
x, 272 p.

Includes a chapter "Spinoza on the social problem" (p. 90-116)

Tex, Jan den
Locke en Spinoza over de tolerantie. Amsterdam, Scheltema & Holkema, 1926.
137 p. 23cm.

Original paper cover bound in.
Bibliography: p. ͺ131ͺ-133.

I-45
POLITICAL IDEAS

Guenther, Louis
Die Idee der Wiedervergeltung in der Geschichte und Philosophie des Strafrechts. Ein Beitrag zur universal-historischen Entwickelung desselben. Erlangen, T. Bläsing, 1891.
2 v.

Includes a reference to Spinoza (v. 2, p. 115-116)

ͺAdelphe, Louisͺ 1879-1914.
La formation et la diffusion de la politique de Spinoza. (Questions et hypothèses fondées sur des documents nouveaux). ͺ1914ͺ
253-280 p.

In Revue de synthèse historique, t. 28, 1914.

Ricco, Cesare
Le dottrine giuridiche e politiche di B. Spinoza e T. Hobbes. Giovinazzo, Tip. del R. Ospizio, 1884.
48 p.

Assarsson, Pehr, 1838-1894.
Om Spinozas statslära och dess förhållande till Hobbes' och Rousseaus ... Lund, Tryckt uti Berlingska boktryckeriet, 1864.
1 p. l., 48 p. 20 cm.
Akademisk afhandling—Lund.

1. Political science—Hist. 2. Spinoza, Benedictus de, 1632-1677. 3. Hobbes, Thomas, 1588-1679. 4. Rousseau, Jean Jacques, 1712-1778.

I-45
4454

Bechhöfer, N
Die Politik des Spinoza. ⌐187-?⌐
⌐149⌐-163 p. 25cm.

1. Spinoza, Benedictus de, 1632-1677.

I-45
4455

Berolzheimer, Fritz, 1869-1920.
The world's legal philosophies. Tr. from the German by Rachel Szold Jastrow, with an introduction by Sir John Macdonell and by Albert Kocourek. Boston, The Boston book company, 1912.
liv, 490 p. 22 cm. (The modern legal philosophy series. II)

Includes a section on Spinoza (p. 127-132) and other references to him.

NNC

I-45
4456

Cohen, Renato
Il pensiero politico dello Spinoza. ⌐1933⌐
241-272 p.

In Pisa. Scuola normale e superiore. Annali; Lettere, storia e filosofia, ser. 2, v. 2, 1933.

DLC

I-45
4457

Eckstein, Walther, 1891-
Zur Lehre vom Staatsvertrag bei Spinoza. (Aus Anlass von Spinozas dreihundertsten Geburtstag) ⌐1933⌐
356-368 p.

In Zeitschrift für öffentliches Recht, Bd. 13, 1933.

I-45
4458

Ferrière, Émile, 1830-
Littérature et philosophie. Paris, Marpon, 1865.
304 p.

Includes a section "Sur la politique de Spinoza" (p. 180-214)

MB

I-45
4459

Fullerton, William Morton, 1865-
Problems of power; a study of international politics from Sadowa to Kirk-Kilissé. London, Constable, 1913.
xx, 323 p. 23 cm.

Includes references to Spinoza.

I-45
4460

Gebhardt, Carl, 1881-1934.
Spinoza als Politiker. Heidelberg, C. Winter ⌐1908?⌐
cover-title, 263-267 p. 25cm.

"Sonderabdruck aus den Verhandlungen des III. Internationalen Kongresses für Philosophie, Heidelberg, 1908."
Bibliographical footnotes.

I-45
4461

Gierke, Otto von, 1841-1921.
The development of political theory. Translated by Bernard Freyd. New York, Norton ⌐c1939⌐
364 p. 23 cm.

I-45
4462

Gierke, Otto Friedrich von, 1841-1921.
Natural law and the theory of society, 1500 to 1800, by Otto Gierke, with a lecture on The ideas of natural law and humanity, by Ernest Troeltsch; translated with an introduction by Ernest Barker ... Cambridge ⌐Eng.⌐ The University press, 1934.
2 v. 24 cm.

A translation of five subsections in the fourth volume of Gierke's "Das deutsche genossenschaftsrecht." *cf.* Introd.
"List of authors cited": v. 2, p. ⌐401⌐-417.
Includes references to Spinoza.
1. Natural law. 2. State, The. 3. Political science—Hist. I. Troeltsch, Ernest, 1865-1923. II. Barker, Ernest, 1874- tr. III. Title.

JA83.G5 320.9 34—29519

Library of Congress ⌐54x1⌐

I-45
4463

Green, Thomas Hill, 1836-1882.
Lectures on the principles of political obligation. Reprinted from Green's Philosophical works, vol. II. With preface by Bernard Bosanquet. London, New York, Longmans, Green and Co. ⌐1937⌐
xxiv, 252 p. 23cm.

Includes a chapter on Spinoza (p. 49-59)

Gumplowicz, Ludwig, 1838-1909.
... Geschichte der staatstheorien ... Innsbruck, Wagner'sche universitäts-buchhandlung, 1905.
xi, 592 p. 23cm.
CONTENTS.—Vorchristliches altertum.—Das christliche Europa.—Das zeitalter der revolutionen.
Includes a section on Spinoza (p. 207-223)

1. Political science—Hist.

Gumplowicz, Ludwig, 1838-1909.
Geschichte der Staatstheorien. Innsbruck, Wagner [1926]
xl, 564 p. (His Ausgewählte Werke, Bd. 1)

Includes two sections on Spinoza (p. 207-223)

Gunn, John Alexander, 1896-
Spinoza and present-day politics. [1921]
83-92 p.

In Contemporary review, v. 120, 1921.

Hartenstein, Gustav, 1808-1890.
Gust. Hartensteinii De notionum juris et civitatis, quas Ben. Spinoza et Thom. Hobbesius proponunt, similitudine et dissimilitudine diss. I-[II] Lipsiae, Typis A. Edelmanni, [1856-57]
2 pts. 26cm.

At head of title, pt. 1: Ordinis philosophorum Lipsiensis decanus et reliqui professores memoriam Ioannis Augusti Ernesti die XX. M. Decembr. A. MDCCCLVI ... celebrandam indicunt.

CONTINUED ON NEXT CARD

Hartenstein, Gustav, 1808-1890. De notionum juris et civitatis ... [1856-57] (Card 2)

At head of title, pt. 2: Ordinis philosophorum Lipsiensis decanus et reliqui professores memoriam Friderici Aug. Guilelmi Spohnii die XX. M. Januar. A. MDCCCLVII ... celebrandam indicunt.

Hoff, Josef
Die Staatslehre Spinoza's mit besonderer Berücksichtigung der einzelnen Regierungsformen und der Frage nach dem besten Staate. Prag, J. B. Brandeis, 1895.
56 p. 22cm.

Thesis, Jena.

Hoff, Josef
Die Staatslehre Spinozas, mit besonderer Berücksichtigung der einzelnen Regierungsformen und der Frage nach dem besten Staate. Berlin, S. Calvary, 1895.
56 p. 22cm.

Bibliographical footnotes.
Issued also as thesis, Jena.

Horn, I E originally Ignaz Einhorn, 1825-1875.
Spinoza's Staatslehre, zum ersten Male dargestellt. Dessau, M. Katz (Gebrüder Katz) 1851.
201 p. 20cm.

Horn, I. E., originally Ignaz Einhorn, 1825-1875.
Spinoza's Staatslehre, zum ersten Male dargestellt. 2. Ausg. Dresden, L. Ehlermann, 1863.
xii, 201 p. 20cm.

Knies, Karl Gustav Adolf, 1821-1898.
Die politische oekonomie vom standpunkte der geschichtlichen methode, von Karl Knies. Braunschweig, C. S. Schwetschke und sohn, 1853.
xii, 355, [1] p. 21cm.

1. Economics.

SPECIAL COLLECTIONS SPINOZA I-45 4474

Kohn, Ernst, 1901-
Spinoza und der Staat; Studien zur niederländischen Staatsauffassung des 17. Jahrhunderts und zur politischen Geistesgeschichte. Berlin, Studentendruck Berlin, 1926.
68 p. 21cm.

Part of thesis, Berlin.
Bibliography: p. 65-67.
Presentation copy to Carl Gebhardt, with the author's inscription.

SPECIAL COLLECTIONS SPINOZA I-45 4479

Malapert, Paulin, 1862-
De Spinozae politica. Paris, F. Alcan, 1897.
91 p. 23cm.

Thesis, Paris.
Bibliographical footnotes.

1. Spinoza, Benedictus de, 1632-1677.

SPECIAL COLLECTIONS SPINOZA I-45 4475

Kriegsmann, Georg
Die Rechts- und Staatstheorie des Benedict von Spinoza. Wandsbeck, F. Puvogel, 1878.
xv p. 27cm.

Thesis, Göttingen.

VOLUME OF PAMPHLETS

1. Spinoza, Benedictus de, 1632-1677.

NNC

SPECIAL COLLECTIONS SPINOZA I-45 4480

[Meijer, Willem, 1842-1926.
Wat is de staat? (Naar Spinoza) [The Hague, 1914]
22 p. 25cm.

Original paper covers bound in.
Signed: W. Meijer.

I-45 4476

Kym, Andreas Ludwig, 1822-1899.
De juris notione Spinozae. Berolini, G. Schade [1846]
62 p.

Thesis, Berlin.

NN

I-45 4481

Meijer, Willem, 1842-1926.
Wat is de staat? (Naar Spinoza) 2. ed. Den Haag, W. P. van Stockum & Zoon, 1928.
31 p.

OCH

I-45 4477

Laurent, François, 1810-1887.
Histoire du droit des gens et des relations internationales. Bruxelles, Meline, Cans, 1861-70.
18 v. 23 cm.

Includes a section on Spinoza (v. 12, p. 239-254)

I-45 4482

Meijer, Willem, 1842-1926.
Spinoza's leer aangaande het beheer der staatsgelden. [1918]
p. 9.

In De Amsterdammer, Weekblad voor Nederland, 7. December 1918.
With reference to an article in De Amsterdammer of 26. October 1918.

NN

I-45 4478

Lauterpacht, Hersh, 1897-
Spinoza and international law. [1927]
89-107 p.

In British year book of international law, 1927.

SPECIAL COLLECTIONS SPINOZA I-45 4483

Meinecke, Friedrich, 1862-1954.
Die Idee der Staatsräson in der neueren Geschichte. 3. durchgesehene Aufl. München, R. Oldenbourg, 1929.
545 p. 22cm.

Includes a section on Spinoza (p. 270-278) and other references to him.
Bibliographical footnotes.

SPECIAL COLLECTIONS SPINOZA I-45 4484

Menzel, Adolf, 1857-
Beiträge zur Geschichte der Staatslehre. Wien, Hölder-Pichler-Tempsky, 1929.
582 p. 24cm. (Akademie der Wissenschaften in Wien. Philosophisch-historische Klasse. Sitzungsberichte. 210. Bd., 1. Abhandlung)

Includes "Die Staatslehre Spinozas" (p. ͵264͵-447)
Bibliographical footnotes.

I-45 4485

Menzel, Adolf, 1857-
Homo sui juris. Eine Studie zur Staatslehre Spinozas. ͵1905͵
77-98 p.

In Zeitschrift für das privat- und öffentliche Recht der Gegenwart, 32. Bd., 1905.

I-45 4486

Menzel, Adolf, 1857-
Spinoza und das Völkerrecht. ͵1908͵
17-30 p.

In Zeitschrift für Völkerrecht und Bundesstaatsrecht, Bd. 2, 1908.

SPECIAL COLLECTIONS SPINOZA I-45 4487

Menzel, Adolph, 1857-
Wandlungen in der Staatslehre Spinoza's. Stuttgart, J. G. Cotta, 1898.
38 p. 25cm.

"Vorliegende Arbeit bilded einen Theil der im gleichen Verlage erschienen 'Festschrift zum siebzigsten Geburtstage Sr. Exzellenz Dr. Joseph Unger'."
Manuscript notes by Carl Gebhardt, with his signature on t.-p.

I-45 4488

Meyer, Eugen, 1871-
Das Verhältnis der Lehren Spinozas zum öffentlichen Recht und zur Volkswirtschaft der Gegenwart. ͵1920͵
72-80 p.

In Deutsche Rundschau,Bd. 182, 1920.

SPECIAL COLLECTIONS SPINOZA I-45 4489

Otto, Eduard, 1862-
Zur Beurteilung und Würdigung der Staatslehre Spinozas. Darmstadt, C. F. Winter, 1897.
31 p. 27cm.

Volume of pamphlets.

1. Spinoza, Benedictus de, 1632-1677.

NNC

SPECIAL COLLECTIONS SPINOZA I-45 4490

Pollock, Sir Frederick, bart., 1845-1937.
Spinoza's political doctrine with special regard to his relation to English publicists. ͵1921͵
45-57 p. 22cm.

Cover-title: Dissertatio ex Chronici Spinozani tomo primo separatim edita.

SPECIAL COLLECTIONS SPINOZA I-45 4491

Pollock, Sir Frederick, bart., 1845-1937.
Spinoza's political doctrine with special regard to his relation to English publicists. ͵1921͵
45-57 p. 22cm.

Cover-title: Dissertatio ex Chronici Spinozani tomo primo separatim edita.
Presentation copy to A. S. Oko with the author's inscription.

I-45 4492

Prantl, Karl von, 1820-1888.
Ueber die geschichtlichen Vorstufen der neueren Rechtsphilosophie, Rede in der öffentlichen Sitzung der königl. Akademie der Wissenschaften am 27 März 1858 zur Vorfeier ihres 99. Stiftungstages. München, J. G. Weiss, 1858.
24 p. 27 cm.

NNU

SPECIAL COLLECTIONS SPINOZA I-45 4493

Ravà, Adolfo
La filosofia del diritto e dello stato alla celebrazione spinoziana dell'Aja. Roma, Presso l'amm.ne della Rivista, 1927.
12 p. 25cm.

"Estratto dalla Rivista internazionale di filosofia del diritto, anno VII, fasc. VI."
Original paper covers bound in.

I-45
4494

Sabatier, Antoine, de Castres, 1742-1817.
De la souveraintě, ou Connaissance des vrais principes du gouvernement des peuples. Altona, A. H. Meyer, 1806.
2 v.

DLC

I-45
4495

Seydel, Max von, 1846-1901.
Grundzüge einer allgemeinen Staatslehre. Freiburg, J. C. B. Mohr [187-?]
vii, 104 p.

SPECIAL COLLECTIONS SPINOZA

I-45
4496

Steffes, Johann Peter, 1885-
Die Staatsauffassung der Moderne; auf der Grundlage der kulturphilosophischen Zeitideen. Freiburg im Breisgau, Herder, 1925.
xv, 169 p. 20cm. (Schriften zur deutschen Politik. 8. u. 9. Heft)

Includes references to Spinoza.
Bibliography: p. xi-xv.

I-45
4497

Taute, Gottfried Friedrich, 1794-1862.
Der Spinozismus als unendliches Revolutionsprinzip und sein Gegensatz. Eine zur Feier der Geburt Sr. Majestät des Königs in der Königl. Deutschen Gesellschaft zu Königsberg in Pr. am 16. Oct. 1848 gehaltene Rede. Königsberg, Tag & Koch, 1848.
48 p.

NN

I-45
4498

Trendelenburg, Friedrich Adolf, 1802-1872.
Die sittliche Idee des Rechts. Ein Vortrag gehalten in der Akademie der Wissenschaften zur Nachfeier des 15. Octbr. 1849. Berlin, G. Bethge, 1849.
24 p.

NN

I-45
4499

[Tullio, Vincenzo de]
Il concetto del diritto nella dottrina di Spinoza. [1884]
[314]-336 p.

In Giornale napoletano di filosofia e lettere, scienze morali e politiche, n. s. v. 9, 1884.

I-46
PSYCHOLOGY

SPECIAL COLLECTIONS SPINOZA

I-46
4500

Carp, J. H
Psychologische beschouwingen in verband met het wezen van het Spinozisme. [1922]
[280]-301 p. 24cm.

"Overdruk uit het Tijdschrift voor wijsbegeerte, ... Jaargang 1922, afl. 4."
"Lezing, gehouden ter gelegenheid van de 25ste jaarvergadering van de Vereeniging 'Het Spinozahuis' te Leiden."

I-46
4501

Dandolo, Giovanni, 1861-
La dottrina della memoria in Cartesio, Malebranche e Spinoza. [1893]
289-320 p.

In Rivista italiana di filosofia, anno 8, v. 1, 1893.

SPECIAL COLLECTIONS SPINOZA

I-46
4502

Godfernaux, André
De Spinoza psychologiae physiologicae antecessore. Lutetiae Parisiorum, Typographia L. Maretheux, 1894.
68 p. 23cm.

Thesis, Paris.
Unbound copy.

NNC

SPECIAL COLLECTIONS SPINOZA

I-46
4503

Gore, Willard Clark
The imagination in Spinoza and Hume; a comparative study in the light of some recent contributions to psychology. Chicago, University of Chicago Press, 1902.
77 p. 24cm. (The University of Chicago contributions to philosophy. Vol. II, no. 4)

Thesis (Ph. D.) - University of Chicago.
Thesis note on cover.
Published also without thesis note.

SPECIAL COLLECTIONS SPINOZA I-46 4504

Kuhn, Heinrich, 1893-
Zur Psychologie Baruch Spinozas; Vortrag, gehalten zur Feier des 300. Geburtstages des Philosophen. Hrsg. vom Interessenverband im Ausland graduierter deutscher Akademiker, Berlin. Berlin, Buchdruckerei Michel, 1932.
16 p. 23cm.

"Wissenschaftliche Sonderdrucke. Heft I."
Original paper covers bound in.

SPECIAL COLLECTIONS SPINOZA I-46 4505

Maudsley, Henry, 1835-1918.
Body and mind: an inquiry into their connection and mutual influence, specially in reference to mental disorders: an enlarged and revised edition. To which are added psychological essays. By Henry Maudsley ... New York, D. Appleton and company, 1874.
x p., ⌊1⌋,-275 p. 19cm.

SPECIAL COLLECTIONS SPINOZA I-46 4506

Maudsley, Henry, 1835-1918.
Physiologie de l'esprit. Traduit de l'anglais par Alexandre Herzen. Paris, C. Reinwald, 1879.
xvi, 500 p. 24cm.

Includes a reference to Spinoza (p. 47)

SPECIAL COLLECTIONS SPINOZA I-46 4507

Maudsley, Henry, 1835-1918.
Responsibility in mental disease. ⌊Authorized ed.⌋ New York, Appleton, 1896.
x, 313 p. 20cm.

Includes references to Spinoza.

I-46 4508

Partzsch, Oscar
Spinozas Lehren über das Wesen der Gefühle. ⌊1895⌋
273-283 p.

In Neue Bahnen, Jahrgang 6, 1895.

SPECIAL COLLECTIONS SPINOZA I-46 4509

Siwek, Paul
L'âme et le corps d'après Spinoza (la psychophysique spinoziste) Paris, F. Alcan, 1930.
xxvii, 202 p. 23cm. (On cover: Collection historique des grands philosophes)

Issued also as thesis, Clermont.
Original paper covers bound in.
Bibliography: p. xxii-xxvii.

I-47 PSYCHOLOGY AND ETHICS

SPECIAL COLLECTIONS SPINOZA I-47 4510

Bidney, David, 1908-
The psychology and ethics of Spinoza; a study in the history and logic of ideas, by David Bidney, PH. D. New Haven, Yale university press; London, H. Milford, Oxford university press, 1940.
xv, 454 p. 24cm.

1. Spinoza, Benedictus de, 1632-1677. 2. Emotions. 3. Ethics. 4. Psychology.

40-4287
Library of Congress B3998.B47
——— Copy 2.
Copyright A 136398 ⌊10⌋ 199.492

SPECIAL COLLECTIONS SPINOZA I-47 4511

Carp, J H
Über das Emotionale und Rationale im Spinozismus. ⌊Hagae Comitis, 1922⌋
130-137 p. 23cm.

Cover-title: Dissertatio ex Chronici Spinozani tomo secundo separatim ecita.
Presentation copy to A. S. Oko with the author's inscription and signature.

SPECIAL COLLECTIONS SPINOZA I-47 4512

Dunham, James Henry, 1870-1955.
... Freedom and purpose; an interpretation of the psychology of Spinoza, by James H. Dunham ... Princeton, N. J., and Lancaster, Pa., Psychological review company ⌊1916⌋
3 p. l., 126 p. 24cm. (Psychological review publications. Philosophical monographs ... vol. I, no. 3. March, 1916)
Published also as thesis (PH. D.) University of Pennsylvania.

1. Spinoza, Benedictus de, 1632-1677. I. Title.

16—11402
Library of Congress B1.P7 vol. 1, no. 3
⌊40b1⌋

SPECIAL COLLECTIONS SPINOZA I-47 4513

Ginsberg, Hugo ~~Wilhelm~~, 1829-
Ueber den einfluss der psychologie des Spinoza auf seine ethik ... Breslau, Druck von H. Lindner ⌊1855⌋
32 p. 19cm.
Inaug.-diss.—Breslau.
Lebenslauf.
Volume of pamphlets.

1. Spinoza, Benedictus de, 1632-1677. 2. Ethics.

18-13734
Library of Congress B3999.E8G5

Gunning, Johannes Hermanus, 1829-1905.
Spinoza en de idee der persoonlijkheid; eene studie door J. H. Gunning Jr. Utrecht, Kemink, 1876.
342 p. 19cm.

1. Spinoza, Benedictus de, 1632-1677.

Gunning, Johannes Hermanus, 1829-1905.
Spinoza en de idee der persoonlijkheid. 2. druk. Met een inleiding van Is. van Dijk. Baarn, Hollandia-Drukkerij, 1919.
iv, 277 p. 21cm.

Original paper cover bound in.
Bibliographical notes: p. 255-272.

Muret, Maurice, 1870-
L'esprit juif; essai de psychologie ethnique. Paris, Perrin, 1901.
320 p. 19cm.

Includes a chapter on Spinoza (p. [52]-92)
On original paper cover, bound in: Deuxième édition.

Richter, Raoul, 1871-1912.
Der Willensbegriff in der Lehre Spinoza's. Leipzig, W. Engelmann, 1898.
136 p. 23cm.

"Separat-Abdruck aus: Wundt, Philosophische Studien, Bd. XIV, Heft 1 u. 2."
Habilitationsschrift, Leipzig.
Carl Gebhardt's signature on t.-p.
Bibliographical footnotes.

Richter, Raoul, 1871-1912.
Der Willensbegriff in der Lehre Spinoza's. Leipzig, W. Engelmann, 1898.
cover-title, [119]-156, [241]-338 p. 23cm.

"Separat-Abdruck aus: Wundt, Philosophische Studien. XIV. Bd., 1. u. 2. Heft."

Benamozegh, Elijah, 1822-1900.
Sopra Spinoza e la teosofia. [1880]
333-336, 365-367 p.

In Il Vessillo israelitico, anno 28, 1880.

Bohrmann, Georg, 1888-
Grundlagen zu einer Untersuchung über Spinozas Stellung zur Religion. Leipzig, Röder, 1913.
44 p. 22cm.

Thesis, Erlangen, 1912.
"Wird nur ein teil der Arbeit als Dissertation gedruckt. Das vollständige Arbeit erscheint unter dem Titel" Spinoza's Stellung zur Religion ... als 9. Heft der ... "Studien zur Geschichte des neueren Protestantismus".

Bohrmann, Georg, 1888-
Spinozas Stellung zur Religion; eine Untersuchung auf der Grundlage des Theologisch-politischen Traktats. Nebst einem Anhang: Spinoza in England (1670-1750) Giessen, A. Töpelmann, 1914.
84 p. 23cm. (Studien zur Geschichte des neueren Protestantismus, 9. Hft.)

Issued in part as thesis, Erlangen.
Original paper covers bound in.
Ms. notes by A. S. Oko.
Bibliographical footnotes.

Burtt, Edwin Arthur, 1892-
Types of religious philosophy. New York and London, Harper [c1939]
ix, 512 p. 22 cm.

Includes a section "Spinoza's philosophy of religion" (p. 180-192) and other references to Spinoza.

Camerini, Donato
Le idee religiose di Benedetto Spinoza. [1905]
498-505 p.

In Il Vessillo israelitico, anno 53, 1905.

I-48 4524

Castelar y Ripoll, Emilio, 1832-1899.
Rede über Religions-Freiheit. Gehalten am 12. April 1869 in der Sitzung der spanischen Cortes. Würzburg, In Commission der Stahel'schen Buch- und Kunsthandlung, 1869.
20 p.

Includes a reference to Spinoza (p. 19)

MH

SPECIAL COLLECTIONS SPINOZA I-48 4525

Central Conference of American Rabbis.
Thirty-seventh annual convention, June twenty-second to twenty-sixth, nineteen hundred and twenty-six, Asheville, North Carolina. Edited by Rabbi Isaac E. Marcuson. [1926]
441 p. facsim. 24cm. (Its Yearbook, vol. XXXVI)

References to Spinoza included in "Jewish champions of religious liberty" by Sidney S. Tedesche (p. 181-212)

SPECIAL COLLECTIONS SPINOZA I-48 4526

Congrès international de philosophie. 5th, Naples, 1924.
Atti del V Congresso internazionale di filosofia, Napoli 5-9 maggio 1924. Promosso dalla Società filosofica italiana pel settimo centenario della fondazione della R. Università di Napol [!] a cura del segretario generale, Guido della Valle. Napoli, Società anonima editrice Francesco Perrella [1925]
lxxix, 1183 p. plates, ports. 26cm.

"Spinozismus und Religion" by Carl Gebhardt: p. 286-295.

I-48 4527

Couchoud, Paul Louis, 1879-
La doctrine religieuse de Spinoza. [1901]
173-195 p.

In Revue des deux mondes, 71. année, 5. période, t. 3., 1901.

SPECIAL COLLECTIONS SPINOZA I-48 4528

Erdmann, Johann Eduard, 1805-1892.
Vermischte Aufsätze. Leipzig, Verlag von Fr. Chr. Wilh. Vogel, 1846.
vi, 192 p. 22cm.

Bibliographical footnotes.
Contents.--Die Universität und ihre Stellung zur Kirche.--Die Religionsphilosophie als Phänomenologie des religiösen Bewusstseyns.--Die Grundbegriffe des Spinozismus.

I-48 4529

Feldkeller, Paul, 1889-
Die Idee der richtigen Religion. Eine Theorie der religiössen Erkenntnis. Gotha, Perthes, 1921.
viii, 147 p.

Includes references to Spinoza.

OCH

SPECIAL COLLECTIONS SPINOZA I-48 4530

Fessler, Ignatius Aurelius, 1756-1839.
D. Fessler's Ansichten von Religion und Kirchenthum. Berlin, J. D. Sander, 1805.
3 v. 17cm.

Includes references to Spinoza (v. 1, p. 45-52)

SPECIAL COLLECTIONS SPINOZA I-48 4531

Gebhardt, Carl, 1881-1934.
Die Religion Spinozas. [1932]
23 l. 29cm.

At head of title: Archiv für Geschichte der Philosophie. XLI. Band. Heft 3.
Galley proof.

SPECIAL COLLECTIONS SPINOZA I-48 4532

Gebhardt, Carl, 1881-1934.
Die Religion Spinozas. [1932]
[339]-362 p. 26cm.

"Sonderabdruck aus dem Archiv für Geschichte der Philosophie ... Band XLI, Heft 3."
Bound with Gebhardt, Carl. Spinoza in der Schule. [1930]

SPECIAL COLLECTIONS SPINOZA I-48 4533

Gehring, Albert, 1870-
The religion of thirty great thinkers; together with miscellaneous essays on religious subjects, by Albert Gehring. Boston, Mass., Marshall Jones company [c1925]
xiii, 268 p. 19½cm.

"Partial list of writings in which the religious views of the men considered in this book are laid down": p. 123-124.
Includes a section on Spinoza (p. 14-17)

1. Religion—Philosophy. I. Title.

25-6871

Library of Congress BL51.G37
Copyright A 823878 [a40g1]

Johnson, Francis Howe, 1835-1920.
What is reality? An inquiry as to the reasonableness of natural religion, and the naturalness of revealed religion. Boston, Houghton, Mifflin, 1891.
xxvii, 510 p. 21cm.

Includes references to Spinoza (p. 225, 228-230)

Maurer, Theodor, 1873-
Die Religionslehre Spinozas im Theologisch-politischen Traktat. Strassburg, Druck der Strassburger neuesten Nachrichten, vrm. H. L. Kayser, 1898.
69 p. 24cm.

Thesis, Strassburg.
Volume of pamphlets.

Krupernik, B
Philosophie und Naturwissenschaft in ihren Beziehungen zur Religion. [1918-19]
102-124 p.

In Jüdisches Jahrbuch für die Schweiz, Jahrgang 3, 1918-19.
Includes a reference to Spinoza (p. 114-115)

Meijer, Willem, 1842-1926.
Over Spinoza en den godsdienst. [1907]
[316]-327 p. 25cm.

From Tijdschrift voor wijsbegeerte, 1. jaarg., 3. aflevering, Sept. 1907.
Volume of pamphlets.

Law, Edmund, *bp. of Carlisle*, 1703-1787.
An enquiry into the ideas of space, time, immensity, and eternity; as also the self-existence, necessary existence, and unity of the divine nature: in answer to a book lately publish'd by Mr. Jackson, entitled, The existence and unity of God proved from His nature and attributes. By Edmund Law ... To which is added, A dissertation upon the argument a priori for proving the existence of a first cause. By a learned hand. Cambridge, W. Thurlbourn, 1734.
2 p. l., 196, 98 p. 20½ cm.
The "Dissertation upon the argument a priori" is by Daniel Waterland.
1. Religion—Philosophy. 2. Jackson, John, 1686-1763. The existence and unity of God proved from His nature and attributes. 1740. I. Waterland, Daniel, 1683-

Meijer, Willem, 1842-1926.
Over Spinoza en den godsdienst. [1907]
12 p. 25cm.

Reprint from Tijdschrift voor wijsbegeerte, 1. jaarg., 3. aflevering, Sept. 1907.
Volume of pamphlets.

Letsome, Sampson, ed.
A defense of natural and revealed religion: being a collection of the sermons preached at the lecture founded by the Hon. Robert Boyle esq. (from the year 1691 to the year 1732). With the additions and amendments of the several authors, and general indexes. London, Printed for D. Midwinter, 1739.
3 v.

[Naigeon, Jacques André] 1738-1810, comp.
Recueil philosophique; ou, Mélange de pieces sur la religion & la morale. Par différents auteurs ... Londres, 1770.
2 v.

Martinetti, Piero, 1872-1943.
Problemi religiosi nella filosofia di B. Spinoza. [1939]
289-311 p.

In Rivista di filosofia, anno 30, 1939.

Newman, Francis William, 1805-1897.
On the relations of theism to pantheism, and On the Galla religion. Ramsgate, T. Scott, 1872.
23 p. 19cm.

Volume of pamphlets.

I-48
4544

Pfleiderer, Otto, 1839-1908.
The philosophy of religion on the basis of its history. London, Williams and Norgate, 1886-1888.
4 v. 23 cm.

Includes a chapter "Benedict Spinoza" (v. 1, p. 31-67)

I-48
4545

Philosophische Betrachtung über Theologie und Religion überhaupt und über die jüdische insonderheit. Frankfurth, 1784.
248 p.

Includes a reference to Spinoza (p. 118-119)

OCH

I-48
4546

Picton, James Allanson, 1832-
The religion of the universe. London, New York, Macmillan, 1904.
x, 379 p. 23 cm.

Includes references to Spinoza.

DLC

SPECIAL COLLECTIONS
SPINOZA

I-48
4547

Powell, Elmer Ellsworth, 1861-
Spinoza and religion; a study of Spinoza's metaphysics and of his particular utterances in regard to religion, with a view to determining the significance of his thought for religion and incidentally his personal attitude toward it. By Elmer Ellsworth Powell ... Chicago, The Open court publishing company; [etc., etc.] 1906.
xiii p., 1 l., 344 p. 20½ cm.

1. Spinoza, Benedictus de, 1632-1677. 2. Philosophy and religion. I. Title.

B3999.R4P8 6—21921

Library of Congress [51d½]

SPECIAL COLLECTIONS
SPINOZA

I-48
4548

Powell, Elmer Ellsworth, 1861-
Spinoza and religion; a study of Spinoza's metaphysics and of his particular utterances in regard to religion, with a view to determining the significance of his thought for religion and incidentally his personal attitude toward it, by Elmer Ellsworth Powell ... Boston, Chapman and Grimes [°1941]
xii p., 3 l., 344 p. front. (port.) 1 illus., diagr. 21 cm.

1. Spinoza, Benedictus de, 1632-1677. 2. Philosophy and religion. I. Title.

41—9708

Library of Congress B3999.R4P8 1941
[49d1] 199.492

SPECIAL COLLECTIONS
SPINOZA

I-48
4549

Prümers, Walther, 1876-
Spinozas Religionsbegriff. Halle a. d. S., Druck von E. Karras, 1906.
43 p. 24cm.

Thesis, Bonn.
Published in full as v. 23 of Abhandlungen zur Philosophie und ihrer Geschichte.
Volume of pamphlets.

SPECIAL COLLECTIONS
SPINOZA

I-48
4550

193Sp4
DP7131 Prümers, Walther, 1876-
Spinozas Religionsbegriff. Halle a. d. S., M. Niemeyer, 1906.
73 p. 24cm. (Abhandlungen zur Philosophie und ihrer Geschichte ... 23. Hft.)

Issued in part as thesis, Bonn.
Bound with Powell, Elmer Ellsworth. Spinozas Gottesbegriff. 1899.

NNC

I-48
4551

Rauh, Frederic, 1861-1909.
Quatenus doctrina quam Spinoza de fide exposuit cum tota ejusdem philosophia cohaereat. Tolosae, ex typis A. Chauvin, 1890.
3 p. l., 67 p. 22 cm.

Thesis, Faculté des lettres de Paris.

NcU

I-48
4552

Reimarus, Hermann Samuel, 1694-1768.
Abhandlungen von den vornehmsten Wahrheiten der natürlichen Religion. Sechste Auflage, durchgesehen und mit einigen Anmerkungen begleitet von J. A. H. Reimarus. Hamburg, C. E. Bohn, 1791.
13 p. l., 700 p., 12 l. port. 20 cm.

Includes a section on Spinoza (p. 160-164)

NNUT

I-48
4553

Reimarus, Hermann Samuel, 1694-1768.
Die vornehmsten Wahrheiten der natürlichen Religion in zehn Abhandlungen auf eine begreifliche Art erkläret und gerettet. Vierte verbesserte und stark vermehrte Auflage. Hamburg, bey J. C. Bohn, 1772.
[16], 766, [24] p. 19cm.

Includes a section on Spinoza (p. 187-191)

I-48
4554

The religion and ethics of Spinoza. [1871]
22-41 p.

In The National quarterly review, v. 23, 1871.

I-48
4555

Renouf, Sir Peter Le Page, 1822-1897.
Lectures on the origin and growth of religion as illustrated by the religion of ancient Egypt. Delivered in May and June, 1879. London and Edinburgh, Williams & Norgate, 1880.
x, 259 p. 22 cm. (The Hibbert lectures, 1879)

Includes a reference to Spinoza (p. 234)

SPECIAL COLLECTIONS
SPINOZA
I-48
4556

Silberstein, Solomon Joseph, 1845-
ספר הדת והתורה; יוכיח שהדת היא
איננה אמונה, כי אם הדעה הטהורה היא
הדת; בחמשה חלקים. מאת שלום יוסף
בן אהרן זילבערשטיין. נויארק, בדפוס
יצחק אהרן בראדי ויעקב צעלימער, תרמ"ז.
[New York, Press of Brody & Chelimer, 1887]
168 p.

Title transliterated: Sefer ha-dath wĕ-ha-tōrā.

CONTINUED ON NEXT CARD

SPECIAL COLLECTIONS
SPINOZA
I-48
4557

Silberstein, Solomon Joseph, 1845-
ספר הדת והתורה. [1887] (Card 2)

Added t.-p. in English: Religion and law, showing: that religion is not faith, but pure knowledge.
Includes section on Spinoza (p. 133-168)
Contents.--א. סוד מציאות יהוה.--ב. תורת משה.--ג. תורת עזרא.--ד. תורות התלמוד.--ה. תורת האדם והמדינה.

I-48
4558

Santayana, George, 1863-1952.
Religión última. [1933]
273-292 p.

In Revista de occidente, año 11, t. 42, 1933.
Includes references to Spinoza.

I-48
4559

Söderblom, Nathan, abp., 1866-1931.
Das Werden des Gottesglaubens; Untersuchungen über die Anfänge der Religion. Deutsche Bearbeitung hrsg. von Rudolf Stübe. Leipzig, Hinrichs, 1916.
xii, 398 p. 24 cm.

Includes references to Spinoza.

SPECIAL COLLECTIONS
SPINOZA
I-48
4560

Thilo, Christfried Albert
Spinozas Religionsphilosophie. Langensalza, H. Beyer & Söhne (Beyer & Mann) 1906.
80 p. 24cm. (Religionsphilosophie in Einzeldarstellungen, hrsg. von O. Flügel. Heft VII)

SPECIAL COLLECTIONS
SPINOZA
I-48
4561

Tarin, Jean Henri
Spinoza théologien. Genève, Imprimerie P. Richter, 1909.
96 p. 24cm.

Thesis, Geneva.
Bibliography: p. [5]

I-48
4562

Valsecchi, Antonio, 1708-1791.
Dei fondamentali della religione et dei fonti dell'empietà libri tre. 2. ed. Padova, G. Manfrè, 1767.
3 v. 25 cm.

NIC

I-48
4563

Watts, Isaac, 1674-1748.
Discourses of the love of God, and the use and abuse of the passions in religion, with a devout meditation suited to each discourse ... London, Printed for J. Clark and R. Hett, 1729.
ix, [3], 304, [1] p. 31 cm.

MB

I-48
4564

Wobbermin, Georg, 1869-
Religionsphilosophie. Berlin, Heise, 1924.
248 p. 20 cm. (Quellen-Handbucher der Philosophie hrsg. von Arthur Liebert. 5. Bd.)

I-49
SCIENCE

SPECIAL COLLECTIONS
SPINOZA
I-49
4565

Aster, Ernst von, 1880-
... Raum und zeit in der geschichte der philosophie und physik, von E. von Aster ... München, Rösl & cie., 1922.
150, [1] p. 16½cm. (Philosophische reihe, hrsg. von dr. Alfred Werner. 45. bd.)

1. Space and time.
A C 33-1701
Title from Columbia Univ. Printed by L. C.
[2]

SPECIAL COLLECTIONS
SPINOZA
I-49
4566

Crommelin, Claude August, 1878-
Spinoza's natuurwetenschappelijk denken. Leiden, E. J. Brill, 1939.
19 p. 24cm. (Mededeelingen van wege het Spinozahuis, VI)

On verso of half-title: Mededeeling no. 49 uit het Nederlandsch Historisch Natuurwetenschappelijk Museum te Leiden.

I-49
4567

Haeckel, Ernst, 1834-1919.
Die Wissenschaft und der Umsturz. [1895]
197-206 p.

In Die Zukunft, 10. Bd., 1895.
Includes references to Spinoza.

I-49
4568

[Pollock, Sir Frederick] bart., 1845-1937.
The scientific character of Spinoza's philosophy. [1873]
567-585 p.

Signed: Frederick Pollock.
In The Fortnightly review, v. 19 (n. s. v. 13), 1873.

SPECIAL COLLECTIONS
SPINOZA
I-49
4569

[Pollock, Sir Frederick, bart.] 1845-1937.
The scientific character of Spinoza's philosophy. [1873]
[567]-585 p. 23cm.

Signed: Frederick Pollock.
From Fortnightly review, n. s., v. 13, 1873.
Volume of pamphlets.

SPECIAL COLLECTIONS
SPINOZA
I-49
4570

Worm, Kurt
Spinozas Naturrecht. [1904]
[500]-515 p. 23cm.

From Archiv für Geschichte der Philosophie, Bd. XVII, Neue Folge, X. Bd.

I-50
STATE AND RELIGION

SPECIAL COLLECTIONS
SPINOZA
I-50
4571

Dessauer, Moritz
Spinoza und Hobbes; Begründung ihrer Staats- und Religionstheorieen durch ihre philosophischen Systeme. Breslau, 1868.
43 p. 23cm.

Thesis, Heidelberg.
Published also without thesis note.

NNC

SPECIAL COLLECTIONS
SPINOZA
I-50
4572

Dessauer, Moritz, 1842-1895.
Spinoza und Hobbes; Begründung ihrer Staats- und Religionstheorieen durch ihre philosophischen Systeme. Breslau, Schletter'sche Buchhandlung (H. Skutsch) 1868.
43 p. 24cm.

Issued also as thesis, Heidelberg.

I-50
4573

Herbart, Johann Friedrich, 1776-1841.
Analytische beleuchtung des naturrechts und der moral, zum gebrauch beym vortrage der praktischen philosophie. Von J. F. Herbart. Göttingen, Dieterich, 1836.
xviii, 264 p. 21cm.

Includes a section "Von der Begründung nach spinozistischer Richtung" (p. 35-43)

1. Natural law. 2. Law—Philosophy. 3. Ethics. I. Title.
35-38232
Library of Congress [2]

I-50
4574

Melamed, Samuel Max, 1885-1938.
Spinoza, the Jew; his conception of the Jewish state. [1927]
336-337 p.

In The New Palestine, v. 12, 1927.

I-50
4575

Mélamed, Samuel Max, 1885-1938.
Der Staat im Wandel der Jahrtausende; Studien zur Geschichte des Staatsgedankens. Stuttgart, Enke, 1910.
xii, 303 p. 26 cm.

Includes a section on Spinoza (p. 241-245) and other references to him.

I-50
4576

Meozzi, Antero
Le dottrine politiche e religiose di B. Spinoza, paralello con T. Hobbes. [Arezzo, Sinatti, 1916?]
216 p. 20 cm.

I-50
4577

[Solari, Gioele] 1872-
La politica religiosa di Spinoza e la sua dottrina del jus sacrum. [1930]
306-344 p.

At head of title: Gioele Solari.
In Rivista di filosofia, anno 21, 1930.

SPECIAL COLLECTIONS
SPINOZA
I-50
4578

Waldauer, Adolf
Spinoza's Hebräerstaat. [1891]
[1]-2, [5]-6, [9]-10, [13]-14 p. 31cm.

From Jüdisches Litteratur-Blatt, Jahrg. XX nos. 1-4, Januar 1891.

I-51
SUBSTANCE

SPECIAL COLLECTIONS
SPINOZA
I-51
4579

Albert, Reinhold
Spinoza's Lehre über die Existenz Einer Substanz. [1875]
41 p. 23cm.

From Programm der Annen-Realschule, Dresden, für 1875.
Bibliographical footnotes.

I-51
4580

Avenarius, Richard Heinrich Ludwig, 1843-1896.
Philosophie als Denken der Welt gemäss dem Princip des kleinsten Kraftmasses. Prolegomena zu einer Kritik der reinen Erfahrung. Habilitationsschrift der philosophischen Facultät der Universität zu Leipzig vorgelegt und als Einladung zu der ... Probevorlesung über die Substanz Spinoza's. Leipzig, Fues's Verlag (R. Reisland) 1876.
xiii, 82 p. 23 cm.

DLC

SPECIAL COLLECTIONS
SPINOZA
I-51
4581

Bidney, David, 1908-
The problem of substance in Spinoza and Whitehead.
574-592 p. 26cm.

"Reprinted from the Philosophical review, November 1936."
Presentation copy to A. S. Oko with the author's inscription and signature.
Original paper covers bound in.

I-51
4582

Bierens de Haan, Johannes Diderik, 1866-1943.
De idealiteit der substantie volgens Spinoza. [1924]
253-272 p.

In Tijdschrift voor wijsbegeerte, 1924.

NN

I-51
4583

Brunschvicg, Léon, 1869-1944.
La révolution cartésienne et la notion spinoziste de la substance. [1904]
755-798 p.

In Revue de métaphysique et de morale, 12. année, 1904.

NNC

⌐Delbos, Victor¬ 1862-1916.
La notion de substance et la notion de Dieu dans la philosophie de Spinoza. ⌐1908¬
⌐783¬-788 p. 25cm.

Signed: Victor Delbos.
On cover: Revue de métaphysique et de morale. Extrait du numéro du troisième Congrès de philosophie, novembre 1908.

⌐Hebler, Karl¬ 1821-1898.
Spinoza's Lehre vom Verhältniss der Substanz zu ihren Bestimmtheiten, dargestellt von C. Hr. Bern, Jenni, 1850.
62 p. 20cm.

Bound with Horn, I. E., originally Ignaz Einhorn. Spinoza's Staatslehre. 1863.

1. Spinoza, Benedictus de, 1632-1677.

⌐Delbos, Victor¬ 1862-1916.
La notion de substance et la notion de Dieu dans la philosophie de Spinoza. ⌐1908¬
⌐783¬-788 p. 26cm.

Signed: Victor Delbos.
From Revue de métaphysique et de morale, 16. année, no. 6, novembre 1908.

Heidmann, Karl, 1858-
Der Substanz-Begriff von Abälard bis Spinoza. Berlin, Druck von Gebr. Unger, 1890.
56 p. 25cm.

Thesis, Berlin.
Imperfect: title-page lacking.

Friedrichs, Max, 1857-
Der Substanzbegriff Spinozas neu und gegen die herrschenden Ansichten zu Gunsten des Philosophen erläutert. Greifswald, J. Abel, 1896.
97 p. 25cm.

Thesis, Leipzig.
Volume of pamphlets.

Hessen, Johannes, 1889-
Das substanzproblem in der philosophie der neuzeit, von d. dr. Johannes Hessen ... Berlin und Bonn, F. Dümmler, 1932.
287 p. 24½cm.
Bibliographical foot-notes.
Includes a section on Spinoza (p. 63-77)

1. Substance (Philosophy)

A C 34-1539

Title from Princeton Univ. Printed by L. C.
⌐2¬

Fürst, Julius, 1805-1873.
Spinozae de substantia doctrina. Heidelbergae, G. Reichard, 1848.
28 p. 21cm.

Thesis, Heidelberg.
Volume of pamphlets.

1. Spinoza, Benedictus de, 1632-1677.

Jolivet, Régis, 1891-
... La notion de substance; essai historique et critique sur le développement des doctrines d'Aristote à nos jours, par Régis Jolivet ... Paris, G. Beauchesne, 1929.
3 p. l., 335, ⌐2¬ p., 1 l. 23 cm. (Bibliothèque des Archives de philosophie)
"Bibliographie": p. ⌐309¬-315.
Includes a section "Le panthéisme spinoziste" (p. 143-152) and other references to Spinoza.
1. Substance (Philosophy) I. Title.

Library of Congress BD331.J6 30—29952
⌐a49b½¬ 111

⌐Hebler, Karl¬ 1821-1898.
Spinoza's Lehre vom Verhältniss der Substanz zu ihren Bestimmtheiten, dargestellt von C. H--r. Bern, C. A. Jenni, Vater, 1850.
62 p. 21cm.

Original paper covers bound in.

⌐Laws, ¬
Beurtheilung der spinozistischen Substanz und der Leibnitzischen Monaden. ⌐Rössel, Druck von F. Kruttke, 1857¬
19 p. 20cm.

Signed: Laws.
From Fünf und zwanzigster Jahresbericht über das Königl. Progymnasium zu Rössel.

Leander, Pehr Johan Herman, 1831-1907.
Om substansbegreppet hos Cartesius, Spinoza och Leipnitz. Lund, Berlingska Boktryckeriet, 1862.
44 p.

Thesis, Lund.

[Swediaur, François Xavier] 1748-1824, ed.
The philosophical dictionary, comprising the opinions of all the best writers on moral, political and theological subjects, such as Locke, Hume ... and others, who have written in favour of the liberties and happiness of mankind. [2d ed.] London, W. Benbow, 1822.
1 v. (unpaged) 22cm.

Includes a reference to Spinoza under the heading: Substance.

Lindemann, Richard, 1860-
De substantiae, attributorum, modorum apud Spinozam ratione et cohaerentia. Halis Saxonum, 1884.
35 p. 25cm.

Thesis, Halle.
Volume of pamphlets.

Thomas, Karl, d. 1873.
De relatione quae inter Spinozae substantiam et attributa intercedit. Regimontii Borussorum, impressit E. J. Dalkowski [1839]
49 p. 21cm.

Habilitationsschrift, Königsberg.
Bibliographical footnotes.
Bound with Thomas, Karl, d. 1873. Spinozae systema philosophicum adumbratum.

Raesfeld, Alphons von, b. 1835.
Symbola ad penitiorem notitiam doctrinae quam Spinoza de substantia proposuit. Bonnae, Formis Carthausii [1858]
33 p. 21cm.

Thesis, Bonn.
Volume of pamphlets.

1. Spinoza, Benedictus de, 1632-1677.

Wahle, Richard, 1857-
Ueber das Verhältniss zwischen Substanz und Attributen in Spinoza's Ethik. Wien, F. Tempsky, 1889.
22 p. 26cm. (Sitzungsberichte der Kais. Akademie der Wissenschaften in Wien. Philosophisch-historische Klasse. Bd. CXVII, Abhandlung VIII)

Rappeport, Ernst, 1889-
Über die Substanzdefinition in Spinoza's Ethik. Wien, 1914.
46 p. 23cm.

Thesis, Basel.

1. Spinoza, Benedictus de, 1632-1677. Ethics

Wahle, Richard, 1857-
Ueber das Verhältniss zwischen Substanz und Attributen in Spinoza's Ethik. [1889]
22 p. 26cm.

From Sitzungsberichte der Phil. hist. Classe der kais. Akademie der Wissenschaften in Wien, v. 117.

Samuel, Otto
Die Substanz - eine reine Anschauung. [1914]
12-40 p.

In Zeitschrift für Philosophie und philosophische Kritik, Bd. 154, 1914.
Includes a reference to Spinoza (p. 23)

Walter, Reinhold
Ueber das Verhältniss der Substanz zu ihren Attributen in der Lehre Spinoza's, mit besonderer Berücksichtigung der Auffassung desselben bei Kuno Fischer, Erdmann und Trendelenburg. Nürnburg, U. E. Sebald, 1871.
39 p. 22cm.

Thesis, Erlangen.

Wolf, Abraham, 1876-
Spinoza's conception of the attributes of substance. [1927]
[177]-192 p. 23cm.

At head of title: Meeting of the Aristotelian Society ... on February 21st, 1927.

Wolfson, Harry Austryn, 1887-
Spinoza on the simplicity of substance. [1923?]
57 l. 29cm.

Typescript.
Manuscript notes.

Wolfson, Harry Austryn, 1887-
Spinoza on the simplicity of substance. [Hagae Comitis, 1923]
142-178 p. 22cm.

Cover-title: Dissertatio Chronici Spinozani tomo tertio separatim edita.
Presentation copy to A. S. Oko, with the author's inscription and signature.
Bibliographical footnotes.

Wolfson, Harry Austryn, 1887-
Spinoza on the unity of substance. [Hagae Comitis, 1922]
92-117 p. 26cm.

On cover: Dissertatio ex Chronici Spinozani tomo secundo separatim edita.
Presentation copy to A. S. Oko, with the author's inscription and signature.

Wolfson, Harry Austryn, 1887-
Spinoza on the unity of substance. [1922?]
35 l. 28cm.

Typescript, with manuscript corrections and footnotes.

Wolfson, Harry Austryn, 1887-
Spinoza's definition of substance and mode. [Hagae Comitis, 1921]
101-112 p. 23cm.

On cover: Dissertatio ex Chronici Spinozani tomo primo separatim edita.
Presentation copy to A. S. Oko, with the author's inscription and signature.

Wundt, Wilhelm, 1832-1920.
Einleitung in die Philosophie. 9. Aufl. Mit einem Anhang: Tabellarische Übersichten zur Geschichte der Philosophie und ihrer Hauptrichtungen. Leipzig, Kröner, 1922.
xviii, 448 p. 22cm.

Includes a section "Spinozas Substanzlehre" (p. 198-204)

I-52 TELEOLOGY

Kratz, Heinrich, 1836-
Spinoza's ansicht über den zweckbegriff dargestellt und beurtheilt von Heinrich Kratz ... Neuwied & Leipzig, J. H. Heuser'sche verlags-buchhandlung, 1871.
49 p. 22cm.
Inaug.-diss.—Göttingen.
Original paper covers bound in.

1. Theology.

Library of Congress B3999.T3K8 6—21188
[a37b1]

Kuske, Erich
Spinoza und die Teleologie. [1918]
20 p. 24cm.

From Preussische Jahrbücher, Bd. CLXXI, Heft. 1.

NNC

Wetzel, Paul, 1842-
Der Zweckbegriff bei Spinoza. Leipzig, Druck von Fr. Andrä's Nachfolger, 1873.
vi, 92 p. 22cm.

Thesis, Leipzig.
Published also without thesis note.
Includes bibliographical references.

Wetzel, Paul Friedrich, b. 1842.
Der Zweckbegriff bei Spinoza; eine philosophische Abhandlung, verfasst von Paul Wetzel. Leipzig, A. Lorentz, 1873.
90 p. 24cm.

Issued also as thesis, Leipzig.
Original paper cover bound in.
Volume of pamphlets.

I-53
TERMINOLOGY

⌐Dunin-Borkowski, Stanislaus, Graf von⌐ 1864-
Stil in der Philosophie, an einem Beispiel erläutert. ⌐1928⌐
⌐335⌐-347 p. 26cm.

Signed: Stanislaus v. Dunin Brokowski.
From Stimmen der Zeit, 58. Jahrgang, 11. Heft, 115. Band, August 1928.
Deals with Spinoza.
Bibliographical footnotes.

⌐Dunin-Borkowski, Stanislaus, Graf von⌐ 1864-
Stil in der Philosophie, an einem Beispiel erläutert. ⌐1928⌐
⌐335⌐-347 p. 26cm.

Signed: Stanislaus v. Dunin-Borkowski.
Deals with Spinoza.
"Sonderabdruck aus den Stimmen der Zeit, Monatsschrift für das Geistesleben der Gegenwart, August 1928, Band 115, Heft 11."

Eucken, Rudolf, 1846-1926.
Geschichte der philosophischen Terminologie, im Umriss dargestellt. Leipzig, Verlag von Veit & Comp., 1879.
iv, 226 p. 23cm.

Includes references to Spinoza.

⌐Navarro, Martín⌐
Gustav Theodor Richter: Spinozas philosophische Terminologie. Erste Abteilung: Grundbegriffe der Metaphysik. ⌐1914⌐
499-505 p. 25cm.

Signed: Martín Navarro.
From Estvdio, año II, tomo V, núm. 15, marzo de 1914.
A review of Richter's book.

⌐Porges, Nathan⌐ 1848-1924.
Das Wort Pharisäer bei Spinoza. ⌐1917⌐
⌐150⌐-165 p. 23cm.

From Monatsschrift für Geschichte und Wissenschaft des Judentums, 61. Jahrgang, Heft 3/6, Neue Folge, 25. Jahrgang, März-Juni 1917.
Bibliographical footnotes.

Unbound copy.

⌐Porges, Nathan⌐ 1848-1924.
Das Wort Pharisäer bei Spinoza. ⌐1917⌐
⌐150⌐-165 p. 23cm.

From Monatsschrift für Geschichte und Wissenschaft des Judentums, 61. Jahrgang, Heft 3/6, Neue Folge, 25. Jahrgang, März-Juni 1917.
Bibliographical footnotes.

⌐Richter, Gustav Theodor⌐ 1886-
Richter, Gustav Theodor. Spinozas philosophische Terminologie, historisch und immanent kritisch untersucht. 1. Abteilung: Grundbegriffe der Metaphysik. 1913. ⌐1914⌐
p. 426.

Signed: G. Th. Richter.
In Kant-Studien, 19. Bd., 1914.
A notice by the author concerning his book.

Richter, Gustav Theodor, 1886-
Spinozas philosophische Terminologie; historisch und immanent kritisch untersucht. Erste Abteilung: Grundbegriffe der Metaphysik. Leipzig, J. A. Barth, 1913.
170 p.

No more published?
Issued also as thesis, Berlin.

Richter, Gustav Theodor, 1886-
Spinozas philosophische Terminologie, historisch und immanent kritisch untersucht. Erstes Kapitel des ersten Teils. ⌐Leipzig, J. A. Barth, 1912⌐
71 p. 23cm.

Thesis, Berlin.
Published in enlarged form without thesis note.
Bibliographical references included in "Anhang" (p. ⌐56⌐-71)

Tönnies, Ferdinand, 1855-1936.
Philosophische Terminologie in psychologisch-soziologischer Ansicht. Leipzig, T. Thomas, 1906.
xvi, 105 p.

Willmann, Otto, 1839-1920.
Die wichtigsten philosophischen Fachausdrücke in historischer Anordnung. [2. Aufl.] München, J. Kösel & F. Pustet [1923]
136 p. 17cm. (Sammlung Kösel, 28)

Includes a section on Spinoza (p. 81-83) and other references to him.

I-54
THEISM

Bühler, Adolph
Theokrisis; Ideen über Gott und Welt zur Versöhnung des Theismus und Pantheismus. Berlin, Nicolaische Verlagsbuchhandlung (G. Parthey) 1861.
vi, 253 p. 19cm.

Includes references to Spinoza.

Flint, Robert, 1838-1910.
Theism; being the Baird lecture for 1876. 7th ed., rev. Edinburgh and London, Blackwood, 1889.
ix, 447 p. 20 cm.

Includes references to Spinoza.

Iverach, James, 1839-1922.
Theism in the light of present science and philosophy. New York, London, Macmillan, 1899.
xi, 330 p.

Includes references to Spinoza.

Newman, Francis William, 1805-1897.
The two theisms. London, T. Scott [1874]
16 p. 19cm.

Volume of pamphlets.

I-55
THEOLOGY

[Ammon, Christoph Friedrich] 1766-1849.
Grundzüge der Theologie des Spinoza. [1813]
16 p.

In Kritisches Journal der neuesten theologischen Literatur, Bd. 1, 1813.

Boedder, Bernard, 1841-
Natural theology. London, Longmans, Green, 1891.
xii, 480 p.

Includes an appendix "Examination of propositions I-VI in Spinoza's Ethics" (p. 449-460) and other references to Spinoza.

Boedder, Bernard, 1841-
Natural theology. Second edition. London, New York, Longmans, Green, 1902.
xii, 480 p. 20 cm. (Stonyhurst philosophical series)

Includes appendix "Examination of propositions I-VI in Spinoza's Ethics" (p. 449-460) and other references to Spinoza.

Dulau, P
Spinoza philosophe et théologien. [1927]
454-483, 684-703 p.

In Divus Thomas; commentarium de philosophia et theologia, series 3., annus 4., 1927.

Garve, Christian, 1742-1798.
Ueber das Daseyn Gottes; eine nachgelassene Abhandlung. Neue Auflage. Breslau, W. G. Korn, 1807.
viii, 250 p.

Includes a section "Ueber das theologische System des Spinoza" (p. 241-250)

Hedge, Frederic Henry, 1805-1890, ed.
Recent inquiries in theology, by eminent English churchmen; being "Essays and reviews". 2d American, from the 2d London ed. With an appendix. Edited, with an introduction, by Frederic H. Hedge. Boston, Walker, Wise, 1861.
xiv, 498 p. 20 cm.

Renner, Johann Gotthold
Das Selbstbewusstsein der Gottheit im Systeme Spinozas. Goldberg i. Schl., O. Collmar, 1906.
27 p. 26cm.

At head of title: Schwabe-Priesemuth-Stiftung (Städtisches Progymnasium) zu Goldberg i./Schl. Wissenschaftliche Beilage zum Jahresbericht über das Schuljahr Ostern 1905 bis Ostern 1906.

Thieme, Karl
Die christliche Demut; eine historische Untersuchung zur theologischen Ethik. Erste Hälfte. Wortgeschichte und die Demut bei Jesus. Giessen, A. Töpelmann, 1906.
xvi, 258 p. 23 cm.

Includes a reference to Spinoza (p. 7-8)

Tulloch, John, 1823-1886.
Rational theology and Christian philosophy in England in the seventeenth century. Edinburgh, W. Blackwood and Sons, 1872.
2 v. 23cm.

Includes a reference to Spinoza in the chapter on Henry More (v. 2, p. 345)
Contents.--v. 1. Liberal churchmen.--v. 2. The Cambridge Platonists.

Walch, Johann Georg, 1693-1775.
Historische und theologische Einleitung in die Religions-Streitigkeiten, welche sonderlich ausser der Evangelisch-Lutherischen Kirche entstanden. Dritte Auflage. Jena, bey Johann Meyers Wittwe, 1733-36.
5 v. 17 cm.

Vol. 5 includes references to Spinoza.

I-56
THEORY OF KNOWLEDGE

Aster, Ernst von, 1880-
Geschichte der neueren Erkenntnistheorie (von Descartes bis Hegel) Berlin, W. de Gruyter, 1921.
vi, 638 p. 24cm.

Includes a section on Spinoza (p. 126-161)

Berendt, Martin, 1849-1903.
Die rationelle erkenntnis Spinozas. Versuch einer erläuterung derselben von M. Berendt ... Berlin, Preussische philologen-zeitung (E. Lazarus) 1889.
1 p. l., 28 p. 18½cm.
Abdruck aus der Preussischen philologen-zeitung.
Volume of pamphlets.

1. Spinoza, Benedictus de, 1632-1677. 2. Knowledge, Theory of.

Berendt, Martin, b. 1849.
Spinoza's Erkenntnisslehre in ihrer Beziehung zur modernen Naturwissenschaft und Philosophie. Allgemein verständlich dargestellt von Martin Berendt und Julius Friedländer. Berlin, Mayer & Müller, 1891.
xix, 315 p. 22cm.

Original paper cover bound in.

Burthogge, Richard, 1638?-ca. 1700.
An essay upon reason, and the nature of spirits. By Richard Burthogge, M. D. London, Printed for J. Dunton, 1694.
3 p. l., 280 p. diagr. 18cm.
Includes references to Spinoza.

1. Knowledge, Theory of. 2. Supernatural.

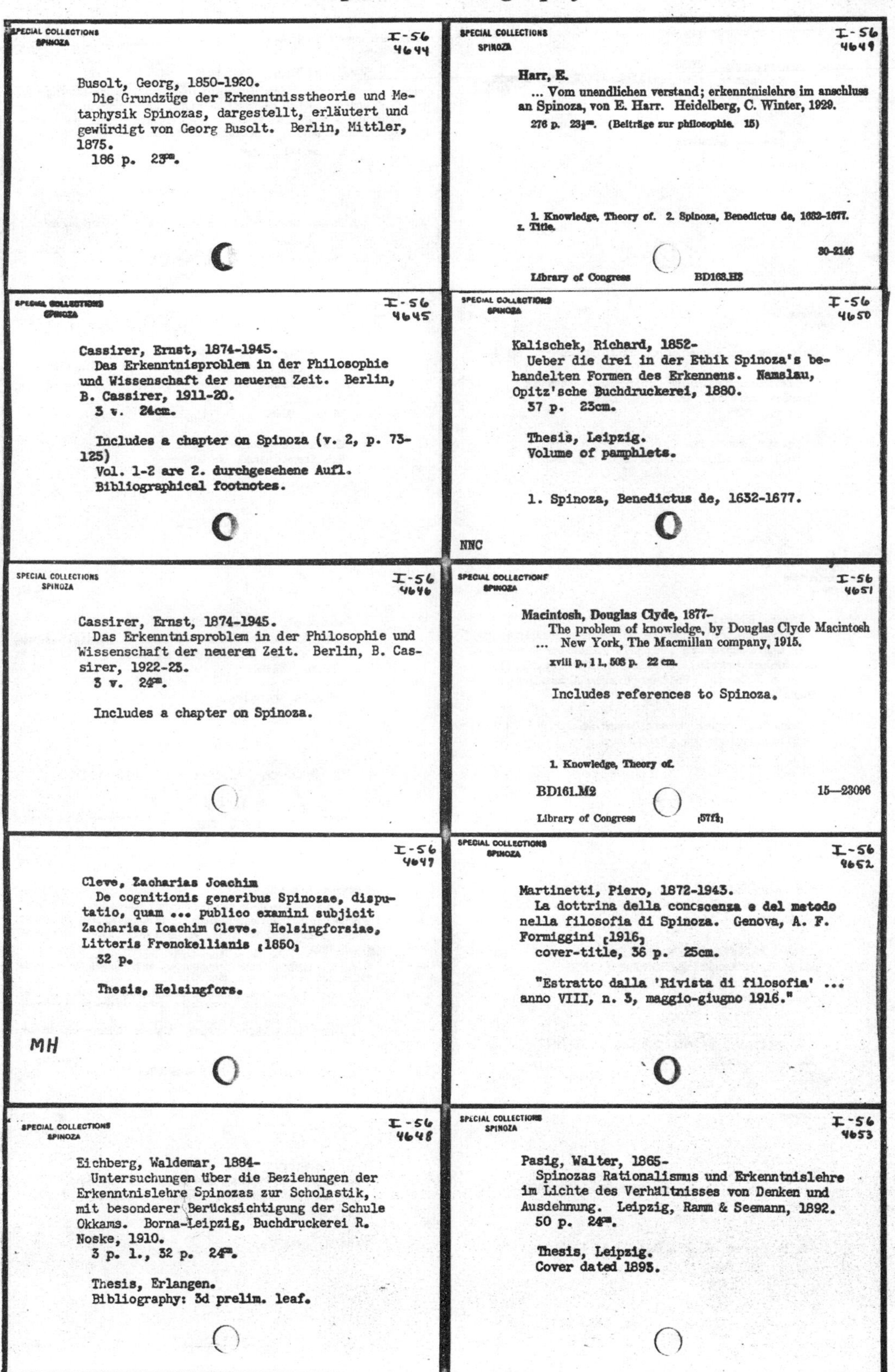

SPECIAL COLLECTIONS
SPINOZA
I-56
4644

Busolt, Georg, 1850-1920.
Die Grundzüge der Erkenntnisstheorie und Metaphysik Spinozas, dargestellt, erläutert und gewürdigt von Georg Busolt. Berlin, Mittler, 1875.
186 p. 23cm.

SPECIAL COLLECTIONS
SPINOZA
I-56
4649

Harr, E.
... Vom unendlichen verstand; erkenntnislehre im anschluss an Spinoza, von E. Harr. Heidelberg, C. Winter, 1929.
276 p. 23½cm. (Beiträge zur philosophie. 15)

1. Knowledge, Theory of. 2. Spinoza, Benedictus de, 1632-1677. I. Title.

30-2146

Library of Congress BD163.H3

SPECIAL COLLECTIONS
SPINOZA
I-56
4645

Cassirer, Ernst, 1874-1945.
Das Erkenntnisproblem in der Philosophie und Wissenschaft der neueren Zeit. Berlin, B. Cassirer, 1911-20.
3 v. 24cm.

Includes a chapter on Spinoza (v. 2, p. 73-125)
Vol. 1-2 are 2. durchgesehene Aufl.
Bibliographical footnotes.

SPECIAL COLLECTIONS
SPINOZA
I-56
4650

Kalischek, Richard, 1852-
Ueber die drei in der Ethik Spinoza's behandelten Formen des Erkennens. Namslau, Opitz'sche Buchdruckerei, 1880.
37 p. 23cm.

Thesis, Leipzig.
Volume of pamphlets.

1. Spinoza, Benedictus de, 1632-1677.

NNC

SPECIAL COLLECTIONS
SPINOZA
I-56
4646

Cassirer, Ernst, 1874-1945.
Das Erkenntnisproblem in der Philosophie und Wissenschaft der neueren Zeit. Berlin, B. Cassirer, 1922-23.
3 v. 24cm.

Includes a chapter on Spinoza.

SPECIAL COLLECTIONS
SPINOZA
I-56
4651

Macintosh, Douglas Clyde, 1877-
The problem of knowledge, by Douglas Clyde Macintosh ... New York, The Macmillan company, 1915.
xviii p., 1 l., 503 p. 22 cm.

Includes references to Spinoza.

1. Knowledge, Theory of.

BD161.M2 15—23096

Library of Congress [57f1]

I-56
4647

Cleve, Zacharias Joachim
De cognitionis generibus Spinozae, disputatio, quam ... publico examini subjicit Zacharias Ioachim Cleve. Helsingforsiae, Litteris Frenckellianis [1850]
32 p.

Thesis, Helsingfors.

MH

SPECIAL COLLECTIONS
SPINOZA
I-56
4652

Martinetti, Piero, 1872-1943.
La dottrina della conoscenza e del metodo nella filosofia di Spinoza. Genova, A. F. Formiggini [1916]
cover-title, 36 p. 25cm.

"Estratto dalla 'Rivista di filosofia' ... anno VIII, n. 3, maggio-giugno 1916."

SPECIAL COLLECTIONS
SPINOZA
I-56
4648

Eichberg, Waldemar, 1884-
Untersuchungen über die Beziehungen der Erkenntnislehre Spinozas zur Scholastik, mit besonderer Berücksichtigung der Schule Okkams. Borna-Leipzig, Buchdruckerei R. Noske, 1910.
3 p. l., 32 p. 24cm.

Thesis, Erlangen.
Bibliography: 3d prelim. leaf.

SPECIAL COLLECTIONS
SPINOZA
I-56
4653

Pasig, Walter, 1865-
Spinozas Rationalismus und Erkenntnislehre im Lichte des Verhältnisses von Denken und Ausdehnung. Leipzig, Ramm & Seemann, 1892.
50 p. 24cm.

Thesis, Leipzig.
Cover dated 1893.

Rosca, Paul, 1884-
Spinoza's Erkenntnislehre. Hermannstadt, Krafft, 1911.
80 p.

Thesis, München.

Schoultz von Ascheraden, Max, Freiherr, 1864-1925.
Die Erkenntnislehre Spinozas. Marburg, Buchdruckerei O. Ehrhardt, 1892.
84 p. 22cm.

Thesis, Marburg.
Published also without thesis note.

Strack, Rudolf
Notwendigkeit und Freiheit; eine Erläuterung der Lehre Spinozas über das relative Verstandesdenken (ratio) Berlin, E. Ebering, 1921.
84 p. 24cm. (Philosophische Abhandlungen, Heft 3)

Original paper covers bound in.
Bibliography: p. [7]-8.

Vloemans, Antoon
Het ideaal der kennis bij Spinoza. [1923]
[61]-72 p. 25cm.

From Tijdschrift voor wijsbegeerte, 17. jaargang, 1. aflevering, Februari 1923.

1. Spinoza, Benedictus de, 1632-1677.

Vloemans, Antoon
Spinoza's leer van de menschelijke kennis. [1928]
[657]-673 p. 25cm.

From Vragen van den dag, Oct. 1, 1928.

1. Spinoza, Benedictus de, 1632-1677.

Vold, John Mourly, 1850-1907.
Spinozas erkjendelsestheori i dens indre sammenhæng og i dens forhold til Spinozas metafysik. En række undersøgelser som bidrag til at fastsætte Spinozismens grundtanker, af J. Mourly Vold ... Kristiania, J. Dybwads forlag, 1888.
1 p. l., xiv, 384 p. 22½cm.

1. Spinoza, Benedictus de, 1632-1677. 2. Knowledge, Theory of.

Voss, Robert von, 1878-
Ueber den Begriff der Erkenntnis, insbesondere der intuitiven, bei Spinoza. [Leipzig, 1901]
39 p. 24cm.

Thesis, Leipzig.
Bibliographical footnotes.

Zeitschel, Richard, 1856-
Die Erkenntnislehre Spinoza's. Langensalza, Druck von H. Beyer & Söhne, 1889.
38 p. 21cm.

Thesis, Leipzig.

1. Spinoza, Benedictus de, 1632-1677.

I-57
TRUTH

Lévêque, Raphaël.
... Le problème de la vérité dans la philosophie de Spinoza. Préface de m. Maurice Pradines ... Strasbourg [etc.] Librairie Istra; [London, New York, H. Milford, Oxford university press, 1923.
viii p., 1 l., 155 p. 25½cm. (Publications de la Faculté des lettres de l'Université de Strasbourg. fasc. 17)
"Ce travail a été présenté comme mémoire pour le diplôme d'études supérieures de philosophie devant la Faculté des lettres de l'Université de Strasbourg le 17 juin 1922."
Original paper covers bound in.
1. Spinoza, Benedictus de, 1632-1677. 2. Truth. 3. Knowledge, Theory of.

Meier, Friedrich, 1875-
Die Lehre vom Wahren und Falschen bei Descartes und bei Spinoza. Leipzig, Richter, 1897.
viii, 54 p. 23 cm.

Thesis, Leipzig.

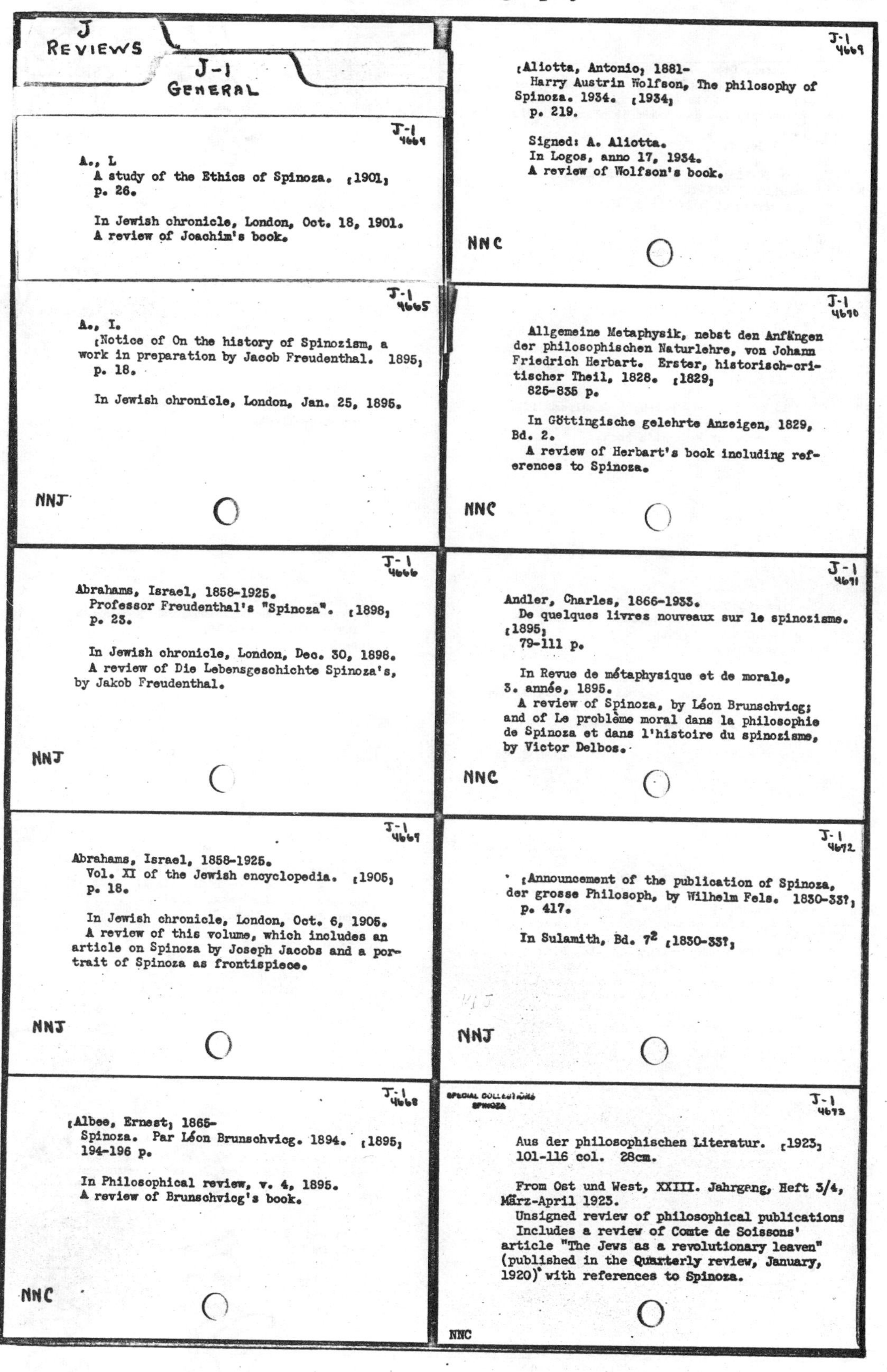

J
REVIEWS

J-1
GENERAL

J-1 4664

A., L
A study of the Ethics of Spinoza. [1901]
p. 26.

In Jewish chronicle, London, Oct. 18, 1901.
A review of Joachim's book.

J-1 4665

A., I.
[Notice of On the history of Spinozism, a work in preparation by Jacob Freudenthal. 1895]
p. 18.

In Jewish chronicle, London, Jan. 25, 1895.

NNJ

J-1 4666

Abrahams, Israel, 1858-1925.
Professor Freudenthal's "Spinoza". [1898]
p. 23.

In Jewish chronicle, London, Dec. 30, 1898.
A review of Die Lebensgeschichte Spinoza's, by Jakob Freudenthal.

NNJ

J-1 4667

Abrahams, Israel, 1858-1925.
Vol. XI of the Jewish encyclopedia. [1905]
p. 18.

In Jewish chronicle, London, Oct. 6, 1905.
A review of this volume, which includes an article on Spinoza by Joseph Jacobs and a portrait of Spinoza as frontispiece.

NNJ

J-1 4668

[Albee, Ernest] 1865-
Spinoza. Par Léon Brunschvicg. 1894. [1895]
194-196 p.

In Philosophical review, v. 4, 1895.
A review of Brunschvicg's book.

NNC

J-1 4669

[Aliotta, Antonio] 1881-
Harry Austrin Wolfson, The philosophy of Spinoza. 1934. [1934]
p. 219.

Signed: A. Aliotta.
In Logos, anno 17, 1934.
A review of Wolfson's book.

NNC

J-1 4670

Allgemeine Metaphysik, nebst den Anfängen der philosophischen Naturlehre, von Johann Friedrich Herbart. Erster, historisch-critischer Theil, 1828. [1829]
825-835 p.

In Göttingische gelehrte Anzeigen, 1829, Bd. 2.
A review of Herbart's book including references to Spinoza.

NNC

J-1 4671

Andler, Charles, 1866-1933.
De quelques livres nouveaux sur le spinozisme. [1895]
79-111 p.

In Revue de métaphysique et de morale, 3. année, 1895.
A review of Spinoza, by Léon Brunschvicg; and of Le problème moral dans la philosophie de Spinoza et dans l'histoire du spinozisme, by Victor Delbos.

NNC

J-1 4672

[Announcement of the publication of Spinoza, der grosse Philosoph, by Wilhelm Fels. 1830-33?]
p. 417.

In Sulamith, Bd. 7^2 [1830-33?]

NNJ

SPECIAL COLLECTIONS SPINOZA

J-1 4673

Aus der philosophischen Literatur. [1923]
101-116 col. 28cm.

From Ost und West, XXIII. Jahrgang, Heft 3/4, März-April 1923.
Unsigned review of philosophical publications
Includes a review of Comte de Soissons' article "The Jews as a revolutionary leaven" (published in the Quarterly review, January, 1920) with references to Spinoza.

NNC

J-1
4674

[Baensch, Otto] 1878-1936.
Alfred Wenzel, Die Weltanschauung Spinozas, 1. Teil: Spinozas Lehre von Gott, von der Erkenntnis und dem Wesen der Dinge. 1907. [1909]
161-166 p.

In Göttingische gelehrte Anzeigen, 171. Jahrgang, 1909.
A review of Wenzel's book.

NNC

J-1
4675

[Baensch, Otto] 1878-1936.
Die Philosophie des Spinoza im Lichte der Kritik, von Franz Erhardt. 1908. [1909]
1019-1028 p.

In Göttingische gelehrte Anzeigen, 171. Jahrgang, 1909.
A review of Erhardt's book.

NNC

J-1
4676

[Barrett, Clifford]
The philosophy of Spinoza, by Harry Austryn Wolfson. 1934. [1935]
452-455 p.

Signed: Clifford Barrett.
In International journal of ethics, v. 45, Oct. 1934-July 1935.
A review of Wolfson's book.

NNC

SPECIAL COLLECTIONS
SPINOZA

J-1
4677

[Baumgarten, Siegmund Jakob] 1706-1757, ed.
Nachrichten von einer hallischen Bibliothek ... Halle, J. J. Gebauer, 1748-49.
4 v. in 2. 18cm.

The first four volumes (1.-24. Stück) of the eight volume set belonging to the first series of the author's Nachrichten von merkwürdigen Büchern, issued monthly, each number with separate t.-p. (Jan. 1748-Dec. 1749)
Includes reviews of books by and about Spinoza.

NNC

SPECIAL COLLECTIONS
SPINOZA

J-1
4678

Baumgardt, David, 1890-
Robinson, Lewis, Kommentar zu Spinozas Ethik. [1933]
p. 440. 24cm.

A review of Robinson's work.
From Kant-Studien, Band XXXVIII, Heft 3/4, 1933.
Bound with Jung, Gertrud. Hallett, H. F., Aeternitas. [1933]

SPECIAL COLLECTIONS
SPINOZA

J-1
4679

Bellaar Spruyt, Cornelis, 1842-1901.
Van Vloten's Benedictus de Spinoza beoordeeld door C. B. Spruijt. Utrecht, J. L. Beijers, 1876.
xi, 100 p. 25cm.

Original paper covers bound in.

NNC

J-1
4680

Bergmann, Hugo, 1883-
Ein neues Spinoza-Buch. [1935]
p. 7.

In Prager Presse, Aug. 4, 1935.
A review of The philosophy of Spinoza, by Harry A. Wolfson.

DLC

J-1
4681

Bergmann, Hugo, 1883-
[Review of The philosophy of Spinoza, by Harry A. Wolfson. 1935]
p. 5.

In Jüdische Rundschau, Jahrgang 40, 1935.

NN

SPECIAL COLLECTIONS
SPINOZA

J-1
4682

[Bierens de Haan, Johannes Diderik] 1866-1943.
Dr. W. Meijer, De Rozekruisers of de vrijdenkers der 17de eeuw. [1917]
107-108 p. 25cm.

Signed: B. de H
A review of Meijer's book.
Includes a reference to Spinoza.
From Tijdschrift voor wijsbegeerte, 11. jaarg., 1. aflevering, Jan. 1917.
Volume of pamphlets.

NNC

J-1
4683

[Bijvanck, W J C]
Spinoza in Utrecht. Een aanteekening op: Spinoza en zijn kring. Historisch-kritische studiën over Hollandsche vrijgeesten door K. O. Meinsma. [1896]
182-193 p.

Signed: B.
In De Gids, v. 60, 4. serie, 14. jaargang, 2. deel, 1896.
A review of Meinsma's book.

NNC

 J-1 4684

[Blumenthal, Walter Hart] 1883-
Spinoza revealed as beacon of Godly enlightenment in new biography by Lewis Browne. [1932]
p. 446. 33cm.

Signed: W. H. B.
From American Hebrew and Jewish tribune, v. 131, no. 25, November 4, 1932.
With Van Son, A. World honors Spinoza. [1932]

J-1 4685

Bolin, Wilhelm, 1835-1924.
[Review of Spinoza en zijn kring, by K. O. Meinsma. 1896]
423-424 p.

In Biographische Blätter, Bd. 2, 1896.

NN

 J-1 4686

[Bréhier, Émile] 1876-1952.
Gustave Cohen. Le séjour de Saint Evremond en Hollande (1666-1672) et l'entrée de Spinoza dans le champ de la pensée française. Paris, Honoré Champion, 1926. [1927]
110-111 p. 26cm.

Signed: É. B.
A review of Cohen's book.
From Revue d'histoire de la philosophie, 1re année, fasc. 1, janvier-mars 1927.

J-1 4687

Broad, Charlie Dunbar, 1887-
Prof. Hallett's Aeternitas. [1933]
151-169, 299-318 p.

In Mind, n. s. v. 42, 1933.

NNC

J-1 4688

[Bruining, Albert] 1846-1919.
Wetenschappelijke metaphysica. [1905]
310-333, 482-506 p.

Signed: A. Bruining.
In De Gids, v. 69, 4. serie, 23. jaargang, 4. deel, 1905.
A review of Einführung in die Metaphysik auf Grundlage der Erfahrung, by Gerardus Heymans, in which Spinoza is discussed.

NNC

 J-1 4689

Brunner, Peter, 1910-
Spinoza. Vier Reden von Carl Gebhardt. [1930]
650-651 p. 25cm.

From Der Morgen, V. Jahrgang, 6. Heft, Februar 1930.
A review of Gebhardt's work.

J-1 4690

Bücher über Spinoza. [1932]
p. 8.

In Prager Presse, Nov. 18, 1932.
A review of Spinoza; slavný a neohrožený filosof státního demokratismu, by J. Dvorský; and of Spinoza; Bildnis eines geistigen Helden, by Rudolf Kayser.

DLC

J-1 4691

[Buonaiuti, Ernesto] 1881-
Ancora Spinoza. [1934]
562-563 p.

Signed: e. b.
In Religio, v. 10, 1934.
A review of Spinoza e due antecedenti italiani dello Spinozismo, by Fausto Meli.

NNC

J-1 4692

[Buonaiuti, Ernesto] 1881-
Spinoza. [1934]
p. 383.

Signed: e. b.
In Religio, v. 10, 1934.
A review of The philosophy of Spinoza, by Harry A. Wolfson.

NNC

J-1 4693

[Busse, Ludwig] 1862-1907.
J. Freudenthal, Die Lebensgeschichte Spinozas in Quellenschriften, Urkunden und nichtamtlichen Nachrichten. 1899. [1899]
1499-1503 col.

In Deutsche Litteraturzeitung, 20. Jahrgang, 1899.
A review of Freudenthal's book.

NNC

[Caird, Edward] 1835-1908.
Spinoza: his life and philosophy, by Frederick Pollock. [1881]
63-65 p.

In The Academy, v. 19, Jan. 22, 1881.
A review of Pollock's book.

[Cantimori, Delio]
Fausto Meli, Spinoza e due antecedenti italiani dello spinozismo. 1934. [1935]
86-88 p.

In Giornale critico della filosofia italiana, anno 16, 2. serie, v. 3, 1935.
A review of Meli's book.

[Carp, J H]
Mystik und Rationalismus, von Christian Janentzky. [1922]
269-272 p. 22cm.

Signed: J. H. Carp.
A review of Janentzky's book.
Includes references to Spinoza.
From Chronicon Spinozanum, v. 2.

[Carp, J H]
Spinoza's leven: Dr. Antoon Vloemans, Spinoza, de mensch, het leven et het werk. [1931]
[225]-228 p. 28cm.

Signed: J. H. Carp.
From Den Gulden winckel, no. 359, November 1931.
A review of Vloemans' book.

Carriere, Moriz, 1817-1895.
Neues über Spinoza. [1892]
4-6 p.

In Allgemeine Zeitung. Beilage, Nr. 42, 1892.
A review of Spinoza's Erkenntnisslehre in ihrer Beziehung zur modernen Naturwissenschaft und Philosophie, by Martin Berendt and Julius Friedländer.

Ch. Appuhn: Oeuvres de Spinoza, traduites et annotées par. Tomo II: Traité theologico-politique. [1914]
387-388 p. 25cm.

Signed: X. X.
From Estvdio, año II, tomo VI, núm. 17, Mayo de 1914.
A review of Appuhn's translation.

Charpentier, T V
Delbos. Le problème morale dans la philosophie de Spinoza. 1894. [1894]
418-428 p.

In Revue philosophique de la France et de l'étranger, 19. année, t. 38, 1894.
A review of Delbos' book.

Churgin, Gershon A
הפילוסופיה של שפינוזה. ניו־יורק, תרצ"ה.

[New York, 1935]
[118]-119 p. 24cm.

Title transliterated: ha-Pilosofiyā ...
A review of Harry Austryn Wolfson's The philosophy of Spinoza.
From Horeb, vol. II, no. 1, April 1935.

Clark, Henry W
[Review of Philosophical treatment of divine personality, by F. Harte. 1913-14]
306-307 p.

In Review of theology and philosophy, v. 9, 1913-14.

Claudius, Matthias, 1740-1815.
Zwei Recensionen &c. in Sachen der Herren Lessing, M. Mendelssohn und Jacobi ... [1882]
421-435 p. (In his Werke, 12. Aufl. Gotha, Perthes, 1882, 1. Bd.)

Reviews of Ueber die Lehre des Spinoza, in Briefen an den Herrn Moses Mendelssohn, by Friedrich Heinrich Jacobi; and of Moses Mendelssohn an die Freunde Lessings, ein Anhang zu Herrn Jacobi Briefwechsel über die Lehre des Spinoza.

SPECIAL COLLECTIONS SPINOZA J-1 4704

[Claudius, Matthias] 1740-1815.
Zwey Recensionen &c. in Sachen der Herren Lessing, M. Mendelssohn, und Jacobi ... Hamburg, In Commission bey C. E. Bohn, 1786.
29 p. 18cm.

Signed: Asmus.
Reviews of "Ueber die Lehre des Spinoza ..." by Friedrich Heinrich Jacobi, and "Moses Mendelssohn an die Freunde Lessings."
Bound with Jacobi, Friedrich Heinrich. Ueber die Lehre des Spinoza. 1785.

J-1 4705

[Cohen, Hermann] 1842-1918.
Freudenthal, J., Spinoza. Sein Leben und seine Lehre. Erster Band. Das Leben Spinozas. 1904. [1904]
1189-1191 col.

Signed: H. Cohen.
In Literarisches Zentralblatt für Deutschland, 55. Jahrgang, 1904.
A review of Freudenthal's book.

J-1 4706

Cohen, Hermann, 1842-1918.
J. Freudenthal, Spinoza. Sein Leben und seine Lehre. 1. Bd. Das Leben Spinozas. [1928]
501-503 p. (In his Schriften zur Philosophie und Zeitgeschichte, 2. Bd.)

A review of Freudenthal's book, reprinted from Literarisches Zentralblatt, 1904.

J-1 4707

[Cohen, Morris Raphael] 1880-1947.
Bidney, David. The psychology and ethics of Spinoza; a study in the history and logic of ideas. 1940. [1941]
p. 238.

Signed: M. R. C.
In Jewish social studies, v. 3, 1941.
A review of Bidney's book.

J-1 4708

[Cohen, Renato]
Giuseppe Roverelli, Il pensiero spinoziano nell'idealismo moderno. 1934. [1936]
118-119 p.

In Giornale critico della filosofia italiana, anno 17, 2. serie, v. 4, 1936.
A review of Roverelli's book.

SPECIAL COLLECTIONS SPINOZA J-1 4709

[Cohen, Renato]
Spinoza nel terzo centenario della sua nascita. Pubblicazione a cura della Facoltà di filosofia dell' Università cattolica del Sacro Cuore. [1935]
[277]-285 p. 26cm.

Signed: Renato Cohen.
A review of the above-named work.
From Giornale critico della filosofia italiana, anno XVI, 2. serie, v. 3, maggio-giugno, 1935.

NNC

J-1 4710

De la veritable religion. A Paris chez Claude Barbin. 1688. [1690]
49-66 p.

In Journal des sçavans, pour l'année 1689, t. 17, 1690.
A review of Michel Le Vassor's book, including references to Spinoza.

J-1 4711

Demonstration ou preuves évidentes de la verité & de la sainteté de la morale chrétienne; ouvrage qui comprend en cinq entretiens toute la morale. Par le R. P. Bernard Lami. 1706. [1707]
285-301 p.

In Journal des sçavans, tome 36., 1707.
A review of the first two parts of Lamy's book, including references to Spinoza.

J-1 4712

Deussen, Paul, 1845-1919.
Ludwig Stein, Leibniz und Spinoza. Ein Beitrag zur Entwicklungsgeschichte der Leibnizischen Philosophie. 1890. [1893]
126-142 p.

In Zeitschrift für Philosophie und philosophische Kritik, n. F. 101. Bd., 1893.
A review of Stein's book.

J-1 4713

Dr. Martineau's Spinoza. [1883]
p. 5.

In Literary world, v. 14, Boston, 1883.
A review of A study of Spinoza, by James Martineau.

Dopp, Joseph
Harry Austryn Wolfson, The philosophy of Spinoza; unfolding the latent processes of his reasoning. 1934. ⌊1934⌋
412-420 p.

In Revue neo-scolastique de philosophie, t. 37, 1934.
A review of Wolfson's book.

Dorner,
⌊Review of Jacobis Spinoza Büchlein, edited by Fritz Mauthner. 1914⌋
col. 541.

In Theologische Literaturzeitung, Jahrgang 39, 1914.

Douwen, W J van
⌊Review of Spinoza en zijn kring, by K. O. Meinsma. 1898⌋
395-419 p.

In Theologisch tijdschrift, jaargang 32, 1898.

⌊Dunin-Borkowski, Stanislaus, Graf von, 1864-1934.
Altes und Neues zum Erkenntnisproblem. ⌊1924⌋
⌊291⌋-300 p. 26cm.

Signed: Stanislaus v. Dunin-Borkowski.
A review of Oswald Külpe's Die Realisierung.
"Sonderabdruck aus den 'Stimmen der Zeit' Juli 1924, Band 107, Heft 10."

⌊Dunin-Borkowski, Stanislaus⌋ Graf von, 1864-1934.
Baruch de Spinoza. Ethik. Übersetzt und mit einer Einleitung und einem Register versehen von Otto Baensch. 7. Aufl. 1910. ⌊1911⌋
262-263 p.

In Archiv für Geschichte der Philosophie, Bd. 24., 1911.
A review of Baensch's translation.

⌊Dunin-Borkowski, Stanislaus, Graf von, 1864-
Benedikt de Spinoza und Niels Stensen. ⌊1926⌋
⌊126⌋-138 p. 26cm.

Signed: Stanislaus v. Dunin-Borkowski.
From Stimmen der Zeit, 57. Jahrgang, 2. Heft, 112. Band, November 1926.
Bibliographical footnotes.

⌊Dunin-Borkowski, Stanislaus, Graf von⌋ 1864-
Chronicon Spinozanum. Tomus primus. ⌊1924⌋
227-228 p. 26cm.

Signed: Stanislaus v. Dunin-Borkowski.
A review of the above-mentioned book.
"Sonderabdruck aus den 'Stimmen der Zeit', Juni 1924, Band 107, Heft 9."
With the author's Die Ethik Spinozas, von Benzion Kellermann. ⌊1924⌋

⌊Dunin-Borkowski, Stanislaus, Graf von⌋ 1864-
Die Ethik Spinozas, von Benzion Kellermann. ⌊1924⌋
226-227 p. 26cm.

Signed: Stanislaus v. Dunin-Borkowski.
A review of Kellermann's book.
"Sonderabdruck aus den 'Stimmen der Zeit', Juni 1924, Band 107, Heft 9."

⌊Dunin-Borkowski, Stanislaus⌋ Graf von, 1864-1934
Die Philosophie des Spinoza im Lichte der Kritik, von Franz Erhardt. 1908. ⌊1909⌋
204-212 p.

Signed: Stan. von Dunin-Borkowski.
In Philosophisches Jahrbuch, 22. Bd., 1909.
A review of Erhardt's book.

Dunin-Borkowski, Stanislaus, Graf von, 1864-
Die Schriften des Uriel da Costa. Mit Einleitung, Übertragung und Regesten hrsg. von Carl Gebhardt ⌊1924⌋
p. 228. 26cm.

Signed: Stanislaus v. Dunin-Borkowski.
A review of Gebhardt's edition.
Includes references to Spinoza.
"Sonderabdruck aus den 'Stimmen der Zeit', Juni 1924, Band 107, Heft 9."

CONTINUED ON NEXT CARD

SPECIAL COLLECTIONS SPINOZA J-1 4924

Dunin-Borkowski, Stanislaus, Graf von, 1864-
Die Schriften des Uriel da Costa. ₍1924₎
(Card 2)

With the author's Die Ethik Spinozas, von Benzion Kellermann. ₍1924₎

NNC

J-1 4929

₍Elbogen, Ismar₎ 1874-1943.
Freudenthal, J. Die Lebensgeschichte Spinoza's in Quellenschriften, Urkunden und nichtamtlichen Nachrichten. 1899. ₍1899₎
329-335 p.

Signed: J. Elbogen.
In Monatsschrift für Geschichte und Wissenschaft des Judenthums, 43. Jahrgang (n. F. 7. Jahrgang), 1899.
A review of Freudenthal's book.

SPECIAL COLLECTIONS SPINOZA J-1 4925

₍Dunin-Borkowski, Stanislaus, Graf von₎ 1864-
Spinozas philosophische Terminologie, historisch und immanent kritisch untersucht von Gustav Theodor Richter. Erste Abteilung. Grundbegriffe der Metaphysik. ₍1922₎
259-262 p. 22cm.

Signed: Dunin Borkowski.
A review of Richter's book.
From Chronicon Spinozanum, v. 2.

NNC

J-1 4930

₍Elbogen, Ismar₎ 1874-1943.
Freudenthal, J. Spinoza, sein Leben und seine Lehre. 1. Band: Das Leben Spinozas. 1904. ₍1905₎
120-128 p.

Signed: I. Elbogen.
In Monatsschrift für Geschichte und Wissenschaft des Judentums, 49. Jahrgang (n. F. 13. Jahrgang) 1905.
A review of Freudenthal's book.

J-1 4926

Edman, Irwin, 1896-1954.
The unique and powerful vision of Baruch Spinoza; Professor Wolfson's long-awaited book is a work of illuminating scholarship. ₍1934₎
p. 6. port.

In New York times. Book review, July 22, 1934.

J-1 4931

Entretien d'un philosophe chrétien et d'un philosophe chinois, sur l'existence et la nature de Dieu. Par l'Auteur de la Recherche de la vérité. 1708. ₍1708₎
1134-1143 p.

In Mémoires pour l'histoire des sciences & des beaux arts, 1708, pt. 3.
A review of Malebranche's book, including a reference to Spinoza.

SPECIAL COLLECTIONS SPINOZA J-1 4927

Edman, Irwin, 1896-1954.
The unity of Spinoza's thought: The philosophy of Spinoza, by Richard McKeon. ₍1929₎
467-470 p. 26cm.

A review of McKeon's book.
From the Menorah journal, vol. XVI, no. 5, May, 1929.

J-1 4932

Erdmann, Benno, 1851-1921.
Spinoza. ₍1889₎
305-315 p.

In Archiv für Geschichte der Philosophie, Bd. 2, 1889.
Reviews of Spinoza und die Scholastik, by J. Freudenthal; Beiträge zur Entwicklungsgeschichte Spinoza's, I., by L. Busse; Die Staatstheorie von Hobbes und Spinoza, by K. Gaul; Die Psychologie des Spinoza, by F. Schneider; Die Affectenlehre Spinozas, by J. Nenitescu; and Spinoza, by J. Bergmann.

SPECIAL COLLECTIONS SPINOZA J-1 4928

Efros, Israel Isaac, 1890-
Wolfson's Philosophy of Spinoza; Bernard's Philosophy of Spinoza and Brunner. ₍1937₎
cover-title, ₍237₎-248 p. 25cm.

Reviews of the above-mentioned books.
From the Jewish quarterly review, New series, vol. XXVII, no. 3, January 1937.

J-1 4933

₍Erdmann, Johann Eduard₎ 1805-1892.
La philosophie de Leibnitz. Fragmens d'un cours d'histoire de la métaphysique donné dans l'Académie de Lausanne par C. Secretan. 1840. ₍1843₎
353-364 col.

Signed: Dr. Erdmann.
In Jahrbücher für wissenschaftliche Kritik, März 1843.
A review of this work, including references to Spinoza.

J-1
4734

Ernst, Simon, 1898-

ספר חדש על שפינוזה(שפינאָזא און זיין סביבה פון ד"ר יעקב שאצקי). [1928]

478-479 p.

Title transliterated: Sefer hadash ʿal Shpinozah ...

In Mizrakh u-maʿarab, v. 3, 1928.

A review of Jacob Shatzky's book.

NNJ

J-1
4735

Ernst, Simon, 1898-

שפינוזה לאור הססתורין העברי. (לרגלי הופעת ספרו של נחום סוקולוב על שפינוזה ותקופתו). [1929]

303-305 p.

Title transliterated: Shpinozah leʿor ha-mistorin ha-ʿibri.

In Mizrakh u-maʿarab, v. 3, 1929.

A review of Sokolow's book.

NNJ

J-1
4736

[Eucken, Rudolf Christof] 1846-1926.

Die Lebensgeschichte Spinoza's. In Quellenschriften, Urkunden und nichtamtlichen Nachrichten, von J. Freudenthal. 1899. [1898]

p. 7.

In Allgemeine Zeitung. Beilage, Nr. 279, 1898.

A review of Freudenthal's book.

J-1
4737

[Flanor, T T]

[Review of Spinoza, by Ernest Renan, an address given at The Hague. 1877]

62-63 p.

In De Nederlandsche spectator, 1877.

DLC

J-1
4738

[Flint, Robert] 1838-1910.

Philosophische Monatshefte, Bd. 12, Hfte. 4, 5, 1876. [1876]

556-558 p.

Signed: R. Flint.

In Mind, v. 1, 1876.

A review of this issue of the periodical, which includes a discussion of Opitz's article "Spinoza als Monist, Determinist und Realist".

J-1
4739

[Franck, Adolphe] 1809-1893.

Antécédents de l'hégélianisme dans la philosophie française; Dom Deschamps, son système et son école d'après un manuscrit et des correspondances inédites du XVIIIe siècle, par Emile Beaussire. 1865. [1866]

609-624 p.

Signed: Ad. Franck

In Journal des savants, année 1866.

A review of Beaussire's book.

J-1
4740

[Franck, Adolphe] 1809-1893.

La morale de Spinoza, examen de ses principes et de l'influence qu'elle a exercée dans les temps modernes, par René Worms. 1892. [1892]

333-347 p.

Signed: Ad. Franck.

In Journal des savants, année 1892.

A review of Worms' book.

J-1
4741

Frederiks, J G

Colerus' Leven van Spinoza herdrukt. [1880]

391-393 p.

In De Nederlandsche spectator, 1880.

A review of Korte, dog waaragtige levens-beschryving, van Benedictus de Spinosa, by Johannes Colerus; preface signed by M. F. A. G. Campbell.

DLC

J-1
4742

[Freudenthal, Jacob] 1839-1907.

K. O. Meinsma, Spinoza en zijn kring. Historisch-kritische studiën over Hollandsche vrijgeesten. 1896. [1898]

143-146 col.

In Deutsche Litteraturzeitung, 19. Jahrgang, 1898.

A review of Meinsma's book.

SPECIAL COLLECTIONS
SPINOZA

J-1
4743

[Freudenthal, Jacob] 1839-1907.

Kuno Fischer. Geschichte der neuern Philosophie. 2. Band. Spinozas Leben, Werke und Lehre. Heidelberg, 1898. [1899]

[300]-310 p. 25cm.

Signed: Freudenthal.

"Sonderabdruck aus Zeitschrift für Philosophie und philosophische Kritik. 114. Bd."

A review of Fischer's work.

NNC

[Freudenthal, Jacob] 1839-1907.
L. Busse. Ueber die Bedeutung der Begriffe essentia und existentia bei Spinoza. [1888]
113-115 p.

In Archiv für Geschichte der Philosophie, Bd. 1, 1888.
A review of Busse's article in Vierteljahrsschrift für wissenschaftliche Philosophie, Bd. 10, 1886.

Freudenthal, J. Die Lebensgeschichte Spinoza's in Quellenschriften, Urkunden und nichtamtlichen Nachrichten. 1899. [1899]
1700-1701 col.

In Literarisches Centralblatt für Deutschland, Jahrgang 1899.
A review of Freudenthal's book.

[Freudenthal, Jacob] 1839-1907.
Léon Brunschvicg: Spinoza. 1894. [1895]
111-114 p.

Signed: J. Freudenthal.
In Zeitschrift für Philosophie und philosophische Kritik, 106. Bd., 1895.
A review of Brunschvicg's book.

[Frothingham, Octavius Brooks] 1822-1895.
The Ethics of Benedict de Spinoza. From the Latin, with an introductory sketch of his life and writings. 1876. [1876]
p. 138.

Signed: O. B. Frothingham.
In Library table, v. 1, 1876.
A review of an American translation of Spinoza's work.

[Fullerton, George Stuart] 1859-1925.
La doctrine de Spinoza exposée et commentée à la lumière des faits scientifiques. Par Emile Ferrière. [1900]
289-290 p.

Signed: G. S. F.
In Psychological review, v. 7, 1900.
A review of Ferrière's book.

[Fullerton, George Stuart] 1859-1925.
Der junge Despinoza; Leben und Werdegang im Lichte der Weltphilosophie. Stanislaus von Dunin-Borkowski. 1910. [1911]
79-82 p.

In Journal of philosophy, psychology and scientific methods, v. 8, 1911.
A review of Dunin-Borkowski's book.

[Fullerton, George Stuart] 1859-1925.
Der junge Despinoza. Leben und Werdegang im Lichte der Weltphilosophie. Stanislaus von Dunin-Borkowski. [1911]
79-82 p. 26cm.

Signed: George Stuart Fullerton.
From the Journal of philosophy, vol. VIII, no. 3, February 3, 1911.
A review of Dunin-Borkowski's book.

Galliner, Arthur, 1878-
Der Jude Spinoza; eine Wiederbegegnung nach hundert Jahren. [1937]
p. 17. 48cm.

From Jüdische Bibliothek; Unterhaltung und Wissen. Nr. 39, 30. September 1937.
An article chiefly about Auerbach's Spinoza.

[Gebhardt, Carl] 1881-1934.
J. Lucio d'Azevedo, Historia dos christãos novos portugueses; Joaquim de Carvalho, Leão Hebreu filósofo; Carolina Michaëlis de Vasconcellos, Uriel da Costa. [Hagae Comitis, 1923]
361-365 p. 22cm.

Signed: Carl Gebhardt.
Reviews of the above-mentioned books.
Includes references to Spinoza.
With the author's Baruch de Spinoza, Ethik ... [1923]

[Gebhardt, Carl] 1881-1934.
Probleme der Teleologie bei Maimonides, Thomas von Aquin und Spinoza, von Peter Brunner. [1929]
533-534 p. 25cm.

Signed: Carl Gebhardt.
From Der Morgen, V. Jahrgang, 5. Heft, Dezember 1929.
A review of Brunner's work.

SPECIAL COLLECTIONS SPINOZA
J-1 4754

Gebhardt, Carl, 1881-1934.
Ein Weg zu Spinoza; unter Bezugnahme auf Stanislaus von Dunin-Borkowski S. J. Aus den Tagen Spinozas ... Erster Teil: Das Entscheidungsjahr 1657. ⌊1936⌋
⌊339⌋-344 p. 26cm.

A review of Dunin-Borkowski's work.
From Philosophia, vol. 1, 1936.

NNC

SPECIAL COLLECTIONS SPINOZA
J-1 4755

Gebhardt, Carl, 1881-1934.
Ein Weg zu Spinoza; unter Bezugnahme auf Stanislaus von Dunin-Borkowski S. J. Aus den Tagen Spinozas ... Erster Teil: Das Entscheidungsjahr 1657 ... 1933. ⌊1936⌋
⌊339⌋-344 p. 26cm.

A review of Dunin-Borkowski's work.
Pencilled note: Off-print: Philosophia, I, 1936 ⟨1937⟩
Bound with Gebhardt, Carl. Spinoza in der Schule. ⌊1930⌋

J-1 4756

⌊Geiger, Abraham⌋ 1810-1874.
Don Chasdai Crescas' religionsphilosophische Lehren in ihrem geschichtlichen Einflusse dargestellt von M. Joel. 1866. ⌊1866⌋
257-261 p.

In Jüdische Zeitschrift für Wissenschaft und Leben, 4. Jahrgang, 1866.
A review of Joel's book, including references to Spinoza.

J-1 4757

⌊Geiger, Ludwig⌋ 1848-1919.
⌊Review of Spinoza im Porträt, by Ernst Altkirch. 1913⌋
161-163 p.

In Allgemeine Zeitung des Judentums, Jahrgang 77, 1913.

NN

J-1 4758

⌊Gentile, Giovanni⌋ 1875-1944.
B. Spinoza, L'Etica - Della correzione dell'intelletto. ⌊1913⌋
139-140 p.

Signed: G. G.
In La Critica, v. 11, 1913.
A review of Mario Rosazza's translation of Spinoza's work.

J-1 4759

⌊Gentile, Giovanni⌋ 1875-1944.
Edmondo Solmi. - Benedetto Spinoza e Leone Ebreo. Studio su una fonte italiana dimenticata dello spinozismo. 1903. ⌊1904⌋
313-319 p.

Signed: G. G.
In La Critica, v. 2, 1904.
A review of Solmi's book.

J-1 4760

Gentile, Giovanni, 1875-1944.
Leone Ebreo e Spinoza. ⌊1923⌋
96-106 p.

From his Studi sul rinascimento. Firenze, Vallecchi ⌊1923⌋
A review of Benedetto Spinoza e Leone Ebreo, by E. Solmi.

J-1 4761

⌊Gentile, Giovanni⌋ 1875-1944.
Spinoza. - L'Etica: nuova traduzione dall'originale latino con introduzione e note di Erminio Troilo. ⌊1917⌋
47-52 p.

Signed: G. G.
In La Critica, v. 15, 1917.
A review of this translation of Spinoza's work.

J-1 4762

⌊Glogau, Gustav⌋ 1844-1895.
Ludwig Stein, Leibniz und Spinoza. Ein Beitrag zur Entwicklungsgeschichte der Leibnizischen Philosophie. 1890. ⌊1891⌋
1444-1446 col.

In Deutsche Litteraturzeitung, 12. Jahrgang, 1891.
A review of Stein's book.

J-1 4763

Glucksmann, Abraham, 1883-1943.
ברוך שפינוזה היהודי... ⌊1924⌋
5 pts.

Title transliterated: Barukh Shpinozah ha-yehudi.
In ha-ʿOlam, v. 12, 1924.
On the occasion of the publication of Jacob Klatzkin's book about Spinoza.

NNJ

Gluecksmann, Abraham, 1883-1943.

[1924] שפינאזא און בערגסאן (א פאראלעל).
38-40 p.

Title transliterated: Shpinoza un Bergson (a paralel)
In Bikher-velt, v. 3, no. 1-2, 1924.
A review of William Nathanson's book.

Goethe und Spinoza, 1783-86. Von Bernhard Suphan. (Sonderabdruck aus der Festschrift zur zweiten Säcularfeier des Friedrich Werder'schen Gymnasiums zu Berlin. 1882.) [1882]
p. 627.

In Philosophische Monatshefte, 18. Bd., 1882.
A review of Suphan's book.

Gorelik, Schmarja, 1877-1942.
Ein Spinozaroman. [1919]
169-174 p. 22cm.

From Neue jüdische Monatshefte, 3. Jahrg., Heft 7/8, Jan. 10/25, 1919.
A review of Erwin Guido Kolbenheyer's Amor Dei.

[Greenstone, Julius Hillel] 1873-
Judaica. Festschrift zu Hermann Cohens siebzigstem Geburtstage. 1912. [1914-15]
466-488 p.

Signed: Julius H. Greenstone.
In Jewish quarterly review, n. s. v. 5, 1914-15.
A review, in an article entitled: Three jubilee volumes, of the Cohen Festschrift which includes an essay "Spinozas Zusammenhang mit dem Aristotelismus" by Julius Guttmann.

Grützmacher, Richard Heinrich, 1876-
[Review of Führende Denker, by Jonas Cohn. 1921]
col. 217.

In Theologisches Literaturblatt, Jahrgang 42, 1921.

[Guzzo, Augusto] 1894-
Spinoza, Opera. Im Auftrag der Heidelberger Akademie der Wissenschaften herausgegeben von Carl Gebhardt. [1926]
219-223 p. 25cm.

Signed: Augusto Guzzo.
"Estratto dal Giornale critico della filosofia italiana, VII, 1926."
A review of Gebhardt's edition of Spinoza's works.

H., M.
Spinoza. [1899]
p. 23.

In Jewish chronicle, London, Dec. 29, 1899.
A review of Die Lebensgeschichte Spinoza's, by Jacob Freudenthal.

[Hallett, Harold Foster]
Aeternitas. To the editor of Mind. [1934]
275-278 p.

Signed: H. F. Hallett.
In Mind, n. s. v. 43, 1934.
A letter to the editor in reply to C. D. Broad's criticism of Hallett's book.

Halpern, J
Despinoza in neuer Beleuchtung. Analyse des Werkes: Stanislaus von Dunin-Borkowski S. J. Der junge De Spinoza. Leben und Werdegang im Lichte der Weltphilosophie, 1910. [1913]
45-71 p.

In Archiv für Geschichte der Philosophie, 27. Bd., Okt. 1913-Juli 1914.

Halpern, J
Despinoza in neuer Beleuchtung. Analyse des Werkes: Stanislaus von Dunin-Borkowski S. J. Der junge De Spinoza. Leben und Werdegang im Lichte der Weltphilosophie, 1910. [1913]
[45]-71 p. 22cm.

"Sonderabdruck aus dem 'Archiv für Geschichte der Philosophie', Bd. 27 H. 1."
Presentation copy to Carl Gebhardt, with author's inscription and signature.
Original paper cover bound in.

Harap, Louis
Harry Austryn Wolfson.- The philosophy of Spinoza; unfolding the latent processes in his reasoning. 1934. [1935]
543-546 p.

In Isis, v. 22, Dec. 1934-Feb. 1935.
A review of Wolfson's book.

Harry A. Wolfson: The philosophy of Spinoza. [1934]
p. 330.

In Jewish forum, v. 17, 1934.
A review of Wolfson's book.

[Hasse, Heinrich] 1884-1935.
Altkirch, Ernst. Spinoza im Porträt. 1913. [1914]
401-402 p.

In Kant-Studien, 19. Bd., 1914.
A review of Altkirch's book.

[Hauser, Otto] 1876-
Der junge de Spinoza. Leben und Werdegang im Lichte der Weltphilosophie. Von Stanislaus von Dunin-Borkowski. [1910]
244-246 p. 26cm.

Signed: Otto Hauser.
From Die Grenzboten, 69. Jahrgang, Nr. 31, 3. August 1910.
A review of Dunin-Borkowski's book.

Hauser, Otto, 1876-
[Review of Der junge De Spinoza, by Stanislaus Dunin-Borkowski. 1910]
244-246 p.

In Die Grenzboten, Jahrgang 69, Nr. 31, 1910.

[Heinemann, Isaak] 1876-
Guttmann, Julius: Die Philosophie des Judentums. [1933]
394-398 p. 23cm.

Signed: Heinemann.
A review of Guttmann's work.
From Monatsschrift für Geschichte und Wissenschaft des Judentums, 77. Jahrgang, Heft 5, September/Oktober 1933.
Includes a reference to Spinoza.

Heinrich, Wilhelm
Eines Spinozaforschers Lebensweg und Lebenswerk. [1935]
541-547 p.

In Scholastik, 10. Jahrgang, 1935.
An account of the work of Stanislaus Dunin-Borkowski.

Heinzelmann,
[Review of Spinozas Stellung zur Religion, by Georg Bohrmann. 1915]
col. 447.

In Theologisches Literaturblatt, Jahrgang 36, 1915.

[Henkel, M D]
Amsterdamer Brief. [1915]
14-18 col.

In Beiblatt der Zeitschrift für Bücherfreunde, n. F., 7. Jahrgang, 1915.
A review of Spinozahuis, Leyden. Catalogus van de boekerij der Vereeniging "Het Spinozahuis".

Herr, Lucien, 1864-1926.
Ludwig Stein. Leibniz und Spinoza. 1890.
Arnoldi Geulincx. Opera philosophica rec. J. P. N. Land. Vol. 1. 1891. [1892]
71-74 p.

In Revue critique d'histoire et de littérature, n. s. t. 33, 1892.
A review of these two works.

Hicks, George Dawes, 1862-1941.
Survey of recent philosophical literature. [1917]
147-152 p.

In Hibbert journal, v. 16, 1917.
Includes a review of Philosophical essays in honor of James Edwin Creighton (p. 147-148) which contains an essay "The confusion of categories in Spinoza's Ethics" by Ernest Albee.

Il problema della libertà e del male in Spinoza e in Leibniz (è il titolo promettente del libro di Ida Somma) [1935]
p. [292] 26cm.

Signed: G. R.
A review of Somma's book.
From Giornale critico della filosofia italiana, anno XVI, 2. serie, v. 3, maggio-giugno, 1935.
With Cohen, Renato. Spinoza nel terzo centenario della sua nascita. [1935]

Hicks, George Dawes, 1862-1941.
Survey of recent philosophical literature. [1921]
165-171 p.

In Hibbert journal, v. 20, Oct. 1921-July 1922.
Includes a review of Spinoza and time, by Samuel Alexander [1921] (p. 170-171)

Jakoby, Günther
Dr. M. E. Gans: Spinozismus. Ein Beitrag zur Psychologie und Kulturgeschichte des Philosophierens. [1909]
p. 275. 26cm.

From Zeitschrift für Philosophie und philosophische Kritik, Bd. 134, Heft II, März 1909.
A review of Gans' work.

A hundred notable books: 1934. [1934]
137-138 p.

In New republic, v. 81, 1934.
Includes The philosophy of Spinoza, by Harry A. Wolfson.

Janet, Paul, 1823-1899.
Un précurseur français de Hegel. [1865]
244-251 p.

In Revue des deux mondes, 35. année, 2. période, t. 58, 1865.
A review of Antécédents de l'hégélianisme dans la philosophie française, by Emile Beaussire.

[Husik, Isaac] 1876-1939.
Spinoza. [1924]
577-579 p.

In Jewish quarterly review, n. s. v. 14, July 1923-April 1924.
A review of Spinozas Leben und Lehre, by Georg Mehlis.

Jelke.
[Review of Johannes Colerus, by Johannes E. B. Blase. 1920]
col. 359.

In Theologisches Literaturblatt, Jahrgang 41, 1920.

[Husik, Isaac] 1876-
Studies on Spinoza. [1929]
305-312 p. 24cm.

Signed: Isaac Husik.
Reviews of v. 2-3 of Chronicon Spinozanum, of Ernst Altkirch's Maledictus und Benedictus, and of Leon Roth's Spinoza, Descartes and Maimonides.

[Joachim, Harold Henry] 1868-1938.
The oldest biography of Spinoza. Edited, with translation, introduction, annotations, etc. by A. Wolf. 1927. [1927]
403-405 p.

Signed: Harold H. Joachim.
In Journal of philosophical studies, v. 2, 1927.
A review of Wolf's edition of the biography attributed to J. M. Lucas.

J-1
4794

[Joachim, Harold Henry] 1868-1938.
Ad Spinozae Opera posthuma. Scripsit J. H. Leopold. 1902. [1902]
p. 579.

Signed: H. H. Joachim.
In Mind, n. s. v. 11, 1902.
A review of Leopold's book.

○

J-1
4795

Jordan, Bruno, 1885-
[Review of Die Schriften des Uriel da Costa, ed. and tr. by Carl Gebhardt. 1924]
88-90 col.

In Theologische Literaturzeitung, Jahrgang 49, 1924.

NNJ

○

J-1
4796

[Jülicher, Adolf] 1857-1939.
Ein moderner Gnostiker und Augustinus. [1920]
386-390 col. 34cm.

Signed: Adolf Jülicher.
A review of Augustinus redivivus.
Includes references to Spinoza.
From Die Christliche Welt, 34. Jahrgang, Nr. 25, 17. Juni 1920.

○

J-1
4797

Jung, Gertrud, 1894-
Hallett, H. F., Aeternitas. A Spinozistic study. [1933]
436-437 p. 25cm.

A review of Hallett's work.
From Kant-Studien, Band XXXVIII, Heft 3/4, 1933.

○

J-1
4798

[Karpeles, Gustav] 1848-1909.
Eine neue Biographie Spinoza's. [1904]
245-248 p.

In Allgemeine Zeitung des Judentums, Jahrg. 68, 1904.
A review of Spinoza, sein Leben und seine Lehre, I. Bd., by Jacob Freudenthal.

○

J-1
4799

[Kilpatrick, William Heard] 1871-
Spinoza's Short treatise on God, man and his well-being. Translated and edited, with an introduction and commentary and a life of Spinoza. A. Wolf. 1910. [1911]
164-166 p.

Signed: W. H. Kilpatrick.
In Journal of philosophy, psychology and scientific methods, v. 8, 1911.
A review of this edition of Spinoza's work.

○

J-1
4800

Klausner, Joseph, 1874-
ספרותנו ... המדעית. [1924]
466-468 p.

Title transliterated: Safruthenu ... ha-mada'ith.
In ha-Shiloah, v. 41, 1924.
A review of Jacob Klatzkin's Hebrew translation of Spinoza's Tractatus theologico-politicus, and of his Barukh Shpinoza.

NNJ

○

J-1
4801

Knight, William, 1836-1916.
[Review of Spinoza's Erkenntnisslehre in ihrer Beziehung zur modernen Naturwissenschaft und Philosophie, by Martin Berendt and Julius Friedländer. 1892]
296-307 p.

In Critical review of theological & philosophical literature, v. 2, 1892.

NN

○

J-1
4802

Koch, Max, 1855-1931.
[Review of Spinoza im jungen Goethe, by Robert Hering. 1898]
175-177 p.

In Freies Deutsches Hochstift, Frankfurt a. M. Berichte, n. F. Bd. 14, 1898.

DLC

○

J-1
4803

Kowalewski, Arnold, 1873-
[Review of Grosse Denker, by Ernst von Aster and others. 1913]
497-499 col.

In Theologische Literaturzeitung, 1913.

NN

○

J-1
4804

[Koyré, Alexandre] 1892-
Ethica more scolastico rabbinicoque demonstrata. A propos d'un livre récent. [1935]
282-294 p.

Signed: A. Koyré.
In Revue philosophique de la France et de l'étranger, 60. année, t. 120, 1935.
A review of The philosophy of Spinoza, by Harry A. Wolfson.

J-1
4805

Krivitzki, I

אַ נאַציִאָנאַל-פֿאַשיסטישע פֿאַלסיפֿיקאַציִע
פֿון ספּינאָזעס פֿילאָזאָפֿיע. [1932]
42-74 p.

Title transliterated: 'A natziyonal-fashistishe falsifikatziye fun Spinozes filozofye.
In 'Afn visnshaftlekhn front, no. 1-2, 1932.
An attack on the interpretation of Spinoza in books by S. I. Stupnitzky and N. Sokolow.

NNJ

J-1
4806

L., S. I. E.
Pantheism. [1926]
p. 14.

Signed: S. I. E. L.
In Jewish chronicle, London, Oct. 22, 1926.
A review of Pantheism and other essays, by Louisa E. Cohen.

NNJ

J-1
4807

[Lagneau, Jules]
Fr. Pollock. Spinoza, his life and philosophy. 1880. [1882]
306-315 p.

In Revue philosophique de la France et de l'étranger, 7. année, t. 13, 1882.
A review of Pollock's book.

J-1
4808

[Land, Jan Pieter Nicolaas] 1834-1897.
Leibniz und Spinoza. Ein Beitrag zur Entwicklungsgeschichte der Leibnizischen Philosophie von Ludwig Stein. 1890. [1891]
602-614 p.

Signed: J. P. N. Land.
In Philosophische Monatshefte, 27. Bd., 1891.
A review of Stein's book.

J-1
4809

Land, Jan Pieter Nicolaas, 1834-1897.
Nieuw licht over Spinoza en zijne eeuw.
's Gravenhage, Nijhoff, 1896.

OCH

J-1
4810

[Land, Jan Pieter Nicolaas] 1834-1897.
Nieuw licht over Spinoza en zijne eeuw.
[1896]
8 p. 21cm.

Signed: J. P. N. Land.
"Overgedrukt uit de 'Nederlandsche Spectator', 1896, no. 14."
Book review of Meinsma, Koenraad Oege. Spinoza en zijn kring.

J-1
4811

Land, Jan Pieter Nicolaas, 1834-1897.
De nieuwe uitgave der werken en de portretten van Spinoza. Amsterdam, 1884.
15 p.

OCH

J-1
4812

[Land, Jan Pieter Nicolaas] 1834-1897.
Spinoza: his life and philosophy, by Frederick Pollock. 1880. [1881]
131-137 p.

Signed: J. P. N. Land.
In Mind, v. 6, 1881.
A review of Pollock's book.

J-1
4813

[Land, Jan Pieter Nicolaas] 1834-1897.
Spinozas Entwicklungsgang, besonders nach seinen Briefen geschildert, von A. Baltzer. 1888. [1890]
76-91 p.

In Philosophische Monatshefte, 26. Bd., 1890.
A review of Baltzer's book.

J-1
4814

[Latta, Robert] 1865-
Spinoza: his life and philosophy. By Sir Frederick Pollock. Second edition. [1900]
241-252 p. 25cm.

Signed: R. Latta.
A review of Sir Frederick Pollock's book.
From the International journal of ethics, v. 10, 1900.

J-1
4819

[Lindsay, James]
Lydia Gillingham Robinson, "Spinoza's Short treatise on God, man, and human welfare". 1909. [1911]
266-267 p.

In Archiv für Geschichte der Philosophie, Bd. 24., 1911.
A review of Robinson's translation.

J-1
4815

[Lee, Arthur Bolles] 1849-1927.
Die Ethik des Spinoza im Urtexte, herausgegeben, etc., von Hugo Ginsberg. Der Briefwechsel des Spinoza im Urtexte, herausgegeben, etc., von Hugo Ginsberg. [1877]
273-274 p. 22cm.

Signed: Arthur Bolles Lee.
From Mind, v. 2, 1877.
A review of the two above-mentioned works.

J-1
4820

[Lovejoy, Arthur Oncken] 1873-
Recent literature in philosophy and ethics. [1904]
395-405 p.

Signed: Arthur O. Lovejoy.
In American journal of theology, v. 8, 1904.
Includes a review of Benoit de Spinoza, by Paul Louis Couchoud (p. 404-405)

J-1
4816

[Lee, Arthur Bolles] 1849-1927.
Die Lehre Spinoza's, von Theodor Camerer. 1877. [1878]
261-262 p.

In Mind, v. 3, 1878.
A review of Camerer's book.

J-1
4821

[Lülmann, Christian] 1861-
Die Affectenlehre Spinoza's. Von Joan Nenitescu. [1888]
366-367 p.

Signed: C. Lülmann.
In Philosophische Monatshefte, 24. Bd., 1888.
A review of Nenitescu's book.

J-1
4817

Levy, Solomon, 1872-
Benedict Spinoza. [1926]
p. viii.

In Jewish chronicle, London; Supplement, Feb. 26, 1926.
A review of Benedict Spinoza, by A. A. Gunn.

J-1
4822

[Lülmann, Christian] 1861-
J. Freudenthal: Spinoza, sein Leben und seine Lehre. Erster Band: Das Leben Spinozas. 1904. [1905]
214-215 p.

Signed: Lülmann.
In Zeitschrift für Philosophie und philosophische Kritik, Bd. 126, 1905.
A review of Freudenthal's book.

J-1
4818

Levy, Solomon, 1872-
Spinoza. [1924]
p. viii.

In Jewish chronicle, London; Supplement, March 28, 1924.
A review of Civilization and ethics, by Albert Schweitzer.

J-1
4823

[McKeon, Richard] 1900-
The philosophy of Spinoza, unfolding the latent processes of his reasoning. Harry Austryn Wolfson. 1934. [1936]
412-418 p.

Signed: R. McK.
In Journal of philosophy, v. 33, 1936.
A review of Wolfson's book.

J-1
4824

McKeon, Richard Peter 1900-
Spinoza. Band III. Aus den Tagen Spinozas ... II. Teil: Das neue Leben. Band IV. Aus den Tagen Spinozas ... III. Teil: Das Lebenswerk von Stanislaus von Dunin Borkowski. 1937.
380-383 p. 26cm.

Signed: R. McK.
A review of Dunin Borkowski's book.
From the Journal of Philosophy, vol. XXXIV, no. 14, July 8, 1937.

J-1
4825

Man and free-will. [1928]
p. 328.

In The Times [London] Literary supplement, v. 27, 1928.
A review of The unique status of man, by Herbert Wildon Carr.

J-1
4826

Martineau's Spinoza. [1883]
506-507 p.

In The Saturday review, London, v. 55, 1883.
A review of A study of Spinoza, by James Martineau.

J-1
4827

Martinetti, Piero 1872-1943.
Celestino Pulcini. L'Etica de Spinoza. Studio critico, gnoscologico, storico. 1914. 1915.
242-245 p.

In Rivista di filosofia, anno 7, 1915.
A review of Pulcini's book.

J-1
4828

[Meijer, Willem] 1842-1926.
Bespreking van prof. B. J. H. Ovink's Spinoza. [1914]
471-474 p.

Signed: W. M.
In Tijdschrift voor wijsbegeerte, jaargang 8, 1914.

J-1
4829

[Meijer, Willem] 1842-1926.
J. Freudenthal, Die Lebensgeschichte Spinoza's, in Quellenschriften, Urkunden und nichtamtlichen Nachrichten. 1899. [1899]
123-126 col.

Signed: W. Meijer.
In Museum. Maandblad voor philologie en geschiedenis, 7. Jaargang, 1899.
A review of Freudenthal's book.

J-1
4830

[Meijer, Willem] 1842-1926.
K. O. Meinsma: Spinoza en zijn kring. Historisch-kritische studiën over Hollandische vrijgeesten (Spinoza und seine Umgebung. Historisch-kritische Studien über holländische Freigeister). 1896. [1898]
124-127 p.

Signed: W. Meyer.
In Zeitschrift für Philosophie und philosophische Kritik, Bd. 113, 1898.
A review of Meinsma's book.

J-1
4831

Meijer, Willem, 1842-1926.
Over de kemmerkende eigenschappen van der leer van Spinoza. [1906]
153-169 p.

In De XXe eeuw, 12. jaargang, 1906.
A review of Einführing in die Metaphysik auf Grundlage der Erfahrung, by Gerardus Heymans, in which Spinoza is discussed.

J-1
4832

[Meijer, Willem] 1842-1926.
[Review of Spinozistisch en modern parallelisme, by Gerardus Heymans. 1915]
366-368 p.

In Tijdschrift voor wijsbegeerte, jaargang 9, 1915.

J-1
4833

[Meijer, Willem] 1842-1926.
Spinoza, Jacobi, Lessing; ein Beitrag zur Geschichte der deutschen Literatur und Philosophie im 18. Jahrhundert. F. C. van Stockum. [1917]
108-110 p. 25cm.

Signed: W. M.
A review of Van Stockum's book.
From Tijdschrift voor wijsbergeerte, 11. jaarg., 1. aflevering, Jan. 1917.

VOLUME OF PAMPHLETS

J-1
4834

ₑMeijer, Willemₑ 1842-1926.
Spinoza's beoordeeling en invloed in Duitschland van 1677 tot 1750. Dr. Th. C. van Stockum. ₑ1917ₑ
110-111 p. 25cm.

Signed: W. M.
A review of Van Stockum's book.
From Tijdschrift voor wijsbegeerte, 11. jaarg., 1. aflevering, Jan. 1917.
Volume of pamphlets.

NNC

J-1
4839

Meunier, F
ₑReview of Réfutation inédite de Spinoza, by G. W. Leibniz. 1854ₑ
153-154 p.

In Revue contemporaine, t. 4, 1854.

NN

J-1
4835

ₑMeijer, Willemₑ 1842-
Spinoza's Ethica; analyse og karakteristik af Harald Høffding. ₑ1921ₑ
303-314 p. 22cm.

Signed: Dr. W. Meijer.
Cover-title: Dissertatio ex Chronici Spinozani tomo primo separatim edita.
A review of Höffding's book.

J-1
4840

ₑMeyer, W ₑ
H. Høffding, Spinoza's Ethica. ₑ1919ₑ
265-271 col.

Signed: W. Meyer.
In Museum. Maandblad voor philologie en geschiedenis, 26. jaargang, 1919.
A review of Høffding's book.

J-1
4836

Meinsma, Koenraad Oege, 1865-
Over Spinoza: J. Freudenthal, die Lebensgeschichte Spinoza's in Quellenschriften, Urkunden und nichtamtlichen Nachrichten. ₑ1899ₑ
4 p. 20cm.

A review of Freudenthal's book.
"Overgedrukt uit 'de Kroniek' van Zondag 19 Maart 1899."

J-1
4841

ₑMillas y Vallicrosa, José Maríaₑ 1897-
Wolfson, H. A., The philosophy of Spinoza, unfolding the latent processes of his reasoning. 1934. ₑ1934ₑ
438-440 p.

Signed: J. M. V.
In al-Andalus, v. 2, 1934.
A review of Wolfson's book.

J-1
4837

Meinsma, Koenraad Oege, 1865-1929.
Over Spinoza: J. Freudenthal, Die Lebensgeschichte Spinoza's in Quellenschriften, Urkunden und nichtamtlichen Nachrichten. ₑ1899ₑ
92-93 p. 41x31cm.

From De kroniek, no. 221 (5. jaargang) 19 maart, 1899.
A review of Freudenthal's book.

J-1
4842

Muenz, Bernhard, 1856-1919.
Eine neue Spinoza-Biographie. ₑ1905ₑ
129-134, 191-196 col.

In Ost und West, 5. Jahrgang, 1905.
A review of Spinoza, sein Leben und seine Lehre. 1. Bd., by Jacob Freudenthal.

J-1
4838

ₑMeinsma, Koenraad Oegeₑ 1865-1929.
Over Spinoza. ₑ1899ₑ
3 p.

In De Kroniek, Sept. 24, 1899.
A review of Spinoza, by Frederick Pollock.

NBuG

J-1
4843

Mulder, W
De jeugd van Despinoza. ₑ1911-13ₑ
5 pts.

In Studien. Tijdschrift voor godsdienst, wetenschap en letteren, jaargang 44-45, dl. 77-79, 1911-13.
A study of Der junge De Spinoza, by Stanislaus Dunin-Borkowski.

ICU

Murti, T R V
[Review of The philosophy of Spinoza, by Harry A. Wolfson. 1935]
180-197 p.

In The Philosophical quarterly, v. 11, 1935.

Muth, Karl, 1867-
Spinoza-Renaissance. [1933]
[346]-351 p. 25cm.

A review of Stanislaus von Dunin-Borkowski's Spinoza nach dreihundert Jahren.
From Hochland, Januar 1933.

[N., E.]
[Review of The philosophy of Spinoza, by Harry A. Wolfson. 1934]
p. 2.

Signed: E. N.
In Boston evening transcript, May 29, 1934.

Natural plays and made pieces. [1932]
p. 461.

In The Times. [London] Literary supplement, v. 31, 1932.
Includes a review of Spinoza: the maker of lenses, by J. Alexander Gunn.

Noble, Edmund, 1853-1937.
Recent books I like. [1934]
p. 4.

In Boston transcript; book section, Dec. 22, 1934.
Includes The philosophy of Spinoza, by Harry A. Wolfson.

Panter, Peter
L'Esprit. [1926]
389-391 p. 22cm.

From Die Weltbühne, XXII. Jahrgang, no. 36, 7. September 1926.
A review of the first issue of the periodical L'Esprit.
Includes a reference to Spinoza.

Paret, Hans,
Pflaum, Heinz. Die Idee der Liebe. Leone Ebreo. Zwei Abhandlungen zur Geschichte der Philosophie in der Renaissance. [1931]
p. 179. 25cm.

A review of Pflaum's work.
From Kant-Studien, Band XXXVI, Heft 1/2, 1931.
Bound with Paret, Hans. Leone Ebreo, Dialoghi d'amore ... [1931]

[Patton, Francis Landey] 1843-1932.
A study of Spinoza. By James Martineau. 1882. [1883]
901-903 p.

Signed: F. L. Patton.
In Presbyterian review, v. 4, 1883.
A review of Martineau's book.

Paulsen, Friedrich, 1846-1908.
Zu Hemans "Kant und Spinoza". [1901]
[471]-472 p. 24cm.

A review of Heman's book.
From Kantstudien, Band V, Heft 4, 1901.

1. Heman, Karl Friedrich, 1839- Kant und Spinoza. 2. Spinoza, Benedictus de, 1632-1677.

Pearson, Karl, 1857-1936.
Martineau's "Spinoza". [1882]
114-116 p.

In Cambridge review, v. 4, 1882-83.
A review of Martineau's book.

J-1
4854

Pearson, Karl, 1857-1936.
Pollock's Spinoza. [1880]
94-96 p.

In Cambridge review, v. 2, 1880-81.
A review of Pollock's book.

DLC

J-1
4855

[Peirce, Charles Santiago Sanders] 1839-1914.
Spinoza's political and ethical philosophy. By Robert A. Duff. [1904]
p. 63.

In The Nation, v. 79, 1904.
A review of Duff's book.

J-1
4856

[Peirce, Charles Santiago Sanders] 1839-1914.
A study of the Ethics of Spinoza. By Harold H. Joachim. 1901. [1902]
36-37 p.

In The Nation, v. 75, 1902.
A review of Joachim's book.

J-1
4857

[Petersdorff, Egon von] 1892-
Gabriel Huan: Le Dieu de Spinoza. [Hagae Comitis, 1922]
[262]-265 p. 22cm.

Signed: Egon v. Petersdorff.
A review of Huan's book.
Cover-title: Dissertatio ex Chronici Spinozani tomo secundo separatim edita.

J-1
4858

Philosophische aanmerkingen ontrent de Christelyke religie ... C'est à dire, Reflexions philosophiques sur la religion chrétienne, par G. F. Meier ... Traduite de l'allemand par J. G. van Haar. Tome 1. 1763. [1763]
406-434 p.

In Bibliotheque des sciences et des beaux arts, tome 19., 1763.
A review of Meier's book, including references to Spinoza (p. 415-416)

J-1
4859

The philosophy of Spinoza, by Harry Austryn Wolfson. [1934]
p. 265

In Boston. Public library. More books, v. 9, 1934.
A review of Wolfson's book.

J-1
4860

The philosophy of Spinoza, unfolding the latent processes of his reasoning, par Harry Austryn Wolfson. 1934. [1935]
7-8 p.

In Revue de métaphysique et de morale, 42. année, Supplément, n° de juillet, 1935.
A review of Wolfson's book.

J-1
4861

Pīnĕḥās ben Amittay, pseud.?
"הגיוני שפינוזה". [1897]
52-53 p. 23cm.

Title transliterated: Heghyōnē Shpīnōzā.
Review of Salomon Rubin. Heghyōnē Shpīnōzā.
From Ner ha'maarabi (The Western light) vol. II, no. 1, July 1897.

J-1
4862

[Pollock, Sir Frederick, bart.] 1845-1937.
Der junge De Spinoza. Leben und Werdegang im Lichte der Weltphilosophie. Von Stanislaus von Dunin-Borkowski. [1910]
575-578 p. 25cm.

Signed: F. Pollock.
A review of Dunin-Borkowski's book.
From the English historical review, vol. XXV, no. 99, July 1910.

J-1
4863

[Pollock, Sir Frederick] bart., 1845-1937.
A new edition of Spinoza. 1880.
p. 311.

In The Academy, v. 18, Oct. 30, 1880.
A letter to the editor about a projected edition of Spinoza's works.

J-1
4864

Pollock, Sir Frederick, bart., 1845-1937.
[Review of A study of Spinoza, by James Martineau. 1883]
104-108 p.

In Mind, v. 8, 1883.

NN

J-1
4865

[Pollock, Sir Frederick] bart., 1845-1937.
[Review of Vom phantastischen Pessimismus zum freudigen Realismus: Schopenhauer und Spinoza, by Hermann Klencke. 1882]
454-455 p.

Signed: F. P.
In Mind, v. 7, 1882.

NN

J-1
4866

[Pollock, Sir Frederick] bart., 1845-1937.
Spinoza: sein Leben und seine Lehre, von J. Freudenthal. 1. Band: Das Leben Spinozas. 1904. [1904]
576-578 p.

Signed: Frederick Pollock.
In Mind, n. s. v. 13, 1904.
A review of Freudenthal's book.

J-1
4867

[Pollock, Sir Frederick] bart., 1845-1937.
Spinoza's political and ethical philosophy, by Robert A. Duff. [1903]
399-402 p.

Signed: F. Pollock.
In Mind, n. s. v. 12, 1903.
A review of Duff's book.

J-1
4868

[Pollock, Sir Frederick] bart., 1845-1937.
Spinoza's wijsbegeerte, door M. C. L. Lotsij. 1878. [1879]
431-439 p.

Signed: F. Pollock.
In Mind, v. 4, 1879.
A review of Lotsij's book.

J-1
4869

[Pollock, Sir Frederick] bart., 1845-1937.
A study of the Ethics of Spinoza, by Harold H. Joachim. 1901. [1902]
246-249 p.

Signed: F. Pollock.
In Mind, n. s. v. 11, 1902.
A review of Joachim's book.

J-1
4870

[Porges, Nathan] 1848-
Gebhardt, Carl: Die Schriften des Uriel da Costa mit Einleitung, Uebertragung und Regesten (Bibliotheca Spinozana Curis Societatis Spinozanae, T. II) [1923]
210-220 p. 22cm.

Signed: N. Porges.
A review of Gebhardt's book.
From Monatsschrift für Geschichte und Wissenschaft des Judentums, 67. Jahrgang, Heft 7/9, Juli/September, 1923.

J-1
4871

Prall, David Wight, 1886-1940.
Spinoza reconstructed. [1935]
476-477 p.

In Saturday review of literature, v. 11, 1934-35.
A review of The philosophy of Spinoza, by Harry A. Wolfson.

J-1
4872

Ravitch, Melech, 1893-
געגען דעם קריטיקער דוד איינהארן.
[Vienna, Union-Buchdruckerei, 1920]
15 p. (געגען און פאר. פאלעמישע בלעטער פאר קלארקייט, 1. העפט)

Title transliterated: Gegen dem kritiker David Einhorn.
Against David Einhorn's criticism of Ravitch's Shpinoza; poetisher priv in fir tsiklen.

J-1
4873

[Read, Carveth] 1848-1931.
Modern philosophy from Descartes to Schopenhauer and Hartmann. By Francis Bowen. [1878]
118-124 p. 22cm.

Signed: Carveth Read.
From Mind, v. 3, 1878.
A review of Bowen's work.
Includes references to Spinoza.

NNC

Recent novels. ₍1882₎
p. 8.

In New-York daily tribune, April 16, 1882.
Includes a review of Spinoza, by Berthold Auerbach, tr. by E. Nicholson.

Renouvier, Charles Bernard, 1815-1903.
La philosophie de Spinoza. Spinoza: his life and philosophy, by Frederic Pollock. ₍1881₎
₍33₎-40 p. 25cm.

A discussion of Sir Frederick Pollock's book.
From La Critique philosophique, politique, scientifique, littéraire, 10. année, no. 29, 20 août 1881.

Renan, Ernest, 1823-1892.
₍Review of Réfutation inédite de Spinoza par Leibniz, précédée d'un mémoire par A. Foucher de Careil. 1854₎
p. 383.

In L'Athenaeum français, année 3, 1854.

₍Review of Die Lebensgeschichte Spinoza's in Quellenschriften, Urkunden und nichtamtlichen Nachrichten, by Jacob Freudenthal. 1898₎
6-7 p.

In De Amsterdammer, Weekblad voor Nederland, 1898, no. 1121.

Renan on Spinoza. ₍1877-78₎
p. 27.

In The Reformer and Jewish times, v. 9, no. 3, 1877-78.
An account of an address by Ernest Renan at The Hague.

₍Review of Die Lebensgeschichte Spinoza's in Quellenschriften, Urkunden und nichtamtlichen Nachrichten, by Jacob Freudenthal. 1899₎

In Journal des débats, Paris, 11. sept. 1899.

Renouvier, Charles Bernard, 1815-1903.
Descartes, Spinoza et Leibniz. Spinoza: his life and philosophy, by Frederic Pollock. ₍1881₎
2 pts. 25cm.

A discussion of Sir Frederick Pollock's book.
From La Critique philosophique, politique, scientifique, littéraire, 10. année, no. 31, 3 septembre 1881, p. 72-80 and no. 34, 24 septembre 1881, p. 120-127.

₍Review of Führende Denker, by Jonas Cohn. 1921₎
col. 217.

In Theologisches Literaturblatt, Jahrgang 42, Nr. 14, 1921.

Renouvier, Charles Bernard, 1815-1903.
Les origines du spinosisme. Spinoza: his life and philosophy, by Frederic Pollock. ₍1881₎
₍49₎-57 p. 25cm.

A discussion of Sir Frederick Pollock's book.
From La Critique philosophique, politique, scientifique, littéraire, 10. année, no. 30, 27 août 1881.

₍Review of L'Esprit des loix, by Montesquieu. 1749₎
161-167 p.

In Nouvelles ecclésiastiques, ou mémoires pour servir à l'histoire de la constitution Unigenitus, pour l'année 1749.
Includes a reference to Spinoza (p. 161)

J-1 4884

[Review of Origines juris naturalis, by J. G. Wachter. 1704]
668-671 p.

In Unschuldige Nachrichten von alter und neuen theologischen Sachen, Bd. 4, 1704.

NjP

J-1 4885

[Review of Spinoza, by Berthold Auerbach]
[1882]
930-931 p.

In The Spectator, v. 55, London, 1882.

J-1 4886

[Review of Spinoza, by Sir Frederick Pollock; 2d ed., 1899] [1899]
209-210 p.

In The Nation, v. 69, 1899.

J-1 4887

[Review of The philosophy of Spinoza, by Harry A. Wolfson. 1938]
p. 34.

In Jeschurun; the organ of S. A. traditional Jewry, v. 2, 1938.

NN

J-1 4888

[Review of A study of Spinoza, by James Martineau. 1882]
1480-1481 p.

In The Spectator, v. 55, 1882.

J-1 4889

[Review of Spinoza and Cartesianism, by Leon Roth. 1923]
p. 13.

In Jewish chronicle, London, June 1, 1923.

NNJ

J-1 4890

[Review of Spinoza, Descartes & Maimonides, by Leon Roth. 1925]
p. 112.

In Journal of religion, v. 5, 1925.

NNJ

J-1 4891

[Review of Spinoza, sein Leben und seine Lehre, by Jacob Freudenthal. 1904]
488-490 col.

In Theologisches Literaturblatt, Jahrgang 25, 1904.

NNJ

J-1 4892

[Review of Spinoza nach dreihundert Jahren, by Stanislaus Dunin-Borkowski. 1932]
p. 452.

In Jüdische Rundschau, Jahrgang 37, 1932.

NN

J-1 4893

[Review of Spinoza's Erkenntnisslehre in ihrer Beziehung zur modernen Naturwissenschaft und Philosophie, by Martin Berendt and Julius Friedländer. 1893]
p. 204.

In Allgemeine Zeitung des Judentums, Jahrgang 57, 1893.

NNJ

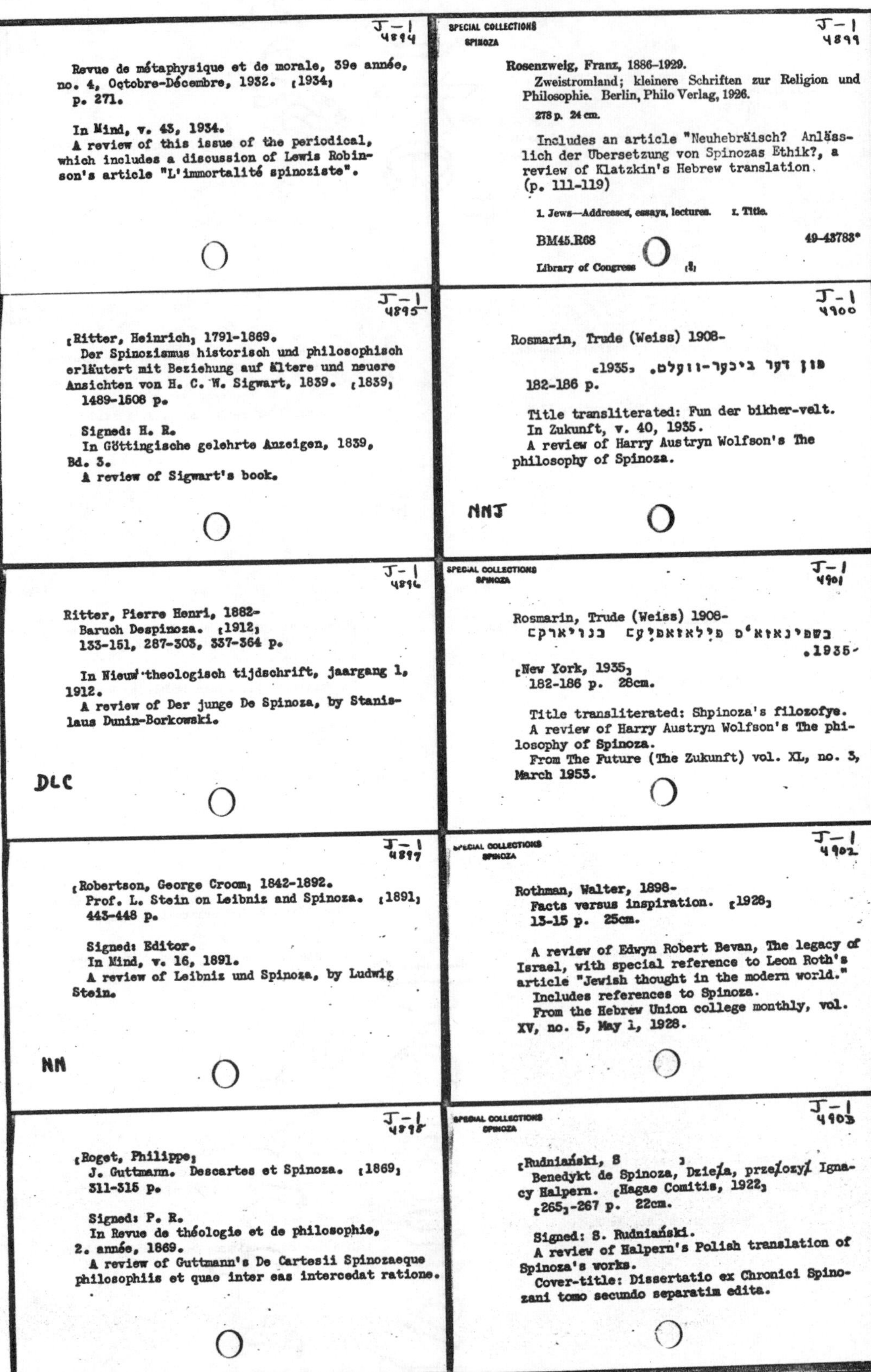

J-1
4894

Revue de métaphysique et de morale, 39e année, no. 4, Octobre-Décembre, 1932. [1934]
p. 271.

In Mind, v. 43, 1934.
A review of this issue of the periodical, which includes a discussion of Lewis Robinson's article "L'immortalité spinoziste".

J-1
4895

[Ritter, Heinrich] 1791-1869.
Der Spinozismus historisch und philosophisch erläutert mit Beziehung auf ältere und neuere Ansichten von H. C. W. Sigwart, 1839. [1839]
1489-1508 p.

Signed: H. R.
In Göttingische gelehrte Anzeigen, 1839, Bd. 3.
A review of Sigwart's book.

J-1
4896

Ritter, Pierre Henri, 1882-
Baruch Despinoza. [1912]
133-151, 287-303, 337-364 p.

In Nieuw theologisch tijdschrift, jaargang 1, 1912.
A review of Der junge De Spinoza, by Stanislaus Dunin-Borkowski.

DLC

J-1
4897

[Robertson, George Croom] 1842-1892.
Prof. L. Stein on Leibniz and Spinoza. [1891]
443-448 p.

Signed: Editor.
In Mind, v. 16, 1891.
A review of Leibniz und Spinoza, by Ludwig Stein.

NN

J-1
4898

[Roget, Philippe]
J. Guttmann. Descartes et Spinoza. [1869]
311-315 p.

Signed: P. R.
In Revue de théologie et de philosophie, 2. année, 1869.
A review of Guttmann's De Cartesii Spinozaeque philosophiis et quae inter eas intercedat ratione.

SPECIAL COLLECTIONS
SPINOZA
J-1
4899

Rosenzweig, Franz, 1886-1929.
Zweistromland; kleinere Schriften zur Religion und Philosophie. Berlin, Philo Verlag, 1926.
278 p. 24 cm.

Includes an article "Neuhebräisch? Anlässlich der Übersetzung von Spinozas Ethik?, a review of Klatzkin's Hebrew translation. (p. 111-119)

1. Jews—Addresses, essays, lectures. I. Title.

BM45.R68 49-43783*

Library of Congress [1]

J-1
4900

Rosmarin, Trude (Weiss) 1908-
פון דער ביכער-וועלט. [1935]
182-186 p.

Title transliterated: Fun der bikher-velt.
In Zukunft, v. 40, 1935.
A review of Harry Austryn Wolfson's The philosophy of Spinoza.

NNJ

SPECIAL COLLECTIONS
SPINOZA
J-1
4901

Rosmarin, Trude (Weiss) 1908-
שפינאזא'ס פילאזאפיע [ניויארק] 1935.
[New York, 1935]
182-186 p. 28cm.

Title transliterated: Shpinoza's filozofye.
A review of Harry Austryn Wolfson's The philosophy of Spinoza.
From The Future (The Zukunft) vol. XL, no. 3, March 1935.

SPECIAL COLLECTIONS
SPINOZA
J-1
4902

Rothman, Walter, 1898-
Facts versus inspiration. [1928]
13-15 p. 25cm.

A review of Edwyn Robert Bevan, The legacy of Israel, with special reference to Leon Roth's article "Jewish thought in the modern world."
Includes references to Spinoza.
From the Hebrew Union college monthly, vol. XV, no. 5, May 1, 1928.

SPECIAL COLLECTIONS
SPINOZA
J-1
4903

[Rudniański, S]
Benedykt de Spinoza, Dzieła, przełożył Ignacy Halpern. [Hagae Comitis, 1922]
[265]-267 p. 22cm.

Signed: S. Rudniański.
A review of Halpern's Polish translation of Spinoza's works.
Cover-title: Dissertatio ex Chronici Spinozani tomo secundo separatim edita.

J-1
4904

[Samter, N]
Spinoza in Deutschland. Gekrönte Preisschrift, von Max Grunwald. 1897. [1898]
143-144 p.

Signed: N. Samter.
In Monatsschrift für Geschichte und Wissenschaft des Judenthums, 42. Jahrgang (n. F. 6. Jahrgang), 1898.
A review of Grunwald's book.

J-1
4905

[Schaarschmidt, Karl Max Wilhelm] 1822-1906.
Benedict de Spinoza's kurzer Tractat von Gott, dem Menschen und dessen Glückseligkeit, von Christoph Sigwart. 1870. [1870]
64-73 p.

Signed: C. Schaarschmidt.
In Philosophische Monatshefte, 5. Bd., 1870.
A review of Sigwart's book.

J-1
4906

[Schaarschmidt, Karl Max Wilhelm] 1822-1906.
Spinoza; his life and philosophy by Fred. Pollock. 1880. [1881]
363-367 p.

Signed: C. Schaarschmidt.
In Philosophische Monatshefte, 17. Bd., 1881.
A review of Pollock's book.

J-1
4907

[Schaarschmidt, Karl Max Wilhelm] 1822-1906.
Zur Spinoza-Litteratur. [1877]
524-529 p.

Signed: C. S.
In Philosophische Monatshefte, 13. Bd., 1877.
A review of ten works by and about Spinoza.

J-1
4908

[Scheller, Will] 1890-
Die Bibliothek der Philosophen. [1913?]
286-[290] p. 20cm.

Signed: Will Scheller.
A review of the series "Die Bibliothek der Philosophen" (München, G. Müller) of which Friedrich Heinrich Jacobi's Spinoza-Büchlein is the second volume.
From Der Brenner, 1913?

J-1
4909

Scherlag, Marek
Ein neuer Spinoza-Roman. [1907]
4-6 p.

In Die Welt, Vienna, 11. Jahrgang, 1907.
A review of Spinoza, by Otto Hauser.

J-1
4910

Schettler, Paul, Verlag, Cöthen.
Der Sokrates der Neuzeit u. sein Gedankenschatz; sämmtliche Schriften Spinoza's, kurz gefasst, mit Hervorhebung aller Lichtstrahlen [von M. Dessauer] [1884?]
[4] p. 18cm.

Reviews from various periodicals of Dessauer's work.

J-1
4911

[Seeligmann, Sigmund] 1877-1941.
De Joden in Nederland. Jac. Zwarts, Hoofdstukken uit de geschiedenis der Joden in Nederland. [1930]
5 p. 24cm.

Signed: Sigmund Seeligmann.
A review of Zwarts' book.
"Overdruk uit: Tijdschrift voor Geschiedenis, 45. jaargang, aflevering I, 1930."

J-1
4912

Seligkowitz, Benzion, 1864-
[Review of Versuch einer praktischen Kritik der Lehre Spinozas, by Alfred Nossig. 1901]
29-30 p.

In Juedisches Litteratur-Blatt, Jahrgang 25, 1901.

J-1
4913

Seligmann, Louis
Spinoza, ein historischer Roman von B. Auerbach. 1837. [1838]
27-28 p.

In Allgemeine Zeitung des Judentums, Jahr. II, 1838; Literarisches und homiletisches Beiblatt, No. 7.
A review of Auerbach's book.

J-1
4914

Seligman, Raphael, 1875-1943.

רשימות(פילוסופים והוגי-דעות...)

[1934]
321-325 p.

Title transliterated: Reshimoth ...
In Moznayim, v. 2, 1934.
A review of Joseph Klausner's Pilosofim, with references to the chapter about Spinoza.

J-1
4915

Sentimens chrêtiens touchant quelques questions de controverse entre les Catholiques & les Protestans, ou Lettre d'un homme desintéressé écrite au sujet de la réponse qu'on voit ici faite de la part de M. de la Chaise à la lettre que M. Spon lui a écrite & qui a ci-devant été donnée au public. 1686. [1686]
595-598 p.

In Nouvelles de la republique des lettres, May 1686.
A review of this book.

J-1
4916

Septimana Spinozana, Acta conventus oecumenici in memoriam Benedicti de Spinoza diei natalis trecentesimi Hagae Comitis habiti. 1933. [1934]
13-14 p.

In Revue de métaphysique et de morale, 41. année, Supplément, n° d'avril, 1934.
A review of this volume.

J-1
4917

Shemueli, Ephraim, 1908-

בשדה ספר(מסרת והיסטוריה) [1935]
502-504 p.

Title transliterated: Bisdeh sefer ...
In Gilyonoth, v. 2, no. 11-12, 1935.
A review of Harry Austryn Wolfson's The philosophy of Spinoza.

J-1
4918

[Siebeck, Hermann] 1842-1921.
Hering, Robert. Spinoza im jungen Goethe. 1897. [1899]
122-124 col.

Signed: H. Siebeck.
In Literaturblatt für germanische und romanische Philologie, 20. Jahrgang, 1899.
A review of Hering's book.

J-1
4919

[Siegel, Carl] 1872-
Gherasim, Vasile. Activismul lui Spinoza. 1928. [1930]
p. 318.

Signed: C. Siegel.
In Kant-Studien, 35. Bd., 1930.
A review of Gherasim's book.

J-1
4920

[Sigwart, Christoph von] 1830-1904.
Benedicti de Spinoza Opera quotquot reperta sunt. Recognoverunt J. van Vloten et J. P. N. Land. Volumen prius [-posterius] 1882-[83]
1340-1344; 185-190 p.

Signed: C. Sigwart.
In Göttingische gelehrte Anzeigen, [144.] Jahrgang, 1882, Bd. 2, p. 1340-1344; [147.] Jahrgang, 1885, p. 185-190.
A review of this edition of Spinoza's works.

J-1
4921

Silva Rosa, Jacob S da, 1886-
Carl Gebhardt, Die Schriften des Uriel da Costa mit Einleitung, Uebertragung und Regesten. [1924]
266-268 p. 26cm.

From Tijdschrift voor geschiedenis, 1924, no. 3.
A review of Gebhardt's edition of Acosta's works.

J-1
4922

Silva Rosa, Jacob S da, 1886-
M. H. Cohen, Spinoza en de geneeskunde. [1924]
268-269 p. 26cm.

From Tijdschrift voor geschiedenis, 1924, no. 3.
A review of Cohen's work.
With the author's Carl Gebhardt, Die Schriften des Uriel da Costa.

J-1
4923

Simcox, Edith
A study of Spinoza. By James Martineau. [1882]
307-308 p.

In The Academy, London, v. 22, 1882.
A review of Martineau's book.

[Singer, Isidore] 1859-1939.
Baruch Spinoza's relation to Judaism. [1904]
262-272 p. ports.

In New era illustrated magazine, v. 5, 1904.
A review of Spinoza, sein Leben und seine Lehre, 1. Bd., by Jacob Freudenthal.

[Singer, Isidore] 1859-1939.
Baruch Spinoza's relation to Judaism. [1904]
262-272 p. ports. 26cm.

Signed: Isidor Singer.
A review of Spinoza, sein Leben und seine Lehre. I. Bd., by Jacob Freudenthal.

[Siwek, Paul]
Intorno alla religione dello Spinoza. [1939]
368-377 p.

Signed: Paolo Siwek and Giorgio Radetti.
In Giornale critico della filosofia italiana, anno 20, 2. serie, v. 7, 1939.
A commentary by Siwek on Radetti's review of his Spinoza et le panthéisme religieux, and Radetti's rejoinder.

[Smidt, B J]
Spinoza en zijn kring. [1896]
513-524 p.

In De Dageraad, 17. jaargang, 1895-96.
A review of K. O. Meinsma's book.

Smith, Preserved, 1880-1941.
Shoes and ships and sealing-wax. [1921]
851-852 p.

In The Nation, v. 112, 1921.
A review of The encyclopaedia of religion and ethics, v. 11.
Includes a reference to the article on Spinoza.

Sokolow, Nahum, 1860-1936.

[1885] ספרות ישראל במשך השנה החולפת.
39-41 p.

Title transliterated: Safruth yisrael ...
In ha-ʿasif, v. 2, 1885.
A review of Salomon Rubin's Hebrew translation of Spinoza's Ethica.

[Sommer, Hugo] b. 1839.
Die Lehre Spinoza's, von Theodor Camerer. 1877. [1877]
696-704 p.

In Göttingische gelehrte Anzeigen, [139.] Jahrgang, 1877, Bd. 1.
A review of Camerer's book.

[Sorley, William Ritchie] 1855-1935.
Spinoza's Erkenntnisslehre in ihrer Beziehung zur modernen Naturwissenschaft und Philosophie. Allgemein verständlich dargestellt von Martin Berendt und Julius Friedländer. 1891. [1892]
132-136 p.

Signed: W. R. Sorley.
In Mind, n. s. v. 1, 1892.
A review of Berendt and Friedländer's book.

Spinoza. [1877]
p. 12.

In The Times, London, April 24, 1877.
An account of a lecture by Frederick Pollock at the Royal Institution on April 20, 1877.

Spinoza. [1877-78]
p. 3.

In The Reformer and Jewish times, v. 9, no. 11, 1877-78.
An account of a paper read by Sir Frederick Pollock before the Royal Institution of Great Britain, April 20, 1877.

J-1
4934

Spinoza. ₍1899₎
p. 140.

In The Saturday review, London, v. 88, 1899.
A review of Spinoza, his life and philosophy, by Frederick Pollock, 2d ed.; and of Ethic, tr. from the Latin of Benedict de Spinoza by W. Hale White, 3d ed., rev. and corr.

J-1
4935

Spinoza als Staatslehrer für die Gegenwart. ₍1864₎
p. 102.

In Deborah, Jahrgang 10, 1864.
A review of Spinoza's Staatslehre, by I. E. Horn.

OCH

J-1
4936

Spinoza and religion. By Elmer Ellsworth Powell. ₍1906₎
487-488 p.

In The Nation, v. 83, 1906.
A review of Powell's book.

J-1
4937

Spinoza - der Demokrat. ₍1932₎
p. 2.

In Prager Presse, Dec. 6, 1932.
A review of Spinoza; slavný a neohrožený filosof státního demokratismu, by J. Dvorský.

DLC

J-1
4938

Spinoza: his life and philosophy, by Frederick Pollock. 1880. ₍1880₎
440-441 p.

In Mind, v. 5, 1880.
A review of Pollock's book.

J-1
4939

Spinoza: his life and philosophy. By Frederick Pollock. ₍1880₎
668-669 p.

In The Athenaeum, Nov. 20, 1880.
A review of Pollock's book.

J-1
4940

Spinoza: his life and philosophy, by Sir Frederick Pollock; 2d ed. Ethic demonstrated in geometrical order; translated from the Latin of Benedict de Spinoza by W. Hale White; translation revised by Amelia Hutchison Stirling; 3d ed. rev. and corrected. ₍1899₎
7-8 p. port.

In The Academy, v. 57, July 1, 1899.
A review of these two books, with a portrait of Spinoza.

J-1
4941

Spinoza nach dreihundert Jahren von Stan. v. Dunin Borkowski. 1932. ₍1934₎
16-17 p.

In Revue de métaphysique et de morale, 41. année, Supplément, nº d'avril, 1934.
A review of Dunin-Borkowski's book.

J-1
4942

Spinoza, par Stanislaus von Dunin Borkowski. Bd. III, Aus den Tagen Spinozas. II. Teil: Das neue Leben. 1935. ₍1936₎
4-5 p.

In Revue de métaphysique et de morale, 43. année, Supplément, nº d'avril 1936.
A review of Dunin-Borkowski' book.

J-1
4943

Spinoza redivivus: Benjamin de Casseres. ₍Berlin, Tagebuchverlag, 1930₎
1277-1280 p. 21cm.

From Das Tagebuch, Jahrgang 11., Heft 32, August 1930.
At head of title: O. L.
A review of De Casseres' "Forty immortals", with a passage on Spinoza quoted in German translation.

J-1
4944

Spinoza's Staatslehre. Zum ersten Male dargestellt. Von J. E. Horn. 1851. [1851]
col. 594.

In Der Orient; Berichte, Studien und Kritiken, 12. Jahrgang, 1851.
A review of Horn's book.

J-1
4945

[Splettstösser, Willi] 1875-
Splettstösser, Willi. Der Grundgedanke in Goethes Faust. 1911. [1911]
509-510 p.

Signed: Willi Splettstösser.
In Kant-Studien, 16. Bd., 1911.
A notice by the author concerning his book.

J-1
4946

Spruijt, Cornelis Bellaar
Van Vloten's Benedictus de Spinoza beoordeeld door C. B. Spruijt. Utrecht, J. L. Beijers, 1876.
xi, 100 p.

Original paper covers bound in.

J-1
4947

Stearn, H T
Spinoza. [1881]
166-167 p.

In Cambridge review, v. 2, 1880-81.
A reply to Karl Pearson's article "Spinoza" in Cambridge review, v. 2, 1880-81.

DLC

J-1
4948

Stephan, Horst, 1873-
[Review of Die Auseinandersetzung Herders mit Spinoza, by Wilhelm Vollrath. 1912]
304-305 col.

In Theologische Literaturzeitung, Jahrgang 37, 1912.

NN

J-1
4949

[Stephen, Sir Leslie] 1832-1904.
Spinoza. [1880]
752-772 p.

In Fortnightly review, n. s. v. 28, 1880.
A review of Spinoza: his life and philosophy, by Frederick Pollock [1880]

J-1
4950

Strauss, David Friedrich, 1808-1874.
Charakteristiken und Kritiken; eine Sammlung zerstreuter Aufsätze aus den Gebieten der Theologie, Anthropologie und Aesthetik. 2. wohlfeilere Aufl. Leipzig, O. Wigand, 1844.
x, 459 p.

Includes a review of Spinoza; ein historischer Roman, by Berthold Auerbach (p. 448-453)

J-1
4951

Stupnitzky, Saul Isaac, 1876-1942.
ברוך שפינאָזא. אין צוזאמענהאנג מיט'ן ארויסגעבן זיינע ווערק אויף יידיש און העברעיש. [1925]
p. 3.

Title transliterated: Barukh Shpinoza ...
In Literarishe bleter, v. 1, no. 40, 1925.
On the occasion of the appearance of Hebrew and Yiddish translations of Spinoza's works.

NNJ

J-1
4952

Szold, Henrietta, 1860-1945.
[A critique of Isaac Mayer Wise's "The cosmic God"]
[1] p. 23cm.

Typewritten letter to A. S. Oko, with Henrietta Szold's critique copied from the Jewish messenger, March 20, 1881.
Includes references to Spinoza.

J-1
4953

[Tarozzi, Giuseppe] 1866-
L'evoluzionismo monistico e le idee-forze. L'évolutionnisme des idées-forces par Alfred Fouillée. 1890. [1890]
740-750 p.

In Rivista di filosofia scientifica, v. 9, 1890.
A review of Fouillée's book.

J-1
4954

Tocco, Felice, 1845-1911.
Delle opere pubblicate in Italia nel 1886 e 1887 intorno alla storia della filosofia. ‹1889›
‹141›-160 p.

In Archiv für Geschichte der Philosophie, Bd. 2, 1889.
Includes a review of La dottrina della realtà del mondo esterno nella filosofia moderna prima di Kant, by Alessandro Chiappelli.

J-1
4955

‹Tönnies, Ferdinand› 1855-1936.
Dr. August Baltzer: Spinozas Entwicklungsgang, besonders nach seinen Briefen geschildert. 1888. ‹1891›
129-132 p.

In Zeitschrift für Philosophie und philosophische Kritik, n. F. 98. Bd., 1891.
A review of Baltzer's book.

J-1
4956

Traité de la verité de la religion chrêtienne ‹par Jacques Abbadie› A Rotterdam chez Reinier Leers 1684. ‹1684›
857-858 p.

In Nouvelles de la republique des lettres, octobre 1684.
A review of Abbadie's work.

J-1
4957

Tumarkin, Anna, 1875-
Erich Becher: Der Begriff des Attributes bei Spinoza in seiner Entwickelung und seinen Beziehungen zu den Begriffen der Substanz und des Modus. ‹1909›
102-104 p. 29cm.

A review of Becher's work.
From Zeitschrift für Philosophie und philosophische Kritik, 135. Bd., 1909.

J-1
4958

Tumarkin, Anna, 1875-
Karl Gebhardt: Spinozas Abhandlung über die Verbesserung des Verstandes. ‹1909›
104-107 p. 29cm.

A review of Gebhardt's work.
From Zeitschrift für Philosophie und philosophische Kritik, 135. Bd., 1909.
With the author's Erich Becher: Der Begriff des Attributes bei Spinoza. ‹1909›

J-1
4959

‹Turner, J E ›
Beyond humanism: essays in the new philosophy of nature. By Charles Hartshorne. (1937) ‹1938›
357-358 p.

Signed: J. E. Turner.
In Philosophy, v. 13, 1938.
A review of Hartshorne's book.

J-1
4960

Ueber die Bedeutung der Einbildungskraft in der Philosophie Kant's und Spinoza's, von J. Frohschammer. 1879. ‹1880›
p. 153.

In Mind, v. 5, 1880.
A review of Frohschammer's book.

J-1
4961

‹Ulrici, Hermann› 1806-1884.
A study of Spinoza. By James Martineau. 1882. ‹1883›
151-153 p.

Signed: H. Ulrici.
In Zeitschrift für Philosophie und philosophische Kritik, 83. Bd., 1883.
A review of Martineau's book.

J-1
4962

Upton, Charles Barnes, b. 1831.
Dr. Martineau's and Mr. Pollock's Spinoza. ‹1882-83›
757-797, 137-176 p.

In Modern review, London, v. 3, 1882 and v. 4, 1883.
A review of A study of Spinoza, by James Martineau; and of Spinoza: his life and philosophy, by Frederick Pollock.

J-1
4963

‹Vexler, Feliciu›
Spinoza Briefwechsel. Lebensbeschreibungen und Gespräche. Übertragen und herausgegeben von Carl Gebhardt. 1914. ‹1915›
501-502 p.

In Journal of philosophy, psychology and scientific methods, v. 12, 1915.
A review of this edition of Spinoza's work.

J-1 4964

La vie de B. de Spinosa ... par Jean Colerus. 1706. La verité de la resurrection de Jesus-Christ, défendue contre B. de Spinosa, &c., par le même auteur ... de la même année. [1707]
102-109 p.

In Journal des sçavans, t. 36, 1707.
A review of these two works by Colerus.

J-1 4969

Vloten, Johannes van, 1818-1883.
Prof. Jhr. van der Wijck's Spinoza getoetst. Haarlem, W. C. de Graaff, 1877.
20 p.

OCH

J-1 4965

[Vivas, Eliseo]
Baruch or Benedictus. [1934]
222-224 p.

In The Nation, v. 139, 1934.
A review of The philosophy of Spinoza, by Harry A. Wolfson; and of Spinoza and Buddha, by Samuel M. Melamed.

J-1 4970

[Vloten, Johannes van] 1818-1883.
Schopenhauer, Kant en Spinoza. [1878]
506-513 p.

Signed: v. Vl.
In De Levensbode, 10. deel, 1878.
A review of Die Lehre Schopenhauer's; Versuch einer kurzen Darstellung ihres Inhaltes, by Ernst Eckstein.

J-1 4966

[Vloten, Johannes van] 1818-1883.
Goethe en Spinoza. [1878]
423-432 p.

Signed: v. Vl.
In De Levensbode, 10. deel, 1878.
A review of Die Beziehungen Goethe's zu Spinoza, by Georg Jellinek.

J-1 4971

[Vloten, Johannes van] 1818-1883.
Spinoza door een geloovig Franschman bekeken. [1867]
71-80 p.

In De Levensbode, 2. deel, 1867.
A review of Spinoza et le naturalisme contemporain by Jean Félix Nourrisson.

J-1 4967

Vloten, Johannes van, 1818-1883.
Ijselkout. Mengelingen en bijdragen. Deventer, A. ter Gunne, 1855.
viii, 256 p.

Includes "Spinoza en Leibnitz", a review of Réfutation de Spinoza par Leibnitz (p. 206-216); and "Spinoza en Shakspere", a review of Geschichte der neuern Philosophie, Bd. 1,Abt. 2, by Kuno Fischer (p. 217-221)

OCH

J-1 4972

[Vloten, Johannes van] 1818-1883.
Spinoza-waardeering in Engeland. [1878]
491-505 p.

Signed: v. Vl.
In De Levensbode, 10. deel, 1878.
A review of Spinoza, by Sir Frederick Pollock, a paper read before the Royal Institution of Great Britain, April 20, 1877.

J-1 4968

[Vloten, Johannes van] 1818-1883.
Mensch en dier; naar Schopenhauer en Spinoza. [1871]
110-121 p.

In De Levensbode, 4. deel, 1871.
A review of Die Solidarität alles Thierlebens; Vortrag gehalten am 31en Mai 1869, by Carl Rokitansky.

J-1 4973

[Vloten, Johannes van] 1818-1883.
Spinoza's vertoog over God en mensch. [1867]
460-471 p.

In De Levensbode, 2. deel, 1867.
A review of Spinoza's neuentdeckter Tractat von Gott, dem Menschen und dessen Glückseligkeit, by Christoph Sigwart.

J-1
4974

[Vloten, Johannes van] 1818-1883.
De wetenschappelijke aard van Spinoza's wijsbegeerte, door een Engelschman ontvouwd. [1873]
267-279 p.

In De Levensbode, 6. deel, 1873.
A review of The scientific character of Spinoza's philosophy, by Sir Frederick Pollock, an article in The Fortnightly review, v. 19, 1873.

J-1
4975

[Walsh, Francis Augustine] 1884-
The philosophy of Spinoza. By Harry Austryn Wolfson. 1934. [1934]
352-355 p.

Signed: Francis A. Walsh.
In The New scholasticism, v. 8, 1934.
A review of Wolfson's book.

J-1
4976

[Walsh, Francis Augustine] 1884-
Spinoza: nel terzo centenario della sua nascita. (Rivista di filosofia neo-scolastica: supplemento speciale al volume XXV, Agosto, 1933). 1934. [1935]
63-65 p.

Signed: F. A. Walsh.
In The New scholasticism, v. 9, 1935.
A review of this volume.

J-1
4977

[Webb, Clement Charles Julian] 1865-1954.
A history of mediaeval Jewish philosophy, by Isaac Husik. 1916. [1918]
102-108 p.

Signed: C. C. J. W.
In Mind, n. s. v. 27, 1918.
A review of Husik's book.

SPECIAL COLLECTIONS
SPINOZA

J-1
4978

Weiss, Paul, 1901-
The philosophy of Spinoza: unfolding the latent processes of his reasoning, by Harry Austryn Wolfson. [1934]
220-221 p. 34cm.

From the New republic, October 3, 1934.
A review of Wolfson's book.

NNC

J-1
4979

Wenzel, Alfred
Ein neues Spinozabuch. [1911]
19 p.

In Zeitschrift für Philosophie und philosophische Kritik, Bd. 143, 1911.
A review of Der junge de Spinoza; Leben und Werdegang im Lichte der Weltphilosophie, by Stanislaus Dunin-Borkowski.

J-1
4980

A wide choice for readers in the Christmas book lists; selected titles from recent months in fiction, biography, travel and other fields. [1934]
8-9, 39-42 p.

In New York times. Book review, Dec. 2, 1934.
Includes The philosophy of Spinoza, by Harry A. Wolfson.

J-1
4981

Wiernik, Peter, 1865-1936.

אונזער פיעל שפראכיגע ליטעראטור. [1934]
p. 6.

Title transliterated: Unzer fi'l shprakhige literatur.
In Morgen zhurnal (Jewish morning journal) May 13, 1934.
A review of Harry Austryn Wolfson's The philosophy of Spinoza.

NNJ

J-1
4982

[Wolf, Abraham] 1876-
[Letter to the editor. 1927]
p. 603.

Signed: A. Wolf.
In Journal of philosophical studies, v. 2, 1927.
A reply to Harold H. Joachim's review of Wolf's translation of The oldest biography of Spinoza, attributed to J. M. Lucas.

J-1
4983

[Wolf, Abraham] 1876-
Professor Freudenthal's "Spinoza". [1899]
490-495 p.

Signed: A. Wolf.
In Jewish quarterly review, v. 11, 1899.
A review of Die Lebensgeschichte Spinozas in Quellenschriften, Urkunden und nichtamtlichen Nachrichten, ed. by Jacob Freudenthal.

[Wolf, Abraham] 1876-
Prof. J. Freudenthal's "Life of Spinoza".
[1905]
390-396 p.

Signed: A. Wolf.
In Jewish quarterly review, v. 17, Oct. 1904-July 1905.
A review of Spinoza, sein Leben und seine Lehre, 1. Bd., by Jacob Freudenthal.

[Wolf, Abraham] 1876-
Spinoza and time, by S. Alexander. London, 1921. [1921]
321-324 p. 22cm.

Signed: A. Wolf.
A review of S. Alexander's book.
Cover-title: Dissertatio ex Chronici Spinozani tomo primo separatim edita.

Wolfson, Harry Austryn, 1887-
A case study in philosophic research and Spinoza. [1940]
cover-title, [268]-294 p. 24cm.

"Reprinted from The New scholasticism, vol. XIV, 3, July, 1940."
A critique of David Bidney's The psychology and ethics of Spinoza.

Wolfson, Harry Austryn, 1887-
Spinoza and his times. [1935]
306-307 p. 34cm.

From the New Republic, January 23, 1935.
A letter to the editor by Wolfson, in answer to Paul Weiss' review of his work "The philosophy of Spinoza" which appeared in the New Republic of October 3, 1934. Includes also Paul Weiss' reply.
With Weiss, Paul. The philosophy of Spinoza. [1934]

[Wolfson, Harry Austryn] 1887-
Spinoza, Descartes and Maimonides, by Leon Roth. [1925]
303-306 p. 25cm.

Signed: H. A. Wolfson.
A review of Roth's book.
From the Philosophical review, vol. XXXIV, 3, Whole no. 201, May 1925.

Wyzewa, Teodor de, 1862-1917.
Ecrivains étrangers. Deuxième série. Paris, Perrin, 1897.
364 p.

Includes "Les amis de Spinoza, d'après un ouvrage hollandais" (p. 319-343), a review of Spinoza en zijn kring, by K. O. Meinsma.

Wyzewa, Teodor de, 1862-1917.
La jeunesse de Spinoza. Der junge Spinoza, Leben und Werdegang im Lichte der Weltphilosophie, par Stanislas von Dunin Borkowski ...
[1911]
[449]-460 p. 25cm.

From the Revue des deux mondes, LXXXIe année, 6. période, t. 2, mars-avril 1911.
A review of Dunin-Borkowski's book.

Zangwill, Louis, 1869-
Pantheism modernised. [1921]
i-iii p. 38cm.

From Jewish Chronicle Supplement, July 1921.
A review of S. Alexander's "Spinoza and time".

Zifroni, Abraham, 1883-1933.

אגרות שפינוזה. [1921]
147-148 p.

Title transliterated: ʿIgeroth Shpinozah.
In Maʿabaroth, v. 3, 1921.
A review of Spinozas Briefwechsel ... übertragen von J. Bluwstein.

J-2
WORKS
IN TRANSLATION

[Aikins, Herbert Austin] 1867-
The principles of Descartes's philosophy. Benedictus de Spinoza. The philosopher's earliest work, translated from the Latin, with an introduction by Halbert Hains Britan. 1905. [1906]
302-303 p.

Signed: H. Austin Aikins.
In Journal of philosophy, psychology and scientific methods, v. 3, 1906.
A review of this edition of Spinoza's work.

SPECIAL COLLECTIONS SPINOZA
J-2 4994

Benedetto Spinoza: L'Etica. Della correzione dell'intelletto. Traduzioni di Mario Rosazza. [1914]
335-336 p. 25cm.

Signed: X. X.
From Estvdio, año II, tomo VI, núm. 14, febrero de 1914.
A review of Rosazza's translation.

J-2 4995

[Brunner, L]
Een wijsgeering codicil. [1871]
113-131 p.

Signed: L. B.
In De Gids, v. 35, 3. serie, 9. jaargang, 2. deel, April 1871.
A review of Benedicti de Spinoza "Korte verhandeling van God, de mensch en deszelfs welstand" ... Edidit et praefatus est Car. Schaarschmidt.

NNC

SPECIAL COLLECTIONS SPINOZA
J-2 4996

Ch. Appuhn: Oeuvres de Spinoza, traduites et annotées par. Tomo II: Traité theologico-politique. [1914]
387-388 p. 25cm.

Signed: X. X.
From Estvdio, año II, tomo VI, núm. 17, Mayo de 1914.
A review of Appuhn's translation.

J-2 4997

The chief works of Benedict de Spinoza. Translated from the Latin with an introduction, by R. H. M. Elwes. Benedik Baruch von Spinoza's Stellung zum Judenthum und Christenthum. Von Alfr. Chr. Kalischer. [1885]
p. 164.

In The Nation, v. 40, 1885.
A review of these two works.

SPECIAL COLLECTIONS SPINOZA
J-2 4998

Espinosa: Ética. Versión castellana de Manuel Machado. [1914]
148-149 p. 25cm.

Signed: A.
From Estvdio, año II, tomo VII, núm. 19, Julio de 1914.
A review of Machado's translation.

J-2 4999

Federbusch, Simon, 1890-
שפינוזה בעברית. [1923-24]
9-11 p.

Title transliterated: Shpinozah be'ivrith.
In ha-Tor, v. 4, no. 33, 1923-24.
A review of Jacob Klatzkin's Hebrew translation of Spinoza's Ethica, and of his Barukh Shpinoza.

NNJ

SPECIAL COLLECTIONS SPINOZA
J-2 5000

[Gebhardt, Carl] 1881-1934.
Baruch de Spinoza, Ethik, übersetzt von Otto Baensch [und] Benedicti de Spinoza Ethica. [Hagae Comitis, 1923]
[358]-361 p. 22cm.

Signed: Carl Gebhardt.
Reviews of the above-mentioned editions.
Cover-title: Dissertatio ex Chronici Spinozani tomo tertio separatim edita.

NNC

SPECIAL COLLECTIONS SPINOZA
J-2 5001

Gebhardt, Carl, 1881-1934.
Die Ethik Spinozas über Gott und Geist, von Benzion Kellermann ... [Hagae Comitis, 1923]
366-367 p. 22cm.

A review.
With the author's Baruch de Spinoza, Ethik ... [1923]

NNC

J-2 5002

[Guzzo, Augusto] 1894-
Spinoza, Opera, im Auftrag der Heidelberger Akademie der Wissenschaften; hrsg. von Carl Gebhardt. [1926]
219-223 p.

In Giornale critico della filosofia italiana, v. 7, 1926.
A review of this edition of Spinoza's works.

SPECIAL COLLECTIONS SPINOZA
J-2 5003

Kilpatrick, William Heard, 1871-
Spinoza's Short treatise on God, man and his well-being. Translated and edited, with an introduction and commentary and a life of Spinoza. A. Wolf. [1911]
164-165 p. 25cm.

Signed: W. H. Kilpatrick.
From the Journal of philosophy, v. VIII, no. 6, March 16, 1911.
A review of Wolf's edition of the Spinoza Treatise.

J-2 5004

Land, Jan Pieter Nicolaas, 1834-1897.
1. Spinozas Entwicklungsgang, besonders nach seinen Briefen geschildert, von A. Baltzer. 2. Inventaire des livres formant la bibliothèque de Bénédict Spinoza, publié d'après un document inédit ... par A. J. Servaas van Rooyen. [1890]
76-91 p. 22cm.

Reviews of the above-mentioned books.
From Philosophische Monatshefte, v. 26, 1890.

J-2 5005

[Land, Jan Pieter Nicolaas] 1834-1897.
Spinoza's Ethica in het Engelsch. [1894]
5 p.

Signed: J. P. N. Land.
Review of William Hale White's English translation of the Ethica.
"Overgedrukt uit 'De Nederlandsche spectator', 1894, no. 19."

J-2 5006

Land, Jan Pieter Nicolaas, 1834-1897.
Spinoza's Ethica in het Engelsch. [1894]
151-153 p.

In De Nederlandsche spectator, 1894.
A review of Ethic, tr. by W. Hale White, 2d ed., rev. & corr.

DLC

J-2 5007

Leopold, J H
Brievan van Spinoza. [1903]
339-341 p.

In De Nederlandsche spectator, 1903.
A review of Nachbildung der im Jahre 1902 noch erhaltenen eigenhändigen Briefe des Benedictus Despinoza, ed. by Willem Meijer.

DLC

J-2 5008

[Lewkowitz, Albert] 1873-
Lewis Robinson: Kommentar zu Spinozas Ethik. 1. Band. [1932]
178-180 p. 23cm.

Signed: Albert Lewkowitz.
A review of Robinson's book.
From Monatsschrift für Geschichte und Wissenschaft des Judentums, 76. Jahrgang, Heft 2, März/April, 1932.

J-2 5009

[Maccall, William] 1812-1888.
French criticism on Spinoza. [1865]
608-626 p.

In Fraser's magazine for town & country, v. 71, 1865.
A review of Oeuvres de Spinoza, par Emile Saisset. Nouvelle edition [1861]

J-2 5010

[Meijer, Willem] 1842-1926.
Spinoza's Ethica; analyse og karakteristik af Harald Høffding. [1921]
303-314 p. 22cm.

Signed: Dr. W. Meijer.
Cover-title: Dissertatio ex Chronici Spinozani tomo primo separatim edita.
A review of Höffding's book.

J-2 5011

[Peirce, Charles Santiago Sanders] 1839-1914.
Spinoza's Ethic. [1894]
344-345 p.

In The Nation, v. 59, 1894.
A review of Ethic, tr. from the Latin of Benedict de Spinoza by W. Hale White, 2d ed., rev.

J-2 5012

[Pollock, Sir Frederick] bart., 1845-1937.
[Review of Benedicti de Spinoza opera, ed. by J. van Vloten and J. P. N. Land, and of The chief works of Benedict de Spinoza, tr. from the Latin by R. H. M. Elwes. 1882-84.
455-456, 313-314 p.

Signed: F. P.
In Mind, v. 7, 1882; v. 9, 1884.

NN

J-2 5013

Ravà, Adolfo
Le opere di Spinoza. [1927]
[273]-316 p.

In Rivista di filosofia, anno 18, 1927.

J-2
5014

[Review of Ad Benedicti de Spinoza Opera quae supersunt omnia supplementum, ed. by J. van Vloten. 1864]
221-222 p.

In Historische Zeitschrift, Bd. 12, 1864.
Signed: v. Vl.

J-2
5019

Solomon, Hannah G
A sheaf of leaves. Chicago, Printed privately, 1911.
270 p. 23cm.

"Review of Spinoza's Theologico-politicus": p. 9-15.

J-2
5015

[Ritter, Heinrich] 1791-1869.
Ad Benedicti de Spinoza Opera quae supersunt omnia supplementum, 1862. [1862]
1841-1851 p.

Signed: H. Ritter.
In Göttingische gelehrte Anzeigen, 1862, Bd. 3.
A review of the supplement to Spinoza's works edited by Johannes van Vloten.

J-2
5020

Spinoza. [1882]
802-803 p.

In The Saturday review, London, v. 53, 1882.
A review of Benedicti de Spinoza Opera quotquot reperta sunt; recognoverunt J. van Vloten et J. P. N. Land, vol. prius; and of Spinoza, by Berthold Auerbach, tr. by E. Nicholson.

J-2
5016

[Ritter, Heinrich] 1791-1869.
Spinoza's neuentdeckter Tractat von Gott, dem Menschen und dessen Glückseligkeit. Erläutert und in seiner Bedeutung für das Verständniss des Spinozismus untersucht von Christoph Sigwart, 1866. [1867]
601-616 p.

Signed: H. Ritter.
In Göttingische gelehrte Anzeigen, 1867, Bd. 1.
A review of Sigwart's book.

J-2
5021

Spinoza: Briefwechsel. Uebertragen und mit Einleitung, Anmerkungen und Register versehen von Carl Gebhardt. [1914]
340-342 p. 25cm.

Signed: A.
From Estvdio, año II, tomo VIII, núm. 23, noviembre 1914.
A review of Gebhardt's edition of Spinoza's correspondence.

J-2
5017

Rosenzweig, Franz, 1886-1929.
Neuhebräisch? Anlässlich der Uebersetzung von Spinozas Ethik. [1926]
105-109 p. 25cm.

Review of Klatzkin's Hebrew translation of Spinoza's Ethics.
From Der Morgen, II. Jahrgang, 1. Heft, April 1926.

J-2
5022

Sternberg, Kurt, 1885-
Gebhardt, Karl. Spinoza. Vier Reden. [1931]
p. 178. 25cm.

A review of Gebhardt's work.
From Kant-Studien, Band XXXVI, Heft 1/2, 1931.
Bound with Paret, Hans. Leone Ebreo, Dialoghi d'amore ... [1931]

J-2
5018

[Simon, M]
Spinoza, his life and Treatise on God and man. Translated, with introduction and commentary, by A. Wolf. [1910]
89-91 p. 26cm.

Signed: M. Simon.
A review of Wolf's edition of the Spinoza Treatise.
From the Jewish review, vol. 1, no. 1, April 1910.

J-2
5023

Tumarkin, Anna, 1875-
Philosophische Bibliothek. Band 91. B. de Spinozas kurzgefasste Abhandlung von Gott, dem Menschen und dessen Glück. Aus dem Holländischen ins Deutsche übersetzt und mit einem Vorwort begleitet von C. Schaarschmidt. [1909]
p. 109. 29cm.

A review of Schaarschmidt's edition.
From Zeitschrift für Philosophie und philosophische Kritik, 135. Bd., 1909.

SPECIAL COLLECTIONS SPINOZA J-2 5024

Tumarkin, Anna, 1875-
Philosophische Bibliothek. Band 92. B. de Spinoza: Ethik. Übersetzt und mit einer Einleitung und einem Register versehen von Dr. Otto Baensch. ₑ1909ₛ
p. 110. 29cm.

A review of Baensch's edition.
From Zeitschrift für Philosophie und philosophische Kritik, 135. Bd., 1909.
With the author's Erich Becher: Der Begriff des Attributes bei Spinoza. ₑ1909ₛ

NNC

SPECIAL COLLECTIONS SPINOZA J-2 5025

Tumarkin, Anna, 1875-
Philosophische Bibliothek. Band 93. Baruch de Spinoza: Theologisch-politischer Traktat. Übertragen und eingeleitet nebst Anmerkungen und Registern von Carl Gebhardt. ₑ1909ₛ
108-109 p. 29cm.

A review of Gebhardt's edition.
From Zeitschrift für Philosophie und philosophische Kritik, 135. Bd., 1909.
With the author's Erich Becher: Der Begriff des Attributes bei Spinoza. ₑ1909ₛ

NNC

SPECIAL COLLECTIONS SPINOZA J-2 5026

Tumarkin, Anna, 1875-
Philosophische Bibliothek. Band 94. Baruch de Spinoza: I. Descartes' Prinzipien der Philosophie auf geometrische Weise begründet. II. Anhang, enthaltend metaphysische Gedanken. III. Aufl. Neu übersetzt und herausgegeben von Dr. Artur Buchenau. ₑ1909ₛ
p. 110. 29cm.

A review of Buchenau's edition.
From Zeitschrift für Philosophie und

CONTINUED ON NEXT CARD

NNC

SPECIAL COLLECTIONS SPINOZA J-2 5027

Tumarkin, Anna, 1875- Philosophische Bibliothek. Band 94 ... ₑ1909ₛ (Card 2)

philosophische Kritik, 135. Bd., 1909.
With the author's Erich Becher: Der Begriff des Attributes bei Spinoza. ₑ1909ₛ

NNC

SPECIAL COLLECTIONS SPINOZA J-2 5028

Tumarkin, Anna, 1875-
Philosophische Bibliothek. Band 95. Baruch de Spinoza: Abhandlung über die Verbesserung des Verstandes. Abhandlung vom Staate. III. Aufl. Übertragen und eingeleitet nebst Anmerkungen und Register von Carl Gebhardt. ₑ1909ₛ
107-108 p. 29cm.

A review of Gebhardt's edition.
From Zeitschrift für Philosophie und philosophische Kritik, 135. Bd., 1909.

NNC

J-2 5029

Verwey, Albert, 1865-1932.
Stille toernooien. Amsterdam, W. Versluys, 1901.
305 p.

Includes a review of Ethica van Benedictus de Spinoza vertaald door H. Gorter. 's Gravenhage, 1895. (p. ₍41₎-60)

K
NOTES ON AUTHORS

K 5030

Adler, Elkan Nathan, 1861-1946.
Dr. Jacob Freudenthal. ₍1907₎
p. 8. port.

In Jewish chronicle, London, June 14, 1907.
An obituary.

NNJ

K 5031

Bernfeld, Simon, 1860-1940.
Jakob Freudenthal. ₍1907₎
14-16 p.

In Die Welt, Vienna, 11. Jahrgang, 1907.

OCH

SPECIAL COLLECTIONS SPINOZA K 5032

Bettelheim, Anton, 1851-1930.
Berthold Auerbach; der Mann, sein, Werk, sein Nachlass. Stuttgart, J. G. Cotta'sche Buchhandlung Nachfolger, 1907.
x, 450 p. port. 23cm.

Includes references to Spinoza.

K 5033

Bradlaugh, Charles, 1833-1891.
The autobiography of Mr. Bradlaugh. A page of his life ... London, C. Watts ₍1873₎
24 p. 18½cm.
Portrait of author on half-title.

NN

Library of Congress DA565.B7A2 4-2669
₍a33b1₎

K 5034

[Bullen, Arthur Henry] 1857-1920.
Bertram Dobell. [1915]
165-166 p.

Signed: A. H. Bullen.
In The Nation, v. 100, 1915.

NNC

SPECIAL COLLECTIONS SPINOZA K 5039

Desmaizeaux, Pierre, 1673?-1745.
La vie de Mr. Bayle: par Mr. Des Maizeaux. Nouvelle edition ... A La Haye, Chez P. Gosse & J. Neaulme, 1732.
2 v. 17cm.

Includes references to Spinoza (v. 2, p. 325)

K 5035

Calamy, Edmund, 1671-1732.
Memoirs of the life of the Revd J. Howe. London, 1724.

NNUT

K 5040

Edelmann, Johann Christian, 1698-1767.
Selbstbiographie, geschrieben 1752; hrsg. von Carl Rudolph Wilhelm Klose. Berlin, Wiegandt, 1849.
xxviii, 457 p.

Includes a reference to Spinoza (p. 334)

SPECIAL COLLECTIONS SPINOZA K 5036

Camerer, Paul
Theodor Camerer, 1833-1909 [von Paul Camerer; Nachschrift von Professor D. Traub. Hagae Comitis, 1921]
285-289 p.

Sketch of the life of the Spinoza scholar.
Cover-title: Dissertatio ex Chronici Spinozani tomo primo separatim edita.

SPECIAL COLLECTIONS SPINOZA K 5041

Elbogen, Ismar, 1874-1943.
Moritz Steinschneider, der Vater der hebräischen Bibliographie. [1926]
155-158 p. port. 33cm.

"Sonderdruck aus den Soncino-Blättern; Beiträge zur Kunde des jüdischen Buches."

SPECIAL COLLECTIONS SPINOZA K 5037

Collins, William Lucas, 1817-1887.
Butler. Philadelphia, Lippincott, 1881.
177 p. port. 18cm. (Philosophical classics for English readers. [v. 2])

Bibliography: p. 176-177.

SPECIAL COLLECTIONS SPINOZA K 5042

[Gebhardt, Carl] 1881-1934.
Jacob Freudenthal (1839-1907) [Hagae Comitis, 1922]
199-219 p. 22cm.

Signed: Carl Gebhardt.
Cover-title: Dissertatio ex Chronici Spinozani tomo secundo separatim edita.

K 5038

Delbrück, Johann Friedrich Ferdinand, 1772-1848.
Der verewigte Schleiermacher. Ein Beytrag zu gerechter Würdigung desselben seinen Verehrern geziemend dargeboten. Bonn, A. Marcus, 1837.
130 p.

NN

SPECIAL COLLECTIONS SPINOZA K 5043

Gebhardt, Carl, 1881-1934.
Juan de Prado. [Hagae Comitis, 1923]
269-291 p. 22cm.

Cover-title: Dissertatio ex Chronici Spinozani tomo tertio separatim edita.
Bibliographical footnotes.

SPECIAL COLLECTIONS
SPINOZA
K
5044

[Geck, Rudolf] 1868-1936.
Carl Gebhardt. [1934]
[1] l. 26cm.

Signed: -ck.
"Sonderabdruck aus der Frankfurter Zeitung, Abdbl./I. Mgbl. vom 31. Juli 1934."
Includes references to Spinoza.
Volume of pamphlets.

NNC

SPECIAL COLLECTIONS
SPINOZA
K
5045

[Geiger, Abraham] 1810-1874.
Samuel David Luzzatto. [1866]
22 p. 21cm.

From Jüdische Zeitschrift für Wissenschaft und Leben, 4. Jahrg., 1866.
Includes a reference to Spinoza (p. 11)

K
5046

Howe, John, 1630-1705.
The works of ... J. H. ... With his funeral sermon by Mr. Spademan. To which are prefix'd, Memoirs of the life of the author, collected by E. Calamy. London, 1724.
2 v. port.

NNUT

SPECIAL COLLECTIONS
SPINOZA
K
5047

Jackson, Abraham Willard, 1843-1911.
James Martineau; a biography and study. Boston, Little, Brown, 1901.
x, 459 p. ports. 22cm.

Includes references to Spinoza.

SPECIAL COLLECTIONS
SPINOZA
K
5048

Jones, Sir Henry, 1852-1922.
Principal Caird; an address, delivered to the students of the Moral Philosophy Class on the opening day of the session 1898-99. Glasgow, J. MacLehose and Sons, 1898.
29 p. 23cm.

Speech in memory of the author of a work on Spinoza.

SPECIAL COLLECTIONS
SPINOZA
K
5049

Joseph, Horace William Brindley, 1867-1943.
Harold Henry Joachim, 1868-1938. [1938]
29 p. 26cm.

Includes references to Spinoza.
"From the Proceedings of the British Academy, volume XXIV."
Bibliography: p. 28-29.

K
5050

[Liebert, Arthur] 1878-1946.
Benzion Kellermann † (1869-1923). [1923]
486-490 p.

Signed: Arthur Liebert.
In Kant-Studien, 28. Bd., 1923.
An obituary of Kellermann including references to Spinoza.

K
5051

Masson, Flora
Robert Boyle; a biography. London, Constable, 1914.
ix, 323 p. port. 23 cm.

NN

K
5052

Minor, Jakob, 1855-1912.
Christian Thomasius. [1888]
9 p.

In Vierteljahrschrift für Litteraturgeschichte, 1. Bd., 1888.

K
5053

More, Paul Elmer, 1864-1937.
Shelburne essays. Fifth series. New York, Putnam, 1908.
v, 261 p. 19 cm.

Includes an essay "James Thomson ('B. V.')" (p. 170-195)

SPECIAL COLLECTIONS SPINOZA K 5054

[Obituaries, in German, of Carl Gebhardt. 1934]
4 articles in 1 v. 26cm.

Clipped from various newspapers.
Include references to Spinoza.
Volume of pamphlets.

NNC

K 5059

Salt, Henry Stephens, 1851-
The life of James Thomson ("B. V."), with a selection from his letters and a study of his writings. London, Reeves and Turner, 1889.
vi, 335 p. port.

SPECIAL COLLECTIONS SPINOZA K 5055

Oko, Adolph S 1883-1944.
Abschiedsworte von Adolf S. Oko, gesprochen bei der Trauerfeier am 30. Juli 1934. [1934]
[3] p. 21cm. in 26cm.

In honor of the deceased Carl Gebhardt.
Includes reference to Spinoza.
Volume of pamphlets.

NNC

SPECIAL COLLECTIONS SPINOZA K 5060

Schopenhauer-Gesellschaft.
Nachruf. Am 25. Juli 1934 starb in Frankfurt a. M. ... Carl Gebhardt ... [1935]
[1] l. 26cm.

From Jahrbuch der Schopenhauer-Gesellschaft, v. 22, 1935.
Volume of pamphlets.

1. Gebhardt, Carl, 1881-1934.

NNC

SPECIAL COLLECTIONS SPINOZA K 5056

Oko, Adolph S 1883-1944.
Abschiedsworte von Adolphe S. Oko, gesprochen bei der Trauerfeier am 30. Juli 1934. II. Aufl. [1934?]
[4] p. 21cm. in 26cm.

In honor of the deceased Carl Gebhardt.
Includes reference to Spinoza.
"Gedruckt in 200 Exemplaren."
Volume of pamphlets.

NNC

SPECIAL COLLECTIONS SPINOZA K 5061

Schopenhauer-Jahrbuch.
Zweiundzwanzigstes Jahrbuch der Schopenhauer-Gesellschaft für das Jahr 1935. Heidelberg, C. Winter, 1935.
ix, 455 p. port. 23cm.

Bio-bibliography of Carl Gebhardt (p. [401]-411) includes references to Spinoza.

SPECIAL COLLECTIONS SPINOZA K 5057

Oko, Adolph S 1883-1944.
In memoriam Carl Gebhardt (1881-1934) [1937]
[331]-338 p. port. 26cm.

Pencilled note by A. S. Oko: "Off-print: Philosophia, I, 1936 [1937]"
Includes references to Spinoza.
Volume of pamphlets.

NNC

SPECIAL COLLECTIONS SPINOZA K 5062

Scott, William Robert, 1868-
Francis Hutcheson; his life, teaching and position in the history of philosophy, by William Robert Scott ... Cambridge, The University press, 1900.
xx, 296 p. 23cm.

Includes a reference to Spinoza (p. 227)

1. Hutcheson, Francis, 1694-1746.

3—2011

Library of Congress B1503.S4 [38g1]

K 5058

Roest, Meijer, 1821-1890.
De "wetenschappelijke moraliteit" van dr. A. van der Linde een poosje maar to luchten gehangen, ten gerieve der lezers van diens Spectator-opstellen en boek over "De Haarlemsche Costerlegende". Amsterdam, Levisson, 1870.
vi, 50 p. 24 cm.

Includes a reference to Spinoza (p. 19-20)

K 5063

Seth Pringle Pattison, Andrew, 1856-
Alexander Campbell Fraser 1819-1914. [1915]
289-325 p.

In Mind, n. s. v. 24, 1915.

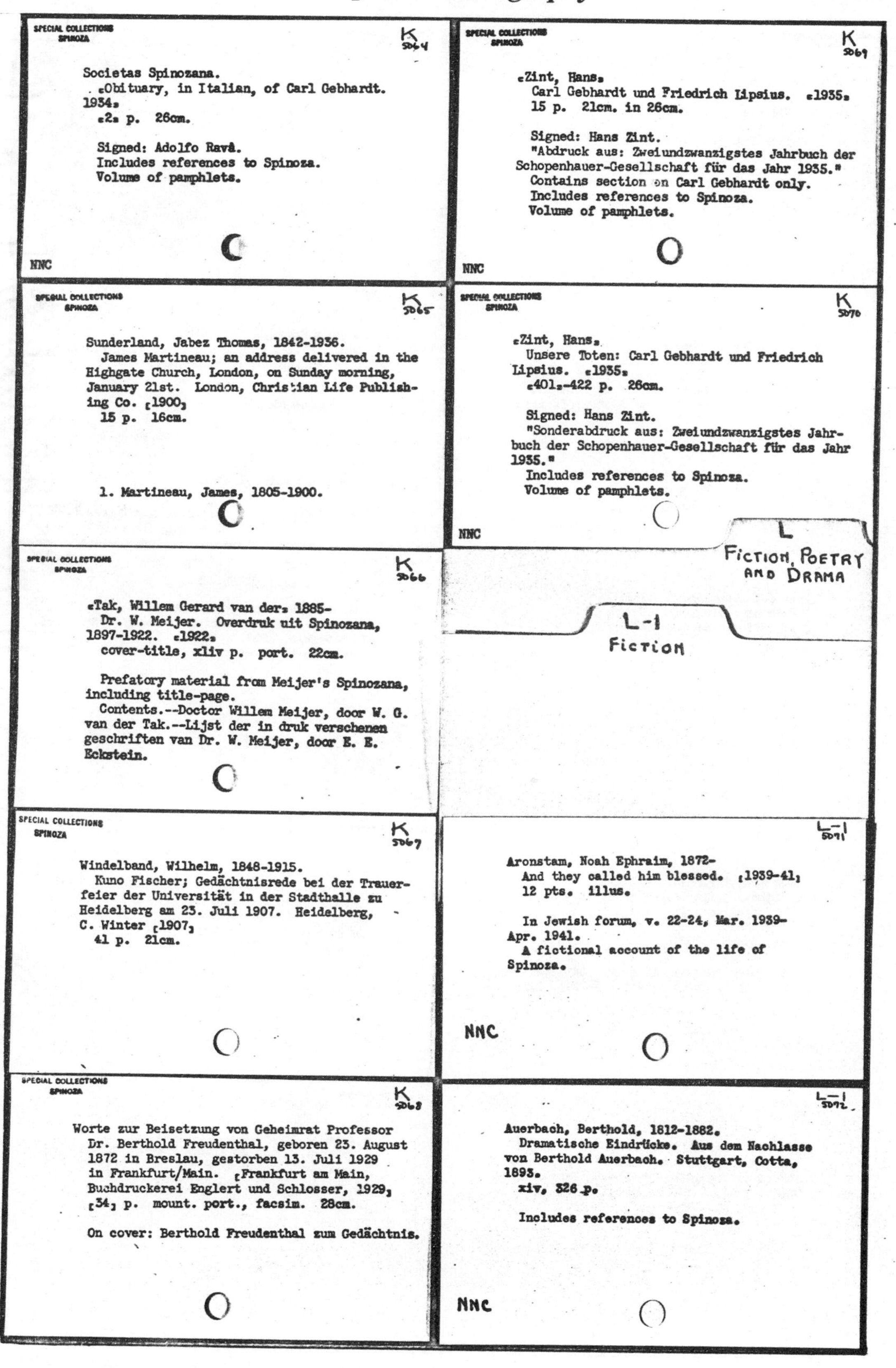

SPECIAL COLLECTIONS
SPINOZA
K 5064

Societas Spinozana.
[Obituary, in Italian, of Carl Gebhardt. 1934]
[2] p. 26cm.

Signed: Adolfo Ravà.
Includes references to Spinoza.
Volume of pamphlets.

NNC

SPECIAL COLLECTIONS
SPINOZA
K 5065

Sunderland, Jabez Thomas, 1842-1936.
James Martineau; an address delivered in the Highgate Church, London, on Sunday morning, January 21st. London, Christian Life Publishing Co. [1900]
15 p. 16cm.

1. Martineau, James, 1805-1900.

SPECIAL COLLECTIONS
SPINOZA
K 5066

[Tak, Willem Gerard van der] 1885-
Dr. W. Meijer. Overdruk uit Spinozana, 1897-1922. [1922]
cover-title, xliv p. port. 22cm.

Prefatory material from Meijer's Spinozana, including title-page.
Contents.--Doctor Willem Meijer, door W. G. van der Tak.--Lijst der in druk verschenen geschriften van Dr. W. Meijer, door E. E. Eckstein.

SPECIAL COLLECTIONS
SPINOZA
K 5067

Windelband, Wilhelm, 1848-1915.
Kuno Fischer; Gedächtnisrede bei der Trauerfeier der Universität in der Stadthalle zu Heidelberg am 23. Juli 1907. Heidelberg, C. Winter [1907]
41 p. 21cm.

SPECIAL COLLECTIONS
SPINOZA
K 5068

Worte zur Beisetzung von Geheimrat Professor Dr. Berthold Freudenthal, geboren 23. August 1872 in Breslau, gestorben 13. Juli 1929 in Frankfurt/Main. [Frankfurt am Main, Buchdruckerei Englert und Schlosser, 1929]
[34] p. mount. port., facsim. 28cm.

On cover: Berthold Freudenthal zum Gedächtnis.

SPECIAL COLLECTIONS
SPINOZA
K 5069

[Zint, Hans]
Carl Gebhardt und Friedrich Lipsius. [1935]
15 p. 21cm. in 26cm.

Signed: Hans Zint.
"Abdruck aus: Zweiundzwanzigstes Jahrbuch der Schopenhauer-Gesellschaft für das Jahr 1935."
Contains section on Carl Gebhardt only.
Includes references to Spinoza.
Volume of pamphlets.

NNC

SPECIAL COLLECTIONS
SPINOZA
K 5070

[Zint, Hans]
Unsere Toten: Carl Gebhardt und Friedrich Lipsius. [1935]
[401]-422 p. 26cm.

Signed: Hans Zint.
"Sonderabdruck aus: Zweiundzwanzigstes Jahrbuch der Schopenhauer-Gesellschaft für das Jahr 1935."
Includes references to Spinoza.
Volume of pamphlets.

NNC

L
FICTION, POETRY AND DRAMA

L-1
FICTION

L-1 5071

Aronstam, Noah Ephraim, 1872-
And they called him blessed. [1939-41]
12 pts. illus.

In Jewish forum, v. 22-24, Mar. 1939-Apr. 1941.
A fictional account of the life of Spinoza.

NNC

L-1 5072

Auerbach, Berthold, 1812-1882.
Dramatische Eindrücke. Aus dem Nachlasse von Berthold Auerbach. Stuttgart, Cotta, 1893.
xiv, 326 p.

Includes references to Spinoza.

NNC

SPECIAL COLLECTIONS SPINOZA L-1 5073

Auerbach, Berthold, 1812-1882.
Spinoza. [1837]
241-261, [300]-324 p. 23cm.

From Europa; Chronik der gebildeten Welt, 4. Bd., 1837.
Excerpts from the author's novel on Spinoza.

L-1 5074

Auerbach, Berthold, 1812-1882.
Spinoza. [1858-59]
6 pts.

In Revue germanique, v. 4-6, 1858-59.
A French translation of Auerbach's novel.

NjP

L-1 5075

Auerbach, Berthold, 1812-1882.
Spinoza. Stuttgart, Cotta, 1871.
xv, 284 p. 16 cm. (His Romane, 1. Bd.)

NNC

SPECIAL COLLECTIONS SPINOZA L-1 5076

Auerbach, Berthold, 1812-1882.
Spinoza. Ein Denkerleben. Neu durchgearb., stereotypirte Aufl. Mannheim, Bassermann & Mathy, 1854.
vi, 395 p. 19cm.

On cover: Zweiter Abdruck. Stuttgart und Augsburg, J. G. Cotta'scher Verlag, 1855.

SPECIAL COLLECTIONS SPINOZA L-1 5077

Auerbach, Berthold, 1812-1882.
Spinoza. Ein Denkerleben. Neu durchgearb., stereotypirte Aufl. Mannheim, Bassermann & Mathy, 1854.
vi, 395 p. 18cm.

SPECIAL COLLECTIONS SPINOZA L-1 5078

Auerbach, Berthold, 1812-1882.
Spinoza. Ein Denkerleben. [Stuttgart, J. G. Cotta, 1858]
2 v. 18cm. (His Gesammelte Schriften, 10.-11. Bd.)

Half-title.

L-1 5079

Auerbach, Berthold, 1812-1882.
Spinoza. Ein denkerleben. Von Berthold Auerbach. 4. aufl. Stuttgart, J. G. Cotta, 1860.
2 v. in 1. 18cm.
Vol. 2 has half-title only.

1. Spinoza, Benedictus de, 1632-1677.

NN
Library of Congress PT1812.A3S6 1860 15-20275
[s26c1]

SPECIAL COLLECTIONS SPINOZA L-1 5080

Auerbach, Berthold, 1812-1882.
Spinoza. Ein historischer Roman. Stuttgart, J. Scheible, 1837.
2 v. in 1. 17cm.

SPECIAL COLLECTIONS SPINOZA L-1 5081

Auerbach, Berthold, 1812-1882.
Spinoza; het leven van eenen denker. Naar de laatste op nieuw bewerkte uitgaaf uit het hoogduitsch. Met een voorberigt van D. Burger, Jr. Te Doesborgh, W. Becking, 1856.
xii, 386 p. 24cm.

SPECIAL COLLECTIONS SPINOZA L-1 5082

Auerbach, Berthold, 1812-1882.
Spinoza. Naar de vierde hoogduitsche uitgaaf bewerkt met toestemming van den schrijver. 's-Hertogenbosch, Van Heusden, 1875.
428 p. 20cm.

Auerbach, Berthold, 1812-1882.
Spinoza; a novel. From the German by E. Nicholson. New York, Holt, 1882.
v, 444 p. 17cm. (Leisure hour series, no. 135)

Auerbach, Berthold, 1812-1882.
Spinoza; a novel. From the German by E. Nicholson. Authorized edition. Leipzig, B. Tauchnitz, 1882.
2 v. in 1. 17cm. (Collection of German authors, 42-43)

Original paper covers bound in.

Auerbach, Berthold, 1812-1882.
Spinoza. Novelle. New York, G. Munro, 1881.
47 p. (Deutsche Library, no. 102)

Auerbach, Berthold, 1812-1882.
שפינוזה.
Warsaw, 1898.
171 p.

Title transliterated: Shpinozah.
A Hebrew translation by T. F. Shapiro of Auerbach's novel.

Auerbach, Berthold, 1812-1882.
שפינוזה; ספור מחיי הפילוסוף ברוך
די-שפינוזה והעתים אשר עברו עליו.
לפי המספר בספרו של הח' ברטהאלד אוי-
ערבאך בשפה אשכנז. מאת ט"ף שפירא.
ווארשא, הוצ' אליהו בערמאן, תרנ"ח.
[Warsaw, 1898.
171 p. 19cm.

Title transliterated: Spinoza.
Hebrew adaptation of Auerbach's novel by T. P. Schapiro.

Auerbach, Berthold, 1868-1925.
ברוך שפינאזא, נאך בערטהולד אוי-
ערבאך, פון ב. גארין.
New York, Hebrew Publishing Company, 1917.
136 p. 21cm.

Title transliterated: Borukh Shpinoza.
Yiddish adaptation of Auerbach's novel.

Bourget, Paul, 1852-1935.
שפינאזא. ניו-יארק, 1913.
[New York, 1913]
14-15 p. 31cm.

Title transliterated: Shpinoza.
From Di literarishe velt. The Jewish literary world, vol. 1, no. 6, Jan. 17, 1913.

1. Spinoza, Benedictus de, 1632-1677.

Dercksen, Jacobus Marinus Everhardus, 1825-1884
Een vondeling uit de zeventiende eeuw. Leiden, De Breuk & Smits, 1879.
3 v. in 1. 24cm.

Vol. 2 and 3 include references to Spinoza.
Ms. notes by Carl Gebhardt on flyleaf.

Dörfler, Peter, 1878-
Judith Finsterwalderin; Roman. 8. Aufl. München, J. Kösel & F. Pustet, 1925.
501 p. 19cm.

Includes references to Spinoza.

Gerchunoff, Alberto, 1883-
ברוך ספינאזא'ס ליבע [פון] אלבער-
טא גערשונאוו. פון שפאניש: יוסף מענ-
דעלסאן. בוענאס איירעס, ארויסגעגעבן
פון דער "סאסיעדאד העבראיקא ארכענטי-
נא", 1933.
[Buenos Aires, 1933]
92 p. port. 17cm.

Title transliterated: Baruch Spinoza's libe.
Yiddish translation of Gerchunoff's los amores de Baruj Spinoza.

L-1
5093

Gerchunoff, Alberto, 1883-
... Los amores de Baruj Spinoza. Buenos Aires, Biblioteca argentina de buenas ediciones literarias, 1932.
99 p., 1 l. incl. 1 illus., port. 16cm. (Babel, biblioteca argentina de buenas ediciones literarias)

Presentation copy to A. S. Oko, with the author's inscription and signature.

1. Spinoza, Benedictus de, 1632-1677—Fiction. I. Title.

33-36011

Library of Congress PQ7797.G4A65 863.6

L-1
5094

Grunwald, Max, 1871-
Monistische Märchen; aus einem Briefwechsel. Berlin, B. Harz, 1921.
199 p. 18cm.

Includes references to Spinoza.

L-1
5095

193Sp4
EG515 Gutzkow, Karl, 1811-1878.
Gesammelte Werke. Frankfurt am Main, Literarische Anstalt (J. Rütten) 1846.
v. 11-12 in 1. 17cm.

Vol. 11 includes a story "Der Sadducäer von Amsterdam" (p. [99]-170) in which Spinoza as a child appears as one of the characters.

1. Spinoza, Benedictus de, 1632-1677 - Fiction.

NNC

L-1
5096

Gutzkow, Karl, 1811-1878.
Uriel Acosta, der Sadduzäer von Amsterdam. München, H. von Weber [1922]
76 p. illus. 26cm. (Dreiangeldruck, 19)

Spinoza as a child appears as one of the characters.

Bound in leather.

1. Spinoza, Benedictus de, 1632-1677 - Fiction.

L-1
5097

Gutzkow, Karl, 1811-1878.
Uriel Acosta, der Sadduzäer von Amsterdam. München, H. v. Weber [1922]
76 p. illus. 26cm. (Dreiangeldruck, 19)

Spinoza as a child appears as one of the characters.

L-1
5098

Hauser, Otto, 1876-
Rasse und Rassenfragen in Deutschland. Weimar, A. Duncker [1915]
134 p.

Includes a reference to Hauser's novel about Spinoza (p. 106)

NN

L-1
5099

Hauser, Otto, 1876-
Spinoza; Roman. Deckel, Titelblatt und Buchschmuck von J. V. Cissarz. Stuttgart, A. Bonz, 1907.
392 p. 17cm.

L-1
5100

Hauser, Otto, 1876-
Spinoza; Roman. Stuttgart, Bonz, 1924.
312 p.

OCH

L-1
5101

Hauser, Otto, 1876-
Spinoza. Roman naar het Duitsch. Met toestemming van den schrijver vertaald door H. A. Lesturgeon. Met portret van Spinoza. Leiden, E. J. Brill, 1907.

OCH

L-1
5102

Hirsch, Leo, 1903-
... Gespräch im nebel; Leibniz besucht Spinoza, von Leo Hirsch. Berlin, Philo verlag und buchhandlung, g. m. b. h., 1935.
47 p. 18cm. (Philo-bücherei. nr. 2)

1. Leibniz, Gottfried Wilhelm, freiherr von, 1646-1716. 2. Spinoza, Benedictus de, 1632-1677. I. Title.

35-35656

Library of Congress B2597.H5
Copyright A—Foreign 28288
[2] 193.1

L-1 5103

Klencke, Hermann, 1813-1881.
Swammerdam; oder, Die Offenbarung der Natur. Ein kultur-historischer Roman. Leipzig, H. Costenoble, 1864.
3 v.

A novel dealing with Spinoza.
Second edition.

OCH

L-1 5104

Kohn, Ahron
הפרידה. ‏[1862]
105-108 p.

Title transliterated: ha-Pridah.
In Kokhbe yizhak, v. 28, 1862.
About Spinoza.

NNJ

SPECIAL COLLECTIONS SPINOZA L-1 5105

Kolbenheyer, Erwin Guido, 1878-
Amor Dei; ein Spinoza-Roman. [3. Aufl.] München, G. Müller, 1912.
389 p. 19cm.

L-1 5106

Kolbenheyer, Erwin Guido, 1878-
Amor Dei; ein Spinoza-roman. 45. Aufl. München, G. Müller, 1917.
v, 389 p.

MH

L-1 5107

Kolbenheyer, Erwin Guido, 1878-
Amor Dei; ein Spinoza-roman. 13.-17. Tausend. München, G. Müller, 1921.
388 p. 19 cm.

ICU

L-1 5108

Kolbenheyer, Erwin Guido, 1878-
Amor Dei; ein Spinoza-roman. Neuauflage. München, Müller [c1913]
364 p.

IaU

SPECIAL COLLECTIONS SPINOZA L-1 5109

Kolbenheyer, Erwin Guido, 1878-
Amor Dei; ein Spinoza-Roman. München, G. Müller, 1919.
389 p. 19cm.

Original paper covers bound in.

L-1 5110

Kolbenheyer, Erwin Guido, 1878-
Amor Dei; ein Spinoza-roman. München, Müller, 1927.
364 p. 20 cm.

L-1 5111

Kolbenheyer, Erwin Guido, 1878-
Amor Dei; ein Spinoza-roman. München, G. Müller, 1908.
vii, 496 p.

NN

SPECIAL COLLECTIONS SPINOZA L-1 5112

Kolbenheyer, Erwin Guido, 1878-
God-intoxicated man, by E. G. Kolbenheyer; translated by John Linton. London, Ivor Nicholson & Watson, ltd., 1933.
319, [1] p. 23cm.

1. Spinoza, Benedictus de, 1632-1677—Fiction. 2. Rembrandt Hermanszoon van Rijn, 1607-1669—Fiction. I. Linton, John, tr. II. Title. *Translation of* Amor Dei.

A 40-284
Northwestern univ. Libr. for Library of Congress [PT2621.O68] [2] 833.91

[Mahon, Patrice], 1865-1914.
Baruch. [1915]
278-293 p.

Signed: Art Roë.
In Revue des deux mondes, année 85, période 6, t. 28, 1915.
A short story based on Spinoza's life.

Sue, Eugène, 1804-1857.
Latréaumont. Paris, Gosselin, 1838.
2 v. plates, facsim. 22 cm.

Spinoza appears as a character in chapter 1.

Meijer, Willem, 1842-1926.
Een theologische roman uit de 17de eeuw. [1898]
172-202 p.

In Archief voor Nederlandsche kerkgeschiedenis, dl. 7., 1898.
Includes references to Spinoza.

Theilhaber, Felix Aaron, 1884-1956.
Dein Reich komme! Ein chiliastischer Roman aus der Zeit Rembrandts und Spinozas. [1.-3. Aufl.] Berlin, C. A. Schwetschke & Sohn [1924]
171 p. 21cm.

L-2
POETRY AND DRAMA

Philippson, Ludwig, 1811-1889.
Jakob Tirado; geschichtlicher Roman aus der zweiten Hälfte des sechszehnten Jahrhunderts. Leipzig, O. Leiner, 1867.
372 p. 19cm. (Added t.-p.: Schriften hrsg. vom Institute zur Förderung der israelitischen Literatur. 12. Jahr: 1866-1867)

Abelson, Alter.
Sambatyon and other poems, by Alter Abelson ... New York, N. Y., The Ariel publications, 1931-
v. port. 21cm.
Author's autograph, v. 1.
Includes two poems on Spinoza.

I. Title.

Schachnowitz, Selig
Die Messiasbraut; die Geschichte einer verlorenen Hoffnung. Historischer Roman aus dem 17. Jahrhundert. Frankfurt am Main, Hermon Verlags-Aktiengesellschaft [c1925]
434 p. 19cm.

Spinoza appears as one of the characters in the novel.

Askanazy, Helene
Spinoza und de Witt; neun Bilder vom Kampf der "Freiheit" um die Republik und ein Epilog. Wien, Amalthea-Verlag [1931]
246 p. 21cm.

Presentation copy to Carl Gebhardt, with the author's inscription and signature.

Sue, Eugène, 1804-1857.
... De Rohan; or, The court conspirator. An historical romance. By M. Eugene Sue ... New York, G. Munro, 1880.
74 p. 32½cm. (Seaside library, v. 39, no. 800)

Spinoza appears as a character in chapter 1.
1. France—Hist.—Louis XIV, 1643-1715—Fiction. I. Title.
[*Name originally:* Marie Joseph Sue]

Bab, Julius, 1880-
Spinoza; zwei Gedichte. [1912]
p. 45.

In Freie jüdische Lehrer-stimme, 1. Jahrgang, 1912-13.

Ball, Benjamin West, 1823-1896.
To Benedict Spinoza.
[1] p. 21cm.

Manuscript copy of poem.
"In Radical review, May, 1877."

1. Spinoza, Benedictus de, 1632-1677 - Poetry

Barrios, Miguel de, 1625-1701.
Coro de las musas, dirigido al excelentissimo señor don Francisco de Melo ... por el capitan don Miguel de Barrios ... En Brusselas, De la imprenta de Baltazar Vivien, 1672.
[40], [3]-648 p. illus., port. 13cm.

Poems.
Several errors in paging.
Includes poems relating to Juan de Prado and Spinoza reference (p. 588)

[Barrios, Miguel de] 1625-1701.
... Epistola censoria respondiendo à otra que le escrivio el Doctor Juan de Prado en tercetos ...
[4] l. 13cm.

Photostat copy (negative) of the poem, from his Coro de las musas, Brussels, 1672, p. 588-592.
Includes Spinoza reference (p. 588)

[Barrios, Miguel de] 1625-1701.
Tercetos en respuesta de obros que me escriviò el Doctor Don Juan de Prado ...
[8] l. 22cm.

Manuscript copy (twentieth century) from Flor de Apolo, by Miguel de Barrios, Brussels, 1665 (cf. label on cover), p. 186-190.

Beale, H B
Spinoza. [1910]
356-357 p. 26cm.

Poem.
Pencilled note: T. P.'s magazine, no. 3, Dec. 1910.

1. Spinoza, Benedictus de, 1632-1677 - Poetry.

[Bernis, François Joachim de Pierre de, *comte de Lyon, cardinal*] 1715-1794.
La religion vengée. Poëme en dix chants. Parme, Palais royal, 1795.
1 p. l., [26], 243, [1] p. front. (port.) 15½cm.
Dedication signed: Jos. Nicolas d'Azara.
Includes a section on Spinoza (p. [77]-95)

I. Azara y Perrera, José Nicolas de, marqués de Nibbiano, 1730-1804, ed.

11—21673

Library of Congress PQ1957.B45A7
[37b1]

Bernis, François Joachim de Pierre de, comte de Lyon, cardinal, 1715-1794.
La religion vengée, poème en dix chants. A Paris, Chez Amand Koenig; A Strasbourg, Chez le même, 1798.
xii, 241 p. 21cm.

Includes a section on Spinoza (p. 77-95)

Blackmore, Sir Richard, d. 1729.
Creation. A philosophical poem. Demonstrating the existence and providence of a God. In seven books. By Sir Richard Blackmore ... The second edition ... London, Printed for S. Buckley and J. Tonson, 1712.
1 p. l., lii, [2], 359 p. 16cm.

Includes references to Spinoza.

Blackmore, Sir Richard, d. 1729.
Creation. A philosophical poem, demonstrating the existence and providence of a God. In seven books. By Sir Richard Blackmore ... The third edition ... London, Printed for J. Tonson, J. Brown, and O. Lloyd, 1715.
1 p. l., lxvi, [3], 237 p. 14cm.

Includes references to Spinoza.

Caroline Louise, pseud.
Baruch von Spinoza; Drama in 5 Aufzügen.
Berlin, F. Schneider, 1855.
147 p. 19cm.

SPECIAL COLLECTIONS SPINOZA
L-2 5133

Delius, Rudolf von, 1878-
Die Feier; Gedichte. Jena, E. Diederichs, 1919.
94 p. 21cm.

Includes a poem "Spinozas Bildnis" (p. 17-18) and a reference to Spinoza in "Die Philosophenstube" (p. 24-25)

L-2 5134

Feinstein, Moshe, 1896-
אֶל בָּרוּךְ שפּינוֹזָה. [1926-27]
p. 309.

Title transliterated: ʿel Barukh Shpinozah.
In ha-Doar, v. 6, 1926-27.
A poem.

NNJ

L-2 5135

Gordon, Leon, 1830-1892.
כל שירי יהודה-לײב גאָרדאָן.
St. Petersburg, 1884.
4 v.

Title transliterated: Kal shirey Judah-Leyb Gordon.
Includes a reference to Spinoza (v. 4, p. 112)

NNJ

SPECIAL COLLECTIONS SPINOZA
L-2 5136

Greene, B M
The God-intoxicated man; a play in three acts. [1922]
298-382 p. 26cm.

From the Menorah journal, vol. VIII, no. 5, October 1922.

SPECIAL COLLECTIONS SPINOZA
L-2 5137

Grelinger, Charles, 1873-
Baruch de Spinoza, biographie lyrique en 4 episodes. Paroles et musique de Charles Grelinger. [19--]
26 l. 28cm.

Typescript of libretto.

SPECIAL COLLECTIONS SPINOZA
L-2 5138

Grelinger, Charles, 1873-
Baruch de Spinoza; suite pour piano, tirée de la biographie lyrique en quatre épisodes. Paris, A. de Smit, 1932.
15 p. of music. 34cm.

Contents.--Prélude (sur deux thèmes hébraïques)--Dialogue.--Tumulte dans la synagogue.--Menuet (style ancien)--Scherzo "Pierlala" (sur un thème hollandais)--La mort de Spinoza.

SPECIAL COLLECTIONS SPINOZA
L-2 5139

Gunn, John Alexander, 1896-
Spinoza, the maker of lenses; a play in three acts. London, Allen & Unwin [c1932]
99 p. 19cm.

L-2 5140

Heller, Seligmann, 1831-1890.
Ahasverus; ein Heldengedicht. Leipzig, D. Wigand, 1866.
xvi, 557 p. 20 cm.

Includes sections on Spinoza (p. 475-486)

OCH

L-2 5141

Heller, Seligmann, 1831-1890.
Ahasverus; ein Heldengedicht. 2. Aufl. Leipzig, D. Wigand, 1868.
xvi, 559 p.

Includes sections on Spinoza (p. 475-486)

NNJ

SPECIAL COLLECTIONS SPINOZA
L-2 5142

Heydenreich, Karl Heinrich, 1764-1801.
Gedichte. Leipzig, F. G. Baumgaertner [1802]
2 v. in 1. plates. 18cm.

Vol. 2: "Nach dessen Tode gesammelt und herausgegeben von A. H. Heydenreich."
Includes a poem "Menschenbestimmung, nach Spinoza" (v. 1, p. 132-134)

Huch, Ricarda, 1864-1947.
Gedichte. Leipzig, H. Haessel, 1922.
viii, 276 p. 19cm.

Includes a poem "Spinoza" (p. 137-140)

Hirschberg, Henriette
Spinoza's Tod (21. Februar 1677). Aus einem teilweise veröffentlichten Cyklus Kanaan.
[1894]
p. 83.

In Allgemeine Zeitung des Judentums, Jahrgang 59, 1894.

Der Kettenträger. Amsterdam [i. e. Cöthen, Aue] 1796.
2 v. plate. 18cm.

Imprint from Weller, Die falschen und fingierten Druckorte.
Pencilled on t.-p.: Klinger, F. M.

Kettner, Frederick, 1886-
Die erste Spinoza-Gemeinschaft, oder, Der Anti-egoist; ein ethisches Drama, und ein Vor-Wort an Constantin Brunner. Wien, A. Wolf, 1929.
xiv, 60 p. 25cm.

At head of title: Dr. Friedrich Kettner.
Presentation copy to Carl Gebhardt, with the author's inscription and signature.

Kronenberg, Moritz, 1865-
Moderne Philosophen; Porträts und Charakteristiken. München, Beck, 1899.
ix, 221 p. 22cm.

Includes a poem "Spinoza" by Hermann Lotze (p. 216)
Contents.--Hermann Lotze.--F. Alb. Lange.--Victor Cousin.--Ludwig Feuerbach.--Max Stirner.

Lenau, Nicolaus, 1802-1850.
Faust; ein Gedicht. 2., ausgeführtere Aufl. Stuttgart, J. G. Cotta, 1840.
207 p. 18cm.

Includes an allusion to Spinoza (p. 143)

Luiken, Jan, 1649-1712.
Stichtelijke verzen. Bijeengebracht en ingeleid door C. B. Hylkema. Zaandam, C. Huig, 1904.
xxiv, 141 p. illus., port. 21cm.

I. Title. II. Hylkema, C B ed.

MacCall, William, 1812-1888.
Moods and memories. London, W. Stewart [188-?]
96 p. illus. 19cm.

Poems.

I. Title.

Mandelkern, Solomon, 1846-1902.
שירי שפת עבר. ספר ראשון. מאת
שלמה מאנדעלקערן.
Hebräische Gedichte. 1. Buch. Leipzig, Selbstverlag des Verfassers, 1882.
110 p. 19cm.

Title transliterated: Shīrē śĕfath ʿEbher.
Includes poem about Spinoza (p. 78)

Morganstern, Abraham
Marranos and other poems. Boston, Badger [c1935]
70 p. 21 cm.

Murr, Christoph Gottlieb von, 1733-1811.
Die jetzige Welt. Ein Lehrgedicht, von C. G. von Murr ... Vierte, sehr veränderte und vermehrte Auflage. Nürnberg, bey Monath und Kussler, 1804.
15 p. 19cm.

Murr, Christoph Gottlieb von, 1733-1811.
Sinngedichte, von Christoph Gottlieb von Murr ... Magdeburg, Bey Johann Christoph Zapffe, 1773.
36 p. 16cm.

Oudaan, Joachim, 1628-1692.
Gedichten van Joachim Oudaan, noit voor dezen in 't licht gezien. Uitgegeven door H. K. Poot. Te Delf, By Reinier Boitet, 1724.
[8], 260, [4] p. 16cm.

Includes a reference to Spinoza (p. 99)

Oudaan, Joachim, 1628-1692.
Joachim Oudaans Poëzy, verdeeld in drie deelen, waar van de inhoud op de andere zyde te zien is. Achter het derde deel komt het leven van den dichter, beschreven door den Heer David van Hoogstraten. Te Amsteldam, By de Wed: P: Arentz, en K: vander Sys, 1712.
3 v. 17cm.

Added engraved t.-p.
Includes references to Spinoza (v. 1, p. 75; v. 2, p. 68-69, 112)

Paulus, Heinrich Eberhard Gottlob, 1761-1851.
Entdeckungen über die Entdeckungen unserer neuesten Philosophen. Ein Panorama in fünftehalb Acten mit einem Nachspiel. Von Magis Amica Veritas. Bremen, A. D. Geisler, 1835.
iv, 46 p. 22 cm.

Paulus, Heinrich Eberhard Gottlob, 1761-1851.
Zur Sicherung meiner Ehre. Aktenstücke als Manuscript für Freunde und unpartheyische Beurtheiler. Heidelberg, K. Groos, 1819.
64 p. 19 cm.

Petzold, Alfons, 1882-1923.
Baruch Spinoza. [1916-17]
p. 123.

In Jüdischer National-Kalender, aus der Jahr 5677, 1916-17.
A poem.

Philippson, Ludwig, 1811-1889.
Saron. 2., gänzlich umgestaltete und verm. Ausg. 2. Theil. Dichtungen in metrischer Form. 2. Bd.: Episches. Voran einige Novellen. Von Ludwig und Phöbus Philippson. Leipzig, O. Leiner, 1860.
vi, 402 p. 19cm. (Added t.-p.: Schriften hrsg. vom Institute zur Förderung der Israelitischen Literatur. 5. Jahr: 1859-1860)

Includes a sketch about Spinoza: "Die Trennung" (p. 205-215)

Philippson, Ludwig, 1811-1889.
Saron. Gesammelte Dichtungen von Ludwig Philippson. 3. Aufl. 1. Theil: Novellenbuch. 1. Bd. Leipzig, J. Wallerstein, 1857.
viii, 409 p. (Novellenbuch von Phöbus und Ludwig Philippson. Bd. 1)

Ravitch, Melech, 1893-
שפינאזא; פאעטישער פריוו אין פיר ציקלען: דער מענש, דאס ווערק, די שפין, קטרת. וויען־ברין, מ. היקעל־פערלאג, ת״רע״ט.
[Vienna, M. Hickl-Verlag, 1918 or 1919]
69 p. 24cm.

Title transliterated: Shpinoza; poetisher priv in fir tsiklen.

Ravitch, Melech, 1893-
שפינאָזא. פּאָעטישער פּריוו...
Vienna, 1919.
60 p.

Title transliterated: Shpinoza. Poetisher priv.

Regelson, Abraham
ניצוצות משפינוזה בשירה האנגליה.
ניו-יורק, תרצ"ג.
[1932]
53-55 p. 32cm.

Title transliterated: Nīṣōṣōth mi-Shpīnōzā ...
From ha-Doar, vol. XIII, no. 4, Nov. 25, 1932
With Goldberg, Abraham. Bārūkh Shpīnōzā. [1932]

Reichert, Victor Emanuel, 1897-
"Spinoza smoked a pipe." [1928]
p. 7. 27cm.

Poem.
From the Rockdale scroll, vol. II, no. 3, May 19, 1928.

Relav, Peter
Jesus Christus und Benedictus Spinoza im Zwiegespräch. Berlin, Verlag des Bibliographischen Bureaus, 1893.
61 p. 23cm.

Original paper covers bound in.

Ring, Max, 1817-1901.
Gedichte. Berlin, H. Steinitz, 1896.
vi, 148 p.

Includes a poem on Spinoza (p. 68-69)

Rolland, Romain, 1866-1944.
Empédocle, suivi de L'éclair de Spinoza. Paris, Éditions du Sablier [1931]
130 p. plates, ports. 20cm.

No. 26 of 180 copies.
Original paper covers bound in.

1. Spinoza, Benedictus de, 1632-1677.

Rubin, Salomon, 1825-1910.
ברוך שפינוזה ברגשי אהבת אלהים.
(Amore Dei intellectualis) [Podgorze, 1910]
31 p.

Title transliterated: Barukh Shpinozah ...
Added t.-p. in German.

Skutch, Robert Frank
"Spinoza", a play in four acts. [1917]
[537]-539 p. 32cm.

From Jewish Comment, vol. XLVIII, no. 26, March 23, 1917.
"Excerpts from each of the four acts of the play."

1. Spinoza, Benedictus de, 1632-1677 - Drama.

Smith, Erwin Frink, 1854-1927.
For her friends and mine: a book of aspirations, dreams and memories, by Erwin F. Smith. Washington, D. C., Priv. print. [by Gibson bros., inc.] 1915.
379, [1] p., 1 l. incl. illus., port. 28cm.

"Five hundred and ten copies ... have been printed on Italian hand-made paper of which this is no. 267." Signed by the author.
Poems.
Biographical sketch of Charlotte May Smith: p. 17-46.
Includes a poem about Spinoza (p. 178)

1. Smith, Mrs. Charlotte May (Buffett) 1871-1906. I. Title.

Sully-Prudhomme, René François Armand, 1839-1907.
Oeuvres de Sully Prudhomme: Poésies, 1866-1872. Paris, A. Lemerre [1872]
243 p. 17cm.

Includes "Un bonhomme", a poem on Spinoza (p. 31)

Teichert, Adolf
Für Israel! Mahn-, Weck- und Trostrufe. München ₍189-₎
xii, 316 p.

Includes a poem "Uriel Acosta und der junge Spinoza" (p. 188)

Vondel, Joost van den, 1587-1679.
J. van Vondels Hekeldigten, met aanteekeningen, uit's digters mondt opgeschreven, nooit voor dezen gedrukt ... t'Amersfoort, By Pieter Brakman, 1707.
1 p.l., 154, 14, ₍4₎ p. plates, ports. 21cm.

"Vertroosting voor de onnozele en bedroefde ingezetenen van Hollandt, over de doodt van zyne Hoogheit Prins Willem den II.": 14 p. following p. 154.
Bound with the author's Vorstelijcke warande der dieren. ₍16--₎

Townsend, George Alfred, 1841-1914.
Poems of men and events, by George Alfred Townsend. Gapland ed. New York, E. F. Bonaventure, 1899.
7 p. l., 328 p. front., plates, ports. 28cm.
No. 307 of an ed. of 500 copies.
Includes a poem on Spinoza (p. 294)

Vondel, Joost van den, 1587-1679.
Vorstelijcke warande der dieren: waer in de zeden-rijcke philosophie, poëtisch, morael, en historiael, vermakelijck en treffelijck wort voorgestelt. Met exempelen uyt de oude historien, in prose; ende uytleggingen, in rijm verklaert, door J. v. V. Verciert met hondert vijf-en-twintig aerdige afbeeldingen, in koper gesneden, door Marcus Gerards ... t'Amsterdam, By d'Erve de Wed: Gysbert de Groot ₍16--₎
₍6₎, cxxv l. 125 illus. 19cm.

CONTINUED ON NEXT CARD

Tuinman, Carolus, 1659-1728.
Rymlust: behelzende I. Het ongerymde pausdom, met eene rommelzode van paapenheiligdom. II. Uitspannings uitspanning. En III. Rymproeve. Alles tot betoog van de rymrykheid der Nederduitsche taal. Noch een byvoegzel van gedichten. Door Carolus Tuinman. Te Middelburg, gedrukt by Michiel Schryver, 1729.
₍12₎, 403, ₍1₎, 16 p. 21cm.

Includes two poems on Spinoza (p. 11 and 16 at end)

Vondel, Joost van den, 1587-1679. Vorstelijcke warande der dieren. ₍16--₎ (Card 2)

Title vignette.
The date of publication is after 1617, for the corrections indicated at end of that edition have been made. The illustrations are the same.

Ursin, Johann Heinrich, 1608-1667.
Novus Prometheus Praeadamitarum plastes ad Caucasum relegatus & religatus, schediasma Iohannis Henrici Ursini ... Francofvrti, Apud Christianum Hermsdorf, 1656.
176 p. 14cm.

Bound with La Peyrère, Isaac de. Praeadamitae. 1655.

Weinschenk, Jakob Hugo
Sonette. Leipzig, Helingsche Verlagsanstalt, 1930.
259 p. 16cm.

Includes a poem "Spinoza" (p. 224)

Vondel, Joost van den, 1587-1679.
J. v. Vondels Palamedes, of Vermoorde onnozelheit. Treurspel, met aanteekeningen uit's digters mondt opgeschreven. Den tweeden druk merkelyk vermeerdert ... t'Amersfoort, By Pieter Brakman, 1707.
₍16₎, 78 p. plates (1 double) port. 21cm.

Bound with the author's Vorstelijcke warande der dieren. ₍16--₎

Wirsén, Carl David af, 1842-
Under furor och cypresser; diktsamling. Stockholm, P. A. Norstedt ₍1896₎
vii, 329 p. 20cm.

Includes a poem "Spinoza" (p. 12-14)

L-2 5183

Zangwill, Israel, 1864-1926.
דער איינזאמער פילאזאף (ברוך שפי-
נאזא) פון ישראל זאנגוויל, איבער-
זעצט פון א. פרומקין. לונדון, ב.
רודערמאן.
[London, B. Rudermann, 19--?]
cover-title, [145]-180 p. port. 23cm.

Title transliterated: Der aynzamer filozof.
Deals with Spinoza.

L-2 5184

Zangwill, Israel, 1864-1926.
Dreamers of the Ghetto. Copyright edition. In two volumes. Vol. I. Leipzig, B. Tauchnitz, 1898.
326 p. 17cm.

Includes "The maker of lenses", which deals with Spinoza (p. [211]-248)

L-2 5185

193Sp4
EZ1

Zangwill, Israel, 1864-1926.
Dreamers of the ghetto. Philadelphia, The Jewish publication society of America, 1898.
iii, 536 p.

Includes "The maker of lenses" which deals with Spinoza (p. 186-[220])

L-2 5186

Zangwill, Israel, 1864-1926.
Dreamers of the Ghetto. New York, Bloch Publishing Company, 1923.
iii, 523 p. 19cm.

Includes "The maker of lenses", which deals with Spinoza (p. 186-[220])

L-2 5187

Zangwill, Israel, 1864-1926.
לוטש הזכוכיות; ספור במאת ישראל
זנגביל, תרגום: פ. ג. בתל-אביב
הוצ' פ. גינזבורג.
[Tel-Aviv, 19--]
31 p. (ספריה קטנה: ב)

Deals with Spinoza.
Title transliterated: Lōṭēsh ha-zĕkhūkhīyōth.

L-2 5188

Zangwill, Israel, 1864-1926.
Marzyciele ghetta; przekład z angielskiego M. Krzeczowskiej. Z przedmową W. Feldmana. Brody, F. West, 1905.
viii, 252 p.

Translation of Dreamers of the ghetto.

L-2 5189

Zangwill, Israel, 1864-1926.
Les rêveurs du Ghetto. Traduction de Madame Marcel Girette. [Paris] Éditions G. Cres, 1920.
265 p. 19cm. (Collection "Anglia")

Includes "Le polisseur de verres", which deals with Spinoza (p. [205]-265)
Original paper covers bound in.

L-2 5190

Zangwill, Israel, 1864-1926.
Les rêveurs du Ghetto; traduction de Madame Marcel Girette. Paris, Les Éditions G. Crès, 1922-26 [v.1, 1923]
3 v. 19cm. (Collection "Anglia")

Includes "Le polisseur de verres", which deals with Spinoza (v. 1, p. [205]-265)

L-2 5191

Zangwill, Israel, 1864-1926.
Träumer des Ghetto; deutsche autorisierte Ausgabe durch Hanns Heinz Ewers, unter Mitwirkung des Verfassers. Berlin, S. Cronbach, 1908.
2 v. 20cm.

Includes "Der Linsenschleifer", which deals with Spinoza (v. 1, p. [228]-269)

L-2 5192

Zweig, Stefan, 1881-1942.
Spinoza. [1903]
218-219 p. port.

In Jüdischer Almanach 5663, 1903.
A poem.

L-2
5193

Zweig, Stefan, 1881-1942.
Spinoza. [1904]
p. 277. port.

In Jüdischer Almanach; Neuausgabe, 1904.
A poem.

M
MISCELLANEOUS
RE SPINOZA

M-1
SPINOZA'S LIBRARY

M-1
5194

Baudius, Dominicus, 1561-1613.
Dominici Bavdi Epistolae semicenturia auctae; lacunis aliquot suppletis. Accedunt eiusdem Orationes et libellvs De foenore. Amstelodami, Typis Ioannis Ianssonii, 1660.
[24], 732 p. port. 15cm.

M-1
5195

Buxtorf, Johann, 1564-1629.
Johannis BuxtorfI Thesaurus grammaticus linguae sanctae Hebraeae duobus libris methodicè propositus ... adjecta prosodia metrica sive poeseos Hebraeorum dilucida tractatio: lectionis hebraeo-germanicae usus & exercitatio. Editio tertia ... In inclyta Helvetiorum Basilea, impensis Ludovici Regis, 1620.
8 p. l., 690, [29] p. 17cm.

M-1
5196

Homerus.
De Iliaden van Homerus, prins der Grieksche poëten; of Beschrijving van d'oorlog tusschen de Grieken en Trojanen, om de schaking en wechvoering van Helena ... Nieuwelijks door J. H. Glazemaker vertaalt en met kopere platen verçiert. t'Amsterdam, Voor Jan Rieuwersz, boekverkoper, 1658.
v. 1. plates. 13cm.

Added engraved t.-p.

M-1
5197

Jelles, Jarig
Belydenisse der algemeenen en Christelyken geloofs, vervattet in een brief aan N. N. Door Jarig Jelles. t'Amsterdam, By Jan Rieuwertsz, 1684.
[6], 161, [7] p. 14cm.

Photostat copy (positive)

M-1
5198

Land, Jan Pieter Nicolaas, 1834-1897.
De bibliotheek van Spinoza. [1889]
117-119 p.

In De Nederlandsche spectator, 1889.
A review of Inventaire des livres formant la bibliothèque de Bénédict Spinoza. by A. J. Servaas van Rooijen.

DLC

M-1
5199

Lansberge, Jacobus van, 1590-1657.
Iacobi LansbergI medicinae doctoris Apologia, pro commentationibus Philippi Lansbergii in motum terrae diurnum & annuum: adversvs Libertvm Fromondvm ... & Joan. Baptistam Morinvm ... Middelbvrgi Zelandiae, Apud Zachariam Romanvm, 1633.
[16], 131 p. diagrs. 19cm.

Closely cropped at bottom.

NNC

M-1
5200

Machiavelli, Niccolò, 1469-1527.
Tvtte le opere di Nicolo Machiavelli, cittadino et secretario fiorentino, divise in V. parti, et di nvove con somma accvratezza restampate. 1550.
5 pts. in 1 v. 22cm.

Title-vignette (port.)
Each work, except the Discorsi and the Asino d'oro, has special t.-p. with port. vignette.

M-1
5201

Mansvelt, Regnerus à, 1639-1671.
Regneri à Mansvelt ... Adversus anonymum theologo-politicum liber singularis, in quo omnes & singulae Tractatus theologico-politici dissertationes examinantur & refelluntur, cum praemissa disquisitione de divina per naturam, & Scripturam revelatione. Opus posthumum. Amstelaedami Apud Abrahamum Wolfgang, 1674.
[4], 364 p. 20cm.

A reply to Spinoza's Tractatus theologico-politicus.

M-1
5202

Martialis, Marcus Valerius.
M. Val. Martialis Epigrammata. Cum notis Th. Farnabii. Amsterdami, Apud Iohannem Blaev, 1644.
492 p. 14cm.

Engraved title-page.

Nourrisson, Jean Félix, 1825-1899.
La bibliothèque de Spinoza. [1893]
577-615 p.

In Académie des sciences morales et politiques, Paris. Revue des travaux et comptes-rendus de ses séances, 140. t., 1893.

[Nourrisson, Jean Félix] 1825-1899.
La bibliothèque de Spinoza. [1892]
[811]-833 p. 21cm.

Signed: Nourrisson.
From Revue des deux mondes, t. CXII, 15. août 1892.

I. Spinoza, Benedictus de, 1632-1677.

Pérez, Antonio, 1583-1672.
AntonI PerezI ... Institvtiones imperiales, erotematibus distinctâe, atque ex ipsis principijs regulisq̂ue juris, passim insertis, explicatâe. Editio novissima, post varias editiones externas denuò secundum exemplar originale Lovaniense revisa & a mendis purgata. Antverpiâe, Apud viduam & filium Joannis Baptistâe Verdussen, 1696.
[8], 468, [4] p. 14cm.

Pérez, Antonio, 1583-1672.
AntonI PerezI ... Ivs pvblicvm, quo arcana & iura principis exponuntur. Amstelodami, Apud Ludovicum & Danielem Elzevirios, 1657.
[16], 338 p. 14cm.

Added engraved t.-p.
Printer's device on t.-p.

Perez, Antonio, d. 1611.
Las obras y relaciones de Ant. Perez ...
[Ginebra] Por Ivan di Tornes, 1644.
[32], 1126 p. 18cm.

1. Spain - Hist. - Philip II, 1556-1598.

Pignoria, Lorenzo, 1571-1631.
Laurentii Pignorii Patavini Mensa Isiaca, qva sacrorum apud Âegyptios ratio & simulacra subjectis tabulis âeneis simul exhibentur & explicantur. Accessit ejusdem authoris de Magna Deum Matre discursus, & sigillorum, gemmarum, amuletorum aliquot figurâe & earundem ex Kirchero Chifletioque interpretatio. Nec non Jacobi Philippi Tomasini Manus Âenea, & de vita rebusque Pignorii dissertatio. Amstelodami, Sumptibus Andreâe Frisii, 1670.
4 pts. in 1 v. illus., fold. plates. 24cm.

CONTINUED ON NEXT CARD

Pignoria, Lorenzo, 1571-1631. Laurentii Pignorii Patavini Mensa Isiaca. 1680. (Card 2)

Added engraved title-page, dated 1669.
Parts [2] and [3] have special title-pages, pt. [4] has half-title.

Pignoria, Lorenzo, 1571-1631.
Magnâe Deum Matris Idâeâe & Attidis initia. Ex vetustis monumentis nuper Tornaci Nerviorum erutis. Auctore Laurentio Pignorio ... Amstelodami, Sumptibus Andreâe FrisI, 1669.
[8], 28 p. illus. 24cm. (In his Mensa Isiaca. 1670)

Quevedo y Villegas, Francisco Gómez de, 1580-1645.
Les oeuvres de D. Francisco de Quevedo Villegas ... Divise'es en deux volumes, dont le premier contient Le coureur de nuit ... l'Avanturier Buscon; et les Lettres du Chevalier de l'Epargne. Et le second, Les sept visions ... Nouvelle traduction de l'espagnol en françois & enrichie de figures en taille douce ... A Brusselles, Chez Josse de Grieck, 1698.
2 v. illus. 16cm.

Added title-pages engraved.

Saavedra Fajardo, Diego de, 1584-1648.
Corona gothica, castellana, y avstriaca, politicamente ilustrada ... Por Don Diego Saavedra Faxardo ... En Amberes, En casa de Ieronymo y Iuan Bapt. Verdvssen, 1658.
[16], 513, [23] p. 23cm.

Saavedra Fajardo, Diego de, 1584-1648.
Idea principis Christiano-politici 101 sijmbolis expressa. A Didaco Saavedra Faxardo ... Amstelodami, Apud Joannem Jacobi fil: Schipper, 1659.
[24], 831, [4] p. illus. 13cm.

Scapula, Johann, 1540-1600?
Ioan. Scapulae Lexicon graeco-latinum, è probatis auctoribus locupletatum, com indicibus, et graeco & latino, auctis, & correctis. Additvm auctarium dialectorum, in tabulas compendiose redactarum. Accedunt lexicon etymologicum, cum thematibus investigatu difficilioribus & anomalis, et Ioan. Meursii glossarium contractum, hactenus desideratum. Editio nova accurata. Amstelaedami, Apud Ioannem Blaeuw, & Ludovicum Elzevirium, 1652.
[8] p., 1790 col., [240], 62 p., 63-366 col. 38cm.

Schooten, Frans van, 1615-1660.
Francisci van Schooten Mathematische oeffeningen, begrepen in vijf boeken ... Waer by gevougt is een Tractaet, handelende van reeckening in speelen van geluck, door d'heer Christianus Hugenius. Desen druck vermeerdert met een korte verhandeling van de fondamenten der perspective. [t'Amsterdam, by Gerrit van Goedesbergh, 1660.
544 p. diagrs. 20cm.

Each book has special title-page.

Servaas van Rooijen, Abraham Jacobus, b. 1839.
Inventaire des livres formant la bibliothèque de Bénédict Spinoza, publié d'après un document inédit, avec des notes biographiques et bibliographiques et une introduction par A. J. Servaas van Rooijen. Notes de la main de David Kaufmann. La Haye, W. C. Tengeler, 1888.
219 p. 26cm.

"La vie de B. de Spinosa ... par Jean Colerus": p. 47-108.

Tacitus, Cornelius.
C. Cornelii Taciti Opera qvae exstant. Ivstvs Lipsivs postremùm recensuit. Additi commentarii aucti emendatíque ab ultimâ manu. Accessit C. Velleivs Patercvlvs cum eiusdem Lipsi auctioribus notis. Antverpiae, Ex officina Plantiniana, Apud Ioannem Moretum, 1607.
[16], 547, [31] p., 1 l., 36, 84, [14] p. 38cm.

"Ivsti Lipsi Dispvnctio notarvm Mirandvlani codicis ad Corn. Tacitvm. Editio

CONTINUED ON NEXT CARD

Tacitus, Cornelius. C. Cornelii Taciti Opera qvae exstant. 1607. (Card 2)

secunda" and "C. Velleivs Patercvlvs cvm animadversionibvs Ivsti Lipsi" have special title-pages and pagination.
Printer's device on title-pages.

Vulliaud, Paul, 1875–
Spinoza d'après les livres de sa bibliothèque, par Paul Vulliaud. Paris, Bibliothèque Chacornac, 1934.
103 p. 22½cm.
"Inventaire de la bibliothèque de Spinoza": p. [99]–103.
Original paper covers bound in.

1. Spinoza, Benedictus de, 1632-1677.

Wolzogen, Ludovicus, 1633-1690.
Ludovici Wolzogen De Scripturarum interprete adversus exercitatorem paradoxum libri duo. Accessere de occasione hujus scripti espistolae duae. Ultrajecti, Apud Johannem Ribbium, 1668.
2 p. l., 274 p., [4] l. 14 cm.

CBPac M-2
SOCIETAS SPINOZANA

[Gebhardt, Carl] 1881-1934.
Societas Spinozana. [1927]
10 p. plate. 23cm.

1. Societas Spinozana. 2. Spinoza, Benedictus de, 1632-1677.

Ravà, Adolfo
La "Societas Spinozana" e il suo "Chronicon". [1923]
310-312 p.

In Giornale critico della filosofia italiana, anno 4, 1923.

Societas Spinozana. ['s-Gravenhage? 1928?]
10 p. illus. 22cm.

Text in German.

1. Spinoza, Benedictus de, 1632-1677. 2. Societas Spinozana.

Tönnies, Ferdinand, 1855-1936.
Societas Hobbesiana - Societas Spinozana. [1931]
78-82 p. 21cm.

From Monistische Monatshefte, 16. Jahrgang, April, 1931.

M-3
SPINOZA HOUSES

Bolland, Gerardus Johannes Petrus Josephus, 1854-1922.
Spinoza; rede tot inwijding van het herstelde Spinozahuis te Rijnsburg op den 24 Maart 1899 uitgesproken door G. J. P. J. Bolland. Leiden, A. H. Adriani, 1899.
54 p. 25cm.

Original paper cover bound in.

1. Spinoza, Benedictus de, 1632-1677.

[Brief account of the purchase of the house at 28, Doublet straat, The Hague, where Spinoza lived 1652-1678. 1878]
p. 3.

In The Times, London, Sept. 3, 1878.

Carp, J H
Het Spinozahuis te 's-Gravenhage (Domus Spinozana) [1928]
73-75 p. illus. 25cm.

From Haagsche Gids, December 1928.

1. Spinoza, Benedictus de, 1632-1677 - Homes and haunts.

[Gebhardt, Carl] 1881-1934.
Domus Spinozana. [Hagae Comitis, 1927]
65-87 p. 22cm.

Signed: Carl Gebhardt.
Cover-title: Dissertatio ex Chronici Spinozani tomo quinto separatim edita.

Gebhardt, Carl, 1881-1934.
Domus Spinozana. [1933]
[309]-321 p. 26cm.

"Reprint from Septimana Spinozana."
Bound with Gebhardt, Carl. Spinoza in der Schule. [1930]

1. Spinoza, Benedictus de, 1632-1677.

Meijer, Willem, 1842-1926.
Gids voor de bezoekers van het Spinozahuis te Rijnsburg. [n. p., 189-]
4 p. 23cm.

Bound with: Spinozahuis, Leyden. Verslag omtrent de lotgevallen ... 1896/99-1920/21.

Meijer, Willem, 1842-1926.
Guide of the Spinoza-House at Rijnsburg. [n. p., 189-]
4 p. 23cm.

Bound with: Spinozahuis, Leyden. Verslag omtrent de lotgevallen ... 1896/99-1920/21.

[Meijer, Willem] 1842-1926.
De woning van Despinoza op de Stille Veerkade. [1902]
[207]-217 p. plan. 19cm.

Signed: W. Meijer.
From Die Haghe; bijdragen en mededeelingen; 1902.

M-3
5233

Spinoza House. ₍1927₎
p. 8, 16. illus.

In Jewish guardian, London, Feb. 11, 1927.

NN

SPECIAL COLLECTIONS
SPINOZA

M-3
5238

Spinozahuis, Leyden.
Verslag omtrent de lotgevallen ...
₍1₎-38.
1896/99-1934/35.
Leiden, E. J. Brill, 1899-1935.

M-4
INEDITA SPINOZANA

M-3
5234

The Spinoza House in Rijnsburg. ₍1902₎
p. 9. illus.

In Jewish chronicle, London, Aug. 29, 1902.

NNJ

SPECIAL COLLECTIONS
SPINOZA

M-4
5239

Gebhardt, Carl, 1881-1934.
... Inedita spinozana, von Carl Gebhardt ... Vorgelegt von Heinrich Rickert. Heidelberg, C. Winter, 1916.

24 p. 24½cm. (Sitzungsberichte der Heidelberger akademie der wissenschaften ... Philosophisch-historische klasse. ₍bd. 7₎ jahrg. 1916, 13. abh.)

1. Spinoza, Benedictus de, 1632-1677. I. Title.

A C 36-56

Title from Univ. of Chicago AS182.H44 vol. 7
Library of Congress [AS182.H44 bd. 7]

SPECIAL COLLECTIONS
SPINOZA

M-3
5235

Spinoza-herdenking. ₍Spinoza appeal. Hagae Comitis, 1927₎
181-187 p. 22cm.

Cover-title: Dissertatio ex Chronici Spinozani tomo quinto separatim edita.
Appeals in Dutch, English, French and German for money to purchase and preserve Spinoza's house at the Hague.

M-5
PSEUDO-SPINOZANA

SPECIAL COLLECTIONS
SPINOZA

M-3
5236

Spinozahuis, Leyden.
Mededeelingen van wege het Spinozahuis.
1-6.
Leiden, E. J. Brill, 1934-39.

Contents.--1. Vaz Dias, A. M. De firma Bento y Gabriel de Spinoza.--2. Vaz Dias, A. M. Uriel da Costa.--3. Coert, J. Spinoza en Grotius.--4. Coert, H. J. Spinoza's betrekking tot de geneeskunde en haar beoefenaren.--5. Jong, K. H. E. de. Spinoza en de stoa.--6. Crommelin, C. A. Spinoza's natuurwetenschappelijk denken.

SPECIAL COLLECTIONS
SPINOZA

M-5
5240

₍Spinoza, Benedictus de₎ 1632-1677.
Lucii Antistii Constantis ₍pseud.₎ De jure ecclesiasticorum, liber singularis. Quo docetur: quodcunque divini humanique iuris ecclesiasticis tribuitur, vel ipsi sibi tribuunt, hoc, aut falsò impièque illis tribui, aut non aliundè, quam à suis, hoc est, ejus reipublicae sivè civitatis prodiis, in qua sunt constituti, accepisse. Alethopoli ₍i.e. Amsterdam₎ Apud Cajum Valerium Pennatum, 1665.
₍15₎, 162, ₍5₎ p. 16cm.

CONTINUED ON NEXT CARD

SPECIAL COLLECTIONS
SPINOZA

M-3
5237

Spinozahuis, Leyden.
Statuten der Vereeniging "Het Spinozahuis."
₍n. p., 1903?₎
4 p. 23cm.

Bound with: Spinozahuis, Leyden. Verslag omtrent de lotgevallen ... 1896/99-1920/21.

1. Spinoza, Benedictus de, 1632-1677 - Societies, periodicals, etc.

SPECIAL COLLECTIONS
SPINOZA

M-5
5241

₍Spinoza, Benedictus de₎ 1632-1677. Lucii Antistii Constantis ₍pseud.₎ De jure ecclesiasticorum. 1665. (Card 2)

Fictitious imprint.
Ascribed also to P. de La Court. cf. Brit. Mus. Cat.
Manuscript note in French ascribing the work to Spinoza appears on page facing t.-p.; "B. Spinosâe" inserted by hand after the pseudonym on t.-p.

Appendix

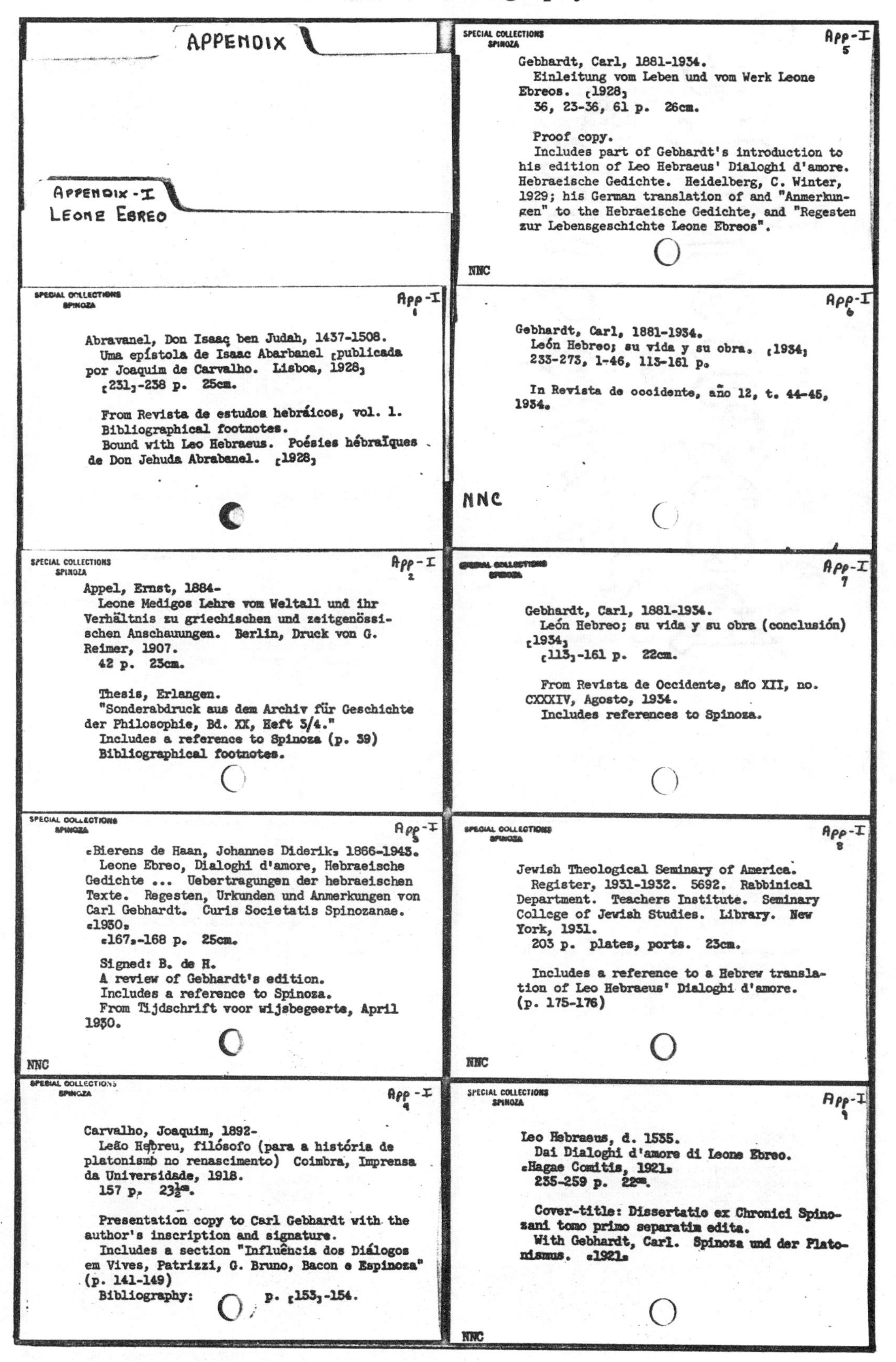

APPENDIX

APPENDIX - I
LEONE EBREO

SPECIAL COLLECTIONS
SPINOZA
App-I 1

Abravanel, Don Isaaç ben Judah, 1437-1508.
Uma epístola de Isaac Abarbanel ₍publicada por Joaquim de Carvalho. Lisboa, 1928₎
₍231₎-238 p. 25cm.

From Revista de estudos hebráicos, vol. 1.
Bibliographical footnotes.
Bound with Leo Hebraeus. Poésies hébraïques de Don Jehuda Abrabanel. ₍1928₎

SPECIAL COLLECTIONS
SPINOZA
App-I 2

Appel, Ernst, 1884-
Leone Medigos Lehre vom Weltall und ihr Verhältnis zu griechischen und zeitgenössischen Anschauungen. Berlin, Druck von G. Reimer, 1907.
42 p. 23cm.

Thesis, Erlangen.
"Sonderabdruck aus dem Archiv für Geschichte der Philosophie, Bd. XX, Heft 3/4."
Includes a reference to Spinoza (p. 39)
Bibliographical footnotes.

SPECIAL COLLECTIONS
SPINOZA
App-I 3

₍Bierens de Haan, Johannes Diderik₎ 1866-1943.
Leone Ebreo, Dialoghi d'amore, Hebraeische Gedichte ... Uebertragungen der hebraeischen Texte. Regesten, Urkunden und Anmerkungen von Carl Gebhardt. Curis Societatis Spinozanae. ₍1930₎
₍167₎-168 p. 25cm.

Signed: B. de H.
A review of Gebhardt's edition.
Includes a reference to Spinoza.
From Tijdschrift voor wijsbegeerte, April 1930.

NNC

SPECIAL COLLECTIONS
SPINOZA
App-I 4

Carvalho, Joaquim, 1892-
Leão Hebreu, filósofo (para a história de platonismo no renascimento) Coimbra, Imprensa da Universidade, 1918.
157 p. 23½cm.

Presentation copy to Carl Gebhardt with the author's inscription and signature.
Includes a section "Influência dos Diálogos em Vives, Patrizzi, G. Bruno, Bacon e Espinoza" (p. 141-149)
Bibliography: p. ₍153₎-154.

SPECIAL COLLECTIONS
SPINOZA
App-I 5

Gebhardt, Carl, 1881-1934.
Einleitung vom Leben und vom Werk Leone Ebreos. ₍1928₎
36, 23-36, 61 p. 26cm.

Proof copy.
Includes part of Gebhardt's introduction to his edition of Leo Hebraeus' Dialoghi d'amore. Hebraeische Gedichte. Heidelberg, C. Winter, 1929; his German translation of and "Anmerkungen" to the Hebraeische Gedichte, and "Regesten zur Lebensgeschichte Leone Ebreos".

NNC

App-I 6

Gebhardt, Carl, 1881-1934.
León Hebreo; su vida y su obra. ₍1934₎
233-273, 1-46, 113-161 p.

In Revista de occidente, año 12, t. 44-45, 1934.

NNC

SPECIAL COLLECTIONS
SPINOZA
App-I 7

Gebhardt, Carl, 1881-1934.
León Hebreo; su vida y su obra (conclusión) ₍1934₎
₍113₎-161 p. 22cm.

From Revista de Occidente, año XII, no. CXXXIV, Agosto, 1934.
Includes references to Spinoza.

SPECIAL COLLECTIONS
SPINOZA
App-I 8

Jewish Theological Seminary of America.
Register, 1931-1932. 5692. Rabbinical Department. Teachers Institute. Seminary College of Jewish Studies. Library. New York, 1931.
203 p. plates, ports. 23cm.

Includes a reference to a Hebrew translation of Leo Hebraeus' Dialoghi d'amore. (p. 175-176)

NNC

SPECIAL COLLECTIONS
SPINOZA
App-I 9

Leo Hebraeus, d. 1535.
Dai Dialoghi d'amore di Leone Ebreo. ₍Hagae Comitis, 1921₎
235-259 p. 22cm.

Cover-title: Dissertatio ex Chronici Spinozani tomo primo separatim edita.
With Gebhardt, Carl. Spinoza und der Platonismus. ₍1921₎

NNC

App-I 10

Leo Hebraeus, d. 1535.
Dialogi di amore, composti per Leone medico, di natione Hebreo, et dipoi fatto Christiano. [In Vinegia, In Casa de' figlivoli di Aldo] 1541.
[2], 261 (i.e. 241), [1] l. 17cm.

Imprint from colophon.
Numbers 135-154 omitted from pagination.
Printer's device on title-page and verso of last leaf.

App-I 11

Leo Hebraeus, d. 1535.
Dialoghi di amore, composti per Leone medico hebreo. In Vinegia [In casa de' figlivoli di Aldo] 1549.
228 l. 17cm.

Printer from colophon. Printer's device on t.-p. and verso of last leaf.

App-I 12

Leo Hebraeus, d. 1535.
Dialoghi di amore, composti per Leone medico hebreo. In Venegia [In casa de'figlivoli di Aldo] 1552.
228 l. 17cm.

Printer's name from colophon.
Printer's device on t.-p. and verso of last leaf.

App-I 13

Leo Hebraeus, d. 1535.
Dialoghi di amore, composti per Leone medico hebreo. In Vinegia, 1558.
228 l. 16cm.

Colophon reads: In Venetia per Isepo Guiglielmo Vicentino, alle spese però del nobil'huomo M. Federico Torresano d'Asola. Nell'anno della salutifera redetione humana. M D LVIII.
Printer's device of Aldus on t.-p. and verso of last leaf.

App-I 14

Leo Hebraeus, d. 1535.
Dialoghi di amore, di Leone Hebreo medico. Di nvovo corretti, et ristampati. In Vinegia, Appresso Domenico Giglio, 1558.
246 l. 17cm.

App-I 15

Leo Hebraeus, d. 1535.
Dialoghi di amore di Leone Hebreo medico di nvovo corretti, et ristampati. In Vinetia, Presso Giorgio de' Caualli, 1565.
246 l. 16cm.

App-I 16

Leo Hebraeus, d. 1535.
Dialoghi di amore di Leone Hebreo medico, di nvovo corretti et ristampati. In Venetia, Appresso Nicolò Beuilacqua, 1572.
246 l. 15cm.

Ms. notes by Carl Gebhardt.

I. Bevilacqua, family of printers. 1572.

App-I 17

Leo Hebraeus, d. 1535.
Dialoghi di amore, di Leone Hebreo medico, di nvovo corretti, et ristampati. In Venetia, Appresso Giouanni Alberti, 1586.
246 l. 16cm.

App-I 18

Leo Hebraeus, d. 1535.
Dialoghi di amore, di Leone hebreo medico. Di nuouo con diligenza corretti, et ristampati. In Venetia, Appresso Gio. Battista Bonfadino, 1607.
295 l. 15cm.

Printer's device on t.-p. and at end.

App-I 19

Leo Hebraeus, d. 1535.
Dialogi d'amore di Maestro Leone medico Hebreo. [Roma, Antonio Blado d'Assola, 1535]
3 pt. in 1 v. 21cm.

Imprint from colophon.

App-I 20

1938p4
FL12519 Leo Hebraeus, d. 1535.
... Dialoghi d'amore, a cura di Santino Caramella. Bari, G. Laterza & figli, 1929.
2 p. l., 457 p. 21cm. (Half-title: Scrittori d'Italia. ⌈114⌉)

At head of title: Leone Ebreo (Giuda Abarbanel)
"Un elenco degli studi che abbiano qualche importanza": p. ⌈413⌉-414.

App-I 21

Leo *Hebræus*, *d.* 1535.
... Dialoghi d'amore. Hebræische gedichte, herausgegeben, mit einer darstellung des lebens und des werkes Leones, bibliographie, register zu den Dialoghi, uebertragung der hebræischen texte, regesten, urkunden und anmerkungen von Carl Gebhardt. Heidelberg, C. Winter; London, Oxford university press; ⌈etc., etc.⌉ 1929.
5 p. l., 3-122 p., facsim. (2 p. l., 37 numb. l., 1 l., 75, 154 numb. l., 2 l.) 41, 36, 66 p. 22½cm. (*Half-title:* Bibliotheca Spinozana curis Societatis Spinozanæ. t. III)
At head of title: Leone Ebreo.
"Einmalige ausgabe in fünfhundert numerierten exemplaren ... Nummer 088."175."

(Continued on next card)
46-45277
⌈2⌉

App-I 22

Leo *Hebræus*, *d.* 1535. ... Dialoghi d'amore ... 1929.
(Card 2)
The text of the "Dialoghi d'amore" is a facsimile of the first edition, Rome, 1535.
"Bibliographie": p. 111-122.

Presentation copy to A. S. Oko, with the editor's inscription and signature.
Ms. notes by A. S. Oko.

1. Love. I. Gebhardt, Carl, 1881- ed. II. Title.

B785.L33D5 1535 a 46-45277

Library of Congress ⌈2⌉

App-I 23

Leo Hebraeus, d. 1535.
... Dialoghi d'amore. Poesie hebraiche. Ristampati con introduzione di Carl Gebhardt. Heidelberg, C. Winter, 1924.
xvi p., facsim. (⌈2⌉, 37, 75, 154, ⌈2⌉ l.) 30, ii p. 23cm. (Bibliotheca Spinozana curis Societatis Spinozanae, t. III)

The text of the "Dialoghi d'amore" is a facsimile of the first edition, Rome, 1535.
Introduction includes references to Spinoza.
Carl Gebhardt's inscription on half-title.

App-I 24

Leo Hebraeus, d. 1535.
Klage gegen die Zeit von dem Weisen Don Jehuda Abrabanel; uebertragen von Carl Gebhardt. ⌈1928⌉
662-668 p. 25cm.

Extract from Der Morgen, III. Jahrgang, 6. Heft, Februar 1928.
Includes references to Spinoza (p. 667-668)

NNC

App-I 25

Leo Hebraeus, d. 1535.
Klage gegen die Zeit von dem Weisen Don Jehuda Abrabanel; uebertragen von Carl Gebhardt. ⌈1928⌉
662-668 p. 25cm.

From Der Morgen, Jahrgang 3, no. 6.
Includes references to Spinoza (p. 667-668)

App-I 26

Leo Hebraeus, d. 1535.
La tradvzion del Indio de los tres Dialogos de amor de Leon Hebreo, hecha de italiano en español por Garcilasso Inga de la Vega ... En Madrid, En casa de Pedro Madrigal, 1590.
⌈12⌉, 313, ⌈31⌉ l. 20cm.

App-I 27

Leo Hebraeus, d. 1535.
La traduzión del Indio de los tres Dialogos de amor de León Hebreo, hecha de italiano en español por Garcilasso Inga de la Vega. ⌈1915⌉
⌈278⌉-459 p. 27cm.

From Menéndez y Pelayo, Marcelino. Orígenes de la novela, t. IV.

App-I 28

Leo Hebraeus, d. 1535.
Leonis Hebraei ... De amore dialogi tres, nvper a Ioanne Carolo Saraceno purissima, candidissimaq; Latinitate donati. Necnon ab eodem et singvlis dialogis argumenta sua præmissa, & marginales annotationes suis quibusque locis insertæ, alphabetico & locupletissimo indice his tandem adiuncto, fuerunt. Venetiis, Apvd Franciscvm Senensem, 1564.
⌈117⌉, 422, ⌈1⌉ p. 15cm.

App-I 29

Leo Hebraeus, d. 1535.
Philosophie d'amovr de M. Leon Hebrev, traduicte d'italien en françoys, par le Seigneur du Parc Champenois ... A Lyon, chez Guil. Rouille & Thibauld Payen, 1551.
675, ⌈42⌉ p. 18cm.

App-I 30

Leo Hebraeus, d. 1535.
Philosophie d'amovr de M. Leon Hebrev, traduite d'italien en françois, par le seigneur du Parc Champenois. A Paris, Chez Claude Micard, 1577.
816, [48] p. 12cm.

Colophon reads: A Roven, De l'imprimerie de George l'Oyselet.

App-I 31

Leo Hebraeus, d. 1535.
Philosophie d'amovr de M. Leon Hebrev. Traduite d'italien en françois, par le Seigneur du Parc Champenois. A Paris, Chez Claude Micard, 1580.
816, [48] p. 12cm.

Colophon reads: A Roven, De l'imprimerie de George l'Oyselet.

App-I 32

Leo Hebraeus, d. 1535.
Philosophie d'amovr de M. Leon Hebrev: contenant les grands & hauts poincts, desquels elle traite, tant pour les choses morales & naturelles, que pour les diuines & supernaturelles. Traduite d'italien en françois, par le Seigneur du Parc, Champenois. A. Lyon, Par Benoist Rigavd, 1595.
816, [47] p. 12cm.

App-I 33

Leo *Hebraeus, d.* 1535.
The philosophy of love (Dialoghi d'amore), by Leone Ebreo; translated into English by F. Friedeberg-Seeley and Jean H. Barnes, with an introduction by Cecil Roth. London, The Soncino press, 1937.
xv, 468 p. 24 cm.
"This is the second book issued in connection with the Soncino Jewish publication society."

1. Love. I. Friedeberg-Seeley, F., tr. II. Barnes, Jean H., joint tr. III. Soncino Jewish publication society, London. IV. Title.

B785.L33D53 181.3 38—12990

Library of Congress [54d1]

App-I 34

Leo Hebraeus, d. 1535.
Poésies hébraîques de Don Jehuda Abrabanel (Messer Leone Ebreo) Texte hébreu revu et annoté, suivi d'une version et d'explications en français par Nahum Slousch. [Lisboa, 1928]
[192]-230 p. 25cm.

Text of poems in Hebrew and French.
From Revista de estudos hebráicos, vol. 1.

App-I 35

Leo Hebraeus, d. 1535.
ויכוח על האהבה, מאת ... דון יְהודה בן יִצחק אברבנאל ז"ל. יִוצא לאור בפעם ראשונה בשפת עברִית מתוך כ"יִ ... ונלוה לו תולדות המחבר מאת דוד גאָרדאָן ...
Lyck, M'kize Nirdamim, 1871.
15 p., 96 numb. l. 22½cm. (Added t.-p.: ספרים היוצאים לאור בפעם ראשונה על ידי חברת מְקיצי נרדמים ...)

Title transliterated: Wikkûah ʿal ahabāh.
Leaves numbered in Hebrew.

App-I 36

Mackehenie, C A
Apuntes sobre las traducciones castellanas de Leon Hebreo. [1940]
[679]-697 p. facsim.

From Mercurio peruano, año XV, no. 165, noviembre y diciembre de 1940.
Includes bibliographical references.

App-I 37

[Nicolini, Fausto] 1879-
Per la biografia di Leone Ebreo. [1930]
312-314 p. 24cm.

Signed: Fausto Nicolini.
A summary of biographical facts about Leo Hebraeus as established in the edition of his Dialoghi edited by Santino Caramella (Bari, Laterza, 1929)
From La Critica, anno XXVIII, fasc. IV (Terza serie, anno IV, fascicolo IV) 20 luglio 1930.

App-I 38

Paret, Hans
Leone Ebreo, Dialoghi d'amore, Hebräische Gedichte. Herausgegeben mit einer Darstellung des Lebens und des Werkes Leones, Bibliographie, Register zu den Dialoghi, Ubertragung der hebräischen Texte, Regesten, Urkunden und Anmerkungen von Carl Gebhardt. [1931]
177-178 p. 25cm.

A review of Gebhardt's edition of these works of Leo Hebraeus.
From Kant-Studien, Bd. XXXVI, Hft. 1/2, 1931.
Includes a reference to Spinoza.

App-I 39

Pflaum, Heinz
Die Idee der Liebe. Leone Ebreo. Zwei Abhandlungen zur Geschichte der Philosophie in der Renaissance. Tübingen, J. C. B. Mohr (P. Siebeck) 1926.
iv, 158 p. 24cm. (Heidelberger Abhandlungen zur Philosophie und ihrer Geschichte. 7)

Includes references to Spinoza.
Bibliographical references.

Pflaum, Heinz
Leone Ebreo und Pico della Mirandola.
[1928]
344-350 p. 23cm.

From Monatsschrift für Geschichte und Wissenschaft des Judentums, 72. Jahrgang, Heft 7/8, Juli/August 1928.
Bibliographical footnotes.

Pflaum, Heinz, 1900-
Der Renaissance-Philosoph Leone Ebreo (Jehuda Abarbanel) [1926]
213-222 p. 32cm.

"Sonderabdruck aus den Soncino-Blättern; Beiträge zur Kunde des jüdischen Buches."
Includes a reference to Spinoza (p. 220)

1. Leo Hebraeus, d. 1535.

[Roditi, Edourd]
The complaint of Jehudah Abravanel. [1932]
81-83 p. 21cm.

Signed: Edourd Roditi.
"Based upon the 'Elegy on destiny', written in 1504, of Leone Ebreo."
From The Jewish review, no. 1, June-August 1932.

Roditi, Edouard
Prison within prison; three elegies on Hebrew themes. Prairie City, Ill., Press of J. A. Decker, 1941.
22 p. plate. 23cm.

Includes a poem on Leo Hebraeus, "The complaint of Jehudah Abravanel" (p. 9-18)

Saitta, Giuseppe, 1881-
La filosofia di Leone Ebreo. [1924-25]
[12]-19, [140]-153, [241]-256 p. 25cm.

Incomplete.
From Giornale critico della filosofia italiana, anno V., fascicolo primo, gennaio 1924; anno VI., fascicolo secondo (aprile 1925) e terzo (luglio 1925)
Ms. notes by Carl Gebhardt.

Saitta, Giuseppe, 1881-
Filosofia italiana e umanesimo. Venezia, "La Nuova Italia", 1928.
157 p. 22cm. (Storici antichi e moderni)

Reprinted from various periodicals.
Contents.--L'originalità della filosofia italiana.--La storia del pensiero come storia nazionale.--La rivendicazione di Epicuro nell'umanesimo.--La filosofia di Leone Ebreo.

Solmi, Edmondo, 1874-1912.
Benedetto Spinoza e Leone Ebreo; studio su una fonte italiana dimenticata dello spinozismo. Modena, Coi tipi di G. T. Vincenzi e nipoti, 1903.
96 p. 23cm.

Manuscript notes by Carl Gebhardt.
Bibliographical footnotes.

[Steinschneider, Moritz] 1816-1907.
Leo Hebraeus, ein jüdischer Philosoph der Renaissance; sein Leben, seine Werke und seine Lehre. Von Dr. B. Zimmels. [1887]
8 (i.e. 14) l. 29cm.

Signed: Moritz Steinschneider.
Typescript copy of a review of Zimmel's book from Vierteljahrsschrift für Kultur und Litteratur der Renaissance, 2. Bd., 1887, p. 290-296.

Zimmels, Bernhard, 1862-1890.
Leo Hebraeus, ein jüdischer Philosoph der Renaissance; sein Leben, seine Werke und seine Lehren. Breslau, Verlag von W. Koebner, 1886.
120 p.

Includes references to Spinoza.

APPENDIX II
URIEL ACOSTA

App-II
49

Acosta, Uriel, 1585 (ca.)-1640.
Leben und unglückliches Ende Uriel Acosta's, ein Warnungsruf für manche Verirrungen underer Zeit. ⌈1859⌉
306-320 p.

An extract from Acosta's Exemplar humanae vitae.
In Jeschurun. Ein Monatsblatt für und über Israel, v. 1, 1859.

App-II
50

Acosta, Uriel, 1585 (*ca.*)-1640.
Die schriften des Uriel da Costa, mit einleitung, übertragung und regesten hrsg. von Carl Gebhardt. Curis Societatis Spinozanæ. Amsterdam, M. Hertzberger; ⌈etc., etc.⌉ 1922.
xl, 285, ⌈1⌉ p. illus. (incl. facsim.) 23 x 18cm. (*Half-title:* Bibliotheca Spinozana curis Societatis Spinozanæ, t. II)
"Zur da Costa-literatur": p. 225-233.
CONTENTS.—Einleitung: Da Costa und das Marranenproblem. Die gründung der sephardischen gemeinde in Amsterdam. Die spaltung des bewusstseins. Das schicksal da Costas. Da Costa und Spinoza.—Propostas contra a tradição. Thesen gegen die tradition.—Sobre a mortalidade da alma. Über die sterblichkeit der seele.—Exemplar humanae vitae. Ein beispiel menschlichen lebens.—Regesten.—Anmerkungen.
I. Gebhardt, Carl, 1881- ed. and tr.

⌈*Name originally:* Gabriel da Costa⌉
25-16284 Revised

App-II
51

Acosta, Uriel, 1585 (ca.)-1640.
Une vie humaine. Traduit du latin et précédé d'une étude sur l'auteur par A.-B. Duff et Pierre Kaan. Paris, F. Rieder, 1926.
138 p. 19cm. (Judaisme. 3)

The introduction includes a section "Da Costa et Spinoza" (p. 58-77)
Bibliography: p. ⌈95⌉-96.

App-II
52

Acosta, Uriel, 1585 (ca.)-1640.
Uriel Acosta, Dokument eines Menschenschicksals; das "Exemplar humanae vitae" aus dem Lateinischen neu übertragen von Oskar Jancke. Einband-Entwurf von W. J. M. Schmitz-Gilles. Aachen, Verlag "Die Kuppel", K. Spiertz, 1925.
43 p. 23cm.

Original paper cover bound in.

App-II
53

Acosta, Uriel, 1585 (ca.)-1640.
Uriel Acosta's Selbstbiographie. Lateinisch und deutsch. Mit einer Einleitung. Leipzig, E. O. Weller, 1847.
47 p. 20cm.

App-II
54

Cassel, David, 1818-1893.
Lehrbuch der jüdischen Geschichte und Literatur. Leipzig, Brockhaus, 1879.
xi, 564 p. 22 cm.

Includes a section "Uriel Acosta und Baruch Spinoza" (p. 466-468)

App-II
55

Cassel, David, 1818-1893.
Leitfaden für den Unterricht in der jüdischen Geschichte und Litteratur. Nebst einer kurzen Darstellung der biblischen Geschichte und einer Übersicht der Geographie Palästinas. 9. verb. Aufl. Frankfurt a. M., J. Kauffmann, 1895.
viii, 146 p. 21cm.

Includes a section "Uriel Acosta und Baruch Spinoza" (p. 105-106)

App-II
56

Friedländer, Max Hermann
Geschichtsbilder aus der nachtalmudischen Zeit. Frankfurt a. M., H. L. Brönner, 1885.
v. 3

Includes a section "Uriel da Costa und Spinoza" (p. 33-36)

App-II
57

Gutzkow, Karl, 1811-1878.
Uriel Acosta. In three acts. From the German of Gutzkow, by H. Spicer. London, K. Paul, Trench, 1885.
viii, 87 p.

Spinoza as a child appears as one of the characters.

App-II
58

Gutzkow, Karl, 1811-1878.
Uriel Acosta; a tragedy in five acts. Translated from the German by M. M. New York, M. Ellinger, 1860.
92 p. 18cm.

Spinoza as a child appears as one of the characters.

App-II 59

Gutzkow, Karl, 1811-1878.
Uriel Acosta. Trauerspiel in fünf Aufzügen. [184-?]
62 p.

Spinoza as a child appears as one of the characters.

OCH

App-II 60

Gutzkow, Karl, 1811-1878.
Uriel Acosta. Trauerspiel in 5 Aufzügen. Mit einer Einleitung von Rud. v. Gottschall. Leipzig, Reclam, 1909.
82 p. (Reclams Universal-Bibliothek, 5051)

Spinoza as a child appears as one of the characters.

MB

App-II 61

Gutzkow, Karl, 1811-1878.
Uriel Acosta. Trauerspiel in fünf Aufzügen. 6. Aufl. Leipzig, Brockhaus, 1866.
116 p.

Spinoza as a child appears as one of the characters.

OO

SPECIAL COLLECTIONS SPINOZA
App-II 62

Gutzkow, Karl, 1811-1878.
Uriel Acosta; Trauerspiel in fünf Aufzügen. 17. Aufl. Berlin, H. Costenoble [191-?]
82 p. 20cm.

Spinoza as a child appears as one of the characters.

SPECIAL COLLECTIONS SPINOZA
App-II 63

Gutzkow, Karl, 1811-1878.
אוריאל אקוסטה; משחק תוגה בחמש מע־
רכות, מחוברת אשכנזית מאת המליץ הנשגב
הנאדר לתהלה ולתפארת קארל גוטצקאוו.
נעתק לשפת עבר מאת שלמה ראבין. וויען,
תרט"ז לפ"ק.
[Wien, Druck von U. Klopf s. und A. Eurich, 1856]
121 p.

Title transliterated: Uriel Acosta.

CONTINUED ON NEXT CARD

NNC

SPECIAL COLLECTIONS SPINOZA
App-II 64

Gutzkow, Karl, 1811-1878.
אוריאל אקוסטה. [1856] (Card 2)

Added t.-p. in German: Uriel Acosta; Trauerspiel in fünf Aufzügen, von Karl Gutzkow, in's Ebräische übersetzt von Salomo Rubin.
Spinoza as a child appears as one of the characters.

NNC

App-II 65

Gutzkow, Karl, 1811-1878.

אוריאל אקאָסטא. טראַגעדיע אין 5 אקטן.
אידיש פון אברהם מאָרעווסקי.
[Warsaw, 1921]
128 p.

Title transliterated: Uriʻel Akosta.
Spinoza as a child appears as one of the characters.

NNJ

SPECIAL COLLECTIONS SPINOZA
App-II 66

Jellinek, Herrmann
Uriel Acosta's Leben und Lehre; ein Beitrag zur Kenntniss seiner Moral, wie zur Berichtigung der Gutzkow'schen Fiktionen über Acosta und zur Charakteristik der damaligen Juden. Aus den Quellen dargestellt. Zerbst, Kummer'sche Buchhandlung, 1847.
viii, 44 p. 17cm.

Includes references to Spinoza.
Bibliographical notes.

SPECIAL COLLECTIONS SPINOZA
App-II 67

[Katzenstein, Julius] 1890-1946.
Uriel da Costa; oder, Die Tragödie der Gesinnung. Berlin, Rowohlt, 1932.
340 p. plates, ports. 21cm.

Author's pseud., Josef Kastein, at head of title.
Includes references to Spinoza.
Bibliography: p. 333-338.

SPECIAL COLLECTIONS SPINOZA
App-II 68

Klaar, Alfred, 1848-
Uriel Acosta; Leben und Bekenntnis eines Freidenkers vor 300 Jahren. Berlin, G. Reimer, 1909.
169 p. 19cm.

Acosta's Exemplar humanae vitae in the Latin original and in German translation: p. [93]-155.
Includes references to Spinoza.
Bibliographical notes.

Levy, Erna
Uriel Acosta zu Gutzkows fünfzigstem Todestag (16. Dezember 1878) ⌊1928⌋
748-757 p. 24cm.

From Blätter der Städtischen Bühnen Frankfurt a. M., Hft. 47/48, Jahrg. 1928, 2. bis 15. Dezember.
Includes a reference to Spinoza as a character in Gutzkow's "Uriel Acosta" (p. 756)

Limborch, Philipp van, 1633-1712.
Philippi a Limborch De veritate religionis Christianæ amica collatio cum erudito Judæo. Govdæ, Apud Justum ab Hoeve, 1687.
⌊16⌋, 364, ⌊14⌋ p. 24cm.

"Urielis Acosta Exemplar humanæ vitæ. Addita est Brevis refutatio argumentorum quibus Acosta omnem religionem revelatam impugnat, per Philippum a Limborch": p. ⌊341⌋-364.

Limborch, Philipp van, 1633-1712.
Philippus van Limborchs Vriendelyke onderhandeling met een geleerden Jood, over de waarheid van den Christelyken godsdienst, nevens Uriels Acostas Voorbeeld van 't menschelyk leven; met de aanmerkingen daar over. Als mede een Kort verhaal wegens de bekeering van eene Juffrouw, die genegen zynde Joodsch te worden, weder tot den Christelyken godsdienst gebragt ist. Alles uit het Latyn vertaalt. T'Amsterdam, By Pieter Visser, 1723.
⌊38⌋, 747 p. 21cm.

Limborch, Philipp van, 1633-1712.
Philippus van Limborchs Vriendelyke onderhandeling met den geleerden Jood Isaac Orobio de Castro, over de waarheid van den Christelyken godsdienst. Nevens Uriëls Acostaas Voorbeeld van't menschelyk leven; met de aanmerkingen daar over. Als mede een Kort verhaal wegens bekeering van eene Juffrouw, die genegen zynde Joodsch te worden, weder tot den Christelyken godsdienst gebragt is. Alles uit het Latyn vertaalt. De tweede druk. T'Amsterdam, By Pieter Visser, 1735.
⌊36⌋, 747, ⌊5⌋ p. 20cm.

Magalhães Basto, Artur de, 1894-
Alguns documentos inéditos sôbre Uriel da Costa. Coimbra, Imprensa da Universidade, 1930.
35 p. facsim. 24cm.

"Separata de 'O Instituto', vol. 79º, nº 1."
Presentation copy to Carl Gebhardt with the author's inscription and signature.

Magalhães Basto, Artur de, 1894-
Novo documento inédito sôbre Uriel da Costa. Coimbra, Imprensa da Universidade, 1930.
17 p. facsim. 24cm.

"Separata de O Instituto, vol. 79º, nº 4."
Presentation copy to Carl Gebhardt with the author's inscription and signature.

Michaëlis de Vasconcellos, Carolina, 1851-1925.
Uriel da Costa; notas relativas à sua vida e às suas obras. Coimbra, Imprensa da Universidade, 1921.
180 p. ports., facsim. 29cm.

On cover: Instituto de estudos históricos e filosóficos.
Includes quotations in Spanish translation from Frederick Pollock's "Spinoza, his life and philosophy" and from Dunin-Borkowski's "Der

CONTINUED ON NEXT CARD

Michaëlis de Vasconcellos, Carolina, 1851-1925.
Uriel da Costa. 1921. (Card 2)

junge De Spinoza" and other references to Spinoza.
Cover dated: 1922.
"Separata da Revista da Universidade de Coimbra, vol. XIII, nºs 1 a 4."
"Lista cronológica de escritos de Uriel ou relativos a Uriel": p. ⌊163⌋-177.
Presentation copy to Carl Gebhardt with the author's inscription and initials.

Michaëlis de Vasconcellos, Carolina, 1851-1925.
Uriel da Costa; notas suplementares relativas a sua vida e sua obra. ⌊1924⌋
5-22, 157-158 p. 25cm.

Signed: Carolina Michaelis de Vasconcellos.
A review of Die Schriften des Uriel de Costa, mit Einleitung, Übertragung und Regesten hrsg. von Carl Gebhardt.
From Lusitania, revista de estudos portugueses, fasciculo 1, Janeiro de 1924.
French summary: p. 157-158.

Paley, Johann
אוריאל אקאסטא, פון יאהאן פאלייא
(בן אסתי?) ניו יארק, היברו פאבלי-
שינג קאמפאני.
New York, Hebrew Publishing Company, 1906.
78 p. 21cm.

Title transliterated: Uriel Acosta.
Spinoza appears as one of the characters.

 App-II 79

Perles, Joseph, 1835-1894.
Eine neuerschlossene Quelle über Uriel Acosta
Krotoschin, B. L. Monasch, 1877.
[193]-213 p. 19cm.

"Aus der Frankel-Craetz'schen Monatsschrift, Mai 1877."
Original paper covers bound in.
Includes references to Spinoza.
Bibliographical footnotes.

 App-II 80

Porges, Nathan, 1848-
Zur Lebensgeschichte Uriel da Costas. [1918]
[37]-48, [108]-124, [199]-218 p. 23cm.

From Monatsschrift für Geschichte und Wissenschaft des Judentums, 62. Jahrg., Heft 1/3, 4/6, 7/12.
Includes references to Spinoza.
Bibliographical footnotes.

 App-II 81

Reznikoff, Charles, 1894-
Uriel Acosta; a play. [1925]
35-42 p. 26cm.

From the Menorah journal, vol. XI, no. 1, February 1925.

 App-II 82

Reznikoff, Charles.
Nine plays, by Charles Reznikoff. New York, C. Reznikoff [°1927]
3 p. l., 113 p., 1 l. 21½cm.
"400 copies were printed and the type distributed; this is number 108."

CONTENTS.—Uriel Acosta.—Abram in Egypt.—Chatterton.—Meriwether Lewis.—Captive Israel.—The black death.—Coral.—Rashi.—Genesis.

Sachar, Abram Leon, 1899-
A history of the Jews [by] Abram Leon Sachar ... New York, A. A. Knopf, 1930.
xv p., 2 l., 3-408, xxiv p., 1 l. front., maps (part double) 24½ cm.
"Selected bibliography": p. 397-408.
Includes a section "Acosta and Spinoza" (p. 245-248)

1. Jews—Hist.

 App-II 84

Silva Rosa, Jacob S da, 1886-
Uriël da Costa en Dr. Samuel da Silva (1571-1631) Haarlem, 1927.
cover-title, 7 p. illus. 22cm.

"Overdruk 'De Vrijdagavond', Jaarg. IV, No. 31."
Author's inscription and initials on cover-title.

 App-II 85

Sonne, Isaiah, 1887-
Da Costa studies. Philadelphia, Dropsie College for Hebrew and Cognate Learning, 1932.
cover-title, [247]-293 p. 24cm.

"Reprinted from the Jewish Quarterly Review, New series, vol. XXII, number 3."
Includes references to Spinoza and to Carl Gebhardt's Die Schriften des Uriel da Costa.
Bibliographical footnotes.

Strauss, Eduard
Uriel da Costa. [1926]
2 p.

In Frankfurter Zeitung, Jan. 7, 1926.

NN

 App-II 87

Vaz Dias, A M 1877-1939.
Uriel da Costa; nieuwe bijdrage tot diens levensgeschiedenis. Leiden, E. J. Brill, 1936.
32 p. facsims. 24cm. (Mededeelingen van wege het Spinozahuis, II)

 App-II 88

Zeitschrift für hebräische Bibliographie ...
Jahrg. 15$^{3-6}$.
Mai/Juni-Nov./Dez. 1911.
Frankfurt a. M., J. Kauffmann, 1911.

Lists a work about Spinoza (no. 3, p. 77) and includes an article "Leon Modena über Uriel da Costa" by N. Porges (no. 3, p. 80-82)

APPENDIX III
DE TRIBUS
IMPOSTORIBUS

App-III
93

De tribus impostoribus.
De impostura religionum breve compendium; seu, Liber de tribus impostoribus. Nach zwei Mss. und mit historisch-litterarischer Einleitung, hrsg. von F. W. Genthe. Leipzig, F. Fleischer, 1833.
62 p. 22 cm.
"Réponse à la dissertation de Mr. de La Monnoye sur le traité: De tribus impostoribus," signed J. L. R. L. [i. e. P. F. Arpe]: p. [27]-40.
Includes references to Spinoza (p.14, 18-20)
1. Rationalism. 2. La Monnoye, Bernard de, 1641-1728. I. Genthe, Friedrich Wilhelm, 1805-1866, ed. II. Arpe, Peter Friedrich, 1682-1740.

App-III
89

[Briggs, Samuel] ed.
De tribus impostoribus, A. D. 1230. The three impostors, translated (with notes and comments) from a French manuscript of the work written in the year 1716, with a dissertation on the original treatise and a bibliography of the various editions. By Alcofribas Nasier, the later [pseud.] Privately printed for the subscribers, 1904.
159 p. facsims. 25cm.
CONTINUED ON NEXT CARD

App-III
94

De tribus impostoribus.
De tribvs impostoribvs. Anno MDIIC. Zweite mit einem neuen Vorwort versehene Auflage von Emil Weller. Heilbronn, G. Henninger, 1876.
39, [1] p. 21cm.
Includes references to Spinoza (p. vi-vii)

App-III
90

[Briggs, Samuel] ed. De tribus impostoribus, A. D. 1230. 1904. (Card 2)

Contains English translations of two works. The first (p. [26]-109) is a translation of the work in French which appeared 1719 as 2d part of "La vie et l'esprit de m. Benoît de Spinosa", and later under title "Traité des trois imposteurs". It is translated from a manuscript copy which includes two preliminary sections (found in some other manuscript copies), "Dissertation on the Book of the three
CONTINUED ON NEXT CARD

App-III
95

De tribus impostoribus.
De tribus impostoribus M.D.IIC. texte latin, collationné sur l'exemplaire du Duc de La Vallière ... augmenté de variantes de plusieurs manuscrits, etc. et d'une notice philologique et bibliographique par Philomneste Junior [Pierre Gustave Brunet] Paris, Gay, 1861.
lv, 57 p. 16 x 9 cm.
References to Spinoza (p. xxx-xl) included in "Notice bibliographique".

App-III
91

[Briggs, Samuel] ed. De tribus impostoribus, A. D. 1230. 1904. (Card 3)

impostors" and "Frederick Emperor to the very illustrious Otho".
The second (p. [11]-144) is a translation of the Latin work with which the former was long confused, "De tribus impostoribus" (translated from 1876 ed. of Emil Weller)
Includes references to Spinoza, p. 10-11.
"Edition 352 copies."
Bibliography: p. [9]-17.

App-III
96

De tribus impostoribus.
Ketzerphilosophie des mittelalters. Das buch genannt "De tribus impostoribus." 1598. Übers. mit einem nachwort und anmerkungen versehen, von Gregor von Glasenapp. Riga, Jonck & Poliewsky, 1909.
58 p. 22½cm.
Includes references to Spinoza (p. 53).
1. Glasenapp, Gregor von, 1855- ed. and tr. II. Title.

App-III
92

De tribus impostoribus.
De imposturis religionvm, breve compendium. Descriptum ab exemplari manuscripto, quod in bibliotheca Joh. Freder. Mayeri, publice distracta Berolini anno 1716. deprehensum, et a Principe Eugenio de Sabaudia LXXX. imperialibus redemptum fuit.
[31] p. 21cm.
Manuscript.

App-III
97

[Diderot, Denis] 1713-1784.
Pensées philosophiques ... A La haye, Aux depens de la compagnie, 1746.
[96] p. 17cm.
Manuscript; apparently a copy of the printed edition, without the table.
Bound with Traité des trois imposteurs. 1777.

App-III 98

Kettner, Friedrich Ernst
De duobus impostoribus B. Spinosa et B. Bekkero dissertatio historica. Lipsiae, 1694.

NIC

SPECIAL COLLECTIONS SPINOZA

App-III 99

Kortholt, Christian, 1633-1694.
De tribus impostoribus magnis liber, cura editus Christiani Kortholti ... Kiloni, Literis & sumptibus Joachimi Reumanni, 1680.
[16], 294 p. 17cm.

An attack on Edward Herbert, Thomas Hobbes and Benedictus de Spinoza (p. 139-225)
"Appendix, qua Hieronymi Cardani & Edoradi Herberti de animalitate hominis opiniones ... proponuntur, ac ... examinantur": p. 227-295.

NNC

SPECIAL COLLECTIONS SPINOZA

App-III 100

Kortholt, Christian, 1633-1694.
De tribus impostoribus magnis liber, cura editus Christiani Kortholti ... Hamburgi, Imprimebat Joachimus Reumann, 1700.
[10], 3-168 p. 21cm.

An attack on Edward Herbert, Thomas Hobbes and Benedictus de Spinoza (p. 75-120)
"Appendix, qua Hieronymi Cardani & Edoardi Herberti de animalitate hominis opiniones ... proponuntur, ac ... examinantur": p. 121-158.
Preface by Sebastian Kortholt.

NNC

App-III 101

[Kortholt, Christian] 1633-1694.
De tribus impostoribus magnis liber; demuo editus cura Sebastiani Kortholti. Hamburgi, literis & sumptibus J. Reumanni, 1701.
[10], 168 p.

An attack on Edward Herbert, Thomas Hobbes and Benedictus de Spinoza.

MH

App-III 102

Marchand, Prosper, d. 1756.
Dictionnaire historique, ou Memoires critiques et litteraires, concernant la vie et les ouvrages de divers personnages distingués, particulierement dans la republique des lettres. La Haye, P. de Hondt, 1758-59.
2 v. in 1. 42 cm.

References to Spinoza included in article "Impostoribus (liber de tribus)" (v. 1, p. 312-329)

SPECIAL COLLECTIONS SPINOZA

App-III 103

[Mehlig, Johann Michael]
Das erste schlimmste Buch, oder historisch-critische Abhandlung von der religionslästerlichen Schrift De tribvs impostoribvs. Chemnitz, Johann Christoph Stössel, 1764.
[12], 100 p. 18cm.

Includes references to Spinoza (p. 32, 34)

SPECIAL COLLECTIONS SPINOZA

App-III 104

MSCPTUM de tribus impostoribus Gallico sermone exaratum ineditum et longe rarissimum.
1 p. l., 129 p. 16cm.

Manuscript copy of the work which appeared as the 2d part of "La vie et l'esprit de m. Benoît Spinosa" (1719) and later under title "Traité des trois imposteurs".
Not a translation of the Latin treatise "De tribus impostoribus".
Attributed by some authorities to J. M. Lucas.

SPECIAL COLLECTIONS SPINOZA

App-III 105

Presser, Jacob, 1899-
Das buch "De tribus impostoribus" (Von den drei betrügern) von dr. J. Presser. Amsterdam, H. J. Paris, 1926.
3 p. l., 169 p. 2 facsim. 25cm.

The author's thesis, Amsterdam.
"Bibliographie": p. 125-135.
With the text (p. 136-146)
Includes references to Spinoza (p. 81-82, 96-98)

1. De tribus impostoribus. I. Title.

[Full name: Gerrit Jacob Presser]

Library of Congress BL2773.D43P7 40-16039
[2] 211

App-III 106

Rosenkranz, Karl, 1805-1879.
Der Zweifel am Glauben. Kritik der Schriften: De tribus impostoribus. Halle, Reinicke, 1830.
viii, 88 p.

NN

SPECIAL COLLECTIONS SPINOZA

App-III 107

Spinoza II. oder Subiroth Sopim ... Rom, bei der Wittwe Bona Spes, 5770 [i. e. Berlin, W. Vieweg, 1787]
xii, 116 p. 17cm.

A translation of the work which appeared as the 2d part of "La vie et l'esprit de Mr. Benoît de Spinosa" (1719) and later under title "Traité des trois imposteurs." Attributed by some authorities to J. M. Lucas.

NNC

CONTINUED ON NEXT CARD

Spinoza II. oder Subiroth Sopim. 5770
[i. e. 1787] (Card 2)

"Das Mscrpt dieser deutschen Uebersetzung ... führte den Titel: Das Buch von denen dreyen Erzbetrügern, Mose, Mesia und Mahomed ... ein überaus rares Manuscript in französischer Sprache. Nunmehro aber ins Teutsche übersetzt ... 1745": Vorrede, p. x.
Van der Linde 103: "Uitgegeven in 1787, bij W. Vieweg in Berlin."

Traité des trois imposteurs ...
[122] p. 22cm.

Manuscript copy of a printed edition; pagination (135, [2] p.) of the printed edition given in margins.
A revision by Vroes, J. Aymon and J. Rousset de Missy of the 2d part of "La vie et l'esprit de m. Benoît Spinosa", a work attributed by some authorities to J. M. Lucas. -Cf. Barbier and British Museum Catalogue.

CONTINUED ON NEXT CARD

Traité des trois imposteurs ... (Card 2)

"Sentimens sur le Traité des trois imposteurs" (par B. de La Monnoye): p. [81-103]
"Reponse à la dissertation de M. de la Monnoye sur le Traité des trois imposteurs" (p. [104-116] signed: J. L. R. L. [i. e. P. F. Arpe]
"Copie de l'article IX. du tome 1er, seconde partie, des Memoires de litterature, imprimés à la Haye chez Henry du Lauzet 1716": p. [117-120]

Traité des trois imposteurs. 1775.
152 p.

A revision by Vroes, J. Aymon and J. Rousset de Missy of the 2d part of "La vie et l'esprit de m. Benoît Spinosa", a work attributed by some authorities to J. M. Lucas. -Cf. Barbier and British Museum Catalogue.
This edition published in Holland, according to Brunet's edition of De tribus impostoribus, p. xxxi; in Amsterdam, according to Barbier.

Traité des trois imposteurs. En Suisse, De l'Imprimerie philosophique, 1793.
1 p. l., 168, iii p.

A revision by Vroes, J. Aymon and J. Rousset de Missy of the 2d part of "La vie et l'esprit de m. Benoît Spinosa", a work attributed by some authorities to J. M. Lucas. -Cf. Barbier and British Museum Catalogue.

Traité des trois imposteurs. A Amsterdam, 1776.
1 p. l., 138, [2] p. 17cm.

A revision by Vroes, J. Aymon and J. Rousset de Missy of the 2d part of "La vie et l'esprit de m. Benoît Spinosa", a work attributed by some authorities to J. M. Lucas. -Cf. Barbier and British Museum Catalogue.
"Sentimens sur le Traité des trois imposteurs" (par B. de La Monnoye): p. 93-119.

CONTINUED ON NEXT CARD

Traité des trois imposteurs. 1776. (Card 2)

"Réponse a la dissertation de monsieur de la Monnoye, sur le Traité des trois imposteurs" (p. 119-134) signed: J. L. R. L. [i. e. P. F. Arpe]
"Copie de l'article IX, du tome Ier, seconde partie, des Mémoires de littérature, imprimés à la Haye ... 1716": p. 135-138.

Traité des trois imposteurs. [Amsterdam] 1777.
152 p. 17cm.

A revision by Vroes, J. Aymon and J. Rousset de Missy of the 2d part of "La vie et l'esprit de m. Benoît Spinosa", a work attributed by some authorities to J. M. Lucas. -Cf. Barbier and British Museum Catalogue.
"Sentimens sur le Traité des trois imposteurs (par B. de La Monnoye): p. [103]-130.

CONTINUED ON NEXT CARD

Traité des trois imposteurs. 1777.
(Card 2)

"Reponse a la dissertation de mr. de la Monnoye, sur le Traité des trois imposteurs" (p. 131-146) signed: J. L. R. L. [i. e. P. F. Arpe]
"Copie de l'article IX du tome Ier, seconde partie des Mémoires de littérature, imprimés à la Haye ... en 1716": p. 147-150.

Appendix IV
Auxiliary Works

Alexander ab Alexandro, 1461-1523.
Alexandri ab Alexandro, jurisperiti Neapolitani, Genialium dierum libri sex, cum integris commentariis Andreæ Tiraquelli, Dionysii Gothofredi, J. C. Christophori Coleri & Nic. Merceri. Accessere indices capitum, rerum & verborum locupletissimi ... Lugduni Batavorum, Ex officinâ Hackiana, 1673.
2 v. 21cm.

Added engraved title-pages; v. 2 has engraved t.-p. only.

Arrianus, Flavius.
'Αρριανοῦ Περὶ ἀναβάσεως 'Αλεξάνδρου ἱστοριῶν βιβλία ζ'. Τοῦ αὐτοῦ 'Ινδικά. Arriani De expedit. Alex. Magni historiarum libri VII. Ejusdem Indica. Ex Bonavent. Vulcanii Brug. interpretatione. Nicolaus Blancardus e veteribus libris recensuit, versionem Latinam emendavit, octo libros animadversionum adjecit. Volumen primum. Amstelodami, Apud Joannem Janssonium à Waesberge, & viduam Elizæi Weyerstraet, 1668.
[14], 617, [35] p. port. 20cm.

CONTINUED ON NEXT CARD

Arrianus, Flavius. Arriani De expedit. Alex. Magni historiarum libri VII. 1668. (Card 2)

Added title-page engraved.
Complete in one volume?
"Photii patriarchæ Constantinopolitani ex Arriani scriptis eclogæ. Andrea Schotto interprete": p. [595]-617.

Bornius, Henricus
Henrici Bornii ... Oratio inauguralis de vera philosophandi libertate, dicta in splendidissimo & frequentissimo auditorio Lugduni Batavorum, die II Novembris anni cIↃ IↃc LIII. ... Lvgd. Batavor., Ex officina Johannis & Danielis Elsevier, 1654.
[4], 35, [4] p. 20cm.

Delmedigo, Joseph Solomon, 1591-1655.
Melo Chofnajim ... Biographie Josef Salomo del Medigo's; dessen Brief an Serach ben Nathan, enthält einen kurzen Leitfaden der hebräisch-jüdischen Litteraturgeschichte, nach dem hier zum ersten Male herausgegebenen Originale übersetzt ... nebst einzelnen Anmerkungen zu andern hebräischen hier zum ersten Male gedruckten Schriften, von Abraham Geiger. Hrsg. von W. Wilzig. Berlin, 1840.
lvi, 104, 80, viii p. port. 21cm.

Added t.-p. and part of text in Hebrew.

Eleutherius, Theophilus
Verklaring over het drie-en-vijftigste kapittel van de profeet Esaias. Door Theophilus Eleutherius. Gedrukt na het jaer onses Heeren 1627.
12, [2] p. 25cm. (In Sozzini, Fausto. Brieven aan zijn vrienden geschreeven. 1666)

Hallewi, Aaron, d. 1293.
ספר החינוך, יבאו בו התרי"ג מצות
יסוד תורת משה ונבואתו: מנימוקן של
גדולי עולם הרי"ף והרמב"ם והרמב"ן
זצ"ל: מסודרות על פי סדר הפרשיות כל
פרשה ופרשה המצות הנמצאות בה, ושורש
המצוה ודיניה ומנהגיה מקומם אנה הוא:
... חובר מימי קדם מאיש לוי ברצלוני
אשר נודע בשערים שמו: גם ברכות יעטה
רודף צדקה וחסד כמ"ר יצחק סג"ל יצ"ו

CONTINUED ON NEXT CARD

Hallewi, Aaron, d. 1293. ספר החינוך.
(Card 2)

בכמהח"ר יעקב סג"ל זצ"ל הערלישהיים
אשר הוציאו לאור ושם עינו עליו להגיהו
בכל עוז: ותהי ראשית מלאכתו סוף שנת מה
נאוו על ההרים רגלי מבשר ליצירה: להוצאה
זואני דגארה ובביתו עה ויניציאה:
[Venice, Giovanni di Gara, 1600-01]
228 l. 22cm.

Title transliterated: Sefer ha-Ḥinnūkh.

Huet, Pierre Daniel, 1630-1721.
Alnetanae quaestiones de concordia rationis et fidei ... Lipsiae, 1692.
[4], 437, [15] p. 25 cm.

App-IV 126

Huet, Pierre Daniel, 1630-1721.
Demonstratio evangelica ad Serenissimum Delphinum. 4. ed. Lipsiae, Apud J. T. Fritsch, 1694.
2 v. in 1. 22 cm.

CtY

App-IV 127

Huet, Pierre Daniel, 1630-1721.
Demonstratio evangelica ad Serenissimum Delphinum. 5a ed. Lipsiae, Apud J. T. Fritsch, 1703.
31 p. l., 1187, [81] p., 2 l., 69, [7] p. port. 22 cm.

CtY

App-IV 128

Huet, Pierre Daniel, 1630-1721.
Demonstratio evangelica ad Serenissimum Delphinum. Sexta editio. Francofurti, 1722.
718 p.

PHC

App-IV 129

Huet, Pierre Daniel, 1630-1721.
Petri Danielis Huetii De interpretatione libri duo: quorum prior est, De optimo genere interpretandi: alter De claris interpretibus. His accessit De fabularum romanensium origine diatriba. Editio altera, priore emendatior. Hagæ-Comitis, apud Arnoldum Leers, M.DC.LXXXIII, M.DC.LXXXII.
2 v. in 1. 16cm.

Title vignette: A. Leers' device.
Vol. [II] has special t.-p.: Petri Danielis Huetii Liber de origine fabularum romanensium, ad Joannem Renaldum Segræsium. Ex gallico latine reddidit Gulielmus Pyrrho ... Hagæ-Comitis, apud Arnoldum Leers, M.DC.LXXXII.

~~(Continued on next card)~~

33-806

[45b1]

SPECIAL COLLECTIONS SPINOZA App-IV 130

Huygens, Christiaan, 1629-1695.
Christiani Hvgenii ... Horologivm oscillatorivm, sive De motv pendvlorvm ad horologia aptato demonstrationes geometricæ. Parisiis, Apud F. Muguet, 1673.
[14], 161, [1] p. diagrs. 33cm.

Title vignette.

SPECIAL COLLECTIONS SPINOZA App-IV 131

Ibn Tufail, d. 1185.
Het leeven van Hai ebn Yokdhan, in het Arabisch beschreeven door Abu Jaaphar ebn Tophail, en uit de Latynsche oversettinge van Eduard Pocock ... In het Nederduitsch vertaald door S. D. B. Waar in getoond wordt, hoe iemand buiten eenige ommegang met menschen, ofte onderwyzinge, kan komen tot de kennisse van zich zelven, en van God. t'Amsterdam, By Willem Lamsveld, 1701.
[21], 293, [17] p. plates. 16cm.

CONTINUED ON NEXT CARD

SPECIAL COLLECTIONS SPINOZA App-IV 132

Ibn Tufail, d. 1185. Het leeven van Hai ebn Yokdhan. 1701. (Card 2)

Added engraved t.-p.
Ms. note by Carl Gebhardt on fly leaf. Gebhardt rejects the possibility that the translator's initials on t.-p. are Spinoza's initials in reverse order.

SPECIAL COLLECTIONS SPINOZA App-IV 133

Jonstonus, Joannes, 1603-1675.
Iohan. Ionstoni Doct. medici Enchiridion ethicvm, ex sententiosissimis dictis concinnatum, et in libros tres distinctum. Lugd. Batavorum, ex officina Elseviriana, 1634.
2 p. l., 228 p. 10cm.

Title-page and one leaf following lacking; title-page supplied in manuscript. Cataloged from title given in Willems, Alphonse. Les Elsevier, 1880.

NNC

SPECIAL COLLECTIONS SPINOZA App-IV 134

Jonstonus, Joannes, 1603-1675.
Ioh. Ionstoni ... Natvræ constantia: seu, Diatribe in qua, per posteriorum temporum cum prioribus collationem, mundum, nec ratione sui totius, nec ratione partium, universaliter & perpetuo in pejus ruere, ostenditur. Amsterdami, Apud Gvilielmvm Blaev, 1632.
[8], 182 p. 13cm.

Bound with the author's Thavmatographia natvralis ... 1632.

SPECIAL COLLECTIONS SPINOZA App-IV 135

Jonstonus, Joannes, 1603-1675.
Ioh. Ionstoni Thavmatographia natvralis, in decem classes distincta, in quibus admiranda I. Coeli. II. Elementorvm. III. Meteororvm. IV. Fossilivm. V. Plantarvm. VI. Avivm. VII. Qvadrvpedvm. VIII. Exangvivm. IX. Piscivm. X. Hominis. Amsterdami, Apud Gvilielmvm Blaev, 1632.
[12], 501, [3] p. 13cm.

Julianus, Apostata, emperor of Rome, 331-363.
Deffense du paganisme par l'empereur Julien, en grec et en françois, avec des dissertations et des notes pour servir d'eclaircissement au texte & pour en refuter les erreurs par Mr. le marquis d'Argens ... A Berlin, Chez Chretien Frederic Voss, 1764.
[4], lxxii, 306 p. 17cm.

Greek text and French translation on opposite pages.

Koran.
Mahomets Alkoran, door de Heer du Ryer uit d'Arabische in de Fransche taal gestelt; beneffens een tweevoudige beschryving van Mahomets leven; en een verhaal van des zelfs reis ten hemel, gelijk ook zijn samenspraak met de Jood Abdias. Alles van nieus door J. H. Glazemaker vertaalt, en te zamen gebracht. t'Amsterdam, Voor Jan Rieuwertsz, 1657.
[16], 692, [4], 125 p. 14cm.

Added t.-p., engr.

[Laet, Joannes de], 1593-1649.
Hispania; sive, De Regis Hispaniāe regnis et opibus commentarius. Lugd. Batav., Ex officina Elzeviriana, 1629.
[16], 498, [1] p. 12cm.

Engraved t.-p.
Dedication signed: Ioannes de Laet.
The first of two editions which appeared in 1629.--cf. Willems, Alphonse. Les Elsevir. 1880.

Leon, Jacob Judah Aryeh, 17th cent.
ספר תבנית היכל, אשר בו נחקר בקצר
אמיץ על תבנית אשר עשה המלך שלמה לה׳
בכל חוקותיו ובכל צורותיו ... חברו
בלשון לעז וגם העתיקו ללשון הקדש החכם
... כמהרר יעקב יהודה אריה ... אמשטרדם,
בבית השותפים יהודה בן מו"הרר מרדכי
זצ"ל שמואל בר משה הלוי שליטא, שנת
ה׳ בהיכל קדשו ה׳ בשמים כסאו לפ"ק.

[Amsterdam, Levi Marcus, 1650]
[6], 3-38 l.

CONTINUED ON [illegible] CARD

Leon, Jacob Judah Aryeh, 17th cent. ספר תבנית היכל. [1650] (Card 2)

Title transliterated: Sefer Tabhnīth hēkhal.
Translated from the Portuguese.
"Dedicacao", in Portuguese: [4] l. at beginning.
Added t.-p. in Latin: Libellus effigiei, Templi Salomonis, in qvo fabricâ Templi & omnium ejus vasorum instrumentorumque ... structurâ ac formâ, breviter describitur ...

Lipsius, Justus, 1547-1606.
Justi Lipsi ... Opera omnia, postremum ab ipso aucta et recensita: nunc primum copioso rerum indice illustrata. Versaliâe, Apud Andraêam ab Hoogenhuysen et Societatem, 1675.
4 v. illus., fold. plates, port. 21cm.

Vol. 1 has engraved t.-p.

Photius, patriarch of Constantinople.
Photii patriarchâe Constantinopolitani ex Arriani scriptis eclogâe. Andrea Schotto interprete. (In Arrianus, Flavius. Arriani De expedit. Alex. Magni historiarum libri VII. 1668, p. [594]-617)

[Quin, Walter] 1575?-1634?
Corona virtvtvm principe dignarvm, cui adjuncta sunt de vita & virtutibus duorum Antoninorum Pii & Marci maximè memorabilia. Editio tertia emendatior & auctior. Lvgd. Bat., Ex Officinâ Elseviriana, 1634.
[16], 242 p. 10cm.

Bound with Jonstonus, Joannes. Enchiridion ethicvm. 1634.

Serrurier, Pierre, 17th cent.
An awakening warning to the vvofull vvorld, by a voyce in three nations; uttered in a brief dissertation concerning that fatal, and to be admired conjunction of all the planets, in one, and the same sign (...) to come to pass the [11] day of December, anno 1662. In which it is clearly evinced, as well by S. Scriptures, as by the nature of the conjunction itself, and other antecedents, concomitants and circumstances, that the glorious

CONTINUED ON NEXT CARD

Serrurier, Pierre, 17th cent. An awakening warning to the vvofull vvorld. 1662. (Card 2)
coming of Jesus Christ is at hand ... Autore Petro Serario. Amsterdam, 1662.
42 p. 19cm.

 App-IV 146

Serrurier, Pierre, 17th cent.
Antwoort, op een Wonderspreuckigh tractaet eenes onbenaemden discipels van Renatus des Cartes; in het welck by de philosophie aen de Christen-werelt voor een onfeilbare regel en richt-snoer opdringht, om de Heylige Schrift uyt te leggen ... Mitsgaders het oordeel eenes voortreflijcken mans, soo over dit dispuyt, als over de stellingen van Des Cartes, soo inde philosophie als theologie. Door Petrus Serarius. t'Amstelredam, Gedruckt by Broer en Ian Appelaar, 1667.
[34], 98 p. 21cm.

~~CONTINUED ON NEXT CARD~~

 App-IV 147

Tomasini, Jacopo Filippo, 1597-1654.
Iac. Philippi Tomasini ... De vita, bibliotheca et museo Laurentii Pignorii ... dissertatio. [1669]
[61]-94 (i. e. 96) p. illus. 24cm. (In Pignoria, Lorenzo. Mensa Isiaca. 1670)

NNC

 App-IV 148

Tomasini, Jacopo Filippo, 1597-1654.
Manus Aeneae, Cecropii votum referentis, dilucidatio. Auctore Jacobo Philippo Tomasino ... Amstelodami, Sumptibus Andreae Frisii, 1669.
[29]-60 p. illus. 24cm. (In Pignoria, Lorenzo. Mensa Isiaca. 1670)

NNC

App-IV 149

Tuinman, Carolus
De heillooze gruwelleere der vrygeesten; in haar grond en tzamenschakeling, uit derzelver schriften aangewezen, ontmaskert, en wederlegt. Tot een Vervolg op J. Kalvijns vertaalde Onderrichting tegen de vrygeesten zynes tijds, en de overeenstemming met de hedendaagsche ... Door Carolus Tuinman ... Te Middelburg, By Johannes op Somer, 1714.
8 p. l., 240 p.

NIC

App-IV 150

Tuinman, Carolus, 1659-1728.
Johan Calvijns onderrichting tegen de vrijgeesten, met de overeenstemming van die vrijgeesten met de hedendaagsche. Middelburg, 1712.

NIC

 App-IV 151

Velthuysen, Lambert van, 1622-1685.
Lamberti Velthuysii, Ultrajectini, Opera omnia. Ante quidem separatim, tam Belgicè quam Latinè, nunc verò conjunctim Latinè edita. Quibus accessere duo tractatus novi, hactenus inediti: prior est De articulis fidei fundamentalibus: alter De cultu naturali, oppositus Tractatui theologico-politico & operi posthumo Benedicti de Spinoza ... Roterodami, Typis Reineri Leers, 1680.
2 v. 21cm.

 App-IV 152

Velthuysen, Lambert van, 1622-1685.
Lamberti Velthuysii, Ultrajectini, Opera omnia. Ante quidem separatim, tam Belgicè quam Latinè, nunc verò conjunctim Latinè edita. Quibus accessere duo tractatus novi, hactenus inediti: prior est De articulis fidei fundamentalibus: alter De cultu naturali, oppositus Tractatui theologico-politico & operi posthumo Benedicti de Spinoza ... Roterodami, Typis Reineri Leers, 1680.
2 v. 25cm.
Large paper edition.

 App-IV 153

Veredicus, Iustus, pseud.
Een oprechten Pharisaeus ontmantelt van zijnen verçierden dobbelden doctoralen titul. Waar ontrent veel vreemde ongerijmde en doortrapte practijcken, van verscheyden Utrechtsche schijnheyligen, naacktelijck ontdeckt, ende uyt publijcke acten klaarlijck bewesen werden. Door Iustus Veredicus [pseud.] Tot Rotterdam, Gedruckt by Jan Francken, 1667.
[4], 64 p. 21cm.

Bound with Blyenbergh, Willem van. De waerheyt van de Christelijcke Godts-dienst. 1674.

APPENDIX V
ORIGINAL CARDS
by OKO (selected)

2 W140

[Letters.- Latin. (Letter 72, to ...)] [cont.]

It then came into the possession of Louis Koch of Frankfort. In 1917 it was auctioned off by Henrici in Berlin and acquired by the firm Lieppmannsohn for a buyer whose name the firm would not divulge. (See Gebhardt, IV, 427.)

O-II-IV X W418a (23)

Prefixed by the "Epistola ad amicum". The comments of T. Goedewaagen, in Dutch, 8 p., are appended at the end.

[A.S.O.: copy no. 23; the "Aankondiging van de Heuvelpers te Hilversum Juni MCMXXVII" [cover]

O-IV-23 ✓ EW44
G-IV-5(1)✓(NC)

[Letters.- English.- 1928.]

The correspondence of Spinoza; translated and edited with introduction and annotations by A. Wolf. London: G. Allen & Unwin Ltd., [1928]. 502 p. [1-2 blank], 1 l., 1 facs., 1 pl., 2 port. 8°.

Portrait of Spinoza. (From the original portrait at Wolfenbüttel.) - Portrait of Oldenburg. (From the portrait at the Royal Society.) - Plate: portraits of Boyle, Hudde, Leibniz, Fabritius.- Facsimili of Spinoza's writing (being Ep- [cover]

G-II-22 ✓ x W359a

[Renati Des Cartes Principia Philosophiae.- German.- 1907.]

Baruch de Spinoza: I. Descartes' Prinzipien der Philosophie auf geometrische Weise begründet. II. Anhang, enthaltend metaphysische Gedanken. Dritte Auflage. Neu übersetzt und herausgegeben von Artur Buchenau. Leipzig: Verlag der Dürr'schen Buchhandlung, 1907. VIII, 190 p. 12°. (Philosophische Bibliothek. Bd. 94.) [cover]

O-IV-23 ✓ 1-a EW45

[Letters.- English.- 1928.] [cont.]

XV; apparently reproduced from W. Meijer's edition of the extant autograph letters of Spinoza, 1903).

Contents: Preface (p. 9-11). - Introduction. §1. The Seventeenth century. §2. Descartes and Spinoza. §3. Oldenburg, Boyle, and Spinoza. §4. The scientific background of Spinoza's correspondence. §5. Hudde, Boxel, Burgh, Leibniz, Tschirnhaus. §6. De Vries, Meyer, Balling, Bouwmeester, Jelles, Schuller. §7. Blyenburgh, Ostens, Velthuysen, Fabritius, Graevius, Steno. §8. The philosophical importance of Spinoza's correspondence. §9. Bibliographical (p. 23-69). - Correspondence (p. 71-366). - Annotations (p. 367-484). - Index (p. 484-502).

p. 483-484: "Suggested emendations in the Heidelberg edition of the Correspondence and in the texts on which it is based." [see next card.]

O-VII-6 ✓ x W359b

[Renati Des Cartes Principia Philosophiae.- German.- 1922.]

Spinoza: Descartes' Prinzipien der Philosophie auf geometrische Weise begründet. Anhang, enthaltend Metaphysische Gedanken. Vierte Auflage. Neu übersetzt und herausgegeben von Artur Buchenau. Leipzig: Verlag von Felix Meiner, 1922. VIII, 190 p. 12°. (Philosophische Bibliothek. Bd. 94.) [cover]

O-IV-23 ✓ 2. EW46
G-IV-5(1)✓(NC)

[Letters.- English.- 1928.] [cont.]

"The present translation is based on the Heidelberg edition, and the version followed is the original one, if still extant, whether in Latin or in Dutch, while deviations of any importance, found in other extant versions, are indicated in the Annotations... The present translation is the only complete English translation. It is more complete than any other translation in any language, and, it is believed, also the most accurate" (p. 62).

p. 441: "The Prince Palatine who sent the invitation to Spinoza was Carl Ludwig, Brother of Christina, Queen of Sweden"... (!) [cover]

W139 (35)

[Letters.- Latin. (Letter 72, to Schuller)]

"Een der brieven, door den Heer van Kempen en mij gefacsimileerd uitgegeven, werd in ms. te Berlijn verkocht. Deze brief uit de verzameling van den Heer Alexander Meijer Cohn bracht naar men mij mededeelde 1200 MK. op en werd gekocht door Pearson en Co. Pall Mall Place London S.W." (Verslag, 1905/06, p. 2.)

no. 2513 of the catalogue fetched, according to the printed "Preis-Verzeichnis", MK. 1175. [cover]

O-IV-23 ✓ 2-a. EW47
G-IV-5(1)✓(NC)

[Letters.- English.- 1928.]- [cont.]

Reviews: Mind; by H.F. Hallett.
New Statesman (June 16, 1928).

O-VI-22✓ W.152a

[Letters.-German.-1871.]

Die Briefe mehrerer Gelehrten an Benedict von Spinoza und dessen Antworten, soweit beide zum besseren Verständniss seiner Schriften dienen. Uebersetzt und erläutert von J. H. v. Kirchmann. Berlin: Verlag von L. Heimann, 1871. XIII, 258p. 12°. (Philosophische Bibliothek. Bd 46.)

[cover]

G-V-6✓ W133a

[Letters.-German.-1897.]

Die Briefe mehrerer Gelehrten an Benedict von Spinoza und dessen Antworten, soweit beide zum besseren Verständniss seiner Schriften dienen. Uebersetzt und erläutert von J.H. v. Kirchmann. Leipzig: Verlag der Dürr'schen Buchhandlung, 1897. 1p.l., (I)VI-XIII, 258p. 12°. (Philosophische Bibliothek. Bd. 96.)

[cover]

O-VI-29✓ G-II-20✓ W154a

[Letters.-German.-1904.]

Spinozas Briefwechsel. Verdeutscht und mit Einleitung und Anmerkungen versehen von J. Stern. Leipzig: Druck und Verlag von Philipp Reclam jun., [pref. 1904]. 295p. 24°. ([Universal=Bibliothek. no. 4553-4555.])

Contents: Vorwort des Übersetzers (p.3-6). Spinozas Briefwechsel (p.

[cover]

O-VII-16✓ W160

[Letters.-German.-1916.]

Spinozas Briefwechsel und andere Dokumente. Ausgewählt und übertragen von J. Bluwstein. Leipzig: Im Insel=Verlag, 1916. XXIII, 353(1)p. 8°.

367p. 3.-5. Tausend 1923 (Same text)

Contents: Einleitung [mainly biographical]. Spinozas Briefwechsel in Auswahl [being 74 letters].

[cover]

O-VII-16✓ 2. W161

[Letters.-German.-1916.] [cont.]

Ergänzende Stellen [zum Briefwechsel] aus den Werken Spinozas [in chronologischer Anordnung]. Anmerkungen zu den Briefen. Sach= und Namenregister.

The translation leaves much to be desired. The arrangement of the Letters is not in chronological order. Bresser and Huygens still figure as addressees; and there are a few wrong dates. "Dokumente" in the title is misleading.

O-VI-30✓ W154c

[Letters.-German.-192-.]

Spinozas Briefwechsel. Verdeutscht und mit einer Einleitung und Amerkungen versehen von J. Stern. Leipzig: Verlag von Philipp Reclam jun., [192-]. 294p. 16°. ([Universal=Bibliothek. no. 4553-4555.])

Prof-1904 (HM)

A reprint.

"Auf holzfreies Papier gedruckt".

O-VII-17✓ W167

[Letters.-German.-1923.]

Spinozas Briefwechsel und andere Dokumente. Ausgewählt und übertragen von J. Bluwstein. Leipzig: Im Insel=Verlag, 1923. XXIII(I), 367(1)p., 1l. 8°.

3. bis 5. Tausend. Being the same text as ed. 1916.

G-2-3✓NC

(A.S.O.)

CtY M Sco-85 3,5M NOS 10112 EW34

Spinoza. [Letters.-English.]

A letter expostulatory to a convert from protestant Christianity to Roman catholicism. (from the Latin.) Ramsgate: T. Scott, 1869. 14p. 16°. [T. Scott's publications, v.3]

See v.d. L: 34.

O-XLII-5✓ W187

[Ethica.-Latin.-1920.]

Benedicti de Spinoza Ethica ordine geometrico demonstrata et in quinque partes distincta. [At end: Zehntes Buch der Rupprecht-Presse zu Muenchen. Im Auftrage von Walther C. F. Hirth unter Druckleitung von F. H. Ehmcke begonnen im Herbst 1919 fertiggestellt im Herbst 1920 in einer Auflage von 150 numerierten Abzuegen

G-L-11✓NC [cover]

O-XLII-5✓ 2. W188

[Ethica.-Latin.-1920.] [cont.]

mit der Hand auf Zanders-Buetten gedruckt.] 2p.l. [blank], 181p., 3l. [last 2 blank]. sq. 4° [no. 141]

The text is that of Vloten-Land, 2. ed., 1895.

Review: Gebhardt, Carl, in Chronicon Spinozanum, tom. 3, p.359-361.

(A.S.O.: copy no. 141; G.: copy no. 128.)

G-L-11✓NC

0-II-22✓ W193

[Ethica.- Latin.- Portions.- 1924.]

Spinoza. [Portions from Ethica, with German translation.] (In: Leitl, Emmeram. Lateinisch für Erwachsene, hervorgegangen aus Unterrichtskursen für Männer und Frauen aller Stände. 2. Teil. München: J. Kösel & F. Pustet, 1924. 12°. p. 75-84.)

0-II-20✓NC W189

[Ethica.- Latin.- 1924.]

Benedetto Spinoza: Etica parti I. e II. ed estratti delle parti III., IV. e V. con introduzione, commento e nota bibliografica a cura di Augusto Guzzo. Firenze: Vallecchi, [1924]. 230 p., 1 l. 8°. (Testi filosofici commentati.)

G-IV-27✓

Ravà, no. 2.

(C.G.) (A.S.O.)

0-II-21✓ W190

[Ethica.- Latin.- 1933.]

Benedicti de Spinoza Ethica ordine geometrico demonstrata. Testo latino con note di Giovanni Gentile. Seconda edizione riveduta da Tommaso Fiore. Bari: Gius. Laterza & Figli, 1933.

3 p. l. [first blank], [V]VI-XVIII, 385 p., 1 l. 8°. (Classici della filosofia moderna; Collana di testi e di traduzioni. [V.] 22.)

(A.S.O.) cover

0-II-21✓ 2. W191

[Ethica.- Latin.- 1933.] [cont.]

A page for page reprint of ed. 1915, with the omission of the list of the "Errata-corrige" (p. XVIII) now corrected in the text. Also the names of the editors of the series are omitted. The paper cover has: Etica.

0-VIII-13✓ W194

[Ethica.- Danish.- 1933.] I hefte 36

Baruch de Spinoza: Etik oversat og forsynet med Inledning og Noter af S.V. Rasmussen. København: Levin & Munksgaards Forlag, 1933. xx, 319 p. 8°.

*Denne første danske Udgave af Ethica udkommer i Anledning af 300 Aaret for Spinozas Fødsel.

G-XV-26✓(NC) Oversaettelsen er foretaget efter Carl [over]

0-VIII-13✓ 2. W195

[Ethica.- Danish.- 1933.] [cont.]

Gebhardt's tekstkritiske Udgave...

(Forord; dated 1932.)

G-XV-26✓(NC)

(A.S.O.)

0-VIII-13✓ W196

[Ethica.- Danish.- 1933.] I hefte 36

Baruch de Spinoza: Etik. Oversat og forsynet med Indledning og Noter af S.V. Rasmussen. København: Levin & Munksgaards Forlag, 1933. XX, 319 p. 8°.

G-XV-26✓(NC) Indledning, p. IX-XX. Noter, p. 211-295. Index til Etikken, p. 297-319.

(A.S.O.- G.: With translator's autograph dedication.)

Barnard D211 C127 Spinoza EW119

[Ethica.- English.- 1904.]

Selections from the literature of theism. Edinburgh, 1904. 8°.

p. 76-113: God as infinite substance by Spinoza. Selections from Spinoza's Ethics translated by the Editor.

D211 C127 Caldecott, Alfred, ed. Sel. from the lit of theism. 1931, 3d ed.

Bodleian Cat. (Not in D.N.L.)

EW55

[Ethica.- English.- 1876.]

Review of: Ethics... New York, 1876. (Library table. New York, 1876. 4°. Nov., p. 138.)

By Octavius Brooks Frothingham.

Anonymous review: Popular science monthly. New York, 1876, v. 10, no. 56, p. 244-245.

EW73

White, William Hale, tr.

Review of his tr. of "Ethic", 3. ed. 1899. (Saturday review. 29 July, 1899, p. 140.)

Reviewed together with F. Pollock, Spinoza, 2. ed., 1899.

EW74

White, William Hale

[Review of his tr. of the "Ethic".] (Westminster review. July, 1883.)

Pref. to 1. ed. is very much different from that of the 2.

G-L-12✓ G-L-13✓ W276 501

[Ethica.— German.— 1920.]

Baruch de Spinoza: Ethik übersetzt von Otto Baensch. [At end: Sechsundzwanzigstes Buch der Ernst Ludwig Presse zu Darmstadt. Hergestellt in 150 Abzügen, davon 50 auf Japanbütten. Begonnen 1914 durch Ch. H. Kleukens. Beendet 1920 durch Karl Simon in Darmstadt.] 320 p. [first l. blank] 2 l. [last blank]. 4°.

[over]

G-V-2✓ W290

[Ethica.— German.— Portions.— 1903.]

Spinoza. Gott ist die Ursache aller Dinge.— Die Natur handelt nicht nach Zwecken.— Die göttliche Liebe.— Erläuterungen [by Paul Menzer]. (In: Dessoir, Max, and Menzer, Paul. Philosophisches Lesebuch. Stuttgart: Verlag von Ferdinand Enke, 1903. 8°. p. 82-96.)

See also Namenverzeichnis.

"Die... Übersetzung schliesst sich

[over]

G-L-12✓ G-L-13✓ 2. W277 501

[Ethica.— German.— 1920.] [cont.]

The Propositions are printed in red.

Review: Gebhardt, Carl, in Chronicon Spinozanum, tom. 3, p. 358-361.

H.U.C.: copy of the ordinary Bütten.
(G.: copy of each.— A.S.O.: copy of Japanbütten; withdrawn.) G12 - ordinary - paper; G-13 - special paper - [illegible]

G-V-2✓ 2. W291

[Ethica.— German.— Portions.— 1903.] [cont.]

an Kirchmann an."

(G.)

O-VI-28✓ G-V-19✓NC W257b 496

[Ethica.— German.— 1923.]

Benedictus de Spinoza: Die Ethik nach Art der Geometrie dargestellt. Neu übersetzt von J. Stern. Dritte Auflage. Mit einer Einleitung von Werner Schingnitz. Leipzig: Verlag von Philipp Reclam jun., [pref. 1923]. 420 p., 1 l. 16°. ([Universal=Bibliothek. no. 2361-2364.])

[over]

G-III-7✓ W256a

[Ethica.— German.— 1887.]

Die Ethik. Von B. Spinoza. Neu übersetzt und mit einem einleitenden Vorwort versehen von J. Stern. Leipzig: Druck und Verlag von Philipp Reclam jun., [pref. 1887]. 408 p. 24°. ([Universal=Bibliothek. no. 2361-2364.])

2te Aufl. (1909) 402 pp.
3te Aufl. (1923) 420 pp.

Contents: Vorwort des Übersetzers (p. 3-18). Ethik (p. 19-389). Führer durch

[over]

G-5-4✓ W279 53

[Ethica.— German.— 1924.]

Baruch Spinoza: Die Ethik [übertragen von Rudolf Borch und herausgegeben von Richard Hirsch]. Berlin und Wien: Hans Heinrich Tillgner Verlag, 1924. 231(1) p., 1 l. 8°.

(C.G. With translator's autograph dedication and corrections in pencil by C.G.)— Printed but not published (withdrawn?).

O-VI-27✓ G-V-18✓(NC) W.257a 496

[Ethica.— German.— 1909.]

Die Ethik. Von B. Spinoza. Neu übersetzt und mit einem einleitenden Vorwort versehen von J. Stern. Zweite Auflage. Leipzig: Druck und Verlag von Philipp Reclam jun., [pref. 1909]. 402 p. 24°. ([Universal=Bibliothek. no. 2361-2364.])

3te Aufl. repr. of the 2nd 420 pp. (1923)

Baer, no. 47.

4th with an introd. by W. Schingnitz (1925) 420 pp.

[over]

G-V-3✓ W293

[Ethica.— German.— Portions.— 1925.]

Spinoza. Der Gottesbegriff. Aus der Ethik. I. Teil. Lehrsatz 15.— Demut und Reue sind keine Tugenden. Aus der Ethik. IV. Teil. Lehrsatz 53 und 54. [Translation Otto Baensch.] (In: Ettlinger, Max; Simon, Paul; Söhngen, Gottlieb. Philosophisches Lesebuch. München: Verlag Josef Kösel & Friedrich Pustet K.-G., [1925]. 8°. p. 237-238.)

[over]

G-V-3 ✓ 2. W 294

[Ethica.- German.- Portions.- 1925.] [cont.]

p. 231: portrait of Spinoza; a drawing by Franz Kotzian (Munich), after the Wolfenbüttel portrait.

(G.)

G-VII-23 ✓ W 319

[Ethica.-Italian.- Selections.-1928.]

B. Spinoza: L'Etica; esposta e commentata da Piero Martinetti. Torino: G.B. Paravia & C., 1928. XII [1-II blank], 150 p., 1 l. [blank], 1 port. 12°. ([Piccola biblioteca di filosofia e pedagogia.])

Blank l. removed by binder.
Port.: Wolfenbüttel; inscription: B. Spinoza.

(G.)

[Contents:] ↔ [cover]

O-VIII-9 W 317

[Ethica.- Italian.- 1933.]

Spinoza: L'Etica. Nuova traduzione dall'originale latino con introduzione e note di Erminio Troilo. Milano: Casa Editrice Bietti, [1933]. 339 (1) p., [1-2 blank]. 16°. ([~~Biblioteca "Réclame". no. 280.~~])

p. 11-49: Introduzione alla filosofia di Benedetto Spinoza. The paper- [over]

O-VIII-1N W 320

[Ethica.-Italian.- Selections.- 1933.]

B. Spinoza: L'Etica; esposta e commentata da Piero Martinetti. Torino: G.B. Paravia & C., [1933]. XII [1-II blank], 150 p., 1 l. [blank], 1 port. 12°. ([Piccola biblioteca di filosofia e pedagogia.])

"Prima ristampa".

(A.S.O.)

O-VIII-9 2. W 318

[Ethica.- Italian.- 1933.] [cont.]

Cover has: Baruch Spinoza.

The translation is based on ed. Vloten-Land, 2. ed., 1895. The notes, few in number, are given at the foot of the p.

(A.S.O.)

O-VIII-14 ✓
G-XV-25 ✓(M) W 335

[Ethica.- Swedish.- 1922.]

Benedikt Spinoza: Etik. Översättning met en inledning av Alf Ahlberg. Stockholm: Björck & Börjesson, [1922]. 299 p., 1 port. 8°. ([Berömda filosofer. [V.] 20.)

Inledning, p. 5-11. The port.: "Benedictus Spinoza", is from the engraving of H. Lips (1803).

(G.- A.S.O.)

O-VIII-10 ✓ W 313

[Ethica.- Italian.- Portions.- 1914.]

Spinoza: Dio. A cura di Nicola Checchia. Lanciano: R. Carabba, [1914?]. 126 p., 1 l. 12°. ([Cultura dell' anima. no. 38.])

Being pt. 1 of Ethica.

Ravà, no. 6, gives 1919; whereas G. Gentile in his ed. of the Ethica (1915 and 1933), p. XVII, footnote, has 1914. The Pref. is dated 1911.

[Prefazione], p. 5-22.- Cenni biografici, p. [over]

O-VII-23 ✓ W 386a

[Korte Verhandeling van God, de Mensch en deszelfs Welstand.- German.- 1869.]

B. de Spinoza's kurzgefasste Abhandlung von Gott, dem Menschen und dessen Glück. Aus dem Holländischen zum ersten Male ins Deutsche übersetzt und mit einem Vorwort begleitet von C. Schaarschmidt. Berlin: Verlag von L. Heimann, 1869. XVIII, ~~XIII p., 1 l.~~ 117 p. 12°. (Philosophische Bibliothek. Bd. 18.)

[over]

1919 ed. not located W 316

[Ethica.-Italian.- 1919.]

Spinoza: Dio [being Ethica, pars I]. A cura di Nicola Checchia. Lanciano: Carabba, 1919. 126 p. 16°. (Cultura dell'anima. no. 38.)

✓ A second ed.?

HARVARD COLL. LIBR.- [1911] - Phil 3819.60 - Also in SCS
same ed., city + publ. 1911 126 p.

Ravà, no. 6. (not seen.)

O-VII-25a. b.
G-II-24 - 24(a) (a) added fr bk-HM W 392a

[Korte Verhandeling.]

Spinoza: Kurze Abhandlung von Gott, dem Menschen und seinem Glück. Übertragen und herausgegeben von Carl Gebhardt. Leipzig: ~~Verlag von Felix Meiner,~~ 1922. XXVIII, 156 p. 12°. (Philosophische Bibliothek. Bd. 91.)

Inhalt: Einleitung (p. V-XXVIII).- Kurzer Abriss der Abhandlung über Gott usw.- Kurze Abhandlung von Gott, dem Menschen und seinem Glück.- Anhang.- Von der menschlichen Seele.- Anmerkungen: Zur Textgestaltung (p. 139-156).

[over]

O-VII-4 (HM) W393

[Tractatus de Intellectus Emendatione.- Latin.-1933.]

Spinoza: De intellectus ementatione. A cura di Augusto Guzzo. Firenze: G.C. Sansoni, editore, 1933. 1p.l., (1)6-49p., 1l. 8°. ([Studi e testi; publicati a cura della R. Scuola Normale Superiore di Pisa. ser. 2, v. 1.)

On last l.: Pisa: Tip. Pacini Mariotti, [over]

W412

[Tractatus de Intellectus Emendatione.-Italian.-1913.]

Benedetto Spinoza: L'Etica. [Also:] Della correzione dell' intelletto. Traduzione sull' edizione di J. V. Vloten et J.P.N. Land di Mario Rosazza. [With a preface.] Milano: Fratelli Bocca, 1913. XXXI, 303 p. 8°. (Biblioteca di scienze moderne. no. 61.)

Reviewed by G. Gentile (Critica 1913, p. 139-140)

Ravà, no. 5: Torino: Bocca, 1913.

G-VII-4 (HM) 2. W394

[Tractatus de Intellectus Emendatione.-...] [cont.]

1933-XI.

"Questa edizione - preparata per rendere più agevole, nei seminari delle Facoltà filosofiche, la lettura di un testo così notevole - è condotta, generalmente, su l'edizione critica più perfetta e più recente delle Opere spinoziane ..." ed. C. Gebhardt.

(G.)

O-II-10 (NC) W466

[Tractatus Theologico-Politicus.- Latin.- 1672.]

Tractatus theologico-politicus continens dissertationes aliquot, quibus ostenditur libertatem philosophandi non tantum salva pietate, & reipublicae pace posse concedi: sed eandem nisi cum pace reipublicae, ipsaque pietate tolli non posse. Hamburgi: apud H. Künraht, 1672. 6p.l., 233(1)p. 4°.

G-I-6b
G-I-21 This ed. shows the several characteristics of issue "B": p. 42 is numbered 24, and p. 207 [over]

O-V-5 EW142

[Tr. de Int. Em.- Eng.- Portions.-1933.]

Benedict de Spinoza: On man's desires. (Golden book magazine. New York, 1933. 8°. v. 17, no. 99, p. 254-256.)

Comprises the first 4 p. of A. Boyle's translation. Woodcut (illustration) by Lucina Smith Wakefield.

[over]

1-a W467

[Tractatus Theologico-Politicus.-...] [cont.]

is numbered 213. The errata on p. 8, 22, 39, 41, 95 (partly) and 121 are corrected in the text, and the dot on the "i" in "dedit" (line 12 of the t.-p.) is lacking.- S. von Dunin-Borkowski is accordingly mistaken when he says that this ed. has the special features of issue "C."

Not in v.d. L.- Copies: H.U.C.; Weg [Cornell], p. 2; N.Y.P.L.; G(2); A.S.O.- The H.U.C. copy is bound in a contemporary parchment binding which contains in addition: 1) Cuperus, Arcana atheismi (1676); 2) Museus, De luminis naturae...

O-V-5 2. EW143

[Tr. de Int. Em.- Eng.- Portions.-1933.] [cont.]

"Spinoza the great philosopher, gentle seventeenth century lens-grinder of Amsterdam, is known to all. Yet what he believed; why the 300th anniversary of his birth has occasioned such deed world-wide celebration, is less well-known. This personal foreword from The Improvement of the Understanding seems to us to embody simply and movingly the essence of these beliefs." (Editorial note.)

(A.S.O.)

2 W468

contra Edoardum Herbert de Cherbury [1667?]; 3) Museus, polemic against the Tr. theol.-pol. (1674).- G.'s copy, likewise bound in parchment, has the so called Op. posth. port. as frontispiece, and contains in addition to the Tractatus: 1) the Op. posth.; 2) Mansvelt, Adversus anonymum Theologico-politicum (1674); 3) Breitenburg, Enervatio (1675); 4) [L. Meyer], Philosophia S. Scripturae interpres (1666). (Being the copy described by D.-B.!)- The A.S.O. copy was [over]

Formerly also bound up with other items.

O-VII-8 x W4096

Baruch de Spinoza. Abhandlung über die Verbesserung des Verstandes. Abhandlung vom Staate. Dritte Auflage. Übertragen und eingeleitet nebst Anmerkungen und Register von Carl Gebhardt. Leipzig: Verlag der Dürr'schen Buchhandlung, 1907. XXXII, 214 p. 8°. (Philosophische Bibliothek. Bd. 95.)

Pub. 1906.

1. ed. (H. Kirchmann): 1871; 2. ed. (durchgesehen von G. Giesserow): 1888. [over]

2-a W469

[Tractatus Theologico-Politicus.-...] [cont.]

p. 3 [unnumbered] of the Pref. bears the sig. "(*)4"; C has "3." (Compare other issues!)

EW152

[Tractatus Theologico-Politicus. - Latin. - 1763.] A

Tractatus / de / Miraculis. / Authore Spectatissimo. / Londini: / MDCCLXIII. / vi, (1)8-48 p. 8

Dedication (iii-iv); Praefatio (v)-vi.

Copy in London Library (formerly in possession of Sir F. Pollock) [over]

0-III-14✓ EW155

[Tractatus Theologico-Politicus. - Eng. - 1683.]

Miracles, / no violations / of the / Laws / of / nature. / Quid non miraculo est, / cum primum in no- / titiam venit? Plinius Histor. Nat. / lib. 7. cap. 1. / London: / Printed for Robert Sollers at the King's Arms and / Bible in St. Paul's Church-yard. 1683. / 3 p. l., 31 p. 4°.

A translation of chap. 6 of the Tractatus theologico-politicus.

l. 2-3: Premonition to the candid reader. (To be quoted.)

copy in London Library.

2. EW153

[Tractatus Theologico-Politicus. - Latin. - 1763.]

See: Land, J. P. N. Bibliographische Bemerkungen: III. Spinozistisches. (A. f. G. d. P. Bd. 7, 1894, p. 374-375) - where this is noted.

(See entry under Land.)

0-III-14✓ EW156

[Tractatus Theologico-Politicus. - English. 1683.]

Miracles no violations of the laws of nature. 1683.

According to Pollock (Athenaeum, March 16, 1889), the above tr. of chap. VI of the Tr. theol.-pol. is "cooked in much the same fashion as the reprint of 1763."

The Deists (or Authorities) picked out this chapter as controversial weapons.

In B. M.

EW154

[Tractatus Theologico-Politicus.

Tractatus de primis duodecim veteris Testamenti Libris, in quo ostenditur eos omnes ab uno solo Historico scriptos fuisse deinde inquiritur quisnam is fuerit & an huic operi ultimam manum imposuerit.

not in HUC

Being chap. VIII & IX of Tr. Theol.-Pol.

See v. d. L. 7 (note).

0-III-14✓ EW157

[Tr. Theol.-Pol. - Eng. - Portions. - 1683.]

Miracles no violations of the laws of nature...

"This has been ascribed, without any good ground, to Charles Blount. It does not seem to me to be in his style." (Robertson, J. M., A short history of freethought, 3. ed., 1915, vol. 2, p. 95, note.) But Blount was the translator only, and not the author.

WH9-1

[Tr. Theol.-Pol. - Czech. - 1922.]

Benedikta Spinozy Traktát theologicko-politický. Přeložil Josef Hrůša. V Praza: "Tribuna", 1922. 364 p. (Knihovny "Obelisk." Čis. 6.)

Tr. from ed. Bruder.

Cont.: Slovo překladatelovo. Z předmluvy vydavatele Karla Hermanna Brudera. Traktat (Spinoza, Spisy filosofické, I, p. v, & xxx.)

Tiskem : nákladem akciové společn...

0-VI-24✓(NC) K W543d

G-V-1d

[Tr. Theol.-Pol. - German. - 1886.]

Der Theologisch-politische Traktat von B. Spinoza. Neu übersetzt und mit einem biographischen Vorwort versehen von J. Stern. Leipzig: Druck und Verlag von Philipp jun., [pref. 1886]. 385 p. 24°. ([Universal-Bibliothek. [no.] 2177-2180])

[1910?] a repr. of the 1st ed. 3rd ed. (repr.) [192-?]

[over]

WH95

[Tr. Theol.-Pol. - Czech. - 1922.]

Benedikta Spinozy Traktát theologicko-politický. Přeložil Josef Hrůša. V Praza, 1922.

Pub. by "Tribuny"? in the ser. "Obelisk"?

✓PPL - Libr. Co... Ridgeway Libr. Brown & Christian - DeWall 5069 EW193a

[Tractatus Theologico-Politicus. - Eng. - 1737.] 9-5M-F

A / treatise / partly / theological, / and partly / political, / containing some few / discourses, / to prove / that the liberty of philosophizing (that is / making use of natural reason) may be allowed / without any prejudice to piety, or to the peace of / any commonwealth. / And that / the loss of public peace and religion itself must necessarily / follow, where such a liberty of reasoning is taken away. / Hereby know we, that we dwell in God, and God in us, / because he hath given us

Sr. 1 (ed. 1689)

[over]

2. EW194 [cont.]

[Tractatus Theologico-Politicus.-Eng.-1737.]

of his Spirit. I John, iv, 13./ Translated from the Latin of Spinoza./ London:/ Printed in the year 1737. And sold by the booksellers of/ London and Westminster./ 15 p. l., 452 p. 8°
(32) p., 452 p.

l. 2-3 (verso blank): The translator to the reader. - l. 4-12: The preface. - l. 13-15: A table of the several chapters.

Copy in London Library. — v. d. L. 14

G-III-10✓ W. 546e

[Tractatus - Theologico - Politicus - German - Selection

Spinoza: Theologie, Vernunft und Glaube. [Sonderausgabe aus: Spinoza. Theologisch-politischer Traktat. Herausgegeben und eingeleitet von Carl Gebhardt. (Kapitel 14)] Leipzig: F. Meiner, ?[~~1926?~~]. 1 l., (1) 250-272 p. 12°. (Taschenausgaben der "Philosophischen Bibliothek". Heft 49.)

O-VI-25✓
G-V-17✓ W. 543e

[Tr. Theol.-Pol-German.- 1909.]

Der Theologisch-politische Traktat von B. Spinoza. Neu übersetzt und mit einem biographischen Vorwort versehen von J. Stern. Zweite Auflage. Leipzig: Druck und Verlag von Philipp Reclam jun., [pref. 1909]. 384 p. 24°. ([Universal=Bibliothek. [no.] 2177-2180a])

[cover]

HUC copy lacks German cover [illegible] W548

[Tractatus Theologico-Politicus.-Hebrew.-Portions.-1883.]

[ch. 1 and 2, in extract, of the Tractatus theologico-politicus; translated into Hebrew by S. Rubin.] (In his: מַעֲשֵׂה מֶרְכָּבָה. Die Thiergebilde ... in der Vision des Propheten Ezechiel. Historisch-Kritisch beleuchtet in zwei Theilen: I. Die Prophetie. II. Die Angelologie.) Wien, 1886 [rather, 1883]. 8°.

[cover]

O-VI-26✓ W 543g

[Tr. Theol.-Pol.-German.- 192-]

Spinoza: Der Theologisch-politische Traktat. Dritte Auflage. Neu übersetzt und mit einem biographischen Vorwort versehen von J. Stern. Leipzig: Verlag von Philipp Reclam jun., [192-]. 384 p. 16°. ([Universal=Bibliothek. [no.] 2177-2180a])

"Holzfreies Papier".

[cover]

---

24 [illegible] W549

[Tractatus Theologico-Politicus.-Hebrew.-...] [cont.]

Thl. 1, p. 6-28.)

The German title taken from paper-cover. The Hebrew t.-p. has: 643 = 1883.
The Hebrew title of Thl. I is ספר הנביאות.

Repr.: השחר, v. 11.

See Introduction to his tr. of Ethica.
Printer: Druck von Georg Brög.

(J.T.S.)

G-III-8✓ W546-c

[Tractatus - Theologico - Politicus - German - Selections]

Spinoza: Prophetie und Propheten. Leipzig: F. Meiner, [1926?] 1 p. l., (1) 16-57 (1) p. 12°. (Taschenausgaben der "Philosophischen Bibliothek". Heft 47.)

Sonderausgabe aus: Spinoza. Theologisch-politischer Traktat. Herausgegeben und eingeleitet von Carl Gebhardt. [chap. 1.] - [2.]

O II-1✓ To copy X W 418a

[Tractatus Politicus.-Latin.- 1928.]

Benedictus de Spinoza: Tractatus politicus. [At end: Hilversumi excudebat Sjoerd H. de Roos prelo sua, cui nomen Heuvelpers, typis dictis Meidoorn, secundum editionem principem Operum Postumorum Benedicti de Spinoza, anno Domini 1677 in lucem missam. Curabat Tobie Goedewaagen, Litt. et Philos.

[cover]

G-III-9✓ W. 546d

[Tractatus. Theologico-Politicus - German - Selections]

Spinoza: Von den Wundern. Sonderausgabe aus: Spinoza. Theologisch-politischer Traktat. Leipzig: F. Meiner, [1926?] 1 l., 111-132 p. 12°. (Taschenausgaben der "Philosophischen Bibliothek." Heft 48.)

[Herausgegeben und eingeleitet von Carl Gebhardt. Kapitel 15.] [6.]

EW147

[Tractatus Politicus.-English. (Maccall).]

Tait's Edinburgh magazine.
Review of Maccall's tr. of Tr. Pol.
July, 1854, p. 445-446.

0-IV-30 ✓ EW148

[Tractatus Politicus.- English.- 1937.]

Writings on political philosophy by Benedict de Spinoza. Edited by A. G. A. Balz. New York [and] London: D. Appleton-Century Company, incorporated, [1937]. xxxv, 197 p. 12°. (Appleton-Century philosophy source-books; Sterling P. Lamprecht, editor.)

(A.S.O.) [over]

0-IV-30 ✓ 1-a. EW149

[Tractatus Politicus.- English.- 1937.]

Contents: Note.- Introduction: Nature, the state of nature, and the state.- Selections from the Tractatus theologico-politicus.- Benedict de Spinoza's Political treatise.

The version is that of R. H. M. Elwes. "A few changes have been made in the translation... Here and there a word or phrase has been altered, and on occasion the Latin has been.

[next]

0-IV-30 ✓ 2 EW150

[Tr. Pol.- Eng.- 1937.] [cont.]

inserted in parentheses in the text, or has been given in foot-notes... The Latin insertions have been drawn from the Gebhardt edition of the Opera".

"The purpose of this volume is to provide under one cover the body of Spinoza's writings on political philosophy" ~~(p. v)~~... Only those portions of the Tractatus Theologico-Politicus... dealing with political theory have [over]

0-IV-30 ✓ 2-a. EW151

[Tr. Pol.- Eng.- 1937.] [cont.]

been selected for inclusion in this volume... These selections... added to the Tractatus Politicus... provide virtually everything written by Spinoza on political theory" (p. v-vi).

G-III-6 ✓ W425a

[Tractatus Politicus.- German.- 1906]

Der politische Traktat von B. Spinoza. Neu übersetzt und mit einem Vorwort versehen von J. Stern. Leipzig: Druck und Verlag von Philipp Reclam jun., [pref. 1906]. 165 p., 1 l. 24°. ([Universal=Bibliothek. no. 4752-4753.])

Vorwort des Übersetzers, p. 3-6. p. 7: full title. p. 9-10: Ein Brief des Verfassers an ei- ~~There are also footnotes and an Alpha-~~ [over]

0-VI-31 ✓
G-V-22 ✓(NC) W425b

[Tractatus Politicus.- German.- 192-]

Spinoza: Der politische Traktat. Übersetzt und mit einem Vorwort versehen von J. Stern. Leipzig: Verlag von Philipp Reclam jun., [192-]. 160 p. 16°. ([~~Rec~~ Universal=Bibliothek. no. 4752-4753.])

A reprint; p. 7-10 (now comprising the "Inhaltsverzeichnis", which previously [over]

W428

[Tractatus Politicus.- Italian.- 1918.]

B. Spinoza: Tractatus politicus. Traduzione e prefazione di Antero Meozzi. Lanciano: R. Carabba, 1918. 124 p., 2 l. [last blank]. 12°. (Cultura dell' anima. no. 55.)

Harvard copy: n. d. ~~but apparently~~ series does not give the number.

Ravà, no. 8. (Not seen.)

0-VIII-12 ✓ W429

[Tractatus Politicus.- Italian.- 1934.]

B. Spinoza: Tractatus politicus. Traduzione e prefazione di Antero Meozzi. Lanciano: R. Carabba, [1934]. 124 p., 2 l. [last blank]. 12°. ([Cultura dell' anima. ~~ser~~ no. 55.])

Also 1918 (124 p.)

Prefazione del traduttore ~~[Spinoza's relation to Hobbes]~~, p. 5-27.

(A.S.O.)

0-VIII-12 ✓ 2. W430

[Tractatus Politicus.- Italian.- 1934.] [cont.]

Foot-note at beginning of Pref.: "Cfr. A. Meozzi. Le dottrine politiche e religiose di B. Spinoza. Confronto con Hobbes. (Op. prem. dalla R. Acc. di Sc. pol. e mor. di Napoli). Firenze, Gonnelli, 1915."

[Tr. ~~Polit~~ Pol.- Russian.- 1910.] W437

B. Spinoza. Politicheskii traktat (Tractatus politicus). Perevod s latinskago i primchaniya [?] C. M. Rogovina i B. [?] V. Chredina. Predislovie pro- [?]. C. A. Kotlyarevskago [?]. Moscow: N. N. Klochkov, 1910. xx, 157 p. 8°.

H.U.C. Kotlyarevskii

W438

[Tractatus Politicus.- Russian.-1910.]

Tr. Regovitch & Tchredin. Moscow: KlotchKor, 1910. xx, 157 p.

(Phil. d. Gegenwart, II, no. 394.)

A

NNUT - 5 V.S. 3

[Abbadie, Jacques (or James)]. 1654?-1727

GW43 A12 Tr 1684

Traité de la verité de la religion chrétienne. À Rotterdam: chez Reinier Leers, 1684. 8°. 2 vols.

BN 059 N85 Review of: in Nouvelles de la république des lettres. Amst., 1684. tom. 2, p. 399-410.

Also 1826 ed. (Dijon) - 4 vol.

(M.L.) See v.d.L. 358 (n.).

NNC LC has Rotterdam 1688 (2 v.) [covers]

37a

A, I.I.V.

Kort en bondig bewys datter een God en een gods-dienst is naar door een salig en onstecfelyk leven kan verkregen worden. Dienende tot vernietiging van... Stellingen der Cartesiaanische philosophen. Door I. I. V. A. Amsterdam: J. de Ridder, 1680. 4°.

Against atheists (Spinozists, Cartesians, &c.).

Engr. frontispiece. - Scarce.

---

2. (copy of card) 4

[Abbadie, Jacques (or James)] [cont.]

A. "strives hard to refute both Hobbes and Spinoza on points of Biblical criticism." (Robertson, I [141])

He settled first in Berlin (where he wrote his Traité) and later in London. The Traité is little known now, but it was much esteemed in its day. Robertson (p.250) instance Madame de Sévigné who "declared that she would not let pass a year of her life without re-reading the second volume of Abbadie."

NN NNJ 5 E-1

A., L.

A study of the Ethics of Spinoza. [Review of: Joachim, H.H. A study of the Ethics of Spinoza. Oxford, 1901.] (Jewish chronicle [London]. 1901, Oct. 18, p. 26.)

---

2. III-b E9

Spinoza, Baruch or Benedictus.

Abrahams, Israel.-Amsterdam... [Cont.]

Chapters on Jewish literature. Philadelphia, 1899. 12. p.(243)-252.)

P.141: Crescas' work influenced the thought of Spinoza who was also a close student of Maimonides.

NN NNJ 5 2525

Joachim, H. H.

A., L.

spec coll spin

A study of the Ethics of Spinoza. [Review of: Joachim, H.H. A study of the Ethics of Spinoza... Oxford, 1901.] (Jewish chronicle [London]. 1901, Oct. 18, p. 26.)

893.2 A68 III-b-2 E8

Spinoza, Baruch or Benedictus.

Abrahams, Israel.

Amsterdam in the seventeenth century: Manasseh ben Israel.-Baruch Spinoza.-The Drama in Hebrew.-Moses Zacut, Joseph Felix Penso, Moses Chayim Luzzatto. (In his:

See next card.

LC 19-1069 rid 8-6

2

Krause, K.C. Friedrich (Christian) 2

[Abaelardus, Petrus.]

"Die Uebereinstimmung der Lehre Spinoza's und Abälard's Theologia christiana hat Fessler, Abälard und Heloise, Bd. II, S. 591, dargelegt." (Krause, K.C.F. Grundr. d. Gesch. d. Phil., p. 260, footnote.)

Correct title?

NN, NNJ 5 1575

Freudenthal, J.

A[brahams], I[srael].

Professor Freudenthal's "Spinoza". [Review of: Freudenthal, J. Die Lebensgeschichte Spinoza's... Leipzig, 1899.] (Jewish chronicle [London]. 1898, Dec. 30, p. 23.)

Short notice.

√c 12

Acri, Francesco.

Una nuova esposizione del sistema dello Spinoza. (In his: Dialettica turbata. Bologna, 1910.)

Firenze, 1877 ed. OCH - 87p.

Ravd, no. 13. (Not seen.) - Guzzo has: 1911.

1\. E30

Spinoza, Baruch or Benedictus

Adler, Felix.

["Even the illustrious figure of a Spinoza, which compels Dühring to evince an unwilling respect, is not safe against indirect detraction. He seeks to belittle the philosophical fame which he cannot wholly deny, and sums up with a per-

SEE NEXT CARD.

2\. E31

Adler, Felix.-["Even the illustrious figure ... [cont.]

fidious assertion (perfidious, because such assertions can never be proved) that Spinoza became what he was, notwithstanding his Jewish origin, and not because of it". (Address 1. p.13.)— "You remember what was done to Spinoza, how he, more than two hundred years ago,

SEE NEXT CARD.

3\. E32

Adler, Felix.-["Even the illustrious figure ... [cont.]

was anathematized and execrated in the name of pure theism:.. And the echo of those curses still lingers in the heart of many a monotheist of to-day, and wrath rises in their breasts when they hear of radical views, and the impulse exists to cry, "Down with the heretic",

SEE NEXT CARD.

4\. E33

Adler, Felix.-["Even the illustrious figure ... [cont.]

as their fathers cried two hundred years ago; and they would also give effect to their impulse, as their fathers did two hundred years ago, if the gentler manners of to-day and a more humane public opinion did not curb them". (Address 2. p.28.)] (In his: "The anti-Jewish agita-

SEE NEXT CARD.

try NNJ Oca Pamph. Vol. #2 Nos 6-27

MH-4 5. 1851-1933 (L.C. cat.) E34

Adler, Felix.-["Even the illustrious figure ... [cont.]

p.1-21; tion in Germany". [Also:] "Larger Tolerance ..." p.23-32. [New York, 1881.] 8.

Two Addresses delivered by Prof. Felix Adler before the Society for Ethical Culture at Chickering hall, December 19 and 26, 1880.

[N.Y. 1880?] 32 pp. 21½ cm. Pamphlet

OCH

PP Drop

No indices.

Harvard Coll. Libr. - Ger 3435.50.5-4

publisher? (not seen)

√Adler, Felix, 1851-1933.

Two addresses etc etc

Includes a ref to Sp (p. 28) in "The anti-Jewish agitation in Germany"

(this form of entry or anal?)

oNNL oLC

√ NNC 893.2643 oGC 56 22 (1856-1927)

Ahad Ha-Am, pseud. of Asher Ginzberg,

[Spinoza's attitude to the Gospels (...) ; letter to Joseph Klausner, with reference to S.'s utterances in Tr. Theol.-Pol.] (In his: ... Tel-Aviv, 1924-1925. 8o. v. 4, p. 216.) 6 v. (1923-25)

pp. 215-

Letter dated, London, March 1, 1911. K. was then in Odessa.

---

12 NNC Nos 4-11 E38

P519 Spinoza, Baruch or Benedictus.

NN-YAR Albee, Ernest. "Editor: George Holland Sabine."

5

The confusion of categories in Spinoza's Ethics. (In: Philosophical essays in honor of James Edwin Creighton... New York, Macmillan co., 1917. 8. p.1-25.)

xii p., 1 l., 356 p. 24½ cm

[over]

---

205 H52 NNC-4 2. in Sp's Ethics E39

Albee, Ernest.—The confusion of categories... [cont.]

The main object of the essay is to show the incompatability of the view of substance as ultimate logical ground and that of a world in some sense determined in infinitum, of the view of logical and that of casual necessity, of the view of psycho-physical parallelism and that of moral freedom. (G. Dawes Hicks, in Hibbert Journal, v.16, 1917, t.p.: 1918, p.147.) IN: "Survey of Recent Philosophical Literature," pp. 147-152.

Alexander, Bernhard.

Spinoza... Mit einem Bildnis Spinozas. München: Verlag Ernst Reinhardt, 1923. 178 p., 1 l., 1 port. 8°. (In: Kafka, Gustav, ed. Geschichte der Philosophie in Einzeldarstellungen. ~~Bd. 18.~~) Abt. II. Die Philosophie der neueren Zeit I, Bd. 18, 1923
port.: "Spinoza. Nach dem Bild eines unbekannten Meisters des 17. Jahrhunderts im Schlosse zu Wolfenbüttel".
[cover]

2. (copy of verso 1) 31
Alexander, Bernhard. [cont.]
Contents: Das Leben Spinozas... Die Werke Spinozas. 1. Der Kurze Traktat... 2. Über die Verbesserung des Verstandes... 3. Die Schrift über Descartes' Prinzipien... 4. Der Theologisch-politische Traktat... 5. Die Ethik. A. Die Lehre von Gott... B. Die Lehre vom Geist (mens)... C. Die Lehre von den Affekten... D. Die Lehre von der menschlichen Freiheit... Zusammenfassung... Bibliographischer Wegweiser [54 numbers]. Anmerkungen.

Alexander, Bernhard.
Spinoza und die Psychoanalyse. (Internationaler psychoanalytischer Verlag. Almanach [no. 3] für das Jahr 1928. Wien, [1928]. 12°. p. 94-103.)

8000 copies printed.
From: Chronicon Spinozanum. tom. 5.

(A.S.O.-G.)

Alexander, Bernhard.
Spinoza és a pszichoanalizis. [Also German:] Spinoza und die Psychoanalyse. (Chronicon Spinozanum. Hagae Comitis, 1927. sq. 8°. p. 88-103.)

(A.S.O.) - ?

1. E46
Alexander, Hartley Burr.
Nature and human nature: essays metaphysical and historical. Chicago: Open Court Pub. Co., 1923. ix p., 1 l., 529 p. 8.

See next card.

2. E47
Alexander, Hartley Burr.-Nature... [cont.]
ch.xiv. Hebraism as a mode of philosophy. (First pub. in The Menorah Journal. v.6. 1920, - there entitled, "The Hebrew contribution to the Americanism of the fu-
See next card.

3. E48
Alexander, Hartley Burr.-Nature... [cont.]
ture." Delivered as the first Leopold Zunz memorial lecture before the Intercollegiate Menorah Association, New York, December, 1919.)
Spinoza p.488-489. a section

1-a. E53
Alexander, S[amuel]. - Spinoza and... [cont.]
In the unbound copies, the (first) blank l. is pasted on to the (stiff) paper-cover, so that the pag. is: 3 p. l., 9-80 p.

(A.S.O.: 1) in original binding; 2) in boards.)

~~3.~~ 2 E54
Alexander, S[amuel].-Spinoza... [cont.]
¶ Afterword as foreword (by Viscount Haldane) I. The world of events: time as intrinsic. II. Spinoza's conception of time. III. The infinite mode of motion and rest. IV. The transition from extension
See next card.

~~4.~~ 3 E55
Alexander, S[amuel].-Spinoza... [cont.]
to this mode. V. Time as an attribute of God: consequences of this hypothesis (1) The ultimate reality as space-time. (2) Modes and the ultimate reality of the same stuff. (3) The grades of reali-
See next card.

5. 4 E56

Alexander, S[amuel].-Spinoza... [cont.]

ty — the hierachy of levels. (4) Thought an empirical character, not an attribute. VI. Spinoza's infinity of attributes. VII. (5) Religion in Spinoza and the intellectual love of God. VIII. Changes

See next card.

6. 5 E57

Alexander, S[amuel].-Spinoza... [cont.]

in the conception of God and religion. The conatus of Spinoza and the nisus. IX. Conclusion.

Author inquires: What consequences would follow from the substitution of time for thought in the Spinozistic attributes.

[cover]

5-a E58

Alexander, S[amuel].- Spinoza... [cont.]

See: Jewish chronicle [London]. May 19, 1922 ~~[1921?]~~, p.11: Spinoza. Lecture by Professor Alexander. [Report.]

46

AltKirch, Ernst.

Benedictus Spinoza. illus. (Ost und West. Berlin, 1909-1910. Jahrg. 9, col. 591-598, 649-650, 653-664; Jahrg. 10, col. 79-100.)

Excer ptd.

I. Vom äusserlichen Menschen Spinoza. II. Die Bildnisse Spinozas. III. Im Lande Spinozas.

1) Spinoza [by] Karl Bauer, München.

[cover]

2 48.

AltKirch, E.

6) Spinoza 1671. Nach dem Oelgemälde von Hendrik van der Spyck, im Besitz der Königin von Holland. 7) Spinoza cr. 1669. Nach dem Kupferstich in 4° der Opera posthuma (1677). 8) Spinoza (zweifelhaftes Bildnis). Nach dem Oelgemälde von Franz Wulfhagen, im Besitz des Hofphotographen A. Schmidt in Pforzheim. 9) Falsches Bildnis Spinozas [Bildnis mit dem Hut].

See also col. 77-78 (preceding article [cover]

2-a. 49.

Alt Kirch, E.- Benedictus Spinoza... [cont.]

III (col. 79ff.)

Article II in part the same as that in A.Z.d.J. (1911). Article III, except for a few minor changes, is the same as that in Westermanns Monatshefte (1907); only that the illus. in the former comprise also facs.: 1) T.-p. of Pentateuch with Spinoza's autograph (Berlin, State Library); 2) T.-p. of Tr. theol.-pol. (Königsberg University Library); 3) 5 marginal notes to the Tr. theol.-pol.

G-XVI-10 VS 59.

AltKirch, Ernst.

Evremond und Spinoza. (Nord und Süd. Breslau, 1919. Bd. 168, p. 88-96, 202-210, 313-319; Bd. 169, p. 92-98, 204-212.)

Fiction.

(G.-Author's copy with many corrections in MS.)

G-XIII-44 VS III-b-5 53.

AltKirch, Ernst.

Die Freunde Spinozas. (Morgen. Berlin, 1927. Jahrg. 3, Heft 1, p. 37-44.)

Posthumously published. (Perhaps same as the article in Zeitgeist?)

G-IX-16, 17 (1) white paper (2) yellow paper

AltKirch, Ernst. VS

Maledictus und Benedictus. Spinoza im Urteil des Volkes und der Geistigen bis auf Constantin Brunner. Leipzig, Verlag von Felix Meiner, 1924. 211 p., [1-2 blank]. 8°.

Contents: Vorrede. Spinoza und seine Zeitgenossen. Spinoza im Urteil der Nachwelt. Namenverzeichnis.

[cover]

G-IX-16/17 1-a (verso 1) 61.

AltKirch, Ernst.-Maledictus... [cont.]

"Meinem Buche 'Spinoza im Porträt'..., das sich mit dem äusserlichen Menschen Spinoza befasst, lasse ich das über den innerlichen Menschen Spinoza folgen" (p.7).

Appeared in 2 issues: 1. on yellowish paper, bound in half cloth; 2. on pure white paper, bound in half parchment.

(A.S.O.: 2 copies on white paper; 1 on yellowish.)

O-IX-16/17 2 ✓ III-b-1 62.

Altkirch, E.- Maledictus ...

[Reviews of.]
Baumgardt, David. (Kant-Studien. Bd. 31, 1926, p. 393-394.)

Hirsch, E. (Theologische Literaturzeitung. Jahrg. 49, 1924, col. 548.)

Taub, Hans. Spinoza im Urteil seiner Zeitgenossen. (Bayerische israelitische
[over]

O-XLIII-6 4. VCS

Altkirch, E. — Im Lande ... [cont.]
— Bronzestatuette Spinozas von J. Mendes da Costa (col. 435).

Excerpted
(A.S.O.: First 2 articles on better paper;
O-XLIII-30, 31
2. copy of article I-II also on ordinary paper.)

VSC III-b-4 52.

Altkirch, Ernst.

Spinozas Freunde. (Zeitgeist. Beiblatt zum "Berliner Tageblatt". no. 20, May 17, 1910.)

?
(A.S.O.-Inserted in his: Die Bildnisse Spinozas, 1911.)

O-IX-18 VS IV-c-22 68

Amzalak, Moses Bensabat.

Spinoza. Lisboa: [Of. Gráf. do Museu Comercial de Lisboa], 1927. 29 p., 1 l. [blank]. 8°.

port.: Opera posthuma engraving, on front paper-cover.
Conferência realizada na Biblioteca Israelita de Lisboa, a convite da Associação de Juventude Israelita "He-
G-VIII-8 [over]

G-XXI-9 VS III-b-6 39.

Altkirch, Ernst.

Im Lande Spinozas. illus. (Westermanns Monatshefte. Braunschweig, 1907. Jahrg. 52, p. 211-222.) excerpted.

Concerning the portraits and abodes of Spinoza.
Bildnis Spinozas aus den Opera posthuma. Bildnis Spinozas von Hendrik van der Spijck.
(G.) [over]

O-IX-18 2. (Kwol) VS 69

Amzalak, Moses Bensabat. [cont.]
haber", na noute de 20 de Fevereiro de 1927, em comemoração do 250° anniversário da morte de Spinoza.

Contents: I. Biografia. II. Doutrinas.

G-VIII-8
(A.S.O. -G.)

G-XXI-9 2. (Dup of version) III-b-6 40

Altkirch, Ernst - Im Lande ... [cont.]
Bildnis Spinozas im Haager Städtischen Museum.
Das Spinozadenkmal im Haag.
Also: Das Spinozahaus in Rijnsburg. Das Spinozahaus in Amsterdam. Das Spinozahaus im Haag (Veerkade 32), vom Garten gesehen. Das Siegel Spinozas.

G-XVI-5 VCS 76

Andala, Ruardus.

Apologia / pro / vera & saniore / philosophia, / quatuor partibus comprehensa, / auctore / Ruardo Andala, / Phil. et S.S. Theol. Doctore & Professore / Ordinario. / Franequerae, / Ex officina Wibii Bleck, Bibliopolae. / MDCCXIX. / 3 p. l., 210 p. 4°.

Only (?) pt. 1 (p. 1-59) and 2 (p. 61-110) relate to Spinoza. pt. 1 is headed:
(G.) [over]

O-XLIII-6 3 VCS 50

Altkirch, E.

— Im Lande Spinozas. Ein Nachtrag. illus. (Ost und West. Berlin, 1911. Jahrg. 11, col. 429-434.)
Excerpted
In part a review of: Dunin-Borkowski, S. von, Der junge De Spinoza.
port.: Spinoza 1671. Medaillonbildnis von Hendrik van der Spyck im Königl. Hausarchiv im Haag. - Das Spinozadenkmal im Haag...
[over]

G-XVI-5 2. VCS 77

Andala, Ruardus.- Apologia ... [cont.]
Philosophia R. Descartes Spinosismo opposita; pt. 2 is headed: Spinosus Stoicismus fons Spinosismi et puritas philosophiae R. Descartes. In a series of numbered heads, in parallel columns, Stoicism and Spinozism are compared.
A refutation of: Regius, J. Cartesius Spinozae praelucens.
Not in v.d. L. Trinius, p. 591, has: 1718. Pollock, p. XXVII. Grunwald (p. 32) refers to the book.

Andala, Ruardus.

Bibl. Parriana, p. 424, has as follows: Andalae (Ruardi) Cartesius, versus[!] Spinozismi Eversor, et Physicae Experimentalis Architectus, 4to, Franequerae, 1719. To which is added a note: "Spinoza professed himself a Cartesian, and Andala's book was designed to prove the fallacy of that profession. S[amuel] P[arr]."

Andala, Ruardus.—Exercitationes ... [cont.]

Recto of l. 8 and last l., a catalogue of books.

Spinosa confutatus, p. 54 (refers to Ethica, pt. 2, prop. 2), and 196-197 (referring to the Tr. Theol.-Pol., ch. 3 and 6, from which he quotes passages): "Pessime Spinosa leges naturae cum Dei Decreto & Providentia confundit".

(G.—full leather: contemporary.)

Andala, Ruardus.

Cartesius / verus Spinozismi / eversor, / et / physicae experimentalis / architectus, / auctore / Ruardo Andala, / Phil. et SS. Theol. Doctore et Professore / ordinario. / Franequerae / Ex officina Wibii Bleck, Bibliopolae, MDCCXIX. 282, 44 p. 4°.

p. 1-282: Cartesius verus Spinozismi eversor. This is followed by 44 p. [over]

NjNbT (to NjNbS—Gardner H. Sage Libr., New Brunswick)

Andala, Ruardus.

Syntagma theologico-physico-metaphysicum, complectens Compedium theologiae naturalis; Paraphrasis in Principia philosophiae Renati Des Cartes; ut & Dissertationum philosophicarum heptada. Auctore Ruardo Andala Philosophiae Doctore & Professore. Franequerae: Apud Wibium Bleck, Bibliopolam, 1711. p?

[over]

Andala, Ruardus.—Cartesius... [cont.]

with a new title: Dissertatio physica qua repraesentatur Cartesius physicae experimentalis architectus, ventilata publicè A.D. 21. Jun. MDCCXIX. Defendente Georgio Szoboszlai, Transylvano-Hungaro.

Reply to: Regius, J. Cartesius verus Spinozismi architectus.

v.d.L. 303 (not seen). Full title in Pollock, p. xxvii (the date MDCCIX is an error)

Andala, Ruardus.—Syntagma... [cont.]

"The Paraphrasis and the Dissertationes are obviously separate books that were brought together under a common title with the Compendium; the title page of the Paraphrasis indicates as year of publication the year 1710.

"The Compendium and the Dissertationes contain numerous references to Spinoza and Spinozism whereas I found in the Paraphrasis only one slight remark. There is prefixed a poem by Cornelius Schellinger which is referred to by Baeck in his thesis, p. 15.

NNUT

Andala, Ruardus, 1665-1727. (dates not seen in LC card)

Dissertationum philosophicarum heptas.... Franequerae, 1711.

(4) p + 292 p.

Contains "at least one incidental ~~reference~~ attack on Spinoza... (p. ~~190~~)". (Pollock, p. xxvii f.)

p. 185-194.

Bound w. his Compendium Theologiae Naturalis Franequerae, ... W. Bleck, MDCCX, (?) p + 224 p.

Andala, R.—Syntagma...

"One of the seven dissertations is a Dissertatio philosophica De Unione mentis cum corpore. I know from my notes that there is a Disputatio philosophica de unione mentis & corporis physica, neutiquam metaphysica, Franeker 1724, which was reprinted the same year at Halle. Christian Wolff had mentioned Andala in his Commentatio luculenta, p. 78, in his Monitum ad Comment. [over]

Andala, Ruardus.

Exercitationes academicae in philosophiam primam et naturalem; in quibus philosophia Renati Des-Cartes clare & perspicue explicatur, valide confirmatur, nec non solide vindicatur. Franequerae: Ex officina W. Bleck, 1709. 8 p. l., 26 p., 1 l., 590 p., 9 l. 4°.

[over]

Andala, R.—Syntagma... [cont.]

and in his Anmerkungen ueber das Bedenken der Theologischen Facultaet zu Halle, p. 35, giving him credit that he was teaching Wolff's philosophy in Holland. Andala who just had read Lange's pamphlets (some of them penes me!) of course was not pleased and wrote his thesis of 1724 revealing the axioms of Wolff's philosophy as Spinozistic and atheistic errors. But I don't know whether the thesis of 1724 is a new one or the Thesis of 1711 enlarged and rewritten." (F. Bamberger, letter of Nov. 23, 1940.)

Anderson, John M. (Berkeley Calif.)

"Change and personality." (Journal of philosophy. v. 35, 1938.), pp 505-517.
Spinoza, esp. pp 508-9; 515-16.

Sp., he holds, had only a mechanistic theory of human personality, and no appreciation of the dynamic nature of human conduct and the autonomous forces of the mind. (See: Bidney, D., Psychol. & ethics of Sp., p. 380f.)

Andler, Charles.

Nietzsche et ses dernières études sur l'histoire de la civilisation. (Revue de métaphysique et de morale. tom. 35, 1928, p. 161-191.)

I. Spinoza (p. 162-166). II. Ernest Renan. III. Gobineau. excerpted

(G.)

Antal, G. von.

Die holländische Philosophie im neunzehnten Jahrhundert. Eine Studie. Utrecht: C. H. E. Breijer, 1888. 8°.

Spinoza, p. 102-106.
Deals with Spinoza studies in Holland during the 'sixties and 'seventies.

(G.) (Subj.: History)

[Abrahams, Israel.] 1858-1925

Professor Freudenthal's "Spinoza". [Review of: Freudenthal, J. Die Lebensgeschichte Spinoza's... Leipzig, 1899.] (Jewish chronicle [London]. 1898, Dec. 30, p. 23.)

Short notice.

Apel, Walter [Georg].

Spinozas Verhältnis zum ontologischen Beweise. Inaugural-Dissertation zur Erlangung der Doktorwürde vorgelegt der philosophischen Fakultät der Universität Leipzig. Leipzig: Druck von Hartman & Wolf, 1911.
77 (1) p., 1 l. 8°.

(A.S.O.-G.) [over]

Apel, Walter [Georg]. [cont.]

Contents: ... I. Teil. Über das Wesen des ontologischen Beweises. 1. Abschnitt. Der ontologische Beweis nach Anselm und Descartes... 2. Abschnitt. Die Grundlage der ontologischen Beweisführung... II. Teil. Spinozas Verhältnis zum ontologischen Beweise. 1 Abschnitt. Spinozas Stellung in seiner früheren Periode. Der Tractatus brevis... 2. Abschnitt. Spinozas Stellung in seiner späteren Periode. Das vollendete System...

Argens, Jean Baptiste de Boyer, marquis d'

The Jewish spy: being a philosophical, historical and critical correspondence, by letters which lately pass'd between certain Jews in Turkey, Italy, France, &c. Translated from the ... French ... into English. London: Printed for D. Browne and R. Hett, 1739.
5 vols

Spinosa, [v. 1], p. 244-246.

(A.S.O.)

Argens, Jean Baptiste de Boyer, marquis d'

La philosophie du bon-sens; ou, Réflexions philosophiques sur l'incertitude des connoissances humaines, à l'usage des cavaliers et du beau-sexe. À Londres: aux dépens de la compagnie, 1737. 12°.
nouv. éd. revue, corrigée et augmentée 1747

Spinosa, p. 234-246, 303-305.
p. 234-239 form part of § V of Réflex- [over]

Argens, Jean Baptiste de Boyer... [cont.]

ion III. § VI (p. 239-246) is headed: Réfutation du dogme de l'âme du monde, et du sisteme de Spinosa. p. 303-305 comprise § XVIII: Que les principales preuves de Spinosa sont tirées du sisteme de Des-Cartes. See also index.

(A.S.O.)

Argens,

Jewish Spy (The): being a Philosophical, Historical, and Critical Correspondence by Letters which lately pass'd between certain Jews in Turkey, Italy, France, &c., translated from the Originals into French by the Marquis D'Argens, and now done into English, port. and engd. titles, 5 vols, 12mo, cf. (some ll. of Vol. 2 slightly wormed), 1739-40 £1 5s

Arnauld, Antoine

(Livre) des vraies et des fausses idées. ch. 14. of Des Vraies et des Fausses Idées

Défense 5. partie. ch. 14: p. 114-129.

See Malebranche's reply, p. 373-376.

Accuses Malebranche of Spinozism.

in Oeuvres philosophiques de A. A. Nouv. Ed., .. par Jules Simon.

Paris, Charpentier, 1845, xii + 563 p.

(Not seen.) LC 19-4,78

Aronstam, N. E. 2

Episode the eight: The herem. (v. 23, Oct., 1940, no. 9, p. 170-171.)

Episode the tenth: Rhijnsburg. (v. 24, no. 1, Jan., 1941, p. 14)

---

052 M NNC-4 E 80

Arnold, Matthew.

The bishop and the philosopher. (Macmillan's magazine. London, ~~1863.~~ 8°. v. 7, 1863, p. 241-256.)

An essay; charges Bishop Colenso and his followers with narrow vision for employing a method of Biblical controversy opposed to that suggested by Spinoza.

G-XXVIII-4 124

Ast, Friedrich. IV.b.5

Hauptmomente der Geschichte der Philosophie. München: A. Weber, 1829. nar. 8°.

Spinoza, p. 61-62.

(G.-Interleaved.)

CtY - KG. Spt - 5 2877a 114.

Arnoldson, K. P. (Klas Pontus), 1844-1916 (LCcat)

Benedikt Spinoza. En Uppsats.. Upsala [1877] 1 p. l., 16 pp. front. (port.) 19 cm.

Dictionary has: Arnoldsson, K. P. Benedict Spinoza. Upsala, 1877. Reprint from Samningsökaren.

The correct name is Arnoldson. - A. was a leading adherent in Sweden of an association of "Believers in Reason", which closely resembled the British Ethical Societies. A. was a well-known peace advocate. (Robertson, 3 ed., II, 418.)

entered

IRA + TxU

oNNC

Aster, Ernst von 1880- NNC 109 125

"Geschichte der neueren Philosophie." (In: Dessoir, Max. Lehrbuch der Philosophie; herausgegeben von M. Dessoir. Berlin, [1925]. 8°. [v. 1], p. 375-548.)

2 vols, both dated [1925]

Spinoza, p. 420-428.

Analytical t.-p. reads: Die Geschichte der Philosophie. Dargestellt von Ernst v. Aster, Ernst Cassirer, Max Frischeisen-Köhler, Josef Geyser. [over]

893.105 J556l NNC-4 E 93

Aronstam, Noah E.

"And they called him blessed." (Jewish forum. ~~New York.~~ 1940. v. 23, ~~no. 2,~~ p. 19-20; ~~no. 3,~~ p. 49-51; ~~[no. 4]~~ p. 68, 72; ~~no. 5,~~ p. 91-92; ~~no. 6,~~ p. 113.) (no. 7) p. 131-2 (no. 8) p. 144, 142; (no. 9) p. 170-171; (no. 10) p. 182

Fiction. v. 24 (no. 1) p. 14; (no. 3) p. 42; (no. 4) p. 50, 70.

The 3. instalment has the sub-title: (Episode the third.) November, the twenty fourth, 1632. Here the author deals with Spinoza and da Costa; Gutzkow's [over]

---

2. 126

Aster, Ernst von. - Geschichte ... [cont.]

Ernst Hoffmann. Im Verlag Ullstein, Berlin.

[L. L.]

1-a. E 94

Aronstam, Noah E. - And they called... [cont.]

Der Sadduzäer von Amsterdam is followed, or "adapted". Spinoza's father was "Alfonso De Espinoza" - "who abbreviated his name to Spinosa," and his mother "Manuela." The last (4.) instalment has the sub-title: (Episode the fourth.) Heritage.

2 port. The one [with 1. article] is by J. A. Kaliff [?], apparently after the engraving of François; the second (p. 113) is a "Bust in Sculpture contest won by Gabriel Kohn."

0-IX-28 130

Aster, Ernst von.

Geschichte der neueren Erkenntnistheorie. (Von Descartes bis Hegel.) Berlin und Leipzig: Vereinigung wissenschaftlicher Verleger Walter de Gruyter & Co., 1921. 8°.

Spinoza, p. 126-161.

1. Erkenntnistheoretische Grundbegriffe. 2. Zur Lehre von der Methode.

G-XXVIII-5 [over]

O-IX-28 2. ✓ 131

Aster, E[rnst] von. - Geschichte... [cont.]

See also Personen- und Sachregister.

(A.S.O.-G.) G-XXVIII-5

G-XVI-17 ✓ 138

Auerbach, Berthold.

Spinoza. Ein historischer Roman. Thl. 1-2. Stuttgart: J. Scheible's Buchhandlung, 1837. 16°.

Thl. 1: x p., 1 l., (1)6-278 p.; Thl. 2: 315 p.

This ed. contains an introduction, headed: Das Ghetto, as well as notes ("Beilagen") at end of Thl. 2 (p. 301-315). The whole consists of 33 chapters. [over]

S.

O-IX-29 ✓ 127

Aster, Ernst v[on]. TT-b-7

Geschichte der Philosophie. 2., verbesserte Auflage. Mit einem Anhang: Wie studiert man Philosophie? Leipzig: A. Kröner Verlag, [1935]. xxiii [I-II blank], 468 p. 12°. (Kröners Taschenausgabe. Bd. 108.)

Spinoza, p. 213-217. - See also Personenregister

[A.S.O.]

G-XVI-17 2. 139

Auerbach, Berthold. - Spinoza. Ein hist- [cont.] orischer...

V. d. L. 126 (note).

Baer, 243.

(H.U.C.)

O-XX-59 ✓ 133

Astrada, Carlos.

Goethe y el panteismo spinoziano. [Santa Fe, Argentina]: Instituto Social de la Universidad Nacional del Litoral, 1933. 23 p. 8°.

(A.S.O.)

Spec Coll Spin (?)

Auerbach, Berthold.

Spinoza / Het leven van eenen denker / door / Berthold Auerbach. / naar de laatste op nieuw bewerkte uitgaaf / uit het Hoogduitsch. / Met een voorberigt van / Dr. D. Burger, Jr. / Conrector aan het Gymnasium te Doesborgh. / te Doesborgh, bij / W. Becking. / 1856. / 2 p. l., XII, 386 p., 1 l. nar. 8°.

[over]

G-XVI-19, 20. ✓ 156

Auerbach, Berthold.

Spinoza. Ein Denkerleben. Bd. 1-2. (In his: Gesammelte Schriften. Erste, neu durchgesehene Gesammtausgabe. Stuttgart und Augsburg: J. G. Cotta'scher Verlag, 1858. 12°. Bd. 10-11.)

Being the 3. ed. Bd. 1: x p., 1 l., 212 p.; Bd. 2: 3 p. l., 232 p. The whole consists of 27 chapters.

(G.) [over]

G-XVI-16 ✓ 141

Auerbach, Berthold.

Spinoza. (Europa. Chronik der gebildeten Welt. Stuttgart, 1837. Bd. 4, p. 241-261, 300-312.)

"Wir geben ... hier einige Bruchstücke [ch. 2-4, 13, 24] aus einem merkwürdigen Buche, das in diesen Tagen ... erschienen ist... Nach einer mündlichen Mitthellung des Verf. sind diese beiden [over]

G-XVI-19, 20 2. ✓ 157

Auerbach, Berthold. - Spinoza ... [cont.]

"Ich habe bei dieser neuen Durchsicht Mehreres bestimmter abgeschlossen, da ich nicht voraussehe, wann und ob ich überhaupt noch zur Ausführung eines ehedem lang gehegten Planes komme: das fernere Leben Spinoza's, nach seinem Weggange von Amsterdam, in ähnlicher Weise zu behandeln." (Preface to this - 3. - ed., dated Dec., 1857.)

G-XVI-16 2. 142

Auerbach, Berthold. - Spinoza. (Europa... [cont.]

ersten Bände jedoch nur als Prolog zu dem grossen Drama 'Spinoza's Tod' zu betrachten, das er sich noch zu schreiben vorgesetzt hat. Das hier [in the 2 volumes] Gebotene endet mit Spinoza's früherer Periode ... (Editorial note, p. 241).

(G.)

0 170

Auerbach, Berthold.

Spinoza. [A novel; tr. into Hebrew by Reisen (Raisen?). Warsaw: Progress, 1900 (?)

Not MH

2-a E104

B[ ], A.E. – The greatest... [cont.]

"Spinoza was preeminent in this select company [of good men who are an inspiring example to all who seek to live bravely, purely, and unselfishly, and of great thinkers whose wisdom and knowledge and intellectual power are a possession for ever to all who seek truth], great and good, as a thinker and as a man."

2 E101

Review of Spinoza, by B Auerbach

Auerbach, B. V 55 nas

[Review.] (Spectator [London]. July 15, 1882, p.930-931.)

V. 55 Missing in NNC

[from D. Hutcheson's slip.]

2-a E105

B[ ], A.E. [cont.]

za as the one modern philosopher who is worthy to be named in the same breath with Plato."

DLC-B3208.P5 1876-3 183

NjP, CtY, PU

Avenarius, Richard [Heinrich Ludwig] 1843-1896

Philosophie als Denken der Welt gemäss dem Princip des kleinsten Kraftmasses. Prolegomena zu einer Kritik der reinen Erfahrung. Habilitationsschrift der philosophischen Facultät der Universität zu Leipzig vorgelegt und als Einladung zu der Probevorlesung über die Substanz Spinoza's. Leipzig: Fues's Verlag [R. Reisland] 1876. xiii, 82 p. 8°

22½ cm.

Habilitationsschrift, LPZ

LC 11-18230

oNNC

2 E106

B[ ], A.E.

Spinoza studied "the philosophers of his own time particularly Descartes and Malebranche". "Spinoza was the last great mediaeval thinker... This comes out characteristically in two ways. First, he was a rationalist... Spinoza was mediaeval rather than modern, also, in that he was certain of God". Quotes at end the Archbishop of York [Wm. Temple]: "I do indeed regard Spino- [over]

2 184

Avenarius, Richard. – Philosopie als... [cont.]

His: Kritik der reinen Erfahrung. Bd.1. Lpz., 1907. 2. ed.

" Der menschliche Weltbegriff... Lpz., 1905. 2. ed.

Also: Bush, W.T. "Avenarius and the standpoint of pure experience. N.Y., [1905]. (Columbia Univ.)

B

G-XVI-25 196

Bab, Julius.

Rembrandt und Spinoza. (Der Morgen. Berlin, 1929. Jahrg. 5, p.393-397.)

"Wie Rembrandt und Spinoza aneinander vorbeigingen, jeder zur Erfüllung seines innersten Wesens, auf das Volk des anderen zu, das scheint nicht Fremdheit und Ausschliesslichkeit darzutun, sondern eine geheimnisvoll verwandte Anziehungskraft, [over]

NNG 2-25-47+ NNUT: LS70 C562 NOS 7-11 E103

AL5-3671

B[ ], A.E.

Verified by photo. "The greatest Jew since St. Paul. Baruch de Spinoza: Nov. 24, 1632 – Feb. 22, 1677." (Church times [London]. Nov. 18, 1932.) p.625-626.

London, Palmer (weekly) 1896. v.35 to date.

PPStC for Signed, A.E.B.

PPP-Divr. Sci.

Vol. 108, 1932, p.625-626. [over]

D-X-2 196

Bab, Julius.

Rembrandt und Spinoza. Ein Doppelbildnis im deutsch-jüdischen Raum. Berlin: Philo Verlag und Buchhandlung GmbH, 1934. 2p.l., 102 p., 1 l., 10 pl., 2 port. 12°.

port.: 1. "Der junge Spinoza" (being the so-called van der Spyck port.); 2. "Spinoza in späteren Jahren" (the Op. posth. port.). (A.S.O.)

O-X-5 V S 206

Baeck, Leo.

Spinozas erste Einwirkungen auf Deutschland. Berlin: Mayer & Müller, 1895. 2 p.l., 91 p. 8°.

"Die schriftstellerische Wirksamkeit der Männer, deren Beeinflussung durch Spinoza dargestellt worden ist, fällt in den Ausgang des 17. und den Beginn des 18. Jahr- [over]

G-XVI-27

O-X-5 2.S 207

Baeck, Leo. [cont.]

hunderts" (p. 84).

Baer, 496.

(G.) G-XVI-27

O-X-5 V 6 205

Baeck, Leo.

Spinozas erste Einwirkungen auf Deutschland. Inaugural-Dissertation zur Erlangung der Doktorwürde von der philosophischen Fakultät der Friedrich-Wilhelms-Universität zu Berlin ... Berlin: Mayer & Müller, 1895. 2 p.l., 91(1) p., 1 l. 8°.

(A.S.O.) – G. G-XVI-27 G-XVI-26

G-CIV-20 ✓ 229

Barrios, Miguel or Daniel Levi de.

Coro de las musas, dirigido al Excellentissimo Señor Don Francisco de Melo... Por el Capitan Don Miguel de Barrios... En Brusselas: B. Vivien, 1672. v.p. 12°.

The pag. is as follows: 22 p.l., (1)4-48, 25-48 [repeated], 49-288, 241-288 [repeated], 389-392 p., [over]

G-CIV-20 1-a ✓ 230

Barrios, Miguel or Daniel Levi de. [cont.]

1 l., [follows] p. 394, 392-648 p. [or 722 p.], 1 port [being that of Francisco de Melo].

The repeated figures are given in ( ). p. 124 erroneously numbered 134, p. 125 is numbered 135; p. 216 is numbered 116; p. 388 is numbered 378; p. 389 is numbered 375; p. 475 is numbered 479, p. 483 is numbered 438.

G-CIV-20 2 ✓ 231

Barrios, Miguel or Daniel Levi de.

The "Epistola censoria, respondiendo à otra que le escrivio el Doctor Juan de Prado en tercetos", contains (p. 588) an allusion to Spinoza ("Agora espinas son las que ayer rosas ..."). See: Gebhardt, C., Juan de Prado (Chronicon Spinozanum, tom. 3, p. 269-291).

(G. Missing: l. 9-10, and p. 25-48 [2. counting] A few p. slightly mutilated.)

G-CIV-20 D 232

323 **Barrios** (Miguel de). **Coro De Las Musas dirigido al Excellentissimo Senor Don Francisco de Melo. Brussels, Baltazar Vivien, 1672. £3 3s**

12mo. Old calf, with the arms of Lord Stuart of Rothesay on sides.

The poems of De Barrios, whose real name was Daniel Leir de Barrios and who was one of the most distinguished Spanish Jewish poets, are very rare. There is a long panegyric of Charles II and other celebrated men of the period. Lacks the portrait of Melo, mentioned by Palau.

(Davis & Orioli, 1935.)

✓ NNC 88Ar31 G62 239

Barthélemy-Saint-Hilaire, Jules.

[Spinoza discussed (or only referred to) in the Introduction to his Aristotle translation (Traduction générale d'Aristote? 2 v. Paris, 1892).

NOS 12-12-57

LC

NNUT: RA42 B28 5 ✓ 240

NNC – Bartholmèss, Christian, 1815-1856 (Enc. Un. Illustrada, v. VII, p. 984)

Histoire critique des doctrines religieuses de la philosophie moderne. Paris: C. Meyrueis & Cie., 1855. 2 v. 8°.

Renaissance du Spinosisme, v. 2, p. 29-82.

Not in v. d. L.

vd 10-27-58

G-XXVIII-6 ✓ V-b 249

Bauer, W.

Geschichte der Philosophie für gebildete Leser, zugleich als Einleitung in das Studium der Philosophie. Halle: G. Schwetschke'scher Verlag, 1863. 8°.

Spinoza, p. 184-194.

(G.)

0-X-19 ✓ 264

Baumgardt, David.

Der Kampf um den Lebenssinn unter den Vorläufern der modernen Ethik. Leipzig: F. Meiner, 1933. XI, 384p. 8°.

Herder und Spinoza 1766-1775, ~~p.~~ - ~~20~~ Herders Eintreten für den Naturalismus der Spinozischen Moral, p.208-210. - Herders Bekenntnis zu Spinozas Utilismus 1787, p.231-233. - Jacobis [over]

0-X-19 2. ✓ 265

Baumgardt, David. - Der Kampf... [cont.]

"Über die Lehre des Spinoza" 1785..., p.321-330. See also Personenregister.

(A.S.O. - unbd.)

NNJ-C ✓ NN NNJ 5 258

Baumgardt, David.

Spinozas jüdische Sendung. (Juedische Rundschau. Berlin, 1932. f° Jahrg. 37, no. 93, p. ~~551~~ 451-452.)

... Der jüdische Geist konnte ~~nicht~~ auf die Dauer nicht an Spinoza vorübergehen... Heute gibt es - neben entschiedenen Gegnern - auch im Judentum eine ganze Reihe von Anhängern Spinozas, die nicht nur seine denkerische Grösse anerkennen, sondern auch das Wesentliche seiner Lehre bejahen. Prof. David Baumgardt hat im vorigen [over]

2. ✓ 259 [cont.]

Baumgardt, David. - Spinoza's jüdische...

Winter an der Hochschule für die Wissenschaft des Judentums einen Vortrag über Spinozas Wirkung in der deutschen und in der jüdischen Gedankenwelt gehalten. Dieser Vortrag, über den die "Jüdische Rundschau" in Nr. 20 d. J. berichtet hat, erscheint nun in dem Spinoza gewidmeten Heft der Zeitschrift "Der Morgen." Der erste Teil der Abhandlung schildert die "Wirkung Spinozas auf deutsche Denker. Den zweiten Teil, der Spinoza's Bedeutung für das Judentum unserer Tage zum Gegenstand hat, geben wir nachstehend mit Erlaubnis des Verfassers und der Philo-Verlags wieder." Red.

✓ 262

Baumgardt, David. 1890- IV.c.24

Spinoza. Zur 300. Wiederkehr seines Geburtstages am 24. November 1932. (Gemeindeblatt der jüdischen Gemeinde zu Berlin. Jahrg. 22, ~~no. 11~~, ~~Nov~~, 1932, p. 266-268.)

NN NNJ-C 4

Being ~~the~~ article I of his:

in Sp. Coll. → Spinoza und Mendelssohn.

(G.) [over]

2. ✓ IV.c.24 263

Baumgardt, David. - Spinoza. Zur 300... [cont.]

illus.: "Inneres der portugiesischen Synagoge in Amsterdam, in der der Bann über Spinoza und Uriel Acosta verhängt wurde."

✓ 273

Bayle, Pierre.

Analyse raisonné de Bayle, ou abrégé méthodique de ses ouvrages, particulierement de son Dictionnaire historique et critique, dont les remarques ont été fondues dans le texte, pour former un corps instructif & agréable de lectures suivies. Tome VII. A Londres, 1770. 8°.

[over]

1-a. ✓ 274

Bayle, Pierre. - Analyse ... [cont.]

Du Spinozisme, p.1-101

§ I. Du Spinozisme avant Spinoza. Spinozisme des Indiens. § II. Spinozisme d'un secte de Chinois. § III. Spinozisme des Japonnais. § IV. Particularités concernant Spinoza. § V. Système de Spinoza. § VI. Eclaircissement sur l'objection emprunté de l'immutabilité de Dieu. § VII. S'il est vrai que Bayle n'ait pas compris la doctrine de Spinoza. Nouvelles observations critiques sur ce système [next]

2 ✓ 275

Bayle, P. - Analyse...

§ VIII. D'un livre de Mr. Stoupp intitulé: La religion des Hollandois & de la réponse à ce livre par Jean Brun. § IX. Sémences d'athéisme découvertes dans le Traité theologico-politique de Spinoza, par ceux qui l'ont réfuté, & développées d'une maniere plus précise par Jean Bredenbourg.

[over]

2-a. ✓ 276

Bayle, P. - Analyse ... [cont.]

V. 1-4 (1755) edited by abbé de Marsy; V. 5-8 edited by Jean-Baptiste René Robinet.

See: Albert, Reinhard. Die Philosophie Robinets (Leipzig, 1903), p. 7. Albert gives Amsterdam as the place of publication. So does Baldwin.

(G)

Bayle, Pierre.

Analyse raisonnée de Bayle; ou, Abrégé méthodique de ses ouvrages, particulierement de son Dictionnaire historique et critique, dont les remarques ont été fondues dans le texte former un corps instructif & agréable de le-etures fuivies. tome 7. A Londres, 1770. 8o.

? Spinoza, p. 1-101. (v. in Gebhardt Coll.)

Bayle, [cont.]

Expressions shou'd drop from him in the heat of Dispute, or decays of his Understanding, which might be made use of against his Principles; that is, lest it should be reported, his Conscience awakening at the sight of Death, had made him renounce his Principles, and bely his former Conduct. Is it possible to conceive a more ridiculous and extravagant Vanity, or a more senseless Passion for the false Idea one forms of Constancy? We shall see more Examples of this Kind." (From: Sect. CLXXXI. A new Observation, shewing [over]

Bayle, Pierre.

Herrn Peter Baylens... verschiedene Gedanken bey Gelegenheit des Cometen... an einen Doctor der Sorbonne gerichtet. Aus dem Französischen übersetzet, und mit Anmerkungen und einer Vorrede ans Licht gestellet von Joh. Christoph Gottscheden... Hamburg: bey sel. Felginers Wittwe und J.C. Bohn, 1741. 8o.

[over]

Bayle, — Miscellaneous Reflections... [cont.]

that Men don't walk according to their Principles.) — p. 359: He [the man of pleasure] breaks not his Brain with Spinosa's crabbed Doctrines, to prove the Universe a simple undivided Being, and Us so many Modifications of the Divinity."

Bayle, Pierre. — Herrn Peter... [cont.]

Spinoza (Umstände von dessen Tode), p. 654-655; note by the translator, quoting Colerus in refutation of the story, p. 644-657

(G.)

Bayle, Pierre.

Oeuvres diverses: contenant tout ce que cet auteur a publié sur des matieres de theologie, de philosophie, de critique, d'histoire, & de litterature; excepté son Dictionnaire historique et critique. tom. 1-3. À La Haye: Chez P. Husson, [and others], 1727-

[over]

Bayle, Pierre

Miscellaneous reflections, occasion'd by the comet which appeared in December 1680. Chiefly tending to to explode popular superstitions. Written to a doctor of the Sorbon, by Mr. Bayle. Translated from the French. To which is added, the author's life. In two volumes. London: Printed for J. Morphew, 1708. xxxviii, 550, 224 p. 8o.

v. 1-2 of the "Reflections" have a cont. pag.

Spinoza, p. 375-376.

[over]

Bayle, Pierre. — Oeuvres diverses:... [cont.]

3 v. only; v. 4 lacking. — v. 3 is divided into 2 pts., with sep. t.-p., but pag. is cont.

Bayle, — Miscellaneous reflections... [cont.]

"But what cou'd outdo [Footnote: He dy'd at the Hague, Feb. 21, 1677.] Spinosa's Vanity a little before his Death? The Account is of fresh date, and I have it from a good hand. He was the rankest Atheist that e'er liv'd, and so bewitch'd to certain Principles of Philosophy, that to meditate on 'em with greater success, he betook himself to a profound Retreat, renouncing all the Pleasures and Vanitys of the World, and intirely occupy'd in his abstruse Reasonings. When he found himself near his end, he sent for his Landlady, and beg'd her to let no Clergyman come near him in that condition. The reason of this Caution, as we are inform'd by his Friends, was, lest any

---

[Bayle, Pierre.]

Pensées diverses, écrites à un Docteur de Sorbonne, à l'occasion de la comète qui parut au mois de Décembre 1680. À Rotterdam: Chez Reinier Leers, 1683. 12o.

Spinoza [circumstances of his death], p. 565-566.

See also p. 541 (" On ne va point [over]

G-XVI-35 2. ✓ 292

[Bayle, Pierre.]—Pensées diverses, ... [cont.]

se rompre la tête à étudier les prétenduës démonstrations de Spinoza, pour tâcher de comprendre que l'Univers est un Être simple, & que nous sommes des modifications de Dieu").

The story of the circumstances surrounding Spinoza's death, Freudenthal, Lebensgeschichte, p.33-34 (from: Oeuvres div., ed. 1727, v.2, p.117).

(G.)

G-XVI-36, 37 ✓ 293

Bayle, [Pierre].

Pensées diverses, écrites à un docteur de Sorbonne, à l'occasion de la comète qui parut au mois de Décembre 1680. Cinquième édition. tom. 1-2. À Amsterdam: Chez Herman Uytwert, 1722. 12°.

Pag. cont.

Spinoza, tom. 2, p. 374-375.

(G.)

G-X-24, 25, 26, 27 ✓ c 295

Bayle, Pierre.

Pensées diverses, écrites à un Docteur de Sorbonne à l'occasion de la comète qui parut au mois de Décembre 1680. Sixième édition. tom. 1-4. À Amsterdam: Chez Meinard Uytwerf, 1749. 12°.

tom. 1-2 cont. pag.

Spinoza, tom. 2, p. 359, 374-375.

(A.S.O.) [cover]

G-X-24, 25, 26, 27 1.a. ✓ 296

Bayle, Pierre. — Pensées diverses... [cont.]

tom. 1-2 consist of the original 263 §.

tom. 2. contains: Addition aux Pensées diverses sur les comètes; ou, Réponse à un libelle intitulé, Courte revuë de maximes de morale & de principes de religion de l'auteur des Pensées diverses sur les Comètes, &c. [by P. Jurieu] Pour servir d'instruction aux juges ecclésiastiques qui en voudront conoître. Par, M. Bayle. Quatrième édition. À Amsterdam: Chez Herman Uytwerf, 1722.

G-X-24, 25, 26, 27 2 ✓ 297

Bayle, P. — Pensées. [1749]

tom. 3-4 (with cont. pag.): Pensées diverses... ou, Réponse à plusieures dificultez que Monsieur *** a proposées à l'auteur. Par M. Bayle. Nouvelle édition. The running title is: Continuation des Pensées diverses.

Spinoza, tom. 1, p. 124; tom. 2, p. 489.

G-XVI-38, 39 ✓ 298

Bayle, Pierre.

Pensées diverses sur la comète. Édition critique avec une introduction et des notes publiée par A. Prat. tom. 1-2. Paris: Société nouvelle de librairie et d'édition, 1911-1912. 12°. (Société des textes modernes.)

Spinoza, tom. 2, p. 134-135.

(G.) [cover]

G-XVI-38, 39 2. ✓ 299

Bayle, Pierre. — Pensées diverses... [cont.]

"La présente édition reproduit exactement le texte de l'édition de 1683" (tom. 1, p. xxx).

NNUT: QK2 B38 ✓ 309

Beaussire, Émile. 1824-1889

Antécédents de l'hégélianisme dans la philosophie française: Dom Deschamps, son système et son école; d'après un manuscrit et des correspondances inédites du XVIIIe siècle par Émile Beaussire. Paris: G. Baillière, 1865. 1 p.l., (5) VI-XVI, 233 (1) p., 1 l. 12°.

Réfutation courte et simple du système de Spinoza, p. 39-43.

(L.L.) [cover]

G-XVI-44 ✓ o 318

Bechhoefer, R.

Die Politik des Spinoza.

Excerpt from a magazine. 1873? p. 149-163.

(G.) [cover]

G-XVI-44 2. 319

Bechhoefer, R. [cont.]

"Es ist das eine gar merkwürdige und lehrreiche Erscheinung, das wie die Bibel so auch Spinoza von der deutschen Nation am reinsten verdolmetscht wurde. Der Schreiber dieser Zeilen kann überhaupt nicht begreifen, wesshalb Spinoza von den Gläubigen immer so heftig angegriffen wurde"... (p. 49).

"Bei dem nachfolgenden Versuche handelt es sich zumal nur um die Lehre vom Staate" (p. 150).

323

Beckkoetter, Oskar.

Hobbes und Spinoza. Diss. München, 1920.

Münster, 1920.

Überweg [1924], p. 662.

---

194 B455 Q32 [1926] ed. E135

Bergson, Henri.

From [I. The metaphysical interpretation of modern science: Descartes, Spinoza, Leibniz.] (In his: Creative evolution. Authorized translation by Arthur Mitchell. New York, (1911.) 8°. p. 345-356.)

p. 345-347: Descartes; p. 347-354 has the running title: Spinoza and Leibniz; p. 355: Parallelism and monism. See also Index.

(A.S.O.)

Bellaar Spruyt, Cornelis, 1842-1901 4731

Spruyt, Cornelius Bellaar.

NNC "Die Geschichte der Philosophie in Holland von 1878-bis 1888." (Archiv für Geschichte der Philosophie. Bd. 3, 1890, p. 495-510.)

Being a continuation of the article in Bd. 2, p. 122-141.

p. 495-502 deals with the Spinoza studies by J. van Vloten, [over]

USE 1901 ed. 192 B45 I2 - Copy in Philos. E164

Berkeley, George, bishop.

192 B45 I 4v. The works... including many of his writings hitherto unpublished. With prefaces, annotations, his life and letters, and an account of his philosophy by A. C. Fraser. Oxford, 1871. 4 v. 8°.

See Index. [Many ref. in v. 1, in the Common-place Book.] Use Johnston's ed. of " " Bk, 1930. See E163. (Incl. refs to Sp)

rd (2) 7-25

---

2. 4732

Spruyt, C. B. — Die Geschichte ... [cont.]

J. P. N. Land, M. C. L. Lotsy, and H. du Marchie van Voorthuysen.

O-XI-6 387

Bernis, F.-J.-P. de, cardinal.

La religion vengée. Poème en dix chants. A Paris: A. Koenig, 1798. 10 p. l., (5)VI-XXI, 241(1) p. 8°.

A posthumous work; ed. by J. N. d'Azara.- port. of author on t.-p.

Chant V: Le spinosisme, p. 77-95.

Notes, p. 223.

Not in v. d. L., B. or W. (A.S.O.)

[over]

---

211 B43 E154

Benn, Alfred William.

The history of English rationalism in the nineteenth century. In two volumes. London: Longmans, Green and Co., 1906. 8°

Spinoza, v. 1, p. 94-103.- See also Index.

ord. 7-11 [over]

---

2. 388

Bernis, F.-J.-P. de, cardinal.- La religion... [cont.]

"De Bernis performance is recommended by Ste.-Beuve as combining vigour with discretion" (Pollock, p. 386).

---

2. E155

Benn, Alfred William.- The history of... [cont.]

Treats on Spinoza in ch. II: History of the relations between rationalism and Christianity to the end of the seventeenth century.

The topics discussed are: Spinoza combines Hobbes with Descartes; God as impersonal power; Miracles, freewill, and final causes excluded; Individualistic character of Spinozism; Spinoza as a Biblical critic; His relation to modern thought; his relation to Descartes.

[Auerbach, B.] O-IX-39 173

Bettelheim, Anton.

Berthold Auerbach: Der Mann - sein Werk - sein Nachlass. Mit einem Bildnis des Dichters. Stuttgart und Berlin: J. G. Cotta'sche Buchhandlung Nachfolger, 1907. 8°.

[chap.] IV. Zwei historische Romane: Spinoza.- Dichter und Kaufmann. See also Namenverzeichnis.

(A.S.O.) [over]

[Auerbach, B.] 2. 174
Bettelheim, Anton. [cont.]
See also [on Auerbach and Spinoza] Grunwald, p. 168-172, 331-334.

---

v c (Gr. NNC cat) 415
Bierens de Haan, David, 1822-1895.
"Bouwstoffen voor de geschiedenis der wis- en natuurkundige wetenschappen in de Nederlanden." (Koninklijke Akademie [van Wetenschappen], Afdeeling Natuurkunde. Verslagen en mededeelingen. Reeks 2, ~~v. 19~~, 1884, p. 78-~~88.~~ 184
2. reeks, 19. deel +p.
Deals with the Stelkonstige reecke- [over]

---

2. v c 416 [cont.]
Bierens de Haan, D.-Bouwstoffen...
ning van den Regenho-[g] and the Reeckening van Kanssen.
(To be revised.)

---

v c II-16 437
Biograph (Der). Darstellungen merkwürdiger Menschen der drei letzten Jahrhunderte... Halle: Verlag der Waisenhaus-Buchhandlung, 1806. nar. 12°. [or 8°.] (Bd. 5, Stück 3 [p. 257 (or 255?)-316: Benedikt Spinoza [by Schaller?].)
Not in v. d. L.
(H. U. C.)- See entry: [Schaller, ?].

E196
Blakey, Robert. 1795-1878
History of the philosophy of mind.... London: Longmans, 1850. 8°. 4 v.
Brown, Green and Longmans, Vol. II
Benedict Spinoza, p. 355-384. - Boulanvilliers, Lamy, Wittich, and Niewentyt [on Spinoza], p. 455-460.
Also: DLC
See v. d. L. 148 (XXVI).
Niewentyt? - Is there another ed.?

---

v c 446
Bleek, W
Giordano Bruno, Goethe und das Christentum. Naturwissenschaft und Bibel. Berlin: Neues Leben, 1911. 192 p. 8°.
"Der V. weist in quellenmässiger wissenschaftlicher Untersuchung nach, das Goethe weniger von Spinoza als von den Elementen der Philos. Giordano Bru- [over]

---

2. v c 447
Bleek, W. [cont.]
nos, die in das System Spinozas übergegangen sind, bestimmt ist."
(Phil. d. Gegenw. III, no. 541.)

---

210 B63 2d ed 1902 (card c.) +p. E206
Boedder, Bernard.
Natural theology. London: Longmans, Green, and Co., ~~1896~~ 1902. 1 p. l., (2) VIII-XII, 480 p. 2. ed. 12°. (Stonyhurst philosophical series.)
1891 ed. in Biblio. LC has only 1921 ed.
Preface dated 1891.
Appendix II: Examination of Propositions I-VI. in Spinoza's Ethics, p. 449-460. - See also p. 112-117: Pantheism ("Spinoza's fundamental [over]

E207
Boedder, Bernard. - Natural theology... [cont.]
errors"); p. 200-205: Spinoza's proof that God is the only substance, and that everything else is a mode of God; and p. 424-427. ("Spinoza's objections against miracles").
"The pantheistic system of Spinoza ... is worked out with so much simulation of mathematical exactness, that to some authors... it appeared to be theoretically irrefutable. We have already argued the absurdity of the two fundamental dogmas of Spinoza's monism [p. 112-117]. Moreover, we have set forth the ambiguity of two of his most important definitions, and pointed out the paralogism introduced by their use in the very first [next]

---

2. E208
Boedder, Bernard. [cont.]
step of his reasoning [p. 200-205]. This, however, we could not do without referring to the connection between the first six propositions of the Ethics. In order now to enable our reader to see this connection, and to judge for himself as to the safety of the road cut by Spinoza to his famous Proposition VI... we will examine thoroughly into the first six propositions of his Ethics" (p. 449). The author (a S. J.) gives his verdict as follows: "Only, I say, by assum- [over]

2-a. E209

Boedder, Bernard. – Natural theology... [cont.]
ing all these false interpretations of ambiguously worded propositions, can any connection be made out between the premises and the conclusion of the demonstration by which Spinoza proves Proposition VI. Consequently this proposition, which is the whole foundation of his pantheistic monism, must be pronounced to be a miserable sophism" (p. 460).

W. S. Lilly, Many mansions (p. 177, footnote) calls Boedder's "Examination" of Prop I-VI "a searching and severe criticism."

(D.W.L.) Also in L.L.

✓c NNC 105 Z 466

Boehmer, Eduard.

Spinozana. I-VI. (Zeitschrift für Philosophie und philosophische Kritik. v. 36, 1860, p. 121-166; v. 42, 1863, p. 76-121; v. 57, 1870, p. 240-277.)

V. d. L. 49 (note) gives instalment 1 & 2 (I-IV).

[over]

1a ✓c 466a

Boehmer, Eduard. – Spinozana... [cont.]

II-III: n. F. Bd. 42, p. 76-121. (Halle, 1863.) [Mit Beziehung auf v. Vloten: Ad Benedicti de Spinoza Opera omnia Supplementum. Amstelod. 1862.] III is really a discussion of the "Frage nach der Stellung Spinoza's zu der Annahme eines vermenschlichen Selbstbewustsein Gottes."

[next]

---

2 ✓c 467

Boehmer, E.

IV: a survey of the Tr. br. literature; also Spinoza's relation to his precursors is discussed.
V: attributes and other concepts are discussed.
VI: a biographical note on the dates of Spinoza's birth and death in the Dutch Colun. (n. F. Bd. 57, p. 240-277. Halle, 1870.)

0-XI-28 ✓ IV-10 468

Boer, Julius de.

Spinoza. Baarn: Hollandia-Drukkerij, [1911]. 48 p. 8°. (Groote denkers. ser. 3, no. 3.)

Title taken from paper-cover.

(A.S.O. – Unbd.)

5-XII-12 ✓ 469

Boer, T. J. de.

Eenige opmerkingen over Spinoza's Amor Dei intellectualis. (Tijdschrift voor wijsbegeerte. Haarlem, 1918. jaarg. 12, p. 380-395.)

Voordracht, op de jaarvergadering van de vereeniging "Het Spinozahuis" 30 Juni l.l. te Amsterdam gehouden.

(G.)

DLC 4 Tjitze de, 1866-1942 E211

Boer, Tj. de.

[Het Spinozisme van Santayana.] (Nieuwe Rotterdamsche Courant. June 5, 1928.)
Jaargang 85, no. 155 (Part 3), p. 2 (ochtendblad)
Report of lecture; superscribed "Vereeniging Het Spinozahuis".
about 2/3 column.
"Een rede van prof. Tj. de Boer."
(G.)

✓c 490

Boerhaave, Hermannus.

Dissertatio philosophia inauguralis de distinctione mentis a corpore. Leiden, 1690. 4°.

"It appears that he had actually disputed against Spinoza in an academical thesis" (Pollock).
(Dr. Johnson wrote a Life of Boerhaave, in the Gentleman's Magazine, Jan.-Apr., 1739).

See v. d. Aa, Biographisch woordenboek der Nederlanden. – See Pollock (1880), p. 376. "Spinozist against his will", B. is characterized by P. in the Index.

---

0 482

Bolin, W.

See: Jodl, F.

DSG (now DAFM) (120/5) MH-A (160) 2 c 493

✓Bontekoe, Cornelis, 1627-1685.

Tractaat van het excellenste kruyd thee:... In 's Gravenhage, P. Hagen, 1679.
14 p. l., 367 pp. 12°. (DSG)

"... Dr. Bontekoe, in the course of an extremely quaint work on the numberless virtues of tea ... took occasion emphatically to renounce Spinozism. Some one had accused him, it appears, of atheism. 'I will one day show the world,'

oNNC
oLC

[over]

1-a. ✓c 494

Bontekoe, Cornelis.— Tractaat van... [cont.]

he exclaims, 'what sort of an atheist I am, when I refute the godless works of Spinoza, and likewise those of Hobbes and Machiavelli, three of the most cursed villains that ever walked this earth' [p. 349; see also p. 199]. The variety of Dr. Bontekoe's other pursuits and quarrels (which were many) appears to have prevented him from fulfilling this rather comprehensive promise." (Pollock, p. 375.)

---

2 ✓c 495

Bontekoe, Cornelis.

Bontekoe, according to S. Kortholt, was one of the "many learned men" who "tried very hard to acquire the books" which Spinoza left. He edited (under the pseudonym of Philaretus) the first complete edition of Geulincx' Ethica (1675). Freudenthal (Lebensg., p. 247) describes him as "ein zur Zeit Sp.s in Amsterdam lebender berühmter Arzt". Gebhardt (Spinoza: Lebensbeschreibungen..., p. 142) writes: "ein berühm [over]

2-a. ✓c 496

Bontekoe, Cornelis. [cont.]

ter Mediziner in Amsterdam." Wolf (Oldest biography of Spinoza, p. 192) says: "Cornelis Bontekoë [!] was a Hague doctor. But see: Land, J.P.N., Arnold Geulincx..., p. 85-86. See also Joecher, Gelehrten-Lexicon.

---

160 Ebd missing NOS 12-12-57 nes 1-30-58 E231

Boole, George.

Analysis of Dr. Samuel Clarke's "Demonstration of the being and attributes of God", and of the "Ethica ordine geometrico demonstrata" of Spinoza. (In his: Collected logical works. Chicago and London: The Open Court Publishing Co., 1940. v. 2, ch. XIII.)

NNC does not have 1940 ed.

A reprint of his: An investigation of the [over]

---

2. E232

Boole, George.— Analysis of... [cont.]

laws of thought... (1854).

OCH ? DLC - A P 82 .S4 Nv-only 1905 1911- E245

Bourget, Paul.

NN (?) RPB ?

Spinoza. (Translated by Jacques Mayer.) (Sentinel. A newspaper devoted to Jewish interests? Chicago, 1912?)

"The feuilleton, of which this is a part, was the first essay of the great French psychological novelist to appear in print. He had quite forgotten its existence, when a few weeks ago, it was discovered in an issue of Renaissance, a literary journal no longer published, found in the newspaper department of the Bibliothèque nationale. M. Bourget was an obscure [youth], barely twenty years of [over]

---

2. E246

Bourget, Paul.— Spinoza... [cont.]

age, when he wrote it".

(A.S.O.)

G-XVI-17,18 ✓ 507

Bouillier, Francisque.

Histoire de la philosophie cartésienne. tom. 1-2. Paris: Durand, Libraire; Lyon: Brun et Ce, Libraires, 1854. 8°.

Spinoza [his life and philosophy], tom. 1, p. 299-408 (being ch. XV-XIX). There are numerous references to Spinoza also in the other chapters.

(G.) [over]

NNUT QK3 XB76 (1842) - S. pagina, same; publ, city ✓ oNNC 506

Bouillier, Francisque. Cyrille, 1813-1899.

Histoire et critique de la révolution cartésienne. Lyon: L. Boitel, 1852. vii, 448p. 8°.

~~Spinoza.~~

Spinosa, p. 201-235.— Rapports de la philosophie de Malebranche avec la philosophie de Descartes et de Spinosa, p. 263-267.

1854 ed 2v. SCS DB6368 284-408

Not in n.d.L. ← this is other title

(L.L.) Copy LC ed. - it is for 1842 but otherwise same

0-XI-38 ✓ 525

Brakell Buys, W. R. van.

Het Godsbegrip bij Spinoza. Een inleiding tot het monisme. Utrecht: Erven J. Bijleveld, 1934. 147p., 1l. 8°.

Contents: Inleiding.— I. De Spinozistische Kenleer. II. De substantie. a. Het begrip bij Spinoza. b. Het begrip bij Shankara. c. Conclusie. III. De verhouding tot de wereld. a. Shankara's instelling. b. Spinoza's instelling. IV. God-natuur. V. God, de [over]

526

Brakell Buys, W. R. van. [cont.]

geest. VI. De menschelijke geest. a. De staat der lijdingen. b. De vrije zelfbepaling. c. Beatitudo. VII. Het Spinozisme als religie.

Bibliography on last f.

529

Brandes, Georg.

..." Georg Brandes in einer interessanten Reisebeschreibung aus Holland [hatte] Spinoza ein paar Seiten gewidmet und ihn bei der Gelegenheit dem dänischen Publicum mit zündenden Worten ins Gedächtnis gerufen." (Karitz, A. Nordischer Spinozismus [Chr. Spin., V, 178-9].)

532

Brasch, Moritz.

Benedictus von Spinoza. Ein historisch-philosophisches Characterbild. (Auf der Höhe. Leipzig, 1885. 8°. Bd. 15, p. 171-183.)

Reprinted from his: Die Klassiker der Philosophie Bd. 2.

541

Braun, Otto.

Spinoza und sein Einfluss auf die deutsche Literatur. (Deutsche Zeitung. Während des grossen Krieges herausgegeben von den in Holland internierten Deutschen. Haag, 1918. Reihe 1, no. 2, p. 1-4.)

"Da mir hier jegliches Material fehlte, ist der Artikel rein aus dem [over]

563

Brochard, Victor.

De l'erreur. Troisième édition. Paris: F. Alcan, 1926. 4 p. l. [first blank], 286 p., 1 l. 8°. ([Bibliothèque de philosophie contemporaine.])

Théorie de Spinoza, p. 69-96.

(A.S.O. - unbd. - G. - unbd.)

[over]

564

Brochard, Victor. - De l'erreur... [cont.]

1. ed. Paris, 1879; 2. ed. 1897. (Überw., IV, 528.)

568

Brochard, V[ictor].

Études de philosophie ancienne et de philosophie moderne. Recueillies et précédées d'un introduction par V. Delbos. Nouvelles édition. Paris: Librairie Philosophique J. Vrin, 1926. XXVIII, 559 (1) p. 8°. ([Bibliothèque d'histoire de la philosophie.])

[over]

569

Brochard, V[ictor]. - Études de... [cont.]

Le Traité des passions de Descartes et l'Éthique de Spinoza, p. 327-331. Le Dieu de Spinoza, p. 332-370. L'éternité des âmes dans la philosophie de Spinoza, p. 371-383.

First published Paris: F. Alcan, 1912. The new ed. is a reprint.

(G. - ½ buckr.)

585

Brockdorff, Cay [Ludwig Georg Conrad,] von, Baron. 1874-

Die Geschichte der Philosophie und das Problem ihrer Begreiflichkeit... Osterwieck/Harz u. Leipzig: A. W. Zickfeldt, 1908. 2. ed. zweite, stark vermehrte Auflage. XX, 154 p. front. (port.), illus. 24 cm.

Spinoza, not in Register. See VI Kapitel. #5+6, p. 97-113. Sp. esp. #5, 97-108; VII, #2, p. 115-116.

"Brockdorff" hat dem Titel seiner 'Philosophischen Anfangsgründe der Psychologie' (Hildesheim, 1905) das Bild [over]

586

Brockdorff, Cay von, Baron. - Die Geschichte... [cont.]

Spinozas vorangestellt und am Schluss des Buches daran erinnert, wie dieser Denker uns zu den Höhen des Erkennens ruft."

Hecke, G., Benedik Spinoza... p. 5-6.)

 E287

Brown, Thomas. [1778-1820.]

Inquiry into the relation of cause and effect. [Being the 3. ed. of his: Observations on the nature and tendency of Mr. Hume concerning the relation of cause and effect, 1005.] Edinburgh, 1818. 4. ed. [2. under changed ti.] 1835. 8°.

Edinburgh: A. Constable & Co., 1818. xvi, 569 p. 8°

C.H.E.L., XIV, 6-7.

[L.L.] NNC has 3d ed., Andover, 1822

LC has Andover, 1822: 39-16013

 Ac.7 4 NNC E293

Broydes, Isaac?. 1903 MDCCCCIII

"Ethics- Philosophical." (Jewish Encyclopaedia, v. 5, pp. 252-255

"The later philosophic writers, e.g., Gersonides and Albo, mainly repeat the ethical views of Maimonides till the epoch-making appearance of Spinoza, who neither in source nor in influence is strictly Jewish."

G-XVII-25 593

Brucăr, I.

Filosofia lui Spinoza. Bucureşti: Societatea Română de Filosofie, 1930. 184 p. [1-2 blank]. 8°.

First pub. in Revista de filosofie, v. 12, together with the Rumanian tr. of the Ethica. In the new issue the paging is in Arabic numerals, and an analytical table of contents was added (p. 181- [over]

G-XVII-25 2. 594

Brucăr, I. - Filosofia lui... [cont.]

184; p. 180 being blank).

(G. ½ buckr.)

591

Brucăr, I.

Personalitatea lui Spinoza. (Sinai. Anuar de studii judaice. Bucureşti, 1928. 8°. p. 50-56.)

Forms part (p. 11-19) of chap. I of his: Filosofia lui Spinoza (1930).

(A.S.O. Extract. ½ cloth.)

G-XVII-26 595

Brucăr, I.

Spinoza: viaţa şi filosofia. Bucureşti: Alcalay & Co., [1933]. 193(1) p. 16°. (Biblioteca pentru toţi. no. 1334-1335.)

Reproduction of Spinoza statue at The Hague on paper-cover.

(G. ½ buckr.)

G-XVII-26 2 596

Brucăr, I. [cont.]

Contents: Prefaţă. Introducere. 1. Viaţa lui Spinoza. 2. Porunca XI. 3. Şlefuitorul de ochielari. 4. Meledictus şi Benedictus. 5. Despre Dumnezeu şi natura lui. 6. Despre ideia de lege şi de libertate individuală. 7. Etica empirică şi sub specie aeternitatis. 8. Psihologia lui Spinoza: sea despre corp şi suflet şi despre pasiuni. 9. Despre eternitatea sufletului şi cunoaştere. 10. Filosofia

---

3 597

Brucăr, I. [cont.]

religiei. 11. Critica filosofiei spinoziene. 12. Influenţele filosofiei lui Spinoza. Incheiere.

Much of the matter was taken over verbatim from author's larger work, Filosofia lui Spinoza.

598

Brucăr, I.

Spinoza und die Ewigkeit der Seele. (In: Spinoza-Festschrift; hrsg. von S. Hessing... Heidelberg, [1933]. 8°. p. 1-7.)

"Aus dem Rumänischen von M. Marcianu"; being cap. XI: "Despre eternitatea sufletului", of author's Filosofia lui Spinoza. 1930.

(A.S.O.)

G-XXXII-10, 11, 12, 13, 14 600

Brucker, Johann Jacob.

Jacobi Bruckeri Historia critica philosophiae ~~a mundi incunabulis ad nostram usque aetatem deducta~~. tom. 1-4^1-2. Lipsiae: B. C. Breitkopf, 1742-1744. 4°.

Spinoza, tom. 4² [or V. 5], 1744, p. 682-706. See also p. 267.

(G.) [over]

G-XXXI-10, 11, 12, 13, 14 2. 601
Brucker, Johann Jacob.- Jacobi ... [cont.]
At end of tom. 4, pars altera: "Finis tomi quinti et ultimi."

G-LI-5, 6, 7, 8, 9, 10 602
Brucker, Johann Jacob.
Jacobi Bruckeri Historia critica philosophiae... Editio secunda volumine VI. accessionum et supplementorum auctior. tom. 1-6. Lipsiae: Impensis Haered. Weidemanni et Reichii, 1766-1767. 4°.
Spinoza, tom. 4² [or v. 5], p. 682-706. See also p. 267. See also [over]

G-LI-5, 6, 7, 8, 9, 10 2. 603
Brucker, Johann Jacob.- Jacobi ... [cont.]
tom. 2, p. 1054-1056, 1067, and tom. 6, p. 922-923 (Spinoza and the Kabbalah).
V. 1 and 6 are dated 1767.
The 2. ed. is a reprint of the first, with the addition of v. 6.
v.d. L. 148 (XIX).
(G.)

~~Spinoza, Baruch or Benedictus.~~ 1. 616
Brunner, Constantin. 1862-1937
Goethes Verhältniss zu Spinoza. (In: Die Zukunft. Berlin, 1912. ~~8. Jhrg. 21,~~ Bd. 81, 1912, p. 386-389. p. 386-389.)
"Alles in dieser Zusammenstellung ist streng wörtlich angeführt; ich habe Goethe über
See next card.

~~Spinoza, Baruch or Benedictus.~~ 2. 617
Brunner, Constantin.-Goethes Verhältniss... [cont.
sein Verhältniss zu Spinoza selber reden lassen; er kann es am Besten. Ich habe ihn deshalb selber reden lassen, weil in jüngster Zeit von den lieben Philologen einige die Philologie besessen haben,
See next card.

~~Spinoza, Baruch or Benedictus.~~ 3. 618
Brunner, Constantin.-Goethes Verhältniss... [cont.]
Goethes Aussagen über sein Verhältniss zu Spinoza, besonders in seinen jüngeren Jahren (vor 1783), einfach Lügen zu strafen. Sie können sich ein solches Verhältniss ohne das genaue Studium Spinozas
See next card.

~~Spinoza, Baruch or Benedictus.~~ 4. 619
Brunner, Constantin.-Goethes Verhältniss... [cont.]
nicht denken; sie wissen nicht, dass von Spinoza als Persönlichkeit und von wenigen seiner Sätze ein ungeheurer sittlicher und praktischer Anstoss auszugehen vermag." (p.387.)
(Not in B.)

NN-*DF 621
Brunner, Constantin. 1862-1937
Ein Idealporträt Spinozas [being the bust by Georg Wienbrack]. (Nord und Süd. Berlin, 1913. Jahrg. 37, p. 27-43.)
Jahrg. 37, Bd. 144, 1913, p. 27-43.
With plate; legend: "Eine Idealbüste Spinozas von Georg Wienbrack".
[over]

---

2. 622
Brunner, Constantin.—Ein Idealporträt... [cont.]
"Constantin Brunner bringt in seinem demnächst erscheinenden Werke 'Die Vereinigung der Künstler mit den Denkern'... die psychologische Analyse von Spinozas Physiognomie. Ein Teil dieser Arbeit gelangt vorher in der Zeitschrift Nord und Süd zum Abdruck" [the only part published] (Altkirch, E., Spinoza im Portrait, p. 111). See also p. 79 (about the bust, done in 1911).
(H.U.C.)

G-XVII-33 662
Brunschvicg, Léon.
Les étapes de la philosophie mathématique. Deuxième édition. Paris: Librairie Félix Alcan, 1922. 8°.
La philosophie mathématique de Spinoza, p. 138-151.
Contents: L'intuition spinoziste et l'intuition cartésienne. La conception spinoziste de la vérité. Le passage du mécanisme au [over]

G-XVII-33 2.✓ 663

Brunschvicg, Léon. — Les étapes ... [cont.]
mathématisme. Le monisme de Spinoza. La limitation technique du spinozisme.

(G.)

G-XVII-34, 35 ✓ 664

Brunschvicg, Léon.
Le progrès de la conscience dans la philosophie occidentale. tome. 1-2. Paris: F. Alcan, 1927. 2 v. 8°.

tom. 1, capitre VII: Spinoza. Section I: Les problèmes nouveaux de la vie religieuse; Section II: La théorie Spinoziste de la conscience; [over]

G-XVII-34, 35 2.✓ 665

Brunschvicg, Léon. — Le progrès... [cont.]
Section III: Spinozisme et Platonisme, p. 162-194. — See also Index.

Pag. cont.

(G. — with author's autograph dedication — unbd.)

C-XII-24 ✓ 660

Brunschvicg, Léon.
Spinoza et ses contemporains. Troisième édition, revue et augmentée. Paris: Librairie Félix Alcan, 1923. 2 p. l., II p., 1 l., 495(1) p. 8°. ([Bibliothèque de philosophie contemporaine.])

Contents: Avant-propos. Première partie: Spinoza... Deuxième partie: Les contemporains de Spinoza. chap. IX. [over]

G-VIII-48

O-XII-24 2. 661

Brunschvicg, Léon. — Spinoza et ... [cont.]
Descartes. chap. X. Pascal. chap XI. Malebranche. chap XII. Fénelon. chap. XIII. Leibniz. chap. XIV. La place du spinozisme dans l'histoire.

pt. 1 is the 3. ed. of his Spinoza; pt. 2 is made up of articles published in the Revue de métaphysique et de morale, 1904-1906.

(A. S. O.) G-VIII-48

G-XVII-31 ✓ IV-3 654

Brunschvicg, Léon.
Spinoza. Ouvrage couronne par l'Académie des Sciences Morales et Politiques. Paris: Félix Alcan, éditeur, 1894. 4 p. l. [first blank], 224 p., 1 l. 8°. ([Bibliothèque de philosophie contemporaine.])

Contents: chap. I. La liberté de [over]

G-XVII-31 1-a.✓ IV-3 655

Brunschvicg, Léon. — Spinoza. Ouvrage... [cont.]
l'esprit. chap. II. La méthode. chap. III. Dieu. chap. IV. L'homme. chap. V. La passion. chap. VI. L'action. chap. VII. L'éternité. chap. VIII. La pratique.

Baer, no. 489.

(G.)

O-XI-23 ✓ IV-13 b 659

Brunschvicg, Léon.
Spinoza. Ouvrage couronné par l'Académie des Sciences morales et politiques. Deuxième édition, revue et augmentée. Paris: Félix Alcan, éditeur, 1906. 3 p. l. [first blank], II, 235(1) p. 8°. ([Bibliothèque de philosophie contemporaine.])

(A.S.O.)

5 NN 1-[3] DLC ✓c IV-c-34 672

Brunschvicg, Léon.
Spinoza. (Revue littéraire juive. v. 1, no. 2, 1927, p. 142-148.)

His Hague address?

G-XVII-32 ✓ 670

Brunschvicg, Léon.
Sur l'interprétation du spinozisme. n.t.-p. [Hagae Comitis, 1921.] 58-62 p. sq. 8°.

Title taken from first p.
Repr.: Chronicon Spinozanum. tom. 1.

(G.)

O-XLIII-37 ✓C 671

Brunschvicg, Léon.

Sur l'interprétation du spinozisme (Menorah. Paris, 1927. année 6, no. 6, p. 84-86.)

also: Le 250° anniversaire de Baruch Spinoza, p. 83, in obvc.

(G.)

NNUT-5 E296

RB42 B91 Buchanan, James.

Modern atheism. Boston: Gould & Lincolm, 1857. 12°.

The system of Spinoza, p. 142-161.

o BM
o NNC
• LC

Divinity professor in the New College, Edinburgh. - See: Ethics. N.Y., 1876

✓ NN NNJ 677

Buber, Martin. 1878-5

Der Chassidismus als Antwort auf Spinoza. (Jüdische Rundschau. Berlin, 1932. f°. Jahrg. 37, no. 93, p. 452.)

"Der Baalschem hat von Spinoza vermutlich nichts gewusst; dennoch hat er ihm die Erwiderung gegeben".

[over]

NNUT: RB45-5 B92 1737 ✓ 691

Buddeus, Johann Franz, 1667-1729.

Ioan. Francisci Buddei... Theses theologicae de atheismo et superstitione variis observationibus illustratae et in usum recitationum academicarum editae. Suas quoque observationes et dissertationem contra atheos adjecit Hadrianus Buurt. Traiecti ad Rhenum: Apud I. H. Vonk van Lynden, 1737. 18 p.l., 625(1)p., 11 l. [last blanks.

NNC+ ... 1717 oLC rBN 8°. over [over]

---

2. ✓ 678

Buber, Martin. - Der Chassidismus ... [cont.]

"Martin Buber hat in den Schriften seiner ersten Periode Spinoza als ein Figür gewertet, in dessen Denken die „Idee der Einheit", eine der grundlegenden Tendenzen des Judentums, sich verwirklichte. In der letzten Periode seines Schaffens hat Buber seine Stellung zu Spinoza geändert. Eine Auseinandersetzung, die zu dem wichtigsten gehört, was in unserer Zeit über Spinoza geschrieben wurde, befindet sich im Geleitwort der Gesammtausgabe der „Chassidischen Bücher" von Martin Buber. Wir bringen hier den ersten Teil dieser Auseinandersetzung zum Abdruck."- Red.

2.✓ 692

Buddeus, - Ioan. Francisci... [cont.]

Spinoza, p. 120-132, 193, 200-203, 209-210, 214-215, 218-226, 248-249; Spinozism, p. 369-379.

(H.U.C.)

G-XVII-37 ✓ 675

Buber, Martin.

Geleitwort zur Gesamtausgabe. [Spinoza, Shabbethai Ẓebi and Israel Ba'al Shem-Ṭob.] (In his: Die chassidischen Bücher. Hellerau, 1928. nar. 12°. p. XI-XXXI.)

(G.)

NN-ZET-5 Johann Franz, 1667-1729. 693

Buddeus, Johannes Franciscus.

Joan. Francisci Buddei... Theses theologicae de atheismo et superstitione variis observationibus illustratae. Quibus suas annotationes adjecit Joannes Lulofs. Lugduni Batavorum: apud J. Le Mair, 1767. XXXII p., 1 l., 568 p., 7 l. 4°. su cd181 (cap. III, § 5-6) p. 172-182

Benedictus de Spinoza, p. 95-105 (cap. I, § XXVI), 351-363 (cap. VI, § VI). - See also Index rerum.

L.L.
oNNC • LC [over]

O-XII-25 ✓ 676

Buber, Martin.

Spinoza, Sabbatai Zwi und der Baalschem. (In his: Deutung des Chassidismus... Berlin, 1935. 12°. p. 42-64.)

Same as the "Geleitwort".

(A.S.O.)

---

2. ✓ 694

Buddeus, Johannes Franciscus. - Joan... [cont.]

The dedicatory epistle of the author is dated 1716.

G-XVII-41 ✓ 695

Buddeus, I ? F ?

Lehr-Sätze von der Atheisterey und dem Aberglauben mit gelehrten Anmerckungen erläutert... ins Teutsche übersetzt durch Th. Eusebium. Jena, 1723. 2. ed.

Spinoza, p. 144-156.

B. was a friend of Stolle. ? Verify.

NN-RBG ✓ NNC 878 -5 B92 718

Burmann, Pieter, 1668-1741, ed.

Sylloges epistolarum a viris illustribus scriptarum, tomi quinque, collecti et digesti per Petrum Burmannum, nomina exhibebit, post tomum quintum index primus. Leidae: apud S. Luchtmans, 1727. 4°. 5 v.

Only 400 copies printed. Vol. 4 cont. 55 epistles of Jac. Prizonius and Nic. Heinsius.

rd 10-20

---

o 697

Buddeus, Johann Franz

Veritas resurrectionis Christi contra impias quorundam, speciatim Benedicti de Spinoza, objectiones, asserta seu meditatio Paschalis anno MDCCIX. proposita. [1725.] p. 47-56. covers

Extract in (Nijhoff Cat. 595, no 4008.)

---

v201 B957; Butler D201 B95; Coll. D201 B95 E302

Burtt, Edwin A.

NNC

Types of religious philosophy. New York and London: Harper & Brothers, Publishers, [1939]. 8°. ix, 1 l., 512 p.

Spinoza's philosophy of religion, p. 180-192. See also Index, p. 511.

cf Rev. ed. [1951] v201 B95 xi, ; Butler D201 B957

(Brentano's)

rd 7-17-58

NN-ZFB- corr title 2. 698

Buddeus, J F - Veritas... [cont.]

(In his: Meditationibus sacris Syntagmati Dissertat. theol. subjectis.)

[Taken from Trinius, p. 428.]

O-XI-33 719

Busolt, Georg.

Die Grundzüge der Erkenntnisztheorie und Metaphysik Spinozas dargestellt, erläutert und gewürdigt. Von der Universität zu Königsberg gekrönte Preisschrift. Berlin: E. S. Mittler und Sohn, 1875. 5 p. l., 186 p. 8°.

B. 368.

(A.S.O.)

covers

G-XXVIII-11, 12 ✓ 706

Bueschíng, Anton Friedrich.

Grundriss einer Geschichte der Philosophie und einiger wichtigen Lehrsätze derselben. Thl. 1-2. Berlin: J. G. Bosse, 1772-1774. 8°.

Spinoza (Benedict von), Thl. 2, p. 674-675 (kann nicht mit Zuverlässigkeit des Atheismi beschuldigt werden); p. 755 (nahm die Ewigkeit der Welt

covers

O-XI-33 2. ✓ 720

Busolt, Georg. - Die Grundzüge... [cont.]

Contents (abbreviated): Vorwort. - Einleitung. Spinozas Stellung in der Geschichte der Philosophie als notwendige Grundlage der Beurtheilung seines Systems. - Theil I. Erkenntnisztheorie und Methode... Theil II. Die Substanz und ihre Attribute oder die Natur als Ursache (natura naturans)... Theil III. Die Modi oder die Natur als Wirkung (natura naturata) und die Lösung der Aufgabe des Systems überhaupt...

G-XXVIII-11, 12 2. ✓ 707

Bueschíng, Anton Friedrich. - Grundriss... [cont.]

an); p. 823 (hielt die Seele für materiel); p. 879 (Erfinder der leibnitzischen vorherbestimmten Harmonie [quoting M. Mendelssohn]).

(G.) Not in Grunwald.

O-XII-38 ✓ III:26 727

Busse, Ludwig.

Beiträge zur Entwicklungsgeschichte Spinoza's. Inaugural-Dissertation... Berlin: G. Schade, [1885]. 88 p., 1 l. 8°.

B. 435.

(A.S.O. - Heavy paper.)

G-XVIII-4 covers

0-XII-38 2. ✓ 728

Busse, Ludwig.- Beiträge zur... [cont.]

"Die nachfolgenden Untersuchungen bilden einen Bruchtheil einer grösseren Abhandlung, die von mir später publicirt werden wird, und in welcher ich die Entwicklung der Grundzüge des Spinozischen Systems von dem ersten, durch die in dem 'tractatus brevis' enthalten 'Dialoge' characterisirten Stadium an bis zum letzten und höchsten der 'Ethik' darstelle" (p.5).

Author places the "Cogitata metaphysica" prior to the "Tractatus brevis."

G-XVIII-4

0-XII-38 3. ✓ 729

Busse, Ludwig.- Beiträge zur... [cont.]

Headings: Tractatus brevis. I. Theil.- Der Anhang Th. I und die Beilage an Oldenburg.- Tractatus brevis. II. Theil.- Der Anhang II. Theil und die Zusätze.

Gebhardt in his translation of the Tr. brevis (Einleitung, p.xxviii) says that Busse's Dissertation is "von sehr bedingten Wert."

G-XVIII-4

✓ 737

Busse, Ludwig.

Beiträge zur Entwicklungsgeschichte Spinoza's. (Zeitschrift für Philosophie und philosophische Kritik. n.F. Bd. 90, 1887, p.50-88; Bd. 91, 1887, p.227-251 ... 1888, p.203-239; Bd. 96, 1889, p.62- ... v.97, 1889, p. ...-222.

I. Die Reihenfolge seiner Schriften. II. Avenarius Ansicht über die Entwicklung des Spinozischen Pantheismus. III. Die Dialoge.

I. (Bd. 90, p.50-88), reviewed in Arch. f. Gesch. d. Phil. Bd. 2, 1889, p. 308-311. By Benno Erdmann. covers

---

2. ✓ 738

Busse, Ludwig.- Beiträge zur... [cont.]

"Ueber der Abhandlung Busses, dessen Erstlingsarbeiten zu Spinoza im vorigen Jahresbericht besprochen worden sind"...

0-XII-39 -NF (not in SCS) ✓ 733

Busse, L[udwig]. 1862-1907

Ueber die Bedeutung der Begriffe "essentia" und "existentia" bei Spinoza. Ein Beitrag zur Entwickelungsgeschichte Spinoza's. (Vierteljahresschrift für wissenschaftliche Philosophie. Leipzig, 1886. Jahrg. 10, 1886, p. 283-306.)

NNC-4 105 ✓

Abridgment of a larger wk in Ztsch. für Phil. u. Phil. Kr. (in SCS) covers

---

Footnote 1, p.283 2. ✓ 734

Busse, L[udwig].- Ueber die... [cont.]

"Der... Aufsatz stützt sich auf eine grössere, die gesammte Entwickelung der Spinozischen Metaphysik und Erkenntnistheorie umfassende Abhandlung, welche ich früher verfasst habe und welche in der 'Zeitschrift für Philosophie und philos. Kritik'... erscheinen wird. Herr Professor Sigwart empfahl mir, die Begriffe 'essentia' und 'existentia' in einem besonderen Excurs zu behandeln. Dem... Winke folgend, habe ich das Resultat meiner Untersuchungen in diesem Aufsatz niedergelegt" (p.283).

(H.U.C.)

C

UCLA (Antiq. Cat. #150, #779) 756

[Charpentier, L.]

C***, M.

Lettres critiques, sur divers ecrits nos jours, contraires à la religion & et aux moeurs. Par M. C***. Partie 1-2. A Londres, 1751. 2 v. 8°. 2 parts, 1 vol.

Part II pp.149-221

Lettre XX-XXII, being p. 149-222 of partie 2, deals with Spinoza. Lettre XX (p. 149-169): Vie de Spinosa. Lettre XXI (p. 170-199): Idée générale du système de Spinosa, & de ses principales connoissances. Lettre XXII (p. [cont.]

---

2 757

C***, M.- Lettres critiques... [cont.]

200-222): Réfutation abrégée du système de Spinosa.- See also Lettre XIX.

Not in v.d.L.

Trinius, no. 4.

Comp. with v.d.L. 109: first & last initial being same.

(B.M. Apr., '35.)

---

804 ✓ NNC E305
C12

Caird, Edward.

Essays on literature and philosophy. v.1-2. Glasgow: J. Maclehose and Sons, 1892. 2 v. 12°.

cont. pag.

Cartesianism. General relation of Descartes, Malebranche, and Spinoza. 3. Spinoza, v.2, p.332-383.- See also Index., II, p. 551. Many references.

Incl. a section on Spinoza (v.2, p.332-383) and other refs to him

E.L.L.S covers

1-a. E306

Caird, Edward.- Essays on Literature... [cont.]

The essay on Cartesianism was published in 1876, in the Encyclopaedia Britannica. Subsequent to this date "there has been in this country much discussion as to the Philosophy of Spinoza... to which, of course, no reference will be found" in this article. (Prefatory note).

p.267: "By Cartesianism is here meant the philosophy developed in the works of DesCartes, Malebranche, and Spinoza. It is impossible to exhibit the full meaning of these authors except in their relation to each other, for they are all ruled by one and the same thought in different stages of its evolution."

2 E307

Caird, Edward.

"Some later writers have gone further, and attempted to show that the main doctrines by which its philosophy is distinguished from that of Des Cartes were due to the direct influences of Jewish writers like Maimonides, and Chasdai Creskas, rather than to the necessary development of Cartesian ideas. And it is undoubtedly true that many points of similarity with such writers, reaching down even to verbal coincidence, may be detected in the works of Spinoza, although it [over]

2-a. E308

Caird, Edward. — Essays on Literature... [cont.] is not so easy to determine how much he owed to their teaching."

Discusses: Spinoza's "relation to Descartes and to the Jewish philosophers; his mathematical method; negation of the finite as the way to knowledge and love of the infinite; distinction of opinion and knowledge; abstractness of opinion and its dependence on imagination; knowledge based upon the idea of God, or of nature as a whole; distinction of ratio and scientia intuitiva;

3 E309

Caird, Edward.

individual: reduced to modes, and mind and matter to attributes of the infinite substance; consequences of the principle that determinatio est negatio; disappearance of evil sub specie aeternitatis; mind matter as parallel attributes; relation of soul and body; whether Spinoza's distinction of attributes is relative to our intelligence; conflict of the ideas of an abstract and concrete unity; imperfect return from the infinite to the finite; ethical consequences of Spinoza's doctrine; [over]

3-a. E310

Caird, Edward. — Essays on Literature... [cont.]

relation of the conatus sese conservandi to the amor Dei intellectualis; identification of intelligence and will; new idea of freedom that freedom is possessed by God, and may be shared by man; his view of the passions; his professed rejection of asceticism, and indirect admission of it as an element in morality; whether he admits degrees in existence; his influence on later philosophy."

804 C12 E701

Goethe,

Caird, Edward.

Goethe and philosophy. (In his: Essays on literature and philosophy. Glasgow, 1892. 12°. v. 1, p. 54-104.)

Only scattered refs. to Sp.

Discusses, among others, Goethe's "Attitude Towards Jacobi, Spinoza, Kant, Fichte and Schelling... Goethe's turning from Rousseau to Spinoza".

[illegible] 7-11

NIC-[illegible] -4 E323

Cairns, John. 1818-1892.

Unbelief in the Eighteenth century as contrasted with its earlier and later history. Edinburgh, 1881. 8°.

Being the Cunningham Lectures for 1880.

Spinoza, p. 50-59.

pp. ix, 309 p.

oAAC
oLC

See CBM, XXX, col. 575.

[over]

1-a. E324

Cairns, John. — Unbelief in... [cont.]

(From a slip by F.P. "Of no particular value.")

NNUT QQ C15 card: 1908 E325

NIC DLC-4 B791. C2 Calkins, Mary Whiton. 1863-1930.

The persistent problems of philosophy. An introduction to metaphysics through the study of modern systems. New York: The Macmillan Co., 1907. xxii, 575 p. 8°. 21cm.

NSP

Sp. — Chapter VIII, p. 282-306. + Index, "Monistic pluralism: the System of Sp." p. 574.

N - *R-YC - NY, 1939 reprint of 5th rev. ed. 1925.

NJ-Mf 1921 ed.

LC 7-11605

NNC has 1929, 1921, 1912 [illegible] 10-28-58

PU; OClW 1 E330

Calkins, Mary Whiton. 1863-1930.

The persistent problems of Philosophy. An introduction to metaphysics through the study of modern systems... New York: The Macmillan Co., 1910. xxiv, 558 p. 2. ed. 8° (12° card - [illegible] - DLC)

First published 1907; reprinted 1908.

chap. VIII. Monistic pluralism: The system of Spinoza. (p. 277-306). - chap. IX. The advance toward monistic spiritualism... (Introduction: The double relation of post-Kantian

oLC [over]

2-a. E331

Calkins, Mary Whiton. — The persistent... [cont.]

philosophy to Kant and Spinoza. p. 307-308). - Appendix: Baruch de Spinoza: The monistic pluralist. I. Life (1632-1677). II. Bibliography. III. Note upon Spinoza's doctrine of the infinite modes. IV Exposition and estimate of parts II-V. of Spinoza's "Ethics." (p. 464-483)

The reference to Spinoza on p. III is not given in the first edition.

Campbell, Archibald. [1691-1756.]

An enquiry into the original of moral virtue wherein it is shewn, (against the author of the Fable of the bees, &c.) that virtue is founded in the nature of things, is unalterable, and eternal, and the great means of private and publick happiness. With some reflections on a late book, entitled, An enquiry into the original of our ideas of beauty and virtue. By Archibald Campbell. Edinburgh: for G. Hamilton, by R. Fleming & Co., 1733. 30 p.l., 546 p., 1 l. 8°.

[Campbell, Archibald.]

Ἀρετη-λογια; or, An enquiry into the original of moral virtue; wherein the false notions of Machiavel, Hobbes, Spinoza, and Mr. Bayle, as they are collected and digested by the author of The fable of the bees, are examin'd and confuted; and the eternal and unalterable nature and obligation of moral virtue is stated and vindicated. To which is prefix'd, A prefatory introduction, in a letter to that author. By Alexander Innes. Westminster: printed by J. Cluer and A. Campbell, for B. Creake, 1728. 4 p.l., XLII, 333 p. 8°. [Over]

2. E335

[Campbell, Archibald.] — Ἀρετη-λογια ... [Cont'd]

Innes "employed to make arrangements for its publication appropriated it to himself."

Campbell, M. F. A. G.

Het sterfhuis van Spinoza. (Nederlandsche spectator. [jaarg.] 1880, p. 206-207.)

Campo, Mariano.

Spinoza e Kant. (In: Spinoza nel terzo centenario della sua nascita; pubblicazione a cura della Facoltà di Filosofia dell' Università Cattolica del Sacro Cuore. Milano, 1934. 8°. p. 33-84.)

Carabellese, Pantaleo.

Il concetto Spinoziano dell' errore. (Septimana Spinozana... Hagae Comitis, 1933. 8°. p. 261-266.)

(A.S.O.)

[Gebhardt, Carl] in Memoriam

Carp, J. H.

Carl Gebhardt en het Spinozisme. n.t.-p. Assen: Alg. Ned. Vereen. voor Wijsbegeerte, [1935]. 227-238 p. 8°.

Title taken from paper-cover.

Repr.: Algemeen Nederlandsch tijdschrift voor wijsbegeerte en psychologie, 1935.

(A.S.O.)

Carpov (Carpow), Paulus Theodorus ?

Animadversiones philologico-critico-sacrae... Accedunt Don Isaac Abarbanelis De creatione angelorum, et Saulis Levi Morterae De aeterno ac indissolubili legis Mosaicae cum gente Israelitica nexu... dissertationes. Leipzig, 1740. pp. 190 4°

p. 37-39: an attack on the Tractatus theologico-politicus.

The little known book was acquired ... in 1928.

Carroll, William. fl. 1706

A dissertation upon the tenth chapter of the fourth book of Mr. Locke's Essay concerning humane understanding; wherein that author's endeavours to establish Spinoza's atheistical hypothesis... are... confuted. To which is subjoin'd: A short account of the sense wherein ... the reasonings in the following pernicious books are to be understood, viz. The reasonableness of Christianity [by J. Locke]; Christianity not mys- [Over]

Carroll, William. — A dissertation... [Cont'd]

terious [by J. Toland]; The rights of the Christian Church [by M. Tindal]. London, 1706. 8°.

4 l., XV, 292 p. No author index

E351

Carroll, William.

A letter to the Reverend Dr. Benjamin Prat, Chaplain in Ordinary to his Grace the Duke of Ormond, J. V. Professor, and Fellow of Trinity College in Dublin: wherein, the dangerous errors in a late book, intituled, An essay concerning the use of reason in propositions, the evidence whereof depends upon human testimony: are detected, confuted, and gradually deduc'd from the very basis of atheism, upon which alone they are bottom'd. By William Carroll. London: R. Sare, 1707. 24 p. 4°.

[over]

2. E352

Carroll, William. — A letter to ... [cont.]

"The very basis of atheism" is what the author calls "Spinoza's hypothesis". He gives several quotations from the Ethica, which he also translates; quotes Ep. 62 [now 58] and the Tr. theol.-pol. "Mr. Locke and Spinoza, two Men of Matter, two Originals of One Only Substance, are Originals of our Author's Opinion" (p. 8).

(See also L.C. entry.)

D.W.L.

E354

Carrol, William.

Spinoza reviv'd. Part the second. Or, A letter to Monsieur Le Clerc, occasion'd by his Bibliotheque Choisie, tom. 21. Wherein Her Majesty's prerogative, and the authority of parliaments, are defended. As also a full confutation of the many calumnies which the said Monsieur Le Clerk hath endeavour'd to throw on the learned and reverend persons that wrote against the seditious and atheistical principles, in a book entituled, The rights of the Christian Church asserted,

[over]

 E411

[Carroll, William.]

Remarks upon Mr. Clarke's sermons, preach'd at St. Paul's against Hobbs, Spinoza, and other atheists... London: for Jonathan Robinson, 1705. 4°.

1 l., 42 p.

(Offered, in a letter of Aug. 2, 1938, by Maggs Bros., for 8s. 6d.)

[Clarke, S.] 2. E412

[Carroll, William.] - Remarks upon... [cont.]

"The "Remarks" are apparently the same to which he replies in the Preface to his "Discourse concerning the unchangeable obligations of natural religion...

Who ascribes the "Remarks" to W. Carroll?

(Zimmerman, Dictionary, & C.H.E.L. & Überw. already consulted.)

 E344

[Carroll, William.] fl. 1706

Spinoza reviv'd; or, A treatise, proving the book, entitled, The rights of the Christian church, &c. [by Matthew Tindal] (in the most notorious parts of it) to be the same with Spinoza's Rights of the Christian clergy, &c. [i.e., Lucii Antistii Constantis De jure ecclesiasticorum, attributed to Spinoza], and that both of them are grounded upon downright atheism. [By William Carroll.] To which is added, A preliminary discourse relating to the said books, by George Hicks.

[over]

2. E345

[Carroll, William.] - Spinoza reviv'd... [cont.]

London: J. Morphew, 1709. 36 p. l., 179 p. 8°

A preliminary discourse, l. 2-30, is signed George Hickes. Author's name appears nowhere in book. - Not in Bohrmann V.d.L. 55. [Does not know author; line divisions do not tally with copy examined.] B.M. [under: Tindal, M.] Weg, p. 5 (L.W.L.)

 E346

[Carroll, William.] fl. 1706.

Spinoza reviv'd:/ or, A/ treatise,/ proving the book,/ entitled,/ The rights of the Christian church, &c./ (in the most notorious parts of it)/ to be the same with Spinoza's Rights of/ the Christian clergy, &c. and that both/ of them are grounded upon downright/ atheism./ To which is added,/ A preliminary discourse relating

NNC LC BM

[over]

1-a. E347

[Carroll, William.] — Spinoza reviv'd... [cont.]

to the said/ books,/ by the Reverend Dr. George Hicks./ — Moveat cornicula risum/ Furtivis nudata coloribus. —/ Horat. Epist. I. Lib. I./ London:/ Printed and to be sold by J. Morphew, near/ Stationers Hall. 1709./ 36 p. l., 179 p. 8°.

The Preliminary discourse is signed George Hickes. The author of the Treatise is William Carroll.

v.d.L. 55. (The line division differs; also

2 E348

[Carroll, William.] - Spinoza reviv'd...

some words. The motto is incorrect. There 36 p. l. = 72 p.)

T.-p.; Preliminary discourse, 29 l.; Contents, 6 l.; Spinoza reviv'd, p. 1-44; Appendix, p. 145-179.

(H.U.C.)

See E350 E353✓

Carroll, William.

Spinoza reviv'd. London, 1709. 8°

[In connection with above:

Hickes, G. Three short treatises. London: W. Taylor, 1709; Christian Priesthood

author? Some considerations concerning the Trinity. Lond.: H. Clements, 1707.

Dr. Potter. Title?

Author? An account of Mr Lock's religion... Lond., 1700.

Lee (Rev.), Antiscepticism. [on Lt Essay] Lond., 1702.

Auth.? The principles of deism truly represented, &c. In an excellent ~~v. d. L. 55. - Way, p. 6.~~ dialogue between a scepthick and a deist. Lond., 1708.

E356

Carroll, William.

Spinoza reviv'd, part the second; or, A letter to Monsieur [Jean] Le Clerc, occasion'd by his Bibliotheque choisie, tom. 21, wherein Her Majesty's prerogative, and the authority of parliaments, are defended. As also a full confutation of the many calumnies which the said Monsieur Le Clerc hath endeavour'd to throw on the learned and reverend persons that wrote against the seditious and atheistical principles, in a book entituled, The rights of the Christian

[over]

---

2. E357

Carroll, William. — Spinoza reviv'd... [cont.]

church asserted, &c. [by Matthew Tindal]. By William Carroll. London: J. Morphew, 1711. 1 p. l., 76 p., 1 l. 8°

(See also L.C. entry.)

Not in v. d. L. (Not in B., W., or Bohrmann.) B.M.? D.W.L.

E358

Carroll [or Caroll], William.

Spinoza revived... 1711.

— A letter to the Rev. Dr. Benj. Pratt. 1707.

O

E363

Caroll, [Spinoza reviv'd...]

[Curll, E]

Memoirs of the life and writings of Matthew Tindall, L.L.D.; with a history of the controversies wherein he was engaged. London: Printed for E. Curll, 1733. ~~4 p. l., 24 p.~~ 8°.

p. 49-53.

[L.L.]

D-XLII-25 799

Carvalho, Joaquim de.

Sôbre o lugar de origem dos antepassados de Baruch de Espinosa. n.t.-p. Coimbra: Imprensa da Universidade, 1930. 29 p. 4°.

Repr.: Miscelânea de estudos em honra de D. Carolina Michaëlis de Vasconcellos.

G-LIII-12 Title taken from paper-cover.

[over]

D-XLII-25 2. 800

Carvalho, Joaquim de. — Sôbre o... [cont.]

(G. Author's autograph letter inserted. with author's autograph dedication to C.G.)

Spec Coll Spin 798

Carvalho, Joaquim de.

Spinoza perante a consciência portuguesa contemporânea. (Chronicon Spinozanum. tom. 5, 1927, p. 138-139.)

G-XVIII-13, 14, 15 807

Cassirer, Ernst.

Das Erkenntnisproblem in der Philosophie und Wissenschaft der neueren Zeit. Bd. 1-3. Zweite durchgesehene Auflage. Berlin: Verlag Bruno Cassirer, 1911-1920. 3 v. 8°.

Bd. 3: Die nachKantischen Systeme, (G.) is of the 1. ed.

[over]

G-XVIII-13, 14, 15 1-a. 808

Cassirer, Ernst. — Das Erkenntnisproblem... [cont.]

Spinoza, Bd. 2, p. 73-125.

I. Die Erkenntnislehre des "Kurzen Traktats". II Der "Tractatus de intellectus emendatione". III. Der Begriff der Substanz. - Die Metaphysik. See also Namen- und Sach-Register.

Bd. 3, p. 17-22: [F. H. Jacobi and Spinoza; also Jacobi"s] Kritik der Spinozistischen Denkform; p. 135-136: Der kritische und der Spinozistische Einheitsbegriff [in Fichte's Wissenschaftslehre].

2 809

Cassirer, E. - Das Erkenntnisproblem ...

— —— [Dritte Auflage.] Bd. 1-3. Berlin: Verlag Bruno Cassirer, 1922-1923. 3 v. 8°.

Bd. 1-2, a reprint of the 2. ed. Bd. 3 [Zweite Auflage], a reprint of the 1. ed.

(A. S. O.)

O-XIII-16 815

Chajes, Adolph.

Ueber die hebräische Grammatik Spinoza's. Promotions-Schrift. Breslau: F. W. Jungfer, 1869. 32 p. 8°.

Review: Jüdische Zeitschrift. Jahrg. 8, 1870, p. 201. [By A. Geiger?]

G-IX-7

v. d. L. 282.

O-XIII-25 825

Chartier, Émile.

Spinoza por Emile Chatier [!]. Traducción revisada por Rodrigo García Treviño. México: Editorial America, 1941. 131 p. [1-2 blank]. 16°. (Biblioteca filosofica. [v.] 2.)

The "Table analytique des matières et des références" and the "Mémento bibliographique" are omitted.

(A.S.O.)

MH - Phil 400.63 - 4 832

✓ Chiappelli, Alessandro, 1857-1931.

La dottrine della realtà del mondo esterno nella filosofia moderna prima di Kant. I. Firenze, 1886. 141 p.

Spinoza, tip. dell'arte della stampa,

capitolo II Il periodo Cartesiano (Geulincx, Malebranche, Spinoza)

pt. 1. Da Descartes a Berkeley. (Only one pt.?) p. 63-110.

Rev. in Arch. f. Gesch. d. Phil. v. 2, 1889, p. 157-160; by Felice Tocco. Sp. esp. p. 70-80.

o NNC copy from BN

o LC

---

see O-XIII-26 833

Chmaj, L.

De Spinoza a Bracia Polscy, odb. z "Reformacji w Polsce". 1924.

Sp. & the Polish Brethren.

(S.'s attitude [relation] towards the Socinians)

See: Kot, Stanislas: Le mouvement antitrinitaire au 16e et au 17e siècle. Paris, 1937. 105 p.

[over]

---

2. 834

Chmaj, L. - De Spinoza a ... [cont.]

p. 100: Un des exiles [?], probablement Jérémie Fellbinger à été son [Spinoza's] professeur de Latin... Ce n'est pas sans fondament que les autorités hollondaises... rattachoient [?] ce traité de S. [Tr. Th.-Pol.] à la bibliothèque des Frères Polonais... (Verify!)

O-XIII-26 SPINOZA ROOM

835 C

Chmaj, Ludwik.

De Spinoza a Bracia Polscy. Kraków: Krakowska Społka Wydawnicza, 1924.

42 p. 8.

Repr.: "Reformacja w Polsce", 1924. no.9-10

NN - ZAE p.v. 991 - 5 1 E 379

Christian (The) free-thinker; or, An epistolary discourse concerning freedom of thought; In which are contained observations on the lives and writings of Epicurus, Lucretius, Petronius, Cardan, Bruno, Vanini, and Spinosa... 2. ed. London: printed fo J. Roberts, 1740. vi, 66 p. 8°. 22 cm.

Spinoza, p. 57-60, 62, 63. (Also p. 51.)

o NNC

o LC

+ BM - no ed. number

[over]

1-a E 380

Christian (The) free-thinker; or... [cont.]

p. 57: "The name of Spinosa, is so famous, as well amongst those who detest, as those who approve his opinions; that I should not have chosen a more proper Person than he, to close the Instances, I offer you, of the uneasiness and want of Tranquillity, incident to Free Thinkers."

p. 58: "That he professed himself a Christian, is the common Opinion, but I know no Grounds for it. He was reserved, spoke by Starts, frequently dissembled his Principles, was of a splenetick, melancholy disposition, vain of his Philosophick Moderation, cautious of discoursing on Religion, and exceedingly averse to any disputes about it."

(See abstract on sheets.) [See next.]

---

2 E 381

Christian (The) free-thinker... [cont.]

p. 59: "He went pretty much on Jordano Bruno's Notions, though he wanted his vivacity, as Vanini copied Cardan, without having his Solidity. There is no Wonder need be made, as to the Reputation Spinosa acquired, for Free-thinking will always make a Noise... Had Spinosa been a Monk, he would have been certainly sainted, for his Temper would have pushed him to extravagant Mortifications; as it is, his Oddities have procured him only the Character of a Philosopher."

843

Chuchmarev, Vladimir.

[The atheism of Spinoza. (Russian.)] Kharkov, 1930.

Ateizm Spinosy... 8°. (B.M.: enty Chumarov.)

(Siwek)

842

Chuchmarev, Vladimir.

Problema pochodzennia religii osvitlenni Spinozy la sucasnoii nauky. Kharkov, 1929. (Étendard du Marxisme.)

(Siwek.)

845

Cipriani, Cipriano.

Spinoza. Sassari: Tip. Libertà, 1914. 78p. 8°.

Not in Ravà.- Überweg [1924], p. 668. (Not seen.)

E 404

Clarke, Samuel 1675-1729

Abhandlung von dem Daseyn und den Eigenschaften Gottes... Braunschweig u. Hildesheim, 1756.

Only Germ. tr. Only the "Demonstration" was translated

E 406

Clarke, Samuel.

Demonstratio existentiae et attributorum Dei adversus Hobbesium, et Spinosam potissimum atque eorum asseclas a Samuele Clarkio ... Anglice conscripta, nunc Latinitate donata. n.p., n.d. [Basle, 1709?] 3 p. l. 78 p. 4°.

NN-1713 All do? N. ed.; OCH; PU (ie. 1713 ed's) + MH

MH: pp. (16), 173.

[over]

2.

E 407

Clarke, Samuel.- Demonstratio... [cont.]

Translated by Jenkin Thomas Philipps, also known as Jenkinus Thomasius. The book, apparently, forms an appendix to the translator's Historia atheismi (Basle, 1709?); the t.-p. has "N. II." (at the bottom).

Weg, p. 8

(H. U. C.,

E 399

2nd ed.? special

Clarke, Samuel.

A demonstration of the being and attributes of God. More particularly in answer to Mr Hobbes, Spinoza, and their followers. [p. 1-55.] ^ - A discourse concerning the unchangeable obligations of natural religion, and the truth and certainty of the Christian revelation. Being eight sermons... in... 1705... [p. 57-196.] (Boyle Lectures. London, 1739. f° v. 2.)

^ 1 p. l., being the t.-p., wanting in the L.L. copy.

[3. ed. 1711]

Clarke, Samuel, 1675-1729. 1st, 2nd ed. E 387

NNUT-5 RD50 B96 1704-5 in his →

A demonstration of the being and attributes of God: more particularly in answer to Mr. Hobbes, Spinoza, and their followers... The third edition. London, 1711. (10)p + 147p.

X

— A discourse concerning the unchangeable obligations of natural religion, and the truth and certainty of the Christian revelation. The third edition. London, 1711. (58)p + 351 p.

(Hellersberger, Cal. XIV, no. 2391.)

BM gives 1706 only

Carpenter D820.9 W211 + R820.9 W21 1919-1931 ed.

E 415

[Clarke, Samuel.] saw: Spec Coll - ref

Sorley, W. R.

(In: Cambridge history of English literature cheap edition.) v. 9, 1932. p. 237-238.) pp 332-333.

NY & Cambridge

"Clarke's Boyle Lectures may be safely reckoned his greatest work. They contain little that is strikingly new; but the arrangement of the separate points and the logical consecutiveness of the whole are masterly; and they show, nearly always, an elevation of tone and clearness of phrase which were often lacking in the controversies of the age. Clarke arranges his arguments in a

[over]

1-a

E 416

[Clarke, Samuel.] - Sorley, W.R. ... [cont.]

series of propositions which he first states and then proceeds to demonstrate; but, otherwise, he did not imitate mathematical method, as Descartes and Spinoza had done. Nor did he, like Descartes, rely on the purely ontological argument. He argued from existence, not from idea: maintaining that there must be a self-existent being to account for existing things, and then going on to show the attributes which must belong to this self-existent being. When he has to prove that

P333

1-0. E417

[Clarke, Samuel.] – Sorley, W.R. ... [cont.]

intelligence and wisdom are among these attributes, he relies expressly on a posteriori reasoning. The whole argument, – therein resembling Locke's belongs to the cosmological variety. Clarke's system has been represented as only a less logical Spinozism; but the comparison is superficial. One salient point of resemblance – the view of space as an attribute of God – means something different in the two systems; for Clarke [next]

---

2 E418

[Clarke, Samuel.] [cont.]

does not identify space with matter. And the method of his argument leaves room for the recognition of freedom and for a distinction of morality from nature, which were impossible for Spinoza". (p. 298.)

853

Coert, J.

Spinoza en Grotius met betrekking tot het volkenrecht. Leiden: E.J. Brill, 1936. 2 p.l., 18 p., 1 l. [blank]. 8°. (Mededeelingen ~~te Het~~ van wege Het Spinozahuis. [no.] 3.)

(A.S.O.)

---

2. 854

Coert, J. – Spinoza en Grotius ... [cont.]

Subj.: Grotius, Hugo. *
International Law. *

851

Coert, H.J.

Spinoza's betrekking tot de geneeskunde en haar beoffenaren. Leiden: E.J. Brill, 1938. 2 p.l., 18 p., 1 l. [blank]. 8°. (Mededeelingen van wege Het Spinozahuis. [no.] 4.)

Voordracht, gehouden ter gewone jaarvergadering van Het Spinozahuis te Rijnsburg in 1938.

---

2. 852

Coert, H.J. – Spinoza's ... [cont.]

Subj: Medicin
Life (?)

NNJ-C 5
NN
1. E421

Cohen, Max.

Schiller and the Jews. (Reform advocate. 1905. v.29, p.325-328.)

Repr.: New era. May, 1905.

p.328: "In respect to the influence of

SEE NEXT CARD.

---

2. E422

Cohen, Max.-Schiller... [cont.]

Spinoza upon Schiller there has been quite a critical controversy, Boas and Gervinus contending that the poet was thoroughly versed in the writings of the Jewish philosopher, while Ueberweg, in

See next card.

---

3. E423

Cohen, Max.-Schiller... [cont.]

'Schiller als Historiker und Philosopher' [sic!], insists that he had but scant knowledge of Spinoza, and that little at only second hand. At all events, we have among his poems an epigrammatic tribute

See next card.

---

4. E424

Cohen, Max.-Schiller [cont.]

that deserves to be remembered in this place:

Spinoza.

Hier light[!] ein Eichbaum umgerissen

Sein Wipfel thaat die Wolken kuessen

See next card.

5.
E 425

Cohen, Max.-Schiller... [cont.]

Er ligt[!] am Grund—warum?

Sein schönes Holz zum Bau'n vonnöthen

Die Bauren hatten, hör ich reden,

Und rissen ihn desswegen um.

ICMILC MIDWEST INTER-LIBRARY CENTER, (Chicago)
892

Cohn, Jonas, 1869- [Grützmacher]

Führende Denker. Geschichtliche Einleitung in die Philosophie. 4. Auflage. Leipzig: B. G. Teubner, 1921. 116 p. 12°. (Aus Natur- und Geisteswelt. Bd. 176)

Reviewed by R. H. Grützmacher in Theologisches Literaturblatt, Jahrg. 42, no. 14 (July 8, 1921), col. 217.

Also: 1917?

Also 5. ed.

883

Cohn, Jonas.

Geschichte des Unendlichkeitsproblems im abendländischen Denken bis Kant. Leipzig: W. Engelmann, 1896. 8°.

Spinoza, p. 152-159.

Der Kurze Traktat. Die Ethik.

Der Brief an Ludwig Meyer [Letter 12]. Die Erkennbarkeit des Unendlichen.

[over]

2.
884

Cohn, Jonas.—Geschichte des... [cont.]

Review: Zeitschr. f. Phil. u. Pädagogik, Jahrg. 9 (Langensalza, 1902), p. 357-358; by Arnold Kowalewski.

Inserted in A.S.O. copy.

(G.)

E 430

Coleridge, S. T.

Consult:

Muirhead, J. H. Coleridge as a philosopher. London, 1930.

Robinson, H. C. Diary. (1869; 3 v. 1872; 2 v.)

Snyder, Alice D. Coleridge on logic and learning. New Haven, 1929.

Wellek, René. Immanuel Kant in England. Princeton, 1931. missing

Winkelmann, E. Coleridge und die Kantische Philosophie. Leipzig, 1933.

[over]

2
E 431

Coleridge, S. T.—Consult: [cont.]

Brandl, A. Samuel Taylor Coleridge und die englische Romantik. Berlin, 1886. [L.L.]

——Eng. tr.: Coleridge and the English Romantic School. 1887. [L.L.]

Brooke, Stopford A. Theology in the English poets. 1874. [L.L.] (10 ed. 1907)

Green, J. H. Spiritual philosophy founded on the teaching of the late S. T. Coleridge. 1865. (2 v.) [L.L.]

Jack, A. A., and Bradley, A. C. Short bibliography of Coleridge. 1912 (English Association leaflet no. 23).

Shepherd, R. H. The bibliography of Coleridge. Revised, corrected and enlarged by W. F. Prideaux. 1900 [L.L.]

NN-5
YBG
1.
936

~~Spinoza, Baruch or Benedictus~~

Colerus, Johannes, 1647-1707.

Iohannis Coleri... Wahrheit der Auferstehung Jesu Christi wider B. de Spinoza und seine An[hänger] vertheidiget: Nebst einer genauen Lebens-Beschreibung dieses berüchtigten Philosophens, die man

third (1734) in B.M. cat. under Coler, Jean

SEE NEXT CARD.

2.
937

Colerus, J.-Iohannis Coleri... [cont.]

nic[ht so] wol aus seinen eigenen Schrifften, als vielmehr aus vieler [glaub]würdigen Leute mündlichen Erzehlung, so ihn im Leb[en] gekant haben, aufgesetzt, aus dem holländischen Original und der frantzösis[chen] Übersetzung

SEE NEXT CARD.

3.
938

Colerus, J.-Iohannis Coleri... [cont.]

verdeutscht, mit benöthigten Anmerckungen u[nd] Register versehen von Wigand Kahl[er]. Lemgo: gedruckt mit Meyerischen Schr[iften, 1734]. 8p. 1 p.L., 256 p., 2 L., 1 pl., 1 port. 8 & nar. 16.

See next card.

4.
939

Colerus, J.-Iohannis Coleri... [cont.]

Parts of t.-p. missing and supplied in ms.

The translator's preface (7 L.) is missing.

Portrait, between p. 114 and 115, with (above left) snake biting its tail; "charac-

SEE NEXT CARD.

5. 940

Colerus, J.-Iohannis Coleri... [cont.]

terem reprobationis in vultu gerens", as part of the inscription beneath. [Altkirch, p.93-94 (no.35): Kommt nur in einzelnen Exemplar vor.]

v.d.L.93.

B.169. — Weg, p.8.

---

2. 922

Colerus, — Vita Spinozae... [cont.]

Dunin-Borkowski, p.11: "A. Gfroerer druckte am Kopf seiner Ausgabe der Werke des Philosophen einfach Köhler und Lucas ab."

941

Colerus, J. Wahrheit d. Auferstehung J. Christi; tr. W. Kahler. Lemgo, 1734.

(Copy defective; wanting tr. preface.)

(1718 ed. Spec Coll. Spin. + 210/2) E 444

Colliber, Samuel, 1718-1737.

NNUT 5 LS64 C699 M

An impartial enquiry into the existence and nature of God: being a modest essay towards a more intelligible account of the Divine perfections. With remarks on several authors both ancient and modern; and particularly on some passages in Dr. [S.] Clarke's Demonstration of the being and attributes of God. In two books. With an appendix concerning the nature and space of duration. The [over]

LC

NNC Spec Coll Spin 945

Colerus,

Die Lebensbeschreibung des Colerus. (In: Zum Charakter Spinozas. Erläuterung der wichtigsten Nachrichten über sein Leben. Vom Verfasser des Spinoza Redivivus und Augustinus Redivivus... Halle, 1919. 8°. p. 52-94.)

A new translation.

---

2. E 445

Colliber, Samuel. — An impartial... [cont.]

third edition. With considerable additions and improvements, made partly with regard to some objections of the Reverend Mr. [John] Jackson. By Samuel Colliber. London: Printed for R. Robinson, 1735. 276 p. 8°

Book 2 has a sep. t.-p.
Frequent references to Spinoza.

(L.L. Leslie Stephen's copy.)

LLC-B 3934.R9 C8 948

Colerus, J.

[Life of B. S. Translated into Russian by L. I. [Y.?] Gurevich [Gurevitch?]. St. Petersburg, 1891.

Together (as an appendix?) to Spinoza's Correspondence by the same translator. Letters first, apparently.

---

128 C69 NNUT LS64 C699 5. E 446

[Colliber, Samuel.] fl. 1718-1737.

Free thoughts concerning souls: In four essays: I. Of the humane soul consider'd in its own nature. II. Of the humane soul compared with the souls of brutes. III. Of the supposed prae-existent state of souls. IV. Of the future states of souls. To which is added, An essay on creation. By the author of the Impartial inquiry, &c. [i.e. S. Colliber]. London: Printed for R. Robinson, 1734. xiii(1), 168 p. 8°.

req 10-20 [over]

0-II-4 921

Colerus, [French.]

Vita Spinozae a Colero scripta cum additamentis ex libello „Refutationf des erreurs de B. de Spinoza par Mr. Le comte de Boullainvilliers," et ex manuscripto Lucae medici depromtis. (In: Benedicti de Spinoza Opera philosophica omnia edidit... A. Gfroerer. Stuttgardiae, 1830. 8°. p. xix-lxiv.)

Allen

[over]

---

2. E 447

[Colliber, Samuel.] — Free thoughts... [cont.]

— p. vii - viii are omitted from pag. — Preface signed S. Colliber.

— The references to Spinoza are found in Essay V (p. 134-168), which deals with: "Sect. I. Six Arguments proving that the Present Form of the Universe was not from Eternity. Sect. II. Three Arguments proposed, tending to demonstrate the Possibility of the Production of a new Substance. Sect. III. The Certainty of the Creation of a new Substance demonstrated by Five several Arguments. Sect. IV. Objections answer'd." — The "most numerous Sect of Unbelievers; I mean the Spinosists." Trinius, no. 31 (Collyber).

NNC E449

[Colliber, Samuel.]

Free thoughts concerning souls; in four essays.... London, 1734.

Spinoza? For R. Robinson Not seen in contents. No author Index.

xiii + 1 p., 168 p. gen'l essays.

956

Corleo, S

Le comuni origini delle dottrine filosofiche di Micel, Malebranche e Spinoza e loro confronto con quelle di Gioberti. 1882.

Not in Rarb.

G-XVIII-22 957

Cornill, Adolph.

Materialismus und Idealismus in ihren gegenwärtigen Entwickelungskrisen beleuchtet. Heidelberg: J.C.B. Mohr, 1858. 8°.

Spinoza, p. 346-355.

(G.)

NNJ-4 E458

Copeland, Arthur.

Spinoza, apostle of emancipated thought. (American Israelite. v. 67, 1921, no. 41, ~~April 7~~, p. 1 [1½ col.].)

1⅓ "

Rev. Dr. A. C., Chaplain Auburn Prison.

G-XVIII-24 967

Costa, Isaac da.

Israël en de volken. Overzicht van de geschiedenis der Joden tot op onzen tijd. Tweede druk. Met een voorrede van A. W. Bronsveld. Haarlem: A.C. Kruseman, 1873. XVI, 550 p.

p. 403-550 contains "Bijdragen", being reprints of articles [over]

G-XVIII-24 2. 968

Costa, Isaac da. — Israël en de... [cont.]

from periodicals (including the Ha-vorscher, where the series "Adellijke geslachten onder de Israëlieten" first appeared).

Spinosa, p. 277-280; of the family, p. 474-475.

A copy in the Jewish Theological Seminary of America is dated 1876.

First ed. 1849. (not seen.)

(G.)

G-XVIII-25 969

Costa, Isaac da.

Israel und die Völker. Eine Uebersicht der Geschichte der Juden bis auf unsere Zeit von Isaak da Costa. Aus dem Holländischen von einer Freundin des göttlichen Wortes ins Deutsche übertragen und zum Drucke befördert von K. Mann. Frankfurt a.M.: H.L. Brönner, 1855. [over]

G-XVIII-25 2. 970

Costa, Isaac da. — Israel und die... [cont.]

2 p. l., (I) IV-XVI, 446 p. 8°

According to the Jewish encyclopedia, the translator was Miss Thumb.

Spinosa, p. 304 [erroneously numbered 204] - 307.

(G.)

893.191 C823 1 E466

Costa, Isaac da.

Noble families among the Sephardic Jews by Isaac da Costa; with Some account of the Capadose family... by Bertram Brewster, and An excursus on their Jewish history by Cecil Roth. With over 40 full-page illustrations. Oxford University Press; London: H. Milford, 1936. vi p., 2 l., 219 p., 44 pl. f°. [over]

1-a. E467

Costa, Isaac da. — Noble families... [cont.]

"The Chapter upon Sephardic History which forms the opening section of this volume [and entitled: The Jews of Spain and Portugal] is a reprint of Book III of the admirable translation by Mary Kennedy of the original edition of Da Costa's well-known Israël en de Volken ... The articles by the same writer upon 'Noble Jewish Families' (originally published [next]

2

E 468

Costa, I. da. - Noble families... [cont.]
in De Navorscher, c. 1857) were reprinted in the second Dutch edition of that work in 1876 [!], and consequently appear now for the first time in English... worked up by me from the rough draft by another hand and indeed almost entirely rewritten ... In the work of Mary Kennedy I have made only slight necessary [over]

2-a.

E 469

Costa, I. da. - Noble families... [cont.]
corrections and emendations." (Preface by B. Brewster.)

Spinoza, p. 89-91; the family of, p. 115-116.
Incl. sections on Spinoza (p. 89-91) and the Spinoza family (p. 115-116)

LC 37-9106 ord 7-16-58
(H.U.C.)

997

Cousin, Victor, ed.

Correspondance de Malebranche et de Mairan [1713-1714]. (In his: Fragments philosophiques pour servir à l'histoire de la philosophie. Cinquième édition. Philosophie moderne. pt. 1 [being v. 3 of series]. Paris, 1866. 8°. p. 404-487.)

[over]

2.

1000

Cousin, Victor, ed. - Correspondance... [cont.]
8 letters, 4 by each of the correspondents; ed. from a MS.
Mairan challenges Malebranche to acknowledge or disavow his relationship with Spinoza especially as regards his conception of extension.

Comp. v.d. L. 312 (n.).

(G.)

G-XXVIII-26

995

Cousin, Victor.

Des rapports du cartésianisme et du spinozisme. [1. Pensées de M. de la Clausure sur les opinions de M. Descartes. 1673. 2. Sur le spinosisme; by the abbé Gaultier. Edited from MSS.] (In his: Fragments philosophiques pour servir à l'histoire de la philosophie. Philosophie moderne. pt. 1 [being v. 3 of [over]

G-XXVIII-26

1-a.

996

Cousin, Victor. - Des rapports... [cont.]
series]. Paris, 1866. 5. ed. 8°. p. 259-296.)
Sur le spinosisme, p. 270-285. Gaultier (Jansenist and Cartesian) endeavours in this epistolary dissertation to refute the view expressed by a doctor (ordon) - name not given - of the Oxford University in a letter to a friend in France, that Descartes' doctrine of continuous creation leads of necessity to Spinozism.

2

997

Cousin, V. - Des rapports...
Janet, P., French thought and Spinozism (p. 1077); would date the MS. of Sur le spinosisme "probably... at the close of the seventeenth century". However, the author refers to [Theodor Ludwig] Lau (he calls him "un Hollandais"), whose Meditationes philosophicae de Deo, mundo et homine, did not appear before 1717.
Comp. v. d. L. 312.

(G.) [over]

2-a.

998

Cousin, V. - Des rapports... [cont.]
Janet, p. 1077, notes a 9. ed., with apparently the same pag.

G-XXVIII-17

986

Cousin, Victor.

Histoire générale de la philosophie depuis les temps les plus anciens jusqu'a la fin du XVIIIe siècle. Paris: Didier et Cie, 1863. 8°.

Leçon 1-10.
Leçon 8. Philosophie du XVIIe siècle. Idéalisme [Descartes, Spinoza, Malebranche]. p. 409-436: Spinoza. [over]

G-XXVIII-17

2.

987

Cousin, Victor. - Histoire générale... [cont.]
p. 430 mentions Leone Ebreo (Léon Hébreu) - the first time that Leone and Sp. have been connected?

(G.)

 988

Cousin, Victor.

Histoire générale de la philosophie depuis les temps les plus anciens jusqu' au XIXe siècle. Huitième édition revue et augmentée. Paris: Didier et Cie, 1867. 12°.

Leçon 1-10.

Leçon 8. Philosophie du dix-septième siècle. Idéalisme [Descartes, [over]

 2. 989

Cousin, Victor. — Histoire générale... [cont.]

Spinoza, Malebranche]. p 421-445.

11. ed. Paris, 1884. 12° (N.Y.P.L.)

(G.)

 991

Cousin, Victor.

Spinoza et la synagogue des Juifs portugais à Amsterdam. (In his: Fragments philosophiques pour servir à l'histoire de la philosophie: Philosophie moderne. pt. 1. Paris, 1866. 5. ed. 8°. p. 121-126.)

Forming v. 3 of the series of 5 v. of the Fragments philosophiques. v. 3 [over]

 2. 992

Cousin, Victor. — Spinoza et la... [cont.]

was first published in 1847.*

p. 124-125 contain Spinoza's letter to L. Meyer (Ep. 15) in the original Latin; first printed in the Fragments philosophiques, in 1847 (p. 60-62).

D.-B., I 43, has: Nouveaux fragments philosophiques, 1847.

Comp. v.d. L. 281.

* But the 5. ed. has an "Avant-propos de l'edition de 1845"!

(G.)

 1003

Covotti, Aurelio.

Relazione sul concorso pel premio annuale del 1912 sul tema: "Il Tractatus theologico-politicus dello Spinoza: attinenze della dottrina in esso svolta con l'Etica dello stesso autore. Rapporto della dottrina politica dello Spinoza con quella dell' Hobbes". (Società Reale di Napoli. - Accademia di Scienze Morali e Politiche. Rendiconto. anno 52, 1914, p. 100-132.)

Ravà, no. 42. (Not seen.) [over]

2. 1004

Covotti, Aurelio. — Relazione... [cont.]

See also Ravà no. 23, 25, 26, and Pref. of no. 8: the result of the "concorso."

Creighton, James E

Spinoza. (In: The Americana; a universal reference library... New York, [cop. 1912.] 4°. v. 19, [nearly 5 col.].)

No pagination.

(1907), " ", almost 5 cols., same author, in Vol. XIV of this ed. — 3 p.

Prof. of Philosophy at Cornell University.

 1012a

Cresson, André.

Spinoza: sa vie, son oeuvre; avec un exposé de sa philosophie par André Cresson. Paris: Alcan; Presses Universitaires de France, 1940. 2 p. l., 142 p., 1 l. 12° (Philosophes. Collection dirigée par Émile Bréhier.) [over]

1015

Crippa, Piero.

Spinoza. Milano: Ist. Artigianelli, 1921. 148 p.

parte I. La teoria della conoscenza.

Ravà, no. 29. (Not seen.)

 1016

Crommelin, C[ ] A[ ].

Spinoza's natuurwetenschappelijk denken. Leiden: E. J. Brill, 1939. 2 p. l., 19 p. 8°. (Mededeelingen van wege Het Spinozahuis. [no.] 6.)

Forms also Mededeeling no. 49 uit het Nederlandsch historisch natuurwetenschappelijk Museum te Leiden. [over]

1-a. 1017

Crommelin, C[ ] A[ ].—Spinoza's ... [cont.]

Voordracht, gehouden ter gewone jaarvergadering van Het Spinozahuis te Rijnsburg in 1939.

"Toch is het gerechtvaardigt van Spinoza's natuurwetenschappelijk denken te spreken, al volgde hij in dat denken veelal Descartes en al was zijn gedachtenleven in hoofdzaak wijsgeerig. Over sommige natuur-

1065

De Conciliis, N.

Sul concetto Spinozistico dello absoluto. Avellino, 1910.

Ravà, no. 20. (Not seen.)

2 1018

Crommelin, C.A.

wetenschappelijke onderwerpen, b.v. de atomistiek, heeft Spinoza stellig diep nagedacht, en ook in zijn wijsgeerig denken speelde de natuurleer een belangrijke rol, zooals de Ethica ons bewijst" (p.19).

In the main the references are to the Epistolae; but towards the end the Stelkonstige Reeckening van den regenboog and Reeckening van kanssen are also discussed.

[over]

NNC 193Sp4 5 G53 1068

De Jong, K.H.E. in Sp. Coll.

Spinoza en de Stoa. Leiden: E.J. Brill, 1939. 2 p.l., 34 p., 1 l. [blank]. 8°. (Mededeelingen van wege Het Spinozahuis. [no.] 5.)

Voordracht, gehouden ter gewone jaarvergadering van "Het Spinozahuis" te Rijnsburg in 1937.

(A.S.O.)

[over]

Claude August 1878 2-a. 1019

✓ Crommelin, C.A.— Spinoza's ... 1939 [cont.]

ICU (at least)

See also his: Het lenzenslijpen in de 17de eeuw. Amsterdam: H.J. Paris, 1929. (Voordracht gehouden den 2den Juni 1929 te Leiden in de algemene vergadering der Vereeniging Het Spinozahuis.)

o NNC D

o LC Het lenzen slijpen in de 17e eeuw. Met 29 afb. 45

+ Brinkman

D

2. 1069

De Jong, K.H.E.— Spinoza en ... [cont.]

Subj.: Stoicism. #

1057

Darjes, Joachim Georg. [1714-1791]

Erste Gründe der philosophischen Sittenlehre. Jena, 1750. 620 p.

"Spinozismus ist aus verschiedenen Schriften der Alten zusammengesetzte Gotteslängnung."

3. aufl. Jena, 1762, 668 p. IU

Not in Grunwald. (Not seen.)

-XI-15 1077

Delbos, Victor.

La notion de substance et la notion de Dieu dans la philosophie de Spinoza. (Revue de métaphysique et de morale. Paris, 1908, année 16, p. 783-788.

Überweg, p. 671. (G.) G-XIX-3 not a repr.

Repr. A.S.O.

G-XIX-1 1059

Daumal, René.

Le non-dualisme de Spinoza; ou, La dynamite philosophique. (Nouvelle revue Française. Paris, 1934. année 22, no. 248, p. 769-787.)

(C.G.)

1096

De Nardi, Pietro.

Della matematica e della fisica nella logica e nella metafisica di Cartesio, Spinoza, Leibnizio e Kant. Esposizione critica. Forli: ~~1905.~~ Tip. Sociale, succ. Bordandini, 1905 68 p. 8°.

Levi & Varisco, no. 149.

Überweg [1924], p. 654.—Not in Ravà.

1117

Deschamps, Léger-Marie.
Réfutation courte et simple du système de Spinoza.
sep. slip

"Les archives des Ormes en possèdent deux exemplaires manuscrits, tous deux de la main de dom Deschamps. Ce ne sont que quelques pages, destinées, dit l'auteur, à servir d'annonce à son grand ouvrage." (Beaussire, É. Antécédents de l'hégélianisme... Paris, 1865, p. 40.)
See: Beaussire.
194D451 OB
[over]

2. 1118

Deschamps, Léger-Marie.— Réfutation... [cont.]
Überweg [1924], p. 432: "Einen modifizierten Spinozismus vertritt der Benediktiner Dom. Deschamps in einem bald nach 1770 verfassten, aber erst durch Émile Beaussire... veröffentlichten Manuskript."
Freudenthal, II, 232: ... "Dam. [!] Deschamps in seinem 1770 geschriebenen, aber erst sehr viel später bekannt gewordenen Werk Réfutation de Spinoza."

O-XV-31, 32, 33, 34 1119

Deslandes, [André François Boureau].
Histoire critique de la philosophie, où l'on traité de son origine, de ses progrès, & des diverses révolutions qui lui sont arrivées jusqu'à notre tems. Nouvelle édition. Par M. Deslandes. tom. 1-4. À Amsterdam: Chez François Changuion, 1756. 4 v. 12°.

Spinosa (Benoît), tom. 1, p. 178-180
[over]

O-XV-31, 32, 33, 34 2. 1120

Deslandes, [André François Boureau]. — Histoire... [cont.]
(Son système sur la création du monde); p. 253 (qu'il n'y a qu'une seule substance dans l'univers: Opera posth., ep. 5 and 6); tom. 2, p. 59 (nom qu'il donne aux ames particulières: Opera posth., ep. 29); tom. 4, p. 32-33 (extrait de sa vie).
1. ed. Amsterdam, 1737. (3 vols.)
[a?]
The first history of philosophy in French.
(A.S.O.)

G-XXVIII-22 1138

Deter, Chr. Joh.
Kurzer Abriss der Geschichte der Philosophie. Fünfte Auflage. Berlin: W. Weber, 1892. 8°.

Baruch Spinosa, p. 63-66.

(G.)

1162

Deurhof, W.
Pleitreeden voor Deurhofs Job...
[2. issue or ed. of v. d. L. 197?]

"Yesterday I received some Dutch pamphlets... the most interesting one... is probably a pamphlet having a long title beginning 'Pleitreeden voor Deurhofs Job' (second print of v. d. Linde 197?)". From a letter of F. Bamberger, May 17, 1940.

O-XVI-1 1166

Deussen, Paul.
Der Idealrealismus des Spinoza. (In his: Allgemeine Geschichte der Philosophie mit besonderer Berücksichtigung der Religionen. Zweiter Band, dritte Abteilung: Die neuere Philosophie von Descartes bis Schopenhauer. Zweite Auflage. Leipzig, 1920. 8°. p. 41-69.)
[over]

O-XVI-1 1-a 1167

Deussen, Paul.— Der Idealrealismus... [cont.]
See also p. 7-8.
1. Vorbemerkungen. 2. Spinozas Leben und Schriften. 3. Die Form der Ethik des Spinoza. 4. Die Metaphysik des Spinoza. 5. Die Ethik de Spinoza.

cop. 1917. This ed. apparently a repr. of the 1.
(A.S.O.)

O-XVI-1 2 1168

Deussen, P.
"Während Descartes, Geulincx und Malebranche nur noch einen Ehrenplatz in der Geschichte der Philosophie beanspruchen können, erstreckt sich der Einfluss des Spinoza noch bis in die Gegenwart hinein, nicht nur auf diejenigen, welche ihn aus esprit de corps als einen ihrer Leute verehren, sondern auch auf den viel weiteren Kreis aller derjenigen, welche heute noch dem Idealrealismus oder, was
[over]

O-XVI-1 2-a. 1169

Deussen, P. — Der Idealrealismus... [cont.]
dasselbe bedeutet, dem psycho-physischen Parallelismus huldigen, einer Richtung, auf welche Kant stark genug eingewirkt hat, um das Zwingende seiner Beweise anzuerkennen, und doch nicht stark genug, um die Heilung von der uns allen angeborenen Krankheit des Realismus zu vollbringen" (p. 41).

 1173

172 Deylingi, D. Salomonis, Observationum Sacrarum pars prima (— tertia), in qua multa Scripturae Veteris ac Novi Testamenti dubia vexata solvuntur, loca difficiliora ex antiquitate, et variae doctrinae apparatu, illustrantur, atque ab audaci recentiorum criticorum depravatione solide vindicantur .... Editio tertia emendatior, ac tertia parte auctior. Lipsiae. Sumptibus Haeredum F. Lanckisii MDCCXXXV. 4°. 3 Teile. Prgt.
I. 1735. Kupfer, 7 Bll., 404 SS. u. 14 Bll.
II. 1737. 7 Bll., 620 SS., 14 Bll. u. 6 Kupfer.
III. Editio altera. 1726. 4 Bll., 576 SS., 19 Bll. u. 6 Kupfer.
Zu den audaces recentiores critici gehört vor allen Spinoza. „In seinen dickleibigen „Observationes sacrae", die heute höchstens noch wegen ihres reichhaltigen Schimpfwörtervorrats gegen Spinoza aufgeschlagen werden, überhäuft Deyling seinen Feind mit Koseworten wie: „doctrinae impietate opinionumque absurditate Atheus percelebris, sacratissimus et exsecrabilis audacissimus et impudentissimus, auctor detestabilis etc." (Grunwald S. 48-49)

1677-1755

Trinius, p. 531: D. Sal. Deylingii veritas resurrectionis Christi adversus Spinosam & Woolstonum adserta in Tom. III. S. Observatt. Miscell. P. 2. Obs. 17. p. 849.

[over]

 1189

Dilthey, Wilhelm.

Die Autonomie des Denkens, der konstruktive Rationalismus und der pantheistische ~~Idealismus~~ Monismus nach ihrem Zusammenhang im siebzehnten Jahrhundert. (Archiv für Geschichte der Philosophie. Bd. 7, 1894, p. 28-91.)

Sp 76-91

 1179

Dictionnaire théologique-portatif, contenant l'exposition et les preuves de la révélation; de tous les dogmes de la foi et de la morale; les points de controverse; les hérésies les plus célèbres... Ouvrage utile pour les jeunes théologiens... À Paris: Chez Didot [and others], 1761. 8°.

Spinosistes, p. 482-483.

(G.)

---

 2. 1190

Dilthey, Wilhelm.— Die Autonomie... [cont.]

The Section 0[?] dealing with "Der konstruktive Rationalismus und der pantheistische Monismus" (p. 74 to end) deals with the influence of Stoic tradition on Spinoza, by way of Telesius, Hobbes and Descartes.

Repr. [Berlin: G. Reimer, 1893.] 28-91 p. 8°

(G.)

✓Deyling, Salomo, 1677-1755 LC gives Salomon 1174

Deylingi, D. Salomonis.—Observationum... [cont.]

Burgersdijk & Niermans, p. 146, no. 3722: Deylingus, S. Observationes Sacrae. Ed. 2. Lips., 1720-1726. 3 v. 4°. — no. 3723: Observationes Sacrae. Lips. 1708, 11. 2 v. 4°

pars I, 1735, Sp. — ... p. (428) 3rd ed.
" II, 1737, Sp. " II. p. (645) 3rd ed.
" III, 1739. — 3rd ed.
" IV, 1757, Sp. " II. p. (940). — 3rd ed.
" II, 1748.

(2d ed. not ...)

---

 no more seen 1191

Dilthey, Wilhelm.

Giordano Bruno und Spinoza. ~~Erster Artikel.~~ (Archiv für Geschichte der Philosophie. Bd. 7, 1894, p. 269-283.)

(B's life to its zenith in Engl.)

Contains only sections I-IV as against I-VI in the Gesammelte Schriften (his sojourn in Germany and the end his death.) The whole treats only of the life of B., and the title is changed in "Giordano Bruno"

 1192

Dilthey, Wilhelm.

'Aus der Zeit der Spinoza-Studien Goethe's.' (Archiv für Geschichte der Philosophie. Bd. 7, 1894, p. 317-341.)

Der Aufsatz Goethe's. (Goethe's Spinoza essay, found in the Goethe-Archiv at Weimar in the hand-writing of Frau von Stein, was first published by B. [over]

 1231

Doerfling, Max.

Die Ansichten Spinozas über das Wesen der Affecte und ihre gegenseitigen Verhältnisse. Eine Studie von Dr. Max Dörfling. Zerbst: C. F. Dörfling, 1873. 2 p. l., (1)4-27 p. 8°.

Verso of t.-p.: Gedruckt bei Sam. Lucas in Elberfeld.

(G.) The dedicatory leaf was ~~apparently~~ added to this ed.

---

2. 1193

Dilthey, Wilhelm.— Aus der Zeit... [cont.]

Suphan in the Goethe-Jahrbuch of 1891, and subsequently included in the Weimar edition of Goethe's works; here reprinted.)—Goethe's Pantheismus in seiner Ausbildung vor der Weimarer Zeit.—Der Aufsatz Natur. (First published in the Tiefurter [?] Journal, 1782.)—Enstehung des Spinoza aufsatzes.—Interpretation des Aufsatzes. The section "Der Aufsatz Natur" contains some additions in the reprint in the gesammelte Schriften.

 1238

✓Drews, Arthur, Christian Heinrich, 1865-1935

Die deutsche Spekulation seit Kant mit besonderer Rücksicht auf das Wesen des Absoluten und die Persönlichkeit Gottes. Bd. 1-2. Berlin: Verlag von Paul Maeter's Buchhandlung, 1893. 2 v. 8°.

LC has 2d ed.

Spinoza. Die Substanz als Subjekt, v. 1, p. 42-47.—Der naive Pantheismus, p. 52-55.—Schleiermacher [and Spinozism], p. 215-228.—Jacobi [and Spinoza], v. 2, p. 4-5.—See also Namenregister. V. 2, p. 632

193 D82 same pagin. as 1895 ed.

Butler B409.3 D82 same Leipzig, 1895 ed. — 2d ed.

1244

Dubislar, Walter. / This title not in NNC or LC

MH → Über die Definitionen. ~~Leipzig~~ Berlin, 1927.
2. ed. — ~~[illegible]~~

*NNC '05 Er 451 #1 — — 3. ed. 1931.

Spinoza, p. 66—
"Die Seiten über Spinoza ... sind freilich unwichtig"... (D.-B. IV, 489.)

Die Definition Beihefte d. Erkenntnis I
Leipzig Felix Meiner
VIII + 160 p. (Sp. - p. 66 ff (66-68)) OK a section
rd 3-13-59

E522

Filleau de la Chaise, Jean, c.1630-c.1693.
Du Bois de la Cour, pseud.
UCLA (Antiq. Cat. 150, #642)
An excellent discourse proving the divine original, and authority of the five books of Moses. Written originally in French by Monsieur Du Bois de la Cour, and approved by six doctors of the Sorbon. To which is added a second part, or an examination of a considerable part of Père Simon's Critical history of the Old Testament, wherein all his objections, with the weightiest of Spinosa's against Moses's being the author of the first five books of the Bible, are
[over]

1-a E523

Du Bois de la Cour, pseud. — An excellent ... [cont.]
answered, and some difficult places of Holy Scripture are explained. By W. L. [corimers 21 (?)] London: Printed for Tho. Parkhurst, 1682. 20 p. l., 168 p. 8° 2 parts, 1 vol. Calf, sm. in — 8.
STC Wing D 2407 (4 copies)

---

2 E524

Du Bois de la Cour, pseud.
Preface by R. B. (l. 2-13). — The epistle to the reader by W. L. (l. 14-21). — A discourse of the proofs of the books of Moses, p. 1-57. — The second part; containing an examination of a considerable part of Père Simon's Critical history of the Old Testament. Wherein all his arguments, with the weightiest of Spinosa's against Moses's being the author of the first five books of the Bible, are fully and clearly answered, and several difficult places of Holy Scripture are explained, by W. L. London: Printed for Tho.
[over]

---

2. E525

Du Bois de la Cour, pseud. — An excellent ... [cont.]
Parkhurst, 1682, p. 59-168 [p. 59-60 being the t.-p. to pt. 2].
The Preface speaks of "the two following Treatises, one written and the other translated by Mr. W. L my greatly valued freind, well known to me to be a man of Learning and Judgement and examplary faithfulness to God and Conscience ... And verily a man that hath well digested the matter of such Controversies, will find that Pomponatius, Vaninus, Hobbes, Spinosa &c. were Ignorant men, that knew not their own Ignorance, nor what they wrote against, and that Simon saith little but what Commentators have often Answered"...

---

3. E526

Du Bois de la Cour, pseud.
p. 61: "What is contained in these following sheets, was first intended for a Preface unto the foregoing Discourse, Translated out of French into English, but when I had finished it, I found it would be too long a Preface unto such a short Discourse; and therefore upon Second thoughts, I concluded it would be better to subjoin it thereunto by way of Appendix, or Second Part. Who was the Author of the Discourse, I do not certainly know: but it is probable, that Monsieur du Bois de la Cour, who wrote
[over]

3-a. E527

Du Bois de la Cour, pseud. — An excellent ... [cont.]
the Discourse on Paschal his thoughts, or Meditations on Religion, &c. was likewise the Author of this Discourse; for they are frequently bound together, and were published, the one in 1671, and the other in 1672, with the approbation of the same Doctors of the Sorbon, excepting one whose name is not subscribed with the other six, unto the approbation of this Discourse."
p. 62-63: "It would ... have been altogether needless for me to have added ... this Second Part, if there had not been lately published in English a Book of
[next]

---

4 E528

Du Bois de la Cour, pseud.
P. Simon's Intituled, A Critical History of the Old Testament, where ... he hath ... [said?] Moses cannot be the Author of the Books which are attributed to him ... I was desirous to know what Arguments he used to prove such an uncouth Assertion, as had seldom been heard of from any before, but such as Hobs in his Leviathan, Pereyre in his Systema Praeadamitiam, and Spinosa in his Tractatus Theologico-Politicus, all Atheists or Infidels".
Is R. B. Richard Baxter? And W. L.: William Lowth?
[over]

4-a. E529

Du Bois de la Cour, pseud. — An excellent ... [cont.]
Gunn, p. 141: "It is interesting to note this as the first English book dealing with Spinoza, being a reply to his Tractatus Theologico-Politicus, prior to its English Translation, which appeared 1689".

8-XVI-11 1249

Duehring, E[ugen].
Kritische Geschichte der Philosophie von ihren Anfängen bis zur Gegenwart. Berlin: L. Heimann, 1869. 8°.

Spinoza, p. 273-313.

v. d. L. 148 (XXXIX).

(G.)
(A.S.O.) 6-XXVIII-24

 1250a

Dujovne, León.
Spinoza: su vida, su época, su obra, su influencia. tom. 1- Buenos Aires, 1941- . (Monografíos Universitarias. Instituto de Filosofia.)

tom. 1. La vida de Baruj Spinoza.

(Communication of J.M. Benardete.)

2. 1310

Dunin-Borkowski, Stanislaus, Graf von.—Spinozas... [cont.]
der Korte verhandeling. II. Zur Textgeschichte der Korte verhandeling. III. Einzelheiten.

 E537

Duncan, George Martin.
Relation of Leibnitz to Spinoza.—Literature on Spinoza's philosophy. (In his translation of: Leibniz, G. W. von.—Philosophical works. New Haven: Tuttle, Moorhouse & Taylor, 1890. 8°. p. 370-372.) also p. 384 ff.

Should we add "and references to Sp in editor's notes"?
nd 7-31

 E557

✓ Durant, William James 1885—
Der Einfluss Spinozas. (Jüdische Presszentrale [Zürich]. Jan. 17, 1930, p. 8-9.) B Jahrg. 13, Nr. 579, 1930, p. 8-9.
Illustrated 17. Januar 1930
"Aus Anlass der am 12. Januar [1930!] erfolgten Einweihung des Spinoza-Museums im Haag, geben wir aus dem Kürzlich... erschienen Werk von Will Durant 'Die grossen Denker', die [over]

 1267

Dunin-Borkowski, Stanislaus, Graf von.
Einige rätselhafte Quellen der Korte verhandeling Spinozas. (Chronicon Spinozanum. Hagae Comitis, 1925-1926. sq. 8°. tom. 4, p. 104-122.)

Parallels between Spinoza and Abelard, Thomas Aquinas, and F. Kuyper (Cuperus) and Spinoza.

2. E558

Durant, Will.—Der Einfluss... [cont.]
nachstehenden Stellen über den Einfluss Spinoza's wieder."

Jüdische Presszentrale Zurich und ~~jüdisches~~ Illustriertes Familienblatt für die Schweiz

(G.)

E

 1256

Dunin-Borkowski, Stanislaus, Graf von.
Der erste Anhang zu De Spinozas Kurzer Abhandlung; von Stan. Dunin Borkowski. (Chronicon Spinozanum. Hagae Comitis, 1921. sq. 8°. tom. 1, p. 63-80.)

—— —— Reprint.

OCH E563

[Earbery, Matthias.]
An/ answer/ to a/ book intitled,/ Tractatus Theologico Politicus./ London:/ Printed for Charles Brome, at the Gun, at/ the West End of St. Pauls. 1697./ 8 p.l., 189 p. 8°.

p. 189, verso, and last l.: Books printed for Ch. Brome, 1697.
"Bishop Boyl [Dr. Boyle, bishop of Cork] in his little Body of Divinity, and almost all our Moderns, who have [over]

 1309

Dunin-Borkowski, Stanislaus, Graf von.
Spinozas Korte verhandeling van God, de mensch en deszelfs welstand; von Stan. Dunin Borkowski. (Chronicon Spinozanum. Hagae Comitis, 1923. sq. 8°. tom. 3, p. 108-141.)

I. Entdeckung und Entstehung [over]

2. E564

[Earbery, Matthias.]—An answer... [cont.]
wrote in Vindication of the Scripture, have taken notice of Divers of its [i.e., the Tractate's] dangerous positions ... a Collective Answer to the whole Book, would be more satisfactory to the world... The author wants also to refute it popularly rather than learnedly, since "Deistical Principles begin to be Popular." "And since this Book [the Tractate] has as I am informed, received lately some impressions in our language; I thought it might not be amiss to administer the antidote, in the same vehicle, in which the Party has presented the Poyson..." (Preface.) Copy in London Library.— See v.d.L. 370
(Also in H.U.C.)

OCH E565
Earbery, Matthias.
Deism examin'd and confuted. In an answer to a book intitled, Tractatus Theologico Politicus. By Matthias Earbery. London: Printed for Charles Brome, 1697. 8 p.L., 189 p. 8°.

p. 189, verso, and last L.: Books printed for Ch. Brome, 1697.

Copy in London Library; with autograph of Leslie Stephen. v. d. L. 370.

NNC 505 F77 4 1320
Ebbinghaus, Julius. 1885-
Über den Grund der Beschränkung unserer Erkenntnis auf die Attribute des Denkens und der Ausdehnung bei Spinoza. (Forschungen und Fortschritte [Berlin]. Nov. 20, 1932.)
Jahrg. 8, 1932, p. 420-421.
"Auszug eines Vortrags, gehalten
(G.) Subtitle [illegible]
covers

---

2. 1321
Ebbinghaus, Julius. — Über den... [cont.]
auf der Spinoza-Woche im Haag (5. bis 10. Sept.) ... 1932..."

JOURNALISM D071 N495 F NNC-4 81-86 E567
Edman, Irwin. 1896-1954
Spinoza's message for a world beset. (Times [New York] Magazine. Nov. 20, 1932, Sect. 6, p. 5, 16.)

"In the following article Spinoza's philosophy is interpreted, its application today is set forth and the career of the man revealed".
With the bust of Spinoza by Huettenbach, in the garden of the Domus Spinozana.
(A.S.O.)

O-XVII-12 1344
Eisler, Rudolf.
Geschichte des Monismus. Leipzig: Alfred Kröner Verlag, 1910. 8°.

Spinozas Pantheismus und Identitätslehre (Okkasionalismus, Geulincx, Malebranche, Spinoza), p. 33-36.)

(G.) A.S.O.
G-XXVIII-25

NNC 103 E1811 1347
Eisler, Rudolf.
"Spinozismus." (In his: Wörterbuch der philosophischen Begriffe und Ausdrücke quellenmässig bearbeitet. Berlin, 1899. 8°. p. 723.)
(a later ed. NNC R031 E184 3v. 1927-30,)
(A paragraph "Spinozismus" p. 723)
103 E18112 V. III, pp. 137-138 (Spinozismus)
(A.S.O.)
[illegible] 7-30-58
Cover

---

2. 1348
Eisler, Rudolf. — Spinozismus... [cont.]
— — (In his: Wörterbuch der philosophischen Begriffe. Historisch-quellenmässig bearbeitet. Zweite, völlig neu bearbeitete Auflage. Berlin, 1904. Bd. 2, p.)
3. ed. 1910. 3 v.
v. III, 1910, p. 1409.

---

194 B455 DE E577
Elliot, Hugh S. R.
[Spinoza: his philosophy and Ethics.] (In his: Modern science and the illusions of Professor Bergson... London, 1912. 12°. p. 151-152.) other refs also
See also Index.

Incl. refs. to Sp.

(A.S.O.)
[illegible] 7-30-58
covers

---

2. E578
Elliot, Hugh S. R. — [Spinoza: his [cont.]
"There is nothing particular to say about him, save that he evolved his system from the depths of his own mind, explaining the Universe as manifestations of an infinite impersonal substance. His system has just as strong a claim on our belief as that of Bergson or any other metaphysician... Spinoza's System is in many ways superior to Bergson's. He was a firm believer in the universality of causation: his exposure in his Ethics of the origin of the fallacies of teleology, makes that work still worthy of general study."

NNC 179 A 1361
Erdmann, Benno.
Spinoza. [Review of:] 1. Freudenthal, J. Spinoza und die Scholastik. — 2. Busse, L. Beiträge zur Entwicklungsgeschichte Spinozas. I. Die Reihenfolge seiner Schriften. — 3. Gaul, K. Die Staatstheorie von Hobbes und Spinoza, in ihren Schriften Leviathan und tractatus politicus verglichen. — 4. Schneider, F. Die Psychologie des Spinoza unter besonderer Bezugnahme auf Cartesius.
pp 305-308; 308-311 SCS; pp. 311-312; pp 312-313
covers

NNC-4 2. 1362

Erdmann, Benno.— Spinoza [Review of: ... [cont.]
p. 313-315
5. Henitescu, J. Die Affectenlehre Spinozas.
6. Bergmann, J. Spinoza, Vortrag gehalten im Goethehause in Frankfurt. (Archiv für Geschichte der Philosophie. Berlin, 1889. Bd. 2, p. 305-315.)
A

O XVII 21 1364

Erdmann, J[ohann] E[duard].

Vermischte Aufsätze. Leipzig: F.C.W. Vogel, 1846. 8°.

Die Grundbegriffe des Spinozismus, p. 118-192.
A. Die Substanz. B. Der Modus. C. Das Attribut.

V. d. L. 425.

(A.S.O.)

O-XIII-19,20 1368

Erdmann, Johann Eduard.

Grundriss der Geschichte der Philosophie. Bd. 1-2. Dritte, verbesserte Auflage. Berlin: W. Hertz, 1878. 8°.

Spinoza, Bd. 2, p. 45-77.—See also Namen-Register to both volumes.

(A.S.O.—F.C.S. Schiller's copy.)

NNUT: QH E66 3v. 1834-53. 5 the same as 1371 1372

Erdmann, Johann Eduard, 1805-1892.

Versuch einer wissenschaftlichen Darstellung der Geschichte der neuern Philosophie. Bd. 1, Abth. 1-2. Leipzig: E. Frantzen, 1834-1836. 2 v. 8°.

Bd. 1, Abth. 1. Darstellung und Kritik der Philosophie des Cartesius nebst einer Einleitung in die Geschichte der neuern Philosophie. (X p., 1 l., CX p., 1 l., 336 p., 1 l.)
Incl. a section on Sp. (v. 1, pt. 2, p. 47-98)
" " 2. Malebranche, Spinoza und die Skeptiker [cover]

G.-XIX-28 1367

Erdmann, Johann Eduard.

Grundriss der Geschichte der Philosophie. Zweiter und letzter Band. Philosophie der Neuzeit. Zweite, sehr vermehrte Auflage. Berlin: W. Hertz, 1870. 8°.

Spinoza, p. 45-74. See also Namen-Register.

(G.)

2. 1373

Erdmann, Johann Eduard.— Versuch... [cont.]
und Mystiker des siebzehnten Jahrhunderts. Darstellung und Kritik ihrer Systeme. (XXII p., 1 l., 257 p.)

Bd. 1¹: Riga und Dorpat. 1834.
G-XIX-21 " 1²: Leipzig, Riga und Dorpat. 1836 (v.d.L. gives: XXII p., 1 l., (258), [X p.]; NYPL: XXII, 257, 1 l., CX p., 1 l. 12° — Apparently, the "Beilagen" are there given in Bd. 1², comprising [(X p.)]

V.d.L. 316

4 E 592

Erdmann, Johann Eduard, 1805-1892
A history of philosophy. English translation edited by Williston S. Hough. London, 1890. 3 v. 8°. (Library of philosophy.)
From the 3. German edition, 1878.
V. II, 1890 - Sp. 66 ... 52 91.
NN - Nf 1892-... Also, see index
Vol. II: ... 1897
NNC ... 1891-1913; 1892-3
BM
... LC (2d ed. 1890-92)

1394 (3)

Ewyck, G. van.

De groote swaerigheid, voortkomende uit de samenschakelingen der denkbeelden, dewelke de zeer vermaerde Heer Jacobus Wittichius, Meester in de vrye Kunsten, Doctor en openbaar Professor in de philosophie, opgemaakt heeft in zyne Wysgeerige twistredeneering over de nature Gods. [cover]

O-XII-22 1363

Erdmann, Johann Eduard.

Leib und Seele nach ihrem Begriff und ihrem Verhältniss zu einander. Ein Beitrag zur Begründung der philosophischen Anthropologie. Halle: C.A. Schwetschke und Sohn, 1837. 8°.

Spinoza, p. 105-109. See also p. VII and 126.

(A.S.O.)

1-a 1393 (4)

Ewyck, G. van.— De groote... [cont.]
Welke swaerigheid (opdat an dezelve opendlyk werde voldan, dewyl ook de gemoederen van veele niet weinig door dezelve gequeld zouden konnen worden) openbaarlyk heeft willen voorstellen, ende te gelyk den voornaemsten Spinosistischen grondregel t'eenemaal omverre werpen, G: van Ewyck, Regtsgeleerde. Uit het Latyn vertaalt door

2 1395

Ewyck, G. van.

P. L. D. W. Te Delft: Gedrukt by Reinier Boitet, 1719. 77(1) p., 1 l. 4°.

Art in V. d. L. (266 gives the original Latin edition).

The Dutch translation contains a "Toegift van den auteur" (p. 63 to end), not found in the original Latin version, with reference mainly to the notes by W. added to his tr. of the Disputatio.

(G.) – Weg, p. 6.

[over]

2-a. 1396

Ewyck, G. van. — De groote... [cont.]

Together with: Leydekker, J. De blyde Spinosist ... Te Rotterdam, 1719

O-XLII-8

[Excommunication.] 1397

Der Bannspruch gegen Baruch Spinoza. [Translated into German by Ludwig Philippson.] (Allgemeine Zeitung des Judenthums. Leipzig, 1862. Jahrg. 26, no. 44, p. 623-624.)

"Vor Kurzem gab J. van Vloten ... mehrere unedirte Fragmente Spinoza's heraus, als ein Supplement zu dessen sämmtlichen Werken. In...

[over]

O-XLII-8

[Excommunication.] 2. 1398

Der Bannspruch gegen Baruch Spinoza. [cont.]

[den Collectomeen] theilt der Herausgeber auch den Wortlaut des Bannfluches in spanischer [really Portuguese] Sprache und mit lateinischer Uebersetzung mit, und geben wir ihn als ein für die Zeit und die Person bezeichnendes Document in deutscher Uebertragung hier wieder."

(A. S. O.)

O-XLII-9

[Excommunication.] 1399

Bannfluch gegen Spinoza. [Druck der Ernst Ludwig Presse zu Darmstadt. Spinoza zu Ehren in einhundert fünfunddreissig Abzügen März 1925 hergestellt. Übertragung von L. Philippson.] 6 f. [first and last blank]. 4°.

G-LIII-4

(A. S. O.)

F

G-XXIX-1 1416

Falckenberg, Richard.

Geschichte der neueren Philosophie von Nikolaus von Kues bis zur Gegenwart. Im Grundriss dargestellt. Leipzig: Veit & Comp., 1886. 8°.

Spinoza, p. 82-103.

[General.] I. Substanz, Attribut, Modus. II. Anthropologie: die Erkennt-

[over]

G-XXIX-2 2. 1417

Falckenberg, Richard. — Geschichte der... [cont.]

nis und die Leidenschaften. III. Praktische Philosophie.

x — — Zweite, verbesserte und vermehrte Auflage. Leipzig: Veit & Comp., 1892. 8°.

Spinoza, p. 94-115.

"Herr Professor A. C. Armstrong in New-York bereitet eine Übersetzung ins Englische vor" (p. vi).

(G.)

Spec Coll Spin (dated 1876) E601

N- Farrar, Adam Storey, 1826-1905.

ET Bampton 1862) 5

A critical history of free thought in reference to the Christian religion. Eight lectures preached before the University of Oxford... on the foundation of the late Rev. John Bampton... London: J. Murray, 1862. lix, 684 p. 1 l. 8°. ↑LC 33-6283 rl 3-5-59

Spinoza, p. 147-162.

39.61 B 162 — — New York, 1863. (The Bampton lectures for 1862.) ↖LC 4-22443

NJ NE NY, 1863 ed. rl 10-23

1422

Faure, A.

Selbsterhaltungstrieb in der Staatsphilosophie Spinozas. Dissertation. München, 1922.

Überweg, p. 672.

1441

Fénelon.

His "Refutation" is an extract from a letter written to Father François Lami, and first published by him in his "Le nouvel athéisme renversé" in 1696. The book "Réfutation" which Dr. Brasch evidently refers to, was published in 1731. This work is known to have been edited by the abbé Lenglet-Dufresnoy (du Fresnoy) though his name does not appear in the book.

→ 1935p4

---

2. 1445

Ferrari, G[iuseppe] M[ichele]. — L'Etica ... [cont.]
ideale dell'uomo...

Ravà. no.17. (Harvard)

NN-YBX - 5

1439

Fénelon, François de Salignac de La Mothe, 1651-1715.

Oeuvres philosophiques de Fénelon. Nouvelle édition collationnée sur les meilleurs textes... par A. Jacques... Paris: Charpentier, 1845. 12°. 1 p.l., LXXII, 484 pp.

Réfutation du spinozisme, p.120-129.

oNNC
oLC
(L.L.)

0-XL-29,30

1453

Ferro, A.

La filosofia di Spinoza e la filosofia ebraica medievale. (Giornale critico della filosofia italiana. Firenze, 1935. 8°. anno 16, ser. 2, v. 3, p. 50-64, 169-180.)

A critical analysis of: Wolfson, H. A. The philosophy of Spinoza (1934). G-XIV-40: fascicolo I only!

NNC

1436

Fénelon, François de...

Oeuvres philosophique de Fénelon... Paris: L. Hachette, 1843. 12°.

Réfutation du spinosime, p.110-118. [From the "Table": L'Etre infini est-il distingué de la collection de tous les être? Absurdité du spinosisme. 1° L'infinie perfection ne peut être changeante et variable. 2° L'infini ne peut être [over]

1482

Fischer, F. ?

Die Schleiermachersche Trennung der Theologie von der Philosophie verglichen mit der Spinozischen. Hamburg, 1848.

not seen DLC catalog (of own holdings)

Reprint? Not in v.d.L. or B. or W.

---

2. 1437

Fénelon. — Oeuvres philosophiques... [cont.]

composé des parties réellement distinguées les unes des autres. Il est absurde d'admettre plusieurs infinis. Résumé de ce qui précède. Prière à Dieu.]

[L. L.] (M. Lowenthal.)

0-XVIII-14

1491 (?)

Fischer, Kuno.

Geschichte der neuern Philosophie. Erster Band, zweiter Theil: Fortbildung der Lehre Descartes; Spinoza. Dritte, neu bearbeitete Auflage. München: Basserman, 1880. 556 p. 8°.

Short notice in: Mind. Oct., 1880. p. 587-588.

First ed. 1854.

MH Phil 3825.6 .5

1444

Ferrari, G[iuseppe] M[ichele]. 1811-1876?

L'Etica di B. Spinoza. Appunti di G. M. Ferrari. Napoli: Stab. Tip. Pierro e Veraldi nell' Instituto Casanova, 1902. VII (1), 157 p., 1 l. 12°.

oNNC
oLC
oBN

Contents: [Prefazione] Libro I. La natura generale della realtà. II. La mente umana... III. La vita [over]

NNC 105 An721 no.7

1514

Fischer, Ludwig.

Die natürliche Ordnung unseres Denkens und der Zusammenhang der Weltanschauungen. Leipzig: F. Meiner, 1927. IX, 359 p. 8°.

Francis Bacon — Spinozas Substanzbegriff — Leibniz Substanzbegriff, p. 210-213.

1 NNC
Box 1 1527
V

Forsberg, N. A.

Jemförande betraktelse af Spinozas och Malebranches metafysika principir. Akademisk afhandling, som med vidtberömda Filosofiska Fakultetens i Upsala samtycke för filosofiska gradens erhållande kommer att offentligen försvaras af N. A. Forsberg... Upsala: Edquist & Berglund, 1864. 2 p.l., (1)4-29 p. 12°.

LC
[over]

---

2. 1528

Forsberg, N. A. — Jemförande betraktelse ... [cont.]

Harvard; Weg, p. 9; Baldwin; Karitz (Chr. Sp. V, 178).

---

052 NNC-4 Incl. discussion of 6 works by Saisset E627
E

[Fraser, Alexander Campbell.]

M. Saisset and Spinoza. (North British review. Edinburgh, 1863. 8°. v. 38, p. 454-489.)

(not signed)

2 1862 ed
SCS 1. Essai de philosophie religieuse (Paris, 1859).
SCS 2. An essay on religious philosophy (Edinburgh, 1863).
SCS 3. Introduction critique aux Oeuvres de Spinoza.
Same cat. Spin 4. Oeuvres de Spinoza; tr. E. Saisset. (3 vols.)
5. Essais sur la philosophie et la religion au XIXe siècle.
SCS 6. Précurseurs et disciples de Des Cartes.

---

2. E628

[Fraser, Alexander Campbell.] — M. Saisset ... [cont.]

p. 459 (note): "Some ... interesting memoranda with regard to the man Spinoza may be found in the simple and touching account of his life by John Colerus... who was personally acquainted with him, and who, while he differed with him in opinion, admired his pure and blameless life. There is a MS. 'Vie de Spinoza' in the Edinburgh University Library which also contains some interesting particulars."

p. 463 (note): "Coleridge thus contrasts Spinozism with 'the Hebrew or Christian Scheme': —

---

3. E629

[Fraser, Alexander Campbell] — M. Saisset ... [cont.]

Spinozism.

'W − G = 0; i.e., the World without God is an impossible idea.

G − W = 0; i.e., God without the world is an impossible idea.

Hebrew or Christian Scheme.

W. − G = 0; i.e., the World without God is an impossible idea.

But G − W = G; i.e., God without the World is God the self-subsistent.'

But this is applicable to the Christian scheme only as popularly understood — not a few thoughtful

---

4. E630

[Fraser, Alexander Campbell.] — M. Saisset... [cont.]

Christians holding by the absolute correlation to God and the world, as an inference necessarily deducible from the moral nature or personality of God."

---

1. E631

Spinoza, Baruch or Benedictus.

[Fraser, Alexander Campbell.]

M. [Émile Edmond] Saisset and Spinoza. (North British review. American edition. New York, 1863. 8. v. 38, p. 240-259.)

Anon.

tried ed. not located

See next card.

---

2. E632

Spinoza, Baruch or Benedictus.

[Fraser, Alexander Campbell.] — M. [Émile Edmond] Saisset... [cont.]

052 E NNC-5 the North British Review
In the Edinburgh ed., p. 454-489.

052 A TB v. 4

See: Pringle — Pattison, A. Seth, The idea of God in the light of recent philo-

cf 2d ed. 1920 Barnard D231 se7

231 Se 7S

See next card.

---

3. E633

Spinoza, Baruch or Benedictus.

[Fraser, Alexander Campbell.] — M. [Émile Edmond] Saisset... [cont.]

sophy (1917), p. 315. — a footnote citing the Fraser article

Review of: 1. Essai de philosophie religieuse. Par É. Saisset. Paris, 1859.

See next card.

---

4. E634

Spinoza, Baruch or Benedictus.

[Fraser, Alexander Campbell.] — M. [Émile Edmond] Saisset... [cont.]

SpC Spin. [3. ed. (rev.) 1862.] — 2. An essay on religious philosophy. By É. Saisset. Translated, with marginal analysis,

See next card.

5. E635
Spinoza, Baruch or Benedictus.

[Fraser, Alexander Campbell.]-M. [Émile Edmond] Saisset... [cont.]

notes, critical essay, and philosophical appendix. v.1-2. Edinburgh: T. & T.Clark,1863.- 3. Introduction cri-

See next card.

6. E636
Spinoza, Baruch or Benedictus.

[Fraser, Alexander Campbell.]-M. [Émile Edmond] Saisset... [cont.]

tique aux Oeuvres de Spinoza. Par É. Saisset.- 4. Oeuvres de Spinoza, traduites en Français pour la première fois.

See next card.

7. E637
Spinoza, Baruch or Benedictus.

[Fraser, Alexander Campbell.]-M. [Émile Edmond] Saisset... [cont.]

Par É. Saisset. v.1-3.—5. Essais sur la philosophie et la religion au XIX siècle. Par É. Saisset. Paris,1845.-

See next card.

8. E638
Spinoza, Baruch or Benedictus.

[Fraser, Alexander Campbell.]-M. [Émile Edmond] Saisset... [cont.]

6. Précurseurs et disciples de Des Cartes. Par É. Saisset. Paris,1862.

[2.ed. 1862.]

Colerus ✓DLC-AP15.N4 903
Frederiks, J. G.

Colerus' Leven va Spinoza herdrukt. (Nederlandsche spectator. [jaarg.] 1880, p. 391-393.)

Review of edition M. F. A. G. Campbell. (over)

Author notes 3 copies of original edition: Collection Prof. Doedes; Universitätsbibliothek Halle; Koninklijke Bibliotheek, The Hague. [over]

So does the Preface by Campbell.

Colerus 2. 904
Frederiks, J.G. – Colerus' Leven... [cont.]

Edition noted also by "Flanor" under the heading "Vlugmaren", p. 371.

0-XIX-8 1612

Freudenthal, J.

Spinozastudien. n.t.-p. [Leipzig, 1896.] 238-282 p., 1 l. blank. 8°.

Title taken from first page.

Repr.: Zeitschrift für Philosophie und philosophische Kritik. Bd. 108.

I. Über den kurzen Tractat. 1. Echtheit des Tractates. 2. Der Tractat kein unreifes ~~Jugend~~werk. 3. Der Tractat ist ein unfertiger Entwurf. 4. Die

G-X-4a,4b G-XX-4: excerpt [over]

0-XIX-8 2. 1613
Freudenthal, J. – Spinozastudien.... [cont.]

Thätigkeit des Redactors. 5. Andere Schicksale der Schrift.

G-X-4a, 4b G-XX-4: excerpt
(A.S.O.-unbd.)

0-XIX-18 1631

Friedlaender, Julius.

Spinoza ein Meister der Ethik. Nach einem Vortrage gehalten in der deutschen Gesellschaft für ethische Kultur in Berlin. Berlin: C. R. Dreher's Verlag, 1895. 30 p., 1 l. 8°.

(A.S.O.) unbd. – Not in B.
G-X-7 [over]

0-XIX-18 2 1632
Friedlaender, Julius. – Spinoza ein... [cont.]

"In der vorliegenden Arbeit habe ich die metaphysischen Begriffe Spinozas ... unberücksichtigt gelassen... Wenn ich die früheren schwierigen Aufschlüsse über Spinoza's Philosophie gemeinsam mit meinem Freunde und Mitarbeiter Herrn Dr. Berendt veröffentlicht habe, so ist auch diese Arbeit im lebhaftesten Gedankenaustausche zwischen uns herangereift und entstanden" (Vorrede).

G-X-7

910.9 F957 cf rev. ed. 1915 940.9 F959I E672

Fullerton, William Morton.

Problems of power... 2. impression. London, 1913. 8°.

p. 62: "The folly of the man who would apply an 'international mind' to the problems of diplomacy has been indicated by Spinoza. He too was a philosopher, but he was well aware that to the historian human passions, love, hate, anger, envy, vanity, pity, and all the other 'movements of the soul', are not [over]

2. E673

Fullerton, William Morton.— Problems of... [cont.] virtues or vices, but merely 'properties', as heat or cold are properties of the air'." [follows a quotation from Tr. Pol. Cap. I, 6, 7].

p. 302: "A lack of intellectual probity is often characteristic of Anglo-Saxon statesmanship, and of late years, in America, Mr Roosevelt alone would seem to have had an inkling of the profound practical truth of Spinoza's remark: "It matters little, as regards the security of the State, what the motives of rulers may be in the successful administration of affairs. Liberty or strength of soul are the virtue of private persons; the virtue of the State is security!"

100 F963 publ 1658

Funck-Brentano, Th

Les sciences humaines: philosophie, médecine, morale, politique. [V. 1.] La philosophie. Paris: (Librairie Internationale) 1868. 8°.
Lacroix

Spinoza, p. 141-152.

G

G-XX-12 1661

Gallucci, Generoso.

La concezione del Cristianesimo nel "Trattato teologico-politico, ed il panteismo di Spinoza. Memoria approvata dalla R. Academia di Scienze Morali e Politiche della Società Reale di Napoli. Napoli: F. Sangiovanni & Figlio, 1915. 11 p. 8°.

Repr.: R. Academia di Scienze Morali e Politiche di Napoli. Atti. v. 44.

(G.) R., no. 23 [over] [over]

1665

Galluppi, Pasquale, baron.

Saggio filosofico sulla critica della conoscenza. Napoli, 1819-1832. 6v.

[Ravà, in Bulletin, p. 53, gives: Napoli, 1832-1836.]

Libro 3, cap. 4: Esposizione ed esame dell dottrina di Spinoza sull' infinito, § 58-75.

NN— —— Iª ed. milanese. Milano, 1846. 5v. 12°. [N.Y.]

XCB; MH; NjP MB 2a ed., .. Napoli: Raffaello. 1833. 6v. 8°

AN LIBR (NNC) 1663

5 Galluppi, Pasquale, barone, 1770-1846

940 62 "Alcune osservazioni sullo spinozismo." (In: Onoranze al prof. Vincenzo Lilla nel suo XL anno d'insegnamento. Messina, 1904. p. 225-226.)

..."publié d'après un autographe de sa jeunesse"...

Ravà in Bulletin de la Société française de Philosophie, année 27, 1927, no. 2-3, p. 53.

V: card made 4M NUS 10/12 1664

Galluppi, Pasquale, baron. † 1846

CtY K8.614 F827 Lettere filosofiche su le vicende della filosofia, relativamente ai principii delle conoscenze umane da Cartesio sino a Kant inclusivamente... Messina, 1827. 290, [2] p., 1 l. 21cm.

— —— 2. ed. Napoli, 1838.

PV (microfilm) —— Firenze, 1842. 352 p. 14cm. ← typed

MH— —— ed. by A. Guzzo. Firenze, 1925. ← typed

Lettera I.

109 G138 French tr.: Lettres philosophiques... Tr. L. Peisse. Paris, 1844. [L. L.] typed for Bibl. 1923-58

Spec Coll Spin 1667

Gancikoff, Leonida.

Aporie del panlogismo (Spinoza e Hegel). (In: Spinoza nel terzo centenario della sua nascita; pubblicazione a cura della Facoltà di Filosofia dell' Università Cattolica del Sacro Cuore. Milano, 1934. 8°. p. 85-98.)

G-XX-13 1670

Gans, M. E.

Spinozismus. Ein Beitrag zur Psychologie und Kulturgeschichte des Philosophierens. Wien: J. Lenobel, 1907. 111 p. 8°.

Baer 623.

(G.) [over]

1-a 1671

Gans, M. E.— Spinozismus. Ein... [cont.]

"Nicht von Spinozas Philosophie, von seinem Philosophieren soll... die Rede sein... Philosophieren heisst zunächst erleben... Ein Erlebnis aber kommt zustande durch die Einsicht in einen Sachverhalt... Erkennen, Wollen und Fühlen sind in gleicher Weise daran beteiligt" (p. 1).

"Logical ethicism" as essence of Spinozistic philosophizing. Spinoza a great "character;"

2 1672

Gans, H.E.

"the Ethica a monument of his personality."

Review: Zeitschrift für Philosophie und philosophische Kritik, Bd. 134, 1909, p. 275. By Günther Jakoby.

---

2. 1685

Gaultier, abbé. – Sur le spinosisme ... [cont.]

Fragm. phil. III, 270-285)" (Erhardt, 496.)

(L.L. Fragments philosophiques, Brussels 1840)

3. ed. 1838

Fragment Philosophiques, III, 1866, p. 270-296.

G-CIV-22 1677

Garve, Christian.

Ueber einen Satz aus der Ethik des Spinoza. Fragment. (In: Neue Miniatur-Bibliothek der deutschen Classiker. Eine Anthologie in 200 Bändchen. Hildburghausen, 1845. nar. 32°. Bändchen 99, p. 45-71.)

On Ethica, pars V, Prop. II. – "Folgende Betrachtungen sind dazu bestimmt, den Sinn [over]

O-XX-27 G1700-5

Gebhardt, Carl.

Domus Spinozana. [Hagae Comitis, 1927.] p. 65-87. sq. 8°.

Repr.: Chronicon Spinozanum. v. 5.

1) Title taken from first page.

Exemplar vitae. - Identität. - Übergang. - Statuten van de Stichting „Domus Spinozana". - Erhaltung. - Bestimmung.

---

2. 1678

Garve, Christian. – Ueber einen ... [cont.]

und die practische Andwendbarkeit dieses Ausspruchs in's Licht zu setzen" (p. 47).

Not in v. d. L.

(G.)

NNC 056 R327 See G-1700-58a for complete entry! G-1700-58

Gebhardt, Carl.

León Hebreo; su vida y su obra. (Revista de Occidente. Madrid, 1934. año 12, Tomo 44, 1934, p. 233-273;

A translation of the "Einleitung: Vom Leben und vom Werk Leone Ebreos" to his ed. of Leone Ebreo (1929).

Tr. by Ortega y Gasset!

1682

Gaul, Karl.

Die Staatstheorie von Hobbes und Spinoza nach ihren Schriften „Leviathan" und „Tractatus politicus" verglichen. (Alsfeld. - Grossherzogliche Realschule. Jahresbericht. no. 589. Alsfeld: H. Düring, 1887. sq. 4°. p. 8-19.)

B. 441.

Review: Archiv für Geschichte der Philosophie. Bd. 2, 1889, p. 311-312. By Benno Erdmann.

(H.U.C.)

O-XLVII-2 B-LVIII-5 G-1700-55

Gebhardt, Carl, ed. & tr.

Die Schriften des Uriel da Costa. Mit Einleitung, Übertragung und Regesten herausgegeben von Carl Gebhardt. Heidelberg: Curis Societatis Spinozanae [at] C. Winters Universitätsbuchhandlung, 1922. xl, 285 (1) p. sq. 8°. (Bibliotheca Spinozana. tom. 2.)

[over]

NNUT QK8 C86 K Same pub. for passage cited. Paris, 1866, 5th ed. 4 1866 ed SCS in Spin Coll 1684

Gaultier, abbé.

p. 257-296 "Sur le spinosisme". (See: Cousin, V. "Des rapports du cartésianisme et du spinozisme".)

"Von einem Jansenisten Gaultier, der zugleich eifriger Cartesianer und auch von Malebranche beeinflusst war, rührt ein Aufsatz 'Sur le spinosisme' her, in dem gezeigt werden soll, dass die Lehre von der Erhaltung der Dinge als einer Kontinuierlichen Schöpfung nicht zum Spinozismus führt, wie ein (uns unbekannter) englischer Gelehrter in einem Brief an einen französischen Freund behauptet hatte. (Cousin, [over]

O-XLVII-2 G1700-56

Gebhardt, Carl.

[See volume - Die Schriften des Uriel da Costa]

— Une vie humaine par Uriel da Costa; traduit du Latin et precedé d'une étude sur l'auteur par A.-B. Duff et Pierre Kaan. Paris: F. Rieder et Cie., 1926. 138 p. 12° (Judaïsme. Études publiées sous la direction de P.-L. Couchoud. v. 3.)

O-XX-26 G1700-20

[Gebhardt, Carl.]

Societas Spinozana. [Its history and achievement during its first 7 years; including its statuts; in German.] n.t.-p. [Heidelberg: C. Winter, 1927.] 10 (1) p. sq. 8°.

p. following (11) being a reproduction of the Spinoza-House, taken in fall of 1926.

O-XX-29 [Gebhardt, Carl] G1700-45
G.LVIII-71

Zint, Hans.

Carl Gebhardt. (Schopenhauer-Gesellschaft. Jahrbuch. Heidelberg, 1935. 8°. [no.] 22, p. 401-411.)

p. III of Jahrbuch contains a "Nachruf", signed, Der Vorstand und die Wissenschaftliche Leitung der Schopenhauer-Gesellschaft.

(A.S.O.)

1686

Gebhardt, Carl.

Spinoza im Portrait; (aus dem Nachlass [herausgegeben von A.S. Oko]). (Philosophia. v. 2, 1927. p. 399-401.)

Extract.

(A.S.O.)

1701

Gehema, J. Abrahamus à.

Den rechten tydkorter waer inne op een philosopische wyse van de vereenigingh der ziele met het lichaem van den mensche gehandelt wordt. 's Gravenhage, 1691.

Many of his works at DSG (now DAFM) National Library of Medicine.

Doubtful!

O-XX-28 G1700-17

Gebhardt, Carl.

Spinoza in unserer Zeit. Rede bei der Spinoza-Feier im Rolzaal in 's-Gravenhage am 5. September 1932. n.t.-p. [The Hague: M. Nijhoff, [1932.]. p. 21-27. 8°.

Title taken from first page.

Repr.: Septimana Spinozana.

G-LVIII-41

---

1. 1702

893.19
G2753

~~Spinoza, Baruch or Benedictus.~~ [~~Tractatus Theologico-Politicus.~~]

Geiger, Abraham.

[Letter, dated 1832, (4 Juli) addressed to Elias Grünebaum (or ~~Grünbaum~~), discussing Spinoza's Tractatus theologico-politicus.] (In his: Nachgelassene Schriften. Berlin, 1878. 8. Bd.5, p.56-57.)

893.19
G2753

See next card.

O-XX-12 G1700-38

Gebhardt, Carl.

Vier Reden, von Carl Gebhardt. Heidelberg: C. Winter, 1927. 3 p.l., 3-80 p. sq. 8°.

Contents: Spinoza. Rede bei der Feier der Societas Spinozana im Rolzaal in 's Gravenhage am 21. Februar 1927.- La dialectique intérieure du spinozisme. Discours prononcé à la Sorbonne le 26 février 1927, à l'occasion de la fête commémorative de la Société française de Philosophie.- [cover]

[Also special paper ed.]-11

G. LVIII-35

---

2. 1703

Geiger, A.-[Letter, dated 1832... [cont.]

See also p.58.- Note on p.40: "Viele Seiten des Tagebuchs [of A. Geiger] sind nun [in the year 1832] mit critischen Bemerkungen...besonders mit Auszügen aus und Bemerkungen zu Spinoza's theologisch-politischem Traktate angefüllt. Letztere

SEE NEXT CARD.

O-XLII-6 G-1700-50

Gebhardt, Carl, tr.

Vom Weg der Erkenntnis. [Abhandlung über die Verbesserung des Verstandes; in extract.] Mit Versen des Angelus Silesius. Zusammengestellt von Carl Gebhardt. Frankfurt a. M., 1927.

[Dritter Druck der Frankfurter Gutenberg-Presse.]

G-LIII-16

---

3. 1704

Geiger, A.-[Letter, dated 1832... [cont.]

bilden auch im Folgenden den Hauptinhalt des Tagebuchs. Diese Bemerkungen, welche auch den Hauptgegenstand der damaligen von Frankfurt aus geführten Correspondenz an die Bonner Freunde ausmachen, schienen, obgleich sie durch Originali-

SEE NEXT CARD.

4. 1705

Geiger, A.-[Letter, dated 1832... [cont.]

tät und Gelehrsamkeit ausgezeichnet sind, zum Abdruck an dieser Stelle ungeeignet".

---

1. 1706

~~Spinoza, Baruch or Benedictus~~

Geiger, Abraham.

[On Spinoza and his philosophy.] (In his: Nachgelassene Schriften. Berlin, 1875. 8. Bd.2, p.208-211.)

Treated under the subject: Allgemeine Einleitung in die Wissenschaft des Judenthums. p. 33-245

See next card.

---

2. 1707

Geiger, Abraham.-[On Spinoza... [cont.]

On p.201 there is quoted, in part, Oldenburg's letter (dated, London, Dec., 1665) to Spinoza.

 1714

Gemelli, Agostino.

Introduzione. (In: Spinoza nel terzo centenario della sua nascita; pubblicazione a cura della Facoltà di Filosofia dell' Università Cattolica del Sacro Cuore. Milano, 1934. 8°. p.1-5.)

(nel [illegible]) 1715

✓ Genovensi, Antonio. [1712-1769.]

Elementi di scienze metafisiche. 1766.

— Latin. 1743.

(Eisler, p.199.)

Überweg (IV, 652): Elementi di scienze metafische (Lateinisch), Neapel 1743, 4 Bde.; 2. Aufl. (ital.) 5 Bde., 1766.

Sarti (p.101) quotes the Latin ed. Neaples, 1756.

[over]

---

2. 1716

Genovensi, Antonio. [...] — Elementi... [cont.]

tr.: Genuensis, Antonius.

(Referred to by B. Nieuhoff, p.260, and towards end of book.)

 1720

Gentile, Giovanni.

Benedetto Spinoza: 21 febbraio 1677-21 febbraio 1927. (Corriere della Sera [Milano]. Prima edizione - mattino. Feb. 22, 1927, p. 3.)

G: Reprint in: Giornale Critico della Filosofia Italiana May 1927

(A.S.O.)

 1719

Gentile, Giovanni.

Spinoza e la filosofia italiana. (Chronicon Spinozanum. Hagae Comitis, 1927. v.5, p. 104-110.)

Ravà, no. 48.

 1725

Gentile, Giovanni.

Studi sul rinascimento. Seconda edizione riveduta e accresciuta. Firenze: G.C. Sansoni, 1936-XIV. 4p.l. [first blank], 311p., 2 l. 8°. (In his: Opere complete. [v.10.])

VII. Leone Ebreo e Spinoza (p. 116-128). - "A proposito del libro

(A.S.O. unbd.)

[over]

---

2. 1726

Gentile, Giovanni.— Studi sul... [cont.]

di Edmondo Solmi, Benedetto Spinoza e Leone Ebreo... Modena ... 1903."

1738

Gerdil, Giacinto Sigismondo

Recuil de dissertations sur quelques principes de philosophie et de religion. Paris, 1760. (Dissertation 4.) —

Sep card → Trad. Sull' incompatibilità dei principii di Descartes e di Spinoza. Napoli, 1853.

See Troilo's tr. of Ethica, p. 40.

G-XXXV-74 1754

Ginsberg, Hugo [Wilhelm].

Ueber den Einfluss der Psychologie des Spinoza auf seine Ethik. Dissertation, welche mit Genehmigung der philosophischen Fakultät zur Erlangung der Doktorwürde ... den 9. August 1855 ... öffentlich vertheidigen wird Hugo Ginsberg gegen die Opponenten: Theodor Bach ... Herrmann Fechner ... Breslau: H. Lindner, [1855]. 32 p. 12°.

Not in v. d. L. – (Not in B.– Wieg., p. 10.)

G-XX-17 1745

Gherasim, Vasile.

in Spin Col. Activismul lui Spinoza (precedat de o expunere a genezei lui istorice) de Vasile Gherasim, Doctor în Filosofie. (Cu un portret al lui Spinoza.) Cernăuţi: Institutul de arte grafice şi editură „Glasul Bucovinei", 1928. 148 p., 1 l. 8°.

port. (p. 3) by J. B. Deshays; reproduced from Dunin-Borkowski, I.

R033 En 1 v. 14 Ak 7-4 NY ed. E 698

Ginzburg, Benjamin. 1898–

f° Spinoza, Baruch. (In: Encyclopaedia of the social sciences. New York [also London], 1934. (1934) v. 14, p. 299–301.)

ud 10-21

A workmanlike article.

Curiously enough, G. omits Duff, but gives Wolfson and Spinoza Mercador et autodidactus in the bibliography.

Duff, R. A., Sp's Polit. & Eth. Philos. (Glasgow 1903)

G-XX-17 1-a 1746

Gherasim, Vasile. — Activismul lui ... [cont.]

(G ½ buckr. With author's autograph dedication.)

NNC 195643 P 1758

(Incl. ref. to Sp.)

Gioberti, Vincenzo.

Opere. Brusselle: Cans e Co., 1844–45. 9 v. 2. ed. 8°. [N. Y. P. L. List]

(See v. 1–4: Introduzione allo studio della filosofia.) see tavola at end of each vol. Sp. scattered

(Name not in Literature)

195643 ✓ LC: 30-8082 — ud (5) 8-8

Intr. allo studio della filosofia. Brusselle, 1844. 4 v. 8°. 2. ed. [L. L.]

—— Capolago, 1849–50. Sulla 2. ed., 4 v. 8° [L. L.] NNC [cover]

---

2. 1747

Gherasim, V. [cont.]

Contents: Către cetitori. Introducere. Partea întâia: Stoicismul, precursor al lui Spinoza. Filosofia creştină şi Spinoza. Filosofia iudaică şi Spinoza. Filosofii arabici. Şi Giordano Bruno, precursor al lui Spinoza. Etica lui G. Bruno. Dependenţa lui Spinoza de filosofia lui Descartes. Şi Thomas Hobbes printre predecesorii lui Spinoza.

---

2. 1759

Gioberti, Vincenzo. — Opere. Brusselle ... [cont.]

X NC — Introduzione allo studio della filosofia. Firenze, 1847–48. 3 v. (Nijhoff Cat. no. 595 (1936).)

193KD K13 v. 35 1930 p. 319 Siegel 3 1748

Gherasim, Vasile [cont.]

4 Partea a doua: Perspective. Necesitate şi libertate. Calea înspre perfecţiune. Felurile de cunoaştere. Cugetarea şi celelalte fenomene sufleteşti. Realizarea perfecţiunii omeneşti. Încheiere. Resumé [in German]. Summary

[Siegel, Carl, 1872– 35. Bd.

193KD K13 Review: Kant-Studien, Bd. 35, 1930, p. 318; by C. Siegel. Signed: Prof. Dr. C. Siegel over

---

104 P549 E 682

Spinoza, Baruch or Benedictus

Gilbert, Katherine Everett.

Hegel's criticism of Spinoza. (In: Philosophical essays in honor of James Edwin Creighton... New York, 1917. 8. p. 26-41.)

[over]

2. E683

Gilbert, Katherine Everett.—Hegel's... [cont.]

Endeavors to refute Hegel's estimate of Spinoza's ethical system as applicable only to a realm of appearance by pointing out the more concrete aspect of Spinoza's philosophy.

Spec Coll Spin 5 1776

[Glatzel, R.W.—Phil. Bibl.]

Review of: Chronicon Spinozanum. tom. 3, p. 351-358. By F. Schlerath.

Lists Bd. 1-7. Spinozahuis, Verslag 1921/22, lists Bd. 1-8.

G-XX-[illegible] 1788

[Glatzel, R.W.]

Augustinus Redivivus. Des heiligen Kirchenvaters philosophisches Weltbild. In Umrissen gezeichnet nach den Bekenntnissen. Vom Verfasser des Spinoza Redivivus. (Der philosophischen Bibliothek zweiter Band.) Halle (Saale): Philosophischer Verlag, 1919. 4 p. l., 189 p. 4°.

[over]

G-XX-[illegible] 1-a. 1789

[Glatzel, R.W.]—Augustinus Redivivus... [cont.]

p. (189) on l. following advertisement and list of series of "Philosophische Weltbibliothek."

Contents: Kapitel I: Menschheitspolitik der Geistesfürsten... Kapitel II: Worte und Bilder... Kapitel III: Das blosse Existieren... Kapitel IV: Hypothetische Früchte. Beilage [List of series].

"In dem... Buche soll gezeigt werden,

G-XX-18 2 1790

[Glatzel, R.W.]—Augustinus... [cont.]

wie ein anderer Vollender der Philosophie... die Welt zum Suchen anleitet. Wie der Spinoza Redivivus ein allererstes Wort über den Philosophen Spinoza war, so ist der Augustinus Redivivus ein solches Wort über den Philosophen Augustinus... Auch dieses Mal ist das Hauptgewicht darauf gelegt worden, dass der zu behandelnde

[over]

G-XX-18 2-a. 1791

[Glatzel, R.W.]—Augustinus... [cont.]

Stoff in einer für den Laien verständlichen Weise dargestellt werde. Denn der sogenannte Laie wird bald Richter über die Philosophie sein müssen" (Vorwort).

G-XX-19 Review of: Juelicher, Adolf. Ein moderner Gnostiker und Augustinus. (Christliche Welt. Marburg i. H., 1920. Jahrg. 34, no. 25. col. 386-390.)

(G.)

G-XX-21 1792

[Glatzel, R.W.]

Gegenstand und Weise von Erfahrung und Transzendenz. Die Grundlagen der Philosophie. Vom Verfasser des Spinoza Redivivus und Augustinus Redivivus. (Der philosophischen Weltbibliothek siebenter Band.) Halle (Saale): Weltphilosophischer Verlag, 1921. 4 p. l., 296 p. 4°.

(G.) [over]

G-XX-21 1-a. 1793

[Glatzel, R.W.]—Gegenstand... [cont.]

Contents: Kapitel 1: Der Merkantilismus der Philosophie. Kapitel 2: Philosophie und Religion. Kapitel 3: Philosophie und Politik. Kapitel 4: Spinozas Abhandlung über die Verbesserung des Verstehens. Kapitel 5: Die Vereinigung zur Pflege der vollendeten Weltanschauung...

G-XX-21 2 1794

[Glatzel, R.W.]—Gegenstand... [cont.]

Kapitel 4 comprises p. 116-278 and consists of 56 "Erläuterungen". In this book the author reveals further his "new knowledge of Spinoza" ("das neue Wissen über Spinoza"); "Spinoza's new knowledge" ("das neue Wissen Spinozas"), he reiterates again, is identical with with the "vollendete Philosophie".

G-LV-21 1777

[Glatzel, R.W.]

Spinoza Redivivus. Eine Fibel für Anfänger und Verächter der Philosophie. Mit 22 Figuren im Text. Berlin: Verlag von Max Rockenstein, 1917. 2 p. l., 135 p. 4°. ~~(Neue philosophische Bibliothek. Bd. 1.)~~

Being v. 1 of a series entitled:

(G.) [over]

1-a 1778

[Glatzel, R.W.]- Spinoza Redivivius... [cont.]

Neue philosophische Bibliothek, afterwards changed to: Philosophische Weltbibliothek.

port.; on t.-p.; after the Hague copy.

Contents: Kapitel 1: Das Schicksal der bisherigen Philosophie, Kapitel 2: Das Schicksal der Philosophie Spinozas. Kapitel 3: Die Hilflosigkeit der gelehrten

G-I-IV-21

0-XX-46 1795

[Glatzel, R.W.]

Zum Charakter Spinozas. Erläuterungen der wichtigsten Nachrichten über sein Leben. Vom Verfasser des Spinoza Redivivus und Augustinus Redivivus. (Der philosophischen Weltbibliothek dritter Band.) Erste Auflage. Halle (Saale): Weltphilosophischer Verlag, 1919. 4 p. l., 143 p. 4°.

(A.S.O.) G-XX-20, G-XX-18 [over]

2 1779

[Glatzel, R.W.]- Spinoza Redivivus...

Wissenschaft gegenüber der Philosophie Spinozas. Kapitel 4: Eine Hilfe, dargereicht von Spinoza in einem Wahrheitsmodell. ~~[Beilage 1. Euklid's Elemente; fünfzehn Bücher, aus dem Griechischen übersetzt (in 1809). Beilage 2 (Aus dem Briefwechsel zwischen Spinoza und Burgh.)]~~

G-I-IV-21 [over]

0-XX-46 2 1796

[Glatzel, R.W.]- Z. Charakter Spinozas...

Contents: 1. Die Quellen. 2. Die Lebensbeschreibung von Lucas [translated by K.F. Heydenreich]. 3. Diejenige von Colerus [translated by the editor; followed by documents no. 68 and 67 of J. Freudenthal's Lebensgeschichte Spinoza's]. 4. Nachlassinventar Spinozas einschliesslich der Bücher [Freudenthal, no. 69]. 5. Die Notizen von Jarig Jelles [translated by C. Gebhardt]. 6. Diejenigen Sebastian

G-XX-20 [over]

2-a. 1780

[Glatzel, R.W.]-Spinoza Redivivius ... [cont.]

"Begonnen ward dieses Werkchen für einen Feldgrauen, der inzwischen dem Vaterlande starb und nunmehr... die ihm zugedachte Gabe seinen noch kampfenden Brüdern weiht" (Vorrede).

G-I-IV-21

0-XX-46 2-a. 1797

[Glatzel, R.W.] - Z. Charakter Spinozas... [cont.]

Kortholts [translated by the editor]. Französische Beleuchtung durch Bayle [from the 2. ed. of his Dictionaire; translated by the editor; followed by Freudenthal, no. 54-55 (Stolle-Hallmann)]. 8. Die Monikhoffsche Lebensbeschreibung Spinozas [being Freudenthal, no. 5]. 9. Öffentliche Verfolgung der Lehre Spinozas [Freudenthal, no. 85; Das Schicksal Adrian Koerbaghs: Fr., no. 30]. 10. Eine Denunziation gegen Spinoza durch einen Teil seiner Mitbürger in Voorburg [Fr., no. 29].

G-XX-2-

0-XX-45 1786

[Glatzel, R. W.]

Spinoza Redivivus. Eine Fibel für Anfänger und Verächter der Philosophie. Mit 22 Figuren im Text. Halle (Saale): Weltphilosophischer Verlag, [cop. 1919]. 2 p. l., 135 p. 4°. ~~([Philosophische Weltbibliothek. Bd. 1])~~

Forms v.1 of the series: Philosophische Weltbibliothek.

(A.S.O.) [over]

DLC 1-27 NjP WNVT KH10 D618 5 1807

Glossner, Michael, 1837-

Divus Thomas; Zur Frage nach dem Einfluss der Scholastik auf die neuere Philosophie. (Jahrbuch für Philosophie und spekulative Theologie. v. 3, 1889, p. 486-493.)

With ref. to Freudenthal's "Spinoza und die Scholastik".

Überweg, p. 669.

0-XX-45 2. 1787

[Glatzel, R.W.]- Spinoza Redivivius... [cont.]

Being the same as ed. 1917, with new t.-p. (without port).

203 H441 1891, c[82-83] E 699

Q Goebel, Julius. 1857-1931

NNC-4 Spinoza, Baruch de. (In: Schaff, Philip. A religious encyclopaedia; or, Dictionary of Biblical, historical, doctrinal, and practical theology... ed. by P. Schaff... New York [cop. 1882-1883]. v. 3, p. 2228-2230.)

(copyright 1883) Funk & Wagnalls Co.

3rd ed. Vol. IV, 1891, p. 2228-2230.

Signed: Dr. Julius Goebel

oLC

 1832

Goethe,

Vloten, Johannes, van.
Goethe en Spinoza. [Review of: Jellinek, G. Die Beziehungen Goethe's zu Spinoza... Wien, 1878.] (Levensbode. Haarlem, 1878. deel 10, p. 423-432.)

~~Signed, v. Vl.~~ D

1834

Goethe

See: Astrada, C.

1835

Goethe.

See: Bayer, Jos.

1836

Goethe,

See: Bleek, W.

1837

Goethe,

See: Goldschmidt, L.

1838

Goethe,

See: Heyder, K.

1839

Goethe,

See: Jellinek, G.

1840

Goethe

See: Schaub, E.L.

1841

Goethe,

See: Splettstoesser, W.

1844

Goldschmidt, Ludwig. 1853–

MN-4 *A "War Goethe Spinozist?" (Frankfurter Zeitung. Jahrg. 54, no. 294, 1909 ~~Oct. 23, 1909.~~) p. 1-2. (bottom half of page. about 6 cols.)

Baer 639.

(A.S.O.)

[over]

2. 1845

Goldschmidt, Ludwig.— War Goethe... [cont.]

"War Goethe jemals Spinozist, so ist von uns ganz sicher nachgewiesen, dass der reife Mann von sich abgestreift hat, was ihm in jungen Jahren ein problematischer Besitz gewesen ist."

1899-1910 ed. 3v. NNUT E 724

UN- YBX 4

Green, Thomas Hill, 1836-1882.

Works of Thomas Hill Green; edited by R. L. Nettleship. London, 1890-1893. 3 v. 8°.

v. 1: 2. ed.; v. 2 and 3: 3. ed.

Also: London, 1906-08.

See Index, Vol. III, p. 479. i.e., II. 355-365; his theory of the state. III. 113, 238.

NNC has other eds.

Spec Coll Spin 1851

Gonella, Guido.

Il diritto come potenza secondo Spinoza. (In: Spinoza nel terzo centenario della sua nascita; pubblicazione a cura della Facoltà di Filosofia dell' Università Cattolica del Sacro cuore. Milano, 1934. 8°. p. 149-180.)

Biliography, p. 179 [16 numbers].

Kiel Universitäts-Bibliothek - Still? 1879

Greyffencrantz, Christian N von.

[Letter to Christian Kortholt; dated, Stockholm, 6th April, 1681.]

"De Spinoza dolentissime miratus fui, hunc virum, quem Philosophiae insignis laude, cum Anno LXXII Haga Comitis cum Mis. Sueciae Regis Legatis per semestre degerem, elatum, semel vidi et aestimavi, tam absonas, et sua nostraque [!] saluti contrarias opiniones in solitudinibus suis [over]

EB.105 E 709

Gottheil, ~~James~~ 5 Richard James Horatio 1862-1936

Some early Jewish Bible criticism. (Journal of Biblical Literature. v. 23, 1904, p. 1-12.)

References to Spinoza; p. 2, 12.

p. 12: "[illegible] hundred years separate him [the author of the Genizah fragment pub. by Schechter in J.Q.R., v. 13, 1901, p. 345-374: The oldest collection of Bible difficulties"] from another great Bible critic; and it is not without interest to see that a number of the things

---

2. 1880

Greyffencrantz, Christian N von.—[Letter... [cont.]

(sibi quippe soli vivere videbatur, semper solitanus et quasi in museo suo sepultus) imbibisse."

(quoted by: Halfmann, Wilhelm. Christian Kortholt... Kiel, 1930. p. 39, footnote.)

S. Kortholt quotes only the words given in ( ).

Halfmann introduces the quotation: "Wie es [C.K.'s De Tribus Impostoribus Magnis Liber] auf einen Bekannten Kortholts, der zugleich Spinoza schützte, zeigt ein Brief..."

Original in Kiel Universitäts-Bibliothek. S.-H. 406, A2; 2.

E 721

Green, Thomas Hill. [1836-1882.]

X His collected Works, 3 vols., ed., with a memoir, by R. L. Nettleship, 1885-8.

See: Fairbrother, W. H. Philosophy of T. H. Green. 1896.

See: Muirhead, J. H. The service of the state; four lectures on the philosophy of T. H. Green. 1908.

Philos. E 3 Ei 82 See: Eisler, Rudolf. Philosophen-Lexikon. 1912, p. 213

Spec Coll See: Cambridge History of English Literature, XIV, 47-4 (over)

Sp Coll Spin [Wachter, J. G.] 1905

Grunwald, M.

Wachter. (In his: Spinoza in Deutschland. Berlin, 1897. 8°. p. 44-45.)

See also Namensverzeichnis.

---

2. E 722

Green, Thomas Hill.— His collected... [cont.]

Prof. of moral philosophy at Oxford. One of the early English Hegelians. He appealed to "Englishmen under five-and-twenty to close their Mill and Spencer and open their Kant and Hegel"; and this appeal [remarks W. R. Sorley (Camb. Hist. of Eng. Lit. XIV, p. 43)] marks an epoch in English thought in the nineteenth century."

In his Lectures on the Principles of Political Obligation he maintains that will, not force, is the basis of the state.

Spec Coll Spin. 1 E 731

Gunn, J[ohn] Alexander.

Spinoza, the maker of lenses. A play in three acts. London: George Allen & Unwin Ltd., [1932]. 99 [1] p. 12°.

The scene is laid in Amsterdam, Rijnsburg, the French Camp outside Utrecht, and The Hague, during the years 1656-1677.

(A.S.O.) [over]

1-a. E732

Gunn, J[ohn] Alexander. — Spinoza. . . [cont.]
Characters: Rabbi David; Rabbi Isaac (heads of synagogues in Amsterdam); Rebekah (Spinoza's sister); Rabbi Saul (Chief Rabbi of Amsterdam); Spinoza; Simon De Vries; A Collegiant (Spinoza's landlord at Rijnsburg); A professor of philosophy of Leyden University; Henry Oldenburg; Hendrik Van der Spijck; his wife; Count Luxembourg; Colonel Stoupe; Dr. Schuller; An attendant of the synagogue; An orderly of the officers' mess.

---

 2 E733

Gunn, J.A.
"This play has been written and published in celebration of the Tercentenary of his birth. Its aim is to present the philosopher in the environment of time and place in which he lived and to convey in some small measure the charm of his personality."
Reviews: Times literary supplement. London, 1932. v. 31, p. 462.
W., M.J., in Views, London, v. 2, January, 1933. (893.105) VCI

 1947

Gunning, J.H.
De eenheid des levens, naar Spinoza's Amor intellectualis. Nijmegen: Firma H. Ten Hoet, 1903. 156p. 8°.
Contents: I. Waar Spinoza staat en wat hij leert. II. Wat wij, die in Jezus Christus gelooven, boven Spinoza ontvangen hebben. Recapitulatie.
[over]

---

 2. 1948

Gunning, J.H. - De eenheid... [cont.]
Samenvatting der hoofdgedachten. Verklaring van uitheemsche woorden.

(A.S.O.)

---

1. 1956

Spinoza, Baruch or Benedictus.
Guttmann, J[akob].

["Ob Haneberg die Bedeutung Gabirol's als Philosoph nicht zu hoch und die seiner jüdischen Mitbewerber auf dem Gebiete philosophischer Forschung nicht zu niedrig anschlägt, wenn er das Urtheil ab-
See next card.

---

2. 1957

Guttmann, J[akob].-["Ob Haneberg... [cont.]
giebt, dass das Judenthum Gabirol seinen einzigen Philosophen nennen durfte, bis Spinoza kam, das mag der Beurtheilung eines Jeden überlassen bleiben... Soviel aber scheint mir an dieser Behauptung doch richtig zu sein, dass die Philoso-
See next card.

---

3. 1958

Guttmann, J[akob].-["Ob Haneberg... [cont.]
phie des Gabirol gleich der des Spinoza mehr der allgemeinen Geschichte der Philosophie als der Geschichte der jüdischen Philosophie angehöre, denn als philosophischer Denker steht Gabirol dem Judenthum kaum weniger fern, als dies bekann-
See next card.

---

4. 1959

Guttmann, J[akob].-["Ob Haneberg... [cont.]
termassen bei Spinoza der Fall ist.- Dürften wir die von einigen neueren Forschern ausgesprochene Vermuthung, dass Giordano Bruno auf die Weltanschauung des Spinoza einen nicht unwesentlichen Einfluss ausgeübt habe, als begründet ansehen, so
See next card.

---

5. 1960

Guttmann, J[akob].-["Ob Haneberg... [cont.]
wäre die Annahme nicht ausgeschlossen, dass die beiden [i.e. Ibn Gabirol and Spinoza] aus dem Schoosse des Judenthumes hervorgegangenen Vertreter des Pantheismus sich auf diesem Wege gewissermassen über die Jahrhunderte hinweg die Hände ge-
See next card.

---

6. 1961

Guttmann, J[akob].-["Ob Haneberg... [cont.]
reicht haben.- Der Dualismus von Materie und Form [of Ibn Gabirol] schliesst eben seinem Begriffe nach die Möglichkeit aus, den Uebergang von dem einen dieser Principien zu dem anderen zu finden. Das Denken geht im Bereiche der Form vor sich.
See next card.

7. 1962

Guttmann, J[akob].-["Ob Haneberg... [cont.]
Form und Materie sind aber in ihrem Wesen von einander verschieden; mithin ist ein Gedachtwerden der Materie eine gar nicht zu vollziehende Vorstellung. Man wird hierbei unwillkürlich an das Verhältniss der Attribute des Denkens und der Aus-

See next card

---

8. 1963

Guttmann, J[akob].-["Ob Haneberg... [cont.]
dehnung bei Spinoza erinnert."] (p.3.)-(p.64-65.)-(p.203.) (In his: Die Philosophie des Salomon ibn Gabirol... Göttingen;1889. 8.)

NOS 17-57
• LC 6-23-58 recalled 6-24-58

Cordoiers brief ref. p.3,65,203.

 1972

Gutzkow, Karl.
Uriel Acosta, der Sadduzäer von Amsterdam. München: Hans von Weber, Verlag, [1922]. 76 p., 2 l. 8°.
p.1-2 blank.
"Als 19. Dreiangeldruck... mit Urzinkzeichnungen von Franz Kolbrand im Auftrage von Hans von Weber bei Breitkopf & Härtel in Leipzig [Cover]

 1-a. 1973

Gutzkow, Karl.— Uriel Acosta ... [cont.]
gedruckt im Sommer 1922. Die einfache Ausgabe wurde in 650 Exemplaren auf Dokumentenpapier, die Vorzugsausgabe in 75 Exemplaren auf deutschen handgeschöpften Bütten abgezogen und numeriert."

(G "Dieses ist ein Abzug der einfachen Ausgabe")

---

 2 1974

Gutzkow, K.— Uriel Acosta...
Drawing: da Costa holding the boy Spinoza on his lap, p.73.

Spec coll Spin 1995

Guzzo, Augusto.
Review of: Rotta, Paolo. Spinoza. Milano, 1923. (Chronicon Spinozanum. v.3, 1923, p. 367-370.)

Ravà, no.54. (Not seen.)

 1994

Guzzo, Augusto.
Spinoza (1632-1932). Firenze: E. Ariani, 1932. 530-546 p. 8°.
Repr.: Scuola e cultura. anno 8.
Title taken from paper-cover.

(G.)

H

 2023

Hannequin, A
Études d'histoire des sciences et d'histoire de la philosophie. Paris: F. Alcan, 1908. 2v. 8°.

Fragment d'une étude sur Spinoza, v.2, p.1-16.

(A.S.O.)

 2033

Hartenstein, Gustav.
De notionum juris et civitatis, quas Bened. Spinoza et Thom. Hobbes proponunt, similitudine et dissimilitudine. 1856. (In his: Historisch-philosophische Abhandlungen. Leipzig, 1870. 8° p. 217-240.)
v.d L. 297 (note).

(L.L.)

 2040

Hartmann, Dr.
Die Lehre des Cartesius De passionibus animae und des Spinoza De affectibus humanis dargestellt und verglichen von Dr. Hartmann, Gymnasial-Lehrer. Wohlau: Druck von Albert Leuckart, 1878. 16p. sq. 8°. (Wohlau.- Städtisches Gymnasium. Programm. no.173.)

(G unbd.)

G-LIV-6 2 2041

Hartmann, Dr. [cont.]

I. Der Geist und der Körper des Menschen nach der Lehre des Cartesius. II. Der Geist und der Körper des Menschen nach der Lehre Spinozas. III. Die "Leidenschaften der Seele" nach Cartesius. IV. Die Lehre von den menschlichen Affekten nach Spinoza. V. Die Lehren beider Philosophen... verglichen.

[over]

G-LIV-6 2-a 2042

Hartmann, Dr. – Die Lehre... [cont.]

"An die Kurzgefasste Darstellung der Lehre des Cartesius... und des Spinoza... Knüpft sich ein Vergleich, in welchem die bedeutendsten Aehnlichkeiten und die auffallendsten Verschiedenheiten der Lehre beider Philosophen in ein und derselben Materie veranschaulicht werden sollen. Zu diesem Versuch reizte nicht wenig die verbreitete Ansicht, dass der Spinozismus die consequente Durchbildung des Cartesianismus sei. Ein Beitrag zur Bekämpfung dieser Ansicht will die folgende Abhandlung sein" (Vorwort).

93Schz IH nos 8-18 2044

Hartmann, E. von.

Schellings philosophisches System. Lpz., 1897. XII, 224 p.

"Eine zusammenfassende Darstellung meiner Ansichten über Spinoza habe ich niedergelegt in meiner... 'Gesch. der Metaphysik', und einen Vergleich mit Schelling in... 'Schellings philosophisches System'. (Grunwald, p. 350, there a letter

[over]

G-XX-45 2056

Hartmann, Hans.

Der Spinozismus. Zugleich eine Betrachtung zum internationalen Spinozakongress. (Preussische Jahrbücher. Jan., 1933. p. 39–49.)

CG. Last p. missing and supplied in typewriting.

[over]

NNUT QU39 433 5 + Brown Libr. QU39 433 E757

✓ Hartshorne, Charles, 1897–

Beyond humanism. Essays in the new philosophy of nature. Chicago, [and] New York: Willett, Clark & Co., 1937. 8°. XIV p., 1 l., 324 p. 20 cm.

○NNC Spinoza, p. 5-7. See also Index.

(Yale)

LC 38-11150 rd 11-7-58 [over]

---

2. E758

Hartshorne, Charles. – Beyond... [cont.]

"The heart of Christendom has been with Jesus – deus est caritas – but its intellect has been with Spinoza – deus sive natura... Spinoza today would not be a Spinozist but a Whiteheadian" (p. 7). The 1. chapter is superscribed "God or nature".

Review: Philosophy. V. 13, p. 357-358.

105 .1826

2058

Hasan, Syed Zafar-ul

Spinozas Monismus. Dissertation. Erlangen, 1922. [Maschinenschrift.] 176 S. 4° [Lag nicht vor, - Auszug soll später ersch.]

not seen BM

" " BN

Erlangen, Phil Diss. V. 30 Juni 1922.

See Jahresverzeichnis der an den deutschen Universitäten... Vol. 38, 1922 1922, p. 174. (* U22, 2018)

Überweg, p. 670. [McKeon, p. 332 ...]

NN-QPT 5 2079

Hauser, Otto, 1876–

[According to his Rasse und Rassenfragen in Deutschland (p. 105), his Spinoza novel was translated into Hebrew.]

Weimar: A. Duncker [1915], 134 p. 12°.

○NNC

○LC

Bijvoog. hoo Spinoza. Roman naar het Duitsch

G-XX-46 2101

Hecke, Gustav.

Benedikt Spinoza, ein Herold des Humanitätsgedankens. (Asträa. Taschenbuch für Freimaurer auf das Jahr 1909. Leipzig, 1909. 12°. n. F. Bd. 28, p. 1-53.)

I. Leben und Charakter. II. Die Lehre.

[over]

G-XX-46 1-a. 2101 a

Hecke, Gustav. – Benedikt Spinoza... [cont.]

"Eine Umschau in dem freimaurerischen Schrifttum erweckt den Eindruck, dass B. Spinoza seltener als andere geschichtliche Grössen, die uns fesseln müssen, der Gegenstand wissenschaftlicher oder erbaulicher Behandlung gewesen ist, obgleich diese doch schon dadurch nahegelegt wird, dass ein Lessing, ein Herder und ein Goethe es wohl mit ihrem freimaurerischen Gewissen haben vereinigen können, jenem Denker des 17. Jahrhunderts ihre Huldigung darzubringen. Jene Vernachlässigung mag teils darin begründet sein, dass der Philosoph wegen

G-XX-46 2. 2102

Hecke, Gustav. – Benedikt Spinoza ... [cont.]

der sachlichen und durch eine spröde Darstellung nach [! noch] gesteigerten Schwierigkeiten, die sein Hauptwerk, die 'Ethik', dem Studium bietet, mehr genannt als gekannt wird, teils aber darin, dass der Fluch, mit dem eine beschränkte oder furchtsame Mit- und Nachwelt den kühnen Denker bedachte, auch bis in unsere Tempel hinein nachhallte" (p. 1-2).

Bei vorstehender Darstellung haben wir [over]

G-XX-46 2-a. 2103

Hecke, Gustav. – Benedikt Spinoza ... [cont.]

es als ausserhalb unserer Aufgabe liegend angesehen, das System Spinozas als Ganzes oder in seinen Einzelheiten einer eingehenden fachphilosophischen Kritik zu unterziehen; denn wir wollten ja in dem Philosophen vor allem den Menschen finden, d.h. erfahren, wie er im Leben und Lehre den Begriff der Humanität zur Geltung gebracht, wie er im Menschen die Menschheit gesehen und auf die Grundlagen ihres wahren Fortschrittes sein Nachdenken gerichtet hat" (p. ii).

335.4 H355 Copy: 0335.4 H35 Butler 0335 H35 E763

Hecker, Julius F.

Moscow dialogues. Discussions on red philosophy by Julius F. Hecker. With a foreword by John Macmurray. London: Chapman and Hall Ltd., [1933]. XVI [I-II blank], 284 p., 2 l. [last blank]. 8°.

nd 9-16-58

Dialogue V: In which the sources of communist philosophy are discussed [over]

---

2. E764

Hecker, Julius F. – Moscow... [cont.]

[the theme being Spinoza's relation to dialectical materialism], p. 55-63.

See also Index.

(Harvard)

NN: YAR-5 2113

Heidenfeld, Albrecht Friedrich Theodor, 1834–

Darstellung der von Cartesius, Spinoza und Leibnitz gegebenen Beweise für das Dasein Gottes. [I.-D.] I. Theil. Breslau: H. Lindner, [1855]. 2 p. l., 34 p. 1 l. 12°.

Not in v. d. L., or B.

(N.Y. P.L., List, p. 37.)

W., p. 10 [gives 33 p.]

---

0 See 2113 2115

Heidenfeld, Albrecht Friedrich Theodor, 1834–

Darstellung der von Cartesius, Spinoza und Leibnitz gegebenen Beweise für das Dasein Gottes. Eine Abhandlung ... mit Genehmigung ... der hiesigen Königl. Universität zur Erlangung der philosophischen Doktorwürde ... Erster Theil. Breslau: H. Lindner, [1855]. 2 p. l., 34 p., 1 l. 8°.

Not in v. d. L. – Not in B. (Weg, p. 10. – N.Y. P.L.)

G-XXXV-101 2125

Heinze, Max.

Leibniz in seinem Verhältniss zu Spinoza. (Im neuen Reich. Wochenschrift für das Leben des deutschen Volkes. Leipzig, 1875. v. 2, p. 921-932.)

Vortrag, gehalten beim Antritt einer ordentlichen Professur der Philosophie in Leipzig.

(Excerpt: G.) [over]

G-XXXV-101 2. 2126

Heinze, Max. – Leibniz in ... [cont.]

"So sehr wir nun auch den strengen Denker in Spinoza schätzen müssen, als welcher er den Schöpfer der Monadenlehre entschieden überragt ... wir sehen doch in der Leibnizischen der Spinozistischen gegenüber berechtigte Begriffe auftreten, namentlich den Individualismus und den Zweck, die wir, um Einseitigkeit zu vermeiden, nicht vernachlässigen müssen ..." (p. 932).

NjP CtY OCH 1 1. 2139

~~Spinoza, Baruch or Benedictus~~ [Poetry]

Heller, S[eligmann], 1831-1890.

Spinoza's Bannung.- Vereinsamung Spinoza's.- Spinoza's Lehre und Ende. (In his: Ahasverus, ein Heldengedicht... Wiens Leipzig, 1866. 12. p. 475-486.)

ONNC CtC xii, 557 p. 19½ cm

"Nur ihre Methode verdankt unsere Philoso-

See next card.

---

2. 2140

Heller, S.-Spinoza's Bannung... [cont.]

phie dem Geiste des Cartesius, nur diese durfte daher auch Gegenstand des Ahasverus werden. Am schönsten ist sie wohl von seinem ihn überragenden Schüler Spinoza dargestellt worden". (p. 554.)

"In dem Aussergewöhnlichen und Unerklärli-

SEE NEXT CARD.

3. 2141

Heller, S.-Spinoza's Bannung... [cont.]

chen seines Auftretens, in dem bescheidenen Dunkel und der Zurückgezogenheit seiner Person, bei dem grossartigsten Sieges- und Selbstbewusstsein seiner Leistung, in der Unendlichkeit seiner Wirkungen und in der hervorragenden Ei-

See next card.

G-XX-48 2159

Herbart, Johann Friedrich.

Gespräche über das Böse. Aufgezeichnet von Johann Friedrich Herbart. Königsberg: bey August Wilhelm Unzer, 1817. VIII, 184p. 12°.

Extracts: Altkirch, p. 137-139. (From: Sämmtl. Werke, Bd. 9 Leipzig, 1851.)

(G.)

4. 2142

Heller, S.-Spinoza's Bannung... [cont.]

genthümlichkeit seines Wesens kann Spinoza nur mit Shakespeare verglichen werden, beide haben vielleicht noch lange nicht den Höhepunkt ihrer Anerkennung erreicht". (p.555.)

"Später haben deutsche Dichter jüdischer

SEE NEXT CARD.

G-XX-49 1 2160

Herbart, [Johann Friedrich].

Zur Lehre von der Freiheit des menschlichen Willens. Briefe an Herrn Professor [F. E.] Griepenkerl von Herbart. Göttingen: In der Dieterischen Buchhandlung, 1836. XXIV, 255p. nar. 12°.

[cover]

5. 2143

Heller, S.-Spinoza's Bannung... [cont.]

Rasse den Plan Goethe's [den Besuch des ewigen Juden bei Spinoza] oft ausgeführt; Berthold Auerbach klein und beschämend, S. Heller mit geistiger Kraft ohne rechte Poesie". (Mauthner, F. Spinoza. Berlin, [1906]. p.75.)

See next card.

G-XX-49 1-a. 2161

Herbart, [Johann Friedrich].-Zur Lehre... [cont.]

Of the 9 "Briefe", 5-7 (p. 100-193) are devoted entirely to a discussion of Spinoza - 6 and 7 to F.H. Jacobi (and partly also Schleiermacher) and Spinoza.

"Abgesehen von allen speculativen Irrthümern, fehlt dem Spinozismus die moralische Wärme und Würde" (Vorrede, p.xxiv).

See Grunwald, p.241-243.

(G.)

6. 2144

Heller, S.-(Spinoza's Bannung)... [cont.]
Ahasverus

A second edition appeared: Leipzig, 1868.
NNJ-R

Heinsius: Ahasverus. Ein Heldengedicht. 2. Aufl. XVI, 559 p. Leipzig, D. Wigand, 1868

NNC
OLC

G-XX-49 2 2162

Herbart, [J. F.]-Zur Lehre... [cont.]

Extracts: Altkirch, E. Maledictus und Benedictus... p.140-141. (From: Sammtl. Werke, Bd. 9 II, 1851.)

G-LII-8 2151

Henke, [Oskar].

Die Lehre von den Attributen bei Spinoza (In: Perleberg.-Städtische Realschule erster Ordnung. Programm. Perleberg, [1875]. sq.4° p.1-18.)

(G.)

O-XLIII-8 2163

Herbertz, R.

Spinoza als Vorläufer Einsteins. (Weltall, Das. Berlin, 1925. v. 25, no. 2, p. 24-26.)

G-LII-17

O-XXII-20 2184

[Herder, J.G.]

Kronenberg, Moritz.
Herder's Philosophie nach ihrem Entwickelungsgang und ihrer historischen Stellung. Heidelberg: Carl Winter's Universitätsbuchhandlung, 1889. XI, 116 p. 8°.

Herder unter dem Einfluss von Leibniz und Spinoza, p. 47-88.

(A.S.O.)

G-XXIX-15 2209

Hermann, Conrad.
Geschichte der Philosophie in pragmatischer Behandlung. Leipzig, F. Fleischer, 1867. 8°.

Der Lehrbegriff des Spinoza.- Der Spinozismus nach seiner weiteren geschichtlichen Bedeutung, p. 273-278.

(G.) With autograph of Wm Bolin on fly-leaf.

O-XXII-19 2186

[Herder, J.G.]

Kuehnemann, Eugen.
Herder. Zweite, neu bearbeitete Auflage. Mit einem Bildnis in Photogravüre. München: C.H. Beck'sche Verlagsbuchhandlung, 1912. 8°.

Herders Gespräche über "Gott", p. 428-441.

(A.S.O.) [over]

G-XX-56 2222

Hessen, Robert.
Die Philosophie der Kraft. Stuttgart: Verlag von Julius Hoffmann, 1913. XI, 367 p. 8°.

Spinoza [: seine Weltanschauung; seine Ethik; sein Leben; seine Vorgänger; seine Mängel; Kants Imperativ und Spinozas Determinismus; vom Bösen], p. 67-74.

[over]

O-XXII-19 2. 2187

[Herder, J.G.] — Kuehnemann, Eugen... [cont.]
First ed. 1894. (Not seen.)

G-XX-56 2. 2223

Hessen, Robert. — Die Philosophie... [cont.]
See also p. 115-116 [Spinoza und der Kirchenglaube], 181-183 [Spinozist Goethe und Kantianer Schiller], 238-239 [Spinoza über den Zweck des Staates]. See also Register.

(G.)

G-XX-57 2191

[Herder, J.G.]

Siegel, Carl.
Herder als Philosoph. Stuttgart und Berlin: J.G. Cotta'sche Buchhandlung Nachfolger, 1907. XVI, 245(1) p. 8°.

Die Spinozagespräche, p. 73-82.
Der Dynamismus zusammenhängend mit Leibniz' und Spinozas Lehre..., p. 131-132.
Gott und Welt, p. 147-155. Begründung

(G.) [over]

NNUT QU38 H59 -5 +NNC 211 H48 2234

Heussler, Hans, 1855-
Der Rationalismus des siebenzehnten Jahrhunderts in seinen Beziehungen zur Entwicklungs-Lehre dargestellt. Breslau: W. Koebner, 1885. 4 p. l., 160 p. 8°.

chapter Spinoza, p. 66-87.- See also section p. 113-114. and "Schluss" p. 128-32
These are all listed in detailed t of c

oLC

G-XX-57 2. 2192

[Herder, J.G.] — Siegel, Carl... [cont.]
der drei Spinozistischen Erkenntnisstufen..., p. 186-187.

---

211 H48 NNC 2230

Heussler, Hans
Der Rationalismus des ~~17.~~ siebenzehnten Jahrhunderts in seinen Beziehungen zur Entwicklungslehre dargestellt von... Breslau, 1885. 4 l., 160 p. No author index. Wilhelm Koebner

II Spinoza S. 66-87. p. 82-85: refutation of K. Fischer's view ~~with~~ in regard to Spinoza's rationalism. (Falckenberg, R. Gesch. d. neueren Phil. 2. ed., p. 98, footnote.)

oLC

2241

5 Heydenreich, Karl Heinrich, 1764-1801.

NNC 212 221 DLC MH

Betrachtungen über die Philosophie der natürlichen Religion. Bd. 1-2. Leipzig, Weygand, 1790-1791. 21 cm

Spinoza (a critical analysis of the main points of his system), Bd. 1, p. 258-272; Bd. 2, p. 168-175. ~~Zufolge~~ Zu folge seines vermittelst der Kritischen Philosophie gewonnenen [over]

1-a. [cont.] 2242

Heydenreich, Karl Heinrich.-Betrachtungen...

strengen und vollständigen Begriffs Gott bekennt Heydenreich in seinen Betrachtungen (Band I, S. 46 und 259), was er in seinem Werke: Natur und Gott nach Spinoza, noch nicht zugab, der Spinozismus zerstöre allen wahren Begriff von Gott und sey daher auch Atheismus (Schelle, p. 280-281, footnote).

2248

2

Heydenreich, K[arl] H[einrich].-Betrachtungen... [cont.]

—— 2. verb. Aufl. 1804.

(Baldwin)

MH phil 8587.14 MH-AH 4

Betrachtungen über die Philosophie der natürlichen Religion. 2 Bde. Leipzig, Weygand, 1804. 8°.

See Vol. I, p. 258-272 Neunte Betrachtung, "Kritik und Widerlegung der ersten Gründe des Spinozismus."

0-XXII-26 2237

Heydenreich, Karl Heinrich.

Natur und Gott nach Spinoza. Von Karl Heinrich Heydenreich. Erster Band. Leipzig: in der Joh. Gottfr. Müllerschen Buchhandlung, 1789. lxxx, 224 p. 8°.

No more pub.-[Preface.]- Leben Benedickts von Spinoza [by J. M. Lucas]. Aus einer französischen Handschrift, mit Anmerkungen vom Herausgeber (p. xix-lxxx).- Einleitungsgespräch über die [over]

G-XXI-1

0-XXII-26 2. 2238

Heydenreich, Karl Heinrich.-Natur... [cont.]

Abhängigkeit des Menschen, über Deismus, Pantheismus und Atheismus.- Ueber das System Spinoza's.

v. d. L. 343.

Weg; N.Y.P.L.; Gebhardt. (A.S.O. Heavy paper.)

Also to be entered under Jacobi-Mendelssohn controversy.

G-XXI-1

G-XXI-3 2245

[Heydenreich, K. H.]

Schelle, Karl Gottlob.

Karl Heinrich Heydenreichs... Charakteristik als Menschen und Schriftstellers ... Mit Heydenreichs Bildniss. Leipzig: G. Martini, 1802. xvi, 499 [1] p., 1 port. 12°.

p. 234-237 deals with Heydereich's Bd. 2 of Natur und Gott nach Spinoza, which [over]

Spec Coll Spin 2270

[History.]

Pollock, Sir Frederick, Bart.

Spinoza and modern thought. [In his: Spinoza... London, 1880. 8°. p. 373-408.]

Being Chapter XII.

Also in 2. ed. (p. 348-382), and in the re-issue of 1912.

2273

Hobbes, Thomas.

See: Battelli, Guido.

2274

Hobbes.

See: Beckkoetter, Oskar.

2275

Hobbes, Thomas.

See: Covotti, Aurelio.

2241

5 Heydenreich, Karl Heinrich, 1764-1801.
Betrachtungen über die Philosophie der natürlichen Religion.
Bd. 1-2. Leipzig, Weygand, 1790-1791.
21cm

Spinoza (a critical analysis of the main points of his system), Bd. 1, p. 258-272; Bd. 2, p. 168-175.
~~Zufolge~~ Zu folge seines vermittelst der Kritischen Philosophie gewonnenen [over]

1-a. 2242 [cont.]

Heydenreich, Karl Heinrich.- Betrachtungen...
strengen und vollständigen Begriffs Gott bekennt Heydenreich in seinen Betrachtungen (Band I, S. 46 und 259), was er in seinem Werke: Natur und Gott nach Spinoza, noch nicht zugab, der Spinozismus zerstöre allen wahren Begriff von Gott und sey daher auch Atheismus (Schelle, p. 280-281, footnote).

2243

Heydenreich, Karl Heinrich.- Betrachtungen... [cont.] 2

—— 2. verb. Aufl. 1804.

(Baldwin)

Betrachtungen über die Philosophie der natürlichen Religion.
2 Bde. Weygand
Leipzig, 1804. 8º.
See Vol. I, p. 258-272 - Neunte Betrachtung, "Kritik und Widerlegung der ersten Gründe des Spinozismus."

2237

Heydenreich, Karl Heinrich.
Natur und Gott nach Spinoza. Von Karl Heinrich Heydenreich. Erster Band. Leipzig: in der Joh. Gottfr. Müllerschen Buchhandlung, 1789. lxxx, 224 p. 8º.

No more pub.- [Preface.]- Leben Benedickts von Spinoza [by J. M. Lucas]. Aus einer französischen Handschrift, mit Anmerkungen vom Herausgeber (p. xix- lxxx).- Einleitungsgespräch über die [over]

---

2. 2238

Heydenreich, Karl Heinrich.- Natur... [cont.]
Abhängigkeit des Menschen, über Deismus, Pantheismus und Atheismus.- Ueber das System Spinoza's.
v.d. L. 343.
Weg; N.Y.P.L.; Gebhardt. (A.S.O. Heavy paper.)

Also to be entered under Jacobi-Mendelssohn Controversy.

2245

[Heydenreich, K. H.]
Schelle, Karl Gottlob.
Karl Heinrich Heydenreichs... Charakteristik als Menschen und Schriftstellers ... Mit Heydenreichs Bildniss. Leipzig: G. Martini, 1802. xvi, 499 [1] p., 1 port. 12º.

p. 234-237 deals with Heydereich's Natur und Gott nach Spinoza, Bd. 2 of which [over]

2270

[History.]
Pollock, Sir Frederick, Bart.
Spinoza and modern thought. [In his: Spinoza... London, 1880. 8º. p. 373-408.]
Being Chapter XII.
Also in 2. ed. (p. 348-382), and in the re-issue of 1912.

2273

Hobbes, Thomas.

See: Battelli, Guido.

2274

Hobbes.

See: Beckkoetter, Oskar.

2275

Hobbes, Thomas.

See: Covotti, Aurelio.

2276

Hobbes, Thomas.
See: Hartenstein, G.

2277

Hobbes, Thomas.
See: Iodice, Antonio.

2278

Hobbes, Thomas.
See: Janet, Paul.

2279

Hobbes, Thomas.
See: Meozzi, Antero.

2280

Hobbes, Thomas.
See: Ricco, Cesare.

2281

Hobbes, Thomas.
See: Rotta, Paolo.

2282

Hobbes, Thomas.
See: Royce, Josiah.

Spec Coll Spin
2299

Høffding, Harald.
A brief history of modern philosophy. By Harald Höffding. Authorized translation by Charles Finley Sanders. New York: The Macmillan Company, [1912]. 12°.

Spinoza, p. 67-78.

(A.S.O.) [over]

2.
2300

Høffding, Harald — A brief... [card 2]
"The original (German) edition from which this translation is made appeared in 1905" (p. V).
2nd 1920 ed Spec Coll Spin

Spec Coll Spin
2305

Høffding, Harald.
Die drei Gedankenmotive Spinozas, von Harald Höffding. (Chronicon Spinozanum. tom. 1, p. 3-13.)

This repeats previous page

2276

Hobbes, Thomas.

See: Hartenstein, G.

2277

Hobbes, Thomas.

See: Iodice, Antonio.

2278

Hobbes, Thomas.

See: Janet, Paul.

2279

Hobbes, Thomas.

See: Meozzi, Antero.

2280

Hobbes, Thomas.

See: Ricco, Cesare.

2281

Hobbes, Thomas.

See: Rotta, Paolo.

2282

Hobbes, Thomas.

See: Royce, Josiah.

2299

Høffding, Harald.

A brief history of modern philosophy. By Harald Höffding. Authorized translation by Charles Finley Sanders. New York: The Macmillan Company, [1912]. 12°.

Spinoza, p.67-78.

(A.S.O.)

[over]

2300

2.

Høffding, Harald. -- A brief...

[over]

"The original (German) edition from which this translation is made appeared in 1905" (p.v).

2nd 1920 ed Spec Coll Spin

2305

Høffding, Harald.

Die drei Gedankenmotive Spinozas, von Harald Höffding. (Chronicon Spinozanum. tom. 1, p. 3-13.)

G-XXI-

2306

Høffding, Harald.

Das erste Buch der Ethica. n.t.-p. [Hagae Comitis, 1922.] 20-53 p. sq. 8°.

Title taken from first p.

Repr.: Chronicon Spinozanum. tom. 2.

"Die Abhandlung im ersten Jahrgan des Chronicon über die drei Gedankenmotive des Spinoza war in meiner [over]

G-XXIX-16 2. 2296

Høffding, Harald. — Histoire de... [cont.]

a) Biographie et caractéristique. b) Théorie de la connaissance. c) Principes fondmentaux du système. d) Philosophie de la religion. e) Philosophie de la nature et psychologie. f) Éthique et politique.

See also "Notes," p. 536-539.

(G.)

G-XXI-9 2. 2307

Høffding, Harald. — Das erste ... [cont.]

...uttersprache die Einleitung zu einer Analyse und Charakteristik der Ethica. Diese Analyse folgt ganz der Darstellung des Spinoza selbst, und in diesem Jahrgang des Chronicon wird im folgenden die Analyse des ersten Buches gegeben werden." (p. 20)

2292

Høffding, Harald.

A history of modern philosophy. A sketch of the history of philosophy from the close of the renaissance to our own day. By Harald Höffding. Translated from the German edition by B. E. Meyer. Authorised translation. V. 1-2. London: Macmillan and Co., Limited. 1915. 8°. [Reprinted?]

G-XXIX-17, 18

2289

Høffding, Harald.

Geschichte der neueren Philosophie. Eine Darstellung der Geschichte der Philosophie von dem Ende der Renaissance bis zu unseren Tagen. Von Harald Höffding. Unter Mitwirkung des Verfassers aus dem Dänischen ins Deutsche übersetzt von F. Bendixen. Bd. 1-2. Leipzig: O. R. Reisland, 1895-1896. 8°. [over]

1-a. 2293

Høffding, Harald. — A history... [cont.]

Benedict Spinoza, v. 1, p. 292-331. Notes, p. 513-517.

(a) Biography and characteristics. (b) Theory of knowledge. (c) Fundamental concepts of the system. (d) Philosophy of religion. (e) Natural philosophy and psychology. (f) Ethic and theory of politics.

(A.S.O.)

---

2. 2290

Høffding, Harald. — Geschichte der... [cont.]

Benedikt Spinoza, Bd. 1, p. 324-372.

a) Biographie und Charakteristik. b) Erkenntnislehre. c) Systematische Grundbegriffe. d) Religionsphilosophie. e) Naturphilosophie und Psychologie. f) Ethik und Staatslehre.

See also "Anmerkungen," p. 577-580. See also Register.

— — [Second ed.] 1921. [Reprinted?]

(G.)

---

2 2294

Høffding, H. — A history...

"In my Spinoza's Liv og Läre ... I have given a popular description of Spinoza and his philosophy. Later, continued study has led me to adopt views on some points other than those advocated in this work" (p. 514).

— — [Another ed.; reprinted?] 1935.

G-XXIX-16

2295

Høffding, Harald.

Histoire de la philosophie moderne par Harald Höffding. Traduit de l'allemand par P. Bordier, avec corrections et notes nouvelles de l'auteur. Préface de M. V. Delbos. Tome premier. Paris: F. Alcan, 1906. 8°.

Benoît Spinoza, p. 306-350.

[over]

O-XXII-39

2297

Høffding, Harald.

Lehrbuch der Geschichte der neueren Philosophie. Von Harald Höffding. Zweite Ausgabe. Leipzig: O. R. Reisland, 1920. 8°.

Spinoza, p. 59-70.

"Dieses Lehrbuch ist eine deutsche Bearbeitung einer kurzen Übersicht über die Geschichte der neueren [over]

O-XXII-39 2. 2298

Høffding, Harald. - Lehrbuch der... [cont.]

Philosophie, die ich bei meinem propädeutischen Kursus ... gebrauche. In der deutschen Bearbeitung ist die Darstellung erweitert und in einigen Punkten geändert"... (Vorrede zur ersten Ausgabe).

This preface is dated Oct. 21, 1906. (Compare note to English translation.)

(A.S.O.)

G-XXI-8 2309

Høffding, Harald.

Spinoza [24. November 1632 - 21. Februar 1677]. [København], 1927. 8 p. 8°.

Repr.: Tilskueren, Marts, 1927.

See: Spinozahuis, Verslag, 1927/28, p. 16-18, according to which account the article first appeared in the February number of Tilskueren, while the paper-cover of the [cover]

G-XXI-8 2. 2310

Høffding, Harald. - Spinoza... [cont.]

reprint, from which the above title was taken, has "Marts".

(G.)

O-XLIII-13 2302

Høffding, Harald.

Spinoza's Ethica. Analyse og Karakteristik. København: Hoved-kommissionaer: Andr. Fred. Høst & Søn, Kgl. Hof-Boghandel, 1918. 97 p., 1 l. sq. 4°. (Kgl. Danske Vidensk. Selsk. Skrifter. Raekke 7. Historisk og filosofisk Afd. [v.] 3, [no.] 3.)

Paged also: 1 p.l., (1) 340-433 p., 1 l.

GLIV-32 (4) (A.S.O.)

---

2 2303

Høffding, H. - Spinoza's Ethica...

Review: Meijer, Willem. (Museum. Maandblad voor philologie en geschiedenis. jaarg. 26, 1919, p. 265 — [in 2 instalments].)

—— —— (Chronicon Spinozanum. tom. 1, p. 303-314.) Also off-print.

See also: Spinozahuis, Verslag, 1910/20, p. 1-3; and: Meijer, W. Spinozana, p. 115-116.

G-LIV-32

O-XXII-42 SPINOZA ROOM 2308

Hoeffding, Harald.

Die Verflechtung der Probleme in Spinozas Philosophie. (In: Kant-Studien. Spinoza-Festheft. Berlin, 1927. 8. p.29-43.)

Repr. A.S.O.

O-XXII-36 2311

Hoelters, Hans.

Der spinozistische Gottesbegriff bei M. Mendelssohn und F. H. Jacobi und der Gottesbegriff Spinozas. Emsdetten: Verlags-Anstalt H. & J. Lechte, 1938. 4 p.l., 92 p., 2 l. [list of publications]. 8°. (Universitas-Archiv. Philosophische Abteilung. Bd. 97.)

[cover]

O-XXII-36 1-a. 2312

Hoelters, Hans. - Der spinozistische... [cont.]

"Diese Arbeit hat der Philosophischen Fakultät der Rheinischen Friedrich-Wilhelm-Universität zu Bonn als Dissertation vorgelegen."

Contents: [Vorwort; by Siegfried Behn.] I. Einleitung. II. Der spinozistische Gottesbegriff bei Moses Mendelssohn... III. Der spinozistische Gottesbegriff bei Friedrich Heinrich Jacobi... IV. Der Gottesbegriff Spinozas kritisch dargestellt... V. Der spinozistische Gottesbe- [next]

O-XXII-36 2 2313

Hoelters, H. [cont.]

griff und der Gottesbegriff Spinozas... VI. Schlussbetrachtung. VII. Literaturverzeichnis.

"In der klassischen Zeit der deutschen Dichtung und in der hochromantischen Epoche der deutsch-idealistischen Philosophie dreht sich eine oft leidenschaftliche Auseinandersetzung um das Werk Spinozas... Da erhebt sich für [over]

O-XXII-36 2-a 2314

Hoelters, H. - Der spinozistische... [cont.]

uns, gerade gegenwärtig, die ernste Frage, ob denn jene deutsche Geistesbewegung... tatsächlich mit dem geometrisierenden Schematismus und der kaltintellektuellen Mystizistik Spinozas innerlich vereinbar und begrifflich vergleichbar sei. Ist 'Spinozismus' dasselbe wie die eigentliche Lehrmeinung Spinozas? Oder ist nicht vielmehr Spinoza in seiner eigentlichen Form dem deutschen Geistesleben unfassbar fern geblieben

C-XXI-36 3 2315

Hoelters, H. [cont.]

ben, um scheinbar angeeignet zu bleiben? ... Von echter Aneignung des weltenfernen andersartigen Systems kann also erst recht nicht die Rede sein, sondern höchstens von einer durchgreifenden, wesenwandelnden, gründlich umschmelzenden Ausdeutung. Der ganze Streit bleibt so eine innerdeutsche Auseinandersetzung zwischen verschiedenen Weisheiten und Gläubigkeiten [over]

C-XXI-36 3-a. 2316

Hoelters, H. — Der spinozistische ... [cont.]

im selben Geistesraum. Wo die Unvereinbarkeiten im einzelnen liegen ... das vermag Hölters ... nachzuweisen, weil er auf Grund der neuesten Forschungen die eigenartige Lehrmeinung Spinozas beurteilen darf, die alles Andere ist, als deutscher 'Spinozismus'" (S. Behn, in Vorwort).

[next]

C-XXI-36 4 2317

Hoelters, H. [cont.]

"Es ist nun hier nicht beabsichtigt, auf dem gesammten Streit um Spinoza zur Zeit Goethes etwa einzugehen. Vielmehr soll hier vor allem die Diskussion Jacobi-Mendelssohn und da wiederum in erster Linie der 'spinozistische' Gottesbegriff in seinem Verhältnis zum Gottesbegriff Spinozas, behandelt werden ... da unter 'spinozistisch' ... Auffassungen anzutreffen sind, die alle möglichen [over]

C-XXI-36 4-a. 2318

Hoelters, H. — Der spinozistische ... [cont.]

nur nicht Spinozas Gedanken darstellen" (p. 2-3).

"Diese kleine Untersuchung ging von dem Gedanken aus, dass Spinozas Lehre im 18. und 19. Jahrhundert einen grossen Einfluss besass und das die Wirkung Spinozas im 19. Jahrhundert eng mit der Jacobischen und Mendelssohnschen Spinoza-Diskussion verknüpft war. Das Spinozabild war ... gerade durch diese Diskussion wie auch das Goethe-Jacobi-Gespräch oft [next]

C-XXI-36 5 2319

Hoelters, H. [cont.]

gefährdet. So wollte diese Abhandlung der Klärung dieser Zusammenhänge dienen und damit dem ewigen Sinn von Philosophie: der Liebe zur Wahrheit" (p. 89).

NjPT - Amsterdam, 1864-69. 2v. 2337

Hofstede de Groot, P. Ver. by phone article + pages ok

Verdediging en bestrijding des Christendoms. [In: Haar, B. ter, and Moll, W. Geschiedenis der christlijke Kerk in Nederland, in tafereelen, onder redactie van B. ter Haar, W. Moll en E. B. Swalue. Met medewerking van P. Hofstede de Groot, [and others]. Rottardam: D. Bolle, n.d. 4°. deel 2, p. 479-509. [over]

2. 2338

Hofstede de Groot, P. - Verdediging... [cont.]

p. 499-506, deals with Spinoza. Reprinted ed. Original ed.: Amsterdam, 1864-1869. (According Burgersdijk & Niermans, Cat. no. 48; no. 5282.)

NjPT → Amsterdam, G. Portielje, 1864-69. 2v., illus., 27 cm

(G.)

2383

Horn, J. E. [originally Ignaz Einhorn].

YO9 NNC 1. 2389
B45 Spinoza, Baruch or Benedictus.
V55 (50-58)
t.p. missing

Horovitz, Aurelie.

Beiträge zu Lessings Philosophie. Inaugural-Dissertation... Bern: Scheitlin, Spring & Cie., 1907. 2 p.L., 89 p. 8.

p88: "In Einem war Lessing Spinozist, indem er

See next card.

° LC

2. 2390

Spinoza, Baruch or Benedictus.

Horovitz, Aurelie.-Beiträge zu Lessings Philosophie... [cont.]

nämlich alles Geschehen in Beziehung zum Unendlichen, zum Ewigen sah."

Not in B.

E821

Howe, John, 1630-1705
NNUT Works. London, 1724. 2 v. f°. oLC rBM
F L516, H856, A, 1724.

Works; ed. H. Rogers. 1862-63. 6 v.
v. 3. The living temple. [v. 6 cont. Index of subjects and authors]
NNUT L516, H856, A, 1862
1702 ed, 2 v. in Spi...
NNUT Calamy, Edmund Memoirs of J. Howe. 1724.
LQ1 H857 C14 oLC rBM
Rogers, H. Life of J. Howe. new ed. 1863. Lond, Rel. Tract Soc.
D.W.L. LC 37-12149
oNNC ord 12-3

E832

USII Hudson, William Henry.
The purple land. Introduction by William McFee, "Modern Library, Pref. date [1904],
Spinoza's message is here invoked (in the penultimate chapter). xvi + 399 p.
Chapter XXVIII "Good-bye to the Purple Land," p. 354-371.
No author Index.
A ref. to Sp (p. 368-9)
ord 3-19

E823

Howe, John. [1630-1705.]

v. 2, pref. discusses Sp. as an Introduction; chap. 1 "refutes" Sp.; chap. 2 refutes the "French writer". - H. speaks also of followers of Sp.
Bohrmann, p. 72-73, and 76. (Quotes: Works, ed. Edmund Calamy, N.Y., 1835, v. 1. Needs verification.)
Pollock, p. 383-384.
[E. Calamy: 1671-1732.]

2403

NN-NKW-5 lxx p., 1 l., 73-400 p. . . 19½ cm.
Hugo, Victor, 1802-1885.
O'Rourke, Lorenzo, tr.
Victor Hugo's Intellectual biography (Postscriptum de ma vie); being the ... of the unpublished works and embodying the author's ideas on literature, philosophy and religion, translated with a study of the last phase of Hugo's genius by Lorenzo O'Rourke. New York and London: Funk & Wagnalls Company, 1907.
oNNC
LC 7-21356 ord 11-7-58 [over]

E812

393.19
H79? Hosmer, James Kendall.
card 1887 The story of the Jews. New York: G.P. Putnam's Sons, 1886 [7] 12°
xxi + 381 p. t.p.
The casting out of a prophet, p. 215-231. port.

Incl. a chapter referring briefly to Spinoza (p. 215-231) and a portrait of him (p. 221)
Is port. in Altkirch?
ord 7-31

1-a 2404

Hugo, - O'Rourke, Lorenzo, tr. . . . [cont.]
On p. lxv of translator's introduction, O'Rourke writes: "Among philosophers he cherished particular admiration for Spinoza, in whose prodigious metaphysical dreams he probably saw reflections of his own. The sublime conception of pantheism which sprang from the brain of the 'God-intoxicated' man made a profound appeal to Hugo's grandiose imagination. It is altogether likely, too, that the profoundly religious idea that underlies Spinoza's system left a deep and permanent impression."

1. E828

Use 1914 ed -NN-AB
Spinoza, Baruch or Benedictus
Hubbard, Elbert. 1856-1915
4 Spinoza. East Aurora, N.Y.: The Roycrofters, 1904. 1 p.L., (1)120-151(1) p., 1 port. 12. (Little journeys [for 1904] to the homes of great philosophers.
Use NN-AB, v. 8 - 14 v. NY., W.H. Wise Co. See next card.
[1916] 21½ cm.

2. 2405

Hugo,
Says Marvin L. (letter of June 22, 1940):
"From the content of the preceding paragraph I gather that O'Rourke bases his statement on a book by Paul Stapfer, called Victor Hugo à Guernsey which details conversations Stapfer had with Hugo in exile. I've not yet got my hands on Stapfer's book.
Possibly Hugo was just blowing-off a few big names. Hugo does have a strong pantheist [over]

2. E829

Spinoza, Baruch or Benedictus
Hubbard, Elbert.-Spinoza... [cont.]
v.14⁵ [of the several ser.])
"Frontispiece portrait from the original drawing made at our shop"; after the port of Hendrik van der Spyck.
9

2-a 2406

Hugo, - O'Rourke, Lorenzo, tr. . . . [cont.]
streak; but I've not yet read enough of his works to know if there is any direct connection between these ideas and Spinoza. I thought that perhaps you had some clues."

2407

Hugo, Victor.

"A Mr. Lorenzo O'Rourke, in a preface to a translation of Hugo's Postscriptum de Ma Vie, says that 'Among philosophers he [Hugo] cherished particular admiration for Spinoza, in whose prodigious metaphysical dreams he probably saw reflections of his own'." [From a letter of Marvin Lowenthal, May 23, 1940.]

9r. Selected Works, 19-- E 846

Huxley, Thomas Henry. [1825-1895.]

His essays on philosophical and ethical topics had an important influence upon English thought, quite apart from his special work in science. He describes his philosophical position as "agnosticism", which term he invented, and which expresses his attit[ude] towards certain traditional questions.

("He regards consciousness as a collateral effect of certain physical causes, and only an effect – never, also, a cause. But, on the other hand, he holds that

---

1-a. E 847

Huxley, Thomas Henry. – His essays on... [cont.] matter is only a symbol, and that all physical phenomena can be analysed into states of consciousness. This leaves mental facts in the peculiar position of being collateral effects of something that, after all, is only a symbol for a mental fact; and the contradiction, or apparent contradiction, is left without remark." (Sorley, in Cambr. Hist. Eng. Lit. XIV, 34.) Comp. Santayana!

The safety of morality lies "in a real and living belief in that fixed order of nature which sends social disorganisation on the track of immorality" ("Science and Morals", 1888). We hear a different tone in his Romanes lecture, where the moral order is contrasted with the cosmic order. Evolution shows constant struggle. He does not look [next]

---

2 E 848

Huxley, T. H. [cont.]

to the historical process for moral guidance, but "repudiates the gladiatorial theory of existence". (Comp. B. Russel!)

See: Pollock (who connects Sp. in direct lineage with this scientific thinker).

I

J

0-XXIII-12 2431

Jacobi, F. H.

Lettere al Signor Mosè Mendelssohn su la dottrina dello Spinoza [1785]. Tr. F. Capra. Bari: Laterza, 1914. (Classici della filos. mod. v. 21.)

Guzzo (Elica), p. 207.

0-XXIII-11 2441

Jacobi, Friedrich Heinrich.

Ueber die Lehre des Spinoza, in Briefen an Herrn Moses Mendelssohn. [2. aufl.] (In his: Werke. Leipzig: G. Fleischer, 1812-1825. 8°. Bd. 4, Abth. 1 [the whole] – 2 [till p. 167].

v. d. L. 344 (m).

2448

Jacobi-Mendelssohn Controversy.

See also: Lessing.

2449

Jacobi-Mendelssohn Controversy.

See: Stockum, T. C. van.

2450

Jacobi-Mendelssohn Controversy.

See: Zirngiebl, E.

XXIII-31 2478

Janet, Paul.

Spinoza et le Spinozisme d'après les travaux récens. (Revue des deux mondes. v. 70. 1867. p. 470-498.)

I. Ad B. de Spinoza opera quae supersunt omnia supplementum (Amsterdam, 1862). – II. [Vloten, J. van.] Baruch d'Espinoza (Amsterdam, 1862). – III. Linde, A. van der. Spinoza (Göttingen, 1862). – IV. Nourrisson, J. F. Spinoza et le naturalisme contemporain (Paris, 1866).

[v. d.] L. 142.

(S.O.) G-XI-10

2468

Jaeger, Wolfgang.
Historia ecclesiastica cum parallelismo profanae ... Hamburg, 1709.

In the long title is also "Spinozismus." Ti. taken from: Nouvelles de la république des lettres (tom. 48? Amst., 1720, 2. rev. ed., p. 593?) [Copy: M.L.]
Perhaps Joh. Wolfg. Jaeger.

2490

Janet, Paul.
Hobbes et Spinosa. (In his: Histoire de la philosophie morale et politique, dans l'antiquité et les temps modernes ... Paris, 1858. tom. 2, p. 167-232.)

Spec Coll Spin

Contents: Hobbes ...-Spinosa. Sa morale: Théorie du bien et du mal. Théorie de la vertu. Objection principale [over]

---

2. 2491

Janet, Paul. — Hobbes et Spinosa ... [cont.]
contre cette morale. — Droit naturel. Principe du droit. De la loi de nature et de la lois de raison. Du droit absolu de la société. Limites de ce droit. Liberté de la pensée. — Système politique de Spinosa. Ses préférences pour le gouvernement populaire. — Rapports et differences de Hobbes et de Spinosa. Critique de la théorie du pouvoir absolu.
(A. S. O.)

O-XXII-32 2497a

Japikse, N.
Spinoza en de Witt. (Bijdragen voor vaderlandsche geschiedenis en oudheidkunde. 's-Gravenhage, 1927. reeks 6, deel 6, afl. 1-2, p. 1-16.)

(G.) unbd. (Afl. 1-2.)
G-XXI-32 - not excerpted - [over]

O-XXIII-24, 25, 26 2499

Jaquelot, [Isaac].
Dissertations sur l'existence de Dieu. Par M. Jaquelot. Nouvelles édition, augmentée de la vie de l'auteur, & de quelques lettres concernant la même matiere. tom. 1-3. À Paris: Chez François Didot [and] Jacq. Barois, 1744. 12°.

(A.S.O.) [over]

O-XXIII-24, 25, 26 2. 2500

Jaquelot, [Isaac]. - Dissertations ... [cont.]

(From Marvin Lowenthal: in exchange; Apr., 1941. Don't find this ed. recorded.)

Spec Coll Spin 2507

Jellinek, Georg.
Die Beziehungen Goethes zu Spinoza. Vortrag gehalten im Vereine der Literaturfreunde zu Wien. (In his: Ausgewählte Schriften und Reden ... Berlin, 1911. 8°. Bd. 1, p. 179-207.)

See also Namen- und Sachregister to Bd. 1.
(A.S.O. - G.)

Spec Coll Spin 2511

Jellinek, Georg.
Vloten, Johannes van.
Goethe en Spinoza. [Review of: Jellinek, G. Die Beziehungen Goethe's zu Spinoza ... Wien, 1878.] (Levensbode. Haarlem, 1878. deel 10, p. 423-432.)

~~Signed, v. Vl.~~

O-XXIII-43, 44 2530

Jodl, Friedrich.
Geschichte der Ethik als philosophischer Wissenschaft. Bd. 1-2. Zweite, neu bearbeitete und vermehrte Auflage. Stuttgart und Berlin: J.G. Cotta'sche Buchhandlung Nachfolger, 1906-1912. 8°.

Spinoza, Bd. 1, p. 487-505. Anmerkungen, p. 670-677. See also Namenverzeichnis.
1. Geschichtliche Stellung Spinozas. [over]

O-XXIII-43, 44 2. 2531

Jodl, Friedrich. — Geschichte der ... [cont.]
2. Spinozas Weltbegriff. 3. Grundlage der sittlichen Urteile. 4. Die sittlichen Imperative. 5. Allgemeine Charakteristik.

(A.S.O.)

 2528

Jodl, Friedrich.

Geschichte der Ethik in der neueren Philosophie. Bd. 1-2. Stuttgart: Verlag der J.G. Cotta'schen Buchhandlung, 1882-1889. 8°.

Spinoza, Bd. 1, p. 322-340. Anmerkungen, p. 436-438.

1. Abschnitt. Persönlichkeit und geschichtliche Stellung. 2. Abschnitt. Das System; [over]

 2. 2529

Jodl, Friedrich. — Geschichte der... [cont.]

§ 1. Aufhebung der objectiven Wertunterschiede; § 2. Die Möglichkeit und das Wesen des Sittlichen; § 3. Versöhnung des Intellectualismus und Emotionalismus. 3. Abschnitt. Verhältniss Spinoza's zur Philosophie seiner Zeit; § 1. Psychologie und Metaphysik des Sittlichen; § 2. Egoismus und Altruismus; § 3. Sittlichkeit und Eudämonismus. 4. Abschnitt. Verhältniss zur Religion.

 2543

Jodl, Friedrich.

Geschichte der neueren Philosophie. Aus dem Nachlass herausgegeben von Karl Roretz... Wien: Rikola Verlag, 1924. 8°.

Spinoza, p. 242-287. See also Namen-Register.

Also 1927.

 2534

Jodl, Friedrich.

Spinoza. Auf Grund einer neueren Darstellung [i.e., Bolin, W., Spinoza... 1894]. (In his: Vom Lebenswege... Stuttgart, 1916-1917. 8°. Bd. 1, p. 22-29.)

First published in: Die Nation, 1894, no. 9.

 2535

Jodl, Friedrich.

Zur Interpretation Spinoza's. (In: Festschrift Theodor Gomperz... Wien, 1902. 4°. p. 342-350.)

A. Hilder

[over]

 1-a. 2536

Jodl, Friedrich. — Zur Interpretation... [cont.]

Rejects R. Wahle's interpretation (in his Kurze Darstellung der Ethik von Spinoza) of Spinoza's teaching as naturalism and positivism, and that substance is the infinite all or the totality of being. J. maintains that "Spinoza's System enthält, wie es auch seine Genesis verräth, eine starke und ursprüngliche Tendenz zum Naturalismus... Aber hinter den starren Formeln seines Systems verbergen sich manigfaltige und widersprechende geistige Einflüsse [next]

 2 2537

Jodl, F. — Z. Interpretation...

... man kann Spinoza nicht rein ablösen von dem theologischen Hintergrunde des ganzen Zeitalters... nicht ablösen von gewissen Tendenzen de Neuplatonismus, welche durch die jüdische Religionsphilosophie und die Kabbala Bestandtheil seiner Bildung geworden waren, wie sie das ganze Renaissance-Zeitalter beschäftigt hatten; nicht ablösen von der echt scho- [over]

 2-a. 2538

Jodl, F. — Z. Interpretation... [cont.]

lastischen Gepflogenheit, Gedankendinge für Realitäten zu nehmen und begriffliche Unterscheidungen für verschiedene Wesenheiten... (p. 350).

See: Wahle, R. Beiträge zur Theorie der Interpretation philosophischer Werke (Zeitschr. f. Phil. u. phil. Kritik, Bd. 122, p. 64 ff.) which contains remarks in reply.

See also Jodl: Geschichte der Ethik, 2. ed., Bd. 1, p. 672-673.

 4794

Jörgensen, A.D.

~~Nich.~~ Nils Stensen. 1884. [Danish.]

København, 1884. 231 p. No author index.

p. 57 "I must also protest against A.D. Jörgensen's reflections (Nich. Steensen [sic], p. 57) on Spinoza's attitude towards experience" (H. Høffding, A history of modern philosophy, London, 1935, I, p. 514).

[over] Dunin-Borkowski, Spinoza, III, p. 382, has "Niels Stensen" and date of 1884.

Steno 2. 4795

Jörgensen, A.D. — Nich. Stensen... [cont.]

According to Høffding (p. 298) Jörgensen "was the first to call attention to the interesting relation between Steno and Spinoza".

Incl. a section on Spinoza (p. 51-57)

2585

Jorna, Bernardus.

Disputatio de quatuor fictis simplicium speciebus... Franeker, 1727.

A pupil of Ruardus Andala. Like his teacher, he accuses Leibniz of having plagiarized Spinoza. (See: Stein, L., Leibniz und Spinoza, p. 3.)

 E896b

Jouffroy, [Théodore Simon].

Introduction to ethics, including a critical survey of moral systems translated from the French of Jouffroy. By William H. Channing. In two volumes. Boston: Hilliard, Gray, and Company, 1841. 8°. (Specimen of foreign standard literature. Edited by George Ripley. v. 5-6.)
Vol. II, 1840, Lecture VI -p.145-174; +, VII -p.175-199.
(Harvard.) [over]

2 E896c

Jouffroy, T. S.

"The two lectures upon Spinoza are entitled to especial praise, as well as for the lucidness of the descriptions and reasonings, as for the humility with which so deep-read a scholar confesses his inability perfectly to comprehend, and his incompetency to pass judgment upon this most abstract of all systems (Translator's Preface, p. XI).

 5 E 900

Jowett, Benjamin, 1817-1893.

[Spinoza in his relation to ancient philosophy.] (In: Plato. The Dialogues of Plato; translated into English... by B. Jowett. Third edition... New York, 1892. 8°. v. 2 [Introduction to Meno], p. 21-22.)

The section: "The 'ideas' of Plato and modern thought" (p. ~~22~~ 13-25) is [over]

2. E 901

Jowett, Benjamin. - [Spinoza in his... [cont.]

an addition to the 3. ed.

"The teaching of Spinoza might be described generally as the Jewish religion reduced to an abstraction and taking the form of the Eleatic philosophy. Like Parmenides, he is overpowered and intoxicated with the idea of Being or God."

(A.S.O.)

 2599

Juengst, W

Verhältnis... 1912.

Review: Theol. Literaturz. Jahrg. 39. 1914. col. 150-151. By P. Lobstein.
Zeitschr. f. Phil. u. philos. Kr. Bd. 154. 1914. p. 103-105. By Max Arthur Jordan.

K

 2609

[Kahler, Wigand.]

Derodon, David.

David Derodons Widerlegter Atheismus worinnen aus der Vernunft erwiesen wird, dass ein Gott sey. Aus dem Frantzöschen [!] übersetzt, mit einer Vorrede von des Auctoris Leben und Schrifften nebst benöthigten Anmerckungen und register herausgegeben von Wigand Kahler. Lemgo: Gedruckt mit Meyerischen Schriften,
(H.U.C.) [over]

2. 2610

[Kahler, Wigand.] - Derodon, David... [cont.]

1733. 13 p. l., 252 p., 4 l., 1 pl. 8°

p. 25, a footnote by the translator in regard to Spinoza's denial of the impossibility of an infinite series of causes whereby he removes one of the premises of the Aristotelian proofs of the existence of God.

Grunwald (p. 51-52) erroneously identifies Kahler's tr. of Colerus (1734) with the anonymous one of 1733. D.-B. (I, 523) already called attention to this error.

 2611

Kahn, Gustave.

Spinoza et Rembrandt. (Menorah. Paris, 1927. année 6, no. 6, p. 86-87.)

(G.)

 E 910

Kantor, H. R., and Kantor, J. R.

Some humanistic elements in Spinoza's thinking. (Biosophical review. New York, 1934. v. 4, no. 1, p. 14-23.)
1934.

Helene J

(H.U.C.) [over]

2. E 911

Kantor, H.R., and Kantor, J.R.— Some... [cont.]

"It is with the viewpoint that Spinoza definitely possesses a more human and practical side than is generally supposed, that we shall point out very briefly some of the evidences of his humanistic and personalistic attitudes. We shall, therefore, attempt to look beyond the formal and metaphysical terminology of his day to find the real man speaking on the basis of his own personality and experience."— Confused (Subj.: Essays?)

Alc 7 E 917

Kellett, Ernest Edward.

Spinoza. (In: Encyclopaedia of religion and ethics; edited by J. Hastings... Edinburgh [also] New York, 1921. f°. v. 11, p. 768-784.)

I. Life. II. Philosophy.— 1. Its aim. 2. Logic and doctrine of method. 3. The geometrical method of of the Ethics. 4. Metaphysical doctrine. 5. Theory of knowledge. 6. Doctrine of the emotions. 7. Human bondage, or the power of the emotions. 8. Human [over]

G-XXI-43 2650

Kayser, Rudolf.

Baruch de Spinoza.— Lessing und Spinoza. (In his: Dichter-Köpfe. Wien, 1930. 8°. p. 7-18.)

First pub. (both essays) and under ti. "Baruch de Spinoza" in Die literarische Welt.

(q.) no

---

2. E 918

Kellett, Ernest Edward.— Spinoza ... [cont.]

freedom, or the power of understanding. 9. Attitude to religion and theology. 10. Political philosophy.

Gives but scanty literature. "Lucas, La vie de Spinoza before 1688, reprinted, Amsterdam, 1719." "La vie" was written before 1688; it was not printed before 1719.

G-XXII-35, 36 2667

Kellermann, Benzion.

Die Ethik Spinozas: Über Gott und Geist. Berlin: C.A. Schwetschke & Sohn, Verlagsbuchhandlung, 1922. VIII, 436 p. 8°.

→ G-XXII-36

Contents: [Vorwort.] Erster Teil. Über Gott. A. Definitionen und Axiome. B. Lehrsätze. Zweiter Teil. Über die Natur und den Ursprung des Geistes. A. Definitionen [over]

"Von diesem Werke wurde auch eine Ausgabe auf holzfreiem Papier ausgegeben."

G-XXIV-37 2674

Kertész, Antal.

Spinoza B. Viszonya a Zsidósághoz és a Keresztenységhez. (Észrevételek egy Rabbi két predikációjához [i.e., Hano Entenz]) Irta: Dr. Košice: „Globus" Könyvnyomda, lapkiadó és irodalmi r.-t., [1927?]. 52 p. 12°.

Kertész Antal.

[over]

G-XXII-35, 36 1-a 2667 a

Kellermann, Benzion.— Die Ethik... [cont.]

und Axiome. B. Lehrsätze.

The author, a disciple of Hermann Cohen, founder of the so-called Marburg school of neo-Kantianism, views the validity of Spinoza's thought from the author's own philosophical standpoint as a basis — or rather discusses Spinoza's doctrines sub specie Hermanni Cohen. "Für unsere Untersuchung handelte es sich ausschliesslich um die Beant

G-XI-22

---

2. 2675

Kertész, Antal.— Spinoza B. ... [cont.]

B. Spinoza. His relation to Judaism and to Christianity. (Observations on two sermons by a Rabbi.) „Globus" Buchdruckerei A.-G.

G-XXII-35, 36 2 2668

Kellermann, B.

wortung der Frage: Welchen objectiv sachlichen Geltungswert enthalten die einzelnen Fundamentalbegriffe in Spinozas Metaphysik, in seiner Psychologie und in seiner Freiheitslehre, inwieweit nähern sich diese Begriffe dem kritischen und kritizistischen Denken, inwieweit entfernen sie sich von ihm?" (p. VII).

G-XI-22 [over]

Spec Coll Spin 2683

Key, Ellen.

..."Lifslinjer (Lebenslinien), deren drei Teile im Anfang unseres Jahrhunderts erschienen. Man findet dort, dass sie durch ein liebevolles Studium Goethes auf Spinoza hingeführt worden ist." (Karitz, A. Nordischer Spinozismus [Chr. Spin., V, 178])

NNJ-M 1926 ed. cf. - [illegible] Soderblom E 903

Kingsley, Mary.

" Miss Mary Kingsley zieht eine Verbindung von ihren Fetisch-Philosophen zu Spinoza. Das mag etwas Kühn sein. Aber ungweifelhaft liegen in den Lehren der verschiedenen Fetisch-Schulen von der Kraft und ihrer Behandlung und ihren Arten Ansätze zu dieser Richtung vor." (Söderblom, N. Das Werden des Gottesglaubens. Lpz, 1916, p. 104-5. See also p. 113.) Sep. card - E 923a

NNJ - Lpz, 1926, XV+361 p.
NN - " " " " 24½ cm.

O-VI-16, 17, 18, 19 x 2703a

Kirchmann, J. H. v[on].

16 Spinoza's Leben und Schriften. (In his translation of: Benedict von Spinoza's Ethik... Berlin, 1868. 12°. p. 1-5.)

17 — — (Zweite Auflage. Berlin, 1870. 12°. p. 1-5.)

— — (Dritte verbesserte Auflage. Leipzig, 1877. 12° p. 1- .)

[over]

O-XXIV-48 2713

Klausner, J.

[illegible] של תורת[illegible]- שפינוזה.
(כנסת. Tel-Aviv, 1929. p. 190-191.)

Repr. (A.S.O.)
Rev. by A. Schlesinger. (Kant-Studien, Bd. 35, 1930, p. 320-321.)

O-XXIV-49 (?) 2717

Klausner, Joseph.

פילוסופים והוגי דעות; מסות ומחקרים.
כרך א. ירושלם, תרצ"ד.

[Jerusalem: Weiss, 1934.] VIII, 244 p. 8°.

Contains: Leone Ebreo and his philosophy of love (reprinted from "Tarbiz", v. 3). - Spinoza: 1) Spinoza and his teaching (reprinted f[illegible] מאזנים, 1933); 2) (repr. from כנסת [illegible] שפינוזה [illegible] ש[illegible] הארפי היהודי
The reprints are revised and enlarged. [illegible] on Leone

(A.S.O.) [over]

G-XXI-45 2727

Klencke, [P. F. H.]

Vom phantastischen Pessimismus zum freudigen Realismus: Schopenhauer und Spinoza von Dr. Klencke. [pt. 1-2.] Leipzig: Verlag der Rossberg'schen Buchhandlung, [1882]. 8°.

Title taken from paper-cover.

[pt. 1.] Pessimismus und Schopenhauer mit Bezug auf Spinoza als Heilmittel des Pessimismus von Dr. Klencke. n.p., n.d. 45 (1) p. [Verso of p. 45: Druck von W. Böhm in Zittau]

[over]

G-XXI-45 2. 2728

Klencke, [P. F. H.] — Vom phantastischen... [cont.]

[pt. 2.] Spinoza mit Rücksicht auf Kant, Schopenhauer, Göthe und die moderne Naturwissenschaft von Dr. Klencke. n.p., n.d. 55 p.

pt. 2, B. 417.

G-XXIX-29 2731

Knauer, Vincenz.

Geschichte der Philosophie mit besonderer Berücksichtigung der Neuzeit. Wien: W. Braumüller, 1876. 8°.

Spinoza, p. 134-138.

(G.)

G-XXI-50 2764

Kolbenheyer, E[rwin] G[uido].

Amor Dei. Ein Spinoza-Roman. München: G. Müller, 1912. 4 p. l. [1-2 blanks], 389 (1) p. [4. ed.] 12°.

(H. 21. C.)

O-XXVI-4 2767

Kolbenheyer, E[rwin] G[uido].

Amor Dei. Ein Spinoza-Roman. München: G. Müller, 1919. 4 p. l. [1-2 blanks], 389 (1) p. 12°.

9.-13. Tausend.

(A.S.O.) [over]

O-XXVI-4 2. 2768 [cont.]

Kolbenheyer, E[rwin] G[uido]. - Amor...

Poem, at p. l. 4a.

C-XXI-5 2771

Kolbenheyer, Erwin Guido.
Gorelik, Shemarya.
Ein Spinozaroman. Von Sch. Gorelik. [Review of: Kolbenheyer, E. G. Amor Dei...] (Neue jüdische Monatshefte. Jahrg. 3, 1918–1919, p. 169–174.)

(A. S. O.)

2788

Kortholt, Chr

Geiffencranz' letter to Kortholt, written in 1681 soon after the publication of De tribus impostoribus, is found at the Kiel University Library (Briefsammlung S.-H. 406, A2; 2).– See: Halfmann, Wilhelm, Chr. Kortholt (Kiel, 1930).

OCH

G-XXI-51 2776

Kortholt, Christian, the elder.
De tribus impostoribus magnis liber [Herbert, Hobbes, Spinoza], cura editus Christiani Kortholti. Kiloni: literis & sumtibus J. Reumanni, 1680. 8 p. l., 304 p. [followed by 4 l. wrongly paged as 287, 288, 279, 290 & 291–294]. 8° & 12°.

v. d. L. 287.

O-XXVI-9 2797

Kovner, Albert [formerly Abraham Uri, or Uriah].
"Der grösste Denker seines Jahrhunderts, Baruch Spinoza, hat sich, bei aller Tiefe seiner von ihm geschaffenen, neuen, rationalen Philosophie, nicht von der Vergangenheit des Judentums lossagen können, die in seinem genialen Geiste tiefe Spuren hinterlassen hatte"... Unter den heutigen Schriftstellern ist Berthold Auerbach die Verkörperung der [over]

MH 1-18 1901-3411? OCH (?) 2786

[Kortholt, Christian]
Halfmann, Wilhelm.
Christian Kortholt. Ein Bild aus der Theologie und Frömmigkeit im Ausgang des orthodoxen Zeitalters. Kiel: W. G. Mühlau, 1930. IV, 2 l., 82 p., port. 8°. (Verein für Schleswig-Holsteinische Kirchengeschichte. [Kiel] Schriften. Reihe 1, Heft 17.)
Port. (frontispiece) is a reproduction by Meisenbach & Riffarth (Berlin) of an engraving in possession of [over]
(H. U. C.)

O-XXVI-9 2. [cont.]

Kovner, Albert [formerly Abraham Uri, or Uriah]. 2798
von uns erwähnten Zwiespältigkeit...
(Grossmann, L., Die Beichte eines Juden [i.e., A. Kovner] in Briefen an Dostojewski; München, 1927, p. 59–60.)

K. wrote the above in the early 1870-ties, in an article (?) "Berlin und Jerusalem." He was called the Pissarev of the Jews.

(G.)

MH- Ger45.1.20 -2W 2786a

Halfmann, Wilhelm
Christian Kortholt. Ein Bild...
(Verein für Schleswig-Holsteinische Kirchengeschichte. Schriften. Reihe 1, Heft 17. – not DLC
ULC – open entry
NNUT ? 82 p. – No index
DLC-BR857.S4V4 (Not Vm. Cat) – S4K5 (DLC cat)

O-XXVI-9 2796

Kovner, Savelii Grigorevich [Saul].
Spinoza, ego zhizn i sochinenya ... Warsaw: M. A. Kovner, 1897. 1 p. l., XIV, C[?]–173 C[?] p., 1 l. 2. rev. ed. 12°.
1 port. of Spinoza; 1 port. of author.
p. 1–XIV a life of author.

(A. S. O. unbd.)
(Essay on Spinoza in Russian)

2. 2787

[Kortholt, Christian] – Halfmann, W.... [cont.]
Historische Landeshalle at Kiel. Another port. is found in the "Beiträge und Mitteilungen" of the Verein, Bd. 7, after p. 168.

Note taken from p. 82.

Spinoza, p. 34–42 (section entitled: Gegen den Deismus"). – See also, p. 37.

-XXI-53 2816

Kraus, Oskar.
Über die Philosophie Spinozas. Aus Anlass seines 250. Todestages. (Euphorion. Stuttgart, 1927. Bd. 28, p. 161–172.)

(G.)

[over]

G-XXI-53 2. 2817

Kraus, Oskar. – Über die Philosophie... [cont.]

I. Ist Spinoza ein Mystiker? II. Die "essentia" des Spinozismus. III. Spinozas Identitätsphilosophie. IV Hauptmängel. V. Vorzüge.

G-XXIX-33 2821

Krause, Karl Christian Friedrich.

Grundriss der Geschichte der Philosophie. Aus dem handschriftlichen Nachlasse des Verfassers herausgegeben von Paul Hohlfeld und Aug. Wünsche. Leipzig: O. Schulze, 1887. 8°.

Spinoza, p. 259-268.

[over]

G-XXIX-33 2. [cont.] 2822

Krause, Karl Christian Friedrich. – Grundriss...

The work was completed in 1828 (see p. xiv).

(G.)

spin Coll Spin 2824

Krejčí, Frant.

O významu spinozovy filosofie. [With German translation:] Über die Bedeutung der Spinozistischen Philosophie. (Chronicon Spinozanum. Hagae Comitis, 1927. Tom. 5, p. 30-39.)

2839

Kroner, D ?

Von Descartes bis Leibniz. (pt. 4 Geschichte der Philosophie) Lpz., 192-

Aus Natur u. Geisteswelt.

G-XXXII-1,2,3,4,5 2847

Krug, Wilhelm Traugott.

Allgemeines Handwörterbuch der philosophischen Wissenschaften, nebst ihrer Literatur und Geschichte. Nach dem heutigen Standpuncte der Wissenschaft bearbeitet und herausgegeben von W. T. Krug. Bd. 1-5. Leipzig: F. A. Brockhaus, 1827-1829. 8°.

Spinosa oder Spinoza (Baruch

[over]

G-XXXII-1,2,3,4,5 2. 2848 [cont.]

Krug, Wilhelm Traugott. – Allgemeines...

oder Benedict von), Bd. 3 (1828), p. 745-755. See also Bd. 5, p. 228-229 ("Zusatz zur Literatur dieses Artikels").

G-XXXII-6,7,8,9 2849

Krug, Wilhelm Traugott.

Allgemeines Handwörterbuch der philosophischen Wissenschaften, nebst ihrer Literatur und Geschichte. Nach dem heutigen Standpuncte der Wissenschaft bearbeitet und herausgegeben. Zweite, verbesserte und vermehrte, Auflage. Bd. 1-4. Leipzig: F. A. Brockhaus, 1832-1834. 8°.

[over]

G-XXXII-6,7,8,9 2. 2850

Krug, Wilhelm Traugott. – Allgemeines... [cont.]

Spinosa oder Spinoza (Baruch oder Benedict von), Bd. 3 (1833), p. 828-839.

v. d. L. 148 (XIII).

(G.)

G-XXI-54 2843

Krug, Wilhelm Traugott.

Spinozae de iure naturae sententia denuo examinata. Symbolarum ad historiam philosophiae particula quarta qua Philosophiae Doctorum et LL. AA. Magistorum creationem annuam d. XVII. Febr. a. MDCCCXXV. in ordinis philosophorum conclavi peractam nuntiat Guilielmus Traugott Krug. Lipsiae: Literis Sta-

[over]

G-XXI-57 2. 2844
Krug, Wilhelm Traugott. - Spinozae de... [cont.]
ritii, typogr. univers., [1825]. 20p. sq. 8°

v.d.L. 414 (not seen).

(G.)

G-XXII-1 2. 2887
Lachièze-Rey, P. [cont.]
II. Spinoza. III. Autres noms et textes.

(G. - ½ buckr.)

G-XXI-55 2870
Kuske, Erich.
Spinoza und die Teleologie. (Preussische Jahrbücher. Berlin, 1918. Bd. 171, Heft 4, p. 1-20.)

Excerpt.

(G.) L Teleology [over]

2895
Lagerlöf, Nils.
Disputatio metaphysica continens cautelas circa examen et refutationem ideae substantiae spinozianae necessarias... Londini Gothorum, 1733.

Kuntz, A. Lorenzo ... Spinozismus (Chr. Spin., I; ...)

ICN + NNC/Paterno/D335/L115 2883
Labriola, Antonio, 1843-1904.
"Origine e natura delle passioni secondo l'Etica di Spinoza." (In his: Scritti varii, editi e inediti, di filosofia e politica, raccolti e pubblicati da B. Croce. Bari, Laterza, 1906. 8°. p. 35-87.)
viii, 507pp... 20½ cm., in 8s.
Published for the first time. The article was written in 1865.
Ravà, no. 9. [L.L.]

NUT QT3 L18 + BROWN LIBR. QT3 L18 E949
Laird, John, 1887-
The idea of value. Cambridge: at the University Press, 1929. xx, 384p. 8°.

Chapter II: Spinoza's account of value, p. 69-91. - See also Index.

NNC
LC 29-27645 rev'd 12-22
(D.W.L. June 1, 1935.) rev'd 3-4 [over]

G-XXII-1 2885
Lachièze-Rey, Pierre.
Les origines cartésiennes du Dieu de Spinoza. Paris: F. Alcan, 1932. XI[1-II Blank], 288p. 8°. ([Bibliothèque de philosophie contemporaine])

Avant-propos. chap. I. Le dialogue entre l'entendement, l'amour, la raison et la concupiscence. chap. II. [over]

1-a. E950
Laird, John. - The idea of... [cont. I]
§1. Introductory. §2. Spinoza's account: the first phase. §3. Comments on the first phase. §4. Spinoza's account: the second phase. §5. Remarks on the second phase. §6. Spinoza's account: the third phase. §7. The rational good: synopsis. §8. Remarks on the above. A. The nature of action. §9. B. The nature of passion. §10. Action and passion in relation to reason. §11. Anticipatory. §12. Spinoza's account: the meaning of good and evil in the third phase. §13. Man's beatitude.
p. xx: "The general outline of the argument in this book is very simple. The first chapter deals with the subordinate (but important) conception of utility, and, at the same time, with economic good.
[next]

G-XXII-1 1-a. 2886
Lachièze-Rey, Pierre. - Les origines... [cont.]
Dieu et l'attribut dans le Court traité. chap. III. La substance et l'attribut dans le Court traité. chap. IV. L'unité divine dans le Court traité. chap. V. La définition de l'essence et la théorie des distinctions. chap. VI. Les preuves de l'existence de Dieu. Conclusion. Index alphabétique des matières. Index des noms propres et de textes: I Descartes

2. E951
Laird, John. [cont. 3]
The main discussion begins with the second chapter, where Spinoza's doctrine of value is considered, and ends with the suggested conclusions of the ninth chapter... The reason for beginning the principal discussion with an account of Spinoza's views is, generally, the catholic prospect of Spinoza's theory, and more particularly the way in which Spinoza plainly suggested the threefold division of the subject which (as I think) all subsequent investigation should follow. The three strands in this thread of Theseus are, firstly, the relative values of natural election; secondly, the relative values of psychological in- [over]

2-a E 952

Laird, John.— The idea of... [cont.]

terest (i.e. of pleasure and conscious appetency): and, thirdly, the absolute values of excellence or of rational perfection. The meaning and the scope of each member in this triple division, together with the relations between them, seem to me to define the entire problem with which we are concerned."

NNC-4 2905

Land, Jan Pieter Nicolaas

109 A

Bibliographische Bemerkungen: III. Spinozistisches. (Archiv für Geschichte der Philosophie. Bd. 7, 1894, ~~p. 374-375.~~) (pp. 362-375. ...)
III Spinozistisches. pp. 374-375.
Notes the Tractatus de Miraculis (London, 1763), the title of which was communicated to Land by Sir Frederick Pollock. (Land erroneously [over]

Lamy 2896

Lami, Bernard.

Demonstration ou preuves évidentes de la verité & de la sainteté de la morale chrêtienne; ouvrage qui comprend en cinq entretiens toute la morale. À Rouen: chez Nicolas Boucher, & chez François Vaultier, 1706. 12°.

NN-3-OA
(Taken from: Journal des sçavans. Amst., 1707. tom. 36, p. 285-301.) [over]

---

2. 2906

Land, J. P. N. — Bibliographische ... [cont.]

suggests that this item belongs after v.d.L. 14; it belongs after no. 7: (where it is actually noted - a note overlooked by both P. & L.) for it brings the Latin original.) — Next the remark that the Opera posthuma were edited by G. H. Schuller, basing it on Schuller's letter to Leibniz of March 29, 1677. Finally the correction of the order of entries 182-185 in v.d.L.: 182-183 are to follow 185.

2897 [cont.]

Lami, Bernard. — Demonstration...

In part a refutation of Spinoza.
Trinius, p. 436, has: Bernhard Lamy, Commentar. in Harm.[?] Evangel. I. 5. c. 41. p. 616 seq.

PLatS ~~Commentarius in ... ... Venetiis, ... 1735.~~
~~XVI, 704 p. ...~~ (or earlier ed.? ... NNC)

2912

Land, J[an] P[ieter] N[icolaas].

SCS

De wijsbegeerte in de Nederlanden. Vertaald en bezorgd door C. van Vollenhoven. Met levensbericht van den schrijver door C. B. Spruyt. Met portret. 's-Gravenhage: M. Nijhoff, 1899. VII, (1)10-230 p., 1 l., 1 port. 8°.

Spinoza [life and philosophy], p. [over]

NNUT-Mc E 953

Lamothe, Claude ~~Grotête~~, ?

5

The inspiration of the New Testament asserted and explained, in answer to some modern writers. London, 1694. 17.7 x 10.9 cm. (11), 178 p.
Printed for Tho. Bennet

The occasion was (Pref., p. 3) Le Clerc's Letters.

NNC
DLC

See v.d.L. 358, note: - De la Mothe: De l'inspiration des livres sacrés[?] du Nouveau Testament. Amsterdam, 1695. 8°. (Acta erud. Lips. 1696, p. ...

1-a. [cont.] 2913

Land, J[an] P[ieter] N[icolaas]. — De wijsbegeerte...

181-230.

A posthumous work; unfinished.
L. wrote it in English, entitled "Philosophy in the Low Countries," and was to form a part of a planned "Series of Books on Philosophy in its National Development" under the editorship of William Knight.
L's MS.

G-XXII-3 2911

Land, J[an] P[ieter] N[icolaas].

Arnold Geulincx und seine Philosophie. Haag, 1895. X [I-II blank], 219 p. 12°.

Schlusswort [Geulincx and Spinoza; a comparison characterization], p. 215-219.

(Cq. unbd.)

---

2 2914

Land, J. P. N. - De wijsbegeerte... [cont.]

contained only the first 3 chap. The chap. on Geulincx (4) consists of L.'s introduction to his ed. of Geulincx' "Van de hooftdeuchden" (1895, p. 1-41), while that on Spinoza (5) is made-up of p. 1-17 of his "Inleiding" to W. Meijer's Dutch tr. of the Tr. Theol.-Pol. [1894] and p. 11-45 of his "Ter gedachtenis van Spinoza" (1877).

PPT; PHC; cf. E957

Carl
Lange, Georg.

PBm LLC- BF531 .E5

G. Lange und W. James: The emotions; ed. by K. Dunlap. Baltimore: Williams & Wilkins Co., 1922.

Psychology classics, v. 1.

G. L. acknowledges in the note: that Spinoza's doctrine comes closest to his own. (See: Bidney, p. 385.)

Ref. to Sp. (p. 83, 90)

2940

Lange, Joachim.

Modesta disquisitio novis philosophiae systematis de deo, mundo et homine et praesertim de harmonia praestabilita. Halae Sax., 1723. 4°

(Spinoza und Leibniz. p. 1274.)

Grunwald, p. 298

DLC - Microfilm (of copy in BM - See XXI, under Geulinck (Arnold)).

B-3 2941

Langenhert, Casparus, fl. 1700, ed.

NNC

Arnoldi Geulincx compendium physicae illustratum à Casparo Langenhert. Franequerae: Ex Officina Leonardi Strick Bibliopolae, 1688.

247, 210.

p. 116: "Quomodo autem Philosophi nonnulli atque Theologi, liberrimum hoc arbitrium cum Deo non competere vaferrimo Spinosae (qui libertatem hanc, [over]

DLC? LH5 .C6 2944

(?)

Larsen, Laurids Johan.

Kjøbenhavns Universitet. Dec. 12, 1873.

At bestemme forholdet mellem Spinozas og Fichtes etik.

Not seen BM

" " BN

L. T. S.

2948

Lasbax, Émile.

La hiérarchie dans l'univers chez Spinoza. Nouvelle édition augmentée d'un préface sur l'application de la méthode d'intuition vitale à l'histoire de la philosophie. Paris: Librairie Philosophique J. Vrin, 1926. 2 p. l., XXIV, 357, VII p. 8°. (Bibliothèque d'histoire de la philosophie.)

G-XI-37 [over]

---

2. 2950

Lasbax, É. [cont.]

Table des matières: Avertissement bibliographique [not found in book]. Introduction: Caractères généraux du spinozisme... Livre I. Les origines phylogénétiques du système. chap. I. Les grands courants de la philosophie antique... chap. II. La révolution cartésienne... Livre II. L'evolution ontogénétique. chap. I. Le thème

G-XI-37 [over]

---

2. 2951

Lasbax, Émile - La hiérarchie... [cont.]

directeur de l'adaptation... chap. II. La détermination de l'etre originaire. Le essence divine et son passage à l'existence... chap. III. L'existence de Dieu: la hiérarchie fondamentale des attributs divins dans la nature naturante... chap. IV. La hiérarchie des modes dans la nature naturée... chap. V. La conversion. - Le panthéisme de Plotin et le panthéisme de Spinoza (schéma comparatif [a table]). - Conclusion.

2955

[Lau, Theodor Ludwig.]

Zwey seltene antisupernaturalistische Manuscripte eines Genannten [i.e. T. L. Lau] und eines Ungenannten. Pendants zu den Wolfenbüttelschen Fragmenten. Berlin [really, Giessen], 1792. 2 p. l., (1)4-94 p. 8°.

The t.-p. does not form part of the sheet.

(H.U.C.) [over]

1-a. 2956

[Lau, Theodor Ludwig.] - Zwey seltene... [cont.]

1. De tribus mundi impostoribus breve compendium. De Moyse, Christo, et Mahumete. Descriptum ab exemplari Mspto. quod in Bibliotheca Io. Frid. Meyeri, Theol. D. publice distracta Berolini anno 1716 deprehensum, et a Principe Eugenio de Sabaudia Lxxx imperialibus redemtum fuit. (p. 1.)

2. Meditationes philosophicae de Deo, mundo, homine. Anno MDCCXVII. (p. 35.) On the p. following a prefatory note on the

---

2 2957

[Lau, T. L.]

author "Ioannes Theodorus Law" [!] and the tract. (De imposturis religionum).

With regard to item 1, F. W. Genthe (De impostura religionum breve compendium, Leipzig, 1833, p. 22) says: "Entweder nach dieser [1753; undated] Ausgabe oder nach einem Mscpt. veranstaltete i. J. 1792 zu Berlin (oder vielmehr Giessen) C. Ch. E. Schmid eine Ausgabe unter dem [over]

2-a 2958

[Lau, T.L.]- Zwey seltene... [cont.]
Titel: De tribus mundi Impostoribus, Mose, Christo et Mahomet, breve compendium. o. J. u. D. Kl. 8. 64S. Allein diese ganze Ausgabe wurde confiscirt und liegt unter Verschluss auf der Universitätsbibliothek zu Giessen." (Apparently, Genthe never saw a copy of this ed.) Weller, p. IX: "Ein neuer [Abdruck] steht in dem von C.C.E. Schmid edirten, aber beinahe vollständig confiscirten Büchlein: 'Zwei [!] seltene antisupernaturatisti-

3 2959

[Lau, T.L.]
sche Manuscripte'. Berlin (Krieger in Giessen) 1792". S. Briggs copies Weller. Presser, p. 122-123: "Die zweite Ausgabe [P. denies the existence of an ed. prior to that of 1753] ist vom Jahre 1792. Damals gab C.C.F. [!] in Giessen einen ~~Abdruck~~ Neudruck heraus unter dem Titel: Zwei [!] seltene antisupernaturalistische Manuscripte...' Die ganze Aufla- [over]

3-a. 2960

[Lau, T.L.]- Zwey seltene... [cont.]
ge wurde beschlagnahmt, nur wenige Exemplare entgingen diesem Lose..."

The typography resembles that of "Spinoza II". The two publications may have emanated from the same circle. The impetus most likely was given by the "Wolfenbüttel Fragments."

4 2961

[Lau, T.L.]
"Sechs Jahre nach L[essing]s Tode veröffentlichte der Kanonikus A[ndreas] Riem [1749-1807] die 'Übrigen noch ungedruckten Werke des Wolfenbüttelschen Fragmentisten [n.p., 1787, 8°] als Lessings Nachlass in acht Kapiteln". (W. Oehlke, Lessing, II, 550.) According to Max Weg, Katalog no. 35, p. 36, the editor was "C.A.E. Schmidt"
M. Weg, Lessing-Bibliothek [being] Katalog [over]

4a. 2962

[Lau, T.L.]- Zwey seltene... [cont.]
No. 31 (1894), p. 21, lists: Zwey seltene anti-supernaturalistische Manuscripte... 1792, with a note: "Eine der seltensten Schriften der 'Fragmenten Litteratur,' von keinem Lessing-Bibliographen erwähnt."
In a letter to Johann Albert Heinrich Reimarus, dated Apr. 10, 1770, Lessing writes that he is returning a parcel of books and MSS. borrowed, among them "Zwey Manuscripta de tribus Impostoribus." (Lessing, Sammtl. Schr., ed. Lachmann, Bd. 17, 1904, p. 319.)

JX 2000 L37H (NNC) 1861 2966

Laurent, François, 1810-1887.
La philosophie du XVIIIe siècle et le christianisme. Paris: A. Lacroix, Verboeckhoven & Cie., 1866. 8°. (In his: Histoire du droit gens et des relations internationales. v. 12.) (v. 12 publ. in 1866.
Spinoza, p. 239-254; 1er 82
18v. 1861-70.

Comp. v. d. L. 148 (XXXVI). [L'humanité
L. gives v. 12 as pt. of ser. of his Études sur l'histoire de [over]

DLC-BL51 .L45 MB; MH; [Clarke, S.] E 413
4 Law, Edmund, 1703-1787.
NIC An enquiry into the ideas of space, time, immensity and eternity, as also the self-existence, necessary existence, and unity of the divine ... Cambridge, 1734. [1703-1787], bishop of Carlisle, ed. of Locke's "Works" (1777).
Cambridge, W. Thurlbourn. 1734.
Against Clarke.
2 p. l., 196, 98 p. 20½ cm
(No index or table of contents. Spinoza ...)
NNC
LC 30-11321 - publ: Thurlbourn

G-XXI-6 2971

Laws,
Beurtheilung der Spinozistischen Substanz. (Koenigl. Progymnasium zu Rössel. Jahresbericht. [no.] 25. Rössel, 1857. 12°. p. 1-7.)

The superscription preceding the text (p. 1) reads: A. Beurtheilung der Spinozistischen Substanz und der Leibnitzischen Monaden. This is followed (p. 7) by: B. Beurtheilung der abso- [over]

G-XXI-6 2. 2972

Laws,- Beurtheilung der... [cont.]
luten Methode, which contains but two passing references to Spinoza.

Not in v. d. L., B., and Überw.- Weg. p. 12
N.Y.P.L. copy apparently a reprint (or lacks t.-p.)
(G unbd.)

893.15 L45 ~~N45.2-57~~ 2974

Lazarus, M.
Ethik d. Judenthums., Frankfurt am Main, 1899

p. 438 f. - L. fondly insists that S. was a past Talmud-jünger.

Includes a section on Spinoza (p. 438-442) in "Anhang" and other references to him.

2977

✓ Leander, Pehr Johan Herman, 1831-1907.
Om Substansbegreppet hos Cartesius, Spinoza och Leibnitz. Akademisk Afhandling... Lund: Berlingska Boktryckeriet, 1862. 2 p.L., 44 p. 8°.

4
MH
MH 4600.3.31
Pp.(4). 44.
no index nor table of contents seen.
oNNC
oLC
✓BM
Not in v.d.L.

PC L
NN- 1880 ed. 2v.
1.
E968
5 Spinoza, Baruch or Benedictus.
1838-1903.
Lecky, W[illiam] E[dward] H[artpole],
+ 1903
1866 ed.
211 L495
[Developments of rationalism and its influence on Biblical interpretation: Spinoza.] (In his: History of the rise and influence of the spirit of rational-
See next card.
NNJ- 1886 ed.
NE

PC L
2.
E969
Spinoza, Baruch or Benedictus.
Lecky, W[illiam] E[dward] H[artpole].-
Developments... [cont.]
D. Appleton
ism in Europe. New York, 1879. 8.
2v. 21cm
rev.ed. v.1, p.305.)

Footnote: Spinoza was, as far as I know,
✓1879 ed. in Philos. Lib NNC
See next card.

PC L
3.
E970
Spinoza, Baruch or Benedictus.
Lecky, W[illiam] E[dward] H[artpole].-
[Developments... [cont.]

the first writer who dwelt much on the possible or probable falsification of some portions of the Old Testament by
See next card.

PC L
4.
E971
Spinoza, Baruch or Benedictus.
Lecky, W[illiam] E[dward] H[artpole].-
[Developments... [cont.]

the insertion of wrong vowel-points, a subject which was a few years since investigated in a work on Hebrew Inter-
See next card.

PC L
5.
E972
Spinoza, Baruch or Benedictus.
Lecky, W[illiam] E[dward] H[artpole].-
[Developments... [cont.]

polations, by Dr. Wall, of Dublin University. Some of the remarks of Spinoza about the Jewish habit of speaking of
See next card.

PC L
6.
E973
Spinoza, Baruch or Benedictus.
Lecky, W[illiam] E[dward] H[artpole].-
[Developments... [cont.]

the suggestions of their own minds as inspirations are still worth reading, but with these exceptions the value of
See next card.

PC L
7.
E974
Spinoza, Baruch or Benedictus
Lecky, W[illiam] E[dward] H[artpole].-
[Developments... [cont.]

the Tractatus Theologico-Politicus seems to me to be chiefly historical.

211 L49
First pub. 1865.
card: 1866

NNUT: DG 559x
5
NNC has Le Clerc
2979
✓[Le Clerc, Jean.], 1657-1736
Sentimens de quelques theologiens de Hollande sur l'histoire critique du Vieux Testament, composée par le P. Richard Simon de l'Oratoire. Où en remarquant le fautes de cet auteur, on donne divers principes utiles pour l'intelligence de l'Ecriteure Sainte[par J. Le Clerc]. A Amsterdam: chez Henry Desbordes, 1685. 2p.l., 457p. 8°.
oNNC
oLC Spinoza, p.92-93, 122, 153, 162.
✓BN
Covers

2.
2980
[Le Clerc, Jean.] - Sentimens de... [cont.]
p. 92-93: with reference to R. Simon (to be quoted).

2981

Le Clerc, Jean [Johannes Clericus].

Sentimens de quelques theologiens de Hollande. 1685.

"These letters excited an immense sensation, especially in England; but they were after all a mere reflection of the ideas of Spinoza. As Père R. Simon truly observed 'En effet, ces Theologiens [from whom Le Clerc's work purported to have proceeded] n'ont fait autre chose pour combattre l'Inspiration de l'Ecriture Sainte, que de mettre en un plus grand jour les raisons de Spinosa, qui a outré cette matière sur de faux [over]

1-a. 2982 [cont.]

Le Clerc, Jean [Johannes Clericus] — Sentimens...

prejugés dont il etoit preoccupé.' [Notes: Histoire critique du Nouv. Test. ch.xxiv p.303. To the same effect Töllner writes: 'Spinoza und Le Clerc begegnen hier einander', p. 314.'] (W. Lee, Inspiration of Holy Scripture, p. 453.)

Note 2 (same p.): "A few of the works which were published in reply may be mentioned: - 'A Vindication of the Divine Authority and Inspiration of the writings of the Old and New Testament. In answer to the Five Letters concerning the Inspiration of Scripture', by W. Lowth

---

2 2983

Le Clerc, Jean.

Oxford, 1692; - 'The Inspiration of the New Testament asserted and explained, in answer to some modern writers', by C. J. Lamothe. London, 1694 (the occasion of which the author states, Pref. p. 3, to have been Les Clerc's 'Letters' to which replies had already appeared from 'M. Witsius in Holland, Mr. Lowth, a divine of Oxford, Father Simon, and Father Le Vassour'); - 'The Inspiration of the Old and New Testament', by Edm. Calamy. London, 1710, who observes in his Preface: 'There is more of subtility and [over]

2-a. 2984

Le Clerc, Jean. — Sentimens ... [cont.]

artifice in these Letters than in anything of that kind I ever yet met with."

---

2. E975

Le Clerc, Jean. — See: ... [cont.]

J. D. Duff, in Cambr. Hist. of Eng. Lit. (IX, 336): "A certain John Le Clerc, who with little real learning of any kind, had contrived to become a considerable figure in European literature"...

Locke's Essay was pub. in Le Clerc's Bibliothèque universelle in 1688.

E783

Hill, Rev. Samuel.

Criticized by Le Clerc.

Rev. Dr. Turner

p. 45-47: passages from the Ethics are translated. (over)

2985

MH - Phil 3831.1 1. 8°. pp. 33.

5 Ledinský, Franz.

Die Philosophie Spinoza's im Lichte der modernen Naturforschung. Betrachtet von Franz Ledinský. Eine von der philosophischen Facultät der Universität Rostock genehmigte Promotionsschrift. Original-Abhandlung. Budweis: Druck von J. Krupička & Comp., 1871. 33p. 8°.

o NNC
o ZC

[over]

---

2. 2986

Ledinský, Franz. — Die Philosophie ... [cont.]

[Contents: Einleitung. Die Naturphilosophie Spinoza's. Vergleich der Spinozistischen Philosophie mit der modernen Naturforschung.]

(Harvard) "Ledinsky ... kenne ich nicht (D.-B., Sp. nach 300 J., p. 168).

NNUT - NY, 1857 + NY 1866 ed's E982

4 Lee, William. 1815-1883

MH The inspiration of Holy Scripture, its nature and proof: eight discourses, preached before the University of Dublin... Fourth edition. Dublin: Hodges, Smith and Co., etc., 1865. lxii p., 2 l., 104-607 p. 8°.

BM lxii [i.e. xliij] p., 1 l., 607 p. 22½ cm.

o NNC Preface to 1. ed. dated 1854; to 2. ed., 1857; to 3. ed., 1864, and postscript, 1865.

LC has NY, 1857, 58

MH-C 1273.25.37

For Sp., see General Index, p. 605: i.e. p. 67, 182, 283, 409, 415, 585, 453. [over]

1-a E983

Lee, William. — The inspiration of... [cont.]

p. 453: "Meanwhile a systematized opposition to the inspiration of Scripture was growing up in another quarter, an opposition suggested by the writings of one through whom, as will presently be seen, the source of every hue and shade of modern scepticism on this question may be ultimately traced." He quotes Quinet, Töllner, R. Simon "with reference to the Tr. Theol.-Pol. — Continuing (p. 464): "But I have said that the writings of Spinoza point out the source to which the several varieties of modern errors respecting Inspiration may be traced. Spinoza, in a word, by bringing the opinions of his nation under the notice of subsequent writers, has introduced into Christian theology the speculation of the mediaeval Jews, and more [next]

2 E 984

Lee, William.

particularly the philosophy of Maimonides [note 3: Baumgarten Crusius (Bibl. Theol., p. 220) having communicated the notion of the 'intellectus agens' put forward by Maimonides, truly says: 'Maimonides ist in diesem Artikel, und überhaupt, die Quelle des Spinoza'.], the master spirit of his race during the Christian era". ["Intellectus agens" (active intellect), according to Wolfson, I, 404, goes back to the Greeks.]
(Grotius, Votum Pro Pace Ecclesiastica, Op., ed. 1679, quotes Maimonides directly.)

cover

2-e. E 985

Lee, William. — The inspiration of ... [cont.]

Again (p. 453): "Spinoza ... was the first, observes Töllner [Die göttliche Eingebung, p. 452], 'who made a tolerably complete collection of the objections against Inspiration. The result was curious. Some theologians gave up the cause as entirely lost; while others attempted still to maintain it, according to the usual theory.' The subject, thus placed upon a new footing, was soon taken up in a kindred spirit by Le Clerc, whose celebrated Letters entitled 'Sentimens de quelques Theologiens de Hollande' were first published in 1685. The Letters excited an immense sensation,

3 E 986

Lee, William.

especially in England; but they were after all a mere reflection of the ideas of Spinoza."

NOS 6-25

Baumgarten-Crusius, L. Fr. Otto (Ludwig Friedrich) 1788-1843 269

"Maimonides ist in diesem Artikel [the notion of the 'intellectus agens'], und überhaupt, die Quelle des Spinoza" (Bibl. Theol., p. 220). — date n vol. ???

Quoted by S. Lee, Inspiration of Holy Scripture, p. 454, note 3.

Comp. Wolfson.

NNC, LC } Lee

2987

Leendertz, W.

Spinoza. (Algemeen Weekblad voor Christendom en Cultuur. jrg. 9, no. 4, 1932, p. 3.)

Sp. & religion. (Not same as article in N. Arnhemsche Courant.)

not seen ULS

(Q.)

S-XXIV-10 2994

Leenhof, Frederik van.

De geest en conscientie des menschen, in haar eygen wezen en werkingen eenvoudiglyk verklaart, tegens de verwarde gedagten en valsche meeningen van veele, byzonder van geene, welke hedendaags dryven dat de conscientie des menschen dwalen kan. Rotterdam, 1691.

~~Use zweite Aufl~~ ~~AAUT~~ 3021

QJ4 L52 A 1915 (1-2) NNC

Leibniz, Gottfried Wilhelm, Freiherr von, 1646-1716.

Hauptschriften zur Grundlegung der Philosophie. Übersetzt von A. Buchenau. Durchgesehen und mit Einleitungen und Erläuterungen herausgegeben von E. Cassirer. Bd. 1. Leipzig: Verlag der Dürr'schen Buchhandlung, 1904. VIII, 374 p., 1 l. 8°. (Philosophische Bibliothek. Bd. 107.)

193L53 J7

Zu Spinozas Ethik, p. 355-374.

From the text of: Gerhardt, C.J. Die philosophischen Schrift- [cover]

LC

2. [cont.] 3032

Leibniz, Gottfried Wilhelm von. — Hauptschriften von G.W. Leibniz. Berlin, 1875-1890.

v. 1, p. 139-150.

1875, 112 "Leibniz und Spinoza"

on 2 sep. yellow sheets - #3021aa + 3021ab

193 L53 ✓ 3024

Leibniz, G. W. von.

Lettres et fragments inédits... (1669-1704); ed. P. Schrecker. Paris: Alcan, 1934. 136 p.

Spinoza? Not in Index des noms".

C-XXII-47 3033a

Leibniz,

Réfutation inédite de Spinoza par Leibniz. Précédée d'un mémoire par A. Foucher de Careil. Paris, 1854 6 p. l., CVI p., 3 l., 1 [unnumbered], 77 p. 8°.

Avant-propos: 4 l. [verso of l. 4 blank]. Mémoire sur la réfutation inédite de Spinoza par Leibniz: 1 l., CVI p. Notice sur le De recondita Hebraeorum philosophia [over]

0-XXVI-47 [Wachter, J. G.] 3033b

Leibniz,

Réfutation inédite de Spinoza par Leibniz. Précédée d'un mémoire par A. Foucher de Careil. Paris, 1854 8.

Notice sur le De recondita Hebraeorum philosophia [Elucidarius cabbalisticus; sive, Reconditae Hebraeorum] de Wachter.
Latin text and French tr. The original ti. in: Animadversiones ad Joh. Georg. Wachter

[over]

0-XXVI-47 2 3033c

Elucidarius cabalisticus; sive, Reconditae Hebraeorum philosophiae brevis & succincta recensio.

—— (In: Foucher de Careil, A. Leibniz, Descartes et Spinoza ... Paris 1862, 8º. p. 179-220.)
French translation only.

[over]

0-XXVI-47 3 3033d

Keine 'Widerlegung' Sp.'s bieten; sie gaben vielmehr nur den erwünschten Anlass, sich vom Standpunkt der Monadenlehre aus mit einigen Grundlehren des Spinozismus auseinanderzusetzen." (Stein, L. Leibniz und Spinoza, 1890, p. 236, note.)

"Was diese Animadversiones wirklich beweisen, ist das genaue Gegentheil von dem, was Foucher de Careil aus ihnen folgern will.

[over]

0-XXVI-47 4 3033e

In a footnote (p. 237) Stein lists the references in the Animadversions to Spinoza's several writings. Apparently, Stein did not have Wachter's Elucidarius before him; for the several references in the Animadversions are taken over by L. from W.'s little book.

3034

Leibniz,

See: Carr, Herbert Wildon.

3035

Leibniz,

See: De Nardi, Pietro.

3036

Leibniz, Gottfried Wilhelm von.

See: Heidenfeld, A. F. T.

3037

Leibniz,

See: Heinze, Max.

3038

Leibniz, G. W. von.

See: Herbart, J. F.

3039

Leibniz.

See: Leander, P. J. H.

3040

Leibniz.
See: Robertson, George Croom.

---

2. E994

Spinoza, Baruch or Benedictus.

Leifchild, John R[ ]. -The higher... [cont.]
New York: G.P.Putnam & Sons, 1872.
xvi, 543 p. 12. (The great problem.)

chap. IX. Pantheism and Spinozism, p.149-172. - chap. X. Spinoza and Leibnits: the

See next card.

3041

Leibniz, Gottfried Wilhelm von.
See: Stein, Ludwig.

---

3. E995

Spinoza, Baruch or Benedictus.

Leifchild, John R[ ]. -The higher... [cont.]

significance of the individual, p.173-196. - Pantheistic immortality [running title], p.450-452.

3042

Leibniz.

See: Volz, L.

3045

Leisegang, Hans.

See: Lessing, G.E. ?

3043

Leibniz.
See: Zimmermann, Robert.

O-XXIX-16 3049

Le Moine, A
Des vérités éternelles selon Malebranche. Paris: Librairie Philosophique Vrin, 1936. 292 p. [1-2 blank], 2 l. [last blank]. 8°.

Malebranche et Spinoza, p. 275-292.

(A.S.O.) unbd.

CtY-L-London, Hodder & Stoughton, 1872 1. E993
xviii, Spinoza, Baruch or Benedictus.
543 p. 20 cm.
Leifchild, John R[ ], 1815-
MH Phil 8591.3 4
The higher ministry of nature viewed in the light of modern science, and as an aid to advanced Christian philosophy. With an introduction by Howard Crosby.

oLC No author index! See next card.
author oDNB oWho's who

G-LV-23 3060

Leopold, J. H.
Spinoza en de Stoa. (Nederlandsche spectator. [jaarg.] 1905. p. 172-174.)

see G XXII - 21 3062

Leroux,

L'indéterminisme latent de Spinoza. (Revue philosophique. v. 49, 1924, p. 301-308.)

G-XXII-32 2 3079

L[euckfeld], J. G.

Franckfurth: Gedruckt bey Joh. Gottlieb Wahrhafft, 1699. 14 p.l., 698 [rather, 684] p., 1 pl. [folded]. 8°.

paged 1-33, 53, 212, 203-636, 621-698.

Spinoza, p. 82-83.

(G.) Not mentioned in Spinoza literature. Name in Jöcher.

[over]

G-XXII-21 3062b

Leroux, Emmanuel.

L'indéterminisme latent de Spinoza.

extrait de Revue Philosophique de la France et de l'Étranger (Sept.-Oct. 1924. p. 301-308).

G-XXII-32 2-a. 3080

L[euckfeld], J. G. – Der verführische ... [cont.]

"Unter andern Atheisten hat sich auch ein gebohrner Jüde nahmens Benedictus besser Maledictus Spinosa ... mit einen [!] solchen Läster=Buch hervor gethan, dergleichen die Welt kaum gesehen, so er Tractatus Theologico politicus ... nennet ... und wie die Unterredner der Monathl. Ergetzlichkeiten P. I. p 991 melden, soll er einer der grösten Atheisten gewesen seyn ..." Follows the fable of Spinoza's orders when dying not to let any clergyman come into his room, quoting the same source, a fable first recorded by Bayle in his: Pensées diverses sur les Comètes (1680).

G-XXII-26 3070

[Lessing, G.E.]

Leisegang, Hans.

Lessings Weltanschauung. Leipzig: Verlag von Felix Meiner, 1931. xi, 205 (1) p. 8°.

Die Gespräche über Spinoza, p. 159-179.

(G.)

Reg. by AH - Not in Un. Cat. 7/23/62 1 3082

not seen BM

Le Vassor, Michel.

1 De la véritable religion. 1688.

Paris, C. Barbin, 1688. In-4°, ..., 710 p. fig.) BN, 96, col. 1075

Tractatus de vera religione. Paris, 1688. (D.)

"Da ... Werk ... (710 Seiten grossen Formats) beschäftigt sich übrigens mit Spinoza nicht genauer, wenn auch oft von ihm gesprochen wird; der author hat es nicht mit der Ethik, sondern nur mit dem theologisch-politischen Traktat zu tun, über den er von seinem theologischen Standpunkt aus in sehr wegwerfender Weise redet." (Erhardt, p. 5, note.)

G-XXII-32 3077

L[euckfeld], J[ohann] G[eorg].

Der verführische Atheisten-Hauffe und das ungöttliche Wesen unter den Christen, worinnen so wohl der Sinn= und thätlichen Atheisterey ausführliche Beschreibungen, als auch drey sonderbahre Haupt=Quellen, nemlich das Hoff= Kriegs= und Universitets=Leben, woraus das ungöttliche Wesen am meisten über die

[over]

O-XXVII-26 3085

Levensbeschryving van eenige voornaame meest Nederlandsche mannen en vrouwen... Uit egte stukken opgemaakt. Tweede deel. Te Amsterdam: by P. Conradi, Te Harlingen, by F. van der Plaats & Junior, 1775. 8°.

Het leven van Benedictus de Spinoza, p. 291-301.

Follows Colerus (date of birth: 1633; removal to Rhynsburg: 1664). The quotation from Spinoza's letter to Jarig Jelles,

[over]

G-XXII-32 1-a. [cont.] 3078.

L[euckfeld], J[ohann] G[eorg]. – Der verführische ...

Länder zu fliessen pfleget, mit einigen Exempeln und dienlichen Anmerckungen dargestellet und gewiesen werden. Auf Veranlassung des itzo in der Christenheit seyenden verwirten Zustandes verfertiget, und mit genehmhaltung einiger Freunde zum Druck übergeben von J. G. L. auff Unkosten Henrici Theophili Steins.

O-XXVII-26 2. 3086

Levensbeschryving van ... [cont.]

given by Bayle, is here given (in Dutch) on p. 301.

Mentioned by B. Nieuhoff, p. 253, "welke levensbeschrijving is overgeschreven in het vaderlands woordenboek door J. Kok, Amst. 1792. XXVII deel, bl. 297 vol 88."

Levi, Adolfo.
Il problema dell'errore nella filosofia di B. Spinoza. Palermo: Industrie Riunite Editoriali Siciliane, 1933. 17 p., 1 l. [blank]. 8°.

Repr.: Sophia. 1933.

Levi, Adolfo. – Il problema ... [cont.]

A. S. O. (unbd.). With author's autograph dedication.

Levisohn, George [also known as Mordecai Gumpel Schnaber].
[Hebrew] ... Hamburg, 1792. 4°.
[see #3094a - may be 1822]

Attacks Spinoza.

Ref.: Grunwald (under Schnaber)
Sokolow, p. (176)
Lachower, P., in [Hebrew], yr. 4, no. 26, Dec. 15, 1932. [See sep. cards.]
MH. Bloch, P., Geschichte der Entwicklung der [over]

Levisohn, George [also known as ...] [cont.]
der Kabbala ... (Trier, 1894), p. 164-165.
The J.E. (v. Levisohn, George) does not mention the [Hebrew]. – Fürst (Levison) does. Bloch.
MH-K6918 Philipp "[?]"

Levy, A.
Spinozas Bildnis. (Archiv für Geschichte der Philosophie. Berlin, 1909. Bd. 23; 1910 Heft 1, p. 117-140.)

Against E. Altkirch; maintains that the portrait does not represent Spinoza.

(in Sp. Coll.)

(H.U.C.)

Levy, J. H.
Religion and theolatry. (Jewish chronicle [London]. Sept. 11, 1903, p. 6.)

Letter to the editor. – See also:

Jewish chronicle, July 17, 1908, p. 16-17; article entitled: A modern Spinoza. Interview for the Jewish Chronicle with J. H. Levy.

[over]

Levy, J. H. – Religion and ... [cont.]
—— Daiches, Sally. Religion and theolatry. (Jewish chronicle. Sept. 18, 1903, p. 13.)
Reply to J. H. Levy in a letter to the editor.
—— S[ ], S. F. Mr. J. H. Levy on Spinoza. (Jewish chronicle. Sept. 18, 1903, p. 13.)
Letter to the editor.

Levy, J. H. – Religion and ... [cont.]
2) —— Levy, J. H. Religion and theolatry. (Jewish chronicle. Sept. 25, 1903, p. 6.)
Reply to S. Daiches.

1) —— Jacobs, Maurice. Mr. J. H. Levy on Spinoza. (Jewish chronicle. Sept. 25, 1903, p. 6.)

[over]

Levy, J. H. – Religion and ... [cont.]
—— Daiches, Sally. Religion and theolatry. (Jewish chronicle. Oct. 2, 1903, p. 8.)
Rejoinder to the above.
—— A[dler?], M[arcus?]. Mr. J. H. Levy on Spinoza. (Jewish chronicle. Oct. 2, 1903, p. 8-9.)
Letter to the editor on the controversy.

NNC has Adler, Marcus Nathan
OLC

Levy, J. H. – Religion and ... [cont.]
2) —— Levy, J. H. Religion and theolatry. (Jewish chronicle. Oct. 9, 1903, p. 6.)
Reply to S. Daiches's earlier [first?] letter.

1) —— Jacobs, Maurice. Mr. J. H. Levy on Spinoza. (Jewish chronicle. Oct. 9, 1903, p. 7.)
Reply to M. A.

Lévy-Bruhl, Lucien.

History of modern philosophy in France ... London: K. Paul, Trench, Trübner &Co., 1899. Xp., 1 l., 5000 p., 23 port. 8°.

Spinoza, see Index, p. 500.: 36, 51, 60, 76, 105, 169, 179, 388, 423, 432, 434.

[L.L.] [over]

2 E1011

Lévy-Bruhl, Lucien.

p. 60: "This [M.'s God-conception] seems to border very closely upon Spinozism, a doctrine which Malebranche himself deemed 'monstrous'. In what does this God, who is at once a unity and an infinite multiplicity of infinite attributes, and who comprises within Himself all real and possible creatures, differ from the divine substance which, according to Spinoza, is the one only being? Is the difference that Malebranche conceives God as spiritual, whereas Spinoza admits of no hierarchy among the [over]

2-a. E1012

Lévy-Bruhl, Lucien. — History of... [cont.]

attributes of the divine Being? But Malebranche himself confesses that reason alone cannot teach us that God is spirit; this is taught us by Holy Scriptures."

p. 76: "An admirable metaphysical system was the fruit of such candid boldness and pious temerity. Malebranche was thereby enabled to say, as a Christian, a great part of what Spinoza said as a free-thinker."

Fénelon and Spinoza, p. 105: "When he [Fénelon] tries to be a philosopher he is a follower of Descartes and the latter's enthusiastic disciple, and if he ceases to follow him, he occasionally goes astray. Thus, when he undertook to refute Spinoza, he opposed his doctrine by one far more akin to real Spinozism than the imaginary Spinozism which he was combatting."

Taine + Spinoza, p. 423-425, 432, 434.

1-a. E1010

Lévy-Bruhl, Lucien. — History of... [cont.]

Spinoza and Descartes, p. 36: "Spinoza adopted the definition which Descartes had given of soul and matter, but in thought and extension he saw only two attributes of one and the same substance."

Spinoza and Malebranche, p. 51, 60-62, 76.

"The hypothesis of the 'vision in God', the most probable and indeed the only probable one, according to Malebranche, seems to our common sense extremely paradoxical... Yet it is a legitimate corollary of the principles established by Descartes; and the theories of Spinoza and Leibniz on this point, though difficult in expression, are not very remote from that of Malebranche." (p. 51).

Lévy-Bruhl, Lucien, 1857-1939. (?)

History of modern philosophy in France. Chicago: The Open Court Pub. Co. [London: K. Paul, Trench, Trübner & Co., Ltd.], 1899. X, 482 p. 8°.

[Tr. G. Coblence.]

Sp.-See Index, p. 500.

[L.L.]

Lévy-Bruhl, L[ucien].

La philosophie de Jacobi. Paris: F. Alcan, 1894. 1 p. l., (I) VI-XXXVIII, 263 p., 1 l. 8°. ([Bibliothèque de philosophie contemporaine])

Capitre VI: Jacobi et le spinozisme (p. 139-173).

[L.L.] (A.S.O.)

[Lewes, George Henry.] 1817-78

Spinoza.- Spinozism. (In: Penny, The, cyclopaedia. London: C. Knight & Co., 1842. fo. v. 22, p. 350-353.) Articles on Spinoza + Spinozism

The authorship of ~~By G.H. Lewes?~~ See v.d.L. 140 (note). these 2 articles was acknowledged by Lewes in a footnote at the end of the Spinoza chapt. in his Biographical hist. of philosophy.

Penny cyclopaedia of the Society for the Diffusion of Useful Knowledge.

Spinoza.- Spinozism. [By G. H. Lewes.] London: C. Knight & Co., 1841. fo. v. 22, p. 350-353.

ad. f-8

Lewkowitz, Julius.

Spinoza's Cogitata metaphysica und ihr Verhältnis zu Descartes und zur Scholastik. Breslau: Druck von Th. Schatzky, 1902. 79 p. 8°.

(G.)

Leydekker, Jacobus.

De blyde Spinosist en De bedroefde Christenleeraar over de Wysgeerige verhandelinge van de natuure Gods, welke de Heer Jacobus Wittichius, thans Phil. Doctor en ordinair Professor te Leiden in den jare 1711. te Duisberg uitgegeven en verdedigt, nu in Maart 1719. in't Nederduits vertaalt, en met aanmerkingen verrykt in't ligt [over]

G-XXII-33 1-a. 3126

Leydekker, Jacobus. — De blyde ... [cont.]
gebragt heeft. Onder beter oordeel opgestelt, door Jacobus Leydekker, Predikant te Middelburg, en uitgegeven op speciaal begeren van de E. Classis van Walcheren. Hier by komt het eenparig oordeel van de Philosophische Faculteit der Academie van Jenen, toegestemt van de Theologische aldaar, over die gemelde Wysgeerige verhandeling. Te Rotterdam:

G-XXII-33 2 3127

Leydekker, J.

By Reinier van Doesburg, boekverkooper, 1719. 6p.l., 101(1)p. 4°.

v. d. L. 270 (not seen).

Contents: Opdragt aan de ... Heeren ... van de vier Classen van Zeeland ... (5 l.). Erste deel: De blyde Spinosist ... (p.1-38). Tweede deel: De bedroefde Chris- [over]

G-XXII-33 2-a 3128

Leydekker, Jacobus. — De blyde ... [cont.]
tenleeraar ... (p.39-82). Advys en oordeel van de theologische en filozofische Faculteit van Jenen ... Latyn en Duits (1. Litterae ... J.F. Buddei; 2. Judicium Theologicae & Philosophicae Facultatis Jenensis, p.83-101).

(G.)

3142

[Library.]

Berliner Lokal-Anzeiger.
Spinozas Bibliothek. [Notice] (1915, no. 213.)

Reprinted in: [Glatzel, R.W.] Zum Charakter Spinozas ... Halle (Saale), 1919. 4°. p.103-104.

Apparently a review of the Catalogus of the Spinozahuis.

3145

Liebreich, Wilhelm.
Examen critique du Traité théol.-pol. de Spinoza. Strassb., 1869.

Not in v. d. L., B., W., or N.Y.
Ueberweg, p.672. (D.)

G-XXIII-34 3162

Lindner, E[rnst] Otto [Timotheus].
De relatione quae inter Spinozae Cogitata metaphysica et Cartesii doctrinam intercedit. Dissertatio... Vratislaviae: Typis Fritzianis, [1844]. 1p.l., 31(1)p. 8°.

Not in v. d. L. or B. — Weg, p. 12. (N.Y.P.L.) (G.)

NN-NAY 4 E1043

Lindsay, James Alexander, 1856-1931
Among the thinkers; leaves from my notebooks. London: H.K. Lewis & Co Ltd, 1931. 12°.

Quotations from Spinoza's writings.
IX, 197p. 12°
See "Index of Authors": p. 8, 30, 58, 151.
(arranged by subject)

ONNC OLC

109 L64 (2.) E1039

Lindsay, James.
Studies in European philosophy. Edingburgh: W. Blackwood and Sons, 1909. XXI, 370p. 8°.
LC 10-8431 nl (4) 9-16-58
Chapter XIII: The philosophy of Spinoza, p.154-170. — See also Index.
A revised and somewhat modified reprint of the preceding article. — "Only certain features of the philosophy of the great and admirable Spinoza, that more especially call for criticism, will be noticed in this chapter" (p.154). "For his fine pedagogic influence we are [over]

2-a E1040

Lindsay, James. — Studies in ... [cont.]
grateful to Spinoza, although a critical study leaves him no more taus than a schoolmaster to bring us to some better form of idealism than his own" (p.170). The sentence (p.160): "One may regard this [Spinoza's influence on subsequent speculation] as the more surprising, considering his confused methods and unclear modes of speech," is not found in the Archiv article.
Contents: Metaphysical setting of Spinoza's philosophy. — His doctrines of God, substance, and causality. — Personality. — Anthropomorphism. — Extension and thought. — Spinoza's psychology. — Attributes and modes — Grandeur of Spinoza's conceptions. — Their lack of consistency. — Deus sive natura. — Spinoza's monism. — Criticism of his harmonisation of attributes and modes with substance. — His ontological position — Natura naturata. — Lack of ethical quality. — Metaphysical basis of ethics. — His scheme too intellectualistic. — His teachings on immortality [next]

(2b.) E1041

Lindsay, James. [cont.]
Treatment of evil. — Ethical versus cognitive activity. — Spinoza on the passions. — On the self. — On Love — Fatal mistake of his philosophy. — Disregard of finite individuality. — His indebtedness. — His influence. — Merits and defects of his system.

(L.L.)

3183

Loewinger, Wilhelm.
Spinoza. Anlässlich der 250. Wiederkehr seines Todestages, 21. Februar 1677. Mit 2 Porträts und 2 Abbildungen. (Menorah. v. 5, no. 2, 1927, p. 117-124.)

Pub. in Wien?

G-XI-55

3187

Longo, Giacomo, 1818-1906.
Il monismo. Catania, 1893.

Grunwald. (Not in Überweg.)

3184

Lo Giudice, Giuseppe.
Un martire della scienza, ovvero Benedetto Spinoza. Milano: Lombardi, 1872. 12 p. 8°.

Ravà, no. 10. (Not seen.)

MH Gov 6605.2 SW E 1059

Lorimer, James, 1818-1890.
The institutes of law; A treatise of the principles of jurisprudence as determined by nature. Edinburgh, London, 1880. xx, 572 p. W. Blackwood and Sons, 2. ed. 8°. 22½ cm
Spinoza, p. 385-387 (et passim). p. 355 See Index, p. 570.

JX 200C L89 In 7 1883 (Int Law-NNC) 1883-84 ed. title differs
NjNbS 1872 ed.

LC 33-13247 nd 3-4 nd 1-6-59

NN-*DA E 1050

NN-*DA ULS gives London guilt by and
Holborn reviews (ref only from this title)

London (The) quarterly review.
Spinoza. London, 1877. 8°. v. 48, p. 124-152.

Literature reviewed or referred to:
Nourrisson, J. F. Spinoza... 1866. ✓ in Bibl.
Lewes, G. H. History of philosophy. ✓ in Bibl.
Hunt, J. Essay on pantheism. 1866. - 1893 in Sp Coll
Times [London]. Feb. 28, 1877. - Sep. cd. ✓ typed
Shelock in Business

[over]

701 L89 3198

Lotze, Hermann.
Geschichte der Aesthetik in Deutschland. München, 1868.

p. 167-? no ref. Sp. not in Namenreg.

LC 2-8755 (Cotta) nd 3-26 L91- no refs seen

(Baldwin, Dictionary.) [L.L.]

2. E 1051

London (The) quarterly review. - Spinoza... [cont.]
"The one correct judgement in a superficial attack published in a denominational review in 1877 is that Spinoza has been loaded with more infamy and extolled with more enthusiasm than perhaps any other personage of modern times. That critic regarded the influence of his doctrine as 'a subtle and deadly malaria,' chiefly on the ground, obviously true but hardly worth proving, that it cannot be reconciled with the popular notion of personal immortality." (Sir F. Pollock, Spinoza. [1935.] p. 15.)

843.19 L9524 E 1076
L9524 relics in the collections (p. 203-06) and
other refs. to him.

Lowenthal, Marvin.
A world passed by. Scenes and memories of Jewish civilization in Europe and North Africa. Fully illustrated. New York and London: Harper & Brothers, 1933. 8°.

nd 7-16-58 Spinoza, p. 203-206. See also Index. Spinoza memorials in Holland. Mainly a description of the

[over]

3188

Longo, Michele.
Spinoza. Torino: Bocca, 1916. 225 p. 16°. (Piccola biblioteca di scienze moderne. [no.] 260.)

Ravà, no. 27. (Not seen.)

2. E 1077

Lowenthal, Marvin. - A world passed... [cont.]
Spinozahuis at Rijnsburg; also the Domus Spinozana at the Hague.

—— [Third printing.] New York: Behrman's Jewish Book House, 1938. 8°
Spinoza, p. 203-206.

NNUT-3rd ... 1821; 245, 41p. E1078

Lowth, William. 1661-1732

A vindication of the divine authority and inspiration of the writings of the Old and New Testament. In answer to a treatise lately translated out of French, entituled, Five letters concerning the inspiration of the Holy Scriptures [by Jean Le Clerc]. By William Lowth. Oxford: Printed at the Theater, and are to be sold by J. Wilmot, 1692. 18 p.l., 288 p. 8°. 16½ cm.

NNC
CtY
BM
William Andrews Clark Memorial Library
CLU (UCLA)

[over]

0-XV-37(1) 3 3205d

[Lucas, J. M.] [1735.]

At the foot of p. 47, in the Collection A.S. Oko is the catchword "L'esprit", which has been pasted over, as in the copy of the Leipzig Stadtbibliothek. Both copies, as well as those in the British Museum and the Munich Staatsbibliothek the footnote at p. 19 reads: "A une lieuë de Leyde", while the 2 copies in the Bibliothèque Nationale, Paris, and the copy in the Vienna Universitätsbiblio-

[over]

2. E1079

Lowth, William.— A vindication... [cont.]

Against the Tr. Theol.-Pol.: Preface (unpag.), p. 39-40, 75, 112, 120-121.

See also l. c.
D.W.L.

0-XV-37(1) 4 3205e

[Lucas, J. M.] [1735.]

Freudenthal knew only of 3 copies of this issue. Dunin-Borkowski knew of 6. We can list 10, as follows: British Museum, London; Bibliothèque Nationale, Paris (2 copies); Halle Universitätsbibliothek; (being ...) Leipzig Stadtbibliothek; Louvain University Library (being Baer no. 171); Spinozahuis, Rhynsburg (Sir Herbert Thompson's copy); A.S. Oko (being no. 43

Munich Staatsbibliothek (von Murr's copy); Vienna Universitätsbibliothek;

[over]

DLC; MWA; CLU (Wm A Clark Memorial) E1080

Lowth, William

A vindication of the divine authority and inspiration of the writings of the Old and New Testament. In answer to the "Five letters concerning the inspiration of Scripture. Oxford. 1692.

Against Le Clerc.
Spinoza?

3206

[Lucas, J. M.] (Jean Maximilien) [MSS.]

F. Mauthner was in possession of "eine saubere Abschrift von Vie und Esprit; der Sammler... klagt in einer Notiz zum 'Esprit', er habe dein Buch 1763 aus einer Handschrift im Besitze eines Stabsarztes vom Regiment Puttkammer abgeschrieben, als eine grosse Seltenheit, und habe dasselbe Werk eben jetzt, im Juni 1795, in einer Auktion für 6 Pfennig erstanden;

[over]

0-XV-37(1) 3205b

[Lucas, Jean Maximilien.] [1735

La vie de Spinosa, par un de ses disciples: nouvelles édition non tronquée, augmentée de quelques notes et du Catalogue de ses écrits, par un autre de ses Disciples &c. A Hambourg, Chez Henry Kunrath. M.DCC.XXXV. 2 p.l., 47 p., 6 l. 8°.

2. SCS 3207

[Lucas, J. M.]— F. Mauthner [cont.]

es habe nun den Titel geführt: des trois Imposteurs." (Der Atheismus ... Bd. 1, p. 320.)

und seine geschichte in abendlande. Stuttgart, Deutsche verlags-anstalt, 1920.

2 vols. 25.5 cm. SCS

NjP, MH-AH; NN; CtY; CLU

0-XV-37(1) 2 3205c

[Lucas, J. M.] [1735.]

Avertissement, 2 p., unnumbered; being, with some omissions and additions, the same as the "Préface" to the ed. in the Nouvelles Littéraires and the "Préface du Copiste" of the Le Vier ed. of 1719.- La vie de Monsieur Benoit de Spinosa, p. 1-44.- Catalogue de ouvrages de Mr. de Spinosa, p. 45-47 (p. 48 being blank).- Recueil

[over]

193 Sp4 SCS
G-BL?
E1081a

[Lucas, Jean Maximilien.]

The oldest biography of Spinoza. [Attributed to J. M. Lucas.] Edited with translation, introduction, annotations, etc., by A. Wolf. London: G. Allen & Unwin Ltd. [1927]. 196 p. [1-2 blank], 2 facs., 2 pl., 2 port. 8°.

3 p. l., [9]-196 p. ...

LC

Contents: Preface.- I. Introduction. II. The life of the late Mr. de Spinosa (translation). III. Additions to the printed texts of 1719 and 1735 (translations).

[over]

2. E 1081b

[Lucas, J. M.] – The oldest biography ... [cont.]

Illustrations: 1. Portrait of Spinoza (frontispiece; a reproduction of that of Wolfenbüttel). 2. Probable portrait of J. M. Lucas (known as a portrait [etching] of De La Fond, one of the names assumed by Lucas). 3. The Paviljoensgracht, in the Hague, as it looked formerly. 4. Pictorial title-page of the Towneley manuscript. 5. The house in the Paviljoensgracht, in which Spinoza lived his last years (1671–1677 [since 1927 known as the Domus Spinozana]). 6. Facsimile of the first page of the Towneley manuscript.

[over]

 E1081

[Lucas, J. M.]

Wolf, A., ed. and tr.
The oldest biography of Spinoza. [Review of.] (Journal of philosophical studies. v. 2, 1927, p. 403–405.) By H. H. Joachim.

"... Professor Wolf's translations, both from the French and from the Latin, are very far from satisfactory ... The real trouble, to speak frankly, is their poor quality".

[over]

---

1. 3210

Lucka, Emil.

Spinoza und Fichte. Eine Betrachtung über das Philosophieren. (Preussische Jahrbücher. Berlin, 1913. 8. Bd. 153. Bd

See next card.

---

2. 3211

Lucka, Emil.-Spinoza und Fichte... [cont.]
Bd. 153, 1913, p. 193–216.)

~~Excerpts.~~

p. 216: "Es ist für einen Denker von der Grösse Spinozas immerhin merkwürdig, dass er die ewige Frage des Warum? aller Existenz ... nicht kennt, dass er niemals an eine Grenze kommt, sondern im naturhaften Dasein völliges Genügen findet. Für den grossen Denker ist dies erstaunlich – aber für den Repräsentanten seines Menschheitstypus kann es nicht wohl anders sein. Und der Mangel an persönlicher Problematik ist vielleicht das letzte Merkmal dieser Geistesart ..."

---

3 3212

Lucka, E.

A psychological study of the relationship between the man and his philosophy. Spinoza belongs to the type of the "Mittelmenschen"; Fichte to that of the "Grenzmenschen". The two are "die grössten Gegensätze, die sich vorstellen lassen". Spinoza's system is absolute rationalism. He is no mystic; not even a pantheist. Goethe was no Spinozist.

[over]

---

4 3214

Lucka, E.

palpable perversion of a saying of Spinoza's reported by Colerus in illustration of the sobriety and frugality of the philosopher. Colerus relates: "And he would say sometimes to the people of the House, that he was like the Serpent, who forms a Circle with his Tail in his Mouth; to denote that he had nothing left at the years end. He added,

[over]

4-a 3215

Lucka, E. – Spinoza und ... [cont.]

that he design'd to lay up no more money than what be necessary for him to have a decent Burying..."

Finally, we are told: "der Mittelmensch ist Monist, der Grenzmensch Dualist."

 3217

Lucka, Emil.

Vom Philosophieren. (In his: Stufen der Genialität. Zweiter Teil der Grenzen der Seele. Dritte bis fünfte erweiterte Auflage. Berlin, 1917. 8°. p. 93–147.)

(A.S.O.)

3223

Luiscius, A.G.

Het algemeen hist. geogr. en genealogisch woordenboek. deel 7. 's Gravenhage, 1737.

art. Spinoza.

(Mentioned in B. Nieuhoff, p. 253.)

3224

Luiscius, A.G.

Het algemeen historisch, geographisch en genealogisch woordenboek. 's Gravenhage, 1724–1737. 8 v. f°.

Spinoza?

Mc

M

052 NNC-4 Maccall E 640
f8 Fraser's Magazine for Town & Country, Vol. 71, 1865 p. 608-626.
French criticism on Spinoza. [Review of: Oeuvres de Spinoza tr. par É. Saisset. Nouv. ed. Paris, 1861.]
London, 1865. 8°. v. 71 1865 p. 608-626.
not signed.
By William Maccall. 1812-88 [See his letter of 23rd May, 1881, addressed to Sir F.P. in possession of A.S.O.]
A rev. of Oeuvres de Spinoza, par Emile Saisset; avec une introduction critique. Nouvelle édition revue et augmentée Paris, Charpentier

UN *DA E 1086
S
M.
Philosophy of Spinoza. (Southern quarterly review. Charleston, 1850. v. 16, p. 76-81.)
[Perhaps by G.S. Morris; ~~or W. Maccall, reprinted?~~]

A67 NNC E1092
McGiffert, A. Cushman Arthur 1861-1933 Ref 4
"Immanence." [In: Encyclopaedia of religion and ethics. v. 7, 1915, p. 169.)
Sp.-p169
The modern conception of Divine immanence had one of its principal roots in the system of Spinoza.
Full Article: p. 167-172.

0-IX-19 3260
Maggid, David.
[Baruch Spinoza.] (In his: הפרופיסור מרדכי בן מתתיהו אנטוקולסקי ... [Warsaw, 1897. 12°. p. 141-147.)
Being chap. 19 of the "Life and work" of Mark Matveyevich Antokolski; description of the Spinoza statue, but deals mainly with his life. He is called "Baruch ben Benjamin de [over]

Carpenter
E1093
MacIntyre, J. Lewis.
Giordano Bruno. London: Macmillan and Co., Limited, 1903. 8°.
Spinoza and Bruno - Bruno and Spinoza - Ratio and intellectus, p. 337-343. See also Index (which, however, does not give all the references to Spinoza).
Ord. 7-16-58
(Yale.)
over

0-IX-19 2. 3261
Maggid, David. — [Baruch Spinoza] ... [Cont.]
Espinoza", and "Olympia" van der Enden changed his name from Baruch to Benedict.
Plate: שפינוזא לפני מותו.
[check]
(A.S.O.)

NNU-T Univ Hts E1099
Mac Question, Rockwood. ?
Higher criticism the philosophical outgrowth of Spinozaism. 1893
card: MacQuesten, Rockwood
Ph. D. thesis, New York University. (1893.)
1 p., 9 l., VII l. 45 l.
typewritten
NNC
LC Not printed.
Author's address: 1673 Eastburn Av., Bronx, N.Y.

MH; OCH; OCH 3264
Mahnke, Dietrich, 1884-1939. Sp-R
"Leibniz und Goethe. Die Harmonie ihrer Weltansichten." Erfurt: Stenger, 1924. 82 p. 8°. (Weisheit und Tat. Heft 4.)
in Spin Coll.
Introductory chapter: Goethes Wahlverwandtschaft mit Spinoza und Ideengemeinschaft mit Leibniz.
Sp. p. 3, 7-11, 17-20, 23, 25

3267

Maier, E.
Die Lehre vom Wahren und Falschen bei Spinoza und Descartes. Diss. Leipzig, 1898.

Überweg, p. 669.

6-XXII-37
3275

Malapert, P.
De Spinozae politica. Thesim proponebat Parisiensi Litterarum Facultati. Paris: F. Alcan, 1897. 91[1]p., 2 ℓ [1 blank]. 8°.

(G.)

3281

Malebranche, N.
See: Cousin, V., ed.

3282

Malebranche.
See: Dandolo, Giovanni.

3283

Malebranche.
See: Fabbri, E.

3284

Malebranche.
See: Forsberg, N.A.

3285

Malebranche.
See: Ragnisco, Pietro.

Spec Coll Spin
3294

Mansvelt, Regner van.
Regneri à Mansvelt Philosophiae, dum viveret, Doctoris & Professoris in Academia Trajectina Adversus anonymum theologo-politicum liber singularis, in quo omnes & singulae Tractatus theologico-politici dissertationes examinantur & refelluntur, cum praemissa disquisitione de Divina per naturam, & Scripturam revelatione. Opus posthu- [over]

2.
3295

Mansvelt, Regner van.— Regneri à ... [cont.]
mum. [Vignette: Quaerendo.] Amstelaedami: Apud Abrahamum Wolfgang Bibliopolam, Anno 1674. 2 p.ℓ., 364 p. 4°.
v.d.L. 363. B.106. Weg, p.13. (N.Y.P.L. B.M. Spinozahuis. H.U.C.)
Spinoza possessed a copy of this work (Inventory, 4°, no. 41). He refers to the book in Ep. 50.— See Dunin-Borkowski, Spinoza, IV, p. 89-90.
(A.S.O. - G.)

0-XLV-13
3309

3) Marcus, Hanna.
Warum musste das traditionelle Judentum Spinoza ablehnen? Ein Nachtrag zur Spinoza-Feier. (Gemeindeblatt der israelitischen Religionsgemeinde zu Leipzig. v.3, no. 16, Apr. 22, 1927, p. 1-2.)

no 21 in folder

G-XXII-40 3311

Maréchal, J.

Le point de départ de la métaphysique. Leçons sur le développement historique et théorique du problème de la connaissance. Cahier II. Le conflit du rationalisme et de l'empirisme dans la philosophie moderne, avant Kant. Bruges (Belgique) C. Beyaert, [1923]. x p., 1 l. [blank], 189 (1) p. 8°. (Museum Lessianum. III. [over]

2. SPINOZA ROOM E1125a M

Martineau, James.-Types... [cont.]

v.2.

Not in Baer.

G-XXII-40 2. 3312

Maréchal, J. - Le point de ... [cont.]

Section philosophique. Publications. [Unnumbered.])

chap. 3. De Descartes à Spinoza: Spinoza et le monisme de la substance. §1. Introduction. 2. Epistémologie de Spinoza d'après le "Tractatus de intellectus emendatione"... chap. 4. (Suite.) §3. La métaphysique de Spinoza d'après l' "Ethique"... 4. Conclusions. (p. 71-94.)

(G. - unbd.)

G-XXII-43 3328

Martinetti, Piero.

La dottrina della conoscenza e del metodo nella filosofia di Spinoza. (Rivista di filosofia. anno 12, 1916, no. 3, p. 289-324.)

According to repr. (G.): anno 8, no. 3, 1916. 36 pp.

Ravà, no. 43.

G-XXIX-24 3322

Maret, H. L. C.

Essai sur le panthéisme dans les sociétés modernes. Troisième édition, revue et augmentée. À Paris: Chez Méquignon Junior et J. Leroux, 1845. 2 p. l., xxII, 494 p., 1 l. 8°.

Spinosa, p. 165-172.

(A.S.O.) C. G-XI-63

Spec Coll Spin 3329

Martinetti, Piero.

La dottrina della libertà in Benedetto Spinoza. (Chronicon Spinozanum. Hagae Comitis, 1926. v. 4, p. 58-67.)

Ravà, no. 45.

NNUT Q120 M37 1. SPINOZA ROOM E1126

Martineau, James, 1805-1900.

Types of ethical theory. v.1-2.

Oxford: Clarendon Press, 1885. 2 v.

8. (Clarendon Press series.)

Spinoza, v.1, p. 234-369.- a chapter See also index of p. [243]-393

See next card.

o NNC

LC 10-2418 vol 1-8-59

3330

Martinetti, Piero.

171.3 M36 La dottrina della libertà in Benedetto Spinoza (In his: La libertà. Milano, 1928. p. 271-282.)

Spec Coll Spin First pub. in Chronicon Spinozanum, v. 4.

(Not seen.)

E1126

Martineau, J.- Types...

"The chapter on Spinoza ... is not a reproduction or abridgment of the monograph on that philosopher which I published two years ago; but a fresh treatment of the given material which is necessarily common to both; marked indeed by no change of interpretation or judgment on important points, but only by such shifting of emphasis as the special exigency of an ethical treatise demanded" (Preface).

X208 M417a2 Note different publisher: Chez Raynal, Libraire,... 3337

Massillon, Jean Baptiste. (b., 1663. 1742)

"Sermon pour le mardi de la quatrième semaine de carême. Des doutes sur la religion." (In his: Oeuvres complètes IV; Sermons pour le carême. Tome troisième. Paris: Méquignon Fils Aîné, 1822. 8°. p. 213-256.) 1848 ed. in Bibliog. o NNC o LC

(Peabody Inst., Baltimore)

M38F Paris, 1821, v.2-6

See also p. 455-461, where an "analysis" of the sermon is given. Oeuvres complètes de Massillon, Tome IV,

(D.W.L.) 1830 ed. in L. L. Sermons pour le carême, Tome troisième. Paris, Chez Raynal... MDCCCXXI. [illegible]

NBuG 6 vols 1823-1825. 3338

Massillon, Jean Baptiste. †1742

Core collect BX1756 M32 1823

Sermon pour le mardi de la quatrième semaine de carême. Des doutes sur la religion. (In his: Oeuvres choisies; Sermons pour le carême. Tome deuxième. Paris: Delestre-Boulage, 1824. 8°. p. 480-429.)

A diatribe against Spinoza.

Spec coll Spin 3341

Matthes, J. C.

De bijbelcritiek van Spinoza. (Teyler's Theologisch tijdschrift. jaarg. 7, 1909, p. 151-173.)

O-XXIX-33 3342

Matthes, J.C.

D bijbelcritiek van Spinoza. n.t.-p. [Amsterdam, 1909.] 23p. 8°.

Title taken from paper-cover. Paged also 151-173.

Repr.: Teyler's Theologisch tijdschrift. jaarg. 7.

(A.S.O.)

O-XXIII-17 3360

Mauthner, Fritz.

Jacobi's Spinoza-Büchlein.

Review: Der Brenner (Innsbruck). Jahrg. 4, p. 289. By Will Scheller.

Theologische Literaturzeitung. Leipzig, 1914 Jahrg. 39, col. 541.

NNJ-ST 3369

5

✓Maybaum, Siegmund, 1844-1919.

Die Methodik d. jüd. Religionsunterrichts.

p. 44, note: the only author who refers to the Jewish dogmas formulated by Spinoza. (Neumark.)

NNJ-ST Breslau 1896 8° xii + 126p.

•NNC

oLC

Spec coll Spin 3374

Mazzantini, Carlo.

Spinoza e l'idealismo contemporaneo. (In: Spinoza nel terzo centenario della sua nascita; pubblicazione a cura della Facoltà di Filosofia dell' Università Cattolica del Sacro Cuore. Milano, 1934. 8°. p. 133-148.)

O-XXX-6-8 3390

Meijer, Willem.

Bestrijding van Professor Erhardt's Kritiek over de philosophie van Spinoza [F. E.: Die Philosophie des Spinoza im Lichte der Kritik; von F. Erhardt. Leipzig, 1908.] (Tijdschrift voor wijsbegeerte. Amsterdam, 1909. 8°. jaarg. 3, p. 371-398, 401-431.

Section II: De leer van God.- De attributen.- Gott und die Natur.- Die Naturphilosophie.- Das Wesen [over]

O-XXX-6-8 2. 3391

Meijer, Willem.— Bestrijding van... [cont.]

der Sittlichkeit.— Religionsphilosophie.— Schluss.

The headings are those of the 2. Teil of the book, entitled "Sachliche Kritik". Teil 1 ("Formelle Kritik") is taken up by the critic in section I.

28p.

(A. S. O.) Repr. in G. (Section I only.) G-XVII-47-2

O-XXX-6-9 3392

Meijer, Willem.

Bismarck en Spinoza. (Tijdschrift voor wijsbegeerte. Harlem, 1912. 8°. jaarg. 6, p. 60-66.)

Being a résumé of: Rosin, Heinrich. Bismarck und Spinoza, in Festschrift Otto Gierke.

(A.S.O.)

G-XXII-50 3393a

Meijer, Willem.

De consensu metaphysicae Spinozanae cum philosophia Arabica sive Moslemitica. (Chronicon Spinozanum. tom. 2, p. 14-19.)

0-XXX-6-3 3395c

Meijer, Willem.
De strijd der refugié's in Holland tegen het staatsbeleid van Lodewijk XIV. (Reprint from: Tijdspiegel. 's-Gravenhage, 1904. no. 9, p.

A monograph on Jean-Maximilian Lucas.
[from the library of F. Pollock]
(H.U.C.: Excerpt.)

0-XXX-6-7 3409

Meijer, Willem.
Over de verhouding van Spinozisme, Boeddhisme en Christendom. (Tijdschrift voor wijsbegeerte. Amsterdam, 1908. 8°. jaarg. 2, p. 331-354.)

(A.S.O.)

3393b

Meijer, W[illem].
De woning van Despinoza op de Stille Veerkade. (Die Haghe. Bijdragen en mededeelingen. [Year book] 's-Gravenhage, 1902. 12°. p. 207-217.)

See also p. 218-259, being an article by C. H. Peters: Een "In memoriam" gewijd aan de Amster-
[cover]

0-XXX-6-5 3399

Meijer, Willem.
Over Spinoza en den Godsdienst. (Tijdschrift voor wijsbegeerte. Amsterdam, 1907. 8°. jaarg. 1, p. 316-327.)

A critique of: Powell, E. E. Spinoza and religion... Chicago, 1906.
According to the Meijer bibliography (p. XXXIX): "Naar aanleiding van E.E. Powell's: Spinoza und Religion."

0-XXX-6-11 3408

Meijer, Willem.
Over de beteekenis en de waarde van het Godgeleerd-staatkundig vertoog van B. Despinoza. (Tijdschrift voor wijsbegeerte. Haarlem, 1917. 8°. jaarg. 11, p. 467-483.)

Against H. Cohen.

6-XXII-47-3

0-XXX-6-6 3400

Meijer, W[illem].
Over Spinoza en den Godsdienst. n.t.-p. [Amsterdam, 1907.] 12 p. 8°.

Title taken from first p.
Repr.: Tijdschrift voor wijsbegeerte. jaarg. 1, 1907.
A criticism of: Powell, E.E. Spinoza and religion... Chicago, 1906.

(A.S.O.)

0-XXX-6-4 3396

Meijer, W[illem].
Over de kenmerkende eigenschappen van de leer van Spinoza. (Voordracht gehouden den 27sten April 1906 in de jaarvergadering der Vereeniging: "Het Spinozahuis".) n.t.-p. [The Hague] 1906.] p. 153-169 p., 1 l. [blank]. 8°.

Repr.: De XXe Eeuw. jaarg. 1906, deel 4.

(A.S.O.)
[cover]

0-XXI-10 3434

Meijer, Willem.
[Review of:] Høffding, H. Spinoza's Ethica; Analyse og Karakteristik. København, 1918. n.t.-p. [Hagae Comitis, 1921.] 303-314 p. sq. 8°.

Title taken from first p.
Repr.: Chronicon Spinozanum. tom. 1.

(G.)

0-XXX-6-4 2. 3397

Meijer, W[illem]. - Over de ... [cont.]
With reference to the criticism of G. Heymans, Einführung in die Metaphysik (Leipzig, 1905), and the reviews by Prof. Bruynings [Bruijnings] in Gids, Nov. & Dec., 1905, and Prof. van der Wijck [Wyck] in Onze Eeuw, 1905. - Bijlage (p. 168-169) refers to Bierens de Haan's Levensleer van Spinoza.

G-XXX-9 3444

Meiners, C.
Grundriss der Geschichte der Weltweisheit. Lemgo: im Verlage der Meyerschen Buchhandlung, 1786. 8°.

Benedictus Spinoza, p. 271-274.

(G.)

 3480

Melamed, S[amuel] M[ax].

Spinoza and Buddha. Visions of a dead God. Chicago: The University of Chicago Press, [c1933]

3491

Melchior, Johannes.

Religio ejusque natura & principium; sive, Epistola qua ad examen vocatur Tractatus theologico-politicus. Ultrajecti, 1672. 8°.

v. d.L. 360. (He has not seen it.) ~~nor is it mentioned elsewhere~~ It is mentioned in Trinius (p. 437, no. 76): "Dieses ist die zweite Ausgabe". The first (1671) is not mentioned.

 3492

Melchior, Johannes, 1646-1689.

Johannis Melchior... Opera omnia theologica, exegetica, didactica, polemica, duobus tomis absoluta, quibus Veteris ac Novi Testamenti libri conferuntur, explicantur, illustrantur: Veritatis religionis Christianae argumentis validissimis asseritur, defenditur: Triplici indice locupletata. Herbornae Nassoviorum: Typis et sumptibus J. N. Andreae, 1693.

[over]

0-XXX-15 3496

not located

Meli, Fausto.

Spinoza e due antecedenti italiani dello spinozismo. Prefazione di Giuseppe Saitta. Firenze: G.C. Sansoni, 1934. VIII, 197p., 1l. 8°. (Pisa, Italy.- R. Scuola Normale Superiore. Studi di lettere, storia e filosofia. [v.] 3.)

Posthumously published.

Contents: Prefazione.- Parte I. Le dottrine religiose e politiche di Fausto Socino e i loro

[over]

---

2. 3493

Melchior, Johannes.— Johannis ... [cont.]

2 v. 4°

The "Religio ejusque natura et principium contra anonymi Tractatum theologico-politicum" or "Epistola ad amicum, continens censuram Theologo-politici", is contained in vol. 2, p. 1-46.

This ed. contains a preface.

Not in v. d. L.

1706 ed. NNUT-2v.- GW23, WS[?], A, 1706

(Spinozahuis, Cat. no. 186.)

0-XXX-15 1-a 3497

Meli, Fausto.— Spinoza ... [cont.]

sviluppi nel pensiero del secolo XVII: Il pensiero religioso e politico di Fausto Socino, Capitolo I. Fausto Socino e la tolleranza religiosa. Capitolo II. Religione e vita morale.— Significato e sviluppi del socinianesimo nel secolo XVII. Capitolo I. Soncinianesimo e suoi sviluppi. Capitolo II. I valori morali e i mistici iglesi. Capitolo III. Il razionalismo. Capitolo IV. Il socinianesimo e lo sviluppo del pensiero politico.— Iacoppo Aconcio.—

3489

M[elchior], J[ohannes]

J[ohannes] M[elchior] V[erbi] D[ivini] M[agister] Epistola ad amicum, continens censuram libri, cui titulus: Tractatus theologico-politicus, in quo demonstratur, &c. Ultrajecti: Ex Officinâ Cornelii Noenaert, Bibliop., 1671. 48p. 4°.

v. d. L. 359.

(G.) [over]

0-XXX-15 2. 3498

Meli, Fausto.— Spinoza ... [cont.]

Parte II. Sulla metafisica razionalistica dello Spinoza: Introduzione.- Il razionalismo. Capitolo I. L'idea chiara e distinta. Capitolo II. Il processo del conoscere. Capitolo III. Il metodo. Capitolo IV. L'immaginazione e l'intelletto.— La metafisica. Capitolo I. Deus seu natura.— Deus sive attributa. Capitolo II. Religione e filosofia. Il trattato teologico-politico.

---

2. 3490

M[elchior], J[ohannes].— J[ohannes]... [cont.]

Spinoza is not named; but it is evident that M. knew that he was the author of the Tractatus: he refers to him as "Zinopsa" or also "Xinopsa". Aside from this anagram, M. refers to the Descartes' Principia as being by the same author. On p. 46, we learn that the Epistola was finished in August, 1670: Daban apud Ubios sextileis, ch b c Lxx (Copies: Royal Library, the Hague; Hamburg [v.d.L.]; Weg; Jerusalem; N.Y.P.L. ["book missing apparently"]; G.

D-B. does not refer to it. Nor Überweg [1924].

G-XXIII-5 3567

Menzel, Adolf.

Beiträge zur Geschichte der Staatslehre. ~~(Ak. d. Wiss. Vienna. Phil.-hist. Kl. 1929.)~~ Wien: Hölder-Pichler-Tempsky A.-G., 1929. 582 p. 8°. (Akademie der Wissenschaften in Wien. Phil.-hist. Kl. Sitzungsberichte. Bd. 210, Abhandl. 1.)

Die Staatslehre Spinozas, p. 264-447.

~~Verify.~~ (G.)

3571

Meozzi, Antero.

Le dottrine politiche e religiose di B. Spinoza — parallelo con T. Hobbes. [Arezzo: Stab. Tipo-Lit. E. Sinatti], n.d. 2 p. l., 216 p. 12°.

[Contents: Capitolo I. Sintesi e significato del Trattato teologico-politico. II. Il metodo. I precursori di Spinoza. III. Della [cover]

1-a. 3572

Meozzi, Antero. — Le dottrine ... [cont.] rivelazione e dei profeti. IV. La ricostruzione ideale, la ricostruzione di Spinoza. VI (rather, V). Dottrine politiche di Spinoza. VI. Dottrine politiche di Hobbes. VII. Confronto tra due logici. VIII. Hobbes e Spinoza nella filosofia del diritto.]

(Harvard)

2 3573

Meozzi, A. — Le dottrine... [cont.]

Apparently a reprint. List of publications by author, following t.-p., contains entry: "Le dottrine politiche e religiose di B. Spinoza 1914, pag. 216, L. 3,00". On back of binding, done at H.C.L., is given 1915. The date of acquisition of book is given as June 11, 1928.

3584

[Meyer, L.] [note.]

F. Kettner ("Exercc. hist.-theolog. de religione prudentum", 1701, Thes. XV, p. 49, 69) declaims against Phil. S. Scr. Interpres, ascribed to Spinoza. (Grunwald, p. 291.)

In Journal de Hambourg [the same as Hamburg. Berichte von gel. Sachen?], Oct. 26, 1694, p. 133, Dartis (the editor), in a criticism of J. La Placette's Traité de la conscience, argues that the book De Jure Eccl. and the Tr. Theol.- [cover]

2. 3585

[Meyer, L.] — F. Kettner... [cont.] Pol. are both the works of Spinoza.

3613

Milan, Italy. — Università Cattolica del Sacro Cuore: Facoltà di Filosofia.

Spinoza nel terzo centenario della sua nascita. Pubblicazione a cura della Facoltà di Filosofia dell' Università Cattolica del Sacro Cuore. Milano: Società Editrice "Vita e Pensiero", 1934. v, 210 p., 1 l., 1 port. 8°. (Rivista di filosofia neo-scolastica. Supplemento speciale al volume 25, agosto 1933) [cover]

2. 3614

Milan, Italy. — Università Cattolica... [cont.]

Contents: Gemelli, A. Introduzione. — Vanni-Rovighi, S. La teoria spinoziana della sostanza e la metafisica tomistica. — Rotta, P. Il Cusano e lo Spinoza. — Campo, M. Spinoza e Kant. — Gancikoff, L. Aporie del panlogismo (Spinoza e Hegel). — Padovani, U.A. Schopenhauer, Spinoza e il panteismo. — Rossi, P. La fisica spinoziana e la fisica moderna. — Mazzantini, C. Spinoza e l'idealismo contemporaneo. — Gonella, G. Il diritto come potenza secondo Spinoza. — Vismara, S. La nullificazione della storia nella filosofia dello Spinoza. — Bestetti, A. La vita di Spinoza in rapporto al suo pensiero.

Wolfenbüttel port.

(A.S.O.)

Millner, Ia. (?)

3616

Millner, Simon (?)

Dr. Millner, in a letter of Oct., 1932, addressed to Sir Frederick Pollock, writes that he had pub. "in the years 1926-7-8 in Russian a number of articles for the popularization of Spinoza. There also appeared at the time in Russian a biography of Spinoza by me."

Ia M... A+MH, a DLC cardseen (B3997. M52) of 1940 ed. B... Спиноза. Москва, 1940. 243 p. 17 cm.

3620

Mirabaud, Jean Baptiste de, 1675-1760 [Holbach, P. H. T.]

Système de la nature; ou, Des loix du monde physique & du monde moral, par M. Mirabaud ~~pt 2~~. Londres, 1770. 2 v. 8°. [Holbach, Paul Henri Thiry, baron d'] 1723-1789.

pt. 2, ch. IV: Examen des preuves de l'existence de Dieu, données par [S.] Clarke (p. 89-137). ch. V. Examen des preuves de l'existence de Dieu, données par Descartes, Malebranche, Newton, &c. "Pub. by the author as the work of Mirabaud" [cover]

2. 3621

Mirabaud, — Système de la... [cont.]

(Spinosa, spinosisme, spinosistes, p. 140-141.)

(D.W.L.)

3633

Moffa, Francesco.
Il "Trattato teologico-politico" di Spinoza.
Napoli: La tipografica, 1916.

Ravà, no. 26. (Not seen.)

WN - *POT
4
E1165
✓ Montefiore, Claude Joseph Goldsmid, 1858-1938

Maintains that the N.T. is vastly more important a book than the writings of Spinoza. [For Jewish study?] (Liberal Judaism and Hellenism[?], p. 80.)
NNJ - Outlines of Liberal Judaism, 1923 - Not seen on p 80

London: Macmillan & Co., Ltd., 1918.
xi, 328 p. 12°.
LC has: Liberal Judaism; an essay, 1903
NNC has: Outlines of liberal Judaism, 1923

Mccarthy [Montesquieu, Charles Louis de Secondat, Baron de la Brède et de.]
3645

[Montesquieu, Charles de Secondat de, baron]
Défense de "L'esprit des loix", à laquelle on a joint quelques éclaircissemens... A Genève: chez Barrillot & Fils, 1750. 207 p. 8°.

LAN LIBR
Amsterdam, 1788
v. 4, p. [195]-280

Spinoza references, p. 5-14, 59, 65.

OCH

(H.U.C.)
✓ BN

3646

Montesquieu, Charles de Secondat de, baron.

not signed
M. was accused of Spinozism in the Nouvelles Ecclésiastiques of Oct. 9 and 16, 1749. He wrote a Défense against this accusation. (See Oudin, p. 64.)

See his: Oeuvres, 1817; 1820; 1859.
" also: Complete works, 1777. — o NNC
+.10
320.1 M761; 320.1 M7612; 320.1 M7631
(Above in L.L.)
o LC

DLC Old Of City
4
E1168
✓ More, Henry. 1614-1687

Ad V. C. epistola altera, quae brevem Tractatûs theologico politici confutationem complectitur, paucáque sub finem annexa habet de libri Francisci Cuperi scopo, cui titulus est, Arcana atheismi revelata, &c. Per Henricum Morum Cantabrigiensem. Londini: Typis J. Macock, impensis Martyn & Gualt. Kettilby, 1679. [In his: Opera philo- [cover]

o NNC
o LC
o BM
DLC-
B1299
.M6
1679
Jefferson
Gill.
✓ EN

1-a
E1169
More, Henry. — Ad V. C... [cont.]
sophica, tum quae Latine, tum quae Anglice primitus scripta sunt, nunc verò partim à scipso, partim ab amico notionum suarum philosophicarum perinde atque Latinae linguae callentissimo, in Latinum versa. Accesserunt scholia, quibus loca quamplurima aut illustrantur, aut emendantur, aut confirmantur deniq; & ab objectionibus quibuscunq; ullius quidem momente vindicantur, ab authore passim adjecta. Londini: Typis J. Macock, impensis J. Martyn & Gualt. Kettilby, 1679.- [Followed by another t.-p. which reads:

2
E1170
More, H.

Henrici Mori Cantabrigiensis Scriptorum philosophicorum tomus prior...] f°. [t.-p.], p. 565-614.)

p. 602-611: Scholia in Epist. ad V. C. Sect. I.

p. 611-614: Adnotationes in antecedentia scholia. Sect. I.

[cover]

2-a
E1171
More, H. — Ad V.C. ... [cont.]
p. 615-635: Demonstrationis duarum propositionum, viz. [Ad substantiam quatenus substantia est, necessarium existentiam pertinere, & unicam in mundo substantiam esse.] quae praecipuae apud Spinozium atheismi sunt columnae, brevis solidáque confutatio.
p. 616-631 are superscribed: Duarum praecipuarum atheismi Spinoziani columnarum subversio.
From the middle of p. 631-635: Mentis statûs post mortem descriptio apud

---

3
E1172
More, H.

Spinoz. perplexa, falsa & frivola".

First t.-p.: Henrici Mori Opera omnia, tum quae Latinè, tum quae Anglicè scripta sunt; nunc vero Latinitate donata instigatû & impensis generosissimi juvenis Johannis Cockshuti nobilis Angli. Londini: Typis impensa J. Macock, sumtibus autem J. Martyn & Gualt. Kettilby, 1679.
[cover]

3-a
E1173
More, H. — Ad V. C... [cont.]
"Anno MDCLXXVII. Scripta est Epistola altera ad V. C. quae brevem Tractatûs Theologico-politici confutationem complectitur. Hujus autem Epistolae scribendae quae fuerit occasioh in ipso Epistolae initio indicatur" (Praefatio generalissima, p. xii). There is a reference to Spinoza on p. xxiii.

v.d. L. 367. See MacKinnon, H. More, p. 241.

G-LII-5,6,7 3675

Muller, P. L.

Onze gouden eeuw. De Republiek der Vereenigde Nederlanden in haar bloeitijd. Geschetst door P. L. Muller, geïllustreerd onder toezicht van J. H. W. Unger. [v.] 1-3. Leiden: A. W. Sijthoff, [pref. 1896]. 4°.

Descartes en Spinoza, [v.] 3, p. 319-324. port. (Wolfenbüttel) on [covers]

G-LII-5,6,7 2. 3676

Muller, P. L. - Onze gouden... [cont.]

p. 322: Baruch Spinoza. Naar een oud schilderij. (Altkirch, p. 84, no. 7.)

(G.)

G-KIX 3685

Muth, Karl.

Spinoza=Renaissance. (Hochland. München, 1933. January. p. 346-351.)

In the main a review of: Dunin-Borkowski, S. von, Spinoza nach dreihundert Jahren.

(G.)

---

105 M74 NNC-4 E1191

Myers, Henry Alonzo. 1906-1955

Systematic pluralism in Spinoza and Hegel. (Monist. Chicago, 1935. v. 45, p. 237-263.)

I: (1) Reflection in Spinoza and Hegel: the key to the similarity of their methods. (2) The infinite and the indefinite in Spinoza and Hegel. (3) The presupposition of concrete system in Hegel and Spinoza. (4) Truth and [covers]

Correct identif. - no title "Systematic ..." in NNC or LC E1192

Myers, Henry Alonzo. - Systematic... [cont.]

adequacy. II: (1) The attributes as systems. (2) The Hegelian categories as systems. (3) Implications of systematic pluralism.

Systematic thinkers agreed that knowledge and reality is one system. But "the trend of modern philosophy has been... gradually away from the classical conception of a single system and toward what may be called systematic [next]

---

2 E1193

Myers, H. A.

pluralism", a striking instance being "the relation between Spinoza and Hegel in the development of the idea of system".

N

893.105 Sh6 NNC-5 NNJ-ST 3713

Neumark, David.

שפינוזה עד עתידות ישראל. (Haschiloah. Berlin, 1897. Bd. 2, p. 287-288.)

Spinoza on the destiny of the Jews; a note with a translation of several sentences of the Tr. theol.-pol. ch. 3 (ed. Gebhardt, p. 56, line 19 - 57, 6). Also reference is made to Oldenburg's letter (Ep. 33), where the ques- [covers]

(A.S.O.)

---

2. 3714

Neumark, David. - [cont.]

tion of the Jew's return to Palestine is raised. This paragraph, too, is translated.

G-XXXT-22 3715

Neumark, David.

Lebensanschauung und Weltanschauung. Historisch-philosophische Skizze... Krakau: Druck von J. Fischer - Verlag des Verfassers, 1903. 1 p. l., 44 p., 1 l. 8°.

Hebrew text and t.-p.

Repr.: Haschiloah. Bd. 11.

Spinoza, p. 30-39.

(A.S.O.)

---

809 N513 NNC-4. 3727

Niceron, Jean-Pierre, 1685-1738.

Joh. Pet. Nicerons Nachrichten von den Begebenheiten und Schriften berühmten [sic] Gelehrten mit einigen Zusätzen herausgegeben von Sieg. Jakob Baumgarten.

24 v. in 13 Halle, 1749-77.

V. 1, 1749.

Spinoza, v. 1 (1749), p. 265-282.

(Taken from D.-B., I, 537.)

G-CII-1-41 3724

[Niceron, Jean-Pierre.]

Mémoires pour servir à l'histoire des hommes illustres dans la république des lettres. Avec un catalogue raisonné de leurs ouvrages. tom. 13. À Paris: Chez Briasson, 1730. 12°.

(G-tom 1-41, 1729-1740)

Benoist de Spinosa, XIII p. 30-52.

See also tom. 20 (1732), p. 59-61: Additions (bibliographical).

[over]

G-CII-1-41 2. 3725

[Niceron, Jean-Pierre.]—Mémoires... [cont.]

Niceron is the first (?) to refer to the Vie by Lucas in the Nouvelles littéraires (tom. 13, p. 52).

v. d. L. 148 (II). No reference to tom. 20.

(G.: compl. set) (tom 1-41 - 1729-1740)

O-KLIII-5 3739

Nieuwentijt, Bernard.

Gronden van zekerheid; of, De regte betoogwyse der wiskundigen so in het denkbeeldige, als in het zakelyke: Ter wederlegging van Spinosaas denkbeelding samenstel; en ter aanleiding van eene sekere sakelyke wysbegeerte, aangetoont, door B. Nieuwentyt. Amsterdam: J. Pauli, 1720. 28 p. l., 456? 458 p. 4°.

With an introduction by Jacob van Ostade.

(A.S.O.—Large paper.)

[over]

O-KL-III-5 2. 3740

Nieuwentijt, Bernard.—Gronden van... [cont.]

This ed. not in v. d. L.—Br. Mus.

— — Den tweden druk. Amsterdam: J. Pauli, 1728. 28 p. l., 456 p. 4° G-LIII-8

This ed. not in v. d. L.—B. 156.—W., p. 13.

— — Den derden druk. Amsterdam: J. Pauli, 1739. 28 p. l. [?], 456 p. 4° G-LIII-9

This ed. not in v. d. L.—Spinoza-huis Cat., no. 216.

— — Amsterdam: Morterre, 1741. 4°

[noted in Blakey? Only?]

— — Den derden druk. Amsterdam: A. Douci, 1754. 28 p. l., 456 p. 4°.

v. d. L. 402.

893.15 v NNC 3719 E1219

Nieto, David. Hallevi, Judah ben Samuel, fl. 1100.

Matte Dan. 1884, Warsaw

Kūsari shēni... vol. of pamphlets.

Contains also a disputation against the Cartesians and Spinozists?

N. was born in Venice in 1654, two years before Spinoza was excommunicated, and died in London in 1728. He studied medicine. Two years after he became Haham of the Portuguese Jews in London (1704), he published a sermon (or treatise) On the Divine Providence which provoked a great controversy amongst his coreligionists.

2. E1220

Nieto, David.—Matte Dan... [cont.]

He was accused of Spinozism

E1221

Nieto, David.

[The first Jew, perhaps, to be accused of Spinozism

G-XXX-11 3751

Noack, Ludwig.

Geschichte der Philosophie in gedrängter Uebersicht. Lehrbuch zum Gebrauche bei akademischen Vorlesungen und zum Selbstunterrichte. Weimar: Druck und Verlag des Landes-Industrie-Comptoirs, 1853. 8°.

Die Philosophie Spinoza's, p. 236-245.

(G.) v. d. L. 148 (XXV).

MH-Phil 3833.3 - pp. 14. 3755

Nordwall, Adolph. Leonh.

Nordvall, Adolf Leonard [dates?] not LC, NNC...

De Spinozismi initiis aphorismi, quos venia reverendissimi et eminentissimi Doct. Joh. Ol. Holmström... nec non consensu Max. Ven. Consit. Strengens. Speciminis loco p.p. Adolph. Leonh. Nordwall... Respondentibus Osc. Magn. Almstedt... Joh. Den. Insulander... in auditorio Reg. Gymn. Strengnes. [?!]

oNNC

oLC

2. 3756

Nordwall, Adolph. Leonh.—De Spinozismi... [cont.]

die XXVII Martii MDCCCLII... Upsaliae: Wahlströ & C., 1852. 14 p., 1 l. [blank]. 12°.

(To be revised!)

Baldwin has erroneously: Nordvall.

(Harvard.)—Subj.: Ethica.

NNUT E1232
MJUB pam 1839

Norton, Andrews, 1786-1853.
A discourse on the latest form of infidelity; delivered at the request of the "Association of the Alumni of the Cambridge Theological School", on the 19th of July, 1839. With notes. Cambridge [Mass.]: J. Owen, 1839. 64p. 8°.
No index

CNNC
LC E13-501
nd 1-23-59
nd 3-4

Microfilm [DCU] - Microfilm of copy in Bibliothèque Nationale, Paris 3801
"Cote 8° R 24728"

Oudin, Charles.
Le spinozisme de Montesquieu. Étude critique.... Paris: Librairie Générale de Droit & de Jurisprudence, 1911. 2p.l., 163p. 8°.
163p.

No table of contents or index. The heading is: "La monarchie et la liberté d'après Montesquieu" (on p. 13), and chap. V (under "V") is superscribed "Montesquieu et Spinoza". - from microfilm, "M. et Sp." looks clearer than ch. II - p12-51; ch. III - p53-93; ch. IV - p. 96-118; text 119-163.
covers

---

2. 3802
Oudin, Ch[ ]. - Le spinozisme... [cont.]
What is the "précédent travail" mentioned on p. 1?

1700
1130
3853
500
900
400
7333

(Sir F. [ ] History [ ] in L. L.)

NNUT E1233
MJUB pam 1839

Norton, Andrews, 1786-1853.
Remarks on a pamphlet entitled "The latest form of infidelity' examined". Cambridge [Mass.]: J. Owen, 1839. 72 p. 8°.

ONNC
LC E13-502
nd 1-23-59

NNUT 4 E1234

Norton, Andrews, 1786-1853.
Tracts concerning Christianity. Cambridge [Mass.]: J. Bartlett, 1852. vi p., 2 l., 3-392 p. 8°.

V. A discourse on the latest form of infidelity. p. 229-268.
VI. Remarks on the modern German school of infide[lity] p. 269-368.

ONNC OLC
covers

CtY 1-12... 3812
1-29+-4

Padovani, Umberto. Antonio, 1894-
Il problema fondamentale della filosofia di Spinoza. Milano: Vita e Pensiero, 1921.
4

Repr.: Rivista di filosofia neo-scolastica. Feb., 1920, p. 3-23. - note other parts. See 3810
v.12?
?

NNC
Ravà, no. 28. (Not seen.) has v. 4-9, 22-49 1912-17, 1930-57
covers

---

2. E1235
Norton, Andrews. - Tracts concerning... [cont.]
VII. On the objection to faith in Christianity as resting on historical facts and critical learning. p. 369-392.

VI and VII are expanded forms of the notes to the 1839 edition of the "Discourse on the latest form of infidelity."
No index

Human Rights Cure

---

2. 3813
Padovani, Umberto. - Il problema... [cont.]
Absolute reality does not belong to the empirical order. It is found in God alone, the knowledge of Whom constitutes the only good of the soul.

3776
Olgiati, Francesco.
Benedetto Spinoza nel 250 anniversario della sua morte. (Vita e pensiero. Milano, 1927. anno 13, v. 18, p. 193-198.)

(9)

Spec Coll Spin 3811
Padovani, Umberto A.
Schopenhauer, Spinoza e il panteismo. (In: Spinoza nel terzo centenario della sua nascita; pubblicazione a cura della Facoltà di Filosofia dell' Università Cattolica del Sacro Cuore. Milano, 1934. 8°. p. 99-116.)

5 Palmedo, Kurt. dates? not seen in LC cat

Der Freiheitsbegriff in der Lehre Spinozas. Ein Beitrag zur Geschichte der ethischen Prinzipien. Inaugural-Dissertation zur Erlangung der Doktorwürde der hohen philosophischen Fakultät der Universität Leipzig eingereicht durch Kurt Palmedo aus Berlin. Weida i. Thür.: Druck

[cover]

2. 3816

Palmedo, Kurt.– Der Freiheitsbegriff... [cont.]

von Thomas & Hubert, 1920. 65p. 8°

Contents: Einleitung. I. Kapitel. Der Begriff der freien Substanz. II. Kapitel. Der Begriff des freien Menschen. Voruntersuchungen zu den folgenden Kapiteln. III. Kapitel. Fundament der Freiheit. IV. Kapitel. Funktion der Freiheit. V. Kapitel. Prinzip der Freiheit. IV. Inbegriff der Freiheit. Anmerkungen.

(Harvard)

Pater, Walter. R7

Sebastian van Storck. (In his: Imaginary portraits. London, 1914. 8°. p. 81-115.)

First published in Macmillan's Magazine, march, 1886, and in Imaginary portraits, of which it forms chap. 3, at London, 1887; often reprinted.

[cover]

2. E1248

Pater, Walter.– Sebastian van... [cont.]

Sebastian van Storck is "the remorseless, Spinozistic idealist, who, by forsaking the actual humanities of life, comes to strange grief..." (Greenslet, Ferris. Walter Pater. New York, 1903. p. 82)

Spinoza is referred to by name at p. 90, 97, 104, and 105.

(A.S.O.) [see also large cards]

 (James) A.M. - BM, Vol. 40 E1250

Paterson, Jac.

Anti-Nazarenus by way of answer to Mr. Toland; or, A treatise proving the divine original and authority of the Holy Scriptures, against atheists, Jews, heathens, Mahometans, papists, Spinoza and other modern errors. London, 1718. 8°.

PPM London, S. Butter, --- (no date given) old Mercantile Libr - now in Storage

Trinius, p. 492. (See B.M. Cat.)

E1287

Pearson, Karl.

Pollock's Spinoza. [Review of: Pollock, Sir Frederick. Spinoza... London, 1880.] (Cambridge review. Nov. 17, 1880, p. 94-95.)

— Spinoza. II. (Cambridge review. Feb. 9, 1881, p. 155-156.)

"I propose in this article to touch on three points, which may perhaps cast some additional light on the views propounded by me in an article on Pollock's Spinoza... these views have been to some extent misunderstood...

[cover]

2. E1290

Pearson, Karl.– Pollock's Spinoza... [cont.]

The three heads of my present discourse shall be as follows:– first, to offer some remarks on Mr. Stearn's objections; secondly, to enter more at length on my view of what Spinoza conceived by Eternity; thirdly, to consider what foundation Spinozism gives us for the construction of a moral code."

1. E1260

Spinoza, Baruch or Benedictus.

Pearson, Karl.

Maimonides and Spinoza. (Mind. London, 1883. v. 8, p. 338-353.)

Incl. in The ethic of freethought... 2d ed. London, 1901 p. 125-142 | See full Spin.

Excerpt.

Argues against "the somewhat one-sided view usually taken of Spinoza's position in

SEE NEXT CARD.

2. E1261

Pearson, K.–Maimonides... [cont.]

the evolution of thought: the importance attributed to the influence of Descartes and the slight weight given to the Jewish writers". K. Fischer "still regards Spinoza as a mere link after Descartes in the chain of philosophical development, rejecting the

SEE NEXT CARD.

3. E1263

Pearson, K.–Maimonides... [cont.]

view that he belongs rather to Jewish than Christian Philosophy. The hypothesis that Spinoza was very slightly influenced by Hebrew thought has become traditional and is to be found in the most recent English works on Spinoza. Mr. Pollock writes that the in-

See next card.

4. E1263
Pearson, K.-Maimonides... [cont.]
fluence of Maimonides on the pure philosophy of Spinoza was comparatively slight (p. 94). Dr. Martineau tells us somewhat dogmatically that 'no stress can be laid on the evidence of Spinoza's indebtedness to Rabbinical philosophy' (p. 56)... Neither Mr. Pollock
See next card.

5. E1264
Pearson, K.-Maimonides... [cont.]
nor Dr. Martineau seems acquainted with Maimonides's Yad Hachazakah. It is to the relation of this work to Spinoza's Ethica that I wish at present to refer". (p. 338.)

First, Maimonides's conception of God as contained especially in Sefer ha-Madda, sec.
See next card.

6. E1265
Pearson, K.-Maimonides... [cont.]
1 [Hilkot Yesode ha-Torah], chap. 1; sec. 5 [Hilkot Teshubah], chap. 10 (following H. H. Bernard's tr. entitled The main principles of the creed and ethics of the Jews, exhibited in selections from the Yad Hachazakah of Maimonides. Cambridge, 1832), is consid-
See next card.

7. E1266
Pearson, K.-Maimonides... [cont.]
ered "which corresponds roughly to Ethica i. and v. of Spinoza... Maimonides and Spinoza strip God of all conceivable human characteristics, they yet hold it possible for the mind of man to attain to some, if an imperfect, knowledge of God, and make
See next card.

8. E1267
Pearson, K.-Maimonides... [cont.]
the attainment of such knowledge the highest good of life... This intellectual relation of man to God forms an all-important feature in the ethics of both M— and S—; it is in fact a vein of mystic gold which runs through the great mass of Hebrew thought". (p. 340-341.)
SEE NEXT CARD.

9. E1268
Pearson, K.-Maimonides... [cont.]
Next, Maimonides's conception of the relation of God to man, premised by what he understands by intelligence, is discussed. (p. 342-345.) The "coexistence of matter and quality [the view of Maimonides] or extension and thought [the view of Spinoza]
See next card.

10. E1269
Pearson, K.-Maimonides... [cont.]
is carried even [by M.], as in Spinoza's case, throughout all being... The parallelism is all the more striking in that in... Scholium [Ethica ii. 13] a classification is suggested based on the degrees wherein the two attributes are present in individu-
SEE NEXT CARD.

11. E1270
Pearson, K.-Maimonides... [cont.]
als. Dr. Martineau... [Spinoza], (p. 190) remarks on a superficial resemblance between G— Bruno and Sp—: 'Bruno animates things to get them into action; S— to fetch them into the sphere of intelligence'." (p. 342.)— A stage "to a far more
See next card.

12. E1271
Pearson, K.-Maimonides... [cont.]
important coincidence" is reached — "the principle, namely, that the knowledge of God is associated always in an equal degree with the love of God: what Spinoza termed the 'Amor Dei intellectualis'." (p. 343.)

Then, the author passes to the subject
See next card.

13. E1272
Pearson, K.-Maimonides... [cont.]
of "God's knowledge and love of himself" (p. 345-347) which, "in the case of both philosophers, is beset with grave difficulties".

A comparison of the views of the two philosophers on the immortality of the soul
See next card.

14. E1273
Pearson, K.-Maimonides... [cont.]
is given on p. 347-348.
"The influence of Maimonides on Spinoza becomes far less obvious when we turn to his doctrine of human affections" — (discussed on p. 348-351). "Nevertheless, we may find several points of contact and even double
See next card.

15. E1274
Pearson, K.-Maimonides... [cont.]
contact".
Finally, a "point of divergence, namely, on the insoluble problem of free-will" is noted (p. 351).
"In the above remarks I have considered only the Yad Hachazakah, because hitherto
See next card.

16. E1275
Pearson, K.-Maimonides... [cont.]
attention seems to have been entirely directed to the More Nebuchim... It is not impossible that in the intervening ten years M— somewhat altered his views. I should not be surprised to hear that the More was held more 'orthodox' than the Yad. The latter, despite
See next card.

17. E1276
Pearson, K.-Maimonides... [cont.]
much Talmudic verbiage...notwithstanding many faults and inconsistencies, yet contains the germs of a truly grand philosophical system, quite capable of powerfully influencing the mind even of a Spinoza... In the second place, I have confined myself en-
See next card.

18. E1277
Pearson, K.-Maimonides... [cont.]
tirely to the Yad on the Ethica. Greater agreement would have been found with the Korte Verhandeling van God &c., while Spinoza's views of Biblical criticism (especially his conception of prophets and prophecy as developed in the Tractatus Theologico-Poli-
See next card.

19. E1278
Pearson, K.-Maimonides... [cont.]
ticus) owe undoubtedly much to the Yad. Yet I wished to show that the study of M— was traceable even in S—'s most finished exposition of his philosophy. Those who assert that S— was influenced by Hebrew thought have not seldom been treated as though they were
See next card.

20. E1279
Pearson, K.-Maimonides... [cont.]
accusing Spinoza of a crime. Yet no great work ever sprung from the head of its creator like Athena from the head of Zeus; it has slowly developed within him, influenced and moulded by all that has influenced its shaper's own character... While recognizing
See next card.

21. E1280
Pearson, K.-Maimonides... [cont.]
many other influences at work forming Spinoza's method of thought, it is only scientific to allow a certain place to the Jewish predecessors with whom he was acquainted... We naturally expect to find considerable divergences between any individual Jewish philoso-
See next card.

22. E1281
Pearson, K.-Maimonides... [cont.]
pher and S—; these divergences have been carefully pointed out by Mr. Sorely, but they are insufficient to prove that S— was not very greatly influenced by Hebrew thought. My aim has been to call in question the traditional view of S—'s relation to
See next card.

23. E1282
Pearson, K.-Maimonides... [cont.]
Jewish philosophy, i.e., that he learnt enough of it to throw it off entirely. I cannot help holding that, while S—'s form and language were a mixture of mediaeval scholasticism and the Cartesian philosophy, yet the ideas which they clothed were not
See next card.

24. E1283

Pearson, K.-Maimonides... [cont.]

seldom Hebrew in their origin. He might be cast out by his co-religionists, but that could not deprive him of the mental birthright of his people — those deep moral and theosophical truths which have raised the Hebrews to a place hardly second to the

See next card.

25. E1284

Pearson, K.-Maimonides... [cont.]

Greeks in the history of thought". (p. 351-352.)

The author before entering upon a comparison of the intellectual relation of M— to S— refers (p. 339-340, n.) "to a close connexion between S—'s method of life and M—'s

See next card.

26. E1285

Pearson, K.-Maimonides... [cont.]

theory of how a wise man should earn a livelihood", and concluding: "Why does S—'s life stand in such contrast to that of all other modern philosophers? Because his life at least, if not his philosophy, was Hebrew!".

Not in B.

E1294

[Peirce, Charles Santiago Sanders.] 1839-1914

[Review of:] Duff, Robert A. Spinoza's political and ethical philosophy. Glasgow: James MacLehose & Sons; New York: The Macmillan Co., 1903. (Nation. New York, 1904. v. 79, no. 2038, p. 63.)

(Not signed) over

Issue of July 21, 1904.

See: Peirce, C. S., Chance, love and logic... London, 104

(A.S.O.) P35 [over]

2. E1295

[Peirce, Charles Sanders.]-[Review of:]... [cont.]

1923, p. 317 (Bibliography of Peirce's published writings).

051 NNC E1293
N 4

[Peirce, Charles Sanders.]

[Review of:] Joachim, H. H. A study of the Ethics of Spinoza. 1901. (Nation. New York, v. 75, ~~no. 1932~~ 1962, p. 36-37.)

(over)

See: Peirce, C. S., Chance, love and logic... London, 1923, p. 316 (Bibliography of Peirce's published writings).

(Not seen.)

051 NNC-4 E1291
N

[Peirce, Charles Sanders.]

Spinoza's Ethic. [Review of:] Ethic. Translated from the Latin... by W. Hale Wright [! White]; translation revised by Amelia Hutchinson Stirling. Second edition... 1894. (Nation. New York, 1894. ~~v. 59, no. 1532, p. 344-345.)~~ v. 59, 1894, p. 344-345

(not signed)

Issue of Nov. 8, 1894. over

See: Peirce, C. S., Chance, love and logic... [over]

2. E1292

[Peirce, Charles Sanders.]- Spinoza's Ethic... [cont.]

London, 1923, p. 315 (Bibliography of Peirce's published writings).

(A.S.O.)

Jüdische Skizzen - 2nd ed. 1920 3844

Perles, Felix.

"Manche ängstliche Gemüter fürchteten von einer kritischen Behandlung der biblischen Schriften eine Schädigung ihres religiösen Empfindens. Sie glaubten, wenn die Sonde der Kritik an die Urkunden des Glaubens gelegt werden, würde der Glaube selbst sich daran verbluten, wenn ein Buch, ein Kapitel oder auch nur ein Wort oder ein Buchstabe angetastet werde, sei das Fundament der Religion erschüttert... Seit Spinoza [Tr. theol.-pol. X: At forte &c., quoted] sucht die Wissenschaft derartige Vorurteile zu zerstreuen." (In his:

2. 3845

Perles, Felix.— "Manche ängstliche... [cont.]

Die Textbibel von Kautzsch. [Repr. in his: Jüdische Skizzen. Lpz. Gustav Engel 1912.] ~~p. 95-96.~~)

Zweite Auflage, VIII+266p. 71-73.

Index, p. 265: 15, 72, 99, 152.

LC

3847

Perrens, F. T.
Les libertins en France au XVIIe siècle.
NNC Paris, 1896.
p. 292-293 especially - for account of influence of Spinoza on the Gassendists - Chapelle in particular - and on the movement of free thought in France.
Spec Coll
Z944.03 P427 1899 ed. different ed. - sep. card.
From a letter of M. L. (Paris, Oct. 22, 1924.)

E579

Peterson, Houston, 1897-
(Ellis, Havelock.)
NNUT: LQ1 E47 + NNC: 825EL592 DP
"Ellis had become rather seriously interested in metaphysical questions about 1880, chiefly through Hinton... He studied... R. Willis's pioneer work on Spinoza... He bought a complete edition of Spinoza in Latin, which he worked through dilligently..." (Peterson, Houston: Havelock Ellis, philosopher of love. Boston; N.Y. Houghton Mifflin Co. [1928] 8° p. 140.)
IX p., 21, 432 p. 21½ cm. 2 l. 23 p. in index ord 1-28-5
Thesis (Ph.D.) - Columbia University.

CLSU 3916

Ploucquet, Gottfried.
... Principia de substantiis et phaenomenis. 2. ed.
Francof. 1764. 399, 72 p. 20 cm.
Lipsiae, In bibliopolio Berger..., Francof. et Lipsiae
"Eine kurze, nicht weiter wichtige Kritik des Spinozismus ~~enthält in ihrem~~ 15. Kap. (S. 203-236) ~~die Schrift see above~~... Der Verfasser beschränkt sich auf die grundlegenden Sätze des ersten Teils der Ethik; im einzelnen bringt er eine Reihe richtiger Bemerkungen; von dem System im ganzen meint er, dass er voller Widersprüche ist und aus [over]

2. 3917

Ploucquet, Gottfried. — Principia de ... [cont.]
willkürlichen und nicht genügend entwickelten Begriffen absolute Folgerungen ableitet; nach seiner Meinung kann es bei der nötigen Aufmerksamkeit jedermann umstürzen (232). (Erhardt, 494)

122 P73 E1323

Plumptre, C E
Natural causation; an essay in four parts. London: T. F. Unwin, 1888. 198 p.
(quotes) Spinoza, on necessity, p. 71-72 - On cheerfulness, p. 91-92.
His History of pantheism was first pub. anon.; later ed. with name of auth.
oLC

MiU-BJ1462.P737 3919
MB
[Pluquet, F. A. Adrien abbé.] 1716-1790.
Examen du fatalisme; ou, Exposition et réfutation des différens systêmes de fatalisme..., Paris, 1757. 3 v. 8°. [Cat. Burgersdijk 1766... [Niermans, no. 12784 [gives: 12°]
oNNC oLC
Anonymous.
See Erhardt, p. 492.
(Same as François A. A. Pluquet, comp. of: Dict. des hérésies. new. ed. 1845, 8°, in L.L. ~~25~~ Vel-M... [over]

1-a 3920

[Pluquet, F. A. A. abbé.] - Examen... [cont.]
"Den Ausdruck Fatalismus nimmt der Verfasser in sehr weitem Sinne, indem er alle möglichen Systeme als fatalistisch ansieht. Sehr eingehend beschäftigt er sich mit dem Spinozismus, von dem er im 1. Bande zunächst eine kurze, sehr allgemein gehaltene Darstellung giebt (349-360), an die sich ein kurzer Abschnitt über den Fortschritt des Spinozismus anschliesst (-371). Der 2. Band führt den Titel 'Exposition et Réfutation du Fatalisme qui ne suppose qu'une substance dans le Monde'. Das erste Buch enthält eine ausführlichere Darstellung und Begründung der Spin. Lehre, ohne sich aber an Sp. selbst näher anzuschliessen (1-137). Das 2. Buch beschäftigt sich mit einem [next]

2. 3921

[Pluquet.] [cont.]
Standpunkt, der nur eine einzige göttliche Substanz zulässt, das dritte entwickelt die Gründe für die Unmöglichkeit einer Mehrheit von Substanzen. Nunmehr folgt in 2 Teilen die Widerlegung dieses ganzen Systems. Der 1. Teil soll den Nachweis erbringen, dass die Existenz einer Mehrheit von Substanzen und die Erschaffung aller übrigen durch eine einzige Substanz nicht unmöglich ist (256-330); der 2. Teil soll zeigen, dass es in Wirklichkeit, mehrere Substanzen giebt, und dass die verschiedenen Wesen, [over]

2-a 3922

[Pluquet.] [cont.]
welche die Welt einschliesst, keineswegs Modifikationen des notwendigen Wesens sind (331-332). Die Körperwelt und die Ausdehnung betrachtet der Verfasser im Anschluss an Leibniz als ein Phänomen, dem eine Vielheit einfacher Substanzen zugrunde liegt, zwischen denen er jedoch eine reale Wechselwirkung annimmt (332-448). Weiter sucht er darzutun, dass sich das Denken und die Körper nicht in einer einzigen Substanz vereinigen lassen (449-499); dabei bringt er gute Auseinandersetzungen gegen die materialistische Auffassung des Seelenlebens, die jedoch gegen Sp.'s Lehre von der einen Substanz mit ihren beiden Attributen nichts beweisen. Den Abschluss dieser Ausführungen [next]

3 3923

[Pluquet.] [cont.]
bildet eine Erörterung über die Notwendigkeit der Annahme einer Mehrheit von denkenden Substanzen (500-518). Der 3. Band des Werkes ist der Widerlegung derjenigen Formen des Fatalismus gewidmet, die mehrere Substanzen annehmen. Die Untersuchungen des Verfassers tragen einen objektiven und wissenschaftlichen Charakter, den sie auch bei der Kritik des Spinozismus in keiner Weise verleugnen; als eine Widerlegung der Lehre Sp's von der einen Substanz kann diese Kritik trotz guter und treffender Ausführungen freilich nicht betrachtet werden." (Erhardt, 492-3.)

NNJ- Nf 5 3927

✓Poiret, Pierre, 1646-1719.

.... Cogitationes rationales de Deo, anima et malo contra Cartesium et Spinoza. Amst.: D. Elzevier, 1677. 4°.

1715, 1635 eds Spec Coll Spin.

1677, 298p. + index (cf. BN, 139, col. 866-7)

1677, 309p. " " (" " ", col. 867)

eds. in Spin Coll. have longer title, wh. incl. ref. to Spinoza

(Burgersdijk & Niermans, Cat. no. 48, no. 12806.)

[over]

2. 3928

Poiret, Pierre. — Cogitationes rationales... [cont.]

Petri Poiret Cogitationum rationalium de Deo, anima & malo libri IV. In quibus, quid de hisce Cartesius, ejusque sequaces, boni aut secus senserint, omnisque philosophiae certiora fundamenta, atque inprimis tuta metaphysica verior, continentur. Amstelodami: Apud Danielem Elsevirium, 1677. 4°.

([Stolle, G. Kurtze Nachricht von den Bücheren und deren Urhebern in der Stollischen Bibliothec Th. 3. Jena, 1734. p. 290-294.) (The 2. ed. is noted p. 294-297.)

C-XXXII-29, 30 1 3939

Polignac, Melchior de, cardinal.

L'anti-Lucrece, poëme sur la religion naturelle, composé par M. le Cardinal de Polignac; traduit par M. de Bougainville. tom. 1-2. A Paris: chez J.-B. Coignard, & A. ~~P.-G. Lem~~ Boudet, [&] P.-G. LeMercier, 1749. 2 v. ~~8°~~ port. 8°.

Spinosa: Son systême exposé & refuté, [over]

C-XXXII-29, 30 1-a 3940

Polignac, Melchior de, cardinal. — L'anti-... [cont.]

tom. 1, p. 153-155 (being livre 3, § V). — Réfutation de son hypothése sur le mouvement, p. 221-229 (being livre 4, § VI). — ... sur l'essence de la matiere, tom. 2, p. 44-49 (being livre 5, § V).

(A.S.O.)

C-XXXII - 31, 32 3 3942

Polignac, Melchior de, cardinal.

L'anti-Lucrece, poëme sur la religion naturelle, composé par M. le Cardinal de Polignac; traduit par M. de Bougainville. tom. 1-2. A Paris: chez Desaint & Saillant, 1750. 2 v. 12°.

Spinosa, tom. 1, p. 284-286, 352-360; tom. 2, p. 41 [erroneously 44 in the Table]-47.

(A.S.O.)

1-a 3944

Polignac, Melchior de, Cardinal. - Anti-... [cont.]

Spec Coll Spin — Lipsiae, 1748. 8°. (G.)

B. Sec 3(1) 4(1) 2 3945

Polignac, Melchior de, Cardinal.

Anti-Lucretius, sive de Deo et natura, libri novem. Eminentissimi S.R.E. Cardinalis Melchioris de Polignac opus posthumum; illustrissimi Abbatis Caroli d'Orleans de Rothelin curâ & studio editioni mandatum. tom. 1-2. Londini: apud J. Nourse, 1748. 8°.

Spinosa, see Index.

In 9 Book... v. 1, lib. 1-4; v. 2, lib. 5-9.

v. 1... [illegible]

3 3946 [Latin]

Polignac

G.CI-17 (1) — — Lugduni Batavorum: Typis E. Luzac, Jun., 1748. 2 v. 8°.

C-XXIII-27 — Lipsiae: Apud B.C. Breitkopf, 1748. ~~2 v.~~ 8°. port.

(G.)

4 3947 [Latin]

Polignac

(1) G.CI-18

— — Parisiis: apud P.-A. Le Mercier, 1749. 2 v. 12°.

P.-A.: Petrum-Aegidium, or Pierre-Gilles

(G.)

3949

Polignac.

"The French ecclesiastic, famous in his day for erudition, polite and skilful diplomacy, and for a collection of Roman antiques, which Frederick the Great bought for Berlin, came across Bayle, who was the purest sceptic of his own, or perhaps of any age. 'I am a protestant,' said Bayle to Polignac, 'for in my soul I protest against all that I hear said, and all that I [over]

1-a 3950

Polignac, — "The French ... [cont.]
see done." Among other things he much impressed the cardinal by his references to Lucretius. Polignac, a sincere and honest man, set to work on a latin poem, Anti-Lucrèce (1747), which made a great stir in the literary world all over Europe. Voltaire in a thoughtless moment too handsomely complimented its author as a mixture of Virgil and Plato, the avenger of heaven and the conqueror of [next.]

2 3951

Polignac [note]

Lucretius. By and by Voltaire changed his mind, and the work speedily became a poem without poetry and philosophy, without reason, a thing of dry bones which everybody praised and nobody could read"... (~~John Morley, Reminis~~ Morley, Recollections, 1917, v. 2, p. 12, footnote.)

105 M (8) NNC-4 1. E1367

Spinoza, Baruch or Benedictus.

Pollock, Sir Frederick. 1845-1937

Notes on the philosophy of Spinoza.

(Mind. vol. II, ~~April~~, 1878. 8. p.195-212.)

~~Excerpt.~~

Reviews first Spinoza's Jewish sources: 1. Avicebron; 2. The Jewish Peripatetics; 3.

SEE NEXT CARD.

2. E1368

Pollock, Sir Frederick.-Notes... [cont.]

Don Chasdai Creskas — then discusses the Ethics. — "The real working parts of Spinoza's system...remain substantially unimpaired"... (p.205.)

"In the spring of last year I had the honou[r] of giving a Friday evening discourse on

SEE NEXT CARD.

3. E1369

Pollock, Sir Frederick.-Notes... [cont.]

Spinoza at the Royal Institution which is printed very nearly as it was delivered in the Proceedings of the Royal Institution (Vol. VIII, p. 363). The wise custom which as a rule confines the length of such discourses to one hour imposed on me

See next card.

4. E1370

Pollock, Sir Frederick.-Notes... [cont.]

an amount of condensation which, however necessary for the spoken word, would be needless and unsuitable in a paper intended for the readers of MIND. The present article contains a more developed statement of points which, at the Royal Insti-

See next card.

5. E1371

Pollock, Sir Frederick.-Notes... [cont.]

tution, I could merely indicate". (p.195.)

p.211-212. "A very brief indication of modern authorities on Spinoza".

E1398

tr. 824 P81 Essay on man. 1733-34

Pope, Alexander. 1st ed.? 1743 (?)

IU Alexandri Pope equitis Anglicani et poetae incomparabilis Commentatio poëtica de homine, ex Anglico idiomata in Latinum translata, et carmine heroico expressa, notisque subjunctis illustrata, per Jo. Joach. Gottlob Am-Ende, Theologiae Doctorum et Antistitem Sacrorum apud Dresonenses. Editio nova et accuratior. Lugduni [over]

1-a. E1399

Pope, Alexander. — Alexandri Pope... [cont.]
Batavorum: Apud Cornelium de Pecker [Pecker?], 1751. 16 p. l., 136 p. 8°. 22cm.
p. l. 11, verso, reference to Crousaz's "Examination" of Pope's poem in which he accuses the poet of Spinozism.

"Natura est corpus. Directrix corporis hujus Mens ratioque Dei est. Deus unus semper & idem

Cum rebus variis varie mutuatur in horas."

Epistola prima, p.29, being verse 470 = line 268

2 E1400

Pope, Alexander.

in the original English [verify!] The tr. gives here a long footnote (p.28-31): "Sunt, qui ex hoc loco Spinozismi accusarunt Poëtam... Epistola tertia, p.70-71, verse 115, re. Sp. he renews his defence of Pope against the charge of Spinozism, in a footnote (p.71). Epistola 3, p.91 (erroneously paged 19) again refers to Spinoza in a footnote.

(Marvin Lowenthal.)

 1856-1931 E1407

Seth Pringle-Pattison, Andrew ~~Seth~~, [formerly A. Seth]

Spinoza, Baruch. (In: Encyclopaedia Britannica. Cambridge [Eng.], 1911. f° v. 25, p. 687-691.) 11th ed.

"Spinoza's philosophy is fully considered in the article Cartesianism" – v. 5 (1910), p. 414-426: The philosophy of Spinoza – Geometrical method applied to metaphysics. – Sense and source of error. – Vices of abstraction and imagination. – Insufficiency of the individual. – The whole dominates the parts. – Finite things modes of infinite substance. – [over]

2. E1408

Pringle-Pattison, Andrew Seth, [...] – Spinoza ... [cont.]

application of nature to matter. – Nature of mind. – Soul and body. – Spinoza's refuge from Descartes' dualism. – Logical difficulties in Spinoza's metaphysics. – Spinoza's ethical system. – Implicit difficulties. (See also Index.) "Cartesianism", Vol. 5, 1910, p. 414-426. latter article by E. C. (Edward Caird)

See Index, v. XXIX, 1911, pp. 747-748.

Q

 4000

Quinet, Edgar. "La Vie de Jésus par le Docteur Strauss."

[On D. F. Strauss.] (Revue des deux mondes. Ser. 4, Vol. 16 ~~tom. 4~~, 1838, p. 585-629.) t. 16. 4. série 1838.

"Ce système conservait fidèlement, comme on le voit, le corps entier de la tradition; il n'en supprimait que l'âme. C'était l'application de la théologie de Spinosa dans le sens le plus borné, à la manière de ceux qui ne voient dans sa métaphysique que l'apothéose de la matière brute". (Lee, S. Inspiration of Holy Scripture, p. 284, note.) [over]

 [Karl Emil Adolf] 3980

Pruemers, Walter.

Spinozas Religionsbegriff. Inaugural-Dissertation zur Erlangung der Doktorwürde bei der hohen philosophischen Fakultät der Rheinischen Friedrich-Wilhelms-Universität zu Bonn vorgelegt von Walter Prümers aus Coblenz. Halle a. d. S.: Druck von Ehrhardt Karras, 1906. 1 p. l., 43(1) p. 8°. [over]

2. 4001

Quinet, Edgar. – [On D. F. Strauss] ... [cont.]

Lee (p. 453): "Meanwhile a systematized opposition to the inspiration of Scripture was growing up in another quarter... Quinet has truly said: L'homme qui de nos jours a fait faire le plus grand pas à l'Allemagne, ce n'est ni Kant, ni Lessing, ni le grand Frédéric; c'est Benedict Spinosa'."

The essay on D.F.S. is entitled "Examen de la vie de Jésus [of Strauss], & is found in his Oeuvres complètes (in 30 v., Paris: Hachette, [1895], in v. [8]). See his Christianity; tr. Cocks. 1846.) R. Heath, Quinet. 1881. (In L. L.)

2. 3981 [cont.]

Pruemers, [Karl Emil Adolf] Walter. – Spinozas...

"Die ... Dissertation bildet die zweite Hälfte einer grösseren Arbeit, die ... mit dem gleichen Titel als Bd. XXIII der 'Abhandlungen zur Philosophie und ihrer Geschichte' ... erscheinen wird."

(G.)

Signed: E. Quinet Edgar 1803-1875

De la Vie de Jésus par le Docteur Strauss.

Incl. refs to Sp

R

 3989

Puenjer, G. Ch. Bernhard.

Geschichte der christlichen Religionsphilosophie seit der Reformation. In zwei Bänden. Erster Band. Bis auf Kant. Braunschweig: C. A. Schwetschke und Sohn, 1880. 8°.

Baruch Spinoza, p. 302-330. (p. 322-330: Gegner und Anhänger des Spinoza.) (G.)

4009

Raciborski, Alexander [Aleksander].

Etyka Spinozy, krytycznie rozebrana i z tegoczesnym materjalizmen zestawiona. Lwów, 1882.

Review: Bill. Warsz. 1882; by Struve [Struveg?]

Ref.: Halpern, I, xl; D.-B., I, 526; Huan (entry: "Die Ethik Spinozas. Weimar, 1882"). [over]

2. 4010

Raciborski, Alexander. — Etyka Spinozy... [cont.]
Tr.: Spinoza's Ethics, critically examined and with modern materialism compared.

G-LIV-31 4015

Radliński, Ignacys.
Spinoza. Notatka historyczna. (Poradnik dla czytających książki. Warszawa, 1902. 4°. rok 2, p. 87-89, 99-105, 111-116, 123-129.)

(G.)

O-XXXIII-28 4016

Radliński, Ignacy.
Spinoza. Rzecz historyczno-społeczna. Warszawa: Skład Główny w Księgarni G. Centnerszwera i S-ki, 1910. 3 p.l., 290 p., 2 l. 8°.

The 2 l. contain a list of the writings of the author.

(A.S.O.)

MH - Phil 4215.2.83 5
" 3998.6 4027

Ragnisco, Pietro, 1839-1920.
Tommaso Rossi e Benedetto Spinoza. Saggio storico-critico del Prof. Pietro Ragnisco. Salerno: Stabilimento Tipografico Migliaccio, 1873. 52 p. 8°.

oNNC
LC
BM

Contents: [Capitolo I. Come il Rossi ha inteso Spinoza: egli è [over]

---

2. 4028

Ragnisco, Pietro. — Tommoso Rossi... [cont.]
fuori del movimento filosofico. Capitolo II. Analisi della dottrina del Rossi: Spinoza e Malebranche. Capitolo III. Nostre conclusioni.]
Rossi, T.
Malebranche,

Ravà, no. 11. (Harvard)

G-XXXV-40 4036

Rappaport, Samuel.
Spinoza und Schopenhauer. Inaugural-Dissertation... der vereinigten Friedrichs-Universität Halle-Wittenberg. Halle a.S., 1899. 4 p.l., 148 p., 1 l. 8°.

See B.549. (G.)

4043

Rauschenplat, A.
Bismarck und Spinoza. Eine Characterskizze. Hamburg, 1893. 19 p. 8°.

(B.M. vol. 45 Rand, p. 498. Not seen.)

O-XX-37 4053

Ravà, Adolfo.
Il pensiero di Spinoza nel terzo centenario della sua nascita. Relazione sul congresso filosofico tenutosi all' Aja dal 5 al 10 settembre 1932.
11 p.

Repr.: Rivista di filosofia. anno 23, no. 4.

Verslag, 1932/33, p. 33, no. 4. G-XIII-10

SCS 4052

Ravà, Adolfo.
Il pensiero di Spinoza e i problemi dell'ora. Discorso tenuto nella Rolzaal de L'Aja per il terzo centenario della nascita di Benedetto Spinoza. (In: Septimana Spinozana... Hagae Comitis, 1933. 8°. p. 28-34.)

(A.S.O.)

LAW LIBRARY 4 ~~Vecchio, Giorgio del, 1878-~~ 4048

Ravà, Adolfo.
Un contributo agli studi spinozani: Spinoza e machiavelli.) Modena: Società Tipografica Modenese, 1931. 15 p.

Repr.: [In:] Studi filosofico-giuridici dedicati a Giorgio del Vecchio nel XXV anno di insegnamento (1904-1929). Modena, Vol. II, 1931, p. 299-313.

Modena, Società tipografica modenese, 1930-1931. 2 v. 28 cm.

Verslag, 1931/32, p. 28, no. 11.

4066

Regius, Johannes

Cartesius Spinozae praelucens. [Dutch. Leeuwarden? 1715?]

"Scripsi ante quadriennium exiguum Tractatum lingua vernacula, cui titulus Cartesius Spinozae praelucens; in quo demonstravi, Cartesium in sua Philosophia ea jecisse fundamenta, quibus [over]

---

2. 4067

Regius, J. – Cartesius Spinozae ... [cont.]

Spinoza impiam & profanam suam Philosophiam inaedificavit." (Regius, J., Cartesius verus Spinozismi architectus, Amst., 1723 [2. ed.], p.5.

D.-B., II, 16, footnote: "Die erste holländische Schrift Regius' 'Cartesius Spinoza vorleuchtend' habe ich nie gesehen."

Not in v.d.L.

4074

Regius, J. [Notes.]

1. Regius: Cartesius Spinozae praelucens (1715?; in Dutch; original title not traced).
2. Andala: Apologia (1719; reply to to 1). Not in v.d.L.; apparently not known to D.-B.; mentioned by Grunwald (p. 32), but seems not to have seen it; Pollock (p. XXVII) gives a full transcription of the title. [over]

1-a. 4075

Regius, J. [Notes.] [cont.]

3. Regius: Cartesius verus Spinozismi architectus (1719; [2. ed.], 1723; a rejoinder to 2, or a defence of 1). v.d.L. 302 is wrong: there is no ed. Leeuwarden, 1718. (See Erhardt, p. 490.)
4. Andala: Cartesius verus Spinozismi eversor (1719; an answer to 3). v.d.L. 303 (not seen); Pollock (p. xxvii) brings a full transcription of the title.

---

2 4076

Regius, J. [Notes.]

5. Andala: Thrasonismus (1719; an "epilogue" to the polemic). v.d.L. 304 (the only item seen by him).

v.d.L.'s note to 303 [our no. 4]: "Hiertegen verscheen een Responsio apologetica" points to Andala's Apologia [no. 2], not known to him, and therefore not in place. Apparently, he followed Stolle, G. (Anleitung z. Historie d. [over]

2-a 4077

Regius, J. [Notes.] [cont.]

Gelahrtheit, 4. ed., 1736, p. 508): "... desgleichen den Jo. Regium, dessen Cartesium verum Spinosismi Architectum (gedruckt zu Leewarden [!] an 1718. in 8.) zwar Ruardus Andala in einem Buche, genannt: Cartesius verus Spinosismi eversor... zu widerlegen gesucht, der aber durch eine Responsionem Apologeticam in 8. absolute vertheidiget worden."

---

3 4078

Regius, J. [Notes.]

This is repeated by Dunin-Borkowski (Spinoza, Bd. 2, p. 16): "Klassische Beispiele dafür [polemics about Spinoza's relation to Descartes] haben wir in der Schrift des Joannes Regius 'Cartesius verus Spinozismi architectus' (Leeuwarden, 1718) und in Ruard Andalas 'Cartesius verus Spinozismi eversor...' (Franeker, 1719). [Footnote: Die erste holländi- [over]

3-a. 4079

Regius, J. [Notes.] [cont.]

sche Schrift Regius' 'Cartesius Spinoza vorleuchtend' habe ich nie gesehen. Von der Linde kennt sie nicht. Von Regius' architectus kenne ich nur eine Ausgabe Franeker 1719. Eine spätere erschien in Amsterdam 1723.] Regius schrieb dagegen eine apologetische Antwort und Andala antwortete (1719) in seinem 'Thrasonismus...'. (Neither Stolle nor v.d.L. states that Regius was the author of the Responsio apologetica.)

G-XXX-16, 17, 18 4117

Reinhold, Ernst.

Handbuch der allgemeinen Geschichte der Philosophie für alle wissenschaftlich Gebildete. Thl. 1-2^{1-2}. Gotha: Hennings'sche Buchhandlung, 1828-1830. 8°.

Spinoza's Pantheismus, Thl. 2, Hälfte 1, p. 222-286.

[over]

G-XXX-16, 17, 18 2. 4118

Reinhold, Ernst. – Handbuch der... [cont.]

Philosophische Methodologie. [Ethica:] 1. Von Gott. 2. [Ethica, pt. 2-5]. Nachfolger des Spinoza.

(G.) Not in v.d.L.

Reinhold, Ernst.

Lehrbuch der Geschichte der Philosophie. Jena: F. Mauke, 1836. 8°.

Spinoza, p. 412-441.
§ 174: Verhältniss der Lehre von Malebranche zu der cartesischen; § 175: Verhältniss der Lehre Spinoza's zu der cartesischen; § 176-177: Synthetische Methode Spinoza's; § 178-185: Die Ethik [over]

Reinhold, Ernst. – Lehrbuch der... [cont.]
des Spinoza; § 186: Spinoza's Ansichten vom Staat u. Recht. Geringer Eingang, den Spinoza's Lehre zu ihrer Zeit fand, Charakter dieser Lehre.

(G.)

Renan, Ernest.

Spinoza. (In his: The poetry of the Celtic races, and other studies. Translated, with introduction and notes, by W. G. Hutchison. London: W. Scott, [1896]. 16°. p. 162-186.)
The Scott library.

ord 7-31

Renan, Ernest.

Spinoza. (In his: The poetry of the Celtic races, and other studies. Translated, with introduction and notes, by W. G. Hutchison. London: W. Scott, [1896]. 12°. ~~[Camelot series.]~~ p. 162-186.)
[Camelot series.] U

Rensi, Giuseppe.

Spinoza. Roma: A. F. Formiggini, 1929. 103 (1) p. 16°. (Profili. no. 107)
An exposition of the philosophy.
Bibliografia, p. 101-102.

Verslag, 1929/30, p. 36, no. 15.
(G.)

Ribbing, Sigurd.

Försök till en framställning af Spinozismens hufvundsatser. Academisk afhandling som med vidtberömda Philos. Facultetens samtycke under inseende af Mag. Sigurd Ribbing... fö philosophiska gradens erhållande till offentlig granskning framställes af Alfred Victor Norinder... [pt. ?] I. Upsala: [over]

oNNC oLC

Ribbing, Sigurd. – Försök till en... [cont.]
P. Hanselli, 1851. 1 p. l., 32 p., [rest wanting in Harvard copy]. 12°.
(Baldwin)

Between p. 16 and 17 is inserted a ti-p. which reads as follows:
[See next card]

Pt. i, ii, paged continuously.

Ribbing, S.

Försök till en framställning af spinozismens hufvundsatser. Academisk afhandling som med vidtberömda Philos. Facultetens samtycke under inseende af Mag. Sigurd Ribbing... för philosophiska gradens erhållande till offentlig granskning framställes af Jonas Widén ... [pt. ?] II. Upsala: P. Hanselli, [over]

Ribbing, S. – Försök till en... [cont.]
1851

(Subj: Descartes & Spinoza.)

Ricco, Cesare. ?

Le dottrine giuridiche e politiche di B. Spinoza e T. Hobbes. [Giovinazzo: Tip. del R. Ospizio, 1884.] 48 p. 8°.

oNNC oLC

Contents: Introduzione. I. Antecedenti storici delle dottrine giuridiche e politiche di Spinoza e di Hobbes. II. Breve analisi delle due dottrine [over]

2. 4171

Ricco, Cesare. – Le dottrine... [cont.]
e cause specifiche che le determinarono. III: Analogie e differenze, loro ragion di essere, ed esame critico-comparativo dell'una e dell'altra dottrina.

Cat. Gen. della Libr. Ital. gives "J. Hobbes" and publ. as Vecchi

Ravà, no. 15. (Harvard)

---

cat. SP. not given in contents.

E 1449

Ripley, George.

, in 1838, Phil. Miscellanies, 2 v. Boston, 1838

Edited "Specimens of foreign standard literature; ~~of which 2 vols~~ philosophical miscellanies from the French" (Boston, 1838). v. 1 cont. V. Cousin's "On the destiny of modern philosophy"; &c. / T. S. Jouffroy, "On philosophy and common sense"; &c. v. 2: Jouffroy, "On the methods of philosophical study"; &c. – H. B. Constant de Rebecque, "The progressive development of religious ideas"; &c.

Ind 3-24 (cont.) No index. No refs. Allen

4175

Richter, F[ranz] Wilh[elm].

Ueber Pantheismus und Pantheismusfurcht. Eine historisch-philosophische Abhandlung. Leipzig: Verlag von R. Hartmann, 1841. IV, (1) 6-71 (1) p. nar. 8°.

Spinoza, p. 34-43.

(G.)

---

2. E 1450

Ripley, George. – Edited, in 1838, ... [cont.]
He translated from the French, with notices, Cousin's "Philosophical essays." (which? Perhaps: "Nouveaux fragments philosophique"? Or are the "essays" the same as in his ed. of the "Specimens"?)
R. was a pupil of Edward Tyrell Channing (at Harvard).
R. was a contributor to The Dial. He was on the staff (?) of the N.Y. Tribune.
His forefathers had been clergymen. The "Transcendental Club" was formed at his house (1836). It never became a formal organization.
He was the leader of the Brook Farm enterprise. (Cambr. H. Am. L. I, p. 339-40.)

4188

Richter, G. T.
[Reviews of his: Spinozas philosophische Terminologie.]

Literarisches Zentralblatt für Deutschland. Jahrg. 65, 1914, col. 1340. By Richert.

Theologische Literaturzeitung. Jahrg. 39, 1914, col. 274-275. By Th. Elfenhaus [Elfenhans?].

---

188 RS1 4210

Ritter, Heinrich.

Die christliche Philosophie nach ihrem Begriff, ihren äussern Verhältnissen, und in ihrer Geschichte bis auf die neuesten Zeiten. Göttingen: Dieterich, 1858-1859. 2 v. 8°.

Spinoza, v. 2, p. 260-274.

LC 21-18617 ordered (4) 9-10-58

v. d. L. 148 (XXVIII).

4206

Rijckius, Theodoor.

Theodori Ryckii ad diversos epistolae ineditae. Ed. G. D. J. Schotel. Hagae Comitum, 1843.

"At p. 6, in letter to Adrian Blyenburg, Aug. 14, 1675: – 'Inter nos rumor est auctorem Tractatus Theologico-politici in promptu habere librum de Deo et Mente multo priore isto peri- [over]

---

109 RS1 cat 4211

Ritter, Heinrich.

Geschichte der Philosophie. Zweite verbesserte Auflage. Hamburg, 1836-53. 12 v. 8

Spinoza: Vol. XI, 1852, pp. 169-291.

(N. Y. P. L.) – Not in v. d. L.

---

2. 4207

Rijckius, Theodoor. – Theodori Ryckii... [cont.]
culosiorem.' Compare Spinoza's Ep. 19 [now 68] of about the same date." (Pollock, p. XXIX.)
See: Freudenthal, Lg., p. 200, no. 16, where the two following sentences are also quoted. F. refers to Meinsma; but Pollock was the first to point it out.
About Rijckius, see Freudenthal, Spinoza, Tl. 1, p. 235 and 341.

QC3 NNU 5 RG1 4212

Ritter, Heinrich, 1791-1869.

Geschichte der Philosophie. Elfter Theil. Hamburg: F. Perthes, 1852. 8°.

Spinoza, p. 169-291.

v. d. L. 148 (XXVIII).

4228

Ritter, P.H.

Schets eener critische geschiedenis van het substantiebegrip in de nieuwere wijsbegeerte. Leiden: E.J. Brill, 1906. 8°.

Spinoza, p.124-150.
a. Kenvormen. b. De substantie.
See als Naamregister.

(G.)

E 1454

Robertson, George Croom, 1842-1892

Elements of general philosophy. Edited from notes of lectures delivered at the [University] College, [London], 1870-1892, by C[aroline] A. Foley Rhys Davids. London: J. Murray, 1896. XVI [I-II blank], 365 (1)p. 12°. (University extension manuals.)

Spinoza, p.59-63, 274-295.

[L.L.]

4229

Ritter, P.H.

Schets eener critische geschiedenis van het substantiebegrip in de nieuwere wijsbegeerte. Leiden: E.J. Brill, 1906. VIII(1), 476p. 8°.

Spinoza. a. Kenvormen; b. De substantie, p. 124-150. (p. 170-173: Spinoza and Leibniz. p. 415-422: [over]

E1468

Roe, E[dward] D[rake], 1859-1929.

The probability of freedom: a critique of Spinoza's demonstration of necessity. n. t.-p. [Oberlin, 1894.] 641-659p. 8°.

Title taken from first page.
Repr.: Bibliotheca Sacra, Oct., 1894.
Contents: [I. Fundamental and requisite positions of Spinoza. II. [over]

2.

Ritter, P.H.— Schets eener ... [cont.
Spinoza and Hegel.) See also Naamregister.

(G.)

2.

E1469

Roe, E[dward] D[rake].— The probability... [cont.]
Impossibility of speculative proof of either hypothesis of necessity or freedom.]
Author's autograph letter addressed to Librarian, inserted in Harvard copy states that the work was "done in Harvard under Professor Royce in 1886, and now revised and published." At time of publication author was Professor of mathematics at Oberlin College.

4234

Rivista di filosofia.

Benedetto Spinoza nel CCL anno dalla morte: MDCXXXII- MDCLXXVII. anno 18, no. 3. 1927.

Contents: Baratono, A. L'unità di Spinoza, p. 205-216.— Fossat, L. Spinoza e la critica moderna della Bibbia, p.217-234.— Goretti, C. Il Trattato politico di Spinoza, p.235-247.— Martinetti, P. Modi primitivi e derivati, infiniti e [over]

4252

Roelofsz, C.

De beteekenis van Christus voor Spinoza. Met een voorwoord van J. H. Carp. Zeist: J. Ploegsma, 1938.

(H.1.25)

2

4235

Rivista di filosofia.— Benedetto ... [cont.
finiti, p.248-261.— Mondolfo, R. Spinoza e la nozione del progresso umano, p.262-266.— Pastore, A. Il principio del metodo sperimentale nella filosofia di Spinoza, p.267-272.— Ravà, A. Le opere di Spinoza, p.273-316.— Solari, G. La dottrina del contratto sociale in Spinoza, p.317-353.— Tarozzi, G. La necessità spinoziana e il determinismo contemporaneo, p.354-360.— Villa, E. La conversione di Spinoza, p.361-369.— Ravà, A. Bibliografia degli scritti italiani relativi a Benedetto Spinoza publicati fino al 250° anniversario della sua morte, p.370-375.
(Verslag. 1927/28, p.47-48.)

4277

Rosenkranz, Hans.

Baruch Spinoza. Zu seinem 250. Todestag. (Jüdische Rundschau. Berlin, 1927. v.32, no.14, p. 95-96.)

Rossi, Paolo.

La fisica spinoziana e la fisica moderna. (In: Spinoza nel terzo centenario della sua nascita; pubblicazione a cura della Facoltà di Filosofia dell' Università Cattolica del Sacro Cuore. Milano, 1934. 8°. p. 117-131.)

Rotta, Paolo.

Il Cusano e lo Spinoza. (In: Spinoza nel terzo centenario della sua nascita; pubblicazione a cura della Facoltà di Filosofia dell' Università Cattolica del Sacro Cuore. Milano, 1934. 8°. p. 21-31.)

4297

Roverelli, Giuseppe.

Il pensiero Spinoziano nell' idealismo moderno. Milano: A. Vallardi [1934]. 118 p. [1-2 blank], 1 l. 12°.

Contents: Dedica. Prefazione. Introduzione. Cap. 1. Il nucleo vitale del pensiero Spinoziano nella fase razionalistica. Cap. 2. La filosofia di B. Spinoza.-Il sistema. Cap. 3. L'originali- [over]

---

2. 4298

Roverelli, Giuseppe. — Il pensiero... [cont.]

tà della filosofia Spinoziana. Cap. 4. La difficoltà implicite nella filosofia Spinoziana e le discussione del sistem Cap. 5. Il pensiero Spinoziano nell' idealismo moderno.

(A.S.O.)

---

 1. E1496

Spinoza, Baruch or Benedictus. [Tractatus Theologico-Politicus.]

Royce, Josiah.

Fugitive essays. With an introduction by J. Loewenberg. Cambridge: Harvard University Press, 1920. 3 p.L., (1)4-429(1) p., 1 port. 8.

1925 ed Spec Coll Spin.

See next card.

LC

---

2. E1497

Royce, Josiah.-Fugitive... [cont.]

Natural rights and Spinoza's essay on liberty [1880], p.290-299.

"Condensation of a lecture still extant on 'Spinoza's Theory of Religious Liberty in the State', read before the Historico-

See next card.

---

3. E1498

Royce, Josiah.-Fugitive... [cont.]

Political Club, March 1, 1878."- Published for the first time.

4309

Rubin, Salomon.

[illegible] (See his Introduction to his tr. of the Ethica, beginning.)

"I also have his Hash'arat ha-Nefesh, a dialogue that has a Spinoza allusion or two." (N. Isaacs, letter of May 23, 1940.)

S

DLC 4IC 480 4 (Priority 4) - pages as white as they can be! 4337 (?)

Sabatier de Castres, Antoine. 1742-1817.

De la souveraineté, ou connaissance des vrais principes du gouvernment des peuples. Altona, 1806. 2 v. in 1. 8°. [Not in L.L. Cat.]

Intr. de A. H. Meyer, .. 358 p.

of NL of LC

His Apologie de Spinosa is said to be a separate publication of a part of this work.

D.-B. (p. 11): "Es war kein neues Buch. Vor vielen Jahren war diese Apotheose als Teil eines grösseren Werkes erschienen". But p. 524: "Den ersten Druck, [over]

---

2. [Cont.] 4338

Sabatier de Castres, Antoine.—De la souveraineté. als Bestandteil eines grösseren Werkes, fand ich nicht. Again, in his "Sp. n. 300 Jahren," p.132: "Seine, Apologie ...' ist nicht erst 1905 und 1810 erschienen..., sondern bereits um 1796."

Freudenthal (II, 257) gives: Paris, 1766. (ditto Baldwin's Dictionary.)

Siwek [1937], 1796.

The following does not contain the "Apologie de Spinosa":

Sabatier de Castres, Pensées et observations morales et politiques pour servir à connaissance des vrais principes du gouvernement. Vienna, 1794. d. rel. 8.—

4339

Sabatier de Castres, Antoine.

["Sabatier (Antoine), dit Sabatier de Castres, littérateur français, né à Castres le 13 avril 1742, mort à Paris le 15 juin 1817." (Larousse.)]

4375

Samtleben, Gustav.

Geulincx ein Vorgänger Spinozas. Inaugural-Dissertation. Halle a.S.: Druck und Verlag von H.W. Schmidt, 1885. 48 p., 2 l. [last blank]. 8°.

Contents: [Introduction.] Geulincx' Verhältnis zu Descartes. Geulincx' Verhältnis zu Spinoza. Geulincx' Verhältnis zu Malebranche. Vita.

 4352

Saisset, Émile.

Maimonide et Spinoza. (Revue des deux mondes. v. 37, 1862, p. 296-334.)

[excerpted]

v.d.L. 279 n.

(Baldwin, Dictionary.) [L.L.]

---

 2. 4376

Samtleben, Gustav. — Geulincx ein ...

Same as the preceding, with a new title-page.

(G)

 + Spec Coll Spin 4353

Saisset, Émile. (both in Sp. Coll.)

La philosophie des Juifs. Maïmonide et Spinoza. (Revue des deux mondes. v. 37. 2. Période 1862. p. 296-334.)

Rev. of Surbe

Spec. in Spin. Reprinted in his: Précurseurs et disciples de Descartes. Paris, 1862.

v.d.L. 279 n.

 4390

Sarti, Christophorus.

Christophori Sarti in Academia Pisana Philosophia Rationalis Artis Criticae ac Metaphysicae P.P. Specimen theologiae naturalis. Lucae: Typis Francisci Bonsignori, 1780. xii, 173 p., 1 l. 8°.

Spinoza, p. ix, 5, 12, 45, 80-81; 92-93 (Deus non est in sensu Spino- [cover]

Entry to be verified.

(H.U.C.)

 4359

S[aisset], Ém[ile].

Spinoza. (In: Dictionnaire des sciences philosophiques. Par une société de professeurs et de savants. Paris, 1844-1852. 8°. tom. 6, p. 729-763.)

v. 1-2 read: Par une société de professeurs de philosophie.

(Seen) Not in v.d.L.

---

2. 4391

Sarti, Christophorus. — Christophori ... [cont.]

sae: Demonstratio 1-3); 101-102 (referring to Antonio Genovensi, Elementi di scienze metafisiche, which contains a discussion of Spinoza's substance); 104, 106; 144-146 (De iis, quae adversus Dei unitatem opponuntur. Oppositio quinta: Pro Spinosismo. Genus argumenti ad instantiam); 154-155 (De oppositionibus adversus Dei attributa physica. Oppositio septima: Adversus miracula pro Spinosa).

 4360

S[aisset], Ém[ile].

Spinoza. (In: Dictionnaire des sciences philosophiques. Par une société de professeurs et de savants sous la direction de M. Ad. Franck. Deuxième édition. Paris, 1875. 8°. p. 1652-1668.)

1875 ed. in Sp. Coll.

1844-52 ed. in Bibliog.

(H.C.O.)

 4396

Savérien, Alexandre.

Spinosa. (In his: Histoire des philosophes modernes, avec leurs portraits gravés par François. Tome premier... [Troisième édition.] À Paris, 1773. 8°. p. 171-193.)

port.: "Spinosa". At the right: C.P.R.

(G. 7 vols. Aetkirch, p. 96, no. 42: 8 vols.) [cover]

2 4397

Savérien, Alexandre. — Spinosa. . . . [cont.]

Altkirch, p 95–96, records: ed. 1761, fo (no. 39); 1762, fo (no. 40); 1773, 4° (no. 41); 1773, 8° (no. 42).

---

101 Sa9 NNC 4394

Savérien, Alexandre.

Spinosa. (In his: Histoire des philosophes modernes avec leur portrait gravé dans le goût du crayon d'après les planches in 4° dessiné par des plus grands peintres. Par M. Savérien. Publiée par François grav., des Des.' du Cab. du Roy &c. Partie 1. À Paris: de l'Imprimérie de Brunet, 1760. 8°. p. 169–191.)

[over]

---

2. 4395

Savérien, Alexandre. — Spinosa. . . . [cont.]

port.: "Spinosa." At right: C[illegible] Privilegie] [illegible] [Regis].

Savérien made use of Lucas in the Nouvelles littéraires.

[illegible] records the 4° [illegible] 1761–1778, which [illegible] appear[illegible] to 1759, 12°.

4536

Securus, Theodorus. — not seen in BM

1) Origo atheismi.

2) Prudentia theologica.

Enumerated in Colerus; not mentioned in v. d. L.

O-XXXVI-5 4538

Segond, J.

La vie de Benoît de Spinoza. Paris: Librairie Académique Perrin, 1933. IX [I–II blank], (1) 12–229 p., 1 l. 12°.

Contents: Prologue. — I. Les origines. II. L'apprentissage. III. L'évolution de l'amour. IV. Du règne de la loi au règne de la vérité. V. L'excommunication. VI. Le polisseur de verres. VII. L'homme libre. VIII. Le cercle spinoziste. IX.

[over]

O-XXXVI-5 2. 4539

Segond, J. — La vie de . . . [cont.]

Le refus de la chaire palatine. X. Le voyage à Utrecht. XI. La persécution. XII La visite de Leibniz. XIII. La mort de Spinoza.

Last l. has: E. Grevin — imprimerie de Lagny – 9-1932.

Siwek, ed. 3. 1933.

(A.S.O.)

O-XXXVI-13 4563

Sérouya, Henry.

Spinoza. (Mercure de France. Dec. 1, 1932. p. 257–313.)

[page-proof — unbound]

Contents: [Introductory note] I. Principaux traits de la vie de Spinoza. II. Sur le sources des spinozisme. III. Le spinozisme. 1. La nature de la connaissance. 2. Dieu. 3. La nature humaine. 4. La vie éternelle. IV. L'ac-

G-XIII-53 [over]

O-XXXVI-13 2. 4564

Sérouya, Henry. — Spinoza . . . [cont.]

tualité et l'influence du Spinozisme.

(G.) G-XIII-53

O-XXXV-23 4410

[Schaller, ?]

Benedikt Spinoza. (In: Der Biograph. Darstellung merkwürdiger Menschen der drei letzten Jahrhunderte . . . Halle, 1806. (Weisenh. Buchh.) nar. 12°. Bd. 5, Stück 3, p. 257–316.) by Prediger Schaller in Magdeburg (Vater von Julius Schaller (1810–1868)

Not in v. d. L.

Could hardly be Julius Schaller, whose "Dissertation" (on Leibniz) was pub. 1833.

(H. U. C.) Entered also: Biograph (Der).

G-XXX-23 4411

D

Schaller, Julius.

Geschichte der Naturphilosophie von Baco von Verulam bis auf unsere Zeit. Thl. 1–2. Leipzig: O. Wigand, 1841–1846. 8°.

Spinoza, Thl. 1, p. 326–343.

(G.) Thl. 2: Halle.

v. d. L. 148 (XXIV). B. 250.

E1522

Schanks, Alexander.
An introduction to Spinoza's Ethic. London: Macmillan and Co., Limited, 1938. v, 103(1)p. 8°.

Contents: Introduction. Section one: Definitions. Section two: Restatement of Spinoza's argument... Section three: Notes. Conclusion.
[over]

2. E1523

Schanks, Alexander.—An introduction.... [cont.]
- Index of principal topics.
Originally a University thesis, approaching "the subject from the point of view of the student, dealing with problems and difficulties peculiar to the novice rather than the larger problems of the expert".
"It has for long been customary to dismiss Spinoza rather curtly on logical grounds, and to overlook the fact that his aim was ethical and not logical. Yet the 'God intoxicated man' who inspired the great English Romantic poets something to say which even if we do not accept it, is too important to be lightly passed over" (p.2).
(A.S.O.)

E1529

Schedd, William T G [1820-1894]
History of Christian doctrine. New York, 1863.

American theologian; prof.

O-XXXV-27 4419

Schelling, Friedrich Wilhelm Joseph von.
F. W. J. Schelling's Denkmal der Schrift von den göttlichen Dingen, etc., des Herrn F. H. Jacobi und der ihm in derselben gemachten Beschuldigung eines absichtlich täuschenden, Lüge redenden Atheismus. Tübingen: J.G. Cotta, 1812. vi, 1 l., 216 p. 8°.
—— Sämmtliche Werke. Stuttgart: J. G. Cotta, 1856-1861. 8°. (v. 8, p. 39-53.)
v. d. L. 347 (n.).
G-XIII-43 Jacobi-Mendelssohn controversy

1924 ed. also DLC B798.S353 5 4430

✓ Schjelderup, Harald Krabbe, 1895-
Filosofiens historie / fra renaissancen til nutiden. Anden forøkede utgave. Oslo: Gyldendalske Bokhandel, 1925. 8°.
5 bl., 228 pages.
First ed., 1924. Kristiania etc.: Gyldendal, 1924
Ger. ed. 1929 5 p. l., 223 p., 22½ cm.
Baruch Spinoza, p. 44-51.
(L.L.) 6 L.L. Sp Coll. have Germ. ed. 1929
LC 25-7011
Une 1924 ed. - NNC
NN - YAL

G-XX-24 4431

Schjelderup, Harald K.
Geschichte der philosophischen Ideen von der Renaissance bis zur Gegenwart. Berlin: W. de Gruyter & Co., 1929. 8°.

Baruch Spinoza, p. 45-52.

Translated from the Norwegian by M. Leixner von Gruenberg.
(B.)

Spec Coll Spin 4441

Schlerath, F
[Review of:] Philosophische Weltbibliothek [by R. W. Glatzel]. (Chronicon Spinozanum. tom. 3, p. 351-358.)

O-XXXV-23 4439

Schlerath, F
Die Spinozafeier im Haag. ("Morgen, Der." v. 3, no. 1, Apr., 1927, p. 120-122.)
Excerpted

O-XXXV-41 4472

Schmoldt, Hans.
Der Spinozastreit. Würzburg: K. Triltsch Verlag, [1938].
2 p. l., 114 p., 1 l. [blank].

Contents: Vorrede. Einleitung. I. Teil: Die Grundlagen. 1. Kapitel: Lage und Aufgabe. 2. Kapitel: Die philosophischen Gespräche um Spinoza. II. Teil: Der geläuterte Spino-
[over]

O-XXXV-41 1-a. 4473

Schmoldt, Hans.— Der Spinozastreit... [cont.]
zismus. 3. Kapitel: Die Vorgeschichte der Morgenstunden. 4. Kapitel: Der Spinozastreit. 5. Kapitel: Zersetzung und Auflösung. III. Teil: Der transzendentale Spinozismus. 6. Kapitel: Vernichtung. 7. Kapitel: Die Gründe des Fortbestehens.

(A.S.O.)

O-XXV-41 2 4474

Schmoldt, H. [cont.]

"Gewöhnlich unterscheidet man in der Geschichte des Neuspinozismus zwei Epochen. Die erste fällt mit der Zeit des deutschen Idealismus zusammen, die zweite erstreckt sich von 1850 bis zur Gegenwart. Schon beim ersten Zusehen ergibt sich nun, dass die Epoche des Idealismus, soweit sie in irgend einem Verhältnis zu Spinoza steht, durch die Gestalt Moses Mendelssohns be- [over]

O-XXV-41 2-a 4475

Schmoldt, H.— [cont.]

stimmt ist, die darauf folgende Epoche durch Karl Marx. Mendelssohn und Marx sind die einzigen Denker, die ein unmittelbares Verhältnis zu Spinoza haben, und der Einfluss, den Spinoza auf den Idealismus und die Neuzeit erlangte, ist nur verständlich, sieht man die Umformung, die er durch jene beiden erfuhr. Die folgende Arbeit will dies bei Mendelssohn aufzeigen... Durch ihn als Menschen wirkt Spinoza auf den Idealismus. Alles, was Mendelssohn jemals tat, hat seine Be- [next]

O-XXV-41 3 4476

Schmoldt, H. [cont.]

ziehungen zu Spinoza... Spinozismus ist für Mendelssohn nicht nur ein philosophisches Lehrgebäude, sondern etwas Lebendiges, zu ihm selbst Gehöriges. Darum geht es der folgenden Arbeit auch nicht um die Philosophie Mendelssohns... sondern um dessen 'Politik'. Weil hierin aber uraltes talmudisches Erbgut durchbricht, steht nicht der 'Philosoph', sondern der Jude Mendels- [over]

O-XXV-41 3-a 4477

Schmoldt, H.— [cont.]

sohn im Vordergrund; Mendelssohn als Jude und Propagandist Spinozas!" (p.3-4).

The history of "Neuspinozismus unter dem Vorzeichen der Frage nach der Vereinbarkeit jüdischen und nicht jüdischen Denkens" begins with Mendelssohn's _Philosophische Gespräche_, 1755 (p.20).

O-XXXV-42 4484

Schoeler, Heinrich von.

Versuch einer intellektuellen Weltanschauung durch Spinoza und Schelling. (In his: Kritik der wissenschaftlichen Erkenntnis... Leipzig, 1898. 8°. p.148-158.)

p.148-154: Spinoza.

(A.S.O.)

4485

Schoenbaum, Mor.

Spinoza. (Českožidovský kalendář. Jahrg. 24[?]. 1922/23.)

NUT 42 5 4489 (?)

Jan Hendrik, 1811-1885.

Scholten, Johannes Henricus.

Manuel d'histoire comparée de la philosophie et de la religion. Traduit du Hollandais par A. Réville. Paris: Treuttel & Wurtz, 1861. 8°

Bénédict de Spinoza, p. 74-76.

p.l., 183p. 24cm.

NNC

LC — h.l. gives Johannes Henricus, 1811-1885

BN — Jan Hendrik, prof à Leide

New Ned. Biog. Woordenboek gives Johannes Henricus

O-XXXV-6 4510

Schulze-Soelde, Walther.

Die Methode Spinozas im Lichte Kants. Eine Studie über Dogmatismus und Kritizismus. Inaugural-Dissertation zur Erlangung der Doktorwürde der hohen philosophischen Fakultät der Grossherzoglich Badischen Ruprecht-Karls-Universität in Heidelberg vorgelegt von Dr. jur. Walter Schulze-Soelde. [over]

O-XXXV-6 2. 4511 [cont.]

Schulze-Soelde, Walther.— Die Methode... Hamm (Westf.): Buchdruckerei Emil Griebsch, 1916. 42p., 1 l. 8°

(G.)

O-XLIII-35 4518

Schwarz, A

Baruch Spinoza. (Jüdisches Litteratur-Blatt. Magdeburg, 1892. 4°. Jahrg. 21, p.45-47, 49-51, 53-54, 57-59.)

Vortrg im Verein für jüd. Geschichte und Litteratur in Karlsruhe am 1. Februar 1892.

(A.S.O.)

[over]

C-XLIII 3 2. 4517

Schwarz, A. — Baruch Spinoza ... [cont.]

Treats on his life and philosophy.

C-XXXVI-3 4517

Schwarz, Hermann.

Gottesvorstellungen grosser Denker. München, 1921. [c.]

nothing:

— Jenseits von Theismus und Pantheismus. Berlin: Junker und Dünhaupt, 1928.

(Perhaps: Schwarz?)

O-XXXVI-5 4532

Schwegler, Albert.

Geschichte der Philosophie im Umriss. Ein Leitfaden zur Übersicht. Vierzehnte Auflage, durchgesehen und ergänzt von R. Koeber. Stuttgart: Verlag von C. Conradi, 1887. IV, 372 p. 8°.

Spinoza, p. 184-191.

G-XXIV-23 4534

Schweitzer, Albert.

Kultur und Ethik. Kulturphilosophie zweiter Teil. Olaus Petri Vorlesungen an der Universität Upsala. München: C.H. Becksche Verlagsbuchhandlung, [cop. 1923]. XXIII(1), 280 p. 8°.

X. Naturphilosophie und Weltanschauung bei Spinoza und Leibniz, p. 113-121. — See also Namenregister.

Spec Coll Spin 4535

Schweitzer,

Kultur und Ethik. Bern: Haupt, 1923.

Spinoza,

4535a

Scotus, Joannes.

See: Erigena, Joannes Scotus.

E1548

Shaftesbury, Anthony Ashley, 3rd earl of Shaftesbury. [1671-1713.]

He is rightly reconed among the Deists.

He lived (resided) in Holland in his early manhood.

He befriended Toland, who in 1699 surreptitiously pub. his benefactor's An Inquiry concerning Virtue, or Merit, S.'s most important work. Here he promulgates his doctrine of "the moral sense" for which he is mostly remembered. "The natural affection of a rational creature", he maintains, will take in the universe, and love all things that have being in the world.

1-a E1549

Shaftesbury, Anthony Ashley, ... — He is rightly... [cont.]

In the universal design of things, "nothing is supernumerary or unnecessary." The whole is harmony; the mind of man is itself in harmony with the cosmic order. But "the virtuoso has obscured the philosopher," says Sorely (Cambr. Hist. Eng. Lit., IX, 300).

His writings are contained in 3 vols. entitled Characteristics of Men, Manners, Opinions, Times (1711).

A 2. ed., rev. & enl., was ready in 1713 (Pub.?)

S. was admired by Leibniz and Diderot.

---

2 E1550

Shaftesbury. [cont.]

Towards the end of the 17. cent., Spinoza's philosophy "had already has been in large part assimilated by S. (– though it was not safe for him to acknowledge it" [Robertson, Pioneer Humanists, p. 178]) in the "Inquiry concerning Virtue or Merit". S. widely affected the ethical thought of the cultured class throughout northern Europe. "It is through him, with Bolingbroke for unconfessed mediator, that Spinozism enters into Pope's Essay on Man ... And there is plenty of evidence that Spinoza was read by many of the English deists and men of science" (Robertson) [over]

893.105 NNJ-C
M878 NN 4577

Shemueli, Ephraim. a

The tragedy of Baruch Spinoza. [Hebrew.] (Moznaim. v. 8, no. 4-5, Feb.-Mar., 1939, p. 445-458; v. 9, no. 3, July-Aug., 1939, p. 332-344.)

In Spinoza Ch., in less complete form

(Taken from: Baron, Salo W., in Jewish social studies, II, no. 3; bibl. [Bibl.], no. 228.)

 4579

Shestov, Léon.

In Job's balances; on the sources of the eternal truths. By Leo Chestov. Translated by Camilla Coventry and C. A. Macartney. London: J. M. Dent and Sons Limited, [1932]. xxxi, 413 p., 1 l. 8°.

"First published in Russian by Annales Contemporaines, Paris, 1929. This Edition, translated from the German and collated with the Russian, first published [over]

 2. 4580

Shestov, Léon. – In Job's balances ... [cont.]

1932".

Children and stepchildren of time; Spinoza in history, p. 247-273.

Spinoza is also discussed [p. xvi-xxi] in the "Foreword: science and free inquiry," p. xi-xxi; and (at p. 371-380) in the essay "What is truth? On ethics and ontology," p. 368-407, being a reply to the criticism made by Prof. Hering on the author's essay "Memento Mori" in Revue philosophique. – See also Index. [L. L.]

 4582

Shestov, Léon.

Kinder und Stiefkinder der Zeit. (Das historische Los Spinozas.) (Die Kreatur. Berlin, 1928. Jahrg. 2, p. 369-396.)

Translated (from the original Russian?) by Hans Ruoff.

(A. S. O.)

4589 (?)

Sibbern, Frederik Ludvig Gabriel.

[Published as a test for the title of "Magisterconferent" of the University of Copenhagen, an article in answer to: At utvikle Grundtanken i Spinozas Ethik. prob. before 1820 city?. yr? see BN

not recognized in BM or BN
verify in monograph on Si, if possible

L. T. S. (not ident. or located)

 4609

Sigwart, H[einrich] C[hristoph] W[ilhelm].

Der Spinozismus historisch und philosophisch erläutert mit Beziehung auf ältere und neuere Ansichten. Tübingen: C. F. Osiander, 1839. iv, 265 p., 1 l. 12°.

v. d. L. 310a–B. 246.

(A. S. O. – in 16°. – N. Y. P. L.: 12°.) [over]

 2. 4610 [cont.]

Sigwart, H[einrich] C[hristoph] W[ilhelm]. – Der...

Contents (abbreviated): Vorrede. – Einleitung. – I. Das historische Verhältniss des Spinozismus. A. Ueber den Zusammenhang des Spinozismus mit der Cartesianischen Philosophie ... B. Ueber den Zusammenhang des Spinozismus mit den orientalischen Lehren. II. Die Grundbegriffe und Grundsätze des Spinozismus ... III. Die Spinozische Lehre von der Welt ...

Review: Ritter, Heinrich, in: Göttingische gelehrte Anzeigen, Sept. 19, 1839, p. 1489-1504; Sept. 21, p. 1505-1508. [not seen]

4631

Silesius

Ellinger, Georg.

Angelus Silesius; ein Lebensbild. Breslau: W. G. Korn, 1927. 8°.

Spinoza and Johannes Scheffler, p. 115, 117-122.

(G.)

 4636

Simon, Ernst.

Zu Hermann Cohens Spinoza-Auffassung. (Monatsschrift für Geschichte und Wissenschaft des Judentums. Breslau, 1935. 8°. Jahrg. 79, p. 181-194.)

Jahrg. 79, Heft 2 forms a "Maimonides-Festschrift. – "Der Aufsatz dient zwar nicht unmittelbar der Maimuniforschung; er schien mir aber wegen seiner Hinweise auf Maimuni und Cohens Maimuni-Auf- [over]

 2. 4637

Simon, Ernst. – Zu Hermann Cohens ... [cont.]

fassung aus dem Rahmen unserer Festschrift nicht herauszufallen. (Note by editor.)

 4639

Simon, Jules.

Spinoza. (Revue des deux mondes. v. 2. 1843. p. 756-786.) excerpted

(A. S. O.)

Comp. v. d. L. 44 n.

Siwek, Paul.

L'âme et la corps d'après Spinoza. (La psychophysique spinoziste.) Thèse pour le doctorat présentée à la Faculté des Lettres de Clermont-Ferrand par Paul Siwek, Docteur en Philosophie. Paris: Libraraire Félix Alcan, 1930. 4 p. l. [the first blank], [I]VIII–XXVII, 202 p., 1 l. 8°. Bibliography, p. XXII–XXVII.

Smith, T.V.

Spinoza's political and moral philosophy. (Monist. Chicago, 1933. v. 43, p. 23-39.)

"A paper read at the tercentenary commemoration of Spinoza sponsored by The Philosophy Club of Chicago and held at The University of Chicago on December 9, 1932".

Slee, J. C. van.

De Rijnsburger Collegianten. Geschiedkundig onderzoek. Bekroond door Teyler Godgeleerd Genootschap. Haarlem: De Erven F. Bohn, 1895. 1 p. l. [blank], XI p., 1 l., 455 (1) p., 4 pl. 8°.

Hoofdstuk IV: De Bredenburgsche twisten (p. 238-266; p. 238-239: Spinoza en de Rijnsburgers). See also p. 126 and 392.

Sokolow, Nahum. 1859-1936

Spinoza the Jew. (Jewish review [London]. Vol. I, 1932-1933, no. 3, Dec. 1932-March, 1933, p. 35-44.)

Same as: Der Jude Spinoza, but somewhat abbreviated.

Slee, J. C. van. — De Rijnsburger... [cont.]

Review: Theologische Literaturzeitung. Jahrg. 21, 1896, Col. 112-115. By Benrath.

"Dass der grosse niederländische Pantheist zeitweise (1661-64) in Rijnsburg Wohnung nahm, mag zwar mit dem jeder Verfolgung abgeneigten Geist, wie er da herrschte, in Zusammenhang stehen, aber weitere Folgen hat Spinoza's Anwesenheit dort nicht gehabt – höchstens dass seine Lehre Anlass zu einer in Cap. 4 dargestellten theologischen Streitigkeit gegeben hat."

Sonne, I.

L'ebraismo di Spinoza. Firenze: "La nuova Italia" Editrice, [1933]. 8 p. 4°.

Repr.: La nuova Italia. no. 7, July 20, 1933.

Smith, Preserved. 1880-1941

[Review of: The encyclopaedia of religion and ethics, v. 11.] (Nation. New York, 1921. v. 112, no. 2919, June 15, 1921, p. 852.)

"The most remarkable biography in this volume is on that most attractive subject, Spinoza. The great beauty of his life and character, as well as of his philosophical ideas, is clearly set forth. Indeed, save in some parts of the Bible, the Jewish race has produced nothing

over

Sonne, I.

Un manoscritto sconosciuto delle "adnotationes" al trattato teologico-politico di Spinoza. (Civilta moderna. 1933?) 1931?

Reprint. 8 p. 8°.

Smith, Preserved. — [Review of:... [cont.]

of equal sublimity to the philosophy of this 'God-intoxicated' man, who learned to view all things 'under the form of eternity'. In contemplation of this universe he finally attained what he aimed at from the beginning, 'the enjoyment of supreme, continuous, and permanent happiness'."

Sonne, I. — Un manoscritto... [cont.]

The MS. described is in the Marucelliana Library in Florence, Italy; written on 25 slips, by an anonymous copyist, and inserted between certain p. in a copy of the Tr. Theol.-Pol. (ed. pr., issue A). In addition to the "Adnotationes", The Tractatus contains also marginal and interlinear glosses, which are reproduced by Sonne in an "Appendice" (p. 7-8), which are reproduced in: Het Spinozahuis. jaarverslag 37, 1933/34, p. 19-20.

2 4686

Sonne, I [cont.]

The author argues against certain conclusions reached by C. Gebhardt with regard to the "Adnotationes" in the latter's ed. of the Opera (v. 3, "Textgestaltung", p. 382-396), in particular that the Marchand-Leyden (ML) MS. is not a copy of Spinoza's autograph but of a copy which combined marginal glosses [over]

2-a. 4687

Sonne, I. — Un manoscritto ... [cont.]

with the "Adnotationes," and which was the source of both, the ML MS. and that of the Marucelliana (MF).

(Date of pub. to be ascertained; also note to be revised.)

4681

Sonne, Isaia.

Spinoza e Pascal. [Per il terzo centenario di Spinoza.] Como: E. Cavallere, 1933-XI. 10p., 1 l., [blank]. 8°.

port. (Op. posth.; Dutch inscription), p. 8.

Repr.: L'Idea Sionistica. anno 3, no. 6-7, Oct.-Nov., 1932. [over]

2. 4682

Sonne, Isaia. — Spinoza e Pascal... [cont.]

Being the same as the Hebrew published on the occasion of the tercentenary of Pascal's birth (1923).

4690

Sophia, Electress of Hannover. [1630-1714.]

"Karl Ludwig war in späteren Jahren ebenso wie seine Schwester, die Kurfürstin Sophie von Hannover, Spinozist." (Freudenthal, I, 342. This statement, found in the "Anmerkungen", is Gebhardt's.)

Sophia was reputed "die Klügste Frau ihrer Zeit" (Überweg). Friend of Leibniz and F. M. van Helmont. Protectress of Toland.

Consult: her Correspondence with her brother (ed. Boden- [over]

2. 4691 [cont.]

Sophia, Electress of Hannover. — "Karl Ludwig... mann, 1886); also her Memoirs (tr. Forrester, 1888); and Leibniz' Correspondence with her (ed. Kropp, 1864-75). Further, M. Mayer in Chronicon Spinozanum, III, 20-44.

4715

Spinozahuis, Het.

Mededeelingen van wege Het Spinozahuis.

[no. 1-5]

Leiden, 1934 -

[no.] 1. Vaz Dias, A.M., and Tak, W. G. van der. De firma Bento y Gabriel de Spinoza. 1934.

" 2. Vaz Dias, A. M. Uriel da [over]

2. 4716

Spinozahuis, Het. — Mededeelingen... [cont.]

Costa... 1936.

[no.] 3. Coert, J. Spinoza en Grotius... 1936.

" 4. Coert, H.J. Spinoza's betrekking tot de geneeskunde... 1938.

" 5. De Jong, K.H.E. Spinoza en de Stoa. 1939.

" 6. Crommelin, C.A. Spinoza's natuurwetenschappelijk denken. 1939.

 4720

Spizelius, Theophilius.

Felix literatus ex infelicium periculis et casibus; sive, De vitiis literatorum commentationes historico-theosophicae, quibus infelicium ex animo, h.e. vitiosorum literatorum calamitates et miseriae, conquisitis exemplis et documentis selectioribus exponuntur, atque eruditis, ad verae et imperturbatae felicitatis sedem tendentibus via tutissima ostenditur. Authore Theophilo Spizelio. Augustae Vindelicorum: Apud T. Goebelium, [over]

1-a. 4721

Spizelius, Theophilius. — Felix Literatus... [cont.]

9 p. l., 1184 p. 8°

Benedictus Spinosa, p. 143-145.

See v. d. L. 358 (n.).

Stitzel, Lutheran theologian, of Augsburg; 1630-1691.

Against the Tr. Theol.-Pol.

D.W.L.

2 4722

Spizelius, Theophilus.- Felix literatus... [cont.]

Freudenthal, Lebensgeschichte Spinoza's, p. 255: ..."Infelix Litteratus ist 1680 zu Rotterdam erschienen. V. d. Linde ... setzt diese Schrift, die er Infelix litterator nennt, in das Jahr 1675, verwechselt sie also mit einem andern Werke Spitzel's, Felix literatus, das im J. 1675 gedruckt ist".

Dunin-Borkowski, Spinoza n. 300 Jahren, p. 125-26: "Der arme Augsburger Spitzel (Spizelius) kam kaum zu einer richtigen Anführung seiner Buchtitel kommen. Einige [over]

2-a 4723

Spizelius, Theophilus.- Felix literatus... [cont.]
sprechen vom 'Infelix literator', andere vom 'Felix L.'; aber auch ein infelix und felix literatus tauchen auf. Von der Linde irrt hier. Freudenthal hat ein Spinoza-Zitat aus dem tatsächlich existierenden 'Felix literatus' (1676, [Fr., above, gives: 1675] 142) gebracht (Ed. Bibl. Spin. I. 342). Aber auch im 'Infelix Literatus'... (Augsb. 1680 [Fr. gives: Rotterdam]) findet sich S. 363 und 364 ein scharfer Angriff auf Spinozas Prophetentheorie."

MH; OCl; CtY - Hkg8 331 4 4724

Splettstösser, Willi.

Der Grundgedanke in Goethes Faust... Berlin: G. Reimer, 1911. viii, 191 p. 8°. 21 cm.
No author index

oNNC - but has both 1875- and 1877-; DLC did give Willy, 1875-; Kayser gives Willi

"Den Grundgedanken des Goetheschen 'Faust' erblickt diese Arbeit im Determinismus Spinozas. Sie will den Nachweis führen, dass Faust prädestiniert ist zur Gnade, und dass seines Lebens Lauf und Ausgang [over]

CtY; MH; DLC; oNNC; oLC E1603

Stearn, H. T. 4"

Spinoza. (Cambridge review. Vol. II, 1880-1881. Feb. 16, 1881, p. 166-167.)

Reply to: Pearson, Karl. Spinoza. II. (Cambridge review. Feb. 9, 1881, p. 155-156.)

"I had intended to close my letter with a brief discussion of some of Spinoza's conclusions; but ... I will ... continue my letter in a later number of the Review. (Verify!) Note S.'s letter re 1. article of P.

G-XXXI-50 4782

Stein, Ludwig.

Neue Aufschlüsse über den literarischen Nachlass und die Herausgabe der Opera posthuma Spinozas. (Archiv für Geschichte der Philosophie. Bd. 1, 1888, p. 554-565.)

Based on H. G. Schuller's letters to Leibniz. Author endeavours to show that Schuller was the editor of the Op. posth. [Berlin: G. Reimer, 1888.]
Repr.: (1) 554-565 (1) p. 8°. (G.)

893.105 I19 1. 4784

Steinschneider, Moritz, 1816-1907
See 4787; 834Au3 BZ II, p. 5

["(Spinoza.) Die k. Bibliothek in Berlin besitzt die Stephanus'sche Pentateuchausgabe 1539-44 in einzelnen Bänden, welchen teilweise ein Amsterdamer Titel vorgebunden ist. Auf Leviticus findet sich der

See next card.

2. 4785

Steinschneider, Moritz.-["(Spinoza.)... [cont.]
fein geschriebene Namen 'Spinosa'. Ist ein Autograph Spinoza's zu einer Vergleichung zugänglich"?] (In: Jahrbücher für jüdische Geschichte und Litteratur. Hrsg. von N. Brüll. ~~Frankfurt a.M.~~, 1889. 8. 9. Jahrg., p. 82-83.)

NNC 893.105 I19 5

See next card.

3. 4786

Steinschneider, Moritz.-["(Spinoza.)... [cont.]

Apparently Steinschneider, as before him M. Philipson, mistook the z for "s" — a mistake, owing to the method of 17. cent. writing, quite common.

"Hier [in the Royal Library at Berlin] ist auch ein Pentateuch in fünf Bänden, der wahrscheinlich das Handexemplar Spinozas [over]

3-a. 4787

Steinschneider, Moritz.- ["(Spinoza.)... [cont.]

Auf einen Titel ist sein Name eingeschrieben, es scheint mir fast unzweifelhaft seine Handschrift, ich habe dieselbe bisher [Feb. 2, 1870] nur in Facsimile gesehen".
834Au3 BZ (B. Auerbach, Briefe an J. Auerbach, II, p. 5.)

AT S 893.105 I19 NNC 4 1. 4788

Steinschneider, Moritz.

Miscellen von Moritz Steinschneider [1. Die Frau und der Narr.- 2. Isak Lathif.- 3. Zur Familie Jachja.- 4. Josef Caspi.- 5. Josef b. Israel.- 6. Meir Daspira?- 7. No'man oder Nu'man.

See next card.

AT
S

2. 4789

Steinschneider, Moritz.-Miscellen...[cont.]
p.82-83
8.Rakuthi.- 9.Spinoza.- 10.Todros aus
Cavaillon.- 11.Teutsch-Benschen.]
[Frankfurt a.M.: H.L.Brönner,1889.]
n.t.-p. p.72-85,1 L. 8.

See next card.

AT
S

3. 1816-1907 4790

Steinschneider, Moritz.-Miscellen...[cont.]

Repr.: Brüll's Jahrbücher für jüdische Geschichte und Litteratur. Jahrg.9. 1889.

Concerning an autograph of Spinoza in the Prussian Staatsbibliothek.

4797

Stern, Daniel, pseud. of Marie d'Agoult.

See: Agoult.

O-XXXVII-24 4800

Stern, J.

Die Philosophie Spinoza's. Erstmals gründlich aufgehellt und populär dargestellt. Zweite, verbesserte Auflage. Stuttgart: J.H.W. Dietz, 1894. VIII, 192 p. port. 12°. (Internationale Bibliothek. Bd. 8.)
B.484.

(A.S.O.)
G-XIV-12 [over]

O-XXXVII-24 2. 4801

Stern, J.— Die Philosophie ... [cont.]

Contents (abbreviated): Vorbemerkung.- Erster Theil. Karakter und Bedeutung der Philosophie Spinoza's. Zweiter Theil. Spinoza's Leben und Schriften ... Dritter Theil. Das System Spinoza's ... - Anhang. I. Das Gesetz der Entwicklung. Darwin, Hegel, Marx und Engels. II. Die Vernichtung der Individualität und die Fortdauer der Gattung ... - Alphabetisches Register.

G-XIV-12

Oct 7-31 E1610

✓ Sterry Peter.) Incl refs to Sp
8235+45
BP Pinto, Vivian de Sola.

Peter Sterry, platonist and puritan, 1613-1672. A
Sp. see biographical and critical study with passages selected
Index, from his writings. (Cambridge University Press.
p.241. [1934] 12s. 6d.) xiii+242p.
"A discourse of the freedom of the will", 1675.
This is his best extended effort. There is discontinuity and confusion in his thought. As a philosophic performance it is not of fine quality. It is also eclectic. Spinozism, Platonism, Calvinism, each contributed to his creed.

G-XXXI-98 4812

Stockum, Theodorus Cornelis van.

Spinoza-Jacobi-Lessing. Ein Beitrag zur Geschichte der deutschen Literatur und Philosophie im 18. Jahrhundert. Proefschrift ter verkrijging van den graad van Doctor in de Wijsbegeerte aan de Rijks-Universiteit te Groningen, op gezag van den Rector-Magnificus Dr. J. van Wageningen, Hoogleeraar in de Faculteit der Letteren [over]

G-XXXI-98 1-a. 4813

Stockum, T. C. van.— Spinoza-Jacobi-... [cont.]

en Wijsbegeerte, tegen de bedenkingen van de Faculteit in het openbaar te verdedigen op Vrijdag 19 Mei 1916, des namiddags te 4 uur, door Theodorus Cornelis van Stockum geboren te Dordrecht. Groningen: P. Noordhoff, 1916. 4 p. l., 108 p. 8°.

Preface and "Stellingen" (p.105-108) in Dutch.

Contents: Einleitung. Kapitel 1. Jacobi vor dem Gespräch mit Lessing. Kapitel 2. Jacobi und Spinoza. Kapitel 3. Jacobi und [next]

G-XXXI-98 2 4814

Stockum, T.C. van.

Lessing. Kapitel 4. Spinoza und Lessing.

"Der Lessing der siebziger Jahre, der Lessing des Gesprächs mit Jacobi zeigt sich vielfach von Spinoza beinflusst. Am wenigsten freilich auf dem Gebiete, wo Jacobi die grösste Uebereinstimmung zu finden glaubte, auf dem der Metaphysik. Um so grösser dagegen ist die Abhängigkeit... in allen Fragen, die die Theologie betref- [over]

G-XXXI-98 2-a. 4815

Stockum, T. C. van.— Spinoza-Jacobi... [cont.]

fen, und hier von einem deutlichen Einflusz der Lehren des theologisch-politischen Traktats zu sprechen, wird nicht zuviel gesagt sein" (p.103).

(G.)

Stockum, T. C. van.
M[eijer], W[illem]. [Review.] (Tijdschrift voor wijsbegeerte. jaarg. 11, 1917, p. 108-110.)
(A.S.O.)

Struve, Burckhard Gotthelf.
Bibliotheca philosophica Struvviana emendata continuatae atque ultra dimidiam partem auctae a L. M. Kahlio. Gottingae, 1740. 8°. 2 v.
I: [VI] l., +76; II - [IV] l., 454 p.
Spinoza, v. 1, p. 104-105, note.
See Index Auctorum at end of II, p. 430.: 139, 247, 274 seq. 67 seq. (II).
(Transcript of note penes me.)

Stolle, Gottlieb. 1673-1744
"Beiträge zur Kenntniss des 17. u. 18. Jahrhunderts aus den handschriftlichen Aufzeichnungen Gottlieb Stolle's. Mitgetheilt von G. E. Guhrauer." (Allgemeine Zeitschrift für Geschichte. Berlin, 1847. Bd. 7, p. 384-436, 481-531.)
v. d. L. 86.
[L. L.]

Sue, Eugène, 1804-1857.
De Rohan; or, The court conspirator. An historical romance. New York: G. Munro, 1880. 74 p. 32½ cm. (Seaside Library, v. 39, no. 800.)
Spinoza is introduced in the first chapter.
LC CA 10-1465 Unrev'd
NN-NKS p.v.14 NY: Harper & Bros., 1845. iv, 5-152 p. 8°.

Strauss, Leo.
Zur Bibelwissenschaft Spinozas und seiner Vorläufer. (Verein zur Gründung und Erhaltung einer Akademie für die Wissenschaft des Judentums. Korrespondenzblatt. Berlin, 1926. no. 7, p. 1-22.)

T

Tarin, Jean-Henri.
Spinoza théologien. Thèse présentée a la Faculté de Théologie de l'Université de Genève pour obtenir le grade de bachelier en théologie. Genève: P. Richter, 1909. 96 p. 8°.
(G.)

Strong, Charles Augustus. 1862-1940
"Final observations." (Journal of philosophy. v. 38, 1941, p. 233-243.)
Sections: "First principles" and "Determinism" (p. 239-243) deal with his relation to Spinoza.
Posthumosly published. "This manuscript was intended to express his final observations on his system of philosophy" (p. 233; editor's note).
(A.S.O.) [over]

Tarin, Jean-Henri. — Spinoza théologien... [cont.]
Chapitre VI: Influence de Spinoza (p. 55-59).

Strong, Charles Augustus. — Final... [cont.]
"In my reply to Montague [Journal of philosophy, v. 36, p. 393-405] I have indicated that my system of metaphysics bears a close resemblance to that of Spinoza. I wish in this essay to make clear what are the points of resemblance and what are the points of difference" (p. 239).

Taylor, A. E. (Alfred Edward) 1869-1945
Some incoherencies in Spinozism. (I-II.) (Mind. n. s. v. 46, 1937, p. 137-158, 281-301.)
I. Contends "that Spinozism can produce no intelligible theory of natural knowledge, because by ignoring the concipient, it has made its 'mind' into one which may be [over]

2. E1630

Taylor, A.E. – Some incoherencies... [cont.]

called a theatre of "psychical occurrences", but really knows nothing." II. Argues that Spinoza's "system, if consistent, is precluded from having any genuinely ethical doctrine at all by its proposed exclusion [Ethica, pt. 3, Preface] of the notion of moral value.

---

105 M E1631

Taylor, A.E.

"Some incoherencies in Spinozism". (Mind, 1937.)

Opposed to the prevalent "attitude of Spinoza-worship". Analysis of the problem of the relation between substance and modes, and evaluation of S's theory of the control of the emotions". Sees many incoherencies and attempts to invalidate the truth of S's conclusions. (1937)

G-XXXI-1 4926

Tennemann, Wilhelm Gottlieb.

Grundriss der Geschichte der Philosophie für den akademischen Unterricht. Vierte vermehrte und verbesserte Auflage oder zweite Bearbeitung von Amadeus Wendt. Leipzig: J.A. Barth, 1825. 8°.

Spinoza, p. 339-344.

(G.)

G-XXXI-1 1-a. 4927

Tennemann, W.G. – Grundriss der... [cont.]

Tennemann, W.G., Grundriss der Geschichte der Philosophie. Lpz. 1829. cart. 6 –

G-XXXI-7 2 4928

Tennemann, W.G. – Grundriss...

— — Fünfte vermehrte und verbesserte Auflage oder dritte Bearbeitung von Amadeus Wendt. Leipzig: J.A. Barth, 1829. 8°.

Spinoza, p. 373- ~~380~~ 380.

(G. & A.S.O.)

DLC - B3974.T5 1922 - 4 E1637

[Thayer, Vivian Trow.] 1886-

A comparison of the ethical philosophies of Spinoza and Hobbes. [Chicago, 1922.] 16 p. 23cm.

Ph.D. thesis, University of Wisconsin, 1922.

"From the Monist, October, 1922"

Printed, it would seem. Thesis note stamped on p. 16

NNC

LC

(L.C. Cat.)

G-XXVI-16 4937

Thilo, Chr[istfried] A[lbert].

Kurze pragmatische Geschichte der neueren Philosophie. Cöthen: O. Schulze, 1874. 8°.

Spinoza, p. 69-89.

[General characterization.]

Spinoza's Ethik. Spinoza's Rechtslehre. Bemerkungen.

(G.)

G-XXIV-55 1. 4966

Til, Salomon van.

Het voor-hof der heydenen, voor alle ongeloovigen geopent, om de selve aldaar door een klare beschouwinge van de betoogde goddelykheyd van Mosis wet-boek tot een eerbiediger ingang in 't heyligdom van Gods wet toe te rusten, door Salomon van Til. Tot Dordregt: D. Goris, 1694. ~~[illegible]~~ 4p.l., 394p. 4°.

G-XXIV-55 2. 4967

Til, Salomon van.

Spinoza, p. 5-7, 152-155, 172-172.

——Verfolg op't Voor-hof der heydenen, waar in de grond-stellingen van Mosis wet en wet-boek met de reeden-leer werden vereffent, en haar vastigheyd tegen de ongodisten nader tot versterkinge des geloofs betoogt. Door Salomon van Til. Tot Dord- [over]

G-XXIV-55 2-a. 4968

Til, Salomon van. – Het voor-hof... [cont.]

regt: D. Goris, 1696. 5 p.l., 251 (1) p., 6 l. 4°

Spinoza, p. 89-110, 200.

v. d. L. 358 (note). – Trinius [he gives Till]: "In diesem Buche ... wird das Ansehen Mosis und seiner Schriften wider die Angriffe des Spinoza gerettet, and der spinozistische Lehrsatz, unam tantum dari substantiam, widerlegt. S. Acta erud. 1695. p. 393. 1696. p. 295." The Acta erud. contain an extract of the book. – See: L'histoire des ouvrages de savans, March, 1696, article 3. – See also: Gebhardt, C., Inedita Spinozana, p. 7-13.

[next]

6-XXV-56 3 4969

Til, Salomon van.

A second ed. [reprint?] : Dortrecht, 1716. Freudenthal, Lebensgeschichte Spinozas (p. 237) quotes from it. (I have not seen it described anywhere.)

CLSU; ~~###~~ Faber du Faur Library - CtY 4960

✓Thomasius, Christian, 1655-1728.

Z917 T36 688 1

Freymüthige, lustige und ernsthafte, jedoch Vernunfft= und gesetzmässige Gedancken; oder, Monaths= Gespräche, über allerhand, fürnehmlich aber neue Bücher, durch alle zwölff Monathe des 1688. und 1689. Jahres durchgeführet von Christian Thomas. Halle: C. Salfeld, 1690. 8°.

oNNC oLC ? 2 v. p. 338-341(?) about Spinoza's Opera posthuma. - p. 342-352(?) about Velthuysen [cont.]

Thomasius, Christian 2 [cont.] 4961

writings and person. - It also cont. a critique of Tschirnhaus' Medicina mentis.

(Stolle, Kurtze Nachrichten ... Jena, 1735, Th. 5, 437-491.)

E 1644

Thomson, James.

"B. V.", i.e. Bysshe Vanolis. Born at Port Glasgow, Nov. 23, 1834; died in 1882, in his forty-eight year.

At an early age he became acquainted with Charles Bradlaugh, the radical politician and atheist, who remained his friend for more than twenty-three years, and who was a strong influence "for good and evil" in the poet's futur life. His meeting with a fair and frail young girl of fourteen, named Mathilda Weller, was another great influence. She was ~~bethr~~ betrothed to T. some year [over]

1-a. E1645

Thomson, James. - "B.V.", ... [cont.]

and a half later. In another six months he received the news of her death. We are reminded of Novalis and his Sophie.

Bradlaugh gave him a means of reaching the public through the National Reformer, a political organ of which he was the editor. For a time the two lodged together. Gradually friends came to T., and even some measure of fame. He corresponded with W.M. Rossetti, George Eliot, George Meredith, the Brownings, and other choice spirits were not slow in recognizing his genius, and even encouragement. His life as a whole was as he noted in his diary "obscure, dismal, bewildered, und melancholy."

---

051 N NNC-S v.100 1915 p.165-6 2 E 1646

Thomson, James. [cont.]

Bertram Dobell, in 1895, undertook to issue a complete edition of Thomson's writings. In that year he brought out the Poetical Works (2 vols. - comprising the 3 original issues of 1880, 1881, and 1884); the volume containing the Biographical and Critical Studies followed in 1896. He did not proceed with the edition. - The Essays and ~~Poem~~ Phantasies (1881) are quite rare, but can still be bought, though at a somewhat forbidding price. There are also a few (2 or 3) minor publications. As a critic T. is judicial in tone, [over]

2-a. E 1647

Thomson, James. - "B.V.", ... [cont.]

clever and original.

T. signed his writings "B.V.," to avoid the name of the older poet and to mark his reverence for Shelley ("B.", ie. Bysshe) and Novalis ("V., i.e. Vanolis = Novalis).

[B. Dobell died on Dec. 14, 1914, in his 73 year. He met T. through Bradlaugh, in 1874, and they quickly became close friends. Due to D's unwearied efforts, 2 vols. of T's poems were published during their author's lifetime. (See: Nation. N.Y., 1915, v.100 p.165-166 - issue of Feb. 11 - being a necrologue of B.D. by A.H. Bullen.)]

---

oLC 4963

Thorild, Thomas. 1759-1808

NcD Thomas Thorilds samlade skrifter; utgifna af P. Hanselli. Upsala, 1874. 2 v. O.

NN- NIQ 4 v. 1819 ed. Upsala

See: Karitz, Anders. Nordischer Spinozismus. (Chronicon Spinozanum. v. 5, 1927, p.165-197.)

Spec. Coll. Spin.

See also his: Tankelinjer hos Thorild. Ungdomsårens filosofi. (Lund. - University. - Årsskrift. N.F. Afd. 1, ~~B~~ v. 9, no 5, p.115-122.) - "Bilaga III. Spinoza Sp. citat ... Thorilds works, appear

Sp. Coll.

4971

Tintner, Moritz.

Abhandlung über Cartesius und Spinoza.

city? yr?

not seen BM

BN only to "Tendlit" (11-4-57)

893.19 Am32

See: American Jewish year book. 1903/04. p. 103. (Author's address: 18 W. 118th St. N.Y.C.)

NNUT: KE66 T641 5 All g. deut. biog. gives Tollner 4975

Töllner, Johann Gottlieb, 1724-1774

Die göttliche Eingebung der Heiligen Schrift untersucht. Vol... XVI, 487, [1]. 21 cm. Mietau u. Lpz., J. F. Hinz, 1772.

p. 453 (according to W. Lee, Inspiration of Holy Scripture, p. 453) T. observes that Spinoza was the first who made a tolerably complete collection of the objections against Inspiration. The result was curious. Some theologians gave up the cause as entirely lost; while others attempted still to maintain it, according to the usual theory."

oNNC p. 314: Le Clerc and Spinoza.

oLC

G-XXV-22a, 22b 4977

Toland, John.

Lettres philosophiques sur l'origine des préjugés, du dogme de l'immortalité de l'ame, de l'idolâtrie & de la superstition; sur le systême de Spinosa & sur l'origine du mouvement dans la matière. Traduites de l'Anglois de J. Toland à Londres [really, Amsterdam, M.M. Rey], 1768. 1p.l., II, 267p. 8°. & 12°.

Translated by Paul Henri Thyri Baron d'Holbach.—See: Barbier, Anonymes, V. 1284.

Not in v.d.L.—B. 184.

G-XIV-24a, 24b

2. E1691

Trueblood, D. Elton.—The influence of... [cont.]

in the Boston Daily Advertiser, signed A.N. Then came his address before the recently formed Alumni Association of the School, entitled "The Latest Form of Infidelity. The Christian Examiner likewise attacked E. also the Princeton Review (Jan., 1839), & a year later it referred to the Address as "a rhapsodical oration in favour of pantheism."

OCH 4988

214 Traité des trois imposteurs. En Suisse, de l'imprimerie philosophique. 1793. 12°. Titelbl., 168 u. III SS. Frz.

V. d. L. 102.

MH Phil 3839.6.15 (LC card): BL2773.V52 1793 1p. l., 168, iii p 14 cm

1

1p.l., 168, III p. 12°.

Contains also: 1) Sentimens sur le Traité des trois imposteurs. Extrait d'un lettre ou dissertation de M. de la Monnoye à ce sujet. 2) Réponse à la dissertation de M. de la Monnoye, sur [over]

NNUT: GW43 T952 A 1774 5 5042

Turretin [Turretinus], Jean-Alphonse.

"Demonstratio Spinozae pro una tantum substantia, miseris equivocationibus nititur". (Opera [1774], vol. 1, p. 4.) omnia, theologica, philosophica et philologica.

Leovardiae et Franequerae, apud ... 1774-1776. 3v.

Quoted in British Quarterly Review, vol. 8, p. 431.

27.5cm.

NNC religion Turretini, Jean Alphonse, 1671-1737 CC [over]

2. 4989

Traité des trois imposteurs... [cont.]

le Traité de trois imposteurs. 3) Copie de l'article IX du tome premier, seconde partie des Mémoires de littérature, imprimés à la Haye, chez Henri du Sauzet, 1716.

(H.U.C.)

2. 5048

Turretin [Turretinus], J-A.—"Demonstratio... [cont.]

T. [1671-1737], Swiss professor," whose Latin work on Christian evidences, translated into French..., we have seen adopted and adapted by the Catholic authorities in France, became a virtual Unitarian"... (Robertson, II 378).

Works perhaps to be examined.

Philosophy

G-XXV-37 5004 (?)

Trendelenburg, Adolf.

Ueber die aufgefundenen Ergänzungen zu Spinoza's Werken und dessen Ertrag für Spinoza's Leben und Lehre. (In his: Historische Beiträge zur Philosophie. Berlin: G. Bethge, 1846-1867. 8°. v. 3, p. 277-398.)

(?)

G-XIV-30a, 30b

109 Ub3611 NNC has NY, Scribner [1871-73] also Ub361 - NY, Scribner, 1876. E1696

Ueberweg, Friedrich.

History of philosophy, from Thales to the present time. Translated from the 4th German edition by G. S. Morris; with... appendix on English and American philosophy by Noah Porter, and appendix on Italian philosophy by Vincenzo Botta. London, 1872-1874. 2 v. 8°. (Theological and philosophical library. Philosophical division. v. 1-2.)

Spinoza: pp55-78

205 H24 NNC-4 [Emerson, R. W.] E1690

Trueblood, D. Elton, 1900—

"The influence of Emerson's Divinity School address." (Harvard Theological Review, v. 32, no. 1, Jan., 1939, p. 41-56.)

No refs seen

It is the controversy around, rather than the influence of, the Address that we read in this article.

Andrews Norton first wrote a critic. [over]

193U/7 NNC 5058

R

Ulrici, Hermann.

Incl. a chapter on Sp (p. 42-66)

Das Grundprincip der Philosophie, kritisch und speculativ entwickelt. Thl. 1-2. Leipzig: T.O. Weigel, 1845-1846. 8°.

Sp. Th. 1, § 10, p. 42-66.

No author indices.

[L.L.] Sp. not seen elsewhere in contents

"Für die subjektivistische Auffassung der Attribute als Sp.'s wahre Meinung tritt auch Ulrici, obwohl nicht mit absoluter Bestimmtheit ein [Thl. I, p. 453]. (Erhardt, 501.)

LC 10-29943 Revised

V

5070

NN - YBG

Valsecchi, Antonio.

Ritratti o vite letterarie e paralleli di G. J. Rousseau e del Sig. di Voltaire, di Obbes, e di Spinosa. E vita di Pietro Bayle. Opera posthuma del pubblico professore P. Antonio Valsecchi. Venezia: Soc. Tip. Pasquali e Curti, 1816. 176 p. 16°.

v. d.L. 120.

(B.M.; N.Y.P.L.; Weg, p. 16.)

[over]

5071

Valsecchi, Antonio. — Ritratti o vite ... [cont.]

B.-B., I, 524: "Das seltene Werk befand sich früher, wie es scheint, in der Wiener Hofbibliothek, wo es auch Ed. Boehmer gesehen hat... Es gelang mir nicht, es dort zu finden. Die Skizze über Despin. ist zweifellos geschöpft aus einem früheren Werk Valsecchis: Dei fondamenti della religione et dei fonti dell' Empieta libri tre (Pad. 1768) III. 25f."...

3306

MH - Phil 1703.3

Marchie van Voorthysen, H. du.

Nagelaten geschriften. Uitgegeven door A. G. de Geer. deel 1-2. Arnhem; 1886-1887. 2 v. 8°.

deel 2: De grondbeginselen van Spinoza's wijsbegeerte, p. 211-259.

"Pas mis dans le commerce" (Cal. B. & N., no. 10252).

oNNC oLC o Princeton cannot verify in notice [over]

1935p4 NNG-5 *in Sp. Cell.* 5086
GS3

[over]

3307

Marchie van Voorthysen, H. du. — Nagelaten... [cont.]

Auth. died Feb. 11, 1885, in his 32nd year.

"In dieser Abhandlung liefert van Voorthysen mit dem ersten Theile der Ethik und mit dem Anfange des zweiten Theiles ein derartiges hand-in-hand fight wie Mill in seinem Buche über Hamilton mit dessen Lehre oder Laas in seinem 'Idealismus und Positivismus' mit der platonisirenden Anschauungen... Ihm scheint die Lehre der Affecte und der Bedingungen des menschlichen Bewusstseins bei Spinoza ebenso unverstandlich wie das Hexen-einmal-eins im Faust." (C. B. Spruyt, in A. f. G. d. P., III, 1890, p. 499-500).

5081

Vaz Dias, A. M., and Tak, W. G. van der.

De firma Bento y Gabriel de Spinoza. Leiden: N.V. Boekhandel en Drukkerij voorheen E. J. Brill, 1934. 2 p. l., 33 p. 8°. (Mededeelingen van wege Het Spinozahuis. [no.] 1.)

Spinozahuis. Mededeelingen van wege het Spinozahuis.

(A.S.O.)

[over]

5082

Vaz Dias, & v. d. Tak. — De firma Bento... [cont.]

Comprising 3 documents: 1) Petition of protest against the refusal of Michael de Spinoza to take up a due bill of exchange, dated Sept. 8, 1638, in which also Hanna Debora, the philosopher's mother, figures; 2) Testament of Spinoza's stepmother, Ester, dated Oct. 23, 1652; 3) Power of attorney conferred by the firm Bento y Gabriel de Spinoza upon its owner's emigra-

[next]

5080

Vaz Dias, A. M., and Tak, W. G. van der.

Spinoza mercator et autodidactus. Oorkonden en andere authentieke documenten betreffende des wijsgeers jeugd en diens betrekkingen verzameld door A. M. Vaz Dias. Uitgegeven en toegelicht en overleg met W. G. van der Tak. 's-Gravenhage: M. Nijhoff, 1932.

5086

Vaz Dias, A. M.

Uriel da Costa. Nieuwe bijtrage tot diens Levensgeschiedenis. Leiden: E. J. Brill, 1936. 2 p. l., 32 p. 8°. (Mededeelingen van wege het Spinozahuis. [no.] 2.)

(A.S.O.)

5091

Velthuysen, Lambert van.

Opera omnia... Quibus acces. 2 tractatus... Prior est De articulis fidei fundamentalibus; alter De cultu naturali, oppositus Tractatui theologico-politico et Operi posthumo B. de Spinoza. [pt. 1-2.] Roterodami, 1680. 1570 p. 4°.

Not in v. d.L. — Weg, p. 16.

Not in B.M., D.M.L., or L.L.

[over]

1-a. 5092

Velthuysen, L. van.- Opera... [cont.]

Dunin-Borkowski Spinoza nach dreihundert Jahren, p.116: "Die Darstellung Lambert Velthuysens (nicht seine Kritik) im Traktat, De cultu naturali et origine moralitatis' (Opera, II [1680], 1371-1390) ist sorgfältig."

Freudenthal, Spinoza, ed. Gebhardt, I, p.340: "Über Velthuysens ... Studium Spinoza's Pref. zu den Opera vol II." p.341: Die späteren Ausserungen Lamberts über Spinoza S. dessen Opera p.1368. — Der meistens durchaus zuverlässige v.d. Linde führt in seiner Bibliographie Spinozas p.91 die im Text genannte Schrift. [p.228: "Über natürliche Gottesverehrung und Ursprung der Sittlichkeit" (against Ethica)]

[next]

2. 5093

Velthuysen, L. van - Opera... [cont.]

unter dem falschen Titel De cultu naturali pudore et dignitate hominis auf und fügt ihr eine andere Schrift Velthuysens De naturali pudore et dignitate hominis bei [after Colerus], die nicht gegen Spinoza gerichtet und schon im Jahr 1676 veröffentlicht ist. Der rechte Titel der ersten Schrift ist: De cultu naturali et origine moralitatis. — Den Irrtum v. d. Lindes teilt Baltzer, Spinozas Entwicklungsgang S. 50."

Meinsma (German tr.), p.444, note, quotes the Opera

[over]

2-a 5094

Velthuysen, L. van.- Opera... [cont.]

omnia, V.1, Praefatio ad Lectorem, "über Spinoza's persönlichen Verkehr mit ... Velthuysen, for the first time. Fr., Lg., p.208 (no.36) quotes from the same Preface. In no. 35 he quotes from the Epistola prefixed to the tractate De cultu naturali.

Erhardt (Philosophie des Spinoza, p.25): "So veröffentlichte ... Velthuysen ... im Jahre 1680 eine längere Abhandlung gegen den theologisch-politischen Traktat und die Ethik. [Im zweiten Teile seiner Opera Omnia, die er selbst herausgab ...] — p. 473 to 474: "Der genaue Titel der Schrift ... lautet, Tractatus de cultu naturali et origine moralitatis. Oppositus Tractatui

[next]

3. 5095

Velthuysen, L. van.- Opera... [cont.]

Theologico-Politico et Operi Posthumo B. D. S.' Die Abhandlung, die einen Text von 200 enggedruckten Quartseiten umfasst, beschäftigt sich lange nicht überall mit Sp.; doch ist ihm ein beträchtlicher Teil des Ganzen gewidmet. Im ersten Kapitel entwickelt der Verfasser in sichtlicher und treffender Weise die Grundgedanken der Spinozistischen Philosophy, denen er dann im folgenden seine eigene Auffassung kritisch entgegenstellt... Die Kritik ... ist überall ruhig, objektiv und sachlich; nicht ein einziges Mal lässt er sich zu einer gehässigen

[over]

3-a. 5096

Velthuysen, L. van. - Opera... [cont.]

Form der Polemik fortreissen; nur in der Widmung spricht er im Hinblick auf die Ansichten Sp.'s und seiner Anhänger von „pestilentibus opinionibus," und in der Verrede sagt er, dass Sp. gewisse Lehren auf eine solche Weise und mit so grosser Schlauheit entwickele, „ut mirer malitiam hominis ad id eniti potuisse: et saepius occurrat animo, num aliquis malus genius ei illa cogitata inieccrit'... Das Wortspiel mit Sp. und spinosias ... findet sich auch bei V.; denn gewiss ist es als Wortspiel zu verstehen, wenn er in der Widmung sagt, dass er in seiner Schrift „spinosas argutias' zurückweisen wolle. Diese Widmung ist datiert vom 1. Febr. 1680, während die Verrede zu-

[next]

O-XLI-1,2. 4. 5097

Velthuysen, L. van.- Opera... [cont.]

Kortholts Buch vom März 1680 stammt. Daher kann V. das Wortspiel nicht aus dem letzteren entlehnt haben; eher wäre die umgekehrte Entlehnung denkbar, obwohl auch sie fraglich ist."

C.G. (small); A.S.O. (large writing paper).

G-XXV-10,11

O-XXXIX-9 5111

Verweyen, Johannes Maria.

[Spinoza und die Scholastik.] (In his: Die Philosophie des Mittelalters. Berlin und Leipzig, 1921. 8°. p. 290-294.)

See also p. 45, 79, 182, 245.

Being Bd.4 of: Geschichte der Philosophie dargestellt von B. Bauch, O. Ewald, [and others].

(A.S.O.)

Cf Ct V sim. title by Engelhard, Heinrich Christ. 5101

Vernuenftige Gedanken von der Natur, was sie sey: Dass sie ohne Gott und seine allweise Beschränkung, ohnmächtig sey, und wie die eine untheilbare göttliche Kraft, in und durch die Mittelursachen, nach dem Maase ihrer verliehenen Wirksamkeit oder Tüchtigkeit, die in der Welt alles allein thätig wirke. Durch fleissiges Nachsinnen, Ueberlegen und Schliessen gefasset, und zur Verherrlichung göttlicher

[over]

1-a 5102

Vernuenftige Gedanken von der Natur... [cont.]

Majestät, auch Förderung wichtiger Wahrheiten herausgegeben, von einem christlichen Gottesfreunde, im Jahre MDCCXLIII. 8°

J.C. Gottsched, at the end of the article "Spinoza" (in his tr. of Bayle's Dictionnaire) notes this, which is "ohne Verleger und ohne Ort des Druckes." He also quotes a paragraph from the "Vorrede", of which I give the first sentence, [next]

Spec Col Spin. 5122

Vismara, Silvio.

La nullificazione della storia nella filosofia dello Spinoza. (In: Spinoza nel terzo centenario della sua nascita; pubblicazione a cura della Facoltà di Filosofia dell' Università Cattolica del Sacro Cuore. Milano, 1934. 8°. p.181-193.)

5129

Vloemans, Antoon.

Het ideaal der kennis bij Spinoza. (Tijdschrift voor wijsbegeerte. Harlem, 1923. 8°. jaarg. 17, p. 61-72.)

(A.S.O.)

G-XXV-16 5125

Vloemans, A

Het leven van Spinoza (den wijsgeer van de stilte). (Het nieuwe leven. Santpoort, 1927. 8°. jaarg. 12, p. 289-299.)

(G.-unbd. Being afl. 11, Maart, 1927.)

G-XXV-17 5126

Vloemans, A

Hoe Spinoza God zocht en de gelukzaligheid vond. (Het nieuwe leven. Santpoort, 1927. 8°. jaarg. 12, p. 321-330.)

(G.-unbd. Being afl. 12, April, 1927.)

G-XXV-15 5124

Vloemans, A

Spinoza's leer van de menschelijke kennis. n.t.-p. [Amsterdam? 1928.] 657-673 p. 8°.

Repr.: Vragen van den tag, 1928.

(G.-unbd.)

5141

[Vloten, Johannes van.]

NNC-4 059 L57

Mensch en dier; naar Schopenhauer en Spinoza. (Levensbode. ~~Haarlem, 1871.~~ deel 4, p. 110-121.) (Vol. IV) 1871

Anonymous.-With reference to C. Rokitansky, Die Solidarität alles Thierlebens... Wien, 1869.

v. d. L. 357 (with date: 1870).

059 L57 NNC-4 4492

Schopenhauer, Arthur.

[Vloten, Johannes van.]

Mensch en dier; naar Schopenhauer en Spinoza. (Levensbode. ~~Haarlem,~~ 1871. ~~deel 4,~~ p. 110-121.) Vol. IV (1871)

Tijdschrift see t.p. ... op onbepaalde Tijden door ...

Anonymous.-With reference to C. Rokitansky, Die Solidarität alles Thierlebens... Wien, 1869.

v. d. L. 357 (with date: ~~1870~~). 1871 ... Vloten.

059 L57 NNC-4 5142

Vloten, Johannes van.

Schopenhauer, Kant, en Spinoza. [Review of: ~~Eckstein, Ernst.~~ Die Lehre Schopenhauers: ~~In~~ (Salon, 1878)] (Levensbode. ~~Haarlem,~~ 1878. ~~deel 10,~~ p. 506-513.) deel 10 (Vol. V)

Signed, v. Vl.

Versuch einer kurzen Darstellung ihres Inhaltes, von Ernst Eckstein. 1878.

NNC-4 059 L57 2626

Kant, Immanuel.

Vloten, Johannes, van.

Schopenhauer, Kant, en Spinoza. [Review of: Eckstein, Ernst. Die Lehre Schopenhauers... ~~In~~ (Salon, 1878)] (Levensbode. ~~Haarlem,~~ 1878. ~~deel 10,~~ p. 506-513.) deel 10 (Vol. V)

Signed, v. Vl.

059 L57 NNC-4 4493

Schopenhauer, Arthur.

Vloten, Johannes, van.

Schopenhauer, Kant, en Spinoza. [Review of: Eckstein, Ernst. Die Lehre Schopenhauers... ~~In~~ (Salon, 1878)] (Levensbode. ~~Haarlem,~~ 1878. ~~deel 10,~~ p. 506-513.) deel 10 (Vol. V)

Signed, v. Vl.

059 L57 NNC-4 5149

[Vloten, Johannes van.] (ed. of periodical)

Spinoza door een geloovig Franschman bekeken. [Review of: Nourisson, J. F. Spinoza et le naturalisme contemporain. Paris, 1866.] (Levensbode. ~~Deventer,~~ 1867. deel 2, p. 71-80.) (Vol. II)

v. d. L. 441 (note). Note: Fascicle 1 only, in which this article appeared, was published in 1866 - the other 3 in 1867.

(C.G.) date on t.p. of vol. - 1867.

5147

[Vloten, Johannes van.]
Spinoza. Geboren 24 November 1632 te Amsterdam, gestorven 21 Februari 1677 te 's Gravenhage. [By J. van Vloten?] [The Hague? 1880?] 8p. 8°.

No title-page. Title taken from first page.

(G.) [cover]

NNC-4 E1353

~~Pollock, Sir Frederick, Bart.~~
[Vloten, Johannes van.]
De wetenschappelijke aard van Spinoza's wijsbegeerte, door een Engelschman ontvouwd. [Review of: Pollock, Sir Frederick, Bart. "The scientific character of Spinoza's philosophy." (Fortnightly review. London, 1873. (Vol. 19) p.567-585.)] (Levensbode. Haarlem, 1873. deel 6, p.267-279.)
6. deel, 1873 not signed

Anonymous.

2. 5148

[Vloten, Johannes van.]—Spinoza. [cont.]
A popular sketch of Spinoza's life and teaching; published anonymously at the time, or shortly after, the unveiling of the Spinoza statue at The Hague.
"Zoo is Spinoza niet alleen de blijde boodschapper der mondige menschheid, neen hij is veel meer, hij is de leermeester der menschheid"... (p.7).

Czech 5159

Vohryzek, Viktor.
Spinoza und Tolstoj. (Českožidovský kalendář. Jahrg. 25. 1905/6.)
not seen ULS

NNC-4 5155

Vloten, Johannes van.
Spinoza-waardeering in Engeland. [Review of: Pollock, Sir Frederick, Bart. Spinoza; paper read before the Royal Institution of Great Britain, April 20, 1877.] (Levensbode. ~~Haarlem,~~ 1878. deel 10 (Vol. X), p.491-505.)

Signed, v. Vl.

5186

Volz, L.
Der Einfluss Leibniz' und Spinozas auf Lessing. Heidelberg: Buchdruckerei Gustav Geier, 1910. 1p.l., 80p. 8°. (Pädagogium Neuenheim-Heidelberg. Beilage zum Jahresbericht 1910.)

(G.) [cover]

057 L57 NNC-4 5154

[Vloten, Johannes van.]
Spinoza's vertoog over God en mensch. [Review of: Sigwart, C. Spinoza's neuentdeckter Tractat von Gott, dem Menschen und dessen Glückseligkeit. Erläutert... Gotha, 1866.] (Levensbode. Deventer, 1867. deel 2, p.460-471.) (Vol. II) deel 2,

v. d.L. 144 (note).

(C.G.)

2. 5187

Volz, L.—Der Einfluss... [cont.]
"Leibniz und Spinoza haben auf Lessing eingewirkt. Jenem verdankt er den Gedanken der Entwicklung ... diesem die strenge Konsequenz des Monismus... Sein Individualismus, der über Leibniz hinausgeht, scheidet ihn von Spinoza ..." (p.80).

059 L57 NNC-4 2867

~~Kuiper, Abraham.~~
Vloten, Johannes van. 1818-1883
Een vermakelijke uitspraak. (Levensbode. Haarlem, 1878. deel 10, p.487-490.)
Signed, v. Vl.
Polemic against Abraham Kuiper (Calvinist clergyman, and, apparently, anti-Semite) who said that "Spinoza heeft zijn hoogen roem aan scheeve voorstelling en kunstmatige opvijzeling te danken".

MH-KSF 458 5184

Volynski, A.
Review of Rubin's Heb. tr. of Ethica. (Voskhod, 1886, 1.)
MH has only #2-4 for 1886 (slavic cat.)!
(NOS 10/11-Lamont Dep)

5189

Vondel, Joost van den.

See: Valk, Th. de.

" Molkenboer, B.H.

NN-YAM p.V.354 5

5197

Vossius, Gerardus Johannes, 1577-1649.

Gerardi Johannis Vossii De philosophorum sectis liber. Cum continuatione & supplementis Johannis Jacobi à Ryssel. Lipsiae: Sumptibus J.C. Meyeri, 1690. 4 p.l., 216 p., 3 l. 4°.

Spec. Coll. has Hague-C., 1657.

cLC Spinoza, p. 203.

" Ex Schola Cartesii derivatur Benedictus de Spinoza, ingeniosissmus Atheos, qui libertate [over]

2.

5198

Vossius, G. J. — Gerardi Johannis ... [cont.]

philosophandi abusus excessit magistri sui limites "... (See: Dunin-Borkowski, Spinoza, II, 195-6.)

[L.L.]

OCH NN- 1690 - paginat. = Lipsiae: ... J.C. Meyeri, ...

5199

Vossius, Gerardus Johannes.

Gerardi Johannis Vossii De philosophorum sectis liber. Cum continuatione & supplementis Johannis Jacobi a Ryssel. Lipsiae: impensis J. C. Meyeri. Jenae: charactere Nisiano, Impr. H. Beyerus, 1705. 4 p. l., 216 p., 2 l. 4°.

Spinoza, p. 203. In the text the name is given "Benedictus de Spinosa". The [over]

... - 4? YAM p.V. 354

2.

5200

Vossius, G. J. — Gerardi Johannis ... [cont.]

"Continuatio" by Ryssel is from p. 122 to end.

NNC - 100, V93 1657-58 ok 2 v. in 1. [VI, 58]

SC, B900.1, V93 also Hague-Comitis, ... MDCLVII 4 p. l., 117, ... 2 l ... Ed. ... Historica, 1653

(H.U.C.)

0-XXXIX-27

5201

Vulliaud, Paul.

Spinoza d'après les livres de sa bibliothèque. Paris: Bibliothèque Chacornac, 1934. 103 p. 8°.

p. 99-103: Inventaire de la bibliothèque de Spinoza.

(A.S.O.) unbd.

0-XXXIX-28

5202

Vulliaud, Paul.

Spinoza. Sa personalité intellectuelle d'apres les livres qu'il a lus. (Revue juive de Genève. année 1, 1932, [no. 1, p. 26-28] no. 3, p. 129-130.)

missing

Being p. 92-97, with the omission of one paragraph, of his: Spinoza... (1934).

(G. - 2. instalment also ...

W

5204

Wa[ ] J.

Spinoza (Baruch, oder wie er sich übersetzte, Benedict). (In: Conversations-Lexicon oder encyclopädisches Handwörterbuch für gebildete Stände. Neunter Band. Stuttgart: bei A. F. Macklot, 1818. 12°. p. 300-305.)

[over]

2.

5205

Wa[ ] J. — Spinoza ... [cont.]

"Nach innen hat sein Geist eine unerbittliche wissenschaftliche Strenge, Beharrlichkeit und Sicherheit, einen unermüdlichen Drang hinweg über das Beschränkte und Endliche nach dem Unendlichen, so dass man das Allgemeine der Vernunft kräftig vorwalten sieht, das freie Verknüpfungs- und Hervorbringungsvermögen aber, die Phantasie, als Quell der Eigenthümlichkeit, zurückstehen; weshalb ihm auch, nach der Bemerkung eines unserer geistreichsten Männer [J. F. Herbart ?], die Idee der Kunst gänzlich abging" (p. 301-302).

(H.U.C.)

0-XXXIX-31

5211

Wachter, Johann Georg.

Elucidarius cabalisticus, sive reconditae Hebraeorum philosophiae brevis & succincta recensio, epitomatore Joh. Georgio Wachtero. Romae [rather, Halle], 1706. 1 p. l., 78 p., 1 l. 8°.

Cap. IV. De Consensu cabalae et Spinozae, p. 39-78.

Weller I, 288: "in Halle gedruckt". C. G. von Murr, B. de Spinoza Adnotationes, p. 31, gives: Rostochii.

(A few p. slightly cropped.)

[over]

2. 5212

Wachter, Johann Georg. – Elucidarius ... [cont.]
Review: Unschuldige Nachrichten, 1709, p417-421. (Baeck, p.75, note 2.)

5210

Wachter, J. Georg [Johann Georg] 1673-1757
Origines juris naturalis; sive, De jure naturae humanae demonstrationes mathematicae. Berlin, 1704.
Baeck, p.76-82. –
See: Grunwald, p. 45. See also Mauthner, Atheismus, III, 250: "Spinoza war nicht ausdrücklich genannt worden".
NjP Review: Unschuldige Nachrichten, 1704, p. 668-671.

ICN fa ; CU (+CBM) 5214

Wachter, Johann Georg, 1673-1757.
Erklärung wegen seines Buches, Elucidarium Cabbalisticum betitelt.) (In: Bayle, P. Historisches und kritisches Wörterbuch... übersetzt von J. C. Gottscheden. Leipzig, 1741-1744. f°. Thl. 4, p. 272.) 4T. Leipzig, 1741-44. fol.
Deutsches Gesamtkatalog, Vol. 13, 1938, col. 712
The "Erklärung" was written at the suggestion of J. C. Gottsched and [over]

O-XXXIX-33 5227

Wahle, Richard.
Kurze Erklärung der Ethik von Spinoza und Darstellung der definitiven Philosophie. Wien: W. Braumüller, 1899. VIII, 212p. 12°.
B.552.
(A.S.O. – Partly pencil-marked.) [over]
G-XIV-44

5209

Wachter, J. G.
[Extract from his: Der Spinozismus im Jüdenthumb; being p. 61-63, abbreviated.] (In: Altkirch, E. Maledictus und Benedictus... Leipzig, 1924. 8°. p.75-77.)

O-XXXIX-33 2. 5228

Wahle, Richard. – Kurze Erklärung ... [cont.]
Contents (abbreviated): Einleitung. I. Buch. Erklärung der Ethik Spinozas. – II. Buch. Über Weltanschauungen.
"Ich gebe die Auffassung der Ethik im Verhältnis zu meinen früheren drei Abhandlungen in knapper Form und ein wenig geändert (p. 6).
G-XIV-44

Spec Coll Spin [Wachter, J.G.] 5217

Mauthner, F.
Wachter. (In his: Der Atheismus und seine Geschichte im Abendlande. Stuttgart, 1922-1923. 4°. Bd.3, p.249-251.)

O-XLIII-34 5245

Waldauer, Adolf.
Spinoza's Hebräerstaat. (Jüdisches Litteratur-Blatt. Magdeburg, 1891. 4°. Jahrg. 20, p.1-2, 5-6, 9-10, 13-14.)
~~"Spinoza selbst hat in dem Hebräerstaat etwas Ideales gesehen~~ Exposition of Tr. Theol.-Pol., chap. ~~17, 18 and 19~~ 17-19.
(A.S.O.)
Subj: Tr.Th.-Pol. [over]

5216

[Wachter, J. G. [Johann Georg]]
Die mit ihr selbst streitende Harmonia der neuen Weltweisen. 1724.
(See Grunwald, p. 45.)
not seen BM

(?) E1725

Watt,
The London Library copy of the Tr. theol.-pol. (1670; issue "B") has the following note on the fly-leaf: "Benedict de Spinoza, was Watt says, an Atheistical Philosopher, was the son of a Portuguese Jew, was born in Amsterdam about 1633, & died in 1677. Of this work, Watt states, 'This laid the foundation of what is called Spinosism'."

 E1733

Webb, Clement Charles Julian, 1865-1954

"Idea." (Encyclopaedia of religion and ethics. v. 7. 1915, p. 85.) article pp81-86

• For the use (or uses) made of the word [idea] by Spinoza the reader must be referred to Spinoza himself (see esp. Eth. II. def. 3, 4, prop. 48, 49) and his commentators (esp. H. Joachim, Study of Spinoza, Oxford, 1901). As the spiritual or psychical correlate of an extended thing or body, a man's mind is described as the "idea" of his body."

 5261

Weichelt, Hans. 1873—

"Spinoza." (Geb. 24. November 1632.) (Allgemeine deutsche Lehrerzeitung. Berlin, 1932. Jahrg. 61, no. 48, p. 873-877.)

also called Paedagogische Ztg. - to 1918

(G.) [over]

---

2. 5262

Weichelt, Hans. – Spinoza... [cont.]

Expository. "Spinoza ist Optimist der Erkenntnis."

 5267

Weimarer historisch-genealogisches Taschenbuch des gesammten Adels jehudäischen Ursprungs. [1920]*

— p. 523 contains the statement that Spinoza was made a noble by the Prince Palatine, Carl Louis [Karl Ludwig].

Verify!!

* 1912 Erster Jahrgang

5269

Weise, Hermann.

Kurze Darstellung von Spinozas Leben. Salzwedel: H. Robolsky, [1876]. 24p. sq. 4°

(Salzwedel.- Koenigliches Gymnasium. 1876. Progr. no. 198.)

(G.)

 5268

Weise, Herm[ann].

Über das erste Buch der Ethik des Spinoza. Inauguraldissertation. Salzwedel: H. Robolsky, [1875]. 36 p. 8°.

^Buchdruckerei von

Contents: Einleitung: Kurze Geschichte der Kritik des Spinozismus. Vorbemerkungen. Kritik. Anmerkungen.

Hist. in B (Vleg. p. 17)

(G.)

5270

Weislinger, [Johann Niklaus, b. 1691]?

Merkwürdigkeiten.

not in BM

city? yr?

no SCS card seen 11-20-57

 5283

Wenzel, Alfred. in Sp. Coll.

"Zur Textkritik von Spinozas Tractatus de Intellectus Emendatione." (Zeitschrift für Philosophie und philosophische Kritik. Leipzig, 1909. Bd. 134, p. 211-231.)

(G.)

 5290

Weyenbergh, H.

Nog iets over Spinoza's tering. (Levensbode. ~~Haarlem, 1878.~~ deel 10, p. 290-297.) (Vol. X), 1878

De Levensbode, deel 10

NNC LC } has Weyenbergh, Hendrik, 1842-85 – an entomologist!

[over]

---

2. 5291

Weyenbergh, H. – Nog iets... [cont.]

: Written from Cordova, in the Argentines.

1.

White, W[illiam] Hale. 1831-1913

"Spinoza's doctrine of the relationship between mind and body." (International journal of ethics. Philadelphia, 1896. 8. v.6, p.515-518.)

"Every student of Spinoza has doubtless

SEE NEXT CARD.

2.

White, W. H.-Spinoza's doctrine... [cont.]

felt the difficulty of reconciling those propositions in the Ethic which appear to make the mind dependent on the body, with other propositions, especially in the fifth part, in which Spinoza maintains, not only the power of the mind over the passions,

See next card.

3.

White, W. H.-Spinoza's doctrine... [cont.]

but its immortality. I propose to offer a few observations, which, if they do not solve the problem, may remove some of its difficulties". (p. 515.)

"It is not my object to defend Spinoza's creed, nor do I pretend that I have com-

See next card.

4.

White, W. H.-Spinoza's doctrine... [cont.]

pletely understood or explained it, but it is a fair reply to the charge of obscurity that all religion in so far as it is speculative, is obscure, and Spinoza's is not more so than the Christian mysteries. Neither is it so obscure as the popular notion as to soul and body, nor as many

SEE NEXT CARD.

5.

White, W. H.-Spinoza's doctrine... [cont.]

other conclusions of common sense which are clear solely because we have so often repeated them. To break down these conclusions is one of the special functions of philosophy". (p. 518.)

Wiarda, J.

De wijsbegeerte en de Kerk. (In: Haar, B. ter, and Moll, W. Geschiedenis der christlijke Kerk in Nederland, in tafereelen, onder redactie van B. ter Haar, W. Moll en E.B. Swalue. Met medwerking van J. Wiarda, [and others]. Rotterdam: D. Bolle, n.d. 4°. deel 2, p. 458-478.)

[over]

2.

Wiarda, J. - De wijsbegeerte... [cont.]

II. Het Spinozisme, p.471-475.

Deals mainly with the F. van Leenhof controversy.

Reprinted ed. Original ed.: Amsterdam, 1864-1869. (See: Burgersdijk & Niermans, Cat. no. 48; no. 5282.)

(G.)

Wielenga, Bastiaan.

Spinozas „Cogitata metaphysica" als Anhang zu seiner Darstellung der cartesianischen Prinzipienlehre. Heidelberg: Carl Winter's Universitätsbuchhandlung, 1899. 4p.l., 59p. 8°.

Contents: Erster Teil. Die Entstehung ... Zweiter Teil. Inhalt und Darstellung ... Dritter Teil. Charakter und Bedeutung. Anmerkungen.

(G.)

Wiener, Max. 1886-

Spinoza. (Gemeindeblatt der jüdischen Gemeinde zu Berlin. Jahrg. 22, 1932, p.263-266.)

port. ("Aus der Erstausgabe der Opera Posthuma.")

(G.)

[Wijck, Jhr. van der.]

B[etz], [H.I.] [Review of: Wijck, Jhr. van der. Spinoza. Groningen, 1877.] (Nederlandsche Spectator. [jaarg.] 1877, p. 43.)

 5313

Windelband, Wilhelm.
Die Geschichte der neueren Philosophie in ihrem Zusammenhange mit der allgemeinen Cultur und den besonderen Wissenschaften. Bd. 1-2. Leipzig: Breitkopf und Härtel, 1878-1880. 8°.

Baruch Spinoza, Bd. 1, p. 186-224.

(A.S.O. - F.C.S. Schiller's copy.)
(v.1: G.) Bd. 1, 1878

 5321

Windelband, Wilhelm. 1848-1915
"Zum Gedächtniss Spinoza's." (Vierteljahrsschrift für wissenschaftliche Philosophie. ~~v.1~~, 1877, p. 419-440.)
1. Jahrgang
(An seinem zweihundertjährigen Todestage gesprochen an der Universität Zürich)

(Baldwin, Dictionary.)

 5314

Windelband, Wilhelm.
Die Geschichte der neueren Philosophie in ihrem Zusammenhange mit der allgemeinen Kultur und den besonderen Wissenschaften dargestellt... Bd. 1-2. Dritte, durchgesehene Auflage. Leipzig: Druck und Verlag von Breitkopf und Härtel, 1904. 2 v. 8°.

[over]

5336

Winkel, Jan te. 1847-
Lijst der afzonderlijke portretten in het legit van de Vereeniging "Het Spinozahuis. s' Gravenhage, 1906.

 2. 5315

Windelband, Wilhelm. - Die Geschichte... [cont.]
Baruch Spinoza, Bd. 1, p. 196-234.

2. ed. 1899 (?)
(G.)

 5337

Wirsén, C. D. af.
Under furor och cypresser. Diktsamling. Stockholm: P.A. Norstedt & Söners Förlag, [1896]. 8°.

Spinoza [a poem], p. 12-18.

(C.G.)

 5329

Windelband, Wilhelm.
Preludii... [Translated from the 2. German ed. by S. Frank.] St. Petersburg, 1904.

Pamyati Spinozi, p. 71-91.

(G)

 ~~NOS 12-10-57~~ 5340

Witte, Henning.
Diarium biographicum, in quo scriptores seculi post natum Christum XVII. praecipui... concisè descripti magnō adducuntur numerō. Gedani [Danzig], 1688. 4°.

"At ~~the~~ sig. Nnnn, fo. 4, verso (the book is unpaged) sub ann. 1677, is the name of Spinoza and a list of his [over]

 5322

Windelband, Wilhelm.
Zum Gedächtniss Spinoza's. (An seinem zweihundertjährigen Todestage gesprochen an der Universität Zürich.) (In his: Präludien... Freiburg i.B. und Tübingen, 1884. 8°. p. 88-111.)

(G)

2. 5341

Witte, Henning. - Diarium... [cont.]
works: the exact date of his death is added in a supplement." (Pollock, p. xxx.)

(Rand, p. 490.) didn't find this in my copy

LC 14-18638
1688-91 - 2 t. in 1

5351

Wittichius, Jacobus.

Disputatio metaphysica de cogitatione, ipsa mente. Quam... sub praesidio... Jacobi Wittichii... publico examini subjicit Petrus Hollebeek, Jos. fil. auctor... Lugduni Batavorum: Apud P. vander Aa, 1719. 3 p.l., 19 p., 3 l. [sig.?]

(Communication of Fritz Bamberger, Chicago; Oct. 18, 1940. Book in his possession)

[over]

2. 5352 [cont.]

Wittichius, Jacobus.- Disputatio metaphysica...

Wy door een andre Geest gedreeven,
Syn bly dat sulke Wittichs leeven,
Die Kragtig de Natuur van Godt
Beschermen tegens bleam en spot.

Van Lasteraars, en Ongodisten,
Van vuile Ketters, Spinosisten,
Wier ongegronde gruwel-leer
In duigen valt, door so een Heer.

(From the rhymes "Ter Eere ..." which comprise the last 3 leaves of the book.)

5349

Wittichius, Jacobus.

Disputatio philosophica de natura Dei. Ed. II. Acc.: J. F. Buddei epistola ad theologos quosdam Roterodamenses, et judicium theol. et philos. facultatis Jenensis de isthac Wittichii disputatione. Hagae Com., 1720. 52 p. 4°.

Not in v. d. L. - Weg, p. 6.

[over]

2. 5350 [cont.]

Wittichius, Jacobus - Disputatio philosophica...

Leydekker, J., De blyde Spinosist, already refers to a 2. ed. in 1719: "... onlangs herdrukt, met lemmata aan den bladrand..." (p. 1 f.). So does Andala, R., Apologia, dated 1719, but printed in the fall of 1718: "Quod captiose & falso in lemmate marginali iterate hujus editionis explicatur ..." (p. 141). See also: Ewyck, G. van, Difficultas maxima, p. 43; tr., p. 41.

5348

Wittichius, Jacobus.

Disputatio philosophica de natura Dei. Duisburg, 1711. 4°.

v. d. L. 254 (not seen). Grünwald, p. 59, gives: Dissert. philolog. de natu Dei contra Spinozam, and p. 302: De nat. Dei.. cum Buddei epistola ad theologos Rotterdamenses.. (Haag 1720).

5353

254. Jacobi Wittichii, Prof. Mathes. in Academia Duisburgensi, Disputatio philosophica de natura Dei. Duisburg. 1711. 4to.

Respond. Gerhardo Nic. Brouwer, Medioburgo Zelando. Cf. Bibliotheca hist.-philolog.-theologica Bremens. I p. 550 e. v. & 939 e. v. B. Glasius: Godgeleerd Nederland. III ('s Hertogenbosch, Gebr. Muller. 1856. 8vo) pp. 619, 620. Deze Jacobus Wittichius werd gewoonlijk (ook door mij in 1861) verward met Christophorus Wittichius, den bestrijder van Spinozaas Ethica en toen reeds lang overleden. Mijn fout werd sedert dikwijls nageschreven.

Wittich, J

According to J. Leydekker (De blyde Spinsist, 1719, p. 1-2) the Disputatio was "onlangs herdrukt, met lemmata aan den bladrand, en door... [J. Wittichius] in 't

[over]

2. 5354

254. Jacobi Wittichii, Prof.... [cont.]

Nederduits vertaalt; met aanteekening vermeerderd, zonder die gemelte lemmata".

Grunwald, p. 59, has: Dissert. philolog. de natura Dei contra Spinozam (Duisburg 1711); p. 302: De nat. Dei... cum Buddei epistola ad theologos Rotterdamenses.. (Haag 1720).

5360

Wittichius, Jacobus.

Philosophisch dispuut of Wysgerige verhandelinge van de natuure Gods. [Translated by the author; to which are added notes.] 1719.

not seen BM

Not in v. d. L. Title taken from: Ewyck, G. van, De groote swaerigheid... p. 63. See also: Leydekker, J., De blyde Spinosist... (the very title, and p. 2).

5355

Wittichius, Jacobus.

Wysgerige ~~twist~~ twistredenering over de natuur van God, welke onder des Heeren bystand onder de bescherming van Jacobus Wittichius, Doctor in de Filozofye, en ordinair Hoogleeraar derzelve, gelyk ook der Wiskunde, in de Koninklyke Academie van Duisburg, op zigh neemt in 't openbaar te verdedigen in Juli 1711, ter gewoner

[over]

2a. 5356

Wittichius, Jacobus.- Wysgerige ... [cont.]

tyd en plaatse, Gerhard Nicol. Brouwer, Mittelburger, beweerder. Hier is tot een Toegift bygevoegt het oordeel van den Heere Ruardus Andala, Professor in de Filozofye en H. Godtsgeleertheid te Franeker, over het Dispuit van den Heere Jak. Wittichius, alles uit het Latyn vertaalt, door A.W.T. en door denzelven uitgegeven. n.p., n.d. [1718.]

2 — 5357

Wittichius, J.– Wysgerige...

2 p. l., 62 p. 4°.

Not in V. d. L.
This translation was suppressed [prohibited struck out] by the Hof van Holland on Dec. 16, 1718, especially on account of the supplement ("Toegift", p. 45–62) in which several professors and theologians are attacked. Wittichius himself was angered by the translation. [cover]

2. — 5376

[Wizenmann, Thomas.]– Die Resultate... [cont.]

"Späterer Dr[uck]", is noted in Max Weg, Lessing-Bibliothek, [being] Katalog no. 31, 1894, p. 21.

2-a. — 5358

Wittichius, J.– Wysgerige... [cont.]

See: Knuttel, W.P.C., Verboden boeken in de Republiek der Vereenigde Nederlanden... 's-Gravenhage, 1914, no. 443.

The extracts from R. Andala (p. 47-50) consist of §xxxii–xxxiv of pt. 3 of his Apologia pro vera & saniore philosophia ... Franequerae, 1719. The

NNCV — 5382

Wolf, Albert.

Die Bedeutung des Kurzen Traktats und der Abhandlung über die Verbesserung des Verstandes für den Aufbau und die Entwicklung des Systems Spinozas. Inaugural-Dissertation zur Erlangung der Doktorwürde der hohen philosophischen Fakultät der Schlesischen Friedrich-Wilhelms-Univer- [cover]

LC

3 — 5359

Wittichius, J.– Wysgerige...

translator states (p. 45) that the Andala book came to his hands just when the printer of his translation was setting the last page. Accordingly, Andala's Apologia must have appeared towards the end of 1718.

(G.) Together with: Leydekker, J.

2. — 5383

Wolf, Albert.– Die Bedeutung ... [cont.]

sität zu Breslau vorgelegt von Albert Wolf. Promoviert: 1. September 1919. Diese Dissertation erscheint später. Breslau: Buchdruckerei H. Fleischmann, 1919. 2 l. 8°.

Consists of t.-p. and "Lebenslauf."

(Harvard)

4897

T., A. W.

[Verse; 4 lines] [In: Wittichius, J. Wysgerige twistredenering over de natuur van God... uit het Latyn vertaalt, door A. W. T. ... [1718] 4°. p. 60.]

Formerly DLC– Now ICMILC, Chicago — 5384

Wolf, Albert 1890–

Die Bedeutung des Kurzen Traktats und der Abhandlung über die Verbesserung des Verstandes für den Aufbau und die Entwicklung des Systems Spinozas. (Dissertation Breslau. [1923])
[Machinenschrift.] Breslau, Phil. Diss. v. [illegible]
83 S. 4° Sept. 1919 [1923]
¶ Nur Titelbl. u. Lebenslauf [2 Bl.] ersch. publ. im 1919. Die Arbeit ersch. später.

G-XXI-25 — 5375

[Wizenmann, Thomas.]

Die Resultate der Jacobischen und Mendelssohnschen Philosophie; kritisch untersucht von einem Freiwilligen. Leipzig: G. J. Göschen, 1786.
255 p., 1 l. 8° [& 16° struck out]

The author was T. Wizenmann.

[: "Vorbericht", inserted after t.-p.] Thus: 2 p. l. (1)4-255 p.

v. d. L. 340. (G.)

[over]

NN-OCH — 5 — E1762

Wolf, A.

The late Poet Laureate [Robert Bridges] and Spinoza (Jewish guardian, London). May 2, 1930, p. 3.

Letter to editor; calls attention to Bridges' anthology, The spirit of man, which opens with a quotation from Spinoza. Then: "Last September Dr. Bridges wrote to me about my edition of The Correspondence of Spinoza... 'I have been reading your book,' wrote Dr. Bridges, 'and I wish to express my gratitude, for I share your affection [cover]

2. E1763

Wolf, A. — The late Poet... [cont.]

ate emotion. But what sets me writing is I confess a selfish motive — which is to ask you if you could get your publisher to send me a single impression of the portrait. I like it better than any I had seen, and should like to frame and hang it up — and I would not damage the book by tearing it out"... It may interest some of your readers to know that my edition of the Theologico-Political Treatise will be ready in the course of this year." (A.S.O.)

 E277

[Bridges, Robert.]

Wolf, A.

The late Poet Laureate and Spinoza. (Jewish guardian [London]. May 2, 1930, p. 3.)

Letter to editor. — "Last September Dr. Bridges wrote to me about my edition of The Correspondence of Spinoza... 'I have been reading your book', wrote Dr Bridges, 'and I wish to express my gratitude, for I share your affectionate emotion. But what sets me writing is I confess [over]

2. E278

[Bridges, Robert.] - Wolf, A. [cont.]

a selfish motive — which is to ask you if you could get your publisher to send me a single impression of the portrait. I like it better than any I had seen, and should like to frame and hang it up — and I would not damage the book by tearing it out!"

 1607

[Freudenthal, J.]

Signed: Wolf, A.

Professor Freudenthal's "Spinoza". [Review of: Die Lebensgeschichte Spinozas... hrsg. von J. Freudenthal. Leipzig, 1899.] (Jewish quarterly review. London, 1899. v. 11, p. 490-495.)

(over)

Examines briefly "one or two points relating to the birth and education" of Spinoza, with special reference to H. Graetz who maintained that he was born in Spain.

 E1764

Wolf, A.

Professor Freudenthal's "Spinoza". [Review of: Die Lebensgeschichte Spinozas... hrsg. von J. Freudenthal. Leipzig, 1899.] (Jewish quarterly review. London, 1899. v. 11, p. 490-495.)

Examines briefly "one or two points relating to the birth and education" of Spinoza, with special reference to H. Graetz who held the view that he was born in Spain.

 E1810

Woodbridge, Frederick J. E., 1867-1940.

Spinoza. By Frederick J. E. Woodbridge. [Also] John Locke and his Essay. By Sterling P. Lamprecht. Tercentenary lectures delivered at Columbia University. New York, 1933. 1 p. l., 29 p. 8°.

Spinoza, p. 1-13.

 A lecture delivered in Havemey- [over]

2. E1811

Woodbridge, Frederick J. E. — Spinoza... [cont.]

er Hall, Columbia University, 26 January, 1933. Theme: Spinoza's convictions as found in the Ethics.

(Harvard)

 5415

Worms, René.

Spinoza. Conférence faite a la Société des Études Juives le 27 Janvier 1894. [Versailles: Cerf et Cie, 1894.] 14 p., 1 l. [blank]. 8°.

Repr.: Revue des études juives, tom. 28.

(A.S.O. With author's autograph dedication [over]

 2. 5416

Worms, René. Spinoza. — [cont.]

to Sir Frederick Pollock. From him to me with slip (inserted).

(Spinoza's thought; no life.)

E 1815

Wuttke, Adolf, 1819-1870.

Christian ethics. Translated by J. P. Lacroix. New York: Nelson & Phillips, 1873. 12°.

v. 1. History of ethics.

Spinoza, p. 281-290.

cf 171.1 W 2v. NY. 1876

3466

Wyzewa, Teodor de.

Le amis de Spinoza. D'après un ouvrage hollandais: [Meinsma, K. O. Spinoza en zijn kring... s'Gravenhage, 1896]. (In his: Écrivains étrangers. Paris, 1896-1897. 12°. ser. 2, p. 319-343.)

NN Repr. from: Revue des deux mondes, Aug. 1, 1896, entitled: Une biographie hollandais de Spinoza.

XYZ

0-XL-55 5439

Zangwill, Israel.

Les rêveurs du ghetto... Traduction de Madame Marcel Girette. [v. 1.] [Paris: Éditions G. Crès & Cie, 1920. 12°.

p. 205-265: Le polisseur de verres.

(A.S.O.)

0-XL-53 5434 [fiction.]

Zangwill, I[srael].

Dreamers of the ghetto. Philadelphia: The Jewish Publication Society of America, 1898. iii(1)p., 1 l., ~~4 p. l.~~, 536 p., 1 l. 12°.

The maker of lenses, p. 186-220.

The quotations from the Ethica are from the version of W. H. White.

(A.S.O.) [over]

G-XXV-46, 47, 48 5440

Zangwill, Israel.

Les rêveurs du ghetto... [tom. 1-3.] [Paris]: Les éditions G. Crès & Cie, 1923. 3 v. 12°. (Collection "Anglia".)

Le polisseur de verres, v. 1, p. 205-265.

Traduction de Madame Marcel Girette.

(G.- unbd.)

0-XL-53 1-a 5435

Zangwill, I[srael]. — Dreamers of the... [cont.]

"The philosophy of Spinoza, though it has affinities both with the logic of Maimonides and the mysticism of the Cabalists and in expression sometimes recalls the grand manner of the ancient prophets, stands nevertheless entirely on its own basis and is a gospel for the world, in which it has worked continuously, whether acknowledged or not, influencing all the best subsequent thinking. But for the ordinary man there is more energizing value in the Cabalistic doctrine that the Messiah could not come until sin had been

[next]

G-XXV-44, 45 5441

Zangwill, Israel.

Träumer des Ghetto. Deutsche autorisierte Ausgabe durch Dr. Hanns Heinz Ewers durch Mitwirkung des Verfassers. Bd. 1-2. Berlin: Verlag Siegfried Cronbach, 1908. 2 v. 12°.

Bd. 1, p. 228-269: Der Linsenschleifer.

(G.- unbd.) [over]

0-XL-53 2 5436

Zangwill [cont.]

worked out from the world, and God himself was thus, as it were, restored to pristine perfection" (p. 527-528; from the "Appendix: To the American Jew").

G-XXV-44, 45 2. 5442

Zangwill, Israel. — Traümer des... [cont.]

The several quotations from the Ethica are taken, with few verbal changes, from Stern's translation.

G-XXV-43 5438

Zangwill, I[srael].

Dreamers of the ghetto. Copyright edition. In two volumes. Vol. I. Leipzig: B. Tauchnitz, 1898. 326 p., 1 l. 16°. (Collection of British authors. Tauchnitz edition. v. 3292.)

V. The maker of lenses, p. 211-248.

B. 516.

(G.- ½ parchment.)

NNC 906 A E1822

Zerffi, Gustavus George.

NNUT LR12 R88 B

The historical development of idealism and realism. IV. Modern period: Descartes-Spinoza-John Locke. (Royal Historical Society, London. Transactions. London, 1880. v. 8, p. 331-355.)

NNC cat: Zerffi, George Gustavus, 1821-1892

Ziehen, Theodor.

Benedictus de Spinoza. Zur 250. Wiederkehr seines Todestages. (In: Kant-Studien. Spinoza-Festheft. Berlin, 1927. 8. p.1-28.)

[over]

2. 5465

Ziehen, Theodor. – Benedictus de... [cont.]

"Im folgenden soll versucht werden, etwas zur Beantwortung dieser Zweifel und Fragen [whether Fichte, Schelling, Hegel, Schleiermach[er] did not form a Spinoza "school" – whether "alle Kernpunkte seiner Gedanken" are not to-day superceded – and so forth] beizutragen und die Bedeutung, die Spinozas System über blosse Anregungen hinaus hat und voraussichtlich noch Jahrhunderte haben wird, festzustellen." (p.2).

5466

Ziehen, Th[eodor].

Die Grundlagen der Religionsphilosophie (Nomotheismus). Leipzig: F. Meiner, 1928. 164p., 1 l. 12°.

Acht Rundfunk-Vorträge.

V. Pantheistische Religionsphilosophie. Giordano Bruno. Spinozas Identifizierung von Gott und Welt. Amor intellectualis

[over]

2. 5467

Ziehen, Th[eodor]. – Die Grundlagen... [cont.]

Die Aufnahme des Spinozaschen Pantheismus (Lichtenberg, Goethe, Schleiermacher u.a.m.). C. Brunner. Haeckel. p. 83-101.

(G.) unbd.

5468

Zifroni, A.

Iggerot Spinoza. [Review of: Spinozas Briefwechsel... übertragen von J. Blewstein.] (Ma'abarot, v. 3, 1921, p. 147-148.)

(N. Isaacs.)

5479

Zimmermann, Robert.

Leibnitz bei Spinoza. Eine Beleuchtung der Streitfrage. Wien: F. Tempsky, 1890. 1p.l., 64p. 8°. (Kais. Akademie der Wissenschaften in Wien. – Philosophisch-historische Classe. Sitzungsberichte. Bd. 122, [Abhandl.] 2.)

(G.)

G-XXV-50 5480

Zimmermann, Robert. – Leibnitz bei... [cont.]

"Die ... Abhandlung hat sich ausschliesslich die Beleuchtung der durch die jüngsten Entdeckungen in ein neues Stadium getretenen persönlichen Beziehungen zwischen Leibnitz und Spinoza zur Aufgabe gestellt. Wenn es ihr gelungen sein sollte, die aus denselben gezogenen, für Leibnitzens Charakterbild nachtheiligen Folgerungen [von L. Stein und A. Baltzer] als unbegründet darzuthun, so wird sie dieselbe als gelöst und die schuldige Pflicht der Pietät gegen das Andenken desselben als erfüllt ansehen dürfen" (p.6).

5477

Zimmermann, Robert, edler von, 1824-1898.

Leibnitz und Lessing.. (Eine Studie) (Kais. Akademie der Wissenschaften in Wien. – Philosophisch-historische Classe. Sitzungsberichte. Wien, 1855. 8°. Bd. 16, p.326-391.)

Treats also on Leibniz and Spinoza, with reference to Foucher de Careil's Réfu-

(Verify pag. &c.)

[over]

0-XL-64 5471

Zimmermann, [Robert].

Ueber einige logische Fehler der Spinozistischen Ethik. (Kais. Akademie der Wissenschaften in Wien. – Philosophisch-historische Classe. Sitzungsberichte. Wien, 1850. 8°. Jahrg. 1850, Bd. 2, p. 451-464.) Excerpted

[Bd. 6 of the series?]

(A.S.O. unbd.)

[over]

2. 5472

Zimmermann, [Robert]. – Ueber einige... [cont.]

Spinoza's concept of substance.

[Zint, Hans.]

[Carl Gebhardt; a necrologue. Frankfurt a. M.: Löber & Co., 1935.] 15 p. 8°.

n. t.-p.

p. 1 reads: Abdruck aus: Zweiundzwanzigstes Jahrbuch der Schopenhauer=Gesellschaft für das Jahr 1935; but in reality it is not an off-print. It was privately printed anew.

(A.S.O.) [See G-1700-45]

Zirngiebl, Eberhard.

Der Jacobi=Mendelssohn'sche Streit über Lessing's Spinozismus. Ein Bruchstück aus der von der philosophischen Fakultät der Ludwig=Maximilians=Universität München gekrönten Preisschrift „Quellenmässige Darstellung und Charakteristik der Philosophie von Friedr. Heinr. Jacobi" als Inaugural=Abhandlung. München: E. Stahl, 1861. 31 p. 8°.

(G.)

Zweifel, Lazar (Eliezer ben Zebi ben David ha-Kohen).

"He endeavored also to give a Jewish coloring to Spinoza's philosophy, and quoted fifty opinions, most of which, including that of Besht (Baal Shem-Tob), were in harmony with the philosopher, while he himself contended that the only difference lay in the fact that Spinoza used words without careful discrimination to explain his system ("Shalom 'al-Yisrael," III. 43, ed. Wilna, 1873)." (J. E.)